WONDERFUL BOOKS

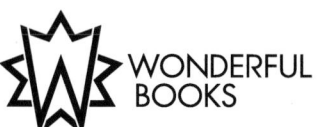

THE TARDIS CHRONICLES

VOLUME 1: BEFORE THE TIME WAR

PAUL MC SMITH

A Wonderful Book
Published in 2020
by Paul MC Smith/Wonderful Books
41A West Valley Road,
Hemel Hempstead HP3 0AN
www.wonderfulbook.co.uk

Copyright © Paul MC Smith 2020
Foreword copyright © Clayton Hickman 2020
The moral right of the author has been asserted

'Doctor Who' series copyright © British Broadcasting
Corporation 2020

Printed by Amazon

ISBN 978-0-9576062-4-1

With special thanks to Clayton Hickman for assistance
and encouragement, and thanks to Alan Barnes,
Richard Bignell, David Brunt, Jonathan Morris,
Jon Preddle and Gavin Rymill

This book is sold subject to the condition that it shall not,
by way of trade or otherwise, be lent, re-sold, hired out, or
otherwise circulated without the publisher's prior consent
in any form of binding or cover other than that in which it
is published and without a similar condition including this
condition being imposed upon the subsequent purchaser

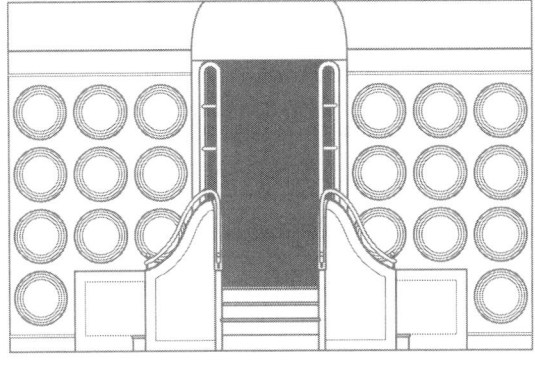
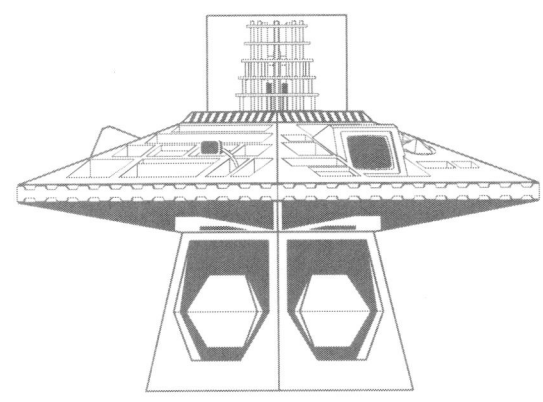

CONTENTS

IT LOOKS JUST LIKE A POLICE BOX

The Brachacki Box 1963-1966	10
The Brachacki Box 1966-1970	76
The Brachacki Box 1971-1975	116
The Newbery Box 1976-1982	182
The Yardley-Jones Box 1 1980-1982	256
The Yardley-Jones Box 2 1983-1989	306
The Yardley-Jones Box 3 1984-1989	352
The Hudolin Box 1996	390

IT'S BIGGER ON THE INSIDE

The Brachacki/Newbery Original 1963-1972	16
The Gleeson Washout 1972	140
The Liminton Throwback 1972-1973	146
The Green Improvisation 1974	160
The Ruscoe Reclamation 1975	168
The Newbery Stateroom 1976-1977	186
The Newbery Classic 1977-1980	206
The Ruscoe Expansion 1980-1983	261
The Thornton Rectification 1983-1988	329
The Hudolin Cathedral 1996	392

WHAT ARE ALL THESE KNOBS?

Console A 1963-1970	24
Panels A 1970	112
Console B 1971-1974	119
Panels B 1972-1974	142
Console Ci 1975	170
Console D 1976-1977	189
Console Cii 1977-1982	210
Panels Cii 1978-1981	236
Panels Cii 1980-1981	264
Panels Cii 1982	286
Console Ciii 1983	309
Console E 1983-1989	332
Console F 1996	394

TARDIS LANDINGS

First Doctor	34
Second Doctor	83
Third Doctor	110
Fourth Doctor	164
Fifth Doctor	288
Sixth Doctor	358
Seventh Doctor	376
Eighth Doctor	405

FOREWORD

THE ACTUAL WORKING OUT IS INCREDIBLY TEDIOUS, LOTS OF FIDDLY COMPUTATIONS

 This is the most important book you'll ever read. Oh no, sorry, you're not me, are you? Let me try that again.

This is an extremely interesting, well-written, immaculately researched, gorgeously designed and illustrated book about the TARDIS. Hmm, not sure that has the same ring to it. Accurate, yes, but lacking in punch. I'll have another think.

In the meantime, a bit of biographical information. Back in the last century I edited *Doctor Who Magazine* for a few years. I also provided about 70% of the covers for the *Doctor Who* DVD range (and 10% of those were actually okay if you squint). Since then I've mainly skulked around on Twitter, endlessly banging on about all things TARDIS. If you're not one of the 0.0205% of the UK population who follow me there, you've missed out on a series of interminable threads delving into Police Box prop minutiae, and maybe 30 tweets a week where my faithful followers send me photos of *appalling* TARDIS props/models/illustrations/bookcases to goad me into a) despair, and b) angrily declaring that the windows are wrong. Maybe you had to be there.

The upshot of all this is that I'm a wee bit obsessed with the TARDIS. Always have been. I mean, I've liked *Doctor Who* for as long as I can remember, but for that entire span I've *utterly adored* the TARDIS. As a kid my sketch pads were stuffed with drawings of roundels and consoles, and I built countless cardboard Police Box miniatures, usually suspended on a cotton thread so I could spin them to recreate the model shot from my treasured *Pyramids of Mars* VHS. As an adult I've spent almost as long trying to accurately recreate roundels in Photoshop, or recapture the typographical quirks of Police Box signage. It's no more productive but it does save money on cotton.

"Just write a book," my weary Twitter pals would urge after the latest 20-tweet thread on photo blowup walls. The problem is I am pathologically lazy: 240-character TARDIS tweets are one thing, but the sheer hard graft of translating them into a useful reference work is quite another. So the blessed relief of *The TARDIS Chronicles* finally existing – without me having to write the bloody thing – cannot be overstated.

Paul and I are by no means the only TARDIS obsessives out there – if you're willing to trawl the backwaters of Google then you'll find a wealth of research and analysis. But it's very scattershot and sometimes contradictory. This book is the first time *everything* has been meticulously compiled and presented in one place (although split over two volumes as there's so much more to cover now). And the sheer amount of new research, cross-checking, document-digging and good old-fashioned legwork that has gone into these pages is astonishing.

I've loved the back-and-forth discussions with Paul over the last few years: all the 'but-what-about's, the 'haven't-we-forgotten's and the 'surely-that-must-mean's as we wrangled with minute details of sets and props. We didn't always agree, but usually I had to admit defeat when faced with some hitherto-unknown scrap of proof he'd somehow unearthed.

And the new facts! The precious new facts. From the two TARDIS lamps that alternated during 1965-66, to details of the *five* 'Police telephone' plaques that featured on the *three* 1980s boxes. Not to mention the totally different cornices of the Season Nine and Ten control rooms, or the truth behind that anecdote involving Jon Pertwee, the console and a hammer.

Of course the quest for obscure TARDIS knowledge never ends. Perhaps we'll never know how often the duplicate Police Box doors made for the pilot appeared on screen. And the alterations made to the Newbery prop between scenes shot on the *same day* of filming for *Logopolis* remain baffling. Strangest of all is the BBC forking out to build a second main roundels wall in 1963 but then hardly ever using the thing.

That brings me to the designers whose work is celebrated in this book. At last the fan 'wisdom' that told us how a resentful Peter Brachacki half-arsed his original TARDIS set designs, or how Barry Newbery's second (not 'secondary') control room set warped in storage between seasons, can be laid to rest. *The TARDIS Chronicles* provides the true story, and cements Brachacki, Newbery, Thornton, Yardley-Jones *et al* as incredible talents who transcended a lack of time and money to craft props and sets that have more than stood the test of time. They remain inspiring – and utterly beautiful – today.

So perhaps I was right the first time and this really is the most important book you'll ever read. It will, at least, give you a new appreciation for the little things that make *Doctor Who* so special: that battered blue Police Box and the impossibly large control room within.

One thing I can guarantee: in this book, *all* the windows are right.

CLAYTON HICKMAN
March 2020

INTRODUCTION

WE HAVE CHARTED YOUR VOYAGES FROM GALAXY TO GALAXY AND FROM AGE TO AGE

To most people the form of a Police Box is now synonymous with *Doctor Who* – indeed, any cuboid blue object is often humorously compared to the Doctor's TARDIS. And for many followers of the programme, that tall blue box has become an object of intrinsic attraction, partly because of the original's elegant design (although never accurately replicated in the programme itself) and partly because of the engaging idea of an advanced space/time ship being impossibly contained within a relatively small box.

This inspired concept forms the focus of much of the very first episode of *Doctor Who*, and the scene where snooping schoolteachers Barbara and Ian first push their way into the Police Box and are astonished by the large space they find inside is as impactful now as it was to the audience in 1963. A new generation of young viewers got their chance to experience this seminal moment when the episode, 'An Unearthly Child', was repeated on BBC2 in November 1981.

By then the inside of the TARDIS was a familiar sight, being featured more often in stories than it had been in the series' early days. Initially, when each episode was recorded week by week, having the large control room set erected in the television studio restricted the space available for other settings, so it was used as little as possible, mainly only for the opening and closing episodes of a serial. By the mid-1970s, however, stories were produced in blocks of scenes based around the same setting, so TARDIS scenes could be recorded all together then edited into whichever episodes the script required.

Dedicated viewers at that time were just being to form an organised fandom, led by the older teenagers and young adults who had been hooked by the series when they were children and were already feeling nostalgia for those early days. With *Doctor Who* unavailable to rewatch on demand as it is now, these fans were keen to catalogue the series' past. Their sources of information were limited, however: photographs, off-air audio recordings of variable quality, for a lucky few some videotapes of more recent stories, but for the most part they were reliant on their collective memories.

The nascent Doctor Who Appreciation Society was at the forefront of this effort, with its Story Information (or 'Stinfo') publications, summarising the Doctor's adventures. It also produced a regular magazine, *Tardis*, with reviews, reports and features. Appropriately, given the periodical's title, coverage of the TARDIS featured early when society founders Jan Vincent-Rudzki and Stephen Payne secured an interview with the series' very first designer Peter Brachacki. Appearing in Volume 1 Number 10 of *Tardis*, dated September 1976, this is the only known interview he gave about his brief work on *Doctor Who*, before he passed away in 1980. As well as providing insight into Brachacki's intentions when designing the TARDIS control room and console, it's also the source of one or two misconceptions that continue to be reiterated.

Then in 1978, across several issues of Volume 3 of *Tardis*, Richard Landen presented a TARDIS 'Instruction Manual', featuring line drawings of each panel of the original 1960s console (although incorporating some aspects introduced on its 1970s replacement) and describing the functions of many of the controls. Five years later, Landen became feature writer for Marvel's *Doctor Who Monthly* magazine and issue 79, dated August 1983, reprinted his console manual verbatim, even using the same drawings. While these were reasonably accurate in their layouts (based on photos rather than screen images), the detail of the controls was more speculative. And in attempting to assign functions to almost every lever, switch and display, the accompanying text was highly imaginative, with only a few items matching information given in the series itself. Indeed, the article's claim that "Hartnell and Troughton invariably used the same switches for instigating the same operations of the Ship" is easily disprovable now we can see the episodes in far better quality than would have been available to fans during the last century. And any claim to catalogue every control falters on the fact that many were never used on screen and fewer still had their functions explicitly given in dialogue.

This reprint was inspired by the publication by Severn House a few months earlier, in March 1983, of Mark Harris's *Doctor Who Technical Manual*, which presented line drawings and cutaways of various gadgets, robots and vehicles from the series. Included were elevations and a plan of the then-current console, although the labelling of control functions was again largely speculative.

At the same time, *Doctor Who Monthly* began serialising 'The TARDIS Log', also written by Landen, a listing of each of the Ship's journeys with brief details of location and date (where discernible). One particular joy for TARDIS-loving readers (like myself) was the use of off-screen images of the Ship from episodes that at the time were never expected to be seen again, and in issue 78 a surprise cache of photos of genuine Police Boxes in real-world locations. For those of us too young to have

INTRODUCTION

ever seen a real Box, this was strangely exciting, almost like seeing evidence of a real TARDIS not just the BBC's fictional prop. The Log continued until issue 83 when it reached the most recent episodes of *The King's Demons*.

As *Doctor Who* continued, and for a time seemed to have concluded, others expanded on the work of these pioneers, unearthing more information about the series' production and the people who made it. As the episodes themselves became available to view by all, on-screen events were analysed in greater detail. Such research has often focused on the TARDIS: where it's been, what it does, how it works and how it was realised on screen.

Doctor Who Magazine updated its 'TARDIS Log' in issue 174 (June 1991), when it was increasingly looking like the Doctor's television travels were over. Even though it devoted nearly the whole edition to a listing of the TARDIS's journeys (or 'journies' as it infamously mis-labelled them), it still only had space to give brief descriptions of landing locations, along with small plans of the original 1960s console (with erroneous control labels from Landen's previous 'Instruction Manual'), its Pertwee-era replacement, the much-altered console from Season 20 (reusing parts of the drawing from Harris's *Technical Manual*) and the most recent model introduced in *The Five Doctors*. The magazine has continued to run occasional features and special issues about the TARDIS, including Gareth Roberts' three-part rundown of its features and functions in issues 340, 343 and 345 (2004); Gavin Rymill's examination of control room design changes in issues 530 and 532 (2018); and an edition of *The Essential Doctor Who* in June 2014 dedicated to the TARDIS, which included more accurate control descriptions by Roger Andrews of the 1960s, late-1980s and mid-2010s consoles. Books devoted to the TARDIS include Steve Tribe's *TARDIS Handbook* (BBC Books, 2010) and the *TARDIS Type 40 Instruction Manual* by Richard Atkinson and Mike Tucker, illustrated by Gavin Rymill (BBC Books, 2018).

THESE ARE THE CHRONICLES

The TARDIS Chronicles draws on all these sources along with my own research to present the most comprehensive charting of the TARDIS's course through the Doctor's television adventures. Every landing seen on screen is listed and numbered in chronological order (if such a term can be used for a time-travelling vessel) – in this first volume, from the Ship's leaving Gallifrey with the Doctor and Susan aboard, to its materialisation on a crashing gunship just before the Doctor gives up his title in order to fight in the Time War.

Where landings are separated by a solid line, they are not necessarily consecutive, so there's the possibility of unseen trips in between; a broken line indicates there could be a gap but the notes discuss why this is or isn't likely. No line means a landing follows directly from the last. Landings that are only mentioned or implied – the Doctor is an incessant name-dropper – are included as 'Previous Landings' at the latest point at which they could have occurred. This is often just before the story in which they're referenced, but if, say, the Doctor is talking to a companion who hasn't shared the experience then it must have been before they boarded the TARDIS so will be placed earlier.

Each landing has a place and time given, with as much precision as can be discerned from on-screen evidence, including duration of the Ship's visit if this is significantly longer than the real-time length of the episode(s). Details in square brackets are speculation or, in the case of historical Earth-based events, inference based on real-world information (although, as we shall see, there can be discrepancies between the *Doctor Who* universe and our own). Also listed are whoever is aboard the TARDIS at the time of each landing, and the television episodes during which the Ship is seen at that location.

There follows a description of each landing. This includes events inside the TARDIS prior to materialisation, details not only of the immediate vicinity but also of the broader environment that it's feasible the Ship's systems could detect, plus any action that occurs within sight of the Police Box. Only information given on-screen is reported here, so can be considered as 'true' (within the fiction of the programme). Where the TARDIS is seen or heard to materialise or dematerialise, from either outside or inside the Ship, this is indicated with a downward or upward pointing icon.

After this are up to three sections of additional information. **CONTROLS** catalogues every use of the console as seen on screen. Where it's said or shown what a control does this is indicated, or else a function may be guessed at based on what subsequently occurs. This section also mentions changes made to the console props. **LORE** cites specific functions and features of the TARDIS that we learn about in the stories. And **NOTES** covers behind-the-scenes information about how the TARDIS is presented on screen (for example, materialisation techniques and model usage), rationale for any speculation about the landing location or date, further supposition about what we see and learn on screen, and any TARDIS-related production errors.

Finally, throughout the book are illustrated histories of each Police Box prop, control room set and console, covering their design, construction, features and modifications. Plans of each console's panels identify which controls perform a specified function, cross-referenced to the Landings during which they're used, and at the back is an index of named controls and components.

Originally the *The TARDIS Chronicles* was to have been a single tome covering all *Doctor Who* to date, but just getting to the end of the original series took 400 pages. So the revived series will be covered in Volume 2, with still much to learn and explore about the operations and destinations of the Doctor's wondrous blue box.

IT LOOKS JUST LIKE A POLICE BOX

THE BRACHACKI BOX
1963-1966

In the earliest discussions about a new science-fiction serial for Saturdays on BBC Television, one key element was a time machine that would transport a team of people into dangerous environments. But what form should it take? A gleaming spaceship was considered too ostentatious for the educational remit of the programme, but a more ordinary object was thought too magical. There was even talk of having no exterior appearance at all – the time machine would be coated in "light-resisting paint" that rendered it invisible.

It was head of drama Sydney Newman – the originator of the *Doctor Who* format – who hit on the idea of combining both options and having a technological control room contained impossibly within a mundane cabinet such as a night-watchman's hut. After further discourse the use of a Police Box was settled on, possibly the suggestion of script consultant Anthony Coburn – an Australian who, being less familiar with British street furniture, found the large blue boxes uncanny when stumbled upon in unexpected places.

The BBC couldn't use a genuine Police Box, even had the Metropolitan Police permitted it. For one, they were made mostly of concrete so were incredibly heavy. Plus they were more than ten feet in height (so the flashing roof lamp could be spotted from a distance), making them far too bulky for moving around a television studio. Consequently, the designer assigned to *Doctor Who* as it prepared for its first recording sessions, Peter Brachacki, had to create his own version of a Police Box – something that would pass for the real thing but which was tailored to the practicalities of television production.

The basis for the TARDIS was the Mark II Metropolitan Police Box, designed by the force's architect and surveyor Gilbert MacKenzie Trench. This style was first deployed in 1931, following trials of similar wooden Mark I boxes, and by 1963 there were close to 700 across London. Although a familiar sight, they weren't that popular. Constables on the beat disliked them for being cold, damp and uncomfortable, while the public were reluctant to use them, assuming they were exclusively for the police or preferring a public telephone kiosk (particularly after the introduction of the 999 emergency call number in 1937). An appropriate disguise, therefore, for a time machine that wants to go unnoticed.

Brachacki's Police Box prop was constructed in wood but visually faithful to the genuine article. The height was reduced to make it more manageable in the studio, by shortening the depths of the base and the lowest rail on the panelled sides, while the roof had only one step rather than two and a much shallower pitch. The projection of the corner posts above the 'Police box' signs was greater, however, to maintain the tall, thin look. The prop also had fidelity in its colouring, not just the overall dark blue but also white window frames and a white 'Police telephone' plaque on the panel below the left-hand front window. (Although there was no phone behind this, there is evidence this panel could be opened.) Other accurate details included the Fresnel-lensed roof lamp

Left Mark II Metropolitan Police Box, front elevation and section through left-hand panels
Right Brachacki prop front elevation (with Met Police Box outline for comparison) and section through left-hand door

IT LOOKS JUST LIKE A POLICE BOX

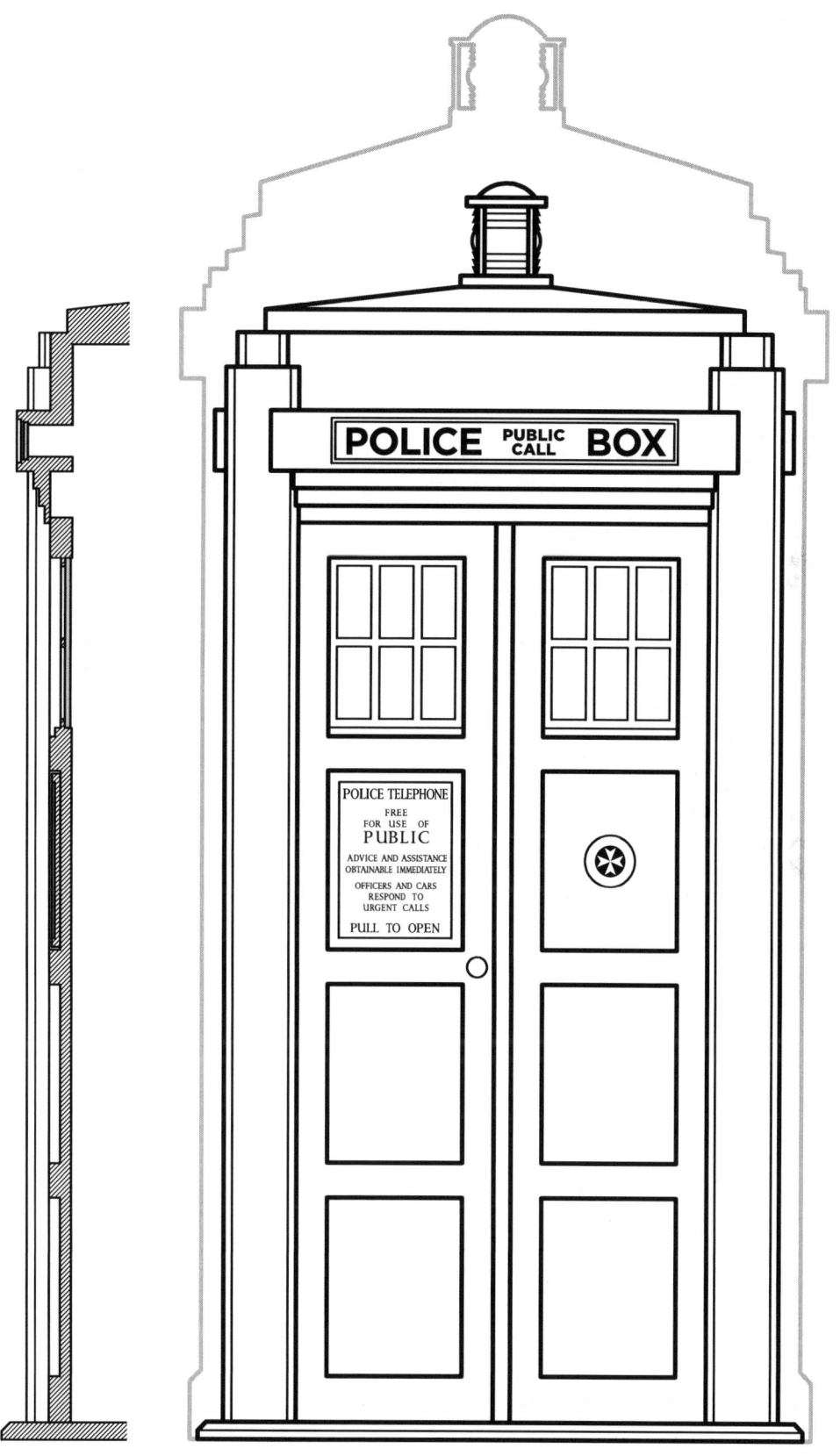

IT LOOKS JUST LIKE A POLICE BOX

Above 'Police telephone' plaque seen on the Brachacki box from 1963 to 1969. This was very faithful to the layout and style of genuine Police Box plaques

Brachacki was assigned to work on *Doctor Who* in the second week of July 1963, shortly after recording of the first episode had been put back from early August to late September. He had an initial meeting with series producer Verity Lambert, associate producer Mervyn Pinfield and director Waris Hussein on Wednesday 10 July to discuss their thoughts on the TARDIS control room – the most crucial set given its use throughout the series. But Brachacki didn't endear himself to the production team by being able to spare them only half an hour and informing them he would be occupied with other productions for the next two weeks. Although Lambert wrote to her department head Donald Wilson a week later to express concern about Brachacki's unavailability, and he passed on her worries to head of television design Richard Levin, by the second week of August design drawings had been produced for all components of the TARDIS control room, including iconic elements like the circular-patterned walls and hexagonal console. Lambert had a second meeting with Brachacki on Wednesday 21 August in which they discussed the TARDIS set in detail and agreed to simplify some of his initial ideas.

FIRST APPEARANCES

It's not known when the design drawings for the Police Box prop were prepared – perhaps after the more crucial interior had been designed but before the junkyard set was drawn up in early September. On Friday 13 September an experimental recording session was held in Lime Grove Studio D to try out various camera effects for the technically complex new series. These included ways of making the TARDIS disappear, for which the new Police Box prop may have been available, although a stand-in might have been used. It seems the efforts had limited success, however, given that for the first decade of the programme the materialisations were achieved either on film or by mixing between still photographs. It has also been reported the Police Box was too large to fit into the lift used for transporting scenery up to Studio D on the fourth floor of the Lime Grove building. Yet no indication of how this was rectified has been given and it seems an unlikely error for an experienced designer like Brachacki to make, so this may be apocryphal.

The prop was definitely completed by the following Thursday, 19 September, as this was when pre-filming for the first story took place at Ealing Film Studios. The prehistoric plain set was erected on Stage 3A and the Police Box was filmed with the shadow of a man (uncredited extra Leslie Bates) falling across it for the cliffhanger of episode one, an establishing shot for episode two, and with spears being thrown at it to be mixed with a shot of the empty set for the Ship's departure in episode four.

It was back in Lime Grove Studio D the following week for the first 'pilot' recording of *An Unearthly Child* on Friday 27 September. The scenes of the Police Box in the junkyard show a very clean prop and reveal some

with domed circular cap, clear acrylic 'Police box' signs with white lettering, windows that opened inwards at the top, and the St John Ambulance emblem on the right-hand door (although this was simplified from the organisation's official badge and omitted its lettering).

One significant point of difference was the doors themselves. Real Police Boxes had only one door, on the right at the front, which opened outwards. The left-hand side was part of the concrete fabric of the box so didn't open, except for the hinged panel behind which was a phone for the public to use. On the Brachacki prop, the front was a pair of doors that both opened inwards, possibly to match the main double-doors of the control room set. The centre post covering the gap between them was attached to the left-hand door, acting as a stop for the right-hand side, so the former could only be opened if the latter was at least ajar. This meant it was easier for the actors to enter and exit the Police Box via the right-hand door, although they did sometimes use the left (proving there was no phone cupboard behind it). The rear side was also given doors, this time opening outwards, for access and so that when all four actors had to be seen going into or emerging from the TARDIS they didn't need to squeeze together inside. The prop was constructed as a single unit and couldn't be taken apart, as would later become the norm, but was instead mounted on castors so it could be wheeled around.

curious details. The sign box on the right-hand side was missing its lettering – very noticeable as the camera pans away from the TARDIS at the start of the episode. A small change to the prop since it was filmed at Ealing is also evident. The shot of it dematerialising in episode four shows three handles on the front: one on each door and another on the right-hand side of the telephone plaque's frame. Before the studio recording a week later, these were removed as by then Ian was scripted to point out the Police Box has no handles. This change may even have been made on the day of recording as the screw holes are clearly visible in close-ups of the Doctor unlocking the door. These shots also reveal the plaque panel was initially hung with hinges on the right and a handle on the left, as was common on genuine Police Boxes. Screw holes can be seen on both sides of this panel's frame, and there are rabbets on its right-hand edge that align with the hinges now positioned on the left.

SECOND CHANCES

This initial recording of the first episode was deemed unfit for broadcast and the production team was told by Sydney Newman to do it again. This had been anticipated, however, and the next episode wasn't scheduled to be recorded until three weeks later to allow time for its slot to be given over to a remount instead, with subsequent episodes then proceeding weekly. The opportunity was taken to refine almost every aspect of the production and modifications were made to the Police Box prop at the instigation of new designer Barry Newbery, who was brought in shortly after the pilot recording when Brachacki was taken to hospital with a stomach ulcer.

One of Newbery's first tasks was to prepare for further filming at Ealing for the rest of the opening story, which was due to take place in the second week of October – barely a week after he had taken over the design remit. This session included the time travellers emerging from the TARDIS in episode two to find they are no longer in London, cavemen blocking their return to the Ship at the end of episode three, and their eventual escape in episode four. By now the Police Box prop had been given a more weathered and dirty appearance to make it look more like it had been travelling for some time. This creates a slight continuity error in the broadcast episodes: when the TARDIS stands on the prehistoric plain as seen by Kal, and when it fades away at the end of the story – filmed in September – its surface is smooth and glossy and its window frames, telephone plaque and St John Ambulance emblem are bright and clean; but in other scenes with the regular cast, filmed in October, it's grubbier and the white highlights are less distinct.

Another difference was that in the pilot recording the inside of the box had been lit, so when the doors were open the white-painted interior looked bright, suggesting the control room within. In the later filmed sequences, and subsequently in the studio, the inside of

IT LOOKS JUST LIKE A POLICE BOX

AN UNEARTHLY SOUND

Brian Hodgson of the BBC's Radiophonic Workshop was assigned to create the special sounds for the new series. For the Doctor's wondrous time machine, he wanted to give a sense of elements both approaching and receding from the listener, as if all of the past and future were being opened up to them.

His initial TARDIS take-off effect, heard in the pilot recording, was more sporadic than the one we're now used to. It starts with a series of beeps that begin to overlap as they increase in frequency. Then some of the rising-falling grinding sounds – famously originated by sliding a key along a stretched piano string – are heard in discrete bursts before being suffused into a high pulsing tone and harsh whooshing. It's an altogether more disorientating sound, appropriately, but not as immediately striking as its replacement.

When it was decided to re-stage the first episode Hodgson had time to rework the effect and give it more structure. After a deep rumble, the grinding establishes a rhythm before the pulsing tone begins, mixed which softer whooshes into a rising pitch more suggestive of a vessel ascending. Even though the TARDIS sound is now a familiar icon of the series, when the full version kicks in at the end of *Doctor Who*'s first episode it's still a heart-thumping moment.

In later years, Hodgson successfully had the effect classified as music, earning him well-deserved royalties whenever it's played.

the prop was dark. Photographs show it was still white when *An Unearthly Child* episode one was remounted but had been painted black by the time *Marco Polo* episode one was recorded in January 1964.

Finally, when the Police Box was returned to Lime Grove Studios for the remount of episode one on Friday 18 October it had undergone further minor modification. Principally, it now had its 'Police box' lettering on the right-side sign and the frame around the telephone plaque was repainted blue, while the whole prop was given a further coat of paint that almost completely obscured the St John Ambulance emblem. It was also daubed with Artex to give it a rougher texture, perhaps more like the concrete of genuine Police Boxes.

This is how the prop remained for the rest of the series' first year in production. Initially it was wheeled into the studio regularly, appearing in all but episode six of *The Daleks* and in most episodes of *Marco Polo* (if only in the background or on a cart). But as the style of the programme developed, the TARDIS was generally seen only at the start and end of a story to deliver its occupants to and from each adventure. The prop did make

IT LOOKS JUST LIKE A POLICE BOX

THE STANDALONE DOORS

For the shot in the pilot episode of Barbara pushing her way into the TARDIS, a duplicate pair of doors was made and placed just outside the control room set in line with its large double entrance doors. This formed a freestanding piece of scenery that Brachacki intended would reinforce the sense of the control room being within the Police Box. It was specified to match the main prop in all details, even down to the hinged windows: the one on the left-hand door is open when Barbara pushes past. The plaque panel (glazed, unlike the main prop) was still hinged on the right, though, and both this and the two doors also had screw holes where handles had been removed, as on the main prop.

When Barry Newbery assumed design duties for the episode's remount, he had the frame for these extra doors split in two so they could be separated and wheeled out of the way when not needed. These are included on the redrawn studio floorplan for the repeat recording so were probably available on the day but director Waris Hussein chose not to use them after all. Instead, when Barbara first enters the TARDIS, the scene cuts directly from her running into the Police Box prop to her staggering onto the control room set, without the close-up of her pushing through the duplicate set of doors as seen in the pilot recording. Instead a black curtain was hung beyond the control room doors and the Police Box doors were not seen from inside the TARDIS. The standalone doors were kept in storage, however, and are believed to have made four on-screen appearances.

Episode one of *The Reign of Terror* was recorded on Friday 10 July 1964 in the narrow confines of Lime Grove Studio G. With sets including three distinct areas of woodland, a farmhouse courtyard and building interiors (all one connected set), space was at a premium. So after recording the TARDIS's materialisation on the main forest area, the Police Box prop was removed and the standalone doors were used for the close-up of the Doctor locking the TARDIS door, as they took up less room. Here they match the full front of the Police Box, with corner posts and a 'Police box' sign. Both Brachacki's and Newbery's design drawings for the doors show them within a plain flat frame, but the view of them in the pilot recording suggests the corner posts at least were included from the start. If not, they may have been added when the doors were revamped for *An Unearthly Child*, as the sign box in *The Reign of Terror* has a split down the middle.

The standalone doors weren't used again until early 1966 during production of *The Massacre*. Although this serial's episodes are missing, photos taken on location at Wimbledon Common show that the Police Box put together for filming (and new companion Jackie Lane's photocall) was only a rough approximation of the main prop. The sides were just painted flats rather than properly panelled, notably with an incorrect arrangement of bars on the windows, and the roof was a simple two-stepped block. But the front of the box had very accurate doors which, together with the muddied but white telephone plaque frame and a visible split in the centre above the sign box, indicates the standalone doors were used to make up the front of this makeshift Police Box. Viewers who recall seeing episode four when broadcast report that in the scene when Dodo bursts into the TARDIS, the Police Box doors were visible beyond the control room doors, as in the pilot episode, so it seems the standalone set was used in the studio too.

The third episode of *The Celestial Toymaker*, recorded in Riverside Studio 1 on Friday 1 April 1966, required three sizeable sets: the Toymaker's office, Mrs Wiggs' kitchen and a ballroom. On the last, Dodo and Steven had to cross a triangular dancefloor to reach what they thought was the TARDIS but which turned out to be a fake. And it was a fake as it seems the standalone doors were used again to save space. Photos of the set show this Police Box had no roof lamp and was up against the backdrop, plus its window frames were notably cleaner than the main prop's and the St John Ambulance emblem more prominent, all suggesting it was the duplicate.

Finally, a similar arrangement to that in *The Massacre* may have been set up for the last episode of *The Tenth Planet*, recorded on Saturday 8 October 1966. The studio floorplan indicates the standalone doors were erected beyond the control room's main doors. So there may have been a shot of Ben and Polly coming through the Police Box doors into the TARDIS to find the Doctor collapsed on the floor. If so, this was the last appearance of these duplicate doors, and the control room would not be visibly connected to the Police Box exterior again until the revival of *Doctor Who* in 2005.

---

it out of the confines of Lime Grove Studios, however, when episode one of *The Sensorites* and all of *Planet of Giants* were recorded at the still-new BBC Television Centre. It even went outdoors as part of *Doctor Who*'s first major location shoot, filmed on Thursday 27 August 1964 beside the Thames under Kew Railway Bridge for the travellers' arrival in *The Dalek Invasion of Earth*.

Yet it was back in the studio – this time the BBC's Riverside Studios a few miles downstream at Hammersmith, where the Daleks' return was recorded – that the Police Box suffered its first significant damage. When in episode one, taped on Friday 18 September, the bridge collapses and blocks the TARDIS's entrance, the falling debris struck the front sign box. This isn't noticeable in the broadcast episode but when the prop was back in the studio on Friday 23 October for the travellers' return to the Ship in episode six, the damage is clearly visible – a large piece of the top-left corner of the sign box is missing and splinters hang down over the lettering. The camera shot is so blatant that it can only have been a deliberate choice not to repair the damage in the intervening weeks so as to suggest it was 'real' within the fiction of the show and not just a production error.

LIGHT SWITCHES
Production on *Doctor Who* took a break after *The Dalek Invasion of Earth* was completed, so the Police Box prop wasn't needed again until episode one of *The Rescue* was recorded on Friday 4 December in Riverside Studio 1. By then the front sign box was finally repaired (although the replacement section of wood is visible from here on as it's slightly paler in colour), and shortly afterwards changes were made to the roof lamp. It's tempting to suppose this was also damaged by falling debris in *The Dalek Invasion of Earth*, although in that story the lamp can't be seen so may have been removed specifically to avoid breaking it. It's shown only briefly in *The Rescue*, where it's hard to make out because it's either obscured by light when on or in darkness when off, but seems to have the original lensed covering still. The prop wasn't required for *The Romans*, and when it was back in the studio for episode one of *The Web Planet*, recorded on Friday 22 January 1965, the lamp had a simpler, straight-sided covering and the rods supporting the cap were placed in line with the roof's edges rather than its corners. This new lamp was also narrower and the dome on the cap was higher. Although the Police Box was on set for later episodes, it's only seen briefly on screen and the lamp isn't shown. However, a photograph taken by the design department shows that by episode three the lamp had been replaced again by a wider cylinder with a new square cap (with supporting rods back in the corners) but again with a high dome.

For the next story, *The Crusade*, the Police Box was taken to Ealing Studios to film its arrival and departure, then back to Riverside Studios for episodes one and four. In the former, recorded on Friday 5 March, there's one brief shot in which the roof lamp can be seen and it looks more like the original version again – certainly the cap is circular, not square. Yet in episode one of the following story, *The Space Museum* (recorded in Television Centre Studio 4 on Friday 2 April), the lamp has a thin straight-sided cylinder as in *The Web Planet* episode one but with the square cap from later in that serial. Come episode four, recorded on Friday 16 April, the circular cap of the original lamp has reappeared. In *The Chase* it has the wider cylinder in episode one, then the narrower one in episode two, then back to the wider one in episode four, but always with the square, high-domed cap. Then in photos of the TARDIS on the beach set for *The Time Meddler*, it appears to have no lamp at all.

The Police Box was considered an item of scenery so was the responsibility of the set designer and his team. Because the flashing lamp was electrical, however, it was handled and maintained by the Visual Effects department. It would seem that at some point around the end of 1964 or start of 1965, the original lensed casing was lost or broken, although the cap and rods caging it were usable. It was replaced, perhaps in a hurry, with a simpler cylinder and a makeshift cap for *The Web Planet* episode one, before a new square cap and a different cylinder were created for its next appearance in episode three. Combinations of these two cylinders and two caps were subsequently used at random, presumably determined by whatever the prop handlers happened to pick up on the studio day. To be fair, the camera rarely tilts high enough to see the top of the Police Box prop so these differences would have been unnoticed by viewers.

Another minor change at this time occurred between recording episodes four and five of *The Chase* in late May 1965. The frame around the telephone plaque became much paler – not white as it originally had been but as though much of the blue paint was rubbed off. The prop displays no other signs of having had its paintwork touched up so why this should be is a mystery.

The third season of *Doctor Who* is something of a Dark Age for the series. Many of the episodes from this run are missing, and incoming producer John Wiles dispensed with the screen-photographing services of John Cura and cut back on the use of BBC photographers to take publicity shots during studio rehearsals. Thus the visual record of those serials in production during the latter half of 1965 and first half of 1966 is slim to non-existent.

What we do know is the Police Box prop was getting shabbier as time wore on. In the last week of April 1965, between the close of *The Space Museum* and the start of *The Chase*, the front sign box was damaged again, losing a strip across the top-right that was only patched a few weeks later, and increasing scuffs and chips to the prop's paintwork are evident. The roof lamp settled on the wider cylinder with the low-domed circular cap, appearing as such in at least *The Daleks' Master Plan* episode twelve, *The Ark* and *The Celestial Toymaker* episode four. Yet the thinner covering and square high-domed cap were used for the makeshift Police Box filmed on location at the end of *The Massacre* (as the main prop was needed in the studio for recording of *The Daleks' Master Plan* episode eleven on the same day, presumably with the circular-capped wide lamp) and for location filming of the TARDIS for *The War Machines* and *The Smugglers*.

After nearly three years of almost weekly use, and with the increasing likelihood the prop would need to be transported to filming locations, the production team decided in the summer of 1966 to give the Police Box its first major refurbishment.

IT'S BIGGER ON THE INSIDE

THE BRACHACKI/NEWBERY ORIGINAL
1963-1972

The first thing that *Doctor Who*'s debut designer Peter Brachacki tackled when he turned his thoughts to the programme at the end of July 1963 was the interior of the Doctor's 'spaceship'. This was the main set for half of the first episode and was to be used throughout the series. But what should this marvel that could traverse all of space, time and matter look like?

During development much thought had been given to its external appearance and by Thursday 16 May the series format document had settled on "a police telephone box standing in the street". But inside was described merely as "an extensive electronic contrivance. Though it looks impressive, it is an old beat-up model." By Friday 12 July this had been updated by story editor David Whitaker to include "comfortable living quarters with occasional bric-a-brac acquired by the Doctor in his travels". Earlier that week design department manager James Bould had assigned Brachacki to work on *Doctor Who*, and on Wednesday 10 July the designer had his first, brief, meeting with the production team, who were keen to outline their thoughts on the Doctor's then-unnamed vessel.

However they described their vision, they probably left Brachacki with Anthony Coburn's latest draft script for the first episode, submitted just two days prior. Beyond being a large space seemingly contained within the Police Box, this gave little description of the ship's interior, although on entering it the two teachers Mr Chesterton and Miss Canning (as Barbara was then named) were subjected to a mind-numbing barrage of light and sound as part of "the process which enables material bodies to make the adjustment between one ratio of Space-Time and another". Referenced are a control panel with dials and levers, seats for the Doctor and Suzanne (later Susan) to strap themselves into on take-off, and a domed screen in the ceiling that uncovers to display their psychedelic journey back through time, while a machine voice counts down the years being traversed.

Brachacki was busy working on prior assignments for the next two weeks – credits in *Radio Times* indicate that in the latter half of 1963 he designed episodes of music show *The Choice is Yours*, lecture series *The Rise of Christian Europe* and editions of the anarchic children's show *Crackerjack* – but once he became free in the last week of July he approached the task with efficient creativity. He wanted something timeless, with a sense of power, and quickly settled on the use of geometric shapes, selecting an arrangement of staggered circles on

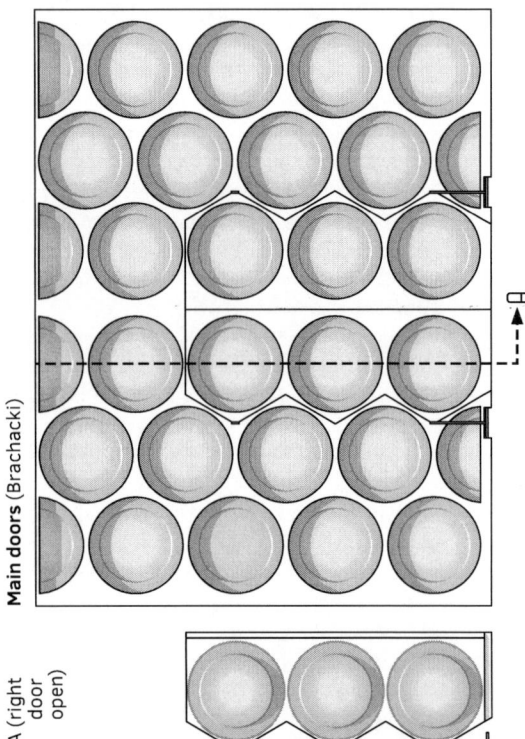

IT'S BIGGER ON THE INSIDE

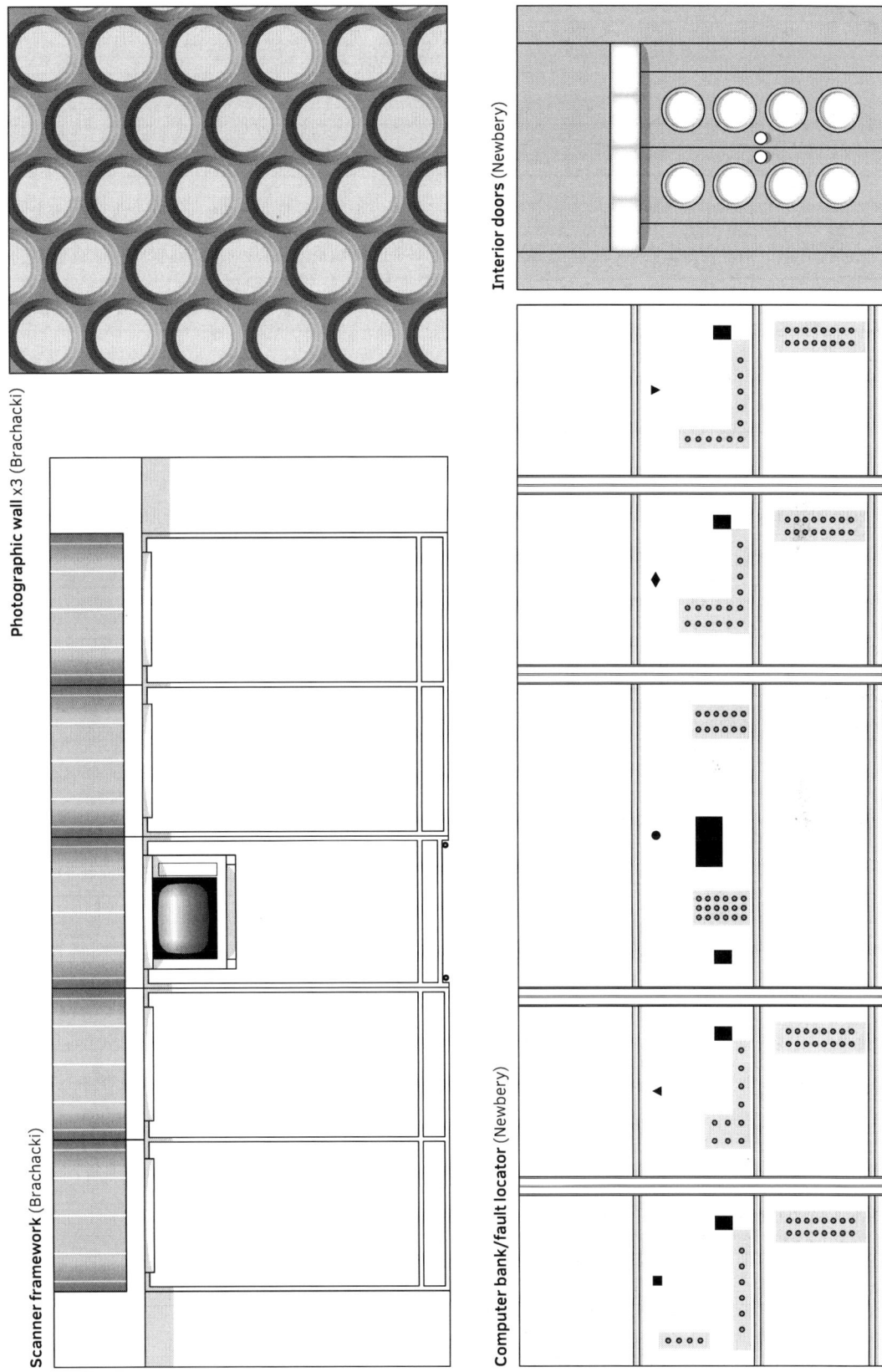

Photographic wall x3 (Brachacki)

Scanner framework (Brachacki)

Interior doors (Newbery)

Computer bank/fault locator (Newbery)

IT'S BIGGER ON THE INSIDE

the walls. These were possibly inspired by the patterning on some plastic sheeting or the skylights in the scenery dock at BBC Television Centre.

By having a freestanding control console that was believably operable by the Doctor alone, Brachacki was able to construct the space around it from separate wall sections that would withstand repeated use in the studio better than a single conjoined set might. He had hoped to make these from fibreglass so they could be lit as if pulsing with energy when the ship was in flight, but this was beyond his budget and he had to scale back his designs. However, Brachacki could afford to add interest to this background of circles with other items positioned around the control room, such as two large perspex cabinets containing lights, a metal framework from which the scanner screen was hung (originally planned to descend through a pair of drop-down doors), metal frames with either tinted perspex or ruched fabric screens, and an overhead light in a hexagonal frame intended to suggest the Ship's power source.

Designs for all these elements were drawn up by Ray London in the middle of August and on Wednesday 21 Brachacki and Verity Lambert met again to go over his plans in detail. This may be when some of the scaling back was agreed, not just for cost reasons but no doubt because the designer would have knowingly provided the producer with a range of options from which to select the ones she thought would work best. Certainly at some point before construction began it was decided to dispense with six internally illuminated columns that would have supported the overhead light, along with the descending scanner and some of Brachacki's ideas for the console. As his final control room designs were approved and sent to the BBC's scenery builders, he continued with planning the other sets for the first episode, namely the schoolrooms and junkyard on Totter's Lane, all of which had to be ready for the scheduled recording date of Friday 27 September.

REMOUNT REFINEMENTS

This initial recording of the first episode was vetoed for broadcast by head of drama Sydney Newman for a number of scripting and technical reasons. Sadly, while that decision was being reached, Brachacki was suddenly hospitalised. Fellow designer Barry Newbery was assigned to replace him on *Doctor Who*, with little time not only to prepare for the remount of episode one in under three weeks but also to organise the sets for the subsequent three instalments of that first serial.

Fortunately the TARDIS set pieces had been kept as it was known they were to be used throughout the series (whereas the other sets had to be rebuilt). There were two identical wall sections each with six columns of deeply indented circles. These were built from plywood in a metal frame on castors, with the recesses backed by vacuum-formed PVC discs that could be lit from behind.

(Brachacki's idea to have some of these removable so cameras could shoot the control room from behind the wall was not implemented.)

Another section like the indented walls had a central pair of doors whose hinged edges zigzagged around the staggered roundels. Initially these were operated manually but after this proved problematic during the first recording, Newbery had a camshaft fitted to the bottom hinges so the doors could be opened more smoothly. Because of their thickness, the touching edges of the two doors had be to chamfered so they wouldn't jam as they opened, and possibly as a result of this the gap between them was off-centre. One idea in the original plans but ultimately abandoned was to paint zigzags between each column of roundels to disguise the outline of the doorway.

Supplementing these was a large backcloth printed with a magnified photo of staggered circles. The original source photo is long reported to have been a pill blister pack but this is unlikely. Blister packs didn't become widely available until later in the 1960s with the introduction of the oral contraceptive. Even if Brachacki had found an early example, they usually had the compartments arranged side by side, with space between them to allow single pills to be pushed out, not the tightly interlocking circles of the TARDIS walls. Also, the original backcloth featured at least twelve columns of six circles, far more than any single blister pack would have had (and it must have been a single image as the circumference ridges exhibit changes in perspective). Brachacki himself said in a 1976 interview that the photo was of a three-inch-square plastic sheet that had circles indented or punched out. The impression of pill packaging comes from the middle of each circle being paler, but this was because these were cut out then covered with fabric so they too could be lit from behind – although in the event this never happened as, being a flat backdrop, it was inevitably placed against to the studio wall. For the pilot this backcloth was a single piece 28 feet wide and hung from a rail, which meant wrinkles could be seen as it bunched up at floor level. For the remount, Newbery had new photographic walls made in three narrower sections (five columns of 5½ roundels), each fixed tautly on a wooden frame. He then used narrow strips of painted plywood to cover where their edges abutted.

The most significant change was to the rear wall of the set. For the pilot, Brachacki had specified a large backcloth be painted based on the same image used for the photographic walls but at even greater magnification. In front of this were placed stand-up cutouts of enlarged photos of glass vacuum tubes and lightbulbs. Lambert felt this scenery was not distinctive enough so Newbery replaced it with a new piece: a multi-section computer bank that became better known as the fault locator. This was comprised of five flats each featuring metal plates with blinking lights and small windows. The framework in front had a lintel with five circular holes in its underside; the scanner monitor was hung below the centre one and the others contained lights shining through segmented diffusers. Above each circle was a curved fascia, although as early as *The Edge of Destruction* this was replaced with a flat cloth painted to look like three-dimensional cylinders.

Brachacki had also designed the overhead light with a segmented diffuser held in a hexagonal frame, hung from the ceiling between the console and main doors. Immediately below this, the floor was painted with a beige hexagon within the otherwise light-blue lacquered floor-space, a detail maintained for the rest of the first serial but afterwards dropped. One other adornment at floor level was a set of six trapezium-shaped metal plates that formed a hexagonal ring around the base of the console.

When setting the studio for the remount of episode one on Friday 18 October, Newbery kept the scanner framework, light-cabinets, some metal-framed screens, the metal plates around the console and the overhead light. He also re-hired the antique furniture Brachacki had dotted around the room, including a large brass candle stand, a pedestal formed from three carved eagles (an armillary sphere was placed on this in place of the carved Chinese dragon in the pilot recording) and a fluted wooden pillar supporting a Westminster Abbey skeleton clock. To these were added a Medieval Spanish wooden armchair with studded leather seat and back, and another wooden chair based on a stone throne at Knossos. Many of these would appear in the control room for years to come (see table, page 22).

The last piece of recurring control-room scenery was a pair of interior doors that first appeared in episode two of *An Unearthly Child*. Designed by Newbery, these tied into the geometric theme with four small roundels in each door, and had an illuminated lintel (although this was only ever switched on in its debut appearance).

SHIFTING SCENERY
The arrangement of control room walls for their first ever appearance on screen was, clockwise from the left: the main doors, one of the indented walls, the three photographic walls in a line, then the computer bank returning at right angles, parallel to the doors. In front of this was the scanner framework with a light-cabinet at each end, then the console and finally the overhead light. This layout was repeated for the third story, *The Edge of Destruction*, with the addition of the second indented wall returning at right angles to the computer bank, followed by the interior doorway leading to the sleeping quarters and two of the metal-framed screens. With episode two of *An Unearthly Child* showing an indented wall to the left of the main doors, then the interior doors, a sense was quickly established of a complete enclosure.

It wasn't to last. As the Doctor's adventures continued, there wasn't always space in the studio to set up the full control room every time it was needed, so just one or two

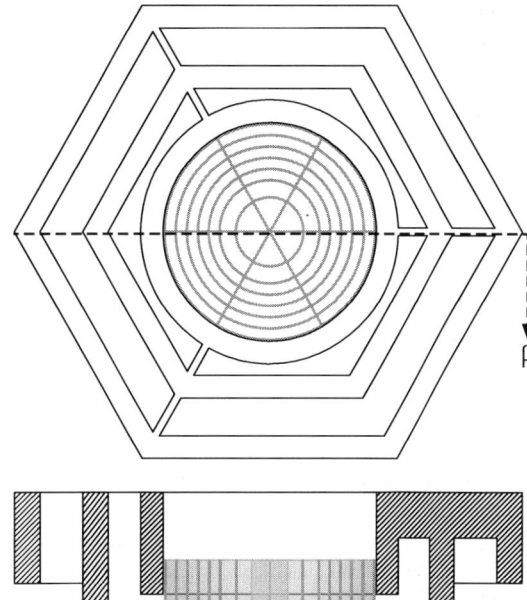

Above Overhead light, plan and section through A

wall sections were used, sufficient to suggest the wider room without needing to show it. These usually included the main doors, as the travellers were generally shown leaving or entering the TARDIS, and one indented wall or a couple of the photographic walls. Early casualties of the repeated shifting between the scenery store and the studio were the skirting boards along the front edges of the doors and indented walls to hide their castors. These were clearly prone to detaching in transit and had disappeared by the time *The Sensorites* episode one was recorded on Friday 29 May 1964. They were refitted for *Planet of Giants* three months later but had gone again by the end of *The Dalek Invasion of Earth*, recorded in October.

During the break in production after this serial the main doors' opening mechanism was upgraded, perhaps allowing them to be powered rather than operated by hand. The part around the bottom of the cam shaft attached to the hinges became more prominent, protruding from under the raised base of the wall. This is noticeable for many years to come – even being shown close up in some episodes, rather spoiling the magic of the TARDIS's operation – as the doors became the longest lasting part of the control room set. Through repaints and redesigns, this original wall was still in use until 1975. Even when the set was redesigned in 1977, the same doors and their mechanics were incorporated into a new wall. They made their last on-screen appearance in *The King's Demons* in 1983 having served faithfully (well, with ongoing repairs) for close on 20 years.

Almost as long-lived was at least one of the six-column indented walls. Like the doors, one of the pair was kept through several control room revamps up to 1975. It

IT'S BIGGER ON THE INSIDE

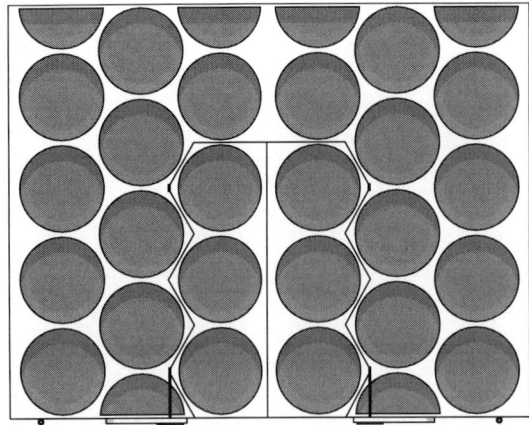 

Above Towards the end of Season 2 the vacuum-formed roundels were replaced by flat discs which were rarely backlit

last appeared in episode one of *The Masque of Mandragora*, recorded on Sunday 6 June 1976, as part of the TARDIS's corridors. Both indented walls were last seen together on screen either in *The Tomb of the Cybermen* (two walls are seen in alternate shots but as the TARDIS scene was filmed this may be the result of editing) or, failing that, in *The Power of the Daleks*. Although only one is used at a time in subsequent stories, it's not possible to tell if this was always the same one or whichever of the two happened to be pulled out of storage.

As noted, the roundels in these walls and the main doors were translucent PVC, vacuum-formed with an inner recess. Being thin plastic these too were prone to damage and, although the original plans indicate spares were to be supplied (and the mould was kept so more could be made), they became noticeably bashed and dented as the series progressed. After *The Space Museum* – in which they look especially crumpled – the roundels in the doors wall and one of the indented walls were replaced with flat fabric backings. When lit from behind these still showed a ring around the edge, perhaps to retain a feel of the original appearance. They tended to be backlit less often from here on, however, leaving the roundels much darker than their surrounds.

The other indented wall's original roundels survived until at least *The Time Meddler*, but eventually these too were replaced with flat ones. At some time during the fourth production block the backings on the walls were changed again, removing the outer ring but still appearing pale or dark if lit or not. Those on the doors wall were replaced gradually, with some ringed backings, particularly on the doors themselves, surviving until 1972's *The Curse of Peladon*. Also in 1966, all three indented walls had about four inches trimmed from their tops for reasons that are unclear (possibly to remove damage).

The three photographic walls were also much used throughout the 1960s and beyond, sometimes even in preference to the indented sections. During the show's third production block, after recording of *The Daleks' Master Plan*, the three photographic sections were remade. The original photo of whatever the source material was had probably long since been discarded, so it seems one of the existing walls was itself re-photographed: the same slight shift in perspective of the circumference ridges towards the edges is evident, but they have noticeably less detail and greater contrast between the light and dark areas (this may have been deliberate of obscure the scuffs and scratches the originals had acquired). One puzzle is that the new photographic walls were slightly larger, having an extra quarter or so of a roundel down both sides. Did the original prints wrap around their timber frames so, when unpicked, more of the roundels were revealed? Close examination of photos and surviving episodes seems to indicate a new pair of photographic walls were produced for *The Mind Robber*, where the roundels at the edge are clearly cropped differently than previously seen, and then a third before *The War Games*. This last is probably the one used in the three appearances of a photographic wall in colour.

SPINNING AROUND

As televisions pictures improved with the move to a higher definition in 1967 and colour in 1970, these photographic sections became less convincing as genuine three-dimensional walls. This wasn't helped by their not always being erected the right way up. Being fixed to a frame rather than hung from a rail meant they could be positioned on any side. The first instance of this occurs in *The Reign of Terror* episode six, where one of the set's three photographic walls is upside down (the shadows are at the bottom of the rings), but is clearer when repeated in *Planet of Giants* episode one. In the first episode of *The Space Museum* one was placed on its side, with the roundels aligned in rows rather than columns. This practice reached its peak in *The Mind Robber* episode one, when the bulk of the control room was composed of photographic walls on their sides. This created the impression of a single wide wall with uniform

IT'S BIGGER ON THE INSIDE

rows of roundels. Clearly by this time no thought was given to whether they even had a correct orientation, and from *The Web of Fear* onwards only once do they appear correctly: shadows at the top. When *Doctor Who* moved into colour production, a photographic wall was usually used discreetly owing to its obvious flatness but once, in *Colony in Space* episode one, it appears quite clearly (fortunately this time it was the right way up but had a big crease across the middle). One last appeared as part of the control room in *The Curse of Peladon* in 1972, but its final use (barely glimpsed on screen) was in *The Time Monster* the same year.

The computer bank wall was used frequently throughout the series' first production block but less so thereafter: only twice each in the second and third blocks (as far as we can tell, given many episodes are missing). Its five sections were not always all used, and might be arranged in different configurations but always with the widest section in the centre as originally designed. It appears to make a reappearance at the start of *The Tomb of the Cybermen* but this is in fact the photographic backdrop first used in *The Dalek Invasion of Earth* so it's possible the original – last seen in *The Celestial Toymaker* episode four – no longer existed by 1967. Then out of the blue, in *The War Games* episode ten the control room gained a simplified reconstruction of the computer bank.

The interior doors were similarly used less and less after the first year, last appearing at the end of *The Ark* as Dodo shows off her latest outfit. These originally had vacuum-formed recessed roundels too, smaller than those on the main walls, but by *The Chase* they had been replaced by flat inserts. The overhead light was abandoned even sooner as it was heavy, tricky to hang and interfered with the studio lighting. After the initial trio of stories, it appears only in episode one of *The Chase*, by when its depth had been reduced to make it lighter.

ONE-OFF WALLS

Further bespoke walls made occasional appearances throughout the 1960s. Other than the framed perspex screens that Brachacki had made but which were little used after the first few stories (last seen in *The Rescue* episode two) and occasional plain flats used to fill in gaps and cover joins, there were some notable additions to the general control room architecture. First came the equipment bay featured throughout *The Web Planet*. This annexe was to the left of the main doors, with the interior doorway on its left, and contained various cabinets and devices including the astral map. It was seen again, without the equipment, in *The Chase* as the area where the Doctor worked on the time and space visualiser, although it was now separated from the main doors by a photographic wall. At some point between *The Daleks' Master Plan* and *The Power of the Daleks*, the floor stopped being painted blue.

Greater variety was introduced during Patrick Troughton's custody of the TARDIS, even as scenes in the control room became scarcer. Off-screen photos from the missing first episode of *The Abominable Snowmen* show panels of dials and meters, stock pieces that were used repeatedly in other sets during this period. Similar ones appear in episode six of *The Wheel in Space* forming part of a new scanner wall. Yet another is used in *The Mind Robber* episode one to the right of the long photographic wall and beside a new corridor leading from the control room directly to the power room. Finally, in *Colony in Space* there was a panel on the far-right of the set with white pushbuttons on coloured strips.

Throughout these variations two things remained constant: Peter Brachacki's six-sided 'mushroom' console and walls pattered with circles – features that would be used in control room designs up to the present day and without which the TARDIS just wouldn't be the TARDIS.

IT'S BIGGER ON THE INSIDE

CONTROL ROOM LAYOUTS AND CONTENTS

	Main doors	Indented wall 1	Indented wall 2	Photo wall 1	Photo wall 2	Photo wall 3	Scanner	Fault locator	Interior doors	Other	Overhead light	Light-cabinet 1	Light-cabinet 2	Brass pillar	Knossos chair	Studded chair	Armillary sphere	Eagles pedestal	Skeleton clock	Fluted pillar	Food machine	Astral map
An Unearthly Child 1	1	2		3	4	5	6															
An Unearthly Child 2	3	2							1													
An Unearthly Child 4	1	2		3	4	5	6															
The Daleks 1	3	4					1	2														
The Daleks 2	1	2																				
The Daleks 7	2	1																				
The Edge of Destruction 1	1	2	7	3	4	5	6	8														
The Edge of Destruction 2	1	2	7	3	4	5	6	8									a					
Marco Polo 3								1														
Marco Polo 5		1																				
Marco Polo 7		1		2																		
The Keys of Marinus 1	1																					
The Aztecs 4				1	2																	
The Sensorites 1	3	2							1													
The Sensorites 6	1	2																				
The Reign of Terror 1	1	2		3	4		5															
The Reign of Terror 6		1		2↻	3		4															
Planet of Giants 1	1	2		3↻	4	5	6															
Planet of Giants 3		1		2	3	4	5															
The Dalek Invasion of Earth 1										b												
The Dalek Invasion of Earth 6	2	1																				
The Rescue 1	1	2		3	4																	
The Rescue 2	4	2	3	1																		
The Romans 4	2	1																				
The Web Planet 1	3							1	2c													
The Web Planet 2	2								1c													
The Web Planet 3	2								1c													
The Crusade 4		1	2																			
The Space Museum 1	1	2		3↷																		
The Chase 1	4			3↻				1	2c													
The Chase 3				1	2	3↻	4															
The Chase 4	1	2		3	4																	
The Time Meddler 1		4	2				1	3											d			
Galaxy 4 1	1	2		3e																		
The Myth Makers 1				1↻	2																	
The Myth Makers 2	1																					
The Daleks' Master Plan 1	1	2		3	4	5	6															
The Daleks' Master Plan 7	1	2		3	4																	
The Daleks' Master Plan 8	3	2							1													
The Daleks' Master Plan 10	1	2																				
The Daleks' Master Plan 11	2	3		1	4														f	f		
The Ark 4				1	2		3															
The Celestial Toymaker 4				1	2↻	4↷	3															
The Smugglers 1	1	2																				
The Smugglers 4	1	2																				
The Tenth Planet 1	1	2																				
The Tenth Planet 4	1	2																				
The Power of the Daleks 1		3	4	1	2																	
The Underwater Menace 1	1	2																				
The Underwater Menace 4	1	2																				

IT'S BIGGER ON THE INSIDE

	Main doors	Indented wall 1	Indented wall 2	Photo wall 1	Photo wall 2	Photo wall 3	Scanner	Fault locator	Interior doors	Other	Overhead light	Light-cabinet 1	Light-cabinet 2	Brass pillar	Knossos chair	Studded chair	Armillary sphere	Eagles pedestal	Skeleton clock	Fluted pillar	Food machine	Astral map
The Moonbase 1		1	2																			
The Moonbase 4		1	2																			
The Tomb of the Cybermen 1		1	2				3[b]															
The Abominable Snowmen 1		1	2					4		3[g]												
The Enemy of the World 6		1	2	3																		
The Web of Fear 1		1	4	3↗	5↶					2[h]												
Fury from the Deep 6				1↶																		
The Wheel in Space 1	3	4		1↶						2[h]												
The Wheel in Space 6		2		3↶					1[i]											j		
The Mind Robber 1		1	5	2↶	3↶	4[k]																
The Invasion 1	2			1↶																		
The Seeds of Death 1	1			2↶																		
The War Games 10	1	2					3↗	4[l]														
The Claws of Axos 3,4	2	3		1↗[m]																		
Colony in Space 1	2	3		4				1[n]		5[o]												
The Curse of Peladon 1	3	2		1↶																		

Notes

- Numbering indicates position of walls clockwise from screen left
- Scanner listed without fault locator indicates monitor positioned off set for cutaway shots
- Arrows indicate rotation of photographic walls when not upright
- a Not seen but likely present
- b Photographic backdrop
- c Lab section
- d Not usual Westminster Abbey skeleton clock
- e Present but may not have been part of set
- f Associated pedestals marked on floorplan so likely present
- g Computer panels
- h Plain flat section
- i In wall with computer panels
- j Holding small vase
- k New interior doorway incorporating scanner
- l Newly built
- m Placed outside main doors
- n In new flat wall
- o Computer panels (different from g)

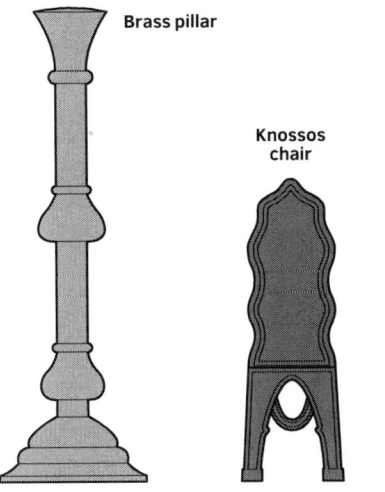

Brass pillar

Knossos chair

Studded chair

Armillary sphere on eagles pedestal

Skeleton clock on fluted pillar

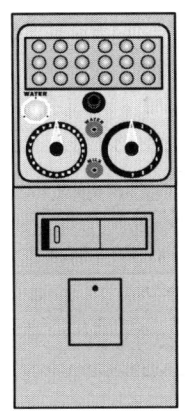

Food machine

Astral map

WHAT ARE ALL THESE KNOBS?

CONSOLE A
1963-1970

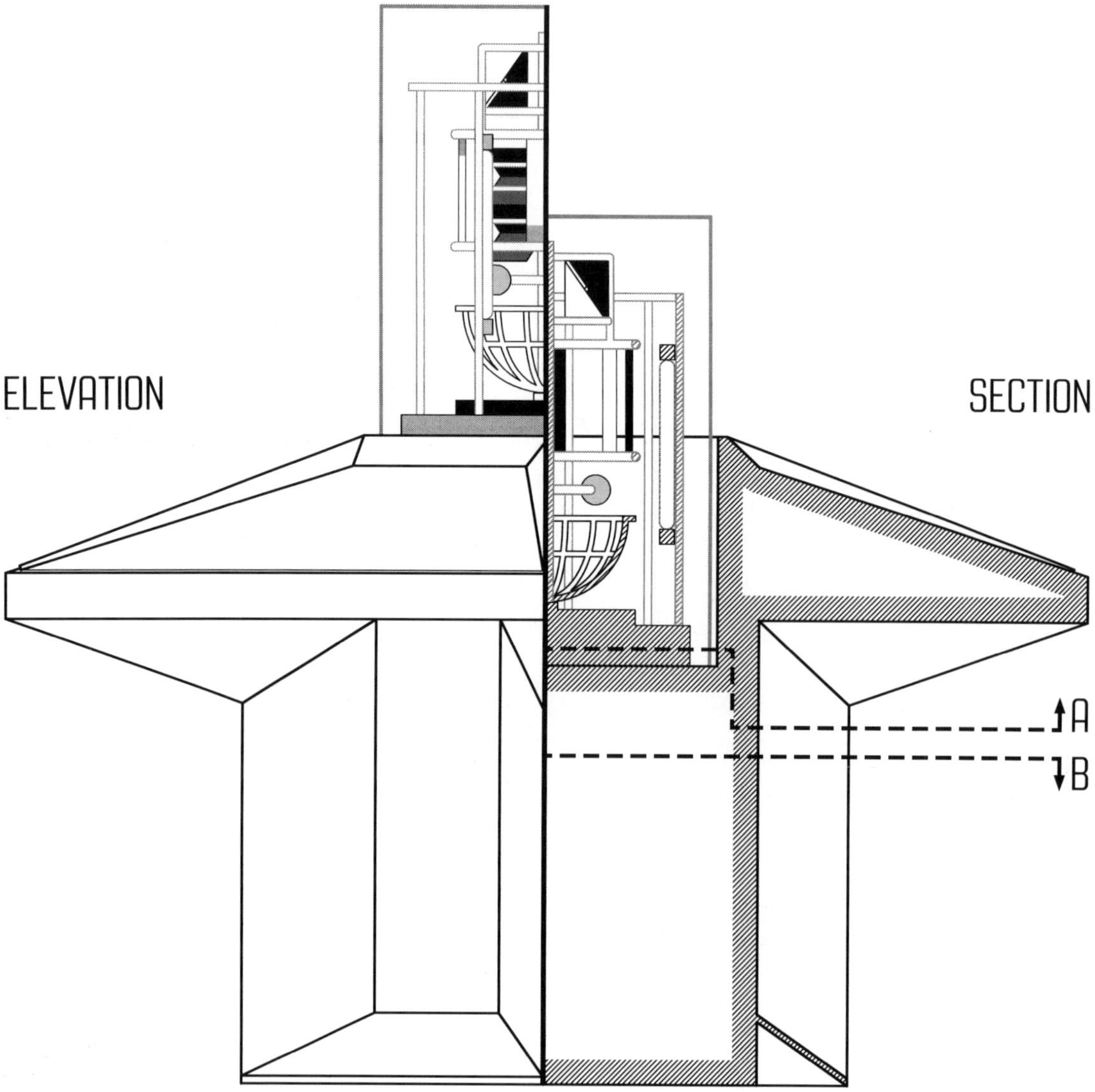

ELEVATION   SECTION

↑A
↓B

A key requirement for Peter Brachacki when designing the TARDIS was to present a craft that could be operated by just one person. His brilliance was in devising a standalone console around which the Doctor would need to move, rather than a desk at which he sat. This was not only unique but placed the console at the heart of the set and allowed for greater dynamism and more varied staging.

The console was one of the first elements Brachacki created and design drawings were prepared by 12 August 1963, six weeks before it would be needed in the studio for recording. These show the familiar hexagonal table with sloping control panels, a narrower pedestal with fins at the corners, and a central clear cylinder. But there are other elements that would ultimately be abandoned. The top edge of each panel was to have acoustic fibre (like on a loudspeaker) covering a microphone. The central

WHAT ARE ALL THESE KNOBS?

PLAN **SECTION A**

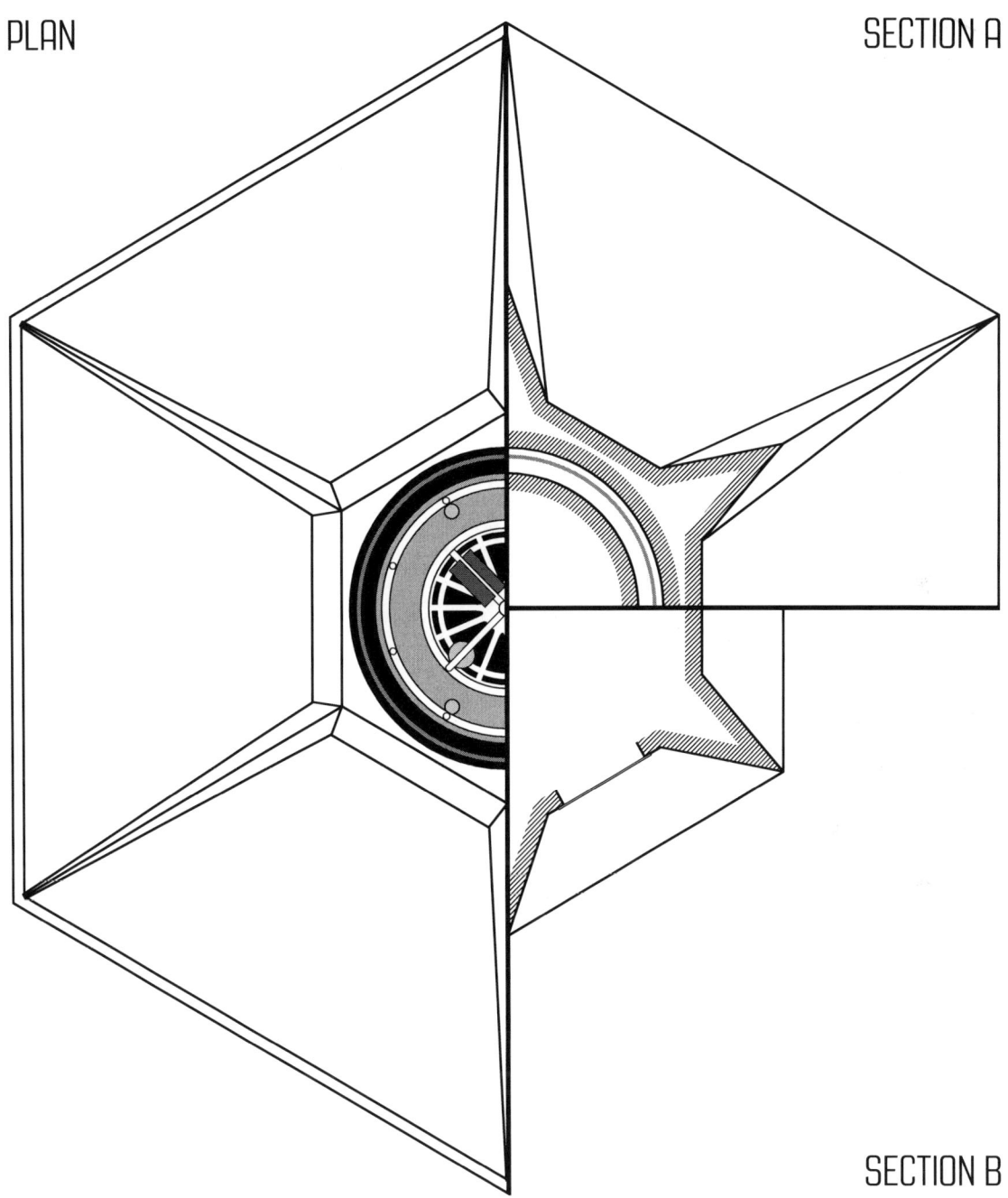

SECTION B

column was in a fixed position and had a curved rim. Finally the console had thick metal handles at each corner to allow the Doctor to spin the required controls towards him, as the whole thing was on six castors. (Initially a round track was placed under the console to guide its rotation but this was discarded after *The Daleks*.)

During construction these elements were refined. The handles were ditched, the microphone shelves became a smaller grille on each panel, and the central cylinder was easier to make with a completely flat top. Two pieces of clear flexible plastic were wrapped around a clear acrylic disc at the top and a wooden disc at the bottom. This looked like a glass drum on the televisions of the time but watching the cleaned-up episodes on DVD now, the seams down either side can sometimes be discerned.

It's not entirely clear who built the original console as the finished prop was a collaboration between several teams inside and outside the BBC. It's generally taken to

WHAT ARE ALL THESE KNOBS?

PILOT EPISODE CONTROLS

The first version of the console's panels had more uniform controls, with a predominance of rotary handles, half-covered lights, black switches and clear plastic levers. All but the last were retained on the final console. Here they are numbered clockwise in accordance with their later refit. The Doctor turns ① to electrify the console; Ian subsequently gets a shock near ②. The Doctor turns ③ (and possibly ① as well) to dematerialise the Ship.

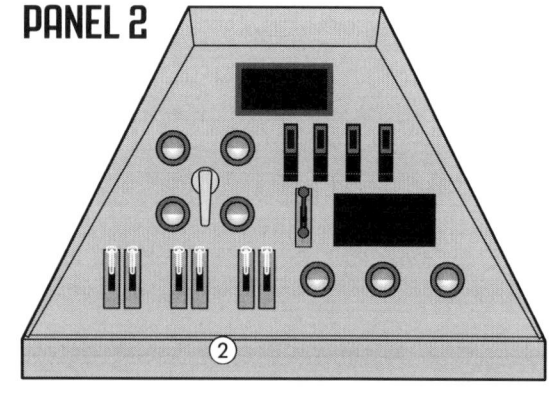

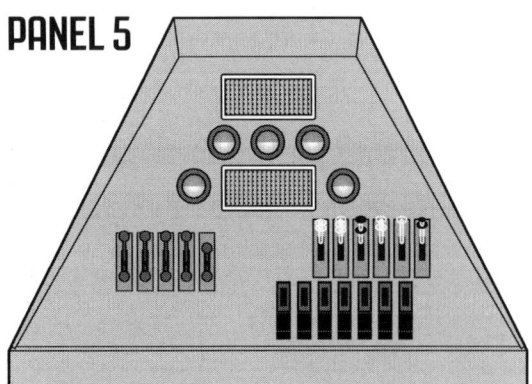

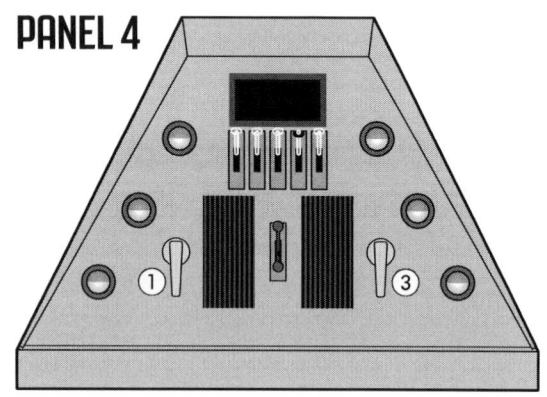

be the work of Shawcraft Models of Uxbridge, run by Bill Roberts, which made models and props for film and exhibition companies, and was later contracted to build the original Daleks. Certainly Shawcraft did some work on the console and became responsible for its storage and upkeep during the early years of the programme, but did it do the initial construction? Brachacki's design drawings are stamped with the words 'Outside contract', yet Jack Kine, head of the BBC's Visual Effects department, recalled the console being "made as a collaborative effort, partly at the scenery workshop, partly by the props department and partly by us at visual effects".

The design drawings do say the six removable control panels were "to be worked on by visual aids" (an earlier term for the Visual Effects department), which was also to make the central column and its "revolving perspex navigation instrument". However, Kine and his staff only recall installing electrical components like lights and an air pump to make the column rise while the TARDIS was in flight then sink back down when the Ship landed. Shawcraft, on the other hand, was expert at working with plastics, so the intricate arrangement of clear rods and rings that made up the central column's inner structure was most likely its work. Equally, after Brachacki's original idea to have the controls moulded to fit the operator's grip was judged too expensive, simpler levers were made from clear acrylic rods and discs to give them an other-worldly feel. These too were something Shawcraft would be best placed to produce.

So it could be the body of the console was constructed by the BBC's scenery crew then passed to Shawcraft to fit the controls and central column, before returning to Visual Effects to wire up the electrics. Or maybe once Shawcraft was involved, it was given the whole project, the design drawings were stamped accordingly, and that's why the company retained possession of the prop.

Its surfaces were painted a pale green, which would look white on monochrome television sets (whereas true white would register too brightly on the electronic cameras of the time). This only became evident when the programme moved to being made in colour and the console made its final appearance in *Inferno* in 1970.

The completed console first went before the cameras in Studio D at Lime Grove, as part of the control room set, on Friday 27 September 1963 for recording of the first episode, 'An Unearthly Child'. Photos taken during studio rehearsals only show one panel; more can be discerned from the episode recording but this only survives as a 16mm film telerecording of a 405-line television picture so detail is limited. Shown above is a best estimate

WHAT ARE ALL THESE KNOBS?

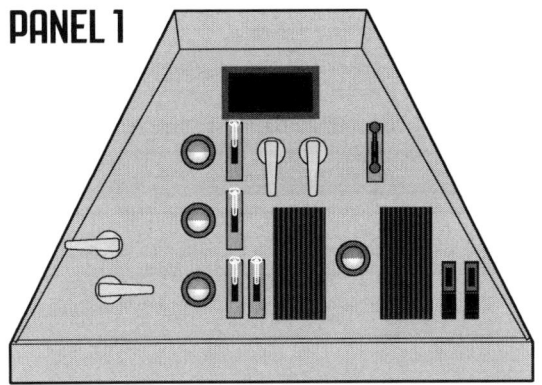

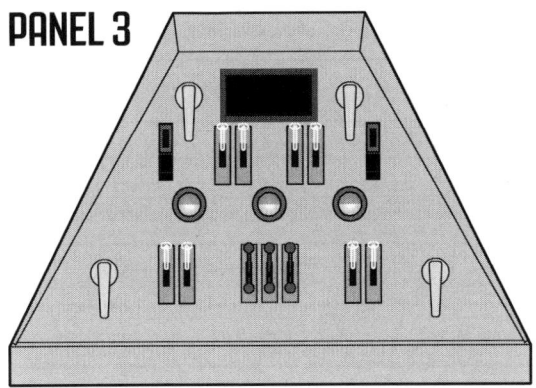

of the arrangement of controls. Panel 1 is only glimpsed from an angle (in particular, it may not have the left-hand black panel), and panel 4 faced the main doors. The sixth panel is not seen on screen but probably matched the final panel layout minus the disc and plate of switches.

Like many other aspects of the programme, when the first episode was scheduled to be re-recorded the console was revamped, probably at the instigation of replacement production designer Barry Newbery. He chose to change the controls almost completely, either because he thought they were too delicate or just to add more variety and make them stand out more on camera. Some elements were kept, such as the half-covered lightbulbs, rotary handles, black slider switches and small levers – although their clear rods were replaced with wooden stems and coloured spherical knob. Notable additions were several large round gauges, illuminated discs, metal plates with dials and flick switches, and the square radiation meter.

Some panel layouts changed more than others. Panel 4 retained its arrangement of lightbulbs, the small levers at the top and the two rotary handles. The centre small lever of the original was replaced by a large sliding knob and two illuminated displays were added. Similarly, panel 5 lost just the left-hand set of small levers, replaced by two large sliders and a red rotary switch.

One aspect not often commented on are the controls *underneath* the panels. Below the front-right edge of panel 2 and the left-hand edge of panel 3 were stuck two pairs of white ridged knobs. These don't appear to have been connected to anything and were probably just there for added interest. As early as *The Edge of Destruction* one of the pair under panel 2 had come off, while both of those below panel 3 were gone by *The Time Meddler*. One is visible underneath the left-hand edge of panel 5 for the first time in this story so, as it wasn't there in *The Web Planet*, it was likely moved from panel 3. Of these remaining two, that under panel 5 survived to at least *The Ambassadors of Death* while the one below panel 2 had gone by *Inferno*, so it's likely both were removed when the console was modified just before the latter story.

The pedestal on which the console stood was a narrow hexagonal column that flared at the bottom, with fins at each corner. It had holes cut in alternate sides (beneath panels 2, 4 and 6) for the electrical cables that powered the lights and air line for the central column mechanism to be connected irrespective of how a director wanted to orient the console. The intention was for the cables always to be behind the console, out of the studio cameras' sights, although occasionally they could be seen on screen. These access holes had hinged covers to hide them when not in use, and sometimes they were used within the show if the Doctor needed to retrieve a component from under the console, such as the fluid link in *The Daleks* or the emergency unit in *The Mind Robber*. At some point in 1966 prior to recording *The Tenth Planet*, metal strips were fixed to the edges of the fins and base to protect them for further knocks during transit, and in January 1968 two metal handles were added under panel 2 for the Doctor and Victoria to hold on to at the start of *The Web of Fear*.

The console understandably suffered wear and tear, losing some controls, gaining others – sometimes only for the episode or two they were required by the script, vanishing as mysteriously as they had appeared. The outer casing of the central column also received running repairs, having the seams down the sides shored up with clear plastic strips and the join with the top disc secured with additional screws between Seasons 3 and 4.

No one in the 1960s gave any thought to clarifying which controls did what or came anywhere close to establishing an instruction manual. William Hartnell may have told colleagues that he had a consistent system of operation, and perhaps he tried to, but watching the episodes themselves shows this to be untrue. Levers are thrown and switches pressed at the convenience of the actors and camera angles, depending on how the console happens to have been positioned, even for such frequent tasks as opening the doors or activating the scanner. The following plans label those controls which we see being used for specified functions, while the main Chronicles detail other uses and changes to the console.

WHAT ARE ALL THESE KNOBS?

PANEL A1

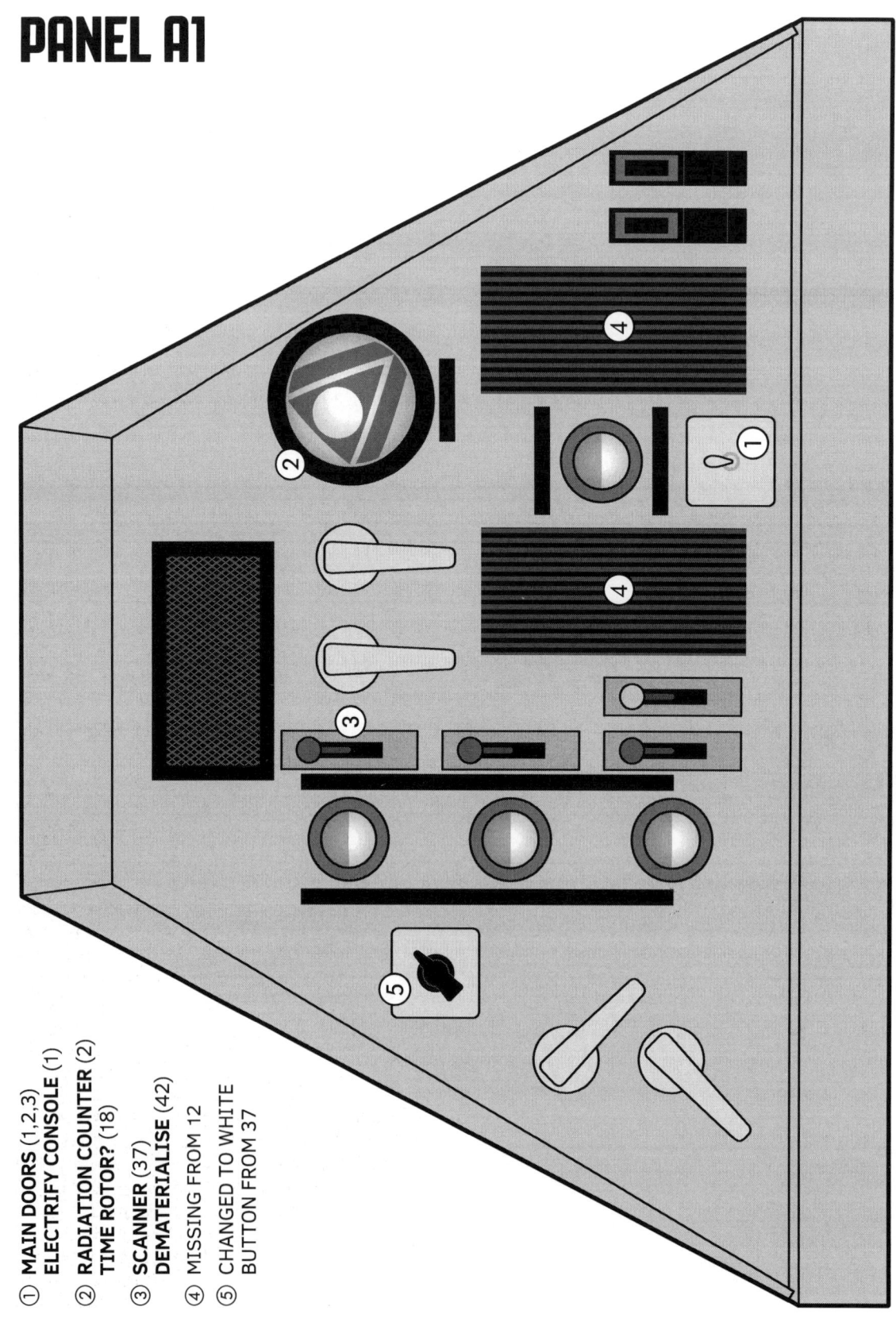

① **MAIN DOORS** (1,2,3)
  ELECTRIFY CONSOLE (1)
② **RADIATION COUNTER** (2)
  TIME ROTOR? (18)
③ **SCANNER** (37)
  DEMATERIALISE (42)
④ MISSING FROM 12
⑤ CHANGED TO WHITE BUTTON FROM 37

PANEL A2

WHAT ARE ALL THESE KNOBS?

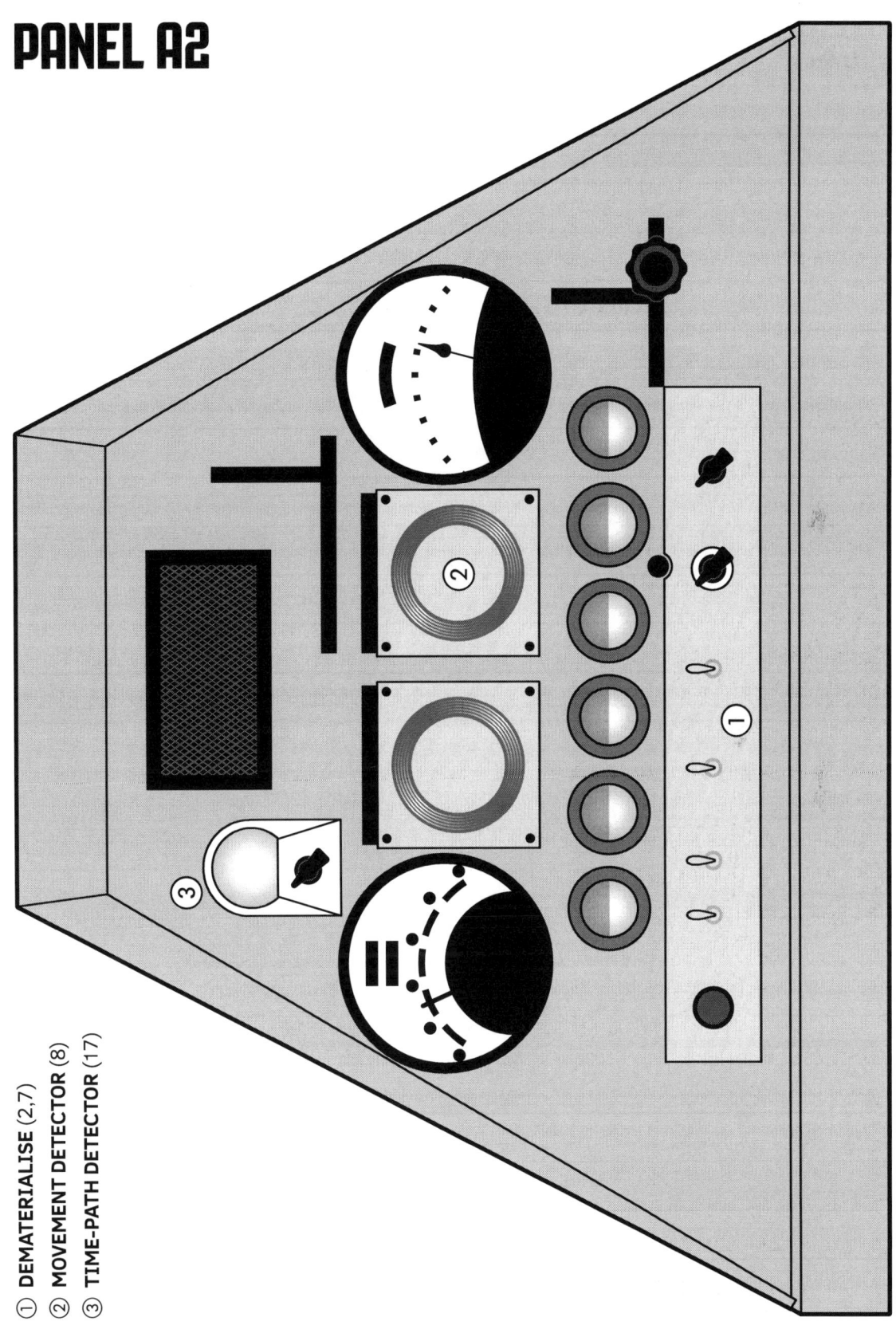

① DEMATERIALISE (2,7)
② MOVEMENT DETECTOR (8)
③ TIME-PATH DETECTOR (17)

WHAT ARE ALL THESE KNOBS?

PANEL A3

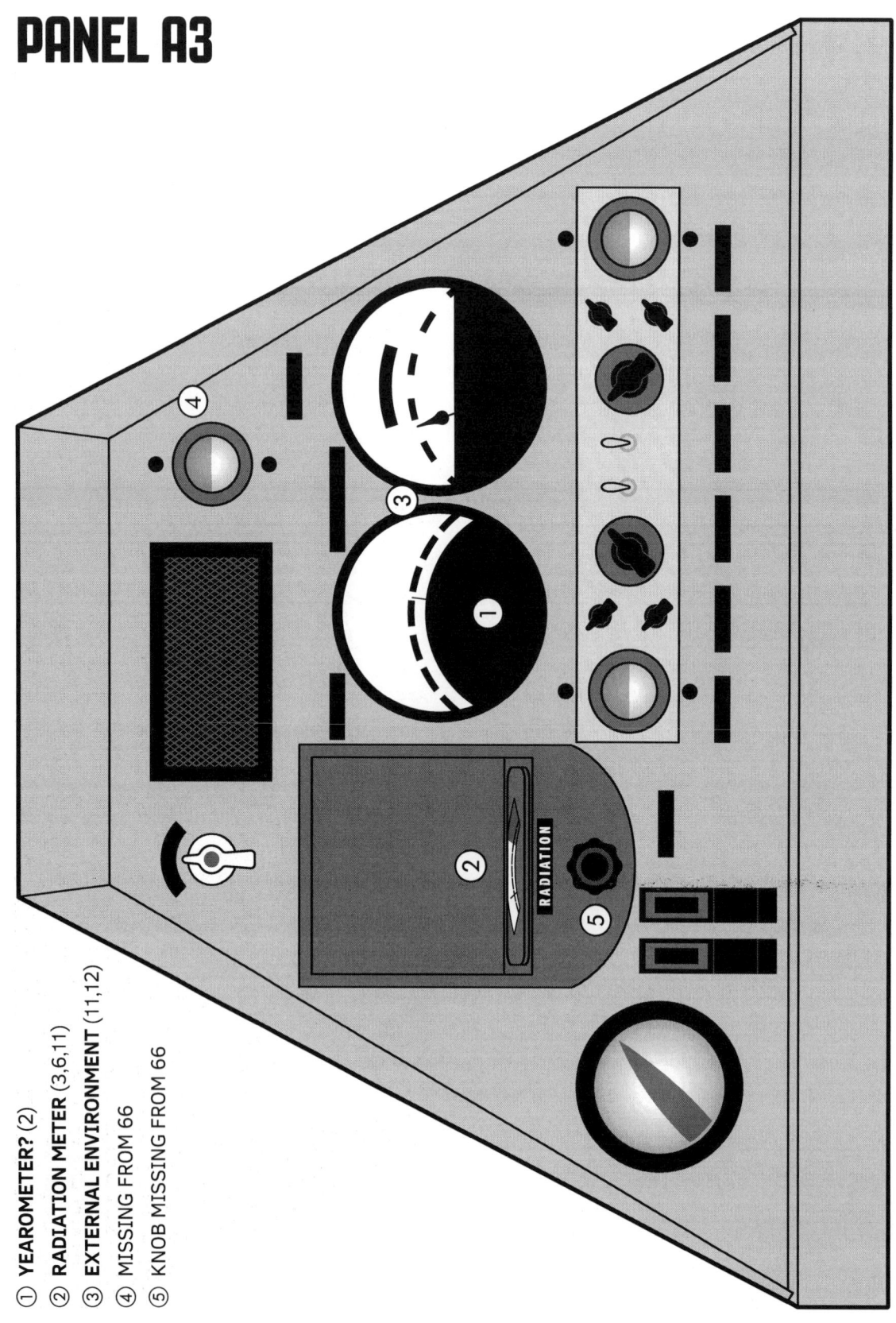

① **YEAROMETER?** (2)
② **RADIATION METER** (3,6,11)
③ **EXTERNAL ENVIRONMENT** (11,12)
④ **MISSING FROM 66**
⑤ **KNOB MISSING FROM 66**

WHAT ARE ALL THESE KNOBS?

PANEL A4

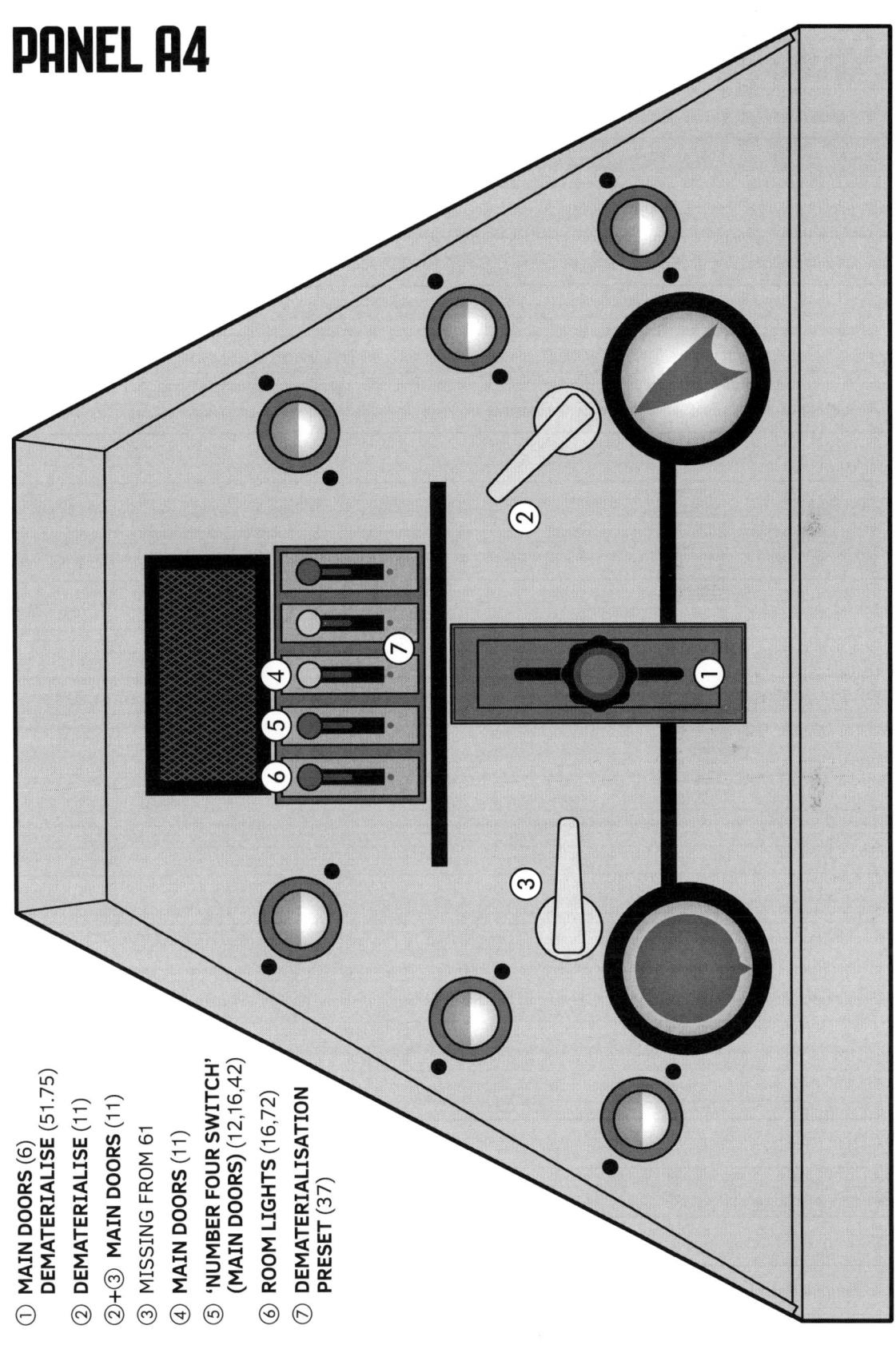

① **MAIN DOORS** (6)
   DEMATERIALISE (51,75)
② **DEMATERIALISE** (11)
②+③ **MAIN DOORS** (11)
③ MISSING FROM 61
④ **MAIN DOORS** (11)
⑤ **'NUMBER FOUR SWITCH'**
   (MAIN DOORS) (12,16,42)
⑥ **ROOM LIGHTS** (16,72)
⑦ **DEMATERIALISATION**
   PRESET (37)

WHAT ARE ALL THESE KNOBS?

PANEL A5

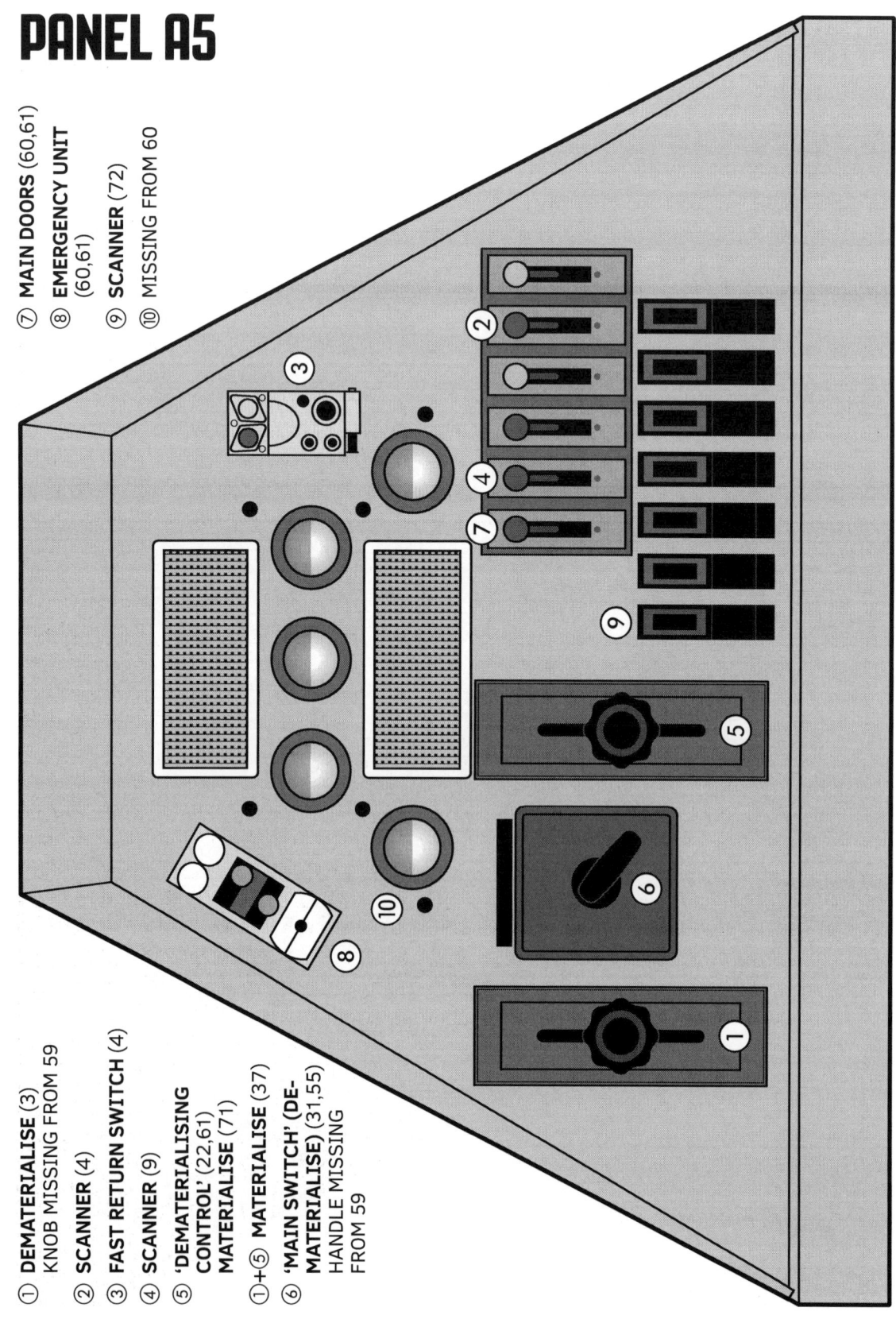

① **DEMATERIALISE** (3)
KNOB MISSING FROM 59
② **SCANNER** (4)
③ **FAST RETURN SWITCH** (4)
④ **SCANNER** (9)
⑤ **'DEMATERIALISING CONTROL'** (22,61)
MATERIALISE (71)
①+⑤ **MATERIALISE** (37)
⑥ **'MAIN SWITCH' (DE-MATERIALISE)** (31,55)
HANDLE MISSING FROM 59
⑦ **MAIN DOORS** (60,61)
⑧ **EMERGENCY UNIT** (60,61)
⑨ **SCANNER** (72)
⑩ MISSING FROM 60

PANEL A6

WHAT ARE ALL THESE KNOBS?

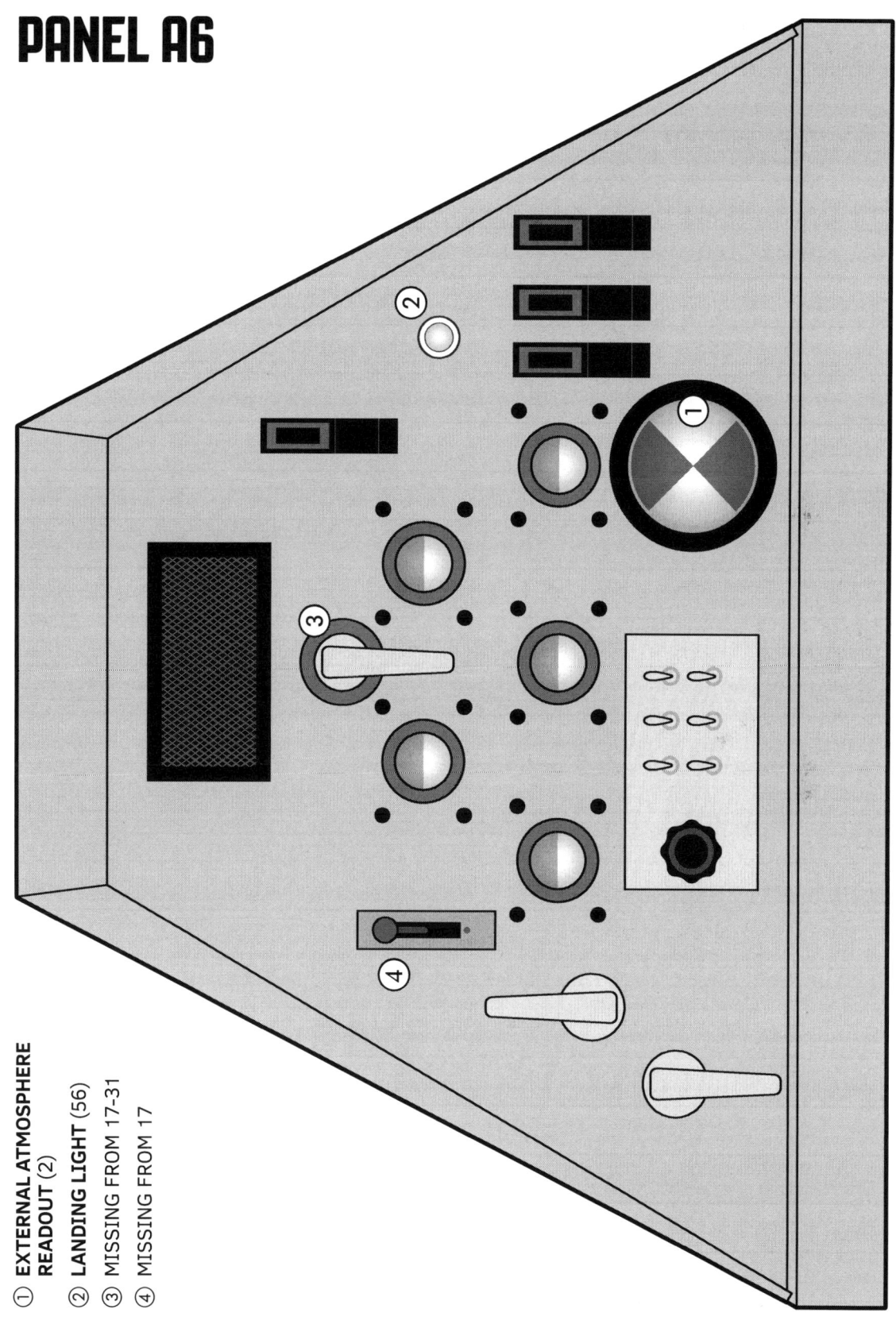

① **EXTERNAL ATMOSPHERE READOUT** (2)
② **LANDING LIGHT** (56)
③ MISSING FROM 17-31
④ MISSING FROM 17

THE JOURNEY BEGINS

SPACE Gallifrey, Citadel, repair shop
TIME Unknown
TRAVELLERS The Doctor, Susan
EPISODES The Name of the Doctor

The Doctor and his young granddaughter have decided they need urgently to leave their home world so he guides her to the lowest levels of the Time Lords' citadel where faulty TARDISes awaiting repair or decommission are left unguarded: after all, who would want to steal them? He has previously selected one of the uncamouflaged time machines – something about it excited him when he first touched its console, as if it wanted him to steal it – and he ushers Susan inside, unaware they have tripped an alarm.

For an imperceptible moment the timeline flickers. It seems a stern man in Victorian gentleman's dress is preventing their egress but then a young woman replaces him and makes sure the Doctor sticks with his original choice of TARDIS, despite its faulty navigation system. Then she too is gone and events continue as if neither was ever there.

The Doctor joins Susan inside. They know if they leave they may never be able to come back, effectively exiling themselves. But their minds are made up and together they set the Ship in motion. Before anyone can stop it, the TARDIS is spinning through the Vortex, away from Gallifrey and towards who knows where.

- **NOTES** When stealing the TARDIS, the Doctor and Susan look as we're used to seeing them: he is already dressed in tailcoat, wing-collar shirt and checked trousers, and has a lined face with long white hair; she appears no younger than when attending Coal Hill School and wears a short skirt. Even given that Time Lords (if indeed Susan is one) may not visibly age as fast as humans, this limits how long they can be travelling alone before first gaining companions from Earth.
- The long shots of the pair use stand-in actors (Kevin Legg and Grania Pickard) but the close-ups of the Doctor are clips rotoscoped from episodes and given muted colour. The shot of him about to enter the TARDIS is taken from episode two of *The Aztecs* as he enters the temple to talk to Barbara; his stern face as he listens to Clara is from episode four as he talks with Cameca for the last time. The dialogue, "Yes, what is it? What do you want?" is lifted from episode five of *The Web Planet*, addressed to the Menoptra Prapillus when planning their attack on the Carsenome.
- The appearance of a row of TARDISes as silver cylinders with inset rectangular doors was scripted as being their 'neutral state'. Cut dialogue had Fabian saying, "Someone is stealing one of the TARDISes. Type forty, malfunctioning cloaking device," which his fellow technician Andro corrected to, "Chameleon circuit." Fabian asked, "What's a chameleon?" to which Andro replied, "Dunno." This would have contradicted what Susan says in *An Unearthly Child*, that the TARDIS had changed appearance during prior landings.

PREVIOUS LANDINGS

SPACE Earth, [Europe]
TIME Various
TRAVELLERS The Doctor, Susan
EPISODES Mentioned by Susan in An Unearthly Child 2

When the chameleon circuit was working and the Ship could change its appearance to blend into its surroundings, it had disguised itself as an ionic column and a sedan chair.

- **NOTES** Both disguises suggest previous visits to Earth before Susan met Barbara Wright.
- Ionic columns have been in use since the 6th century BC, originating during Greece's Archaic Period, a time of great cultural development that the Doctor is sure to have been interested to visit (see below for one possible occasion).
- The sedan chair is a form of litter – a seat suspended on two poles so it can be carried – used across Europe from at least the Renaissance until the early-19th century, when horse-drawn hackney carriages became more popular.

SPACE Earth, England
TIME Late-19th century
TRAVELLERS The Doctor, Susan
EPISODES Mentioned by the Doctor in The Edge of Destruction 2

The Doctor acquired a rather large tweed Ulster coat from comic-opera writers William Gilbert and Arthur Sullivan.

- **NOTES** This was before he met Ian Chesterton so must be before Landing 1.
- The implication is the Doctor met Gilbert and Sullivan although this may be apocryphal. His use of the term "acquired" could mean he was given the coat or bought it, or even that he stole it. Gilbert and Sullivan collaborated from 1871 to 1896.

SPACE Venus
TIME Unknown
TRAVELLERS The Doctor, Susan
EPISODES Mentioned by Susan in Marco Polo 2

Susan has been to Venus, where the seas are composed of a liquid metal.

- **NOTES** When Ping-Cho describes the moonlit desert as like "a great silver sea" it reminds Susan of the metal seas of Venus, suggesting she has seen these herself (although it's possible she has only heard of or read about them).
- Although Susan is talking to Ping-Cho, there's no time since Ian and Barbara joined Susan and the Doctor that they could have travelled to Venus, so this must be before Landing 1.
- In his third incarnation, the Doctor was partial to practising Venusian aikido, knew a Venusian

lullaby and mentions how untrustworthy a Venusian shanghorn is with a perigosto stick, all possibly learned during this visit. By his fourth incarnation, the Doctor had a pilot's licence for the Mars-Venus rocket run but this may have been acquired sometime after the 40th century as it's suggested in *The Daleks' Master Plan* that humans had colonised Venus by that time.

SPACE Earth, [Greece]
TIME [4th century BC]
TRAVELLERS The Doctor, Susan
EPISODES Mentioned by the Doctor in
 The Keys of Marinus 6

The Doctor met the Ancient Greek philosopher Pyrrho, who founded Scepticism.

- **NOTES** This was before the Doctor met Ian so must be prior to Landing 1. It could be the occasion when the TARDIS disguised itself as an ionic column (see above).
- Born about 360BC on the Mediterranean island of Elis, Pyrrho travelled to the East with Alexander the Great, a figure the Doctor is very likely to want to know, so perhaps he met them both on that expedition. Shortly after his third regeneration, the Doctor does imply he has met Alexander, and a script featuring an encounter with the Macedon king was in preparation while *The Keys of Marinus* was in production, although it didn't feature Pyrrho as a character.
- It's odd the Doctor recommends Ian "should read Pyrrho" as the philosopher produced no writings himself. What we know of his ideas is derived from reports of accounts made by his follower Timon and, for his being a proponent of scepticism, the later interpretations of Sextus Empiricus – although perhaps the Doctor knows something we don't.

SPACE Earth, England, London
TIME Early-16th century
TRAVELLERS The Doctor, Susan
EPISODES Recalled by the Doctor in
 The Sensorites 1

The Doctor deliberately quarrelled with King Henry VIII in order to be sent to the Tower of London where the TARDIS was – whether it had landed or been taken there is unknown.

- **NOTES** The Doctor recalls this trip – which Susan also remembers so it's not apocryphal for once – as happening "long before [Barbara and Ian] appeared on the scene", suggesting they were travelling alone for some time before Landing 1.
- The Doctor later encounters Henry VIII again during his twelfth incarnation (see Landing 551 in volume 2).

SPACE Esto
TIME Unknown
TRAVELLERS The Doctor, Susan
EPISODES Described by Susan in The Sensorites 2

On this planet the plants communicate using thought transference. If they detect another mind interrupting their connection they begin screeching (possibly telepathically rather than audibly).

- **NOTES** The visit to Esto must have been before Susan met Barbara.
- This may also be where Susan heard a sound like that made by time-accelerated foliage on Marinus, although on that occasion she couldn't remember where she previously heard it.

SPACE Earth
TIME Early-19th century
TRAVELLERS The Doctor, Susan
EPISODES Claimed by the Doctor in
 The Sensorites 5

The Doctor met the socialite and fashion trendsetter George 'Beau' Brummell, who told him he looked better in a cloak.

- **NOTES** This was before the Doctor met Ian.
- When in his sixth incarnation, the Doctor mentions how Brummell was ridiculed for his fashion sense, something he may have witnessed here.

SPACE [Earth, Europe]
TIME [Mid-1910s]
TRAVELLERS The Doctor, Susan
EPISODES Mentioned by Susan and the Doctor in
 Planet of Giants 3

At some location the Doctor and Susan dodged shrapnel during an air raid by Zeppelins.

- **NOTES** This was before the Doctor and Susan met Ian and Barbara.
- If the Doctor is being precise in his use of the term Zeppelins ("What infernal machines") then this was most likely during the First World War. While Germany carried out a bombing campaign across Britain, it did target other Allied countries too.

SPACE Dido
TIME Before 2493
TRAVELLERS The Doctor, Susan
EPISODES Discussed by the Doctor in The Rescue 1

The Doctor visited Dido when the planet was sparsely populated, with barely a hundred humanoid inhabitants, whom he found peaceful as any violence would jeopardise their society's survival. He learned something of their ceremonial traditions and that they had just perfected a handheld tool that projected a powerful ray, which they used in construction. He did not encounter any sand beasts or the traps in the cave.

- **NOTES** This was before Ian and Barbara were travelling in the TARDIS.

■ By the time *The Rescue* was shown, the TARDIS had been seen to land on Earth repeatedly at different points in human history, so it's perhaps not surprising the Doctor should also have been to Dido before. Something about the rock he analyses must indicate the time period as he's certain his return (see Landing 12) post-dates this visit.

SPACE Earth, Italy, Rome
TIME Unknown past
TRAVELLERS The Doctor, Susan
EPISODES Mentioned by the Doctor in The Romans 1
The Doctor went to Rome and considered it to be a "fascinating" city.
■ **NOTES** The Doctor begins telling Vicki a tale of his previous visit to Rome as they go to pack for their journey but is out of earshot before we hear any details. As Ian and Barbara are also keen to see ancient Rome, this previous visit of the Doctor's is probably before he met them.
■ The Doctor may have visited the city at any time in its history but, in the context of telling Vicki what to expect, he probably means Ancient Rome, so some time between the 8th century BC and the 5th century AD.

SPACE Earth, [America, Montana]
TIME [After 1864]
TRAVELLERS The Doctor, Susan
EPISODES Claimed by the Doctor in The Romans 2
The Doctor says he taught the Mountain Mauler of Montana how to wrestle, suggesting a visit to that North American region at some time after it was first named Montana Territory.
■ **NOTES** This may be apocryphal to impress Vicki. Our history doesn't record such a wrestler but if he was a local hero he may be the inspiration for the name of current Montanan junior ice hockey team the Missoula Maulers. Alternatively, the Doctor's visit may have been in the future.
■ If it did occur, it was before the Doctor met Vicki; while there are potential gaps for unseen landings prior to *The Rescue*, it's more likely this encounter was before Landing 1. Perhaps the Doctor taught the Mauler a form of Venusian aikido.

SPACE Earth, Denmark, Copenhagen
TIME [1837]
TRAVELLERS The Doctor, Susan
EPISODES Claimed by the Doctor in The Romans 3
The Doctor met author of fairy tales Hans Christian Andersen and gave him the idea for the story 'The Emperor's New Clothes'.
■ **NOTES** Again, this was before Vicki joined the Doctor's travels and thus likely prior to Landing 1.
■ Andersen acknowledged that he adapted his story of a ruler fooled into going out naked by swindling weavers from *Das Novellenbuch*, a German anthology of old European fables edited by Edvard von Bülow and published in 1836. The particular story, 'So ist der Lauf der Welt', was itself translated from the 1335 Spanish book of morality tales by Don Juan Manuel *Libro de los Ejemplos del Conde Lucanor y de Patronio*. So perhaps the Doctor directed Andersen to a copy of the former, or even the latter, and recommended the tale for his own *Eventyr, Fortalte for Børn*. He may also have been instrumental in Andersen's last-minute change to the ending of 'Kejserens nye Klæder' so that a child now spoke out about the emperor's nakedness.

SPACE [Earth, Scotland]
TIME [Mid-18th century]
TRAVELLERS The Doctor, Susan
EPISODES Mentioned by the Doctor in The Space Museum 2
The Doctor met a man who was inspired by steam from a kettle to make a great discovery.
■ **NOTES** Barbara infers that the Doctor is talking about James Watt and the story of how as a child he watched the vapour from a boiling kettle and was inspired to develop the steam engine. Yet when she offers this as the name the Doctor is struggling to recall, he barely acknowledges her and certainly doesn't confirm it. Watt is indeed renowned for developing more efficient steam engines that went on to power the Industrial Revolution. His key contribution was to condense steam in a separate chamber from the piston so that the latter didn't waste energy by being constantly reheated – an insight arrived at in 1765 while he was working as an instrument maker for Glasgow University, so perhaps the Doctor met Watt there. Is this one of the "greatest discoveries", though, given the power of steam was known about long before Watt? Indeed, his own work was based on improving existing steam engines, in particular the atmospheric engine created by Thomas Newcomen. The story of Watt's childhood interest in steam may not be apocryphal, however. It seems to originate from his cousin Marion Campbell, who grew up with him in Greenock, and was promulgated by his son James Watt Jr in the 1830s to establish his late father's attention to the heat properties of steam (rather than just its already well-known power) long before anyone else. Watt Sr's own notes from 1765 and later also show he did use tea-kettles in his experiments. It has been suggested, however, that while Watt's understanding of the properties of steam may have helped in his development of better steam engines, it was his thoughts on the chemical composition of water, perhaps in advance of his contemporaries Henry Cavendish and Antoine Lavoisier, that were inspired by his

childhood kettle-watching. Could this be the great discovery the Doctor is thinking of? Was he there in Greenock in the middle of the 18th century to see (or even cause) the moment of that spark in the young Watt's mind?

SPACE Rings of Akhaten, Tiaanamaat
TIME Unknown
TRAVELLERS The Doctor, Susan
EPISODES Mentioned by the Doctor in
    The Rings of Akhaten

The Doctor brought his granddaughter to the marketplace orbiting the gas-giant planet of Akhaten. He very much enjoyed the diversity of alien lifeforms living and trading in harmony.

▣ **NOTES** The Doctor tells Clara in *The Rings of Akhaten* (Landing 576, vol.2) that he previously visited the bazaar on Tiaanamaat (a name for the asteroid used in production documents but not on screen) with his granddaughter "a long time ago". This means for him personally, but it may not have been very long before that story as he and Dor'een know each other (depending on how long-lived her species is).

SPACE Earth
TIME Unknown
TRAVELLERS The Doctor, Susan
EPISODES Seen on the scanner in
    The Edge of Destruction

The TARDIS arrived in a temperate countryside on a sunny day with birdsong in the air.

SPACE Quinnis
TIME Unknown
TRAVELLERS The Doctor, Susan
EPISODES Seen on the scanner in
    The Edge of Destruction

According to the Doctor, the planet Quinnis is "of the fourth universe". The TARDIS arrived in a misty jungle where Susan and her grandfather were separated from the Ship and had difficulty recovering it.

▣ **NOTES** The trip to Quinnis is specifically said to be recent – "Four or five journeys back," according to Susan – so it must have been just before the TARDIS arrived in Totter's Lane. She also recalls the pastoral location (and doesn't contradict Barbara's assertion it could be England). If the sequence is in order, then the countryside visit was before Quinnis. Alternatively, it's possible that after Quinnis the TARDIS landed in 20th-century England and was physically transported to London when Susan decided she wanted to stay on Earth for a while; it's unlikely the Doctor successfully performed a short hop within the same timezone given his apparent inability to control the TARDIS at this stage. Then again, it's suggested in episode two of *An Unearthly Child* that it's the loss of his notebook that causes the Doctor to have problems directing the Ship, so perhaps before that he was in full control.

▣ The TARDIS's visit to Quinnis is later recounted by Susan in the Big Finish audio play *Quinnis* by Marc Platt. It arrives in the township of Bridgetown, built high above the surface jungle, during a severe drought. The Doctor successfully makes it rain but the Ship is washed away in the resulting flood.

LANDING 1

SPACE Earth, England, London, Shoreditch,
    76 Totter's Lane
TIME Five months in [1962 to] 1963
TRAVELLERS The Doctor, Susan
EPISODES An Unearthly Child 1

The Doctor has been travelling with the Hand of Omega – a stellar manipulator developed by the Time Lords – and needs somewhere safe to conceal it. When the TARDIS arrives in England in the mid-20th century, Susan is keen to learn more about the culture and the Doctor agrees to stay awhile. Susan enrols at Coal Hill School in Shoreditch, London while the Doctor makes arrangements to have the Hand of Omega buried in a nearby graveyard. He also tries to repair some faulty components in the TARDIS with the technology available to him, although he seems yet to notice that the chameleon circuit is showing its first signs of malfunctioning: although a Police Box is a suitable contemporary disguise, it is out of place in a junkyard.

After five months, Susan returns to the TARDIS at the end of another day at school. Her grandfather is not there so she settles down to read a book about the French Revolution while listening to pop music. Unknown to her, two of her teachers have followed her, curious about why her home appears to be a scrapyard. Ian Chesterton and Barbara Wright enter the yard to look for her and are surprised to find a Police Box among the bric-a-brac, especially as this one is humming with power and feels alive to the touch.

They hide when the Doctor returns but as he opens the box's door they hear Susan call out to him and inadvertently reveal themselves. The Doctor quickly shuts the door and denies hearing anything or the possibility of there being anyone inside. Finding him obstructive, the teachers are about to leave to find a policeman when Susan, puzzled by what is keeping her grandfather, opens the door again and the two teachers push their way in, thinking to rescue her.

They are bemused to find themselves within the large bright control room of the TARDIS, which Susan says is her home and the Doctor admits is a vessel that can travel anywhere in time and space. The teachers cannot take it all in and believe it to be an illusion, part of a game the girl and her grandfather are playing.

The Doctor, however, refuses to let them out, fearing they will talk about what they have seen, leading others to investigate. He insists that if the teachers are released then he and Susan must leave Earth. She is not ready to give up her life on Earth and petulantly threatens to stay behind without him, so the Doctor makes a hurried dematerialisation. Susan tries to wrestle him away from the controls, causing a bumpy take-off that knocks both teachers unconscious. The scanner shows an aerial view of London receding as the Doctor and Susan stand by the console.

- **CONTROLS** The main doors are here controlled by the flick-switch at the bottom of panel A1. The Doctor appears to use the same switch to electrify the control on panel A2 (far-right switch at the bottom) that Ian tries when attempting to open the main doors – presumably a function to prevent the console being tampered with. When the Doctor tries to take off surreptitiously, he first flicks switches on panel A2 although the dematerialisation sound doesn't begin until he operates a control on panel A4 (possibly the large slider), where Susan tries to pull him away from the console.
- The flick-switch at the bottom of panel A1 actually operates the lightbulb immediately above it. It's a popular control: Susan flicks it off and on to close the main doors; when the Doctor mentions finding "a replacement for that faulty filament" he takes something (presumably said item) from his pocket and attaches it under the console then flicks the same switch off and on; and when Ian is trying to find the doors control on the console, the Doctor reaches for this switch. He isn't seen to operate it but the implication is he has electrified the console, or at least the part of it Ian touches, to prevent unauthorised use. As Ian is nowhere near the right control to open the main doors anyway, this looks like the Doctor is just being malicious.
- Similarly, the switches at the bottom of panel A2 are wired to the row of lightbulbs above them and to the two central rotating-light units.
- **LORE** From outside, the TARDIS makes a low hum and touching it reveals a slight vibration.
- The Doctor makes his first attempt at explaining how the TARDIS is bigger on the inside than the outside. He compares it to displaying a large building on a television screen in a small sitting room, thereby making it seem like the former is inside the latter. Given that he's trying to discredit Ian's insistence that the TARDIS is an illusion, this is a weak analogy as the television image is only a representation of the real object. So he's suggesting the Ship's interior is similarly a representation, image or, indeed, illusion.
- Susan claims she coined the name TARDIS from the initials of Time And Relative Dimension In Space. Given that later in the series TARDIS seems to be the accepted name for all of the Time Lords' time-space machines, some have speculated that Susan (and thus the Doctor) must have been involved in their initial creation on Gallifrey.
- It's established that the central column of the console stays in its lowest position when the TARDIS is stationary, then oscillates up and down when the Ship dematerialises. However, this action was not applied consistently in the series' early years.
- If Susan is still listening to her transistor radio while waiting in the Ship for the Doctor to return, then radio waves must be able to penetrate its outer shell. Alternatively she may have tuned the scanner to her preferred radio station.
- As the TARDIS takes off, images from the programme's opening titles are superimposed over shots of the Doctor and Susan, the first suggestion that these are intended as a representation of travel through the dimensions.
- **NOTES** It's established in *Remembrance of the Daleks*, although not stated here, that Coal Hill School is in the Shoreditch area of London. It's not clear how far away Totter's Lane is: Susan is happy to walk home from school (and her teachers let her, so it can't be an unsafe distance) but they themselves drive, as do the Doctor and Ace during their return to the area shortly after. Decades later there is a sign for IM Foreman's junkyard placed right outside the school entrance but this is perhaps a souvenir to commemorate the area's industrial past, since lost to redevelopment. When the TARDIS takes off, the scanner shows a view of the City (see below), certainly a walkable distance from Shoreditch but an unlikely location for a junkyard, particularly one between houses and a big wall.
- Susan tells Barbara, "I love your school. I love England in the 20th century. The last five months have been the happiest of my life." It's not clear if she's referring to her time in England or specifically at the school – the TARDIS might have landed some time before she enrolled – but she must have been attending for much of that time for her teachers to become so intrigued by her. (Although arguably, if she has been mixing with teenagers and blissing out to pop music for five months, surely she would have figured out the pre-decimal currency by now – or has she been using psychic paper to get anything she wants for free?) We might also wonder what the Doctor has been doing with himself all this time.
- It's confirmed in episode two of *An Unearthly Child* that it was 1963 when the TARDIS left the junkyard at Totter's Lane, but there's nothing to say it was November, as is often assumed because that's when the first episode was broadcast. (Indeed, when the scripts were initially being written the intention was for the series to begin in September.) All we know is that it's dark shortly after school finishes for the day and that there has been fog recently, so certainly in the colder months but at which end of the year? The winter of 1962/63 was famously severe, with heavy snows and freezing temperatures across Britain – even the sea around the south-east coast froze, something surely the Doctor would be interested to witness. There's no sign of snow on the ground when Ian and Barbara drive to Totter's Lane, but in the first week of March 1963

temperatures in London rose and the snow thawed. Also note that Ian warns Susan, "There'll probably be fog again tonight," although come the evening there is none, suggesting the nights are getting warmer. November 1963, on the other hand, was very wet, with 114mm of rain falling in London during the month.

▮ Most significantly, when the Doctor returns to London at least a month later (see Landing 291) the weather is hardly typical of December or January. It's dry, bright and seemingly warm. It remains daylight long after the school day is over and the children wear blazers with no overcoats, scarves or gloves. If Susan had begun at Coal Hill at the start of the school year in September, it would still be mid-winter six months later. So perhaps the TARDIS arrived in late-1962 (to catch the sea freeze), Susan started school in January 1963 and it's now March. Alternatively, given evidence in *Remembrance of the Daleks* that the Doctor's return after a month is in November, it could now be October (the risk of fog is just plausible although sunset was around 6pm, rather late for school to be finishing). That would mean the TARDIS arrived around May but Susan has only been attending Coal Hill since the new term in September – just long enough for two of her teachers to notice her oddness but not for the school authorities to get suspicious about her address, perhaps.

▮ It's later established that the Doctor has deposited the Hand of Omega at a local undertaker's during this visit to London and departs before he can finalise arrangements for it to be buried. It could therefore be inferred that he had been travelling with the Hand since leaving Gallifrey; indeed, that taking it was part of his reason for running away from his planet. Yet *The Name of the Doctor* shows the Doctor and Susan absconding from the citadel repair shop in a TARDIS apparently chosen at random (perhaps with a little prompting from Clara Oswald) with no sign of the Hand's casket. Had they already hidden the Hand aboard (and Clara was just reversing the Great Intelligence's interference of misdirecting them to a different capsule), or did the Doctor come across the stellar manipulator during his early travels? As we have seen, he and Susan make numerous landings both on Earth and elsewhere before arriving in 1963, so why decide to leave the Hand in a populous place like London and not, say, sink it in a swamp on Quinnis? Perhaps, therefore, he only discovered the Hand on 20th-century Earth after he arrived there and did what he could to make it harder for others to find. Either way, suddenly leaving before finishing the job becomes far more irresponsible. Why not let Barbara and Ian go, quickly deal with the burial of the Hand, then persuade Susan they must leave for fear the two teachers will expose them?

▮ As *Remembrance of the Daleks* requires us to rethink events prior to *An Unearthly Child* anyway, why not go even further? Could it be that, one day while Susan is at school, the Doctor is struck by an idea trickling back down his timeline about how to save a besieged Gallifrey? He takes the TARDIS into the maelstrom of the Time War and initiates the intricate calculations that will allow him and the Ship, many centuries in their personal futures, to successfully translate the entire planet and its population into a frozen instant of time, thus escaping the Dalek onslaught. Afterwards he returns to Totter's Lane with no memory of his involvement, except perhaps a vague sense of now being cut off from his own planet but that one day he shall get back, one day… Perhaps the subconscious computations limit the Doctor's and/or the Ship's ability to navigate from here on, even the latter's capacity to blend into its surroundings. Or the TARDIS, having seen that it retains its Police Box shape throughout its own future, might realise that it now must not change; note, the fault locator never indicates the chameleon circuit as being impaired. And maybe on his return, the Doctor discovers he has mysteriously acquired an ancient Gallifreyan weapon that he must now hide as best he can. It's probably going a step too far to suggest the Hand of Omega and the Moment are actually one and the same, although the latter isn't seen again in *The Day of the Doctor* after the rescue of Gallifrey, and there's a pleasing symmetry to the idea the Hand is used both at the start of the Time War, with the destruction of Skaro, and to bring it to a close.

▮ The image on the scanner of London receding, followed by the opening shot from the title sequence of a rising white streak, rather suggests the TARDIS is lifting off vertically, as would a rocket. The view is actually from the top of St Paul's Cathedral, looking east across the then-new Bank of England building on New Change and along Watling Street.

LANDING 2

SPACE Earth, [Africa or the Levant], rocky plain
TIME Two days in 100,000BC
TRAVELLERS The Doctor, Susan, Barbara Wright, Ian Chesterton
EPISODES An Unearthly Child 1-4

The TARDIS relocates almost instantly to the same planet but far in its past, arriving on a cold, barren plateau edged by woodland beyond which are caves inhabited by primitive humans. One is hunting near the TARDIS's landing site and sees it arrive, casting a long shadow as the sun rises behind him.

As the Doctor and Susan evaluate where they have landed, Barbara and Ian regain consciousness but are still incredulous, even though the scanner shows they are no longer in the junkyard. To prove they have moved, the Doctor leads them all outside to establish where and when they are. The Ship remains in the now-incongruous form of a London Police Box. Nearby, Barbara finds the skull of a horse-like animal half-buried in the freezing-cold sand.

Later in the night the travellers attempt to return to the TARDIS but the tribesmen have got there first and surround the Police Box. They lead their prisoners back to the caves at spear-point.

Shortly after dawn the next day, the dishevelled travellers successfully regain the safety of the Ship, narrowly escaping the pursuing tribe who wish to sacrifice the strangers to their sun god Orb. The Doctor throws the TARDIS into a rapid dematerialisation and the spears of the cavemen pass harmlessly through the fading Police Box.

○ **CONTROLS** Susan establishes that "the base [of the Ship] is steady" from panel A1. The Doctor operates switches on panel A2 while the yearometer on panel A3 (seemingly one of the large gauges) registers zero, which the Doctor interprets as a fault. He assesses the atmospheric quality from panel A6 (apparently from the round display at the bottom) while Susan gets a radiation reading from panel A1 (seemingly from the round display at the top right). When they prepare to leave the Ship, the Doctor turns the left-upper and top rotary handles on panel A6 while Susan opens the doors with a double-flick of the switch on panel A1.

○ Before dematerialising, Susan pushes levers at the top of panel A4 and the centre large slider, perhaps to lock the main doors. The Doctor operates the switches at the bottom of panel A2 to initiate take-off.

▮ **LORE** The instrumentation in the central column continues to rotate and illuminate after the TARDIS has landed. (The original intention was that this provided the pilot with navigational information.)

▮ It's established that the scanner shows the immediate view outside the Ship.

▮ The Police Box doors can close automatically. The implication here and throughout the early years of the programme is that the control room's big double doors and the wooden Police Box doors are one and the same, and their appearance depends on whether you're looking at them from inside or outside. This suggests the Ship's camouflage works to some extent on a perceptual level.

▮ **NOTES** The TARDIS has almost certainly moved in relative space as well as time (assuming it's still on Earth, which is never stated but was the intention; the date is given in the title of the script and Ian later recalls it as "prehistoric times" – see Landing 8). Ice sheets covered the northern-most regions of modern Europe 100,000 years ago, even though the area that would become southern England was probably ice free. More significantly, anatomically modern humans (which the cave-dwellers encountered here clearly are) had barely migrated out of Africa at this time. Za talks of tribes on "the other side of the mountains" but his group seems to be distant from those, possibly venturing towards the south of Africa or across the Levant. Hominid remains discovered in caves at Skhul in Israel date from about this time, although it has been suggested this line of migrants died out about 80,000 years ago – perhaps they just couldn't retain the knowledge of how to make fire.

▮ The Doctor confirms, "We've gone back in time all right," but without the yearometer he can't determine how far. "One or two samples [from outside] and I shall be able to make an estimate," he says but when he adds, "I do wish this wouldn't keep letting me down," he seems to indicate the console in general rather than the yearometer specifically – an early indication the Ship as a whole is somewhat unreliable.

▮ The control room's interior doors are seen for the first time, although it's not yet shown that they lead to further areas of the TARDIS.

▮ The term 'chameleon circuit' is not coined at this time, just that the TARDIS should have altered its appearance. The Doctor finds its remaining a Police Box "very disturbing". Presumably it was the sudden take-off that put paid to the circuit. It can't have been one of the things the Doctor was trying to repair in London as both he and Susan are surprised by the TARDIS's failure to change shape this time.

▮ This is the first time the TARDIS is seen to fade away when it dematerialises. This was shot on film and then processed as a dissolve from a view of the plateau with the Police Box to one of the empty set.

▮ It's not yet established that the TARDIS is invulnerable to outside attack (particularly feeble spears) but the Doctor should know this so he doesn't really need to make the rushed take-off he does. Presumably he's agitated from his recent exertions and Ian's unwitting insistence they leave immediately.

LANDING 3

SPACE Skaro, petrified forest near Dalek city
TIME Six days in unknown future
        [between 1963 and 2540]
TRAVELLERS The Doctor, Susan, Barbara, Ian
EPISODES An Unearthly Child 4; The Daleks 1-5,7

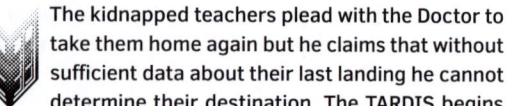

The kidnapped teachers plead with the Doctor to take them home again but he claims that without sufficient data about their last landing he cannot determine their destination. The TARDIS begins rematerialising straight away, arriving in an ashen alien forest that has been petrified by nuclear fallout. The high radiation level registers on the console, unnoticed by any of the travellers.

There is no evidence of life outside; even a small metallic creature seems to have been killed in its tracks by whatever detonation irradiated the planet. Some distance beyond the edge of the forest is an intact, technologically advanced city which appears deserted.

The travellers explore but return to the Ship as night falls. Barbara comforts Susan, who is sure someone was out in the forest with them, while Ian tries to understand the TARDIS's operation. Tired of his questions, the Doctor distracts him with some food – although a flavoured bar from a machine is not what the teacher was expecting. They are all startled by a knocking from outside but the scanner reveals nothing.

Reluctantly the Doctor agrees to leave the planet without exploring the city. As the TARDIS begins to take off, however, he reaches into the console's pedestal and dislodges a fluid link. This causes the power to fluctuate and the Ship to shudder as it cancels the dematerialisation. Susan checks the fault locator, situated in the computer wall, which indicates the problem is in component K7. The Doctor removes the offending fluid link and claims all the mercury has leaked out and he has none to replace it with. Their best chance of finding some, he asserts, is in the city and come the morning all four travellers head out, the Doctor taking the fluid link with him. Immediately outside they find a metal box containing vials of liquid, which Susan places on a chair in the Ship.

Later that evening, as a storm breaks, Susan returns to collect the box, having learned the vials contain an anti-radiation drug which she and her friends need to cure their contagion. When she sets out again she meets a Thal, Alydon, who gives her an extra supply. As Susan makes her way back to the city, more Thals set up camp beside the TARDIS.

The travellers help the Thals evade a Dalek ambush and they all make it out of the city, returning to their camp by the Ship. The Doctor learns of Skaro's history and finds the Thals have star maps, from which he hopes to determine the planet's position. Unable to convince their new friends of the need to fight the Daleks to preserve their way of life, the travellers plan to leave Skaro only to realise the creatures have confiscated the vital fluid link. The Doctor attempts to make a replacement but discovers he genuinely has run out of mercury.

The Doctor and Susan spend two days at the Thal camp devising a way to disable the Daleks' scanners, while Ian and Barbara find a route through the mountains at the rear of the city. They exhaust the city's power, preventing the Daleks from exploding another atomic device and saving the Thals from further irradiation. Some time later, after the Doctor has performed some soil tests and Susan has changed her outfit, the travellers say their goodbyes. The Thals give gifts of gratitude, while Ganatus is particularly sad to see Barbara go. The Doctor refits the recovered fluid link and the Thals watch amazed as the Police Box fades away.

○ **CONTROLS** As the Ship lands, the Doctor operates the small levers on panel A5 while Susan flicks one of those on panel A4. This probably activates the scanner as the Doctor throws an adjacent lever when later checking it. The radiation meter is the large square display on panel A3 (labelled 'Radiation') and takes a moment to register the dangerous level outside. When the travellers return from exploring the forest the needle has dropped back into the safe zone. The Doctor checks a wall of computer banks to try to determine where the Ship has landed.

○ The TARDIS contains a food machine that produces foil-wrapped nutrition bars which can be programmed for flavour. Two large dials on the front – one lettered from A to Z, the other numbered 1 to 9 – are used to enter an alphanumeric code to select the flavouring of choice. J62L6, for example, produces bars that taste of bacon and eggs. The bars are dispensed on small trays.

○ The left-hand large slider on panel A5 begins the dematerialisation process, the Doctor making further adjustment on panel A6. The fluid link is a thumb-sized silver tube encircled by four discs, housed in the pedestal beneath panel A6 behind a cover hinged along its bottom edge. It takes a few seconds before the link's removal disrupts the dematerialisation process. When the take-off fails, the Doctor throws the right-hand large slider on panel A5 and the right-hand gauge on panel A3 (labelled 'Pressure') fluctuates wildly as the power is interrupted. When Susan leaves after collecting the drugs, she opens the doors with the flick switch on panel A1.

○ The fault locator includes a mechanism with nine sensors scribing ink traces on a roll of paper.

○ The delicate controls of the console were prone to damage as the prop was manhandled in and out of the studio (or just by an overenthusiastic actor). Already the small lever on the left of panel A6 and those on panel A1 have lost their knobs.

○ The Doctor moves all round the console operating controls as the TARDIS takes off, including the large slider on panel A4.

▮ **LORE** The Doctor admits he cannot fully control the TARDIS's flight, saying, "This isn't operating properly. Or rather, the code is still a secret." He suggests having precise temporal and spatial information about the point of departure would allow him to fix a specific destination, and Susan confirms that when leaving prehistoric Earth they took off too quickly. There's also "a meter fixed to a great big bank of computers" that can "take over the controls of the Ship and deliver you to any place you want to go" but only if fed with the right information. Yet when Barbara asks the Doctor if he can work the Ship he replies, "Of course I can't, I'm not a miracle worker."

▮ The sound of the TARDIS taking off is audible inside the Ship. Here the descending tones of its materialising again are also heard for the first time (simply the take-off sound effect played in reverse), although it fades out before reaching the familiar grinding part.

▮ Someone knocking on the Police Box door is audible inside the control room.

▮ The lock on the TARDIS door is key operated but inside are 21 "holes", only one of which opens the door. If the key is used incorrectly then the inside of the lock melts to prevent access. How the right hole is selected is unclear; the Doctor and Susan know how to do so but as she is worried Ian might get it wrong it's possible some form of telepathic influence is involved. Susan also says the whole lock can be removed from the door, again to stop unwanted entry (prefiguring the events of Landing 8).

▮ **NOTES** The Doctor recalls this trip to Skaro in *Planet of the Daleks*, which is set in 2540 (see Landing 94). The Thals in that story say the events were "generations ago", so perhaps only a few hundred years earlier. Although he suggests in *The Dalek Invasion of Earth* that his first encounter with the Daleks was "a million years ahead of us in the future", he's merely speculating. An early outline for *The Daleks* set events in the 23rd century; although this was removed in later drafts it would fit with the Doctor's using the fast return switch when leaving Skaro because he believed it was in Barbara and Ian's future.

- When Barbara comforts Susan in the TARDIS, it's implied they're talking in a separate room from the control area. Although the scene was recorded on the control room set – the wall against which the table is positioned is that housing the main doors – the background hum of the control room is faded down to suggest a different area of the Ship. This scene, therefore, is arguably the first time we see beyond the control room. The location of the food machine is again just a corner of the main control room set.
- When the chameleon circuit was working, presumably the lock was still visible on the exterior – discrete enough on a sedan chair but rather conspicuous on an ionic column.
- This is the first time the effect of the TARDIS dematerialising was performed in the studio, mixing from a shot of the Police Box on the jungle-clearing set to a carefully lined up photo of just the set (taken earlier in the recording day during camera rehearsals).

LANDING 4

SPACE Space, Skaro's solar system
TIME Moving backwards
TRAVELLERS The Doctor, Susan, Barbara, Ian
EPISODES The Daleks 7; The Edge of Destruction 1-2

Attempting to return the two teachers to 20th century Earth, the Doctor activates the fast return switch but a burst of energy knocks them all unconscious. The TARDIS is silent and the console inactive when the travellers recover. Their memories are muddled and they all seemed confused about where they are. They begin to fear the Ship has crashed or some force has got inside, but the Doctor soon suspects the two teachers of sabotage. Whenever one of them tries to approach the console they get an unbearable head pain, unless it is the section with the scanner control. Yet all the screen shows are images of past landing sites taken from its memory bank, while the doors open and close on their own. The Ship itself seems to be trying to alert them to an impending danger. It somehow melts the faces of their clocks and watches, then sounds a klaxon and illuminates the whole of the fault locator every fifteen seconds to indicate time is running out before the TARDIS is destroyed.

At Ian's insistence, the Doctor checks the fast return switch – on the same panel as the scanner control – and discovers that a broken spring has caused it to stick as if still pressed, sending the TARDIS hurtling back in time to the creation of Skaro's solar system. The Doctor repairs the switch and the power immediately returns to normal, allowing the Ship to dematerialise and escape the danger.

- **CONTROLS** The Doctor references a "main unit". The fault locator has a three-character display of a letter and two numbers, plus an adjacent light. When testing the safety of the console, the Doctor throws one of the small levers on panel A5 (second from the right), which he later confirms is the scanner switch. The fast return switch is at the top-right of panel A5.
- The buttons for lowering the beds are numbered one to six, suggesting there are that many beds (at least in this room. No controls are visible in the second room where Ian sleeps, so perhaps all beds are controlled from one panel). When putting Susan to bed, Ian seems to press button one yet the second bed along tips down.
- The food machine is slightly different from the one seen previously, with additional buttons specifically for water and milk, dispensed in plastic pouches.
- The readout of the fault locator is seen displaying A12 with the last digit rotating up to A17. This could be a hexadecimal system (A12 would be 2,578 in decimal) or even, as it has previously identified a component K7, base 21. More likely is that each of the three digit wheels contains letters A to Z and numbers 0 to 9, allowing identification of up to 46,655 components.
- The fast return switch doesn't appear on the console until the second episode of *The Edge of Destruction*, so how did the Doctor previously operate it? Famously, it has 'Fast return' handwritten above it on the console, presumably as an aid for the actors to identify the right control. This is cleaned off or painted over after this story.
- **LORE** The source of the TARDIS's power, the "heart of the machine" as the Doctor calls it, is housed beneath the console. The rising and falling of the central column reflects the strength of the power thrust. Were any of the energy to escape the occupants would "be blown to atoms in a split second".
- Susan claims it's impossible for the Ship to crash.
- Ian refers to the console as the 'control column', a term Susan later also uses.
- The TARDIS has a memory bank that records its landing sites and can display images of them on the scanner.
- The Ship has a "built-in defence mechanism" to protect itself (and any passengers?) from accidental or intentional destruction.
- **NOTES** A new sound effect is created for the TARDIS breaking down. After an explosion, part of the standard grinding sound is repeated with added echo.
- The behaviour of the TARDIS in this story is (deliberately?) obtuse but then the exact nature of its flight has never been clearly shown in the series. Sometimes we see the Police Box spinning through a star field as if it moves through space like a regular spaceship; at other times it's shown in a swirling tunnel, often that used in the title sequence of the time, later dubbed the space-time vortex or continuum. In either case it's usually traversing time as well as distance. So when the TARDIS dematerialises from the surface of a planet, where does it go? Into space or some form of hyperspace that tunnels between discrete points of the four-dimensional universe as we perceive it? Or

both? Clearly other dimensions are involved but they may not be totally separate from the four that we can perceive. In *The Edge of Destruction* it must be travelling backwards in time under the command of the fast return switch but it's still influenced by the forces outside in 'real' space. Equally, in *The Web Planet* the Animus is able to entrap the Ship in flight and force it to land on Vortis (see Landing 14), as perhaps does the Gravitron in *The Moonbase* (Landing 49) and the Great Intelligence in *The Web of Fear* (Landing 56). For this book we'll assume that whenever the TARDIS is in flight, whether it's seen against a starry background or in a vortex, then it's travelling across dimensions. Even if it appears to be in deep space without moving through time (other than at the normal rate all of us are subject to), we'll assume that if it's spinning and/or flashing its light then it's in some form of extra-dimensional travel.

▣ The Doctor doesn't believe the Ship can think as a human does but "must be able to think as a machine". This and other stories, notably *The Doctor's Wife*, show that it has conscious thought processes and an awareness of its surroundings, so is not merely reacting programmatically. Nonetheless, it can't tell the difference between a loose spring and someone holding down a control. After shutting down the power and knocking everyone out, does it still think someone is pressing the switch? Even if not and it's trying to alert the crew to a problem with the control, can it not deactivate or disregard the fast-return system?

▣ So what about the fast return switch, how does that work? The Doctor merely says, "I had hoped to reach your planet Earth. Skaro was in the future and I used the fast return switch." This might suggest it simply sends the Ship back along its most recent trajectory through space as well as time, returning it to prehistoric Earth from where, perhaps, the Doctor was more confident of making the relatively short hop back to the 20th century. So would keeping the switch permanently pressed, as the broken spring effectively does, push the TARDIS back through all its journeys? This is what the views on the scanner imply. The Ship itself seems to think this would be a bad idea (realising it would eventually lead it back to Gallifrey from which, according to *The Doctor's Wife*, it was as keen to escape as the Doctor) and so forces a materialisation in 'real' (three-dimensional) space within Skaro's solar system but is still moving backwards through time towards that system's creation, as the Doctor explains: "Outside the atoms are rushing towards each other, fusing, coagulating, until minute little collections of matter are created... A new birth of a sun and its planets." Once the faulty switch is repaired it can dematerialise again (as it's heard to do) and resume its journey towards Earth.

▣ We definitely see further rooms beyond the control room this time. Just outside is a corridor containing a couch, a small round table, an upholstered chair and a food machine. Immediately behind this is a bedroom with a half-hexagonal table, a Dahlen egg-shaped wire chair and three recliners that swing down from the wall – although only two were constructed. (This room backs onto the control room and light can be seen bleeding through its roundels onto the fabric screen that forms the wall of the bedroom.) Further along the corridor is another bedroom with two more recliners.

▣ The sequence of images on the scanner is obscure. In trying to get the occupants to understand the danger they're in, the TARDIS shows recent landing sites: a country scene, then the creepy planet Quinnis, then Skaro receding into the distance. (It's implied to be Skaro when the Doctor later describes how the fast return switch works, and confirmed when the same planet is seen at the end of *The Space Museum* as the Daleks track the TARDIS.) However, it doesn't show London or the Stone Age plateau on which it recently materialised. Is missing these out supposed to indicate to the Doctor he's misusing the fast return switch?

LANDING 5

SPACE Earth, China (Cathay), Pamir Mountains; transported by cart to Peking
TIME Several months in 1289
TRAVELLERS The Doctor, Susan, Barbara, Ian
EPISODES The Edge of Destruction 2; Marco Polo 1-7

With the fast return switch unjammed, the TARDIS completes its return journey to Earth and, although it gets the date wrong, arrives closer to the 20th century than 100,000BC at least. It materialises on a snowy pass high in the Pamir mountain range – observed by the Mongol warlord Tegana – and the travellers wrap up against the cold before exploring. Immediately outside the Ship they find a footprint, enlarged by the melting snow.

Just then a circuit burns out causing the Ship's lighting and heating systems to fail, possibly because of the calamity just avoided. The damage also affects the food machine, leaving the travellers with no water. The Doctor removes a circuit which he is unable to repair so must make a replacement from scratch.

Nearby a party of humans is crossing the mountains: Mongols led by the Venetian explorer Marco Polo. He gives the travellers food and shelter and the next day examines the TARDIS, intrigued by Ian's claim that it moves through the air. He has it brought down from the pass on a sledge and takes it, and the travellers, with him as they journey down the mountain through the Kashgar valley and join the Silk Road along the edge of the Taklamakan desert to the town of Lop. He denies the travellers access to the Ship, however, planning to present it to the Khan in return for permission to go home to Italy.

The Doctor sulks while the group sets out across the Gobi desert, the Police Box secured on a cart. Owing to the heat and lack of water, Polo allows him and Susan to rest in the Ship. After a cold night, the Doctor is woken by condensation dripping from the walls and he and Susan collect it in a cup. Polo, believing the Doctor has been hoarding water, decides that when they set off again towards Tun-Huang the TARDIS will be locked and he will hold the key, so the Doctor spends his rest time making a spare to hand over. Thus he is able to enter the Ship secretly and build a new circuit while the caravan continues through Su-Chow, Kan-Chow and Lan-Chow to Sinju. There he completes and installs the repaired circuit but is discovered leaving the TARDIS and Polo confiscates the Doctor's key.

When the caravan reaches Cheng-Ting, Polo receives instruction to make haste to attend the Khan in his summer palace at Shang-Tu and insists they must all ride ahead of their possessions, including the TARDIS, unaware that Tegana is planning to steal the 'magic caravan' and deliver it to his master Noghai. Ping-Cho recovers one of the keys from Polo's room and returns it to Susan. That night, the Doctor, Ian and Barbara successfully enter the Ship but Susan loiters to say goodbye to Ping-Cho and is caught by Tegana, forcing the others to abandon their escape. Polo again takes custody of the keys and the next day they all set off on horseback for Shang-Tu, leaving the Ship behind.

Before it can be collected for transportation to the palace, however, the TARDIS is stolen by Tegana's hired thief. Ian finds it being handed over to the warlord. As they confront each other, the Khan's soldiers arrive and order they all be taken to their ruler, now at his Peking palace. There the Doctor has won great wealth playing Kublai Khan at backgammon but wagers it all in return for the TARDIS. Unfortunately this time he loses.

The TARDIS is deposited in the throne room of the Khan's Imperial Palace at Peking and he is pleased with his prize. While Polo brings the keys, the Khan is attacked by Tegana. Polo saves his leader's life, then duels with the Mongol warlord outside the Ship. Defeated, Tegana takes his own life. In the commotion, Polo hands the Doctor the keys and the four travellers hurry inside, Susan bidding a last farewell to Ping-Cho. The court is bemused as the Police Box fades away.

- **CONTROLS** The Doctor reports they are "several thousand feet above sea level" so there must be an altimeter in the Ship.
- **LORE** The TARDIS interior is normally heated but if that control fails the temperature eventually equalises with the exterior environment. If this is colder than the ambient temperature inside then condensation will form on the control room walls.
- The TARDIS has an extensive wardrobe.
- The Doctor insists that someone else using the key incorrectly would "destroy the Ship" (he is likely exaggerating to deter Polo from trying, worried it would nevertheless disable the lock, as explained by Susan in *The Daleks*).
- The exterior of the Ship is light enough to be lifted by a handful of men.
- **NOTES** The opening shot of *Marco Polo* is a filmed pan across a model of snowy mountains that, an off-screen photo reveals, included a miniature Police Box. It's hard to tell if this is the same one seen more clearly in *The Keys of Marinus* (Landing 6) but it's likely to be given the mountains themselves are reused from two serials earlier, where they backed the model Dalek city.
- It's a bit of a design flaw that just one circuit burning out can knock out all the TARDIS's power. Although the Doctor says only the lighting, heating and water production are affected, the implication is that the whole Ship is disabled as he doesn't simply depart in search of a better place to perform repairs.
- It's not clear if the 2LO the Doctor mentions is the designation of the faulty circuit or not. He initially says the lights have gone out because "the whole circuit has burnt itself to a cinder". Shortly after he sends Susan back into the Ship to fetch the 2LO, saying she knows what it is, while he worries whether he can "find the fault" – as he already knows a circuit has burnt out, he must mean whatever caused it to do so. We next see him outside the TARDIS holding a small black box with loose wires hanging from it and discussing with Susan how he will have to make a replacement. This can't be the entirety of the lighting circuit, and doesn't look like it's "burnt to a cinder", so must be the faulty component that caused the Ship-wide failure. But if this is the 2LO it's remarkable the Doctor asked for it before knowing it was the cause of the problem. A lucky deduction, or is the 2LO a tool with which he planned to detect the fault? He does poke at the box of wires with what looks like a screwdriver, but we know how deceptively simple some of the Doctor's gadgets appear, especially the screwdrivers…
- The failure of the food machine to supply water may be related to this latest power failure. However, as Susan was having trouble with it a few hours previously – registering empty even though it was still dispensing – it may already have been on the blink.
- This is the first time the interior of the TARDIS is shown to be affected by exterior environmental conditions, as the hot days and cold nights in the Gobi desert cause condensation to form inside.
- In episode two, it's a little odd that Barbara's claim, "When we're in [the TARDIS] we feel safe and secure," is intended to reassure Susan given the paranoid experience they've just been through inside the Ship.
- Here Barbara refers to the Ship without the definite article – "Look, TARDIS is the only home we have at the moment" – a form usually limited to early literature about the series, such as the first novelisations and annuals. In episode seven both the Doctor and Marco Polo do the same, as if it's a proper name.
- The studio floorplan for episode three shows a small set comprising the interior doorway, two of the metal-framed screens and a couch in front of a blue backcloth was used for the scene of condensation dripping on the Doctor. Episode four's camera script indicates two close-ups of the Doctor working on the circuit in the Ship were recorded but there is no visual evidence to show what if any set pieces were seen. The floorplan for episode five and an off-screen photo show an indented wall and one of the illuminated pillars,

plus the console, formed the control room set as the travellers prepare to depart. Finally, in episode seven an indented wall and a photographic wall formed a corner backdrop for the cast around the console for the final shot of the serial, although off-screen photos suggest they could barely be seen.

- In scenes where the TARDIS is only glimpsed in the background, a full-size photo cutout was positioned at the rear of the set, as the Police Box prop was usually already in use on another set.
- The departure of the TARDIS was filmed ahead of the episode's studio recording, with a dissolve to show the Police Box disappearing. Off-screen photos show the prop was filmed from above (via an angled mirror) looking down onto the roof with its light flashing.

LANDING 6

SPACE Marinus, island amid an acid sea
TIME At least nine days in an unknown future
TRAVELLERS The Doctor, Susan, Barbara, Ian
EPISODES The Keys of Marinus 1,6

The TARDIS arrives on a small island on the planet Marinus. Around it are large jagged rocks and by the shore the sand is worn into sharp shards of glass. There is no sound of wildlife although there is some scrub-like vegetation (despite Barbara's claim to the contrary). The surrounding sea and pools on the beach are highly acidic, capable of dissolving fabric in seconds. In the centre of the island is a large flat-topped pyramid.

Susan briefly returns to the Ship to get a fresh pair of shoes, unaware that prowling around it is a wetsuited Voord, one of four just arrived on the island in acid-proof submersibles. She does notice its footprints when she emerges, however, and follows them to the pyramid. Barbara looks for her inside the Ship, carefully locking the door when she re-emerges.

Having investigated the pyramid and met its sole occupant, Arbitan, the travellers return to the TARDIS only to find the old man has erected an invisible circular barrier around it to prevent their leaving until they agree to help him recover the micro-circuit keys to his mind-controlling Conscience machine.

Having recovered the keys but destroyed the Conscience machine to prevent the Voord leader Yartek from dominating everyone on Marinus, the travellers return to the TARDIS with their new friends Altos and Sabetha. The Doctor checks the force barrier is gone and that the Ship is unharmed, then he, Susan, Ian and Barbara say goodbye to the young couple and the Police Box leaves the beach as silently as it came.

- **○ CONTROLS** The Doctor is looking at panel A3 when checking the radiation level outside and activates the scanner from the same panel. Susan opens the doors using the large slider on panel A4.
- **LORE** The scanner currently shows a monochrome image; when Barbara bemoans the lack of colour the Doctor claims it's a temporary fault.
- The time mechanism is one of the Ship's faulty systems.
- **NOTES** This landing probably follows directly from the last as Ian is wearing the jacket, shirt and boots he acquired in China, although Barbara and Susan have had time to change their clothes. If there have been intervening landings Ian may just be re-wearing an outfit he likes. In *The Sensorites* the travellers fondly mention the places they've visited, suggesting perhaps that all the landings up to then are strictly sequential (see Landing 8). However, they may just be picking some highlights and there could be unseen destinations before and after their visit to Marinus.
- The TARDIS's arrival is shown using a filmed model, probably that glimpsed at the start of *Marco Polo*. This time it's seen materialising, though, complete with flashing light. The materialisation sound is not heard on screen but incidental music is playing so it may just be that the diegetic sound is turned down. Its departure is the same silent model footage shown in reverse.
- Barbara is seen locking the TARDIS door after looking inside for Susan, so presumably the Doctor has shown her how to use the key without melting the lock.

LANDING 7

SPACE Earth, Mexico, Temple of Yetaxa, tomb
TIME Five days in 15th/early-16th century
TRAVELLERS The Doctor, Susan, Barbara, Ian
EPISODES The Aztecs 1,4

The TARDIS arrives at the top of an Aztec temple, inside the tomb of Yetaxa, an honoured priest whose remains are laid out in jewelled finery. Barbara idly puts on one of the priest's bracelets while Susan discovers a large slab can be swung upwards to allow the priest to exit should he be reincarnated. They, Ian and the Doctor emerge from the tomb only to discover that, once closed, the slab cannot be opened again from outside.

However, a panel in the base of Yetaxa's altar leads to a series of tunnels within the pyramid and exits in the neighbouring garden. Ian later uses this to climb from the garden into the tomb where the Ship is shrouded in darkness. He takes a length of bindings from the corpse, ties them through a loop above the slab and trails it under the lip when he exits, to provide leverage from the outside.

The Doctor places the strip over a pulley he has carved and pulls on it to open the tomb, while Ian holds off warrior Ixta. He joins the others as the slab swings up and they all rush into the tomb. Tlotoxl arrives with more warriors but abandons the chase as the sun is eclipsed, returning to the platform outside of complete his bloody sacrifice. Barbara bemoans her failure to change the Aztecs' beliefs. She takes off her ceremonial robes and places Yetaxa's bracelet back beside his body. The Doctor reassures her she at least helped the priest of knowledge Autloc to become more enlightened about his people's practices.

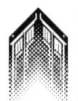

As Barbara enters the Ship, the Doctor takes out the brooch given him by his fiancée Cameca. He places it with the other jewels on the altar and turns to leave, then retrieves it and puts it back in his pocket before entering the TARDIS and taking off.

- **CONTROLS** The Doctor operates the switches at the bottom of panel A2 and the dial in its bottom-right corner as the Ship dematerialises.
- The small lever on the left of panel A6 has had its missing top replaced with a much larger knob like those on the large sliders, possibly from elsewhere on the console. The upper two of the small levers on panel A1 are now missing their stems altogether.
- **NOTES** *The Aztecs* begins with a repeat of the model shot of the TARDIS disappearing from the beach on Marinus before fading to black and cutting to the Ship already in Yetaxa's tomb, suggesting a single journey. However, at least some short time has passed as the travellers have changed their outfits and there's nothing in the narrative to rule out further landings between the two stories.
- Assuming Barbara is right to date Yetaxa's death around 1430, this must be between then and the arrival of Hernán Cortés in 1519. Ixta's father built the temple pyramid to house Yetaxa's body but design and construction may not have begun until after the priest's death. This likely took several decades to complete and Ixta may not have been born until after. There's nothing to say his father wasn't old when a younger Cameca knew him. From the view at the top of the temple, this is a sizeable city, with other temples visible. Autloc has Susan learn from the annals of Cuautitlan, a city north of the capital Tenochtitlan, so perhaps this is where they are. Yetaxa is probably the deity of one 'calpolli' or clan within this 'altepetl' or city state, as Tlotoxl and Autloc seem to have authority only within the temple and its province, and we meet no ruler.
- We don't see the TARDIS dematerialise, only hear it from inside as the Doctor operates the controls.

LANDING 8

SPACE Earth spaceship orbiting Sense-Sphere, flight deck
TIME 28th century
TRAVELLERS The Doctor, Susan, Barbara, Ian
EPISODES The Aztecs 4; The Sensorites 1,6

The TARDIS comes to rest but even the Doctor is confused that some instruments say it has stopped while others show it is still moving, as if on or inside something. The scanner shows only static so – after reminiscing about their experiences together – the travellers venture outside.

They discover they are aboard a spaceship from Earth. Its two crewmembers appear to be dead but in fact are in a deep sleep that suspends their bodily functions. They have been placed in that state by the telepathic Sensorites from the planet below while their ship is held in orbit. One of the aliens is aboard and to prevent the travellers from leaving it removes the TARDIS lock from the door using a handheld energy device. The Doctor demands the lock be returned but the Sensorites insist they cannot leave and instead take all but Barbara and Captain Maitland down to the Sense-Sphere.

In gratitude to the travellers for discovering what was killing their people and apprehending those responsible, the Sensorites (under the Doctor's supervision) refit the TARDIS lock. The Doctor and Susan board the Ship while Ian and Barbara say goodbye to the Earth crew as they prepare to return home. Susan is despondent her heightened telepathic abilities were just a result of the Sense-Sphere's ultra-high frequencies; the Doctor consoles her with a promise to develop her talents when they return home, whenever that may be. She looks forward to settling down somewhere one day.

Ian and Barbara finish their farewells and enter the TARDIS, and the four travellers watch on the scanner as the rocket finally breaks orbit. When Ian remarks that at least they know where they are going, the Doctor interprets this as an insult to his piloting skills and takes offence, insisting that the two teachers must leave the Ship wherever they next land. He sets the TARDIS in motion.

- **CONTROLS** Susan looks towards panel A1 when she mentions the instruments that indicate the Ship has materialised, while the Doctor points to panel A3 as having others which suggest it's still moving. He indicates the right-hand rotating-light unit on panel A2 when he says, "This says everything has stopped but the Ship," although both units are illuminated. Susan operates both the scanner and the main doors from panel A6, but later operates the scanner from panel A3.
- The right-hand gauge on panel A2 is labelled 'Oxygen' and registers zero. Nevertheless, the Doctor can determine that there is "fresh air" and a "normal" temperature outside.
- One of the black-and-white squares at the top of the central column's inner structure is missing in episode one. By episode six it's back but has been rotated so it no longer mirrors the other.
- **LORE** The scanner image can be affected from outside, such as by an unsuppressed motor or a magnetic field. The scanner can also show a view which is not immediately outside the Ship.
- With the door's opening mechanism removed, the Ship is permanently locked. Breaking down the door would disturb the field dimensions inside the TARDIS.
- **NOTES** Although the last scene of *The Aztecs* shows the TARDIS has landed again this doesn't prove it follows immediately after leaving 15th-century Mexico (although that was undoubtedly the intention when it was made). All the travellers bar the Doctor have changed their clothes and at the start of *The Sensorites*, when the Doctor refers to Barbara's experiences with the Aztecs, she says, "I've got over that now," suggesting

some time has passed. While they later recount the places the Ship has taken them – citing prehistoric times, the Daleks, Marco Polo and Marinus – with Barbara concluding, "And the Aztecs," as though that's the most recent, she may be highlighting that trip because the Doctor just brought it up.

- Is this the first time the TARDIS has landed aboard a spaceship or vessel of any kind? The Doctor seems genuinely puzzled by the conflicting readouts saying the Ship has landed but is still moving: surely he can differentiate between the Ship itself being in flight and the movement of wherever it has landed? The TARDIS isn't moving relative to the spaceship any more than when it lands on a planet.
- It's often claimed this story features the first time the camera follows the cast out of the control room and turns to show the Police Box, but this is not true. Yes, the doors open directly onto the spaceship flight deck, but the sets have been positioned this way previously, such as with the prehistoric plain in *An Unearthly Child* episode two and the jungle in *The Daleks* episode three. Although here the camera does follow the actors through the control room doors, there is then a shot change (indeed, a recording break was taken) before Susan is seen turning to lock the TARDIS door.
- The Sensorite manages to remove the TARDIS lock unnoticed even though the travellers are plainly standing just a few feet away and smell burning while it's doing it. It removes not just the exterior plate with the keyhole but the cylindrical opening mechanism behind it too, leaving a circular hole in the door. Although the process produces smoke and a burning smell, it seems to simply loosen the lock rather than damaging the fabric of the door. Nonetheless, that must be an amazingly powerful device the Sensorites have, able to disable the TARDIS in a way more advanced beings will be incapable of in the future. Perhaps because of this event the Doctor reinforces the Ship.
- When the Doctor and Susan are waiting to leave, Ian and Barbara walk into shot as if they've just entered the control room from outside, yet the closed main doors are clearly visible right behind them.
- Once everyone is aboard, the first thing the Doctor does is check the scanner to "have a look at Maitland and see him off", and this shows the Earth ship flying away. But the TARDIS hasn't taken off yet so how is the scanner getting this view from outside the rocket? One explanation is that the Ship was taken down to the Sense-Sphere along with Barbara; after the discovery of the deranged humans in the aqueduct, perhaps Carol and John decided to stay on the planet as ambassadors, so Ian and Barbara were saying goodbye to them there. Note the Doctor only talks of seeing off Captain Maitland, not all their new friends. Alternatively, Maitland believed he needed to 'undock' the TARDIS before he left, so once Ian and Barbara had stepped into the Police Box he had it ejected out of an airlock and it's actually adrift in space as they watch the rocket zoom away.

LANDING 9

SPACE Earth, France, Île-de-France, woodland 12km north of Paris
TIME [24 to 28 July] 1794
TRAVELLERS The Doctor, Susan, Barbara, Ian
EPISODES The Reign of Terror 1,6

The TARDIS materialises, again silently, nestled among trees at dusk in the French countryside. The Doctor is confident that he has successfully brought Barbara and Ian home and prepares to depart again as soon as they have left the Ship. Susan is upset at the thought of travelling on without the teachers, who have become her friends, but the Doctor affects an air of indifference and distracts himself with a book. When Ian and Barbara ask if he is sure they are in the right place, he activates the scanner to convince them. This shows trees and cultivated fields, reminding Barbara of a holiday in Somerset. Just in case the Doctor is wrong, however, Ian persuades him to come for a drink so they can part on friendlier terms. Sure enough, moments later they hear musket fire and encounter a young boy lurking in the bushes who tells them they are near Paris.

After three days in Paris, the travellers escape the city as riots break out following the overthrow of Robespierre and his reign of terror, travelling by carriage to where the TARDIS waits. Back in the safety of the control room, as they change out of their period clothes, they discuss the futility of trying to change established historical events.

- **CONTROLS** After the Ship has landed the Doctor throws the large slider and some of the small levers on panel A4, then adjusts controls on panel A5 and the right-hand rotary handle on A4. He activates the scanner with one of the small levers on panel A5 (second from the left) and reaches across the same panel, possibly to the rotary handle at bottom-left, to extend the scanner view beyond the immediate surroundings. He seems to switch it off with one of the small levers on panel A4 but may be opening the main doors (see below).
- In episode one, the top grilles on panels A2 and A4 are missing, as are the two domed lightbulbs on either side of the strip at the bottom of panel A3. By episode six, the grille on panel A4 has been replaced with a paler cover like that on panel A5.
- **LORE** The scanner can display more than just what's immediately outside, here showing a view beyond the intervening trees.
- **NOTES** This story takes places during the last days of Maximilien Robespierre's leadership of the French Revolution, climaxing with his arrest on 27 July 1794. The TARDIS must therefore arrive on the evening of the 24th, the travellers reach Paris the next day, visit the physician on the 26th before Ian and Barbara pose as pub keepers that night, then witness Robespierre's downfall the following evening before returning to the Ship, arriving on the morning of the 28th.

- The TARDIS's arrival is a mix from a photo of the woodland set to a shot of the set with the Police Box in position. This is the first time the full-size prop has been shown materialising. The interior light flashes in time with the roof lamp, illuminating the windows and 'Police box' signs. The materialisation sound is not used, however, just the interior hum fading in slightly before the TARDIS actually appears.
- While the full-size prop is used for the materialisation, in the shot of the Doctor locking the TARDIS the duplicate standalone doors created for *An Unearthly Child* make their first on-screen appearance. Note that we don't see anyone coming through the doors, and there appears to be a split up the centre of the lintel, most notable on the 'Police box' sign where the 'P' in 'Public' is clearly displaced from the rest of the word. It's also much more closely surrounded by foliage than in the shot of the TARDIS arriving. It's evident that the Police Box prop was moved off the forest set in the recording break after the control room scene, as examination of the painted backdrop reveals the landing site is the same bit of set as where Ian later drags Jean-Pierre from the bushes. It would be quicker to have the standalone doors already set up among the bushes for the brief shot of the Doctor by the Ship. Note, these doors can later be glimpsed behind Barbara when soldiers lead her, Susan and Ian away from the burning farmhouse.
- The hum of the scanner stops when the Doctor flicks a lever, but William Hartnell looks and gestures towards the doors and says his line, "Well, if you're going, be off with you," as though he has operated the doors control. The doors are not shown opening until several seconds later, however, while William Russell continues with his next line. Was the vision mixer a bit slow at changing camera shots?
- Although Susan says the Reign of Terror is the Doctor's favourite period of Earth history (perhaps it was the hats), and she herself spotted an inaccuracy in the book on the French Revolution that Barbara loaned her in *An Unearthly Child*, this doesn't necessarily mean they have been to this time before. They may both simply have learned about it and only now have the chance to experience it themselves. One can't imagine they'd be in a hurry to come back after their perils on this visit.
- When the travellers return to the TARDIS at the end of the story, the shot of the Police Box is a photo taken during recording of episode one to avoid having to re-erect the woodland set.

LANDING 10

SPACE Earth, England, near south coast
TIME [Early-1960s]
TRAVELLERS The Doctor, Susan, Barbara, Ian
EPISODES Planet of Giants 1,3

The TARDIS is coming in to land when part of the console overheats, a yellow warning light on the fault locator illuminates and a hooter sounds as the main doors accidentally open before the Ship has fully materialised. Ian, Barbara and Susan succeed in pushing them closed and once the TARDIS has settled everything seems fine, the fault locator reporting no problems. Yet when they turn on the scanner the screen shatters. Outside are what appear to be large heavy stone blocks cemented to the ground, with channels between them. But the travellers soon realise they have been shrunk to about an inch in height and are in a household garden; the stones are cracked paving slabs. When the doors opened during materialisation, the space pressure was too great and compressed the Ship.

When the travellers get back to the diminished Ship some hours later, Barbara is fast succumbing to the DN6 pesticide that has killed all the insect life in the area. The TARDIS dematerialises and its dimensions return to normal. A seed the Doctor brought with him shrinks to its usual size and similarly the effect of the chemicals on Barbara's skin are reduced to harmless levels. As she, Susan and Ian go to clean themselves up, the Doctor checks the scanner but finds it still inoperative as the Ship begins to land again.

- **CONTROLS** As the TARDIS prepares to materialise, the Doctor operates the large slider on panel A4 and the two right-most small levers above it, both of the large sliders on panel A5 simultaneously then the right-most small lever next to them, switches on panels A6 and A1, a knob at the bottom of panel A2, one of the left-hand rotary handles on panel A1, and finally the left-hand rotary handle on panel A4. Barbara burns herself on panel A6. When the doors open the Doctor tries to close them with the two left-most small levers at the top of panel A4. Afterwards the right-hand large slider on panel A5 is back in its upper position so must have been operated during the emergency, but is then in its lower position again after the Doctor has checked the fault locator. He can determine the exterior temperature from a control on the far-left of panel A6. Susan turns on the scanner from panel A3 and opens the doors from panel A4. The Doctor flicks switches at the bottom of panel A2 prior to dematerialising, then again to operate the scanner as the Ship begins to rematerialise.
- The fault locator now has two four-character readouts – showing QR18 and A14D – next to green, amber and red lights labelled respectively 'Green normal', 'Yellow stand by' and 'Red alert'.
- From this story the top grille on panel A2 is replaced with a paler cover like those on panels A4 and A5. The levers on panel A1 have also been repaired and that on A6 has regained its proper spherical knob. The missing lightbulbs on panel A3 have also returned.
- **LORE** The Doctors says that in order to "side-step" the Ship from the late-18th century to the 20th, he "tried another frequency".

- The main doors can be physically pushed closed when they're trying to open [the mechanism cuts outs when it detects resistance – see also Landing 198].
- The point of materialisation is the most dangerous moment in the TARDIS's flight.
- Despite the TARDIS being shrunk, the fault locator shows no problems, suggesting the Ship can operate perfectly well in its reduced circumstances. The scanner can't cope with the unexpected scale, however, as if the image is "too big for its frame".
- Although the Police Box appearance is only a disguise, its windows open, tilting inwards on hinges along the bottom like a real Metropolitan Police Box.
- **NOTES** This serial was produced immediately after *The Reign of Terror* so, when the Doctor says he is trying to nudge the TARDIS from the late-18th century to the middle of the 20th, it's clear the intention at the time was that this was the very next journey. However, given this story was ultimately held back to start the second season of *Doctor Who* (and the Doctor is wearing a snazzy new cloak, not the one given him by the Sensorites) it's possible they've just visited somewhere else in the 1700s on a completely different adventure.
- Farrow visits Forrester while on leave from his ministry, heading to France to tour its rivers (what, all of them?). He says he has "a small boat down in the harbour", which Forrester says is ten miles away, and Farrow is planning to leave that day (sailing across the Channel alone), so Smithers' house must be near a coastal town.
- The TARDIS materialising is shot on film using the same model as in *The Keys of Marinus* (Landing 6). As then, it appears and disappears silently.
- It's not entirely clear whether it's the excessive "space pressure" or the doors opening mid-materialisation that causes the Ship to be shrunk. Perhaps the former caused the latter which disrupted the relative dimensions in (physical) space.
- When the scanner explodes, rather than ruin the screen (and risk injuring cast and crew with flying glass), it simply shows film footage of glass smashing – a clever effect but diminished by the resultant smoke being confined to the screen image (and its losing horizontal hold when the image flashes).
- As the Doctor notes, it's odd that the scanner doesn't show what's outside, even if it is at a magnified scale. This suggests it's not just a direct camera feed but that the scanner needs to interpret the visual data (see Landing 188) and in this instance is overwhelmed with data. Or it's just another glitch.
- As Ian and the Doctor exit the TARDIS, the left-side windows of the Police Box have been left open. This prevents the left-hand door from opening fully, requiring the actors to use both doors. Note how William Hartnell has to push the right-hand door inwards to allow the left, with the centre post, to close first.
- When the TARDIS dematerialises and returns to normal size, the lights in the control room dim but the central column remains stationary. It only starts rising, and the take-off sound is heard, as the Ship begins to rematerialise.
- The closing TARDIS scene as recorded – before the fourth episode was cut down when being combined with the original episode three – began with the Doctor hurriedly repairing the scanner so he can take off and restore the Ship's size, with Ian badgering him as Barbara's condition worsens. This is why in the broadcast episode, when the Doctor checks the scanner and finds it showing only static, he says, "Now that is irritating. I had to repair that wretched thing and now look at it," even though as broadcast he doesn't seem to have had time to fix it since it exploded in episode one. That would also have made it less strange that the Doctor is checking the scanner while the Ship is still in flight.

LANDING 11

SPACE Earth, England, London, under a bridge spanning the Thames
TIME At least several days (maybe a week or more), [around 2167]
TRAVELLERS The Doctor, Susan, Barbara, Ian
EPISODES The Dalek Invasion of Earth 1-2,6

The TARDIS appears silently beneath a dilapidated bridge next to the Thames in London. Pasted to the wall behind the Ship is a sign that reads: 'Emergency regulations. It is forbidden to dump bodies into the river'. Nevertheless, floating in the stinking water is a man in torn clothes and wearing a heavy metal head-piece. The travellers can see nothing of distinction on the scanner but the readings are consistent with Earth so they venture outside.

There is no sound of wildlife, people or traffic and all around is debris and overgrown vegetation, but the teachers recognise it as London. The bridge itself is weak and when Susan climbs up to see better, parts of the structure collapse and a large girder blocks the entrance to the Ship. While the Doctor and Ian search a nearby warehouse for cutting equipment, Barbara bathes Susan's injured ankle. The women are taken by rebels to protect them from patrols, and sure enough when the Doctor and Ian return they are soon surrounded by Robomen as one of their Dalek masters emerges from the river and orders them taken to landing area one.

The travellers return to London after defeating the Dalek invasion and, with help from Wells, Tyler and David Campbell, clear the debris from in front of the TARDIS doors. Susan sits under the bridge, massaging her foot where her shoe has worn through during the journey from Bedfordshire. The Doctor offers to mend it but becomes aware his granddaughter is rather subdued and fears he knows why. He leaves her (taking her shoe with him) to prepare the Ship for take-off, noting David nearby. As Ian says goodbye to their friends, Barbara has to pull him away to let Susan and David talk alone. The young man proposes but Susan cannot choose between the settled life she wants with him and the duty she feels to her grandfather. In the TARDIS, Barbara and Ian watch solemnly as the Doctor comes to a difficult conclusion. He locks the doors and speaks to Susan outside via the scanner, telling her this is her chance to belong somewhere and live a normal life. Promising to return one day, he sets the Ship in motion and the Police Box fades away leaving Susan behind.

- **CONTROLS** The Doctor tries to clear the static on the scanner by flicking a switch on panel A2. Susan reads the external radiation, oxygen and pressure readings from panel A3, and opens the doors by turning both rotary handles on panel A4. The Doctor pulls the central small lever at the top of panel A4 to close and double-lock the doors. He flicks a lever and turns the right-hand rotary handle on the same panel to dematerialise the Ship.
- **LORE** The scanner incorporates a speaker system allowing those inside the Ship to be heard outside.
- The doors can be "double-locked", preventing access even with a key.
- **NOTES** *The Dalek Invasion of Earth* was produced immediately after *Planet of Giants* and is clearly intended to follow directly, with the Doctor tutting at the scanner. However, he has had time to clean himself up and is now wearing his jacket, and the scanner is no longer showing static as it was at the end of *Planet of Giants*, just an indistinct image. Given the repeated problems with the screen, it's possible there are landings between the two television stories, especially as two consecutive visits to Earth (even in different times) is unusual for the Ship at this stage.
- Where does the TARDIS land? London of the 22nd century must have a very different layout to that of today, at least in the *Doctor Who* universe. Because of the variety of filming locations used, the geography shown on screen appears wildly at odds with the real world. The arrival of the TARDIS was filmed beneath the southern end of Kew Railway Bridge in West London but, when the travellers emerge, the shot that is clearly meant to be what they're seeing across the river is of Butler's Wharf on the south bank way downstream to the east. Kew Railway Bridge is arguably nondescript enough to represent any bridge (although the studio set was designed to match it), so perhaps the intention was the TARDIS landed under the northern end of Tower Bridge, across from the wharves on the south. Indeed, Barbara asks, "Are we down by the docks?" which were mainly downstream of Tower Bridge, including the adjacent St Katherine's Dock where some of the shots of the warehouse the Doctor and Ian explore were filmed (although if they are at the northern end of Tower Bridge, then they head west towards the warehouse whereas St Katherine's Dock is east). Yet when Ian looks out the warehouse window he can see Battersea Power Station, which is further upstream beyond Westminster. (Note that this shot – a photo augmented with a futuristic globe-shaped nuclear reactor – is reversed. Battersea is south of the river and Grosvenor Bridge is west of it, but as seen here, apparently from the east, the bridge is in front of the power station.) So is the warehouse actually in Pimlico on the opposite bank to Battersea and the TARDIS arrived under the northern end of Vauxhall Bridge? Moments later the Doctor and Ian watch a Dalek flying saucer crossing the skyline, which we see passing east-west across the rooftops of the Foreign & Commonwealth Offices as we look south towards Victoria Tower and Westminster Abbey. That viewpoint is from the heart of Westminster, which can't be where the travellers are. When the Doctor and Ian return to the TARDIS, the latter suggests the saucer landed "somewhere over the other side of the river, in the direction of Sloane Square." That's north of the river in Chelsea, which means the TARDIS is definitely on the south bank after all. And Ian can only have made that estimation if he were somewhere in Battersea, placing the Ship under Chelsea, Albert or, at a pinch, Battersea Bridge. In any case, his earlier view of Battersea Power Station would be impossible (unless in this universe it was built on the north side of the river in Churchill Gardens). Finally, when the Dalek rises from the water, this was filmed close to the northern end of Hammersmith Bridge (near Riverside Studios, where much of the series' pre-filmed studio scenes were staged).
- In *The Daleks' Master Plan*, the Doctor advises Bret Vyon to look to historical records of the year 2157 for details of the last time the Daleks attacked Earth. This could be when the Daleks initiated their invasion by bombarding Earth with plague-bearing meteorites, said to be about ten years prior to the Doctor's arrival, their main attack beginning six months later. Although the Doctor finds a calendar for 2164, this is in a long-disused warehouse so unlikely to be the current date.
- The TARDIS materialises – filmed on location for the first time – with its right-side windows open, a detail carefully matched when the scene moves into the studio a moment later (although now the Police Box is at a different angle to the wall behind it). When the bridge collapses, the 'Emergency regulations' poster can be seen through these open windows (perhaps because, as a set photo shows, the right-hand rear door was missing its window entirely. Although the back of the box is seen in episode six it's not clear if this has been refitted).
- In episode one, the fault locator, including the scanner framework, is a large photo of that wall section and part of the floor, hung as a backdrop (the bottom edge of which can be seen as the camera pulls back). This was to save space in the studio as only one brief scene in the TARDIS was required. So despite the Doctor saying the fuzzy scanner image could be "moving water" it is in fact perfectly still.
- In the studio the Police Box prop had its roof light removed to avoid it breaking when the bridge girder was dropped. Indeed, the 'Police box' sign above the

doors is damaged by the falling beam, as clearly seen in episode six when the debris has been cleared away. Note that the side windows are now closed, when they were open in episode one. The telephone plaque panel is also ajar, confirming it was indeed hinged.
- For the first time the TARDIS is seen to dematerialise while an actor is also on screen. To achieve this a photo of the Police Box was superimposed using inlay onto the shot of Susan on the bridge set and then faded out.

LANDING 12

SPACE Dido, cave
TIME After 2493
TRAVELLERS The Doctor, Barbara, Ian
EPISODES The Rescue 1-2

The TARDIS materialises on the planet Dido while the Doctor sleeps in a chair in the control room. When Barbara and Ian wake him, he shuts off the power to complete the landing and checks the external environment. When the scanner shows they are in a cave or underground, Barbara fears they could be trapped but the Doctor assures her the Ship can take off again quite easily. With Susan gone, he shows Barbara how to open the main doors and they head outside.

The Doctor recognises an unusual smell in the cave but is not intrigued enough to investigate, instead returning to the Ship to continue his nap – although he can hear Ian and Barbara talking via the scanner and pops back out to collect a stone sample. As the couple find a way out of the cave via a tunnel, the TARDIS is examined by what appears to be a creature with spiky spines and protruding eyes. It follows the two travellers and shortly afterwards Ian returns alone, just before the tunnel collapses in an explosion. The noise brings the Doctor out of the Ship, where he has examined the stone and determined he is back on Dido. He fetches a large torch from inside and discovers Ian stunned by the rockfall. Finding the previous route blocked and worried about Barbara, they hurriedly seek another way out of the cave.

Later, an unconscious Doctor is left outside the TARDIS by two surviving Didonians. Ian and Barbara find him there and Ian uses the Doctor's key to open the Ship and take him inside. Vicki is waiting in the cave and the recovered Doctor goes out to speak to her. She has no one left to look after her so the Doctor invites her aboard the TARDIS. He leaves her a moment to consider and, back in the Ship, learns that Ian and Barbara have had the same idea. Amazed by the Ship's larger interior, Vicki agrees to join them. The Police Box vanishes from the cave as the Doctor explains to Ian that not all the Didonians are dead and he doubts they will let the approaching rescue ship land.

○ **CONTROLS** The Doctor shuts off the power after landing by turning the rotary handle on panel A5, moving the two large sliders downwards and flicking the small levers upwards. He checks the external air quality and temperature from panel A3 and operates the scanner with one of the small levers at the top of panel A4. He teaches Barbara to open the main doors using "number four switch": the fourth lever from the right at the top of panel A4. When he prepares to dematerialise the Ship, the Doctor turns the rotary handle on panel A5 as the doors close then flicks switches and levers on the same panel. He operates controls on panels A3, A4 and A5 as the TARDIS takes flight.

○ One of the small levers on panel A5 really controls the centre lightbulb between the two grilles.

○ From this story onwards the two dark grilles at the bottom of panel A1 are missing (although their screw holes are still visible). These are never replaced, leaving a conspicuously blank area on this panel.

▮ **LORE** Travellers in the TARDIS can feel a trembling when the Ship is in flight, which stops when it lands. Sometimes, as here and previously briefly seen at the end of the very first episode, the Police Box roof lamp can continue to flash after the TARDIS has materialised.

▮ The Ship can travel through solid matter.

▮ **NOTES** This was the first serial produced in *Doctor Who*'s second recording block, after a month's break since completing *The Dalek Invasion of Earth*. Even so, the intention was that this story followed directly from the last. Although not absolute proof, the Doctor's sleeping through the landing, absent-mindedly asking Susan to open the main doors, and then Barbara and Ian's musing about her and David all strongly suggest little time has passed since they said goodbye to her.

▮ When Barbara asks Vicki what year she left Earth, she says, "2493, of course," as if it should be obvious. Without knowing how far Dido is from Earth or how long it is since the spaceship crashed, for all Barbara knows Vicki left when she was a baby and has spent her life in space. Then again it seems quite a small ship, suitable only for short journeys, so perhaps Dido is fairly close to Earth and Vicki thinks it's clear it can't be more than a year since they left and she's basically saying, "Well, this year, duh!" Learning Barbara is from 1963, Vicki estimates her age as "about 550", which must be an overestimation as a 2513 date would make Vicki at least 20 years old.

▮ The arrival of the TARDIS was achieved by mixing from a photo of the empty cave set to another of the same view but with the Police Box prop in position. The latter had the roof lamp cut out and a light was waved behind the hole to animate the flashing lamp. Its departure uses the same photo dissolve only in reverse and slightly zoomed out. In both shots, the rising take-off sound effect is heard, with the preceding rumble for the actual take-off.

▮ The inside of the Police Box prop has been lined with a crinkled foil-like material, perhaps a curtain to prevent the rear doors being seen. This can be seen again in *The Space Museum* (Landing 16).

▮ Barbara notices the Ship has stopped even though the central column is still oscillating and the landing sound

can be heard. The roof lamp also keeps flashing long after arrival, presumably a directorial choice to explain how the travellers can see inside the dark cave.
- Why is she now worried about being trapped underground when the Ship has previously landed inside an Aztec tomb and a spaceship without impediment?
- When the travellers return to the Ship, the left-hand door's window is open. This causes a continuity error because it's closed in the photo sequence of its take-off.
- Oops! Just before Vicki first enters the control room, a camera can be seen reflected in the acrylic screen at the back of the set.

LANDING 13

SPACE Earth, Italy, Umbria, hillside near Asisium
TIME Mid-June to a few days after 18 July 64
TRAVELLERS The Doctor, Barbara, Ian, Vicki
EPISODES The Rescue 2; The Romans 1,4

The TARDIS begins to rematerialise straight away, the Doctor hoping for a chance to rest. But the Ship arrives on a narrow cliff path, sways momentarily then topples over, throwing the occupants across the control room. It comes to rest at the bottom of the hill, unharmed but at an angle on some rocks. Nevertheless, the travellers leave it there hidden by branches and take up residence at the nearby empty villa of Flavius Guiscard for a well-earned holiday.

The Doctor and Vicki return to the villa having escaped Rome ahead of the Great Fire, unaware Ian and Barbara have themselves only recently got back from their own adventures in the city. All four head back to the TARDIS, Ian bringing a jug and goblet with him as souvenirs. They clear away the branches from the roof and in front of the doors and board. The Ship dematerialises, its engines not even disturbing the chirping birds. As the Doctor monitors the console, Vicki tells Barbara and Ian about how he fooled Nero's court by only pretending to play the lyre. The women change out of their Roman clothes, Vicki disbelieving the teachers' claim that not even the Doctor knows where they will land next.

- **CONTROLS** As the Ship settles the Doctor flicks levers at the top of panel A4 and turns back the rotary handle on panel A5. After take-off he operates a switch along the bottom of panel A2.
- **LORE** The orientation of the Police Box exterior directly affects the interior.
- **NOTES** The TARDIS on the cliff edge features a newly made model, much larger (just over three feet tall) than the one previously used during the first production block. While reasonably faithful to the full-size prop, its roof is less deeply stacked, the window frames and bars are blue instead of white, its St John Ambulance emblem is more prominent and the rail below the lowest panels is taller.
- The actors throw themselves backwards towards the main doors to simulate the control room tipping, but in the model shot the Police Box falls to its left with the front doors facing sideways.
- It's indicated by the centurion in episode one and by Barbara in episode four that the story starts in the vicinity of the Roman town of Asisium (modern-day Assisi) but it would appear this is not the location of the market Barbara and Vicki visit. That is generally referred to as a village and the slaver Sevcheria is confident it's too small a place for any law enforcement to interfere with his kidnapping plans. Also, the real Maximum Petullian is seen playing there during the day, yet that evening the centurion who encounters the Doctor tells him Petullian was expected in Asisium the previous day but did not arrive. The most likely explanation is the villa the travellers squat in is just north of a village that itself is an hour or so's walk north of Asisium. Thus Petullian passes through behind schedule and is murdered as he approaches Asisium, where the Doctor and Vicki later find his body as they head south towards Rome. The centurion explicitly escorts them to Asisium that evening, from where they continue to Rome the next morning.
- The travellers have been staying at the villa for "three or four weeks" according to Barbara; "nearly a month" by Vicki's reckoning. The night the latter and the Doctor leave for Rome (it's odd they don't wait for morning but then the Doctor can be impetuous), Ian and Barbara are taken by slave traders. Barbara is forced to walk the 80 or so miles to Rome – at least three or four days' journey on foot – and arrives about the same time as the Doctor (so do he and Vicki also walk rather than finding a carriage?). Ian's journey is less clear. Assisi is about as far from the sea as you can get in Italy so why is someone looking to buy galley slaves in the vicinity? Ancona on the eastern Adriatic coast is probably the nearest port, yet Ian washes up on a beach a day's walk from Rome from the wreck of a ship that was sailing south. Any river journey from Assisi would eventually lead into the Tiber and thence to Rome, but the buyer says he's going nowhere near the city. Yet the main ports on the western Tyrrhenian coast are Ortia and Portus – just outside Rome. So did he take his charges all the way across land to a smaller port further north, such as Tarquinii or even Populonium, just to then sail south along the coast within swimming distance of Rome? If so, when Ian indicates it has been five days since (presumably) he was taken, he can have spent only the last of those actually rowing. He arrives in Rome and ends up in the gladiatorial school the day before Nero implements his (or rather the Doctor's) plan to burn down the city, which occurred on the night of 18 July. Ian and Barbara and, separately, the Doctor and Vicki all leave Rome that night, presumably another three- or four-day journey (unless this time they do secure some wheeled transport). The former pair arrive at least several hours ahead of the latter – they've had time to tidy and freshen up and take a long sleep. So in all they spend just over a month in 1st-century Italy.

LANDING 14

SPACE Isop galaxy, Vortis; dragged into Carsenome
TIME Unknown [future]
TRAVELLERS The Doctor, Barbara, Ian, Vicki
EPISODES The Romans 4; The Web Planet 1-4,6

The Doctor notices the TARDIS has materialised and instantly been enveloped by a powerful force from which he cannot break free. He claims the Ship is "being slowly dragged down" although it makes a seemingly normal materialisation on the barren, rocky surface of Vortis. The air is thin but breathable.

The others change into their regular clothes while the Doctor tries to deduce what force is holding the Ship. Outside, man-sized ant-like Zarbi approach the TARDIS making incomprehensible chirruping sounds. Inside, Vicki is pained by a humming in her head; the Doctor presumes it is an "extrasonic" sound audible only to the young.

He tries to overcome the force holding the TARDIS on Vortis and for a moment it begins to silently dematerialise but re-solidifies as the power drains away and a wispy web envelops it. The Ship is shaken, causing the image on the scanner to sway wildly, and the travellers are thrown to the floor as the sound of the Zarbi is heard inside. When things settle, Barbara takes Vicki to recover from her headache, while Ian and the Doctor don atmospheric density jackets to sustain them while they explore the planet. Without power to operate the main doors, the Doctor activates a light in the equipment area and by eccentrically waving his jewelled ring in front of it he makes the doors open. Outside the web has cleared from the Ship and the Doctor discovers the rocks contain mica. The force holding the TARDIS also attracts gold objects, plucking Ian's pen from his hands and, even in the Ship, pulling on the gold bracelet Barbara is wearing. As the Zarbi's chirruping crescendoes, the doors are forced open, a table is upset and the console itself spins. Barbara is overcome and in a trance is led from the control room by the pull on her bracelet. Vicki is alone in the TARDIS as it again is shaken. Thrown against the console, she panics and operates levers, unwittingly realigning the fluid link and restoring the power.

However, the force is still too great for the Ship to dematerialise and it is dragged away, shepherded by the twittering Zarbi. Vicki watches helplessly on the scanner as the Police Box is drawn into the Carsenome – a structure of dense creepers that has grown around the Animus. The doors open on their own and she ventures out only to be surrounded by Zarbi. One tries to enter the TARDIS but is repelled. Ian and the Doctor are brought in having also been captured, and the latter communicates with the Animus. It believes he is part of a Menoptra invasion spearhead and, to show its power, has a wall-mounted weapon fire at the TARDIS but it is unharmed. The Doctor negotiates access to the Ship to recover the astral map with which to detect the massing Menoptra forces. He and Ian bring it out, being careful not to unplug its power cable as that would break the time and relative dimension link.

Pretending to gather information for the Animus, the Doctor sends Vicki into the TARDIS for a red box containing "a recording compound" but when she returns with it he insists he asked for a white box and that she has brought one of his specimens – a dead spider – which Vicki discovers frightens the Zarbi.

The Doctor sends Vicki into the Ship for his walking stick, which he uses to get close enough to one of the Zarbi's gold control collars to examine it without falling under the Animus's influence, while Vicki distracts their Zarbi guard with the boxed spider. The Doctor attaches the collar to the astral map and uses the power from the TARDIS to disable its effect. Now able to control the collar with the power of his ring, the Doctor slips it round the neck of the Zarbi guard and has it lead him and Vicki out of the Carsenome.

Once the Animus has been destroyed by the Menoptra's isop-tope device, the Carsenome dies also and quickly rots away, leaving the TARDIS in the open air. The ground is still rocky but water is returning to the surface, as are the subterranean Optera. The Doctor leads the others back into the Ship and it fades from the surface of Vortis, leaving only a legend of how Earth people came to defeat the dark power.

- **CONTROLS** The Doctor operates two switches on panel A6 to gauge the power response. He adjusts the small levers on panel A4 as the power builds and switches on panel A5 when checking the motors. As the TARDIS tries to dematerialise, the Doctor turns the rotary switch on the left of panel A1. He uses the row of levers on panel A5 to try to counteract the interference, and flicks one of the same to try to open the main doors. Vicki frantically throws levers on panels A1 and A6, which initiate the dematerialisation sound, although the Ship doesn't take off.
- The control at bottom-right of panel A2 has been replaced with a smaller black knob and the vertical strip next to it is missing. The hatch in the console's pedestal below panel A6 is missing its cover.
- **LORE** The console is freestanding and can be moved.
- The TARDIS has a forcefield that can repel intruders.
- **NOTES** Although the travellers encounter no other humans on Vortis, it's likely their landing there is at a time in Earth's relative future as the Animus plans to use the knowledge it extracts from them to "pluck from Earth its myriad techniques and take from man his mastery of space".
- The shot of the TARDIS materialising on Vortis used the new 3-foot miniature made for *The Romans*.
- It's not clear how the TARDIS is trapped by the Animus. It doesn't appear to have materialised in orbit around Vortis and been physically pulled to the surface, as the dialogue perhaps suggests, because the Police Box fades into view as usual rather than descending from the sky. So did the Animus somehow reach out into the Vortex and pluck the Ship from there, particularly as the Doctor says they have been dragged off course?
- The control room now has a small equipment area with scientific instruments on metal shelves, a first-aid box, an old dentist's equipment tower (forgotten about or

lost before *The Gunfighters* – Landing 38), a stool on wheels, plus the free-standing astral map. The light the Doctor uses to open the doors is a Cobra table lamp designed by Angelo Lelli in 1964.
- The electrical cables powering the console are clearly visible snaking across the studio floor in episode one.
- The TARDIS fading in and out was achieved by superimposing a shot of the Police Box prop over another of the Vortis backdrop, although the mask for the inlay effect is poorly aligned. The prop has a new roof lamp for the first episode, more slender than before with the rods supporting the more rounded cap in line with the roof's sides rather than its corners. By episode three this has been replaced by a wider, straight-sided lamp with a square cap and rods back in the corners.
- Barbara puts her goblet (the one Ian purloined from the villa in Roman Italy) on the console when she comforts Vicki and it's still there after everyone falls about as the TARDIS is shaken. It has gone by the time the console starts spinning.
- When the Doctor operates the main doors with his ring (has it some power of its own that he transfers to the TARDIS?) he and Ian look round to watch them, but the right-hand door is already wide open.
- The bedroom with fold-down recliners first seen in *The Edge of Destruction* appears again.
- Oops! As Barbara grabs hold of the spinning console, the studio's illuminated exit sign can be seen beyond the edge of the set. To be fair, this was probably not visible on televisions of the time.
- The shots of the TARDIS being drawn across the surface of Vortis and into the Carsenome are on film and feature the 3-foot model.
- It's not clear why the Zarbi is repelled from entering the TARDIS when the travellers can come and go as they please. Perhaps it's a result of the creature's dominance by the Animus, some form of mental control that's antipathetic to the dimensional forces in the Ship, or simply that the TARDIS doesn't want to let the Zarbi in.
- In this scene, the long cylinder of the lock – as seen when removed in *The Sensorites* (Landing 8) – can be seen projecting from the back of the left-hand door of the Police Box prop, along with what may be a latch on the inside of the door. Note the window in this door is hinged open throughout (although not when the model is used, of course), as is one of the side windows when the TARDIS dematerialises at the end of the story.
- Given its name, the astral map is presumably a navigation aid, although it can also receive and record audio transmissions. It appears to be something the Doctor has acquired (there is another in Eldred's rocket museum in *The Seeds of Death*) but it does plug into the control room wall so must be compatible with Time Lord technology. The time and relative dimension link he cautions mustn't be broken perhaps aligns the map with the Ship's location in order to present relevant star charts.
- When the Doctor and Ian wheel the astral map out of the Ship, the actors clearly push it from behind the Police Box prop, rather than from inside it, presumably to avoid it clattering over the doorstep.
- In episode six, with the Police Box prop erected on the Vortis surface set for the final scenes, the shot of it in the Carsenome is a photo (of the rear of the box, probably taken during the studio day for episode three when the prop was last on that set), and the scenes of Barbara and the Menoptra in the Zarbi centre finding the astral map are shot to avoid showing the corner where the TARDIS should be standing. Its departure is a dissolve from a shot of the Police Box to a photo of the Vortis set, although a very different area so the rock formations change as the Ship departs. A recording break allowed the prop to be removed from the set before the final scene.

PREVIOUS LANDINGS

SPACE Earth, South Africa, Mafeking
TIME May 1900
TRAVELLERS The Doctor, [unknown companions]
EPISODES Mentioned by the Doctor in
  The Daleks' Master Plan 8
The Doctor witnessed the celebrations following the Relief of Mafeking.
- **NOTES** As the Doctor is telling Steven and Sara about Mafeking, his trip must have been before they (particularly the former) came aboard the TARDIS, so before Landing 15, after which landings are sequential until Steven's arrival.
- The siege of Mafeking (now called Mahikeng) during the Second Boer War was a significant victory for the British after Colonel Robert Baden-Powell (later to found the Scouting Movement) defended the town from Boer attack for seven months until reinforcements arrived. Baden-Powell employed some ingenious methods to convince the enemy his position was stronger than it really was, ideas that could have been suggested by the Doctor were he there.
- Note, however, that when observing the New Year's Eve crowds the Doctor says, "I've seen them behave in a fashion like that on a former occasion." The Relief of Mafeking was widely celebrated back in Britain so the Doctor may not have been there in person but was in England when the welcome news came through.
- The Doctor mentions the Relief of Mafeking again in *The Invasion of Time*, although only to compare it to the relatively quiet victory over the Vardans, not to suggest he was there.

SPACE Toymaker's domain
TIME None
TRAVELLERS The Doctor, [unknown companions]
EPISODES Recalled by the Toymaker in
  The Celestial Toymaker 1

The Doctor briefly arrived in the Toymaker's domain but did not stay long enough to succumb to any of his devious games.

NOTES The Doctor's first encounter with the Toymaker was before he met Steven. It's possible he wasn't even in the TARDIS – during Landing 37 the Toymaker is able to hijack the Ship and tamper with its scanner operations to lure the Doctor out; either he wasn't quick enough to do this previously or the Doctor was using a different form of transport, perhaps a different TARDIS on a mission for the Time Lords before he left Gallifrey with Susan.

LANDING 15

SPACE Earth, Palestine, woodland near Jaffa
TIME Two days in [October 1191]
TRAVELLERS The Doctor, Barbara, Ian, Vicki
EPISODES The Crusade 1,4

The TARDIS arrives in woodland overlooking the coastal town of Jaffa, fortunately materialising with just a quiet whirr as a Saracen soldier has passed its landing spot moments before. He and his squad are stalking a nearby early-morning hunting party of European knights, suspecting that one of them is the English king Richard. The travellers leave the Ship and are soon embroiled in a fight between the two parties, both Ian and the Doctor taking up swords to hold off the attacking Saracens. The Doctor's life is saved by the injured William de Tornebu but Barbara is carried away. As Ian searches for her, the Doctor gets drugs from the Ship for Vicki to apply to the knight's arrow wound. After an hour Ian returns empty handed, but de Tornebu is carrying a valuable belt of the king's and the Doctor is confident they can use it to gain Richard's favour and so secure help in finding Barbara. Ian stays by the Ship to make a stretcher for de Tornebu while the Doctor brings out two cloaks to hide his and Vicki's anachronistic clothing so they can head into Jaffa to find more suitable attire. Returning with stolen garments, they carry the wounded knight to Richard's headquarters in the town.

The day after their arrival, Ian and Barbara return to the wood where the TARDIS stands. Tired by their ride from Lydda, they hide among the tall bushes around the Ship and wait for their friends. As dusk falls, the Doctor and Vicki approach but find their way barred by the Earl of Leicester, who has followed them, convinced the Doctor is a spy for the Saracens. The pair try to slip past but although Vicki reaches the TARDIS, the Doctor is caught. Ian steps out into the clearing and claims he has a prior right to be the Doctor's executioner. The condemned man asks to look upon Jaffa one last time, to which Leicester agrees and allows Ian to lead him through the bushes. As the travellers bundle into the TARDIS, Leicester realises he has been tricked but can only mourn the fate of brave Sir Ian as he is spirited away in the vanishing blue box.

NOTES While Barbara tells Saladin, "I could say I'm from another world...ruled by insects," she doesn't mean directly; she also mentions being "in Rome at the time of Nero. Before that we were in England, far, far into the future" so she isn't listing all landings in sequence.

Although dates and events often differ in *Doctor Who* from our own history, King Richard I captured the town of Jaffa (now part of Tel Aviv-Yafo) in September 1191 (after the Battle of Arsuf, mentioned in episode three) and in the following weeks offered to marry his sister to Saladin's brother. However, dialogue suggests he has yet to march on Ascalon as he seems unaware that the town was demolished by Saladin.

While the Police Box prop was present in the studio on the woodland set, its arrival and departure were pre-filmed as this was easier to achieve on film than videotape. It doesn't appear with the usual grinding noise but a softer whirr (different from that in *The Reign of Terror* – Landing 9); birdsong is heard at the same time so this must be a diegetic sound.

LANDING 16

SPACE Xeros, close to Morok museum
TIME Unknown future
TRAVELLERS The Doctor, Barbara, Ian, Vicki
EPISODES The Crusade 4; The Space Museum 1,3-4

The TARDIS has barely left Earth when it jumps a time track. In the control room, the lights go out and the background hum fades, although the console still works. Stood around it, all four travellers are momentarily frozen in position. The Ship materialises on the sandy surface of the planet Xeros, a short distance from a number of disused spaceships of different design and sophistication, positioned beside the planet's museum of space exploration.

When the travellers are free to move again they find they are suddenly wearing regular clothes, not their medieval outfits, which Vicki finds hanging in the wardrobe as if they had changed without remembering. The Doctor is unperturbed and puts it down merely to a case of "time and relativity". Vicki fetches him a glass of water from the food machine but when she accidentally drops it she is shocked to see the shattered tumbler reform and spring back into her hand.

With no signs of life visible on the scanner, the travellers venture outside. Although the area is highly eroded, suggesting great age, the atmosphere is temperate. However, Ian notices they are not leaving any footprints in the deep dust.

As the travellers explore the museum, the time tracks realign. The TARDIS becomes visible to the Morok guards, the travellers' footprints appear in the sand, and inside the Ship the glass falls again and stays broken. The Moroks cannot get into the TARDIS so move it to just outside the museum's entrance, shooing away curious Xerons.

The commanding Morok, Governor Lobos, and his deputy examine the Police Box and order cutting equipment be brought to force open the door. Before they can, Ian, Barbara and Vicki are found trying to get out of the museum. Ian fights off two Moroks outside the Ship as they try to take him to the governor's office. He hides behind the Police Box and overcomes the lone guard, forcing him to reveal where the Doctor is being held.

Three Moroks bring a handheld drill attached by cable to a power pack but as they start to use it on the TARDIS door the deputy governor arrives and notices the entrance to the museum is unguarded. He takes two of the soldiers with him to find out what happened to the relief guard, leaving the other standing sentry.

When Barbara and Dako emerge from the gas-filled building, the guard holds them at gunpoint but is himself shot by Sita, whom Vicki has helped break into the Morok armoury. The deputy returns with a guard, gunning down Sita and knocking out Dako before taking Barbara and Vicki to face the governor. But the armed Xerons are revolting and shoot down more Moroks as they try to take refuge in the museum building. The Xeron leader Tor revives Dako, learns of the women's capture and heads off to rescue them.

With the Xerons' uprising a success, they begin dismantling the museum and reclaiming their planet. Among the exhibits is an inoperative time and space visualiser, which Tor allows the Doctor to take as a souvenir. Once it has been manoeuvred into the Ship, the Doctor checks the controls and discovers a small component got stuck, causing the TARDIS to land and the travellers to exist on a separate time track until the element released itself – he likens it to the delay in a lightbulb's element reaching incandescence after an electrical current is applied. He removes the component to show Ian and Barbara outside, then has them take it back inside. There they see the visualiser and re-emerge to ask the Doctor what it does but he tells them they will see once he has repaired it. Vicki says her goodbyes to Tor and joins the others in the Ship and it vanishes from Xeros. But its journey is being tracked from afar…

- **CONTROLS** The Doctor sets the ship in motion from panel A5. He restores the control room's lights using the far-left lever at the top of panel A4 and opens the main doors with the lever next to it. The unnamed component that caused the dimensional trouble is an inch-long silver rod.
- **NOTES** The presence of a time and space visualiser – a human device given it's labelled with planets from the Solar system – in the Morok museum indicates this landing is at a time in Earth's relative future (see Landing 17).
- The arrival of the TARDIS was filmed using the 3-foot model. Note it doesn't have the white window frames of the full-size prop and the ledge above the 'Police box' signs is shallower.
- The TARDIS's wardrobe is seen for the first time, or at least a cupboard with a rail on which hang the costumes worn in *The Crusade*. The door is recycled from the spaceship set built for *The Sensorites*.
- This is the last appearance of the original TARDIS food machine. Instead of dispensing a pouch of water as it did in *The Edge of Destruction*, it fills the glass Vicki places in its slot.
- This scene of Vicki getting a glass of water was pre-filmed ahead of the studio recording of episode one. As well as the food machine, it features the original interior doors last seen in *The Web Planet* episode one (although they've lost their translucent roundels) plus one of the indented walls and a photographic wall (positioned on its left-hand side so the roundels are aligned in rows rather than columns).
- The Police Box the travellers find inside the museum is again the model (or a photo of it), not the full-size prop (which was on the exterior set), superimposed over the shot of the actors. Even before the Doctor walks through the image, you can see the bottom edge of the wall and the actors' shadows where the TARDIS appears to be standing.
- What does jumping a time track mean? From what we see here, it seems to be a discontinuity in the process of cause and effect. The TARDIS has skipped ahead in time resulting in a delay before the effects of the travellers' actions are felt by the rest of the universe. Thus when the travellers arrive on Xeros, their footprints in the sand, their contact with objects in the museum, even their very presence are not perceived immediately. Similarly, they can see the Moroks and Xerons talking but not hear their speech (although why this should be restricted to audible phenomena is unclear. Why aren't the inhabitants invisible to the travellers too?). Eventually the time tracks realign and effect follows cause as normal. Rather than a gradual re-synchronising, they appear to snap back suddenly and the effects of actions made earlier (although on a different time track) are now perceptible, but not their causes. Thus to the Moroks the TARDIS and the travellers' footprints appear from nowhere. Presumably the exhibit Vicki and Ian tried to touch suddenly falls off its pedestal and a guard outside the museum is startled by a sneeze from nowhere. The time the TARDIS skipped is when the travellers (would have) changed their clothes, and as they re-sync with the rest of the universe there's a suggestion they now have some awareness of that period, as though it happened but then didn't because the TARDIS jumped ahead. So if they've been walking around in advance of their actual arrival (from the perspective of the rest of the universe), how do they see themselves already in cabinets? The Doctor suggests this is a glimpse of a possible future and the travellers spend the rest of the story fretting over whether they are bound to that future or can change it. However, perhaps they are actually viewing the effects of causes that now never happened. The Doctor says, "We must have arrived here sometime in the TARDIS. These

people saw us and thought we were worthy people to be put in their space museum." As they are seeing this from their position ahead of the rest of the universe, it has already happened. So did the TARDIS foresee its occupants being captured on Xeros and deliberately jump a time track to delay their arrival and avoid that outcome? (Either this dislodged the component or its misalignment saved them by mere happenstance.) The travellers are thus witnessing events as they would have happened – they got changed, landed and were captured and frozen – but when their time track realigns that past is erased and they are no longer in danger of being exhibited in the museum.

▪ The Police Box prop is lined with shiny material, as in *The Rescue* (Landing 12), visible when Ian and Barbara emerge to ask about the time and space visualiser.

▪ According to documentation, the departure of the TARDIS was pre-filmed and edited together with the following zoom towards Skaro as a single film insert. However, the only pre-filming done for the story was of Vicki dropping the glass of water (so it could be shown in reverse) and model shots of the space museum exterior. The latter include 'TARDIS dematerializing' but this must be the shot of it arriving in episode one, which is otherwise un-noted in the schedule and definitely uses the 3-foot model, whereas the shot of the Ship departing in episode four is demonstrably the full-size prop. There seems to be no indication that the Police Box prop and two sections of museum wall were included in the pre-filming at Ealing Studios. Other sources, including the production notes on the story's DVD release, indicate the roll-back-and-mix technique was used. After shooting the Police Box on the set, the video recording was rewound slightly while the prop was removed, then the tape was restarted and a shot of the empty set was gradually mixed in to make it appear as if the TARDIS were fading away. This was actually difficult to achieve in the studio at the time but is perhaps the sort of thing technically minded director Mervyn Pinfield would attempt. Certainly the alignment of the background as the TARDIS vanishes is precisely maintained, an effect rarely achieved on film as film cameras don't produce as steady a picture as electronic cameras. (It's hard to be sure from watching the episode as it only survives as a film copy anyway so the tell-tale differences between filmed and taped material are less clear.)

LANDING 17

SPACE Aridius, Sagaro desert
TIME Two days in unknown
TRAVELLERS The Doctor, Barbara, Ian, Vicki
EPISODES The Chase 1-3

The TARDIS flies through the Vortex as the Doctor works in the control room to repair his newly acquired time and space visualiser, although distracted by Vicki's tuneless whistling. He gets it working and uses it to view Abraham Lincoln's speech at Gettysburg, Shakespeare at Queen Elizabeth's court, and a Beatles performance in 1965.

As the travellers dance to the Fab Four, the TARDIS materialises on the planet Aridius, which orbits two suns with a low rotational period and has slightly greater gravity and more oxygen in its atmosphere than Earth. There are only sand dunes around the Ship – once the bottom of the ocean before the approaching suns dried up the waters. As Vicki and Ian explore, the Doctor gives the latter a "TARDIS magnet" – a homing device to lead them back to the Ship.

Barbara and the Doctor stay by the TARDIS to sunbathe. When the visualiser begins whining they return to the control room to switch it off, only to find it has tuned in to the Daleks preparing to set off in their own time machine in pursuit of the TARDIS. Before they can find Ian and Vicki to warn them, night falls and a sandstorm blows up. By the morning the Ship is completely buried.

The Daleks have arrived on Aridius and use seismic detectors to locate the TARDIS. They take two Aridians prisoner and force them to dig out the Police Box, then exterminate them. They fire on the Ship too but their weapons are insufficient to destroy it. Vicki watches from a nearby hatchway to the Aridians' underground city.

After sunset, the reunited travellers cover the edge of the open hatchway and lure the lone Dalek guard to pass over it and fall down into the city. They rush into the Ship as more Daleks arrive and ineffectively fire on the departing Police Box.

The travellers rejoice at their narrow escape but soon the time-path detector on the console indicates another time machine is following them.

◉ **CONTROLS** The time-path detector – which surveys the path through the Vortex along which the TARDIS is travelling and warns of other time machines on the same route – is located in the top-left corner of panel A2. It doesn't appear until needed in episode three even though the Doctor claims it has always been in the Ship, and disappears again after this story.

◉ The rotary handle at the top of panel A6 and the small lever to the left of it are missing, their places covered with foil, which also seems to have been used to cover part of the grille at the top of the panel. The handle will eventually be replaced but the small lever never returns and the foil marking its position also disappears, both sometime before *The Tenth Planet*.

▪ **LORE** The TARDIS can be located with a homing device, a spherical unit with a spinning attachment.

▪ The TARDIS is invulnerable to Dalek firepower.

▪ **NOTES** The story opens with the series' first representation of the TARDIS in the Vortex, with moving kaleidoscope patterns superimposed over a shot of the smaller Police Box model seen in *The Keys of Marinus* and *Planet of Giants*.

▪ The time and space visualiser appears to have been built specifically to spy on our solar system as the dials around the screen are labelled with the names of Earth's fellow planets. Although Pluto is included,

Mercury is not – perhaps it's too close to the Sun for its radiated light neutrons to be detected. Vicki says scientists of her time were working on a device to convert light neutrons to electrical impulses so they could view historical events. The Doctor's response, "That's exactly what this is," could mean it's either that type of device or specifically the one humans were developing in the 25th century. As it can tune in to Dalek headquarters, do they have a base in the solar system or has the Doctor widened the visualiser's range?

- The bedroom is seen again with its angled recliners, this time with a wall of roundels (one of the indented walls). The visualiser is by the equipment area introduced in *The Web Planet*. The interior doors have had just one of their roundels refitted since *The Space Museum* episode one; there's a poor camera move revealing the internal framework of this set piece when Vicki leaves Ian to his book and enters the bedroom. Shots of the visualiser also show the edge of a photographic wall, exposing the fact its roundels were flat.
- The arrival of the TARDIS on Aridius was filmed on location using the 3-foot Police Box model, its first use outside a studio so now fitted with a battery to power the flashing roof lamp. Its departure was achieved in the studio by mixing from a shot of the Police Box prop (in negative while being fired upon) to another camera pointed at a different area of the desert set.
- To avoid taking up too much studio space with the control room set, which already had to incorporate the bulky visualiser prop, the console was not present and a low camera angle was used to suggest the Doctor operating the controls. This unfortunately shows the top of the main doors wall and the studio lights beyond.
- After its foil-like backing in the last story, here the Police Box prop appears completely open at the back. This may have been a deliberate attempt to suggest the bright interior of the Ship. Note the painted backcloth of the sand dunes of Aridius is not visible behind the emerging time travellers, suggesting the open rear of the prop is covered by a backlit sheet of white material (the shadows at the base of the Police Box indicate there is a light behind it).
- In episode two, when the Daleks have uncovered the Ship and attempt to destroy it, the camera shows the left-hand side and back of the Police Box prop, with the rear doors closed of course. When a Dalek turns its back to the Ship to guard it, it bumps against the prop and the rear doors can be seen to wobble.
- What is the point of introducing the TARDIS magnet? Obviously it's a handy device but Ian never needs to use it. The intention seems to be to set up the irony of the Doctor giving it to Ian but then needing it himself when the TARDIS is buried. But even then the Daleks easily trace the Ship and kindly have it exhumed just so they can attempt to destroy it.
- It's hard to make out (Barbara must have amazing eyesight to notice it on the visualiser's tiny display), but the TARDIS is displayed on a screen in the Dalek headquarters on (presumably) Skaro, so they have some

incredibly powerful telescopes. It's the commanding black Dalek that names the Ship's location as the Sagaro Desert on Aridius; assuming this is its Aridian name from when the species was more technologically advanced before their world dried up, presumably it was then known as the Sagaro Ocean.
- When the TARDIS is in flight after leaving Aridius, the central column remains stationary in its lower position, although the inner workings flash and rotate.
- The Doctor's line about the time-path detector, that "it's been in the Ship ever since I constructed it," has been taken to suggest the Doctor built the TARDIS itself. However, as he calls it "my time-path detector" and that's the subject of the sentence, it's more likely this is what the Doctor is saying he made.

LANDING 18

SPACE Earth, America, New York, Empire State Building, observation deck
TIME 12.03pm, 1966
TRAVELLERS The Doctor, Barbara, Ian, Vicki
EPISODES The Chase 3

While his companions change out of their sandy clothes and refresh themselves with guava-flavoured bars from the food machine, the Doctor struggles vainly to shake off their pursuers. He needs to maintain at least a twelve-minute lead in order for the Ship's computers to reorientate after a landing, but dismisses Ian's suggestion that they could simply fly faster and outrun their enemies. Vicki notices the time rotor slowing down as the TARDIS begins to land, materialising on the open-air observation deck on the 86th floor of the Empire State Building. Visiting Alabaman Morton Dill is surprised as one by one the four travellers emerge from the Police Box.

The travellers quickly realise this is no place to confront the Daleks as people would get hurt so they swiftly return to the TARDIS, bidding farewell to a befuddled Morton, who misses the Ship's departure while fetching his movie camera.

- **CONTROLS** The Doctor operates controls on panels A1 and A2 as he tries to elude the Dalek time machine. The time rotor appears to be on panel A1. As the Ship prepares to land the Doctor presses one of the switches at the bottom right of panel A1 and adjusts the two rotary handles at the top.
- When Vicki points out the time rotor is slowing down, she seems to be looking and pointing towards the circular display on the right of panel A1, and the Doctor glances at this as he adjusts the two rotary handles next to it. So the rotor is not the central column at this stage (later stories take them to be the same thing based on misinformation from fans).
- **LORE** Once the TARDIS has materialised it takes [up to] twelve minutes for the computers to "reorientate and gather power" before the Ship can dematerialise.

- The time rotor slows down moments before the TARDIS starts to materialise somewhere.
- **NOTES** The shots of the TARDIS in the Vortex use a photo of the Police Box prop superimposed over the kaleidoscope background.
- Again the central column remains stationary even before the Ship has materialised.
- Although the tour guide claims to be on the 102nd storey, it's clear the set is more like the observation level on the 86th. There is another viewing area on floor 102 but it's much smaller, being at the top of the pinnacle, and enclosed by glass. The building's height as given by the guide, 1,473 feet, is now out of date as the antenna has since been reduced by nineteen feet.
- The arrival of the TARDIS (and its subsequent departure) is a camera shot of the Police Box prop (already in position of the set) inlaid over a photo of the empty set. You can see the misaligned inlay mask cuts off the left-hand edge of the prop.
- This landing is the first time the familiar grinding sound is played in reverse. The same effect is used again for the next two landings before reverting to the usual rising take-off sound.
- This is the first time someone expresses incredulity at how many people can fit inside the Police Box. Certainly a real Police Box couldn't hold four people because half the floorspace was taken up by a desk (on the side behind the panel containing for telephone for public use, which wasn't actually a door as it is on the TARDIS). But an American like Dill wouldn't know that, and four people in a 4ft-square space surely isn't that incredible (cramped but not impossible).
- This is also the first time the TARDIS's Police Box disguise is confirmed to be blue, possibly not obvious to viewers living outside London who may never have seen a genuine Metropolitan Police Box.
- Although the Doctor claims it takes twelve minutes for the TARDIS computers to ready the Ship for departure, it only remains on the Empire State Building for a little over three minutes. The scene is played out continuously and there's no real gap, even between camera shots, for nine minutes of unseen action. However, later in the story that twelve minutes is taken as the lead they have on the Daleks rather than a minimum time between landing and taking off.

Santa Maria in the Azores island group. Barbara cannot resist looking around to indulge her love of sailing ships despite Ian's protestations, and sure enough she is discovered by first mate Albert Richardson. Vicki comes to her rescue by clubbing the sailor on the head.

The TARDIS is soon ready to leave, this being an unsuitable place to face the Daleks. Ian, yet to find his sea legs, goes to fetch the two women but is unwittingly clobbered by Vicki too. She and Barbara help him back into the Ship and it dematerialises in front of a recovered but startled Richardson.

On board, Barbara treats Ian's head and he tells her he spotted the name of the vessel they were on. The Doctor has tried altering the curve along which the TARDIS is travelling but the Daleks have detected the change and are still on their trail, now just eight minutes behind – a gap that will be reduced further after their next landing.

- **NOTES** The Mary Celeste was discovered abandoned on 4 December 1872 and the last entry in the ship's log was dated 25 November. At 8am its position was logged as 37°01'N 25°01'W, which is just two miles off the coast of Santa Maria.
- Although the central column is again stationary during the scene in the control room, all other indications are that the Ship is in flight. So when Barbara asks, "Why don't we just stay where we are?" she doesn't mean they have landed somewhere but that they should keep going indefinitely. The Doctor's assertion, "The vacuum in space, we should all be dead in no time," would seem to suggest that they'd run out of air and heat. We've seen before, in *Marco Polo*, that the exterior environment can affect the interior of the TARDIS, so does it need to land on a suitable planet at regular intervals to replenish its atmosphere?
- The TARDIS is not seen materialising, just heard as the camera pulls back to reveal the Police Box already on deck. It is seen taking off, filmed with the evacuation scenes that used the water tank at Ealing Film Studios.
- Given how confused the travellers were in *The Sensorites* to have landed but still be moving, imagine how frenzied they would have been had they first materialised on a boat at sea.
- Oops! In the episode's closing TARDIS scene, a member of the production crew can be seen through a gap in the control room set, just behind Barbara.

LANDING 19

SPACE Earth, Atlantic Ocean, Mary Celeste
TIME [25 November 1872]
TRAVELLERS The Doctor, Barbara, Ian, Vicki
EPISODES The Chase 3

As the Ship moves on the Doctor begins work on a device with which to combat the Daleks. He dismisses Barbara's suggestion that they remain in flight indefinitely and moments later the TARDIS lands again anyway. It materialises on the deck of the Mary Celeste as it sails a calm Atlantic about six miles from

LANDING 20

SPACE Earth, Festival of Ghana, Frankenstein's House exhibit
TIME 1996
TRAVELLERS The Doctor, Barbara, Ian, Vicki
EPISODES The Chase 4

The TARDIS materialises in what appears to be the hallway of a large old house. It is rather eerie, though, with cobwebs, flickering lights, bats and a fireplace shaped as the gaping maw of a monstrous face with glowing eyes. The Doctor and Ian venture up the creaking stairs while a spooked Barbara and Vicki remain by the Ship. However, they are confronted by a cloaked, fanged man who claims to be Count Dracula.

When the Doctor and Ian return, having decided they have landed in a manifestation of the dark recesses of the human mind – somewhere the Daleks can never reach them – they find the women have vanished. They return upstairs to find them, just as the Dalek time machine appears in a corner behind the staircase.

When the travellers realise the Daleks have landed in the apparently haunted house, they head back to the hallway but are spotted. The Dalek is distracted by the appearance of Dracula to greet it, giving the travellers the chance to rush into the TARDIS. Vicki hangs back to warn the count of the danger, though, and is cornered by Daleks as the Ship leaves without her.

In the control room, the Doctor insists to Ian that they have just been "lodged for a period in an area of human thought", but the teacher is doubtful.

The Doctor continues to work on his device and it is only when Barbara brings four cups of water that they realise Vicki is missing. The Doctor blames himself for departing so swiftly. Even if he could repair the Ship so that he could control its flight, it would take months or even years and the Daleks are in close pursuit. Ian suggests capturing the Daleks' time machine and using that to recover Vicki. The Doctor agrees their next landing place will be where they confront the Daleks.

- **LORE** If the time mechanism were working correctly it would be possible to direct the Ship to specific locations. Repairing it requires the work of months or even years, however.
- **NOTES** The true location of this landing is as confusing as the Doctor's mistaken explanation that "millions of people secretly believing…makes this place become a reality". It's revealed to the viewer to have been 'Frankensteins [sic] House of Horrors' at the Festival of Ghana. If that means it's in Ghana, why has the exhibit been 'Cancelled by Peking' – what jurisdiction do the Chinese have in Africa in 1996? Perhaps, therefore, it makes more sense to consider it an exposition *about* Ghana *in* Peking. In either case, why is the entrance fee given in dollars? And what on earth has a Transylvanian-style haunted castle got to do with the culture of Ghana? (Perhaps that's why the Chinese government cancelled it, because it was so out of keeping with the festival.)
- The arrival of the TARDIS is achieved by inlaying a shot of the Police Box over a photo of the empty set. Note how the scene switches to a different camera view before Barbara can move beyond the edge of the inlay mask. However, this has the effect of making the TARDIS appear to land in front of, or even around, a large candle stand that in the next shot can still be seen just to the left of the Police Box prop on the set. When it dematerialises, again using inlay, the superimposed TARDIS half-obscures the candle stand giving the impression that it's now right behind the Ship.
- The TARDIS also materialises with its left-hand door ajar (the white-painted inner edge of the right-hand door is visible). This is so the centre post doesn't catch on the right-hand door as Barbara exits via the left.
- After taking off, the central column is again stationary. Was the console prop broken or did the director just choose not to have the (noisy) mechanism switched on (or forget to)? In these scenes the usual Medieval Spanish studded armchair has been swapped for a similar vintage crossed-leg chair, while the Westminster Abbey skeleton clock is sitting on the floor rather than its usual fluted pillar.

LANDING 21

SPACE Mechanus, jungle below Mechanoid city
TIME Two days in unknown future
TRAVELLERS The Doctor, Barbara, Ian
EPISODES The Chase 4-6

The TARDIS sets down on Mechanus amid a dark, swampy jungle with dense vegetation. This includes tall toadstools that can move and capture animals by lowering their wide, veined caps over their prey and smothering it. Light makes them retreat. Some 1,500-feet above is a large elegant city on stilts. The three travellers set out with the Doctor's device to find a suitable place to confront the Daleks, following a nearby pathway indicated by a row of lights.

Vicki is also on Mechanus, having arrived in the pursuing Dalek time machine. Venturing out into the jungle, she finds the TARDIS. There is no one inside to let her in, however, and she runs when attacked by a fungoid.

The Daleks also locate the Ship and are menaced by fungoids, which retreat under Dalek fire. With no trace of the travellers they decide to wait by the TARDIS and search once the sun rises. When an advance guard discovers their quarry in a cave at the far end of the pathway, the lead Dalek orders section four to enter and attack while section two prevents anyone escaping. They all move off to exterminate the travellers.

Later, with the city above on fire and crumbling as the Daleks and Mechanoids annihilate each other, the travellers escape back to the jungle below. Following them is stranded astronaut Steven Taylor, who staggers through the smoky vegetation, avoiding fungoids, until he stumbles across the TARDIS. The Doctor and Vicki return, having reluctantly allowed Barbara and Ian to try getting back to Earth in the Daleks' time machine. In the control room, they use the time and space visualiser to see that their friends made it home safely before dematerialising from Mechanus.

- **CONTROLS** The Doctor turns a dial on panel A3, then flicks a lever on panel A4 apparently to turn off the scanner (and/or possibly open the main doors). As the doors are heard to open, he adjusts further switches on panels A3 and A2.

- **NOTES** The time and space visualiser, seen here for the last time, is shot against a plain flat wall rather than one of the control room walls.
- The departing TARDIS is the smaller Police Box miniature filmed on a simple model of the jungle set. The final shot of the story is the photo of the TARDIS prop previously used against the Vortex footage this time superimposed over a star field.
- It's not clear how Steven gets into the TARDIS; it was clearly locked when Vicki battered on the door. Steven must have found the Ship while the Doctor was programming the Dalek time machine to take Barbara and Ian home, but it's not even as if the teachers left the door open after returning for some souvenirs – they take nothing with them from their travels. Perhaps the Daleks succeeded in opening the TARDIS but then abandoned it when they were all called upon to fight off the Mechanoids, and the Doctor was just too upset at losing his friends to notice the door was unlocked.

LANDING 22

SPACE Earth, England, Cleveland coast
TIME Three days in [September] 1066
TRAVELLERS The Doctor, Vicki, Steven Taylor
EPISODES The Time Meddler 1,4

The Doctor talks to Vicki to make sure she doesn't also want to return home but she assures him she has nothing to go back to. They are interrupted by noises from the living quarters and are startled to discover Steven Taylor. He collapses to the floor as the TARDIS materialises on a beach at the foot of some cliffs on the Northumbrian coast in 11th-century England. Standing above looking out to sea is a cowled monk, who peers down at the incongruous Police Box with suspicion. Its arrival is also spotted by local Saxon Eldred, who runs to tell village headman Wulnoth.

Inside Steven recovers and explains how he wandered through the jungle on Mechanus until he came across the TARDIS. He is incredulous, however, when Vicki claims it is smaller on the outside than inside and is a time machine. The Doctor gets her to show Steven where he can wash and get some fresh clothes before they head outside to prove to him the Ship's capabilities.

Freshly shaven, Steven joins the Doctor and Vicki on the beach, where the latter has found a rusty horned Viking helmet. The young man is still not convinced, although he admits the TARDIS is "a little unusual". The Doctor confesses a "slight technical hitch" prevents him from directing the Ship with accuracy, while its appearance is designed to blend in with its surroundings; Vicki concedes its failure to do so is another technical hitch. They are unaware that the monk is crouched behind a rock eavesdropping. As twilight falls, the Doctor sets off along the beach to find a gentle way to the top of the cliffs, while Steven and Vicki attempt a more direct route up. The monk approaches the incongruous Police Box and seems to recognise it.

Later, Eldred leads Wulnoth to the clifftop above the TARDIS but as they look over they see the tide has come in and bemoan that what they hoped might be a valuable find has probably been washed away. The next night, Vicki and Steven finally make it back to the cliff and also fear the Ship has been swept away by the sea – either that or the Doctor has dematerialised and left them stranded.

When the travellers return to the clifftop the next day they find the tide is now out and the TARDIS is still safe and sound on the beach below. They find a way down the cliff and depart before the area is overrun by invading Vikings.

- **CONTROLS** The Doctor adjusts the left-hand rotary handle on panel A4 and presses switches at the bottom of panel A5 before asking Vicki if she wants to go home. While she explains to Steven about the TARDIS, the Doctor is at the console flicking levers on panel A5. When Steven asks what the large central lever on that panel does, the Doctor says it's the dematerialising control. He then throws the left-most four of the five levers at the top of panel A4.
- The dimensional control of the Monk's TARDIS is located beneath panel A3 of his console, so presumably the Doctor's is the same (although the two time machines are of different types, their control layouts are exactly the same).
- The pale grilles at the top of panels A2 and A4 have gained black rims.
- **LORE** Vicki says the word TARDIS is an initialism for "Time And Relative Dimensions In Space" (the line was scripted as 'Dimension', as originally given by Susan in *An Unearthly Child*).
- The TARDIS can survive underwater without flooding or being washed away. As it's light enough to be loaded onto a cart (see Landing 5) this might be just because the incoming tide isn't strong enough.
- The Monk's TARDIS, or possibly just its console, is a 'Mark 4'. The implication that there have been marks 1 to 3 must mean the Doctor's people have been developing TARDISes since he left – it's not that the Monk has simply built his own too. The Doctor declines to answer Vicki's question about whether his TARDIS is an earlier mark but does admit the Monk's has had "quite a few changes", and estimates he left his home planet some 50 years before the Monk.
- The Monk doesn't use the term 'TARDIS' but refers only to his time ship or time machine. It has an automatic drift control to enable safe materialisation in space, something the Doctor must add to his TARDIS as later it can also do this.
- Removal of a TARDIS's dimensional control shrinks its interior dimensions, possibly to a size that fits into whatever object the TARDIS is currently disguised as.
- **NOTES** The Monk's plan is to destroy the Viking fleet ahead of the Battle of Stamford Bridge, so this story definitely takes place before 25 September 1066. Edith tells the Doctor there hasn't been much sight of Vikings this year, "except for that one raid that was beaten off

just north of here," so it doesn't sound like Harald Hardrada has yet landed in Cleveland and begun his plundering, which heralded the invasion. That was shortly after he had gathered his fleet at Tynemouth on 8 September. As the Vikings who come ashore here are an advance party taking the lay of the land, this is presumably shortly before Hardrada's main fleet arrives, so early in the second week of September. The Doctor says the Humber is to the south, and the invading fleet landed at the Tees before sailing down the coast, so the village and monastery are on the North Yorkshire coast.

- The arrival of the TARDIS is a dissolve between two photos (featuring the full-size prop), but the Monk's view from above was filmed using the 3-foot model Police Box. This was used again for the TARDIS's departure, filmed against a photo of the cliffs. On-set photos suggest the Police Box prop was missing its roof lamp during studio recording.
- The scenes in the Monk's TARDIS use the same set as the Doctor's, although the console is raised on a dais. Both indented walls appear, one still with its original recessed PVC roundels, whereas those on the other wall and main doors had been fitted with flat discs prior to production of *The Chase* – here, without backlighting, they are noticeably darker than the originals in the third wall.
- The Monk assigns the incongruous appearance of the Doctor's "modern Police Box" to a broken camouflage unit and is proud that he can direct and land his own ship precisely. This might suggest he knows of the Doctor's peripatetic wanderings, but he could just be guessing from the TARDIS's appearance and the Doctor coincidental presence here – at no point does he worry the Time Lords have sent an agent to stop him meddling with Earth history.

LANDING 23

SPACE [Galaxy Four], unnamed planet
TIME Three days in unknown time
TRAVELLERS The Doctor, Vicki, Steven
EPISODES Galaxy 4 1-2,4

The TARDIS materialises on an unknown planet orbiting three suns. The even surface of dark sandy ground is interrupted only by occasional branchless, segmented trunks with scrubby bushes and fragrant rose-like flowers at their bases. The atmosphere is conducive to humanoid life yet the area is deserted, reminding the Doctor of the planet Xeros.

Inside the Ship, Vicki finishes trimming Steven's hair as the Doctor surveys their landing site. As they prepare to explore, a short domed robot approaches the Police Box and blindly bumps into it. The travellers listen as it feels its way all around the TARDIS, then as it moves away they see it on the scanner. Vicki christens it a 'Chumbley' on account of its bumbling movement.

When they emerge the Chumbley returns and tries to communicate, but becomes wary as Steven tries to get behind it. The Doctor deduces that, although blind, the robot can detect them through sound and heat. When it demonstrates its power by blasting one of the trees with a light ray, the travellers allow themselves to be led away.

Two more Chumblies glide up to the TARDIS and try to gain entry using a drill, unsuccessfully. The Doctor and Steven return and watch from a distance as the robots apply their light rays to the door lock instead, but the Ship's force barrier holds and the Chumblies give up. When they have gone, the travellers go inside where the Doctor consults his astral map. He is disturbed to find that the planet they are on is due to explode in just two days' time.

They are about to leave to fetch Vicki, who is being held by Drahvins in their crashed spaceship nearby, when a Chumbley returns. It places a black rod beside the Ship and edges away before touching two wires. An explosion rocks the TARDIS, throwing the Doctor and Steven to the floor; as they recover there is a second detonation. The Ship is unharmed, however, as the blind robot discovers when it bumps into it. It departs, allowing the two men to head out to recover Vicki.

As the suns begin to set on the planet's final day, the Doctor, Vicki and a Chumbley return to the TARDIS to connect a cable from a Rill spaceship so they can feed it the power needed to take off. Distant earthquakes begin to shake the ground but the Doctor has completed the connection and they hurriedly return to the Rill ship.

Three to four hours later, the Doctor, Vicki and Steven are escorted to the TARDIS by a Chumbley, which holds off the pursuing Drahvins with its light ray. Once inside, the Doctor disconnects the power cable and Steven throws it out the door. The Drahvins make a last-ditch bid to reach the Ship but it dematerialises as the planet breaks up around them.

The travellers are unable to view the destruction as the TARDIS is already beyond that galaxy, but on the scanner is another planet. As the Doctor attends to Vicki's injured ankle, they wonder what might be down there.

- **CONTROLS** The Doctor monitors the TARDIS's arrival from panel A5.
- **LORE** Not only can knocking on the Police Box doors and walls be heard inside the control room but the direction of the sound is relative to its position around the much smaller exterior.
- The forcefield can withstand energy rays (so perhaps upgraded since Landing 8) and explosions.
- The power of the TARDIS can be transferred to other systems and converted into a form they can use.
- **NOTES** The arrival and departure of the TARDIS were filmed on the planet set at Ealing Studios using the Police Box prop.
- Although the script indicates the planet is in Galaxy Four, this is not stated on screen. Indeed, the Drahvins declare themselves as coming "from the planet Drahva, in Galaxy Four", which is perhaps an odd distinction if they're still in that galaxy. Then again, they're searching

- for suitable planets for colonisation so it's unlikely they would explore an entirely different galaxy when there must be worlds much closer to home they could settle.
- Although Maaga says there is no life on the planet, the presence of fragrant flowers suggests there may be insects. She no doubt means sentient life.
- Without the episodes to view we can't be sure what control room walls appeared. Publicity photos of William Hartnell believed to be taken during camera rehearsals of episode one show the main doors wall and an indented wall at right angles. In the surviving clip from that episode, when a Chumbley approaches the Drahvin spaceship one of the photographic walls can be seen through the windows in the background of one shot, but it's not clear if this was part of the TARDIS set or an unused piece of scenery accidentally caught on camera.
- Here the astral map can be used to determine how long a planet will persist for; either it can detect whatever internal forces are building that cause the planet's destruction, or the Doctor can ascertain from its position among three suns how long it'll be before their gravity pulls it apart.
- The scanner shows an image of the planet Kembel but the Ship flies on. Yet after its very next landing, the TARDIS will arrive on Kembel as if it knows there is a significant danger there that needs the Doctor's attention. Either its flight through space-time while leaving the doomed planet in *Galaxy 4* took it into the vicinity of Kembel, making its return there shortly afterwards suspiciously quick (only Earth has been honoured with swift return visits so far, and then usually in very different periods of human history) or the TARDIS was deliberately presenting a view of the planet to entice the Doctor to go there. We know from *The Edge of Destruction* and later stories that the Ship has a form of sentience so perhaps it was trying to tell the Doctor that the Daleks are on Kembel, and after he fails to recognise the message the TARDIS takes him there anyway. Or did the Doctor deliberately avoid going straight there by having Vicki "put that third switch forward" (without being able to view the episode we can't know which switch this was)? From concern about Vicki's inured ankle, objection to being told where to go, or just worry about what he might find there, does he decide to go elsewhere only for the TARDIS to later insist on landing on Kembel?

LANDING 24

SPACE Earth, Anatolia, plain near Troy; carried into Troy
TIME Three days in [1190s BC]
TRAVELLERS The Doctor, Vicki, Steven
EPISODES The Myth Makers 1-2,4

The TARDIS appears on a wide sandy plain where two men in skirts and sandals with swords and shields goad and fight each other. The travellers watch them on the scanner, the Doctor noting their Grecian apparel and deciding to go out alone to ask where they are. Steven objects but is told to stay and look after Vicki.

The Doctor emerges from the TARDIS just as Hector invokes Zeus to appear and save his adversary; unfortunately for him, the distraction allows Achilles to run the Trojan through instead. The Doctor is appalled, although flattered when Achilles takes him for the Father of the Gods and appeals for his help with the Greek siege of Troy. When Odysseus comes across the pair, however, he is less than awed, either by Zeus's appearance or his "travelling temple". He orders the Doctor be taken to the Greek camp, suspecting there is more of deceit than divinity about him. Vicki and Steven see the Doctor being led away so the latter, having already changed into appropriate clothing, heads out to rescue him.

The following morning, Trojan prince Paris is supposed to be seeking Achilles to take revenge for the death of his brother Hector but, discovering the TARDIS, uses it as an excuse to return to the city. He has a patrol tie it to a cart and take it to the main square of Troy, claiming to have captured it from the Greeks. Both his father King Priam and sister Cassandra are unimpressed and fear it may be a ploy to get Greeks inside the city walls. As they prepare to set fire to the box as an offering to the gods, Vicki searches the wardrobe for a suitable gown and exits the Ship just as the pyre is about to be lit. Her claim to be from the future offends the priestess Cassandra but intrigues Priam, who takes Vicki – redubbed Cressida – into his protection.

In the evening of the following day, as Greek soldiers pour through the gates of Troy, killing the city's occupants, the Doctor finds Vicki by the TARDIS. She sends Katarina, one of Cassandra's servants, to find Steven and bring him here, while she urges the Doctor into the Ship. She tells him she has fallen in love with Priam's youngest son, Troilus, and wishes to stay in this time to be with him. Hurrying off to find him on the plain, where she sent him to evade the massacre, Vicki bids a final farewell to the Doctor.

No sooner has she gone than Katarina returns with a semi-conscious Steven, who has been wounded in the shoulder by a Trojan. They help him into the Ship as Odysseus spots them and demands the Doctor's temple as his spoils. However, the Doctor slams the door shut and the TARDIS fades away before a finally awestruck Odysseus.

Inside, the Doctor is concerned by Steven's worsening condition and has little time to deny Katarina's supposition that she is dead and travelling through limbo to the afterlife. He can only hope they land somewhere he can find drugs to treat his friend's septicaemia.

- **LORE** The Police Box can be moved by manpower alone but is suggested to be heavier than it looks.
- **NOTES** Vicki still has a sore ankle, as she indicated at the end of *Galaxy 4*, so despite viewers being shown *Mission to the Unknown* in the interim, this is clearly intended to be taken as the TARDIS's next landing.
- The seventh level of habitation at Troy, dated to 1300-1190BC, is generally believed to be that, if any, besieged and destroyed by the Greeks.

- Previously the TARDIS has been stocked with at least some medical facilities – a first aid kit and various ointments. What happened to the medicated bandages from *The Edge of Destruction*? Has something previously happened to deplete the Ship's stocks, has the Doctor merely forgotten about them, or is he at a loss without Susan or Barbara around to apply them?
- The TARDIS isn't heard to materialise on the soundtrack of episode one despite the camera script indicating it should be, leaving the impression it's already in situ while Achilles and Hector fight. Its departure in episode four used inlay to allow the Police Box prop to fade out while Odysseus looks on in astonishment. A model shot of the TARDIS within Troy is also documented as being filmed for episode four.
- Surviving clips from the story show at least two photographic walls were used as part of the control room set in episode one. One of the indented walls may be seen in episode two but it's not clear. Vicki looks for suitable period clothing in the TARDIS wardrobe – last shown in *The Space Museum* (Landing 16) – which in the script is given as being 'a cupboard in the living quarters'. This might indicate the room with beds last seen in *The Chase* was used; the script and a surviving clip suggest this reappears in episode four where the injured Steven is laid. If so, by the next episode he has been moved to a couch in the control room.
- The Doctor recalls witnessing the fall of Troy in *The Unquiet Dead* (Landing 324, vol.2).

LANDING 25

SPACE Kembel, jungle
TIME Several days in 4000
TRAVELLERS The Doctor, Steven, Katarina
EPISODES The Daleks' Master Plan 1-2,6

The TARDIS arrives in the dense, steamy jungle of the planet Kembel, the sounds of strange creatures all around (including Varga plants from Skaro). It is witnessed by dishevelled Space Security agent Bret Vyon, who approaches the Police Box but ducks out of sight as the Doctor and Katarina emerge. The Doctor tells the girl to close the doors behind him – he has shown her which switch controls them – and to look after Steven while he seeks help. As he moves off through the jungle, Vyon follows him.

Inside Steven regains consciousness but is confused about where Vicki is. Vyon has taken the Doctor's key from him and returns to the Ship, determined to find a way back to Earth and warn them of what he has learned on Kembel. He leaves the key in the lock, however, as he steps inside and is amazed by the control room within. Convincing Katarina he has been sent by the Doctor to cure Steven, he has her close the doors but she insists only the Doctor can work his temple. While Vyon contemplates the controls, Steven recovers enough to knock him out from behind.

The Doctor gets back to the Ship, angered at Vyon's overpowering him but amused to find the key still in the lock. He prepares to enter and confront the man when a spaceship roars overhead, heading for the city beyond the jungle. Inside the TARDIS he finds Vyon has already been subdued and sits him in a 'magnetic chair' of the Doctor's invention. When the agent wakes, he finds he cannot move, held in a forcefield "strong enough to restrain a herd of elephants". Assuring Katarina their guest is quite powerless until released by pressing a switch on the back of the chair, the Doctor heads out again for the city.

With Steven unconscious and feverish, Vyon persuades Katarina to take some tablets from his belt and give them to her patient, promising they will cure him. As she does so, he notices on the scanner a Dalek is just outside. Unaware that they are safe in the TARDIS, Vyon convinces Katarina to release him from the chair so they can escape "the evil ones". Together they carry Steven out of the Ship and into the bushes before the Dalek spots them. Shortly after, the Doctor returns having also discovered the city is run by the Daleks, and is disturbed to find they have found the Ship. He slips back into the jungle as the Daleks prepare to set fire to the area to flush out the intruders.

The TARDIS sits in the jungle for several days before the Doctor and Steven are able to return, now with Space Security agent Sara Kingdom (Vyon's sister). They are also accompanied by a squad of Daleks and Mavic Chen, guardian of Earth's solar system, who are keen to recover the box of taranium the Doctor has stolen from them. Sara and the Doctor go inside the Ship while Steven waits outside. Over the speaker, the Doctor tells him to hand the taranium – actually a fake sample the Doctor has made – to Chen. As soon as Steven does so the Daleks open fire on him, unaware he is protected by a field of gravity force and reliance power. It absorbs their fire, freeing Steven to duck into the TARDIS which dematerialises immediately.

- **NOTES** The TARDIS's arrival was filmed on the jungle set at Ealing Studios – the 35mm footage of which survives – with the take-off sound effect played over it when the episode was recorded at Television Centre. Although its departure in episode six can be heard, the camera script suggests is wasn't shown dematerialising, the shot instead staying on the confused Daleks.
- Judging from the audio recording of episode one, the sound effect for the control room doors is played when the outer Police Box doors are opened and closed.
- Photos show a flat padded couch and footstool were added to the control room set for episode one, for Steven to lie on while Katarina tends to him. Beyond the main doors was a photographic backdrop showing the Kembel jungle. The studio floorplan shows the set included the computer wall, scanner framework and illuminated pillars.
- These Daleks don't recognise the TARDIS as their greatest enemy's time machine, so are presumably from an earlier time period than those in *The Chase*.
- The Doctor gives Sara his key and has her open the door of the TARDIS. This is the first time she has even seen the Ship and it hardly seems likely he has

had any opportunity to explain to her how to operate the lock correctly so that it doesn't melt (see Landing 3), so presumably he has simplified the mechanism by now (a wise move given the rotation of humans he's had travelling with him recently). Note that Bret Vyon was able to open the door with the key against the Doctor's wishes.

▣ This is the second time the Doctor has spoken from inside the TARDIS to someone outside, by some unseen speaker system, the first being his farewell to Susan (see Landing 11).

LANDING 26

SPACE Earth, [north-east] England, police station yard
TIME 25 December [1965]
TRAVELLERS The Doctor, Steven, Sara Kingdom
EPISODES The Daleks' Master Plan 6-7

The Doctor and Steven argue over the risky use of gravity force and the Doctor insists his friend must give up any notion of experimenting with it again or be put off the Ship. Meanwhile the TARDIS lands in the yard of a police station somewhere in the north of England, for once its Police Box form being an appropriate disguise. When Sara points outs the central column has stopped oscillating, the Doctor tries the scanner only to find it is suddenly not working. To repair it means checking the whole circuit but as Steven moves to open the main doors the Doctor alerts him to readouts on the console showing high levels of toxins in the atmosphere. Because Steven and Sara are both from the future where the air is purer, they are at risk from the pollution here, so the Doctor insists on going out to repair the scanner alone.

Outside, the TARDIS has been noticed by a police sergeant and two constables. The sergeant leaves the others to guard it just as the Doctor emerges but ducks back in when one of the constables spots him. He tells his friends they are on Earth and that he will distract the policemen while they repair the scanner. He exits again and is immediately apprehended and escorted into the police station.

Minutes later Steven emerges but hides when an officer passes by. He finds a police uniform in a car and puts it on before heading into the station to find the Doctor. When neither returns for some time, Sara exits to fix the scanner herself. At first she is moved on by a constable but doubles back and climbs up onto the roof to effect the repair.

Sara is caught climbing down from the TARDIS roof and taken into the station, where Steven is pretending to have been seconded from G Division. He persuades the officers to free the Doctor and Sara into his custody and they all hurry back into the Ship, which disappears before a startled constable.

With the scanner repaired, the Doctor turns his attention to the taranium. He is confident the Daleks will not attack the solar system with their Time Destructor until they have tested it, at which point they will discover their taranium is fake and will hunt down the travellers. He hopes to destroy the real taranium before that happens.

▮ **LORE** It's hard to be sure because the episode is missing but this seems to be the first time it's indicated that the scanner camera is in the lamp on the Police Box roof. Previous times someone has been seen in close-up on the scanner – a Zarbi in *The Web Planet* and King Priam in *The Myth Makers* – they seem to have been peering in the windows.

▮ The Doctor tells the police inspector that the Police Box outside is "a machine for investigating time and relative dimensions in space".

▣ **NOTES** The usual grinding sound isn't heard as the TARDIS lands, nor does the background hum of the control room change; the only indication is the central column stops moving. Its take-off was recorded as a mix from a shot of the full-size prop to a photo of the empty police station yard.

▣ There's no visual evidence of what control room walls were used at the end of episode six, but publicity photos of Jean Marsh as Sara Kingdom taken during studio rehearsals for episode seven show the main doors, an indented wall and two photographic walls.

▣ The TARDIS has been in 1960s England before and not registered a poisonous atmosphere. Is this the London-based writers mocking northern cities?

▣ The original plan was to have the policemen played by actors from the popular series *Z Cars*, which was set in the fictional northern town of Newtown. This idea fell through but the accents of the cast suggest the location was retained, and Steven adopts a Liverpudlian lilt when pretending to be from nearby G Division.

▣ Newcomer Sara knows the scanner circuity is in the roof lamp and how to repair it, without any opportunity for instruction from the Doctor.

LANDING 27

SPACE Earth, America, California, Hollywood film stage
TIME About 1920
TRAVELLERS The Doctor, Steven, Sara
EPISODES The Daleks' Master Plan 7

The TARDIS soon lands again, somewhere with much better air quality. When the travellers check the scanner they see a woman screaming as she is dragged by a man in a cape towards a giant circular saw, and rush outside to help. They find they are on a movie set, however, and have just ruined a take. The director orders they be removed only to be wowed by the way Sara and Steven fight off the stagehands. He chases after them keen to sign them up as his newest stars.

The Doctor is the first to get back to the TARDIS, where he encounters a downhearted comic who cannot make an impression in Hollywood because Charlie Chaplin has done all the best routines. The Doctor commiserates but is more interested in getting past him and into the Ship. When Steven and Sara appear with a string of people in pursuit, all three bundle into the Police Box and it dematerialises – the best special effect the movie makers have ever seen.

The Doctor recalls it was Christmas at the police station they visited so, to calm them after their hectic experience, he hands his friends glasses of champagne and wishes them (and everyone at home) a happy Christmas.

▤ **NOTES** The TARDIS lands silently once more and Sara is again the first to notice the Ship has stopped. It's take-off was probably a mix to a photo of the empty set.

▤ Among the nods to early Hollywood movies included in this episode are the Keystone Kops, a man looking very much like Charlie Chaplin, a film much like 1921's *The Sheik* starring Rudolph Valentino, and references to actors Douglas Fairbanks and Mary Pickford and director Cecil B DeMille. All were active in Hollywood during the 1910s and 20s, although not necessarily at the same studio. (The Arabian film in production might be a cash-in following the success of *The Sheik*, or even an early attempt at that film before the lead was recast, given the low opinion of the actor seen here.) The only anachronism is a clown thinking of changing careers and becoming a singer by the name of Bing Crosby. In our history, Harry 'Bing' Crosby is not known to have had an early career as a comic, only as a singer, and did not travel to Los Angeles until 1925.

▤ Unless the food machine has gained a button for champagne, the Doctor has acquired a bottle of bubbly from somewhere, which he has kept outside the control room (so it's not from the drinks cabinet revealed in *Twice Upon a Time* – see Landing 43).

▤ The Doctor's turn to camera to address the viewers was not an ad lib but a late addition to the camera script, probably by director Douglas Camfield as story editor Donald Tosh disliked the idea. Given this was the first episode of the series to be broadcast on Christmas Day (and the last until *Doctor Who* returned in 2005), this indulgence can be understood. But perhaps the Doctor is merely turning aside and remembering Barbara, Ian and Vicki – companions he has returned home or who have found a new home in the past year – and hoping they too are having merry Christmases.

LANDING 28

SPACE Earth, England, cricket ground
TIME 2½ minutes in [20th century]
TRAVELLERS The Doctor, Steven, Sara
EPISODES The Daleks' Master Plan 8

The Doctor is disturbed to discover from the time-curve indicator that the TARDIS is being followed. Steven and Sara assume it must be the Daleks but the Doctor doubts they can have tested their Time Destructor so quickly and refuses Sara's demands to return to Kembel. With their pursuer getting closer, he decides to try to shake them off by landing, and the Ship materialises in the middle of a cricket test match between England and Australia, disrupting play but barely phasing the placid commentators.

With no sign of whoever might be following, the TARDIS dematerialises again just two-and-a-half minutes after landing. Their pursuer is still on their tail, however.

▤ **NOTES** Although it's reasonable to assume all the journeys within the epic *The Daleks' Master Plan* are consecutive, there's no narrative continuity for the TARDIS travellers between the previous episode and this. The Doctor is expecting the Daleks to take some time testing the fake taranium he gave them before they become an immediate threat again and ignores Sara's insistence they should return to Kembel straight away, which may suggest they've already been putting off dealing with the Daleks' invasion plans.

▤ The time-curve indicator – named in the next episode although it's not seen then – seems to function much like the time-path detector seen in *The Chase*. If this was writer Dennis Spooner's intention (and he was story editor on the earlier serial) he nevertheless renamed it in his rehearsal script as the 'time-space curve machine'. Here it's not a component on the console but a freestanding white monolith with a large yellow circular screen on which are etched criss-crossing lines. It makes a high warbling sound when tracking another time machine.

▤ The commentators are English and Australian so it's likely the match is between teams of those nationalities. Scott, the Australian, refers to "your ground staff", suggesting the game is taking place in England. The cricket ground isn't named but the production team had hoped to film the TARDIS's arrival at the Oval; in the end it was achieved using photos of a model Police Box in Hammersmith Park (probably the 3-foot prop but possibly a new model created for the scenes on Tigus – see next landing).

▤ The Doctor says he "must do something drastic" and then that "my plan hasn't worked" but it's not clear how landing and taking off minutes later is either drastic or much of a plan to discover who's following them. We're not shown if the Monk (for it is he) also lands on the cricket pitch, delaying the game a second time.

LANDING 29

SPACE Tigus
TIME Unknown
TRAVELLERS The Doctor, Steven, Sara
EPISODES The Daleks' Master Plan 8

The Doctor tries another landing, this time on the young planet Tigus, which is still cooling and volcanically active. The Ship materialises amid large smooth solidified lava flows while in the near distance vents pour out steam and fresh magma. Viewing the bubbling surface on the scanner, the Doctor plans to leave as soon as possible but Sara notices the time-curve indicator has stopped – whoever has been following them has landed somewhere nearby.

The travellers venture outside, stepping gingerly across the hot rocks. As they move away from the Ship to search for their pursuer, the Monk sneaks round behind them. He kicks the Police Box door but only succeeds in stubbing his toe. Then he dons goggles and aims a small laser device at the lock. There is a beam of light and, although the TARDIS door appears unharmed, the Monk chuckles and heads off after the travellers.

When they return, the Doctor discovers his key no longer works – the Monk has "reset the lock mechanism". Steven tries pushing on the door to no avail. The Doctor, however, has devised a solution. He uses his ring to refract the light from the planet's sun into the keyhole and the lock is released. His key now works and they all enter and take off.

Inside the Doctor explains the "unusual powers" of the sun combined with the "certain properties" of his ring counteracted the Monk's interference with the lock. The meddler will still be after them, however, and he asks Steven to monitor the time-curve indicator.

▪ NOTES A new model Police Box was built for the shots of the TARDIS on Tigus – or possibly two. The first attempt at filming the volcano model was rejected by the director because the TARDIS miniature used was out of proportion, and the shots had to be remounted. So what changed: the setting or the box? Photos exist of *a* miniature Police Box on the volcano model, and this matches the 12-inch one that reappears through to the mid-1970s (and in film footage taken at Shawcraft's studio where it stands next to the 3-foot model). This doesn't look especially out of scale with the background so is taken to be the one ultimately seen on screen, although without having the episode to view we can't be certain. But there was another model, never used in the series but shown in a 1971 schools documentary going behind the scenes at BBC Television Centre and later photographed for the Fourth Doctor title sequence. When auctioned at Christie's in December 2005 this was described as seventeen inches tall. It's remarkably similar to the 12-inch model, and indeed they have often been thought one and the same, but there are details that differentiate them, as well as the evidence of their different sizes. But the similarity does suggest they were made around the same time, so is the larger the unused first model, deemed too big for the volcano set so replaced with a smaller one?

▪ The Doctor has used his ring to open the door before, in *The Web Planet*, although that was from the inside when the Ship had no power (see Landing 14). Still, he used the ring in combination with a light source as here, so clearly some form of electromagnetic radiation is involved in the operation of the lock and doors.

▪ The lock certainly seems to be a weak point in the TARDIS's defences. While sometimes protected by the Ship's forcefield (see Landing 23), it can be reset or even removed completely (see Landing 8). This may not damage the Ship itself but is highly inconvenient to any legitimate crew trying to get in.

LANDING 30

SPACE Earth, England, London, Trafalgar Square
TIME 31 December 1966
TRAVELLERS The Doctor, Steven, Sara
EPISODES The Daleks' Master Plan 8

The TARDIS materialises in a crowded Trafalgar Square shortly before midnight on New Year's Eve. Church bells are ringing and revellers stagger past the innocuous Police Box. Watching on the scanner, the Doctor likens the boisterousness of the celebrations to the Relief of Mafeking.

However, the Doctor needs to repair the TARDIS lock after the Monk's interference and busy central London is not the ideal place so he prepares to move on.

▪ NOTES This episode was broadcast on 1 January 1966 and, like the previous week's toast to Christmas, the TARDIS's arrival in Trafalgar Square at midnight is a nod to the contemporary New Year celebrations (as the travellers watch the revellers on the scanner, on Kembel the Daleks are counting down to the launch of their time machine, mimicking the traditional countdown to midnight on New Year's Eve). Note, however, that the Daleks specifically say the TARDIS has landed in 1966 (well, "one-nine-six-six" in Dalek speak). As the new year doesn't begin until *after* midnight (obviously), the crowds must be seeing in 1967 and therefore this interlude is set a year after its real-world broadcast.

LANDING 31

SPACE Earth, Egypt, pyramid construction site; moved into tomb
TIME [About 26th century BC]
TRAVELLERS The Doctor, Steven, Sara
EPISODES The Daleks' Master Plan 9-10

The TARDIS arrives in Ancient Egypt near the foot of a newly completed pyramid, although work is still ongoing in the enclosure as all around are construction materials. There is no sign of workers, however, so the Doctor takes the opportunity to finish repairs on the exterior lock using a tool called a diatrab, while Steven seeks a higher vantage point from which to spot the inevitable arrival of the Monk. He soon spies something materialising – although it doesn't blend in like a working TARDIS should – and warns the Doctor as Sara emerges from the Ship to say the time-curve indicator has stopped registering their pursuer. The Doctor doesn't want to leave the TARDIS unlocked so he continues with his work while the others go in search of the Monk.

The Doctor completes the repair and heads off to find his friends. The Egyptians begin moving their pharaoh's burial treasures into the tomb for safety, including the TARDIS. Fortunately the Doctor finds it inside the tomb having followed the Monk, who is tracking it with an energy counter. With the Daleks nearby, the Doctor has no time to deal with the Monk's childishness so ties him up in bandages and secures him inside a sarcophagus before setting out again in search of Steven and Sara.

They, however, have found the Ship themselves but it is locked and there is no sign of the Doctor. They find the swaddled Monk but are not sympathetic to his claim of being unfairly attacked. He tries to convince them to let him into the TARDIS, hoping to get hold of the taranium, but only the Doctor has a key. Steven and Sara leave again to look for him, taking the Monk with them.

Later, having learned his friends are prisoners of the Daleks, the Doctor enters the TARDIS and collects the taranium to swap for the hostages.

The three travellers hurry into the tomb as the Daleks and Egyptians fight. The Doctor is annoyed he was unable to trick the Daleks and had to hand over the real taranium – they can now complete their Time Destructor. He has stolen the directional unit from the Monk's TARDIS, however, which he hopes will get them back to Kembel to stop the Daleks' plan. The Doctor fits the unit into the console but is concerned it might not work in his older TARDIS: the increased energy rate could destroy the central column. The only way to test it is to switch it on. Steven operates the main switch to dematerialise the Ship and there is a flash of energy.

- **CONTROLS** The directional unit is a transparent block with embedded circuitry and a metal section at one end. It fits into the console underneath panel A6. The 'main switch' that Steven turns seems to be the rotary handle on panel A5.
- The top grille on panel A6 has been replaced by this point – although with a lighter mesh that reveals parts of the structure of the console through the hole beneath – as has the rotary handle below it.
- **LORE** The Doctor's inability to pilot the TARDIS is clearly indicated to be because it lacks a directional unit, not because he's forgetful or incompetent, or because the Ship is generally unreliable.
- **NOTES** Whose pyramid is being built? The model, although based on the Pyramid of Khufu at Giza according to designer Barry Newbery, does not seem to match the arrangement and number of pyramids there, or at any other known site. The rehearsal script suggests it's an earlier edifice that inspired Khufu's tomb. Certainly the main pyramid seen here is the only one visible in the area so was the first to be built there, as Khufu's was at Giza but so too was the Pyramid of Sahure at Abusir or the much later Pyramid of Amenemhat I at Lischt. Indeed, tombs from the later dynasties (20th century BC onwards) have survived less well into the modern day, so that seen here may have long since been plundered. (It may even have been abandoned and demolished after being visited by deadly war machines – an ill omen if ever there was one.)
- The large model of the pyramid and its surrounding enclosure included a tiny model Police Box – about the same size as the first miniature TARDIS made for season one but probably not the same one – which was used to show the Ship arriving. Similarly sized miniatures of the Dalek time capsule and the Monk's TARDIS disguised as a block of stone were also used.
- The Monk refers to the Doctor's TARDIS as such but only after he has heard the Doctor himself do so (and he was present when Vicki used the term in *The Time Meddler*). He later calls his own time machine "my TARDIS", however, the first time the name has been applied to another ship.
- After the Doctor has adjusted the Monk's TARDIS to take on the appearance of a Police Box, the usual prop was used to represent both time machines. In episode ten, a break in recording after the shot of the Doctor, Sara and Steven entering the TARDIS allowed the box to be moved from the tomb set to the outdoor set for the Monk's escape from the Daleks. The latter dematerialisation was achieved with sound only, the camera closing in on the Daleks firing as the take-off sound effect is heard.

LANDING 32

SPACE Kembel, jungle
TIME 4000 (some time after Landing 25)
TRAVELLERS The Doctor, Steven, Sara
EPISODES The Daleks' Master Plan 11-12

The directional unit has burnt out, fortunately taking the brunt of the excess energy rather than the console itself, but not before the TARDIS successfully reaches Kembel. Indeed, the Doctor initially thinks the plan has failed and they are still in Egypt, until he checks the scanner and sees jungle. The travellers head out to search for the Dalek city, Steven taking an impulse compass with him to guide them.

Steven and Sara briefly return to where the Police Box stands having been separated from the Doctor. Unsure whether he is lost in the jungle, has already found the city or been captured by the Daleks, they decide all they can do is find the city and try to stop the Daleks' plan themselves. They head back into the jungle.

The Doctor activates the Time Destructor and slowly but surely time on Kembel accelerates. Steven is first to recover the safety of the TARDIS, Sara having gone back to help the Doctor. He paces the control room impatiently waiting for the others. Checking the scanner shows no sign of them and he thumps the console in frustration. Outside the environment is changing faster and faster, the jungle withering and the landscape turning to desert. The Doctor and Sara come in sight of the Ship but both are weak, Sara in particular now aged and wrinkled. The Doctor collapses and she tries to help him with the last of her strength but cannot.

Steven spies them on the scanner and rushes out to help but is buffeted by the howling wind. By the time he reaches Sara's body she is nothing but dust. Beginning to struggle against the aging effects himself, he finds the Time Destructor and tries to smash it then, failing that, to turn it off but there seems to be no change. In fact he has thrown it into reverse and time is now racing backwards. With Steven's help, the Doctor recovers slightly and pleads with his friend to get back to the Ship. Together they stumble into the TARDIS and close the doors with relief.

The pursuing Daleks catch up but they too are being affected by the Time Destructor. They fire but to no effect. Their casings disintegrate into their raw components and the mutant creatures inside flail around in the sand until they too are gone. The ground heaves as time rolls backwards until finally the taranium powering the Destructor is exhausted and the planet falls silent, barren and dead.

The Doctor and Steven step from the TARDIS onto the dusty surface. All that is left of the Time Destructor itself is a twisted lump of metal, and of the Daleks there is only a tiny dead embryo in the sand. Lamenting the great cost of defeating the Daleks – the deaths of Vyon, Katarina and now Sara – they return to the Ship and level Kembel to its ghosts.

- **CONTROLS** When Steven operates the scanner towards the end of episode twelve, the sound of a lever bouncing and coming to rest suggests it could be one of the large sliders on panel A4 or A5.
- **LORE** The console has a built-in safety measure to prevent damage from surges of energy.
- Quite understandably but worth noting, the TARDIS is unaffected by the shifting flow of time around it.
- **NOTES** This is the TARDIS's most instantaneous flight yet. There's no indication of the Ship dematerialising as light fills the control room the moment Steven throws the switch. The travellers may have been briefly knocked out, or at least dazzled, but even they are unaware the Ship has moved so presumably there was no movement of the central column or sound of engines. Perhaps this is how TARDISes should operate when being piloted properly.
- According to studio plans, the time-curve indicator was not included on the control room set for episode eleven. The Doctor must therefore have tidied it away when working in the TARDIS during Landing 31, it no longer being needed once the Monk had caught up with them. The set comprised the main doors and an indented wall, with a photographic wall on either side. For episode twelve it may have been smaller as there are only brief scenes inside the TARDIS. On the soundtrack the doors can be heard closing (a physical clunk as well as the added sound effect) so they must have been present.
- Although it's the first we've seen of it, Steven seems familiar with the operation of the impulse compass. This suggests an unseen adventure in which he used it, perhaps between Landings 22 and 23.

LANDING 33

SPACE Earth, France, Paris, Rue de Béthisy
TIME [20] to 24 August 1572
TRAVELLERS The Doctor, Steven
EPISODES The Massacre 1,4

The TARDIS arrives in Paris again, materialising discreetly behind the gate to a yard beside the Hôtel de Rohan-Chabot on the Rue de Béthisy. The Doctor and Steven step out to find where they are, deducing the location from a street sign and the time period from people's clothing. The Doctor knows of an apothecary in the city at this time – Charles Preslin, who has a pioneering theory about germs – and determines to visit him. They both return to the Ship to find suitable attire for the period and for the Doctor to check some old documents. Steven refuses to stay while the Doctor pays his respects, so they visit a nearby tavern and agree to meet again there that evening.

It is only a few days later that the Doctor discovers the date and hurries Steven back to the TARDIS. Their way is blocked by guards outside the hotel where the wounded Admiral de Coligny has his rooms. They wait impatiently through the night then, as the bell sounds for the end of curfew early the next morning, the guards are relieved by soldiers come to kill de Coligny. The Doctor and Steven take their chance to slip by and into the Ship. It dematerialises ahead of the slaughter that is to come.

- **NOTES** There is no explicit indication that this follows directly from Landing 32 but Steven does tell Gaston he has been in Egypt so it's unlikely there have been many landings in between and probably none on Earth.
- Henry III of Navarre was married in Paris on 18 August 1572, which Steven is told was "yesterday". Yet the next day Steven overhears plans for de Coligny to be assassinated "tomorrow", which occurred on the 22nd. There's no room for an extra day in Steven's storyline, so the TARDIS must have landed on the 20th and presumably Nicholas Muss had been celebrating a little too hard or was simplifying things when he told Steven the wedding was yesterday rather than the day before that.
- According to the camera script, the TARDIS was heard but not seen to materialise, the Police Box prop already in position on the set. Its departure from Paris was similarly represented by just the sound effect, with the camera quickly cutting away to images of the massacre.

LANDING 34

SPACE Earth, England, London, [Wimbledon] Common
TIME [Mid-1960s]
TRAVELLERS The Doctor, Steven
EPISODES The Massacre 4

Steven is angry at the Doctor for leaving his friend Anne Chaplet behind in Paris, knowing she will likely be killed. The Doctor's argument that they cannot know for sure and must not interfere with the course of history does nothing to placate Steven and he determines to leave the Ship for good wherever it lands next. As they quarrel the TARDIS materialises on a common in London. Steven checks the scanner and opens the doors but even a last plea from the Doctor cannot stop him storming out, leaving the old man to muse on all those who have left him and his own inability to go home.

A young girl runs across the common and, mistaking the TARDIS for a real Police Box, bursts into the control room looking for a telephone. She needs to ring the police about an accident in which a boy is hurt. She seems totally unfazed by the Ship's larger interior and is gazing around when Steven returns to warn the Doctor of two approaching policemen. The Doctor hurriedly closes the doors and dematerialises the Ship, which is seen disappearing by a woman walking her dog.

Only then does Steven notice the girl. She is blasé about the notion of never seeing her home again as she is an orphan and claims no one, not even her great aunt, will miss her. The Doctor is taken by her similarity to his granddaughter Susan. Only when she tells them her name – Dorothea 'Dodo' Chaplet – and that her grandfather was French do the Doctor and Steven take comfort that perhaps Anne survived the Paris massacre after all.

- **LORE** The Doctor explains to Dodo that "this machine is for travelling through time and relative dimensions in space".
- **NOTES** Although Dodo's approach to the TARDIS was filmed on Wimbledon Common, it's not stated as such on screen. Steven does confirm that they've landed on *a* common.
- It's generally assumed that Dodo came from contemporary England (as this was the intention of the production team at the time), placing this brief arrival in 1966, or arguably late-1965. However, when she later returns to modern-day London in *The War Machines* (Landing 40), Dodo expresses surprise that construction of the Post Office Tower is complete, suggesting it wasn't at the time she left. In our history, the building was officially opened in October 1965, and was structurally complete as early as 1964, so perhaps this landing is earlier than supposed.
- The TARDIS lands without its usual grinding being heard inside the control room, only the background hum falls silent (although the squeaking of the central column continues for several moments after).
- Without being able to watch the episode, we can't be sure how Dodo's entrance into the TARDIS was depicted but from the soundtrack she seems to run straight inside. Real Police Boxes were usually locked and were for the exclusive use of the police, apart from the telephone accessible to the public from outside by opening the panel below the front left-hand window. Yet Dodo doesn't even try to use the external phone and runs in as though she's expecting there to be a lot of room inside, not a 2-foot-square space. According to those who remember watching the original broadcast, the Police Box doors were visible outside the control room doors – a rare appearance of the standalone doors created for *An Unearthly Child* (see page 14) – and the soundtrack does feature what sounds like these being pulled shut when Steven leaves the Doctor alone, and opened when Dodo enters. It seems the inside double doors remain open until they are heard closing just before the TARDIS takes off.
- The scenes of Dodo entering the Police Box and the woman watching it vanish were filmed on Wimbledon Common on Friday 7 January 1966. However, the TARDIS prop was needed in the studio that day for recording of *The Daleks' Master Plan* episode eleven, so a duplicate was hastily thrown together. Publicity photos taken during the location filming show this was a very rough approximation of a Police Box. The front used the standalone doors, which matched the main prop, but the two sides were simple painted flats and far less accurate, notably the arrangement of bars on the windows (but possibly not visible on screen). These all supported a two-stepped flat roof.

LANDING 35

SPACE The Ark (within visual range of Earth), jungle zone
TIME Far future (57th Segment of Time)
TRAVELLERS The Doctor, Steven, Dorothea 'Dodo' Chaplet
EPISODES The Ark 1-2

The TARDIS seemingly lands in a steamy jungle which Dodo is keen to explore, ignoring Steven's calls for caution. Around them is an unusual range of flora and fauna from all across the Earth, including toucans, chameleons, monitor lizards, locusts and elephants. Dodo believes they are simply at Whipsnade Wild Animal Park in England, although when the Doctor exits the Ship he tells Steven there is something strange about his instrument readings. The two men briefly re-enter the TARDIS to double-check, unaware that nearby is an alien one-eyed creature.

Staying in sight of the Ship, the travellers notice the ground is vibrating and the sky is a wide, metal, illuminated roof. They find paintings of two-headed zebras on a rock wall, convincing Steven they cannot be on Earth. An electronic alarm sounds and he spies two of the monocular creatures by the TARDIS. He warns the others and they hide in a crevice in the rock as the aliens search for them – not helped by Dodo's having a cold and sneezing. When the coast is clear, they move out and come to a clearing overlooking a vast complex of buildings beneath the same metal roof. The Doctor realises they are on an enormous spaceship before they are captured by more of the one-eyed aliens and taken away.

Later, as the inhabitants of this ark begin to succumb to Dodo's cold virus, against which they no longer have any immunity, one of the alien Monoids collapses and dies in front of the TARDIS. The Doctor eventually persuades the humans to let him devise a vaccine, and he sends Dodo to the Ship to collect some testing equipment.

With the disease killing the Ark's population cured by the Doctor, the travellers depart on friendly terms. A Monoid takes them on one of the loading vehicles to the Ship and watches as it fades away.

- **NOTES** Although the intention of the production team at the time was that his story followed directly from *The Massacre*, Dodo shows no surprise that the TARDIS has moved from London. While this is consistent with her earlier lack of bewilderment at the Ship's interior, it's equally possible she has already had an adventure or two and now believes they are simply back on Earth in her own time. Notably she has had time to go "footling about" in the TARDIS wardrobe and is "beginning to enjoy this space travel or whatever it is". The Doctor is also confident of sending her to the Ship alone to collects specific pieces of equipment.
- The Doctor estimates the 57th Segment of Time must be "at least ten million years" ahead. We know that in the *Doctor Who* universe the Earth is consumed by the Sun some five billion years from now (see Landing 322, vol.2). So either the Doctor is way out or he has just had an adventure around the year 4990000000.
- The TARDIS's arrival and departure (and swift return – see next Landing) were filmed at Ealing Studios along with the other jungle scenes.
- This is only the second time the TARDIS has been seen to land on a spaceship so could the Doctor's "really very strange" instrument readings be similar to the we've-stopped-but-we're-still-moving quandary faced in *The Sensorites* (Landing 8)? Not exactly the same, though, as surely the Doctor would have figured that one out by now, and here he doesn't realise they're on a spaceship for some time.
- The Ark's commander describes the appearance of the TARDIS as a "black box". He has only seen it on a monitor so perhaps they only show a black-and-white image. Steven doesn't correct him but then he's being interrogated so maybe thought it wasn't diplomatic to say, "It's dark blue, actually." He also says the Ship "has a mind of its own" – merely implying that it's uncontrollable or has he had experience we didn't see of the TARDIS's sentience?

LANDING 36

SPACE The Ark (approaching Refusis Two), jungle zone
TIME Far future (57th Segment of Time), 700 years after Landing 35
TRAVELLERS The Doctor, Steven, Dodo
EPISODES The Ark 2-4

Almost immediately the TARDIS materialises again and the travellers are surprised to find themselves seemingly back in the place they just left. Indeed they are aboard the ark from Earth but it is now 700 years later and the vessel is nearing its destination.

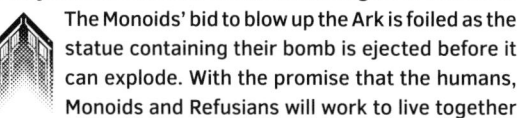

The Monoids' bid to blow up the Ark is foiled as the statue containing their bomb is ejected before it can explode. With the promise that the humans, Monoids and Refusians will work to live together in peace on Refusis, the travellers take their leave. Dassuk and Venussa watch on their command console as the TARDIS disappears from the jungle.

- **NOTES** Given the essentially random nature of the TARDIS's landing sites (apart from its predilection for Earth), this return to the Ark must simply be a fluke. Or has some higher power, or even the Ship itself – Steven does say, "The TARDIS made the decision" – deliberately directed the Doctor here to deal with the ramifications of his past disruption?
- The TARDIS's departure is seen on a monitor, showing a mix between two (poorly aligned) photos of the jungle set with and without the Police Box prop.

LANDING 37

SPACE Toymaker's domain
TIME None
TRAVELLERS The Doctor, Steven, Dodo
EPISODES The Ark 4; The Celestial Toymaker 1,4

Steven brings the TARDIS in to land while Dodo changes into more contemporary "fab" clothing. Suddenly the Doctor fades from view, although his voice can still be heard. He seems unaware of any difference but when his friends insist they cannot see him he deduces they are under attack from some power able to penetrate the Ship. The scanner shows nothing – Steven thinks it is not working but the Doctor points out the screen is too clear: the image is being blocked. Rather than leaving, he decides they must go outside and orders Steven to open the main doors because he is disembodied.

On leaving the Ship the Doctor becomes visible and tangible again. The travellers find themselves in a large room with a patterned floor and a big cupboard at one end. When Steven spots a man-sized tin toy robot with a screen in its chest showing images from his past, the Doctor warns him not to watch. He realises they are in the domain of the Celestial Toymaker, a powerful being who wishes to dominate their minds with his trickery. On cue, the Toymaker appears, standing in place of the TARDIS, which vanishes. When they demand its return the robot's screen displays a long line of Police Boxes on a conveyor belt. The Toymaker tells them they can only recover the genuine TARDIS by winning his games.

Steven and Dodo complete their final game and reach the genuine TARDIS just as the Doctor makes the second-to-last move of his own trilogic game. Now visible, tangible and audible again, the Doctor holds off placing the final counter in order to check on the Ship. He lets his friends inside but the Toymaker is confident he will still win. When the Doctor finds the TARDIS will not dematerialise, the Toymaker explains he must finish his game first – but doing so will instantly destroy this domain and the time travellers along with it. From inside the Ship, the Doctor mimics the Toymaker's voice to instruct the last piece to move. The TARDIS dematerialises as the counter slots into place and the Toymaker's world disintegrates.

Although they have escaped the Toymaker this time, the Doctor warns that he is indestructible and they are sure to meet again. To celebrate this victory, however, Dodo offers the Doctor one of the sweets she was given by the overgrown schoolboy Cyril. But when he bites into it, the Doctor clasps his jaw in agony.

- **CONTROLS** Steven pulls the two large sliders on panel A5 downwards as the TARDIS begins to materialise. He later closes the doors with one of the small levers at the top of panel A4. Moments later he uses the same set of levers to "preset for dematerialisation" having first moved the large slider downwards. The Doctor turns on the scanner with the top-most small lever on panel A1. When his first attempt to control the trilogic game fails, the Doctor operates a control on panel A5 (his hand makes a twisting motion so this is probably the rotary handle at bottom left); on the second attempt, Steven reaches across to that panel to throw the "master switch" (one of the small levers).
- The small dial switch on the left of panel A1 has by this time been replaced with a larger white button while the right-hand of the two lower small levers has gone missing. The fault locator wall is missing all its light panels, leaving holes where they were positioned, and only the central part of the scanner framework (holding the monitor) is used. Little wonder this was their last appearance.
- **LORE** The TARDIS forcefield (or "safety barrier") can be penetrated by a sufficiently powerful force, such as that of the Toymaker.
- The scanner image can be blocked or suppressed.
- **NOTES** Although the scene of the Doctor vanishing comes at the end of The Ark, the two companions have had time to change their clothes so this journey may not be consecutive with leaving the Ark. Indeed, the Doctor says, "The gravitational bearing must have rectified itself," a problem not noted before so may be the result of a further adventure. Dodo does mention the Refusians as a possible cause of the Doctor's invisibility, however, so it's likely not much time has passed.
- This is the first time someone other than the Doctor is seen operating the console to materialise the TARDIS. Previously he has asked Steven to open the main doors or activate the scanner but never land the Ship. Obviously Steven has become a trusted companion, more so even than Susan.
- The usual Police Box prop was used for the fake TARDIS found by Steven and Dodo at the end of their first game. We can't be sure without the episode to view, but it's possible the inside of the prop is shown in full for the first time when they find it's just an empty cabinet. The image on a monitor of a conveyor belt with multiple TARDISes was a pre-filmed model shot.
- In episode two Steven and Dodo encounter four white cupboards in the shape of the TARDIS. Photos show these had plain rather than panelled sides, but the fronts were accurate replicas of the main prop – usefully so as two were later used to refurbish the Police Box prop. The main difference (apart from the colour) was that the doors opened outwards and had mushroom-shaped knobs rather than handles. One had a square window cut in the panel below the right-hand window, through which was viewed the counter for the Doctor's moves in the trilogic game.
- In episode three, the standalone doors are believed to have been used as the fake TARDIS at the far end of the triangular dance floor, to save space. (It's possible they were also used for the false TARDIS at the end of episode two, with a regular telephone box placed behind for the Toymaker to ring with the next clue.)

LANDING 38

SPACE Earth, America, Arizona, Tombstone, livery store yard
TIME [24 to 27 October 1881]
TRAVELLERS The Doctor, Steven, Dodo
EPISODES The Gunfighters 1,4

The TARDIS materialises amid sacks and barrels in the yard of one of Tombstone's seven livery and feed stores, close to the entrance of the OK Corral. When Steven and Dodo discover they are in the Wild West, they head back into the Ship for appropriate attire, emerging in rather theatrical interpretations of American Western fashion, including a wide-brimmed hat for the Doctor. Before he can see if there is a local dentist who can help with his toothache, the travellers are discovered by sheriff Wyatt Earp, who leads them away at gunpoint to account for themselves.

Following the infamous gunfight, the travellers return with Doc Holliday and Kate to the livery yard where the TARDIS waits. The gambler-cum-dentist is set to leave town as there is a $2,000 reward on his head for murder and treason. He gives the Doctor a copy of his Wanted poster and bids the travellers goodbye. The Doctor discards the poster as he ushers his friends into the Ship, eager to be on his way also.

- **NOTES** As usual, events in Doctor Who don't quite match up with history as we know it. For one, the real gunfight took place around 3pm, not early in the morning as portrayed here. But if we can assume the shoot-out at least took place on the same day, Wednesday 26 October, then the TARDIS arrives two days earlier. It's also unclear how soon afterwards the travellers are able to get away, although they don't appear to be in a hurry to avoid the subsequent inquiries. In our history, Ike Clanton wasn't involved in the gunfight and four days after filed murder charges against Wyatt and Virgil Earp and Holliday, and the three were arrested. The following hearing took a month before acquitting the accused. With Ike dead in the Doctor Who version of events, Holliday seems to be at some liberty to leave Tombstone before too many questions are asked (although the reward for his capture dates from July – sadly the year is obscured but begins with 18) so the time travellers may have enjoyed a few more days in town before departing.

PREVIOUS LANDINGS

SPACE Earth, Scotland, Glasgow
TIME 1888
TRAVELLERS The Doctor, [unknown companions]
EPISODES Claimed by the Doctor in The Moonbase 2
In his first incarnation, the Doctor acquired a medical degree from the University of Glasgow, possibly under the tutelage of Joseph Lister.

- **NOTES** As Polly is unaware of the Doctor's qualification, he must have gained it before meeting her, which means he would have been in his first incarnation. The Doctor only says he "took a degree", which could mean he just sat the exams while his companions were busy elsewhere – perhaps visiting the International Exhibition of Science, Art and Industry held in Glasgow that year.
- The Doctor's memory may be at fault here (or he could just be making it up to reassure Polly – in The Krotons he tells Zoe he's not a doctor of medicine) as although Lister spent much of his medical career in Glasgow, by 1888 he was at King's College Hospital in London. Yet the Doctor's actual words are, "Glasgow. 1888, I think. Lister," which might not mean he met Lister, just that the degree course covered the pioneering surgeon's techniques.

SPACE Unnamed planet
TIME Unknown
TRAVELLERS The Doctor, [unknown companions]
EPISODES The Three Doctors; The Five Doctors
At some point during his first incarnation, the Doctor was wandering alone in some formal gardens when he was twice lifted from his time-stream in order to assist his future incarnations.

The first time he was taken by the Time Lords, who transported him in a transparent diamond-shaped capsule. But their energy was being drained into a black hole and the capsule was caught in a time eddy. The Doctor could only talk to his next two incarnations via the TARDIS scanner, even after the Time Lords projected his capsule into the black hole. After the black hole was destroyed, the Doctor was returned to his own time.

Back in the gardens, the Doctor was then plucked out of his time-stream again by the Time Scoop, a long-forgotten device of the Time Lords', which deposited him in the Death Zone on Gallifrey. There he helped three of his next four incarnations (and several companions, including Susan) to overcome President Borusa's bid to gain immortality. Afterwards everyone was returned to their original times and places by the consciousness of Rassilon.

- **NOTES** There's no period while the Doctor is in his first incarnation when he is seen travelling alone, so we must assume that he is taken while his companions are elsewhere then returned to the exact same moment, probably with no memory of his detour. Given this, and the similarity of locations from which he is taken in both stories, it makes some sense to assume the two kidnappings are almost consecutive. This is not certain but it's plausible that Borusa knew of the earlier extraction so Time Scooped the Doctor from the same point in his time-stream. The second kidnapping at least must come after The Dalek Invasion of Earth (Landing 11) as the Doctor clearly hasn't seen Susan for some time, and both are probably before The Savages (Landing 39) as subsequent landings before his regeneration are consecutive (although Twice Upon a Time showed how it's possible to insert whole new adventures in the gaps between scenes).
- Another possibility is that the Doctor is taken during a televised adventure. Although there are times when he doesn't appear in an episode because William Hartnell was on holiday (owing to the year-round production schedule of the time), narratively his whereabouts are mostly known. However, there is one notable absence. During The Massacre (Landing 33) the Doctor disappears for three days, leaving Steven on his own. When he returns he makes no attempt to explain where he has been, saying only he was "unavoidably delayed". Could he have been visiting a chateau near Paris and admiring its gardens when his assistance was needed in his future? Returned with no memory of events, but perhaps aware something unusual had happened, he might be understandably confused (especially if it had happened twice in quick succession), so is unforthcoming when Steven asks where he has been.

LANDING 39

SPACE Unnamed planet
TIME Two days in unknown future
TRAVELLERS The Doctor, Steven, Dodo
EPISODES The Gunfighters 4; The Savages 1,4
The TARDIS arrives on a planet which the scanner shows to be rocky but with some tree cover. The Doctor claims to know where they are, a time in the future, "the distant horizon of an age of peace and prosperity." As all three travellers head out, the Doctor carrying his Reacting Vibrator instrument over his shoulder, the scanner shows a man wearing animal skins and carrying a club approaching.

The Doctor leaves Steven and Dodo to wait by the TARDIS while he takes some readings. When he doesn't return, Steven follows but a cry from Dodo brings him back to the Ship. She claims to have seen a primitive-looking man on the ridge above them but there is no sign of him now. They both move off to find the Doctor but more figures appear and throw spears at them so they run back to the TARDIS for cover. The attack stops when the primitives are frightened away by Exorse, a soldier from the nearby city, who offers to take Steven and Dodo there to be reunited with the Doctor.

Some time later, Steven and Dodo return to the Ship with the Doctor's RV device. They leave it behind after taking a container of capsules marked D403 from the emergency cabinet.

Early the next day the Doctor and Dodo return to the TARDIS without Steven, who has been persuaded to stay and help the two factions on the planet work together to build an equal society. Dodo is tearful at leaving him behind but the Doctor is confident Steven will be a great leader. The Ship fades away.

- **NOTES** Although the scene of the Doctor declaring they have landed in a future age of peace and prosperity comes at the end of *The Gunfighters*, it follows a fade-to-black after he was seen entering the TARDIS in Tombstone, during which Steven and Dodo have changed their clothes, so there's no narrative continuity between the two landings.
- The ability of the elders of this world to follow the course of the TARDIS is surprising. Exorse tells the Doctor they have "been plotting the course of your space-time ship for many light years", while Jano says, "We have charted your voyages from galaxy to galaxy and from age to age." This is quite an achievement given even the Doctor doesn't know where he's going to land next. While the Daleks and the Monk have previously followed the TARDIS's course, they were in time machines of their own. How, then, have these people been able to track the Doctor's erratic flight to different parts of the universe in vastly different times? Equally unclear is why they are doing it. Did they invent the technology specifically to find the Doctor? Jano says he never expected to actually meet him, so presumably not. Having devised a means to survey all of time and space, then, did they just stumble across the Doctor's adventures and get hooked? It's almost like they've been watching half-hour snippets of his life weekly for the past two and a half years… Actually, could this be the answer? We've previously seen a television-like device that could tune in to events anywhere in the past: the time and space visualiser. Have the elders of this world created their own version and, in gathering light neutrons from distant stars (which, of course, originated far in the past), kept noticing a man in a blue box appearing on different planets in different times? This could even be a future Earth and the origin of the Doctor's visualiser.
- The establishing shots of the TARDIS at the start of the story and departing at the end were still photos taken on location using the 3-foot model, even though the full-size prop was also present in the sandpit in Surrey used to represent the planet in the story. A behind-the-scenes photo of the crew filming a scene from episode one shows both props (and also proves that the full-size Police Box had rear doors, as they can be seen to be ajar). Director Christopher Barry chose to show the Ship in a long shot, which was easier to achieve with the model rather than getting the camera a suitable distance from the larger box. Surviving off-screen photos show that episode one's title and writer credit were displayed over a shot of the Police Box that, while small in the frame, looks like it's the miniature and is clearly not in the same location as later shots of the actors with the full-size prop. At the end of the serial the TARDIS is seen to fade away by mixing between two photos, although they're misaligned so the background shifts as the box vanishes.

LANDING 40

SPACE Earth, England, London, Camden, Fitzroy Square
TIME 12 to [15] July 1966
TRAVELLERS The Doctor, Dodo
EPISODES The War Machines 1,4; The Smugglers 1

For the first time in a long time the TARDIS fits perfectly into its surroundings when it materialises on a 20th-century London street, beside the fence surrounding Fitzroy Square Gardens, and startling a flock of pigeons. Both travellers immediately recognise where they are; Dodo in particular is happy to be back home. The Doctor hangs a sign reading 'Out of Order' on the TARDIS door to deter anyone trying to enter, thinking it a real Police Box – a timely precaution as a policeman soon approaches but continues on his beat when he sees the notice. The Doctor's attention is caught by the nearby Post Office Tower, about which he senses something alien and heads off with Dodo to investigate.

Days later, the Doctor waits for Dodo outside the TARDIS, getting increasingly impatient. Instead his recent acquaintances Polly and Ben arrive with a message from Sir Charles Summer that Dodo has decided to stay in London. The Doctor thanks the two youngsters and encourages them to be on their way. A suspicious Polly looks back, however, and spots him entering the Police Box. Ben is reminded he earlier picked up a key the Doctor had dropped and Polly insists they return it now. There is no response when they knock on the door so they use the key and venture inside just before the Ship dematerialises.

The Doctor is angry at Polly and Ben's intrusion, telling them they are now travelling through time and space and that it may be a long time before they see their home again. He admits he has no control over when or where the Ship lands.

- **LORE** Dodo asks Wotan what the word TARDIS means and reads out the printed response: "Time and relative dimensions in space." Neither she nor the Doctor suggests that the machine has got it slightly wrong by citing the plural 'dimensions'.
- **NOTES** Although there is nothing in the narrative to say this landing immediately follows Landing 39, Dodo

is wearing the same outfit she had on in *The Savages* and briefly mentions Steven as if she's still missing him.

- The intention was for the TARDIS to land in Fitzroy Square and narratively that must be where it is for the Doctor and Dodo to have the view of the Post Office Tower they do (plus Ben says so in the next story). However, in order to achieve the high shot of the Police Box materialising, the prop had to be positioned in nearby Bedford Square to be visible from the Centre Point building, from which the opening panorama was filmed. Subsequent shots of the travellers emerging and the policeman approaching were also filmed in Bedford Square, although that of the Doctor and Dodo heading towards the tower at the end of the first scene was filmed in Conway Street, which leads from the southern corner of Fitzroy Square.

- Watch the driver getting out of his car on the left of the screen just as the TARDIS materialises, only to mysteriously vanish into thin air.

- Between this location filming and the later studio recording, the Police Box prop was refurbished and repainted (see page 76). Note that in the shots on film – the TARDIS arriving and the two travellers emerging – the window frames are still white and the St John Ambulance emblem is visible on the right-hand door (although painted over), whereas in the shots recorded in the studio – those with dialogue – the frames are blue and the emblem is gone.

- In episode one, Sir Charles Summer declares that Wotan will take control of all computers in the country "next Monday, July the sixteenth, that is in four days' time". That places the TARDIS's arrival on Thursday 12 July. The choice of date would seem to be an attempt to make the series appear contemporary as the final episode of *The War Machines* was scheduled to be broadcast on 16 July 1966. Yet surely the production team would therefore have known that date was a Saturday, not a Monday. In our history, 16 July fell on a Monday in 1962 but then not again until 1973. The latter would have been a plausible setting for the story at this point in the series: it's only Dodo who's surprised the Post Office Tower is complete, no one else mentions its being new, so it may have been standing for years before the decision to install Wotan there (although would the very Sixties Inferno club still be the "hottest nightspot in town" by 1973?). However, in the next story Ben confirms he comes from "good old nineteen sixty-six". If only Sir Charles had said Monday the 18th then Wotan's planned attack would have come at noon on the 16th, tying in to episode four's broadcast.

- Two days go by between the Doctor's arrival and his defeat of Wotan, but it seems likely he stays around to help clean up for once, if only because after the first day he put Dodo to sleep for 48 hours to recover from Wotan's control. It's probably Sunday 15 July, then, that he plans to reunite with Dodo and leave – there's not much traffic on the street and Polly isn't at or dressed for work. It could be as late as 20 July given that when Polly and Ben return to London in *The Faceless Ones* he declares, "July the twentieth, nineteen sixty-six is when it all began. We're back to when it all started," but adds, "Well, I think." He might be talking broadly rather than being specific to the day, and would the Doctor really stick around for a whole week?

IT LOOKS JUST LIKE A POLICE BOX

THE BRACHACKI BOX
1966-1970

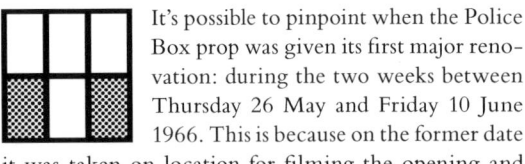

It's possible to pinpoint when the Police Box prop was given its first major renovation: during the two weeks between Thursday 26 May and Friday 10 June 1966. This is because on the former date it was taken on location for filming the opening and closing scenes of *The War Machines*, while on the latter it was in Riverside Studio 1 for recording of the first episode, by which time its appearance was noticeably different. The alterations weren't about making the prop look better but to ensure it stayed in one piece.

It's likely the box was completely dismantled and put back together to strengthen the joins after three years of manhandling. Most noticeably, it was reduced in height by cutting away the sides above the corner posts. The reason for this was that the front and rear of the box were replaced with fascias from the fake-TARDIS cupboards constructed for *The Celestial Toymaker* earlier that year. These were shorter than the TARDIS proper, with the corner posts rising only slightly above the sign boxes, so the old sides were trimmed to match.

In other respects these cupboards were close copies of the main prop, with only minor differences. The signs themselves had a semi-opaque film applied to the acrylic with black lettering, instead of white letters on translucent acrylic, in keeping with the inverted colours of their original purpose. The windows lacked the additional strip along the bottom sill, meaning the proportions of the panes were ever so slightly different. And the doors opened outwards, with small wooden doorknobs.

The fronts of two cupboards, including corner posts, were attached to the panelled sides from the original prop and its base, with battens along the bottom of the sides to secure them more sturdily. Although the quarter-round beading down the outer corners and inner edges of the posts was replicated from the original prop, it had been omitted from the plain cupboard sides. This meant the sides now butted tighter against the new front and back posts, and weren't as deeply recessed, making the plan of the box no longer a true square, being shallower than it was wide. The base therefore had a deeper sill at the front and back, and the sign boxes on the side were trimmed to account for the shorter width, making the edges of the recess markedly closer to the lettering. (Those on the front and back were slightly lower too.)

The pitched roof had little left to support it with the top of the box and particularly the corner-post caps cut away – large gaps can be seen when the TARDIS lands on its side in *The Ice Warriors*.

While these changes made the prop lighter and easier to manoeuvre in studio and on location, they took it further away from the tall, multiple-stepped-roof design of the original Metropolitan Police Box.

A problem then arose with the new doors. Because these had been made to open outwards their tops were below the level of the stepped lintel. This wasn't an issue for the rear of the box, where the doors had always opened out (and here they retained the cupboards' round knobs), but at the front the steps no longer acted as a doorstop. So even though these doors were now hinged to open inwards, they could still bow outwards. By the time *The Power of the Daleks* episode six was recorded on Saturday 26 November, two clover-shaped brackets had been screwed into the lowest lintel step either side of the centre post to restrain the doors.

More noticeable on screen than these structural alterations were the cosmetic changes. The window frames on all sides were painted blue instead of white, the St John Ambulance emblem disappeared completely, and the front door lock was now positioned on the right-hand rather than left-hand door. The roof lamp and telephone plaque were transferred from the old prop. The latter's frame got a fresh coat of paint (although still slightly paler than the rest of the box) and even though the white *Toymaker* pieces were of course painted blue the condition of the paintwork was still very rough, with scuffs and missing flakes evident even in *The War Machines*. If this was deliberate distressing it only made the prop look as worn out as before.

This wasn't helped by its soon suffering further damage. At least by the time of location filming for *The Highlanders* in November 1966, the bottom six inches of the centre post on the right-hand side of the box had broken off (see page 78). This was never replaced and would get worse before the prop was finally scrapped.

PLAQUE PLACING

With much of the fourth season of *Doctor Who* missing, we're reliant on photographs to spot further changes to the Police Box. The clearest is that towards the end of this production block the telephone plaque was moved onto the right-hand door. This doesn't appear to have happened when the prop was filmed at Gatwick Airport on Monday 13 March 1967 for the first episode of *The*

Right Refurbished Brachacki prop front elevation and section, with reduced height and replacement doors

IT LOOKS JUST LIKE A POLICE BOX

IT LOOKS JUST LIKE A POLICE BOX

Left The box's sides (right-hand pictured) were now narrower than its width and retained unrepaired damage
Below The original telephone plaque was replaced during *The Seeds of Death* in 1969 with a completely new style. The wording was the same but this introduced ampersands and arranged the lines differently. It would remain this way for the remainder of the Brachacki prop's use

POLICE TELEPHONE
FREE
FOR USE OF PUBLIC
ADVICE & ASSISTANCE
OBTAINABLE
IMMEDIATELY
OFFICERS & CARS
RESPOND TO
URGENT CALLS
PULL TO OPEN

Faceless Ones, but by the time the TARDIS's theft at the start of *The Evil of the Daleks* was filmed a month later on Friday 21 April behind-the-scenes photos show the plaque had been relocated. Had it come off and was simply put back on the wrong side? Whatever the reason, it remained this way until *The Wheel in Space* episode one, recorded on Friday 5 April 1968 (although the episode is missing, a photograph of the Servo Robot with the TARDIS behind it shows the plaque still on the right-hand door). When episode one of *The Dominators* was recorded on Friday 17 May, the plaque had been returned to the left-hand door, although by now very dirty and almost illegible. As this serial was designed by one of the debut set designers, Barry Newbery, it could be he was the first to notice the mistake and had it corrected.

The prop appeared the same in *The Mind Robber* which, with *The Dominators*, was recorded directly after *The Wheel in Space* but their broadcast was held back to be the first stories of *Doctor Who*'s sixth season. After a summer break in production, the Police Box was next required on location for filming of *The Invasion* on Tuesday 3 September 1968, but in the meantime its use in another programme had introduced further changes.

The third series of BBC2's science-fiction anthology *Out of the Unknown* concluded with an adaptation of Peter Phillips' short story 'Get Off My Cloud', which featured the TARDIS (plus some Daleks) in a representation of a comatose writer's fevered imagination. As *Doctor Who* was taking its break, the props were available for the recording at Ealing Studios on Thursday 8 August. The script called for the Police Box's phone to be used, so for the first time the telephone plaque became a genuine cubbyhole, with a box added behind for the phone. The plaque itself was cleaned and two handles were added to the prop, one on the right-hand door above the lock and the other at the same height on the left-hand side of the plaque's frame. Pleasingly, this episode of *Out of the Unknown* was designed by Raymond P Cusick, one of the original designers on *Doctor Who*. Although 'Get Off My Cloud' wasn't broadcast until Tuesday 1 April 1969, this series of *Out of the Unknown* was its first made in colour so this would have been the first time the TARDIS was seen on screen to be blue (by the few who yet had colour TVs). Sadly the episode is no longer known to exist.

These changes are evident in the film sequences for *The Invasion*. In particular, at the end of the story when Patrick Troughton enters the Police Box through the right-hand door, the box behind the telephone plaque is clearly visible. The plaque and shiny new handles get a nice close-up in *The Krotons* episode three, but this would be the last appearance of the original 1963 plaque. In *The Seeds of Death*, although the front of the Police Box is only glimpsed as the travellers exit in episode one (recorded on Friday 3 January 1969), the plaque has gone missing – perhaps a consequence of having been converted into a proper door – revealing the inside of the recently added cubbyhole. By the prop's next appearance in studio on Friday 7 February, for episode six, a completely new plaque had been added. No attempt was made to match the original, which itself closely approximated a genuine Police Box plaque. The new sign had no frame and was all blue with hand-painted white sans-serif lettering. This altered the arrangement of some words – most notably 'for use of public' was now on one line – and replaced both instances of 'and' with ampersands. The final line, 'Pull to open', was rendered in italics. The panel was hinged on the right and had a small square handle on the left. In the next story, *The Space Pirates*, the front 'Police box' sign is much more legible, having become increasingly indistinct over the years. It may have had its lettering reapplied or simply been cleaned, possibly for its *Out of the Unknown* appearance or perhaps when the telephone plaque was replaced during *The Seeds of Death*.

Despite this work, after three further years of regular use the Police Box prop was in a poor state once again. Surprisingly, no work was done to smarten it up for its first *Doctor Who* appearance in colour, in *Spearhead from Space*. Jon Pertwee almost takes the door with him as he stumbles out of the TARDIS after landing on Earth, and when the scenes in UNIT's makeshift laboratory were filmed a month later, in October 1969, the box was raised up on blocks with a strip of black fabric round the base to hide the gap. The prop wasn't needed for the rest of the show's seventh season as the Doctor began his exile on Earth, and even though it would be seen the following year, with the format requiring the TARDIS to be used less often it seems an attitude of make do and mend was taken as the box underwent further maintenance rather than being replaced altogether.

LANDING 41

SPACE Earth, England, [Cornwall] coast, cave
TIME Two days in late-17th century
TRAVELLERS The Doctor, Polly, Ben Jackson
EPISODES The Smugglers 1,4

As the Doctor explains their predicament to a startled Polly and an incredulous Ben, the Ship begins to materialise again. The scanner is dark but suggests they have landed in a cave. The Doctor checks the external conditions before allowing his new travelling companions to leave, slightly wistful that he will not be alone for once.

The TARDIS stands in the mouth of a cave at the foot of a cliff. The travellers set off along the beach, Polly excited but Ben stubbornly determined to return to London as soon as possible. They make their way up a cliff path, unaware that at the back of the cave behind the Ship is a passageway leading to the church on the cliff-top.

Although the tide comes in and a storm brews, flooding the cave, the TARDIS remains safely on the beach, and is discovered by perplexed smugglers when they later bring their contraband ashore.

As the Doctor confronts the vicious Captain Pike in the church above, Ben and Polly take the secret passage through the cliff to the cave where the TARDIS waits. Polly is attacked outside the Ship by smugglers Spaniard and Daniel but saved by Ben and the arrival of Blake with a squad of militiamen. She waits by the TARDIS as Ben returns to the church with Blake to rescue the Doctor. Her two friends arrive in the cave safe but exhausted and all three hurry into the Ship and take off, noting that all those who sought to recover Avery's hidden treasure are dead, as the curse foretold.

▮ **LORE** The Doctor admits he has no control over where or when the TARDIS lands.

▤ **NOTES** Polly only speculates they have landed in Cornwall so they could be anywhere on the coast of south-west England as smuggling wasn't restricted to the West Country. Similarly, only the Doctor identifies this as the 17th century, although he usually knows his stuff. Even so, it's probably towards the very end of the 1600s (certainly after the Civil War). Although smuggling had been going on since the first custom duties were imposed in the 14th century, 1688 saw the expansion of both import taxes and the more recent excise duties to cover not just beverages like tea, coffee and spirits but also more essential goods like salt and soap. This increased the motivation to evade them by smuggling goods into the country, as did more draconian laws throughout the 18th century. Blake identifies himself as a "king's revenue officer", likely one of the landguards who patrolled the coastline on horseback, established in 1698. This would place *The Smugglers* between that date and 1702, when King William III died and was succeeded by Queen Anne.

▤ The travellers arrive at Kewper's inn seeking rooms for the night, although it's still daylight when Cherub kidnaps the Doctor shortly after. Pike's meeting with the Squire is in the morning so the Doctor must spend a night on Pike's ship while Ben and Polly are in jail. The Squire's scheme is then for Pike to unload his contraband "tomorrow night" but the captain has his own plans to sneak ashore before dark. Thus the rest of the story plays out on that day and the TARDIS leaves before sundown.

▤ The tide must have come in and out at least twice during that time but the TARDIS is not washed away, as established in *The Time Meddler* (Landing 22).

▤ The TARDIS is not seen materialising, only heard from inside the control room. Its departure was filmed on location using the full-size Police Box prop. Photos show only the main doors and an indented wall forming the control room in both episodes one and four; this was probably the extent of the set, a common minimal configuration for the brief TARDIS scenes topping and tailing many stories in *Doctor Who*'s fourth year.

LANDING 42

SPACE Earth, Antarctica, South Pole
TIME [1] December 1986
TRAVELLERS The Doctor, Polly, Ben
EPISODES The Smugglers 4; The Tenth Planet 1; Twice Upon a Time

Immediately after leaving the 17th century, the TARDIS lands again. Even inside Polly notices the temperature has dropped and the Doctor points to the scanner and announces they have arrived at "the coldest place in the world". The screen shows nothing but icy ground and snow swirling through the air.

Polly finds the wardrobe and brings fresh clothes, including a fur coat and hat for herself, a parka for Ben and for the Doctor a cloak, scarf, gloves and his karakul hat. Outside they are buffeted by the biting wind as they examine aerials and a periscope protruding from the ground. Sure enough they have been spotted by soldiers in the military base beneath the snow and three emerge from a hatch and take the travellers below at gunpoint.

Suspicious of his visitors, base commander General Cutler sends men up to search the Doctor's "hut", unaware that a spaceship has just landed a short distance away. The sergeant finds the TARDIS door locked so sends Private Tito back for a welding torch to cut their way in. While he waits, three tall, silver figures emerge through the snow. The sergeant fires his pistol at them but they are unharmed and chop him down with one strike. When Tito and another soldier return these Cybermen kill them too. They don their victims' hooded coats in order to infiltrate the base, leaving the bodies to be covered by the snow.

Some hours after, more Cybermen approach the base's entrance near the TARDIS but are cut down with weapons taken from their own advance squad. Soldiers emerge to collect the additional weapons.

Later, freed by Ben from the now-powerless Cybermen ship following the destruction of their planet Mondas, the Doctor staggers through the swirling snow desperate to reach the TARDIS. He can feel his first regeneration beginning but is scared of the change and fights to resist it, although his face is already subtly renewing.

A second iteration of the TARDIS, from many centuries in its own future, arrives nearby and the presence of two incarnations of the same Time Lord, both trying to suppress their incipient regenerations, causes a temporal disturbance that drags a Testimony time vessel off course. It was returning a First World War soldier to his point of death but accidentally deposits him at the source of the error. Testimony uses its ability to suspend time to attempt to recover the English Captain but he escapes in the TARDIS with the two Doctors and a glass avatar disguised as Bill Potts.

- **CONTROLS** The Doctor is standing at panel A5 when the Ship materialises and would appear to have his hand on the fast return switch. Has he used it again to try to get his new friends back to their time? If so he hasn't done too badly, being only 20 years out. He reaches across to panel A4 to seemingly turn off the scanner and opens the doors with the second small lever from the left on that panel. He takes off again using the top-most small lever on panel A1.
- **LORE** The inside of the Ship is affected by the exterior temperature again, as it was in *Marco Polo* (Landing 5). Then it had lost all power but here it seems to have no interior heating.
- **NOTES** Usually the audience follows the Doctor's journeys in sequence but here, for the first time, we jump back a bit. At the end of *The Smugglers* the TARDIS has already landed but at the start of *The Tenth Planet* we're introduced to the personnel of Snowcap Base before witnessing, with them, its arrival (filmed at Ealing Studios using the Police Box prop). However, the cut to inside the Ship must include a time jump as Ben and Polly are still in 17th-century clothes when they first notice the cold but have changed into coats when we see them in *The Tenth Planet*. The roof lamp keeps flashing for a short time after materialisation.
- This is one of the Ship's shortest journeys yet. It dematerialises and Polly wonders where they'll land next, then without hearing it rematerialise she is shivering with cold and the Doctor announces they have arrived.
- For once we get a nice close-up of a calendar to show us the date (and the days and dates actually match with our history). There's no indication which day in December 1986 this is, but none is crossed off so perhaps it's Monday the 1st.
- The Doctor misidentifies their location in describing the weather outside as "quite an Arctic storm" when, of course, they are at the South Pole.
- The next few landings are inserted into the original narrative of *The Tenth Planet* as part of 2017's Christmas special *Twice Upon a Time*. The console used is a mostly faithful replica built for the 2013 docudrama *An Adventure in Space and Time* about William Hartnell's time as the Doctor, and which had subsequently been on display at the Doctor Who Experience in Cardiff and used again on screen in 2015's Series 9 finale *Hell Bent* (suggesting it's either the default configuration of all TARDIS consoles, even way into the Time Lords' future, or the Doctor has chosen it out of nostalgia as he's escaping Gallifrey in a stolen time machine again). The control room was also a faithful reproduction, although as a complete 360-degree set for the first time. In place of the photographic walls, however, was a new section made for the undergallery in *The Day of the Doctor* with indented circles within interlocking raised hexagons; a second like it was placed opposite. The fault locator and scanner framework were recreated, the floor was painted with a hexagon around the console (mimicking the original floor plates) and another in front of the main doors, and ornaments were sourced to match those in the original control room: two brass pillars, the wooden Knossos chair, a wooden armchair, an armillary sphere (but on a tapered square pedestal) and a Westminster Abbey skeleton clock on a fluted wooden pillar. Even the astral map and the large overhead light were recreated, although the latter only with CGI. The Police Box exterior was also rebuilt, based on a replica from This Planet Earth but adapted to match the post-1966 remodelled prop incredibly accurately thanks to input from fan Tony Farrell.

LANDING 43

SPACE Centre of the universe, Villengard
TIME Far future
TRAVELLERS The Doctor (two incarnations), Bill Potts, Captain Archibald Lethbridge-Stewart
EPISODES Twice Upon a Time

The TARDIS flies randomly through the Vortex to elude Testimony. The older Doctor uses his sonic sunglasses to connect with the Ship via the scanner and access its database to identify the Glass Woman, but at this stage in its travels it does not hold enough information. He therefore pilots the TARDIS – much to his younger self's astonishment – to the ruined weapons forges of Villengard, now home to the one Dalek that might allow him to access the store of all accumulated Dalek knowledge.

As they venture out, the Captain is attacked by a Dalek mutant. The others pull it off his face and the younger Doctor escorts the shocked soldier back into the TARDIS to revive him with brandy, while Bill tries to persuade the older Doctor she is who she appears to be. She agrees to sit with the bemused Captain as the Doctors head off to seek the information they need. However, she follows them after revealing to the Captain that she is one of Testimony's glass avatars.

Shortly after, time freezes again as Testimony catches up with the fugitives. It has agreed to let the Doctors return the Captain to the front line and his impending end, and the soldier goes with the older incarnation in his TARDIS while the younger Doctor follows in his younger Ship.

- **CONTROLS** The older Doctor is standing at panel A1 when the TARDIS lands although we don't see him operating any controls, the main doors opening automatically; they do so again when the younger Doctor leaves Bill and the Captain in the TARDIS. He looks over panel A5 to determine where they are.
- **LORE** The Doctor stores bottles of alcoholic beverages in the control room, in a cabinet behind a roundel. These include brandy and a drink from Aldebaran.
- **NOTES** According to the younger Doctor's reading of the console, Villengard is at "the very centre of the universe". His older incarnation says it was once "the nightmare of the seven galaxies".
- The Doctor says it's billions of years since he encountered Rusty the rebel Dalek (see Landing 611, vol.2). It's also implied to be after the year 5000000012, when Dr Helen Clay founded Testimony, although the Daleks have time-travel capabilities so their information could be from the future.
- The future Doctor's successful piloting of the TARDIS suggests that its unreliability is due to the younger Doctor's inexperience rather than the Ship itself being at fault. Or the former has just learned a few tricks for bypassing any temperamental systems.
- This retrospectively becomes the first time we see that some wall roundels can be opened, in this case for storage space. We'll be seeing several more examples later (that is, earlier).
- The older Doctor tries to distract his younger, less enlightened self with the blinking lights of the astral map, unseen since *Galaxy 4* (Landing 23).

LANDING 44

SPACE Earth, Belgium, Flanders, no man's land
TIME 24 December 1914
TRAVELLERS The Doctor
EPISODES Twice Upon a Time

The TARDIS journeys back to Europe during the First World War, materialising alongside its future iteration on a muddy bank between the British and German front-line trenches. Time is still frozen as the two Doctors help the Captain back to the crater where he was facing off against a frightened German soldier. Before events resume, they promise him they will look in on his family, the Lethbridge-Stewarts.

Testimony restarts time and the Doctors, hidden by a perception filter, watch as miraculously the enemy forces put down their weapons and join in singing Christmas carols and playing football – at least for one night. The older Doctor reveals he "adjusted the time frame" by a couple of hours to coincide with the Christmas armistice, thus saving both the Captain and his opponent.

The Doctor is reassured that, allowed a future, he will perform noble acts and save lives, so he yields to his regeneration. He takes his leave of his later incarnation and departs in his TARDIS. His hands begin to glow with energy as he sets the Ship in motion.

- **CONTROLS** During the journey to Earth, the Doctor flicks two switches at the bottom of panel A2. He operates two unseen controls at the bottom-right of panel A1 to dematerialise.
- **NOTES** Given the two TARDISes materialise in unison even after the older Doctor has tweaked their destination, we can assume that before leaving Villengard he slaves the earlier TARDIS to follow his, as it wouldn't be wise to rely on the younger Doctor's navigation. Either that or, like the two Doctors, the two TARDISes recognise themselves as one and the same and work together. The older Doctor can't have pre-programmed it as he doesn't decide to slip forward by a couple of hours until after the journey is underway. We might also infer that some control beyond the Doctor's – either his future self's or the Ship's – successfully takes him back to the South Pole to collect Ben and Polly. While this episode is careful to slot into the narrative of *The Tenth Planet* at the start, here we must impose a gap between the Doctor's last words and his lying on the floor, to allow us to get back to where we were…

LANDING 45

SPACE Earth, Antarctica, South Pole
TIME December 1986, moments after Landing 42
TRAVELLERS The Doctor
EPISODES Twice Upon a Time; The Tenth Planet 4

In the instant after it left and time resumed, the TARDIS materialises back at the South Pole, as though it had never left. Following the Doctor from the Cybermen's spaceship, Ben and Polly fear being left behind and hammer on the closed doors as they call to the Doctor to let them in.

Inside, the room is in uproar with lights flashing and the controls seeming to operate themselves. The Doctor leans wearily against the console but summons enough strength to open the main doors before collapsing to the floor. Polly rushes to his side but Ben urges her back when the Doctor's features glow and blur as the TARDIS dematerialises.

- **CONTROLS** The Doctor leans on panel A4 with his hands either side of the central large slider, while the small levers of panel A5 move on their own. It's unclear from the few clips that survive, but if it's the Doctor who opens the doors for Ben and Polly then he probably uses one of the small levers on panel A4. Judging from the soundtrack, he has already collapsed to the floor by the time the dematerialisation sound begins, so it's likely the TARDIS takes off by itself.
- **LORE** It's deliberately obscure what's happening when the Doctor regenerates (not that it was called that at the time) as this was the first time he had been shown to do so, so it's unclear what part the TARDIS plays in the change. Although the controls haven't been seen to move of their own volition before, certainly the console has demonstrated some odd abilities, such as

its spinning in *The Web Planet* (Landing 14), and by now it's reasonably well established that the Ship has something of a mind of its own. The warbling sound heard during the final scene may be to do with the TARDIS or may be a sound in the Doctor's head as his body begins to change (given we also hear and see his inner experience in the next story).

- **NOTES** The staging of *Twice Upon a Time* just about fits into previous continuity although it resequences events slightly. In *The Tenth Planet*, Ben and Polly are shown knocking on the Police Box doors while inside the Doctor is at the console, the controls going wild. They then enter to find the Doctor on the floor. In the Christmas special, the Doctor has already collapsed before a shot is inserted of the TARDIS materialising back at the South Pole (a clip of its arrival from *The Tenth Planet* episode one). This indicates the box did briefly vanish but Ben and Polly may not have noticed in the blizzard, although their worry could be because they heard the grinding sound as it returned and thought it was leaving without them.
- The studio floorplan for episode four of *The Tenth Planet* suggests the standalone doors were erected beyond the control room doors. If so, they may have been seen one last time when Ben and Polly enter the TARDIS.

LANDING 46

SPACE Vulcan, mercury swamp
TIME Three days in unknown future
TRAVELLERS The Doctor, Polly, Ben
EPISODES The Power of the Daleks 1,6

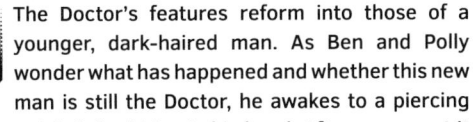

The Doctor's features reform into those of a younger, dark-haired man. As Ben and Polly wonder what has happened and whether this new man is still the Doctor, he awakes to a piercing shriek and dull throbbing in his head. After a moment it fades, his vision settles and he declares, "It's over." He rises, still wearing his long cloak (although his other clothes have also changed), and leans on the console for support. He activates the controls and the TARDIS materialises, coming to rest among the strangely shaped rocks and bubbling, steaming pools of a mercury swamp on the planet Vulcan.

The Doctor, still getting used to his new body, rummages through a large trunk for a replacement coat. He pulls out a mirror, in which he briefly sees his former face, plus a dagger he claims came from Saladin, a lump of metal that reminds him of the Daleks, and a magnifying glass with which he examines his hands. Referring to himself in the third person and giving evasive answers to Ben and Polly's questions frustrates them but he admits only that he has been renewed, saying, "It's part of the TARDIS. Without it I couldn't survive." He returns to the trunk to search for the Doctor's diary but finds instead a recorder and plays a jaunty tune. Locating the diary, he begins reading while opening the doors to head outside; when Ben objects, the Doctor reveals he has already checked the conditions. The sailor is still suspicious of the man's identity but Polly is starting to believe he is the Doctor and they follow him out.

Days later, the travellers cross the mercury swamp to reach the TARDIS, eager to get away from Vulcan before the colonists bill them for the damage the Doctor has caused in defeating the Daleks. Polly and Ben discuss whether the Doctor really knew what he was doing or not, but when they ask him he just chuckles and winks. Outside the Ship are the remains of a Dalek, its casing buckled and collapsed. They edge around it and enter the TARDIS but as it dematerialises the creature's eyestalk lifts upwards as if watching it go.

- **CONTROLS** Without being able to see the episodes we can't say for certain what controls were operated, but off-screen photos show the Doctor leaning on panel A6 and reaching across to panel A5. The soundtrack has the sound of small levers and possibly one of the large sliders like those on the latter panel being operated just before the TARDIS lands.
- Photos from the story show the grille is missing from the top of panel A3.
- **NOTES** This story is often said to be set in 2020 but this date is not in the scripts nor mentioned on screen. It originates from a trailer for the serial shown on BBC1 after the evening News the day before episode one's broadcast, although who wrote the narration for this is unknown. It's best ignored, therefore, especially as we clearly haven't colonised other planets yet. Even in the *Doctor Who* universe man has barely ventured beyond the Moon by now. If the date did come from one of David Whitaker, Dennis Spooner or Gerry Davis, all of whom worked on the scripts for *The Power of the Daleks*, then it could be because in 1966 the idea of off-world colonies within half a century seemed highly feasible given the money being spent on the Space Race at the time. Particularly if it was on another planet in our solar system, and for many years a world within the orbit of Mercury was indeed postulated, named Vulcan by its proponent the French mathematician Urbain Le Verrier (who had correctly predicted the orbit of Neptune, so he had credibility). Although the idea was largely abandoned after Einstein's theory of relativity explained the idiosyncrasies in Mercury's orbit that had led to the suggestion of another planet, it seems the sort of idea that would appeal to David Whitaker. A script about a similar undiscovered planet hidden beyond the Sun had been in development during the first year of *Doctor Who*, and perhaps his having Vulcan covered in mercury swamps is a hint to its location. If he had included more detail in his original scripts, this was probably removed because the preceding story already featured an extra planet in the solar system. The date is also cited in later series guides, notably the 1973 *Radio Times Tenth Anniversary Special* and the 1976 Target edition of *The Making of Doctor Who*, probably copied from contemporary production documentation.

- Quite what role the TARDIS plays in the Doctor's "renewal" is not expounded on, but then the whole regeneration process is kept deliberately obscure at this early stage in the series. Indeed, it's not even a regeneration, strictly speaking – that term isn't applied until much later. It seems the producers at the time intended that the Doctor had been rejuvenated, literally knocking some 200 years off his age and consequently undergoing a physical change. Tying such manipulation of time to the TARDIS is an obvious connection to make in the circumstances; it's only later that regeneration becomes treated as a biological process. Note that for the Doctor's first four bodily changes, an external factor is involved – the TARDIS, the Time Lords, another Time Lord and the Watcher. Only with his fifth regeneration in 1984 (when fans who thought they had all this figured out were influential on the production) did it become simply an automatic result of injury. Even that and his next change occurred inside the TARDIS, as have all regenerations since the series returned in 2005, making its presence still arguably a requirement. Only the Doctor's seventh and eighth regenerations happened nowhere near the TARDIS.
- With or without the TARDIS, there seems to be no rational explanation for how the Doctor's clothes change when his body does. The tradition of showing the new Doctor select his outfit won't begin until his next incarnation; here all we get is him pulling a jacket not dissimilar from his old one out of a trunk and comments on his ring no longer fitting. The one glimmer of opportunity is that when we first see them in *The Power of the Daleks*, Polly and Ben have already removed the coats and gloves they were wearing when they rushed to the collapsed Doctor's side in *The Tenth Planet*. So although the former story starts with a restatement of the regeneration, the action is not strictly continuous. However, the Doctor is clearly unconscious throughout and even if his companions decided to get him out of his wet clothes, at most they'd remove his cloak and shoes, surely – they wouldn't go so far as to change his shirt and trousers and tie a new bow around his neck. One other possibility is that the Doctor's clothes aren't real but holographic, as in *The Time of the Doctor* (see Landing 596, vol.2), but the idea that William Hartnell's Doctor was really walking around naked doesn't bear thinking about.
- This is the largest the control room set has been since *The Daleks' Master Plan*, with two indented walls and two photographic walls, plus most of the regular ornaments. The next few landings will be back to the minimal main doors and one wall.
- The TARDIS dematerialising was achieved using inlay of a photo of the Police Box prop over the shot of the Dalek twitching its eyestalk. The original photo used survives and suggests a hole was made in the roof lamp so a light could be shone through to simulate its flashing, an effect the director Christopher Barry had previously utilised in *The Rescue* (Landing 12).

PREVIOUS LANDINGS

SPACE Earth, Ukraine, Crimean peninsula, Balaklava district
TIME 25 October 1854
TRAVELLERS The Doctor, [unknown companions]
EPISODES Recalled by the Doctor in
The Evil of the Daleks 3

The Doctor witnessed the charge of the British cavalry's Light Brigade against the Russian artillery in the Battle of Balaclava near Sevastopol during the Crimean War.

- NOTES This was before he met Jamie. If he was in his second incarnation then Polly may have spent the visit dressed as a man as she complains of having to do this "last time we went back to the past" in *The Highlanders* (Landing 47). Otherwise the Doctor was in his first incarnation and saw the battle sometime before Landing 39.
- The Doctor may also have met Florence Nightingale at this time, although she didn't arrive in the region until a week or two after the Battle of Balaclava and was based across the Black Sea at barracks near Istanbul (see Landing 124).

SPACE Earth, Tibet, Himalayan foothills
TIME 1630
TRAVELLERS The Doctor, [Polly, Ben]
EPISODES Recounted by Thomni in
The Abominable Snowmen 4

The Doctor visited the Detsen monastery at "a time of trouble" after which he was entrusted with the holy ghanta for safekeeping (who or what it needed keeping safe from is unknown). He met the monk Padmasambhava.

- NOTES The Doctor gives the date of his first visit, which Thomni confirms is when the ghanta was taken. Padmasambhava recognises the Doctor, saying it's "good to look upon your face again". Although it's not impossible that the Intelligence-controlled lama might be able to identify the Doctor in any incarnation, it's simpler to assume he's being literal. Jamie hasn't been to Detsen before so this visit must take place between *The Power of the Daleks* (Landing 46) and *The Highlanders* (Landing 47), when the Doctor was travelling with Ben and Polly. Again, she might have disguised herself as a boy novice to fit into the all-male monastery given her line in the next story.

SPACE Dulkis
TIME Unknown future
TRAVELLERS The Doctor, [unknown companions]
EPISODES Recalled by the Doctor in The Dominators 1

The Doctor spent time on Dulkis, a planet where there is nothing unpleasant and the Dulcians are an advanced, gentle, friendly race who have outlawed

war and abolished all "aggressive weapons". He found it so peaceful he did not want to leave.
- **NOTES** The Doctor has been to Dulkis but Jamie hasn't so this must have been before Landing 47. While the Doctor says his first visit was "some time ago" this probably means for him personally so could have been before or after the Dominators' attack. However, on his second visit (Landing 60) he recognises the island but doesn't know it has been irradiated, so his earlier trip wasn't within the previous 172 years. He also knows of the Dulcians' weapons ban but not their atomic testing, so it's likely he first went there some time between the second and seventh councils.

LANDING 47

SPACE Earth, Scotland, Culloden Moor
TIME [16 to 18 April] 1746
TRAVELLERS The Doctor, Polly, Ben
EPISODES The Highlanders 1,4; The Underwater Menace 1

The TARDIS materialises among trees on the edge of Culloden Moor, where the Jacobite army has recently been routed by British government forces. The ground is wet from the day's rain and the air is chill, convincing Ben they are back on Earth. The three travellers suddenly throw themselves aside as something whistles through the air and thumps into the ground nearby. Investigating, the Doctor recognises it as a ten-pounder cannonball and is for once anxious to leave, but Ben heads up a rise to discover if they are indeed home and Polly persuades the Doctor they must follow.

Not willing to leave Scotland for a life in France, Jamie McCrimmon offers to escort the three travellers back to the cottage on the moor where they met. With government soldiers still on the prowl for survivors of the battle, Polly is worried about leaving the young Scot behind and asks the Doctor if he can join them. The Doctor is happy to concur so long as Jamie teaches him to play the bagpipes. They all cross the moor to the wood where the TARDIS stands. Ben and the Doctor enter but Jamie holds back, suddenly unsure of what he is letting himself in for. Polly gently takes his hand and leads him inside, and the Ship dematerialises.

Jamie is unnerved by the large, bright interior and has second thoughts, but the Ship has already left Scotland. He is incredulous that they do not know where they are going or even what year it will be when they arrive. "Nae man can tether time nor tide," quotes the Doctor from Robert Burns' 'Tam o'Shanter' before realising Jamie will not have heard of the yet-to-be-born poet.

- **CONTROLS** Judging from off-screen photos, the Doctor operates the left-most small switch on panel A4 as the TARDIS dematerialises.

- **NOTES** This is the first landing since Polly and Ben joined the Doctor not to explicitly follow on from the previous one. If they have had further adventures since Landing 46 it's perhaps unlikely any were in Earth's history. Polly says here, "Last time we went back to the past I had to wear boys' clothes all the time," referring to *The Smugglers* (Landing 41), although it's not impossible she had to cross-dress on another unseen occasion.
- Although the date is not given on screen, this story is set in the aftermath of the Battle of Culloden on 16 April 1746. The following story confirms Jamie comes from that year.
- Both the arrival and take-off of the TARDIS were filmed with the Police Box prop on location in Surrey. The latter was shot twice, the second time a week after the first to include Jamie leaving with the Doctor.

LANDING 48

SPACE Earth, Atlantic Ocean, island south of the Azores
TIME [20 or 21 March] sometime after 1968
TRAVELLERS The Doctor, Polly, Ben, Jamie McCrimmon
EPISODES The Underwater Menace 1,4

Immediately after leaving 18th-century Scotland, the TARDIS begins materialising again. Polly hopes they will find themselves back in Chelsea 1966; Ben just does not want to meet the Daleks again; the Doctor would like to see prehistoric monsters; while Jamie is still bewildered by his situation. The Ship comes to rest on the rocky shore of a volcanic island in the Atlantic Ocean, formed some 25 million years ago in the Miocene epoch. While the Doctor sees what he can find among the rock pools, his friends climb higher up the slopes towards the peak. But soon all four are captured by the island's occupants and transported into its depths.

Later that day, or possibly the next morning, the four travellers return to the TARDIS. They enter just as their friends Sean and Jacko emerge from the cave further up the cliff and look down amazed, first at the sight of a Police Box on the shore and then at its disappearance.

Inside the Ship everyone is glad to be on their way again, none more so than Jamie, who is growing to like his new life. He asks if they really have no control over where they go and an insulted Doctor insists he could if he wanted to. The others are derisive so he decides to take them to Mars.

- **CONTROLS** In off-screen photos the Doctor can be seen operating controls on panel A5 as the TARDIS takes off.
- **LORE** Travellers in the TARDIS can sense when it's moving from flight to materialisation (presumably because the trembling diminishes – see Landing 12).
- **NOTES** Professor Zaroff identifies the island as being "west of Gibraltar, south of the Azores. The Atlantic Ridge," so perhaps about 36°N and 25-30°W. The Doctor disputes Zaroff's plan to drill through the crust,

claiming it's "more than a hundred miles thick", but only parts of continental crust are that deep – the mid-Atlantic oceanic crust is nearer 30-40 miles thick. The Doctor's dating of the island's rocks to 25 million years ago is also slightly overestimated if they were formed in the Miocene epoch, which began about 23 million years ago.

▌ Polly guesses the year to be 1970 based on a bracelet she finds, a souvenir from the 1968 Mexico Olympic Games, so it's certainly after that date but exactly how long is unknown. The travellers' arrival is welcomed as being "in time for our festival of the vernal equinox" and they are promptly prepared for sacrifice, so the equinox is presumably that day. That makes it 20 or 21 March, depending on the exact year.

▌ The full-size Police Box prop was not taken on location, the Ship's arrival and departure represented by the 3-foot model. Notice this still has the St John Ambulance emblem and caps on the corner posts, both recently removed from the main prop, although its flatter roof and blue window frames are now closer to the revamped prop.

LANDING 49

SPACE The Moon, near Gravitron base
TIME 2070
TRAVELLERS The Doctor, Polly, Ben, Jamie
EPISODES The Underwater Menace 4; The Moonbase 1,4

The Doctor moves to set the controls for Mars when the room shudders and the engines groan as the TARDIS goes haywire. He struggles at the console as the lights flicker. Slowly he brings the Ship under control and sets it to materialise. On the scanner forms a barren, rocky, starlit image and the TARDIS comes to rest on the surface of the Moon. Polly thinks the Doctor has successfully piloted them to Mars but Ben recognises where they are from pictures. The Doctor admits his failure and prepares to move on but the others insist on taking a look around. He allows them half an hour's exploration and says they will find spacesuits in his trunk.

Unaware that just behind a ridge is hidden a saucer-shaped Cyberman spaceship, the travellers step outside the TARDIS wearing lightweight quilted spacesuits, heavy boots, clear bubble-shaped helmets and dark goggles to protect their eyes from surface glare. Polly thinks she spies a glow on the horizon but the others see nothing. Instead they have fun leaping high due to the Moon's low gravity, although the Doctor warns them about damaging their suits. When Jamie jumps a little too hard he drops over the edge of a crater and out of sight. The others follow and discover a glass-domed base in the crater. Jamie is unconscious from his fall and, as two men emerge from the base to collect his body, the others hurry down to join them.

When the travellers return to the TARDIS, Polly spots a light streaking across the sky which the Doctor confirms could be the Cybermen floating away through space. He leads Polly, Jamie and Ben into the Ship and it fades away from the Moon's surface.

Inside, as they take off their spacesuits, the Doctor suddenly decides to try using the time scanner to see where they will land next, even though he admits it is not very reliable. On the screen appears the image of a giant crab-like claw.

◉ **CONTROLS** In off-screen photos, the Doctor can be seen at panel A5 as the Ship goes out of control.

▌ **LORE** An image of the TARDIS's destination can form on the scanner before the Ship has actually materialised. Judging from the soundtrack, this seems to zoom in as though the TARDIS is physically moving towards the Moon.

▌ The TARDIS interior is a sterile environment.

▌ The main doors can be opened onto an airless environment without any apparent depressurisation.

▌ **NOTES** The sound effect of an explosion and then the TARDIS engines grinding is the same as used at the end of *The Daleks* (Landing 3).

▌ The TARDIS is seemingly affected by the Gravitron on the Moon before it has even landed. Given the apparent scanner image showing the surface getting closer, perhaps the Ship briefly materialised in space near the Moon (the Doctor's best try at reaching Mars), was caught in the Gravitron's influence and pulled down so the Doctor swiftly dematerialised and rematerialised safely on the surface. Alternatively, given gravity is one of the basic forces of the universe and therefore may affect even the extra dimensions through which the TARDIS travels, perhaps it's pulled out of the Vortex by the Gravitron. This would tie in with the similar ability of the Animus in *The Web Planet* (Landing 14), which is said to have drawn new moons to Vortis.

▌ The 3-foot Police Box model was used for the TARDIS's landing, shot on film at Ealing Studios. However, the standard take-off sound effect is played, even beginning with the deep thump and rumble. This and other model shots of the Cybermen's spaceship were filmed on an area of the same lunar landscape set as the live action scenes. The miniature Police Box was also used in the background of some of those shots to suggest the TARDIS was some distance away from the actors. Its take-off was filmed using the full-size prop.

▌ When the TARDIS landed at the South Pole the low temperature outside was immediately felt inside the control room. Yet here, arriving on the much colder Moon, there's no such effect. Has the Doctor done something to insulate the Ship since Landing 45?

▌ This is the only mention of the TARDIS's time scanner – which seems to be a function of the regular scanner – perhaps little used because it's unreliable (although it's accurate in this instance). However, in *Image of the Fendahl*, when the Doctor discovers someone else has invented a time scanner, he's keen to stop its use in case it causes a direct continuum implosion, so perhaps by "unreliable" he means really flipping dangerous.

▌ Why does everyone assume the claw on the scanner is gigantic and not just a close-up of a regular crab?

LANDING 50

SPACE Unnamed planet, near colony settlement
TIME Two days in unknown future
TRAVELLERS The Doctor, Polly, Ben, Jamie
EPISODES The Macra Terror 1

The TARDIS materialises on a rocky ridge above grassy sand dunes, startling a man called Medok, who is trying to escape the guards of a nearby colony. Jamie emerges from the Ship, vigilant for signs of the clawed-creatures glimpsed on the time scanner and picking up a stick to defend himself with. The Doctor, Polly and Ben follow, the sailor mocking the Scot's caution. Suddenly Medok leaps on Jamie. Ben wrestles him to the ground just as police chief Ola arrives. His men take custody of Medok while Ola invites the strangers back to the colony to receive the personal thanks of their leader.

Initially happy to spend some time in the newly freed colony, the Doctor changes his mind when he hears he is in line to be their next leader. He gets his friends to pretend they are joining in the celebrations but while no one is looking they all dance out of the door and make for the freedom of the TARDIS.

- **NOTES** Judging from off-screen photos, when the TARDIS materialises (filmed on location using the full-size prop) it's on an exposed ridge, yet when the travellers emerge (recorded in the studio) it's nestled against a rock face near some buildings.
- This is the first time the travellers are not shown returning to the TARDIS and departing at the end of a story. The filming schedules indicate a shot of the Police Box dematerialising was planned so either it wasn't completed, necessitating the ending as shown, or was filmed but dropped from the final episode.

LANDING 51

SPACE Earth, England, West Sussex, Gatwick Airport runway; transported to Skaro, Dalek city
TIME 20 July 1966; two days in unknown future
TRAVELLERS The Doctor, Polly, Ben, Jamie
EPISODES The Faceless Ones 1,6; The Evil of the Daleks 1,6-7; The Tomb of the Cybermen 1

The TARDIS materialises at the intersection of runaways two and five at Gatwick Airport, right in the path of an incoming jumbo jet. Jamie and the Doctor emerge and, startled by the approaching plane, run in the opposite direction, followed by Ben and Polly. Its landing obstructed, flight SDX quickly pulls up and returns to the stack of planes waiting to land. Two motorcycle police riders investigate the report of a Police Box on the runway and have it loaded onto a lorry and taken to hanger four, where Ben happens to be hiding.

After exposing the Chameleons' kidnapping scheme, the Doctor and his friends are driven to the hangar where the TARDIS is being stored. Realising they are back in their own time, Polly and Ben elect to stay, bidding a sad farewell to the Doctor and Jamie. Once they have gone, the Doctor admits the Ship should be outside the hanger but is missing. Just then the pair see a truck leaving with the TARDIS strapped to the back. They give chase but the vehicle is soon out of sight.

The Police Box is unloaded in the rear yard of Edward Waterfield's antiques shop then later that night is transported using the Daleks' own time-travel technology to their city on Skaro in the far future. The Daleks use their possession of the TARDIS to force the Doctor to assist them in their plan to isolate the Human Factor. When he follows them to Skaro, he encounters the huge Emperor Dalek, which reveals the Doctor's work has enabled it to identify the opposing Dalek Factor. The Emperor shows him the TARDIS, which the Doctor will be forced to use to spread the Dalek Factor to everyone on Earth throughout its history.

The Daleks move the TARDIS outside the city to lure the Doctor through the arch that applies the Dalek Factor, unaware that it will not affect him. As civil war breaks out between the Emperor's Daleks and those the Doctor has imbued with the Human Factor, Waterfield sacrifices himself to save the Doctor, who promises to look after his daughter. He follows Jamie and the now-orphaned Victoria Waterfield to where the TARDIS has been left. Looking down on the chaos engulfing the city, the Doctor wonders if this is the final end of the Daleks.

The travellers hurry into the Ship, lit by the flickering flames engulfing the Dalek city, and introduce Victoria to her new home. She is awed by the TARDIS's greater size within but laughs out loud when Jamie tells her it can travel anywhere in time and space. He takes her to find less restrictive clothes than her Victorian crinoline while the Doctor sets the Ship in motion, offended by Jamie's request for a smooth take-off so as not to frighten their new companion.

- **CONTROLS** When showing Victoria the console, the Doctor throws all five small levers at the top of panel A4 with one sweep of his hand (without discernible effect). When preparing to take off he flicks switches at the bottom of panel A2 and A3, then initiates dematerialisation using the large slider on panel A4 before adjusting the small levers above it and those on panel A5.
- **LORE** The Doctor says the TARDIS has been his home for "a considerable number of years" and, for the first time, gives his age: about 450 years (in Earth terms). He tells Victoria he has "perfected a rather special model" of the sort of time machine her father was trying to build, suggesting perhaps that he himself created the TARDIS. Although we know from *The Time Meddler* (and later events) that other TARDISes exist, it has never been clearly stated that the Doctor *didn't* have a hand in their original development.
- **NOTES** The Doctor says the date is 20 July (perhaps he spotted a calendar in air traffic control at some point), which Ben declares is "when it all began. We're back to when it all started." He might not mean the exact day he and Polly first entered the TARDIS (see Landing 40).

- The events of *The Faceless Ones* take place within one day. It's already daylight when the TARDIS arrives: sunrise on 20 July 1966 was at 5:06am although the shadow cast by the Police Box suggests it's later than that, perhaps about 8am. In *The Evil of the Daleks*, Bob Hall says the TARDIS was due to be collected at three o'clock (we can presume in the afternoon). So the Doctor brings down the Chameleon's whole plan in under ten hours.
- When the travellers spot the incoming plane, instead of just ducking back into the TARDIS and taking off again they scatter in all directions leaving both doors wide open. We must assume these close automatically before the police arrive to remove the obstruction as no one reports it as being anything other than an ordinary Police Box (beyond noting its unusual location).
- When the TARDIS materialises on the runway (accompanied by the take-off sound effect), it's clear the prop has castors under the base and Jamie noticeably steps down when he exits. In the ground-level shot as the others run from the Ship, however, the base is missing and the sides of the prop rest directly on the runway concrete. With Ben and Polly emerging from the Police Box already running, it may be that either it would roll around if on castors or they might trip as they ran through the prop, so the wheeled base was removed altogether.
- The flatbed truck that moves the TARDIS from the runway is not the same as the one Bob Hall hires to make off with the Police Box on behalf of Waterfield. So when do the Daleks become aware of the Doctor's presence in 1966 in order to spring their trap? If they've been tracking the TARDIS (which they've done before), why wait until now? Why not grab it while the Doctor was fighting Macra, or send a saucer to swing by and pick it up off the Moon? Have they, therefore, been staking out 1966 in the vague hope the Doctor will come along one day? It's often remarked how *The War Machines* and *The Faceless Ones* take place within days of each other, explaining why in the former the Doctor gets a tingling feeling that he associates with Daleks. Indeed, Waterfield's antique shop must have been established for some time before he acquires the TARDIS, and presumably the transmat device was installed by Daleks, so they were probably present on Earth earlier in July. But if so, why not steal the TARDIS while everyone's distracted by Wotan's takeover bid? (Did the Daleks have a hand in Wotan's development in the hope of luring the Doctor to 1966?) Perhaps the Daleks only detected the TARDIS once it had landed in Fitzroy Square so they quickly had Waterfield set up shop as a front for being able to acquire the time machine whenever it happened to return, only to get lucky when it turns up again a little over a week later (they couldn't possibly know the Doctor would, for once, drop his companions back more or less where he found them). There is some suggestion that Perry is a very recent employee as he doesn't know much about the business, but if so the Daleks' luck is his misfortune. He's just started a new job when he suddenly has to account to the police for a dead body, a shop full of suspicious antiques and no sign of the supposed owner.
- The Daleks believe they have the ability to destroy the TARDIS (by some means other than their built-in weaponry, which was ineffective in *The Chase* – see Landing 17). Even though the threat to do so appears to coerce the Doctor into helping with their experiments, he may not believe the Ship is at risk and is simply cooperating until he has a chance to recover it.
- Photos from the filming for episode one of *The Evil of the Daleks*, of the Police Box prop being driven away on a flatbed truck, show that the telephone plaque had been moved from its usual (and correct) position on the left-hand door to the right-hand door. This is confirmed in off-screen photos from episodes six and seven. While this was undoubtedly just a mistake, it indicates the sign was removable.
- The shot of the TARDIS at the beginning of *The Tomb of the Cybermen* is the 3-foot model, which still features the St John Ambulance emblem, unlike the full-size prop. The flickering lighting is to represent the burning city of the Daleks.
- Although *The Tomb of the Cybermen* was broadcast as the opening serial of the fifth season of *Doctor Who*, it went into production directly after *The Evil of the Daleks*. Victoria's introduction to the TARDIS was scripted as a direct follow-on from the preceding story, and Jamie and Victoria are wearing the same clothes. The scene was pre-filmed at Ealing Studios (which is why the sound is more echoing than normal), rather than recorded with the episode's other interior scenes in Studio D at Lime Grove, in order to maximise space for the impressive Cyber-tomb sets. Even so, only a minimal control room set it erected, featuring the console, the main doors, one indented wall and the photographic backdrop of the fault locator wall, first seen in *The Dalek Invasion of Earth* (Landing 11).
- Faintly audible when the travellers enter the control room here, but clearer in episode one of *The Abominable Snowmen*, the hum of the main doors is now slightly lower in pitch and dips down at the end as the doors swing open or closed.
- The Doctor is right to be affronted by Jamie's request for a smooth take-off. As far as we've seen, all the dematerialisations Jamie has experienced have been calm. In fact, the only rough journey he's had is when landing on the Moon, which was due to the influence of the Gravitron, not the Doctor's piloting skills.

LANDING 52

SPACE Telos, near Cybermen tombs
TIME Two days in unknown future
TRAVELLERS The Doctor, Jamie, Victoria Waterfield
EPISODES The Tomb of the Cybermen 1

The TARDIS materialises on Telos, close by the just-uncovered entrance to the Cybermen's city. The sound of the Ship's engines is heard by a group of human archaeologists seeking the last remains of the Cybermen, and the crew of the rocket they have hired. Suspicious of a rival expedition, they accost the Doctor, Jamie and Victoria at gunpoint as they make their way over the dunes behind which the TARDIS landed.

The next day, after successfully refreezing the Cybermen, the travellers bid goodbye to the surviving explorers as they return to their repaired rocket, eager to leave Telos behind. The Doctor seems less sure that they have seen the last of the Cybermen than he was about the Daleks. Indeed, as he, Jamie and Victoria head off for the TARDIS, behind them a lone Cybermat crawls across the sand.

▪ **NOTES** After Victoria's introduction to the TARDIS, there's then a break before the travellers arrive on Telos in which further landings could have occurred. Jamie claims not to have had much exercise recently, which at least suggests some time has passed since his clear exertions during the Daleks' tests to determine the Human Factor. Later, the Doctor asks Victoria if she is happy being with him and Jamie, which she can't really have had time to decide if this is her very first trip with them. She is still missing her father, which is to be expected, but notably "only when I close my eyes", perhaps indicating at least some time has passed since she last saw him.

▪ The explorers spend the night inside the Cybermen's city while Captain Hopper and his men repair Toberman's sabotage of their rocket. It's daylight again at the end of the story, by which time the rocket is fixed despite Hopper having previously claimed it would take 72 hours. He presumably adopts the Montgomery Scott method of estimating engine repair times.

▪ The surface of Telos must be temperate as Victoria and several of the humans appear comfortable in light, short-sleeved outfits. So why does the Doctor bring a cape with him from the TARDIS? He hasn't worn one since before his regeneration. Does he know he'll shortly be descending into the Cybermen's frozen hibernation vaults?

LANDING 53

SPACE Earth, Tibet, Himalayan foothills, near Detsen monastery
TIME Three days in [1935]
TRAVELLERS The Doctor, Jamie, Victoria
EPISODES The Abominable Snowmen 1,4

The TARDIS arrives on a hillside in a remote valley in the Himalayas. The scanner shows a grassy, snow-free vista that the Doctor immediately recognises with glee. He begins searching for a 'ghanta' in his trunk, finding instead an odd gadget he recognises but is not sure what it is, a set of damaged bagpipes and a large fur coat. Donning this last item, he decides to take a look outside to confirm their location while leaving Jamie and Victoria to find the ghanta – a Tibetan ritual bell. They watch him on the scanner as he heads over a ridge, then discover the ghanta in a small bag marked 'Detsen monastery'.

Outside the Doctor has spotted just the cloister he was expecting, perched on a ledge lower down the hillside. Returning to the TARDIS he finds large footprints in the mud and examines them, unaware he is being watched.

Back in the Ship, Victoria has changed into warmer clothes while Jamie is confident that as a sturdy Highlander he will be fine in his shirtsleeves. The Doctor returns, clearly distracted, and taking the ghanta heads out again alone. Victoria is soon bored, however, and persuades Jamie to take a quick look outside. As she admires the view he shivers in the cold. When Victoria spots the footprints all round the Ship she decides to track them, so Jamie pops back inside for a coat and the scimitar he earlier found in the trunk. They set off up the hillside.

The following morning as the sun rises, the Doctor and Jamie make their way from the monastery to the TARDIS to collect equipment with which to trace the signals controlling the robotic Yeti. When they arrive, however, they find one of the creatures guarding the Ship. The Doctor throws a rock at it and determines it is inactive, so boldly walks up to it and removes the control sphere from its chest, handing it to Jamie. He goes into the TARDIS and emerges shortly after with a tracking device. Just then the sphere starts bleeping and tries to get back into the Yeti. The Doctor and Jamie can barely hold onto it and only when Jamie places a rock into the Yeti's chest cavity does the sphere go silent again. Realising the dormant Yeti in the monastery could similarly awaken by itself, the Doctor and Jamie rush back there.

The mountain peak above where the TARDIS stands is consumed in a massive explosion as the entity forming within is destroyed, showering the valley in debris. At first light, before the evacuated monks can return to the monastery, Travers accompanies the three travellers back towards the Ship. They find a deactivated Yeti on the hillside, which the anthropologist considers a poor trophy as no one will believe it is genuine. Just then they spot a shaggy creature among the rocks, a real yeti, and Travers dashes off to try to capture it. As the others approach the TARDIS, Jamie hopes for a warmer destination as his knees are turning blue but the Doctor can promise nothing, merely tootling on his recorder.

⊙ **CONTROLS** Victoria operates a rotary control to adjust the scanner image.
⊙ The TARDIS scanner has a new housing in this story. Rather than being just a monitor hanging from the ceiling, it's now behind a flat upright panel with two large circular holes in. Behind it is a new bank of instruments and dials.
⊙ Part of the cover is missing from the fast return switch. The two spheres at the bottom of the central column's inner mechanism have gone missing.

- **NOTES** This most likely follows directly from Landing 52 as Victoria is initially wearing the same dress as in *The Tomb of the Cybermen* and Jamie mentions the Cybermen's tombs, suggesting that's a recent encounter.
- The year is given in *The Web of Fear* but may not be accurate (see Landing 57). The Doctor and Thomni both say it's 300 years since the former's previous visit in 1630, yet Padmasambhava reckons the ghanta has been absent from Detsen for "two hundred years or more" – an odd underestimation if it's actually 305 years. If this landing is closer to the late-1920s, that has implications for dating the Doctor's later exile.
- The materialisation sound effect is the slow echoing version first heard at the end of *The Daleks* episode seven. It's used again at the start and end of *The Enemy of the World* and in *The Web of Fear* episode one.
- Off-screen photos show the main doors are not fully closed when the TARDIS lands. They and photos taken during the location filming confirm the prop still has its 'Police telephone' plaque on the right-hand door.
- The Doctor's trunk appears again, this time containing the ghanta, a scimitar, a large fur coat, a set of bagpipes and a strange jangling contraption. It's beginning to seem likely the trunk is bigger on the inside. Jamie says the Doctor never mentioned he had bagpipes and the Doctor seems worried the Scot might try to play them, yet when he invited Jamie aboard the TARDIS he was keen to learn the instrument. Did Polly and Ben make him think better of it?

LANDING 54

SPACE Earth, Europe, beside Brittanicus Base
TIME Two days in [about 3000]
TRAVELLERS The Doctor, Jamie, Victoria
EPISODES The Ice Warriors 1,6

The TARDIS lands on a drift of snow against the side of a large segmented plastic dome, on its side and slipping top-first down the slope. Fortunately the doors are uppermost, although the Doctor has to climb onto Jamie's shoulders to reach them. The travellers clamber awkwardly out of the Ship, luckily still dressed for the cold after their visit to Tibet. Indeed, Jamie thinks they might have returned there. In fact they are in the future when a new 'ice age' has gripped the Earth. Inside the dome is Brittanicus Base, a converted Georgian mansion, one of several establishments around the world using ionisers to slow the flow of the glaciers that are engulfing more and more of the planet.

The travellers duck behind the TARDIS as a hatch in the dome opens and two bearded men dressed in furs emerge. They carry packets of food but are confident they are not the cause of the alarm sounding inside the dome. When they have passed by, the Doctor and his friends enter.

The next day, the Doctor and Victoria escape the Martian spaceship and return to the ioniser base having used the aliens' own sonic weapon to force them to retreat. The Doctor sends Victoria back to the TARDIS for safety in case using the ioniser causes the Martian craft to explode. Fortunately its engines are inactive and its destruction causes minimal damage. As the humans face operating without computer assistance for the first time, the Doctor and Jamie slip quietly out of the control room and back to the TARDIS. Now upright, it vanishes from the frozen landscape.

- **NOTES** This follows directly from Landing 53: Jamie believes they may even be in the same location and all three travellers are wearing the same clothes, including the Doctor in his shaggy coat (although Victoria has had time to add a cloak with a fur collar). Later the Doctor explains their ignorance of the situation as down to their having "been on retreat in Tibet".
- Although the name of Brittanicus Base is taken to indicate it's in Britain – and *Radio Times* coverage claimed it was in England – this isn't confirmed on screen. The only talk is of it protecting Europe, and the computer calls it "Brittanicus Base Europe". Indeed, given the spelling, it's perhaps more likely to be in Brittany (otherwise it would surely be Britannicus Base). Then again, at one point Miss Garrett mentions being on an island: an unusual if not inaccurate way to refer to the British mainland. Perhaps the base is on the Isle of Wight or one of the Channel Islands, holding back the glacier from reaching mainland Europe. The map seen on screen unfortunately gives no indication of where the ioniser bases are located.
- Similarly, the date is not established on screen. There is a direction in the script saying Miss Garrett is 'dressed in the style of the year 3000AD' and that date was given in the introductory feature to this story in *Radio Times*. Leader Clent talks of the glaciers wiping out "five thousand years of history". If he's dating from early Bronze Age cultures in Western Europe, that could place him in 3000AD; if he's talking of recorded history in the region, then he's nearer 4500AD. Indeed, in *The Talons of Weng-Chiang* the Doctor mentions an "Ice Age around the year five thousand", leading some to consider *The Ice Warriors* is set in the same era. Despite talk of "a second ice age", this must be a colloquialism as true ice ages occur on a timescale of millions of years and we're currently in at least the fifth in the Earth's history. Even the periods of greater glaciation within an ice age cover tens of thousands of years. Clent gives a man-made cause for the drop in world temperature anyway, so his calling it an ice age must just be a vernacular choice.
- The Doctor blames a "blind landing" for the TARDIS materialising on its side, but in what way does this differ from most of his usual landings? At first it appears as though the Police Box prop has lost its 'Police telephone' plaque altogether, but in fact the box is resting on its front and the cast climb out the back doors of the prop, as they opened outwards. Note the knob handles just like those on the fake-TARDIS cupboards in *The Celestial Toymaker* (Landing 37), evidence they were used in the main prop's refit.

The TARDIS dematerialising is the 12-inch model – not used since its first appearance in *The Daleks' Master Plan* (Landing 29) – superimposed over a photo of snowy mountains. This model has the telephone plaque on the left-hand side as usual, even though in the previous and following stories the full-size prop has it on the right-hand door. How the Ship was righted is unknown. It's unlikely the Doctor and Jamie alone would be strong enough to lift it (and why bother if they were about to take off anyway?), so perhaps some of the base personnel found it and set it upright.

LANDING 55

SPACE Earth, Australia, Esperance region, beach
TIME At least two days in 2018
TRAVELLERS The Doctor, Jamie, Victoria
EPISODES The Enemy of the World 1,6; The Web of Fear 1

The TARDIS arrives on a windy shoreline in south-western Australia, ten miles west of Cape Arid. The Doctor immediately bounds across the grassy sand dunes towards the sea, encouraging his friends to find buckets and spades in the Ship with which to build sandcastles. He spots a hovercraft a short distance along the shore, waves, then strips down to his long-johns and throws himself into the warm waters of the Southern Ocean. Jamie and Victoria join him on the beach as he dresses after his swim, but run when the hovercraft approaches, its crew firing guns at them and cutting them off from the TARDIS.

Late the next day, Jamie and Victoria return to the TARDIS having left the Doctor at the research centre to expose Giles Kent and Salamander. Night falls and Jamie waits impatiently outside, lit only by the light from the open TARDIS door. He sees what looks like the Doctor approaching, dishevelled and exhausted. Jamie helps him into the Ship where Victoria is eager to leave. But this is Salamander, who followed them to the beach, and he hesitates over the array of controls on the console. He indicates for Jamie to operate them for him, but the lad objects that he has been told never to touch the controls.

Just then the real Doctor appears in the doorway and tells Salamander he will be put outside to answer for his crimes. The would-be dictator fights off the Doctor and Jamie when they try to stop him operating the controls, and he throws the dematerialisation switch. But the main doors are still open and Salamander is sucked out into the Vortex. The others hold on desperately as they too are pulled towards the doorway. Jamie manages to clamber to the console and operate the doors control just in time to prevent being sucked out too. No sooner has the TARDIS settled down than the Doctor is preparing for a new destination.

◉ CONTROLS Salamander walks up to panel A5 when he enters the TARDIS but doesn't know what the controls do. Jamie puts his hand on the rotary switch but doesn't turn it. Salamander then operates this handle when trying to escape, which dematerialises the TARDIS. When Jamie is trying to close the doors, he falls against panel A5 (now facing away from the entrance) and works his way anti-clockwise round the console to panel A3. Once the Ship has stabilised, the Doctor flicks small levers on panels A4 and the three right-most ones in unison on panel A5.

◉ Panel A5 is facing the main doors when Salamander sets the TARDIS in motion but panel A2 is thereafter.

◉ Two of the six small levers on panel A5 have lost their knobs, while the top-most small lever on panel A1 is missing its stem completely. The panel of switches at the bottom of panel A6 has been reversed so the rotary knob (which has been replaced with a slightly smaller control) is on the right, and a light has been added above the three switches on the right (see Landing 56 for why). Two grab handles have been added to the pedestal below panel A2 for the Doctor and Victoria to hold onto.

📕 LORE The TARDIS can dematerialise even with its main doors open. Unsecured occupants are sucked out into the Vortex (but if the air is too there is sufficient for the travellers to survive for several minutes).

📓 NOTES The Doctor makes a pun about having been "on ice" and Jamie mentions the ioniser, but otherwise there's nothing to suggest this landing comes immediately after Landing 54.

📓 The year is shown on the registration plate of Astrid Ferrier's helicopter, which is valid until 31 December 2018. The torn newspaper Swann finds is dated 'Friday, August 16, 2017', which is said to be "last year's date". (16 August 2017 was a Wednesday in our universe but we know from *The War Machines* (Landing 40) that the *Doctor Who* universe can differ slightly.)

📓 The central column is stationary after the doors have closed, so it's possible the TARDIS has resolved the problem of flying with the doors open by landing somewhere. The column rises only when the Doctor decides to show he's still in control, although the usual grinding noise is not heard, there's just change in the background hum.

📓 A roundel on the far right of the main doors wall is missing its backing throughout episode one of *The Web of Fear*, although as the walls aren't backlit this is easy to miss. It was replaced by *The Mind Robber*.

LANDING 56

SPACE Space [Solar System, near Earth]
TIME Several hours in [early-1970s]
TRAVELLERS The Doctor, Jamie, Victoria
EPISODES The Web of Fear 1

The TARDIS materialises unexpectedly, although it takes both Jamie and Victoria pointing out a flashing light on the console before the Doctor notices. Checking the scanner, they see they are suspended in space as strands of a web-like substance form around the Police Box. All the controls appear to be operating normally so the Doctor wonders if the time-lock has slipped, but it becomes evident the TARDIS is being held by some force.

The Doctor constructs a control box with a lever and dial. When the web starts to clear, he connects this to the console via a cable and pulls the lever which succeeds in moving the TARDIS.

○ **CONTROLS** The lightbulb that indicates the TARDIS has landed is on panel A6. This was added specifically for this episode and remains on the console until Landing 59. The Doctor operates small levers on panel A5 when trying to get the TARDIS moving again. James attaches the Doctor's device seemingly to the collar above panel A3. To get the Ship moving again, the Doctor pushes the large slider on panel A4 upwards (although it springs back as soon as he lets go) before throwing the lever on his control box.

○ The access panel in the pedestal below panel A6 is open.

○ The upper rotary handle on the bottom-left of panel A1 has been replaced with a black circular button by this point. The circular knob on the large slider on panel A4 has been replaced with a smaller sphere.

▌ **LORE** (Sometimes) a light flashes on the console to show the TARDIS has materialised.

▌ The TARDIS has provisions for making sandwiches. (Previously the only food eaten inside the Ship has been in the form of nutrition bars from the food machine. Even if the Doctor has used, say, a cheese-flavoured bar as his filling, the machine didn't seem capable of producing an actual loaf of (sliced) bread, so he must have stocked up at some point.)

▌ **NOTES** Not much time has passed since Salamander's demise. Jamie has changed his clothes and the Doctor has prepared some sandwiches, but the cut on his left cheek – caused by debris from the explosion at the research centre in Australia – is still visible, although healed sufficiently that he no longer needs the plaster he was wearing at the end of *The Enemy of the World*.

▌ The Great Intelligence appears to pluck the TARDIS out of the Vortex, much like the Animus did (see Landing 14). The Ship itself is clearly confused as the landing light on the console flashes while still in flight, the central column moves erratically, then the light flashes again as the TARDIS materialises. Two engine groans are heard and the background hum of the control room changes, suggesting this is a materialisation, although the central column continues to rise and rotate even while the TARDIS is trapped by the web, and the Police Box's roof lamp flashes. It's evidently unusual at this stage for the Ship to materialise in deep space (perhaps the Doctor hasn't yet fitted an automatic drift control – see Landing 22). When Jamie says, "We've landed and yet we haven't landed," he might just mean they're not on a planet, the sort of landing he's used to.

▌ The shots of the TARDIS in space being coated in web used the 12-inch model Police Box. Although the Ship has materialised, its roof light continues flashing.

LANDING 57

SPACE Earth, England, London, Covent Garden underground station
TIME [Early-1970s]
TRAVELLERS The Doctor, Jamie, Victoria
EPISODES The Web of Fear 1

With the web gone, the TARDIS resumes its flight and materialises in the London Underground, although the Doctor's device has placed it around half a mile from where it would have landed. The travellers emerge with electric torches into a dark, tiled tunnel, one end blocked by a metal gate. The other way leads them down some steps to a platform where they discover they are in Covent Garden station. It is dark and empty so the Doctor assumes it is the middle of the night, but when they find another way up to the ticket hall they discover it is daytime. The station is locked up, however, so they head back to the platform to find another way out via the rail tunnels.

With the Great Intelligence repelled, the fungus filling the tunnels evaporates. The Doctor, Jamie and Victoria make their way from Piccadilly Circus back towards Covent Garden, keen to get off the tracks before anyone decides to turn the power back on.

▌ **NOTES** The Doctor says he has moved the TARDIS "perhaps half a mile from where we were expected to land", so he seems to know the web was used to trap the Ship intentionally. This suggests the Great Intelligence detected the TARDIS already on its way to London and suspended it in space to delay it so the Doctor wouldn't arrive before the Intelligence was ready for him. It does say it has been observing the Doctor through time and space, and when they arrive the Doctor mentions to Jamie, "Funny, isn't it? How we keep landing on your Earth." Is the implication that the Intelligence is behind the string of landings on Earth since the TARDIS left Tibet?

▌ When Jamie and Victoria encounter Professor Travers again, he says it's "over forty years" since they first met in Tibet. Travers' daughter Anne later says that was 1935, but she seems to have been given this date by Victoria. At no point during *The Abominable Snowmen* is Victoria seen to learn the date. Was she told by Travers on their way back to the TARDIS, and could she have misremembered or misheard? If he said 1925 (see Landing 53 for why that might be), then 40-plus years on could be any time after 1965. Then again, Anne hears her father say it's 40 years since he met the Doctor and accepts 1935 as a plausible date. Even if Travers made multiple trips to Tibet, Anne doesn't question his maths, so it must be at least within a few years of 1975. Julius Silverstein says he bought the deactivated Yeti from Travers 30 years ago but the latter clearly spent some time studying it before selling it (did he have to dispose of it during the Second World War to keep it out of the hands of people who might have used its technology for despicable ends, or did he just need the money?). Production documents about the costume and make-up requirements specified the date of the story as 1970. The army's wall map of the Tube system doesn't include the Victoria Line; although this was opened in stages between 1968 and 1971, tunnel construction had begun in the early 1960s. Surely in an emergency like this the army would have a map of all the tunnels? Presumably in the *Doctor Who* universe the Victoria Line wasn't begun until the 1970s.

LANDING 58

SPACE Earth, England, North Sea, near coast
TIME At least two days in [1990s]
TRAVELLERS The Doctor, Jamie, Victoria
EPISODES Fury from the Deep 1,3,6

In one of its most unusual landing choices ever, the TARDIS materialises in mid-air above the choppy waters of the North Sea before slowly descending until it rests on the surface of the waves. The three travellers haul out an inflatable dinghy and, donning lifejackets, row their way to the nearby shore. As the men pull the boat up onto the beach then help Victoria out, the Doctor gauges from the chalk cliffs that they are in England – the drizzly weather confirms it for Jamie. Nearby is an unusual amount of sea foam, in which the travellers frolic before investigating a large pipeline that emerges from the sea, crosses the beach and disappears into the cliff face.

A few hours later, the three travellers row back out to the TARDIS with a sample of strange gas-emitting seaweed. They perform tests on it in the laboratory and discover it is a living organism. The Doctor digs out a large book about legends and superstitions, in which he finds a picture of the tendrilled creature that attacked Victoria at the EuroGas compound, originally spotted by North Sea sailors in the 18th century. The seaweed sample suddenly erupts from the glass tank it is in, exuding toxic gas. The Doctor and Jamie manage to contain it, not realising that Victoria's screams weaken it. They head out in the dinghy once more and back to the compound.

The next morning the three travellers walk to the beach with Mr and Mrs Harris, who have agreed that Victoria can stay with them. They say a final goodbye, then the Doctor and Jamie head across the beach to the dinghy, turning for one last wave. They paddle out to the TARDIS and clamber aboard. Jamie is still not convinced they should leave Victoria but the Doctor assures him it is what she wants. A despondent Jamie does not care where they go as the Doctor sets the TARDIS in motion. The Police Box hovers upwards from the surface of the sea then dematerialises, and they watch on the scanner as the image of Victoria, standing alone on the beach, slowly recedes and fades.

▮ **LORE** The TARDIS can float.
▮ It has a laboratory and possibly a library.

▮ **NOTES** The Doctor identifies their location as England from the white cliffs. The most famous chalk escarpments are along the south coast, of course, notably around Dover. North Sea gas fields are much further north, however, so it's more likely the TARDIS lands just off Flamborough Head in East Yorkshire, or possibly on the north Norfolk coast. The Doctor is leaping to conclusions anyway (even if correctly) as there are also white cliffs in Northern Ireland and northern Europe.
▮ Robson says, "I've been drilling gas in the North Sea for most of my life," and that he has a 30-year reputation. The gas fields in the North Sea were first exploited in the mid-1960s so assuming Robson first worked on gas rigs then, it must be the 1990s by now.
▮ The main action of the story seems to take place within one day. The Doctor and Jamie then stay overnight to give Victoria a chance to reconsider staying behind. Their departure without her appears to be the next morning, but earlier the Doctor did say, "Jamie and I will stay for another day, just in case you want to think again," so it could be some time later.
▮ The 3-foot Police Box model was lowered on a line from a helicopter for the shot of the TARDIS arriving. It then cuts to the Doctor's party already in the dinghy approaching the shore, so we don't get to see how they got it through the TARDIS doors. Part of the same film was shown in reverse at the end of episode six to represent the TARDIS taking off again.
▮ Even though it may just be a consequence of being dangled on a rope, this is the first time the Police Box is seen spinning as it travels.
▮ The sound of the TARDIS engines continues as it drops from the sky. For only the second time (since *The Chase* – Landing 18) the effect is a reverse of the usual take-off sound, this time edited into a repeating loop.
▮ Although we haven't seen the TARDIS head up into the sky when taking off before, the image of Victoria on the scanner (filmed from a helicopter) is reminiscent of London receding during the first dematerialisation in *An Unearthly Child* (Landing 1).
▮ No reason for the TARDIS's unusual arrival is given and it's hard to see why it would land in this peculiar manner (beyond the production team's whim: it was initially scripted to land at the top of a cliff from which the travellers climbed down to the beach, but this was changed in consultation with the director). Previously the Ship has been too heavy to be washed away by the sea (see Landings 22 and 41) yet here it can settle on the surface, maintaining a centre of gravity above the level of the water. The Doctor says, "The TARDIS is perfectly capable of floating, you know," but it must surely be a function he has specifically set for it to hover on the surface like this.
▮ Victoria's complaint that "every time we go anywhere, something awful happens" suggests any unseen landings are as dangerous as the ones we do see.
▮ The laboratory is the first indication of there being rooms in the TARDIS beyond living quarters or a wardrobe. Shame we can't actually see it.

LANDING 59

SPACE Spaceship Silver Carrier (approaching Space Station W3 near Earth orbit), main corridor
TIME [21st century]
TRAVELLERS The Doctor, Jamie
EPISODES The Wheel in Space 1,6

As the TARDIS makes its next landing, the Doctor has to wake a dozing Jamie. They look at the scanner but it shows no image, even when the Doctor boosts its power. There is no indication of damage on the fault indicator and the external environment is registering as safe. Suddenly the scanner shows a succession of different images – hippos in a lake, a flock of cranes, a waterfall – which the Doctor realises cannot be what is outside. The TARDIS is trying to tempt them to move on as there is danger here, but before the Doctor can respond there is a power overload and the fluid link beneath the console fails, filling the room with acrid mercury vapour. Choking on the fumes, the Doctor opens a hatch in the wall and pulls out the time-vector generator, causing the room around them to shimmer and shrink. He bustles Jamie out of the TARDIS, where they find themselves in the motor section of a small spaceship with standard air, temperature and gravity. The Doctor gives Jamie a lemon sherbet sweet to clear his throat as they follow a trail of freshly spilled oil further into the seemingly motionless and deserted craft.

As the two travellers explore, a service robot emerges from the ship's control centre and seals the door to the motor section using a chest-mounted laser. Later, a concussed Doctor, keen to get back to the TARDIS to recover, uses the time-vector generator as an energy source to release the welded door but is cornered by the robot before he can enter. Jamie rescues him and uses the generator to destroy the robot.

After the Cybermen are defeated, Zoe accompanies the Doctor and Jamie back to the Silver Carrier. While the two youngsters say goodbye, the Doctor refits the time-vector generator and restores the inside of the TARDIS. He replenishes the evaporated mercury with some he took from the Wheel and checks the fault indicator to ensure all is working normally. When Jamie joins him in the control room, the Doctor catches Zoe hiding in his trunk – she wants to go with them, so to make sure she is aware of the risks she would be letting herself in for, the Doctor dons a headset that allows him to project his thought patterns onto the scanner and shows her his most recent encounter with the Daleks.

When the tale is over, Zoe is still adamant she wants to travel with the Doctor so he dematerialises the TARDIS.

- **CONTROLS** Judging from off-screen photos, the Doctor is standing at panel A4 when he operates the scanner. The fault indicator is a square black box fitted to the top of panel A1 (in place of the grille, which is missing hereafter) with a large red light to its right (like the ones on the Servo robot's shoulders). Beneath the lid of the box is an oscilloscope display. When the power overloads, the grille on panel A6 explodes and emits smoke. Vapour emerges from the hatch in the console pedestal beneath panel A6, tying in with the location of the fluid link in *The Daleks* (Landing 3). The hatch's cover is now hinged on the right.
- The time-vector generator is a foot-long golden rod with gold and white tips. It's housed behind a circular hatch covering one of the indented wall roundels adjacent to the main doors – the clips for it can still be seen in subsequent stories up to *The War Games*, although not the component itself. This is not the same roundel as the one from which the Doctor later gets his memory projector, which is on the other indented wall, although the covering hatch may have been reused.
- The Doctor replenishes the vaporised mercury by fitting a metal funnel into panel A6 and simply pouring in liquid mercury. He then operates the second switch from the left at the bottom of panel A5, which turns on the lights in the central column.
- The hole the Doctor pours mercury into is that created for the landing light in *The Web of Fear* (Landing 56), which once removed here is not replaced. The left-hand large slider on panel A5 has lost its handle, as has the rotary switch next to it, leaving just the spindle sticking up. The lightbulb immediately above this has lost its domed cover and more knobs are missing from the small levers on the right. The lower left-hand rotary handle on panel A1 has also now been replaced with a large black dial and the white button that replaced the switch above it has itself been swapped for a black knob.
- The scanner screen is now embedded in a plain wall above a pair of wall-mounted control panels.
- **LORE** The TARDIS can warn of danger at a location by showing pleasant images on the scanner to tempt the occupants to go elsewhere.
- When the fluid link overheats it leaks toxic mercury vapour into the control room.
- Zoe tells Jamie she asked the Doctor what TARDIS meant and he said, "Time And Relative Dimensions In Space."
- **NOTES** It's possible but unlikely that much time has passed since Landing 58. Jamie is wearing the same clothes and still has Victoria's departure on his mind.
- This is the first time the TARDIS has materialised aboard a spaceship (not counting the massive space ark in *The Ark*) since *The Sensorites* (Landing 8). The Silver Carrier is drifting close to the Wheel space station. When talking about how far away Venus is, machine-taught Zoe gives two measurements: "24,564,000 miles at perihelion and 161,350,000 miles at aphelion." These don't match the distance of the planet itself from the Sun at the closest and furthest points in its orbit (very roughly 67 million miles), so presumably they are its distance from the Wheel at those times. This suggests the Wheel is at a stationary point in space (as much as anything in space is stationary) to which Venus is closest when it's at perihelion and furthest at aphelion. This broadly places the Wheel close to Earth's

orbit (93 million miles). The Silver Carrier is said to be a supply ship for Station Five and around 80 million miles off course. As the Wheel is Station Three, there may be fourteen or fifteen such stations positioned along Earth's orbital path some 40 million miles apart.

▪ Although no dating evidence is given in this story, in *The War Games* Zoe says she was born in the 21st century. This might, therefore, be around the time the Cybermen attack the Moonbase (Landing 49), implementing one invasion plan after the other fails. It would seem their infiltration of the Wheel comes first as here no one has heard of the Cybermen, whereas in *The Moonbase*, "There were Cybermen, every child knows that, but they were all destroyed ages ago." Did stories of Cybermen spread after the Wheel incident, becoming common knowledge by 2070? The Cybermen recognise the Doctor in his second incarnation, possibly from *The Invasion* (Landing 63).

▪ This story was written by David Whitaker, who had been story editor during *Doctor Who*'s first year, so it seems likely the fault indicator that the Doctor directs Jamie to check was intended to be the same as the fault locator (last seen for real in *Planet of Giants* – Landing 10 – and as a photographic backdrop in *The Tomb of the Cybermen* – Landing 52). Instead the production team added the device to the console rather than have a separate piece of scenery.

▪ As in *The Edge of Destruction* (Landing 4), the TARDIS has an exotic way of trying to communicate with its occupants. To warn them of danger outside, it shows them scanner images of attractive locations (including bathing hippos?), expecting this to persuade them to go elsewhere rather than, say, immediately rush outside to see the lovely place they've apparently landed. In the initial script (and Target novelisation) this was expanded upon. The Doctor describes it as an automatic defence network, an optional extra in this model of TARDIS that he usually leaves disconnected because it's so sensitive to even the smallest danger that it would warn them on every landing and they'd never leave the Ship. This seems to be an early attempt to explain why the Doctor always ends up in trouble wherever he goes, yet ties in nicely with later lore about the Time Lords only observing, never acting. Having developed TARDISes, they presumably used them to visit other times and places, but made sure there was a system to deter the crew from ever actually leaving the vessel. It's suggested the Doctor accidentally turns the defence mechanism on when trying to get the scanner working – "I must have pushed the wrong switch," he says.

▪ The TARDIS can't be warning about the imminent fluid link failure, however – the scanner images appear before the power overloads and there's no sign of a problem from the fault indicator. Besides, surely just moving the TARDIS somewhere else wouldn't prevent the fluid link from blowing, unless the overload is somehow caused from outside. Indeed, Jamie later says, "The warning mechanism obviously thought there was something wrong out here." The TARDIS must therefore have detected the presence of Cybermen aboard the spaceship. If so, maybe the Doctor *should* leave the defence network switched on.

▪ Without being able to see the episode, we can't be sure what happens when the Doctor disengages the time-vector generator. He says, "Once removed, it alters the size of the TARDIS. The inside becomes an ordinary telephone box again." Does that mean the control room physically shrinks? Previously this has happened to the Monk's TARDIS when the Doctor removed its dimensional control. Or does it dislocate the internal dimension from the Police Box exterior, as happens in *Father's Day* (see Landing 332, vol.2)? It's not clear how either would solve the problem of the control room being filled with toxic vapour. There's also no indication of how the Doctor and Jamie get back into the TARDIS to restore the interior to its proper size. Is there a slot for the time-vector generator inside the empty Police Box? Or does the Doctor devise a clever way of bypassing the component – it's empty slot in the roundel by the doors is evident right up to the Doctor's capture by the Time Lords.

▪ It's implied the Doctor is projecting his own memories of an encounter with the Daleks for Zoe to watch. Yet the very first scene she sees is of events at which the Doctor wasn't present (as will be many of the others during the subsequent repeat of *The Evil of the Daleks*). So is the Doctor actually tapping into the TARDIS's record of events in its vicinity, as utilised in *The Trial of a Time Lord*? (His claim that his "older model" TARDIS shouldn't have this feature may simply be more of his time-wasting bluster.) If so, there are still incidents the Ship wasn't in the vicinity of – all those in 1866 in particular – so it may also have absorbed the Doctor's and Jamie's memories via the telepathic circuits.

LANDING 60

SPACE Dulkis, Island of Death
TIME Unknown future
TRAVELLERS The Doctor, Jamie, Zoe Heriot
EPISODES The Dominators 1,5; The Mind Robber 1

Tired from projecting his memories for Zoe, the Doctor lands the TARDIS, hoping for a holiday. He is therefore pleased to find they are on Dulkis, a peaceful planet he has visited before. The Ship materialises on an island in the southern hemisphere surrounded by sea mist. It is not far from the coast where a Dulcian travel capsule has recently come ashore, and close to the dilapidated remains of a weapons museum. After the three travellers emerge to survey their location, unaware that until very recently there were deadly levels of radiation in the air, the Doctor retrieves from the TARDIS a fishing net on a pole and a deflated beach ball for Zoe and Jamie, and a fold-up chair for himself to relax in. But they are immediately startled by the sound of the travel capsule exploding and set off to investigate.

Meanwhile robotic Quarks mark the ground near the

TARDIS as the eastern-most of four drilling sites centred on the museum. Hiding from the Quarks, the sole surviving Dulcian from the travel capsule, Cully, comes across the Police Box and is bemused by it and the marking. He ducks out of sight behind the TARDIS as two Dominators arrive to examine the site. The senior, Rago, notices the "crude box-like structure" but dismisses it and rebukes his junior Toba for almost wasting Quark power by destroying it when it presents no disruption to their plans.

Fearing a threat to the Ship, the Doctor and Jamie return to check it is safe. They notice square footprints leading away from the marking and follow them.

Quarks place an upright device with a domed top and pointed base above their marker. They attach their arms to its power inputs and it begins emitting a high-energy pulse into the ground, drilling a hole. Once the bore is complete, they mount a small rocket into the hole, primed to fire once the central hole at the museum is complete.

Jamie and Zoe wait by the TARDIS while the Doctor disposes of the Dominators' atomic seed device by placing it aboard their spaceship just before it takes off. He joins them just as the perimeter rockets fire and explode deep in the mantle. The island is turned into a volcano and Jamie pulls the Doctor into the Ship as lava erupts all around them.

Zoe watches the scanner admiringly as a river of lava rolls towards the TARDIS, but as the Doctor tries to take off the fluid link overheats and a pall of mercury vapour escapes from the console. Jamie is worried the lava will harm the TARDIS; although the Doctor is unconcerned, he cannot be certain as the Ship has never been buried in lava before so he is persuaded they should leave at once. The fluid link gets too hot again as the power rises, however. The Doctor struggles with a jammed control but finally manages to stop the mercury from vaporising so they will not suffocate.

With lava now all around them, the only way to take off is to use the emergency unit. The Doctor is reluctant but the others convince him they have no choice. He retrieves the unit from under the console and affixes it to the control panel. Immediately the Ship, now almost completely covered in molten rock, shifts out of space and time altogether.

◉ **CONTROLS** Jamie appears to close the main doors with the left-most small lever on panel A5 while the Doctor flicks the switches below. The Doctor adjusts controls in the bottom-left corner of this panel as the fluid link overheats, and once it has cooled down he seems to turn the rotary handle. Zoe reads from a gauge on panel A1 (see below) which is marked in tenths of a unit up to 1,000, the danger level. The jammed switch the Doctor wrestles with is a new control stuck to the lower-right button on the fast return switch on panel A5. The emergency unit is stored in the console's pedestal behind a hatch under panel A4. The unit clips onto two white connectors in the top-left corner of panel A5 (added for this story).

◉ The small levers on panel A5 have had their knobs replaced, although they're black and silver rather than red and yellow like the originals. The left-most lightbulb on this panel is now missing while the new lever on the fast return switch is clearly loosely attached as Patrick Troughton has to hold the base in place while wiggling the top. The right-hand gauge from panel A3 has been placed at the top of panel A1 (where the fault indicator was in *The Wheel in Space*). This appears to be a directorial choice to get the desired camera angle when Zoe reads from the gauge, but may have also been to cover the hole from the missing grille (see Landing 59). The middle of the three small levers below it is missing its stem.

◉ Photos taken during studio rehearsals for *The Mind Robber* show a silver disc on panel A4 between the lower two lightbulbs on the left-hand side. This is not there in the broadcast episodes.

▉ **NOTES** We don't hear the TARDIS taking off at the end of *The Wheel in Space*, and as the Doctor is giving Zoe the chance to change her mind presumably he doesn't leave until after he has finished replaying *The Evil of the Daleks* for her. When they arrive on Dulkis, however, the Doctor is still "a little bit weary" from projecting the mental images, so this must be their first landing since leaving the Silver Carrier. Zoe and Jamie are also wearing the same clothes (the latter for the third story in a row).

▉ It's not clear if the Doctor deliberately pilots the TARDIS to Dulkis. To do so would be unheard of at this point in the series but he has already identified the planet before leaving the Ship, which is equally unusual, and does seem to be planning a holiday. Alternatively, he simply recognises Dulkis from the image of the Island of Death on the scanner – "An island of some sort surrounded by a sea of mist," says Zoe – which would be pretty impressive as it's an entirely nondescript place.

▉ The shot of the TARDIS materialising uses the 3-foot model Police Box, filmed on location to save transporting the full-size prop. Brian Hodgson created a new version of the TARDIS landing sound effect, beginning with a descending tone that mixes into the standard grinding with added echo, then cutting out after the first few groans.

▉ The telephone plaque is back on the left-hand door of the Police Box prop but positively filthy.

▉ From episode one of *The Mind Robber*, the sound effect of the main doors operating keeps the lower pitch introduced in *The Tomb of the Cybermen* but cuts off before it dips at the end.

▉ Although the Doctor seems confident the lava won't harm the TARDIS, despite never having been in such a situation, we know that external conditions affect the Ship's interior so it's at least likely to get very hot in there – as Jamie says, "If you don't hurry up and get us out of here we'll be fried by that lava." This seems to be the reason for the fluid link overheating.

▉ The model shot of the TARDIS being overwhelmed with lava (well, foam) also uses the 3-foot miniature.

LANDING 61

SPACE Nowhere
TIME None
TRAVELLERS The Doctor, Jamie, Zoe
EPISODES The Mind Robber 1,5

The emergency unit takes the TARDIS of out space and time altogether. The scanner is blank and all the gauges on the console register zero. The Doctor goes to the power room to make repairs and when Zoe comes to ask him about where they are he warns her there are dangerous forces outside and they must stay in the TARDIS. However, Jamie and Zoe each see an image of their home on the scanner, convincing them they have landed somewhere. Zoe is keen to go out and look but Jamie will not do so without the Doctor and goes to fetch him. Left alone, Zoe sees her home city again on the screen and, unwilling to wait, opens the doors and goes outside, seeming to vanish in a mist. The Doctor is suspicious when Jamie tells him he and Zoe saw different things on the scanner and hurries back to the control room only to find the girl is gone. The Doctor warns Jamie not to follow as there is unknown danger out there, but when the emergency unit flashes a first warning that its time is almost up, the Scot runs out to find Zoe and he vanishes too. The unit gives a second warning as a piercing pulsing sound penetrates the Ship, trying to force the Doctor out but he resists…

He hears Zoe screaming and a voice encourages him to save his friends. The Doctor is reluctant to succumb but cannot risk any harm coming to them so he steps out into the void. Outside, the Ship appears totally white. He sees Jamie and Zoe, similarly dressed completely in white, surrounded by white robots. He assures them only they and the TARDIS are real and helps them to re-enter the Ship.

When they do everything appears normal and the Doctor sets the TARDIS in motion. Jamie takes a nap but has a nightmare about a white unicorn charging straight at him. The power beings to fluctuate and as the Doctor tries to steady it with the use of an emergency power booster he hears a throbbing vibration in his head. The others hear it too and as it swamps their minds the TARDIS appears to break apart. Jamie and Zoe cling to the console as it spins away into a dark void.

Apparently trapped in a land of fiction, the Doctor is later duped into believing the TARDIS has been recovered. But when he goes inside he finds it was an illusion and he is trapped inside a glass case.

With the creator of the world of fictional characters overcome, the Doctor can only hope he and his friends will be returned to reality. As the dimension collapses, the walls of the seemingly destroyed Police Box come back together.

- **CONTROLS** When Jamie is checking if the control that warns of danger is switched off, he points to the small levers on panel A4. Zoe opens the main doors with the left-most small switch on panel A5 and the Doctor closes them from the same panel. He then flicks the switches at the bottom and seemingly sets the TARDIS in motion with the right-hand large slider. He looks at the gauge added to panel A1 and is concerned it has dropped below 1,000 (even though above that meant danger when Zoe previously checked it); this means the Ship is using more power than it's storing. The emergency power booster seems to be part of, or at least controlled from, the console; we can't see all the controls the Doctor tries but he is seen using the middle small lever on panel A4.
- The circular hole left in panel A3 by moving the right-hand gauge has a plain cover over it. The covering of the lightbulb just above it has slipped down, leaving a hole next to the grille, and the front of the radiation meter has also dropped down inside, leaving a gap above it and obscuring part of the curved display window. The left-hand rotary handle on panel A4 is missing and the right-hand gauge on panel A2 has sunk into its hole so that it's sitting almost flush with the surface (possibly from when Wendy Padbury climbed on the console for the pre-filmed shot of it spinning in the void).
- In the filming of the console in the void, Zoe lies across panel A1 while Jamie clings to panels A5 and A6. As this was filmed before the studio recording, panel A1 still has the fault indicator unit at the top, but not the large light that was next to it in *The Wheel in Space*.

LORE Attaching and activating the emergency unit shifts the TARDIS out of the time-space dimension – "Out of reality," claims the Doctor, perhaps pompously – but only for a limited amount of time as it's dangerous to remain among the strange forces outside of time and space. The unit gives increasingly insistent warnings if it's not disengaged before that time.

The TARDIS has a 'power room' (a monitoring centre for its energy output).

NOTES The void the TARDIS arrives in bears many similarities to the Toymaker's domain (see Landing 37). Environments and people can be brought into being at the whim of a controlling intelligence, here the computerised Master Brain operating through a magazine writer who was somehow been transported here. Is the Toymaker someone who similarly found himself in such a dimension – perhaps even a Time Lord who used his TARDIS's emergency unit – and was seduced by the power to create anything he could imagine?

It's often noted how the first episode of *The Mind Robber* had to be produced on minimal budget when it was written at the last minute, and according to writer/story editor Derrick Sherwin used just "a white cyclorama, the TARDIS prop and what was left of the tatty TARDIS interior set", plus some robot costumes from an earlier episode of *Out of the Unknown*. Except little of the control room set was pre-existing. The two photographic walls that make up most of it appear to be newly created as the arrangement of roundels at the edges is different from any photo wall seen before. Plus there's a whole new section incorporating the scanner, plus the power room. While these were no doubt formed from stock pieces, it's not quite the "use only what we've used before" approach frequently quoted.

- Jamie talks of a "wee gadget" on the console that "warns you to go elsewhere if there's any danger". The only time we've seen such a function was when the TARDIS showed tempting images on the scanner at the start of *The Wheel in Space* (Landing 59). The Doctor assumes the images of Jamie's and Zoe's homes are projected by an outside force to entice them to leave the TARDIS, but could it be the Ship again trying to encourage them to return to their 'home' universe as it senses danger here? Has the Doctor unwittingly left the defence mechanism on again? The switch Jamie points to is on the same panel the Doctor was at when he seemingly activated it by accident in *The Wheel in Space*. The two companions see their homes again after leaving the TARDIS but this could be because the images are fresh in their minds – this story is called *The Mind Robber*, after all.
- The roundel to the left of the main doors still has the disc with clips to hold the time-vector generator (although not this component itself) fitted for *The Wheel in Space* (Landing 59). The power room contains the freezing machine used by the Moroks in *The Space Museum* but without its clear dome (did the Doctor nick it when he took the time and space visualiser?).
- When Zoe and Jamie run out of the TARDIS and disappear into the void, a white mask was cut in the shape of the doorway and faded in over the actors. Look closely and you can see it doesn't precisely fit the zigzag edges of the doors.
- The white TARDIS the Doctor emerges from was not the main prop repainted, nor was it one of the false boxes from *The Celestial Toymaker*, but specially built. The stepped lintel above the doors is simpler, as are the corner posts and windows. The 'Police box' sign is deeper and has no lettering, and there's no telephone plaque on the door. Just two sides were made rather than a complete box; the white background cyclorama is thus visible through the open door.
- Although the Doctor appears to dematerialise the Ship and the central column begins oscillating, it stops again before the take-off sound has faded and is stationary even as the Doctor increases power with the emergency booster. So is their departure another illusion?
- Oops! In episode one, when the Doctor gets Jamie and Zoe back into the TARDIS, look closely at the scanner: it's showing the caption slide crediting producer Peter Bryant set up for the end titles.
- The exploding Police Box was a new model built for this sequence. The parts were held together by a taught elastic band inside. The model was hung from a wire and then a small charge severed the band, causing the sides to fly apart. The final shot of it reforming is the same footage in reverse. This model survives in a private collection (see thepropgallery.com/in-detail-TARDIS-filming-miniature).
- The shot from above of Jamie and Zoe on the console is also a model. Note the panels are out of proportion, creating a wide collar around the central column, and the controls bear no resemblance to the full-size prop. The close-up of the actors clinging to the console was filmed ahead of studio recording. From the movement of shadows, it seems the console itself was rotated rather than the camera circling around it.
- When the Doctor is tricked into thinking the TARDIS has been recovered in episode five, he walks into the standard prop but this becomes a photo cutout of a genuine Police Box that falls away to reveal him plugged into the master computer.
- It's possible nothing after the sonic attack on the Doctor halfway through episode one really happens but is all in his mind. At the start of the next story Jamie and Zoe are in the outfits they change into only after the TARDIS has seemingly landed, so it must materialise somewhere for a time. But we've already noted how the views on the scanner could be caused by the Ship itself, and it's only after the Doctor is assailed that he hears a voice – or at least thinks he does. This is why the Police Box appears to have changed colour when the Doctor goes out to rescue his friends, and how their clothes can change colour. It would also explain why the scale on the gauge that Zoe reads from seems to be different between the first and second halves of the episode. So perhaps the TARDIS doesn't really break up, we never see or learn the true nature of the intelligence controlling this realm, and once the Doctor has successfully overcome its attempt to absorb his mind, Jamie and Zoe – who have been sharing the same illusions – find themselves safely in the TARDIS and back in the normal universe.

LANDING 62

SPACE Space, Solar System, near the Moon
TIME [Mid-1970s]
TRAVELLERS The Doctor, Jamie, Zoe
EPISODES The Invasion 1

The travellers awaken in the TARDIS back in the normal universe. Checking the scanner, they find the Ship has materialised in space close to the far side of the Moon. Hidden on the shadowed surface is a Cyberman spaceship that fires a missile at the TARDIS.

The Doctor spots it approaching and tries to move the Ship but the landing circuit has jammed. He attempts to fix it with the missile getting closer and closer. It explodes just as the TARDIS finally dematerialises.

- **CONTROLS** Without being able to view this episode it's not known whether the landing circuit was a new or existing control, and whether the thumps on the soundtrack are the Doctor hitting the console with his fist or (as depicted in the animated version on DVD) trying to reattach a control that has come off in his hand.
- A photo taken during studio rehearsals shows the right-hand gauge is back in its usual position on panel A3 but placed on top of the console rather than fitted through a hole from underneath. This makes it sit much taller than the gauge next to it.

- **LORE** A jammed landing circuit prevents the TARDIS from dematerialising.
- **NOTES** The studio photo shows that, unusually, the main doors of the control room were positioned to the right of the set, with one of the photographic walls on their left (turned on its side). The roundel that had clips fitted to hold the time-vector generator in *The Wheel in Space* (Landing 59) can still be seen adjacent to the left-hand door, although we can't know if it would have been visible on screen.
- The attack on the TARDIS from the Moon's surface is later directly connected to the presence of Cybermen, so this materialisation is in the same time period as the next landing (see this for dating evidence).
- A model shot was filmed of the TARDIS hovering above the Moon, but with the first episode of this serial missing we can't know what miniature was used.
- As the TARDIS does successfully dematerialise just before the missile strikes, what causes the latter to explode? Perhaps it was primed to detonate after a set time rather than on impact, or was it caught in some kind of time-wake from the disappearing TARDIS?

LANDING 63

SPACE Earth, south-east England, field in International Electromatics compound
TIME At least two days in [mid-1970s]
TRAVELLERS The Doctor, Jamie, Zoe
EPISODES The Invasion 1,8

The TARDIS makes a jittery landing in a field of cows. The travellers are relieved to have survived the missile attack and puzzled as to who would want to destroy them. They check the scanner and laugh at the inquisitive cow it displays. The lights flash and a low drone sounds to indicate the visual stabiliser circuit is faulty. Jamie is weary of the continual problems the TARDIS develops but the Doctor tells him it just needs servicing. Checking further afield on the scanner suggests they are in 20th-century England so the Doctor decides to visit Professor Travers in London to see if he can help supply spares with which to repair the Ship. He removes the faulty landing circuit and visual stabiliser circuit, the latter rendering the Police Box invisible.

The travellers emerge into the field as if from nowhere, pass the indifferent cows and exit via a gate beside a road, where the Doctor waves down a passing truck. The driver agrees to take them to London.

After destroying the Cybermen's invasion fleet, the Doctor spends a few days making replacements for the damaged TARDIS circuits, while Jamie recovers from a bullet wound in his leg. Captain Turner drives the Doctor, Jamie and Zoe, plus Isobel Watkins, out to the now-abandoned International Electromatics compound and delivers them, as requested, to an apparently empty field. Their new friends watch bemused as the three travellers feel around for the invisible TARDIS. The Doctor finds it and disappears inside. He refits the visual stabiliser circuit and the Police Box reappears. Jamie and Zoe join him inside and the TARDIS fades away.

- **LORE** The Doctor blames repeated malfunctions on the TARDIS's need for an overhaul, "just like any piece of machinery".
- The exterior of the TARDIS can be rendered invisible by detaching the visual stabiliser circuit.
- **NOTES** The International Electromatics compound is said by Londoner Isobel Watkins to be in south-east England, so probably Kent or Sussex.
- Brigadier Lethbridge-Stewart tells the Doctor it's four years since they last met "in the underground". See Landing 57 for possible dates of *The Web of Fear*; four years on puts *The Invasion* between 1969 and 1979. In episode two, Vaughn views a surveillance photo of the Doctor and Jamie which is labelled E091/5D/78 – could the last two digits indicate the year? Curiously, he has been working with the Cybermen for five years, so their plan predates the Great Intelligence's take-over of London. What would they have done had the Intelligence been successful?
- New TARDIS materialisation sound effects were created for this story. When the Ship first lands on Earth (filmed on location with the full-size prop) the usual grinding sound is barely audible behind a descending whooshing tone (different from that used for Landing 60). When it becomes visible at the end of episode eight, the usual grinding is played in reverse with lots of echo, ending on the deep thump that begins the full take-off effect – close to what will later become the standard materialisation effect. The final dematerialisation effect is also new, with added echo.
- It's strange that reactivating the visual stabiliser circuit seems to make the TARDIS engines operate as the Police Box reappears. After all, it has been there all along, just invisible.
- The TARDIS prop has handles on the doors for the first time – one on the right-hand door and one on the left edge of the telephone plaque's frame. These were added when the box was used in a episode of *Out of the Unknown* recorded during *Doctor Who*'s break in production in the summer of 1968. Also installed for its extracurricular appearance was a box behind the plaque to contain a telephone, which can be seen when Patrick Troughton emerges from the Police Box.

LANDING 64

SPACE Unnamed planet, near Gond settlement
TIME Unknown future
TRAVELLERS The Doctor, Jamie, Zoe
EPISODES The Krotons 1,3

The TARDIS materialises at the foot of a high cliff on a desolate, rocky planet orbiting twin suns. Gravity is standard and the air is breathable but has a strong sulphur and ozone content, plus traces of hydrogen telluride, the remnant of contamination thousands of years ago. When the travellers step outside they immediately notice the smell of "bad eggs", as Jamie puts it; Zoe is worried it could be poisonous but the Doctor seems to find it bracing and assures them the TARDIS instruments would have warned them were it dangerous. Armed with a black umbrella as protection from the heat of the suns, he sets off to explore while humming 'The Lincolnshire Poacher'. There are deposits of magnesium silicate on the surface, which Zoe classifies as mica but is more accurately forsterite – a lump of which the Doctor puts in his pocket. Climbing a ridge, they see below them a community of wedge-shaped dwellings clustered around a much larger domed crystalline structure. On the side of this structure nearest to them is a doorway and Jamie leads the way down a slope of scree to investigate.

A few hours later, the Doctor and Zoe return to the TARDIS to analyse a sample of the Krotons' constituent slurry. They learn it is largely composed of the metalloid tellurium. In the Dynatrope, it is stored in a polarised centrifuge and can be activated by sufficiently high mental power to reform the Krotons themselves. The Doctor searches around the landing area for some samples of sulphur, placing them in a large carpet bag, unaware that a Kroton has been sent to locate the TARDIS. It corners the two travellers and orders them to return to the Dynatrope but when its direction instructions are interrupted they slip past it, climbing the rocks to evade pursuit. Re-establishing its link to the Dynatrope, the Kroton is instructed to destroy the TARDIS and fires its dispersal unit. Fortunately, the Doctor has sets the HADS control and the Ship dematerialises out of danger.

- **NOTES** The TARDIS's arrival uses the same sound effect as Landing 60. To maintain the appearance of being destroyed by the Kroton, it makes no sound when dematerialising.
- Its roof lamp continues to flash for some time after materialising.
- Although all sequences involving the TARDIS were filmed on location using the Police Box prop (including the images displayed on the Dynatrope's monitors), those of the Kroton firing at it were deemed unusable so that scene was restaged in the studio. The November filming was performed in light drizzle and it may be that the required smoke effects were compromised by the rain. (This might also be why the planet was given two suns, as an excuse for Patrick Troughton to use an umbrella on location.) In the end, the only shot used of the Kroton on location was it leaving just before the TARDIS rematerialises.
- It's nice that the original telephone plaque gets a big close-up in episode three as this was its last sighting. Over the Christmas between production of this serial and the next it went missing and wasn't replaced with a new plaque until *The Seeds of Death* episode six was recorded in February (see Landing 66).

LANDING 65

SPACE Unnamed planet, short distance from previous landing
TIME As above
TRAVELLERS None
EPISODES The Krotons 3-4

Under automatic control by the hostile action displacement system, the TARDIS relocates to a ledge higher up the cliff, out of reach of the departing Kroton's dispersal weapon.

The Doctor, Zoe and Jamie return to the Ship, leaving the Gonds to rebuild their society now they are free of the Krotons' control. The TARDIS dematerialises from the cliff ledge.

- **LORE** The TARDIS has a hostile action displacement system (HADS) that automatically relocates the Ship to a nearby safe position if it comes under attack. This can be switched off.
- **NOTES** This time the echoing materialisation sound effect with thump from Landing 63 is reused, and is heard again for the next two landings.
- This is the first time the TARDIS is seen to operate without anyone aboard. As the Doctor ruefully points out, it doesn't select a very convenient place to land. "You can tell that the captain is not at the helm," he says, although it's not like he usually has any control over where the Ship lands anyway.
- Before working out how the hostile action displacement system works we probably need to define what constitutes hostile action. Up to this point the TARDIS itself has rarely come under immediate threat but it has generally been considered to be indestructible, and later in the series this is stated outright. The most direct attack to date is in *The Chase*, when three Daleks fire at the Police Box without effect (see Landing 17). Also, in *The Sensorites* the lock is cut from the door; in *The Dalek Invasion of Earth* it's struck by rubble from a collapsing bridge; in *The Romans* it falls off a cliff; in *The Time Meddler* it's submerged beneath the incoming tide; in *The Daleks' Master Plan* the Monk disables the lock; in *The Faceless Ones* a jumbo jet almost collides with it; in *The Web of Fear* the Great Intelligence holds it in space and smothers it in web; and in *The Mind Robber* it's buried in lava. Either the HADS was on and these situations didn't register as threatening enough to relocate, or the system was off and the TARDIS is capable of withstanding these dangers. (If some of these seem trivial risks, note that the next time we see the HADS used, in *Cold War* (Landing 578, vol.2), it activates just because the TARDIS gets a bit wet aboard a sinking submarine.) In either case, it suggests the Krotons' dispersal weapon *is* powerful enough to harm the Ship, which makes them a much more formidable foe than they're generally considered to be. Perhaps more likely is that, like the defence mechanism in *The Wheel in Space* (Landing 59), the HADS is so sensitive that were it left on the TARDIS would be constantly moving on

before the Doctor had a chance to explore anywhere it landed – one can imagine the timid Time Lords would install a system that activated at the first sign of danger. The question then is why the Doctor has it switched on now. Perhaps after being buried in lava and having to escape by using the emergency unit, which led to a very strange experience, and then being almost blown up by a Cyber-missile, he decided to give it a try.

- The shot of the Police Box on the ledge appears to be the 3-foot model as its windows are much lighter than the full-size prop's and the 'Police box' signs more legible. If so, this was presumably used in preference to lugging the main prop halfway up the cliff. The final shot of the departing TARDIS uses the same miniature, filmed on a rocky model set (although it doesn't look like a ledge – did the TARDIS relocate to its original position after the Kroton left?). It had now been adapted slightly to match the full-size prop: the two handles recently added to the latter were replicated and the St John Ambulance emblem was finally gone.

LANDING 66

SPACE Earth, England, [London], Eldred's museum
TIME [21st century]
TRAVELLERS The Doctor, Jamie, Zoe
EPISODES The Seeds of Death 1,6

The TARDIS returns to Earth, arriving in a museum of aeronautics and rocketry. When the travellers first check the scanner, however, the image of an ion-jet rocket followed by a close-up view of a cosmonaut make them believe they are stationary in space and someone is trying to climb aboard. Each is from a different century, however, and further images of Leonardo da Vinci's design for a flying machine, aviation pioneer Edwin AV Roe's first triplane, the American Gemini 3 capsule, an early 'Charlière' hydrogen balloon, a clipped-wing Mk 5 Spitfire, a Concorde supersonic transport (in an unused 1960s American Airlines livery) and an American Saturn 1B rocket confirm that they are viewing exhibits in the museum. They head outside for a closer look.

The museum's owner, rocket engineer Professor Daniel Eldred, is alerted to their presence and confronts them, thinking they have broken in to laugh at his antiquated exhibits. The Doctor is shocked to learn no one travels into space since the invention of T-Mat, a worldwide transmat system controlled from the Moon. He is particularly impressed with Eldred's design for an ion rocket that was built but never used.

A short time later, Commander Julian Radnor and head technician Gia Kelly visit Eldred to enlist his help with a failure in the T-Mat system. They need his rocket to get to the Moon but the jilted scientist refuses, insisting the vehicle is not ready and there is no one trained to pilot it. The Doctor offers to fly the rocket and Radnor is forced by the circumstances to accept. After a briefing from a still-reticent Eldred, they all leave for the launch site.

Dashing through the rain that has successfully neutralised the attacking Martians' foamy fungus, the travellers return to Eldred's museum, keen to avoid questions about themselves. When Zoe asks where they are going next, Jamie reminds her the Doctor has "no more idea than the Man in the Moon". Affronted, he ushers them into the Ship and immediately takes off.

- **CONTROLS** The Doctor wrestles with the scanner control on panel A5. Although unseen, it looks like a new switch added between the right-hand large slider and set of small levers (unless Patrick Troughton's just miming). He opens the main doors from the same panel.
- There is now a hole at the top of panel A1 where the grille was, and on panel A3 where the top-right light-bulb is missing altogether. The radiation meter on the same panel is missing its control knob. For no obvious reason, there's an extra disc sitting on top of the central column that's sightly larger than the column's casing.
- The exhibits in the museum include an astral map unit exactly like the Doctor's (see Landing 14).
- **LORE** Despite having very recently travelled from the Moon's orbit to Earth, here the Doctor isn't confident of using the TARDIS to get from Earth to the Moon, claiming it's "not suited to short-range travel" and liable to overshoot by a few million miles or a few million years. This is due to his piloting skills at this time rather than the TARDIS's abilities, as it managed perfectly well on its own with Landing 65.
- **NOTES** There's nothing in the narrative to suggest this immediately follows Landing 65. Zoe is wearing the same outfit but Jamie has had time to change into a fresh shirt, so she could just have chosen to put on the vinyl jacket again after other adventures.
- T-Mat Control is explicitly stated to be in London, but is Eldred's museum? There's no way to tell how long it takes Radnor and Miss Kelly to get there after T-Mat stops working but they don't appear to have walked, so presumably there are still vehicles of some sort for local transport. After all, how else does everyone reach the rocket launching site, which clearly isn't in a built-up area? That doesn't mean they travelled far, though, and the Doctor and Eldred nip back to the museum easily enough to run tests on the seed pod, while at the end of the story it's strongly suggested the three travellers have walked all the way in the rain – even though T-Mat is working again, they don't leave via the cubicle in the control centre and clearly don't arrive in Eldred's cubicle else they wouldn't be wet at all. It's not impossible these trips are made in a vehicle, with the Doctor and company dropped off outside the museum and left to dash indoors (they're not *that* wet, after all), but on balance it seems Eldred also lives in London.
- The only indication of a date within the story is the Doctor identifying an ion-jet rocket as heralding from the 21st century, which Eldred later reveals he designed, so presumably he's living in that century. Another story set in this period is *The Moonbase*, which also features a form of weather control, using the Gravitron on the

Moon (see Landing 49). That was installed in 2050, so placing *The Seeds of Death* depends on whether weather control progressed from local influence to a global application, or from a crude worldwide system to a more finessed national one (assuming the local control isn't used in tandem with the broader influence from the Moon). There's talk in *The Moonbase* of using rockets to travel to and from the Moon, so certainly that must come before the invention of T–Mat – even if rockets make a comeback after the Martian's attempted takeover, there's no indication that T–Mat is to be abandoned altogether and would surely continue to be used to get people to the Moon. It therefore seems likely this story comes after 2070. Zoe was also born in the 21st century but has no knowledge of T–Mat, which supports the supposition that *The Wheel in Space* is set before *The Moonbase* (see Landing 59). One contradiction to this is that the Wheel space station acts as "a halfway house for deep-space ships", according to Zoe, whereas Eldred says his ion rocket "was to have been the vehicle to take Man beyond the Moon". One could argue that the deep-space ships are unmanned probes, or perhaps they're test ships for further travel but haven't yet reached another planet, which Eldred's propulsion method would have allowed had it not been abandoned as interest in space exploration declined (as a result of encounters with the Cybermen?). Of course, all this is thrown into further confusion by the events of *Kill the Moon* (see Landing 637, vol.2).

▤ A mirrored surface is placed beyond the control room doors. It reflects the back of the main doors wall – giving the impression of more roundels outside – the console and Patrick Troughton putting on his jacket.

▤ The Police Box prop was in a state when episode one was recorded on 3 January 1969. It had lost its 'Police telephone' plaque, leaving the cubbyhole added for *Out of the Unknown* visible (see Landing 63), and the roof is way off centre, as the shot from Eldred's viewpoint shows clearly. This shows the prop's left-hand side. For the TARDIS's next appearance in episode six, recorded on 7 February, a new plaque was made, although it's nothing like the original. Instead of dark blue serif lettering on a white background, it has white sans-serif letters on a blue panel, plus some minor changes to the wording (see page 78). The new plaque has no frame and a small D-shaped handle on the left-hand side.

▤ The departure of the TARDIS was achieved by mixing from a camera shot of the Police Box prop on the museum set to a photo of just the set.

LANDING 67

SPACE Space, fourth sector of Earth's galaxy, Pliny system, beacon Alpha 4
TIME Unknown future
TRAVELLERS The Doctor, Jamie, Zoe
EPISODES The Space Pirates 1

The TARDIS materialises in the cramped computer bay section of Alpha 4, a modular navigation beacon constructed from argonite, in a region of space some 50 days' flight from Earth. On emerging, the Doctor realises this is not where he expected to be but decides to explore anyway, intrigued by a sophisticated computer system. Jamie would rather leave but the Doctor assures him the craft is unmanned. However, Interstellar Space Corps soldiers are aboard, guarding the beacon from argonite pirates. Hearing the sound of the TARDIS landing, they burst into the computer bay and shoot at the three travellers, who escape through a hatch to the adjacent section. The soldiers are in turn shot down by Caven's pirates, who place scissor charges around the hull of the beacon and detonate them, breaking the magnetic connections between the eight sections and detaching them from the beacon's framework.

Rockets attached to the beacon sections propel them in formation towards the planet Ta. However, when the Doctor tries to re-magnetise them, the section he is in is flung away from the others. The remaining seven, including that containing the TARDIS, continue for several hours until they are intercepted by pirate Dervish in a Beta Dart. His men reset the rockets and send the sections on a new course to the nearby planet Lobos. Once there they settle into orbit where they are discovered by ISC Major Warne in a Minnow ship.

Once the pirates have been exposed and defeated, Milo Clancey gives the Doctor, Zoe and Jamie a lift in his ship, the Liz 79, back to Lobos where the beacon section containing the TARDIS is waiting.

▤ **NOTES** The only location information given on screen is that General Hermack's V-ship is "fifty days and many billions of miles out from Earth" as it enters "the fourth sector of our galaxy". Writer Robert Holmes undoubtedly meant billion to mean a million million (the American definition of a thousand million wasn't adopted in Britain until 1974 and even then took time to become common usage), in which terms 50 light days is only 800 million miles, so the ship must travel faster than light. The nearest star to the Sun is around 25 billion miles away, or 1,550 light days, so the V-ship must be capable of at least 31 times the speed of light. Its manoeuvring within the Pliny system seems quite slow, however, taking several hours to get from one planet to another. There's talk of a 'main boost', the use of which is limited; perhaps this is the faster-than-light engine for travelling long distances but which would be impractical within a solar system.

▤ It's said mining prospectors like Clancey, who has been piloting the Liz 79 for about 40 years, were among the first men to explore deep space, suggesting this is early in Man's development of interstellar travel. Based on spaceship technology seen in other datable stories, this would place it around the 22nd or 23rd centuries.

▤ According to the camera script, the TARDIS's arrival was achieved by fading in an image of the 3-foot Police Box model over a shot of the empty beacon set.

PREVIOUS LANDINGS

SPACE Planet Fourteen
TIME Unknown (before 1970s)
TRAVELLERS The Doctor, Jamie, [unknown others]
EPISODES Mentioned by the Cyberplanner in The Invasion 2

While in his second incarnation, the Doctor, along with at least Jamie, encountered and resisted the Cybermen on a world they designate Planet Fourteen.

- **NOTES** Photos of both the Doctor and Jamie are recognised by the Cybermen, although they believe both men to be human. They are considered hostile and dangerous, so evidently caused the Cybermen some trouble. As the Cybermen have no access to time travel at this point, the encounter must have been before their attempted invasion of Earth aided by Tobias Vaughan (see Landing 63), although for the Doctor and Jamie it could have been after.
- If the Cybermen in *The Invasion* are an advance force from the approaching Mondas (still at least seven years from reaching Earth), might Planet Fourteen be a distant member of the Solar System which Cybermen from Mondas investigated on passing, only to be repelled by the Doctor? Indeed, David Banks' 1988 book *Cybermen* proposes Planet Fourteen was colonised by a group of Mondasians as their home world drifted away from the Sun and developed into a different form of Cybermen from those on Mondas, launching their own attacks on Earth in the 20th and 21st centuries.
- 'The World Shapers', a comic strip in issues 127 to 129 of *Doctor Who Magazine* (1987), suggested Planet Fourteen was an alien designation for Marinus, where the Voord evolved into a breed of Cybermen. While the Doctor confirms in *The Doctor Falls* that Cybermen did arise on Marinus, he cites this separately to those originating on Planet Fourteen, so the two cannot be the same.

SPACE Earth, Indonesia
TIME August 1883
TRAVELLERS The Doctor, [unknown companions]
EPISODES Recalled by the Doctor in Inferno 2

The Doctor heard a noise like the guttural growl made by Harry Slocum – the Inferno project engineer who touched slime from the bore hole and was transforming into a Primord – during the 1883 volcanic eruption of Krakatoa.

- **NOTES** As most of Krakatoa was obliterated when it erupted on 26/27 August 1883, one hopes the TARDIS hadn't landed on the island itself but in Java or Sumatra. Then again, the Doctor is surely not comparing Slocum's growl to the noise of the main explosion itself, which was loud enough to burst the eardrums of sailors 40 miles away. Perhaps the earlier eruptions drew up the same green slime which infected some of the islanders, whom the Doctor encountered.
- In *Rose*, Clive has a sketch that he claims washed up on the coast of Sumatra on the day Krakatoa exploded, showing the Doctor in his tenth incarnation standing before a smoking mountain. Although the drawing has 'August 26th 1883 Krakatoa erupts' written on it, that may have been added later after its discovery; who would stand around sketching while a volcano erupted before them? The volcanoes on the island were active and belching smoke as early as May so the Doctor could have visited weeks before the catastrophic eruption.

SPACE Earth, France, Paris
TIME [Mid-19th century to early-20th century]
TRAVELLERS The Doctor, [unknown companions]
EPISODES Claimed by the Doctor in Inferno 3

The Doctor formed a friendship with Prince Albert Edward, the future King Edward VII, while they were both in Paris.

- **NOTES** It's unlikely the Doctor befriended Bertie during one of the prince's many visits in mid-life to Paris's brothels, so it may have been when as a teenager he accompanied his parents on their state visit in 1855, or his own as king in 1903. However, perhaps their most likely time to meet was at the Exposition Universelle in May 1889 for the opening of the Eiffel Tower.

SPACE Earth, China
TIME [Early] 20th century
TRAVELLERS The Doctor, [unknown companions]
EPISODES Claimed by the Doctor in The Mind of Evil 2

The Doctor met Mao Zedong, "many years" prior to his time of exile on Earth, and was given permission to refer to him by his personal name.

- **NOTES** Assuming the Doctor isn't lying to ingratiate himself with the Chinese politician Fu Peng, his meeting with Mao Zedong must have been on fairly friendly terms. Given the Chinese premier's controversial reputation, maybe we shouldn't presume to judge the Doctor's choice of friends, although it's perhaps wiser to suppose he met Zedong in his youth. The early 20th century was a period of major upheaval for Chinese society, events the Doctor is likely to have been interested in witnessing, and may have tried to influence Zedong's thinking on how to modernise his country.

SPACE Earth, England, London
TIME [1592]
TRAVELLERS The Doctor, [unknown companions]
EPISODES Recalled by the Doctor in The Mind of Evil 5

The Doctor was imprisoned in the Tower of London during Elizabeth I's reign and met Sir Walter Raleigh there, who talked of his discovery of the potato.

◪ **NOTES** Raleigh didn't visit the Americas until late in the 16th century, having previously instigated and sponsored expeditions to the New World but remained himself in England and Ireland. It's possible colonists in the 1580s funded by Raleigh brought back the potato but it was already known of in Europe by then, so not a discovery as such. If so, the Doctor probably met him when imprisoned in the Tower in the summer of 1592 after the queen learned of his secret marriage a year earlier.

SPACE Earth, Europe
TIME Early-19th century
TRAVELLERS The Doctor, [unknown companions]
EPISODES Claimed by the Doctor in Day of the Daleks 1 and The Wedding of River Song

The Doctor met Napoleon Bonaparte and advised "Boney" that an army marches on its stomach. The general threw a bottle of wine at him.

◪ **NOTES** The Doctor's advice is, of course, popularly attributed to Napoleon himself although there is no evidence the French emperor ever said it. Some sources say it derives from the *Mémorial de Saint Hélène*, the memoirs of Napoleon dictated to his follower the Count de Las Cases while imprisoned on St Helena. However, the phrase doesn't appear verbatim in the *Mémorial*, which anyway is an unreliable record of Napoleon's actual words. The aphorism doesn't appear in print in English until 1904 in an edition of *Windsor Magazine*. The principle, that an army needs to be well fed in order to operate effectively, was well established anyway and not an insight exclusive to Napoleon; Frederick II, king of Prussia in the 18th century, is credited with the similar 'An army, like a serpent, travels on its belly'. It may be that the maxim became associated with Napoleon ironically, given his invading army's retreat from Moscow owing to lack of food in the harsh Russian winter. The Doctor's claim is almost certainly apocryphal, therefore, but if he did meet Napoleon it was more likely to have been during or after the Napoleonic Wars (1803-15), in the early years of which the British press coined the soubriquet 'Boney' (which became corrupted to Bogey and hence bogeyman).

◪ Napoleon featured in episode six of *The Reign of Terror*, although the Doctor didn't meet him then.

◪ In the Big Finish audio play *Mother Russia* by Marc Platt, Steven Taylor recalls the TARDIS landing in Russia in 1812. He, the Doctor and Dodo witnessed the French army's march on Moscow and saved Napoleon from an alien shapeshifter.

◪ In the BBC Books novel *World Game* by Terrance Dicks, the Doctor in his second incarnation meets Napoleon several times during his lifetime. He even impersonates Bonaparte in order to ensure the correct outcome at the Battle of Waterloo.

◪ The bottle incident may have been a separate encounter, although by the time the Doctor opens it at Lake Silencio it's encrusted with dust so could have been in his possession a long time.

SPACE Earth, England, London
TIME 15 January 1559 and/or 28 June 1838
TRAVELLERS The Doctor, [unknown companions]
EPISODES Mentioned by the Doctor in The Curse of Peladon 1

The Doctor was in attendance at the coronation of either Elizabeth I or Victoria. Although unsure at first, he seems to later decide it was Victoria's but may have been to both. He has not seen a coronation since.

◪ **NOTES** When Jo suggests watching Queen Victoria's coronation as they will have to miss King Peladon's, the Doctor decides that was the one he previously attended (so not Elizabeth's). However, he quite happily agrees to go again, which surely he would know might be dangerous if he's already been there in an earlier incarnation, so perhaps he's just joking about having "already seen" it (or he's still mixing it up with Elizabeth's). Then again, he clearly expects the Time Lords to "whip us straight back to Earth" so is probably just having a laugh with Jo anyway (although see Landing 83 for why this might not happen).

SPACE Earth
TIME Late-18th/early-19th century
TRAVELLERS The Doctor, [unknown companions]
EPISODES Claimed by the Doctor in The Sea Devils 1

The Doctor was a personal friend of Horatio Nelson, who was one for taking necessary action rather than waiting for orders.

◪ **NOTES** Assuming the Doctor isn't exaggerating to intimidate Captain Hart, he could have met Nelson at any time during the British Navy officer's lifetime and become friends with this charismatic and daring seaman.

◪ In Terrance Dicks' novel *World Game*, the Doctor during his second incarnation meets Nelson in London in September 1805 and saves both him and the Duke of Wellington from being killed by a bomb planted by time-meddling immortals.

SPACE Unnamed planet
TIME Unknown
TRAVELLERS The Doctor, Jamie, Zoe
EPISODES Glimpsed in The Three Doctors 1

The Doctor is on the run through billowing smoke when he is lifted from his time-stream by the Time Lords to assist his future incarnation combat a force draining their energy into a black hole. After that issue is resolved, he is returned to his own time.

◪ **NOTES** The Doctor's extraction from his time-stream occurs sometime after the events of *The*

Invasion (Landing 63) as he recognises Benton and says, "I haven't seen you since that nasty business with the Cybermen." From that time to his capture by the Time Lords he's travelling with Jamie and Zoe, but he appears to be taken mid-adventure so presumably they're just elsewhere. This could be during an unseen adventure or, at a pinch, a televised one – perhaps when the Doctor's running to the weather control bureau in *The Seeds of Death*; the smoke in the background could be the Martian fungus. He's calm and collected when he arrives and isn't anxious about the situation he's left behind, but then he has clearly been briefed by the Time Lords on the way so must know that they'll send him back to complete whatever he was doing.

SPACE Metebelis Three, Acteon group
TIME Unknown
TRAVELLERS The Doctor, [unknown companions]
EPISODES Recalled by the Doctor in Carnival of Monsters 1

The Doctor visited Metebelis Three, "the famous blue planet of the Acteon group", at some point before his exile on Earth. The air there smells like wine.
- **NOTES** Acteon is probably a solar system or group of nearby systems. It's often cited as a galaxy, but this term is coined by Jo – "The Acteon galaxy you said, Doctor?" (well, no, he didn't actually). True, the Doctor uses the word himself in episode four, but he has just escaped from the Miniscope so may still be a little dazed.

SPACE Earth, America, [Massachusetts]
TIME Late-19th century
TRAVELLERS The Doctor, [unknown companions]
EPISODES Claimed by the Doctor in Carnival of Monsters 2

The Doctor was given boxing lessons by bare-knuckle heavyweight champion John L Sullivan.
- **NOTES** If the Doctor is not bluffing to put off his opponent, he perhaps got a few tips from Sullivan while at the peak of his career in the late-1880s after winning fights against Charley Mitchell and Jake Kilrain. Neither the Doctor nor Andrews understands the Queensberry rules they invoke, however, as these stipulate the use of gloves.

SPACE Unknown
TIME Unknown
TRAVELLERS The Doctor, [unknown companions]
EPISODES Recalled by the Doctor in Frontier in Space 2

The Doctor was once captured by Medusoids – "A sort of hairy jellyfish with claws, teeth and a leg" – while on his way to the Third Intergalactic Peace Conference. The Medusoids interrogated him to learn where he was going but released him after they ran out of mind probes, which kept failing because his description of the delegates he was meeting – "a giant rabbit, a pink elephant and a purple horse with yellow spots" – was true but so bizarre they could not accept it.
- **NOTES** This story is almost certainly made up by the Doctor to put Jo at ease about being subjected to a mind probe. At best his description of the delegates is disingenuous: while some aliens in *Doctor Who* have resembled Earth animals, none has been so garish as the Doctor's descriptions here.

SPACE Draconia
TIME Mid-21st century
TRAVELLERS The Doctor, [unknown companions]
EPISODES Discussed by the Doctor and Draconian Emperor in Frontier in Space 5

The Doctor landed the TARDIS on Draconia during the reign of the 15th emperor and helped save the planet from a space-borne plague. The emperor ennobled him in gratitude.
- **NOTES** This was 500 years before the events of *Frontier in Space* (Landing 93).

SPACE Earth, Egypt
TIME Mid-1st century BC
TRAVELLERS The Doctor, [unknown companions]
EPISODES Mentioned by the Doctor in The Masque of Mandragora 3

The finest swordsman the Doctor ever saw was a captain in Cleopatra's bodyguard, from whom he learned some pointers on how to fight.
- **NOTES** It's likely the Doctor means Cleopatra VII, the last ruler of the Ptolemaic Kingdom of Egypt, as she's by far the most famous.
- Although this landing is only confirmed as being before *The Masque of Mandragora* (Landing 123), it's probably much earlier as the Doctor was first seen to be an effective swordsman in *The Sea Devils* (although he was capable of holding off an attacker in *The Crusade*). He further demonstrates his sword skills in *The Time Warrior*, *The Androids of Tara*, *The King's Demons* and *The Christmas Invasion*.

SPACE Unknown
TIME Unknown future
TRAVELLERS The Doctor, [unknown companions]
EPISODES Mentioned by the Doctor in The Five Doctors and Attack of the Cybermen 1

The Doctor encountered Zodin, known as 'the Terrible'. She was a cunning hairy creature that hopped around like a kangaroo.
- **NOTES** The Doctor first mentions Zodin when reminiscing with the Brigadier before realising his friend wasn't involved in the confrontation as it was in the future. He later mistakes Peri for Zodin after his fifth regeneration and calls her "a woman of rare guile and devilish cunning".

LANDING 68

SPACE Unnamed planet, facsimile of First World War battlefield
TIME Unknown future
TRAVELLERS The Doctor, Jamie, Zoe
EPISODES The War Games 1, 9-10

The TARDIS lands among the debris of what seems to be no man's land during the First World War on Earth. The Doctor and Zoe are amused as Jamie is first to step out into the mud. They climb to higher dryer ground and find rolls of barbed wire and an infantryman's tin helmet. A barrage of shell and machine-gun fire sends them diving into a crater. Once it has passed, they are spotted by passing British ambulance driver Lady Jennifer Buckingham, but before they can even think of returning to the TARDIS all four are captured by German soldiers and taken in the ambulance towards their lines.

In fact this is an alien planet where multiple battlegrounds are populated by soldiers from different periods in Earth's history, separated by mist-like forcefields. Space-time machines similar to the TARDIS have been used to transport them here but their function is almost exhausted and to return everyone home the Doctor is forced to contact his own people for help.

Keen to escape before the Time Lords arrive, the Doctor hurries Jamie, Zoe and Lieutenant Carstairs back to the 1917 Zone, where the sounds of fighting have already stopped. The Doctor says a quick goodbye to Carstairs and heads down into the gully where the Ship stands. Zoe and Jamie bid farewell before following, only the latter noticing when the soldier fades away. But all three travellers find themselves struggling as they approach the TARDIS, their movements sluggish as time itself slows.

The Doctor reaches the Ship first and manages to get his key into the lock before succumbing, entreating his friends to concentrate and overcome the Time Lords' forcefield. Zoe slumps against the Police Box but Jamie pushes himself on and helps the Doctor open the door. They crawl inside. Even there the effect can be felt but the Doctor manages to close the doors, boost the power and dematerialise the Ship.

○ CONTROLS The Doctor closes the doors by flicking the switches at the bottom of panel A5 then operates the right-hand large slider, whether to increase the power and/or take off is unclear. On take-off the central column briefly oscillates before coming to rest until the Ship next starts to land again.

▮ LORE Under the influence of the Security Chief's interrogation machine, Zoe says TARDIS means Time And Relative Dimensions In Space.

▮ The Doctor stole the TARDIS in order to leave the Time Lords, his own people from whom he is now a fugitive.

▮ To the Doctor's knowledge, a TARDIS can't be remote controlled or have adjustable internal dimensions without reducing the life of the time control unit, without which it wouldn't be able to operate.

▮ NOTES Director David Maloney gives us one of the most stylish TARDIS materialisations ever, the Police Box appearing reflected in a pool of water, followed by a close-up of the travellers' feet as they step out into the mud. He mirrors this when the TARDIS departs, with a low-angle shot looking up at the Police Box against the sky. Both use the standard take-off sound effect.

▮ We're told the soldiers are kidnapped from Earth and brought to this planet to fight, but what about the environments of each zone? Did the War Lords scoop up great chunks of the landscape as well? The areas of each zone appear quite large. The 1917 Zone, for example, is big enough to encompass both British and German trenches and the officers' residences, which were usually several miles behind the front lines, while the American Civil War and Roman Zones cover large areas of countryside. Surely someone back on Earth would have noticed their disappearances. So did the War Lords create accurate replicas of each combat zone before depositing the kidnapped humans there to unwittingly continue their fighting? The soldiers appear to be individually hypnotised when they're seen being transported in Sidrats, so perhaps they were initially just let loose in an area of Earth-like countryside but perceived it as the battleground they were taken from. If that's the case, how long have they been fighting in the 1917 Zone that it already represents the desolate killing fields of Western Europe?

▮ The name Sidrat is only used once on screen (when the War Chief pronounces it 'side-rat'); otherwise they're referred to as space-time machines or, by the Doctor, TARDIS travel machines. When questioning Zoe, the Security Chief doesn't know what the term TARDIS means, although he is aware that the secret of space-time travel is known only to the Time Lords. He says the War Chief has told them how to operate the machines but not build them, while the War Chief tells the Doctor he brought the machines with him, calling them "a variation on the old models". It seems, then, that the War Chief stole several TARDISes and donated them to the War Lord but didn't tell his people what they're called, simply that they're space-time capsules.

▮ He also hasn't told them that by adding remote control and dimensional flexibility he has limited the lifespan of their time control units. "In my day," the Doctor says, this problem was impossible to solve, although later even his TARDIS is seen to operate via remote control so a solution must have been discovered since he began his travels. What use dimensional flexibility has anyway isn't clear – perhaps the War Chief planned to take over after disposing of the War Lord by squishing him. The Sidrats are bigger on the inside like a TARDIS but appear to have no console, just a panel of controlling 'circuit rods' by the door (even though the Doctor calls it only "a slightly different design to the TARDIS"). They also don't utilise any kind of camouflage (which surely would be useful, given the apparent need to hypnotise any human who accidentally sees one) so presumably they don't have

chameleon circuits or perception filters. In fact, they seem quite basic compared to the Doctor's TARDIS: did the War Chief not want to give away too much sophisticated technology, or did he actually steal some old TARDISes that were waiting to be scrapped?
- The Doctor says the Sidrats are "impregnable against outside attack" to which Jamie replies, "You mean like the TARDIS?" – a different attitude from when the Ship was being buried in lava on Dulkis (see Landing 60).
- The materialisation sound of the Sidrats uses the familiar TARDIS grinding speeded up and mixed with the rising warble from later in the full take-off sequence.
- Here the TARDIS control room doors open with the same sound as those of the Dalek city on Skaro in *The Daleks*, perhaps because this effect has been used for the Sidrat's doors throughout the serial.

LANDING 69

SPACE Unnamed planet
TIME Unknown
TRAVELLERS The Doctor, Jamie, Zoe
EPISODES The War Games 10

As the TARDIS moves on, the Doctor explains the Time Lords are after him because he ran away from his home world out of boredom, fed up with their refusal to use their great powers – like near immortality and space-time travel – to help others and instead merely observe and gather knowledge. He preferred to explore the universe, although he does admit he tends to get into trouble, something else the Time Lords cannot forgive. As he talks he sets the controls for a distant planet on the edge of the galaxy, but the Ship begins to land sooner than expected.

Materialising in the air above a shallow sea, the TARDIS descends to rest on the surface. Zoe is confident it will float but it soon sinks. On the scanner, tropical fish swim past then scatter as a shark darts through the water.

The TARDIS shudders and the engines groan, and when Zoe notices water dripping onto the console the Doctor realises the Time Lords are attacking its defences and hurriedly takes off again.

- **CONTROLS** When discussing his past, the Doctor adjusts switches on panel A6, all three black dials on the left of panel A1 (as well as fiddling with the bottom lightbulb), and switches at the bottom of panel A2 (some of which turn on four of the lightbulbs above them and the lights of the left-hand rotating-light unit; he later turns some of these off again). He also flicks the switch at bottom-right of panel A1, which turns on the lightbulb immediately above it. Before taking off the Doctor flicks switches on panel A5, then operates the small levers and reaches over to panel A4, moving either the right-hand rotary handle or the central large slider. Water drips onto panel A4.
- On panel A3, the glass cover on the left-hand gauge is badly cracked. The holes at the top of panels A1 and A6 where grilles should be have been partially covered with white tape, while the grille on panel A5 now has a black border like those on the remaining three panels. Also on panel A5, the extra toggle switch used in *The Mind Robber* (Landing 60) has gone but the two white connectors for the emergency unit are still present. The inner structure of the central column is missing on of the black-and-white squares at the top.
- **NOTES** The control room is the largest it has been in quite some time, perhaps intended as a valedictory appearance given the Doctor's impending exile. Next to a single wall of back-lit indented roundels is a photographic wall, positioned on its side. Most impressive is the new computer bank/fault locator wall. This is a reconstruction as the original was long gone – last seen in *The Tomb of the Cybermen* (Landing 51), in photographic form, and before that at the end of *The Celestial Toymaker* (Landing 37) – but the arrangement of panels and lights is pretty much the same, and the layout of metal strips gives a sense of the scanner framework that used to stand in front of the computer bank. Even some familiar bits of furniture reappear: the wooden Knossos chair, studded armchair and armillary sphere (although on a new tapered square plinth).
- The arrival of the TARDIS onto the sea reuses footage from *Fury from the Deep* (Landing 58).

LANDING 70

SPACE Deep space
TIME Unknown
TRAVELLERS The Doctor, Jamie, Zoe
EPISODES The War Games 10

Hoping to be untraceable in its vast emptiness, the Doctor materialises the TARDIS in deep space. However, a Time Lord voice demands he return to their home planet and face judgement for his actions. It advises cooperation and the Doctor seems to acquiesce but then dashes around the console to make a quick transference jump.

- **CONTROLS** The Doctor hurriedly adjusts controls on all six panels.
- **NOTES** The materialisation in space reuses footage from *The Web of Fear* (Landing 56), cutting away before too much of the covering web appears.
- The Time Lords use the term TARDIS unprompted but only refer specifically to the Doctor's machine as "the TARDIS". However, earlier the War Chief recognises it as "a TARDIS" implying there are others.

LANDING 71

SPACE Unnamed planet [Earth]
TIME Unknown
TRAVELLERS The Doctor, Jamie, Zoe
EPISODES The War Games 10

As the TARDIS makes a swift relocation, the scanner shows crocodiles thrashing in water. But before the Doctor can dematerialise again the Time Lords take control of the Ship. The travellers are thrown to the floor as the room shakes violently. The Doctor reaches for the console to try to override the power but the controls do not respond.

- **CONTROLS** The Doctor pulls on the right-hand large slider on panel A5 as the TARDIS lands. When it takes off again, the same control keeps springing up when the Doctor tries to pull it down.
- **NOTES** As the Doctor makes a hurried relocation, the materialisation sound flutters and changes speed. This was later reused with added explosion noises for the failed dematerialisation in *Spearhead from Space* (Landing 73).

LANDING 72

SPACE Gallifrey, [Citadel], landing bay
TIME Unknown
TRAVELLERS The Doctor, Jamie, Zoe
EPISODES The War Games 10

The TARDIS finally comes to rest as the Time Lords bring it back to their planet. The scanner initially appears to be broken but slowly the image resolves into a TARDIS landing bay and the Time Lord voice informs the Doctor his travels are over. Jamie suggests trying to escape again but the Doctor is resigned to facing his people and leads his friends out of the Ship. They are greeted by a black-and-white-robed Time Lord who leads them away to the courtroom.

While the Doctor stands witness to the War Lord's trial, two technicians enter the TARDIS and assess the console. The sound of a Sidrat arriving draws one of them outside, where he is gunned down by the War Lord's troops. The sound of gunfire brings out the other technician and he too is shot. The troops rescue the War Lord, who has the Doctor and friends taken hostage, forcing them into the TARDIS and threatening Zoe's life if the Doctor does not take him to his home planet in galactic sector 973. The Doctor tricks them, however, by turning the lights up to full brightness, dazzling the spectacle-wearing aliens. The travellers dash out of the Ship but when the War Lord and his troops follow they are encased in a forcefield by the Time Lords and dematerialised out of existence as punishment for the war games. Hoping they can now leave, Jamie and Zoe find themselves held by the forcefield while the Doctor is returned to the courtroom to face his own trial.

While the Doctor's plea is considered, a Time Lord releases Jamie and Zoe and informs them they are to be returned home to their own times. They insist on seeing the Doctor and the Time Lord escorts them to him.

In one last escape bid, the three travellers make it back to the TARDIS in the landing bay but are met by Time Lords who inform them it is time for the Doctor's friends to say goodbye. He shakes them by the hand and watches sadly as they enter the Sidrat to be taken home, although they will each be left with the memory of their first encounter with him. The Time Lords lead the Doctor away to face his sentencing.

- **CONTROLS** Zoe turns on the scanner (even though they have just been looking at it) with the far-left switch at the bottom of panel A5. The main doors open without anyone touching the console, presumably activated remotely by the Time Lords. The technicians examine the upper and underside of panel A2. The Doctor pushes the two left-most small levers on panel A4 to turn the control room lights on full.
- **NOTES** Gallifrey is not named in this story, only referred to as the 'home planet'.
- The capsules in the landing bay on Gallifrey have the same shape and outward-sliding entrances as the Sidrats, but are a lighter colour, suggesting this is the uncamouflaged form of this model of TARDIS.

PREVIOUS LANDINGS

SPACE Earth, England, UNIT headquarters, grounds
TIME [Mid-1980s]
TRAVELLERS The Doctor
EPISODES The Five Doctors

Having seen a copy of *The Times* newspaper reporting on retired Brigadier Lethbridge-Stewart's speech as guest of honour at a Ministry of Defence gathering, the Doctor popped back to the day of the speech to see his old friend. He landed in the grounds of UNIT's UK headquarters and blustered his way past security.

The Doctor was just about to take his leave of the Brigadier when they were both taken out of time by the Time Scoop.

- **NOTES** This appearance is notorious for having the Doctor aware of the outcome of his trial by the Time Lords seemingly before it has happened. He is still in his second incarnation yet knows that Jamie and Zoe had their memories of their travels with him erased. This, and this incarnation's appearance in *The Two Doctors* (see below), has led to the theory that somehow the Doctor evaded immediate exile to Earth and was used for a time as an agent of the Time Lords. Certainly there's no point during his second incarnation when he's travelling alone, as he seems to be here – if Jamie were with him he'd surely want to meet the Brigadier again too. If he is currently working as an envoy of the Time Lords (no doubt reluctantly), perhaps what he means by "for once I was able to steer the TARDIS" is that he has managed to get where he wants to go, not where he has been directed. It would explain why he can't stay long.
- Curiously, he also remembers battling Omega, yet clearly has no memory of confronting Borusa when

in his first incarnation, and has forgotten both encounters again when he re-experiences them in his third incarnation. It's generally assumed that adventures involving multiple incarnations of the Doctor are somehow erased from his memory afterwards – at least for all but the most recent incarnation involved – so that he can't know his own future. This is usually attributed to whatever time manipulations were required to bring them together in the first place. However, in *The Two Doctors* this incarnation's encounter with the Sontarans is forgotten by the time of his sixth incarnation even though they just happened to cross each other's paths without any temporal juggling. This suggests the memory loss is a function of regeneration and that the Doctor remembers meeting his future selves up until he turns into one of them.

- Presumably Rassilon returns the Doctor and Brigadier to a moment after they were snatched by the Time Scoop. They appear to leave the ex-president's tomb in a temporally fused TARDIS but this may be an illusion (see Landing 244).

SPACE Earth, America, Florida, Miami Beach
TIME [Late-20th/early-21st century]
TRAVELLERS The Doctor, [unknown companions]
EPISODES Seen in The Name of the Doctor
The Doctor was unknowingly witnessed by Clara Oswald as he ran along the beach front.
- **NOTES** This may have been around the time he visited the retired Brigadier as he looks the same age and is wearing his big fur coat (in Miami!).

SPACE Earth, France, Paris
TIME After 1890
TRAVELLERS The Doctor, [unknown companions]
EPISODES Mentioned by the Doctor in
The Two Doctors 3
The Doctor visited the French capital and ate pressed duck at the Tour d'Argent restaurant.
- **NOTES** While the restaurant is older, pressed duck only became a speciality under owner Frédéric Delair at the end of the 19th century. This must therefore be a separate visit to those in Landings 9 and 33. It could have been an unplanned landing before the Doctor was put on trial, or intentional if he was subsequently relieved for a time.

SPACE Space, Third Zone, near space station Camera
TIME [1980s]
TRAVELLERS The Doctor, Jamie
EPISODES The Two Doctors 1
The TARDIS hovered in space beyond the detection beams of the space station where a time-travel capsule was being developed by scientists Kartz and Reimer. Their tests had already registered 0.4 on the Bocca scale and the Time Lords feared they could unravel the fabric of time. They sent the Doctor to negotiate an agreement to have the technology examined. He and Jamie observed the station on the scanner, having dropped off Victoria to study graphology. The Doctor was affronted to find a Stattenheim teleport control had been added to the console, enabling the Time Lords to co-pilot the TARDIS. However, he decided to land discreetly on the station to avoid any clamour for autographs from the assembled scientists.

SPACE Space station Camera, kitchen
TIME As above
TRAVELLERS The Doctor, Jamie
EPISODES The Two Doctors 1
The Doctor consequently landed the TARDIS in the station kitchens and took the Stattenheim's recall disc with him. Head chef Shockeye o' the Quawncing Grig was offended to have the Police Box cluttering up his galley but mollified when the Doctor revealed himself to be a Time Lord. Instead, on learning Jamie was human, the Androgum begged to buy him as he had never cooked an animal from Earth. As the Doctor hurried his companion towards station administrator Joinson Dastari's office they heard the TARDIS dematerialising, the Time Lords wary of leaving it on the station in case anyone should divine its secrets.

SPACE Earth, Spain, hacienda 4km from Seville, cellar
TIME As above
TRAVELLERS None
EPISODES The Two Doctors 3
Recalled by the Doctor's activation of the Stattenheim remote control, the TARDIS materialised in the cellar of the hacienda near Seville where Dastari and the Sontarans had taken the Time Lord to extract his symbiotic nuclei and get the Kartz-Reimer time machine working. But the module was now a wreck and outside were the disintegrated remains of the Sontarans' battle sphere (and Group Marshal Stike). Jamie bid a fond farewell to Peri before he and the Doctor took their leave of the latter's envious sixth incarnation.
- **CONTROLS** For the scene in the earlier Doctor's TARDIS, the panels and central column from console Ciii were used (luckily kept in storage after console E was introduced). The Doctor operates the scanner with a switch on the triangular plate on the left of panel C4 and sets the Ship in motion from panel C1. The Stattenheim remote is on the right of panel C5. The Doctor uses the large slider next to this (taken from panel C3) to rematerialise after applying a few drops of oil. He opens the main doors with the red-handled lever on panel C1.
- **LORE** The TARDIS can now be operated by remote control.
- **NOTES** *The Two Doctors* provides more evidence that the Doctor's second incarnation had further travels after the tribunal had supposedly exiled

him to Earth. Not only is he working for the Time Lords but even Jamie knows the Doctor is one of them. Arising simply from writer Robert Holmes misremembering (or not caring) that the Doctor didn't run missions for the Time Lords until his third incarnation, it's impossible to slot this adventure in among the 1960s stories. Even though the Doctor is travelling with Jamie and, we're told, Victoria, his confidence in being able to return to pick up the latter after her graphology studies goes against everything said about his ability to control the TARDIS in this incarnation. Jamie is also noticeably older which, while possible to disregard as a real-world factor rather than being a deliberate part of the fiction, does add weight to the suggestion that, for a time after the tribunal, the Doctor worked as a deniable agent for the Time Lords. Perhaps initially alone (as in *The Five Doctors*), he may have insisted on some company and so the Time Lords unblocked an older Jamie's memory and reunited him with the Doctor. Victoria seems an odd choice over Zoe so perhaps they simply met her again during an assignment on Earth and invited her to rejoin them. Could this be why the Time Lords appear to have suddenly added a dual-control to the TARDIS, to make sure the Doctor stays on mission rather than being tempted back into his nomadic lifestyle? It's unlikely he would stand for this so perhaps it's not long before the Time Lords realise they'll have to enforce the Doctor's regeneration and exile after all.

- Even though the console and control room walls were from the 1970s and 1980s respectively, Dick Mills used 1960s sound effects for the TARDIS in flight and stationary to help suggest these scenes were from the Doctor's second incarnation.
- As the scenes on Earth seem to have a contemporary 1980s setting, those on the space station must be the same because the Sontarans explicitly don't yet have the ability to time travel.
- The Doctor has met Dastari before at the inauguration of space station Camera, "bearing fraternal greetings from Gallifrey". This suggests it was before the Doctor went on the run; he says it was before he "fell from favour" and became "a bit of an exile", although this could arguably pertain to his tribunal (would Dastari necessarily have "heard something about" the Doctor's fleeing with his granddaughter?).
- It's possible, even likely, that the TARDIS dematerialising from the space station and arriving in the hacienda on Earth is the same journey. It's a time machine, after all, so however long the Doctor has been a prisoner of the Sontarans doesn't matter. And it's likely that the Time Lords would programme the remote control not to leave the TARDIS hanging around unattended.

LANDING 73

SPACE Earth, England, Essex, Oxley Woods; transported to London, UNIT headquarters
TIME [Mid-1970s]
TRAVELLERS The Doctor
EPISODES Spearhead from Space 1-4; The Ambassadors of Death 1

The Doctor's exile to Earth begins and the TARDIS lands in a woodland clearing near the Ashbridge Cottage Hospital, close to where 50 or so Nestene control spheres recently came down through a funnel of super-heated air. The newly regenerated Doctor stumbles from the Police Box and promptly collapses into the heather. He is found by UNIT soldiers, looking for what they believe to be meteorites, and taken to the hospital, while a corporal and private are posted to guard the TARDIS. They encounter local poacher Sam Seeley, who has found one of the 'meteorites' – actually a Nestene energy sphere – but he convinces them his bag contains only rabbits and they let him pass.

A few hours later, the Doctor evades a kidnapping attempt by Nestene facsimiles and tries to return to the safety of the TARDIS. Still disoriented and with his mouth gagged, however, he fails to respond when the guards on the Police Box challenge him and they shoot at him. His head is grazed by a bullet and he collapses again. With the Doctor back in hospital, Brigadier Lethbridge-Stewart has the TARDIS transported to UNIT headquarters in London.

On arrival it's deposited in the laboratory that has been set up for newly recruited scientific advisor Elizabeth Shaw. The Brigadier is unable to open it, however, even with the key he took from the Doctor. The Doctor arrives, having tracked the TARDIS using a wrist-worn homing device, but the Brigadier refuses to give him the key unless he helps discover what the 'meteorites' are.

While working with Liz, the Doctor convinces her that inside the TARDIS is equipment that could help them and that she might be able to get the key from the Brigadier. She successfully retrieves it and the Doctor enters the Police Box. The TARDIS engines begin to groan but then they grind to a halt and smoke seeps from the Ship. A coughing, shame-faced Doctor emerges and reveals the Time Lords have changed the dematerialisation code, disabling the TARDIS and trapping him on Earth.

Some time later, the Doctor removes the console from the TARDIS to work on it separately in his rooms at UNIT headquarters. Trying to reactivate the time-vector generator he gets himself and Liz caught in the time warp field, projecting them each a few seconds into the future.

◉ CONTROLS While talking to Liz about the console in *The Ambassadors of Death*, the Doctor operates switches at the bottom of panel A2; the upper rotary handles on panel A1; two switches at the bottom of panel A6 (which turn off some of the lightbulbs above them) and the lower-left rotary handle; the second- and third-from-left small levers on panel A5 and a switch (which turns on two of the lightbulbs above); the middle and right-most small levers on panel A4 (the first of which turns on the two top-most lightbulbs, the second the bottom-right bulb); a switch on panel A3 (which turns on the left-hand lightbulb next to it); and more switches on panel A2. After Liz disappears, he readjusts the top rotary handles on panel A1, one of the bottom-right switches and another control on the left. Finally he twists the top-right rotary handle on panel A1 again.

- All panels have been given matching dark grey grilles at the top. The missing left-most lightbulb on panel A5 has been replaced with the black dial from the bottom-left of panel A1, while a larger spherical lightbulb has been added to the top-right of panel A3.
- **LORE** The TARDIS being able to fit a large space into its small appearance – that is, being bigger on the inside than the outside – is for the first time attributed by the Doctor to its being "dimensionally transcendental". This seems to be more a sesquipedalian delineation than an explanation.
- **NOTES** *Spearhead from Space* takes place at least six months after *The Invasion* (Landing 63). In *Planet of the Spiders* the Brigadier recalls, "One time I didn't see him for months. What's more, when he did turn up he had a new face," suggesting less than a year goes by between *The Invasion* and *Spearhead from Space*. The first wave of Nestene spheres arrived six months previously, however, which must have been after the Cybermen's invasion attempt else they would probably have been dismissed as part of that attack. (Did the Nestene expect Earth to be weakened by the Cybermen's assault?)
- It's perhaps odd that the Time Lords exile the Doctor to Earth but leave him the TARDIS as well. Even though he can't operate it, they must know its presence will give him cause to try: are they just taunting him with his imposed ignorance? Or are they acknowledging that the Ship is as much to blame for taking the Doctor places where he was bound to interfere, and thus punishing it with exile also?
- The materialising TARDIS is the 12-inch model – still with white telephone plaque and St John Ambulance emblem – the inaccuracies of which are rather highlighted by immediately cutting to the full-size prop on location. The echoing materialisation sound effect first heard with Landing 60 is used. A new sound effect was created for the TARDIS later failing to take off, with the standard grinding sound changing speed and fluttering, although it seems to be a reworking of that used for Landing 71.
- One consequence of *Doctor Who* now being made in colour is that we get visual confirmation that the Police Box is indeed blue. To date it has only ever been mentioned in *The Chase* and *The Daleks' Master Plan*, and described as black in *The Ark*.
- The key only working for the Doctor, not the Brigadier, harkens back to *The Daleks* when Susan insisted only she not Ian could get into the Ship (see Landing 3). Later others were seen to open the door, even without the Doctor's consent, so it seems he initially made the lock simpler to use once he started having more travelling companions, but then tightened up security again at some point – perhaps when he repaired the lock after the Monk damaged it in *The Daleks' Master Plan* (Landing 31). Here the Doctor says it's fitted with a metabolism detector, the implication being the lock is tuned to his biorhythms. Either he later simplifies it again to allow others to enter or perhaps has it recognise their metabolisms too.
- When the Doctor makes his failed attempt to take off, the rear doors are open, presumably to allow Jon Pertwee to step out while smoke is pumped into the box. The arm of the visual effects assistant providing this is also glimpsed (although this wouldn't have been visible when the story was first broadcast; only thanks to the original film being scanned for the DVD release can the full picture now be seen).
- The intervening story, *The Silurians*, is the first of a mere handful of serials to feature no mention or sight of the TARDIS. Previously only *Mission to the Unknown*, the single-episode prelude to *The Daleks' Master Plan*, hadn't included the TARDIS or its occupants.
- *The Ambassadors of Death* provides our first view of the console in colour, and sadly it's looking rather drab. The panels are revealed to be a pale green (deliberately so as on black-and-white cameras this appeared white, whereas true white would have created glare) with mostly grey controls. Even those with some colour, like the lightbulbs, red rotary switch on panel A5 and the red and yellow knobs on the small levers, are muted.
- It's not explained how the Doctor gets the console out of the TARDIS but we know it's a standalone unit (see Landing 14). It can't have fitted through the Police Box doors (unless he adjusted the dimensional control first to shrink it). Could the answer lie in the time-vector generator he's trying to "reactivate". This suggests it has been disengaged, which it's said in *The Wheel in Space* "alters the size of the TARDIS. The inside becomes an ordinary telephone box again." We speculated under Landing 59 that this means the interior dimension is dislocated from the Police Box exterior, so perhaps if done properly (rather than in a rush, like last time it was removed) the console can be relocated to outside the Ship. This would provide a more obvious means for then reconnecting the interior and exterior of the TARDIS (although the Doctor manages it in *The Wheel in Space* seemingly without access to the console). So perhaps at this stage the Police Box is just an empty cabinet while the Doctor works on the console in more comfortable surroundings. Being separated from the TARDIS presumably limits the console's power reserves, however, which is why the Doctor subsequently uses the Inferno project's nuclear reactor.
- Then again, perhaps the ornate room in which we see the Doctor working on the console is actually a redecorated or alternative control room. It does hum, after all (although it's the same hum as heard in the UNIT lab in *Spearhead from Space*).

WHAT ARE ALL THESE KNOBS?

PANELS A
1970

When the TARDIS console was brought out of storage for use in *The Ambassadors of Death*, it hadn't been in a studio for eight months. As it was only required for one scene in this story, little work was done to smarten it up. The controls look much as they last appeared in *The War Games* (only in colour, of course). Panel 3 was still intact (see below) but with the right-hand gauge sitting proud and a new spherical lightbulb replacing the missing half-covered bulb in the top-right corner. The missing bulb on panel 5 was replaced with a black dial but the two controls below were still without handles. The central column was missing most of its inner structure, with just the outer ring on its supporting struts and the strips lights (now green rather than white).

As the console made a more significant appearance in the next story, *Inferno*, more effort went into making it presentable – to an extent. The workings of the central column returned but were in a very poor state, and the whole thing wobbled when the column was in motion. Some controls went unrepaired, such as the small levers on panel 1, but several new ones were added. On the same panel, the long-empty space below the two rotary handles was filled with a large black switch; on panel 2 a red square with two black buttons was added left of the row of lightbulbs, and a dial and gauge fitted either side of the top grille; and on panel 4 a square silver box was placed to the left of the centre large slider.

The biggest change was to panel 3. In the two months since *The Ambassadors of Death* episode one was recorded, the bulk of its controls were replaced by a large metal plate. On this were a few dials, a row of small lights and some flick switches. Some have linked the appearance of this plate to an anecdote about Jon Pertwee asking for the console to have some bits for him to tinker with and a stagehand taking to the prop with a hammer and smashing a large hole in it. This is actually a mix-up with a situation that happened with the replacement console the following year (see page 119) but clearly something happened to this panel for it to require such a major patch. With two large holes already for the circular gauges, and possibly another where the radiation meter sat, it could be that this panel was always weak and placing a metal plate over the top was a quick way to strengthen it.

Finally, to give the mostly grey controls some colour, lines of red tape were added to several panels connecting various switches, like a printed circuit board. Some were also labelled with stick-on letters. All these changes would influence the console's first replacement.

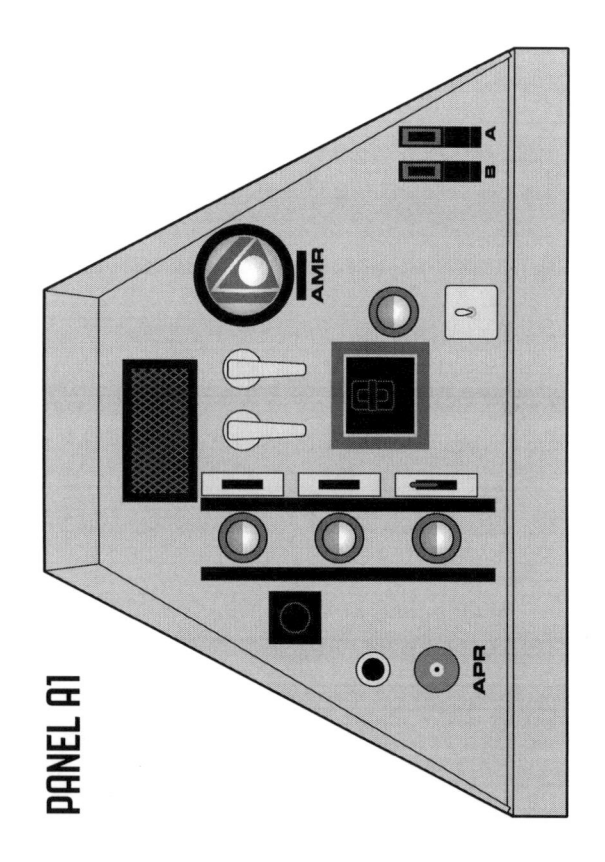

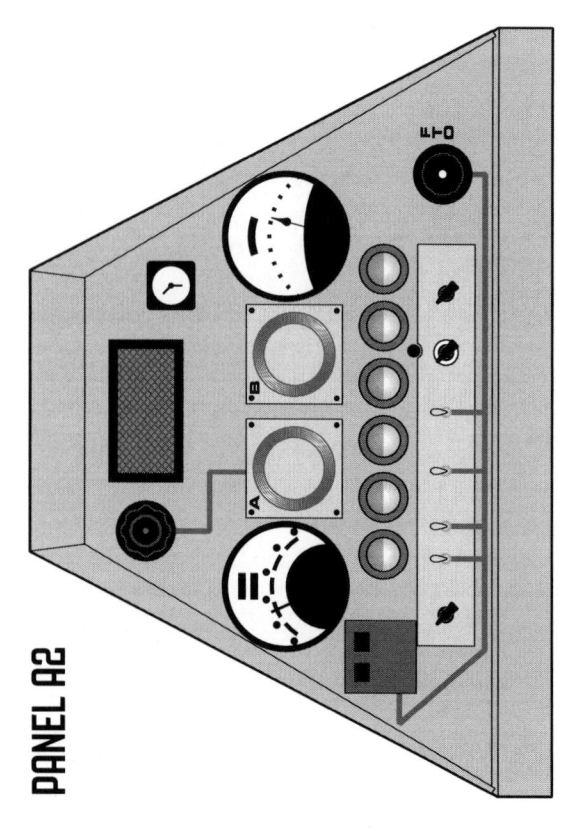

WHAT ARE ALL THESE KNOBS?

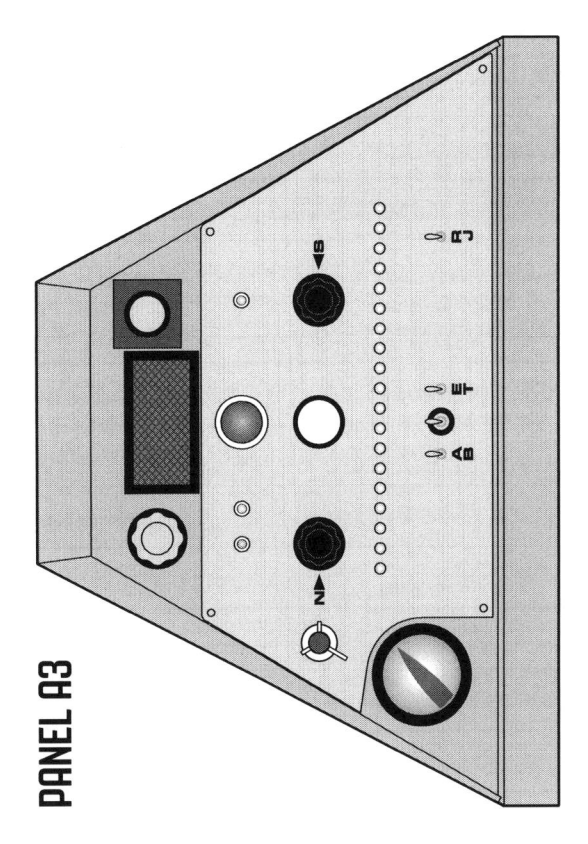

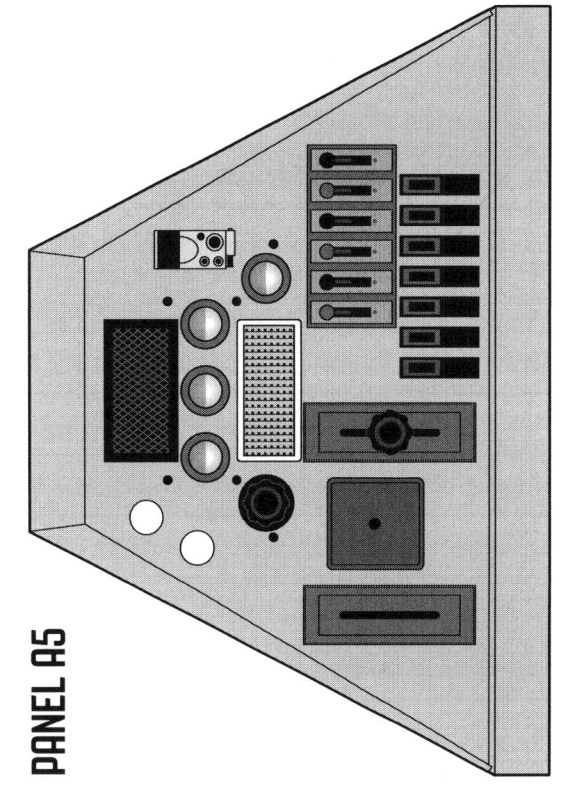

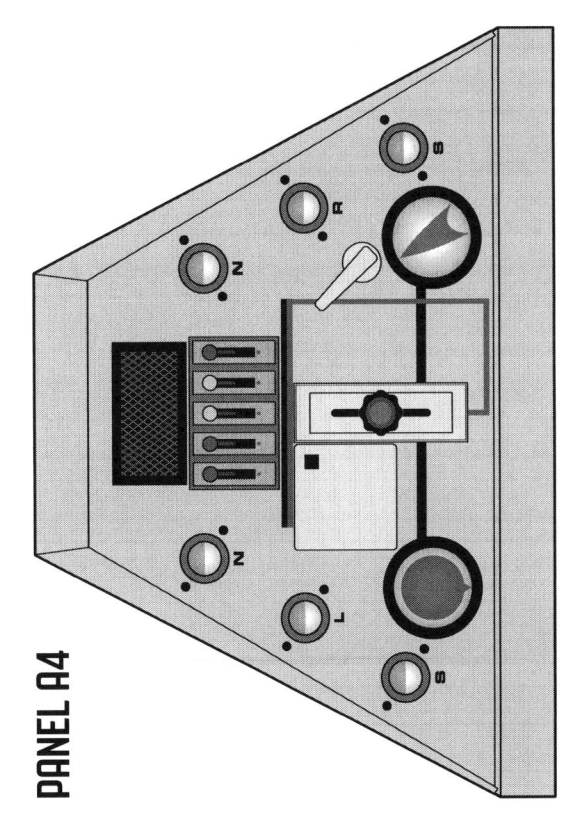

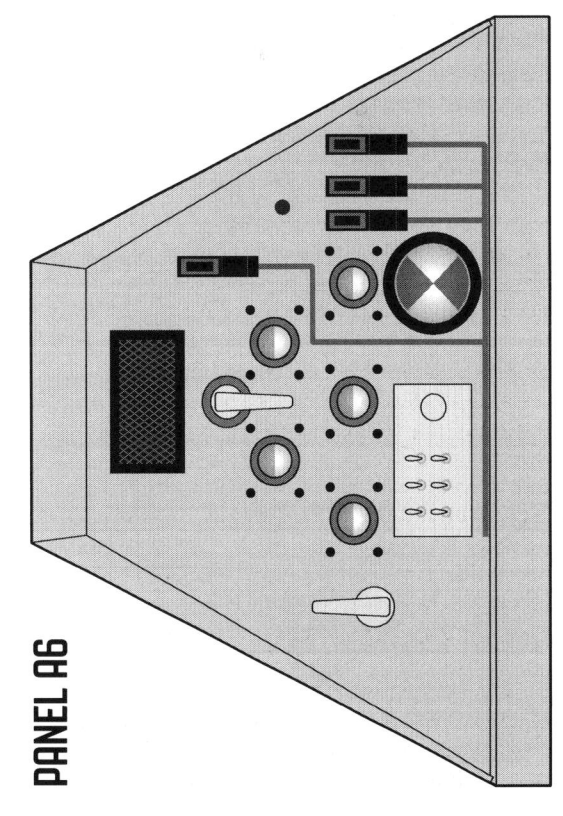

PANEL A3

PANEL A5

PANEL A4

PANEL A6

LANDING 74 console only

SPACE Earth, England, Eastchester, drilling complex, hut
TIME [Mid-1970s]
TRAVELLERS The Doctor
EPISODES Inferno 1

After further work on the console, the Doctor expresses an interest in advising on Professor Eric Stahlman's project to drill through the Earth's crust. Really it's an excuse to set up a small lab in a hut within the drilling complex, where the Doctor transports the TARDIS console and links it to the project's nuclear reactor, hoping to use its power to reactivate the console and escape his exile.

When he and Liz run their first test, however, the output of the reactor is ramped up by the infected technician Slocum and the Doctor loses control of the console. Both he and it disappear from the hut and are transported to a disorienting limbo.

Only when Liz succeeds, after some effort, in cutting the power do they return to the hut. The Doctor is intrigued by his experience and eager to replicate it but is interrupted by an alarm from the drill-head control area and they both go to investigate.

- **CONSOLE** The Doctor flicks one of the small levers on panel A5 when preparing to test the console, then the top three switches on the plate at the bottom of panel A6. As the console shakes he holds onto the top-right switch and bottom-left rotary handle on panel A6.
- **LORE** The console can travel on its own if given a sufficient input of power, although too much can push it into a parallel dimension.
- **NOTES** The location of the industrial complex where Stahlman's drilling project is taking place is named in a radio announcement in the parallel universe, although the scene was cut from the UK broadcast as it was too obvious the announcer's voice was that of Jon Pertwee.
- This is the first time the console is referred to as such on screen, by both Liz and later the Doctor. Previously it has been called the control column or just the controls.
- The limbo the Doctor finds himself in is presumably the same as the Void that he later claims separates parallel universes, as seen in *Rise of the Cybermen* (Landing 350, vol.2) and discussed in *Army of Ghosts*.

LANDING 75 console only

SPACE Parallel Earth, England, Eastchester, drilling complex, hut
TIME 23 July [mid-1970s]
TRAVELLERS The Doctor
EPISODES Inferno 2-3,5

Liz makes further repairs to the console while the Doctor resolves the reactor's power surge. When he returns to the hut he asks Liz to work out some calculations using the computer in central control. This is just a ruse, however, so he can run another trial with the console by himself. He resets the power feed and, just as a vexed Liz returns, the console, the Doctor and his car Bessie all dematerialise.

Stahlman cuts the power to the Doctor's hut, which forces the console to rematerialise. It seems to land in the same place it left, but all the Doctor's equipment has gone and a sign on the hut door says it is a technical store. The Doctor heads out in Bessie and soon discovers this is a parallel Earth where Britain is a republic governed by a military dictatorship.

Captured by Republican Security Forces under Brigade Leader Lethbridge-Stewart, the Doctor is unable to prevent Stahlman's drill penetrating this Earth's crust and unleashing horrendous forces. He tries to persuade Section Leader Shaw that if he can get back to his Earth he may be able to delay the project there, and agrees to show them how he arrived here. They are unimpressed by the console, however, so he uses the last of its stored energy for a demonstration. He shifts himself and the console a few seconds into the future, leaving the console's power reserves exhausted.

- **CONTROLS** Liz replaces a circuit in the pedestal under panel A6. After she has gone, the Doctor operates the rotary handles on panel A1, switches on panel A6, the right-hand large slider and several small levers on panel A5, and an unseen control on panel A4. As the console begins to shake he holds on to controls on panel A6 but by the time he dematerialises he is at panel A4. When showing the console to the Brigade Leader and Miss Shaw, the Doctor flicks small levers on panel A4, causing the central column to move. He operates them again and the large slider below to briefly dematerialise.
- **LORE** The grinding noise can still be heard when just the console dematerialises.
- The console has tri-gamma circuits and a storage unit to retain energy fed into it.
- The Doctor says he removed the console in order to "make some trial runs". It seems at this point that his inability to leave Earth in the TARDIS is simply a mechanical issue which the Doctor is confident of being able to repair. The implication is the console alone is the operative part of the TARDIS and that the control room and the rest of the Ship is merely a container for the comfort of travel.
- **NOTES** In the cut scene, a calendar on the Brigade Leader's desk shows the date. It's likely to be around the same time in the 'home' universe – it's suggested just the drilling is more advanced in the parallel universe rather than time being different.
- The console makes the familiar grinding noise when it moves ahead by a few seconds, so either that's not the sound of the TARDIS engines or they're contained within the console.
- The central column is really showing its age by now. Many of the perspex rings and rods inside are broken or missing, and the pneumatic mechanism for its rising and falling makes an audible hissing sound.
- When the Brigade Leader suggests the Doctor could take people from this Earth back to the one he came

from, the Doctor claims this "would create a dimensional paradox" and "shatter the space-time continuum of all universes". He doesn't seem that familiar with parallel universes yet so could be guessing, or just lying because he isn't keen on saving this Lethbridge-Stewart. When he discovers another parallel Earth while travelling with Rose Tyler and Mickey Smith, there's no problem with people crossing over, and Mickey even meets his counterpart Ricky. Although travel between universes causes dangerous fractures in the fabric of space-time, there's no apparent paradox resulting from the people themselves relocating.

LANDING 76 console only

SPACE Earth, England, Eastchester, drilling complex, hut
TIME As Landing 74
TRAVELLERS The Doctor
EPISODES Inferno 6-7

With the parallel Earth beginning to break up, the Doctor persuades the last few people at the drilling site to help him return to his Earth. He and Greg Sutton connect a cable from the nuclear reactor to the TARDIS console but then must wait for the power to be fed through.

When it does, the console begins charging but the Brigade Leader threatens to shoot the Doctor unless he take the others with him; instead Section Leader Shaw shoots him. The drill head explodes and magma erupts across the complex. As the Doctor struggles with the erratic power flow to the console, lava rolls towards the hut. At the last moment he manages to dematerialise.

The console, Bessie and an unconscious Doctor reappear in his hut, where Liz has been waiting for him. He remains in a coma for a short time but eventually awakens and learns that events have progressed slightly differently here, giving him hope the catastrophic outcome of the parallel Earth can be avoided.

- **CONTROLS** When preparing the console for the power feed, the Doctor operates unseen controls on panel A5. He then works under panel A3 and flicks switches on the same panel when trying to dematerialise.

LANDING 77 console only

SPACE Earth, England, Eastchester, drilling complex, dump; transported to UNIT headquarters
TIME As above
TRAVELLERS The Doctor
EPISODES Inferno 7

As the 'Inferno' project is wound down, the Doctor and Liz complete repairs to the TARDIS console. Before the nuclear reactor is fully dismantled, the Doctor plans to use it one last time to power the console and, he is confident, leave Earth. The Brigadier is dismissive, blaming the console for the Doctor's earlier disappearance in the middle of the crisis. The Doctor takes offence and decides to leave immediately. Switching through the feed from the reactor, he says a fond goodbye to Liz and has a few choice words for the Brigadier before he and the console vanish.

The journey is a short one, however, just a few hundred yards east of the hut, where the console reappears perched precariously atop a rubbish tip. The Doctor clambers down and heads back to the hut to seek help with recovering the console and returning it to his lab at UNIT headquarters.

- **CONTROLS** Liz adjusts the new switch on panel A1 with a screwdriver while the Doctor calibrates controls on panel A3. He turns a dial on the latter panel as the console dematerialises.
- **NOTES** This time the console disappears in an instant with no grinding sound, just a whistle, presumably indicative of its not working correctly after all.
- Although he says his goodbyes – or rather, burns his bridges – the Doctor is surely not planning to travel around the universe just clinging on to the detached console? He must intend to take a quick journey back to his lab at UNIT headquarters in order to return the console to the TARDIS shell and then make a proper getaway before the Brigadier and Liz can get back from Eastchester.
- This is the last appearance of the original TARDIS console in the series. Its fate is unknown but, bar the handful of controls that were cannibalised for its replacement, it was most likely scrapped.

IT LOOKS JUST LIKE A POLICE BOX

THE BRACHACKI BOX
1971-1975

Doctor Who's eighth season began in January 1971 with *Terror of the Autons*. Although the Police Box prop wasn't needed for the scenes filmed on location, it was taken along to the Roberts Brothers Circus on Friday 18 September 1970 for a photoshoot with the new regular cast. In these pictures the box is missing its base altogether but by the time it was required in studio on Saturday 10 October, for recording of episodes one and two, a new one had been fitted. This was narrower than before, little wider than the corner posts, but with a deeper skirting to hide the castors. The battens along the bottom of the side walls were removed, perhaps replaced by stronger fixings on the inside, although two large chips were now ominously visible at the bottom of the right-hand side – we'll keep an eye on those. The telephone cubbyhole had definitely been removed by this time as the left-hand door is wide open throughout *Terror of the Autons*, and a new roof has finally been made (which may have been detachable). This was wider so it would rest more comfortably on the walls but was still made square, which meant it created an overhang at the front because of the box's narrower sides.

The prop received a much-need lick of paint before production began on *The Curse of Peladon* in January 1972 as it had been looking very grey and speckled; its new blue was considerably lighter than previously, although this would darken over time. The roof lamp's cap and supports were painted black, as was the telephone plaque (traces of blue around the white lettering indicate just the surrounding areas were painted over). The new base gets some rough handling when the prop is rocked about on the cliff set in *The Curse of Peladon*, a close-up shot clearly showing a flexing gap between the base board and its skirting. This also reveals angle brackets of the kind used to support bookshelves now fixed the corner posts to the base.

SIGNS OF AGE

A close-up of the front 'Police box' sign in *The Mutants* episode one (recorded in February 1972) shows the lettering was becoming indistinct, either because the film over the acrylic had lost its adhesion or just from accumulated grime. By *The Time Monster* episode six (recorded three months later) the word 'Police' can be read but in another close-up in *Frontier in Space* episode one 'Box' can hardly be made out at all. In *Planet of the Daleks* episode one (recorded in January 1973) the front sign is clearer although not totally, suggesting its legibility was reliant on the studio lighting. Meanwhile, the left-hand side of the box lost its sign altogether. The lettering can be seen in *Spearhead from Space* but is not clear by *Colony in Space*, possibly due to the grubby condition of the box. After its redecoration prior to *The Curse of Peladon*, the left-side sign is not seen until *The Time Monster*. When the prop was taken on location on Thursday 6 April 1972 to film its recovery from a bomb crater, the acrylic insert on this side was removed so a wooden brace could be attached to assist with lifting the box upright. In subsequent studio scenes the sign has a pale insert with no evident lettering on it, suggesting the original was damaged or lost. That side of the box is rarely seen in later stories but when it is there appears to be no 'Police box' lettering. The sign on the right-hand side of the prop was therefore the sole remaining original from 1963.

Also noticeable from *The Time Monster* episode six is that the chips in the bottom rail on the right-hand side have become a large crack. This can still be seen in the next two stories produced – *Carnival of Monsters* and *Frontier in Space* – but by *The Three Doctors*, recorded in November 1972, it was covered by a plank across the full width between the corner posts up to the bottom of the lowest panel. A similar batten was added to the left-hand side, although not as tall, while the front of the base, where the skirting was detaching from the base board, was repaired (but began to split again by the following year).

LAST LEGS

The removal of the expanded foam stuck to the Police Box to represent the fungus in *Planet of the Daleks* left the prop in a poor state. Scrapes to the telephone plaque are noticeable from *The Green Death* onwards, particularly on the bottom-left corner, and the front doors were discoloured. This is evident in *The Green Death* episode one, especially the filmed sequences, but is very obvious in *The Time Warrior*, recorded two months later in May 1973. In fact the plaque is decidedly green and almost illegible, as if some genuine mould had infected the prop. This was cleaned up in the break before production restarted on the rest of Season 11. Design plans indicate the prop was to be repainted, the base re-clad with hardboard, the doors rehung, the window panes on the right side replaced and the 'Police box' signs repainted.

Right Refurbished Brachacki prop front elevation and section with new roof, base with brackets, and handles

IT LOOKS JUST LIKE A POLICE BOX

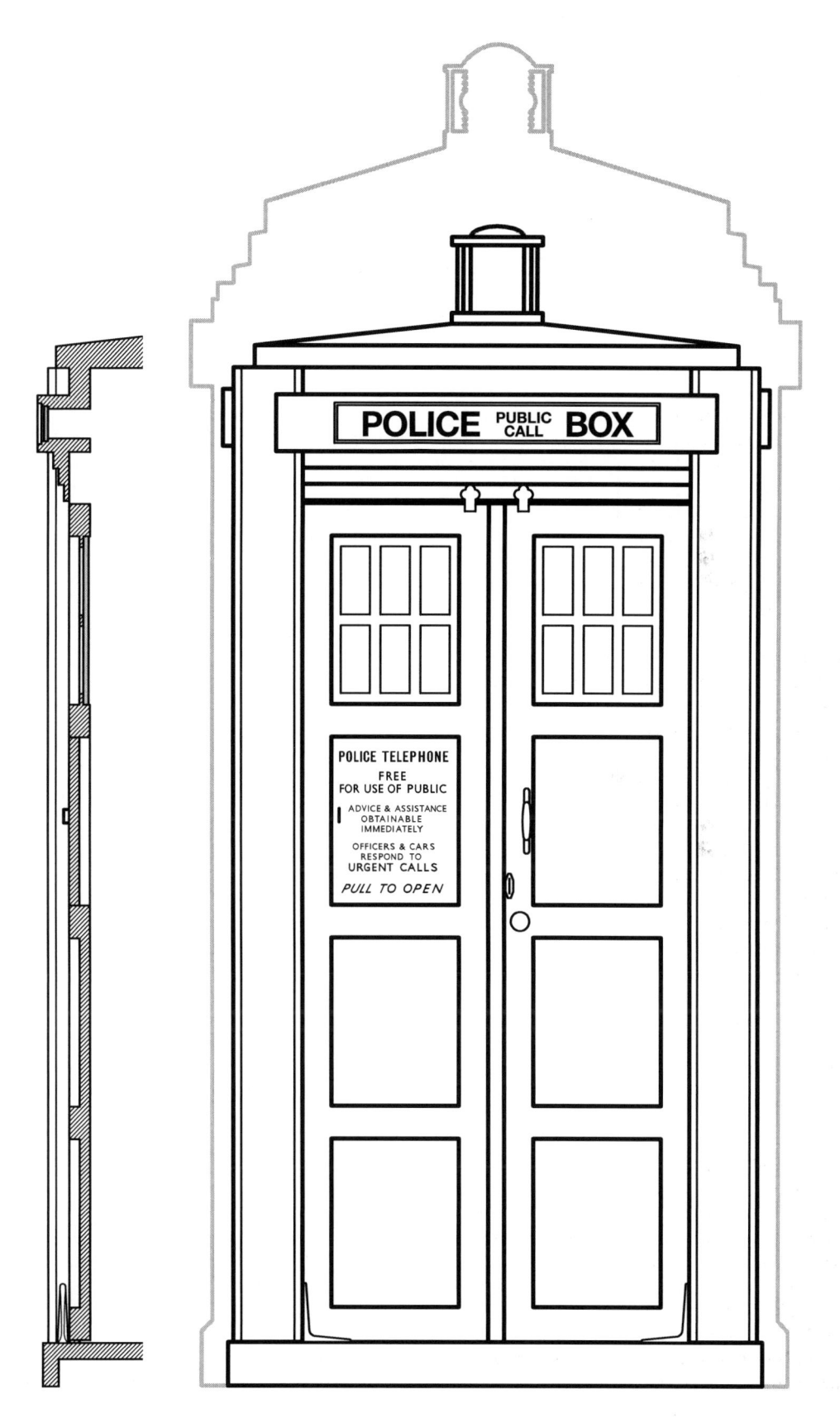

POLICE PUBLIC CALL BOX

POLICE TELEPHONE
FREE
FOR USE OF PUBLIC

ADVICE & ASSISTANCE
OBTAINABLE
IMMEDIATELY

OFFICERS & CARS
RESPOND TO
URGENT CALLS

PULL TO OPEN

IT LOOKS JUST LIKE A POLICE BOX

Above During Season 10 the right-hand side of the prop had cracks at the bottom covered by a plank the same thickness as the corner posts. A similar, shorter board was added on the left-hand side

In *The Time Warrior*, a new shield-shaped TARDIS key was introduced, proposed by Jon Pertwee with an eye to merchandising opportunities that never materialised (until fan-made replicas in the 1980s). A slot was made in the right-hand door for this, between the handle and the Yale lock (which had been painted over since the prop's last redecoration). The Police Box is not seen much in the rest of the 1974 season, and then usually on film or in low light, so it's not until *Planet of the Spiders* that we get clear views of it again. Ongoing wear and tear was evident: a crack in the box's left-side left-hand window and a break in its frame, one of the bars on the rear right-hand window was missing, the roof lamp had lost its cap and supporting rods, and the telephone plaque had lost its handle.

After being little used during the twelfth production block while the Doctor travelled via Time Ring, the prop was repainted again before recording began on *Pyramids of Mars* in May 1975 (in a darker, glossier blue) although the new paintwork was already chipped again by episode four – clearly the prop was never handled very gently. For *The Android Invasion*, filmed the following July, a metal surround was added to the slot previously made for the shield-shaped key, presumably to look better in close-ups when Sarah accidentally cancels the pause control, and the roof lamp was temporarily back to a round-capped lensed cover very much like the original. In *The Brain of Morbius* it returned to a plain cylinder, although with a new flat round cap (but no supporting rods).

The long-serving prop's final appearance was a brief scene at the end of *The Seeds of Doom*, recorded on location on Monday 8 December 1975, battered but perhaps no more so than might be expected for a time machine that had been bouncing around the universe for twelve years. Sadly it was no longer as strong as it looked and, famously, while Tom Baker and Elisabeth Sladen were waiting in the box for their cue to emerge, the roof fell in on their heads. To what degree this anecdote has been built up in the telling is uncertain but clearly it was time for the old prop to be retired and a new prop built for the following season.

The last known sighting of *Doctor Who*'s original Police Box was in a photoshoot by Douglas Morrison for the *Daily Express*, to accompany an interview with script editor Robert Holmes in its Friday 11 February 1977 edition. Seemingly taken in the BBC's prop store, Holmes is standing beside three Daleks while behind him a Dum robot emerges from the TARDIS. The box, unused for fourteen months, was in a sorry state, with peeling paintwork and splitting joints. The roof was missing, perhaps understandably, but so too were both windows on the right-hand side and the Police Box signs were in especially poor condition. It's perhaps surprising the prop survived at all by this stage, with a replacement already in regular use, and was likely scrapped shortly after (although rumours it was rescued persist).

WHAT ARE ALL THESE KNOBS?

CONSOLE B
1971–1974

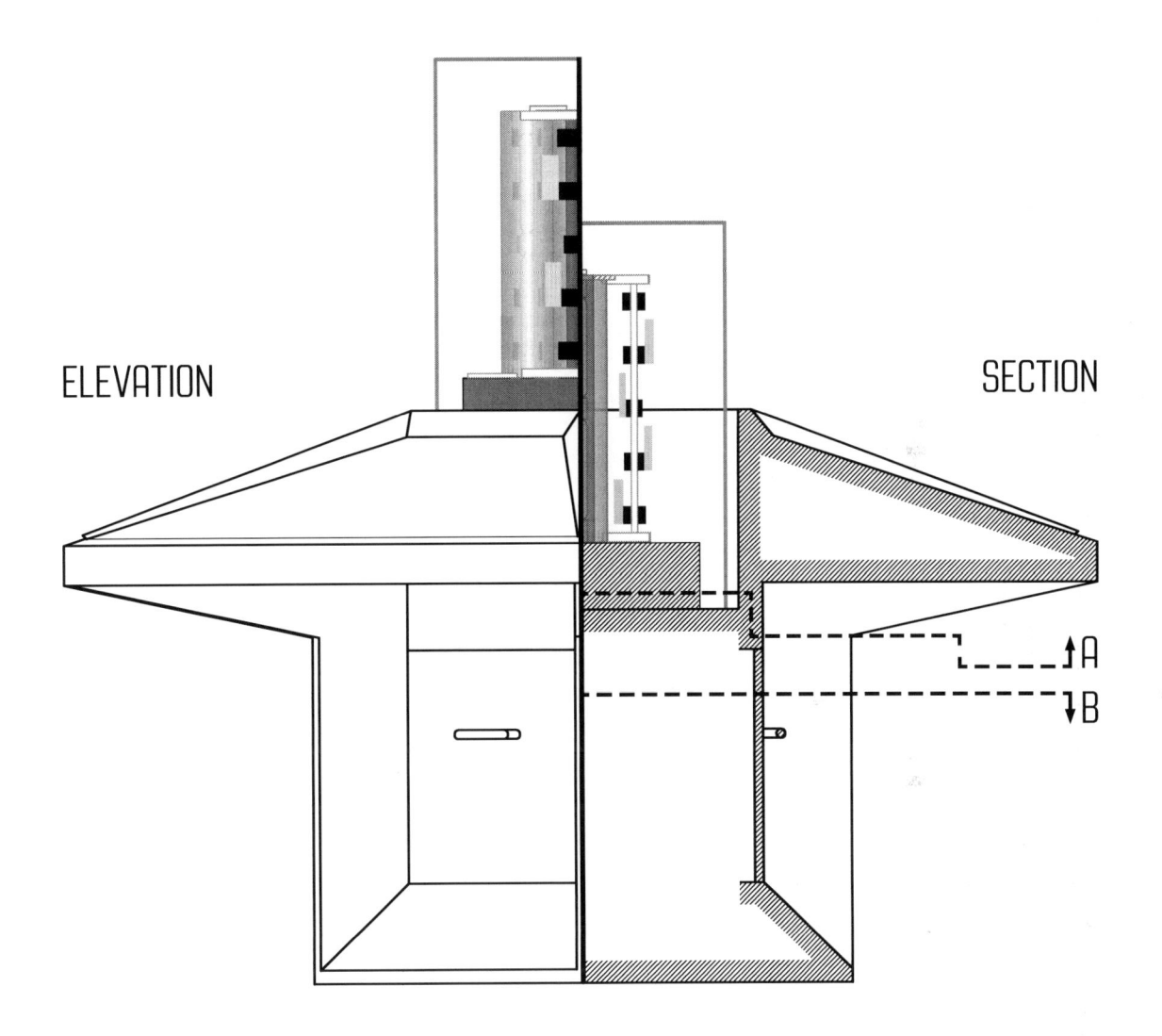

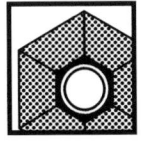

ELEVATION

SECTION

↑A
↓B

Having seen the state of the original console while standing in for director Douglas Camfield on *Inferno*, producer Barry Letts decided it was time for a new prop to be constructed. The opportunity arose later that year as the developing script for 'The Vampire from Space' (later retitled *The Claws of Axos*) included several scenes set inside the TARDIS. The story's designer, Kenneth Sharp, was therefore given budget to produce a new console for this and future serials.

The job was contracted to an outside company, Magna Models, run by Ted Dove, which mostly made resin model train and aircraft kits for experienced hobbyists but had produced display models for the Science Museum in London and spaceships for *The Space Pirates* (it later built the IMC Robot for *Colony in Space*). The new console was wider than the old by just a few inches but the same height, which meant the pitch of the panels was slightly shallower. The fins on the pedestal were flat rather than tapered like the original console's, so the inset panels were wider, and each had a D-shaped handle fitted horizontally near the top so they could be removed for access to the workings of the central column. On top, the tapered dividers between each control panel were now separate screw-on pieces to hide the framework supporting the panels themselves. These

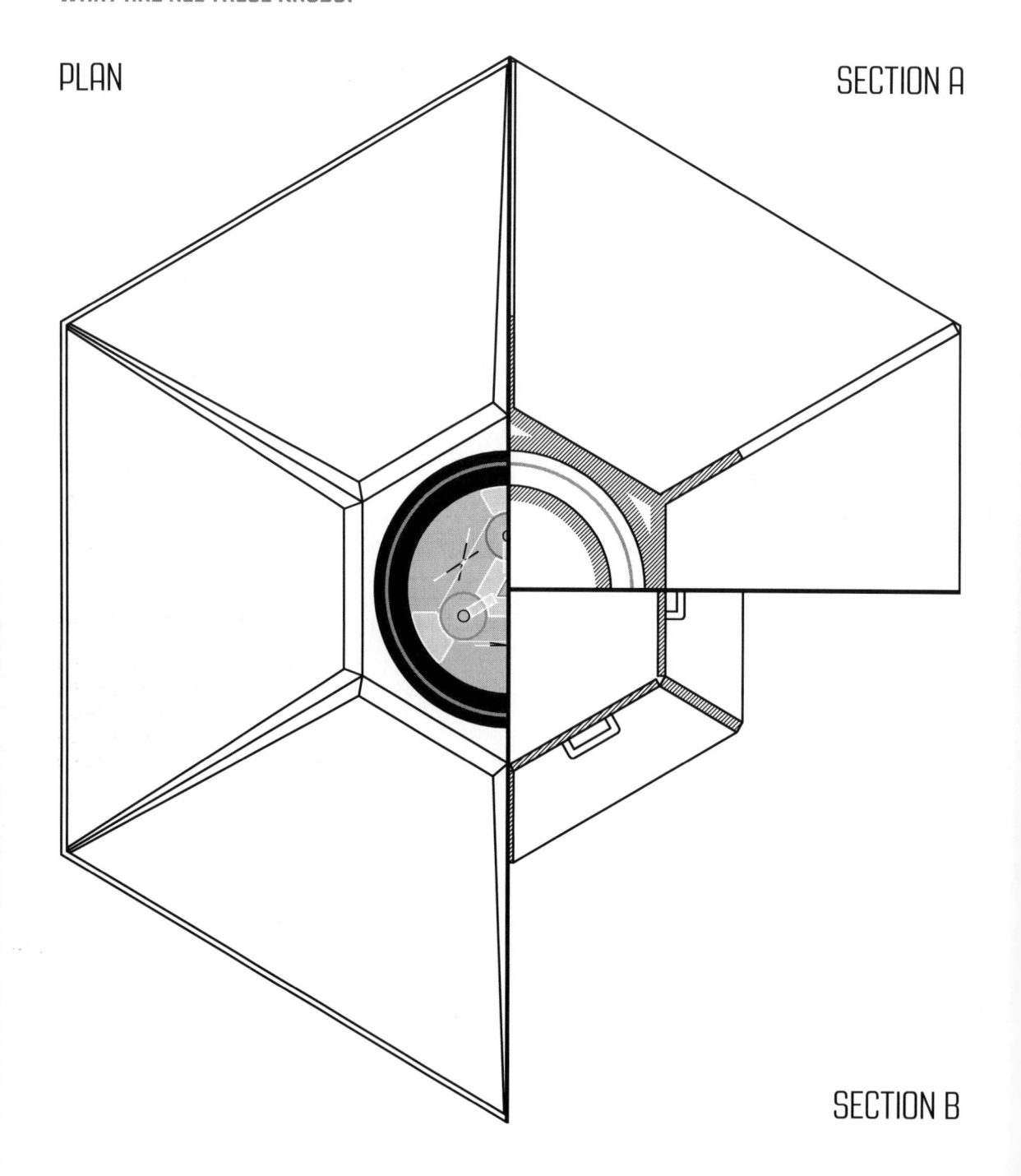

WHAT ARE ALL THESE KNOBS?

PLAN

SECTION A

SECTION B

could be removed for easier storage, while the bevelled collar around the central column was now formed of two sections. The whole console was again painted pale green, either just because it previously had been or because the majority of viewers in the early-1970s would still be watching on black-and-white televisions. The edges of the pedestal's fins and base were again covered with thin metal to protect them from knocks, as was the rim of the upper console.

As the complex arrangement of rods and rings within the original central column had more or less collapsed by the time of *Inferno*, its replacement was a simpler design. This comprised three green plastic tubes containing strip lights positioned around a pink triangular core, with translucent blue and yellow plastic blocks on three sides. The outer casing may have been remade or reused; either way it still had two seams down the sides, now covered by reflective metal strips, and was screwed to the top disc around its rim. A motorised cam mechanism was fitted that made it rise and fall but no longer rotate.

The layout and style of controls were based on the existing console, in its *Inferno* layout, and remained remarkably faithful. Some pieces were actually reused, such as the two large gauges and rotating lights on panel 2 and the illuminated discs. Even the metal plate that had lately been added to panel A3 was reproduced, rather than reverting to the more familiar look with the radiation meter. The new console also had connecting lines in red and black tape, and stick-on letters and numbers labelling various controls, as had been done for *Inferno*. One element not the same, although looking very similar, were the thin black switches. On the original console these had a sliding button on the upper sloped part; on the new console they were a solid moulding with a ridged mound that didn't actually slide. The silver rotary handles were also of a slightly different design. Two stickers bearing the Magna Models logo, address and telephone number were placed on panels 3 and 6.

One unusual new feature was the housing for the dematerialisation circuit on panel 6, featured several times during the console's first appearance in *The Claws of Axos*. This was not initially included – in episode three, as the Master tests the console, that top-left corner of the panel is seen to be empty – so the next day when episode four's TARDIS scenes were being rehearsed in the studio prior to recording, the director asked for the console to be amended with somewhere to place the demat circuit. Jon Pertwee was horrified by the cavalier manner in which a stagehand began smashing into his brand new console with a hammer and chisel, and remonstrated with the man (one account says a punch was thrown and the man needed medical attention but let the matter rest after an apology from the star). Still, a hole was made for the cylindrical housing and its surrounding plate. The latter didn't quite fit, however, and required notches to be cut around the top grille and top-left lightbulb.

The panels would be modified over the years, from minor decorative changes to complete replacement with brand new controls (giving the appearance of it being a different console), but the body of the prop and the central column remained in use through to *The King's Demons* in 1983.

WHAT ARE ALL THESE KNOBS?

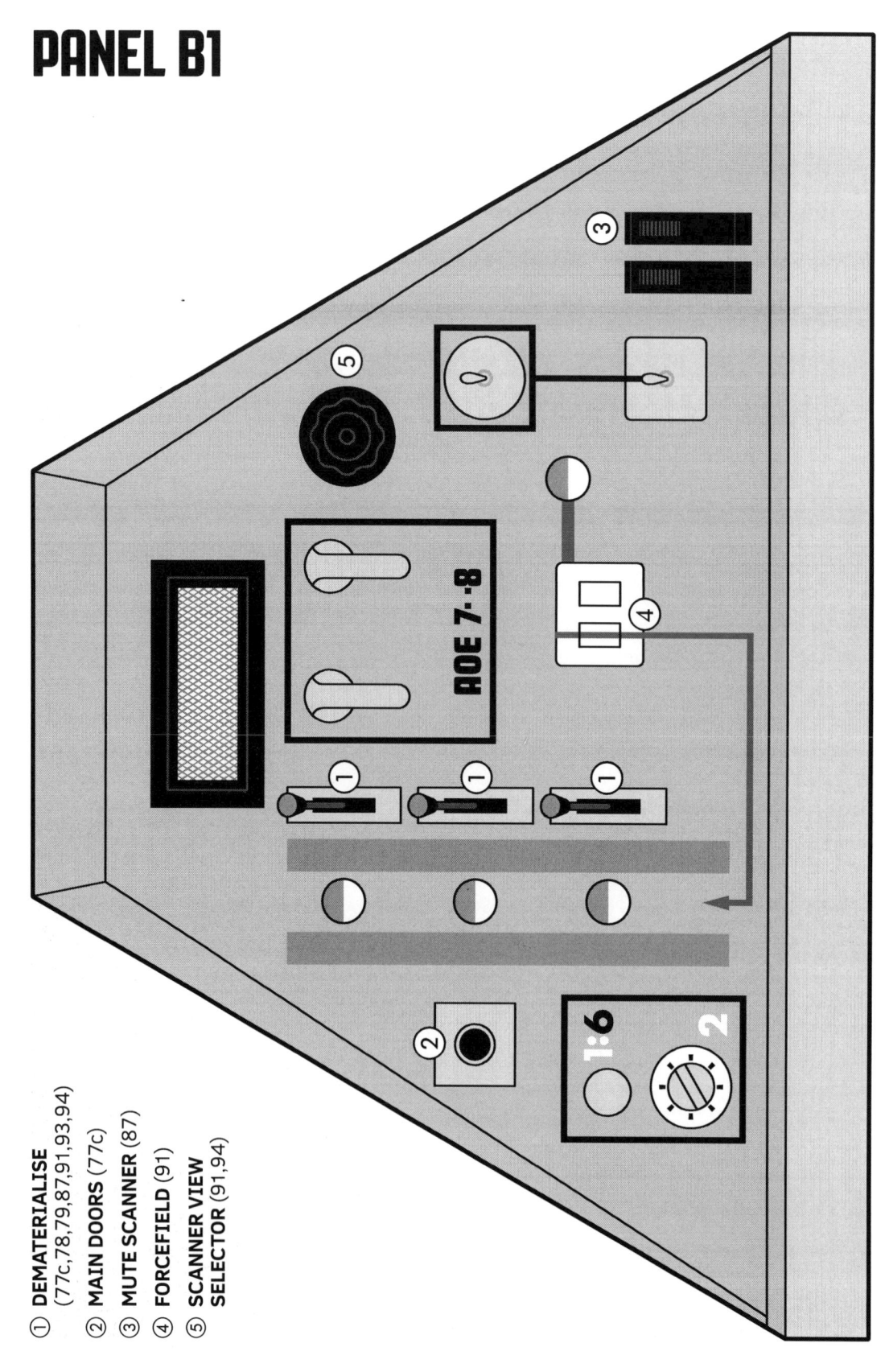

PANEL B1

① **DEMATERIALISE** (77c, 78, 79, 87, 91, 93, 94)
② **MAIN DOORS** (77c)
③ **MUTE SCANNER** (87)
④ **FORCEFIELD** (91)
⑤ **SCANNER VIEW SELECTOR** (91, 94)

WHAT ARE ALL THESE KNOBS?

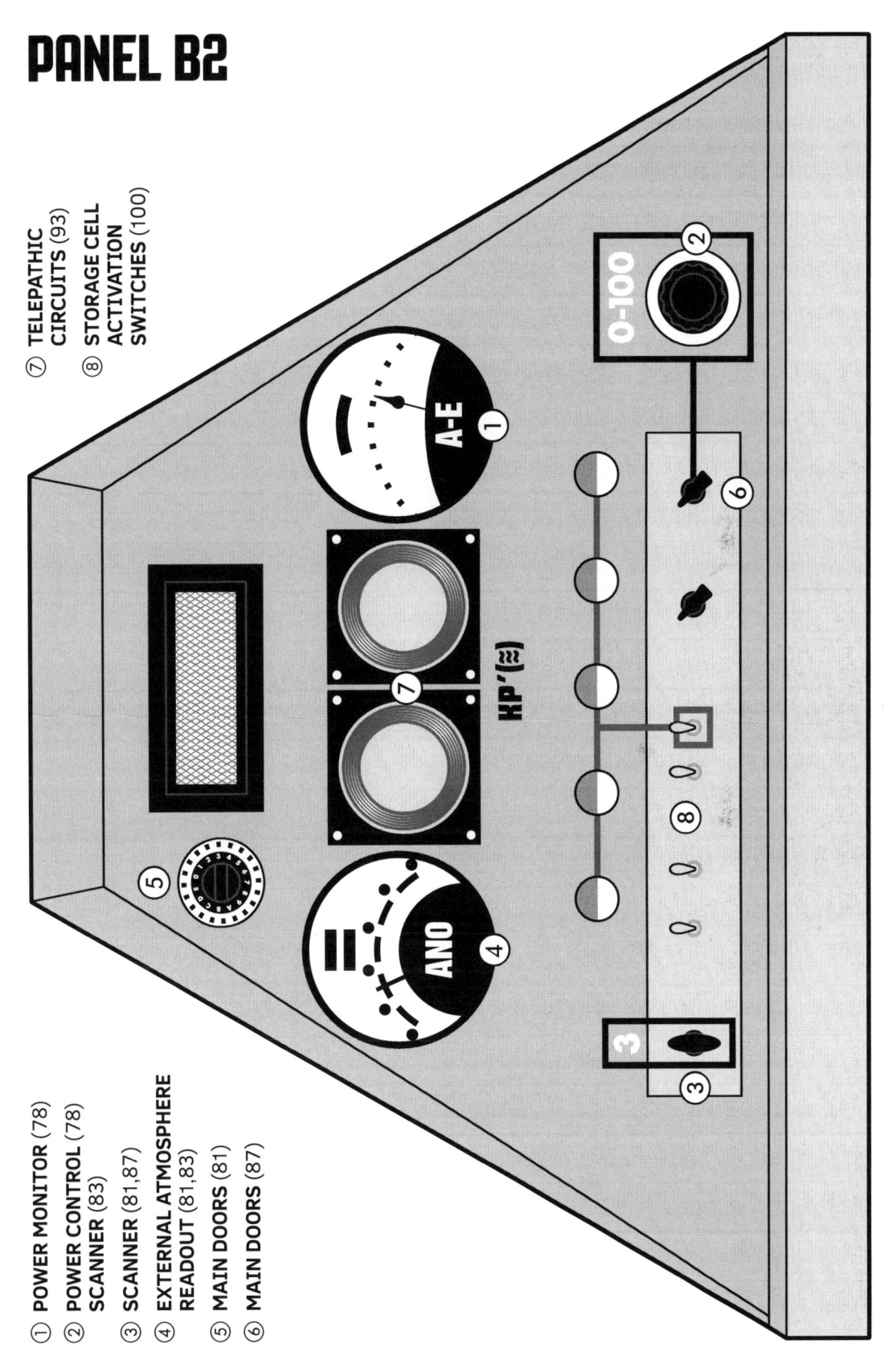

PANEL B2

① POWER MONITOR (78)
② POWER CONTROL (78)
③ SCANNER (83)
④ EXTERNAL ATMOSPHERE READOUT (81,87)
⑤ MAIN DOORS (81,83)
⑥ MAIN DOORS (87)
⑦ TELEPATHIC CIRCUITS (93)
⑧ STORAGE CELL ACTIVATION SWITCHES (100)

WHAT ARE ALL THESE KNOBS?

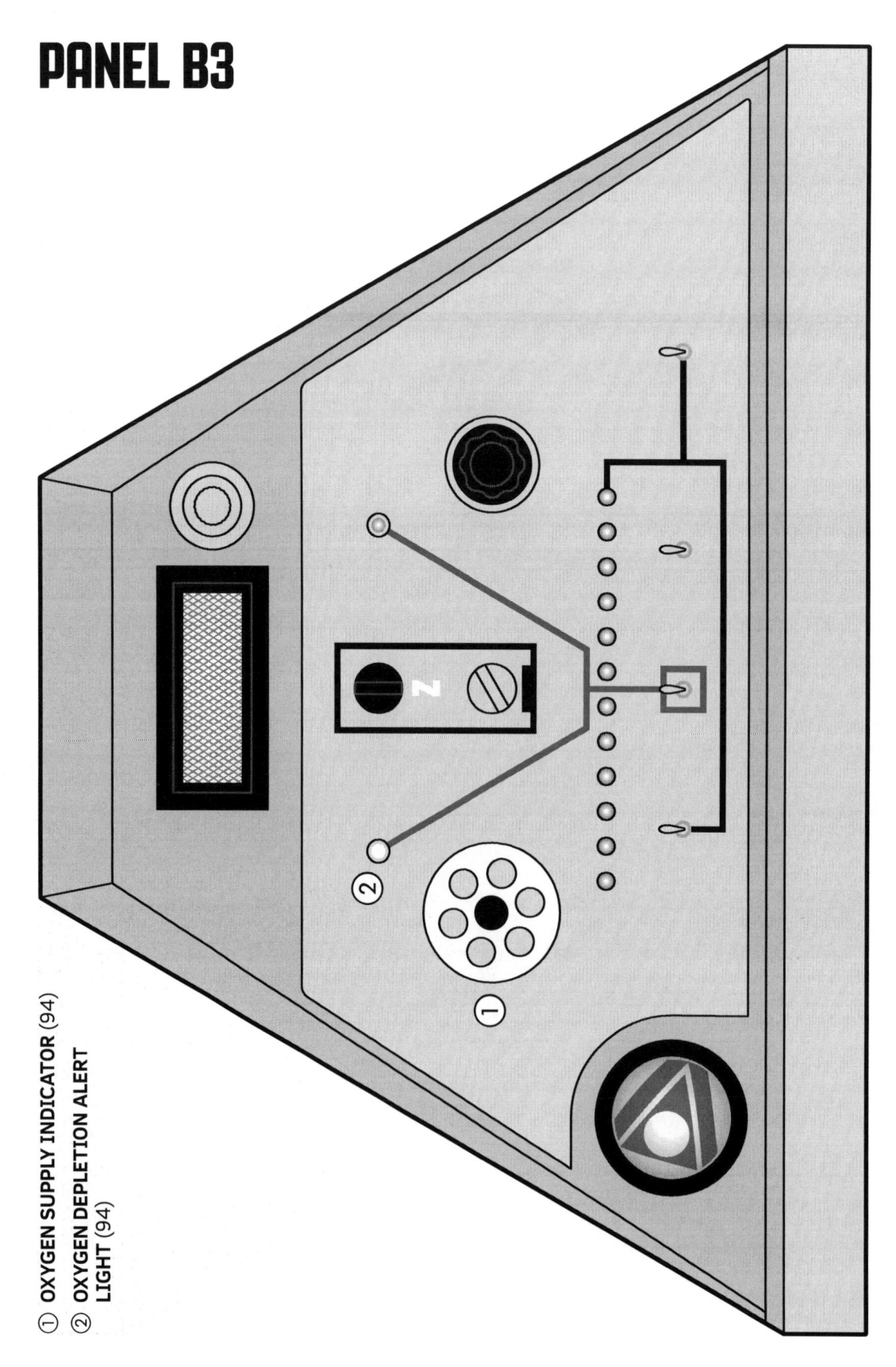

PANEL B3

① **OXYGEN SUPPLY INDICATOR** (94)
② **OXYGEN DEPLETION ALERT LIGHT** (94)

PANEL B4

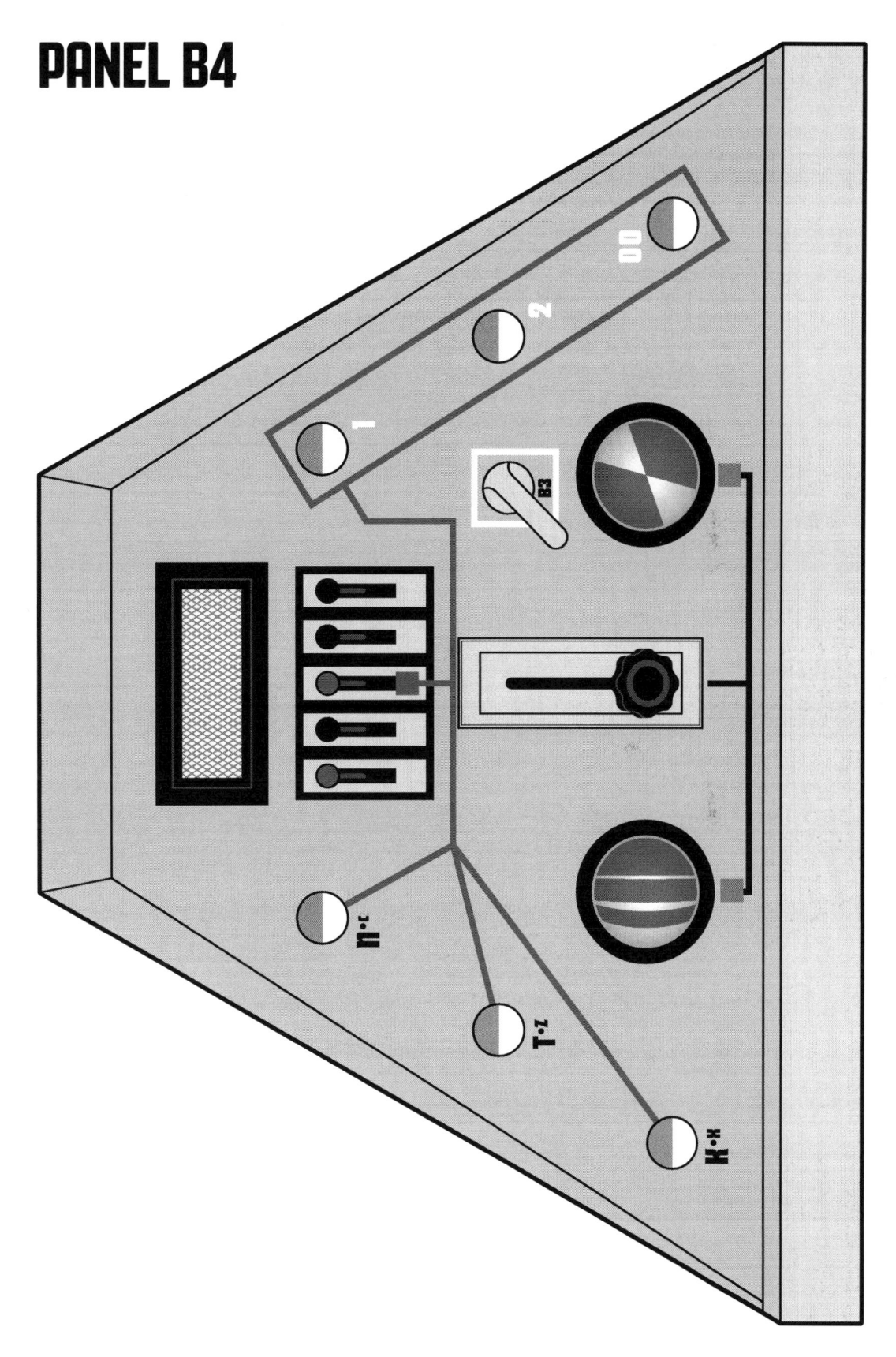

WHAT ARE ALL THESE KNOBS?

WHAT ARE ALL THESE KNOBS?

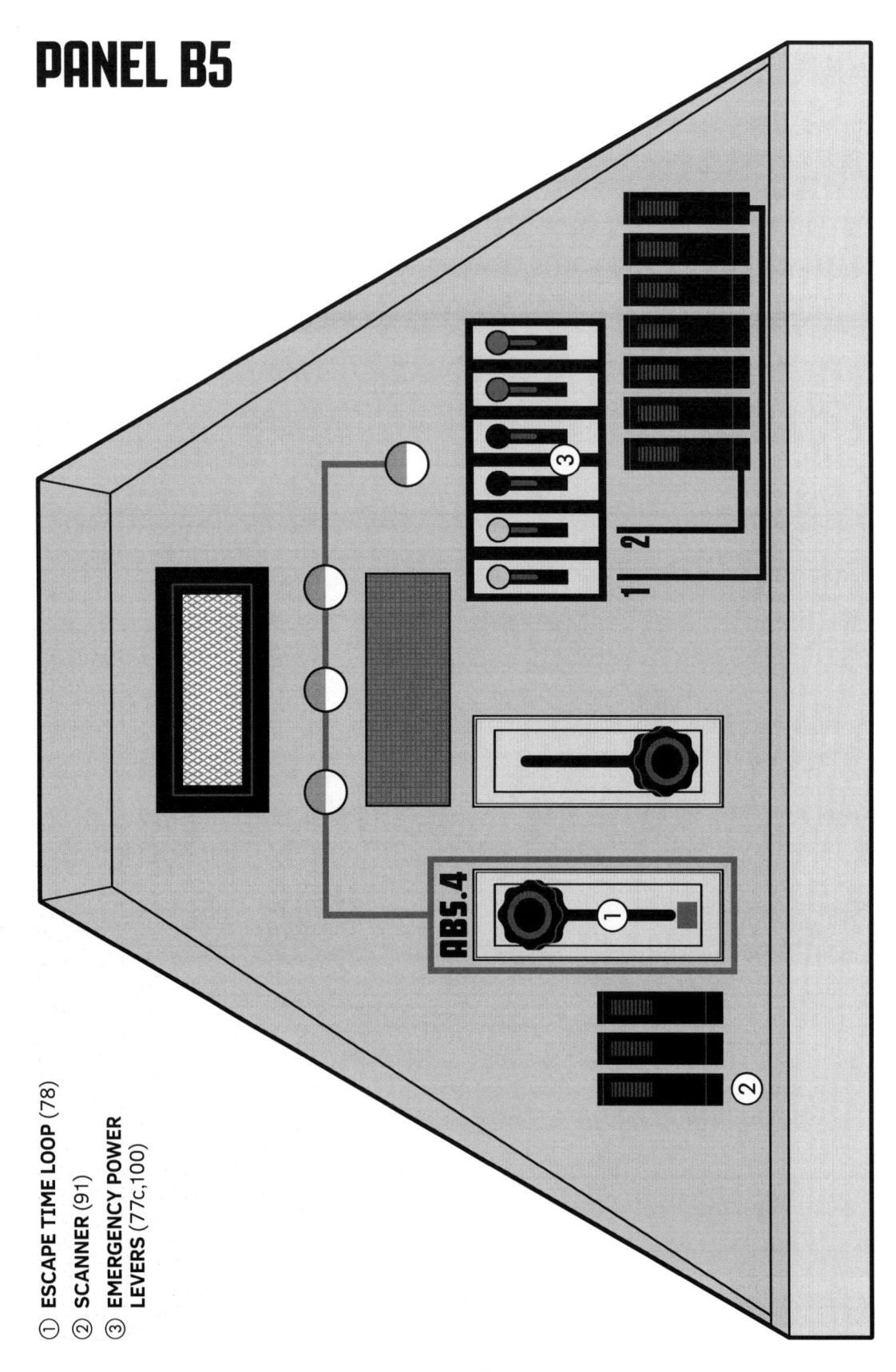

PANEL B5

① **ESCAPE TIME LOOP** (78)
② **SCANNER** (91)
③ **EMERGENCY POWER LEVERS** (77c,100)

WHAT ARE ALL THESE KNOBS?

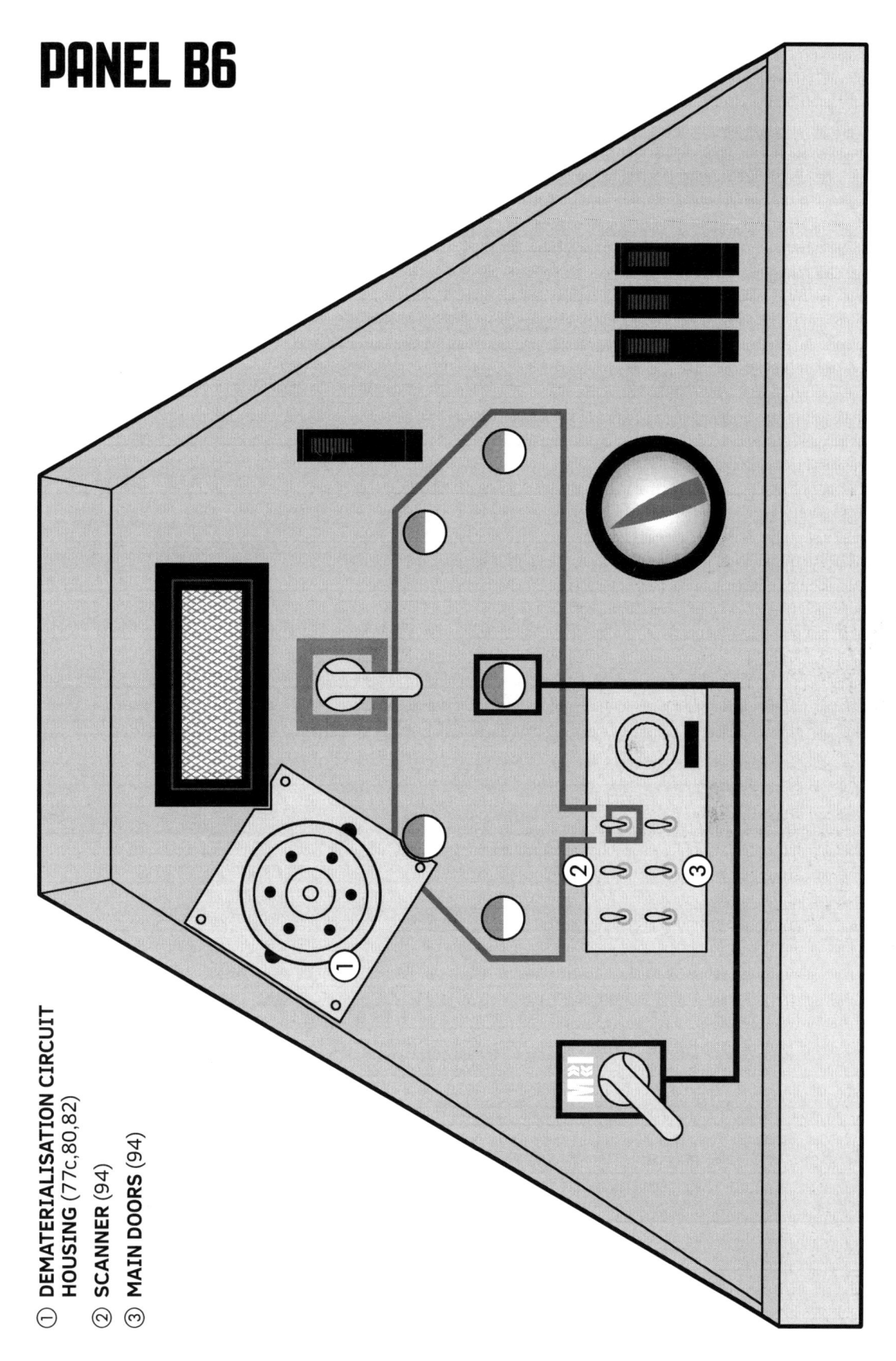

PANEL B6

① **DEMATERIALISATION CIRCUIT HOUSING** (77c, 80, 82)
② **SCANNER** (94)
③ **MAIN DOORS** (94)

LANDING 77 continued

SPACE Earth, England, UNIT headquarters; transported to south-east coast, Nuton Power Complex, cyclotron lab
TIME More than three months in [mid-1970s]
EPISODES Terror of the Autons 1-4; The Mind of Evil 6; The Claws of Axos 3-4

The TARDIS is moved to the Doctor's laboratory at UNIT's new headquarters, somewhere in the south of England, next to a body of water. The Doctor returns the console to the control room and takes the opportunity to reconfigure some of the controls. He thinks he has narrowed down the problem of the Ship's inoperability to the dematerialisation circuit and spends three months trying to repair. He uses the Lamadine technique of steady-state micro-welding but is still not successful, causing a small explosion in the TARDIS even before some over-enthusiastic fire-fighting by Jo Grant undoes all his progress.

Returning to the lab after investigating sabotage at the Beacon Hill radio telescope, the Doctor defuses a lethal volatiser – left there by the Master, recently arrived on Earth – by boiling away its contents in a pressure oven. Some hours later, the box that contained a stolen Nestene energy sphere is brought to the lab where a hypnotised Jo tries to open it, triggering a bomb. The Doctor tosses it out the window into the water below before it explodes. While waiting for the Brigadier to track down the Master's base of operations, the Doctor goes back to working on the dematerialisation circuit, only lured away by the prospect of visiting a travelling circus.

The next day (or possibly later), the Doctor attempts to reactivate his TARDIS, for what he claims is just a proving flight, using the dematerialisation circuit he took from the Master's at the circus. Despite looking the same, however, it is a Mark 2 model instead of a Mark 1 and thus incompatible; the TARDIS attempts to dematerialise but fails, causing the lab to shake and smoke to fill the control room.

While the Doctor is investigating the death of retired plastics factory owner John Farrell, the Master infiltrates UNIT headquarters disguised as a telephone engineer and installs in the lab a new phone with an extra-long cord. The Doctor returns from interviewing Farrell's widow with a plastic troll doll, which comes to life when left on a bench beside a flaming bunsen burner. It attacks Jo before Captain Yates shoots it to pieces. Shortly after, the Master telephones the lab and uses a sonic device to energise the plastic cord, which wraps around the Doctor to strangle him, until the Brigadier rips it from the wall.

The following day, the Doctor is examining a plastic daffodil found at Farrell's abandoned factory when Jo accidentally activates it by using a short-wave radio. He saves her from suffocation when the fake flower spits a plastic film over her face, but they are then confronted by the Master. The Doctor bargains for their lives with the stolen dematerialisation circuit but when Jo blurts out the Brigadier's plan to bomb the Autons, the Master instead takes both her and the Doctor hostage. After the Master's plan has been foiled and the Nestene repulsed, the Doctor reveals that although his nemesis escaped custody, he is stuck on Earth as it was actually the Doctor's malfunctioning circuit he took.

Some time later, a UNIT dispatch rider collects the Master's dematerialisation circuit from the lab and takes it to the Doctor in order to lure the villain into a trap. The Master escapes with the circuit, however, and is able to reactivate his TARDIS and leave Earth.

When the alien biomass Axos lands close to the Nuton nuclear power station, the Doctor persuades its head of research Winser to arrange for the TARDIS to be brought there from UNIT HQ, ostensibly to use the Doctor's equipment to analyse the nature of Axonite rather than risk Winser's particle accelerator. Although the Master hypnotises the driver sent to collect the TARDIS in order to infiltrate UNIT HQ, he still has the Police Box loaded onto a lorry and transported to the power station. Wearing a mask, the Master poses as an army general and orders Sergeant Benton to place the TARDIS in the chamber housing the cyclotron. Once alone, he easily forces open the door with a small electronic device.

Inside, the Master is dismayed to find the console in a state of disarray, covered in cables from the Doctor's attempts to repair it. He tries to get the Ship operational, clearing up the console and attempting a take off, but is unsuccessful. He thinks he may be able to get it working with components from the particle accelerator outside but as he leaves the Ship to cannibalise the machinery he is spotted and captured by the Brigadier and his men. After negotiating his freedom in return for preventing the reactor from going critical as Axos absorbs its output, the Master attaches a cable from the particle accelerator to the TARDIS so the Ship can absorb the reactor's power then feed it through to Axos in one devastating surge.

With Axos temporarily stunned, the Doctor recruits the Master to help repair the TARDIS, convincing him they can escape Earth together. While the Master adapts the accelerator's trigger mechanism to bypass the faults in the dematerialisation circuit, the Doctor steps outside to work out course coordinates, taking a component from the console to prevent the Master leaving without him.

Once the TARDIS is ready, the Doctor bids farewell to Jo, the Brigadier, Mr Chinn and Bill Filer as he and the Master take off together (on the second attempt after the Doctor has remembered to replace the component he removed).

✪ CONTROLS When the Master surveys the console in *The Claws of Axos*, the topmost of the three small levers on panel B1 comes away in his hand. After clearing off most of the loose cabling, he attempts a take-off by operating these levers then, when nothing happens, he presses the two rocker switches adjacent. He pushes the left-hand large slider on panel B5 upwards (which illuminates all four bulbs on that panel), then pulls four of the small levers downwards, causing the engines to groan; he angrily pushes them back up and pulls the large slider back down when the central column fails to move. He tries again to take off, pressing the left-hand rocker switch on panel B1 and slowly moving the three levers downwards. A loose component resting on the console next to them short-circuits and the Master pushes the levers back up. He flicks the left-hand rocker switch again, which this time appears to activate the scanner (or possibly just his thumping the console does so by accident). He is heard to press further switches (probably the same ones) then opens the doors with the upper control on the far left of panel B1. When he uses the TARDIS to store the reactor output, he controls the flow with the two rotary handles on the same panel.

- When the Doctor dematerialises the Ship, he presses one of the rocker switches on panel B1, twists the top-right black dial, adjusts the two rotary handles, then pulls the three small levers downwards in unison (repeating the last after replacing the component under the grille on panel B6).
- The dematerialisation circuit is a hand-sized unit with a core of complex electronics surrounded by four discs at tetrahedral vertices. It slots into a cylindrical casing that rises from the top-left of panel B6. Another component is fitted under the top grille of this panel, the removal of which prevents dematerialisation.
- In episode four of *The Claws of Axos*, the main doors repeatedly open and close without any control on the console being operated.
- **LORE** The Doctor's TARDIS uses a Mark 1 dematerialisation circuit. The Master is in possession of a presumably later model of time capsule that uses a Mark 2 circuit, which isn't backwards compatible.
- According to the Master, the Doctor's TARDIS has no proper stabiliser, is an "overweight, underpowered old museum piece" and operating it is like trying "to fly a second-hand gas stove".
- **NOTES** It would take a whole other book to divine where UNIT's latest headquarters is, but clearly the Doctor has settled in. Not only does he appear to have rooms above his lab (so is perhaps not sleeping inside the TARDIS, assuming he sleeps much at all) but he's also comfortable leaving the TARDIS door wide open throughout *Terror of the Autons*.
- The events of that story take place over at least three days (Jo changes outfits twice), possibly more as early in episode three the Doctor refers to "days of exhaustive investigation by the Brigadier's band of bloodhounds".
- When the Doctor tries to activate the TARDIS with the Master's dematerialisation circuit, the failing take-off sound effect is different from that heard in *Spearhead from Space* (Landing 73), with no fluttering, just slowing down at the end. The arrival of the Time Lord in episode one, however, is accompanied by the echoing materialisation sound first heard in *The Invasion* (Landing 63), although in overlapping loops to extend it and ending on a pop instead of a thump.
- This is the first time we've seen or heard mention of a dematerialisation circuit, although it's possibly the same as the landing circuit mentioned in *The Invasion* (Landing 62). The suggestion continues to be that the TARDIS has merely been disabled to keep the Doctor on Earth and if he can repair it he can leave. He seems confident that just replacing the dematerialisation circuit will reactivate his Ship, and although he attempts what he calls a "proving flight" it's likely, given similar previous opportunities, that had the circuit worked he intended to leave Earth for good. He later tells Winser the TARDIS has "a certain malfunction of the drive system…but the other components are all right", so he at least believes the Ship's inoperability is simply a technical problem. But this doesn't quite tie in with the Time Lords' sentence in *The War Games*, when it's said, "The secret of the TARDIS will be taken from you." Only after Axos has probed the Doctor's mind to learn the secret of time travel, and told him, "We have explored the blocks the Time Lords have imposed upon your memory and can free them," does he admit to the Master, "The Time Lords have put a block on my knowledge of dematerialisation theory." So it seems they also blocked the knowledge that his knowledge had been blocked, disabling both the TARDIS and the Doctor's ability to operate it. Only after Axos pokes around in his brain does he realise this and perhaps start to regain some of that knowledge.
- The incompatibility of components from different TARDIS models was demonstrated explosively the last time the Doctor tried it in *The Daleks' Master Plan* (Landing 31).
- Because it's said Professor Emil Keller installed his mind-purifying device at Stangmoor Prison "nearly a year" ago and the Master is now posing as Keller, it's often assumed he has been stuck on Earth for a year or more since the events of *Terror of the Autons*. This adds tension to the already taut timeline for UNIT stories, so it's more likely Keller was a real person whose identity the Master stole. How Keller came to be in possession of the mind parasite is open to speculation – perhaps it was spontaneously created from the "negative impulses" extracted by the Keller process – but the Master, trapped on Earth, would surely have been looking for opportunities to gain power and recognised the potential in using the parasite. It would be easy for him to take Keller's place and hypnotise anyone who knew the professor into accepting him.
- The Master hypnotises the UNIT driver returning to headquarters and on arrival instructs him to load the TARDIS onto the lorry as though that's his idea. Yet surely that's what the driver was ordered to do anyway. Even if the Master's simply saying, "Get on with what you're supposed to be doing while I spread word of Axonite," why wouldn't he frustrate the Doctor by *not* having the TARDIS taken to him. If he's planning to steal it because the Axons are holding his own TARDIS, then wouldn't that be easier to do at UNIT HQ while all the senior staff are away dealing with Axos? The script seems to acknowledge this when the Master is later caught by the Brigadier, who asks why he brought the Police Box to the power station if he plans to steal it anyway, to which the Master's weak reply is, "I

knew the Doctor would soon return to his TARDIS and I very much wanted to meet him just once more." It could be he's trusting the Doctor to defeat Axos, enabling the Master to regain his own TARDIS.

- ▪ The Master gains access to the TARDIS using a small silver tube (not unlike a sonic screwdriver) that makes the same sound as his laser gun.
- ▪ Given that *The Claws of Axos* is the first time the control room has been seen in almost two years (not since *The War Games*) and thus its debut in colour, it's a sadly minimal set: just two walls (main doors and indented roundels) and the console (which is initially covered in cabling, hiding the fact it's a new prop). They're quite tightly positioned too (with panel B1 facing the doors), presumably because the large laboratory and Axos sets left little space for the TARDIS. With no room for the usual wall-mounted or ceiling-hung monitor for the scanner, this is achieved by inserting a translucent blue disc into one of the wall roundels so that, when lit from behind, an image can be placed there using colour separation overlay (CSO, also known outside the BBC as Chromakey). There is room for a little furniture, however, notably the wooden Knossos chair used since *An Unearthly Child*, a wooden lectern in the shape of an eagle, the studded chair seen often during the Doctor's first incarnation and, in episode four, a computer cabinet (as it isn't there initially, presumably the Doctor wheels it out when working on the TARDIS with the Master). Unusually, in episode four the photographic wall (incorrectly placed on its right-hand edge) can be seen beyond the main doors. Normally these lead straight to whatever's outside (as they will again in the next story) so even if there wasn't space in the studio to erect the TARDIS set adjacent to the laboratory, surely a simple flat of the grey-painted brickwork would have sufficed. Either the TARDIS has temporarily gained a short hallway between the inner and outer doors or this isn't the primary control room.
- ▪ There are lots of problems with the main doors in these episodes. When the Doctor and the Master enter to consult on repairs, the right-hand door doesn't open fully whereas the left one swings right back then has trouble closing again, clattering away in the background (Roger Delgado even pauses in the delivery of his line, as if making sure the noise has stopped before continuing). When the Doctor leaves, only the right-hand door opens (Jon Pertwee seems to expect this so it may be deliberate owing to the cramped staging), but then when he ushers the Master out into Axos only the left door opens. Although it isn't heard every time the doors operate, a new sound effect is introduced.
- ▪ A new control room hum is also debuted in episode four when the Master has got the TARDIS working. Although it will be heard again in *Day of the Daleks*, *The Three Doctors* and *Planet of the Daleks*, other stories feature different sounds.
- ▪ The mid-shot of the TARDIS in the lab in episode three, when Hardiman quizzes the Brigadier about it, uses the 3-foot model (not seen since *The Krotons* – see Landing 65), even though the full-size prop was already on set. It's noticeably a different shade of blue from the main prop and has damage around the 'Police box' sign, although the colour and wording of the 'Police telephone' plaque now match the full-size box. The same shot appears in episode four when the TARDIS dematerialises from the lab, using CSO to overlay the model onto a view of the lab set (and for its later return). This would have been quicker than achieving the effect with the full-size prop, and presumably during editing the shot was added to episode three to clarify what everyone was looking at.
- ▪ The Master takes the Doctor's dematerialisation circuit from its housing in the console, but the last time we saw it, in *Terror of the Autons*, the Doctor gave it to the Master. He subsequently recovered his own working circuit in *The Mind of Evil*, so where has this one in the TARDIS come from? The only explanation is that the Master, for some reason, kept the Doctor's faulty circuit, carried it with him during this story and reinstalled it when trying to get the TARDIS working. Somewhat fortuitous, but perhaps when he formed his bargain with Axos (and we don't know the circumstances of that – the Master may have been at a disadvantage) and it impounded his TARDIS, he retrieved the Doctor's dematerialisation circuit from within hoping he might get a chance to steal his rival's time capsule, as he indeed later claims.
- ▪ The take-off sound effect cross-fades after the first few groans to the later rising notes.

LANDING 78

SPACE Inside Axos
TIME [Mid-1970s]
TRAVELLERS The Doctor, the Master
EPISODES The Claws of Axos 4

Before the Ship has even entered space-time, the Doctor rematerialises it aboard Axos, inside its command centre, where the Master's TARDIS stands nearby. Leading his rival outside at gunpoint, the Doctor claims he is willing to provide Axos with the ability to travel in time by linking it to his TARDIS, on condition that its next target for absorption is the planet of the Time Lords. The Master wants no part of this and tries to leave in his own TARDIS but Axos blocks him until the Doctor has completed the connection.

The Doctor attaches an Axon tendril to the console having secretly set the coordinates for a time loop. The Master realises his plan and rushes outside to warn Axos that the Doctor is betraying it, before dashing into his TARDIS and taking off.

The Doctor ramps up the Ship's power and successfully dematerialises, taking the whole of Axos with it. The Doctor is pinned to the console by two Axons but with effort manages to reach the control to separate the TARDIS from Axos and break free of the time loop, leaving the alien organism trapped forever.

- **CONTROLS** When landing, the Doctor spins the black dial and uses the three small levers on panel B1, resetting the rocker switches once the central column has come to rest. The Master meanwhile holds on to the top-left dial on panel B2.
- The Doctor sticks the Axon tendrils to panel B1. As the TARDIS prepares to dematerialise along with Axos, he turns the dial at the bottom-right of panel B2 and studies the right-hand gauge. To escape from the time loop, he reaches across to the left-hand large slider on panel B5 and pulls it upwards.
- **LORE** The course circuit can display its setting on the scanner. This shows a dot of light moving in the shape of an infinity symbol when set to create a time loop.
- The TARDIS is capable of breaking free of a time loop (at least one it has created).
- **NOTES** The Master's TARDIS appears to be in its undisguised state: a plain white cuboid of similar dimensions to a Police Box, a single hinged door with curved corners taking up most of one face. Note the door doesn't quite fit its frame and the Axos set can be seen through the gap.
- Oops! The Police Box can be seen on the cyclotron set during the attack by Axons even though the TARDIS is supposed to be in Axos at this point.
- The Axon tendril is draped around the central column but doesn't appear to be coming from the direction of the doors. These are very slightly ajar, though, so presumably it enters out of view at floor level and winds around the console.
- The shot of the TARDIS emerging from the time loop is a photo of the 12-inch model, still with a white telephone plaque and traces of the St John Ambulance emblem. This image is familiar to fans of a certain age from its use on the cover of the 1978 *Doctor Who Sound Effects* LP. Its flashing lamp is either a light behind a cutout or an optical effect laid over the image.

LANDING 79

SPACE Earth, England, south-east coast, Nuton Power Complex, cyclotron lab
TIME As above
TRAVELLERS The Doctor
EPISODES The Claws of Axos 4

The Ship returns to its previous departure point in the cyclotron lab, now evacuated as the particle accelerator runs out of control. On emerging, the Doctor sees the accelerator is beyond five-times light speed and so hurries back into the TARDIS.

With the building already beginning to collapse, the Doctor hurriedly takes off again just as the particle accelerator reaches overload and the lab is engulfed in an enormous explosion.

- **CONTROLS** Jon Pertwee maintains continuity by using (roughly) the same controls for take-off: turning the top-right black dial on panel B1, then pulling the three small levers downwards in unison, before adjusting the two rotary handles and pressing the rocker switches.
- **NOTES** The materialisation in the lab is achieved using CSO and the 3-foot Police Box model. The TARDIS also finally gets its most familiar and enduring landing sound effect: similar to earlier ones in that it's basically the take-off sound reversed, but with less echo than previous renditions and ending on a shorter rumble. For this landing it's actually played twice (did the sound mixer cue it too early, or the vision mixer fade in the TARDIS too late?) and ends before the rumble, but the next landing has the straightforward effect.
- A rising whine is heard in the control room as the TARDIS takes off but listen very carefully and some of the usual groans can be discerned in the background.
- The TARDIS's indestructibility seems still to be uncertain as the Doctor clearly thinks it wise to dematerialise from the exploding laboratory rather than just sitting it out inside the Ship. Or is this simply an instinctive reaction to danger?

LANDING 80

SPACE Earth, England, south-east coast, Nuton Power Complex, cyclotron lab (ruins); transported to UNIT headquarters
TIME Minutes after Landing 79
TRAVELLERS The Doctor
EPISODES The Claws of Axos 4; Colony in Space 1

The Doctor discovers the Time Lords have anticipated his getting the TARDIS working again and have programmed it to always return to Earth. It rematerialises moments later among the smoking ruins of the laboratory building.

The Police Box is transported back to UNIT HQ and placed in the corner of the Doctor's new laboratory. Having made progress in getting it working again, the Doctor concentrates on building a new dematerialisation circuit that is not subject to the Time Lords' "homing control".

After some time – during which the Brigadier has agents keeping an eye out for the Master's return, despite his scientific advisor's assurances that the renegade could be anywhere in the universe – the Doctor completes the circuit and invites Jo into the TARDIS for the first time while he tests it. No sooner has he placed the unit into the console, however, than the doors close and the Ship dematerialises under Time Lord control.

- **CONTROLS** The Doctor fits the dematerialisation circuit into the raisable cylinder on panel B6, as in *The Claws of Axos*. He seems to use the dial at the top-left of panel B2 to try to open the automatically closed doors, and adjusts the three levers on panel B1, its bottom-left dial and bottom-right switches when trying to prevent the remote take-off.
- The control room is silent when the TARDIS is stationary. The background hum begins and the central column oscillates for around 25 seconds before the

grinding sound of take-off is heard and the TARDIS actually dematerialises.

- **LORE** The TARDIS can be piloted by remote control, at least by the Time Lords. (The Stattenheim remote used by the Doctor in *The Two Doctors* was no doubt removed prior to his exile, and his memory of it likely erased – when he's in his sixth incarnation he doesn't recall ever having had one.)
- **NOTES** It may just be unnoticeable with the prop on location in daylight, but the Police Box lamp appears not to flash when the tardis materialises.
- So despite disabling some of the TARDIS's workings and blocking the Doctor's knowledge of how to reactivate them, the Time Lords still foresaw the possibility he would get the Ship working and programmed it to "always return to Earth". Do they not trust their own measures to enforce his exile? And what does 'always *return* to Earth' mean exactly: that the Doctor can go somewhere else but when he tries to move the TARDIS again it'll jump back to 20th century England, or that any attempted take-off will only result in rematerialising on Earth? He managed to move the Ship into Axos successfully – the TARDIS didn't just bounce back to the lab, like it does here. This landing is in the same location but the Doctor does manage to shift the TARDIS forward in time to avoid the explosion, so can it only do one or the other? Alternatively, have the Time Lords been keeping an eye on the Doctor, detected he's moved the TARDIS into Axos, then remotely piloted it back to its starting point in the lab (rather than having pre-programmed it, as the Doctor supposes)?
- Although some time has passes after the Axons are repelled – enough for the Brigadier's agents to make at least one mistaken arrest of someone they thought was the Master – it's unlikely the Doctor has been anywhere else in the TARDIS as he's only just finished building a new dematerialisation circuit to override the Time Lords' homing control.
- The Doctor's lab at UNIT HQ is much smaller than that seen in *Terror of the Autons* but could be in the same building – the window and door styles are the same (although the latter has a different handle from the one leading to his old lab). And it's not just a previously unseen corner of the same room as the walls are plastered rather than brickwork, although painted in the same colours: white with a peach dado. Nevertheless, when the phone rings, Jo answers simply, "Laboratory," suggesting this is the only one. Is the move to a smaller room to downplay the Doctor's presence at HQ after the unwelcome attentions of the Ministry of Defence?
- Although Jo has obviously been aware of the Police Box in the Doctor's lab and seen him going in and out of it, she's never looked inside herself or seemingly questioned him about what it contains until now. She's even surprised it's bigger inside than out (the Doctor uses the "dimensionally transcendental" explanation he first did with Liz – see Landing 73) and doesn't seem convinced it's an actual time machine – "I mean, it's just a sort of hobby, isn't it? A kind of game?" – despite having not long ago watched both the Doctor and the Master go inside and the box vanish, convinced the Doctor was somehow leaving Earth for good. Sure, she's supposed to be naive, but here she seems positively blinkered. Then again, she accepts being on a different planet pretty quickly so she's clearly not one to overthink things.

LANDING 81

SPACE Uxareius
TIME 2-5 March 2472
TRAVELLERS The Doctor, Josephine Grant
EPISODES Colony in Space 1

The Doctor admits to Jo that he has no idea where they are going, and they can only watch the streaks of light on the scanner as the TARDIS travels through the Vortex. Slowly the image resolves into that of a planet, which the Doctor recognises as Uxareius.

The Ship makes an abrupt landing on the rocky grey surface. Jo is not convinced that they have travelled to an alien world and demands proof, but the Doctor insists on checking the atmosphere is safe for them before he will open the main doors. Finding the air breathable ("Similar to Earth before the invention of the motor car") he lets Jo out but she is overwhelmed by the truth and immediately wants to return home. The Doctor, however, after being stuck on Earth for so long, is keen to explore and persuades Jo to join him for what he promises will be a quick look around.

She spots an unusual flower with different coloured petals and plucks it from the stony ground, while the Doctor's attention is drawn to the tracks of some machine. Neither notices a green-skinned alien with a spear watching them. As they climb a rise for a better view, the alien approaches the TARDIS. He is soon joined by three others who push the Police Box onto its side, tie a rope around it and drag it away to one of their dwellings.

The human colonists discover the Doctor's blue box stored with other items stolen by the Uxareians in one of their dwellings a few miles away, and bring it back to their main dome. The Doctor evades questions about what it is, merely saying it is an antique of great sentimental value, and as the colonists await a genuine adjudicator to assess their claim, he and Jo slip aboard. Moments later the TARDIS vanishes.

- **CONTROLS** The Doctor uses the left-most switch on the plate at the bottom of panel B2 to operate the scanner, having first flicked the two switches to its right, perhaps to adjust the scanner to work while in flight. When checking the external atmosphere, he flicks the centre switch at the bottom of panel B2 and adjusts the bottom-right dial while referring to the left-hand gauge, then definitely opens the doors with the dial at top-left of that panel.

- **LORE** The Doctor says that, when in flight, the TARDIS is "outside the space-time continuum", which he describes as "nowhere".
- The scanner can display an image while the Ship is in flight, showing streaks of coloured light and a view of the destination planet prior to materialisation.
- **NOTES** Mary Ashe tells Jo the colonists left Earth in 2471 and that they've been on Uxareius just over a year, so it's at least 2472. Indeed, a calendar shows Mon 2/Tues 3 March 2472, which is two days ahead of our real-world calendar but would have been right for 2471. The colonists are unlikely to have brought a stock of future calendars with them so might be reusing the one from their year of departure (by ignoring the shifting day of the week), except that Jane Leeson screws up the older page and throws it on the floor – perhaps she's not expecting them to be there this time next year. If it's accurate and they've been on Uxareius for more than a year, then the flight from Earth took no more than two months, which seems incredibly fast for a journey in a ship that was "obsolete when we bought it" to a planet that's distant enough the voracious IMC are only now aware of its mineral riches. The chart of the colonists' crop yields covers sixteen months from April (2471 at the earliest) to July the following year, with results up to June. So if it is March, the last few results must be projections as it's unlikely Ashe would have let the chart not be updated for eight months given their subsistence living.
- The control room is of more imposing proportions again, with three roundels walls: main doors, indented and photographic (sadly with a very noticeable crease across it). To the left of the doors is a section containing the scanner (a television monitor again), which appears to be part of the new computer bank constructed for *The War Games* (Landing 69), judging from the arrangement of metal strips. A new narrow section on the far right has white buttons on coloured strips – an updated fault locator? The console is positioned with the corner of panels B3 and B4 facing the main doors. Only the right-hand door opens when Jo and the Doctor enter the TARDIS (a directorial choice to match the Police Box in the preceding shot?), but both do when they exit to explore the planet (again, perhaps to match the exterior filming where both Police Box doors are open). A vertical strip has been added down the edge of the right-hand door to cover the gap when both are shut. The doors once more lead directly to the outside environment (a not entirely convincing painted backdrop). The only furniture is a freestanding silver knobbly cylinder of unknown purpose.
- The TARDIS appears and disappears in an instant, rather than fading out and in, and the grinding sound can be heard even before it appears and cuts off sharply once the Ship has gone. It has been suggested that because the TARDIS hadn't been seen in action for a while, everyone on the production team had forgotten how its transference was achieved. Except, of course, many of them had worked on the programme for several years, and in just the previous story the TARDIS's take-offs and landings were in the usual form. A key person who *was* new to the show on *Colony in Space* was director Michael Briant, who possibly didn't know the standard effect or just wanted to try something different. So those working with him who knew better either didn't notice his choice until it was too late or, perhaps more likely, were happy to go along with it. It has since been rationalised that the effect is different because the TARDIS is being operated by the Time Lords, which would be reasonable were it not for the fact that the Master's TARDIS later dematerialises in the same abrupt manner.
- The sound effect for the main doors opening returns to that used in *The War Games*, namely the same as the doors of the Dalek city on Skaro in *The Daleks*.
- You can tell the Time Lords aren't accustomed to interacting with the outside universe. Instead of giving the Doctor any instructions, they just whip him away to Uxareius the moment he happens to step into the TARDIS. They know the Master has information on the Doomsday weapon but how do they know when in the planet's history he intends to acquire it? Even if they have traced his TARDIS to 2472, why drop the Doctor there days before the Master arrives? And only in the vague vicinity of the Uxareians' city? They have improved their aim by the time they send the Doctor to Solos (see Landing 85).
- The Doctor is clearly unused to or over-excited by being able to explore a new planet as he wanders away from the TARDIS leaving both doors wide open. True, he claims to be having just "a quick look around" and is taken at gunpoint before he can return to the Ship, but he should know better. They have closed by the time the Uxareians investigate yet are wide open again when the TARDIS is brought to the colonists' dome.
- When the Uxareian approaches the newly arrived TARDIS he does so from the back and the rear doors wobble as he reaches out to touch them. The Police Box is seen falling forwards onto its front, but in the long-shot of it being dragged away it appears to be on its side as the pale writing of the 'Police telephone' plaque is visible. Perhaps the Uxareians had to roll it over to tie the rope around it.
- The Master's TARDIS reuses the regular console and walls (main doors and photographic), while the flat containing the scanner is the one seen in the Doctor's TARDIS in episode one repainted. There are also five metal filing cabinets containing documents, and two large cylindrical cubicles in which the Master imprisons the Doctor and Jo, behind which is a wall of coloured blocks. Another section of wall is covered in a knobbly gold panel where the nozzle emitting sleeping gas is housed. The reverse side of the main doors and surrounding wall is covered over and painted red to represent the exterior of the Master's TARDIS (disguised as a spaceship), which means the roundels are no longer translucent. Those immediately around the doorway have silvery circles pasted into them. In

episode five, panel B3 is facing the doors and the Master uses the switches at the bottom to operate the scanner and doors; by episode six (recorded the following day) the console has been rotated so panel B1 is facing the doors. Caldwell fiddles with controls on this panel to try to release Jo from the cubicle, and the Master uses the now-standard three small levers to take off, after pressing the adjacent rocker switches and turning one of the rotary handles. When his TARDIS dematerialises the last three groans of the landing sound effect are heard before the ship vanishes on the final thump.

LANDING 82

SPACE Earth, England, UNIT HQ, lab
TIME [Mid-1970s], moments after previous departure
TRAVELLERS The Doctor, Jo
EPISODES Colony in Space 6, Day of the Daleks 1

The Ship arrives back in the Doctor's lab at UNIT HQ, in a different corner from which it left but seemingly mere seconds after departing. When the Doctor and Jo emerge they find the Brigadier still there, unaware they have been gone for days.

The Doctor goes back to working on the dematerialisation circuit to overcome the Time Lords' override that restricts the TARDIS to Earth. He removes the console from the TARDIS again. On one occasion in September, after working through the night with help from Jo, he accidentally causes an overlap with a future point in time when he and Jo are returning to the lab. The effect is brief and ends when part of the console short-circuits.

After investigating reports of a mysterious vanishing man at diplomat Sir Reginald Styles' country home, the Doctor returns to his lab and sets up a test of the futuristic handgun UNIT soldiers found in Styles' grounds. He determines that while it fires a disintegrating energy ray, it is in fact from Earth, its iron content mined in North Wales. Also recovered is a black box into which fits a miniature dematerialisation circuit like the Doctor's. He accidentally activates it but the temporal feedback circuit overloads and the box goes dead.

○ **CONTROLS** When working on the console in his lab, the Doctor places the dematerialisation circuit back into its raised cylindrical housing then flicks a switch at the bottom on panel B6. He takes the circuit out again as it's clearly not working, and when the temporal apparitions vanish he flicks more of the same switches.
○ The left-most of the six small levers on panel B5 has had its silver knob swapped for a black one.
▮ **NOTES** The repeat of the Brigadier's call for the Doctor to "come back at once" suggests the TARDIS returns immediately after leaving, and the dialogue makes clear this was the intention. However, the room is not quite as the TARDIS left it: the wall to the left of the window is shorter, the glass partition in the adjacent wall is different and the chair that was in the corner where the TARDIS reappears is gone (fortunately), as is the map hanging on the wall behind it. Opposite, the light switches next to the green door have disappeared, replaced by a wall-hung barometer and plaque, the map is now hanging to the right of the window, and the desks are in different positions. In fact, the only logical conclusion is that the Doctor and Jo have returned to a subtly different parallel Earth from the one they left. Either that or they've been gone awhile and the Brigadier is in the habit of coming in every day and calling for the Doctor's return just on the off chance.
▮ In *Day of the Daleks*, the Doctor is working on the console in yet another lab room although it's clearly in the same building as his previous one: brick walls painted white with a peach dado, and wooden panelled doors painted olive green, although the wall outside the lab doors is a garish yellow – one wouldn't expect the military to go in for feature walls. Also the control room hum introduced in *The Claws of Axos* can be heard in all laboratory scenes, so presumably it emanates from the console itself.
▮ The Doctor still hasn't overcome the Time Lord's ability to direct the Ship (or, presumably, its limitation to Earth-bound destinations) so it's unlikely he goes anywhere after returning from Uxareius, at least under his own steam. He's still tinkering with the dematerialisation circuit so either the one he constructed from scratch in *Colony in Space* had the same problem as the original – suggesting the limitation may not be in the unit itself – or didn't work at all so he's gone back to repairing the original. Alternatively, the new circuit did work – how else could even the Time Lords operate the TARDIS without a working dematerialisation circuit? It can't be coincidence they took control the minute the Doctor inserted the unit, so has he removed it to avoid being dragged into further missions? "No one's going to turn me into an interplanetary puppet," he tells Jo. Perhaps he thinks he can get the original circuit working without ceding control.
▮ The scene of the Doctor and Jo encountering their future selves was intended to be repeated at the end of episode four of *Day of the Daleks* from the reverse perspective, but was cut by director Paul Bernard as he felt it was anticlimactic. The implication is not that either pair has slipped forwards or backwards in time, but that the Doctor's tinkering with the console has caused two points in time to occur simultaneously, briefly and presumably just in the vicinity of the console. In the cut 'future' section the Brigadier was to have entered saying, "For one ghastly moment I thought I saw two of you," but the 'past' Brigadier's comment, "Glad you're still here," doesn't mean he too saw a second Doctor and Jo, despite the look the pair exchange. He doesn't enter for some time after the duplicates have vanished, and even if he had seen them they would have been heading towards the lab so the Brigadier wouldn't be surprised to find them there. He's clearly just noting that the Doctor's been there all night, which the Doctor and Jo misinterpret owing to their experience.

LANDING 83

SPACE Peladon, cliff below citadel; carried into citadel
TIME Two days in unknown future
TRAVELLERS The Doctor, Jo
EPISODES The Curse of Peladon 1,4

The Doctor believes he has finally got the TARDIS working and persuades Jo to join him on a test flight, even though she is dressed for a date with Captain Yates. They make a successful journey to the planet Peladon but the Ship materialises halfway up a mountainside during a storm. Carved into the rock face above is the royal citadel. Jo is anxious about being late for her night out and is not convinced the TARDIS has really moved, particularly as the scanner is not working, which the Doctor traces to a tiny fault in the interstitial beam synthesiser. He checks the external environment and finds atmosphere, temperature and gravity the same as for Earth. Just then the room gives a lurch and, venturing outside, the Doctor discovers they are not at UNIT HQ. As the TARDIS rocks dangerously on the narrow ledge, the Doctor helps Jo out of the Ship, just before it plummets down the mountainside in a hail of dislodged rocks.

Believing the Doctor to be an official sent from Earth, Peladonian high priest Hepesh sends men to retrieve the delegate's crashed 'space shuttle'. They find it on the lower slopes of the mountain and haul it through the tunnels to the visitors' chambers in the citadel.

With Hepesh's scheme to discredit the Federation delegation foiled, the Doctor checks the TARDIS is undamaged before revealing to Jo they are able to leave. He suspects the Time Lords were responsible for his arrival on Peladon at this turning point in the planet's history and seems unsure whether he and Jo will now be returned to Earth or sent on a further mission. They plan to stay to watch King Peladon's coronation first, however. The royal beast Aggedor has been following the Doctor around since he hypnotised it, so he leads the creature away to be locked up while King Peladon renews his marriage proposal to Jo, but she insists she cannot stay.

The Doctor and Jo are about to join the coronation procession when the arrival of the genuine Earth ambassador forces them to make a swift departure. The other Federation delegates look on in astonishment as the TARDIS fades away before their eyes.

○ **CONTROLS** When the TARDIS has landed, the Doctor throws the four flick-switches at the bottom of panel B2 and checks both large gauges as he performs "routine landing procedures". He activates the scanner with the black dial in the bottom-right corner of the panel.

○ Panel B2 has undergone some minor additions since its last appearance. There are two rings to the right of the grille at the top, and beneath it two black paper dials. Three small gauges have also been added, two at the bottom left and one on the right, although these are simply the paper inserts from some electrical meters stuck onto the console. Beneath the rotating-light units are two similar paper inserts from some sort of bearing gauge; each has two circular scales marked 'Speed' and 'Latitude' (the latter split into 'North' and 'South'), while between them reads 'Lighting fuses', so they're perhaps from an aeroplane dashboard. On panel B1, the knob on the left labelled '1:6' was raised with a red edging but is now just a flat silver disk.

▮ **LORE** The interstitial beam synthesiser is a metal and plastic unit housed in the base of the console (below panel B2). If faulty, the scanner won't operate.

▮ The TARDIS is indestructible, according to the Doctor.

▮ **NOTES** In *Day of the Daleks* the Doctor felt he was "so nearly there" in getting the TARDIS under his control so it's hard to tell how much time and effort have passed that he now believes he has "got it working again". As this is his first test flight it's unlikely there have been unseen trips in the meantime. He comes to suspect even this trip was at the Time Lords' direction, a conviction that would surely be stronger if he had undertaken any further missions since *Colony in Space*.

▮ For the TARDIS materialising, the last four groans of the landing sound effect are looped three times. When dematerialising at the end of the story, the take-off sound fades in at a point just after the initial groans.

▮ A new model Police Box was made for the filming of the TARDIS's arrival and its plunge down the cliff-face. The miniature was built by visual effects designer Ian Scoones from plasticard rather than wood and was about six inches tall. It was closely based on the 12-inch model used since *The Daleks' Master Plan* (and seen here in the shot of the TARDIS teetering on the cliff edge) rather than the full-size prop. The proportions are broadly the same, including the oversized bottom rail, but the roof has a steeper pitch. The model even retains the white 'Police telephone' plaque long since changed on the main prop.

▮ For its one scene, the control room is again accorded a minimal set, with just the main doors and the indented and photographic roundels walls (the latter incorrectly placed on its side). The roundels in the doors wall are dark and those around the doorway filled with reflective paper, as seen when representing the Master's TARDIS in *Colony in Space*, as this wall still had the solid backing added for the earlier story.

▮ The TARDIS's departure is the first definite instance of this effect being achieved using the roll-back-and-mix technique (here with an additional split-screen effect), rather than a filmed insert or a method such as inlay or CSO. The Doctor and Jo were recorded entering the TARDIS, with the shot held for a while after. The Police Box was then removed while the vision mixer rewound the tape and replayed the recording. Once the actors had cleared the right-hand side of the picture, this was masked off with an electronic wipe and the live camera feed of the now-empty room faded in. Note that as the new recording is mixed in the torch flames blur (barely noticeable to the viewer as they're flickering anyway) but also there's a slight change in lighting levels. If you look closely at the floor to the left of the centre pillar you can see a difference in tone indicating where the soft edge of the mask is, across which the shadow of Izlyr's outstretched arm disappears. The delegates were given their cue to enter and seem to be looking at the TARDIS. The left-hand side of the image was then faded out, revealing the empty space the actors were really looking at (and Izlyr's shadow reappears).

▌ The Doctor only speculates the Time Lords directed the TARDIS to Peladon. If he's right, it's odd they should materialise the Ship halfway up a mountainside rather than, say, inside the palace, and that they give him no goal as they do in *The Mutants* (Landing 85). And why should the Doctor be suspicious that he arrived to help the Peladonians "at this precise crisis in their history" when that sort of thing happened all the time before his exile? So maybe on leaving Peladon the Doctor discovers he *has* got the TARDIS working again and he and Jo *do* (re)visit Queen Victoria's coronation. That he does ultimately return to Earth could simply be at Jo's request or because the Time Lords' override eventually kicks back in.

LANDING 84

SPACE Earth, England, UNIT HQ, lab
TIME [Mid-late-1970s]
TRAVELLERS The Doctor, Jo
EPISODES The Mutants 1

The TARDIS (eventually) returns to the Doctor's lab at UNIT HQ, although whether Jo is in time for her night out with Mike Yates is unknown.

Some time later, the Doctor is working on a minimum inertia superdrive for his car Bessie when the Time Lords send him a spherical message container. He explains to Jo that it will open only for its intended recipient and that he has no choice but to deliver it. The TARDIS begins humming and the roof lamp flashes to indicate it is time to go, and although the Doctor tells Jo it is likely to be too dangerous for her to join him, she insists and follows him into the Ship before the doors close and the Police Box dematerialises.

▌ **NOTES** If the Doctor has indeed succeeded in repairing the TARDIS (see Landing 83) then he could have made unseen journeys before this one. Note he's spending his time tinkering with gadgets for Bessie rather than working on the TARDIS, suggesting the latter is no longer a priority (although he has taken time out before to spruce up his car, such as in *The Dæmons*). Also, this time the Time Lords recruit his help by sending a message container, used only "in a real emergency… It's top priority, a three-line whip", and the Doctor is happy to be their delivery boy – surely he'd be demonstrably more opposed to being used thus if he hadn't already regained some measure of freedom. So it's possible that his connections with Jo and UNIT are now keeping him on Earth voluntarily for much of the time.

▌ Although the Doctor's laboratory seen here is arranged differently, it's decorated the same as those seen previously so is probably the same UNIT HQ building. It could be the opposite side of the smaller lab seen in *Colony in Space*.

▌ The sound effect used in *The Claws of Axos* for the control room's main doors operating is here played as the Police Box door opens by itself (and again when Jo emerges after its next landing). The Ship hums loudly and its roof lamp starts flashing before it has started taking off; this is taken to denote its remote operation by the Time Lords but could be caused by the message capsule and for all we know the Doctor then connects that to the console to direct their flight – note the Doctor isn't still carrying it when he exits the TARDIS and has to be reminded by Jo to bring it with them.

▌ This is the first straightforward roll-back-and-mix dematerialisation (without additional video trickery). The actors were recorded entering the TARDIS, then taping was stopped while they and the Police Box were removed from the set. The tape was rewound and replayed, with a new camera shot of the empty room being faded in at the appropriate point. For the effect to be totally convincing, the camera shouldn't move so that the only change is the absence of the Police Box, but here a slight shift causes the background to slip as the picture mixes from one shot to the other.

LANDING 85

SPACE [Cyclops nebula], Skybase One orbiting Solos
TIME Two days in 30th century
TRAVELLERS The Doctor, Jo
EPISODES The Mutants 1,6

It rematerialises in the 30th century inside storage area four on Skybase One, a space station in orbit around Solos from which humans rule the indigenous people of the misty planet. The Doctor and Jo hear an announcement for a visiting party to be taken to the decontamination hall and assume it refers to them.

While they wait for their escort, the Doctor checks the TARDIS instruments to find where and when they are, explaining to Jo that Earth has an interplanetary empire by now. They decide not to wait to be shown around and the Doctor uses his sonic screwdriver to force open the door. Jo reminds him to bring the message box, which the Doctor retrieves from the TARDIS. As they leave, an announcement calls for investigation of the malfunctioning storage area door.

When the Doctor and Jo return to the storage area where the TARDIS arrived they find the door lock has been repaired, forcing the Doctor to short it out again with his sonic screwdriver. An announcement immediately alerts that the door is malfunctioning again while the TARDIS dematerialises.

▌ **NOTES** In *The Brain of Morbius*, the Doctor says the Mutts are a "mutant insect species widely established

in the nebula of Cyclops" so that might be where Solos is. As he goes on to suggest Karn and Gallifrey are in the same region, perhaps that's why the Time Lords were concerned enough about the Solonians' evolution to send the Doctor to ensure it wasn't disrupted by the human imperialists.
- The TARDIS's arrival on Skybase One was also done via roll-back-and-mix, but from a shot of the empty set to one with the Police Box (with actors inside) in position, although again the camera shifts sightly between the two.
- The roof lamp continues flashing for a few moments after materialisation.
- When the TARDIS leaves Skybase we hear the grinding sound but the Police Box doesn't begin to fade before the picture cuts to outside the space station.

LANDING 86

SPACE Earth, England, UNIT HQ, lab
TIME [Mid-late-1970s]
TRAVELLERS The Doctor, Jo
EPISODES The Time Monster 1,3-4

The TARDIS returns to its corner in the Doctor's laboratory at UNIT's UK headquarters.

The Doctor builds a time sensor to alert him should the Master return. One morning, having been working through the night, the Doctor wakes from a nightmare of volcanoes and earthquakes, a glowing crystal and the Master dominating him. Jo points out that she was reading to him the previous night from a newspaper report of an eruption in the Greek islands but he dismisses the matter until she mentions the area is a theorised location of Atlantis. The Doctor warns the Brigadier to be on the alert for sightings of the Master; Lethbridge-Stewart assures him all UNIT personnel are already under such orders. For now they are due at the Newton Institute near Cambridge to observe a demonstration of TOMTIT, a device enabling the transmission of matter through interstitial time. The Doctor refuses to go so the Brigadier takes Sergeant Benton.

The Doctor completes the time sensor, which detects disturbances in the time field. It correctly registers activity in the TARDIS (even though it is calibrated in Venusian units of length, which are just over 4.44 times longer than human equivalents), but then starts responding to another time machine. The Doctor estimates on a map that it is in the region of Cambridge, between 50 and 100 miles away, so he and Jo head off in Bessie to triangulate a more accurate position.

Captain Yates gathers a squad to join the Brigadier at the Newton Institute, where the Master has been discovered as the man behind TOMTIT. At the Doctor's request, Yates also brings the TARDIS, loading it onto the back of an army truck. However, the Master learns of their approach and uses the power of the Kronos crystal to bring elements from the past to attack the convoy. A knight on horseback runs them off the road, then a company of Parliamentarians from the English Civil War pins them down with musket fire. Finally the Master brings a German V-1 flying bomb forward in time from 1944 and it falls on the motorcade. Warned in time, the UNIT soldiers survive but the TARDIS is stuck on its side in the crater. With help from a local farmer and his tractor, they haul it upright.

The time sensor indicates the Master is preparing to make a move so the Doctor and Jo hurry into the TARDIS to follow, the Doctor using the sensor to home on the Master's TARDIS. He plans to materialise his inside it so that they will go wherever the Master does. He warns Jo of the incredible dangers of this but she insists on going with him.

- **CONTROLS** The Doctor closes the main doors by turning one of the knobs on the plate at the bottom of panel B2. When inputting the readings from the time sensor, he adjusts the lower dial (labelled '2') at the bottom-left of panel B1, referring to the gauge above this as the "time setting".
- Panel B1 gains a new grille and gauge (this one with a plastic cover) in the bottom-right corner in place of the two flick switches; another gauge on the left replaces the black button, while the right-hand bearing chart from panel B2 has been moved to under the two rocker switches. Two further gauges have been added either side of the top grille, above which a microphone on a flexible stalk now projects. On panel B6, the cylinder that houses the dematerialisation circuit is missing and the resultant hole is used by the Doctor to hold the time sensor when it's not in use. And the last silver-knobbed small lever (second from left) on panel B5 becomes black. All these changes apply, of course, to both the Doctor's and the Master's consoles.
- **NOTES** We know the Doctor does return to Earth from Skybase as he's back in his lab at the start of *The Time Monster*. If the journey to Skybase was directed by the Time Lords then presumably the return was too, but if the Doctor has got the Ship working again he might take Jo on a few jaunts first. He is confident in his use of it in this story.
- The Doctor's laboratory is more like the one seen in *Terror of the Autons*, with the doorway to the left, window at the back and between them a spiral staircase leading to an upper level. The doors are different, though, taking up more space and located further into the room. Perhaps the Doctor was moved to a smaller lab space while this area was being remodelled. It also has the background hum heard in *Spearhead from Space* and *The Ambassadors of Death*.
- Jo asks if the Doctor is building a "super dematerialisation circuit" and he says that will have to wait, the implication (and no doubt intention) being that he still hasn't got the TARDIS working. Yet her addition of the adjective leaves open the possibility that the regular dematerialisation circuit does work and the Doctor is now working on an improved version, perhaps to guarantee he can travel without Time Lord interference. It could be that, as well as his attachments to

Jo and UNIT, he feels a responsibility to stick around on Earth in case the Master tries another takeover.

- The castors on the unpainted bottom of the Police Box prop are visible when it's lying in the bomb crater. The 'Police box' sign is missing from the left-hand side as a piece of wood is fitted into the sign box to assist with pulling the prop upright.
- Somewhat undercutting the big reveal of the new-look control room, we're shown it first as the Master's TARDIS. Here the central column of the console is replaced by a metallic tiered unit that pulses with light and sits on a cylindrical base (actually an upturned dustbin sprayed silver), with no glass covering. It's only shown rising and falling during flight in episode five; at other times it's stationary even when the Master's TARDIS is in motion.
- Unlike previous changes, the new look of the control room is commented on by the characters (ad libbed by Jon Pertwee and Katy Manning), Jo pointing it out and the Doctor saying, "Just a spot of redecoration, that's all." (So she hasn't been inside since the Doctor – or the TARDIS itself – selected this new 'desktop theme', in 21st century *Who* parlance.) Would he really concern himself with interior decor before he'd got the Ship working properly? How curious that the Master has redecorated his in the exact same manner. Is there an unseen adventure between *The Curse of Peladon* and this when either the Doctor or the Master sees the other's control room and thinks "Ooh, that's nice"?
- When the Doctor and Jo first enter the control room the main doors don't close properly. Despite the new look, they have the same sound effect used in *The Claws of Axos*. The roof lamp doesn't flash when the TARDIS takes off from the bomb crater.
- Furniture in the Doctor's control room comprises a brass lectern (which Jo uses as a coat stand) and a carved-oak cabinet. The Master's has a table with a smoked-glass top (raised on a black block to get the right camera angle for when the Master places the crystal's control unit on it) and a clear plastic globe with a red base on a shorter glass table..

LANDING 87

SPACE Earth, England, Cambridgeshire, Wootton, Newton Institute, inside the Master's TARDIS
TIME As above
TRAVELLERS The Doctor, Jo
EPISODES The Time Monster 4

After what seems to the travellers like just a few minutes, the TARDIS materialises again with a jolt. Yet the Master's TARDIS, disguised as a large computer bank, appears inside the Doctor's control room. When the scanner shows just a swirling pattern – a view of the Vortex through interstitial time – they venture outside only to find they are inside the Master's control room, and exiting that brings them back into their TARDIS: both vessels are inside each other.

The Master can still enter his TARDIS from outside and, when he dematerialises, the Doctor's control room is buffeted violently until the Doctor gets both vessels into phase. The Master addresses him and Jo via the scanner to inform them he has put a time lock on their TARDIS so it cannot leave, but the Doctor has done likewise. He tries to persuade the Master of the folly of his plans but the villain mutes his scanner to lure the Doctor out, knowing he will be infuriated by being ignored. When the Doctor realises this, he pulls a component from beneath the console and adjusts it so he can override the Master's sound receiver. The Master has anticipated this, however, and uses the telepathic circuits to divine the Doctor's words before he speaks them and have them come out backwards. Against Jo's protestations, the Doctor is forced to leave the safety of his control room in order to confront the Master, who releases Kronos, a time-eating Chronovore, from the crystal. The creature engulfs the Doctor, transporting him into the Vortex, and the Master separates the two TARDISes, leaving Jo alone and stranded.

- **CONTROLS** Jo uses the right-most knob on the plate at the bottom of panel B2 to open the doors; the Doctor uses the same or a nearby control to open the doors of the Master's TARDIS. He materialises, as usual, by pulling the three small levers on panel B1 downwards. Jo operates the scanner with a switch at bottom-left of panel B2 (probably the same as in Landing 81). Once the Master's TARDIS has taken off, the Doctor gets his in phase with it from panel B1, including use of the black dial at top-right. He pulls a component from beneath panel B1 to override the Master's muted scanner, and presses the right-hand black switch at the bottom-right of that panel to cut out the scanner microphone so he can speak normally.
- The Master tests the power levels of his TARDIS using the small levers, left-hand rocker switch and right-hand rotary handle on panel B1 usually used for take-off, then later operates the same to actually dematerialise. He presses one of the rocker switches to mute the scanner, then uses these, the levers and the handles, plus the top-right black dial, to feed the Doctor's words back at him. He also expels the Doctor's TARDIS using control on this panel.
- From the last scene of episode four (recorded with episodes five and six two weeks after the rest of episode four had gone before the cameras) the microphone only just added at the top of panel B1 is different, now with a stand, placed on the console and wired through the hole. This suggests it was a working prop (used for recording dialogue to avoid the risk of boom shadows on the new set?). Presumably in the gap between the two recording blocks the original microphone was lost or damaged and a replacement hurriedly provided.
- **LORE** One TARDIS can materialise inside another, although this is a very dangerous manoeuvre. The two time machines must be operating on the same frequency and the time setting must be accurate to within an attosecond: too low and the materialising

TARDIS will miss altogether; too high and it will cause a time ram, where its atoms try to occupy the exact same space and time as the other vessel's, annihilating both. Alternatively, it's possible for both TARDISes to end up inside each other in an infinite progression.

- According to the Doctor, the time a journey appears to take for the occupants varies depending on the "mood" of the TARDIS, which in some sense is alive. In reality, because the Ship is travelling outside the space-time continuum of the universe, it takes "no time at all".
- TARDISes have circuits that allow a telepathic means of communicating. For a childish trick, these can be used to intercept an occupants' thoughts between brain and mouth and make them be spoken backwards.
- **NOTES** It's suggested here and for Landing 88 that the Doctor can only pilot the TARDIS because the time sensor enables him to go wherever the Master is. But his use of it as a "homing device" may mean it's just a way to accurately track the Master's TARDIS (by isolating its operating frequency). Certainly the Ship takes off and lands perfectly under the Doctor's control.
- The Master's TARDIS is disguised as a large computer bank, with an entrance in the right-hand side which slides outwards. Rather sweetly, this has roundels painted on the inside. Its take-off sound is a higher-pitched version of the regular groaning.
- Jon Pertwee and Katy Manning don't do a very good job of staying still as the prop of the Master's TARDIS is wheeled onto the set for the mix shot of it materialising. While the camera shifts very slightly anyway, both actors' poses change more noticeably, making them blur as the computer bank appears.
- The scanner is realised by replacing one of the roundels (top row, second column from the left on the central new wall) with a translucent disc that when lit from behind by a blue light could be used to superimpose an image via CSO. The Master can hack into the Doctor's scanner, appearing on it and eavesdropping without either the Doctor or Jo having activated it. This is probably a function of the two TARDISes operating on the same frequency as the Doctor does the same during Landing 89.
- The two TARDISes are said to be inside each other yet the Master can still enter his from outside, even though the Doctor can see it inside his control room. When the Doctor first checks the scanner it shows the Vortex ("through the TOMTIT gap") yet once he has gone out into the Master's TARDIS and then out again back into his own, the scanner displays the Master's control room. When the Master's TARDIS dematerialises from the lab, it doesn't disappear from the Doctor's control room. Perhaps while the Master's Ship is in the real world there is a starting point to the sequence of alternating TARDISes, but once both are in the Vortex it becomes an infinite loop.
- The last surviving photographic wall was positioned beyond the control room doors when the Doctor's TARDIS was supposed to be inside the Master's. It can be glimpsed through the zigzag edge of the main doors when the Doctor goes out, and through the semi-transparent roundels of the doors wall in later shots. This is its last use in the series.
- When the Doctor and Jo first step out into the Master's control room, the crystal of Kronos is sitting on a table right in front of them – we don't see it but we know the Master brought it in earlier. If they had just thought to nab it and take off again this whole adventure could have been over a lot sooner.
- Although the component the Doctor pulls from under the console to override the Master's speakers comes from beneath the same panel as the interstitial beam synthesiser in *The Curse of Peladon* (Landing 83), it's a different prop.
- For scenes where characters talk via the scanner to those in the other TARDIS, an extra section of roundels was set up with the relevant central column from the console on a table in front of it. The character on the scanner was recorded against this and the image fed onto the CSO scanner disc on the main control room set where the other half of the conversation was being recorded. When the camera pans down with the Doctor as he bends to reach under the console, the image of the Master on the scanner doesn't match the movement.
- The Doctor says TARDISes are telepathic and this is how they communicate. It's not clear if he means communicate with other TARDISes or with their occupants (or both). Certainly the previous attempts by the Doctor's TARDIS to communicate with him have been less than explicit (see Landings 4 and 59). Here the Master uses the telepathic circuits to take the words forming in the Doctor's mind and reverse their sounds before the signal from his brain reaches his mouth and vocal cords.
- While the Police Box is inside the Master's TARDIS, it stands next to the desk with the crystal on it beside the main doors. However, after the Master has banished the Doctor, the desk is suddenly on the other side of the room – notice the scanner roundel in the top-right corner when the Master deactivates the crystal. He then proceeds to look across the console to address Jo supposedly on the scanner (actually behind him). This was probably just to give the director the camera angle he wanted on the Master, but it gives the impression of further walls to the left of the main doors. The fact they also went to the trouble of rotating the console so that Roger Delgado is still standing at panel B1 suggests the stalk microphone was indeed being used to pick up dialogue rather than use a boom.
- The shot of the two TARDISes separating uses the new six-inch model Police Box built for *The Curse of Peladon* and a to-scale miniature of the Master's computer bank. This is the first time the TARDIS is intentionally seen spinning while in the Vortex.

IT'S BIGGER ON THE INSIDE

THE GLEESON WASHOUT
1972

The concluding story of the 1972 season, *The Time Monster*, had more scenes than usual (and much of episode four in particular) set inside the TARDIS, which doubled as both the Doctor's and the Master's vessels. The previous serials that year had included only one brief control room scene, in *The Curse of Peladon* episode one, recorded on Monday 17 January 1972. That had been a minimal set – main doors, an indented wall and one of the photographic walls – which may have been all that was left of the original wall sections.

When designer Tim Gleeson was assigned to work on *The Time Monster*, he would have been aware what set pieces were still in storage as he had been the designer on the previous year's *Colony in Space*, which had also used the regular control room walls to represent the Master's TARDIS. With the photographic walls in particular no longer passable as major scenery, at the very least some new walls would need constructing. With producer Barry Letts already planning to free the Doctor from his exile and have him travel the universe once more, it was agreed that now would be a good time to refresh the TARDIS's interior.

As the main doors had their opening mechanism that would be expensive to replace altogether, this section was reused. For his previous serial Gleeson had clad the rear side with red-painted plywood so it could be shot as both the inside and outside of the Master's TARDIS disguised as a spaceship. This backing had remained since (which is why the roundels are opaque in *The Curse of Peladon*) but was now removed except for the two pieces on the reverse of the doors, which were repainted white. The backing of the roundels and the strip on the front edge of the right-hand door (which Gleeson himself had previously added) were also removed. To complement this and the (likely sole surviving) indented wall, which was also to be reused, Gleeson had two new wall sections built from plywood with the same staggered-circles pattern but only two-thirds as wide. While the cut-out circles were the same size as on the existing sections, they lacked the deep cylindrical indents.

This was because Gleeson's main innovation to tie the new and old sections together was a series of vacuum-formed plastic roundels that had shallow curved sides and a round hole in the centre fitted with clear textured plastic so they could be backlit as before. These roundels were slightly larger than the holes in the walls and were inserted from the front, projecting back through the holes and fixed around their rims. Only whole roundels

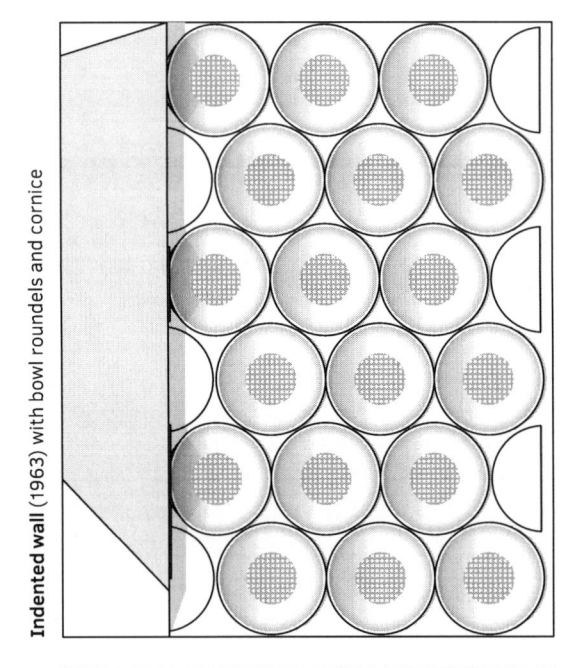

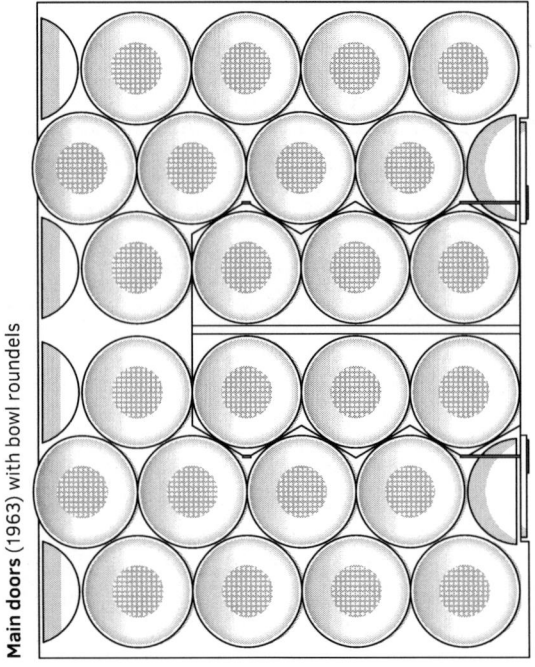

IT'S BIGGER ON THE INSIDE

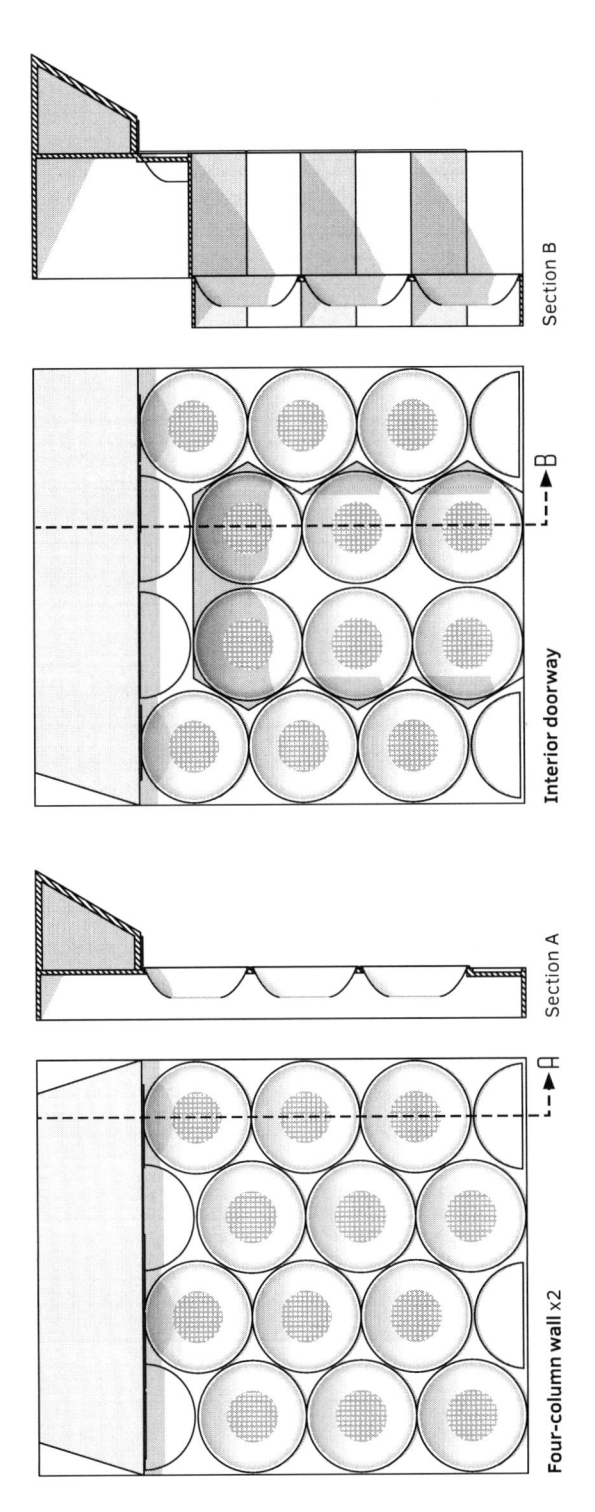

were made so the semicircular cut-outs were backed with solid ply on the new walls and covered with thin sheeting on the original indented wall to hide its deeper recesses. Those on the doors wall were left exposed.

A third new section was constructed in the same style, again four columns of roundels wide but with the centre two aligned rather than interlocking. A section was cut with a zigzag outline, mirroring the main doors, and the sides filled in so this part could slide backwards. This would represent the main doors when the set was used as the Master's TARDIS to differentiate it from the Doctor's.

Finally, all sections bar the main doors had a full-width horizontal cornice added that projected into the room. This had a sloping front face and plastic vent covers attached to its overhanging underside. As well as making the walls feel more solid and connected, this also reduced the risk of camera shots accidentally exposing the tops of the walls. For the newly built sections, the circular cut-outs only went up as high as this cornice whereas on the existing indented wall it necessarily sat in front of the pre-existing recesses, which in behind-the-scenes photos can be seen poking above the top of the entablature. In fact this caused a minor, presumably unforeseen problem. The cornice just touched the tops of the upper roundels on the new walls, but these sections had no castors and stood directly on the studio floor. This meant the roundels on the indented wall were a couple of inches higher and thus pushed up against the underside of the cornice, distorting their tops slightly.

With the new console that had been built the previous year, Gleeson's control room provided a distinctive and fresh look that suited the style of the programme at the time – perhaps only diminished by having to represent two TARDISes, implying both the Doctor and the Master just happened to redecorate in exactly the same style. Nevertheless, it was not to last. Barry Letts and Jon Pertwee weren't keen on the curved roundels, likening them to washing-up bowls, and their clear centres meant that if an exterior set was placed beyond the main doors, as in *The Time Monster* episode four, it could be seen through the roundels. So when the prospect arose of another TARDIS-focused episode the following year, the producer decided to rework the control room again.

Although the full Gleeson style only made this one appearance, reports of the set being replaced because it was damaged in storage are clearly untrue as the new wall sections were all used again (although the unpopular roundels probably were binned). One was seen in *Death to the Daleks*, with boards placed behind its cut-out circles to produce very shallow, solid roundels, along with the overhanging cornice. Then the entire set, with modifications, was reused as the main control room for Season 13 (see page 168). The final appearance of Gleeson's walls was in episode one of *The Masque of Mandragora*, recorded in early June 1976, when they were used to form the TARDIS corridors leading to its second control room.

WHAT ARE ALL THESE KNOBS?

PANELS B
1972-1974

Magna Models closed down in 1972 so storage and maintenance of the console prop was contracted to Westbury Design and Optical, run by Clifford Culley. Some small gauges were added ahead of Season 9, but two specific additions were required for the closing story, *The Time Monster*. The first was an 'Extreme emergency' control, for which a red-knobbed rod was inserted through the hole for the black dial on the right of panel 3 and covered by a flip-up lid. The second was the time ram control dial, which suddenly appeared when needed for episode five, replacing the black dial at bottom-right of panel 2 that's there during episode four, in both the Doctor's and Master's TARDISes. The hole for the dematerialisation circuit housing was here used as a receptacle for the Doctor's handheld time sensor.

For *The Three Doctors* the 'Extreme emergency' control was moved to the right-hand side of panel 6, requiring a new hole to be drilled along with one for the red light above it (a yellow light was also added on the left). This panel then saw a further change for *Death to the Daleks*. The metal plate with flick switches at the bottom was replaced with a larger one featuring small multi-coloured lights and a big red domed light that could flash to indicate the power drain caused by the Exxilon city. Also, a gauge with a square black surround was used to cover the hole in the dematerialisation circuit housing.

Although that was the controls' last appearance in this form, it was not the console's. While the panels were revamped in 1975 for Season 13, the underlying console was retained and would last many years yet.

Only newly added controls are labelled here. See the diagrams on pages 122-127 for further uses of existing controls

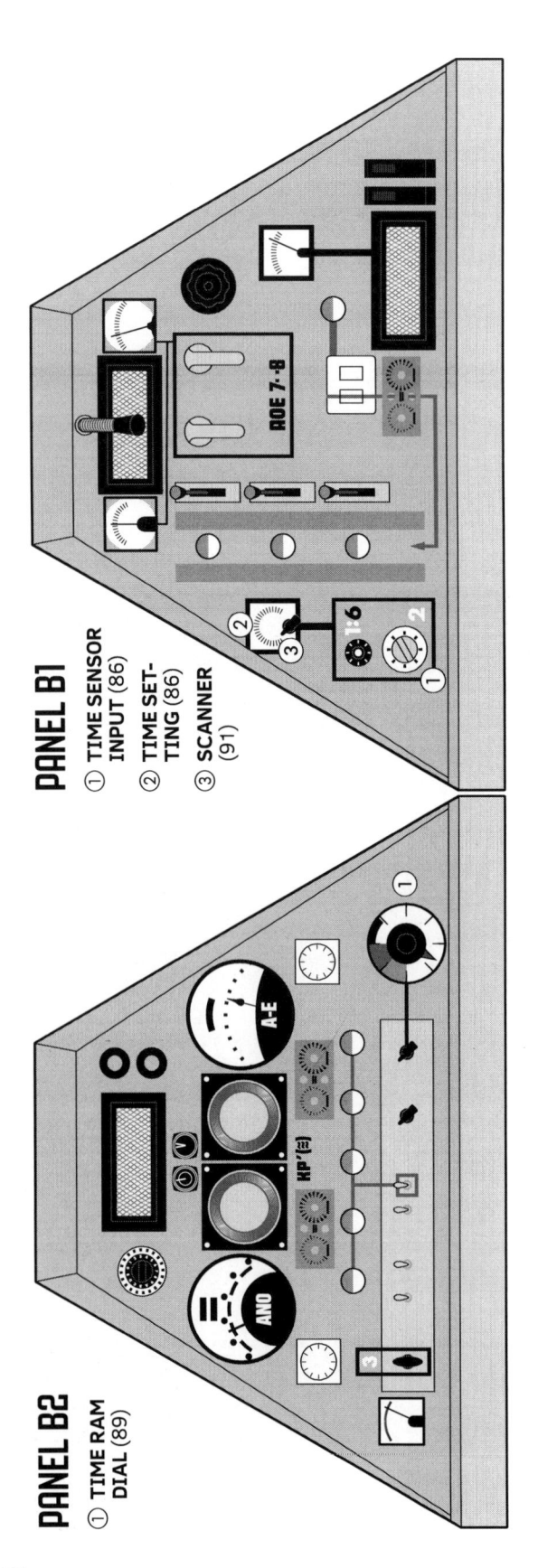

PANEL B1
① TIME SENSOR INPUT (86)
② TIME SETTING (86)
③ SCANNER (91)

PANEL B2
① TIME RAM DIAL (89)

WHAT ARE ALL THESE KNOBS?

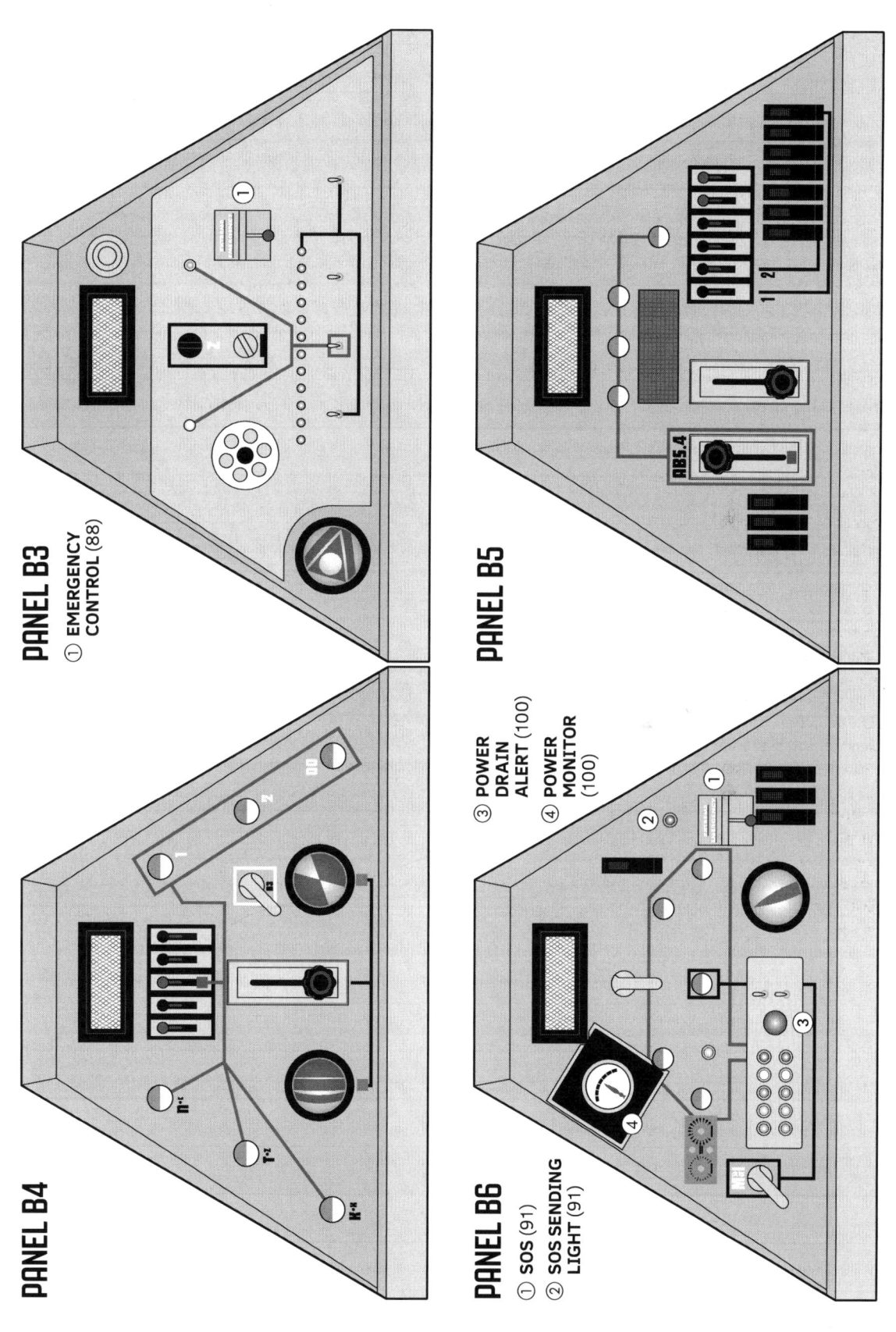

PANEL B3
① EMERGENCY CONTROL (88)

PANEL B5
③ POWER DRAIN ALERT (100)
④ POWER MONITOR (100)

PANEL B4

PANEL B6
① SOS (91)
② SOS SENDING LIGHT (91)

LANDING 88

SPACE Earth, Mediterranean, Atlantis
TIME Two days in late-16th century BC
TRAVELLERS The Doctor, Jo
EPISODES The Time Monster 5-6

The TARDIS relays the Doctor's thoughts to Jo, allowing him to instruct her to use the 'Extreme emergency' control to bring him back into the control room. He uses the time sensor to follow the Master to Atlantis, materialising in a courtyard alongside his rival's TARDIS. High priest Krasis, loyal to the Master, tries to have the Doctor and Jo killed but Lord Hippias intervenes and they are taken to King Dalios.

The next day, the Master gathers the councillors of Atlantis in the courtyard and releases Kronos from the crystal. He is unable to control the creature any more, however, and it rampages through the city causing death and destruction. Jo tries to stop the Master escaping with the crystal but he takes both into his TARDIS and departs. Queen Galleia frees the Doctor and he hurries in pursuit in his own Ship, leaving Atlantis to its terrible fate.

- **CONTROLS** The 'Extreme emergency' control that Jo operates is a red handle under a hinged square metal covering. This has been added to the right-hand side of panel B3 (which the Doctor explicitly calls "control panel number three"), replacing the black dial in the same position; the handle slots into the existing hole for the original dial's spindle. A new dial with a pointer and circular scale replaces the black dial in the bottom-right corner of panel B2 (see next landing).
- **LORE** The Doctor states it's the TARDIS that has enabled him to contact Jo telepathically. This is the first explicit indication of the Ship thinking and acting for itself. Activating the 'Extreme emergency' switch retrieves him from the Vortex and he appears (materialises? reforms?) inside the control room.
- **NOTES** This serial clearly goes along with the hypothesis that the story of Atlantis and its destruction is derived from the eruption of the Greek volcanic island Thera (yet the Master plots his TARDIS's landing site on a map of Athens), which archaeologists estimate occurred around 1500BC, although some evidence indicates it may have been over a century earlier. On their return to the 20th century, the Doctor tells Jo, "It all happened three thousand five hundred years ago."
- The high-angle tracking shot of Jo gives us a nice overview of the console but unfortunately makes the power cable running from it to the back wall very noticeable. Further attention is drawn to this as it's where the Doctor reappears.
- Why doesn't the Master's TARDIS change its appearance when it materialises in Atlantis?
- Jo thinks the Doctor still can't travel where he likes, although she's unsure; the Doctor says he has "not entirely" fixed the TARDIS, suggesting he has repaired it to a degree. As speculated earlier, this could mean he does now have free use of the Ship but is aware that so do the Time Lords, who could send him on a mission or even re-enforce his exile if they become aware of him jaunting around the universe again. Or it may be that he can pilot the TARDIS but not navigate precisely (as in his pre-exile days), which is why he needs the time sensor to accurately locate the Master's TARDIS.
- On arriving in Atlantis, cut dialogue had Jo realising she couldn't speak ancient Greek, so the Doctor activated a translation device under the console. This would have been the first time the question of language had come up in the series.
- The TARDIS's roof lamp doesn't flash when it materialises in Atlantis. When it departs, debris on its roof vanishes along with it. The arrivals and departures of both the Doctor's and the Master's TARDISes were achieved with the roll-back-and-mix technique. When they each arrive, they do so among groups of people who are very bad at staying still between the two set-ups. Alignment of the departure shots is better but look to the bottom left corner in both instances: when the Master takes off, rubble by the crystal holder moves position, and when the Doctor dematerialises the moving shadow of a production crew member appears.
- When Krasis releases Kronos, a shot is reused from the end of episode four set in the Master's TARDIS. This means it's suddenly his black-gloved hand on the release handle, the crystal reverts to the smaller shard, and the Police Box is in the background.

LANDING 89

SPACE Nowhere
TIME None
TRAVELLERS The Doctor
EPISODES The Time Monster 6

The Doctor contacts the Master via the scanner and threatens to time ram his TARDIS if he does not destroy the crystal. With the two vessels still on the same frequency their controls are locked together, and to prove this the Doctor edges a dial towards the danger zone. However, the Master calls his bluff, certain he will not kill Jo, so she twists the dial herself and the two TARDISes collide.

Fortunately, rather than mutual obliteration, the energy discharged releases Kronos from the crystal and suspends the two time machines in a void. Jo recovers consciousness first and crosses to the Police Box to wake the Doctor. Outside they are faced by Kronos in human form, who tells them they are on "the boundary of your reality and mine…the threshold of being". It is grateful for its freedom and agrees to send them home in the TARDIS, but wishes to punish the Master for holding it prisoner. The Master begs for help from the Doctor, who asks Kronos to release the villain into his custody. It agrees, but when the Master escapes in his TARDIS the creature capriciously allows him to go free.

The Doctor and Jo leave in the TARDIS. She cannot understand why he saved the Master from Kronos's punishment; he explains he could never condemn someone to an eternity of torment, not even the Master, despite his causing the destruction of Atlantis.

- **CONTROLS** The Master's TARDIS suddenly has an 'Extreme emergency' control and a time ram dial too. The new dial reacts when the Doctor threatens to time ram the two TARDISes, the implication being that the Doctor is twisting the same control in his TARDIS and the Master's reacts accordingly. The scale goes from -16 to 112, with 96-112 being the red 'Danger' zone (80-96 is shaded amber). Note in the close-up of this control, the glue marks from the black tape that framed the previous dial on this panel are horribly obvious.
- In mid-shots of the Master's console, a piece of unpainted wood can be seen underneath the time ram control, presumably part of the mechanism used to turn the dial remotely in the close-up shots.
- **LORE** A TARDIS can be used to control another if they're operating on the same frequency.
- **NOTES** The Master handcuffs Jo to panel B3 of his console, right next to his own 'Extreme emergency' control. Why does she never think to pull that to stop him?
- The Master is at a loss to prevent the Doctor ramming his TARDIS; he doesn't even try to get it operating on a different frequency (whatever that means) to break the Doctor's control of his console. Is this how the Time Lords can operate the Doctor's TARDIS remotely?

LANDING 90

SPACE Earth, England, Cambridgeshire, Wootton, Newton Institute, TOMTIT lab
TIME Shortly after Landing 87
TRAVELLERS The Doctor, Jo
EPISODES The Time Monster 6

The TARDIS materialises in the TOMTIT lab at the Newton Institute as Ruth Baxter and Stuart Hyde try to release the time lock the Master has left the outside world in. They succeed but the equipment overloads, rendering it useless. The Brigadier bursts in at last only to find the Master long gone and Sergeant Benton returned to adulthood but naked.

- **NOTES** The TARDIS lands where the Master's had stood (more or less) so is it returning to where it had previously materialised except the Master's TARDIS is no longer there to land inside, or is the Doctor controlling it? Or is Kronos just sending him where it assumes he wants to be?
- How does the Doctor get the TARDIS back to UNIT HQ? Well, if we follow the intention of the time that he has yet to regain control of the Ship, then he must have the Brigadier transport it by lorry. But if, as we've speculated, the Doctor repaired the TARDIS prior to *The Curse of Peladon*, he might pilot it there himself, and who knows where else before the next story?

IT'S BIGGER ON THE INSIDE

THE LIMINTON THROWBACK
1972-1973

The Three Doctors was the opening serial of the tenth season of *Doctor Who* and, although strictly speaking a year early, thoughts were very much on the programme's being a decade old. When it came to revamping the TARDIS control room after the unpopularity of Tim Gleeson's attempt for the previous story, therefore, designer Roger Liminton took inspiration from photos of Peter Brachacki's original set.

Cost, as ever, was an issue so he again reused the two original 1963 sections that survived: the main doors and indented wall. These had Gleeson's 'washbowl' roundels removed and replaced with flat translucent plastic discs at the back of the recesses, akin to their appearance during the Troughton years. The doors retained their solid backing, however, now painted blue (to mimic the Police Box doors?). The semicircles of the indented wall were also uncovered and given translucent backings.

From measurements of these existing pieces, Liminton had two new matching sections made, just two columns of circles wide. One was placed to the right of the pre-existing indented wall while the other was intended to go to the left of the main doors. In studio, however, it was positioned on the far right of the set to allow the director the camera angles he wanted. Between these two new sections was the most notable addition: a flat translucent screen with a ceiling piece that contained four circular lights aimed downwards through segmented diffusers. With a monitor hung in front, this was deliberately reminiscent of the original computer wall and scanner framework, although much simpler.

All sections bar the doors again had overhanging cornices that, although similar to those introduced by Gleeson, were newly made. They were shallower than the previous version, while the section on the main indented wall had a square end at the left where it abutted the main doors wall; in *The Time Monster* the cornice here had a tapered end.

The scanner returned to being a hanging television monitor, as in the 1960s, slung from the cornice on the screen wall in front of the downlights. In Liminton's design drawings, however, this is shown encased in a square block that descended from the cornice. Below this, with a gap between, is a square white column (inspired by the illuminated pillars in the original control room?). While the scanner was later placed into the cornice for *Planet of the Daleks* (recorded directly after *The Three Doctors*), its casing wasn't the same as in the set designs and the pillar below was never made.

As part of his homage to Brachacki's set, Liminton also planned to reintroduce the large overhead light, to be hung between the console and the screen wall. His design drawings show this would have been faithful to the original, with two hexagonal outer rings around a circular light with segmented diffuser. But this was also abandoned before construction, or at least never appears on screen.

Finally, the studio floor was painted a medium grey around the edges of the set and white in the centre where the console was positioned – possibly inspired by the hexagons painted on the floor of the 1963 set. The design drawings also indicate an "existing PBU" – that is, one of the photographic walls – was to be placed beyond the main doors. We don't see through the doors in *The Three Doctors*, and when we do in *Planet of the Daleks* there are set pieces appropriate to the TARDIS's location. But this does suggest at least one of the photo walls survived as of late-1972.

Planet of the Daleks also required a bed for the Doctor to recover on. Rather than attempt to reintroduce the TARDIS's living quarters (not represented since *The Chase*), this was situated in the control room itself. A standard self-assembly storage cupboard in white was used, adapted so that a divan could slide out from a deep floor-level drawer (pushed out by a stagehand behind the set). This was positioned to the right of the screen wall in place of the second narrow indented wall, but slightly away from it so that the gap suggested a way through to further TARDIS rooms.

Although Liminton's set was heavily influenced by the original, it didn't last beyond the tenth season. When the control room was next seen in *Death to the Daleks* it may have been thought the bright look didn't suit the requirement for the TARDIS to appear in darkness as its power is drained. Yet even in 1975, when the production team reintroduced the control room after a season's absence, they returned mostly to Gleeson's walls. There's a good chance Liminton's screen wall no longer existed, but one of the narrow indented sections makes a brief appearance in *Pyramids of Mars* and a final one in *The Masque of Mandragora* episode one forming part of the TARDIS corridors.

IT'S BIGGER ON THE INSIDE

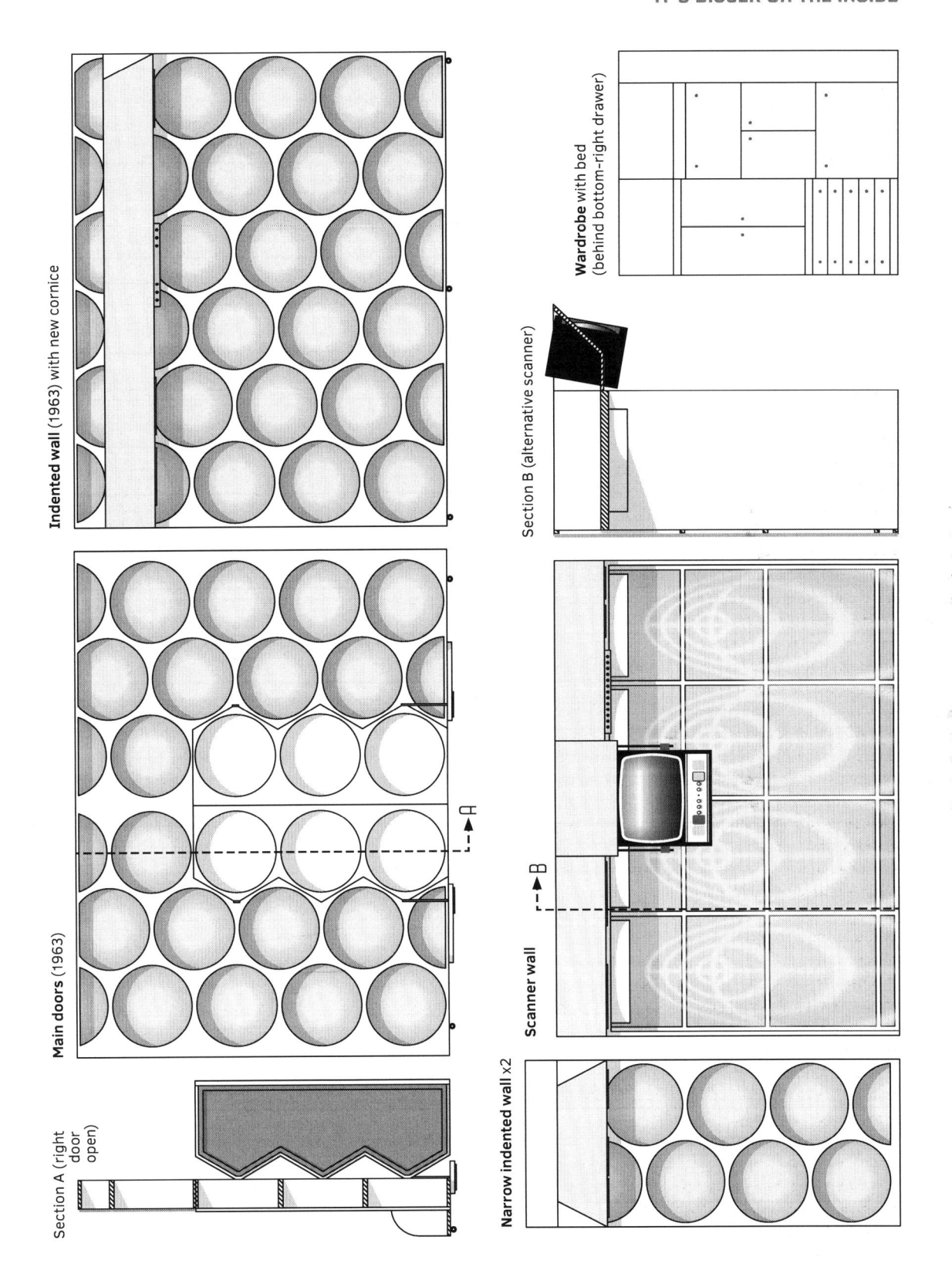

Indented wall (1963) with new cornice

Main doors (1963)

Section A (right door open)

Section B (alternative scanner)

Scanner wall

Wardrobe with bed (behind bottom-right drawer)

Narrow indented wall x2

147

LANDING 91

SPACE Antimatter world inside black hole, Omega's palace; transported back to Earth, England, UNIT HQ, lab
TIME None; [late-1970s]
TRAVELLERS The Doctor (two incarnations), Jo, Brigadier Alister Lethbridge-Stewart, Sergeant Benton, Dr Tyler, Arthur Ollis
EPISODES The Three Doctors 1-4

UNIT is approached by Dr Tyler of Wessex University regarding the sudden disappearance of Arthur Ollis, warden of the Minsbridge wildlife sanctuary, shortly after he had recovered one of Tyler's cosmic ray detectors. The professor has already been getting inexplicable results that he planned to consult UNIT on, suggesting an energy beam directed at the Earth and travelling faster than the speed of light. The Doctor and Jo leave to investigate where the balloon-borne detector came down, leaving Tyler to develop the photographic plate from it in the Doctor's lab. The image shows the distorted face of Ollis, and when Tyler tries to open the detector he too vanishes as an amorphous organism emerges and slides away down the lab sink.

When the Brigadier brings some satellite reports to show Dr Tyler and finds him gone, he worries the professor is wandering around UNIT HQ unescorted and has Sergeant Benton organise a search. There is no sign of him but Benton does report a flash of light in the garage, which the returning Doctor explains was a release of kinetic energy as the organism made Bessie disappear. They deduce the energy beam brought the organism, which is specifically hunting for the Doctor.

Suddenly the building is surround by one-eyed gelatinous creatures that shoot energy pulses from their claws. The UNIT soldiers try to fight them off but their weapons are ineffective. The organism corners the Doctor, Jo and Benton in the lab, taking out part of the wall, so the Doctor bundles them into the TARDIS, turning on its forcefield for safety as the organism continues to expunge pieces of the lab. The Doctor tries to dematerialise the Ship but the organism has somehow immobilised it, so he calls on the Time Lords for help.

The assistance they provide is most unexpected, as a younger version of the Doctor, still in his second incarnation, appears from nowhere. He explains the Time Lords' power is being drained but they summoned enough temporal energy to bring him into his own future. Benton is pleased to see him again, Jo is confused and the older Doctor is rather put out at having his younger self about. The two Doctors telepathically bring each other up to speed on the situation but then squabble over the younger's recorder playing, so the Time Lords try to bring his first incarnation forward in time to mediate. Their lack of energy only permits him to appear on the scanner, and he informs them the energy beam is a bridge that they should cross. The Doctors toss a coin to choose who should go, the older losing, but as he exits the TARDIS Jo runs after him and they are both transported by the organism.

Having achieved its goal, the organism goes dormant so the younger Doctor and Benton risk leaving the TARDIS. They try to keep the thing subdued with a device of the Doctor's construction but it has the opposite effect because the organism is composed of antimatter. The Doctor bundles Benton and the Brigadier back into the TARDIS as the organism becomes agitated again and expunges the Doctor's device.

The Brigadier is anxious to return to his men fighting the gel creatures outside but the Doctor insists he would not get past the organism. He needs to think but cannot find his recorder. To soothe the agitated Brigadier, the Doctor patches his radio through the TARDIS's communication circuit so it will transmit through the forcefield, allowing him to issue orders to his corporal. The Doctor's first incarnation reappears on the scanner to warn them that the Time Lords are fast losing power and tells his future self to turn off the forcefield. This he does, allowing the organism to transport the TARDIS through a black hole, along with the whole of UNIT HQ.

As the scanner still shows the lab, but no organism, they venture outside. The Brigadier is outraged to find the building has been moved, although he cannot comprehend just how far and heads out to find a telephone. The Doctor wants to look again for his recorder but gel creatures arrive and lead him and Benton away.

Some time later, the Brigadier, Benton, Jo, Dr Tyler and Ollis make it back to UNIT HQ. As they debate what to do next, the two Doctors arrive with gel creatures close behind and they all take refuge in the TARDIS, but are trapped there. The Time Lords make a final effort to project the Doctor's first incarnation through the black hole, and he makes telepathic contact with his future selves to devise a plan. This involves dismantling the forcefield and when the Doctors remove the generator they find the younger's recorder has fallen into it, and thus has not been converted to antimatter. They contact Omega via the scanner and offer to help free him from the black hole, persuading him to release the TARDIS so they can travel to his palace.

The Ship instantly rematerialises within Omega's throne room. The Doctors offer Omega his freedom in return for sending their friends home. Omega knows now he can never leave this antimatter universe but promises to release the others and spare their universe if the Doctors stay with him forever. They agree and persuade their friends to step into the singularity. The Doctors then try to make Omega take the forcefield generator but he knocks it away. They dash into the TARDIS as the recorder touches the floor, annihilating Omega and his universe.

With Omega's will gone, the TARDIS is transported back to 20th century Earth, appearing in the Doctor's lab at UNIT where his friends and all the missing items have just reappeared. The earliest Doctor appears on the scanner one last time to say goodbye before fading, as does his second incarnation. The Brigadier and Benton go to check everything has indeed returned, followed by Dr Tyler, leaving Jo and the Doctor in the control room, the latter saddened by Omega's unavoidable fate. Just then a new dematerialisation circuit appears on top of the central column and the Doctor finds his "knowledge of time travel law and all the dematerialisation codes" has returned. The Time Lords have lifted his exile, although he assures Jo he won't be rushing off straight away – he has to build a new forcefield generator first, at least.

○ **CONTROLS** The Doctor turns on the forcefield with the rocker switches on panel B1 (which his second incarnation also uses later) and tries to take off using the three small levers as standard, doing the same in episode four. He sends an SOS to the Time Lords using the red handle under the cover labelled 'Extreme emergency', which has been repositioned on panel B6 above the three switches in the bottom-right corner (its old position on panel B3 is now covered with black tape). A new red bulb above it flashes when the handle is pulled out. The Doctor activates the scanner with one of the switches in the bottom-left corner of panel B5, whereas later his younger self twists the knob on the gauge to the left of the lightbulbs on panel B1. As the two Doctors squabble, the younger adjusts the large black dial on panel B1, and again to try to recover the image of his first incarnation on the scanner.

○ The forcefield generator is located in the console's pedestal beneath panel B1.

○ The new dematerialisation circuit looks, not surprisingly, exactly like the old one the Doctor has been tinkering with for ages. It appears with a speeded up version of the standard materialisation sound effect.

○ The dematerialisation circuit housing is back in its slot at the top left of panel B6 and a yellow bulb has been added above the group of switches at the bottom. The bearing chart has been moved from panel B1 to B6, to the left of the left-most bulb. The hole above the grille on panel B1, where the microphone was fitted in *The Time Monster* (Landing 86), has been covered by a pale circular patch (looking suspiciously like a sticking plaster) and a new black dial has been added at bottom-left (next to the '1:6' label).

▮ **LORE** The Time Lords can remotely provide the TARDIS with additional power.

▮ The scanner can receive visual transmissions (at least from the Time Lords).

▮ External communications devices (at least simple ones using radio waves) can be boosted through the TARDIS's own communication circuit so they can operate from within the Ship's forcefield.

▮ The forcefield not only keeps dangers out but locks occupants in and must be switched off for them to leave the TARDIS.

▤ **NOTES** It's not explicitly stated that UNIT has moved to new headquarters but the building seen in *The Three Doctors* is situated within wooded grounds that cannot possibly match the urban view from the lab window in *Terror of the Autons* and *The Time Monster*. As we've seen, although the Doctor seems to have used several lab spaces over the last few years, they always looked like rooms in the same building. In *The Three Doctors*, the Doctor's lab is clearly on the ground floor, not a higher storey as in *Terror of the Autons*, and there's no staircase to an upper level. There are cosmetic changes too, with blue doors and a green/grey dado.

▤ The TARDIS control room has another redecoration by designer Roger Liminton. The main doors and six-column wall section are both Brachacki originals, the latter now missing its skirting. A deliberate attempt was made to recall the look of the original control room so it's a little strange that the younger Doctor notices and says he doesn't like it. Was the line written under the assumption the previous 'washing-up bowl' design would still be in use, as an in-joke about the production team's dissatisfaction with that look?

▤ Oops! When the Doctor, Jo and Benton first enter the control room, look closely at the scanner on the far-right of the screen: it's showing the same camera feed as the one you're watching.

▤ The main doors make no sound when opening or closing in this story.

▤ Jo's admonishment in episode one that the Doctor was "going off without me" and his admission he was "planning to lure that stuff away from Earth" suggest he's already able to pilot the TARDIS to some degree.

▤ The TARDIS forcefield is first seen in action in *The Web Planet* (Landing 14).

▤ The Doctor is surprisingly willing to call in the Time Lords given how little he knows about the organism. Could he be starting to get a sense of the seriousness of the situation from his previous incarnations' memories?

▤ The younger Doctor appears with the TARDIS's usual grinding sound, much as the Time Lord in *Terror of the Autons* did. So is this noise that of the time continuum being disrupted rather than the Ship's engines?

▤ The Doctor's appearance was achieved using a split-screen effect, with a view of the empty control room overlaid on the left-hand side of the picture – the join runs vertically along the right edge of the central column; note how shadows on the console are cut off, as are Jon Pertwee's fingers when he picks up the recorder. This was then faded out to reveal Patrick Troughton already in position. Similarly, for his departure at the end of episode four the right-hand side of the image had a shot of the empty set faded in to gradually obscure Troughton; note the change in tone on the console's rim and you can still see the Doctor's raised arm reflected in the scanner even after he has 'gone'.

▤ Oops! The edge of the control room set and studio cameras can be seen reflected in the scanner screen during close-ups.

▤ Curiously, the TARDIS scanner shows a view of the lab including the Police Box itself, as if from a camera several feet away. This is also the first time the scanner is used as a remote communications device, rather than simply a 'window' to what's outside. Or, if the Doctor's first incarnation is in some sort of capsule transporting him from his time stream into his future, perhaps he is just outside but in some higher dimension ("I seem to be stuck up here.") that the scanner can visualise – is the view of the Police Box then his viewpoint (it's not seen until after he has made contact)? Then again, how he can see and hear those inside the TARDIS isn't shown, but if his capsule has some form of display perhaps it's just connecting via the scanner like a videophone. The Doctor later calls up Omega on the scanner, who may be using the screen previously seen in his throne room, although that like everything else inside the black hole is just a projection of his will.

- In episode three the Police Box doors are left wide open affording a clear view of the inside: painted black with covers over the rear windows. The fact that the back wall also has doors is clear as there's a gap between them through which can be seen the stripes of the Venetian blind behind the prop. Patrick Troughton exits the Police Box with a piece of equipment he wasn't holding in the preceding control room scene; it's not the pacifier control he used earlier and looks too big to have been in his pocket. It then disappears while the Brigadier checks outside and is never referred to.
- The TARDIS doors are again left open when the Doctor and Benton are taken away by gel creatures, yet are somehow locked by the time everyone returns.
- In episode four, the side of the console's pedestal below panel B5 is loose and the studio floor can be seen through the gap.
- When the TARDIS dematerialises from the lab, the take-off sound effect is the echoing version with leading thump, not heard since *The Seeds of Death* (Landing 66). Similarly, when it rematerialises in Omega's palace the effect introduced in *The Invasion* (Landing 63) is used. In both instances, the Police Box fades in and out of view before finally disappearing/reappearing. Is the TARDIS struggling to operate within the antimatter universe?
- The shot of it dematerialising uses a split-screen effect, with the two gel creatures on the left facing an empty set and a shot of the Police Box in position superimposed on the right. The latter is then faded out. A hard-edged mask was used, rather than a soft wipe, and the line of this can be seen down the centre of the screen betraying a difference in the intensity of the shadows in each shot. Oddly, the shadows on the TARDIS indicate the gel creatures were in position for that shot too, and these don't shift when the right-hand picture is faded out, so if the actors in the gel costumes could stay that still why not use the simpler roll-back-and-mix technique (as with its arrival in Omega's palace)?
- The Police Box's roof lamp doesn't shine when it materialises in Omega's palace but is illuminated from above by a flashing light.
- When the TARDIS is returned to the UNIT lab on Earth, watch the window on the far right of the screen. As the Police Box appears, so does a section of wall outside the window. This is the piece of set directly behind the box, which was designed to swing outwards so that the rear doors of the prop could be used when multiple people needed to go in and out.
- Now the Doctor is free to roam the universe again, where do we stand on when he actually repaired the TARDIS? We've remarked on events and dialogue that indicate he hasn't been trapped for as long as is generally accepted (and no doubt intended by the production team at the time) but also possibly not free or willing to completely resume his nomadic lifestyle. Perhaps it was his imposed ignorance of time travel laws that made him unsure about making too many journeys even though he could, worried he might inadvertently cause temporal damage. His lack of knowledge about dematerialisation codes doesn't seem to have prevented him making trips in *The Time Monster*, and possibly *The Curse of Peladon*, so maybe the key word here is "all": he knew enough to make limited journeys but not for complete navigational control. Maybe he never knew all the codes, which is why his earlier travels were so random and why from now on he'll have much greater command over where he goes. So with Jo happy to travel with him, the Master leaving 20th century Earth alone after his close shave with Kronos, and UNIT well established, it seems he's finally willing to loosen his ties with Earth and explore the universe once more.

LANDING 92

SPACE [Acteon group], Inter Minor, city space port, inside compression field of a Miniscope
TIME Unknown [future]
TRAVELLERS The Doctor, Jo
EPISODES Carnival of Monsters 1–4

The TARDIS arrives in what seems to be the hold of the SS Bernice on Friday 4 June 1926 as it crosses the Indian Ocean – not Metebelis Three, as the Doctor was anticipating. For one thing, the air smells more of sulphur than wine; for another, the crates around them are stencilled 'Bombay' and one containing chickens is bound for Singapore. Hearing the rumble of engines and the tremor of movement, the travellers climb out of the hold to determine where they are.

With time aboard the ship looping through the same hour, the Doctor and Jo return to the TARDIS to fetch a magnetic core extractor with which to open an anachronistic metal plate only they can see. Jo waits outside the Ship, calling out when the whole deck above appears to open up. The Doctor emerges just as a giant hand reaches down and picks up the TARDIS.

The Ship has actually landed inside a Miniscope, caught in the compression field of one of its miniaturised zoological environments: circuit three, a collection of humans (and one plesiosaur). The Scope's owner, a showman called Vorg, thinks the tiny TARDIS is a piece of bric-a-brac that was causing a malfunction, but he places it back inside the machine while he tries to persuade a tribunal of Inter Minorian officials to let him stay on their planet.

Suspicious that Vorg is a spy, Kalik and Orum of the tribunal check the Scope for a transmitter. All they find is the

TARDIS, which taken outside the compression field rapidly returns to normal size, much to the tribunal's alarm. They observe on the Scope's screen that the Doctor and Jo have found their way into the circuit five environment: a marshy landscape from a moon of Grundle, where they are soon being tracked by vicious omnivorous Drashigs. Vorg reluctantly reaches into the machine to distract the creatures while the Doctor and Jo escape back into the workings of the Scope. However, the Drashigs have their scent and break out of their circuit in pursuit.

Kalik plans to allow the creatures to escape from the Scope and rampage through the city to discredit the president, his brother. He dismisses the Functionaries guarding the eradicator weapon and has Orum disarm it. Vorg's assistant Shirna notices the Scope's power is failing and as Vorg tries to repair it a panel at the base opens and the miniaturised Doctor stumbles out. He returns to normal size and is relieved to see the TARDIS safe and sound. He deplores Vorg's use of the Scope and browbeats the tribunal into allowing him to rescue Jo and the other 'specimens' before the Scope's power fails.

The Doctor connects the Scope to the TARDIS via a piece of equipment that compensates for the Scope's faulty omega circuit. It has two levers, one to transpose him back into the machine and the other to send all the lifeforms inside back to where they were taken from. Vorg activates the first lever but tribunal leader Pletrac shoots the equipment as the Doctor vanishes. Vorg hurries to repair it before the Scope's power fades, unaware that Kalik is working to release the Drashigs. The official succeeds but with the creatures grown to full fearsome size he realises his folly just before being eaten. Vorg re-arms the eradicator and shoots the Drashigs but during the distraction the Scope has died. He throws the second lever anyway and with the last vestige of power the specimens are returned home. The Scope goes kaput just as the Doctor and Jo appear beside it.

Vorg regales Pletrac with tall tales of his bravery at gunning down the Drashigs while the Doctor and Jo move the equipment cabinet back into the TARDIS. As the showman introduces the grateful official to the concept of gambling, the travellers leave him to it and take off in the Ship, watched by Shirna.

▪ NOTES This may not be the Doctor and Jo's first journey in the TARDIS since the Time Lords lifted his exile. The Doctor says there's "no need for a test", probably intended at the time to mean a test flight as he gets used to the TARDIS working again. But as he follows this immediately with, "I've been here before and the air is perfectly—" he's just as likely to be talking about no need for testing the environmental conditions – noted as "routine landing procedures" in *The Curse of Peladon*. Jo does ask, "Are you sure you can steer that TARDIS properly?", however, suggesting she hasn't yet made enough trips to have reached a conclusion on that point.

▪ It's possible Inter Minor is in the same group of planets or solar systems as Metebelis Three and that the TARDIS was just drawn off course when caught (somehow) in the Miniscope's compression field. The Doctor says, "We may have slightly overshot the blue planet but we must be on one of the planets in the group." But equally, knowing the TARDIS, they might be nowhere near their intended destination. No one on Inter Minor seems to recognise the name Metebelis when the Doctor mentions it in episode four.

▪ There's no evidence the Miniscope involves time travel when collecting specimens so this could be any time after June 1926, although probably quite a bit of time as the Scope is clearly a run-down piece of kit. Then again, the Time Lords' involvement in the devices' prohibition, regardless of the Doctor's ethical concerns, might suggest they use some illicit time technology and the humans could have been taken from the relative future. The Doctor doesn't consider that he might have arrived at a point in time before Miniscopes were banned, so they must have been disposed of in such a way that they never existed at any point in time, as happened to the War Lords in *The War Games*.

▪ The TARDIS materialises with the now-standard sound effect, but when it leaves at the end of the story an earlier version used during Season 6 is heard (see Landing 63). This story was recorded at the end of the series' ninth recording block and was the last for which Brian Hodgson provided the special sounds. Did he choose to revert to an earlier effect he preferred for his final track? It might explain why his successor, Dick Mills, also uses TARDIS sounds from Season 6 for much of the rest of Season 10 (including *The Three Doctors*, produced after *Frontier in Space*), if that was the tape most recently used.

▪ The miniature Police Box handled by Vorg and later Orum was a new model about two inches tall. At this scale the detail is limited: note the windows and panelling are painted rather than three-dimensional. The TARDIS's return to full size was achieved with three models: this small one starts out in Orum's palm, then he places the six-inch version on the floor and finally the 3-foot model is used for the shot of the Police Box growing.

▪ The TARDIS door is open when the Doctor exits at the end of episode one, but closed when Vorg examines the miniature Ship and when it returns to full size.

LANDING 93

SPACE Earth spaceship C982, cargo hold; transported to Ogron homeworld, Master's base
TIME At least four days in 2540
TRAVELLERS The Doctor, Jo
EPISODES Frontier in Space 1,5-6; Planet of the Daleks 1

To avoid a collision with another spaceship as it enters hyperspace, the Doctor has to make a last-minute course correction to materialise the TARDIS inside the vessel instead. It lands in the cargo hold among hoppers of flour. The Doctor emerges behind Jo, who is a little shaken by their near miss, then he goes back to the control room to find out when and where they are so he can get the Ship back to Earth. Jo looks out a porthole to see another spaceship coming alongside emitting a high-pitched throbbing noise. The Doctor decides to find the crew to confirm the current date for his calculations.

However, the two-man crew believe they are being boarded by Draconians, members of a rival empire to Earth's, and lock the Doctor and Jo in a cell in the hold. The Doctor converts his sonic screwdriver into an electromagnet by reversing the polarity of its power source so he can unbolt the cell door, only for a crewman to come for them anyway, to use as shields against the boarders. The attackers are really Ogrons, however, who stun the Doctor and the crew, lock Jo in the cell, then depart with the cargo and the TARDIS.

The Ogrons return with their spoils to their home planet on the remote fringes of the galaxy at coordinates 2349 to 6784, where the organiser of their raids, the Master, is waiting. Surprised to have the TARDIS delivered to him, he sends Ogrons to bring him the Doctor. When they fail he forges the credentials of a commissioner from Sirius Four and sets off for Earth to find the Doctor himself.

The Master returns to the Ogrons' planet days later with Jo his captive, knowing the Doctor will follow to rescue her. He tries to hypnotise Jo but she has learned how to counter this by reciting nursery rhymes. She even resists his hypnotic sound device, so the Master has Ogrons take her to a cell. Another of the ape-like mercenaries reports on further raids of Earth cargo vessels and the Master is sure war between Earth and Draconia is imminent.

The Doctor arrives only to discover the Daleks are behind the plan to cause interplanetary war so they can take over the remains of both empires. He rescues Jo and they make for the TARDIS to follow the Daleks to their base of operations, but are intercepted by the Master and Ogrons. The Doctor uses the hypnotic sound device to make the Ogrons see the huge predatory monster they fear and they scatter in panic. As the Master is bundled away in the melee his gun fires, catching the Doctor a glancing blow to the forehead. He is dazed so Jo helps him into the TARDIS. He dematerialises the Ship then sends a request for help to the Time Lords via the telepathic circuits. Jo helps him to a bed in the control room and he slips into a restless coma.

- **CONTROLS** The Doctor closes the main doors from panel B6 then takes off with the standard levers on panel B1. (Note the control room brightens as the Ship is set in motion.) The telepathic circuits are the two rotating-light units on panel B2, which the Doctor places both hands on.
- **LORE** The Doctor claims he didn't steal the TARDIS when he left his home planet, just borrowed it, intending to return it even though it was an older model.
- **NOTES** The Doctor is trying to get Jo back to Earth, and in episode four Jo says how they "keep landing up in one terrible situation after another". At that point she's just waffling on in order to distract the Master yet she seems generally to be telling the truth, so there's a good chance there have been several landings since leaving Inter Minor. Has the Doctor been making repeated failed efforts to reach Metebelis Three until finally Jo gets fed up and asks to be taken home? After their next journey, she insists Earth is the only place she wants to go.

- The Doctor estimates they have landed in the 26th century. The cargo ship pilot records, "Preparing to enter hyperspace at twenty-two oh nine seventy-two, two thousand five hundred and forty EST." This is presumably 22:09, 72, 2540 Earth Standard Time. The time of day concurs with the clock on the bridge (having been scripted as 22:17 – although given this display at one point goes from 22:59 to 22:01 it may not actually be a clock), but what's the time of year supposed to be? It was scripted as 'seven two' not 72, so it could be the seventh of February. Then again, according to the catalogue of the Doctor and Jo's crimes on Sirius, there's an apparent date of '52nd smalk', so perhaps this journey takes place in the 72nd smalk. Other dialogue refers to there still being months, however, so maybe the smalk is a uniquely Sirian measurement of time. Moments later the cargo ship pulls out of hyperspace at "twenty-two thirteen seven two seven two four zero"; although the time was again changed from the scripted 22:19, the second "seven two" is as written so, by the above logic, that would make it four minutes and 4,700 years later. Did scriptwriter Malcolm Hulke mistakenly type 'seven two' again instead of 'two five' and no one noticed?

- The glimpses of the Police Box on the cargo ship's monitor and on the interrogation screen in episode three are the six-inch model. These and the shot at the end of the story (see next landing) cement the idea that the TARDIS spins on its vertical axis when it's travelling.

- When the Master reveals to Jo he has the TARDIS, its right-hand side is facing out of the alcove. But in the re-shot scene for the end of episode six, the front of the prop is facing outward.

- When Jo helps the Doctor into the TARDIS, the 'Police telephone' plaque is slightly ajar, proving that the panel actually opened, although what was behind it is not known (possibly still a hole from when a phone cubby was added – see Landing 63).

- The view through the control room doors at this point is the last time physical scenery was placed beyond the doors to show what was directly outside the Ship until the 2005 series. The next time we see through the doors, CSO is used to simulate the space beyond (see Landings 114 and 115).

- The Doctor has only just been freed from Time Lord oversight and already he's calling on them for help to make sure the TARDIS successfully reaches the Daleks' base, further evidence that he's still getting used to piloting the Ship again. He doesn't use the 'Extreme emergency' control this time (as in Landing 91) but places his hands on the rotating-light units. Is this so he can, as he says, "[send] a message" rather than just a general alert? (Perhaps he's telling the Time Lords, "Please don't send that annoying previous incarnation of mine again.")

- The final shot of *Frontier in Space*, of the TARDIS spinning away (reused in *Planet of the Daleks* episode one), features the 12-inch model. It's the last use of this miniature in the series. The model shot and scenes of Jo helping the injured Doctor into the TARDIS were recorded after the rest of the serial was complete to provide a new ending as it was decided the original no longer tied into the following story sufficiently.

LANDING 94

SPACE Spiridon, jungle
TIME Two days in 2540
TRAVELLERS The Doctor, Jo
EPISODES Planet of the Daleks 1,6

Jo records the Doctor's condition in a handheld audio log. An alarm sounds on the console and the TARDIS materialises on Spiridon just before dawn.

It is surround by jungle although there are marked stones that suggest a past civilisation, and nearby a cryovolcano that vents freezing sludge from the planet's core. Finding the Doctor so cold his face is now covered with frost, Jo determines to venture outside to seek help. She tries the scanner but the view is obscured by squirts of fluid. Donning a raincoat and woollen mittens, she leaves the TARDIS, which is already half covered in a spongy fungus. As she moves away, plants with large petals spray her with a thick yellow liquid.

Back in the Ship, the Doctor recovers and is puzzled to find the automatic oxygen supply on even though the air outside is breathable. He tries to open the main doors but they won't move, sealed shut by the fungus. The console alerts him the oxygen supply is exhausted so he wheels out the emergency supply: a trolley containing three gas canisters. The first two are already empty and the third runs dry while the Doctor is changing his clothes. He checks circuits under the console but finds no fault with the doors and deduces the obstruction must be outside. However, he collapses as the scanner displays 'Cabin Atmosphere Unable to Sustain Life'. Just then a squad of Thals wearing protective hoods cut away the fungus from the Police Box doors and help the fainting Doctor out, alerted to his predicament by Jo. They sit him down away from the spurting plants to recover, spraying his skin with a treatment against the fungus. He tells them he is the same Doctor who helped the Thals long ago when they "were in their greatest peril". He learns he is on Spiridon, a planet with extreme temperature shifts from day to night, aggressive vegetation and invisible inhabitants. The Thals will not tell him their mission here but admit they are down to three men. The Doctor offers to help and they lead him back to their ship where they left Jo.

By the next day the fungus is building up again on the TARDIS exterior. The Doctor and Jo hurry back as, although the Daleks' main force has been frozen in the heart of the cryovolcano and the Thals are on their way home to Skaro in a stolen Dalek spaceship, the Dalek Supreme and his retinue are close behind. They cover their faces against the spurting plants then dash into the Ship and take off just as the Daleks open fire.

The Doctor brings up an image on the scanner of Skaro, where one of the Thals invited Jo to join him, but she sets the view to the only planet she wants to go to: Earth.

- **CONTROLS** Jo activates the scanner with the upper middle switch of the cluster at the bottom of panel B6. The Doctor uses the same switch, and the one below it to open the main doors. He notices the automatic oxygen supply is on from the pale disc on the left of panel B3 while the small bulb just above it flashes when this is depleted. On his return, the Doctor closes the doors with the same switch used in episode one. To dematerialise the TARDIS he presses a rocker switch on panel B1 then pulls the three small levers as standard. He activates the scanner by pressing a switch out of sight but which could be at the bottom of panel B6, then uses the top-right black dial on panel B1 seemingly to select its view. He twists both rotary handles next to this when agreeing to take Jo home.
- **LORE** The TARDIS can take in air from outside if breathable by its occupants, but if not or this is blocked in some way it has a limited internal oxygen supply. (See Landing 19 for more of Terry Nation's ideas about how the TARDIS air supply works.)
- If the exterior doors are sealed by an outside force or substance, the interior doors will not open.
- The scanner can show images from locations a great distance away. It's not clear if these are stills or live. It can also show text warnings.
- **NOTES** Although the journey appears to take some time, to allow the Doctor to recover from his injury, presumably the TARDIS still arrives shortly after the Daleks left the Ogrons' planet, or possibly even earlier to ensure their scheme is foiled before war breaks out between Earth and Draconia. There's no suggestion, however, that the Daleks are operating from a different timezone so this is still the mid-26th century.
- The control room has a new wall section to the right of the scanner wall, with drawers, cupboards and a bed that slides out into the room. (Self-assembly furniture was only just taking off in the UK in the early-1970s with the rise of low-cost retailers like MFI and Texas Homecare.) There is a gap between this and the scanner wall allowing access to more rooms, whereas in *The Three Doctors* there was another wall with roundels there. The two-column wall has lost its skirting, revealing its castors. Otherwise the room maintains the same layout as in *The Three Doctors*, the most consistent it's been in a long time.
- After Jo changes her outfit, the control room walls are not lit from behind so the roundels and scanner wall

are dark, but from the Doctor's recovery onwards they are illuminated (perhaps the TARDIS was keeping the lighting down so he could sleep). Unfortunately this means that in the shots of the Doctor accessing the console's pedestal, the weights holding the wall behind him in place are blatantly silhouetted in the roundels.

- The TARDIS materialises with the echoing sound effect not heard since *The Space Pirates*, although the more usual version plays quietly underneath it. Was this to suggest the Ship was under Time Lord control?
- The typeface used for the scanner warning display is Amelia, designed by Stan Davis in 1964 for the Visual Graphics Corporation. It was famously used on artwork for the 1968 Beatles film and soundtrack album *Yellow Submarine*, as well as the 1973 single release of the *Doctor Who* theme in stereo (the picture sleeve of which featured the same photo of the 12-inch model Police Box seen towards the end of *The Claws of Axos*).
- The outer and inner doors are still treated as one and the same, with the fungus covering the former preventing the latter from opening.
- A model shot of the TARDIS completely engulfed in fungus was planned but never filmed for cost reasons.
- Although the doors are stuck shut, the Doctor's repeated switch flicking must have left them unlocked and trying to open for the Thals to be able to get in from outside. Taron must see the large control room within the small Police Box but never mentions this when later questioning the Doctor's credentials. As he and Codal help the Doctor from the TARDIS, the rear doors of the prop can be seen to be ajar.
- Owing to the limited size of the jungle set, the Police Box can be glimpsed in the background of some shots in episode one that aren't necessarily supposed to be set near the TARDIS.
- The Thals left the TARDIS doors wide open when they pulled the Doctor out, but when he and Jo return they're closed again (a good job else the control room would be full of fungus). When they get back inside, they come into the control room like they've been running some distance. As these scenes were recorded before those on the jungle set, it seems the actors expected just to be running from the Daleks, not standing around scraping off fungus first.
- This story is often said to be a reworking of the very first Dalek serial but the ending as the Daleks fire on the disappearing TARDIS is a straight copy of the end of episode two of *The Chase* (Landing 17).
- The bed-and-cupboard unit is still in place in the control room at the end of the story, even though it wasn't required for this episode. This isn't a case of good continuity by the production team, just that these TARDIS scenes were recorded along with those of episode one to save re-erecting the set.
- Sadly the image of Skaro on the scanner is not the same one used in *The Edge of Destruction* and *The Space Museum* — now that *would* have been impressive continuity keeping.
- The top of the central column is getting very dusty.

LANDING 95

SPACE Earth, England, UNIT HQ, lab
TIME [May, late-1970s]
TRAVELLERS The Doctor, Jo
EPISODES The Green Death 1

The Doctor agrees to Jo's request and returns the TARDIS to his lab at UNIT's headquarters for a well-earned rest.

He decides to ensure he can take her to Metebelis Three as promised by wiring its location into the Ship's space-time coordinate programmer. He tries to excite her interest but she is focused on a report in the newspaper about Global Chemicals, angered that no one is supporting a Professor Jones in his protests about the pollution the company is producing. She decides to go to Llanfairfach in South Wales to join his campaign.

As it happens, the Brigadier also has cause to visit Llanfairfach to investigate a dead miner whose body is glowing green, but he cannot persuade the Doctor to accompany him. He therefore offers Jo a lift as she is adamant about helping Professor Jones. Even the Doctor's offer of all of space and time does not tempt her, so he sets off on his trip alone.

- **LORE** The Doctor is able to hardwire a location into the space-time coordinate programmer to guarantee reaching it.
- **NOTES** Given Jo's frame of mind, we can assume the Doctor yields to her desire and takes her straight home after leaving Spiridon. They certainly return to Earth at some point as *The Green Death* begins with them back at UNIT HQ. But there's nothing to say they didn't take further journeys together before the events of this story.
- There's a calendar at the Llanfairfach colliery office showing Thursday 5 April but the mine has been closed for around a year so this is unlikely to be the current date. In our history this would fit 1973 or 1979, meaning it's now 1974 or 1980 – the latter would fit with later statements made by Sarah Jane Smith. Then again, we've seen how days and dates in the Doctor Who universe rarely match those in ours so we shouldn't now treat this one as reliable. For example, there's also a calendar in the guards' hut at the entrance to Global Chemicals that displays a 29-day month starting on a Tuesday, for which 1972 would be the closest match. The calendar in Mark Elgin's office – arguably most likely to be accurate – says it's May, but then the next day in Yates' office there's one set to 28 April. The first day of the week is marked but this could be Sunday or Monday, which again would make it 1974 or 1980. Perhaps Yates has been given a lesser-used room and this calendar hasn't been updated for a week or so.
- The Doctor's lab is the same as seen in *The Three Doctors*, although equipment has been moved and the TARDIS is standing in a different corner. Its dematerialisation also reveals a telephone that had hung on the back wall is no longer there.

- It's unusually dim of Jo to ask the Doctor if the component he's tinkering with is the dematerialisation circuit as it looks nothing like it. Not so long ago she was considered "top of the class" for recognising a smaller version used in the future humans' time-travel devices. Maybe she's just humouring him, knowing he likes her to take an interest.
- In fact it's the space-time coordinate programmer, a grey L-shaped panel with dials on the front connected to a circuit board with thick red and blue wires. As the Doctor says it's "nearly worn out" it has presumably developed a margin of error, which could be why, as Jo points out, they never got to Metebelis Three.
- The Doctor confirms he can now pilot the TARDIS "wherever and whenever I like" and has "absolute control over her" (a likely story) since the Time Lords lifted his exile.
- The two shots of the lab, with and without Police Box, used for the mix to make the TARDIS disappear are well aligned. However, a shadow appears on the far left of the back wall – was the prop just moved six feet to the left and still cast a shadow over the set? Perhaps they didn't want to move it far as they knew they'd need it back for the TARDIS's return.
- The roof lamp doesn't flash as the TARDIS dematerialises or when it lands on Metebelis.

LANDING 96

SPACE Acteon group, Metebelis Three
TIME Unknown (before Landing 103)
TRAVELLERS The Doctor
EPISODES The Green Death 1

The Doctor's preparations are successful and the TARDIS materialises at dusk on Metebelis Three, the rocky surroundings lit by blue moonlight. He has barely stepped out of the Ship, however, when a screeching creature with a long tentacle attacks him. He breaks free and runs, determined to find a Metebelis sapphire before he leaves.

By the time the Doctor gets back to the TARDIS he is dishevelled and being bombarded by rocks and spears, but has managed to find one of the famed blue crystals. As animals howl in the darkness and the Ship is thrashed by tentacles, the Doctor dashes inside.

LANDING 97

SPACE Earth, England, UNIT HQ, lab
TIME A few hours after Landing 95
TRAVELLERS The Doctor
EPISODES The Green Death 1

He returns to UNIT HQ several hours after he left and, pleased to be back in some level of civilisation, he answers the ringing telephone on his lab bench and agrees to speak to whoever is calling. He's connected to the Brigadier who insists he come to Wales.

PREVIOUS LANDINGS

SPACE Florana
TIME Unknown
TRAVELLERS The Doctor, [unknown companions]
EPISODES Recalled by the Doctor in Death to the Daleks 1

The Doctor visited Florana, one of the most beautiful planets in the universe, with air like a magic potion, fields of perfumed flowers, clear sparkling streams, soft sandy beaches and warm effervescent seas that made him feel "a hundred years younger".

- **NOTES** The Doctor describes the planet to Sarah so must have been sometime before he met her. He says he "always" comes away feeling younger so may have been more than once.

SPACE Earth
TIME Early-20th century
TRAVELLERS The Doctor, [unknown companions]
EPISODES Claimed by the Doctor in Planet of the Spiders 5, Revenge of the Cybermen 4 and The Witchfinders

The Doctor was taught by Harry Houdini, with whom he was friends, how to compress his muscles to escape from confinement. He also learned to tie a tangle Turk's head eye-splice knot with a grommet. In her fourteenth incarnation, the Doctor recalled this as having been over a wet weekend.

- **NOTES** Houdini's career as a stage escapologist took off in the early-1900s and the Doctor could have met him on any of his tours of Europe, America or Australia. His claim to be an "old friend", however, is countered by the Doctor's struggling to recall his first name, and the later suggestion they only met for a couple of days.
- In the BBC/Big Finish audio story *Destiny of the Doctors: Smoke and Mirrors* by Steve Lyons, the Doctor during his fifth incarnation meets Houdini at an English fairground in the 1920s. They recall an earlier meeting in New York in the 1890s when the Doctor was in his first incarnation travelling with Ben and Polly; this could be how Ben knows how to escape being tied with rope in *The Highlanders* (Landing 47).

SPACE Earth, England
TIME [Late-16th century]
TRAVELLERS The Doctor, [unknown companions]
EPISODES Claimed by the Doctor in Planet of Evil 2 and City of Death 4

The Doctor met William Shakespeare and considered him a charming fellow but a dreadful actor. This might have been when the Bard was writing Hamlet but, having sprained his wrist while composing sonnets, had to dictate a portion for the Doctor to transcribe. The Doctor disliked the mixed metaphor "to take

armes against a sea of troubles" but Shakespeare insisted on keeping it.
- **NOTES** The Doctor met Shakespeare only once before Sarah Jane Smith joined him in his travels. The dating of Hamlet's authorship is uncertain. Although it was not published in printed form until 1603 (and is not included in a 1598 list of Shakespeare's plays) there is some evidence a play of this title was performed before 1589, referred to as the Ur-Hamlet. As Countess Scarlioni believes her husband's copy is a first draft, which the Doctor says has "been missing for centuries", could it be this earlier script? The version of the Act III 'To be, or not to be' soliloquy the Doctor reads out matches that from the 1604 Second Quarto, which differs from the earlier First Quarto ("Ay there's the point"), perhaps confirming the theory that the former is as Shakespeare wrote and the latter another's misremembered transcript (particularly if the Doctor is quoting from the Ur-Hamlet).
- During his eleventh incarnation, the Doctor met Shakespeare again, in 1599 while he was preparing to stage Love's Labour's Won (see Landing 370, vol.2). That encounter leaves the Bard considering writing "about fathers and sons, in memory of my boy, my precious Hamnet", which could be taken as implying he has yet to write the tragedy of the Danish prince. Some consider the similarity of names a coincidence, however, as Hamlet is based on older sources. Of course, the time and space visualiser (see Landing 17) shows Francis Bacon suggesting to Shakespeare he pen "the history of Hamlet, prince of Denmark" around 1597, as Barbara seemingly tunes the visualiser to a time between the writing of Henry IV, Part 2 and The Merry Wives of Windsor.
- Between Landing 112 and Landing 161 the Doctor may have encountered Shakespeare again during his childhood, finding him a taciturn boy.

SPACE Earth, France
TIME 18th century (before 1793)
TRAVELLERS The Doctor, [unknown companions]
EPISODES Mentioned by the Doctor in
Pyramids of Mars 1

The Doctor met Marie Antoinette and considered her a "charming lady". He acquired a picklock that had belonged to her.
- **NOTES** As the Doctor is describing Marie to Sarah, this encounter must have been before Landing 98. His knowledge that the French queen was beheaded doesn't necessarily indicate that he was there at her demise – although Susan did claim the French Revolution was "his favourite period in the history of Earth" so it's not impossible (see Landing 9) – and it's not clear if he was given the picklock by her or if it came into his possession later.

SPACE Earth, England, London
TIME September 1666
TRAVELLERS The Doctor, [unknown companions]
EPISODES Mentioned by the Doctor in
Pyramids of Mars 4

The Doctor was blamed for starting the Great Fire of London.
- **NOTES** This was before the Doctor met Sarah. We know from *The Visitation* (Landing 212) that he was indeed partly responsible for causing the outbreak of fire in Pudding Lane that ultimately devastated much of the 17th century city of London, but he was then in his fifth incarnation so couldn't know of it while travelling with Sarah in his fourth. Assuming he's not simply joking (and he does laugh immediately after making the claim), the Doctor could have previously arrived in London during or after the fire and been accused of starting it, particularly if Richard Mace was still around talking drunkenly about how a doctor was involved. His later incarnation does seem to know exactly what he's done – "I have a sneaking suspicion this fire should be allowed to run its course" – and is keen to leave sharpish, so may be talking from personal experience of its aftermath.

SPACE Earth, France, Malplaquet
TIME 11 September 1709
TRAVELLERS The Doctor, [unknown companions]
EPISODES Recalled by the Doctor in
The Android Invasion 1

The Doctor was with the Duke of Marlborough at the Battle of Malplaquet during the War of the Spanish Succession. He remarked on something unusual to the general, which he was later reminded of when he and Sarah were shot at by Kraal androids.
- **NOTES** We don't hear what the Doctor said to Marlborough as he's interrupted by Sarah slipping over the edge of a quarry, but as he's commenting on the oddity of being fired upon unexpectedly, presumably it was a similar situation at the Battle of Malplaquet. He's relating this to Sarah so it was probably before he met her.

SPACE Karfel
TIME Around 50 years before Landing 273
TRAVELLERS The Doctor, Jo, [unknown others]
EPISODES Mentioned in Timelash 1 and
The Death of the Doctor 1

The Doctor took Jo and at least one other person to Karfel, where they visited a leisure garden with singing plants. The Doctor might have posed for a portrait (or this may have been done from memory after his departure) and he gave a locket containing a photo of Jo and a lock of her hair to a Karfelon man. He also befriended a scientist called Megelen but reported him to the planet's ruling council when he discovered the

unethical experiments the scientist was performing on the native Morlox creatures. The Doctor departed promising to return one day.

- **NOTES** In *Timelash*, Katz has a locket given to her grandfather by the Doctor, suggesting this visit was two generations earlier. Kendron says his father talked of the Doctor's return, so he might have been a young boy at this time or was told of the Time Lord by his parents.
- When the Doctor returns to Karfel with Peri, Tekker asks, "Only the two of you?" to which the Doctor replies he's "travelling light this time". This suggests he had more than one person with him on this earlier visit. The Karfelons have a painting of the Doctor in his third incarnation from his first visit, and it's confirmed in *The Sarah Jane Adventures* story *The Death of the Doctor* that Jo accompanied him, so it must take place before she leaves UNIT to marry Clifford Jones and travel up the Amazon. However, this could be after *The Green Death* as it's unlikely the Doctor's driving off into the sunset at the end of that story was the last time he saw Jo. He would surely have attended her wedding, and maybe the trip to Karfel was a parting treat for the newlyweds. Alternatively it could have been earlier once the Doctor had regained control of the TARDIS and any or all of the Brigadier, Captain Yates and Sergeant Benton went with the Doctor and Jo.

LANDING 98

SPACE Earth, England, Wessex, woodland near Irongron's castle
TIME Two days in [12th/early-13th century]
TRAVELLERS The Doctor, Sarah Jane Smith
EPISODES The Time Warrior 1,4

The Brigadier gathers a number of pre-eminent scientists together in a top secret research centre to guard them following a number of recent disappearances. Naturally this includes the Doctor, who has the TARDIS brought along too. He finds himself bunked with Professor Rubeish and Sarah Jane Smith, a journalist who has bluffed her way in using the invite sent to her virologist aunt, hoping for a news story.

That night the Doctor sets up a rhondium sensor to alert him to the presence of delta particles. While he dozes in a chair the sensor reacts and Rubeish disappears. The Doctor uses a handheld device to scan the landing outside and sees a ghostly armoured figure that fades away. He deduces the scientist has been taken via a matter transmitter but one operating from several centuries ago. He fetches a suitcase from the TARDIS and packs away his equipment while telling the Brigadier what he has learned. Unseen, Sarah slips into the Police Box believing Rubeish might be inside. The Doctor tells the Brigadier he has to hurry before the trail fades and takes off in the TARDIS.

The sound of its engines echoing around the surrounding woodland, the Ship materialises in medieval England, close to the castle held by the bandit Irongron. The Doctor exits and heads off, not noticing Sarah emerge from the Police Box behind him. Confused by the TARDIS's inner dimensions, she takes a different direction in search of a telephone.

After noon the next day the Doctor returns to the Ship to collect a fan of metal strips with which to protect himself from the Sontaran Linx's weapon.

Irongron's castle is totally destroyed when Linx's spaceship explodes. The Doctor, Sarah and Hal the archer escape into the woods just in time, then head straight to the nearby TARDIS. Hal praises the Doctor as a great magician, which the Time Lord denies (Sarah is not so sure) but proceeds to astonish the archer by dematerialising the TARDIS before his eyes.

- **LORE** The TARDIS has coffee-making facilities (presumably the food machine is still around somewhere).
- **NOTES** This is the first journey we see the TARDIS make since Jo got engaged but that doesn't mean the Doctor hasn't been places on his own, or even with her given Professor Jones wasn't due to venture up the Amazon for a month.
- In fact, considering the size of the doorway to the Doctor's assigned room at the research centre, how did the TARDIS get in there unless the Doctor piloted it there? Professor Rubeish says he hasn't seen his family in three days, suggesting he has already been detained there that long. As the accommodations are still being set up in the first scene between the Doctor and the Brigadier, the next time we see the former meeting Rubeish and Sarah could be three days later, leaving him plenty of time to have popped back to UNIT HQ and returned in the TARDIS.
- The Doctor berates Rubeish for chalking equations on the side of the TARDIS, although there are already smudges of chalk dust presumably from studio rehearsals prior to recording. The equations have been rubbed off before the later scene of the Doctor preparing his rhondium sensor – by him or did he make the professor do it? Even the residual marks are gone once the Ship materialises in the Middle Ages (filmed earlier on location) so we can surmise chalk dust doesn't survive a flight through the Vortex (although see Landing 169).
- The Doctor tells Rubeish he has been transported back to "the early years of the Middle Ages". This period runs from the end of the 5th century to around the 15th, so the "early years" should be at least before the 10th century. Yet Irongron calls Sir Edward a Norman so it must be after the Conquest; presumably the Doctor meant what historians call the High Middle Ages, from 1066 to the death of King John in 1216. This period covers the Second and Third Crusades (see Landing 15), which are reasonably taken to be what Sir

Edward is referencing when he bemoans his men being taken to fight in the king's "interminable wars". Not that wars were a rarity in those days and the comment could equally apply to the Anarchy (1135-54) when the throne was in dispute (making Edward a supporter of Stephen), the Norman invasion of Ireland (1169-75) in the reign of Henry II, or King John's war against France (1202-14) – perhaps this last as Sarah at least believes it's the 13th century, or so she tells Styre in *The Sontaran Experiment*.

- The TARDIS materialises off screen and the sound effect cuts off sharply after the final groan.
- The Doctor tells Sarah he can go anywhere he likes in the TARDIS "within reason". Does he mean there are physical, legal or moral limitations?

LANDING 99

SPACE Earth, London, park; transported to Acton school
TIME Two days in [late-1970s], some weeks after previous departure
TRAVELLERS The Doctor, Sarah
EPISODES Invasion of the Dinosaurs 1,3-4

The Doctor programmes the Ship to return to UNIT HQ rather than the research centre it left from, although the space-time coordinates are a little out and the TARDIS arrives in a park somewhere in London. He is confident it cannot be more than a few weeks since he and Sarah left the 20th century and, despite her misgivings, they go in search of a telephone to call the Brigadier.

While the Doctor assists with discovering how dinosaurs are appearing and disappearing all over Central London, the Brigadier assigns some of his men to transport the TARDIS to UNIT's temporary headquarters in a school in Acton, setting it down in the biology lab the Doctor has commandeered.

After capturing a tyrannosaurus and chaining it up in an aircraft hanger, the Doctor returns to the school to collect some equipment from the TARDIS. While there, Charles Grover, the minister in charge of evacuated London, reports that the missing scientist Whitaker, suspected of being behind the dinosaur appearances, was a harmless crank. Sarah is not convinced, however. She persuades General Finch to let her photograph the captive creature.

Having been rescued from the escaped tyrannosaurus, Sarah insists someone deliberately tried to get her killed. When the Doctor finds his tracking instruments from the hangar have been sabotaged and Sergeant Benton reports the chains on the creature were cut, they realise there is a mole in UNIT. Knowing that whoever is behind the time manipulations must need a great deal of power, the Doctor and Sarah each pursue their own ways to locate it, the former working in the TARDIS to build a portable detector.

Despite it leading him to a secret bunker beneath an Underground station, the Doctor returns without proof but a suspicion that even Grover is involved in some plot. While the Brigadier seeks permission from Finch to blast their way into the bunker, the Doctor receives a call from Whitaker luring him to the hangar.

The next day time briefly reverses for the entire world before the machine causing it is itself flung back to an earlier era. With London now free from the risk of a dinosaur invasion, the Doctor tempts Sarah with another trip in the TARDIS to Florana.

NOTES This likely follows straight on from Landing 98 as the Doctor has promised to get Sarah home safely. However, her statement, "We set off from the research centre," could just mean 'when we left Earth' rather than 'when we last took off' if they have been to other destinations in the meantime. At the end of episode six she does says, "Alien monsters, robber barons, then dinosaurs: be a long time before I get in that TARDIS again," suggesting she hasn't encountered any other nasties in between. Any additional trips would have to have been peaceful, therefore, and not more than one or two or she wouldn't be assuming the dangers of TARDIS travel outweigh the pleasures. The Doctor has had time to change his clothes, and while Sarah is in the same outfit her hair is noticeably shorter.

- The Brigadier says dinosaurs started appearing in Central London "just after" the Doctor and Sarah "went off on your last little jaunt" and since then there has been time to evacuate eight million people from the area – no mean feat even if the Brigadier is pleased it was "carried out without a hitch". In our history, the population of Central London at the end of the 1970s was only around 2.5m and less than 7m people in the whole of the capital (even now the former figure is under 4m), so in the *Doctor Who* universe London is a much more crowded city. There are 87 dinosaur sightings marked on Benton's map, from Highgate in the north to Battersea in the south, and White City in the west to Mile End in the East, an area of around 123 square kilometres. That gives a population density of some 65,000 people per square kilometre: more than seven times current estimates for Central London's density in our world.
- The TARDIS prop was refurbished prior to the studio recordings for *Invasion of the Dinosaurs* (see page 116).
- The appearance in episode two of a peasant from the time of Richard I, who reigned at the end of the 12th century, is unusual given all the other time transferences bring forward creatures from millions of years ago. Given the TARDIS has just visited that period, could its return to London have coincided with one of Professor Whitaker's scheduled transferences, disrupting it and causing a man from the 1100s to be pulled through time? The fact that time resets and he's (presumably) sent back only when he comes into contact with the Doctor could be significant. And the Doctor does later say he thinks the man's appearance was "an accident".
- The Doctor is plain that time did begin rolling back outside the protective field around Whitaker's

machine. It's only active for 20 seconds but surely it must be designed to reverse time at a faster rate, otherwise the participants in Operation Golden Age would be waiting thousands of years for the Earth to reach pre-civilisation again. So more than 20 seconds were 'undone' but not so long as to erase this whole dinosaur incident. UNIT is still established at the school, General Finch is still to be tried (hard to prove if no one had experienced what he was supposed to have done; in fact, he wouldn't have done any of it yet), and Captain Yates is still made to resign – if the betrayal had no longer been committed, even if the Brigadier remembered it surely he would give Mike a second chance?

LANDING 100

SPACE Exxilon
TIME Two days in unknown future
TRAVELLERS The Doctor, Sarah
EPISODES Death to the Daleks 1

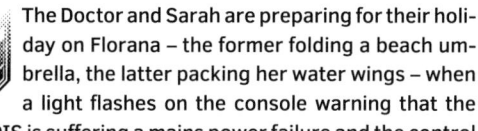

The Doctor and Sarah are preparing for their holiday on Florana – the former folding a beach umbrella, the latter packing her water wings – when a light flashes on the console warning that the TARDIS is suffering a mains power failure and the control room lights dim. The Doctor cuts in the emergency backup units but these too are soon drained and the Ship is forced to make a shaky materialisation on Exxilon.

With the last vestiges of power, the Doctor activates the scanner to see where they have landed but it shows only swirling fog before the image fades. The last lights go out and the control room falls quiet. The Doctor switches in the storage cells but these too are quickly exhausted. Even a battery-operated torch Sarah finds goes dead so the Doctor resorts to lighting an oil lamp. He has to open the main doors by hand using a crank handle.

Outside it is night and a chilling fog swirls through the air. The rocks around them are supplemented by humanoid figures that the Doctor speculates are petrified lifeforms. Dressed in only her bathing costume, Sarah is feeling the cold so returns to the TARDIS for some warmer clothes as the Doctor wanders off against her wishes.

While she searches for him, an Exxilon native sneaks into the Ship. When Sarah returns alone, she thinks she hears someone in the control room but is distracted by more Exxilons approaching outside and hurries to wind the main doors shut. The creature inside attacks her and she beats it off with the crank handle. Terrified, she reopens the doors and rushes out into the darkness, leaving the Exxilon for dead.

The next day, with the beacon atop the Exxilons' living city destroyed, the power is restored to the TARDIS, but also to the Daleks and their ship. They take off but their craft explodes before even reaching space. The damage inflicted by the Doctor to the city's brain systems causes the entire edifice to dissolve. Saddened by the loss of one of the 700 wonders of the universe, the Doctor returns to the Ship with Sarah and departs.

- **CONTROLS** A new set of lights on panel B6 flash when the Ship's energy starts being drained. The Doctor notes the power drain from the new gauge in place of the dematerialisation circuit housing, then activates the emergency power units using the small levers on panel B5 and the storage cells using the four flick switches at the bottom of panel B2. Sarah is standing at panel B1 when she activates the scanner.
- On panel B6, the set of silver switches at the bottom is replaced with a wider plate containing five pairs of small blue, yellow, green, white and red bulbs, one larger domed red light and two flick switches. The whole of the section where the dematerialisation circuit housing once slotted is now covered by a black square with a silver-rimmed circular gauge set into it.
- This is the last appearance of console B in the series, although the body of the prop will return, with new control panels, as console C.
- **LORE** The TARDIS's energy source should never stop. The Doctor calls it "a living thing". Even so, it has emergency power units and backup storage cells.
- The main doors can be opened manually using a crank handle, for which there is a slot to their left.
- **NOTES** This story is the last to feature the control room for some time. The room was slimmed down since last seen in *Planet of the Daleks*, with just three wall sections: main doors, six-column indented roundels and one of the Gleeson walls from *The Time Monster* (see page 160), plus a plain flat on the far right. A hexagonal light was added to the left of the main doors for the shot of it dimming, with a hole drilled further down for the crank handle. There was no mechanism connected to the doors, just the actors suggesting the effort to turn it while a stagehand pushed the door open from behind the set.
- As well as the holiday paraphernalia the Doctor and Sarah are packing – beach umbrella, inflatable swan and lounger, straw hat, water wings and, er, a pair of wellingtons – the control room contains the wooden eagle lectern seen in *The Claws of Axos*, a chest of drawers, a wooden cabinet (not the same as the one in *The Time Monster*) and a wooden room divider with three embroidered panels.
- Although the Doctor has been piloting the TARDIS accurately since his exile was rescinded, it's possible his intention to visit Florana was already off course. Unless the Exxilon city's influence extends into the Vortex, the Ship must have been close to the planet for it to be affected, so was it about to land there by accident anyway? Its loss of power is most unusual given what we later learn about the TARDIS getting its energy from a black hole. If the Exxilon city had absorbed all that it would be unstoppable. Perhaps the Ship's dimensional complexities protect the source itself but energy directed to the control room can be tapped.
- The shaking of the Police Box as it materialises was achieved by the simple method of having someone inside it rocking about. The landing sound effect was also given a warbling quality to match.

IT'S BIGGER ON THE INSIDE

THE GREEN IMPROVISATION
1974

Colin Green, the designer for *Death to the Daleks*, had only one control room scene to stage so he used existing set pieces. The main doors and indented wall were the key sections from the most recently used Liminton set. As the TARDIS needed to appear powered down, these were not back-lit as usual so their roundels were dark and opaque.

Joining them was one of Gleeson's walls – surprisingly still in storage – its washbowl roundels gone and the resulting holes now backed with plywood to create shallow opaque circles. This was in two pieces (you can see the join on screen) and painted a mid-grey to match the unlit roundels of the other walls. This and the indented wall regained the projecting cornice from the Gleeson redesign rather then Liminton's replacement – if the latter still existed it was never seen on screen again.

This set was less of a conscious redesign than even Christine Ruscoe's for Season 13 (see page 168), more a use of stock pieces as designers throughout the 1960s had done. Yet Green's innovation with the shallow roundels would be retained and is the first proof Gleeson's walls weren't junked along with his unpopular roundels.

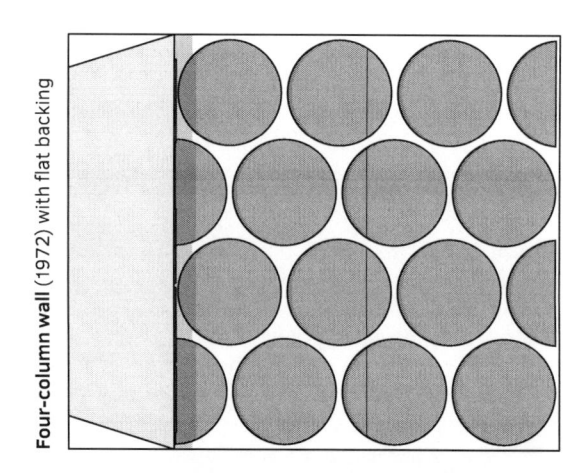

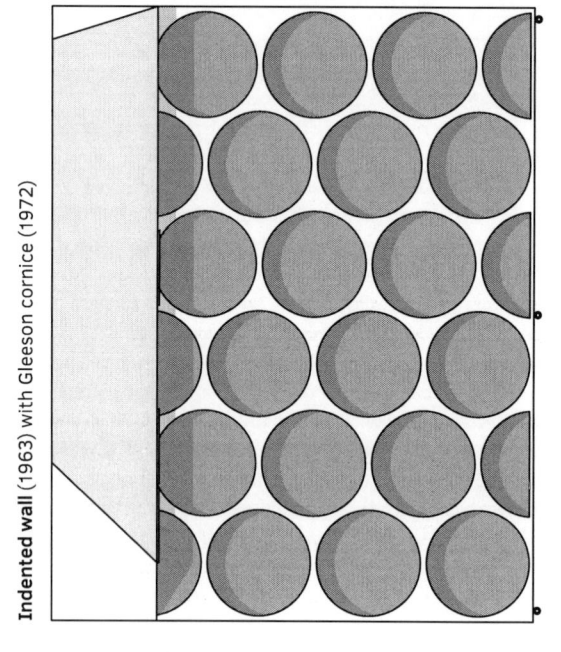

Four-column wall (1972) with flat backing

Indented wall (1963) with Gleeson cornice (1972)

Main doors (1963) with added light and crank slot

- The control room was given a low oscillating drone to suggest it was "dying".
- For the brief view of the scanner, a shot of smoke was superimposed onto a monitor-shaped CSO cutout.
- It has been noted by others that we never learn what happens to the Exxilon in the TARDIS, and some have speculated it's been aboard ever since. However, Sarah is unlikely to have killed the creature, only stunned it, and fortunately she left the door open, so it probably recovered and left the Ship to nurse its sore head.
- Sweetly, the Daleks use a model Police Box as target practice when testing their replacement projectile guns.
- The Doctor says he has seen symbols like those on the exterior of the Exxilon city "on the walls of a temple in Peru". Although he discusses the mystery "that no primitive man could possibly have built such a structure", indicating the temple he's referring to is an ancient rather than modern one, that's not to say he saw it in its heyday and could have visited the site during his exile on Earth.

LANDING 101

SPACE Peladon, tunnel beneath citadel
TIME Unknown future (50 years after Landing 83)
TRAVELLERS The Doctor, Sarah
EPISODES The Monster of Peladon 1,6

The TARDIS returns to Peladon, materialising in the third gallery off the main cavern within the mountain into which the royal citadel is carved. Not only has it missed the palace but 50 years have passed on the planet since the Doctor was last there with Jo. Sarah is not impressed by "another rotten gloomy old tunnel" but the Doctor is sure they must be close to the citadel and they set off to find it, unaware that they are observed by a guard.

By the time they return to the Ship they have successfully averted a miners' uprising and an invasion plan by rebel Ice Warriors. Nonetheless, the Doctor turns down the offer to become Queen Thalira's chancellor. Sarah jokes about the position's perks and the Doctor bundles her into the TARDIS, deciding it's about time he took her home. After a last look round, he follows her in and the Ship dematerialises.

- **NOTES** It's not entirely clear whether the Doctor has intentionally brought them to Peladon or not. He says he has "been meaning to pay a return visit… for ages" but that doesn't rule out the landing being a happy accident. Before the travellers emerge from the TARDIS they know they're on Peladon and the Doctor is expecting to be in the citadel, which could be because that's what he aimed for or his instruments tell him so after landing. He blames the faulty scanner for not knowing sooner they are in the tunnels.
- Sarah is first to note it's 50 years since the Doctor's last visit, but the Doctor and Ortron independently corroborate this later, so how did she know? Most likely from the TARDIS instruments – the Doctor says, "I think my spatial coordinates must have slipped a bit too," suggesting he's already aware of the time gap (and that "my" does imply he deliberately programmed the TARDIS for Peladon). Although he's still hoping to meet King Peladon again, a half-century delay is no reason to presume the monarch won't still be alive. Alternatively, Alpha Centauri might have mentioned the time difference when first escorting the Doctor and Sarah from the throne room.
- The Police Box's right-hand window is visible from the inside when the Doctor opens the door to leave.

PREVIOUS LANDINGS

SPACE Earth, England, London
TIME Mid-1660s
TRAVELLERS The Doctor, [unknown companions]
EPISODES Implied by the Doctor in Planet of the Spiders 2

The Doctor drank coffee prepared by Elisabeth (Mrs Samuel) Pepys, which was the finest he ever tasted.

- **NOTES** Elisabeth Marchant de Saint Michel married Samuel Pepys in October 1655 but died of typhoid fever in November 1669, so the Doctor must have sampled her delicious coffee between these dates.
- The Doctor only says Mrs Pepys made fine coffee, not specifically that he met her, although he would presumably have had to visit the home of the famous diarist in order to be served by his wife. If it was after 1666, it could have been the occasion on which he was blamed for starting the Great Fire of London (see Previous to Landing 98).

SPACE Earth, America, Massachusetts, Boston
TIME Mid-1870s
TRAVELLERS The Doctor, [unknown companions]
EPISODES Claimed by the Doctor in The Android Invasion 2

The Doctor met Alexander Graham Bell while he was developing the telephone and warned him that using overhead wires to transmit sound was unreliable.

- **NOTES** While Bell is generally credited with inventing the telephone, the signals were transmitted over pre-existing telegraph wires, a network of which had spread across America, and the Atlantic, during the previous 30 years. The Doctor, therefore, was perhaps trying to persuade Bell to develop a device using radio waves or even light, which he did a few years later.
- As the Doctor appears to recognise Bell's voice making "the very first phone call" in Father's Day, he may have been present at that occasion on 10 March 1876.

LANDING 102

SPACE Earth, England, UNIT HQ, lab
TIME [Late-1970s]
TRAVELLERS The Doctor, Sarah
EPISODES Planet of the Spiders 1-3

The Doctor takes Sarah back to Earth, landing in his lab once more, and spends some time with his friends at UNIT.

While there, he does some research into extra sensory perception that brings to his attention Herbert Clegg, a stage mind-reader who, the Doctor notices, has genuine clairvoyant ability. He invites Clegg to his lab at UNIT HQ one evening to help prove such psychic powers are a natural, if rare, faculty. The Doctor connects Clegg to an electroencephalograph to display his brainwaves while he studies the Brigadier's watch – a gift from a lady friend called Doris, Clegg divines – then to an image reproduction integrating system, or IRIS, that will show his thoughts on a monitor. When Clegg handles the Doctor's sonic screwdriver he sees Drashigs.

A package arrives from Jo Jones in the Amazon, so the Doctor has Clegg predict its contents: the blue crystal that the Time Lord took from Metebelis Three and gave to Jo as a wedding gift. She has returned it because it disturbs the natives, and when Clegg examines the crystal a powerful force sweeps through the lab and the man dies. The recording on the IRIS monitor shows hideous spiders. The Doctor risks looking into the crystal himself and goes into a trance, revived only by the smell of Sergeant Benton's coffee. All he could see in the crystal, however, was the face of the old hermit who mentored him as a young man.

The next day Sarah tells the Doctor about suspicious goings-on at a Tibetan meditation centre near Stratfield Mortimer in Berkshire. He is more focused on his tests on the crystal until she mentions the appearance of giant spiders. As the Doctor ponders the connection between the crystal and the spiders, the sapphire vanishes. One of the men from the meditation centre, Lupton, has infiltrated UNIT HQ and used the power of the spider hidden on his back to steal the crystal. He shoots Benton with a bolt of electricity and makes off in the Doctor's futuristic car.

When Sarah is later accidentally transported to Metebelis Three in pursuit of Lupton, the Doctor follows her in the TARDIS. He is certain of reaching the right planet as the coordinates are still hardwired into the programmer.

- **LORE** While the Doctor can (now) pilot the TARDIS where he wants, more or less, the Ship itself usually chooses exactly where to land. We later learn the TARDIS itself often decides to take the Doctor where he's needed (see Landing 508, vol.2).
- **NOTES** Although the Doctor is threatening to take Sarah home at the end of *The Monster of Peladon*, given his and the TARDIS's reliability there's no guarantee they make it back straight away. Once they eventually do, there's no telling how long they stay nor what other trips they might have taken in the TARDIS before the Doctor starts developing an interest in ESP and Sarah goes back to work (presuming she's a freelance journalist, if her absence is noted by any commissioning editors she can claim to have been working on a story).
- The Doctor's lab is the same set introduced in *The Three Doctors*, with the TARDIS now back, as then, in the corner by the window. Other furniture has been moved around, and the doors have been repainted a blueish-grey colour.
- The TARDIS is again indicated to be alive, with some form of intelligence. Presented with following Sarah to Metebelis Three, the Doctor is sure of reaching the right planet but relies on the Ship to find the correct region and timezone. Perhaps Lupton's teleportation by the Eight Legs' mental powers left a trace through space-time that the Ship could follow. Or now that Sarah has travelled in the TARDIS for some time and had her brain adapted for things like universal translation (see Landing 322, vol.2), maybe the Ship can pinpoint her location.
- So the space-time coordinate programmer is hardwired only for the planet, not anywhere more precise like a time or place. Bit vague. Even so, if it has been set all this time, how did the Doctor expect to navigate anywhere else? Exxilon and Peladon may have been random landings, particularly if he was having to bypass the coordinate programmer, but he managed to get back to Earth at the correct point in Sarah's time-stream. Perhaps the programmer isn't the main coordinate entry system but just a memory unit for pre-setting a number of destinations.
- Between its transportation to Ealing Studios for filming of *The Monster of Peladon* and its erection in the studio three months later for recording of *Planet of the Spiders*, the Police Box prop has lost the cap and support struts from its roof lamp. The translucent cylinder around the bulb has had a black stripe painted or taped around the top to suggest a cap. This is especially obvious in the overhead shot of the TARDIS leaving Metebelis Three in episode five.

LANDING 103

SPACE Acteon group, Metebelis Three, village
TIME Two days in [26th century or later] (after Landing 96)
TRAVELLERS The Doctor
EPISODES Planet of the Spiders 3-5

The Ship arrives in a village of human settlers who are ruled by the Eight Legs. Their queen, Huath, has Sarah under arrest and orders her guards to bring the Doctor for questioning also. When he resists, the guard captain fires a bolt of electricity at him and he collapses beside the TARDIS. Assuming the Doctor is dead and with Sarah having slipped away to hide among the villagers, the queen leaves frustrated.

Sarah rushes to the Doctor's body and finds he is still alive, barely, so she moves him to the hut of villager Arak and his family as night falls. After some hours, the Doctor briefly wakens and sends Sarah to the TARDIS to collect an old leather satchel containing a machine that will revive him. She takes the key from his pocket and sneaks past the night guards to reach the Ship. As she exits, she is caught by Lupton and taken to the Eight Legs, leaving the satchel by the TARDIS. Arak recovers it, returns to the hut and by dawn the Doctor is fully recovered. Later that morning he leaves the village to seek out Sarah while Arak gathers a force of men who, protected by stones that disperse the Eight Legs' energy bolts, march on their dwellings.

With the attack seemingly successful, the Doctor is transported from the Eight Legs' dwellings by Sarah, unaware she is under the influence of the queen hidden on her back. They reappear in the village and Sarah hustles the Doctor into the TARDIS, which dematerialises.

NOTES The Doctor's return to Metebelis Three must be after his first visit in *The Green Death* (Landing 96) as on that occasion he took the one perfect crystal that the Great One subsequently needs to complete her mental amplifier. How much later is impossible to determine. Although the Metebelis seen here seems a much more peaceful environment than that in *The Green Death*, it could be an entirely different part of the planet uninhabited by any of the vicious creatures that previously attacked the Doctor. Some of those had basic intelligence as they could make spears but it's unlikely these were the ancestors of the villagers the Doctor meets here, who crashed 433 years previously – unless they reverted to barbarism and wiped out all the giant snakes and birds. Judging from other stories, humans didn't begin exploring other worlds until at least the 22nd century, so this can be no earlier than the 26th.

- The shot of the TARDIS materialising on Metebelis Three shows the poor state the Police Box prop was in. The roof is not straight, the left-hand window on the left-hand side is bulging, has a cracked pane and a broken bar, and there is a large split in the front 'Police box' sign. A brief, rare view of the back of the prop moments later shows its right-hand window is missing one of its bars.
- At some point during his exile on Earth, the Doctor has produced a new key for the TARDIS, shield-shaped with a raised design on one side. Alternatively, the key may be linked to the chameleon circuit so it can change appearance depending on what form the TARDIS takes, and the Doctor temporarily disabled this function while he was trying to repair the Ship.
- The departure of the TARDIS from Metebelis Three is an ambitious split-screen effect, but instead of just a simple vertical join the mask follows the shape of the Police Box so actors in the centre background are not accidentally obscured. Note at the very start of the shot a disconnect in the window frames at the top-right of the picture. As the overlaid shot of the TARDIS is faded out, the actors on the left of the screen run forward into the previously obscured empty space.

LANDING 104

SPACE Earth, England, Berkshire, meditation centre, cellar
TIME Early March, [late-1970s], day after Landing 102
TRAVELLERS The Doctor, Sarah, Queen Huath
EPISODES Planet of the Spiders 5-6

The TARDIS lands in the cellar of the meditation centre where Eight Legs have arrived and taken possession of Lupton's naive followers. The Doctor and Sarah find Mike Yates and the centre's head monk Cho-Je unconscious before they too are attacked with electricity bolts from Lupton's men. The Doctor uses a dispersing stone to protect them and they escape upstairs, with help from the centre's dogsbody Tommy. He locks the men in the cellar but they soon break free.

Cho-Je and Yates recover and hurry upstairs. Shortly after, the Doctor appears in the cellar holding the blue crystal, transported by the mental power of the abbot K'anpo. He quickly takes off in the TARDIS before Lupton's men can capture him.

NOTES In *Robot*, set just over three weeks later, Sarah has a day visitor's pass for the National Institute for Advanced Scientific Research dated 4 April, meaning this story takes place early in March.

- The TARDIS's arrival is another split-screen shot, this time with a straight join down the centre. While the actors run to the left of the screen, a shot with the Police Box in place is faded in on the right. Once the actors are off screen, the left-hand side is faded in also ready for Elisabeth Sladen to move across when she exits the TARDIS. Fortunately both the camera and Richard Franklin lying on the floor stay perfectly still between the two shots. The same technique is used, not quite as perfectly, for the Doctor's departure with the crystal. Jon Pertwee stands on set with the Police Box and he is then obscured by a shot of the empty set on the left. The hard-edged mask is aligned with the kink in the background wall but is visible at the bottom of the picture where Pertwee's shadow makes the right-hand side darker. The overlay is then faded, making the Doctor appear, and he runs into the TARDIS on the right. This side then has the empty-set shot faded in over it as the other actors run in on the left, carefully stopping before they reach the edge of the mask.
- The door of the TARDIS is left open yet again.

LANDING 105

SPACE Metebelis Three, near Eight Legs' dwellings
TIME [26th century or later], shortly after Landing 103
TRAVELLERS The Doctor
EPISODES Planet of the Spiders 6

The TARDIS returns to Metebelis Three so the Doctor can confront both the Great One and his fear of her. It materialises on the plain outside the Eight Legs' dwellings and the Doctor is greeted by

Arak and his brother Tuar, who claim to have overcome the spiders. They agree to show him a way into the mountain containing the Great One's cave of crystal.

His body badly irradiated by the amplified energies of the crystal cave, the Doctor staggers back to the TARDIS and departs as the Great One's crystal web intensifies her mental powers until they explosively destroy both her and the mountain.

NOTES CSO-advocate director Barry Letts uses three layers of imposition for the shots of the 'exterior' where the TARDIS materialises: Police Box and actors over a model of the spiders' towers and the mountain, over a photographic slide of a cloudy sky. Note how the model shot doesn't change when the foreground shot of the actors moves in closer but the sky does. The model had a blue backdrop while the actors were in front of a yellow one so the different colours could be used to key all three elements into one.

LANDING 106

SPACE Earth, England, UNIT HQ, lab
TIME 3-6 April, [late-1970s]
TRAVELLERS The Doctor
EPISODES Planet of the Spiders 6, Robot 1-4

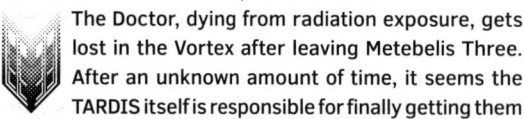

The Doctor, dying from radiation exposure, gets lost in the Vortex after leaving Metebelis Three. After an unknown amount of time, it seems the TARDIS itself is responsible for finally getting them both back to 20th century Earth, to what has become their second home. Over three weeks have gone by since Sarah last saw him, so she and the Brigadier are relieved when the TARDIS rematerialises in the UNIT lab. The Doctor emerges, weak and grey-faced, and collapses to the floor. Although he tries to reassure Sarah, his strength gives out and he appears to die.

However, the regenerated K'anpo appears and tells the Doctor's friends that the Time Lord is not dead and can renew himself. He gives "the process a little push" and warns them that the Doctor will look and act differently. He vanishes as the Doctor's features change into those of a younger man with dark curly hair. The Brigadier phones for the medical officer, Lieutenant Harry Sullivan, as the Doctor begins to recover, murmuring about random elements of his recent escapades. Sullivan has him taken to the sickbay for observation.

The next day Sarah returns to UNIT HQ to check on the Doctor and, learning he is still unconscious, asks the Brigadier to arrange for her to visit the National Institute for Advanced Scientific Research, known as Thinktank. As he takes her to his office to sort out a pass, the Doctor sneaks into the lab in a nightgown. He is about to enter the TARDIS when Sullivan finds him and insists he return to the sickbay. The Doctor assures him he is fully recovered and to prove it ties up the medic with a skipping rope and bundles him into a cupboard. Sarah and the Brigadier return having found the Doctor's bed empty, just as the TARDIS engines begin to groan. Sarah bangs on the doors and the Police Box falls silent. The Doctor pokes his head out to say goodbye but Sarah coaxes him into staying with a mystery about the theft of plans for a secret weapon.

Before he begins investigating, he must get dressed. As the Brigadier brings news of a second robbery, the Doctor tries on various outfits from inside the TARDIS – Viking battle gear, a playing-card king costume and a Pierrot (with face make-up) – before settling on a less outlandish red corduroy jacket, long striped scarf and felt hat.

Having failed to prevent a further robbery of parts needed to build the weapon, the Doctor deduces the thieves must be from Britain using something that doesn't need to breathe, is resistant to electric fences, leaves deep tracks, will kill casually yet is intelligent – just as Sarah returns to report meeting a huge walking, talking robot at Thinktank. To gather more evidence, Sullivan is nominated to go undercover at the Institute while the others visit ex-Thinktank robotics expert Professor JP Kettlewell.

By the time they return to the lab that night there has been another theft: the firing codes for all of America's, China's and Russia's atomic missiles. The only oddity about the people at Thinktank, though, is that many are members of the Scientific Reform Society, a lobby group calling for a more rationally ordered society.

Following a fruitless visit to Thinktank the next day, the Doctor receives a telephone call from Kettlewell telling him the robot is at his house. He speedily types a note saying he has gone to meet the professor, aware that it may be a trap, and pins it to the TARDIS. Soon after, Sarah reads it and hurries after him, not waiting for Sergeant Major Benton to organise backup. They return with an unconscious Doctor and Kettlewell, who tells Sarah that Hilda Winters, the head of Thinktank, reprogrammed his robot to commit the thefts, but that doing so is perilous to its sanity. When Sarah discovers he was made a member of the Scientific Reform Society, she convinces him to sneak her into their meeting that evening.

The Doctor doesn't awaken until then, having worked out in his sleep that Winters and her SRS cronies plan to blackmail the world by threatening to use the stolen missile codes. He is particularly disturbed to hear Sarah is with Kettlewell and hurries to the SRS meeting.

The following day the Doctor – having told the Brigadier he is planning to move on but leaving him a space-time telegraph in case of emergency – finds Sarah in his lab. She is sad the robot had to be destroyed, so the Doctor asks her to come with him in the TARDIS. As they are about to leave Sullivan arrives and sneers at the idea of a Police Box going anywhere. The Doctor invites him to look inside, just to prove his point, and laughs with Sarah at Harry's startled response. They follow him in and the TARDIS dematerialises.

NOTES The return of the TARDIS is again a split-screen effect so Elisabeth Sladen and Nicholas Courtney can be seen reacting as it appears. They are on set with the Police Box, which is initially obscured by an overlaid shot of the empty lab. Unfortunately this is not precisely aligned, so the right-hand background shifts slightly as the TARDIS appears. Its departure at the end of *Robot* uses the same technique. Harry, Sarah and the Doctor are recorded entering the Police Box as the camera pulls back. It's then locked in position and the left-hand side of the picture has a shot of Nicholas Courtney walking onto the empty set overlaid – a difference in lighting reveals the join just to the left of the TARDIS. The right-hand picture is then faded out leaving the Brigadier alone in the lab.

- The Doctor says, "I got lost in the time vortex. The TARDIS brought me home," suggesting it was his navigation at fault but that he was trying to get back to Earth. In light of what we later learn during his twelfth regeneration – when despite receiving a similarly lethal dose of radiation he is able to revisit many of his past companions before succumbing – we can't be sure he travelled directly from Metebelis Three to UNIT HQ.
- Who locks the TARDIS? The Doctor is too busy regenerating after stumbling from the Police Box, so does Sarah or the Brigadier take the precaution of locking up? (Isn't UNIT HQ secure enough?) But why would they then secrete the key in one of his boots? Or does the Doctor always keep a spare in his shoe, as one was there in *Spearhead from Space* too?
- Sarah's Thinktank pass is dated 4 April, so the Doctor must return on the 3rd. Two nights then pass before he departs again.
- Sarah bangs on the TARDIS as it begins to make its take-off sound and the noise stops. This is the first time it's indicated a dematerialisation can be suspended once it has begun (without a fault interrupting the take-off).
- Although the Doctor mentions Alexander the Great and Hannibal when trying to identify the Brigadier as someone he has "met before", his post-regeneration mind is still erratic so it's unclear if he has indeed encountered these ancient leaders. However, see Previous to Landing 1 for when he could have met the former.
- The Doctor changes his clothes very quickly when selecting a new outfit. It's possible time passes slower in the TARDIS so that he changes in what, from outside, seems like an instant. But given what we learn in *The Time of the Doctor* (Landing 596, vol.2), it's possible the Doctor is naked throughout the scene and donning holographic clothes while he makes up his mind. His final selection is probably real (thank goodness).

LANDING 107

SPACE Nerva space station in Earth orbit, control room
TIME [At least 151st century]
TRAVELLERS The Doctor, Sarah, Harry Sullivan
EPISODES The Ark in Space 1-4

The Doctor is planning a quick trip to the Moon to prove to Harry the TARDIS's abilities but the clumsy medic meddles with the helmic regulator, sending the Ship far into the future. It materialises in a dark, airless control room on the Nerva space station. There is gravity but most systems are powered down, including the oxygen supply. The Doctor activates the lights, at least, and Harry unwittingly opens a door, but when Sarah goes through to explore it seals shut behind her. By the time the others find her she is unconscious from lack of air and they too become trapped. The Doctor gets the oxygen flowing again but when he and Harry head for the TARDIS to get some brandy for the recovering Sarah they discover the circuits the Doctor repaired have reactivated an automatic defence system. They hide from its electrical bolts under a desk, working out it is targeted on organic material. The Doctor unscrews the desk from the floor with his sonic screwdriver so they can shuffle it towards the control panel on the wall and deactivate the auto-guard. Returning for Sarah, they find the couch they had placed her on was actually a short-range transmat device. They leave to find where it has sent her.

The Doctor comes back to the control room to complete repairs to the power systems so Vira can continue reviving the hibernating humans aboard Nerva. He detects a fault in the main solar stack and goes to investigate. He returns to shut down the stack as there is something growing inside it, but station commander Lazar (nicknamed Noah) suspects the Doctor of sabotage and stuns him with a laser pistol. Noah tells Vira she must continue with the revivals while he checks the solar stacks. Sarah and Harry arrive to check on the Doctor and find him unconscious. He suddenly awakens with a blinding headache and, learning where Noah has gone, hurries after him.

Noah has been infected by a Wirrn grub and returns to the control room to stop the humans from being woken so the Wirrn can feed on them. Technician Libri has been sent to apprehend him but Noah takes his gun and shoots him dead. His arm is now completely transformed into Wirrn flesh. An automatic message from the Earth High Minister plays and Noah's humanity reasserts itself; he orders Vira to speed up the revival schedule. But the Wirrn infection starts to affect his mind again and he battles with his mutated arm to keep it away from the controls. With a last effort, he staggers out of the control room.

Trapped in the cryogenic chamber, the Doctor plans an escape by reversing the transmat from the control room. He manages to send Harry and technician Rogin through before the power fails. However, with Noah and the Wirrn grubs entering their pupal stage, the Doctor, Sarah and Vira can get to the control room on foot. Harry suggests they all escape in the TARDIS but that would leave the sleepers to the Wirrn. To protect them they plan to lead a power cable from Nerva's transport shuttle through the infrastructure to the cryogenic chamber, to establish an electrical barrier that will keep the Wirrn out.

The Wirrn restore the power and the swarm leader that was Noah offers to let the Doctor and company go if they abandon the sleepers. The Doctor tries to appeal to the vestiges of Noah's human memory but he is now fully Wirrn and switches off the oxygen supply again.

Sarah, Harry and Vira watch from the control room as the shuttle takes off with all the Wirrn aboard, believing the Doctor has perished in its exhaust blast. But he was saved by Rogin and joins them in time to see the shuttle explode – Noah's final act to save his true kin. Without the shuttle, Vira intends to use a transmat cubicle to get her people to Earth but the Doctor finds a fault in the diode receptors and offers to pop down to fix it. Sarah and Harry insist on going with him and bring coats from the TARDIS.

After they have gone, the TARDIS dematerialises under Time Lord control as they send it to rendezvous with the Doctor after he has completed a mission for them on Skaro.

- **LORE** The helmic regulator is a rotating control on the console, unexpected operation of which during flight can disrupt intended landing parameters.
- The TARDIS carries brandy (see Landing 43).
- **NOTES** The Doctor estimates Nerva was built in the late-29th or early-30th century but that they have arrived "several thousand years at least" after that. We learn in *Revenge of the Cybermen* that the station was in use as a beacon near Jupiter "thousands of years before" it was converted into an ark to save the elite from solar flares, which scientists calculated would leave the Earth uninhabitable for 5,000 years; the Doctor concurs this would be the "absolute minimum". Yet we know from *The Daleks' Master Plan* that the Earth is inhabited until at least the 41st century, and later stories mention activity in the 51st (an ice age, so unlikely to be a time of solar flares). Owing to Wirrn sabotage, the Nerva sleepers have been in suspension for "several thousand years" longer than intended, and the Doctor later settles on 10,000 years as the total period of their hibernation. So they must awaken no earlier than the 151st century. (Much later, in *The Beast Below*, the Doctor tells Amy, "Twenty-ninth century. Solar flares roast the earth and the entire human race packs its bags and moves out till the weather improves." See Landing 444, vol.2 for why this must be a different, much less severe period of solar activity.)
- As the TARDIS materialises in the dark, there is no fade in. The roof lamp flashes in the darkness as the sound effect plays then the 'Police box' signs are illuminated as it finally 'lands' (although the white lettering is faintly visible before then). This is the first time the light inside the box has been on since *The Reign of Terror* (Landing 9). The front of the right-hand sign-box has either been painted black or got very dirty.
- The TARDIS arrives with its left-hand side against the wall and the doors facing the doorway to the main control room. But by the time it leaves it has rotated so its front is at a right angle to the doorway, to which it is also now closer. In reality this is because the first two and last two episodes were recorded two weeks apart and the Police Box prop was positioned differently for the latter. But we can postulate the Time Lords initially took control of the TARDIS a little too early and, worried the Doctor would notice and be distracted from defeating the Wirrn, hurriedly put it back again – in a slightly different position – until after he had transmatted down to Earth.

LANDING 108

SPACE Nerva space station above Voga in Jupiter orbit, forward control room
TIME [At least early-30th century]
TRAVELLERS None
EPISODES Revenge of the Cybermen 4

The Doctor has just re-established Nerva's orbit around Voga, after the Cybermen's attempt to crash the station into the planetoid, when the TARDIS materialises in the forward control room. He nips inside to set the drift compensators before the Ship leaves without them and finds the Brigadier has sent him a request for help via the space-time telegraph.

Fortunately, when the Doctor emerges to fetch Sarah, Harry has just transmatted up to the station and he tells the pair they are needed. The TARDIS engines are already sounding as Sarah pulls Harry into the Ship and it dematerialises.

- **NOTES** See Landing 107 for dating discussion but note that, if it was decided to use a space station already "thousands of years" old as the vessel for saving "the entire body of human thought and achievement" (rather than, say, building a brand new one), and that it lasted a further 10,000 years, then Nerva was certainly a sturdy construction. So it may have been in use even before being assigned to warning space traffic of Jupiter's latest moon and this story itself could be set long after the 30th century.
- When the Doctor and friends arrive on Nerva via the time ring and see the TARDIS isn't there, he says they're "a little early" and the Ship is "drifting back through time… We just have to wait for it to turn up." When it does he "set[s] the drift compensators" so it doesn't "[slip] through our fingers". Is the TARDIS therefore just moving backwards through time but not (relative) space until it happens to coincide with the Doctor aboard Nerva? That seems rather random, not to say risky. We know the Time Lords lifted the Doctor and his companions from the transmat beam taking them from Earth back to Nerva and deposited them on Skaro at the dawn of the Daleks' creation. They give the Doctor a time ring that "will return you to the TARDIS when you've finished here" but which actually transports them back to Nerva, yet not in the time period they left. Does that mean the Doctor's encounter with the Cybermen is also orchestrated by the Time Lords? Perhaps they thought, while they had him stopping the Daleks being made, why not have him destroy the last of the Cybermen too? If the TARDIS, then, is under Time Lord control and they set it to materialise only after the Doctor has completed this second mission, presumably he never realises he has been manipulated and just supposes the TARDIS is drifting back to meet them.
- The space-time telegraph doesn't seem to be part of the TARDIS but a separate device the Doctor has left with the Brigadier (seen briefly in *Terror of the Zygons*)

with which to contact him through the Ship's usual communications system. Its message is output onto yellow ticker tape; this can be seen hanging inside the Police Box prop when the Doctor first enters.

LANDING 109

SPACE Earth, Scotland, Inverness-shire, near Loch Ness
TIME Two days in 1980
TRAVELLERS The Doctor, Sarah, Harry
EPISODES Terror of the Zygons 1,4

Responding to the Brigadier's summons, the TARDIS materialises in a forest in the Scottish Highlands, not far from Loch Ness, but a fault renders it invisible. The three travellers do not notice when they first emerge, but when Sarah alerts them that the Ship seems to have gone, the Doctor pops back inside to fix the problem. As Sarah and Harry wonder in which country they might be, the familiar Police Box reappears with a groan. The Doctor checks the coordinates and learns they are in Scotland so dons appropriate attire: a tartan scarf and a tam-o'-shanter. He gives his usual scarf and hat to the others then leads them to find the Brigadier, using a handheld detector to track the syonic signal from the space-time telegraph.

Late the next day, the genuine Duke of Forgill escorts the Doctor, Sarah, Harry and the Brigadier through the forest to where the TARDIS is waiting. The Doctor offers to take them all back to London, claiming they can be there five minutes ago, but both the Brigadier and Harry feel safer with the train. Sarah hesitates but when the Doctor promises they will go straight to London she accepts his offer of a lift.

▌ **NOTES** It's just feasible (if you wanted to imagine additional adventures with the Doctor, Sarah and Harry – and who wouldn't?) that the TARDIS doesn't return to Earth straight away, as the Doctor would know he could respond to the Brigadier's call at any time, what with having a time machine. However, the clear intention is that he has answered the call immediately as the Doctor is sure they're on Earth before he checks the coordinates and is later stern with the Brigadier for having been called back – an unlikely attitude if he was only responding at his leisure (although he may just be laying into Lethbridge-Stewart so he doesn't use the telegraph too often).

▌ Two stories later, in *Pyramids of Mars*, Sarah explicitly states several times she is "from 1980". As *Terror of the Zygons* is the most recent occasion she was in her native time, that's surely what she's referring to. Some assign the date to her first meeting the Doctor in *The Time Warrior* (and dating evidence in *The Green Death* might support this – see Landing 95), but that seems an odd reference point for her given she has been home at least twice since then. Either every Earth-bound adventure between *The Time Warrior* and *Terror of the Zygons* happens in 1980, in which case all those up to *Planet of the Spiders* must occur before March, which is pushing things, or we're now into at least 1981, in which case surely Sarah would give that date in *Pyramids of Mars*.

▌ The Doctor doesn't explain why the TARDIS materialises invisibly, only saying it "must have gone on the blink again" (although in the script he says, "I thought I'd fixed that fusion plate."). The last time it did this, in *The Invasion*, was because of a faulty visual stabiliser circuit (see Landing 63). Although Sarah can't see the Ship so naturally assumes "it's gone", the Doctor can tell it's there, just not visible, so can he sense it? In *The Invasion* he has to feel around to find the TARDIS again whereas here he walks straight through the doorway.

▌ According to the script, the Police Box was supposed to appear "quite quietly", not with the usual sound.

▌ The scene of the TARDIS arriving was cut from the original broadcast of *Terror of the Zygons* because the split-screen effect used for the travellers emerging from nowhere was considered ineffective as the light on location had changed too much between each element being filmed. For many years the scene was thought to no longer exist, until a copy of the sound recording rushes was discovered, and shortly afterwards a copy of the film that together allowed the scene to be reconstructed and included on the 2013 DVD release of the story.

▌ It's feasible the Brigadier had to return to Scotland to wrap up UNIT operations there, but did Sarah and Harry really need to go too? The Doctor implies he's just fetching the TARDIS as he's "going to pilot it all the way to London", so it's not like they're expecting him to disappear without saying goodbye. Arguably they don't trust him to make it back (not that either has particular experience of the TARDIS being unreliable) but if they didn't intend to join him anyway, why not just say goodbye in London? Plainly Sarah was always up for more trips despite her coyness, but Harry's just adding to the wasted UNIT travel budget.

IT'S BIGGER ON THE INSIDE

THE RUSCOE RECLAMATION
1975

Pyramids of Mars, the first story made for Season 13 (*Terror of the Zygons* being held over from the previous production block), required several scenes inside the TARDIS. The interior had not been used since *Death to the Daleks*, recorded seventeen months earlier, so it fell to designer Christine Ruscoe to dig out of storage whatever was left of the TARDIS set pieces and prepare them for use.

The console itself was refurbished by the BBC Visual Effects department (see page 170). As for the walls to go around it, there were the main doors and an indented wall, originals from 1963 that had most recently been refreshed for Season 10. All three of Tim Gleeson's new walls from *The Time Monster* survived (minus their 'washbowl' roundels), one of which had its round cut-outs backed with flat plywood, as seen in *Death to the Daleks*. Finally, at least one but likely both of Roger Liminton's narrow indented walls were also available.

Ruscoe used most of these pieces arranged in a semicircle that was basically a recreation of Gleeson's set for *The Time Monster* – main doors, six-column indented wall, two four-column walls and sliding-arch wall – plus one of the narrow sections on the far right (glimpsed briefly when the TARDIS is dragged off course). All three of Gleeson's walls were given a solid backing to create shallow indented circles, as Colin Green had introduced, and were painted 'TV white' – actually a pale grey that reflected less light than pure white and so didn't exceed the brightness limits of studio cameras. The inner edges of the arch were coloured blue, like the back of the main doors had been although these were now painted white again. With the sliding section placed at a slight angle, this now acted as an interior doorway. Gleeson's cornice also had to be used as his walls were too short without it. (It's not clear whether the narrow wall had a cornice but as Liminton's were seemingly junked after Season 10 it probably didn't.) The set wasn't given any scanner screen, however, probably because the script didn't specify the need for one.

Along with the updated console, the control room appeared newer than its components actually were. Having some walls with roundels that aren't translucent gives the set a greater feeling of solidity, helped by the deep recess of the sliding-arch wall. The set appeared the same in *Planet of Evil*, which would ultimately be broadcast first, but when the TARDIS control room was seen again the following year it had a radical new look.

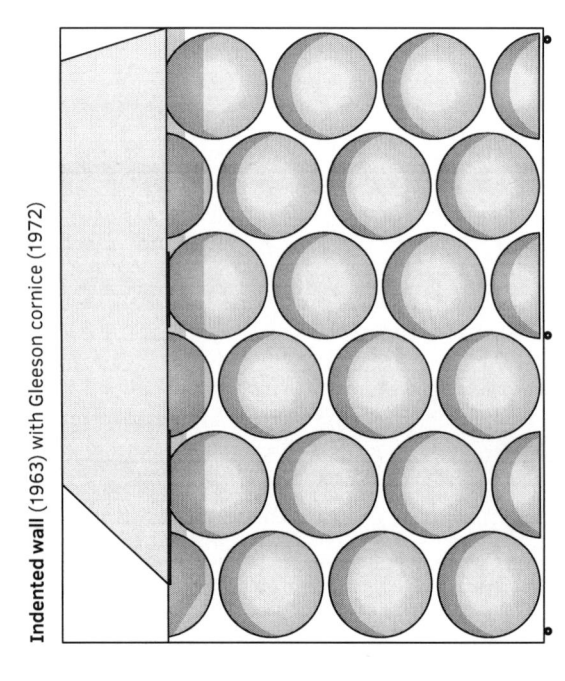

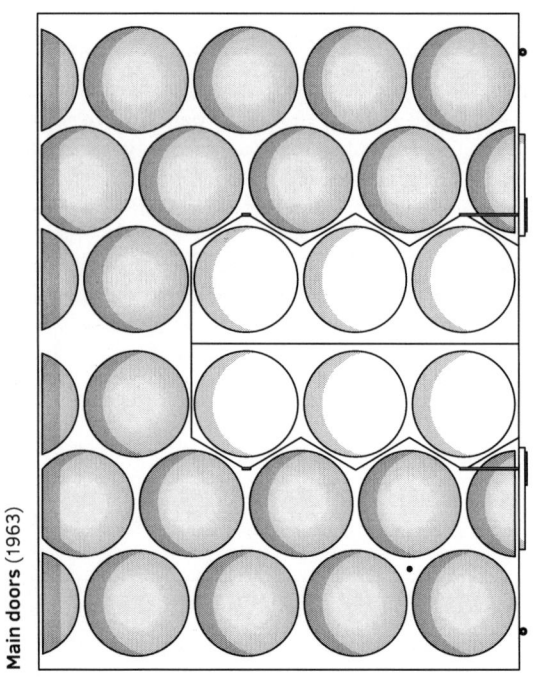

Indented wall (1963) with Gleeson cornice (1972)

Main doors (1963)

IT'S BIGGER ON THE INSIDE

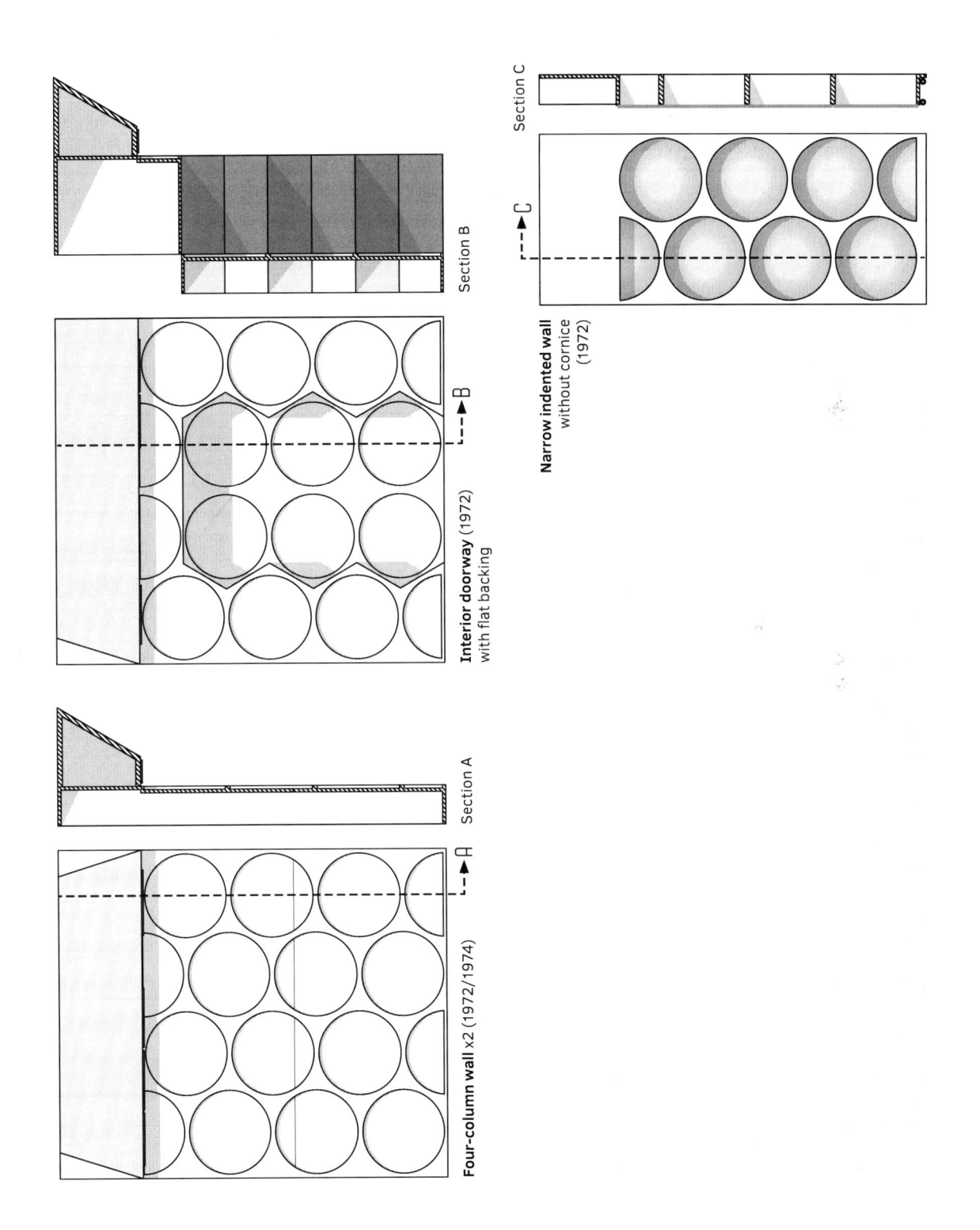

Four-column wall x2 (1972/1974)

Section A

Interior doorway (1972)
with flat backing

Section B

Narrow indented wall
without cornice (1972)

Section C

WHAT ARE ALL THESE KNOBS?

CONSOLE Ci
1975

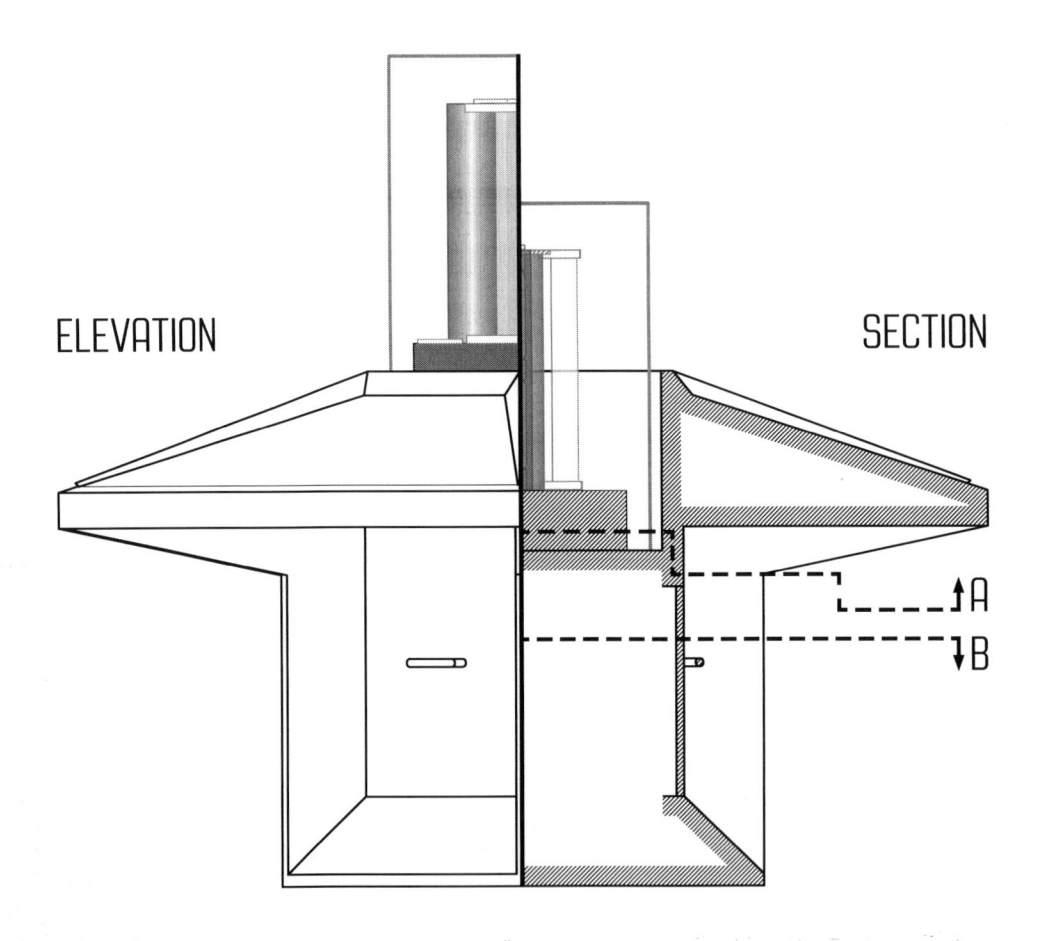

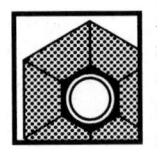

ELEVATION   SECTION

↑A
↓B

After a sole appearance in Season 11 and none at all the season after, the TARDIS control room was required for scenes in two stories of Season 13. First into production was *Pyramids of Mars*, and while designer Christine Ruscoe refreshed existing wall sections for the set, the console was dispatched to the Visual Effects department for refurbishment, probably under the supervision of that serial's effects designer Ian Scoones.

This was Console B, built by Magna Models for Kenneth Sharp in late-1970. Although the changes made in 1975 were more cosmetic than structural, this looked like a new console to viewers, hence its designation here as Console C. The prop was repainted in the same off-white as the set walls, retaining the metal edging on the rim and pedestal. The central column had its green plastic tubes swapped for red ones and the coloured plastic blocks removed to give it a simpler, less garish appearance.

The main change, however, was to the control panels (here numbered in accordance with their more consistent arrangement when they returned in 1977 – see page 210 – but ordered as they first appeared in *Planet of Evil*). It's possible the old ones had been damaged during their seventeen months in storage but more likely, with a new production team running the programme, it was decided a fresh look was in order. There was no attempt to recreate the layout of the previous consoles; instead chunkier, more colourful (although with a predominance of red and silver) items were selected. A few of the old controls were reused, however: some of the long black switches (placed upside down with the thicker end at the bottom) and the casings from the spinning-light units.

After its use in just four episodes, the console went back into storage as a completely new style was adopted for the following season. But this was not its last appearance by a long chalk.

WHAT ARE ALL THESE KNOBS?

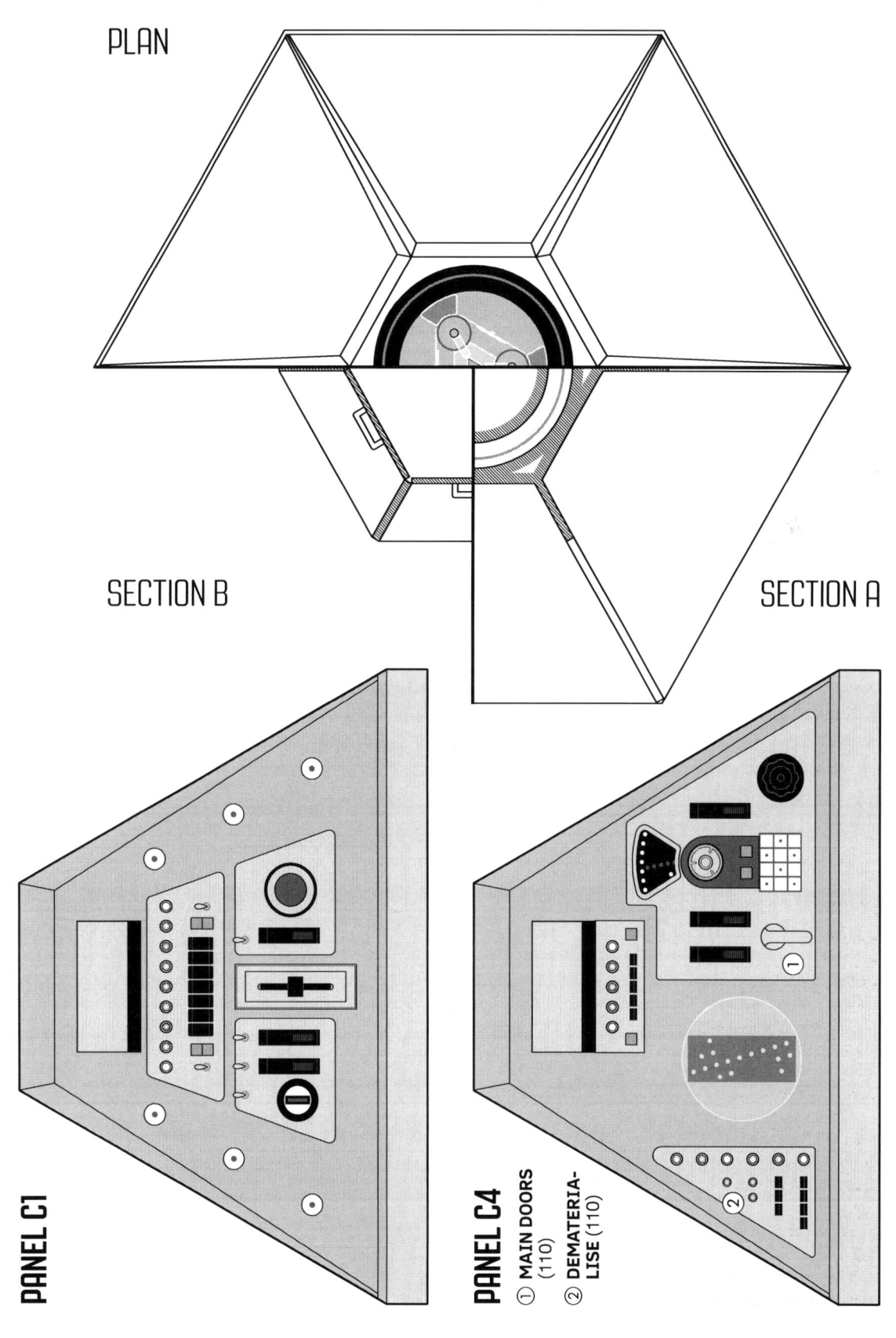

PLAN

SECTION B

SECTION A

PANEL C1

PANEL C4
① MAIN DOORS (110)
② DEMATERIA-LISE (110)

WHAT ARE ALL THESE KNOBS?

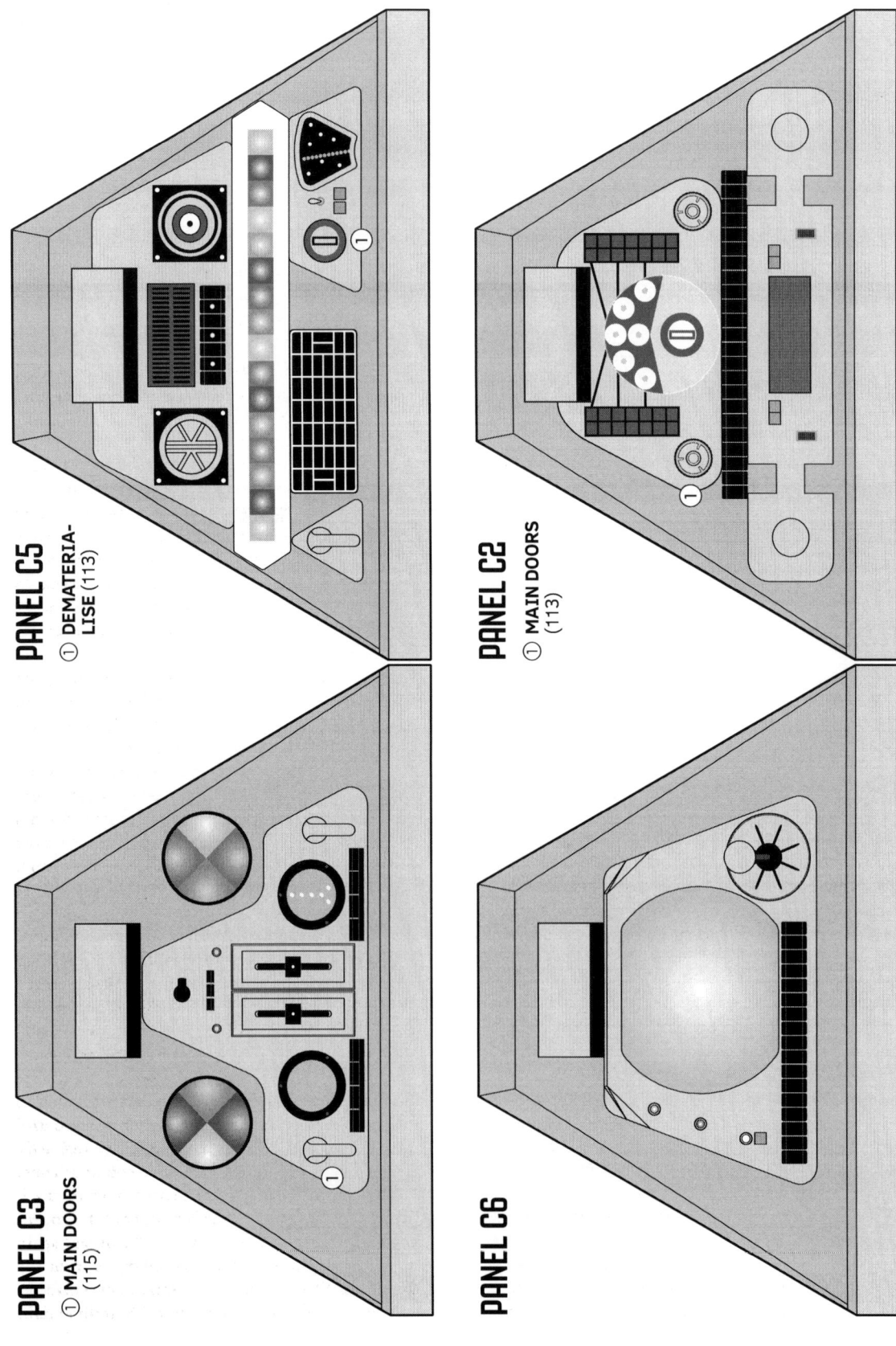

PANEL C5
① DEMATERIA-
LISE (113)

PANEL C2
① MAIN DOORS
(113)

PANEL C3
① MAIN DOORS
(115)

PANEL C6

LANDING 110

SPACE Zeta Minor; transposed to Morestran probe ship
TIME Around 31980 [or 37166]
TRAVELLERS The Doctor, Sarah
EPISODES Planet of Evil 1-4

After travelling for notably longer than expected for a quick hop from Scotland to London, Sarah gets suspicious that something has gone wrong.

The Doctor tries to bluff it out but eventually admits there has been a "slight overshoot" and they have come out of the Vortex some 30,000 years too late. The console picks up a distress call and the Doctor makes an emergency materialisation amid a steamy jungle at night on Inter Minor. The Doctor has a small handheld detector with which he takes a bearing on the signal and they head off in the direction of a small scientific outpost.

Not long afterwards, expedition leader Professor Sorenson finds the TARDIS and hides among the foliage as Sarah returns to collect a spectromixer with which to establish the planet's location, carrying with her a hand tool the Doctor found in the forest. Just after she has gone inside, a Morestran military landing party – searching for Sorenson's missing team – discovers the Police Box and prepares to have it transposed to their orbiting spaceship. They clip two of their transmat armbands onto the TARDIS, one across the doors so that when Sarah tries to leave the Ship she finds the control room doors will not open. Unaware the TARDIS has been moved, she tries again and this time the doors operate normally. She exits to find herself in an airless quarantine berth aboard the Morestran ship. Controller Salamar informs her she is his prisoner and has oxygen pumped in when he realises she cannot breathe. His subordinate Morelli completes quarantine procedures before taking Sarah away for questioning.

The next day, the Morestran ship lands close to the expedition base and Sorenson has his mineral samples from the planet loaded aboard. Crewmen place the canisters in the quarantine berth beside the TARDIS. After being questioned by Salamar, the Doctor and Sarah are detained there also. She returns the TARDIS key to him but he cannot leave yet as the forces on Zeta Minor could destroy the entire universe if mishandled. They examine the mineral samples, which change colour as they emit energy, and the Doctor keeps some in an empty Farrah's Original Harrogate Toffee tin from his pocket. The spaceship's engines start up but the Doctor knows it will not be allowed to leave the planet with the minerals aboard. Sure enough, when it fails to lift off crewman De Haan comes to take the two prisoners to the command deck.

On Salamar's orders, Morelli and De Haan begrudgingly carry the mineral samples outside the ship again. However, Sorenson sneaks into the quarantine berth and takes one of the canisters for himself.

Although the probe ship eventually manages to leave the planet, it is soon suspended in space as the forces on Zeta Minor try to pull it back. Salamar believes the TARDIS is draining his ship's power and forces the Doctor at gunpoint to open it. When a scream from Sarah distracts the commander, the Doctor knocks him out with a punch and rushes out to find her. Salamar recovers and follows him.

With the Morestran ship now being pulled faster and faster towards the planet, a crazed Salamar hunts for Sorenson with a handheld neutron accelerator. He corners the creature the professor has become in the quarantine berth and opens the accelerator, but is killed by Sorenson as the released particles react to produce dozens of antimatter duplicates. The Doctor discovers Salamar's desiccated corpse and closes the neutron accelerator before heading back to the command deck.

Shortly afterwards the Doctor returns to the darkened quarantine berth in search of Sorenson, repelling three of the duplicates with a canister of minerals. A bestial Sorenson emerges from behind the TARDIS and the Doctor stuns him with a laser pistol, drags him into the Ship and dematerialises.

- **CONTROLS** The control panels are arranged (clockwise) 1-4-5-3-2-6, with panel C2 facing the main doors.
- The Doctor operates pushbuttons on the triangular plate at bottom-left of panel C4 and the rotary handle to their right; touches the switch and dial by the gauge at bottom-right of panel C5 but doesn't appear to adjust them; the right-hand large slider and left-hand rotary handle on panel C3; and unseen controls on panel C6. Both he and Sarah examine the screen on panel C6 when the alert sounds and the Doctor seems to initiate the emergency materialisation from here. Sarah uses the rotary handle on panel C4 to operate the main doors. The Doctor dematerialises the TARDIS by pressing two pushbuttons on the triangular plate of panel C4 (the same as he operated in episode one).
- **LORE** The TARDIS can automatically receive distress calls if it's in the same space-time region.
- **NOTES** Although Sarah has changed her clothes while waiting for the Doctor to get her to London, the dialogue in the first TARDIS scene, and later when Sarah is being questioned by Salamar, leaves little room for the possibility of unseen landings since they left Scotland.
- Indeed, when do the control room and console get redecorated? There's no apparent opportunity since the Doctor regained the TARDIS on Nerva beacon, so did the Ship itself fancy a makeover while it was travelling alone, or did the Time Lords install some updates while they had control? Maybe the Doctor's third incarnation let out a burst of regeneration energy after leaving Metebelis Three (accounting for his subdued change when he gets back to Earth) that required the control room to be reconstructed while he recovered in UNIT's sickbay? It could even have been earlier as the control room layout is more or less the same as in *Death to the Daleks*, just with a slightly different colour scheme, although the console then was yet to be reconfigured.
- Zeta Minor is said to be "the last planet of the known universe", "beyond Cygnus A" and "as distant again from the Artoro galaxy as that galaxy is from the Anterides". Of these, only the first is a name currently assigned to a genuine galaxy, some 600 million light

years from Earth. This is relatively close to us given the size of the observable universe is some 91 billion light years across. From our point of view, then, there are lots of things beyond Cygnus A, making that seem an odd marker for a planet "on the very edge of the known universe". There's nothing other than their appearance to suggest the Morestrans are descended from Earth humans, however, so they might be from a planet way beyond Cygnus relative to us. Perhaps their home galaxy is the Anterides, Artoro is halfway to their observable edge of the universe, and to them Cygnus A is the most distant object they have recorded. This edge-of-the-universe stuff might all be hyperbole, anyway. Morestra's sun is dying so they send an expedition across billions of light years to find an alternative energy source? Is there really nothing closer? If they're that advanced, wouldn't it be easier to move to a new planet around a more stable star? Assuming Professor Sorenson has somehow detected a promising energy emission from billions of light years away (and it's hard enough to discern entire galaxies let alone one planet at that distance, but let's say he narrowed his focus the closer he got), the source would no longer be where it seemed even if he were able to travel there instantaneously. Alternatively, if Morestra is actually much closer to Zeta Minor, say an outpost of a civilisation originating a couple of galaxies away – so by 'edge of the universe' they mean 'as far as our people have ever travelled' – why should Salamar be so surprised to find the Doctor and Sarah there? If the Morestrans are within a reasonable travelling time of it, why shouldn't others be?

▪ Wherever Zeta Minor is, it orbits its own sun and at least one other star is visible in the night sky. Although the days seem temperate they're not much brighter than night so the sun may be quite dim.

▪ The Doctor estimates the TARDIS has come out of the Vortex about 30,000 years "too late", presumably meaning beyond the 20th century he was aiming for. Assuming he's talking in relative terms for Sarah's benefit, that makes it the 320th century back home. At the start of episode one, we see Braun place a grave marker reading 'Egard Lumb died here 7y2 in the year 37,166'. Despite seeming close enough to the Doctor's estimate, if the TARDIS was closer to 35,000 years out than 30,000 surely he would have said that? So this is more likely a Morestran dating system, as suggested by the unusual day or month notation.

▪ This is the first appearance on screen of console C, although it was designed for the following serial, *Pyramids of Mars*, which was recorded first. The control room itself is composed of pre-existing walls – from left to right: main doors, six-column deep-indented roundels (still missing its skirting), then the three new walls built for *The Time Monster*. The wall with the sliding cut-out section now forms an interior doorway. On the doors wall, the holes drilled prior to *Death to the Daleks* (Landing 100) for the crank handle and hexagonal light fitting are still visible.

▪ It's not clear whether their overshooting 20th century London is a fault with the TARDIS's navigation or the Doctor's piloting, although Sarah's assertion that the Doctor "always get[s] rude when you're trying to cover up a mistake" perhaps implies the error lies with him. Always assuming he hasn't deliberately taken them far from Earth as a ploy to keep Sarah with him for longer.

▪ The wavering hum in the control room heard here and in *Pyramids of Mars* was previously used in *The Time Monster*, although then only when the TARDIS was in flight.

▪ The Police Box roof lamp keeps flashing after the TARDIS has materialised.

▪ In the Gladstone bag containing the spectromixer (not the same as the satchel seen in *Planet of the Spiders*), Sarah also finds the etheric beam locator the Doctor had in his pocket in *Genesis of the Daleks* (and so was presumably carrying with him throughout Season 12). The spectromixer itself is a small square of red plastic with three metal strips on one side.

▪ A recorded scene, cut for time but retained in Terrance Dicks' novelisation of the story, had Salamar and Morelli discussing the Police Box when it's transposed to the quarantine berth. The latter reports, "The photonic analysis of the exterior indicates an amalgam of elements similar in composition to relics discovered on the Telerian planet in the second era," and, "I've tried to establish age, but there are some confusing trace elements which interfere with the readings." Salamar points out, "The Earth planet has been uninhabited wasteland since the start of the third era." This is probably an intentional reference to the solar-flare-ravaged Earth seen in *The Sontaran Experiment*, although it doesn't help with dating that event. While the scene's inclusion would have established that the Morestrans knew of Earth it doesn't prove they're descended from humans, and their 'eras' don't seem to relate either to the segments of time mentioned in *The Ark* (Landing 35) or the numerous great and bountiful human empires discussed in *The Long Game* (Landing 329, vol.2). Morelli suggests the Police Box's owners are "perhaps alien infiltrators? Operating an undiscovered base there [on Earth]", which could be taken to mean the Morestrans are aware of some of the events of *The Mysterious Planet* (Landing 281). Cut dialogue also established the TARDIS was encased in a magnetic field, presumably as part of the transposing process and to explain why the doors wouldn't open.

▪ The Doctor removes his scarf and leaves it beside the TARDIS when he's a prisoner in episode two. This is because the pre-filmed shots of him floating in the pit for episode three were more convincingly achieved without him wearing it. Within the story, though, there's no obvious reason for it. He must put the scarf inside the TARDIS before being taken back to the bridge, however, as it's not on the floor of the quarantine berth when De Haan and Morelli collect the professor's canisters.

LANDING 111

SPACE Zeta Minor, beside pool
TIME As above
TRAVELLERS The Doctor, Professor Sorenson
EPISODES Planet of Evil 4

The Doctor secures the transformed Sorenson with a bar connecting manacles on his wrists and ankles. But as he returns his attention to the console, the professor awakens and breaks free. The TARDIS materialises beside the dark pool that is a gateway to the antimatter universe and the Doctor hurries outside as Sorenson lumbers after him.

With the bar still attached to the creature by one wrist, the Doctor uses it to keep him out of arm's reach as they circle the pool. Sorenson pulls free and raises the bar to strike the Doctor down, but he falls backwards and tumbles into the blackness. The Doctor throws the canister of minerals in after him.

As the Doctor returns to the TARDIS he spots a restored Sorenson lying unconscious by the side of the pool. He picks up the scientist, carries him into the Ship and dematerialises as the shimmering antimatter energy creature rises from the pool.

✪ CONTROLS After manacling Sorenson, the Doctor flicks a switch on the left of panel C1. When the TARDIS lands he presses unseen controls which could be the same pushbuttons at the bottom-left of panel C4 that he used for take-off.

▤ NOTES The journey back to Zeta Minor seems to take an oddly long time. The Doctor knows the Morestran ship is about to crash and Sarah is under siege from antimatter creatures, yet he calmly spends time shackling Sorenson then fiddling at the console. Of course, however long the trip seems to take to those inside, the TARDIS can still land moments after taking off, but why not do so quickly while Sorenson is unconscious?

▤ As the camera pans up from Sorenson on the floor to the Doctor taking off, the cables powering the console can be seen entering the pedestal beneath panel C1.

▤ The departing TARDIS is the 3-foot miniature (its last appearance in the series) but shot on the full-size set. This was to give the antimatter monster a greater sense of size, and it could be positioned closer to the pool.

LANDING 112

SPACE Morestran probe ship, quarantine berth
TIME As above
TRAVELLERS The Doctor, Sorenson
EPISODES Planet of Evil 4

Sorenson is dazed and confused but alive: the Doctor tells him he is lucky to have been released and only was because the Doctor returned all the antimatter to the pool. As the professor wonders where he is, the TARDIS returns to the quarantine berth aboard the Morestran spaceship.

With the probe ship now freed from Zeta Minor's pull and Sorenson subtly steered towards pursuing an alternative source of energy, the Doctor and Sarah return to the TARDIS to resume their journey to London.

▤ NOTES The Doctor has found a chair from somewhere for Sorenson to sit in. It wasn't in the control room when they landed so he must have brought it from another room after take-off. Nice of him not to leave the professor lying on the floor, even after all the danger he has been responsible for. From what we glimpse of the chair, it has a metal frame and appears to be a fold-up type.

▤ The TARDIS's arrival back on the probe ship is a reversal of the shot of its departure. The materialisation sound effects begins with its early warbling tones and barely gets to the familiar groans before the end thump kicks in.

▤ The final shot of the TARDIS in flight is a new model first used in *Pyramids of Mars* (recorded before *Planet of Evil* but broadcast after). This is actually flipped horizontally – note the white 'Police telephone' plaque appears to be on the right-hand door and, if you look closely, the 'Police box' signs are reversed.

LANDING 113

SPACE Earth, England, Scarman's house, storage room
TIME Two days in 1911
TRAVELLERS The Doctor, Sarah
EPISODES Pyramids of Mars 1-2

The TARDIS is heading to Earth – although the Doctor no longer thinks of it as his home – when a powerful mental force rocks the Ship, causing the relative continuum stabiliser to fail. The console sparks and Sarah sees an image of Sutekh the Osiran's malevolent face. The control room steadies and the Doctor is all for returning to the end of the spectrum where the incident occurred, but a frightened Sarah dissuades him.

The TARDIS materialises with a bump. The energy from a nearby time-space tunnel has drawn it off its temporal course, however. It is in the right spatial location but the year is 1911, before the building used as UNIT HQ was built. Standing there now is the manor house, originally a priory, currently owned by the Egyptologist Professor Marcus Scarman. The TARDIS stands in a ground-floor room in a disused wing of the building, hidden among shipping crates and Ancient Egyptian sarcophagi. As the Doctor senses something very wrong, the sound of ominous organ music drifts from elsewhere in the house.

The Doctor and Sarah are discovered by Scarman's elderly butler Collins, who takes them for friends of a Dr Warlock and warns them of Ibrahim Namin, the Egyptian currently in charge of the house while Professor Scarman is away in Cairo. Collins ushers them out the window but as he watches them go one of the sarcophagi opens and a bandage-wrapped robotic Mummy steps out and strangles the old man. His dying scream brings Namin and Warlock running as the Mummy returns to its coffin. Warlock wants to inform the police but Namin recognises the sign that Sutekh is rising and pulls a pistol on the doctor. His shot is deflected when the Doctor creeps up behind and throws his scarf around the Egyptian, although Warlock is still caught in the arm so Sarah helps him from the room. Namin is about to give chase but instead opens the sarcophagus, activates the Mummy using his ring and sends it after the three fugitives.

Having called off the hunt when an organ sound indicates his master is returning, Namin returns to the storage room to activate two more Mummies.

The next morning, Scarman – now possessed by Sutekh's will and having killed Namin – has the Egyptian's body dumped in the storage room. With two Mummies hunting the poacher Clements, Scarman activates a fourth to help unpack the crates containing parts for a missile and to carry them outside. While they are gone, the Doctor, Sarah and Scarman's brother Laurence sneak in to take Namin's ring so the Doctor can trace the power it uses back to Sutekh's location. They examine some of the crated equipment and deduce Scarman plans to fire the missile at the power source on Mars that is holding Sutekh captive in Egypt. When they hear Scarman and the Mummies returning, all three take refuge inside the TARDIS.

While an astonished Laurence takes a look around the Ship, Sarah suggests they can leave safely as she knows Sutekh did not destroy the world in 1911. So the Doctor offers to show her what 1980 will be like if they were to leave without defeating Sutekh.

- **CONTROLS** The control panels are arranged (clockwise) 1-3-5-4-2-6, with panel C5 facing the main doors.
- When the TARDIS is struck, there are small explosions on panels C6 and C1, one presumably being where the relative continuum stabiliser is housed. The Doctor turns the left-hand silver dial on panel C2 to open the main doors. When jumping ahead to 1980, he turns the bottom-right dial on panel C5 to move the Ship and adjusts the rotary handle bottom-left of panel C3.
- **LORE** Nothing should be able to enter the TARDIS while it's in flight, although an extremely powerful mental force might.
- **NOTES** Given that Sarah has been rummaging around in the wardrobe and the Doctor (himself wearing a new coat) is in a sullen mood that doesn't seem related to his recent experiences on Zeta Minor, there's the possibility unseen landings have occurred. The Doctor is supposedly still trying to get Sarah back to Earth, and she's under the impression they're "going home", but as he doesn't manage it for some time yet it may be an even longer absence than we're shown.
- Scarman's house, originally a priory, is said to be on the same site as UNIT HQ – given its wooded estate, presumably the later headquarters first seen in *The Three Doctors*. When leaving Loch Ness the Doctor said he was heading for London, whereas he now seems to be aiming for UNIT HQ. Of course, that may be in London, although if so it must be towards the outskirts to have that much space around it (particularly if London in the *Doctor Who* universe is as crowded as suggested in *Invasion of the Dinosaurs* – see Landing 99). If not, has their destination changed? Perhaps the Brigadier has used the space-time telegraph again, which is why the Doctor is suddenly grumpy about having to "run around after" him. As Scarman's house burns down in 1911 and UNIT isn't formed until the 1960s, was another residential property built that was eventually sold on, or did the government snap up the estate soon after the fire (Scarman leaves no apparent heirs) to build a wartime establishment away from prying eyes? Either way, it's impressive of Sarah to know the site's history so well. Did she check it out before first infiltrating UNIT in *The Time Warrior*?
- The shot in episode one of the TARDIS spinning through space is not the same as the one at the end of *Planet of Evil* but was filmed at the same time – note the background pattern of stars is the same (only here not reversed). This new model Police Box was built by one of visual effects designer Ian Scoones' team from wood and card, with internal electrics for the flashing light. It was about seven inches tall and replaced the one made for *The Curse of Peladon*. It still matched other models rather than the full-size prop, with a deep bottom rail on the side panelling, white window frames and a white 'Police telephone' plaque.
- The control room layout is the same as in *Planet of Evil* although there is an extra wall section to the right of the interior door (which may have been present but unseen in the previous story). The other indented wall and main doors have white tape across the bottoms in place of the missing skirting to hide the castors, and tape covering the cables powering the console is conspicuous in several shots. Although Sarah appears to be looking towards a wall behind the camera when she sees Sutekh, her point-of-view shot was recorded separately, with the camera pointing at the right-hand side of the indented wall, and inserted during editing.
- Although characters have been seen to change clothes while aboard the TARDIS, this mention of the wardrobe is the first since *The Tenth Planet* (Landing 42).
- Oops! When the control room tilts, a camera can be briefly glimpsed on the left of the screen. This is the one that has just been taking the preceding close-up shot of Tom Baker.
- The engine groans are not heard within the control room when the TARDIS lands, just the end thump from the materialisation sound effect.
- In episode two, when the Doctor is trying to avoid being sucked into the time-space tunnel to Sutekh's tomb, he disables it by throwing the TARDIS key into it, suggesting this has some temporal properties of its own. Even so, Sutekh is able to send the key through the tunnel without any problems in episode four.

LANDING 114

SPACE Parallel Earth, wasteland
TIME 1980 (alternative timeline)
TRAVELLERS The Doctor, Sarah, Laurence Scarman
EPISODES Pyramids of Mars 2

After a brief journey, the TARDIS materialises on an alternative 1980s Earth in a timeline where Sutekh broke free and turned the planet into a blasted wasteland. The Doctor opens the doors so Sarah can see what would happen if they do not at least try to stop Sutekh.

Aghast, she realises they have to go back to 1911, and the Doctor sets the TARDIS to return.

- **CONTROLS** The Doctor seems to open the main doors with an unseen control on panel C5.
- **LORE** The TARDIS can travel into potential timelines that are different from those previously visited by it and its occupants.
- **NOTES** A model shot was filmed showing the TARDIS materialising on the barren future Earth. It was cut from the final episode so as not to lessen the impact when Sarah looks out the doors. It can be seen on the DVD release of *Pyramids of Mars*.
- A blue CSO screen outside the main doors enabled the model footage of the wasteland to be superimposed (a possible reason why the back of the doors had to be repainted from blue to white). Note the background doesn't move when the camera does.
- *Doctor Who* has addressed the question of how actions affect the future on several occasions. Under original story editor David Whitaker, an already known future was immutable, with the Doctor telling Barbara in *The Aztecs*, "You can't rewrite history, not one line." The suggestion was that any action the travellers took in the past would only contribute to the course of history as they already knew it. This is bolstered in *The Romans* when it's the Doctor who gives Emperor Nero the idea for burning Rome, implying that if the travellers hadn't been there then our history would or could have been different. Yet shortly after this, in *The Time Meddler* (by the same writer) it's considered a real possibility that the Monk could alter the future by changing the outcome of the Battle of Hastings. It can feel dramatically unsatisfying if characters are tied to ensuring known outcomes, and raises the question of why they can seemingly do what they like in situations where they don't happen to know the future. According to the Doctor at the time, it's fine to stop the Daleks wiping out the Thals on Skaro, but not to even try to save the Aztecs from being massacred by the Spanish. Presumably, therefore, if the Doctor arrived on early 22nd-century Earth he would have to let the Dalek invasion succeed, having already seen it. And yet by the time of *Day of the Daleks*, he is shown to directly contribute to averting a future he has already experienced. As he concludes in *Inferno*, "Free will is not an illusion after all." Our choices do affect the future and we're not bound by a predetermined outcome. That's why, in *The Time Warrior*, the Doctor is concerned about Linx giving advanced weapons to medieval folk: there's no suggestion that he can't rewrite history, and thus he must be stopped. And here in *Pyramids of Mars* the Doctor says the future can be "shaped", by most people "to a small extent" but to a devastating degree by a powerful figure like Sutekh. And the TARDIS is able to visit just such a future so it must exist somewhere. Is it a parallel world, like that visited in *Inferno*? Adopting the multiverse theory, where every possible choice is played out somewhere in an infinity of parallel universes, can be equally unsatisfying for drama. Who cares if Sutekh wins if the Doctor can just travel to a different universe where he didn't? Actions are as free of responsibility as if they were predetermined to suit a fixed future. Perhaps this, then, is what makes Time Lords special: they exist outside all possible permutations of universal history (the Doctor does say, "I walk in eternity."). Note how there's no version of the Doctor on the parallel Earth of *Inferno* (or later in *Rise of the Cybermen/The Age of Steel*). So uniquely, the Doctor's actions do materially affect which future comes into existence. Here, the universe where Sutekh wins is possible only in the brief time between the TARDIS leaving 1911 and returning. The Doctor can't now visit 1980 and slip sideways into that parallel world, as he did in *Inferno*, because he stopped it ever happening, in any universe. Is this why the Time Lords have a policy of non-intervention, because their actions can eliminate entire universes?
- In episode one Sarah categorically states that she's "really from nineteen eighty" and that's why the Doctor now takes her to that year. She's clearly not rounding up from 1975 or estimating what year it would be by now if she hadn't been travelling with the Doctor. That later stories contradict this requires them to be explained away, not this one.

LANDING 115

SPACE Earth, England, Scarman's house, storage room
TIME Shortly after Landing 113
TRAVELLERS The Doctor, Sarah, Laurence Scarman
EPISODES Pyramids of Mars 2-4

The TARDIS materialises back in the storage room in Professor Scarman's house. Fortunately there are no Mummies about so the Doctor, Sarah and Laurence exit once more through the window and head for Laurence's lodge to begin work on the signal jammer.

Some time after, with Sutekh keen for the missile to be completed, Scarman supervises as two Mummies unpack the warhead trigger charge. He instructs them where to install it and follows them out.

The missile is destroyed so Sutekh plans to use the TARDIS to reach Mars. With his mental powers he projects an image of the Police Box on the screen in his tomb, then possesses the Doctor's mind to force him to pilot the Ship. Scarman escorts the Doctor and a Mummy into the Police Box, bringing Sarah along as a hostage, and it dematerialises.

- **○ CONTROLS** The possessed Doctor closes the doors using the left-hand rotary handle on panel C3.
- **▯ LORE** The Doctor claims the TARDIS controls are isomorphic and respond only to him. As we've seen companions operating the console several times in the past, this is clearly a lie the Doctor tells to preserve his life. (Although it has been argued the Doctor couldn't maintain the lie once Sutekh possesses his mind, the Osiran is aware the Time Lord could yet show signs of free will so his influence is clearly not absolute.)
- **▯ NOTES** It's not certain how much time has passed while the TARDIS has been away. Clements is still evading the Mummies but the missile is almost completed, so it could be anything up to a few hours.
- ▯ CSO is again used to place a shot of the storage room outside the control room doors, although the view doesn't match the position of the Police Box on the storage room set. This is the last time we see what's outside the Ship from inside until the 2005 series.
- ▯ This is also the last we see of these control room wall sections (at least as the control room), some of which have been in use since 1963. When we next see inside the TARDIS things will be very different. It's the last appearance for now of the revamped console too after just two stories, but that will return.

LANDING 116

SPACE Mars, Pyramid of Horus, antechamber
TIME As above
TRAVELLERS The Doctor, Sarah, Marcus Scarman, Mummy servicer
EPISODES Pyramids of Mars 4

The TARDIS travels directly to Mars, materialising in an outer chamber of Horus's pyramid from where the force holding Sutekh prisoner emanates. Scarman emerges and locates the hidden entrance to the control centre. The others follow him out and he orders the Mummy to kill the Doctor as he is no longer needed. It strangles the Time Lord then departs with Scarman. Sarah believes the Doctor is dead but he was still able to breathe thanks to his respiratory bypass system, and is now free of Sutekh's possession. He makes the same gestures as Scarman and the doorway opens.

Once the Eye of Horus is destroyed, all the doorways in the pyramid open, leaving the way back to the TARDIS clear of traps. Realising the force holding Sutekh prisoner on Earth will still be effective for two minutes, the Doctor rushes Sarah back to the Ship and they take off again for Earth.

- **▯ NOTES** Unusually, the interior of the Police Box prop is lit – the inside light was last used on screen in *The Ark in Space* (Landing 107). Unfortunately this means the shadows of the actors inside are cast on the windows as they wait their cue to emerge – worse when Tom Baker dashes into the box then clearly just stands there while it's recorded dematerialising.
- ▯ The shot of the Mars pyramid doorways opening is a model with the new Police Box miniature in the distance. This was filmed with the doors closing one by one, then shown in reverse (and speeded up).
- ▯ The time for radio waves to get from Mars to Earth when the planets are at their closest is nearer to three minutes than two, so the Doctor has a bit more time than he realises.

LANDING 117

SPACE Earth, England, Scarman's house, storage room
TIME As above
TRAVELLERS The Doctor, Sarah
EPISODES Pyramids of Mars 4

During the journey the Doctor disconnects the TARDIS's time control unit and rushes outside with it the moment the Ship rematerialises, hurrying to get to the time-space tunnel's exit in the organ room before Sutekh can escape his tomb.

The thermal balance of the time-space tunnel equalises, causing fires to spring up all through the house. The sarcophagus containing the tunnel explodes, demolishing the organ room, as Sarah and the Doctor dash back to the storage room and into the TARDIS. The Police Box fades away as burning beams collapse around it.

- **▯ NOTES** The time control unit is a white briefcase-sized device with carry handles on each end and a reflective black panel on top. On this are a number of buttons connected by circuit lines, two cable connectors and a central blue dial. The Doctor uses it to shift the threshold of Sutekh's time-space tunnel into the far future, but its purpose in the TARDIS is unknown (see also Landing 68).
- ▯ Curiously, when the TARDIS dematerialises at the end of the story, its flashing roof lamp is an overlaid video effect rather than the actual bulb. Perhaps with the focus on the fire effects – reportedly the largest fire staged in a BBC Television Centre studio at that time – no one remembered to turn on the Police Box prop lamp, so this was added in post production.

LANDING 118

SPACE Oseidon, mock-up of woodland near English village of Devesham
TIME [Early-1980s]
TRAVELLERS The Doctor, Sarah
EPISODES The Android Invasion 1

The Doctor has set the coordinates for Earth and on first appearance the TARDIS has successfully arrived there, in a pleasant summer woodland clearing. An unusual reading on the linear calculator makes the Doctor uncertain, however, so he nips out to check the surroundings while the Ship remains on pause. The ground is dry despite the smell of recent rain and a handheld meter detects high energy levels, but the presence of acorns does suggest this is Earth so the Doctor and Sarah head off to see if they are anywhere near UNIT HQ. The high level of radiation betrays the fact this is actually the planet Oseidon and the entire environment for the surrounding few miles is artificial, created to match Earth in almost every detail.

Sarah is separated from the Doctor and later that afternoon she returns to the TARDIS alone. She inserts the key into the door but is then distracted by a large black capsule a short distance away. As she examines it, the TARDIS dematerialises, the key having cancelled the pause control.

- **LORE** The TARDIS has a pause control that allows it to land temporarily en route to a programmed destination until the key is inserted into the lock to release it.
- The Ship should be serviced regularly, at least every 500 years.
- The TARDIS carries bottles of ginger beer.
- **NOTES** Again, there's the general intention that the Doctor is trying to get Sarah home, but neither seems especially anxious about their repeated misses. Here Sarah even waits inside the TARDIS while the Doctor confirms their location, suggesting she's not really expecting him to have succeeded, possibly owing to further unseen trips since Landing 117.
- It's not explained whether the "space-time warp" through which the Kraals beam their invasion force is artificial or natural. Although their technology is advanced, there's no indication they have conquered time travel, so the 'time' aspect of the warp may simply be that it allows them to cross the distance between Oseidon and Earth near-instantaneously. Guy Crayford isn't returned just after he first disappeared but two years later, suggesting he has been on Oseidon for that amount of time. Although a calendar in the pub shows Friday 6 July, this is unlikely to be the current date; the village is based on Crayford's memories so this is probably the last time he visited the Fleur de Lys. The day and date fit 1979 so if that was just before Crayford disappeared, it would now be 1981 (but we know how mismatched dates can be in the *Doctor Who* universe). The console must give some indication of the year as Sarah states her previous visit to Devesham was "about two years ago" (later confirmed), so whatever the linear calculator does perhaps it threw some doubt on when they'd landed. It's often assumed that Sarah reported on Crayford's disappearance before she met the Doctor, which is just about feasible, but we know she was still working on stories whenever she returned to Earth (as in *Planet of the Spiders*). The Benton android, based on Crayford's pre-flight memories, has the Warrant Officer badge that the real Benton received around the time of the Doctor's last regeneration, so the most likely time for the XK5 launch is during the three weeks the Doctor was absent from UNIT after confronting the Great One on Metebelis Three – this would explain how he's unaware of the flight and why he and Crayford don't recognise each other.
- The space-time warp is something that spaceships can be projected through so is presumably like a wormhole, whether natural or Kraal-made, which could feasibly have diverted the TARDIS right at the moment of materialisation. The Kraal training ground might even be established at a point on the surface proximate to the Oseidon end of the warp for convenience; either that or the TARDIS has time at least to select the one area of the planet that won't kill its occupants in which to land. Nevertheless, both the Ship and the Doctor seem to be aware the coordinate programme hasn't been properly completed, so is the pause control an automatic function or something the Doctor sets (for the one and only time)? We might suppose the former given there seems to be no allowance for ensuring at least a pilot is aboard before resuming the set journey. Okay, there's a delay of a few seconds between the key being inserted and the TARDIS dematerialising, so if Sarah hadn't been distracted she could have boarded in time, but surely you'd programme the Ship to check?
- The Police Box prop's roof lamp is, strangely and for this story only, back to being a Fresnel lens with a round cap, before reverting to the plain cylinder in *The Brain of Morbius*. This is so close to the original lamp from 1963 that it's tempting to believe they're the same one but are probably just very similar. Yet if the visual effects or props department had this to hand here, why couldn't it be used earlier? That it was swapped back for the following story perhaps suggests it was no longer considered the correct one when in fact it was the most accurate seen since 1964.

LANDING 119

SPACE Earth, England, woodland near Devesham
TIME As above
TRAVELLERS None
EPISODES The Android Invasion 4

The TARDIS completes its original course programming and arrives on Earth, this time close to the genuine Devesham. With UNIT overseeing activity at the nearby Space Research Centre ahead of the return of astronaut Guy Crayford, a patrol soon finds the Police Box in the woods and reports it to Sergeant Major Benton. He is puzzled to find the key in the door and instigates a search for the Doctor and Sarah, but neither can be found.

Later that day, having stowed away with the Doctor aboard Crayford's rocket, Sarah safely makes it back to Earth in one of the Kraal androids' ejection pods.

Searching for the Doctor she comes across the TARDIS, the key still in the door. She opens it to see if he is inside but is startled when he taps her on the shoulder. Sarah quickly realises, however, this is an android double of the Doctor and runs. The android helps a duplicate of Sarah out of a nearby pod and they head for the research centre.

The Kraal invasion is averted when the android vanguard is disabled and chief scientist Styggron is killed by his own virus. The Doctor and Sarah return to the TARDIS in the woods. Initially she refuses to enter, telling the Doctor she plans to take a taxi home, but when he offers her a lift again she accepts.

- **NOTES** When materialising on the real Earth, the TARDIS arrives in a different clearing to that it had landed in on Oseidon, although still in Devesham Woods. Where it clearly is not is UNIT HQ. Earlier the Doctor told Sarah, "The coordinates were set for your time," so having been at the right place but in the wrong year, did he try to move the TARDIS forwards in time only? Even after being diverted to Oseidon, why does it still not arrive at UNIT HQ? Landing outside the real Devesham is either an enormous coincidence or the Ship somehow made the connection and figured this would be the most likely place the Doctor would look for it.
- So UNIT soldiers find the TARDIS with the key in the door and just leave it there? Okay, Benton is probably thinking the Doctor's up to something so best not interfere. But then Sarah comes across it, *opens the door* to check the Doctor isn't inside, and *still* leaves the key in the lock, even if she is spooked by seeing duplicates of herself and the Doctor (all the more reason to take it with her). The Doctor should consider himself lucky it's still there when he finally returns to the woods.

LANDING 120

SPACE Kasterborous constellation, Karn, valley near Solon's castle; teleported to Sisterhood's shrine
TIME Two nights in unknown [future]
TRAVELLERS The Doctor, Sarah
EPISODES The Brain of Morbius 1-2,4

Seemingly under the control of the Time Lords, the TARDIS materialises at night on Karn amid an ominous lightning storm. Not far away is a plain where at least fifteen crashed spaceships lie. The Doctor is angry and suspects there is something on Karn his people want him to deal with rather than handle it themselves. He refuses to do their bidding, however, and sits down to play with his yoyo while Sarah takes a look around. Nearby she finds an ejection bubble – an escape pod from a spaceship – then spots the wrecked ships illuminated by a flash of lightning. Only when he hears Sarah call out in fright does the Doctor make sure she is all right. Both are unaware that their arrival has been seen by one of the Sisterhood of Karn.

Concerned that the strangers have arrived without their craft being detected by the Sisterhood, their leader Maren convenes the Sisters and uses their mental powers first to locate the TARDIS and then to teleport it to their shrine. Maren recognises it as a time machine and realises the Doctor must be a Time Lord, the Sisterhood's only equals in mind power. Afraid he has come to Karn to steal their elixir of eternal life, they teleport him also from surgeon Mehendri Solon's castle in order to elicit a confession. His claims to have sensed the living mind of Morbius, executed long ago, hold no sway and the Sisters build a pyre on which to burn the Doctor at dawn. Solon arrives to plead for the Doctor's head and while the Sisters are distracted Sarah sneaks in and unties her friend. Although Sarah is blinded by a flash from Maren's ring, the pair escape and the Sisters give chase.

The Doctor returns to the shrine to request some elixir to restore Sarah's sight only to learn that Solon lied to him and the effect is temporary. He convinces Maren he has not been sent to steal their elixir, and in fact revives the flames that produce it. She agrees to let him return to Solon's castle to rescue Sarah and discover if Morbius really has survived.

When one of the Sisterhood is killed by the creature Solon has stitched together as a body for Morbius's brain, Maren agrees to let her deputy Ohica lead the others and help the Doctor fight it.

That night Sarah and Ohica carry an unconscious Doctor back to the Sisterhood's shrine. He has been mortally wounded in a mind-bending contest against Morbius and only the elixir can save him. Maren gives him the last of the supply, in spite of her own need, and as he recovers she sacrifices herself to rekindle the sacred flame.

Ohica confirms Morbius has been killed so the Doctor hurries Sarah into the TARDIS, leaving the bewildered new head of the Sisterhood with two fireworks to use should the flame dwindle again. He calls out instructions from within the TARDIS before it vanishes from the shrine with a bang and a cloud of smoke.

- **LORE** The TARDIS has calibrators, although they can be unreliable.
- **NOTES** For once there's no suggestion that this follows directly from Landing 119 or that the Doctor is trying to take Sarah home. When she is later blinded she moans, "I could always sell flowers…if I ever get back to Piccadilly," perhaps suggesting she doesn't expect to return there any time soon. At the end of the story the Doctor is eager to leave as he and Sarah "have an engagement" to which she replies, "We have?" so clearly the offer to take her home has been postponed.
- The Doctor tells Sutekh in *Pyramids of Mars* that his home planet Gallifrey is in the constellation of Kasterborous and here says, "I thought I recognised the stars. I was born in these parts," indicating Karn is in the same region given it's "within a couple of billion miles".
- Solon says Earth is his home and the Doctor calls him "one of the foremost neurosurgeons of your time. Considerably after your time, Sarah." So he at least is

from our future. But as he was a follower of the Time Lord Morbius, who likely had access to time travel, the events and history described in this story could have occurred at any time.
- The Police Box prop's roof lamp is back to the standard straight-sided cylinder, although it does regain a round cap after eighteen months of going topless.
- The TARDIS's unusual departure was a directorial choice by Christopher Barry to follow from the discussion of fireworks. The usual take-off sound plays speeded up as a flash charge is ignited in front of the Police Box prop. A video white-out is applied, which then fades to a shot of the smoke-filled shrine.

LANDING 121

SPACE Earth, [England, UNIT HQ]
TIME [Early-1980s]
TRAVELLERS The Doctor, Sarah
EPISODES The Seeds of Doom 1

The TARDIS returns to Earth, possibly finally getting the Doctor and Sarah to UNIT HQ as they originally intended. Certainly the Doctor is available when Sir Colin Thackeray of the World Ecology Bureau contacts UNIT with a mystery about a plant pod that has been discovered deep in the Antarctic ice. Recognising it as a Krynoid seed pod, the Doctor agrees to investigate, fearing it may yet germinate.

LANDING 122

SPACE Earth, Antarctica
TIME [As above]
TRAVELLERS The Doctor, Sarah
EPISODES The Seeds of Doom 6

After saving the world from domination by the Krynoid, the Doctor is ready for a holiday and offers to take Sarah to Cassiopeia. They set off in the TARDIS but the Doctor forgets to cancel the coordinate programme and it materialises amid the snowy wastes of Antarctica. Sarah is dressed for much warmer climes so before she suffers frostbite they head back into the Ship and try again.

NOTES As broadcast, it seems odd that the TARDIS is programmed for Antarctica when it wasn't seen to go there in the first place. In the original script for the scene this was explained: the Doctor reminds Sarah they had first intended to travel there by TARDIS but then changed their mind as "an aeroplane would be less conspicuous". He compares the Ship's operation to a lift: "If you press the button for the second floor and then the button for the basement, you've got to go to the second floor [first]." The dialogue was made more playful during recording on location, however, and this reasoning was lost. Given that, and the fact we only see them arriving by helicopter at the remote Camp Five, it's possible they did travel by TARDIS to a larger base on Antarctica, perhaps South Bend, and then took the helicopter out to the research camp. After all, having recognised the risk posed by the Krynoid pod, would the Doctor really want to spend the best part of a day flying from England to Antarctica when he could get there instantly? If so, they must have also made the return journey to London by TARDIS.
- Equally, it's likely the coordinate programme included directions for the TARDIS to arrive in Antarctica in the appropriate timezone (whether it was initially implemented or not). So this landing is probably in Sarah's time, but knowing the Ship it could be at any point in Earth's history.
- This is the last appearance of the original Police Box prop, refurbished a couple of times but in use for just over twelve years since 1963. Famously, the roof of the box collapsed onto Tom Baker and Elisabeth Sladen inside. The implication is that this was due to the prop being worn out, but (if true) given it was lugged out on location for this one scene and shot at the end of the recording day as the light was fading, it may simply have been badly set up in haste.

IT LOOKS JUST LIKE A POLICE BOX

THE NEWBERY BOX
1976-1982

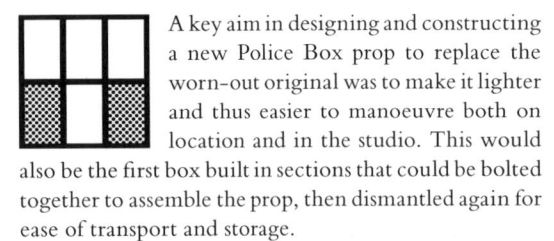

A key aim in designing and constructing a new Police Box prop to replace the worn-out original was to make it lighter and thus easier to manoeuvre both on location and in the studio. This would also be the first box built in sections that could be bolted together to assemble the prop, then dismantled again for ease of transport and storage.

To these ends, the wooden box had no rear wall at all. It was formed of five main sections: base, two sides, front with door and corner posts, and roof. The 'Police box' sign boxes, along with the ledge above them between the corner posts, also detached. The lack of a back made the prop not only lighter but also easier for the actors to use. A black curtain was hung across the gap to make the inside appear dark when actors emerged at the front, although often in publicity photos (and occasionally on screen) this would be dislodged or omitted, revealing the absence of a rear wall. There was no sign box on the back either, just a brace to support the roof and sides, a fact that can be spotted by eagle-eyed viewers whenever the Police Box is shown on screen from the side.

Designer Barry Newbery said in a contemporary interview that he "tried to make it more like the original box than it has been recently", but whatever the intent the final prop was further from matching a genuine Police Box than even the remodelled Brachacki box. While Newbery's blueprints show a slightly more accurate look than was constructed, such as an intention to reinstate the St John Ambulance emblem, even these indicate smaller dimensions than the previous box.

Underscored on Newbery's plans is the instruction 'To be as light as possible' and it would seem to be in pursuance of this goal that several revisions were made. The height of the sides was reduced by shortening the space between the windows and the sign boxes. As the latter also projected further out than previously, thus casting deeper shadows below, this gave the box a sort of 'frowning' appearance. The inset panels were more oblong but the corner posts were wider; with the low roof – just one stack above the corner posts and a very shallow pitch – this made the box look very squat. The windows were covered on the reverse to prevent them being seen from inside the box.

Subtler differences from the previous box included the inset panels having bevelled edges and the centre posts being chamfered. The 'Police telephone' plaque did not open and had no handle. The lettering, white on a blue background, correctly had the word 'public' on a separate line but retained the ampersands introduced on the 1969 plaque and reduced the response to a single 'officer' (although still in multiple 'cars' somehow). Only the right-hand door opened (actually like a real Police Box but still inwards instead of outwards) and this had a Yale lock placed high up beside the panel under the window, with a latch on the inside. It too had no handle, requiring the actors to pull it shut with the key or their fingertips. The design reinstated smaller caps on the corner posts but only very shallow ones before the pitched roof piece. The roof lamp sat on a thicker base than before, which the plans indicate was hinged to allow access to the electrics for the bulb. This once again had a lensed covering, topped with a thin metal domed cap supported by just three rods. The box was painted Prussian Blue using a textured paint, although the lamp cap and rods were white. The 'Police box' signs had white lettering on a black background.

Left The telephone plaque offered only a single 'Officer'
Right Newbery prop front elevation and section

IT LOOKS JUST LIKE A POLICE BOX

IT LOOKS JUST LIKE A POLICE BOX

Perhaps because it was built to be collapsible, the box suffered no major structural damage during its three and a half years of regular use. Small changes were made, however. As early as *The Deadly Assassin* a vertical slot appears in the door next to the middle rail. It's possible this was made to receive a special Gallifreyan key when the Chancellery Guard is trying to get into the TARDIS, or the shield-shaped key previously used, but in the event the guards use a Yale key in the regular lock. Tom Baker does use the shield key in this slot in *The Robots of Death*.

Between recording of that and *The Talons of Weng-Chiang*, the right-hand end of the front 'Police box' sign was repaired, with the black inset area now extending further so that the blue frame was narrower on the right than the left. It remained this way for the first three serials of Season 15 to be produced – *The Invisible Enemy*, *Horror of Fang Rock* and *The Sun Makers* – before getting a new frame fascia that restored the inset width. The prop also received a new coat of paint at this point which was darker, glossier and had a rougher texture.

More significant damage occurred during recording of *The Armageddon Factor* in November 1978 as rubble was dropped in front of the box in episode one. When the prop next appears in episode three, the door window's bottom-left pane is missing a large shard, those above it are scuffed and the bars now overlap the surrounding frame. By episode six a hole is evident in the right-hand window on the left side of the box, presumably sustained at the same time as the front.

The stories of the following season were recorded in a different order to broadcast so the prop was next taken from storage for filming *The Creature from the Pit* at Ealing Studios in March 1979. The door window was repaired (by patching the hole rather than replacing the whole pane) but not that on the left-hand side. The centre post on the front was replaced (no longer chamfered) but the box was not repainted, showing the same patterns of dirt it received in *The Armageddon Factor*. During filming on location for *Destiny of the Daleks* in June, photos of Tom Baker with the TARDIS were taken for a series of birthday and greetings cards from Denis Alan Print. These involved writing messages in chalk on the Police Box, which were simply rubbed rather than washed off after; the prop's next appearance in studio for *Nightmare of Eden* clearly displays chalky residue on the front panels and corner posts. Also by then the repairs to the door window were no longer holding the bottom-right pane in place. The centre post on the front had a large chunk missing at the bottom, and for some reason (perhaps to disguise damage) the base of the box was painted black.

The main vulnerability of the prop, however, was the roof lamp. A photo from *The Deadly Assassin* episode one shows the box without its lamp; this was taken during studio rehearsals so the prop may not have been fully set up, yet in the recorded episode it looks like the lensed covering has been replaced with a plain cylinder as on the previous box. By the time episode four was recorded two weeks later the correct lamp had been reinstated. This survived throughout Season 15 except during location filming for *Image of the Fendahl* in August 1977, when the lamp was missing altogether. After appearing as standard in *The Stones of Blood*, when *The Androids of Tara* was filmed six weeks later the lamp had an additional base that was wider than the roof block on which it sat. Eight weeks later the prop was taken to Suffolk marshes for filming *The Power of Kroll* were the lamp, whether damaged or missing, had to be replaced by a completely different lantern. Subsequently, for studio recording of *The Armageddon Factor* it was fitted with a domed blue police light with a spinning reflector that made it appear to flash. The usual lensed lamp with white metal housing was back in place for *The Creature from the Pit* and *City of Death*, then on location for filming *Destiny of the Daleks* the lamp had to be removed to fit the Police Box under the rock ledge used for its landing site. This might be where it went missing for good as from *Nightmare of Eden* onwards the spinning police light made a permanent return.

NOT SO OBSOLETE

The Newbery box's last appearance would have been in *Shada* had it been completed. The prop wasn't discarded when a replacement was made for Season 18 (see page 256), but passed to BBC Enterprises for promotional use – luckily so. For the closing story of that season, *Logopolis*, two Police Boxes were needed, and when an idea to use the last surviving Metropolitan Police Box on the Barnet bypass in Hertfordshire was scuppered by its being demolished a month before the scheduled filming dates, the old Newbery box was called up for duty.

The prop was modified slightly, although it's not clear if this was to make it more closely match a genuine Police Box or the current Yardley-Jones prop. It was given a new roof with two stepped levels and a steeper pitch like its replacement. This retained the deep block under the roof lamp and a similar block was now added to the Yardley-Jones box. The lettering of the 'Police box' signs was repainted (in a different, bolder typeface compared to the newer prop, although that had one of its signs replaced with the same font). The sign box on the right appears to have been remade as it was thinner than the usual Newbery sign boxes and had an even narrow frame in which the sign was fixed flush. As the Newbery prop would now be acting as a real Police Box, its telephone door was made practical, hinged on the left and with a handle on the right, and a cubbyhole attached behind it to hold a phone. It wasn't otherwise refurbished and still had the hole in its left-side window, badly fitting bars on the door window and a black base.

After filming the opening scene of *Logopolis*, where a policeman using the Police Box is killed by the Master, the prop underwent further adaptation, most notably the conversion of the fixed left side of the front into a

IT LOOKS JUST LIKE A POLICE BOX

Left Front elevation and section of remodelled box for *Logopolis*

Right Further subtle changes were made for *Castrovalva*

practical door (see Landing 196). The box was used again in the studio in early January 1981 for scenes of the Police Box within the TARDIS control room.

It seems, having been retrieved from BBC Enterprises for further use, the Newbery prop was now kept by the scenery department, as it made two further appearances in Season 19. In *Castrovalva*, the Yardley-Jones box was used for the post-regeneration scenes set at the Pharos Project, but for the TARDIS's lopsided landing on the alien world, filmed just three days later, the Newbery box was taken on location. It's generally assumed this was because it was sturdier than the fibreglass prop and so better suited to the actors clambering in and out while it was lying at an angle on its rear side among soft foliage. There must have been a specific reason to use the older box given the newer prop was surely more readily accessible; perhaps the closeness of the filming dates meant the latter was still being transported back to the scenery store while the other was need on location.

Although not clearly visible on screen, photographs taken during the location filming show the box had been refitted with Yardley-Jones-style doors. It's possible these were the wooden formers used to produce the moulds for the fibreglass doors of the newer prop – there's a faint impression of a join between the rails and stiles suggesting

the doors were made from wood. This meant the proportions of the panels on the front were now different from those on the sides. The centre post was attached to the right-hand door and had a handle on it, although off-centre and slightly higher than those on the Yardley-Jones box. The box was also fitted with a new telephone plaque to match that on the newer prop, and similarly the sign boxes were given acrylic inserts with updated lettering. It also regained all three of its original deep sign boxes.

The box was seen on screen for the last time in *Black Orchid*, filmed a month after its use in *Castrovalva*. This was the first time a Police Box prop had been needed since then, so perhaps this box was simply more easily accessible in the scenery store as there's no evident reason the newer prop couldn't have been used. Here its left-side sign box was missing, having been lost or left behind.

For the Newbery box's final public appearance the left side carried a fibreglass Yardley-Jones sign box complete with steps below. This was at the Longleat 20th anniversary celebration weekend on the 3rd and 4th of April 1983. The box was set up in the grounds for visitors to take photos. It was without its roof lamp and the right-side sign box's frame had a large part missing, but this was a rare and exciting opportunity to get up close to the actual TARDIS. Its fate after that is unknown.

IT'S BIGGER ON THE INSIDE

THE NEWBERY STATEROOM
1976-1977

For producer Philip Hinchcliffe's third year in charge of *Doctor Who* he decided a new-look TARDIS control room was in order. This was perhaps a surprising concern given only two of the ten serials he had produced to date had featured scenes inside the TARDIS. But with the first three scripts for the new season requiring the Doctor to be seen piloting the Ship, Hinchcliffe wanted a smaller set that would leave more studio space available for a story's other settings.

As the designer assigned to the season's first story, *The Masque of Mandragora*, the task fell to Barry Newbery who, coincidentally, had been involved in staging the first ever TARDIS scenes in 1963 and so had an understanding of the aesthetics established for the Ship. It was his choice to move away from the bright, futuristic feel of the original control room and instead introduce a Victorian sailing ship look – what he called "a Jules Verne style" – with dark wood-panelled walls, brass fittings and porthole-like stained-glass windows. This suited the darker tone the series had adopted and appealed to Hinchcliffe's affection for Gothic literature and film.

For the first time the set had a fixed layout (rather than being a collection of separate sections) arranged in a U shape around the central console, with the entrance at the back, scanner on the left and interior door on the right. The main wall sections retained a pattern of circles that was symbolic of the TARDIS interior but aligned in rows and columns rather than staggered. Newbery said in a contemporary interview, "These make it easier to put doors around them [as] you didn't get half-circles."

Five basic walls were made, each with three columns of four circles. The roundels themselves, smaller than in previous sets, were cast in fibreglass and given more detail, with a series of ridges around the indentation. The outer lip of these sat on the rim of the circular holes cut in the wall flat, with the roundels then projecting back through them (like the earlier 'washbowl' ones). The walls and roundels were painted dark brown with a mottled effect to suggest a mahogany-like material. The flat centre of each roundel was scored with a diamond pattern to simulate a veneer inlay, as on the console.

On three of these walls, the centres of two or all three roundels on the third row up were cut out and replaced with coloured acrylic discs in one of three Art Deco designs. When lit from behind these gave the impression of stained-glass windows, although sometimes they were unlit and just appeared as dark circles. Newbery also said, "The panels on the wall can be converted at any

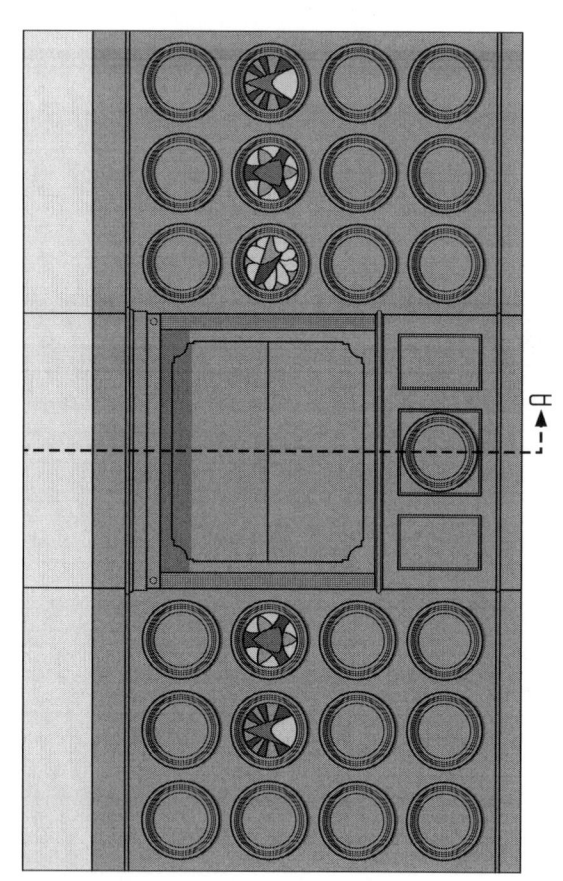

IT'S BIGGER ON THE INSIDE

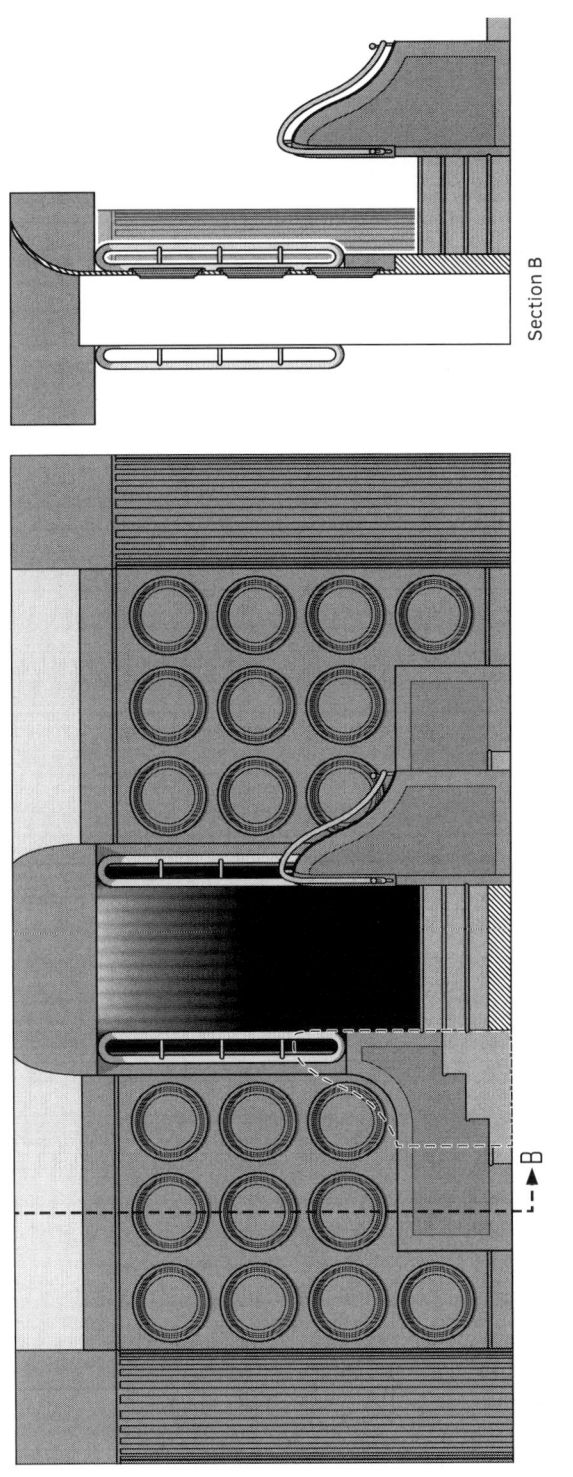

Section B

Main entrance

Interior door

IT'S BIGGER ON THE INSIDE

Three designs of stained-glass (well, coloured translucent acrylic) were made and added to the side walls and interior door

time to be a door with a cupboard or controls behind it." This idea that roundels were access points for storage or circuitry would not be implemented until the 1980s.

Newbery decided to ditch the large double doors of the main entrance as they were now close to thirteen years old and the opening mechanism often caused problems. Instead he had no doors at all, just steps leading up to a dark opening. Above this was a circular lintel that contained a light shining downwards through a grid, reminiscent of the scanner framework in the original control room. Either side of the entrance were four brass trombone-like rails, although the two at the front disappeared after *The Hand of Fear*. Box constructions covered part of the bottom row of roundels where the side steps overlapped the walls, while solid curved balustrades with brass handrails were positioned alongside the front steps leading to the console platform.

The scanner became a large window within the wall, with a yellow CSO backing onto which camera images or graphics could be superimposed, giving a clearer image than a television monitor allowed. This was covered by two shutters which slid vertically, connected by a chain drive. Newbery's initial idea was to have a large handle that the Doctor would turn to open these, but in the end they were operated from behind by a stagehand. While the scanner window was deeply recessed, the wall itself projected slightly beyond those either side. Below were three panels, the centre one with a roundel, and at the sides were narrow square fluted columns.

Opposite the scanner wall was the interior door. This had three panels with beaded edges, the top one featuring a roundel with a stained-glass centre. The door opened into the room and was plain white on the reverse. The last feature was two round columns at the rear corners of the set connecting the roundels walls either side. These were not full cylinders but had a curved span of about 160 degrees, with battens fixed vertically around this arc.

Apart from the disappearing ornamentation by the entrance, the set remained consistent throughout its four appearances in Season 14. In *The Masque of Mandragora*, the fifth roundels wall was placed to the right of the interior door for shots of the Doctor and Sarah discovering the second control room. Outside this was one of the Gleeson/Ruscoe shallow-indent walls to represent the corridor beyond. Although in *The Deadly Assassin* a fourth side of the set is implied, this was actually shot in the back left-hand corner, as the stained-glass roundels prove. In *The Robots of Death*, the fifth roundels wall was now placed to the left of the scanner. A canvas ceiling was also stretched across the right-hand corner in case low-angle shots director Michael Briant was planning accidentally showed beyond the top of the set.

The original wooden Knossos chair made a return to the control room, possibly because Newbery recalled it from his early days on the programme. This had last been seen in *The Claws of Axos*, suggesting the Doctor moved it to the second control room during his exile on Earth. It was actually made use of in *The Deadly Assassin* for the Doctor to seat his dummy on, and was joined in *The Robots of Death* by an oval wooden table, a cabinet where the Doctor kept the cubes used for explaining transdimensional engineering, and a branched coat stand.

Contrary to popular belief, the second control room was *not* replaced because its walls warped in storage. The following year, new producer Graham Williams chose to return to the more familiar white-walled control room as a better fit for the direction he was taking the programme in. However, the roundels walls were simply painted white and made numerous reappearances for several years. The scanner and interior door walls were stripped down and incorporated into the new control room, as were the corner columns (see page 206) – features that were retained in control room designs through to the end of the 1980s.

WHAT ARE ALL THESE KNOBS?

CONSOLE D
1976-1977

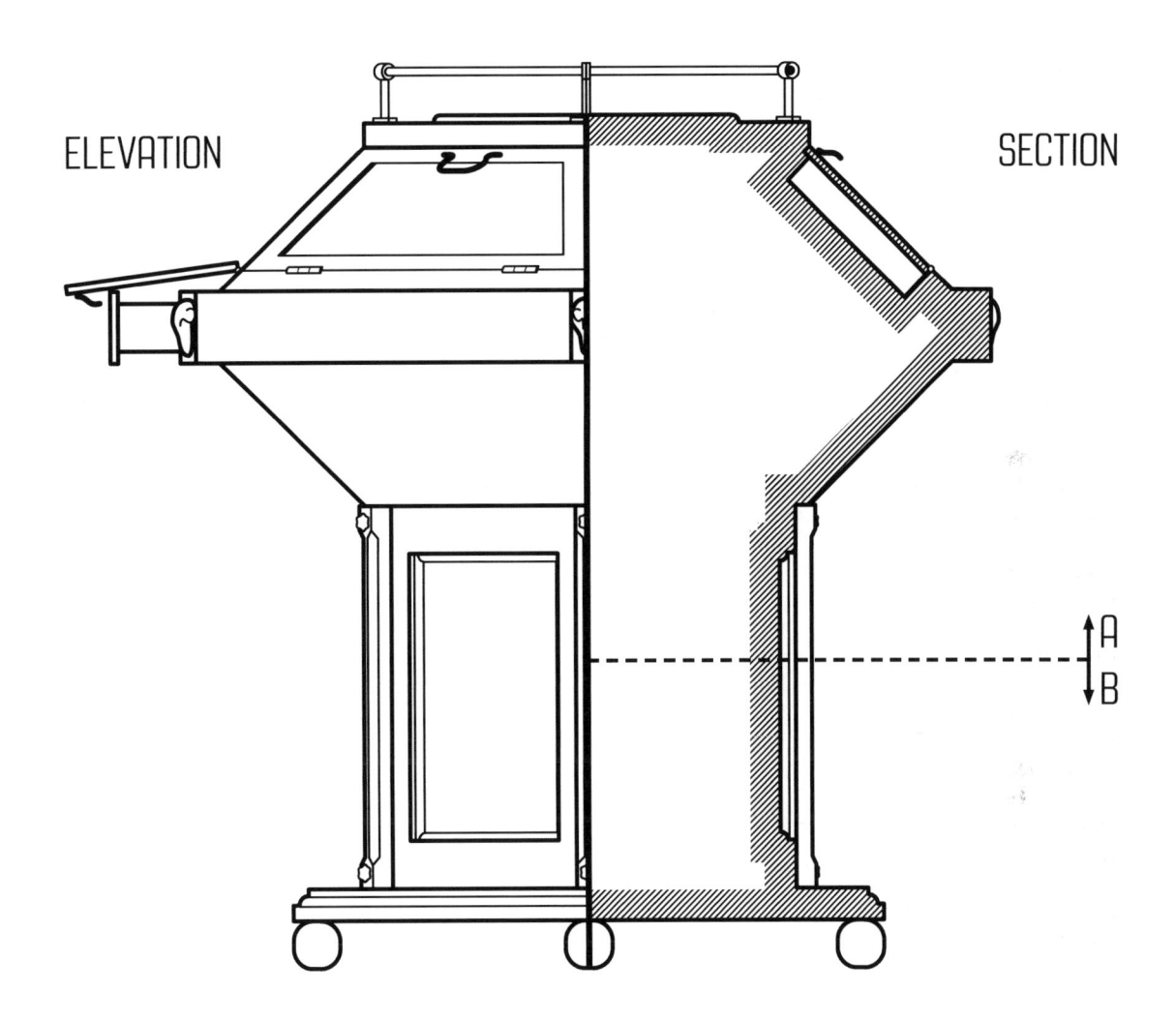

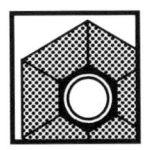

ELEVATION   SECTION

↕ A
  B

To go with his Jules Verne-style control room set, Barry Newbery designed a harmonious console. One aim, as with the set itself, was to make the prop smaller than previous versions, so it was easier for directors to compose shots with two people on either side. Newbery therefore developed something akin to a Davenport bureau, with sloping flaps that hid the controls beneath. Like the set, the console was coloured to give the appearance of being made of a dark wood.

He retained the hexagonal shape of the original but with a much smaller diameter. The six trapezium-shaped panels were steeply pitched, at around 40 degrees from the horizontal, with brass handles at the top and hinges along the bottom edge so they would fold down and rest on the wider rim. The outer faces had a shallow recess into which a pattern of concentric diamonds was scored to imitate veneer inlay (see page 194).

Only one compartment initially had any contents: a drawer with pigeonholes above and space for writing implements in front. The inside of this flap had a faux-leather writing surface while a hidden shelf pulled out from the rim below so the flap was supported at a flatter level than the others. This was probably included as a nod to the prop's bureau-like appearance, although it was made use of in *The Deadly Assassin*. The scripts for this were still being written while the console was being constructed so it's possible Robert Holmes indicated the

WHAT ARE ALL THESE KNOBS?

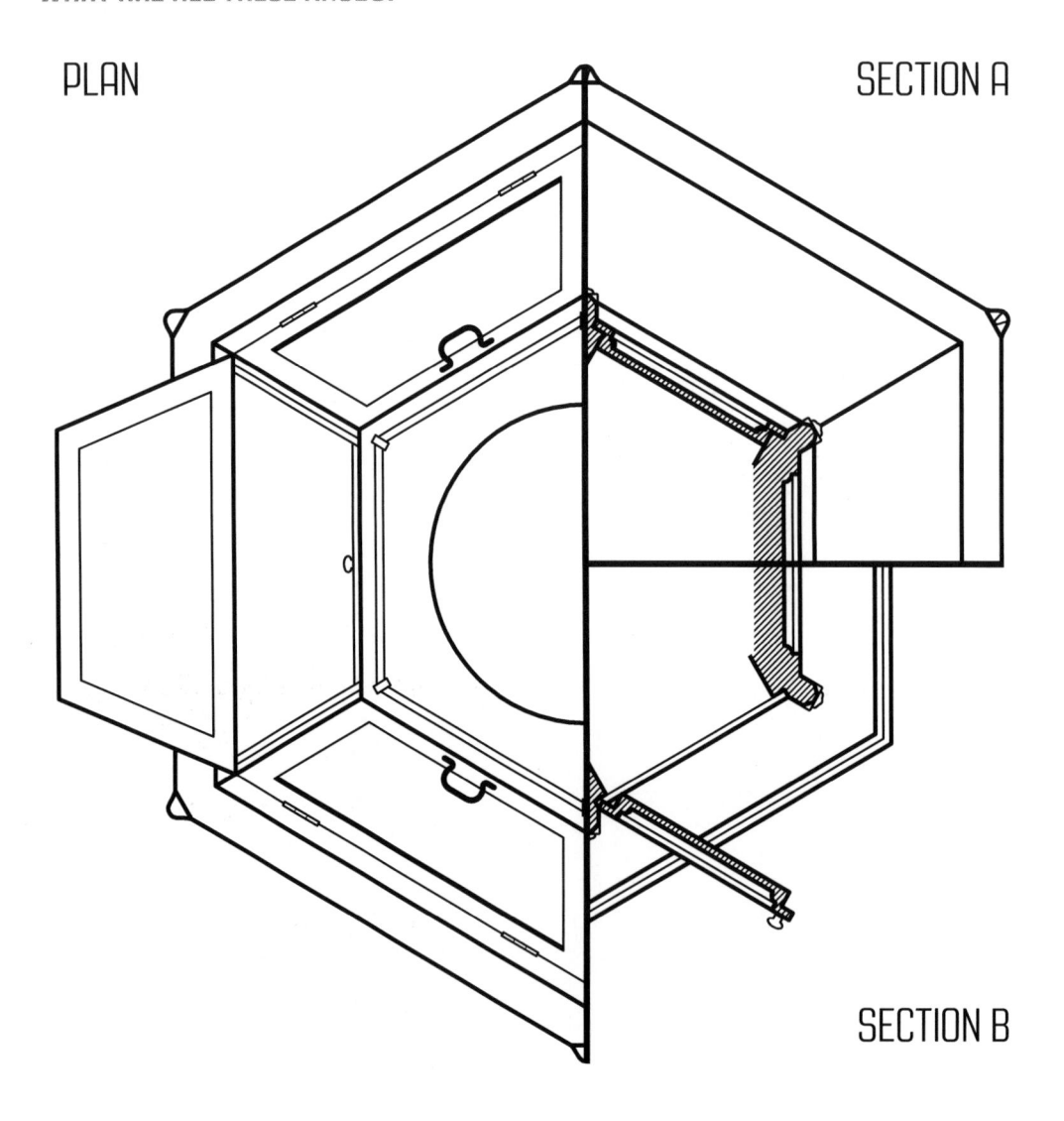

PLAN

SECTION A

SECTION B

Doctor would need to write a note during the course of the story; equally he may have included it after seeing plans for the console to have a desk section, or it was just a handy coincidence.

Newbery left the other five compartments empty as the Visual Effects department was assigned to create the actual controls, although he specified simple controls to suggest advanced technology, saying in a contemporary interview, "The more sophisticated equipment becomes the less obviously complicated it is." For the first serial requiring the console, *The Masque of Mandragora*, just one control panel was made: a black acrylic trapezium onto which where stuck rows of coloured illuminated buttons (yellow, green, red and blue), black press-and-click switches above and a striped speaker-like grille to one side. This slotted into any of the console's compartments, allowing directors to use whichever best suited their camera angles. For *The Hand of Fear* a second panel was needed and a black panel with a grid of flat red, green and blue dots was produced. Later a third panel, a mirror image of the first with the rows of coloured buttons in a different order (blue, green, yellow red), was added permitting four compartments to be used, although no more than three were ever seen open on screen at any one time.

Because the three control inserts were interchangeable, and the console could be rotated, no two stories presented the same arrangement. However, a fixed layout can just about be inferred with some imagination. For *The Deadly Assassin*, the initial panel (2) had orange stickers applied to some of its buttons. If we interpret this as a second panel with the same configuration of buttons as the first, and assume the console has two desk compartments (1), then the layout shown opposite satisfies all scenes on screen except one. In *The Hand of Fear* episode three, panels 2 and 3 are opposite each other but this cannot fit with subsequent stories where we see different combinations of three consecutive panels.

WHAT ARE ALL THESE KNOBS?

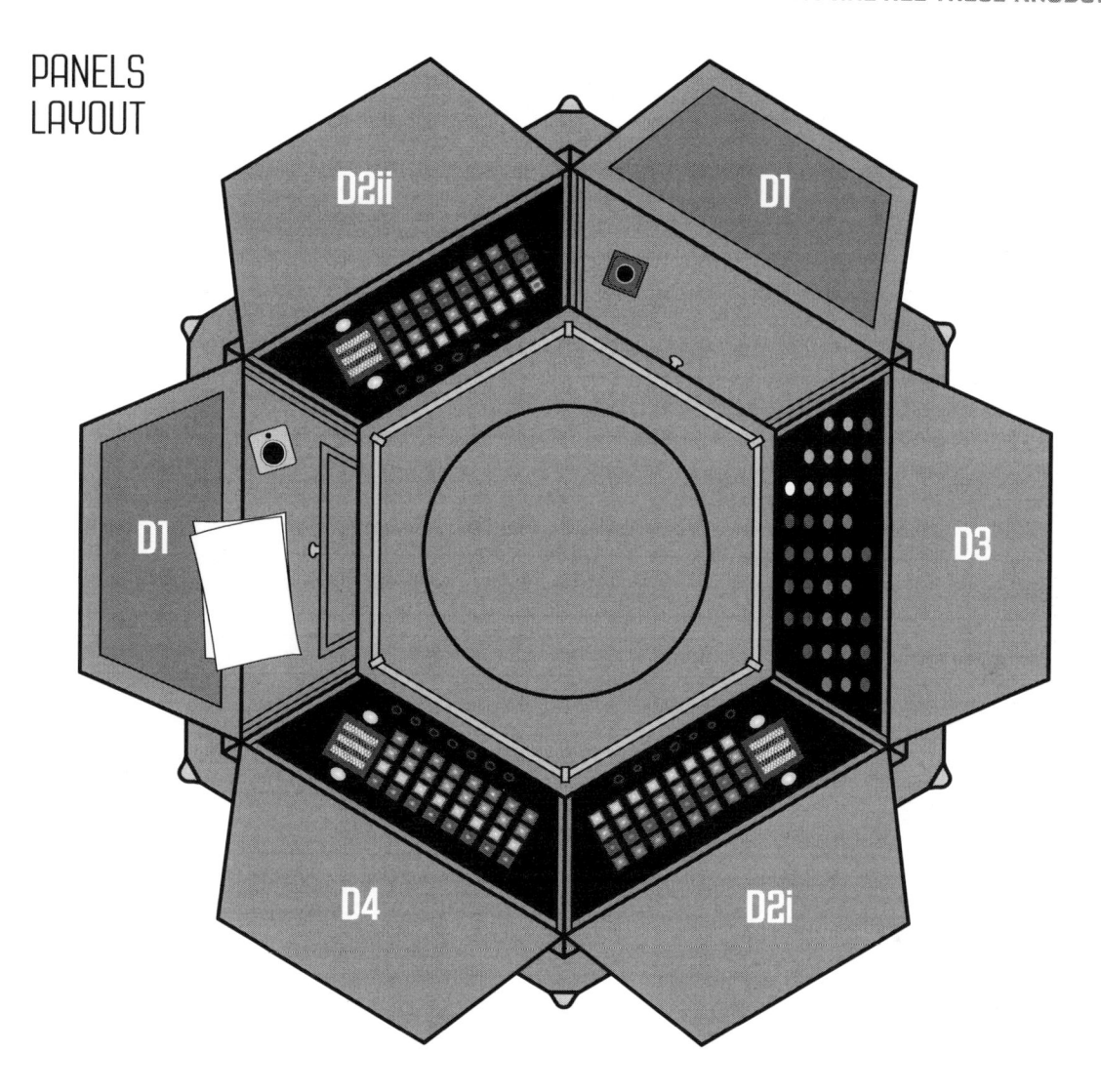

PANELS LAYOUT

(Diagram showing hexagonal console panel layout with labels: D2ii, D1, D1, D3, D4, D2i)

The rim of the console had chamfered corners on which were brass ram's head fittings (possibly door knockers with the rings removed from their mouths). The underside then tapered at an angle as steep as the upper panels to a slender pedestal. The corners of this had square, chamfered columns with brass bosses at top and bottom. Three of the sides opened, the hatch under the desk compartment hinged on the right (this is the one the Doctor delves into at the end of *The Hand of Fear*) and the two on alternate sides hinged on the left. The three-tiered base sat on six clawed feet.

The top of the console had a brass rail and a raised circle in the centre. It has been claimed the latter was to cover the hole from an abandoned attempt to install a rising central column like the old console, but Newbery himself denied this. While he admitted *The Masque of Mandragora*'s director Rodney Bennett suggested having an iris on top through which a dome could rise, Newbery ruled this out on cost grounds. Besides, producer Philip Hinchcliffe had briefed him not to have a central column as its mechanics often caused problems in the studio. The script for that story did mention "a little swivel mirror set into the console" so a freestanding shaving mirror was placed on top. It's doubtful this was ever intended as a permanent feature as it wasn't retained in later episodes.

To give the smaller console more presence, and allow for better camera angles, Newbery positioned it on a circular 2.2m-diameter platform in the middle of the set, which connected to the steps leading to the entrance. Around the edge of this were four brass handrails with gaps aligned with the entrance, interior door, scanner and 'fourth wall'. Nonetheless, Tom Baker's height exaggerated the console's low stature as he had to hunch over to operate the controls.

After Season 14 the previous console was reinstated in a new control room modelled more on the original look. While Newbery's aligned-roundels walls were reused, the console was reportedly scrapped.

WHAT ARE ALL THESE KNOBS?

PANEL D1

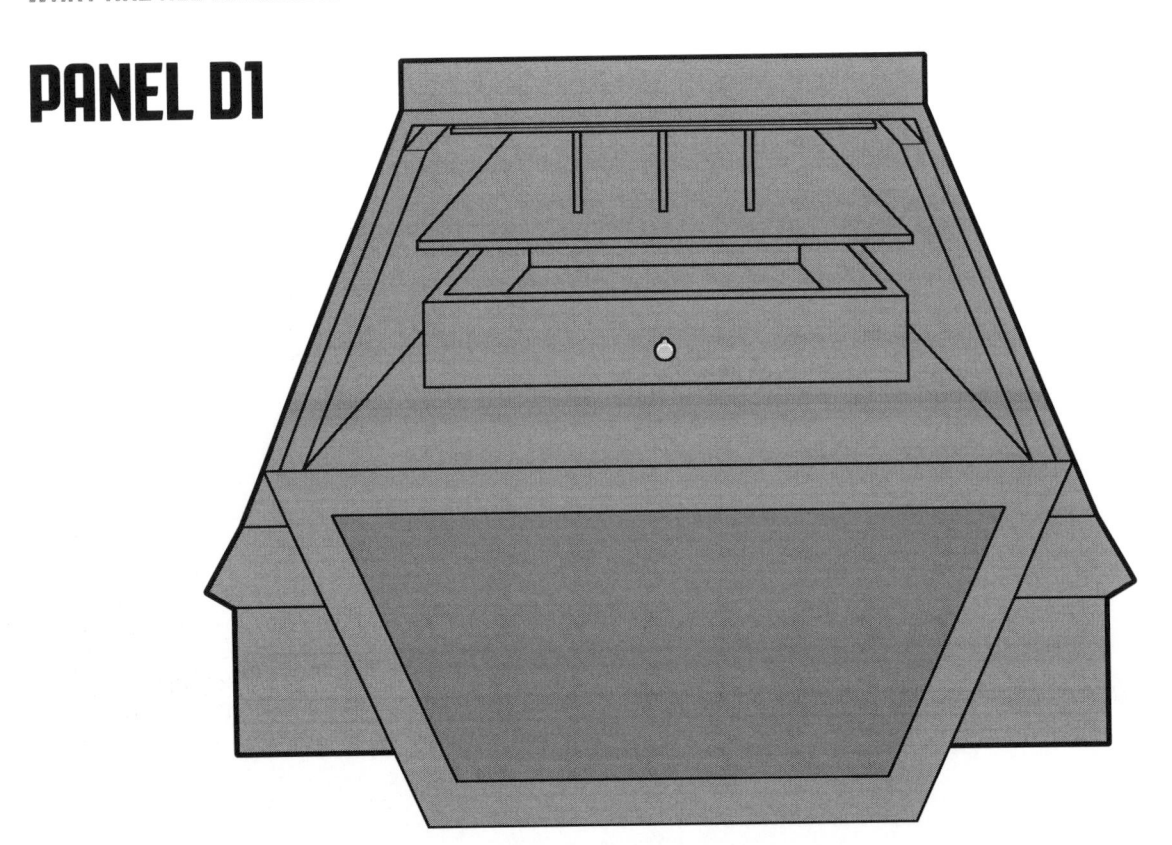

PANEL D2i

① **POWER UP** (123)
   DEMATERIALISE (126)
② **SCANNER** (123)

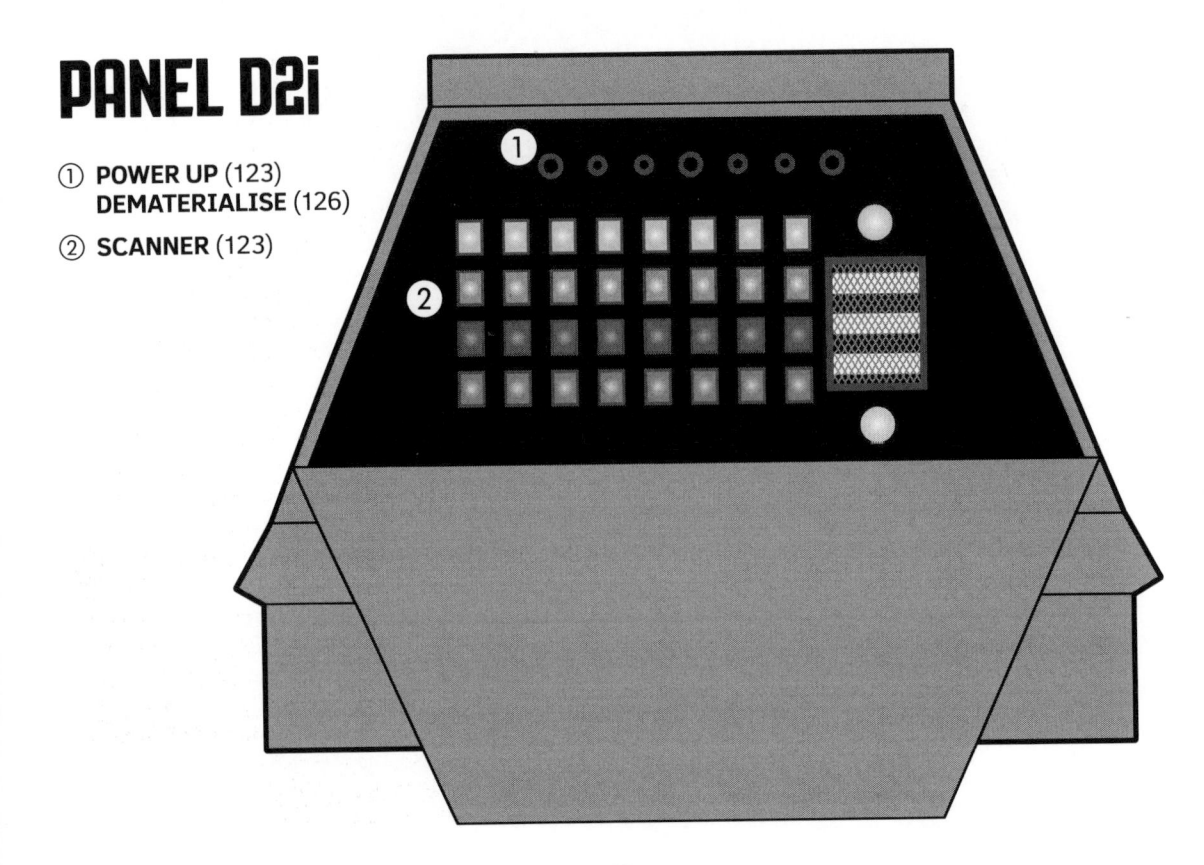

WHAT ARE ALL THESE KNOBS?

PANEL D2ii

① **SCANNER RETUNE** (128)
② **SCANNER** (130)

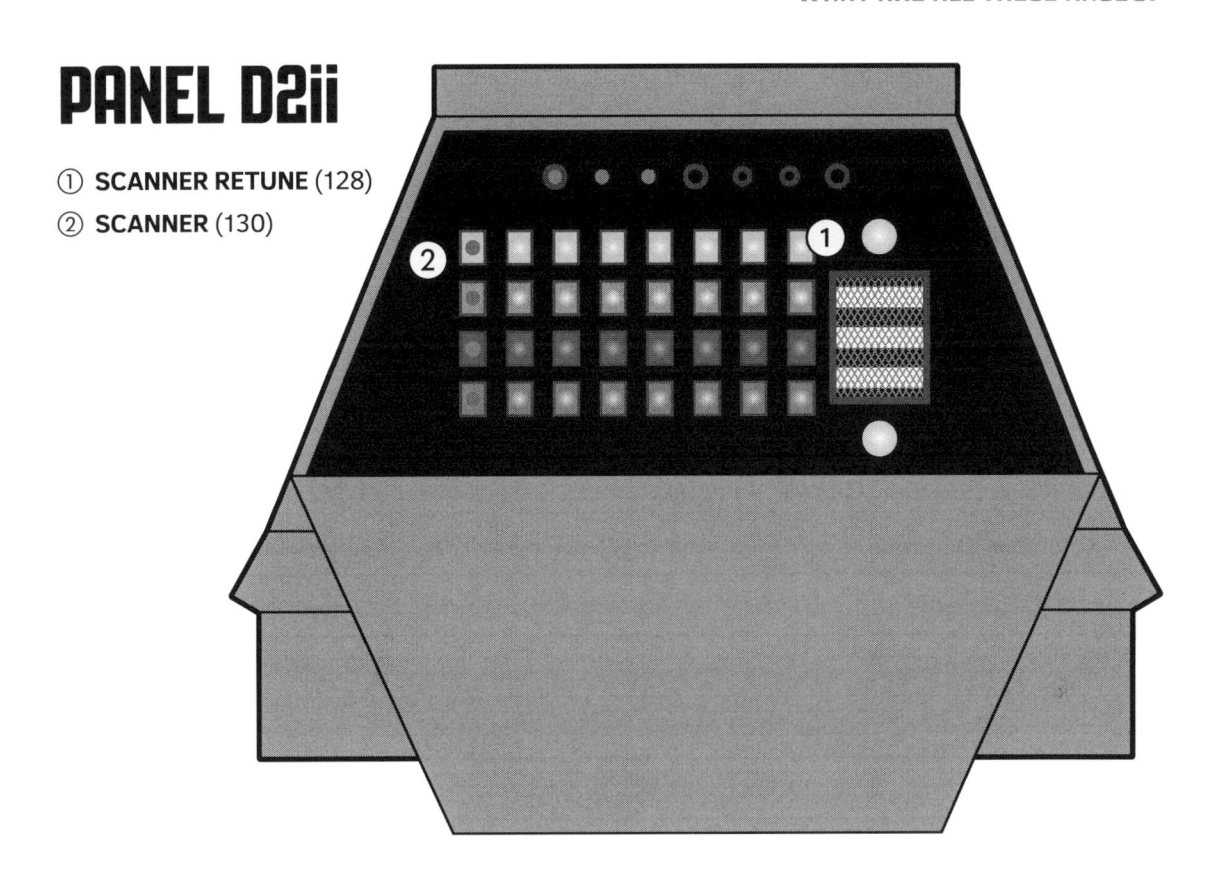

PANEL D3

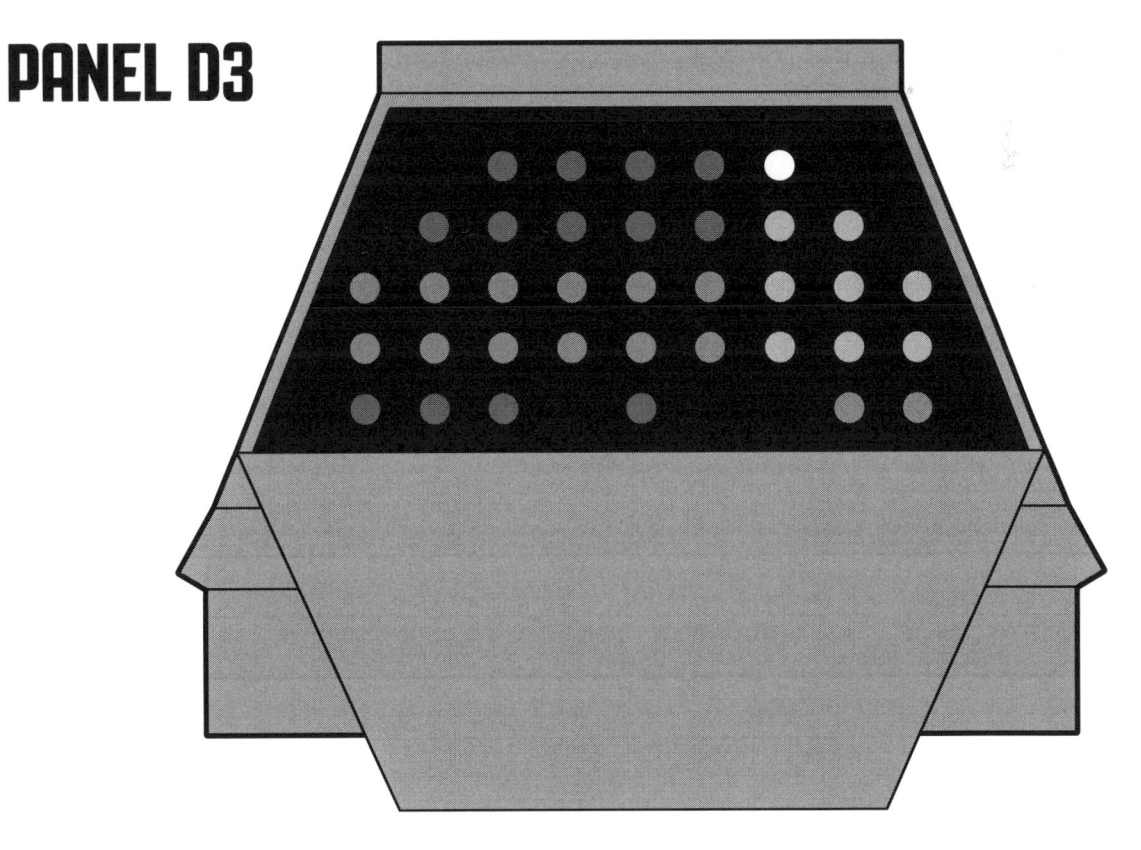

WHAT ARE ALL THESE KNOBS?

PANEL D4

① **SCANNER CHANNEL SELECT** (128)

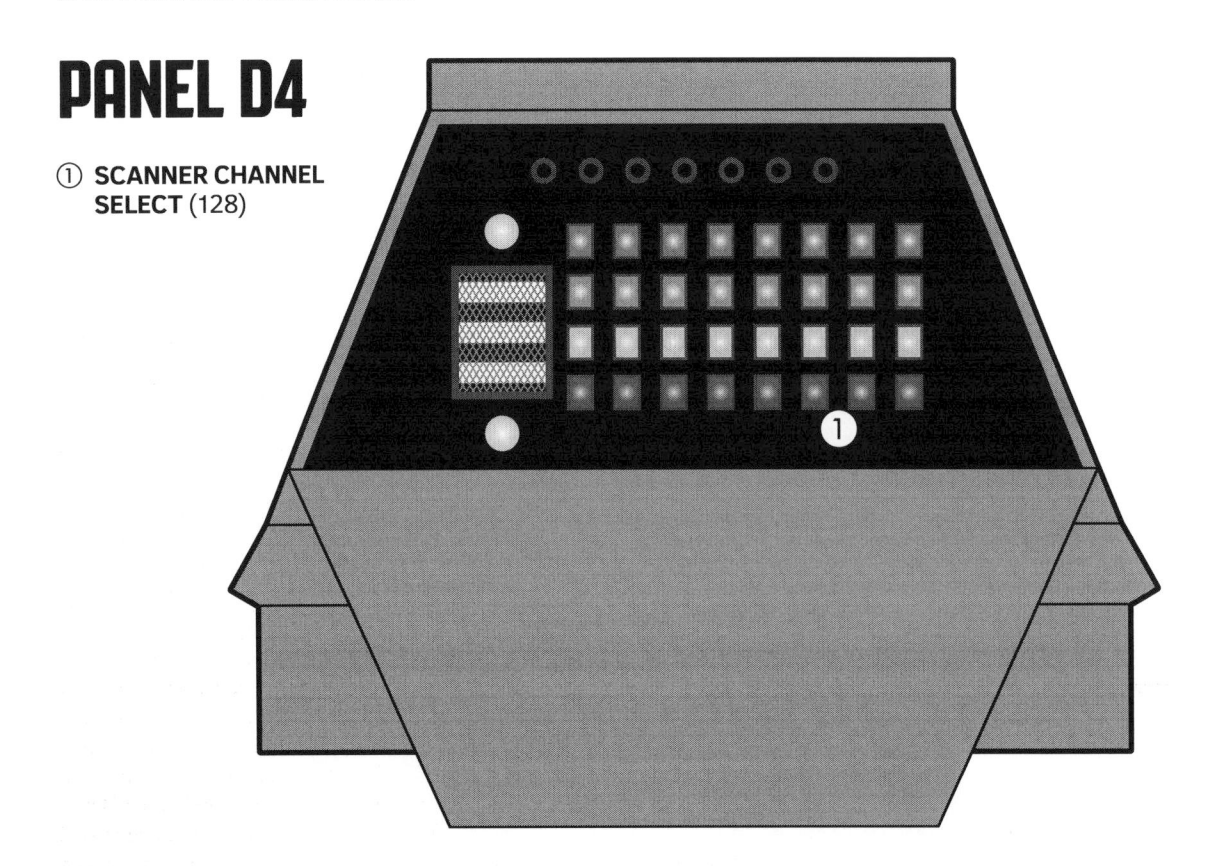

PANEL D
Closed

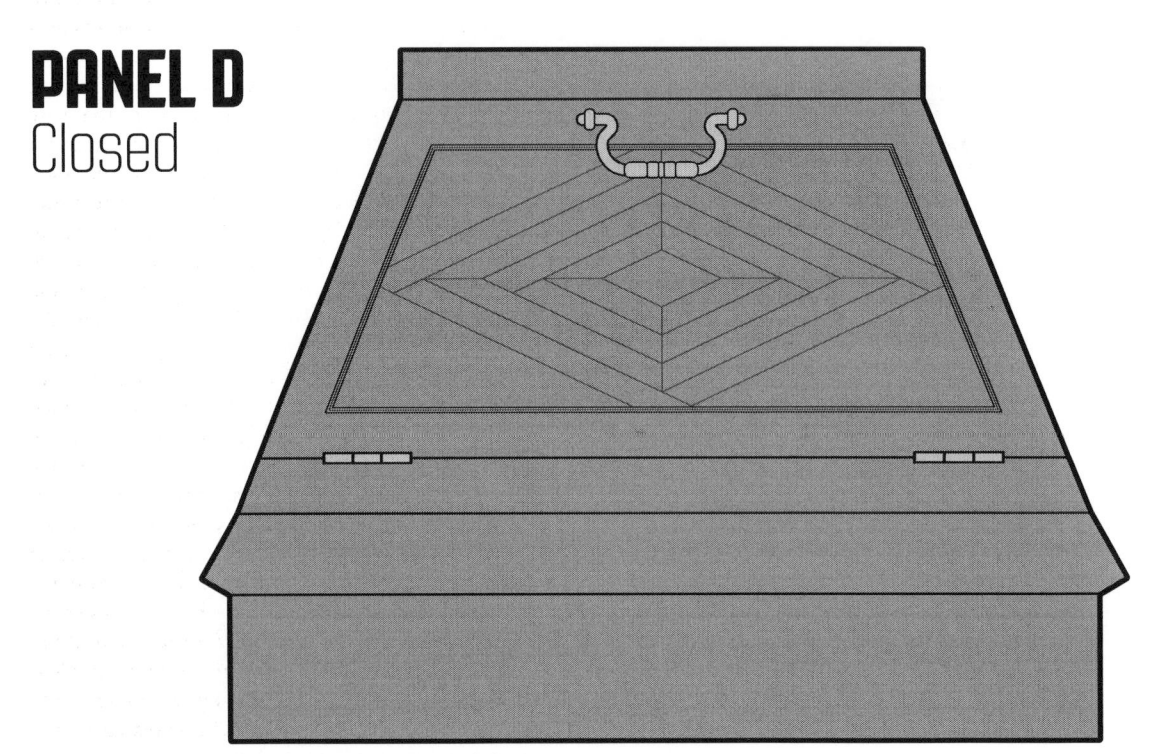

LANDING 123

SPACE Mandragora Helix
TIME [1492]
TRAVELLERS The Doctor, Sarah
EPISODES The Masque of Mandragora 1

The Doctor leads Sarah through TARDIS corridors, passing a large furnished room with a pair of wellingtons by the door, which he calls the boot cupboard. Sarah opens another door leading into a dark wood-panelled room with a central hexagonal bureau-like console, which the Doctor says is a second control room. Sarah finds a recorder inside one of the console's covered compartments and tootles 'The British Grenadiers' while the Doctor dusts with one of his old frilly shirts.

The Doctor brings up the lights and operates the scanner, discovering they are dangerously close to the Mandragora Helix, a mysterious energy emission controlled by a living intelligence. The room starts to shudder as the Helix sucks the TARDIS towards it. The Doctor tries to counter-magnetise the Ship but it is pulled into the whirlpool of energy and he can only hope they can ride through it. However, the TARDIS materialises within a black void encircled by giant crystals.

With the astro-sextant rectifier out of phase, the Doctor cannot tell where they have landed so goes outside to see, insisting Sarah stay inside. She follows, however, joining him in an echoing arena where they can walk around even though there is no discernible surface. A fizzing ball of Helix energy approaches them and the Doctor pulls Sarah behind the TARDIS while it passes.

Thinking they have had a narrow escape, the Doctor bundles Sarah back through the open door and makes a hurried departure, unaware that the Helix energy is inside the TARDIS.

- **CONTROLS** Panel D1 is open when the Doctor and Sarah enter the room. The Doctor uses panel D2, two places anti-clockwise (facing the interior door). Sarah finds the recorder in the compartment to its right.
- The Doctor reactivates the room using the top-left switch on panel D2 and opens the scanner with the far-left button on the second row. He uses further buttons on this panel while trying to counter-magnetise to resist the Helix's pull.
- Panel D2's rows of coloured buttons are, from top to bottom: yellow, green, red, blue.
- **LORE** The TARDIS contains much more than just the control room and a living space, with multiple rooms connected by corridors, although owing to "relative dimensions" it's impossible to say exactly how big it is – "There are no measurements in infinity."
- The TARDIS has a second control room that also provides full piloting functions.
- An out-of-phase astro-sextant rectifier affects readings of the TARDIS's landing site.
- **NOTES** This is the first time since the series began that a new Police Box prop, control room set and console have debuted in the same episode. It won't happen again until the TV movie in 1996.
- The Helix intelligence directs the TARDIS to Earth and plans to rob mankind of his curiosity, afraid that one day he will venture into space and threaten it. The implication, then, is that the Doctor and Sarah first encounter it in the same time period. Despite hijacking a time machine, there's no suggestion that the Helix is attempting to go back and change a known future. Having established a bridgehead with the energy that stows away aboard the TARDIS, it plans to transfer more during the solar eclipse, so appears to be operating in the same time frame (no doubt having some 'astral' way of overcoming general relativity).
- This is the first time we've seen beyond the control room since *The Mind Robber* (Landing 61) and the first indication the TARDIS has lengthy corridors. These are composed of walls from old control rooms in their last ever appearances, notably one of the original 1963 indented walls. Also used are the two shallow-roundels walls built for *The Time Monster* (the joins in their later-added backings still noticeable) and one of the two-column sections from *The Three Doctors*. The two doorways, to the boot cupboard and at the rear of the first corridor, are from stock. Note the Doctor says he'll give Sarah "a guided tour some day", meaning that isn't what he's doing now. So is he taking her somewhere specific? If so, presumably he forgets when distracted by the second control room and the Mandragora Helix.
- The scenes in the new control room were recorded on a different day from the corridor scenes so the two sets didn't link up. Outside the interior doorway is one of the shallow-roundels walls again. The Doctor calls this "the second control room", not *a* second, implying there are only two; we later learn there are in fact many more (see Landing 508, vol.2). Also, it's not the 'secondary' control room, as fans often misname it. The Doctor's remark, "Come to think of it, this *was* the old one," could mean it was only in use before the Doctor acquired the TARDIS, although he later adds, on realising he wasn't in control of the next landing, "Maybe that's why I stopped using the old control room." (Then again, that may be a response to Sarah's noting they have landed somewhere pleasant for once.) Was this the default when he first absconded from Gallifrey and switching to the white-walled room enabled him somehow to stop the Time Lords regaining control of the Ship? The presence of a recorder indicates the Doctor was in here during his second incarnation (hanging by the doorway, barely noticeable on screen but visible in set photos, is an outfit much like that incarnation's) and it has been suggested he used this control room for a time between his trial and exile, although it's not the one he's using in *The Two Doctors*. Again, did he try changing control rooms to escape Time Lord interference? The frilled shirt, as he commonly wore during his third incarnation, suggests he may have tried using this control room to get the TARDIS working again during his exile.

- The shaving mirror standing on top of the console is noted in the dialogue as being exactly that, and it's not there in later episodes, so this is *not* this console's equivalent of the central column. It's probably there because the script did mention "a little swivel mirror set into the console". Hanging on one of the railings around the console are two pairs of headphones. They appear prominently on screen as the TARDIS is pulled into the Helix, so if they were left there by accident surely someone would have removed them. Yet if they are part of the set, why doesn't Sarah don them instead of putting her hands over her ears?
- Deepening hums are heard as the Doctor and Sarah progress through two corridors and then enter the second control room. When the Doctor switches on the lights a new warbling hum starts, which will become the standard sound effect for when the TARDIS is stationary, although here it's still in flight; when it does land within the Helix just a low flat tone is heard. There's also a new sound effect for the scanner opening.
- The TARDIS seen being sucked into the Helix is the model built for *Pyramids of Mars*. It was filmed reflected in a sheet of flexible mirrored material that was pulled from behind to create the distortions. The camera was facing another mirror reflecting this so that the final image was the right way round. The same technique was used for shots in the control room. The miniature was used again in the studio for the shot of the TARDIS materialising in the heart of the Helix, with CSO combining it with a shot of the model crystal spiral.
- The scenes in the Helix void were shot with the Police Box and actors on a green CSO stage. A model shot of crystals against a black cloth was keyed into the background during recording.
- Although the Doctor appears to drag Sarah round the back of the TARDIS, because the new Police Box only had three sides the shot of them sheltering is actually the right-hand side of the prop.

LANDING 124

SPACE Earth, Italy, San Martino, near orange grove
TIME Four days in 1492
TRAVELLERS The Doctor, Sarah, Helix energy
EPISODES The Masque of Mandragora 1,4

The Helix energy takes control of the TARDIS and forces it to land in Italy during the Renaissance, materialising on a warm day in woodland close to an orange grove. As Sarah explores, the Doctor finds a glass flask from which he deduces their location, before following his friend.

Shortly after, the Helix energy emerges from the TARDIS and moves away through the undergrowth.

Four days later, the morning after a lunar eclipse, the Doctor and Sarah return to the TARDIS with a salami sausage as their reward for preventing the Helix intelligence from establishing itself on Earth. Sarah waves farewell to the new duke Giuliano and the Doctor assures her he will not be troubled by Mandragora again, although it will be in a position to attack the Earth again around the end of the 20th century. Giuliano watches bemused as the Police Box fades from view.

- **NOTES** The Duchy of San Martino appears to be one of the many city-states that developed in Northern Italy following the fall of the Roman Empire, although by the mid-15th century most of these had been conquered by the dominant states of Florence, Milan and Venice. It's significant enough that the leaders of these three plus Naples and Padua are willing to travel there for Giuliano's investiture.
- The Doctor estimates the date as late-15th century and only he and Sarah subsequently reference that, although in one scene they're with Giuliano who doesn't contradict them. Sarah later asserts, in The Sarah Jane Adventures story *The Death of the Doctor* that she visited San Martino in 1492, a date adopted from producer Philip Hinchcliffe's novelisation of *The Masque of Mandragora*. Yet the Doctor also says he could have used Galileo's telescope had he arrived in "another fifty years", which would require them to be nearer the middle of the 16th century as Galileo didn't develop his telescope until the early 1600s (either way, it's precocious of Giuliano to have one at all). Perhaps the Doctor knows something about Galileo that we don't, or is simply being flippant, as from 1494 to 1559 the city-states were involved in the Italian Wars so their leaders would hardly come together for a masque. (Is Federico seeking power because he expects war and wants San Martino to be strong enough to survive, which he believes would be less likely under the conciliatory Giuliano?) It must be before 1519 anyway as Leonardo da Vinci is coming to the ball, and after 1482 when he started working in Milan under the patronage of Duke Regent Ludovico Sforza. So the 1492 date is plausible. There was indeed a lunar eclipse at 9:43pm, as the Doctor calculates, but in 1488, and it was only a penumbral eclipse in December, which doesn't tie with Sarah's claim of a warm day. On 2 June 1490, however, there was a total eclipse at 9:49pm, which is surely within the margin of error of the astrolabe the Doctor uses. There were two lunar eclipses visible in Italy in 1492, in April and October, but again both penumbral, so not quite "swallowing" the moon.
- The Doctor supposes, "Helix forcefields must have distorted the coordinates," suggesting he had programmed the TARDIS for somewhere specific before it was diverted. In the next story Sarah is expecting them to arrive in South Croydon so presumably the Doctor is still/again trying to get her home.
- The Doctor may previously have met Florence Nightingale (prior to Landing 47), although he doesn't explicitly say so, merely cites her as someone who could judge the quality of his dressing of Giuliano's wound.
- Sarah queries her comprehension of Italian, the first time a companion has raised the issue of language (but see Landing 88). It's not stated that the TARDIS

is involved, as will later be the case, but the Doctor's explanation that it's "a Time Lord's gift I allow you to share" doesn't rule it out.

LANDING 125

SPACE Earth, England, quarry
TIME [Early-1980s]
TRAVELLERS The Doctor, Sarah
EPISODES The Hand of Fear 1,3

The TARDIS materialises in a working quarry just as a detonation is being prepared. Despite the warning siren, the Doctor and Sarah casually discuss the merits of South Croydon, their intended destination, while the Doctor practises his cricket bowling. Only when they see a workman waving his arms do they realise the danger. A wall of rock explodes above them. The TARDIS stands just beyond the rubble field but the travellers are closer; the Doctor is unharmed but Sarah is buried under boulders. Quarrymen help the Doctor dig her free, finding her unconscious and clasping a fossilised hand. An ambulance takes them both to hospital.

A few hours later the Doctor returns to the quarry to look for fragments of a crashed spaceship the hand might have come down in some 150 million years ago, but finding nothing he returns to the hospital.

Later that same day, the Doctor and Sarah return to the TARDIS with Eldrad, a silicon-based creature from Kastria that has regenerated its body by absorbing radiation from the core of the nearby Nunton nuclear power station. Suspicious of Eldrad's past, the Doctor has agreed to take her back to Kastria to get her away from Earth. She is impressed by the TARDIS but discovers her mental powers have no effect here as the interior of the Ship is multi-dimensional – what the Doctor calls being in a state of temporal grace. He has Eldrad enter the coordinates for Kastria, allowing for the passing of 150 million years, and takes off.

- **CONTROLS** The Doctor performs all operations from panel D3 (facing the interior door) while Eldrad programmes the coordinates from panel D2 opposite.
- The flap for panel D3 has a leather backing, indicating this is actually the desk compartment (D1) with the control panel placed inside (note it's not as deeply inset as panel D2 and flexes when the Doctor presses on it).
- **LORE** The TARDIS has no armaments other than its pilot's wits. Equally, weapons won't affect people inside owing to their being in a state of temporal grace and multi-dimensional.
- The scanner can be used as a display of alphanumeric information.
- **NOTES** This is the first story on contemporary Earth not to feature UNIT since the Doctor's exile was lifted, so there's no guarantee it follows the previous timeline and could be anytime in the late-20th century. It would be awkward if there were records of Sarah being in hospital at a time when she was provably elsewhere, however, so it's perhaps safer to assume this visit comes after the events of *The Seeds of Doom* (Landing 121).
- Although the Doctor tells Eldrad, "Your weapons won't work in here," his subsequent explanation suggests he means they will lack effect rather than fail to operate. He says "*we're* in a state of temporal grace" and "*we're* multi-dimensional" (my italics), applying those conditions to the occupants rather than the TARDIS itself. He goes on to say, "In a sense…we don't exist while we're in here. So you can't hurt us," perhaps implying that because they're in the Vortex and outside the normal flow of time they're subject to different physical laws. The Doctor later admits the whole thing is a "clever lie" (see Landing 519, vol.2), which could itself be a lie, of course. So perhaps here he's simply bluffing to avoid another bout of Eldrad's mind-reading or, as her eyes glow for some time without effect, he has surreptitiously operated a control that blocks her particular form of mental power.
- This time the warbling hum used in *The Masque of Mandragora* (Landing 123) is heard in the control room before take-off, rising to a higher-pitched trilling when the TARDIS is in flight. Both will become familiar to listeners of the 1978 *Doctor Who Sound Effects* LP.
- The scanner displays what are presumably the coordinates for Kastria: 78b REF.66735 144328X 66e 8 0257634 RD=77 144092R 31751 246X56. (These were produced with the BBC's Anchor text generator, an analogue system that created characters electronically and was first used in coverage of the 1970 General Election.) This, along with the instructions the Doctor gives Eldrad for counteracting the expansion factor – "Just punch up 7438000 WHI1212 7272911 E8EX4111 309115 and then see what happens" – indicates the console has an alphanumeric entry format, although the buttons bear no symbols. (The digits Tom Baker reels off were different from the scripted '370222' and incorporated the telephone numbers of BBC Television Centre's switchboard, Scotland Yard and the Doctor Who production office.)

LANDING 126

SPACE Kastria, outside Dome Six
TIME As above
TRAVELLERS The Doctor, Sarah, Eldrad
EPISODES The Hand of Fear 3-4

After a brief bout of turbulence, causing the Doctor to double-check Eldrad's coordinate programming to ensure there is no symbolic resonance in the trachoid time crystal, the TARDIS arrives on the freezing wind-blasted surface of Kastria, some 150 million years since Eldrad was sentenced to obliteration for destroying the solar barriers that protected the planet. The scanner shows the devastation and, a short distance away, a habitation dome. The atmosphere is similar to Earth's although with a higher radiation level. The Doctor lends Sarah his coat as they and Eldrad hurry across the icy surface to the dome.

He does so again when they return to the TARDIS having outwitted a regenerated Eldrad and left him in pieces at the bottom of a deep abyss. The Doctor makes a welcome departure from Kastria as Sarah nurses her frozen fingers.

The Ship has also been affected by the cold and gives the travellers a jolt, so the Doctor opens the pedestal of the console to check the thermo couplings. He has Sarah pass him an astro-rectifier, multi-quantiscope, ganymede driver (in preference to a mergin nut), and the sonic screwdriver (in place of a zeus plug) from the pockets of his coat, oblivious to her claims that she is fed up with being menaced by monsters. In a huff at being ignored by him, Sarah asserts that she is going home and leaves the control room to collect her belongings. The Doctor finishes working under the console, having found nothing wrong after all, but suddenly gets a mental signal recalling him to Gallifrey.

- **CONTROLS** The Doctor operates the scanner by pressing a button on the right of panel D3. On returning to the TARDIS, he dematerialises by pressing the top-left switch on panel D2 (now facing the interior door). After taking off, he is seen standing at panel D3 one position to the right, although the console has been rotated so this panel is now facing the interior door, presumably to get the required camera angle when the Doctor accesses the console's workings through the hatch in the pedestal below this panel. This hatch hinges on the right, proving it's really the desk section above covered by the panel D3 controls.
- **LORE** Symbolic resonance in the trachoid time crystal would destroy the TARDIS (or possibly just prevent it from ever materialising).
- The thermo couplings are housed in the console's pedestal. They can be affected by sub-zero temperatures outside the Ship.
- **NOTES** The Doctor specifically agrees to take Eldrad back to Kastria only if they stay in the same (relative) time, as to travel back to the time of her departure would "contravene the first law of time, a distortion of history". This only makes sense if he knows Eldrad never returned to Kastria when it was populated, which isn't borne out by the rest of the story – at best it's possible he has heard of the planet in a legendary way as he's quite interested in seeing it but is unsure of the exact coordinates. It's more likely he's simply suspicious of Eldrad and doesn't want to risk taking her back to her people, reasoning the Kastrian civilisation won't have survived 150 million years.
- The moment of turbulence is not really explained. Sarah asks if the TARDIS has gone off course but it hasn't. Is it intended to suggest Eldrad has tried to take them back in time after all, which the Doctor has to correct? And does it account for why the Ship lands outside the dome rather than inside?
- Sarah comes back into the control room eating a banana, so clearly the Ship still has provisions beyond those provided by the food machine.
- The model shots of the TARDIS on Kastria feature a new miniature probably built by Steve Drewett, who was assisting this serial's visual effects designer Colin Mapson. This had roughly the same proportions as the model built for *Pyramids of Mars* but was slightly smaller, had an extra step in the roof, the 'Police box' signs were closer to the windows with no stepped lintel between them, and the very bottom rail was deeper still. The windows and 'Police telephone' plaque (again white) were stuck-on paper, slightly larger than the indented panels. The TARDIS's arrival and departure are not the same shot with one reversed as the smoke blows in the same direction in both.
- The new control room in-flight hum continues after the TARDIS has landed.
- When the Doctor accesses the pedestal of the console, it's quite clear there's nothing inside. In fact, there's a round hole in the base that the floor shows through.
- If Sarah hasn't had a bath or washed her hair in a while, has the Doctor not shown her where the TARDIS's bathroom is? Or does it not possess such facilities yet? If not it's surprising she hasn't spent every adventure bursting for a wee (see Landing 764, vol.2).
- When the Doctor says, "I don't know why she goes on like this," is he referring to Sarah's tantrum or the TARDIS's frequent bouts of turbulence?

LANDING 127

SPACE Earth, Scotland, Aberdeen
TIME Before 1981
TRAVELLERS The Doctor, Sarah
EPISODES The Hand of Fear 4

The Doctor must follow the summons but knows he cannot take a non-Time Lord there. He will have to get Sarah home first, so sets the controls for (he hopes) Hillview Road in South Croydon. Sarah returns to the control room with a suitcase and an armful of souvenirs including a tennis racquet, a potted flower and a stuffed toy owl, but soon retracts her insistence on leaving when she learns the Doctor is going to Gallifrey. The Doctor is adamant that he must return alone, however, as the TARDIS materialises in the middle of a quiet suburban cul-de-sac.

Sarah is a little astonished to finally have made it back home. She gives the Doctor back his coat and they promise not to forget each other. She leaves feeling richer for her experiences and sure she will see the Doctor again, turning to watch with sadness nevertheless as the TARDIS fades away without her.

- **CONTROLS** The Doctor sets the coordinates from panel D3.
- **NOTES** It's not until Sarah's return in *School Reunion* (Landing 347, vol.2) that we learn the Doctor didn't drop her off in South Croydon as promised, but in

Aberdeen. Let's hope she had some money for a train, or at least 2p to call the Brigadier and ask for help.

▪ It's fair to assume the Doctor returns Sarah to Earth at a point in time sequential to their previous visits – he probably simply reverses course from Kastria. Sarah assumes so, at least, as she promises to give his regards to Professor Watson at the Nunton power station they recently visited. We've established that *Terror of the Zygons* is set in 1980 (see Landing 109) and Sarah has returned to Earth thee times since then; as we later learn that *K9 and Company* takes place in December 1981, by which time she seems to have settled back into life on Earth, presumably not much time passes between those three occasions. According to *K9 and Company*, she met Commander Pollock in 1979 and her Aunt Lavinia moved to Moreton Harwood around the same time, which could have been during the weeks the Doctor was missing prior to his third regeneration.

LANDING 128

SPACE Gallifrey, perimeter of Capitol, sector seven near communications tower; transducted to Capitol museum
TIME Unknown
TRAVELLERS The Doctor
EPISODES The Deadly Assassin 1,4

The Doctor is en route to Gallifrey when he has a vision of the President's assassination in the Panopticon, apparently by his own hand. He staggers around the control room in confusion and collapses, recovering as the TARDIS materialises in a corridor on the very edge of the Capitol. Having detected its approach, the Chancellery Guard are already in attendance and surround the unauthorised capsule. The Doctor watches on the scanner as Castellan Spandrell and Commander Hilred examine the TARDIS, the former ordering its occupants be arrested.

While the guards bring a variety of keys with which to try opening the TARDIS, the Doctor writes a note warning of the impending assassination attempt. He retrieves a leather medical bag from elsewhere in the Ship and takes from it a hookah, which he lights and places with a cushion wrapped in his hat, coat and scarf on a high-backed chair. He dims the control room lights and leaves the note pinned to this dummy, then hides just outside the main entrance. When Hilred finally unlocks the Police Box door, he and four guards rush in, stasers at the ready, and while they are duped by the dummy the Doctor slips out to warn the President. Hilred finds the note and looks up at the scanner in time to see the Doctor getting away. He leads his guards in hurried pursuit.

After giving them the slip, the Doctor sneaks back into the TARDIS, unaware it is being watched by the Master, who has anticipated the Doctor's trickery. Inside he tunes the scanner to the public register video showing a live broadcast from the Panopticon, but soon tires of Commentator Runcible's fawning discourse. When he switches back to the outside view, he sees Chancellor Goth and Spandrell examining the Ship. Goth suggests transducting it into the Capitol to prevent the Doctor regaining access so Spandrell orders it be sent to the museum.

The TARDIS is relocated and the Doctor staggers out, disoriented by the transduction. He fails to notice a second TARDIS close by, disguised as a dusty grandfather clock. Instead he finds the traditional robes of Gold Usher on display and changes into them, knowing they will grant him unhindered access to the Panopticon.

Not long after, Spandrell, Hilred and a guard check on the TARDIS, suspecting the Doctor of having been inside when it was moved to the museum. A tracking device leads them from the Ship to his discarded clothes, left in place of the Usher's, and they leave to find him.

The planet comes close to destruction when the Master attempts to unleash the powers of the Eye of Harmony, but once the threat is over the Time Lords are keen to brush the whole affair under the carpet, which includes the speedy departure of the Doctor. While Coordinator Engin is sure any past misdemeanours could be overlooked, the Doctor is keen to resume his travels. Spandrell and Engin escort him to the museum, grateful for his defeating the Master, although the Doctor warns that the dying renegade could have used some of the Eye's power to survive. Indeed, as the TARDIS dematerialises, so too does the grandfather clock.

○ **CONTROLS** While the TARDIS is in flight to Gallifrey, the Doctor presses the top-left button on panel D2 (now facing the scanner), causing the row of yellow buttons to light up, the first time they have been seen to do this. He also discerns his landing site and operates the scanner from this panel. The next compartment anti-clockwise is the desk (D1), from which he takes pen and paper to write his note. It also contains letters, an ink well, sealing wax and a seal stamp. To the right is panel D4; the Doctor later presses two buttons on its bottom row to tune the scanner to "the local news programme". He switches the scanner back to normal function with the far-right yellow button on panel D2.

○ Circular orange stickers have been placed on the far-left square button in each row and the left-most three switches at the top of panel D2. Two positions anti-clockwise from this is a new control panel, D4, in the same style – four rows of coloured buttons and a grille at the side – but flipped so the grille is on the left. The buttons are, from top to bottom: blue, green, yellow, red.

▪ **LORE** The Doctors TARDIS is designated a Type 40 TT capsule by the Time Lords, long since decommissioned and considered obsolete. Its outward shape was infinitely variable. Originally 305 were registered, of which all but the Doctor's are now de-registered and non-operational.

▪ The double-curtain trimonic barrier on a Type 40 requires a cypher-indent key.

▪ The scanner can receive local audio-visual transmissions.

▪ **NOTES** It's never made clear, here or later in the series, whether the Capitol is the whole of the Time Lords' city or just one building (or complex of buildings) within it, akin to the US Capitol in Washington DC. Certainly in *The Invasion of Time* and 21st century episodes 'citadel' is used to denote the glass-domed metropolis, so perhaps the Capitol is just the part where the political elite operate. Only Coordinator Engin's response that the APC control is used "to monitor life in the Capitol" might suggest the term relates to all Time Lord habitation.

- The Doctor appears surprised to have materialised just outside the Capitol – "I'm in trouble now" – yet seemingly set the coordinates himself in *The Hand of Fear*. Is this another instance of "[leaving] the actual landing to the TARDIS herself" (see Landing 103)?
- The Police Box roof lamp keeps flashing after the TARDIS has materialised.
- The removal of the Doctor's TARDIS from the register was by order of a malfeasance tribunal. This is generally taken to be a reference to the Doctor's trial in *The War Games*, and one might suppose that striking the TARDIS from the record was because, while it wasn't formally decommissioned, it was out of operation while on Earth. But this again raises the question of why the Time Lords allowed the Doctor access to the TARDIS during his exile, even with the restrictions put on them both. Why not send the Doctor to Earth alone and keep the TARDIS on Gallifrey? They could still have loaned him another or a Time Ring when they needed to use him as an agent. Perhaps the Type 40s weren't obsolete at that time and they didn't want to put it back into the pool of available TT capsules – further evidence that they were exiling the Ship as well for aiding and abetting the Doctor (see Landing 73 *et seq*). The apparent date of the tribunal order, 309906, is unlikely to correlate to Earth dating (that is, not the 310th millennium), but if it's a Time Lord calendar then it's a long way off the "ten million years of absolute power" they have notched up by the time of the Doctor's sixth incarnation.
- Hilred's box of angular metal keys includes a Yale one, so is that actually a standard Time Lord key type?
- The wooden Knossos chair gets used for only the second time, since the Doctor sat on it to take off his shoes in *The Reign of Terror* episode six. Not sure his using a hookah here is a good example for younger viewers, however.
- The guards enter the control room from the right of the doorway, as has become the norm, but when the Doctor sneaks out he moves across the gap from right to left (and one of the guards is looking right at him). So there must be some space between this entrance and the exterior doors, with a nook for the Doctor to hide in as the guards pass and such that it doesn't matter if one turns left or right when leaving the control room.
- Spandrell says a Type 40 capsule's "shape was infinitely variable", implying perhaps that the chameleon circuits of later models were restricted to certain forms. Chancellor Goth expresses surprise that such an old capsule is still operational and in "remarkably good condition", so either he's not the same Time Lord who sentenced the Doctor and his TARDIS to exile on Earth, despite appearances, or he's dissembling as part of the plan to frame the Doctor.
- The transduction effect was not achieved digitally even though it looks like the image is being pixellated (it's too early for such techniques). It's an overlay of three separate camera shots of the Police Box prop – a wide shot of it in position plus two close-up views from different angles – mixed together using a matte of shifting blocks in three different colours from a pattern generator. This had been built for use on Saturday morning children's programme *Swap Shop* and was adopted by this serial's visual effect designer AJ Mitchell to mix the different images together as director David Maloney wanted a more interesting effect than just the normal fade in. (The pattern generator had previously been used for King Rokon's screen in *The Hand of Fear*.)
- The Doctor doesn't retrieve his coat, scarf, waistcoat, shirt or trousers from the museum display before leaving. In fact, when he's arrested he's wearing a white Henley shirt and long-johns under his stolen robes, but when being interrogated he's suddenly in a loose open-necked shirt and belted maroon breeches. Do the Time Lords let all their prisoners pick out new outfits in which to be tortured?
- The shot of the TARDIS dematerialising shows the left-hand side of the prop, revealing that there is no 'Police box' sign box on the rear.

PREVIOUS LANDINGS

SPACE Earth, Switzerland
TIME Early-14th century
TRAVELLERS The Doctor, [unknown companions]
EPISODES Claimed by the Doctor in The Face of Evil 2
The Doctor met William Tell, who taught him to fire a crossbow with great accuracy.
- **NOTES** Although there is no historical evidence for the William Tell legend, now the Doctor has met Robin Hood (Landing 616, vol.2) we know such meetings are possible. Perhaps the Doctor was there to witness the origin of the Swiss Confederacy, or maybe just fighting off robots seeking fuel for their apple-powered spaceship.

SPACE [Unnamed planet, Mordee colony ship]
TIME Unknown future, prior to Landing 129
TRAVELLERS The Doctor, [unknown companions]
EPISODES Mentioned in The Face of Evil 2-4
While in his fourth incarnation, the Doctor encountered a stranded Mordee colony ship on which the master computer was malfunctioning. In fact, generations of work to upgrade the system had resulted in it becoming sentient. Not realising this and believing the data core to be damaged, the Doctor connected

his brain to the computer to perform a variation of the Sidelian memory transfer and restore it. Unwittingly, he left it with a complete imprint of his own personality that, after the Doctor had left, would begin to clash with its own developing mind and cause it to go insane.

- **NOTES** There's no indication whether the TARDIS materialised on the same planet as in *The Face of Evil* where the Doctor then met the Mordee, or inside their ship after it had landed on the planet, or while it was still travelling through space. The Doctor doesn't seem familiar with the jungle and while he does recognise the exterior of the ship, he's pretty good at identifying spaceships (perhaps a Starfall Seven like the spacesuit, possibly called the Imelo if Neeva's litany is any indication). His face must have been carved into the mountain after Xoanon developed dissociative identity disorder, whether that was before or after landing. He says the ship was stranded but this could be in space or on the planet. One could argue the Doctor is more likely to help with computer problems if the colonists still needed it to reach their destination safely, rather than after they'd made landfall when he might encourage them to manage without it and rely on their own fortitude.
- In his novelisation, Terrance Dicks places this trip during the events of *Robot* (Landing 106). A freshly regenerated and still erratic Doctor sneaks off in the TARDIS one night, fixes the colonists' computer, then returns to Earth minutes after he left and forgets about it like a dream. However, the botched memory transfer is as plausible a reason as post-regenerative wooziness for his not remembering straight away what happened. So it could have been while he was travelling with Sarah, or even immediately before the TARDIS brings him back to fix his mistake, as it did in *The Ark* (Landing 36). It might explain why he's talking to himself at the start of the story and could be what the knot in his hankie was supposed to remind him about.

SPACE Korlano Beta
TIME Unknown
TRAVELLERS The Doctor, [unknown companions]
EPISODES Mentioned by the Doctor in
The Robots of Death 1

The Doctor visited this planet where sandminers scour the surface searching for valuable minerals and ores, helped by sandstorms stirring up heavier elements from deeper strata.

- **NOTES** The Doctor is talking to Leela when he mentions Korlano Beta so his visit must have been before he met her. As they seem to go directly from her home world to Storm Mine Four, it would be quite a coincidence if he had seen examples of desert stripping in close succession so this was probably some considerable time before Landing 129.

SPACE Earth, [Iceland]
TIME 51st century
TRAVELLERS The Doctor, [unknown companions]
EPISODES Recalled by the Doctor in
The Talons of Weng-Chiang 6

The Doctor was with the Filipino army as it advanced on Reykjavik during the ice age of the early-51st century. He also became aware of (but didn't necessarily encounter) the Peking Homunculus, an electronic toy doll with the cerebral cortex of a pig, made around the year 5000 as a gift for the children of the Icelandic Alliance's commissioner; and of Magnus Greel, the minister of justice for some unspecified government and reviled as the Butcher of Brisbane, who disappeared around the same time.

- **NOTES** This was before the Doctor met Leela as she is unaware of the events he relates.
- The world is clearly a very different place in the 51st century. Iceland appears to be the leader, or at least originator, of an alliance of unspecified countries – Northern Europe, perhaps, or even Greenland and North America – that is ranged against another power that includes the Philippines, China and possibly Australia (if Greel led a massacre in Brisbane rather than being from there – the name Magnus might imply a Nordic lineage). The Doctor was on the side of the latter, although this may be from expediency rather than choice, particularly if elements in China were responsible for starting the fight with Iceland. In the Big Finish audio play *The Butcher of Brisbane*, the Doctor witnesses events leading up to Greel's disappearance while in his fifth incarnation.
- Despite later interpretations, in the context of *The Talons of Weng-Chiang* the existence of Time Agents is clearly a figment of Greel's paranoia. Believing the zygma experiments to be a success in enabling him to escape justice, he expects others to use the same technology to come after him. But as the Doctor later explains, the experiments were a failure and "nothing came of them".

LANDING 129

SPACE Unnamed planet, jungle
TIME At least three days in unknown future (after 5000)
TRAVELLERS The Doctor
EPISODES The Face of Evil 1,4

The Doctor is aiming for Hyde Park but when the TARDIS materialises he finds himself in an alien jungle, where voracious rat-sized Horda scuttle across the sandy forest floor. He suspects a nexial discontinuity is to blame and pulls out his handkerchief to tie a knot in it as a reminder to overhaul the tracers, only to find it is already knotted for a reason he has forgotten.

He decides to explore the location anyway and heads off into the jungle. Some distance away is a line of low-intensity sonic disruptors that deter the vibration-sensitive invisible creatures that roam the jungle from approaching the tribal village beyond. At the edge of the forest is a low mountain range on the far side of which is a flat plain where a tower-like spaceship stands.

Several days later the Doctor returns to the TARDIS, whistling a tune as he unlocks the door. To avoid being made leader of the shaky alliance between the Sevateem and the Tesh, Leela follows him, intrigued by this man who has shown her new ways of thinking. She has brought the energy weapon the Doctor constructed to protect them from the invisible creatures but he assures her that, as projections of the computer Xoanon's disturbed mind, they are gone now it is cured. Leela asks the Doctor to take her with him and when he demurs she slips past him and into the Ship. He follows protestingly but before he can do anything she touches a control and the TARDIS dematerialises.

▪ **NOTES** This is the first time in the series that the Doctor has been explicitly travelling alone for an unknowable amount of time. It's not impossible that after his exile was lifted he made numerous solo journeys, particularly after Jo Grant left UNIT, but as he had formed a bond with the Brigadier, who was clearly still in need of his services, it's unlikely he was ever away from Earth for long prior to his regeneration.

▪ While the Doctor talks of "the Mordee expedition" and reprogramming Xoanon "for the Mordee" as if they're a species, he also says the Sevateem and Tesh were "all human beings from this colony ship". That could be taken as a generic term for human-looking people, but when the Doctor and Leela later find themselves in the Solar System in the year 5000, he refers to it as "the time of [her] ancestors", so he at least believes she's descended from humans. That might place this in a future where humans are so spread throughout the stars some have adopted new distinctions, perhaps like the Morestrans (see Landing 110).

▪ A slow pan up to the arriving TARDIS allows us to hear the full 20 seconds of the now-standard materialisation sound effect introduced with Landing 79.

▪ The Doctor has acquired a new outfit exactly like the one he left behind on Gallifrey.

▪ For Leela to press the dematerialisation switch by chance is especially lucky with the current console. Even if the Doctor has left the relevant compartment open, it's not like there's one obvious control that suggests 'launch'. In fact, the simpler, more uniform layout of this console's controls suggests each is multi-purpose (and you can take the actors' random button pressing as further evidence of this if you like), perhaps with a telepathic interface that senses what the operator wishes to achieve. Maybe, therefore, the TARDIS likes Leela and would have taken off whichever button she pressed; the Doctor does say in *Image of the Fendahl* that Leela's "primitive thought patterns" appeal to the Ship.

LANDING 130

SPACE Unnamed planet [Kaldor], desert, Storm Mine Four, forward scoop; moved to storage deck section 52
TIME Unknown future
TRAVELLERS The Doctor, Leela
EPISODES The Robots of Death 1-2,4

The Doctor distracts Leela with a yoyo while he works at the console, not realising that she assumes its motion is part of the operation of the TARDIS. When he confesses it is just a fun toy, she lets it fall to the floor in embarrassment and asks how the Ship is bigger inside than out. The Doctor takes two different sized boxes from a cabinet, places the larger on top of the console, then holds the smaller up in front of her over by the scanner. He explains that if the distant box could be kept further away, where it appears smaller, *and* coincident with the other, the bigger would fit inside the smaller – a principle he calls transdimensional engineering but which Leela says is silly.

Just then the TARDIS materialises in the scoop of a sandminer crossing an alien desert in search of precious minerals beneath the surface. The scanner shows only a metal wall so the Doctor dons his coat and scarf before heading out to discover where they are. Leela scoffs at his inability to operate the Ship and he ruefully admits he is not always fully in charge. He tells her to leave the energy weapon behind as people tend not to harm unarmed strangers – usually.

The pair examine the large chamber they are in, noting extensive scratch marks on the hardened alloy walls. At the far end is a slatted opening giving them a view of the vivid landscape across which the sandminer is travelling. Leela thinks she hears a noise behind them but the Doctor is focused on the realisation they are in a scoop that draws in sand under high pressure. Unseen, a large claw descends above the TARDIS and lifts it out of the scoop, leaving the travellers trapped as a sandstorm approaches.

The Ship is deposited on an access walkway among the ore storage hoppers, where not long after the Doctor finds it while exploring the Mine. He opens the hatch on one of the hoppers to explain to Leela how it works, only to realise she is no longer with him. As he passes another hopper on his way back to look for her, he notices the hatch is ajar and, peering inside, discovers the body of one of the crew. When he climbs inside to examine it, the hatch closes and ore comes flooding in from above, burying both the body and the Doctor. He manages to breathe for a while through a handy snorkel, and fortunately command robot SV7 soon arrives, notices a high level of impurity in the sample, and drains the hopper. It releases the Doctor and identifies the body as crewman Kerril before calling for another Voc robot, V17, to restrain the intruder and take him away for questioning.

Later, one of the robots whose programming has been adjusted meets its controller by the storage hoppers. It is given a deactivation disc and ordered to kill Zilda.

After the reprogrammed robots have taken control of the Mine, Leela and Toos pass the TARDIS as they try to avoid being captured. Hearing robots approaching, they hide in an empty hopper, which fortunately the unimaginative automatons do not search as they have previously done so. When the coast is clear, Leela and Toos emerge and head for the control deck.

Once the murderous robots have been destroyed, the Doctor and Leela head back to the TARDIS, leaving survivors Toos and Uvanov awaiting a rescue ship. The Doctor explains that his respiratory bypass system allowed him not to breathe the helium that altered Dask's voice and broke his control of the robots – a trick the Time Lord has learned during his 750 years. The Doctor teases Leela that she, on the other hand, sounded like a mouse. They enter the Ship and depart.

- **CONTROLS** The Doctor presses the top-left button on panel D2 to operate the scanner. Panel D3 is to the right of this, facing the interior door, then the desk compartment D1. Initially the next compartment opposite D2 is open but the Doctor closes it before we can see what controls are within (probably none in reality).
- This is the last appearance of console D in the series, and of its matching control room set, although its wall sections will be repainted and reused in future TARDIS sets through to 1983.
- **LORE** The Doctor makes only his second attempt at explaining how the TARDIS is bigger on the inside (hand-waving statements that it's "dimensionally transcendental" aside) by comparing a large cube far away with a smaller one nearer the observer. While this hints that different dimensions are involved, it also suggests perception is key, similar to his previous television analogy (see Landing 1). Such transdimensional engineering was a key Time Lord development.
- **NOTES** It's unlikely there have been additional landings since meeting Leela. She is unfamiliar with both the TARDIS's operation and the Doctor's navigational abilities, and when she picks up the gun the Doctor tells her to leave it behind, suggesting they haven't ventured outside the Ship since Landing 129 (or they'd have had this conversation before).
- In this serial Kaldor is only named as a city where a Voc therapist malfunctioned. It's taken to be the Storm Mine's place of origin but may not even be on the same planet if these are space-faring humans. Subsequent non-television stories have taken it to be the name of the planet seen here, however.
- The model shot of the TARDIS in flight before the first scene in the control room is reused from *Pyramids of Mars* episode one (Landing 113). The view on a monitor of the TARDIS being lifted out of the scoop uses the same Police Box miniature.
- The control room has gained an oval table as well as the sideboard from which the Doctor takes the two cubes to explain transdimensional engineering. There is also, for the first time, a coat rack on the far left of the room. The Doctor retrieves his coat and scarf from this before heading out, leaving behind his red jacket (from Season 12) and grey coat (last worn in *The Seeds of Doom*). There is also another jacket, which could be the one he wears in *The Talons of Weng-Chiang* – is the Doctor already planning a visit to Victorian London?
- When the TARDIS materialises the right-hand side of the prop is facing the camera, again revealing that there is no 'Police box' sign box on the rear.
- The rather nice long shot of the storage deck was achieved by shooting the TARDIS on the small hopper set from a distance then inserting it via CSO into a view of a model of the Mine's inner structure.
- For the only time with this Police Box prop, when leaving the Doctor unlocks the door using his shield-shaped key in the slot below the Yale lock.
- This is the last time we see the second control room. The Doctor uses it at least until *Horror of Fang Rock* (Landing 132), however, and possibly beyond as there is space for unseen journeys between that and *The Invisible Enemy* (Landing 133).

PREVIOUS LANDING

SPACE Earth, Britain, Essex, London
TIME Early-8th century
TRAVELLERS The Doctor, [unknown companions]
EPISODES Mentioned by the Doctor in
  The Talons of Weng-Chiang 3

The Doctor caught a large salmon in the river Fleet, which he shared with the Venerable Bede, who adored eating fish.

- **NOTES** The Doctor says he caught the salmon "once", suggesting it was some considerable time before Landing 131. However, his fourth incarnation has been the only one to express an interest in fishing (his sixth later indulges in the pastime) so it may have been after Landing 119.
- Bede spent almost his entire life in a Northumbrian monastery and there is no record of him travelling so far south. But he mentions the Anglo-Saxon trading settlement of Lundenwic (west of the old Roman town) in his writings and could have been to visit its bishop. Alternatively the Doctor may have taken the salmon to him, knowing his penchant for fish.

LANDING 131

SPACE Earth, England, East London
TIME Three days in [February 1892]
TRAVELLERS The Doctor, Leela
EPISODES The Talons of Weng-Chiang 1,6

The Doctor decides to show Leela how some of her human ancestors lived (or uses this as an excuse to visit the music hall) by taking her to Victorian London. They dress appropriately – the Doctor ditching his hat and scarf for a deerstalker cap and Inverness cape, Leela swapping her animal skins for a tight jacket and breeches (stashing a blowpipe and janis thorn in her pockets) – as the TARDIS materialises after dark in a foggy street not far from the river. The blast of a ship's horn startles Leela but the Doctor is more interested in a nearby poster advertising the act of magician Li H'sen Chang at the Palace Theatre. Although he would prefer to see Little Tich, they head for the theatre hoping to catch the evening's second performance.

Early in the morning of the second day after, the Doctor leads the way to the TARDIS as, munching on fresh muffins, Professor Litefoot tries to explain to Leela the formalities of drinking tea. The two travellers bid a fond farewell to their new friends Jago and Litefoot, who watch in admiration and astonishment respectively as the Police Box groans and vanishes before their eyes like the ultimate magic trick.

NOTES Where does the TARDIS land? A nearby poster for the Palace Theatre might suggest that's not very far away. The river Fleet is said by the theatre's owner Jago to run "right under the foundations" but by the 19th century this had long been a covered sewer running directly under Farringdon Street as far as Clerkenwell Road. So if the theatre is literally above it then it would have to be in the Mount Pleasant area. However, directly beneath the theatre's cellar is a brickwork cavern with access to a conduit leading to the main sewer, so we can assume Jago is being over-precise and the Fleet actually runs close by. So the theatre may be near Holborn Viaduct or around Ludgate Circus if the "clang and the rush of water as they closed the sluice gates down on the Thames" is audible in the cellar. On the other hand, not long after leaving the TARDIS, the Doctor and Leela are taken to a police station within earshot of a riverside whistle blast and which gets "a lot of [Chinese] in… Limehouse being so close". Limehouse police station itself was on the Isle of Dogs under Metropolitan Police K Division, but the Limehouse area was close to the border with H Division, covering Whitechapel, Wapping and Stepney, so maybe they're at Shadwell or Arbour Square station, each under half a mile from the Thames. (It's possible the two divisions share the services of the Limehouse Mortuary and Coroner's Court.) Except neither Sergeant Kyle nor Constable Quick has letters on his collar, just numbers, indicating they're City Police. Even if they're stationed near Aldgate, Limehouse is over a mile away – not exactly "close". However near to Limehouse the police station is, would Jago be placing posters that far from his theatre? Perhaps, if Chang has been a big enough hit to perform before Queen Victoria at Buckingham Palace, or maybe he's just promoting Chang's act to the Chinese population of the East End. Ultimately, the geography of London might be very different in the *Doctor Who* universe (see also Landing 11) as Litefoot claims Rundall Buildings is "somewhere between Whitechapel and St George's in the East", which puts it near the Commercial Road, yet the laundry based there is called Limehouse Laundry and its label clearly says it's on the Causeway, a mile east. All in all, it's likely the TARDIS materialises among the warehouses in Wapping or Shadwell, and not far from Greel's base at the House of the Dragon given everyone's still chomping on the muffins they buy outside when they get back to the Ship. The Doctor is overconfident when he imagines reaching the Palace Theatre before the second house, not realising it's on the other side of the City. Perhaps, had they not been attacked by the Tong of the Black Scorpion, they would simply have called in at a much closer music hall instead and never met the irrepressible Jago and Litefoot.

The story is set after 1888 as Casey mentions "Jolly Jack at work again", "the Ripper, Mister Jago", in relation to the missing girls. The edition of *Blackwood's Edinburgh Magazine* that Professor Litefoot is reading in episode four is number 916 (volume 151), which was published in February 1892. He may be taking a while to get through it if he's busy with work, but the days seem quite short in the story and the nights are foggy so it's not likely to be more than a month after that. If this dating is correct, the Doctor could have indeed seen Little Tich on stage at the Theatre Royal, Drury Lane had he not been distracted by giant rats and time-travelling tyrants.

LANDING 132

SPACE Earth, England, south coast, Fang Rock
TIME [1910]
TRAVELLERS The Doctor, Leela
EPISODES Horror of Fang Rock 1,4

The Doctor plans to take Leela to Brighton but the TARDIS materialises at night on Fang Rock, a barren outcrop in the English Channel. It is swathed in a chilling fog, which the Doctor blames for their being off course – unaware that it is caused by a Rutan scout ship recently crash-landed just offshore. Joking that they could be in Worthing, he is about to return to the Ship to try again when he notices the lighthouse towering over the island and its inoperative lamp, so decides to call in, ostensibly to ask for directions but really out of curiosity. As he and Leela clamber over the rocks, the light comes on and a foghorn blares out mournfully. The Doctor presses on but Leela hangs back, sensing something dangerous.

A short while later she scouts the area around the lighthouse, hunting for whatever has killed the head keeper. She finds a rock pool with dead fish floating on the surface – electrocuted by the Rutan, which watches her from a distance. Leela hears it crackling but cannot find it and returns to the lighthouse, just as a yacht approaches the island at high speed and crashes on the craggy shore. The Doctor and two of the lighthouse crew head out over the rocks to help any survivors, returning with two gentlemen and a young lady. They are followed by the boat's coxswain, who has found the keeper's body floating in the sea.

As the newcomers recover, Leela shows the Doctor the pool of dead fish and he uses a compass to confirm there is a strong electrical field. They return to the lighthouse, unaware the Rutan is close by.

Some hours later the sun is beginning to rise as a Rutan mother ship approaches in response to its scout's distress call. The Doctor has converted the lighthouse's carbon arc lamp into an amplified carbon oscillator focused through a diamond. He activates it and then he and Leela – the only survivors of the Rutan's attack – run from the building and hide among the rocks. A high-power beam fires from the lamp when the ship comes into range, locks onto its carbon resonator knocking out its anti-gravity system and, with its energy shields lowered for landing, the crystalline vessel explodes. Against advice, Leela cannot resist watching and is temporarily blinded by the flash. Her sight soon returns but the pigment in her irises has been dispersed, turning them from brown to blue. The Doctor recites from Wilfred Gibson's poem 'Flannan Isle' as he leads her back to the TARDIS and it dematerialises.

- **LORE** The visual orientation circuits come into action during a landing. They can perhaps be incapacitated by weather conditions at the landing site, although the Doctor may be being flippant about this.
- **NOTES** Leela asks if the TARDIS "has failed again" as they haven't arrived where the Doctor expected. We haven't seen it land in an unintended place since she joined the Doctor, suggesting they've made further trips since Landing 131. Nevertheless, the Doctor notes how Leela saw ships on the Thames as if this was recently, and she is unfamiliar with spaceships other than the TARDIS.
- Although the Doctor mentions that "on Pharos" slaves were used "to keep the bonfires going", it's not implicit that he has visited the ancient lighthouse of Alexandria himself. If this was a previous journey, it could have been to the Egyptian city any time between the lighthouse's construction in the 3rd century BC and its abandonment in the early-1300s.
- Lord Palmerdale's yacht was heading from Deauville on the Normandy coast to Southampton, so Fang Rock is probably in the eastern reaches of the Solent, perhaps off the tip of the Isle of Wight (as the yacht approaches from the east). If so, it's even further west of Worthing than that is of Brighton, so the TARDIS really did get lost. The island is close enough to land for the use of semaphore, and perhaps within telescope view of a beach if Ben's teasing of Vince is plausible.
- The script doesn't indicate a precise date but BBC documentation places the story at the "turn of the century" and "in 1910". A suggestion that the king is currently Edward (VII) would put it between January 1901 and May 1910, and the last reported sighting of the Beast of Fang Rock "eighty year ago" (sic) was "back in the Twenties". Colonel Skinsale names "Salisbury [and] Bonar Law" as men who make him nervous; as he's comparing them to Lord Palmerdale, it's fair to assume he means Lord Salisbury (either the Third Marquess who was British Prime Minster from 1895 to 1902 and who died in August 1903 or, perhaps more likely, his son the Fourth Marquess, who was also a senior Parliamentarian and closer in age to Skinsale, whom he could have met during their army days). During the decade, Andrew Bonar Law was a Conservative MP for Glasgow then Dulwich, focused primarily on reforms to trade tariffs. The lighthouse has an "early Schermuly" (a reference added by Tom Baker during rehearsals). This was a safety device that fired a small rocket with a rope attached so ships in trouble near the coast can get a line ashore. It was invented in the 1890s by William Schermuly, a former sailor and fireman, with the first production model available by 1897 but not taken up by a shipping company until 1912. He did, however, spend the 1900s demonstrating his invention to potential buyers and made a few sales, so one could have ended up on Fang Rock.
- The TARDIS's arrival and departure are model shots using the miniature built for *The Hand of Fear*. It's position on a rocky ridge doesn't tally with the main prop's placing on the studio set of the island. When departing, the sound effect begins midway through.
- What was the Doctor hoping to show Leela in Brighton? He later claims in *The Leisure Hive* (Landing 182) to have twice "missed the opening of the Brighton Pavilion" (more correctly the Royal Pavilion) but this may not have been the first attempt. Assuming he means its opening to the public in either June 1850 when it was purchased from the Crown or January 1851 after some restoration work had been done, that would make this landing 50 years late. Yet he says to Leela, "We're on the right planet in the right time," which suggests he was aiming for the turn of the century. More likely, then, is a trip to Brighton in the early-1900s, possibly to visit the Palace Pier which had been opened in 1899 and quickly became a popular entertainment venue. Having recently missed seeing Little Tich, perhaps he was hoping to catch a young Charlie Chaplin, who performed on the pier as part of Fred Karno's troupe before he went to America.

IT'S BIGGER ON THE INSIDE

THE NEWBERY CLASSIC
1977-1980

Incoming producer Graham Williams decided a return to the traditional style of TARDIS control room better fitted the brighter tone he was instructed to bring to the series and, once more by chance, Barry Newbery was the designer on the first story for which the new set would be required, *The Invisible Enemy*. It had been less than a year since he created the previous control room, so rather than start entirely from scratch he took some of the ideas and even the walls from that set and reworked them.

Only three new walls were constructed. Two featured the familiar circles, using the same style of ridged fibreglass roundels designed for the 1976 set but now unpainted and pinned behind shallow circular cutouts. They also returned to a staggered arrangement although not as tightly interlocked as previous designs. Despite Newbery's previously expressed aversion to semicircles, these walls had 3½ columns of 4½ roundels each, creating for the first time a quarter-circle roundel. The two walls had their half-roundels on opposite sides so that when placed next to each other they formed a single roundel, although this required a joining piece – three strips of wood in a Y shape that supported the walls at a 120-degree angle – which diminished the effect.

The third new wall was for the main entrance doors, although the double doors themselves were the originals taken from storage (proved by their having the off-centre gap as seen way back in the pilot recording). As such, their circular indentations were larger and deeper than those of the new walls so these were each filled with a ring around two new-style translucent roundels stuck back to back, so they could be seen when the doors were closed or open. From the start of Season 17 in 1979 these were painted over. The doors were fitted into a newly constructed wall cut to accommodate their zigzag edges and given roundels down each side, although these too were painted so not translucent. Plans show there were to be two half-roundels above the doors but these were omitted and, oddly, there was a join between the main part of the wall and the flat upper section, running midway between the top of the doors and the horizontal strip above. This became weak over time and is clearly visible in *Destiny of the Daleks*. A new mechanism for opening the doors was installed, connected to the top pair of hinges where the workings could be more discreetly covered than the floor-level system of old. Beyond the doors was simply a black void (that is, a curtain) like the previous set – no longer would they lead directly to 'outside' scenery.

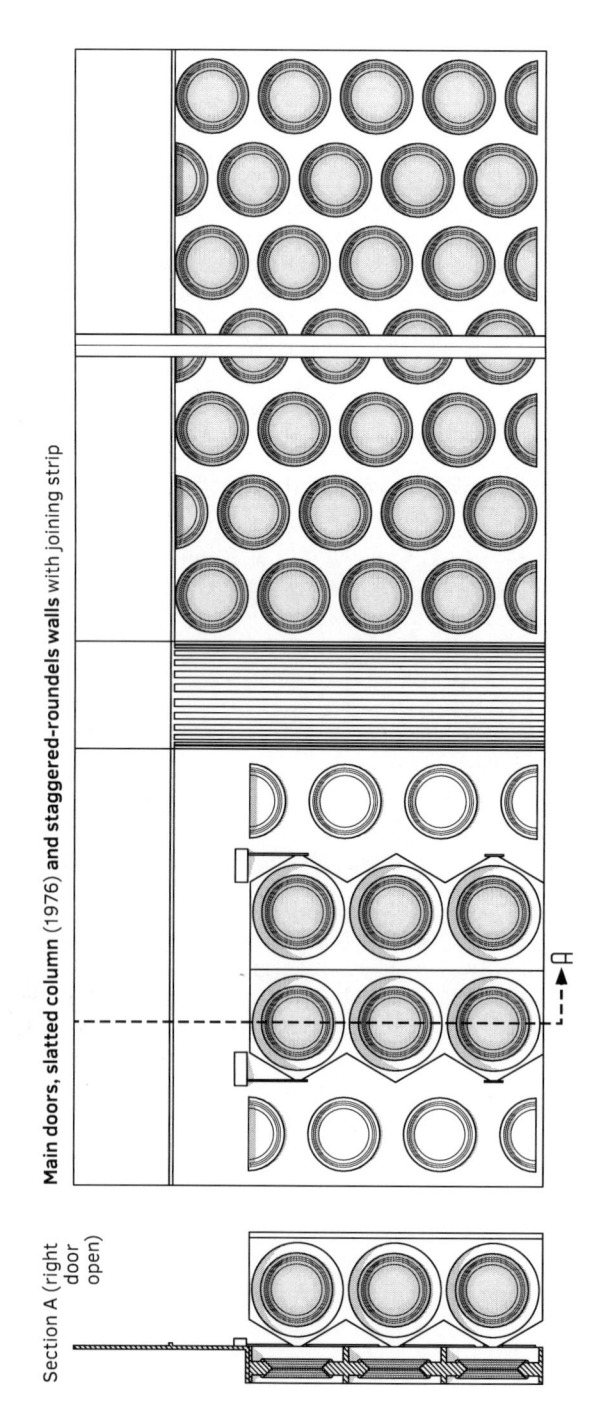

Main doors, slatted column (1976) and staggered-roundels walls with joining strip

Section A (right door open)

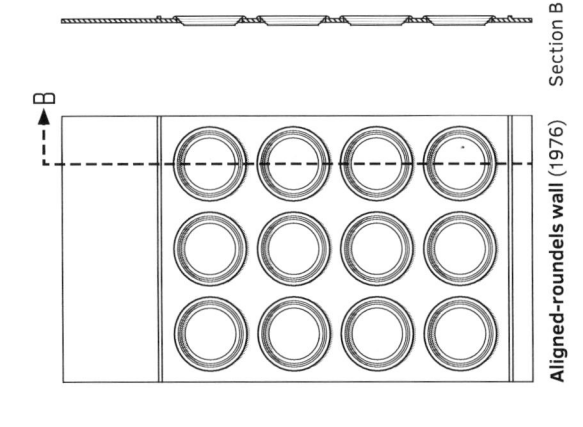

IT'S BIGGER ON THE INSIDE

Section B

Aligned-roundels wall (1976)

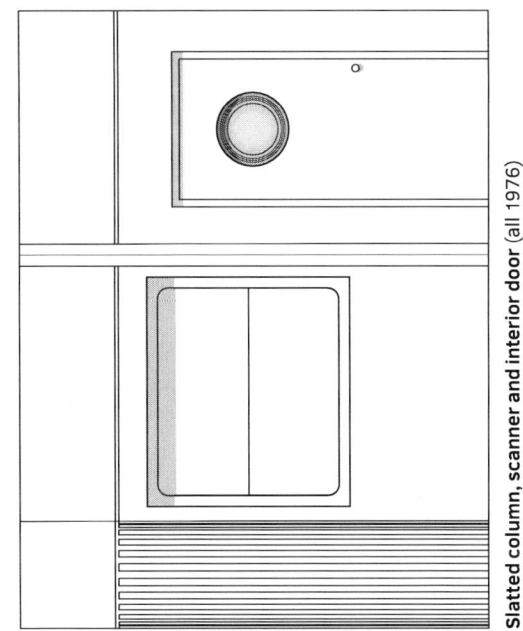

Slatted column, scanner and interior door (all 1976)

The scanner and interior door were from the previous set with all the mouldings removed and painted TV white like the new roundels walls. The scanner window was given a simpler shape with curved corners but retained the double shutters and their opening mechanism. The interior door now opened outwards from the control room, its stained glass replaced with a standard translucent roundel. Also retained were the two round slatted columns, again repainted. The walls were designed with edges that fitted between the battens on the columns so they could be positioned at various angles.

These walls were arranged in a semicircle with the main doors on the left, then a slatted column, the two roundels walls (with joining strip), the second column, the scanner, another joining strip, the interior door and a plain white flat on the extreme right to prevent the cameras accidentally showing the edge of the set (a second flat was required for some shots in *The Sun Makers* episode one). Occasionally for the same reason, one of the 1976 walls (with aligned rather than staggered roundels and repainted white) was positioned to the left of the main doors, more often behind the interior door to represent the corridor beyond, and during Season 17 to the right of the interior door instead of the plain flat.

This layout, with narrower walls at obtuse angles, created a more enclosed feel than the original 1960s set – almost cramped with the return of the larger console. The only furniture was the wooden Knossos chair and the coat stand from *The Robots of Death*, although the latter was swapped for a slimmer hatstand from *Underworld* (see page 208), after which the chair also disappeared.

The set arrangement remained remarkably consistent throughout its three years of use, making this the most uniform control room since the programme began. Only when recording episode one of *Image of the Fendahl* were the two staggered-roundels walls erected the wrong way round, so their half-roundels abutted the columns; this was rectified in the later recording of scenes for episode three. In *The Horns of Nimon* these two walls appear without their joining strip, presumably mislaid, while the strip between the scanner and interior door walls also disappeared from *Destiny of the Daleks* (so not including *The Creature from the Pit*, which was recorded first). Throughout Season 17 the coverings over the workings of the door mechanism were missing, revealing a slot and the head of the cam shaft attached to the hinges. Otherwise the set survived surprisingly well given it was featured in fourteen out of eighteen stories, and elements would be reused in the room's next incarnation.

IT'S BIGGER ON THE INSIDE

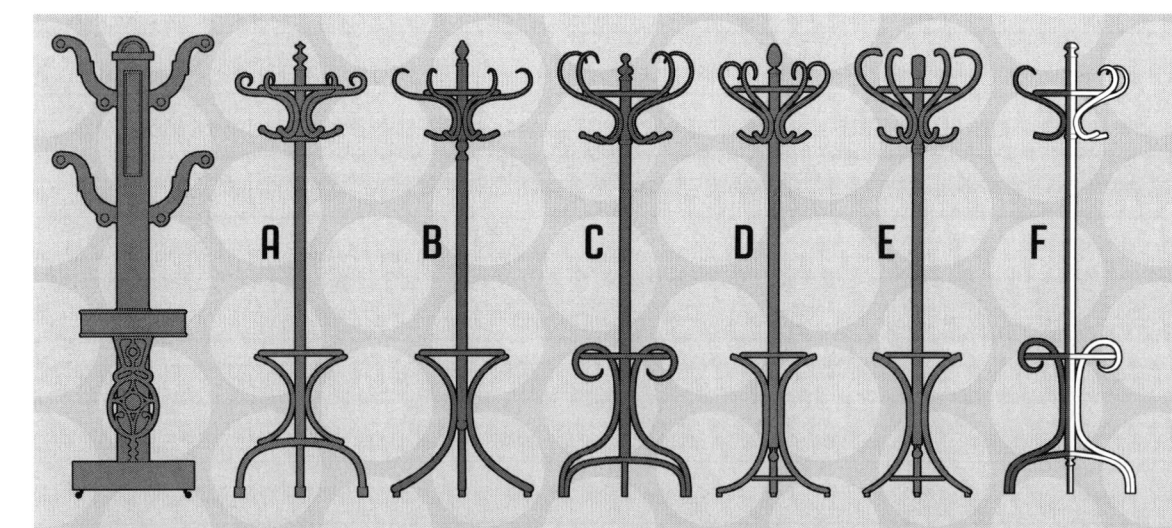

I WOULD LIKE A HAT(STAND) LIKE THAT

Although the Doctor had occasionally donned various forms of headgear, it was only in his fourth incarnation that he started customarily to wear a hat. Even then, it wasn't until Tom Baker's fourth year in the TARDIS that a hatstand became a fixture of the control room. Once introduced, a single hatstand stood in the corner until he gave it away on Frontios, right? Wrong.

We see Leela carrying a traditional bentwood-style hatstand into the newly refurbished control room at the start of *The Invisible Enemy*, but this wasn't the first time the Doctor's coat collection was seen hanging up. In *The Robots of Death* a wooden branched coat rack is seen holding the short red jacket with elbow patches worn throughout Season 12 and the mottled grey coat with dark collar and cuffs first seen in *The Android Invasion*. A similar rack, known as a hall tree, made a return in *Image of the Fendahl* and *The Sun Makers* (not quite the same one, missing the round mirror on its stem).

These and subsequent stories quickly make it apparent that there wasn't a consistent hatstand put aside for use on *Doctor Who* but that any one of no doubt many held by the BBC's props department would be selected at random. In fact, as we'll see, there's one episode in which two hatstands appear, changing between shots.

In *The Invisible Enemy*, although it's obscured by past coats and the Doctor's cape worn in *The Talons of Weng-Chiang*, the hatstand (**A**) has six shallow, tightly curled hooks supporting a wide hoop, with a second narrower one below. One notable feature is that two of the hooks are broken, with just the flat stems sticking out. It has a double bulb at the top and rather bandily arched legs.

After the brief return to a hall tree, a bentwood hatstand was back in *Underworld*. This one (**B**) had six loosely curled hooks, a single ridged bulb at the top of the stem plus a spherical one at the bottom between its splayed legs. Come *The Invasion of Time* and a third hatstand was used (**C**) with eight much larger, looser hooks, a droplet-shaped bulb and arched legs. These split, with the upper part curling around the umbrella holder.

Stand A returned for *The Ribos Operation* at the start of Season 16 but was replaced in the very next story by stand C (for the last time). Stand B was the back in *The Stones of Blood* and *The Armageddon Factor* then is seen no more, with no hatstand appearing in the control room in *The Androids of Tara* and we don't see inside the TARDIS in *The Power of Kroll*.

The Creature from the Pit was the first story into production for Season 17, for which a new hatstand was used (**D**). This had an egg-shaped bulb above six steeply sloping hooks. Its curved legs flattened where they joined the stem before splaying almost to the horizontal, and encircled an extra hoop at the base. Although initially looking very similar, the stand (**E**) in *The Horns of Nimon* had subtle differences. The splayed legs were more steeply and smoothly curved, the six hooks larger with flat rather than tapering tips, and the top of the stem ended with a thicker section but no bulb. In *Destiny of the Daleks*, recorded between these two stories, the hatstand is largely obscured by coats and a multi-coloured umbrella, but a glimpse of the legs suggests this was stand E rather than D. Neither was used again.

Production of Season 18 began with *State of Decay*, with stand A again being first choice. Next up was *Meglos* and, perhaps because the hatstand featured in the action of the repeating chronic hysteresis, a new one was chosen (**F**). This was similar to stand C but with just four smaller hooks, a flattened bulb at the top of the stem and a doorknob-shaped one at the bottom. It was retained for *Full Circle* and, initially, *Warriors' Gate*. However, the latter serial's TARDIS scenes had to be split across two days' recording when director Paul Joyce ran out of time to complete them in one session. For the second day stand

IT'S BIGGER ON THE INSIDE

F was replaced with stand A, so after Biroc commandeers the TARDIS the hatstand suddenly transforms (although the items of clothing hanging on it remain the same). Continuity was maintained for *The Keeper of Traken*, however, which used stand A again but by *Logopolis* the Doctor had reverted to stand F.

The start of 1982 saw a new season, new Doctor and another new hatstand. *Four to Doomsday*, Season 19's first serial into the studio, introduced what almost becomes the first consistent TARDIS hatstand (**G**). The stem had conical bulbs at top and bottom, six (for now) loosely curled hooks surrounded the upper hoop, while the lower hoop encased the tops of the splayed legs rather than resting on them. The legs also had flat ends rather than feet. Stand G was used throughout most of this season and the next, but not exclusively. Stand F popped up again in *The Visitation*, and stand A in *Time-Flight* (its last appearance). In *Castrovalva* there's no hatstand in the control room but the Doctor finds one in a corridor holding his new coat. This was another new stand (**H**) with an acorn-shaped bulb, six tightly curled hooks, and arched legs that curled round the umbrella holder.

The beginning of Season 20 briefly saw a ninth hatstand used (**I**), similar to stand B but with six larger, more steeply angled hooks, spherical bulbs at top and bottom of the stem, and an additional hoop lower down the splayed legs. This appeared in *Arc of Infinity* and *Snakedance* before stand G returned for the rest of the season. One of its hooks had snapped off prior to *Earthshock*, and by *Mawdryn Undead* it had lost a second, before the stand bowed out in *The King's Demons*.

The Five Doctors saw the first white hatstand but this was simply stand F repainted and with extra hooks added, taking it from four to eight. Yet even though the demise of the TARDIS hatstand was already being planned, this refreshed model couldn't make it to the end and was seen no more. *Warriors of the Deep* featured no hatstand, and in *The Awakening* stand I was painted the same grey as the walls as if camouflaged. *Frontios*, of course, gave the hatstand a glorious swansong. Yet in a snub to previous models, this was yet another new stand (**J**), presumably chosen to be more convincing when wielded as a weapon. It had a ribbed bulb similar to stand B's, six very shallow, tightly curled hooks (although one was already snapped off) with the hoop below rather than above them, and no umbrella holder but a base hoop between the splayed legs. Curiously it also had five heart shapes painted along the stem, a send-off from the production team?

While the Doctor's sixth incarnation mostly eschewed headwear, his seventh regained his fondness for wearing a Panama so the control room regained a hatstand for a while, but none as we'd seen before. In *Paradise Towers* the stand (**K**) was a cluster of five chrome tubes curved over at the tops and formed into circular hooks. Very 1980s. This was replaced in the last two stories of Season 24 by a simpler stand (**L**) of four white metal stems bent over at top and bottom to form hooks and feet, each with a further bracket on the stem. This is seen on-screen in *Dragonfire* but also features in a cut scene from *Delta and the Bannermen*, the TARDIS scenes for both stories being recorded on the same day. The innovation in Season 25's sole TARDIS scene in *The Greatest Show in the Galaxy* was that the hatstand became just the upper crown section suspended from a coiled cord (**M**). The short stem was intricately turned and the six flat hooks ended in bars.

The 20th-century series' final control room scene was in *Battlefield*, when the lighting was turned way down to disguise the fact the walls were not the regular set. Yet careful viewing reveals a hatstand was still considered a necessary part of the dressing. It's too dark to be sure but close examination suggests this was stand J as it has the horizontal hooks with hoop underneath and the same pinch in the stem just below. If so, then the Doctor was correct when he said in *Frontios* it was one of a pair.

WHAT ARE ALL THESE KNOBS?

CONSOLE Cii
1977-1982

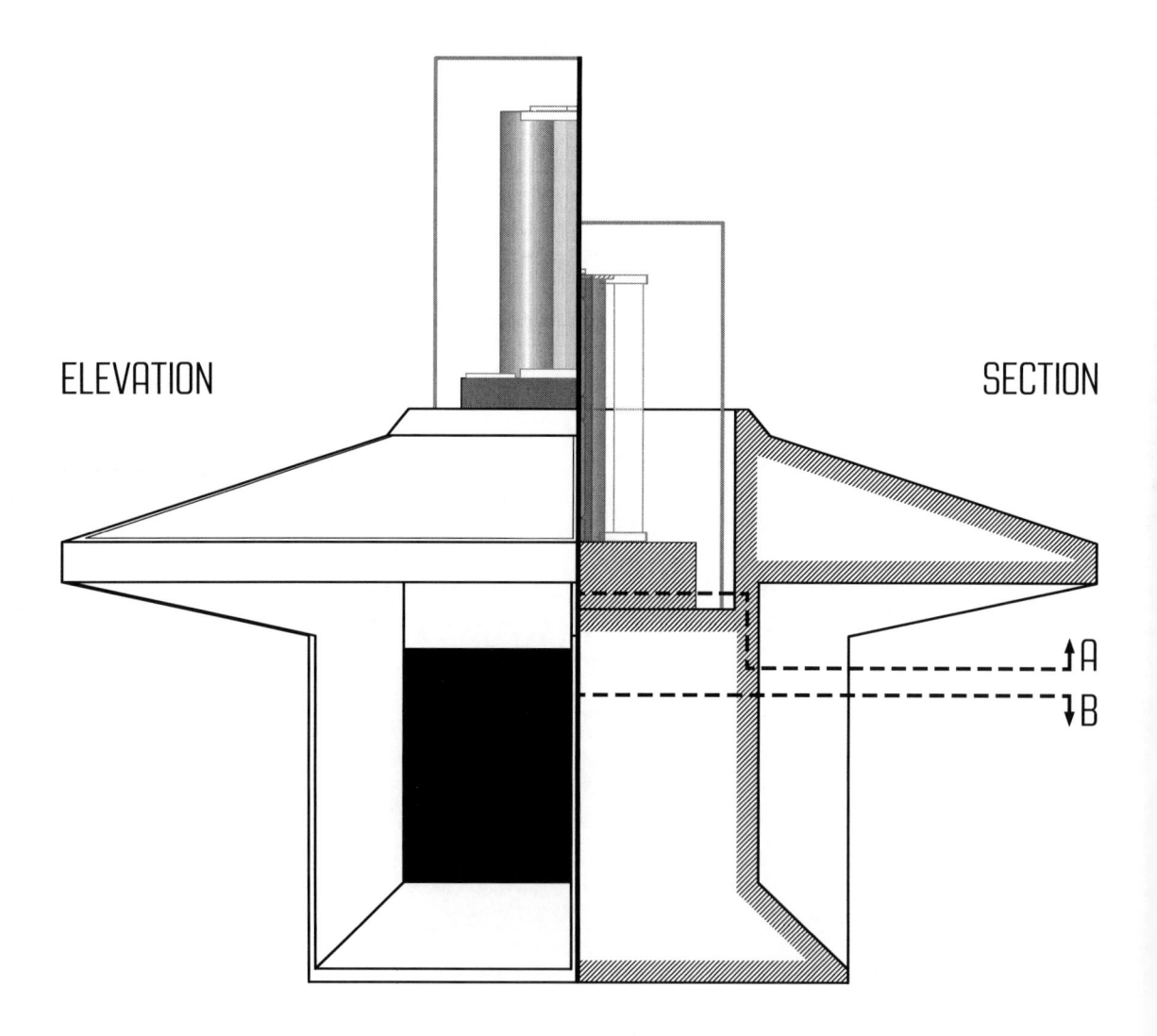

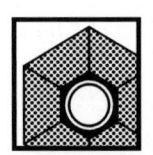

ELEVATION

SECTION

↑A
↓B

With the return to a traditional white-walled control room for Season 15 in 1977, the old console also made a comeback, having fortunately been kept in storage for the past 21 months. This was the one built for Season 8 in 1971 but with new control panels added for its previous, brief appearances in Season 13. The prop understandably required a bit of refurbishment and this went beyond a fresh coat of paint.

The pedestal kept its off-white colour except for the recessed faces between the fins, which were painted black for the first time. They also had their handles removed. The panels and collar were painted a pale grey (with the top of the collar a darker grey), perhaps to give them a more metallic appearance, despite most controls already being on metal plates screwed to the wooden panels. The metal strip around the rim also remained. One notable change was the loss of the tapered dividers between each panel, whether through choice, damage or loss. As a consequence, the internal wooden supports for the control panels were now visible so red tape was applied along these and the edges of the collar. The column itself was unchanged although the mechanism to make it oscillate was probably overhauled.

The controls were largely as had been created for Season 13 but with a few differences. Only panel 5 had

WHAT ARE ALL THESE KNOBS?

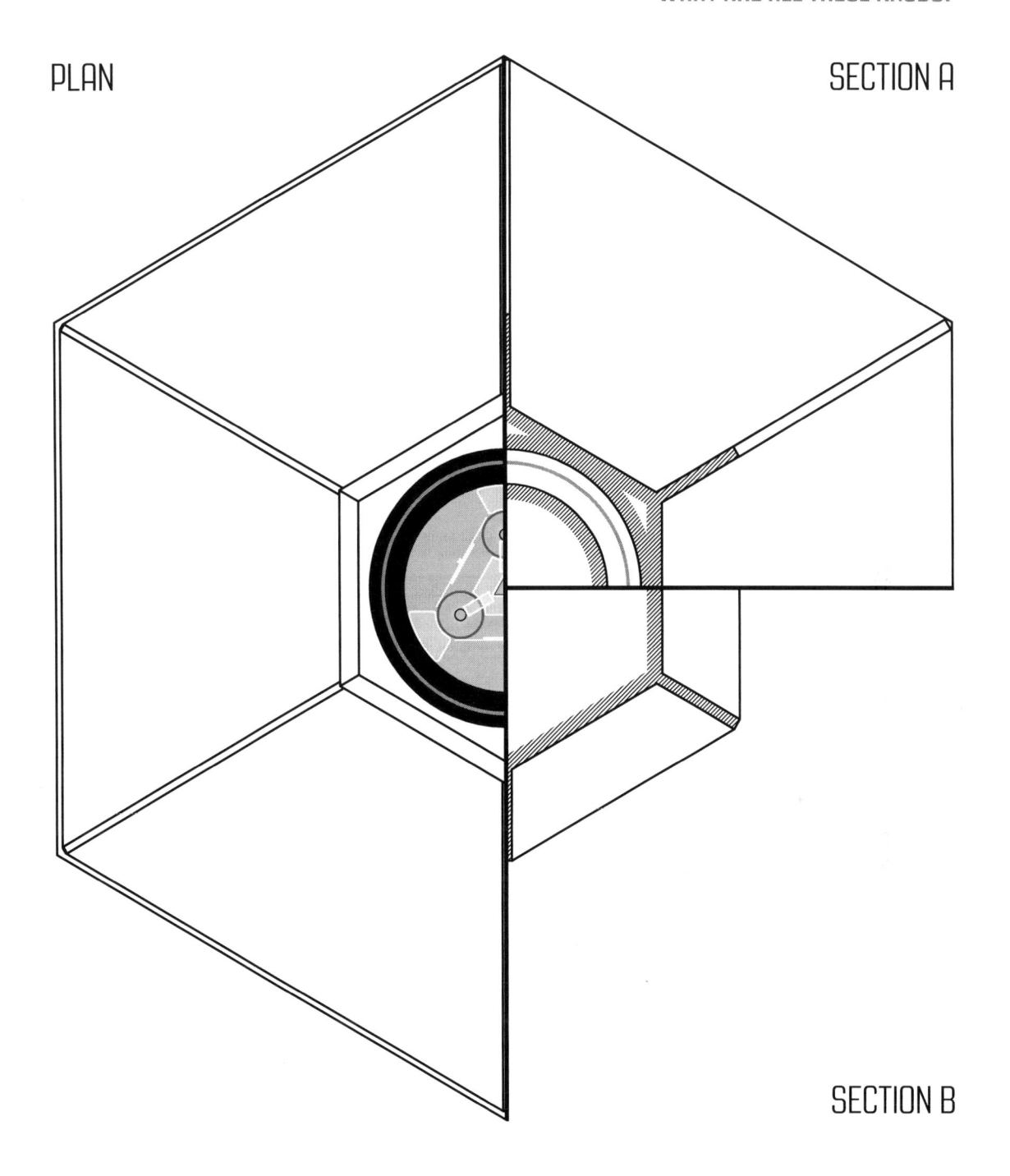

PLAN

SECTION A

SECTION B

a new arrangement of its controls. This lost the two small metal plates at the bottom and the strip of lights was moved down in their place, with the keypad-like block moved up and centred in the gap. Some of the black controls above this (actually fixed wooden pieces rather than operable buttons) were repainted to add a bit of colour, and the red dome on the right lost its cowl and the white disc that had crowned it.

Changes to the other panels were more subtle. Panel 1 lost its black buttons on the upper plate, replaced with a small grey grille. On the plates below, either side of the central large slider, the black switches kept from Console B were swapped for simple black strips of plastic with upturned edges. The dial on the left plate was moved to the right replacing the cowled red button and in its place was a square gauge similar to ones on Console B. The domed lights down each side of the panel were removed and flat blue and green discs added

WHAT ARE ALL THESE KNOBS?

instead (although not quite in the same positions), with strips of red tape between them.

Panel 2 lost the translucent hood in the centre and the two dials either side were painted black instead of silver. In contrast, the row of switches below was given some colour and the silver dome in the bottom-left corner was painted black, while that on the right was replaced with a large red button. This bottom plate was reattached upside down as the black sliding switches moved from the bottom to the top, now with two additional pushbuttons below them, and in the middle was a brass grille in place of the red one taken from Console B.

Panel 3 was essentially unchanged, while the main change to panel 4 was to replace the clear dome centre-left with an illuminated disc held on by a black ring with six raised fixings. The three black switches from Console B were again replaced with simpler black strips. Lastly, panel 6 lost the hood above its display screen and the row of black buttons beneath it. Two flick switches were added in the top-left corner and the rubber base of the silver lever at bottom-right became black.

When the new panels were created not much attention was paid to what order they should be positioned on the pedestal, and their arrangement differs in the console's two appearances in Season 13. Now they were to be used more regularly, small tally marks were placed at the top of each panel and around the bottom edge of the collar so they could be easily matched. Although the console might be rotated so different panels faced the camera, their order around the console stayed the same for most of the next four seasons. The only exceptions were in *Underworld* and *The Invasion of Time*, when panels 3 and 5 were swapped, due either to the director's preference or simple carelessness.

While the basic layout of the console remained the same throughout its use until 1983, its decoration was tweaked almost every year. It generally got a fresh coat of paint at the start of each season and any controls that had been knocked off would be replaced. More obvious changes were made when scripts called for specific controls, most notably the additions (sometimes temporarily) of the randomiser in *The Armageddon Factor*, the emergency transceiver in *The Creature from the Pit*, the records print-out in *State of Decay*, the chameleon circuit programmer in *Logopolis* and the Information System in *Castrovalva* (see pages 236, 264 and 286).

WHAT ARE ALL THESE KNOBS?

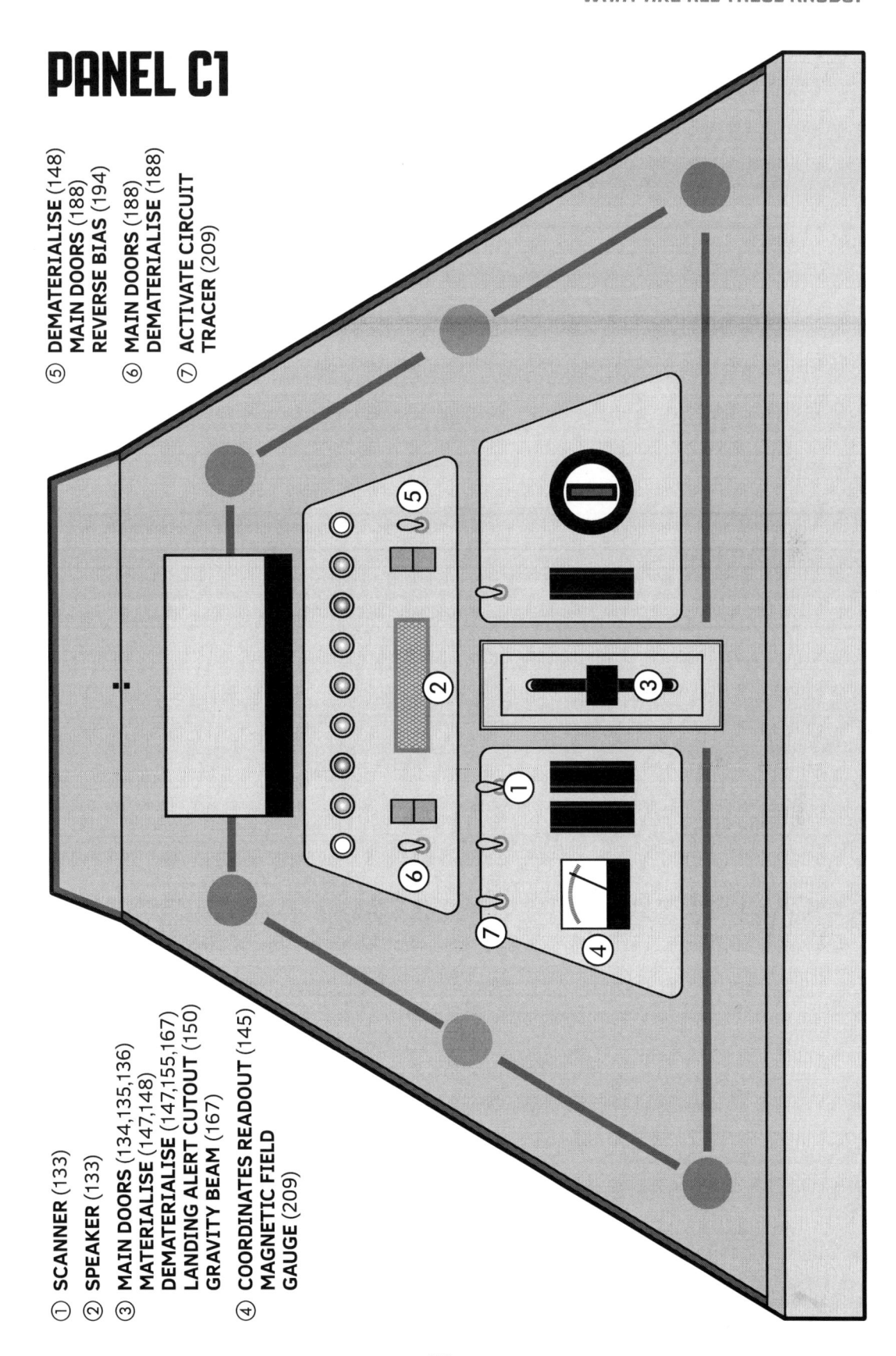

PANEL C1

① **SCANNER** (133)
② **SPEAKER** (133)
③ **MAIN DOORS** (134,135,136)
   MATERIALISE (147,148)
   DEMATERIALISE (147,155,167)
   LANDING ALERT CUTOUT (150)
   GRAVITY BEAM (167)
④ **COORDINATES READOUT** (145)
   MAGNETIC FIELD GAUGE (209)
⑤ **DEMATERIALISE** (148)
   MAIN DOORS (188)
   REVERSE BIAS (194)
⑥ **MAIN DOORS** (188)
   DEMATERIALISE (188)
⑦ **ACTIVATE CIRCUIT TRACER** (209)

WHAT ARE ALL THESE KNOBS?

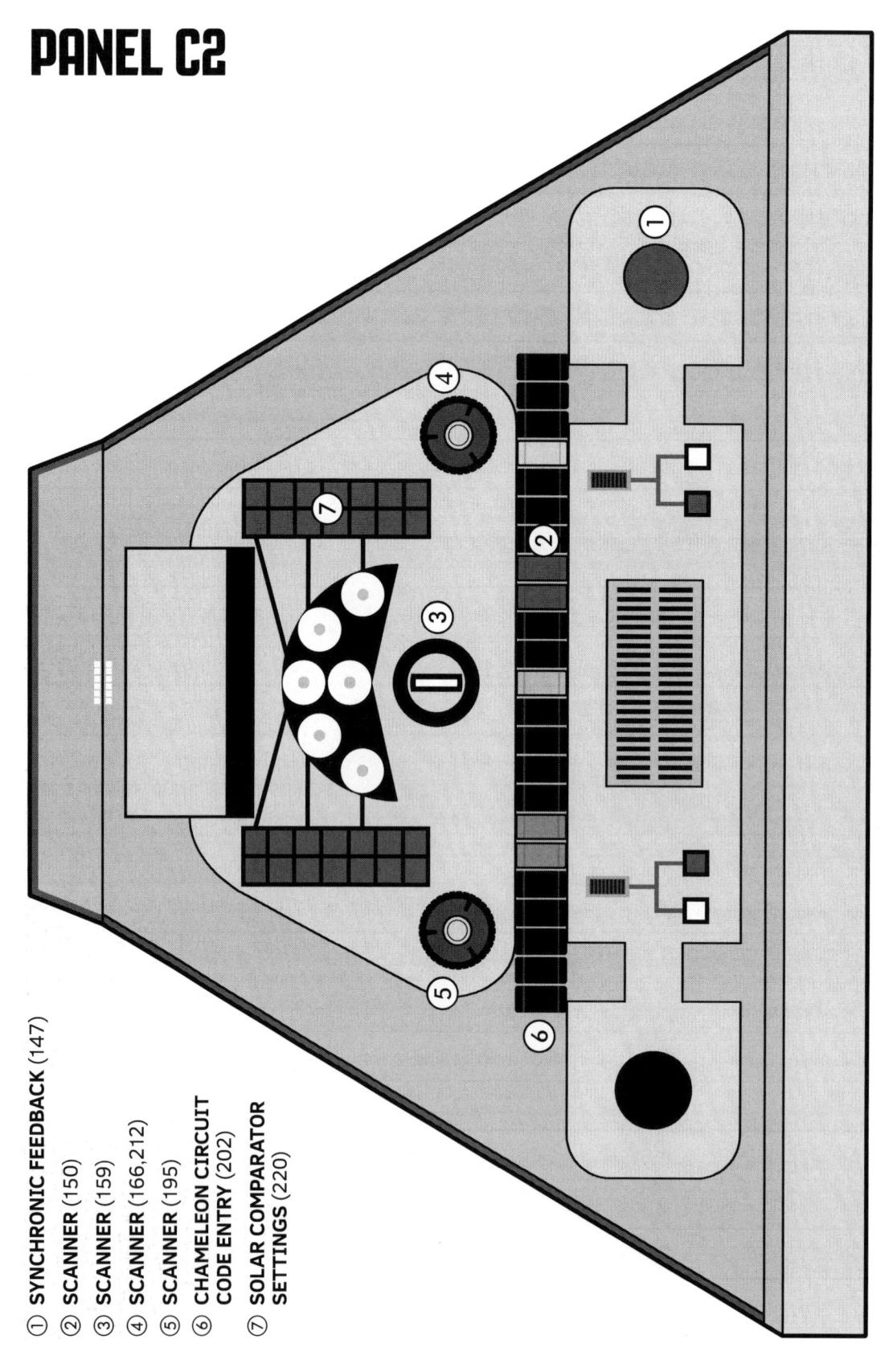

PANEL C2

1. **SYNCHRONIC FEEDBACK** (147)
2. **SCANNER** (150)
3. **SCANNER** (159)
4. **SCANNER** (166, 212)
5. **SCANNER** (195)
6. **CHAMELEON CIRCUIT CODE ENTRY** (202)
7. **SOLAR COMPARATOR SETTINGS** (220)

WHAT ARE ALL THESE KNOBS?

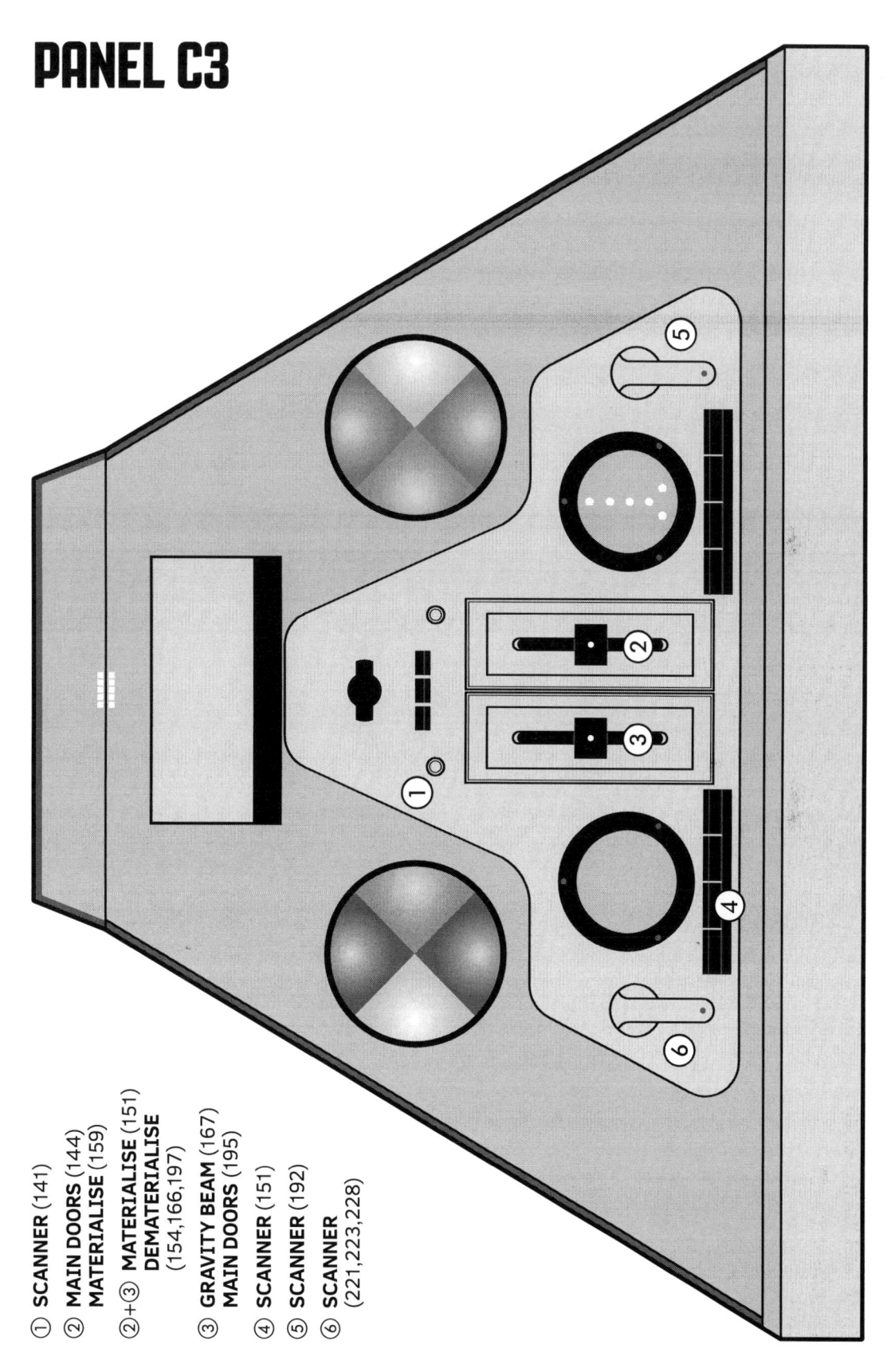

PANEL C3

① **SCANNER** (141)
② **MAIN DOORS** (144) **MATERIALISE** (159)
②+③ **MATERIALISE** (151) **DEMATERIALISE** (154,166,197)
③ **GRAVITY BEAM** (167) **MAIN DOORS** (195)
④ **SCANNER** (151)
⑤ **SCANNER** (192)
⑥ **SCANNER** (221,223,228)

WHAT ARE ALL THESE KNOBS?

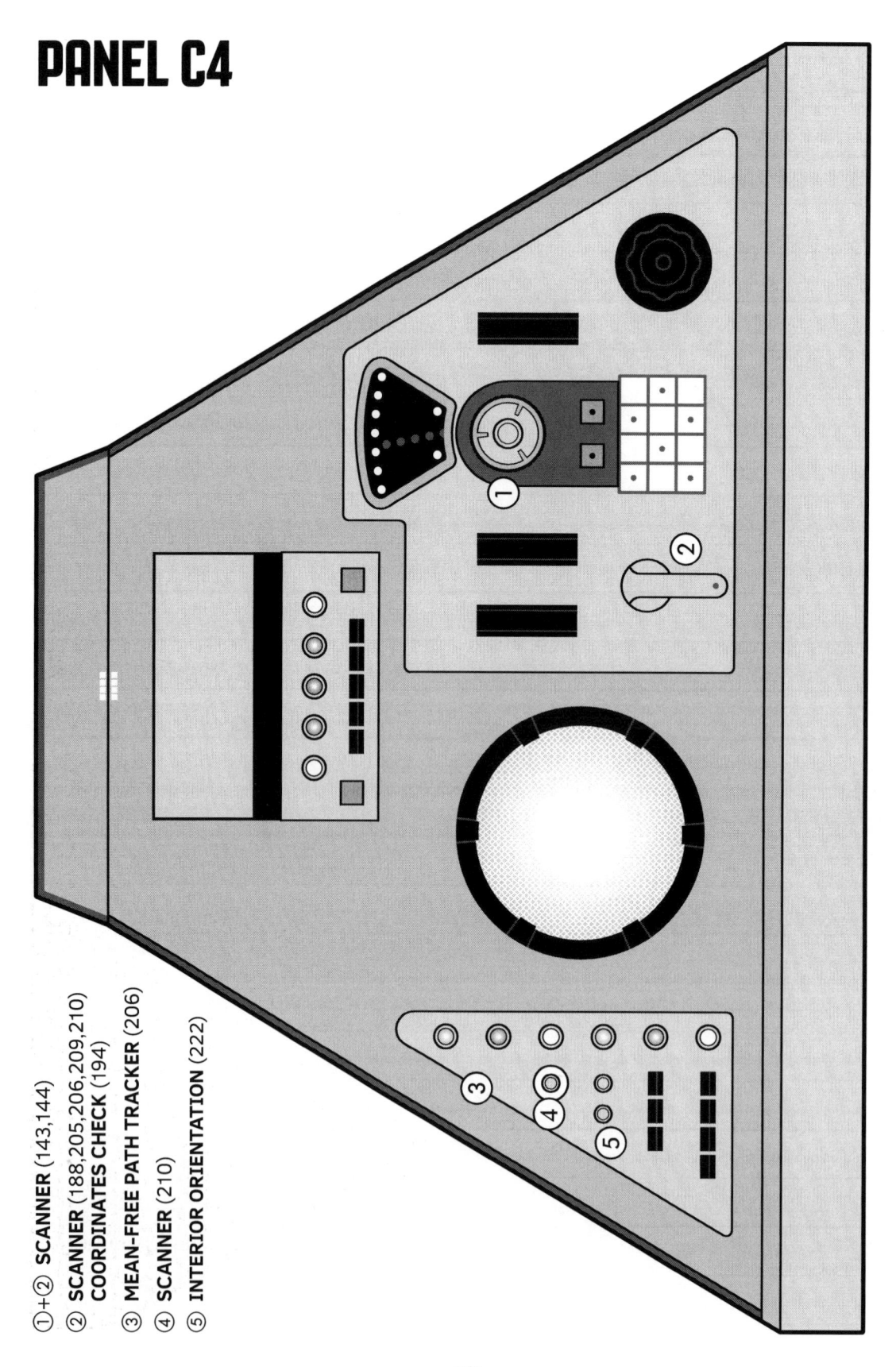

PANEL C4

① + ② **SCANNER** (143,144)
② **SCANNER** (188,205,206,209,210) **COORDINATES CHECK** (194)
③ **MEAN-FREE PATH TRACKER** (206)
④ **SCANNER** (210)
⑤ **INTERIOR ORIENTATION** (222)

PANEL C5

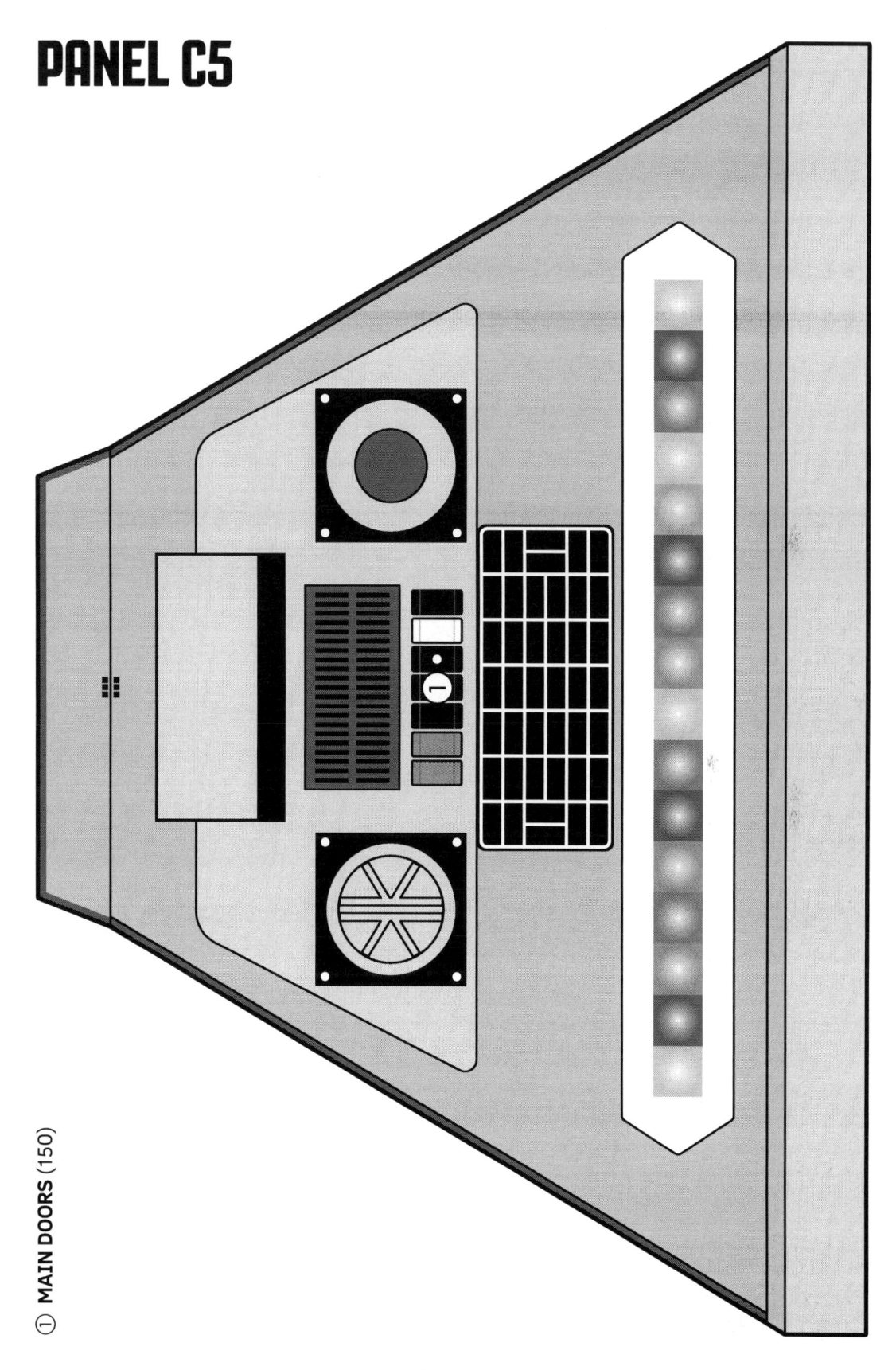

WHAT ARE ALL THESE KNOBS?

① **MAIN DOORS** (150)

WHAT ARE ALL THESE KNOBS?

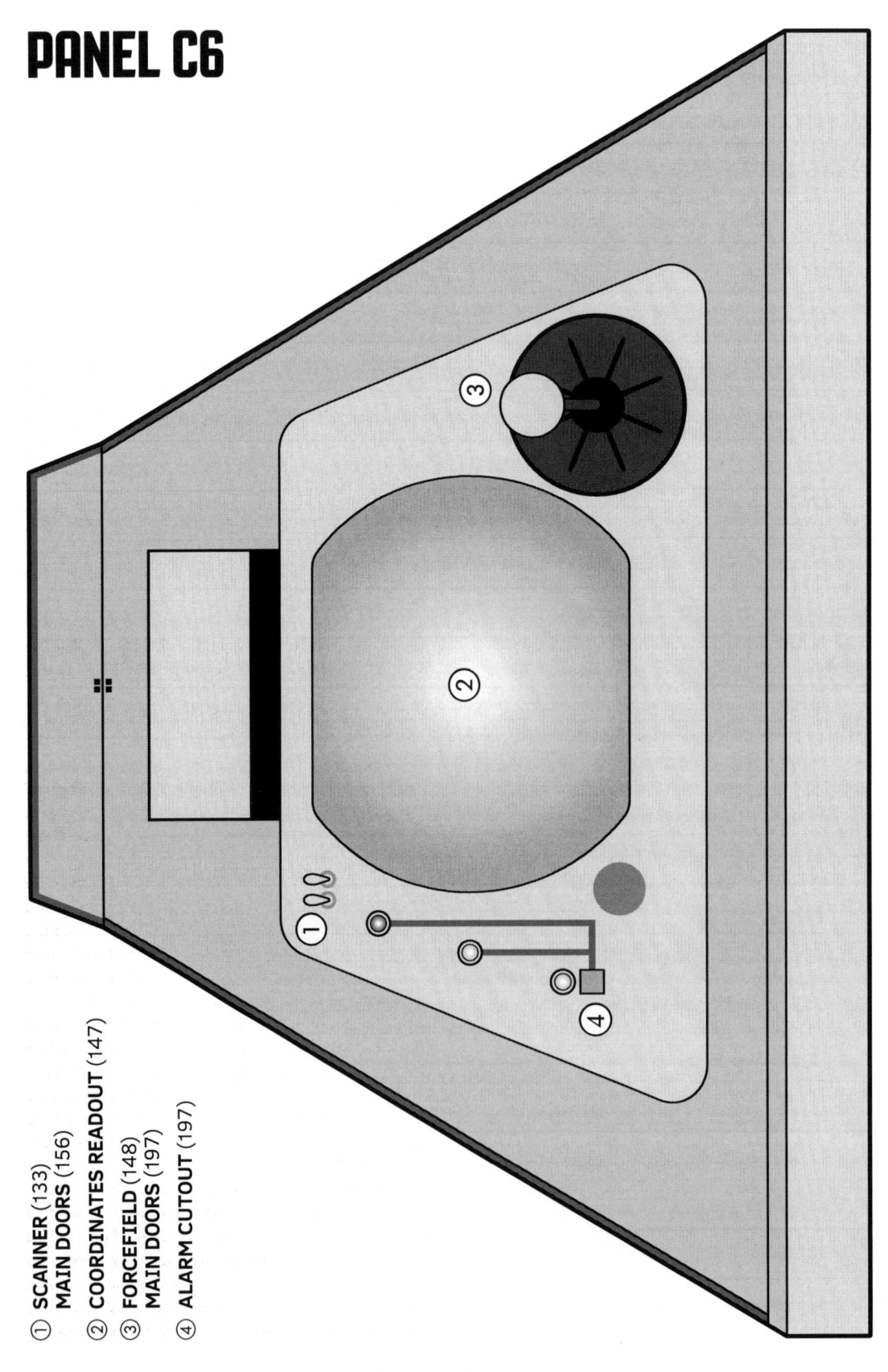

PANEL C6

① **SCANNER** (133)
   MAIN DOORS (156)
② **COORDINATES READOUT** (147)
③ **FORCEFIELD** (148)
   MAIN DOORS (197)
④ **ALARM CUTOUT** (197)

LANDING 133

SPACE Space, Solar System, between Jupiter and Saturn
TIME About 5000
TRAVELLERS The Doctor, Leela
EPISODES The Invisible Enemy 1

Leela helps the Doctor move furniture back into the primary control room, which he has decided to start reusing – even though he professes not to like the colour of the walls, preferring something in blue or aquamarine. Perhaps to test the console, he makes a random landing in space, materialising in the region of Saturn around the year 5000, which is still before Leela's time. He tells her this is when humans began venturing into the further reaches of the Solar System.

They tarry awhile as the Doctor tinkers with the console [reacquainting himself with the controls] and Leela practices writing her name on a blackboard. Just as the Doctor promises to take them "somewhere really interesting" the Ship picks up a mayday call from a manned base on Titan, Saturn's largest moon. The Doctor hurriedly sets the coordinates but before he can implement them another message is received from Titan claiming the emergency is over. Leela is troubled, however, sensing evil and declaring the second voice was not a human speaking.

As the TARDIS moves towards Titan it drifts through a cloud of organic matter that bombards it with energy pulses, attracted by the Ship's mental activity. Inside, the Doctor is at the console checking the computer for static build-up when a component explodes and he is bathed in a purple glow. He feels nothing and dismisses it, but when the element sparks again he examines it more closely and is struck by a burst of the organic energy. He is momentarily disoriented before falling to the floor unconscious.

CONTROLS The Doctor knocks the silver lever on panel C6, the two black sliding switches at the bottom of panel C2, then the three flick switches at bottom-left of panel C1. As he discusses the room's colour, he pushes the large slider on panel C1 up after pressing some switches above it and twists the dial to its right – this possibly materialises the Ship. He operates the scanner from the same panel, seemingly with the flick switch immediately to the left of the large slider, then moves this back down as he turns to look at the screen. He appears to close the scanner with a switch at top-left of panel C6, however. As he talks about humanity's future he turns the right-hand dial on panel C2 repeatedly. He does so again when the distress call is received as well as, on panel C1, flicking a switch, moving the large slider down from mid position and turning the bottom-right dial. The voice emanates from the same panel, probably the grille on the upper plate. When setting coordinates he turns all three dials on panel C2 then unseen switches on panel C1. The block at the top of this panel is flipped open just before something in the space beneath it explodes, and it's from here that the Swarm's bolt emanates and infects the Doctor.

LORE The TARDIS can receive audio [radio] transmissions and relay them via the console rather than the scanner.

The Ship's computers exhibit mental activity similar to an organic brain.

NOTES "Between Jupiter and Saturn" would put the TARDIS about 500 million to 900 million miles away from the Sun. The distress call from Titan takes 30 minutes to reach it, indicating the Ship is some 335 million miles away from the moon. Yet without moving the TARDIS is caught in the same virus cloud as the shuttle on approach to Titan; the cloud is either very big or can move very fast.

The Doctor, seemingly reading from the console, says the date is "about five thousand AD". According to *The Talons on Weng-Chiang*, in this period the Earth is in the grip of an Ice Age, which might be what spurs mankind to go "leapfrogging across the Solar System", although in the earlier story he also says this was "a scientific dark age". He could just be talking about specific applications like catalytic extraction and zygma energy, as the technology on Titan and at Bi-Al seems advanced enough – and Professor Marius is able to create K9. In earlier times humans were travelling to other planets and had an empire, such as in *Frontier in Space* and *The Mutants*, so it seems that after the retrenchment suggested by the latter story mankind retreated to Earth, lost some knowledge, went down a few blind alleys trying to regain it, but eventually was able to venture back into the wider galaxy. Magnus Greel's bid for power may have been short-lived, while narrowly avoiding another world war perhaps encouraged the various alliances to work together towards a brighter future.

The Doctor calls this the "number two control room", presumably picking up on his line in *The Masque of Mandragora* on rediscovering the second control room: "I could run the TARDIS just as easily from here as I could from the old one. Come to think of it, this was the old one." His comment that computers have no imagination and think only in black and white would seem to confirm that the TARDIS itself has done the redecorating, rather than the Doctor programming it to. In later life it will be more adventurous in its control room decor, including the use of blue.

It's not entirely clear whether the Doctor or the Ship itself chooses to materialise. He operates controls while talking to Leela but there is a pause before the central column stops. It's almost as if the TARDIS takes offence at the Doctor's insult about its lack of imagination and so comes to a halt. This might be why the column stays in its upright position.

The hatstand Leela brings into the control room is the first of a surprisingly long line of bentwood-style stands the Doctor will use (see page 208). The wooden Knossos chair is already in the room (are there two or has the Doctor brought it from the second control room? Leela can't have done it as this is the first time she's seen this control room). The Doctor is wearing his grey coat and all of the previous ones worn by this incarnation are on the stand: the red jacket from Season 12, the dark coat first worn in *Pyramids of Mars*, and his jacket, Inverness cape and deerstalker donned in *The Talons of Weng-Chiang*.

▪ The hum that plays while the TARDIS is in flight and winds down when it materialises is a higher pitch than the similar hum in *Death to the Daleks* (Landing 100) but could be the same effect speeded up. The scanner opens with a different sound effect to that used for the second control room the previous year (although that will become the norm in later series).

▪ The shot of the TARDIS being attacked by the Swarm cloud uses the model Police Box built for *Pyramids of Mars* – note the white 'Police telephone' plaque. Although this shows the TARDIS spinning it must still be in normal space in order to pass through the cloud. The last time the Ship was penetrated while in flight was by Sutekh's immense mental force (see Landing 113) and while the Swarm isn't portrayed as being as powerful as he was, the facts its energy can penetrate the TARDIS at all and it infects people's minds suggests the Ship is vulnerable to this type of force – see also Landings 14 and 56.

▪ When giving the coordinates for the base on Titan – quadrant 62, WHI1212 9990 EX41 – Tom Baker strays only slightly from the scripted 'W.H.I. 1,2,1,2 Ex 9990 Quadrant 6T'. As this includes the phone number for Scotland Yard, writers Bob Baker and Dave Martin had presumably noted Baker's substitution in their previous script, *The Hand of Fear* (Landing 125), and pre-empted him.

LANDING 134

SPACE Titan, refuelling base, corridor
TIME As above
TRAVELLERS The Doctor, Leela
EPISODES The Invisible Enemy 1-2

As the Doctor lies unconscious, the TARDIS relocates as programmed to the base on Titan. It materialises beside an airlock, watched from outside the base by Supervisor Lowe in a spacesuit. Three other humans, infected by the Swarm virus, approach and wait for the Doctor, whose brain now hosts the Nucleus of the Swarm.

Inside the TARDIS, the Swarm tries to infect Leela as well but she proves immune to it. The Doctor wakes up but is confused and disoriented, sensing there is something in his head. Dismissing it, he prepares to go out to respond to the mayday but Leela closes the doors and insists there is something evil outside and that he has been affected.

As the Doctor tries to persuade her he is all right, Lowe re-enters the base to arrest the three infected men. A gunfight breaks out in which one of the Swarm's carriers is killed and the other two chase the fleeing Lowe. The Doctor peers out the TARDIS door checking for danger and emerges when he sees there is no one there, followed by Leela wielding her knife. They find the dead body and the Doctor tells Leela to stay by the TARDIS while he investigates, but unafraid she heads off in a different direction.

Contact with the other infected crewmen strengthens the power of the Nucleus over the Doctor's mind and they give him a gun and instruct him to kill Leela. He calls to her from the corridor where the TARDIS has landed, trying to lure her into the open, but when he has her in his sights he is able to resist the Nucleus and warn her. To fight the invader in his mind, the Doctor puts himself into a trance after telling Leela he needs help. She seeks Lowe's assistance – unaware he has now also been infected by the Swarm – who suggests taking the Doctor to the Centre for Alien Biomorphology. They both help the Doctor into the TARDIS and set the coordinates he gives them.

◉ CONTROLS The Doctor opens the main doors with the large slider on panel C1. Leela closes them with an unseen control on panel C2 (possibly the centre dial) but then keeps her hands over the two large sliders on panel C3 to prevent the Doctor from leaving.

▪ **NOTES** Who lands the TARDIS? After setting the coordinates, the Doctor isn't seen to operate any further controls before he's attacked by the Swarm and collapses, and the central column stays stationary throughout. However, the Police Box is spinning when it passes through the Swarm cloud. We must assume, therefore, that the Doctor does set the Ship in motion (unseen after Leela expresses her suspicions about the second message) but because he doesn't want to move in time he just shifts the TARDIS in space. The central column doesn't move because the Ship isn't in full flight, it's affected by the damage caused to the console by the Swarm or it's just being temperamental (or the production team forgot to switch it on).

▪ The doors open with a warbling sound effect, although not quite the same as the more familiar one from later years and the 1978 *Doctor Who Sound Effects* LP.

▪ For the first time, there is only blackness beyond the open main doors. This is how the doorway was represented on the second control room set, which had no doors of course, whereas previously the double doors led directly to whatever was outside (with the occasional suggestion of a short corridor). The black interspace will become the norm from now on, although future producer John Nathan-Turner will later insist that the camera never shows the immediate view through the doors.

▪ Now the Doctor is using a control room with entrance doors again, it's not clear if these are connected to the exterior Police Box door. Here the latter opens and slams shut as the interior doors are operated. Moments later, however, when the Doctor emerges he clearly opens the door himself. More often than not we'll see the interior doors open, then the exterior door open separately as an actor steps out. However, some connection between inner and outer doors is still implied, notably whenever K9 leaves the TARDIS as he's unable to pull open the Police Box door himself.

LANDING 135

SPACE Solar System, asteroid belt, Asteroid K4067, Bi-Al Senta, resepshun
TIME As above
TRAVELLERS The Doctor, Leela, Lowe
EPISODES The Invisible Enemy 2,4

The TARDIS arrives in the reception hall on level X2 at the Bi-Al Senta. The comatose Doctor is secured to a gurney and taken to level X4 for examination by Professor Marius, the centre's specialist in extraterrestrial pathological endomorphisms, while Leela registers his arrival with the receptionist. She soon tires of waiting for news, however, and makes her way to Marius's isolation ward.

Marius plans to operate on the Doctor so the Swarm in space, sensing danger to its Nucleus, infects the crew of a nearby shuttle and has them crash it into the Bi-Al asteroid, demolishing the level between the TARDIS and the isolation ward. Nevertheless, not long after the crash, a short-lived clone of the Doctor makes his way back to the Ship and disconnects the relative dimensional stabiliser, planning to use it to shrink himself and a clone of Leela so they can be injected into the Doctor's body.

The microscopic Nucleus from the Doctor's mind is magnified by the stabiliser and its lackeys bring it to the airlock by reception. Marius is left to infect more staff while Lowe takes the Nucleus back to Titan in a medical shuttle. Leela and the now-uninfected Doctor take refuge with K9 in the immobilised TARDIS. K9 stuns the professor so the Doctor can recover the dimensional stabiliser.

The Doctor has isolated the antibodies that Leela's clone passed on to him and used them to cure Marius. They return to the TARDIS with a batch of the antidote and the Doctor reconnects the dimensional stabiliser. Before departing for Titan, he asks if he can take K9 with him and Marius agrees.

- **CONTROLS** The Doctor again opens the doors with the centre large slider on panel C1.
- **LORE** The relative dimensional stabiliser, a briefcase-sized box with a black control panel, is part of the TARDIS control system. It allows dimensional barriers to be crossed. The Ship can't travel anywhere without it.
- **NOTES** Who pilots the TARDIS? Although the Doctor revives enough to give the coordinates – vector 19, quadrant 3, 743800 (Tom Baker again adding the BBC's phone number to the scripted dialogue; see Landing 125) – he's otherwise withdrawn in order to fight off the Nucleus in his mind. It's unlikely Leela could programme and activate the Ship despite having seen the Doctor do so, particularly as she's now working with an unfamiliar console (although see Landing 141). It's possible that Lowe does so, using knowledge from the Doctor that the Swarm has accessed, but this would surely raise Leela's suspicions. As the Swarm does nothing to stop its host being taken to the Bi-Al Senta, recognising the opportunity to infect more people, perhaps it loosens its grip on the Doctor's mind enough for him to direct the TARDIS.
- How the Doctor's clone gets to the TARDIS to collect the relative dimensional stabiliser is unclear, given the way is supposed to be blocked by the crashed shuttle and Lowe has the isolation ward under siege. The service shaft they came up is behind them and was slower than going on foot, so even if the Doctor has found another way down to reception he'd have to be very quick as the clone only has a lifespan of just under eleven minutes (in fact, once he gets back to the lab Marius talks of him having ten minutes left, so he must get to the TARDIS and back in under a minute). But when could the Doctor discover such a route? He's been unconscious most of the time since arriving at Bi-Al and has only seen the isolation ward.
- The relative dimensional stabiliser is of similar design to the time control unit seen in *Pyramids of Mars* (Landing 117) but is slightly smaller and has simpler controls. On the top panel are red and blue buttons, a pink box and two square silver handles. Underneath are six red connectors or fastenings which attach the stabiliser to a wall-mounted control panel in the lab. The TARDIS can't take off without it but people can enter and leave, so whatever the "dimension barrier" the stabiliser allows one to cross is, it's not to do with the different dimensions inside and outside the Ship.
- Note how the camera zooms into a closer shot of Tom Baker as K9 moves towards the TARDIS. This is because the K9 prop couldn't mount the Police Box's base so Baker acts as if he's letting the robot dog in.

LANDING 136

SPACE Titan, refuelling base, supervisor's office
TIME As above
TRAVELLERS The Doctor, Leela, K9
EPISODES The Invisible Enemy 4

Rather than returning to its previous landing site in the base on Titan, the TARDIS materialises in the supervisor's office. The Doctor emerges with the case of antidote and notices on a monitor that the eggs in the hive are starting to hatch. As he tries to leave the office a medic blocks the way. Leela's gun is ineffective as the Swarm infection has strengthened the man's cells to resist its radiation blast, but K9's blaster successfully stuns him. They leave to find the hive.

Leela and an exhausted K9 return to the office to wait for the Doctor. He comes running past them, straight into the TARDIS and begins to dematerialise. Leela calls out to him and the Ship quickly resolidifies as the take-off is cancelled. She pulls K9 inside, berating the Doctor for not waiting, but he hurriedly sets the TARDIS in motion.

They watch on the scanner as the base explodes, the Doctor having rigged a gun to fire as the Swarm emerged from the hive, igniting the methane in the hatching tanks mixed with the base's oxygen atmosphere. He takes credit for the idea of blowing up the base until Leela points out that was her suggestion all along.

- **CONTROLS** Although the doors are already opening, the Doctor pulls the centre large slider on panel C1 downwards, perhaps setting them to close straight away. He turns the centre and right-hand dials on panel C2.
- **NOTES** As Tom Baker runs into the TARDIS it doesn't half shake. His trailing scarf is trapped in the doors and he has to pull it inside.
- The TARDIS dematerialising was done as a split-screen effect so Louise Jameson didn't have to stay still as it reappears. The left-hand side of the picture had a shot of the empty office faded in over the Police Box. You can see the join down the side of the office window and across the floor.
- The Police Box doesn't fade out completely before Leela calls out and the Ship resolidifies, so it's fair to assume this is an interrupted take-off rather than a full departure and immediate return. The rising dematerialisation sound does switch abruptly to the last groans of the landing effect, however. It's not clear if the Doctor actually hears Leela call his name or whether he has noticed her absence and was cancelling the take-off anyway.
- This is the first time the scanner shows a view of the location the TARDIS has just departed from. So although the Ship is in flight, it must still be in the space-time vicinity of Titan.
- The Doctor hasn't been seen to sit on the wooden Knossos chair since the end of *The Reign of Terror* (Landing 9). He must move it across the control room immediately after taking off, anticipating a desire to sit and pet K9.
- The shot of the TARDIS in space again uses the *Pyramids of Mars* miniature.

LANDING 137

SPACE Solar System, asteroid belt, Asteroid K4067, Bi-Al Senta, resepshun
TIME As above
TRAVELLERS The Doctor, Leela, K9
EPISODES The Invisible Enemy 4

The Doctor returns to the Bi-Al Senta in order to return K9 to Professor Marius. Both he and Leela have taken a liking to the robot dog, praising him for helping to defeat the Swarm, and Marius notices K9 has started calling Leela 'mistress'. As he is due to return to Earth he wonders if the Doctor would take K9 with him. Leela is especially keen, but K9 himself settles the matter by trundling aboard the TARDIS. The Doctor and Leela follow him inside, leaving a slightly wistful Marius, and the Police Box departs.

- **NOTES** Again the camera craftily avoids showing K9 actually entering the Police Box; the actors simply look down as though watching him go inside.
- The shot of the TARDIS dematerialising is the same footage as seen earlier in the episode when it departed for Titan.

LANDING 138

SPACE Earth, England, Fetchborough
TIME 30 July [1977]
TRAVELLERS The Doctor, Leela, K9
EPISODES Image of the Fendahl 1,3

The Doctor is attempting to repair some corrosion in K9's circuits when the TARDIS is suddenly dragged towards a relative continuum displacement zone – a "hole in time" – caused by someone operating a sonic time scan. He wrestles with the controls and manages to break free, perhaps also helped by Leela's placations. The Doctor must disable the source of the time scan to prevent a direct continuum implosion but cannot calculate the coordinates, so he traces it back to its point of origin: with dismay he discovers it is on Earth.

The TARDIS materialises in the vicinity of the time scanner, in a cow field just over a mile from the village of Fetchborough. In the woods nearby is a time fissure and beyond the village is Fetch Priory. It is early morning and church bells can be heard ringing. Deciding that the cows are not responsible for the time scan, the Doctor and Leela set off to find who is.

Late that night they return to the TARDIS and set off on a journey 107 million miles from Earth and twelve million years into the past, looking for the planet on which the Fendahl originated.

- **CONTROLS** When the TARDIS is affected by the sonic time scanner, the Doctor turns the silver dial on panel C5, uses the silver lever on panel C6 and reaches over to move the large slider on panel C1.
- While heading for the fifth planet, the Doctor flicks a switch at the top-left of panel C6, reaches across to another on panel C1, and repeatedly adjusts the silver dial on panel C5. He opens the scanner with a switch on either panel C6 or C1.
- This is the first time we hear sound effects as controls are activated (special sounds creator Dick Mills first did this for *The Sun Makers*, which was produced before *Image of the Fendahl* but broadcast after).
- **LORE** The TARDIS generates a low-intensity telepathic field that allows it to detect the thought patterns of its occupants.
- The Ship contains data banks that can access all Time Lord knowledge. The information is stored as white dots and lines on clear plastic squares.
- **NOTES** One might reasonably assume that Professor Marius would keep K9 well maintained, so the fact his circuits are corroding could imply he has had a few adventures with the Doctor by now. Certainly the Doctor is confident about tinkering with his insides, but then he's like that with all machinery. When Leela says, "Professor Marius would not be pleased," she might not be talking about the Doctor opening up K9 but getting him damaged in the first place.
- This is the first story set on contemporary Earth with no relation to the UNIT timeline so there's no reason

not to assume it's 1977, the year of broadcast. If this means a younger version of the Doctor is also on Earth working with UNIT, who might perhaps be expected to notice someone inventing and operating a dangerous time scanner, we can presume he's too busy trying to find the Master.

- The two staggered-roundels walls have swapped their usual positions, with the half-roundels edges against the ribbed columns either side rather than next to each other in the middle.
- After the TARDIS has materialised, Leela and the Doctor set the coat rack upright, but it didn't fall over during the earlier disturbance. Did the Ship land with a bump? This rack is similar to the one last seen in the second control room in *The Robots of Death* but lacks a mirror on the stem. Other than the hat and scarf the Doctor dons before going outside, it's bare. It seems rather mean of the Doctor to switch to this stand having had Leela bring in a different one laden with coats at the start of *The Invisible Enemy*.
- The Police Box is missing its roof lamp, probably left behind when the prop was taken on location. It also has a slightly darker but noticeably rougher-textured paint job, which will revert in the next story as that was filmed first.
- The TARDIS lands in the morning, judging from the sound of church bells, and they're still ringing after the Doctor has relaxed under a tree awhile. He and Leela then arrive at the boundary of Fetch Priory during daylight but decide to wait until dark before breaking in. So what do they do for what could be eight or nine hours? Climb a tree? Nip back into the village for a pub lunch? The Doctor's evidently not that anxious about disabling the time scanner (he knows it can only be used at night and wants to see it in operation before deciding how best to dismantle it).
- Ted Moss says Fetchborough village is "about a mile" from where he meets the Doctor and Leela, but they have already been walking for a short time. It would make sense for them to head towards the sound of church bells, so the TARDIS probably lands further away than that.
- The Doctor says the fifth planet is "a hundred and seven million miles out" – if he means from the Sun then it would be roughly midway between Earth and Mars, so presumably he means 107 million miles from Earth (where his journey starts), which would position it on the very inner edge of the asteroid belt. It's often assumed that the asteroid belt is the remains of the fifth planet but this isn't explicitly stated in the story. The Doctor does says the planet "broke up" and later that "the Time Lords decided to destroy the entire planet", but if "all memory of the planet's been erased by a circle of time", even from the Time Lords' own data banks, to "[hide] the fact from posterity", how can its remains be the asteroid belt? Then again, the Doctor clearly remembers the planet and where it was, and knows of the Fendahl as being "a creature from my own mythology".

LANDING 139

SPACE Earth, England, Fetchborough
TIME 31 July [1977]
TRAVELLERS The Doctor, Leela, K9
EPISODES Image of the Fendahl 3-4

During the journey the Doctor speculates on how the Fendahl skull might have projected itself across space to reach Earth. He decides to check some data banks elsewhere in the Ship. Leela falls asleep on the control room floor and dreams of something chasing her from which she cannot run. She wakes with a start and almost stabs the Doctor when he returns, having found no information about a fifth planet at all.

The scanner shows only a green vortex which the Doctor recognises as the impression of a time loop, something only his own people could have effected. The planet and all memory of it have been erased. Realising they have been on a wasted journey, he resets the coordinates for Earth.

The journey takes some time, which makes Leela anxious. The Doctor contemplates where the Fendahl skull can be getting the enormous amount of power needed to recreate its body from. He thumps the console when he suddenly realises it must be using the energy released when Fendleman's scanner probes the time fissure.

Eventually the TARDIS lands after nightfall on the day after it left, still some distance from Fetch Priory. The Doctor and Leela hurry through the woods.

The priory, the gathering Fendahleen inside and the time scanner are all destroyed as the building implodes. The Doctor and Leela escape, carrying the Fendahl skull in a lead-lined box. They return to the TARDIS and quickly leave before people start demanding explanations.

Once more in flight, the Doctor finds an imminent supernova in the constellation Canthares in which to dump the skull, destroying it once and for all. After that he plans to finish repairing K9.

- **CONTROLS** The Doctor uses the same controls on panels C5, C6 and C1 as in Landing 138.
- **NOTES** Martha Tyler notes that it's now Lammas eve. Lammas day, celebrating the end of the wheat harvest, falls on 1 August.
- While the amount of time that passes for those inside the TARDIS doesn't always correlate with how far they're travelling, either in space or time, it's not surprising that going back twelve million years might seem to take a while. It's also suggested proximity to the time loop may extend the journey. But why does the Doctor not return to Earth moments after leaving? Even before the trip he doesn't expect to be back before "tomorrow sundown". He might be confident the sun will soon be up, preventing Fendleman from using the time scanner while he's away, and although he has heard Max Stael plotting with Ted Moss he doesn't know they're preparing a ritual. But he knows the Fendahl is attempting to recreate itself and that Thea Ransome is at risk, so why waste a whole day? Also, why not land closer to the Priory to save walking

through the woods, where a Fendahleen has already tormented the Doctor once and killed someone else?
- Is the Doctor keen to get away quickly because he knows the vanishing priory is likely to attract the attention of UNIT and his younger self? Indeed, does he remember investigating the incident?
- Oops! At the end of episode four, the interior door is ajar but no set piece is placed behind it so part of the studio wall can be seen.
- We'll assume the Doctor won't want to risk fully materialising the TARDIS in space near a star that's about to explode, so probably just hovers in the vicinity and chucks the skull out the door.

LANDING 140

SPACE Pluto, Megropolis One, District Four, Block 40
TIME Unknown future
TRAVELLERS The Doctor, Leela, K9
EPISODES The Sun Makers 1,4

The Doctor plays chess with K9 to prove the limitations of the machine mind, but when K9 starts winning he is so flustered that he does not notice the TARDIS has materialised. When Leela points out the central column has stopped moving, the Doctor blusters around the console to hide his vexation at losing the game. The readings indicate they are on Pluto but there is a breathable atmosphere, and the scanner shows a high-rise city. Leaving K9 behind, to the robot dog's disappointment, the Doctor and Leela head outside.

They find they are on a thousand-metre-high rooftop. There is a breeze and clouds hide the sun – actually one of six in-station fusion satellites positioned above each Megropolis – but the temperature is around 20 degrees and the atmosphere is humid. The air is also scented, either with or to hide the presence of the anxiety-inducing chemical pento cyleinic methyl-hydrane. They venture to the parapet and as the Doctor surveys the city spread out below through a telescope, Leela spots a man about to leap from the rooftop. She rushes over to stop him and as the Doctor distracts him with the offer of a jelly baby she pulls him away from the edge.

The man, Cordo, explains about the exorbitant levels on taxation the citizens of Pluto are subject to and how his father's death has made his financial burden untenable. The TARDIS's arrival has been detected and an alarm sounds. Cordo leads Leela and the Doctor into an access stairwell to hide, fearing further fines if they are caught.

Gatherer Hade and his assistant Marn examine the TARDIS, guessing it is a container dropped onto the roof from an illegal air freighter. Hade suspects a major criminal enterprise against the ruling Company is in progress so they leave to set up surveillance of the box. Shortly after, K9 exits the TARDIS despite his instructions and follows the trace of his master, unaware he is being watched.

Some hours later, as the concentration of PCM in the air drops, workers across Pluto are rising up against the Company. A handful of those in Megropolis One make their way to the rooftop of Block 40 to enjoy the sunlight, a hitherto forbidden act. Gatherer Hade orders them down but they are no longer intimidated by him and instead lift him up and toss him over the edge of the building, cheering and promising the same for the Collector.

With the Company bankrupt and the Collector literally liquidated thanks to the Doctor feeding a two percent growth tax into its computers, the workers of Pluto are free. They gather on the rooftop to bid farewell to the Doctor, who encourages them to return to Earth and resettle their true home. Leela says goodbye to Veet as she lets K9 into the TARDIS and the Doctor raises his hat to the crowd before following them.

Inside K9 is keen to resume the chess game but the Doctor operates a control that causes the room to tilt, scattering the pieces across the floor. He apologises and promises that once they are on their way they can replay the game. K9 growls with exasperation.

- **CONTROLS** When the Doctor leaps towards the console he spins the right-hand rotary handle on panel C3 (possibly to prevent going right through the time spiral). He then moves the large slider on panel C1 down and turns the lower-right dial, while twisting an unseen dial on panel C2 (probably the right-hand one), to determine where they've landed. He also flicks a switch on panel C1. The scanner is not seen or heard opening but the Doctor is standing at panels C1 and C2 so its control must be there. He must discreetly operate the doors from the same section.
- When preparing to take off, the Doctor flicks two switches on panel C1. To shake the room he throws a control on panel C3 (probably the right rotary handle).
- **LORE** A control on the console can destabilise the gravity in the control room, causing it to feel like it's tilting even though the Ship is stationary.
- **NOTES** There's nothing to suggest this follows directly from the previous landing other than the Doctor stating, "We're still in the Solar System." Given the previous four stories have all been in our Solar System, this doesn't rule out further landings since *Image of the Fendahl*.
- The little column the chess board is resting on last appeared on the Sand Mine in *The Robots of Death*. Did the Doctor steal it before he left? He's sitting in the wooden Knossos chair for the third time this season, though: nice to see it getting some use at last.
- Given the TARDIS has already landed, the Doctor's fears about going "right through the time spiral", blaming paint for "always jamming things up" and claiming he's "going to materialise" can be taken as exaggeration to distract from his losing to K9 at chess.
- The image of the city on the scanner (artwork rather than a model) is from a low angle, yet from the rooftop outside no other buildings can be seen. Is the screen showing a detailed graphic of the city derived from its scans rather than the immediate view outside? (They could have used the high-angle view seen later when the Doctor looks down at the city through a telescope.)

- Although we don't see through the open doors, light from outside casts shadows of the Doctor and Leela into the control room. The Doctor heads out first while Leela apologies to K9, but then she is the first to step out of the Police Box.
- In the first shot of the TARDIS on location, the black curtain covering the rear of the prop can be seen poking out behind the right-hand 'Police box' sign, then in the following long shot it can just be made out billowing at the bottom.
- When the Doctor re-enters the TARDIS the black void can be seen through the main doors, although there is still a light shining from beyond them. The doors close without a control being operated.
- As the TARDIS has not yet taken off when the Doctor upsets the control room, can we assume this action doesn't affect the outside of the Ship? Otherwise Cordo and company will be startled to see the Police Box lurch to one side. The top of the set and a camera pedestal are briefly visible as the shot tilts, and one of the branches of the coat rack breaks off when it falls over. This was repaired before recording *Image of the Fendahl* (the previous story but made after *The Sun Makers*) but in broadcast order it can be taken as the reason the hatstand in the next story is different.

LANDING 141

SPACE Edge of space
TIME Unknown
TRAVELLERS The Doctor, Leela, K9
EPISODES Underworld 1

While the Doctor is occupied with painting somewhere in the TARDIS, Leela is at the controls when the Ship comes to an automatic halt at the "edge of the cosmos" (or at least an area of null space) where matter can spontaneously coalesce. Viewing the empty blackness on the scanner, the Doctor is awed by the possibilities while Leela sees it as literally nothing. Yet K9 detects a spaceship with an ion drive in the vicinity, at coordinates 34-701-17-50-05.

The Doctor confirms his readings. However, the TARDIS has drifted too close to a swirling nebula that is collapsing towards an unseen centre of gravity. It begins pulling the Ship in so K9 suggests materialising aboard the spaceship as a way to escape and the Doctor concurs.

- **CONTROLS** The control panels are arranged (clockwise) 1-2-5-4-3-6, with panel C5 facing the main doors.
- Leela idly wiggles the silver lever on panel C6, flicks a switch on panel C1, another on panel C6 and unseen controls on panel C3, repeating the last when the central column stops. The Doctor then operates the two pushbuttons and the left-hand rotary handle on panel C3 and the silver lever on panel C6 – the scanner opens after he presses the second button, fractionally before he touches the lever. When trying to detect the spacecraft, the Doctor presses a pushbutton and turns the rotary handle on panel C3, then reaches across to the switch on panel C1 that Leela flicked earlier. She simultaneously operates a pushbutton on panel C3, turns the silver dial and rotary handle on panel C4 and the silver dial on panel C5. To escape the spiral nebula, the Doctor turns the two controls on panel C4 Leela just used, presses unseen buttons on panel C3 and grips but doesn't turn the silver dial on panel C5. Leela also holds this while turning the left-hand black dial on panel C2, and touches the red dome on panel C5 and the black dome at bottom-left of panel C2.
- The inner mechanism of the central column has gained a white band around the top.
- **NOTES** The opening shot of the TARDIS beyond the edge of space and the later one of it evading the nebula feature photographs of the Police Box miniature built for *Pyramids of Mars*. The static shot of the TARDIS and nebula, however, uses the second model built for *The Hand of Fear*. Here its flat, stuck-on windows are very noticeable. These shots were all taped on video during the studio recordings.
- Is Leela flying the TARDIS or just pretending? She continues to operate controls later in the scene, although the Doctor readjusts some of the same ones so might be undoing her tinkering. But it's possible he has been teaching her some basic TARDIS operations, which would mean she may have piloted the Ship to the Bi-Al Senta after all (see Landing 135).
- The hatstand is back to being a bentwood style but different from that in *The Invisible Enemy* (see page 208).

LANDING 142

SPACE Minyan spaceship R1C (at edge of space), storeroom
TIME As above
TRAVELLERS The Doctor, Leela, K9
EPISODES Underworld 1,4

The TARDIS materialises in a long-disused storeroom aboard the R1C, although the sound of its arrival echoes throughout the ancient spaceship.

The Doctor finds a piece of equipment originating from Minyos, a planet far across the universe visited by early Time Lords whose attempts to help the Minyans led to them destroying their world some 100,000 years previously. K9 gauges the isotope decay of the item which indicates it was made that long ago. Leela disintegrates the locked door with a Liebemann maser weapon she finds, and they venture out to discover if any of the crew can possibly still be alive.

After the Minyan ship has narrowly escaped being buried by surrounding matter, then has survived ploughing into and lifting off from the still-forming planetoid at the centre of the nebula, it is finally thrown clear by the shockwave from the explosion of its sister ship the P7E at the core of that planetoid. As the Minyans set course for a new home, taking refugee Trogs with them, the Doctor, Leela and K9 return to the TARDIS.

The Doctor dons his painter's smock but recent events have reminded him of the myth of Jason and the Argonauts' search for the Golden Fleece. He wonders whether such legends could be prophecies, only for K9 to pooh-pooh the idea, so he sullenly returns to his decorating.

- **CONTROLS** While putting on his smock, the Doctor pushes the right-hand large slider on panel C3 up.
- **LORE** The relative dimensional stabiliser operates during materialisation and contributes to the grinding sound.
- **NOTES** The shot of the Doctor and Leela viewing the void on the scanner was taken from behind the set through the open scanner window.
- The Minyans' computer recognises the sound of the TARDIS, so either the Doctor's dates from around the period the Time Lords were on Minyos or their time machines' operation hasn't changed much since. Of course, we don't know how old the TARDIS was when the Doctor 'borrowed' it, but equally it's possible the Minyos incident was within his lifetime.
- The Doctor says Minyos was "on the other side of the universe" yet the R1C has only been travelling for 100,000 years. There's nothing to suggest the ship can travel faster than light – later the crew don't anticipate getting to Minyos Two any faster than four-sevenths light speed – so the distance they've gone must be far less than even the span of the Milky Way. So perhaps the Doctor means "the other side of the galaxy" and the void they enter is inter-galactic space.
- At the start of the final TARDIS scene the central column isn't moving, suggesting the Ship hasn't taken off yet – even though the Doctor is already preparing to return to his painting and Leela is emerging from the interior door (was she really desperate for the loo?). Although the room's hum doesn't change, it's likely the Doctor's control movements are to dematerialise.
- The bottom-right half-roundel in the wall next to the scanner has been removed so the cables powering the console can pass through the hole.

LANDING 143

SPACE Vardan spaceship
TIME Unknown (after Landing 128)
TRAVELLERS The Doctor, Leela, K9
EPISODES The Invasion of Time 1

The TARDIS materialises aboard a Vardan spaceship. The Doctor knows of these aliens' ability to travel along any broadcast wavelength and to read minds, so he disables the scanner to keep them from penetrating the TARDIS and insists Leela remain inside with K9.

The Doctor returns to the Ship, where Leela is vexed by not being told what is happening. He is distracted, however, and tricks her into silence under threat of being stunned by K9, before setting course for Gallifrey.

- **CONTROLS** The control panels are arranged (clockwise) 1-2-5-4-3-6 (as in *Underworld*), with panel C3 facing the main doors.
- Leela turns the silver dial on panel C4 and the rotary handle just below it to try to activate the scanner.
- A microphone on a flexible silver stalk has been placed on panel C1 to the left of the top block. This is to give the Doctor's voice an echo when he speaks to K9 via the console in the scene at the end of episode three.
- **LORE** The scanner can be immobilised.
- **NOTES** As the Vardans are presumably invading Gallifrey to acquire the ability to time travel, the Doctor must encounter them in the same time period as his following return home, which is after his previous visit in *The Deadly Assassin*.
- The Doctor seems to be aware of the Vardans and at least some of their plan before leaving the TARDIS, so there may have been a prior landing where he discovered some of this information and realised the only way to stop them would be to appear to assist them.
- Oops! The Doctor is wearing his scarf when talking to the Vardans but isn't when he returns to the TARDIS, where it's hanging on the hatstand. (He has two and leaves one with the Vardans as collateral?) This is the fourth stand seen since the Doctor returned to using this control room: can he not decide which he likes most?
- Owing to industrial action, *The Invasion of Time* was allocated only three days in the studio and had to complete its other interior scenes on location using an Outside Broadcast video unit. A disused geriatric hospital in Redhill, St Anne's, was chosen as it was close to the sand-pit location being used for filming the Outer Gallifrey scenes, it had large rooms in which sets could be erected and numerous corridors for the TARDIS interior. The studio days were used primarily for scenes on the large Panopticon set, which was then redressed as the courtyard where the TARDIS materialises, plus the small Vardan bridge set. All other sets were erected at St Anne's: the various Citadel offices and corridors, and, it was long thought, the TARDIS control room. Certainly this is shot in an atypical way, most notably the lighting being at floor level rather than overhead. Although the set is the same as seen throughout Season 15, it's shot from low angles and close in, making it feel more cramped than usual. However, it now seems the control room scenes were shot in the studio and these differences were just choices by the director – the low lighting perhaps to reflect the Doctor's apparent perfidy at the start, and low angles to accommodate K9. The BBC's broadcast documentation supports this, as the timings for how much of each episode was recorded in studio or OB only tally if the control room scenes are included in the former. Some viewers also seem to have been taken in by the corridor leading off the control room looking so convincing and assumed it was part of the location. However, this was a set, made to look like brickwork to soften the transition to the location corridors used for the TARDIS interior.

▌ We later learn the Doctor keeps the scanner closed as the Vardans can travel along any "broadcast wavelength", suggesting they could get into the TARDIS by virtue of its receiving a visual image from outside.

LANDING 144

SPACE Gallifrey, Citadel, plaza
TIME As above
TRAVELLERS The Doctor, Leela, K9
EPISODES The Invasion of Time 1-6

The TARDIS is detected en route to Gallifrey and the commander of the chancellery guard issues an amber alert, which is picked up in the control room. The Doctor nibbles on jelly babies, while Leela takes a dip in the Ship's swimming pool to relax.

Commander Andred and eight of his guards line up outside the TARDIS when it materialises in a courtyard within the Citadel, ready to arrest whoever is inside this unauthorised time capsule. The Doctor behaves inconsistently, first acting pleased to see he has a retinue then criticising them. He invites Leela to follow him and Andred, then immediately tells her stay by the Ship. Later the guards lead her away to find suitable attire for the Doctor's investiture as president. K9 is left alone inside, getting no satisfactory answer from the TARDIS regarding the Doctor's whereabouts.

The Doctor returns to the Ship after his inauguration wearing the Sash of Rassilon under his scarf. Leela tries to join him but he regretfully locks her out because her honest thoughts are easy for the Vardans to read, so he cannot confide in her. She moves away when guards led by Andred come looking for her. He thinks she might have gone back into the TARDIS and orders a set of cypher indent keys be brought. Inside, the Doctor discusses with K9 his plan to shut down Gallifrey's defences to allow the Vardans in. He will distract Space Traffic Control by reflecting a transmission beam off the security shield, feeding it back through a linked crystal bank and boosting it through the transducer, while K9 destroys the transduction barriers. The Doctor leaves first but finds Andred still waiting outside the TARDIS. He assures the commander Leela is not inside and sends him away to search for her, then goes his own way. A guard returns with a selection of keys, eventually finding one that opens the TARDIS door. K9 emerges and stuns him before heading for the barrier controls.

After completing his mission, K9 returns to the TARDIS. He uses his probe to open a panel in the console's pedestal and interface with its systems. When the Doctor eventually comes back he finds K9 so engrossed he has to speak via a microphone on the console to get his attention. He places the Matrix interface coronet on K9's head as his machine mind will not be detected by the Vardans that now control Gallifrey and the Matrix.

Outside, Andred and a small group of supporters arrive to assassinate the traitorous Doctor. He shoots the bodyguard Castellan Kelner has assigned to the president and uses the key to get into the Ship.

Before Andred can shoot the Doctor, K9 stuns him. He then interfaces with the console again and begins tracing the channel the Vardans are using. When Andred recovers he tries to shoot the Doctor but his staser gun does not work inside the TARDIS. His supporters are also cut down by Kelner's guards. The Doctor explains that the Vardans cannot read his mind while he is in the TARDIS but outside he has to constantly shield his thoughts as he pretends to go along with their invasion until he can determine their point of origin and time-loop it. While he adapts Andred's helmet to help the commander muffle his own thoughts, K9 succeeds in identifying the Matrix channel the Vardans have infiltrated but there is too much radiolactic interference to locate their planet. The Doctor decides he must dismantle the forcefield around Gallifrey in order to convince them it is safe to fully materialise. Andred and K9 remain in the TARDIS to disable the vulnerable channel – and feel the entire Citadel shudder as the Doctor creates a hole in the forcefield above it – then they leave to meet the Doctor in the president's office.

Leela returns with Outsiders to rescue the Doctor but finds the Ship is still locked. She kicks it angrily before they too head for the president's office to seek him there.

The Doctor, Leela, K9, Andred, Chancellor Borusa and technician Rodan retreat to the TARDIS when a troop of Sontarans take advantage of the gap in the forcefield to invade Gallifrey. The Doctor sends K9 and Andred to a workshop and has Leela escort Borusa to the VIP suite, giving her the Great Key to look after. He then helps Rodan switch the TARDIS's stabiliser circuits into Gallifrey's secondary defence barrier to take control of it and seal the hole. Kelner tries to override this remotely by destabilising the TARDIS interior dimensions and propelling them into a 'black star', but the Doctor manages to activate a fail-safe switch that fixes the Ship in its current state perpetually.

The Doctor, Leela and Rodan make their way through various storerooms, service tunnels and a conservatory before joining K9 and Andred in the workshop. The Doctor uses the coronet to connect K9 to the Matrix again and instructs him to build a Demat gun – an ancient Time Lord weapon activated by the Great Key – assisted by Rodan, whom he hypnotises so she will not remember the procedure. An alarm warns them the Sontarans have broken into the TARDIS so the Doctor, Leela and Andred leave to find Borusa, who is relaxing by the swimming pool, before Commander Stor and his troopers do.

They evade the Sontarans in the sickbay and head back to the workshop. Stor is unable to trace their life signs with his instruments so Kelner suggests finding the ancillary generator and cutting the power to the interference barrier. Stor sends him with a trooper to do so while he makes his way back to the control room, having decided to cut his losses and destroy the entire planet.

In the workshop, the Demat gun is complete and the Doctor arms it with the Great Key. When Kelner and the Sontaran find them, the latter is disintegrated with the gun. Kelner tells them Stor has gone to the Panopticon and the Doctor follows him. Not long after, he returns having used the Demat gun on Stor, but doing so has also wiped his memory of the Vardans and everything that has happened since meeting them.

Some time later, Andred, Borusa and a handful of Outsiders gather outside the TARDIS to cheer the Doctor on his way (having reset the fail-safe switch). Leela and K9 have decided to stay, however, so the Doctor sadly departs alone. Before long, though, he brings out a box marked 'K9 MII'.

- **CONTROLS** The console's inner workings that K9 accesses are beneath panel C4. A hole was cut in the pedestal and a cover placed behind that slid upwards. Behind this was a flat panel with electronic components and flashing lights attached.
- When the Doctor returns to the TARDIS the second time, he flicks a switch at top-left of panel C6 and turns the left rotary handle on panel C3. He appears to turn the right handle when being quizzed by Andred. After popping outside, he closes the main doors with the right-hand large slider on panel C3. Andred seems to use the same controls for the scanner as Leela did above.
- Rodan works at a circuit board that drops down from under panel C5 and she too operates the scanner with the rotary handle and silver dial on panel C4 (the Doctor must have reactivated it while she was working).
- Trying to reset the systems, Kelner turns the black dial at bottom-right of panel C4 and presses further buttons at the top.
- After leaving Gallifrey, the Doctor again turns the handle and dial on panel C4 (without appearing to open the scanner this time) and the left-side silver dial on panel C5. As he looks down at the box with K9 II in, he holds the black dial on the former panel.
- Part of the right-most of the four black switches at bottom-left of panel C4 has snapped off, revealing these are simply wooden pieces not moving switches.
- **LORE** Time Lord time capsules have a molecular patina that identifies them as Gallifreyan (suggesting other species may have time-travel capabilities also).
- The TARDIS is capable of some form of electronic communication with other mechanical intelligences.
- Gallifreyan stasers don't operate within a TARDIS's relative dimensional stabiliser field [a safety feature]. As Andred doesn't know this, it may be an outdated function of older models like the Doctor's Type 40.
- The TARDIS's primary and secondary stabiliser circuits can be used to bypass Gallifrey's transduction barrier controls and take over operation of the planetary forcefield. Its safety circuits can be overridden remotely [only via Time Lord technology]. Reversing the stabilisers propels the interior into a black star.
- A fail-safe switch located in the corridor just outside the control room locks the TARDIS into it a perfect state of inertia, although it can still be entered and exited. Removing the primary refraction tube prevents the fail-safe being reset.
- The TARDIS has, or can be set with, a barrier that prevents any occupants' biological signs being traced. This can be deactivated by removing a circuit housed in the ancillary power station.
- The model of TARDIS the Doctor has (Type 40) was withdrawn centuries ago.
- **NOTES** The TARDIS is revealed to have a swimming pool in a large tiled room, surrounded by garden furniture and potted ferns. Inflatable frogs are also available. There are two large circular openings (one might call them roundels) in one wall. While the Doctor and Leela both call this the bathroom, it's possible they're being facetious, although there are probably shower and toilet facilities attached (possibly only added since Sarah left – see Landing 126). Given the number of times the TARDIS gets knocked about, might we assume the pool is only filled when needed, or has a forcefield over it to prevent spillage? The pool was filmed at British Oxygen Company's building in Hammersmith, London.
- After the TARDIS materialises, the roof lamp stays illuminated throughout the first two episodes.
- The guard uses a key that fits in the upper Yale lock on the Police Box doors, not the slot lower down that we last saw the Doctor use (see Landing 130). Later, when leaving the TARDIS in pursuit of Stor, the Doctor also uses his key in this lock.
- At the end of episode three we finally get the warbling main doors opening sound effect familiar to listeners of the 1978 *Doctor Who Sound Effects* LP and which will be used consistently through to *Paradise Towers* episode one in 1987.
- The Doctor offers Andred a banana, which appears to have just been left on the hatstand. Is this from the same stock as Sarah found (see Landing 126)?
- It's often claimed that Andred's staser doesn't work in the TARDIS owing to the state of temporal grace but this is not stated in the programme. The Doctor's explanation that it "doesn't operate, you see, not in a relative dimensional stabiliser field" could be expounding on how temporal grace works but seems more to be describing a standard function of Gallifreyan patrol stasers, a valid safety feature. Alternatively, the Doctor may have disabled the staser while Andred was unconscious and is just bluffing. K9 was able to stun Andred with his nose laser moments before, after all.
- When Rodan activates the scanner it shows the Sontaran battle fleet in space. This is a greater range than has been displayed before – usually just the immediate surroundings – so has a part of her adjustments been to retune the scanner, or is this a result of linking the console to the planetary defence barrier controls?
- The roundel in the interior door is now dark, almost black, rather than the pale yellow of the wall roundels. It's also fitted from the front of the door so the centre indentation projects into the control room, while on the reverse it has a metal ring edging it. The door has three metal hinges that span its full width and can be barricaded with a beam than drops across the doorway. The corridor beyond is brick with numerous pipes running along it (some of which should emerge into the control room but don't). A box on the wall

- conveniently contains the fail-safe switch and the primary refraction tube that when removed prevents the systems being reset.
- Despite talk of being in a "perfect state of inertia" and "fixed in its present state for eternity", the fail-safe switch appears merely to stop the TARDIS taking off.
- The Doctor sends K9 and Andred to "room twelve-oh-seven on the right" (scripted as, "You go to room 1207, 62nd on the right,") but if this is the workshop where we next seem them, how come the control room is "upstairs" from there?
- The VIP or Chancellor's suite is left off the control room corridor, up three levels and down one, then four left turns to a door marked 'No entry'. As these directions suggest, space in the TARDIS may not be rational (prefiguring the MC Escher influence on the writing of *Castrovalva*); the Doctor himself passes through at least four storerooms that, while he claims they are different (naming three as 23A, 23B and 14D), could be the same one despite him always entering on the upper level and leaving via the lower. He also reckons not to have walked along the "blue section two-five" service tunnel twice but Leela and Rodan both insist they have. Similarly, the Doctor's friends take different exits leading off a corridor but all end up in the sickbay. As Borusa says, "I do wish you'd stabilise your pedestrian infrastructure."
- There is also a conservatory with potted plants, classical murals, metal benches and a large carnivorous plant. As the Doctor pauses for a lie down here, we can assume he's just killing time while he devises a plan, and only heads to the workshop once he has one in mind. He does seem genuinely surprised when the alarm signals the Sontarans have broken into the TARDIS.
- The workshop is like that of a mid-20th century Earth institution, with wooden benches, wall-mounted power sockets and black plastic sheeting over the doors and windows. One of the latter is actually a display and a light flashes behind it when the intruder alarm sounds.
- The ancillary power station, three levels above the workshop, is a white-painted brick corridor disguised as an art gallery featuring a [holographic] copy of the Venus de Milo (as recovered in 1820, missing her arms, rather than as it was originally carved); behind it is Henri Matisse's 1953 collage 'L'escargot'. On the left are JMW Turner's 1844 painting 'Rain, Steam and Speed', Jan van Eyck's 1434 painting 'The Arnolfini Portrait' (of the Italian merchant and his wife) and Pablo Uccello's painting 'Saint George and the Dragon' from around 1470. Opposite this is Edgar Degas' 1878 painting 'L'Étoile'. There is also an early-20th century Mutoscope. The control to deactivate the holograms is in the rear of the Venus statue, while the power circuit is where the Van Eyck was.
- After just a brief glance around the control room, Stor declares, "This machine is a load of obsolete rubbish." What's he basing that judgement on? It's better than any time machine he has otherwise the Sontarans wouldn't be invading Gallifrey. Even if he's seen a report of the Kartz-Reimer module (this story likely post-dates *The Two Doctors*), the TARDIS way outclasses that rickety bucket. It's fair to assume grumpy old Stor says the same thing about any craft he comes across.
- Stor calls the life-signs barrier a "biological barrage". As Kelner successfully cuts the power to this, it's not just Sontaran technology being too primitive to work inside a TARDIS, there must be some dampening field in operation (the Doctor later has a ring that does the same thing – see Landing 362, vol.2). Stor supposes the Doctor has activated this on purpose but he hasn't really had an opportunity to do so, so it's probably an automatic precautionary measure.
- If the Doctor loses his memory of preceding events, why does he go back to the workshop? He should have forgotten everyone is gathered there. Is he just looking for Leela and uses the console to detect her life-signs, now the dampening barrier is deactivated? After all, he does seem surprised to find Borusa there too.
- The departure of the TARDIS used a split-screen effect, with a pre-recording of the Police Box overlaid on the left of the shot of Leela and Andred looking at the empty set. This was then faded out before the camera panned to the right. Note Leela's shadow on the floor is initially cut short just to the right of the TARDIS, then appears when it dematerialises (the two shots are also misaligned so the background shifts too).
- When did the Doctor build a second version of K9? The editing of the episode implies he brings it out soon after leaving the original behind, but those TARDIS scenes could be set much later than the Gallifrey scenes they're intercut with. However, having it all boxed up suggests he's had it a while and has been keeping it out of the way to avoid offending K9. Perhaps while tinkering around inside K9 prior to *Image of the Fendahl* (Landing 138) he realises this unit's lifespan is limited (it's already showing signs of corrosion and its motors whirr alarmingly) so decides he could construct a better one. Knowing how fond Leela is of the robot dog, he makes his new one in private and packs it away for the inevitable day when K9 breaks down for good. In fact, it may not be a completed K9 in the box but a work in progress that he forgot about but now decides is worth completing.

PREVIOUS LANDINGS

SPACE Earth, England
TIME Late-19th/early-20th century
TRAVELLERS The Doctor, [unknown companions]
EPISODES Claimed by the Doctor in
   The Ribos Operation 4
The Doctor was trained in sleight of hand by [John Nevil] Maskelyne.
- **NOTES** The most likely time for the Doctor to have met Maskelyne was during his long engagement

at the Egyptian Hall in Piccadilly, London during the last quarter of the 19th century, but it could have been at any time up to his death in 1917. That's assuming the Doctor isn't referring to his son Nevil or grandson Jasper, both of whom were accomplished stage magicians in the 20th century.

SPACE Earth, England, Lincolnshire, Woolsthorpe-by-Colsterworth
TIME 1666
TRAVELLERS The Doctor, [unknown companions]
EPISODES Claimed by the Doctor in
The Pirate Planet 4

The Doctor tried to lead Isaac Newton towards the truth about gravity by climbing a tree and dropping an apple on the mathematician's head. Newton merely told him to get out of his tree so the Doctor instead gave him some pointers over dinner.

- **NOTES** Newton was away from Cambridge University (which was closed as a precaution against plague) and working at his family home when a falling apple turned his thoughts to the attraction between two bodies of matter, according to colleagues' later reports. They don't mention a doctor explaining things to him in more detail, of course, but given Newton focused on optics in the years immediately after and didn't return to formulating a law of gravitation until the 1680s, perhaps the Doctor felt obliged to manipulate his memories, leaving just a hint of the truth to emerge later.
- One can hardly picture the Doctor in his first or third personas sitting in a tree and dropping apples on Newton's head, so he was likely in his second or fourth incarnation at the time.
- The Doctor later mentions fondly how "there was no limit to Isaac's genius" while punting in Cambridge (see Landing 173), although this by itself doesn't prove they met.

SPACE Earth
TIME Early-20th century
TRAVELLERS The Doctor, [unknown companions]
EPISODES Claimed by the Doctor in
The Stones of Blood 3

The Doctor attempted to convince Albert Einstein that his special theory of relativity was only "nearly right" as it failed to take account of space warping or other dimensions like hyperspace. Einstein insisted he knew better.

- **NOTES** Einstein published his paper 'On the Electrodynamics of Moving Bodies', which discussed what was later called his special theory of relativity, in 1905 while working and studying in Bern, Switzerland, so the Doctor may have met him around then or at any point in his later life.
- The Doctor meets Einstein twice again, during his seventh and twelfth incarnations.

SPACE Earth, Argentina, Buenos Aires
TIME Autumn 1927
TRAVELLERS The Doctor, [unknown companions]
EPISODES Mentioned by the Doctor in
The Androids of Tara 1

The Doctor saw at least one of the 34 games held between 16 September and 26 November of the 1927 World Chess Championship played by title holder José Raúl Capablanca and successful challenger Alexander Alekhine.

- **NOTES** Although K9 doesn't correct him, the Doctor may be bluffing to put the dog off his game by claiming to copy one of Capablanca's moves, or just misremembering (given he seems unaware Alekhine won). The Doctor is playing black and moves his rook from queen's rook four to queen's bishop four, using the English descriptive notation (which he sort of does); in the now common algebraic notation this is a5 to c5. Capablanca never made that precise move while playing black during the 1927 Championship, nor the equivalent of h4 to f4 while playing white. Only in the fifth match of the tournament, on 27 September, did he move his rook from a5 to c5, although he was playing white, so maybe that's the game the Doctor saw (which ended in a tie).

SPACE Earth, England
TIME 17th century
TRAVELLERS The Doctor, [unknown companions]
EPISODES Mentioned by the Doctor in
The Androids of Tara 1

The Doctor went fishing with Izaak Walton.

- **NOTES** The Doctor is perhaps most likely to have been interested in meeting Walton around the time he wrote the first edition of *The Compleat Angler* (published 1653) from which he quotes: that angling is "an art worthy the knowledge and practice of a wise man". Walton was living in London at that time but had shortly beforehand been in Staffordshire keeping a low profile, being a royalist during the interregnum.

SPACE Earth, Bali
TIME Unknown
TRAVELLERS The Doctor, [unknown companions]
EPISODES Claimed by the Doctor in
The Armageddon Factor 2

The Doctor was taught by Balinese firewalkers to withstand great heat.

- **NOTES** Firewalking relies on keeping exposed skin in contact with hot embers for as short a time as possible, not crawling along a hot metal walkway, so the Doctor may be being flippant.

SPACE Earth, Crete
TIME [17th to 12th century BC]

TRAVELLERS The Doctor, [unknown companions]
EPISODES Claimed by the Doctor in The Creature from the Pit 1 and hinted at in The Horns of Nimon 4

The Doctor was present when Ariadne led Theseus to the Minoan labyrinth where the Minotaur dwelled. They suggested unravelling his scarf to provide a trail through the maze so Theseus could find his way back. Affronted, the Doctor provided them with a ball of twine to use instead. After Theseus returned having killed the Minotaur, the couple gave it back to him with a note of their thanks. However, the Doctor forgot to remind Theseus to swap black sails for white on his homeward ship.

▪ **NOTES** This was before the Doctor met Romana but evidently during his scarf-wearing fourth incarnation, so after Landing 119.

SPACE Earth, England, Cambridge
TIME 1955, 1958, 1960, 1964
TRAVELLERS The Doctor, [unknown companions]
EPISODES Mentioned by the Doctor in Shada 1

The Doctor made several visits to Professor Chronotis at St Cedd's College. During the 1960 visit he received an honorary degree from the college.

▪ **NOTES** Chronotis is introduced to Romana in *Shada* (Landing 173) so the Doctor's previous trips to Cambridge must be before she joined him. He may not have met the professor on every previous visit – we only know he asked the porter about him – but has done on at least one occasion as they're friends and the Doctor is aware of his "Milk? One lump or two? Sugar?" joke.

▪ The 1958 visit was prior to Landing 103 ("[I was] in a different body") but likely after Landing 92 as before then the Doctor couldn't reliably pilot the TARDIS. The others were during his fourth incarnation, so after Landing 119.

SPACE Tigella
TIME [Early-20th century] (around 50 years prior to Landing 184)
TRAVELLERS The Doctor, [unknown companions]
EPISODES Mentioned in Meglos 1

The Doctor was shown around the Tigellans' underground city by a young Zastor. He was not allowed to view their power source, the Dodecahedron, owing to religious objections. Although the vegetation on the surface was aggressive, the Doctor had no problematic encounters with it. He did help the Tigellans with some issue, though, as Zastor recalls his ability to solve the insoluble by the strangest means.

▪ **NOTES** When the Doctor later returns to Tigella, Zastor recognises him in his fourth incarnation, so this first visit must be after Landing 119. Romana is unfamiliar with the planet, however, so it's before he met her.

LANDING 145

SPACE Skytha constellation, Ribos, Shur city
TIME Two days in unknown [future]
TRAVELLERS The Doctor, K9, Romanadvoratrelundar
EPISODES The Ribos Operation 1-4

The Doctor has programmed K9 to respond to the high-frequency sound of a dog whistle, and now suggests a holiday for the pair of them on Harlagon Three. His plans are interrupted when the TARDIS is suspended in time by the powers of the White Guardian. The main doors open and a dazzling golden light floods into the dark control room. The Doctor is ordered to an audience with the Guardian.

While he is gone, the Time Lady Romanadvoratrelundar is transported to the TARDIS to act as the Doctor's assistant in his search for the six segments of the Key to Time; she believes she has been assigned by the Time Lord President. She has been given the core to the Key: a wand that can locate then convert the disguised segments into their real form. She makes a socket for it in the console.

When the Doctor returns and time resumes, he is dismayed by both having an assistant forced upon him and her addition to the console. However, he inserts the locator core into its slot and it identifies the planet Cyrrhenis Minima at coordinates 4180 as the location of a Key segment. Yet almost immediately the reading changes to the planet Ribos some 116 parsecs distant at coordinates 4940.

With the location of the segment now stable, the TARDIS materialises in a street in the city of Shur in the early hours of the morning. The planet is currently in its 32-year winter: light snow covers the flagstones and a bitterly cold wind blows between the stone buildings. Unlike the inexperienced Romanadvoratrelundar, the Doctor has anticipated this and brings out a fur-lined cape for her to wear over her flimsy gown. She uses the locator core to get a bearing on the segment, but before heading off the Doctor issues some ground rules: to do as he says, stay close to him and let him do all the talking. He also decides to call her Romana for short, even though she prefers his alternative of Fred. As the Doctor moves off he steps into an animal trap and is hauled up in a rope net; Romana pulls the release lever to let him down.

That evening – having deduced the Key segment is disguised as a lump of the valuable mineral jethrik that two conmen are using to convince deposed despot the Graff Vynda-Ka to buy the planet from them – the Doctor and Romana return to the TARDIS with Garron to get from him the whereabouts of his partner Unstoffe, who has the stone. But the Graff has rumbled the scam and intercepts them, ordering his guards to take them for questioning. Shortly after, K9 picks up the sound of the Doctor's dog whistle and leaves the TARDIS to find his master.

The morning after, with the Graff disposed of and the jethrik recovered, the Doctor returns to the TARDIS, bidding Garron goodbye. The hustler tries one last switch to regain the valuable stone but the Doctor notices and surreptitiously reverses the swap-over. He departs with Romana and K9, leaving Garron to discover his failure as the Police Box fades away.

Inside, Romana touches the locator core to the jethrik and it transmutes into a clear, purple-tinged irregular fragment of a cube: the first segment of the Key to Time.

- **CONTROLS** A slot for the locator core (later referred to as the tracer) is added to the console on panel C3 in the top-right corner.
- The Doctor reads the coordinates for the location of the Key segment from panel C3 then, when they change, he adjusts a control at the top of panel C4. Romana later reads new coordinates from panel C1 – seemingly the bottom-left gauge.
- **NOTES** While the TARDIS is in flight the central column remains raised rather than oscillating. The hatstand is still in the control room but the wooden Knossos chair is missing; instead Romana sits on a Harry Bertoia-style chrome wire-grid chair.
- The TARDIS isn't seen in the place where the Guardian appears, so it probably hasn't landed as such. It seems the Guardian suspends time in order to talk privately to the Doctor, and the audience is probably all an illusion much as his appearance to Romana as the President is later implied to be. It may even be in the Doctor's mind as he's back in the Ship when we next see him.
- Romana does say she made the hole in the console for the tracer but even if she has the technical know-how to adapt the TARDIS, the wand itself is part of a mystical object. Either it has been realised in a form of technology a Time Lord can understand, or Romana has been made to believe she installed the interface for it, like she believes the President sent her on this mission.
- Speaking of the Time Lord President, last we saw that was the Doctor. Clearly he was not who appeared to Romana, and indeed he says, "That President, I should have thrown him to the Sontarans." Given the Doctor's memory of the Sontaran invasion of Gallifrey was wiped, someone must have filled him in on the events of *The Invasion of Time*. Perhaps he was persuaded to hang around after Landing 144 while a new president was selected and inaugurated, and to properly repair and reinstate the transduction barrier (giving Leela some proper time to fall in love with Andred).
- The main doors wall is extended to the left with a white-painted section from the second control room, with aligned rather than staggered roundels.
- The Doctor presumably introduces Romana to K9 and has him recognise her as a friend en route to Ribos, as when the robot dog rendezvous with the others in episode three he readily calls her mistress.

LANDING 146

SPACE Unknown
TIME Unknown
TRAVELLERS The Doctor, K9, Romana
EPISODES The Pirate Planet 1

The Doctor parks the TARDIS while he stows the first segment of the Key to Time in an old refrigerator, hidden among a bunch of random objects. Romana, meanwhile, has been studying the Ship's operating manual to better acquaint herself with what to her is a vintage time capsule.

Inserting the tracer into the console, the Doctor is disappointed to learn the next segment is on the planet Calufrax, a place he considers "paralysingly dull, boring and tedious". Nevertheless, he takes the opportunity to show Romana how an experienced traveller pilots a TARDIS, dematerialising and plotting the coordinates – although without setting the synchronic feedback checking circuit or activating the multi-loop stabiliser, as the manual instructs.

- **CONTROLS** The socket for the tracer is now at the top-right of panel C5. The previous hole in panel C3 still has its black surround but the white edging has been removed. (If the director was unhappy with the camera angle, could the console not have been rotated?)
- Uniquely, in this story the rectangular blocks at the top of each panel are fitted upside down, with the sloping edge at the top rather than the bottom. The left-hand quartered display on panel C3 has lost its black cowl and the inner mechanism of the central column has lost the white band around its top.
- After the Doctor inserts the tracer, he turns the left-hand dial on the same panel. To set the coordinates he pushes up the large slider on panel C1, flicks four of the switches on this panel, turns the centre dial on panel C2 and slides the two black switches at the bottom. (The central column starts moving after he flicks the switch immediately to the left of the large slider on panel C1 but this could be a delayed effect of operating the slider itself – see Landing 147.)
- **LORE** The TARDIS comes with a manual, which states that it's essential to set the synchronic feedback checking circuit when entering coordinates and that the multi-loop stabiliser should be activated to ensure a smooth materialisation.
- The Type 40 is now considered a veteran and vintage vehicle. According to Romana, the Doctor has been operating this TARDIS for 523 years.
- **NOTES** The central column is stationary at the start of the episode and only begins moving once the Doctor has laid in a course for Calufrax, so he must have previously materialised somewhere (possibly in space) while getting some rest and storing the first segment. At least a day has gone by since leaving Ribos as the Doctor and Romana wish each other a good morning (whatever that means in the TARDIS) and she has a new outfit. The hatstand – the model last seen in *The Invasion of Time* – holds not only the Doctor's hat and scarf while he's not wearing them but also two other coats plus three canes, a cricket bat and an umbrella, whereas during the previous landing it was empty. So it's unlikely but not impossible there have been other landings – perhaps on Harlagon Three after all, to warm up on its sunny beaches following the chill of Ribos.

- The Doctor stuffs the first segment of the Key to Time into one of a pair of wellington boots and stores it in a 1927 General Electric 'monitor-top' fridge (white with a mint-green door). This also contains the other boot, a pair of children's red wellies, a 1937 GPO No.332-model black Bakelite telephone, a hardback book, and a china butter dish and milk jug – the latter suggesting this could be a working fridge, not just an old one the Doctor's using as a cupboard. Beside it is a child's red three-wheeled scooter. The fridge is in a black-walled area just beyond the control room's interior door, which the Doctor later claims is a "limbo closet" (see Landing 155).
- Romana reads the TARDIS manual on a brass eagle lectern. The book itself is a large hardback that appears to have handwritten pages.

LANDING 147

SPACE Zanak (at coordinates of Calufrax)
TIME Unknown [late-20th century]
TRAVELLERS The Doctor, K9, Romana
EPISODES The Pirate Planet 1,4

The Doctor's attempt to land on Calufrax unwittingly coincides with the space-hopping hollow planet Zanak materialising around it at precisely the same moment, jamming the TARDIS's materialisation field. Romana assumes the Doctor's piloting skills are at fault, and he graciously allows her to try "by the book".

She sets the synchronic feedback and multi-loop stabiliser and (now that Zanak has completed its transposition) the TARDIS lands smoothly. A look at the scanner, however, shows not the cold, icy surface of Calufrax but the tiered stone archways of the main township of Zanak. As mining equipment begins to extract the mineral deposits from the enveloped Calufrax and crush the remains, some of the energy released causes K9 to spin uncontrollably.

The Doctor determines they have arrived at the correct space and time coordinates but, somehow, not the right planet. As the three travellers go outside to discover where they are, the tracer's reaction confirms that the Key segment is in the vicinity.

Zanak's Captain is preparing to materialise the planet around Earth, so the Doctor and Romana return in an aircar to the TARDIS, intending to disrupt the process as when they first landed. The Doctor sets the coordinates for Earth – 58044684884 – and Romana monitors the warp oscilloscope and the gravity dilation meter to anticipate Zanak's moment of transposition. As the planet initiates its jump the Doctor dematerialises the TARDIS.

- **CONTROLS** The Doctor flicks four switches on panel C1 then moves the large slider down to materialise. When the landing fails he bumps his lip on the edge of panel C6. He then flicks the switches on panel C1 again as he talks to Romana.
- She presses the two grey buttons on the right of the upper plate on the same panel, sets the synchronic feedback by turning the red button at bottom-right of panel C2, then operates unseen controls on panel C1 and possibly C6 to materialise successfully. She opens the scanner from either panel C1 or C2.
- When checking their location, the Doctor uses the screen on panel C6 and turns the right-hand dial on panel C1.
- When returning to the TARDIS, the Doctor pushes the large slider on panel C1 upwards (perhaps to close the doors although we don't hear them), flicks switches and turns the bottom-right dial on the same panel, and turns the right-hand dial on panel C2. Romana reads the coordinates for Earth off panel C6's screen, then grips both black dials on panel C2 when preparing for dematerialisation, suggesting this is where the warp oscilloscope and gravity dilation meter are located.
- When Romana tells him to dematerialise, the Doctor moves the large slider on panel C1 down and presses a button at top-right.
- The central column lights up and rises while Romana is still monitoring for Zanak's dematerialisation, and is already oscillating when she tells the Doctor to take off.
- **LORE** According to Romana "putting it terribly simply", the TARDIS travels by dematerialising from one location, passing through a space-time vortex, then rematerialising in a new location.
- **NOTES** There's no suggestion that Zanak jumps in time, only space (although it has some of the same instruments as the TARDIS, like a warp oscilloscope and gravity dilation meter). The Doctor says Earth is currently inhabited by "billions and billions of people". The world population is estimated to have reached two billion in the first half of the 20th century, and was over four billion by the time *The Pirate Planet* was made in 1978. At present growth rates, the Doctor would surely have said "tens of billions" if this was dated beyond the 21st century, so in all likelihood events are taking place contemporarily with the story's broadcast.
- The disturbance during the failed landing was created by filming the reflection in a sheet of flexible mirrored material while rippling it, then electronically flipping the image back the right way round.
- Although the Doctor's attempted materialisation seems to fail, the control room hum changes to its lower-pitched 'stationary' sound and the central column stops moving. The latter then oscillates as Romana tries again to land. Did the TARDIS rebound and materialise back where it started in Landing 146, with Romana then performing a simultaneous take-off and landing to return to Zanak?
- While the Captain's instruments record electromagnetic disturbance, gravity dilation and "the entire fabric of the space-time continuum [being] ripped apart" when Zanak and the TARDIS try to materialise at the same coordinates, that's likely a factor of their confluence and isn't necessarily the case when the TARDIS lands normally.

- The shot of the Doctor and Romana returning to the control room is taken through the main doorway, looking across to the interior door. Sadly this reveals the taped-over power cable feeding the console.

LANDING 148

SPACE Zanak, Bridge, Queen Xanxia's chamber
TIME As above
TRAVELLERS The Doctor, Romana
EPISODES The Pirate Planet 4

The Doctor attempts to materialise the TARDIS at the same coordinates as Zanak, jamming the engines of both. Romana struggles with the controls as the Doctor makes mental contact with the Mentiads on Zanak. But to reach them he must turn off the forcefield, increasing the risk of the TARDIS exploding. As the control room shudders alarmingly, the Doctor directs the Mentiads to use their telekinetic powers to smash the megaphoton discharge link with a spanner, causing Zanak's engines to explode.

The TARDIS is saved, if a little smoky. The Doctor and Romana pick themselves off the floor and materialise the Ship back on Zanak. It arrives in the Bridge complex beside the aged Queen Xanxia, her body held in the last moments of life by two time dams.

Shortly after, Romana finds K9 and they wait in the TARDIS for the Doctor. He joins them and explains how he has adapted the Bridge controls to create a hyperspatial force shield around the dense shrunken remains of Zanak's previous planetary victims. By remotely accessing the planet's dematerialisation controls from the TARDIS, he activates them for a millisecond or two, inverts the gravity field of the force shield and the condensed planets expand to fill Zanak's hollow centre. The remains of Calufrax – the whole planet was actually the second segment of the Key – are flung off into the space-time Vortex.

- **CONTROLS** The Doctor reverses the controls he used to take off (see Landing 147) when trying to materialise, as well as possibly working the grey lever on panel C6. As the Ship struggles, Romana is at panel C1 where she turns the right-hand dial, flicks the three switches on the left-hand plate and moves the large slider down again.
- She turns off the forcefield using the grey lever on panel C6. There are small explosions on panels C4 and C5.
- When the Doctor returns to the TARDIS he operates unseen controls on panel C1 and C6. He dematerialises by flicking the top-right switch on panel C1.
- **NOTES** The TARDIS last tried to materialise at the same space-time location as another time vessel in *The Time Monster* (Landing 89). Then it was saved by a Chronovore; here Zanak's engines are destroyed before the TARDIS can be. As there's no mention of damage to Earth, we can presume (and it's later implied) Zanak returns to its previous coordinates (that is, where Calufrax was) when it's rebuffed by the TARDIS.
- During shots of the TARDIS shuddering several pieces of flash paper can be seen on the console, which are ignited as the Doctor talks to the Mentiads (note how Mary Tamm steps away from the console first).
- This is the first mention of the TARDIS forcefield since *The Three Doctors* (Landing 91).
- When the Doctor returns there's no black void beyond the main doors; in fact, you can see the white backcloth used as a reflector to illuminate the wall roundels.

LANDING 149

SPACE Zanak
TIME As above
TRAVELLERS The Doctor, K9, Romana
EPISODES The Pirate Planet 4

The TARDIS returns once more to Zanak, materialising at the foot of the mountain into which the Bridge complex is embedded. The Doctor trails a cable from the Ship to where the Mentiads are gathered and Romana hooks it up to a detonation plunger. The Mentiads use their minds to press it and the Bridge above them explodes satisfyingly.

The Doctor and Romana leave the people of Zanak to rebuild their society on a planet now in a fixed orbit, while they head off in the TARDIS to recover Calufrax from the Vortex and convert it back into the second segment.

- **NOTES** It's not entirely clear on screen but the Doctor must be trailing the electrical cable from the TARDIS (why else take the Police Box prop on location for one brief shot?). How it's connected up to destroy the Bridge is not explained. The Doctor has previously "put [the Captain's] dematerialisation control into remote mode" so he can operate it from the TARDIS, so there might be a link he's, say, sending an energy pulse along. Alternatively he may have set something to overload before he left the Bridge and the plunger is just a pretence to give the people of Zanak the satisfaction of feeling they have destroyed their oppressor's domain.

LANDING 150

SPACE Earth, England, [Cornwall], Boscombe Moor
TIME Two days in [late-1970s]
TRAVELLERS The Doctor, K9, Romana
EPISODES The Stones of Blood 1-2,4

With two segments of the Key to Time now in their possession, the Doctor leaves Romana to work out if they fit together while he slots the tracer into the console to see where the next is located. He is pleased to discover it is on Earth but en route, as Romana picks out fresh clothes and shoes, they hear the voice of the White Guardian warning them of his dark counterpart. The Doctor feels obliged to reveal to Romana that she was not sent on this mission by the Time Lord President but by the Guardian, and explains the purpose of the Key and the imminent chaos its recombination will hopefully avert.

234

As they talk, the TARDIS materialises in the English countryside on a drizzly afternoon, not far from a 4,000-year-old stone circle. The Doctor takes a multi-coloured golfing umbrella from the hatstand and heads outside followed by Romana, leaving K9 on "guard duty". While Romana gets a direction on the next segment with the tracer, the Doctor decides the rain is easing and throws his umbrella into the long grass. They head off along a track towards the stone circle.

The sun has set when K9 detects the sound of his master's dog whistle and heads outside in response. Shortly after they both return with a barefoot Romana so she can freshen up after hanging from a cliff for some hours. When she is ready, all three set out again for the stone circle.

Later that night, Romana carries an exhausted K9 back to the TARDIS in order to link his circuit frequency modulator to the Ship's molecular stabiliser and halt the deterioration of his circuits. She leaves him connected to the console as she heads back outside, noticing a pair of crows perched on the Police Box's roof.

The Doctor returns to collect some components with which to build a device to project himself into a hyperspatial dimension. K9's circuits have regenerated by 75 percent so the Doctor disconnects him from the console and they both leave for Professor Rumford's cottage in the nearby village of Boscawen.

The next morning, K9 waits by the TARDIS as the criminal Cessair of Diplos is transformed into an obelisk to become part of the stone circle in perpetuity. The Doctor uses the Seal she stole – the third Key segment – to send the officiating Megara justice machines back to their hyperspatial craft before they can enact his death sentence. He returns to the TARDIS with Romana and Professor Rumford following behind. The elderly archaeologist realises the circle will need surveying anew and the Doctor suggests she write a monograph. He takes the projector device from Romana and boards the Ship while she says goodbye to the professor with a kiss on the cheek. Rumford watches in confusion as the Police Box fades away.

Inside, Romana takes the first two segments from the fridge while the Doctor converts the Seal into the third and attempts to fit all three together.

- **CONTROLS** After the Doctor inserts the tracer (in panel C5) he flicks a switch on panel C6 and operates controls including the large slider on panel C1. He also reaches to his left so may adjust the right-hand dial on panel C2.
- He moves the larger slider on panel C1 down again while Romana is changing her outfit, then further unseen controls on that panel and the centre dial on panel C2.
- After the TARDIS has landed – and, uniquely, sounded a buzzer to alert the travellers – the Doctor moves the large slider on panel C1 back up, shutting off the alarm, and turns the dial to its right. Romana touches two of the row of buttons in the middle of panel C2, the first of which operates the scanner. She reads the atmospheric conditions from the same panel and presses one of the buttons at bottom-right, while the Doctor opens the doors with a switch on panel C1.
- Romana connects K9 to the console with two leads which she inserts into fresh holes in the second and fourth of the top row of white buttons at bottom-right of panel C4. She then opens the doors with one of the row of buttons beneath the red grille on panel C5.
- **LORE** All Type 40 TARDIS's were fitted with a molecular stabiliser.
- **NOTES** The opening scene implies the second segment has just been recovered and Romana is still in the outfit she wears during *The Pirate Planet*, so it's unlikely there have been further landings since leaving Zanak.
- Boscombe Moor is said to be in Damnonium, the Roman province of south-west Britain - covering modern-day Cornwall, Devon and Somerset. In the 7th century the Damnonii were pushed westwards by Saxons into Cornwall. Vivien Fay says she lives in Boscawen, and there is a Boscawen-un stone circle just off the A30 from Penzance to Land's End – although this has nineteen rather than nine stones. In a deleted scene, Plymouth is said to be two hours' drive away.
- Vivien Fay estimates it's "seven hundred odd years" since the Convent of the Little Sisters of Saint Gudula was founded in the 12th century (and she was there). Even if the convent was built in 1200 and Fay considers '700-odd' to be as much as 750, that only gets us to 1950, so either her maths is terrible or this story's set earlier in the 20th century than it otherwise seems.
- The opening shot uses the Police Box miniature built for *Pyramids of Mars* (still with its white 'Police telephone' plaque). The model sequences for this story were recorded in the studio on videotape, rather than being pre-filmed. This is the first representation of the TARDIS in the Vortex (rather than just flying through space) since *The Time Monster* (Landing 87).
- During filming at the Rollright Stones in Oxfordshire, the Police Box prop was erected the evening before it was needed, but come the morning it was missing. It was discovered at the nearby Little Rollright Quarry (used for filming the clifftop scenes) having been moved there overnight as a prank by students from Reed College (also filmed as De Vries' manor house).
- The cam mechanism for the console's central column broke down during studio recording and had to be manually pushed up and down by one of the visual effects crew. To be fair to him, it oscillates no less smoothly than usual. The hatstand is back to the model last seen in *Underworld*, here holding an umbrella before the TARDIS even lands in rainy England. Romana later hangs her discarded shoes on it.
- The scanner's view is unusually blurry. Is it affected by the drizzle? The main doors open with a different hum to the now-usual warbling sound. They remain open even when the outer Police Box door is closed.
- At the end of episode four, the side-on shot of the TARDIS prop again shows the lack of a 'Police box' sign on the rear.

WHAT ARE ALL THESE KNOBS?

PANELS Cii
1978-1981

For Season 16, the panels were repainted a slightly darker grey and the metal rim of the console was painted black, as was the top of the collar. This now had a line of red tape along each bottom edge instead of the top. The knob of the lever on panel 6 was painted grey instead of silver. A hole also needed to be added for the tracer to fit into, initially in panel 3 but then a second was made in panel 5. During early August 1978, prior to recording of *The Androids of Tara*, the prop was given a further spruce-up. Extra tape decoration was added to several panels, notably 3 and 6, and the supports between them were covered with black instead of red tape. The coloured circles on panel 1 had paler centres added, making them look like rings instead of discs.

Little was changed for Season 17, although there is noticeable damage to the bottom corners of some panels. The first story recorded, *The Creature from the Pit*, required somewhere for an emergency transceiver to attach so panel 1 was modified, and this remained in subsequent stories. Conversely, the randomiser unit added to that panel at the end of *The Armageddon Factor* was not permanent and only reappears in *Destiny of the Daleks*. The large red lever added at the same time to engage the randomiser consequently disappears during *The Creature from the Pit* but was otherwise retained (although not yet used as the main doors control).

After the aborted shooting of *Shada*, when the control room had been set up in the studio but not recorded, the console was put back in storage for another six months until needed for *State of Decay*. The only cosmetic change was to repaint the rim silver (although the black undercoat gives it a dark tone). Panel 5 was heavily modified to include a mechanism for the Doctor to print out the Record of Rassilon (see page 264).

Full Circle saw the missing dial in the centre of panel 2 replaced with a large shiny red dome – although this disappeared during production of *Warriors' Gate* and was replaced from *The Keeper of Traken* by a shallower clear dome over a red circle – with two smaller blue discs either side. The top block on panel 1 had its silver cover removed and a slot added for the image translator. Then in *Warriors' Gate* the silver segmented dial (now on the right of panel 5) was swapped for a translucent green plastic cable holder with a grey tubular core.

Only newly added controls are labelled here. See the diagrams on pages 213-218 for further uses of existing controls

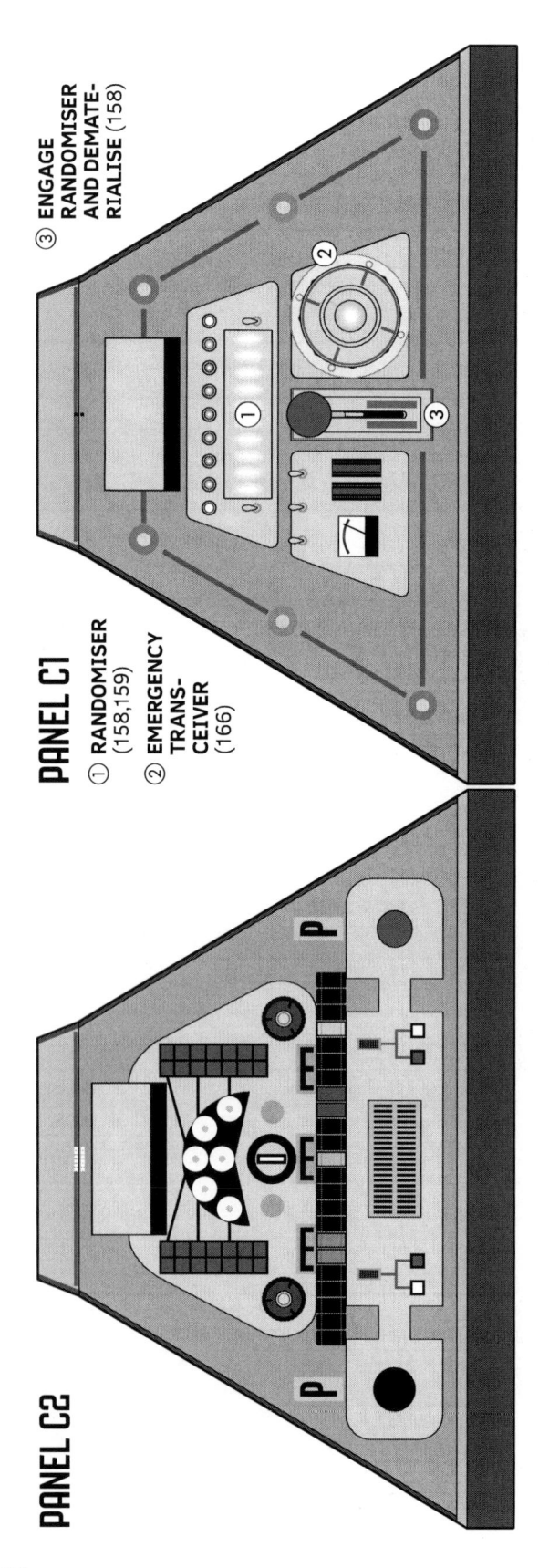

PANEL C1
① RANDOMISER (158,159)
② EMERGENCY TRANSCEIVER (166)
③ ENGAGE RANDOMISER AND DEMATERIALISE (158)

PANEL C2

WHAT ARE ALL THESE KNOBS?

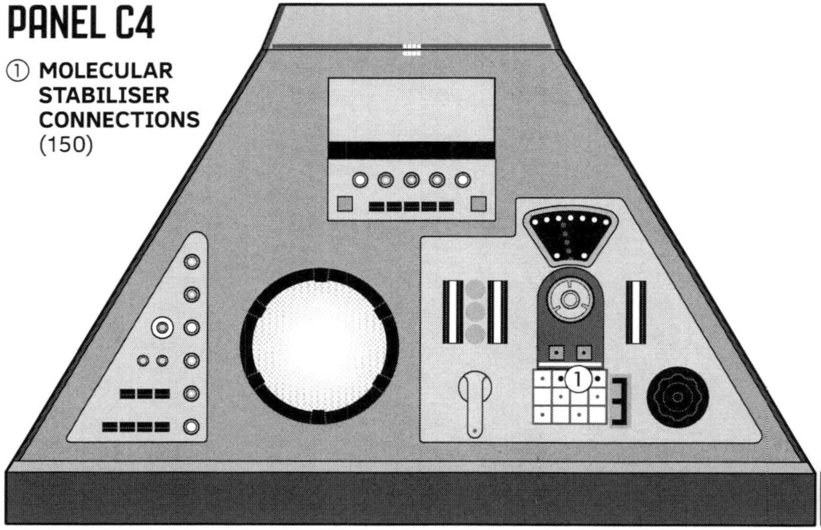

PANEL C3
① **TRACER** (145, 151, 154)

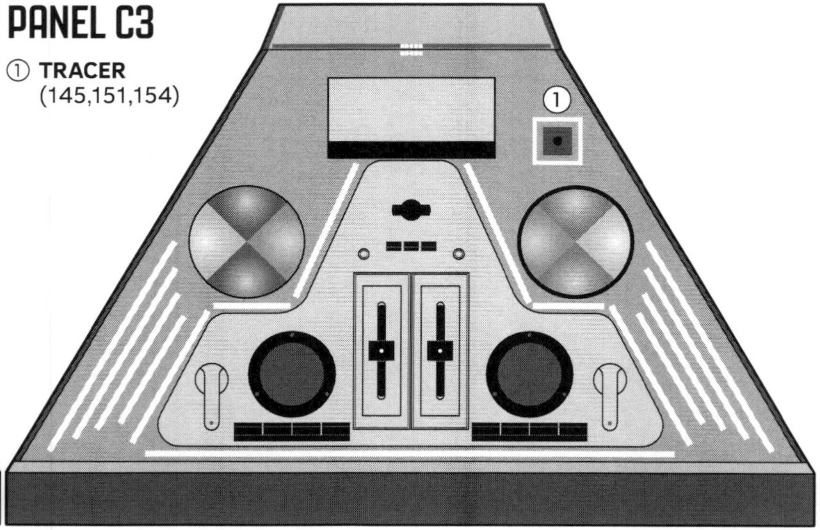

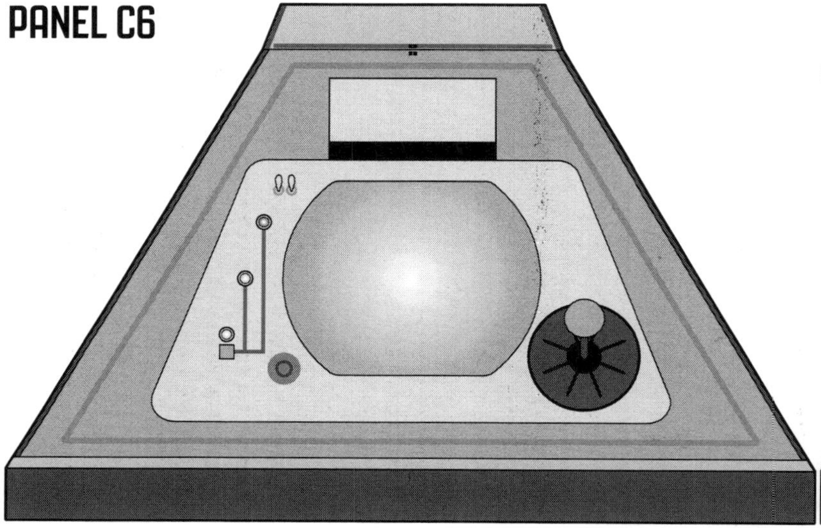

PANEL C5
① **TRACER** (146, 150)

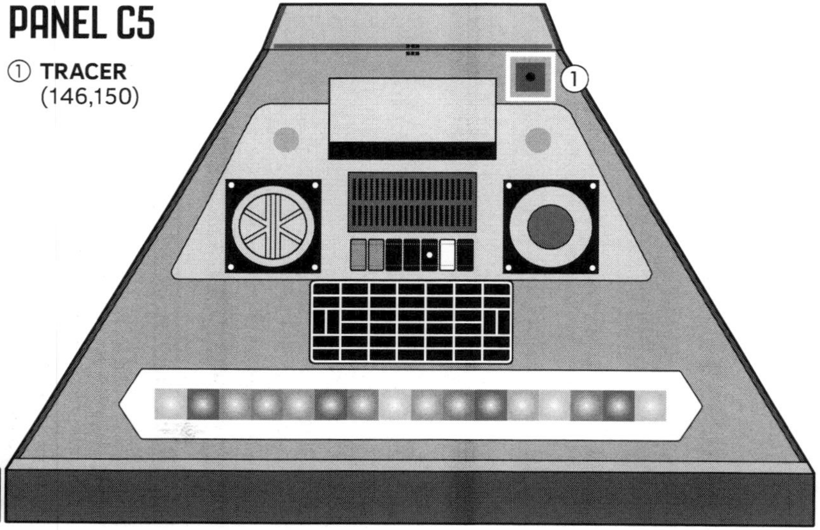

PANEL C4
① **MOLECULAR STABILISER CONNECTIONS** (150)

PANEL C6

LANDING 151

SPACE Tara, estate of Prince Reynart
TIME Three days in unknown [future]
TRAVELLERS The Doctor, K9, Romana
EPISODES The Androids of Tara 1-2

The Doctor is taking a break from searching for the Key to Time and relaxes by playing chess with K9. Romana reminds him of their mission and, pointing out he is about to lose the game anyway, plugs the tracer into the console and smoothly materialises the TARDIS in a warm, shady glen on the planet Tara.

Viewing the pleasant surroundings on the scanner, the Doctor decides to indulge in a spot of fishing while leaving Romana to find the next segment. He digs out an old rod from a cupboard in the control room while she changes into suitable local attire in the TARDIS wardrobe.

Leaving K9 in the Ship, Romana gets a bearing on the segment with the tracer but the Doctor heads off in the opposite direction towards a river. He tells her he is taking the day off, making up a Time Lord rule to justify it.

Early the next morning K9 is awoken by the Doctor's whistle and he dutifully leave the TARDIS.

Another night passes before the trio return to the Ship with the fourth segment of the Key and take off from Tara.

- **CONTROLS** Romana inserts the tracer into its original slot in panel C3 and turns the right-hand rotary handle below, plus either the same on the left or possibly the black dial on panel C4. She then operates further controls on that panel (likely the two dials and rotary handle) and the left and centre dials on panel C2 before materialising by slowly pulling the two large sliders on panel C3 downwards. She opens the scanner with one of the black buttons to the left of these.
- Panel C2 gains some new decals: yellow rectangles with black lettering on them, two 'P's at either end of the middle row of switches and three 'E's on their side above this. Panel C3 is given extra strips of white tape around its metal plate and in the bottom corners, while panel C4 also gets an 'E' decal and some white tape on its switches. Panel C5 now has two silvery circles on its metal plate either side of the top block, and panel C6 has a line of blue tape framing its controls.
- **LORE** The scanner can change its angle of view without being operated from the console.
- The wardrobe contains alphabetised rails of clothing from various planets.
- **NOTES** Although it was doubtless not the intention at the time, there's a plausible gap for further landings since leaving Earth. The Doctor is relaxing and thinks he deserves a break having collected half the Key segments, and Romana has to remind him (and the audience) of their task and the White Guardian's call for urgency, as is they've been neglecting it.
- The chess board is the same as that seen in *The Sunmakers* (Landing 140) but the pieces are very different, being smaller and less ornate.
- The Doctor makes a flippant comment about being allowed a 50-year rest every 400 years and twelve parsecs travelled ("You just made that up," says Romana), but if that's how far they've gone from Earth, they might be visiting Tara in the 24th century.
- The rear of the interior door still has the additional bracing and support for the barricading beam added for *The Invasion of Time* (Landing 144). Just outside the control room now is a wardrobe (a single clothes rack and a white aligned-roundels wall) instead of the dark area where the segments are stored. This suggests the arrangement of TARDIS rooms is mutable, or at least that the storage room can be temporarily hidden.
- The wardrobe hasn't been mentioned since *Pyramids of Mars* (see Landing 113) and not seen since *The Myth Makers* (see Landing 24). Is the cabinet in which the Doctor keeps his fishing gear the same as in *Death to the Daleks* (Landing 100)? It also contains a 1940s British government-issue civilian respirator, a feather duster, an oar, a mop and metal bucket, a besom broom, a cricket pad, a vehicle's brake light and a wicker basket. The hatstand is missing from the control room.
- The main doors open (back with their usual warbling sound effect) automatically for K9. He has, perhaps, by now got a remote link with the console.

PREVIOUS LANDING

SPACE Binaca-Anada
TIME Unknown
TRAVELLERS The Doctor, [unknown companions]
EPISODES Suggested by the Doctor in
The Power of Kroll 1

Methane catalysing refineries are common on this world, with each town using one to produce protein. The Doctor saw hundreds when he was there.

- **NOTES** The Doctor is talking only to the crew of the refinery so this landing could have been while he was travelling with Romana.
- The Doctor says he has seen hundreds of methane refineries before and cites Binaca-Anada as somewhere they are common. The implication is this is where he's seen them but it's not stated outright.

LANDING 152

SPACE Third moon of Delta Magna
TIME Two days in unknown future
TRAVELLERS The Doctor, K9, Romana
EPISODES The Power of Kroll 1,4

The TARDIS materialises among tall reeds on a patch of dry ground amid the marsh around the edge of a large lake. Some distance away is a refinery drawing up methane from the lake bed to convert into protein. K9 is stuck inside the Ship owing to the swampy ground, and even the Doctor and Romana struggle to push through the reeds. The reading from the tracer is diffuse and covers a wide area, so Romana heads for higher ground to see if she can get a clearer bearing.

The next day, after a force 20 storm has swept across the marshes, the Doctor and Romana return to the TARDIS with the fifth segment. K9 is excited to see them as the Ship dematerialises.

▤ **NOTES** Other than the ongoing quest to recover the Key to Time, there's nothing to confirm this landing immediately follows the visit to Tara.
▤ The Police Box prop has a new lamp in this story only, looking like a garden lantern of some kind. It's probable the correct lamp was simply left behind when the box was taken on location. The replacement didn't have a flashing bulb so this had to be simulated with a video effect during editing.
▤ If the Delta Magna moon's escape velocity is "about one point fives miles a second", as the Doctor estimates, that's around a fifth that of Earth's, making the satellite approximately 600km in diameter. For this to have roughly the same surface gravity as Earth, as it seems to – retaining an atmosphere and surface water – its mass must be around one five-hundredth that of Earth.
▤ Given the soggy ground and massive storm, it's lucky the TARDIS hasn't sunk completely by the time the Doctor and Romana return. Or maybe it has been set to float mode as in *Fury from the Deep* (Landing 58).
▤ When the Doctor pitches his voice to shatter a window, he notes this was "Nellie Melba's party piece, though she could only do it with wine glasses". This doesn't confirm he learned the trick from the operatic soprano herself, just that he's heard about it, but he could have met her anytime during her career in the late-18th/early-19th centuries in Australia, Europe or America.

LANDING 153

SPACE Space, Helical galaxy, Atrios/Zeos's solar system
TIME Unknown
TRAVELLERS The Doctor, K9, Romana
EPISODES The Armageddon Factor 1

The tracer directs the TARDIS towards Atrios on the edge of the Helical galaxy and it materialises at the planet's coordinates of 0069. However, the Ship is not in orbit as expected, the scanner showing just stars. Suspecting there has been a time shift, the Doctor takes another reading and locates the planet millions of miles off at coordinates 008-01-0040, but there is still no sign of its twin planet Zeos on the scanner.

The Doctor decides to make a discrete manual landing. As the TARDIS approaches Atrios, Romana detects very high levels of radiation on the planet, suggesting a nuclear war is in progress. If so, the Doctor suspects it must have something to do with the sixth segment.

◉ **CONTROLS** On approach to Atrios, Romana turns an unseen control on panel C4 and presses buttons below the red grille on panel C5, then more on panel C4.
◉ As the TARDIS materialises, the Doctor turns the centre dial on panel C2 then operates the sliding switch at bottom right. Romana also operates controls at the top and right of panel C4. Either the Doctor opens the scanner with the right-hand large slider on panel C3, or Romana does by pressing a control to its left. The Doctor checks the coordinates from panel C3, also moving one of its large sliders and pressing one of the pushbuttons; he presses the last again when the scanner focuses on Atrios. Romana meanwhile presses buttons at the top and left of panel C4.
◉ Romana takes a radiation reading from panel C4. While talking to the Doctor, she presses two pushbuttons on the left of the panel.

▤ **NOTES** Again there's nothing to rule out the possibility of further landings since Delta Magna's moon but with five of the six segments of the Key to Time found one imagines the Doctor would be keen to get his task over with and not delay unnecessarily.
▤ The TARDIS's materialisation in space was filmed using the Police Box miniature built for *Pyramids of Mars* then enhanced with a video effect.
▤ The tracer seems to work by giving a readout of co-ordinates for a segment that the travellers must then input into the console. So why does it not give the coordinates for where the sixth segment on Atrios actually is rather than where the planet should be? In *The Ribos Operation* (Landing 145) it was able to detect and report the first segment moving so why does it not redirect now? Perhaps it did but Romana only read as far as 'Atrios' and, having learned about it at the Time Lord Academy, just gave the Doctor the coordinates she assumed were correct rather than the new ones the tracer was reporting.
▤ The hatstand is back, here draped with the Doctor's cape worn in *The Talons of Weng-Chiang* (although this disappears later in the serial – see below).

LANDING 154

SPACE Atrios orbit
TIME As above
TRAVELLERS The Doctor, K9, Romana
EPISODES The Armageddon Factor 1

The TARDIS rematerialises above Atrios in its new orbit, unaware it has been detected by the Atrions. They fire a nuclear warhead towards what they believe is an enemy surveillance device. As the missile looms on the scanner, the Doctor plans to dematerialise at the last minute to make it appear they were hit. K9 counts down to impact and when he reaches 'one' the Doctor moves the Ship.

◉ **CONTROLS** Romana reaches for the two large sliders on panel C3 to dematerialise and inserts the tracer in the hole on this panel.

● All the control room scenes for this story were scheduled to be recorded on Tuesday 21 November 1978 but time in the studio was cut short owing to a union dispute and these scenes were rescheduled for Tuesday 5 December. It seems some TARDIS scenes for episode one were completed in the earlier studio session, however, as the lighting, console orientation and hatstand items are different from those in later episodes. Also between the two sessions, the yellow decals added to panel C2 prior to *The Androids of Tara* were removed. Of the four control rooms scenes in episode one, all but the third were completed on the earlier date, meaning between the second, third and fourth scenes the decals disappear then reappear.

LANDING 155

SPACE Atrios, war bunker, outside K block; transmatted to Zeos
TIME As above
TRAVELLERS The Doctor, K9, Romana
EPISODES The Armageddon Factor 1, 3-4

Using the tracer, the Doctor puts the Ship down close to the location of the sixth segment. It materialises in a gloomy, long-disused passage in a bunker 400 metres underground, which nevertheless shudders from missile impacts on the surface. Radiation levels are not an immediate threat but round the corner the three travellers find the body of a recently killed guard and a heavy lead door that suggests there is a high-radiation zone beyond – as well as the segment, according to the tracer.

K9 burns a small exploratory hole in the door which reveals a young woman, Princess Astra, trapped on the other side. The breach is detected in the war operations room and the Marshal himself investigates. He arrests the Doctor and Romana for the guard's murder and leads them away. Unspotted, K9 begins to follow but another bomb strike causes the roof of the passage to collapse, blocking the way back to the TARDIS. K9 retreats, then heads for the war room in response to the Doctor's dog whistle.

When a Mute transmats from Zeos and abducts Astra, the TARDIS is also transported to the other planet. Not long after the Doctor too is brought to Zeos and interrogated by the Shadow, an agent of the Black Guardian, to reveal the location of the segments of the Key to Time. When he sees the Shadow has the TARDIS he admits they are inside but refuses to hand them over. The Shadow is patient, however, and confident the Doctor's restless nature will lead him to make a mistake, so he and his Mutes depart. The Doctor makes for the Ship but decides instead to explore Zeos while he is here.

Reunited with Romana and K9, all three return to the TARDIS as Mentalis, the computer controlling the Zeon war effort, begins counting down to planetary obliteration while the Atrion Marshal approaches to deliver a final missile strike. The Doctor collects the five segments of the Key and fits them together to reveal the shape of the missing final piece. He then creates a replica from chronodyne and locks it in place with the tracer. Although the material is only 74 percent compatible with the Key, meaning it will eventually deteriorate, it is sufficient to put the entire universe outside the TARDIS into a three-second time loop. K9 estimates this will only last for three and a quarter minutes, however, so the Doctor commands the Key to localise the effect to the Marshal's spaceship and the Zeon computer room. The decaying chronodyne means the loop is stretching by point three milliseconds every second.

As the Doctor and Romana try to deactivate Mentalis, K9 encounters Princess Astra and her lover Merak, seemingly pursued by two Mutes. As K9 chases the creatures away, Astra is strangely drawn to the TARDIS but cannot get in. The couple leave to find the Doctor.

When he and Romana return to the Ship, K9 is missing and Astra claims Zeons pursued her after Merak had transmatted back to Atrios. The Doctor lets all three of them into the TARDIS, where Astra is enthralled by the Key but does not seem to know anything about the sixth segment. The Doctor notices one of the Shadow's control devices on her neck. Romana locates the Shadow's base and the Doctor dematerialises the Ship.

● **CONTROLS** When locating the Shadow's domain, Romana turns the rotating handle on panel C4 and the silver dial (which squeaks). The Doctor dematerialises using the large slider on panel C1 while Romana operates unseen controls on panels C3 and C4 and buttons below the red grille on panel C5.

▤ **NOTES** The Police Box prop now has a blue emergency vehicle light with a rotating reflector causing it to flash, suggesting the original had been mislaid. This is the first time such a lamp has been used but it won't be the last.

▤ The TARDIS can be glimpsed in the darkness behind the Doctor when the Shadow tries to control him with a device on his neck, slightly undermining the reveal when it's illuminated moments later.

▤ Was the Doctor's line about the Shadow trying to break into the TARDIS added to explain the damage to the front right-hand window and scorch marks on the door (in reality likely caused by falling rubble in episode one)?

▤ The Doctor may be exaggerating when he says the TARDIS is "covered with automatic defence mechanisms" although we know it has a forcefield. Then again, how powerful is the Black Guardian if he can't help his agent get into the TARDIS, say by procuring a cypher indent key? At the end of episode six the Doctor is said to "have fully activated all the TARDIS's defences".

▤ Although he may be bluffing to fool the Shadow, the Doctor's claim the Key segments are kept in a "limbo closet" that can only be accessed when in possession of another segment matches the black void shown in previous episodes. This is usually seen when the Doctor has just recovered a segment and is placing it with the others; at other times, without a segment in hand, the interior door of the control room leads to the TARDIS wardrobe. Only in *The Stones of Blood* episode one do the Doctor and Romana get back into the limbo without a segment (and after she has just changed her outfit, so presumably the door then led to the wardrobe).

- Oops! The entire main doors wall is not properly attached to the column beside it and leans back as the Doctor, Romana and Astra enter and the doors close. The shot of the Doctor commanding the Key to Time, taken from a low angle up through the glass table on which the Key sits, reveals the top of the control room walls and the white cyclorama behind them.

LANDING 156

SPACE Shadow's base, between Atrios and Zeos
TIME As above
TRAVELLERS The Doctor, Romana, Princess Astra
EPISODES The Armageddon Factor 4-6

The TARDIS materialises in a rocky alcove in the Shadow's domain. The time loop has now stretched to six seconds and Romana points out they cannot use the tracer to locate the sixth segment as it is holding together the Key, which is generating the loop. The Doctor asks Astra to help them find the Shadow but she is mesmerised by the Key and wants to stay with it. She receives instruction from the Shadow to bring him Romana, however, so agrees to the Doctor's request. As the two women leave, the console picks up an intergalactic computer distress signal which the Doctor presumes must be K9. He exits the TARDIS with a portable signal detector, takes a bearing and heads off.

The chronodyne segment is starting to vaporise and the time loop has extended to seven seconds. When the Doctor returns he is escorted by one of the Shadow's Mutes to collect the Key. He unlocks the door but, as he tries to bargain with the Mute, Time Lord technician Drax shoots first the Doctor then himself with the repaired dimensional stabiliser from his own TARDIS, which shrinks them to just a few inches in height. They escape from the Mute's stomping feet through a crevice in the rock wall.

The Shadow comes to the unlocked TARDIS but when the door is opened the bright light from within is too much for this creature of darkness. He orders the Mute to enter and bring out the Key, then leaves with it in victory, not noticing or caring that the false segment is disintegrating.

The time loop is slackening and close to enabling Mentalis and the Marshal to obliterate both Zeos and Atrios. The Doctor and Romana have recovered the Key and the sixth segment from the Shadow and make it back to the TARDIS with Merak, but he wanders off in search of Astra, unable to understand that she was the sixth segment all along. Romana is disgusted at their part in ending Astra's life but the Doctor reminds her they must get to Zeos before the loop stretches too far.

○ **CONTROLS** After landing, the Doctor slightly turns the right-hand dial on panel C2. He touches it again when the distress signal is received, having opened the doors with the left-hand switch at top-left of panel C6.

- **NOTES** Although it's referred to in dialogue as the "third planet", the model for the Shadow's domain looks more like a space station. It has a central hub linked to four large, cleft, egg-shaped sections. The original storyline had an extra planet that had shifted Atrios and Zeos out of their orbits, where the Shadow had his 'Castle of Evil', but there was also a mirrored platform in space that was used to direct the Atrion's deadly mega-ray laser; perhaps the final script retained elements of both leading to a slight misunderstanding by the visual effects team.

- The Doctor leaves the TARDIS apparently empty-handed, then outside suddenly has a gadget for tracing the distress signal. As all the control room scenes were recorded on the final studio day the prop could have been introduced when the Doctor first hears the signal, but its absence might explain why Tom Baker plays much of that post-landing scene with his hand in his coat pocket, as if to suggest that's where he was keeping the device.

- A strong light was set up behind the Police Box for the shot of the Shadow being dazzled, with a cloth across the open back of the prop to diffuse the glow (briefly visible as the door opens). It's odd if this is meant to be the bright interior of the Ship as this generally hasn't been visible from outside (see Landing 17 for a possible exception), and certainly not since the dislocation of interior and exterior doors suggested since *The Invisible Enemy* (Landing 134). But nor can it be the effect of the Key as the Shadow is unaffected by it once the Mute has brought it out of the TARDIS.

LANDING 157

SPACE Zeos, Mentalis control room
TIME As above
TRAVELLERS The Doctor, Romana
EPISODES The Armageddon Factor 6

The TARDIS materialises beside the dismantled remains of Mentalis and the Doctor delves into its wiring. Moments later Drax arrives – having transmatted to Zeos with K9 and Merak – and the Doctor demands to know which wire to cut to deactivate the computer. It is five years since Drax built it and he hesitates to remember before affirming the green wire is the correct connection. The Doctor cuts it and the computer system goes dead just as the countdown reaches zero.

Romana reminds them the Marshal will soon be firing his missiles at the planet. They dash into the TARDIS and the Doctor throws up a forcefield between Zeos and the Marshal's ship, just for a millisecond but enough to deflect the missiles, which strike and destroy the Shadow's base. The Doctor offers Drax a lift but the enterprising engineer plans to help with the reconstruction of Atrios.

With the Key complete, Romana presumes they will be returning to Gallifrey, but the Doctor seems consumed with a lust for power now he controls the Key. Fortunately he is just making a point about the dangerous potential of the object. The White Guardian appears on the scanner screen, congratulating the Doctor and requesting he hand over the Key. However, his disregard for the fate of Astra makes the Doctor suspicious and he commands the Key to remain while activating all the TARDIS's defences. The figure on the scanner reveals it is truly the Black Guardian but his threats are meaningless while the Doctor controls the Key. The Doctor orders Romana to dematerialise the Ship as he snaps the tracer in two, thereby dispersing the segments across space and time again.

- **CONTROLS** Romana moves to panel C6 to set the coordinates for Gallifrey. She places her hand on the right-hand controls on the upper plate of panel C1 when instructed to be ready to dematerialise.
- **LORE** The TARDIS can project a forcefield [or extend its own]. It has multiple defences.
- **NOTES** Romana pushes the main doors closed after Drax leaves but they still make the warbling sound.
- When does the full Key get put together? The Doctor says he doesn't have time to fit the sixth segment before dealing with Mentalis, then the next time we see it after the destruction of the Shadow's base the Key is complete. Did Romana slot in the last piece, in place of the decayed false segment, while the Doctor was deflecting the missiles? Or did the Key assemble itself once all six pieces were placed in close proximity?
- Romana expects to be returning to Gallifrey and is surprised when the Guardian and not the Time Lord President appears. But the Doctor explained to her in *The Stones of Blood* (Landing 150) how she had been duped and about the true instigator of their mission.
- The Guardian notes the Doctor has "fully activated all the TARDIS's defences" suggesting there's more than just the forcefield. Then again it seems to be more the Doctor's possession of the Key that's keeping the Black Guardian at bay.

LANDING 158

SPACE Unknown
TIME Unknown
TRAVELLERS The Doctor, K9, Romana
EPISODES The Armageddon Factor 6

The Doctor rematerialises somewhere while he fits a new control to the guidance systems that generates coordinates at random. That way he cannot know where he is going so neither can the Black Guardian.

As the Doctor explains to Romana the operating principle of this 'randomiser', as he calls it, he activates the device and the TARDIS takes off, destination: who knows?

- **CONTROLS** The randomiser is fitted to panel C1 on the upper plate, below the row of lights and between the two flick switches (replacing the buttons and grille). The slider below it now has a lever with a large red spherical knob. This engages the randomiser and dematerialises the TARDIS.

- **NOTES** The Doctor tells Romana to dematerialise as he breaks the tracer and although we don't see or hear the TARDIS taking off we can assume it leaves Zeos at this point. The central column is then stationary and the control room hum low as the Doctor shows off the randomiser, and the take-off sound is heard as he activates it. So he must have materialised somewhere while he fits the device.
- Since the Doctor regained control of the TARDIS at the end of *The Three Doctors* (Landing 91) he has generally been able to pilot it wherever he wants. The show's writers, and more strangely script editor Terrance Dicks, seemed to take some time to appreciate this development given that during Seasons 10 and 11 there are instances of seemingly misguided landings. In the very next story, *Carnival of Monsters* (Landing 92), the Doctor fails to get Jo to Metebelis Three, then needs the Time Lords' help to reach Spiridon in *Planet of the Daleks* (Landing 94). He seems to mis-time his and Sarah's return to London in *Invasion of the Dinosaurs* (Landing 99), and misses Florana in *Death to the Daleks* (Landing 100). The first and last of these can perhaps be explained by the TARDIS being pulled off course, by the Miniscope and Exxilon city respectively, and the others by the Doctor getting used to piloting the Ship. After the Doctor regenerates, missed or unexpected landings can be put down to temporary faults or outside influence, but when the Doctor wants to get to specific places, as in *The Invisible Enemy* (Landings 134-137), *Image of the Fendahl* (Landings 138-139) and *The Pirate Planet* (Landings 148-149), he can and does. Even during his quest for the Key to Time, although the tracer indicated where to go, it appeared down to the Doctor to get there. This is confirmed by the need for the randomiser to revive the early series' approach of never knowing where the TARDIS would land next. Yet even with this device fitted the Doctor is seen to make intentional landings, and after it is removed he still arrives in the wrong place sometimes. Basically, if a writer needs to have the TARDIS land somewhere specific then the Doctor can pilot it successfully, and if it needs to go wrong then the Doctor can't.

PREVIOUS LANDING

SPACE None
TIME The Big Bang
TRAVELLERS The Doctor, [unknown companions]
EPISODES Claimed by the Doctor in Destiny of the Daleks 1

The Doctor witnessed the beginning of the universe.

- **NOTES** While reading *The Origins of the Universe* by Oolon Coluphid, the Doctor suggests the author should have asked "someone who was there". The implication is he's talking about himself but his knowledge might be from Time Lord records.

LANDING 159

SPACE Skaro
TIME [4500]
TRAVELLERS The Doctor, K9, Romana
EPISODES Destiny of the Daleks 1,4

While the TARDIS is in flight, the Doctor tinkers with K9's brain and discovers that his voice unit is malfunctioning, a condition he likens to laryngitis. Unbeknown to him, Romana has regenerated and now looks like Astra. Indeed, the Doctor initially mistakes her for the Atrion princess and so insists she change. After dismissing three further suggestions, he is pleased when Romana returns in a copy of his own outfit. Beneath the hat, though, is the same face as Astra and the Doctor accepts Romana's new look. She goes to change her clothes as the randomiser engages and the TARDIS materialises on a ledge beneath an overhanging stone escarpment, its occupants unaware this is the Daleks' home world Skaro. There is a breathable atmosphere but a high level of radiation and all around is rubble and desolation. The periodic ground tremors that the Doctor initially takes to be seismic activity are actually the result of deep-level high-impact phason drilling.

Before leaving the Ship, the Doctor gives Romana some anti-radiation pills and a bleeper to alert her when she needs another dose. They check the scanner but can see only a rock wall. Before going outside, the Doctor replaces K9's brain but inserts it back to front causing the robot dog to spin on the spot. He swiftly takes it out again and decides to leave K9 immobilised for now.

A short time later Romana approaches the TARDIS to collect K9 but the drilling below causes a rockfall that blocks the entrance to the Ship. Unable to get inside and with her bleeper indicating she is due further anti-radiation pills, Romana returns to where she left the Doctor, unaware she is being followed.

When the Doctor and Romana return they are together able to move the rubble away from the TARDIS door. He explains how the warring Daleks' and Movellans' logical computers were locked in stalemate so the first to take irrational action would have won, and concedes that sometimes he triumphs by making a mistake. They enter the Ship and it dematerialises.

○ **CONTROLS** The Doctor moves the right-hand large slider on panel C3 downwards immediately before the TARDIS materialises but seems surprised at the result. The Doctor is looking at panel C1 as he reads out the atmospheric conditions but he's adjusting the right-hand dial on panel C2 at the same time so may be getting some tactile feedback. He activates the scanner with the centre dial on panel C2 and Romana opens the doors with a flick switch on the left of panel C1.

○ The keyboard on panel C5 is upside down (fitted that way for *The Creature from the Pit*, recorded first – see Landing 166), as is the block at the top of panel C1. The top-right blue disc on this panel has gone missing. The randomiser and red lever are still in place (or rather back after being removed for *The Creature from the Pit*), and the controls on the bottom-right plate of this panel have been replaced with a connector for the emergency transceiver (added for the previously recorded story). The dial that had been on that plate is now in the top-right corner of panel C5.

▤ **NOTES** No date is given for this story but in *Resurrection of the Daleks* Davros says he has been frozen for 90 years. That story is also not dated on screen but the script indicates the Daleks' time period is 4590. Of course, Davros's imprisonment on the space station in the later story could be some indeterminate time after his initial capture at the end of this serial, which might therefore be set some years before 4500.

▤ To the right of the interior door is a section of white-painted wall from the 1976 control room, with aligned rather than staggered roundels, in place of the plain flat wall that had previously been used to extend the control room. The room is given a (partial and poorly fitted) ceiling, just across the scanner wall, for the upward shot of the very tall Romana. There is also, conveniently, a wooden-framed full-length mirror in the control room. The hatstand is largely obscured by an open multi-coloured umbrella (bad luck indoors) as well as the Doctor's brown coat, waistcoat and a white shirt hanging on it. The main doors have had their translucent roundels painted over.

▤ Sure, the scene of Romana trying out different bodies is just a light-hearted way of explaining the change of actor and we should just smile and not think too hard about it. But where's the fun in that? So first, is the Doctor surprised that Romana has regenerated or simply that she now looks like Astra? Neither talks about why she has changed. If she'd done so on a whim or been keeping a health issue secret, surely the Doctor would ask about it? This suggests they both knew she needed to regenerate and he has let her do so in private. He's then perplexed when Astra seems to turn up before quickly grasping that she is Romana, and it's this duplication he objects too (unfairly as he himself has already looked like two different humans and will do so again). So does Romana deliberately take on Astra's appearance? *The War Games* indicates Time Lords can select their new faces so perhaps there's some environment or equipment in the TARDIS that she utilised (has she been in the Zero Room? See Landing 204). The question would then be why choose to look like Astra – "I thought it looked very nice on the princess," seems a touch frivolous. We later see that the Doctor's regenerations can be unconsciously influenced by people he has met (notably in *Deep Breath* but possibly also *The Twin Dilemma*) so perhaps looking like Astra – whose existence was threatened by cosmic forces – was to remind herself that their adventures sometimes have a human cost that's not worth paying. Or it was simply coincidence. Either way, discovering she has regenerated into Astra's form, Romana's arguments that it's attractive and unlikely to be an issue if they stay away from Atrios could be simple rebuttals to the Doctor's initial unease rather than justifications for a choice. It's just about plausible the TARDIS contains an exact replica of Astra's dress – The Androids of Tara suggests the wardrobe contains attire from a wide selection of planets – and we can only assume Romana dons it deliberately to tease the Doctor having found herself, by choice or fluke, looking like the princess. And so to Romana's fashion show of figures. If she is able to choose her post-regenerative form then maybe these are actually her in new bodies, either using up further regenerations or utilising the residual energy from the first to remodel the outward appearance – we later learn in stories like The Christmas Invasion and Let's Kill Hitler that Time Lords are still mutable for some time after regenerating. However, given she starts and ends with the Astra look, the likeliest explanation is that these are mental or holographic projections, deliberately outrageous to wear down the Doctor's objections and resign him to Romana's true new form, while she hides just outside the control room (note her voice doesn't change and neither we nor the Doctor directly see any of the body options speak).

- The Police Box prop had to have its roof lamp removed to fit it in the rocky alcove on location. The shots of it materialising and dematerialising therefore had the flashing light added electronically. Note how the light stays still as the film footage jiggles slightly.
- The lower shutter of the scanner is not fitted correctly, allowing the light illuminating the blue CSO screen behind to leak through the gap.
- The Doctor seems to have the anti-radiation pills and bleepers in his pocket before learning of the conditions of the planet they're on, so does he always carry them around? We also don't see him take any until later.

LANDING 160

SPACE Skaro
TIME As above
TRAVELLERS The Doctor, K9, Romana
EPISODES Destiny of the Daleks 4

The TARDIS is barely in flight when the Doctor – inadvertently proving his point about occasionally making mistakes – presses the wrong switch and it returns to Skaro in the exact spot it just left.

Romana points out the Doctor's error and with a chuckle – perhaps it was not inadvertent after all – he takes off again. This time the Police Box dematerialises for good.

- **NOTES** The Police Box and take-off sound fade completely, then the landing sound is heard as the TARDIS reappears, so this has to count as a second landing rather than merely an interrupted take-off. Perhaps the Doctor is subconsciously reliving the first time he left Skaro and presses the (very) fast return switch.

PREVIOUS LANDING

SPACE [Jagaroth home world]
TIME 400 million BC
TRAVELLERS The Doctor, [unknown companions]
EPISODES Recalled by the Doctor in City of Death 3

The Doctor witnessed the destruction of the Jagaroth in a massive war.

- **NOTES** The Doctor says this was "on one of my trips" so it's fair to assume he was present towards the end of the Jagaroth war – perhaps a civil war given they "all destroyed [themselves]". He at least knows that Jagaroth have "one eye and green skin". Romana seems to have heard of the Jagaroth so she may have been present.
- The war was likely on their planet but as they clearly had some interstellar travel capability it may have been waged across space.

LANDING 161

SPACE Earth, France, Paris, Denise René art gallery
TIME Spring 1979
TRAVELLERS The Doctor, K9, Romana
EPISODES City of Death 1-2

The randomiser lands the TARDIS in the French capital one morning in 1979 – not a vintage year, the Doctor tells Romana. The Police Box materialises in the art gallery of Denise René on the left bank, not entirely out of place among the modern art and sculptures on display. The two Time Lords decide to take in the city's bouquet with a visit to the Eiffel Tower, leaving K9 to guard the Ship.

Around lunch time, and again a short while later, there is a slip in time and two seconds repeat as somewhere in the city a primitive time machine without a relative dimensional stabiliser is tested.

That evening, after sunset, the Doctor returns alone, using his sonic screwdriver to unlock the front door of the gallery. He takes a torch from his pocket to find his way to the TARDIS, pausing only to straighten a lopsided painting on the wall. He greets K9 as he enters and takes off immediately.

- **NOTES** The Doctor states the year, and passes a poster for an exhibition at the Muséum National d'Histoire Naturelle, '3 Millions d'Annes d'Aventure Humaine', running from 26 January to 31 May 1979. (This was a genuine advertisement the film crew spotted while on location in early May and included because it tied in nicely with the story's opening and closing scenes.) While this could be an old poster and the Doctor and Romana are there later in the year, the blossom on the trees near the Eiffel Tower indicates it's spring.
- The TARDIS may arrive on a day when the art gallery is closed as no one seems to wonder what it's doing

there. Then again, the next day it's being admired by two visitors, so the owner must know it's there. A card has been placed in front of it, presumably giving a title and artist; perhaps the Doctor put this up on arrival to deflect suspicion, or convinced the owner the Police Box was a legitimate artwork.

- Professor Kerenski's construction in 1979 of a time machine that can (unwittingly to him) roll back time, returning the Earth to an earlier era, is surprisingly coincident to the activities of Professor Whitaker in *Invasion of the Dinosaurs* (Landing 99). As the former's efforts appear to be totally destroyed and the latter's are sent back in time with their inventor, it's unlikely either built on the work of the other. Kerenski believes himself "the foremost authority on temporal theory in the whole world" and Count Scarlioni must agree or he would have chosen the higher authority, so either they don't know of Whitaker's theories or think them inferior (despite leading to the same result).
- Although it seems unlikely the Doctor would travel for long without reactivating K9, the fact he doesn't tour Paris with his master and mistress – and later doesn't rescue the Doctor when he's in danger from Captain Tancredi's guard – suggests he is still incapacitated.

LANDING 162

SPACE Earth, Italy, Tuscany, Florence, Leonardo's studio
TIME 1505
TRAVELLERS The Doctor, K9
EPISODES City of Death 2-3

The Doctor travels back to Renaissance Italy to quiz Leonardo da Vinci about his apparent painting of seven copies of the Mona Lisa. The TARDIS materialises in a curtained alcove off his studio, around which are scattered artworks in progress.

As the Doctor peruses the studio, he is accosted by a soldier whose commander, Captain Tancredi, looks exactly like Count Scarlioni back in 20th-century Paris. Tancredi reveals he is in fact Scaroth, the last surviving Jagaroth, who was splintered into twelve facets across Earth's history when his spaceship exploded 400 million years ago. The Doctor is less forthcoming when questioned so Tancredi leaves to fetch torture equipment. The soldier is easily overcome, distracted by the flash of a Polaroid camera then knocked out with a punch. The Doctor writes 'This is a fake' with a felt-tip pen on a set of blank boards and leaves a note telling Leonardo to simply paint over the writing. Before he can escape, however, Tancredi returns with thumbscrews. To avoid being tortured, the Doctor confesses both he and Romana are Time Lords.

Tancredi insists the Doctor explain how to stabilise the continuum interface of Scarlioni's time machine, but he becomes distracted by his other splinters making contact. The Doctor is able to slip past the solider and into the TARDIS. He watches on the scanner as Tancredi declares, "The centuries that divide me shall be undone," then dematerialises the Ship.

- **NOTES** The TARDIS's arrival in Florence was shot using the roll-back-and-mix technique. Its subsequent departure was done with a split-screen effect, though, the Police Box on the right being obscured by fading in a view of the empty alcove as Julian Glover continues to act on the left. A soft join was positioned to the right of the chair in the background.
- The Doctor must override the randomiser in order to pilot the TARDIS to a specific destination, so he's not overly worried about the Black Guardian finding him. However, he says the original Mona Lisa was completed in 1503 (a contentious claim) so why didn't he land then? In fact it's quite a coincidence he arrives just as Tancredi is about to commission Leonardo, so perhaps the Ship can detect Scaroth's various iterations.
- It's often assumed the Doctor has met Leonardo before this story (but after Landing 124 as he hadn't at that point), mainly because he talks of Mona Lisa as "that dreadful woman with no eyebrows who wouldn't sit still". However, only hours earlier he was shocked to have it pointed out to him that she had no eyebrows, something he would surely have noticed had he met her, so it's likely the sitting-still comment is a joke (given most portrait sitters get a bit fidgety). The other indicator is he signs off his message to Leonardo 'See you earlier'. This only makes sense if he means it'll be before 1505 but later in the Doctor's timeline, so he clearly intends to revisit the artist in his future (perhaps to forewarn him about Tancredi and persuade him to play along). This may be soon after leaving Paris while it's still fresh in his mind, but certainly before his seventh regeneration as shortly after that he recalls Leonardo having a cold when he sketched the face of a young woman (see Previous to Landing 307).
- For the brief shot of the Doctor watching the scanner, only the scanner wall and one column were erected in the studio, not the whole control room. Curiously, the shot used in the final episode is a single still frame, with only the superimposed image on the scanner moving.

LANDING 163

SPACE Earth, France, Paris, Denise René art gallery
TIME One day after Landing 161
TRAVELLERS The Doctor, K9
EPISODES City of Death 3-4

The TARDIS returns to its previous spot in the Parisian art gallery, arriving in the early morning after its last departure. The Doctor is disturbed by Tancredi's assertion and leaves the gallery, heading towards the Louvre where he had sent Romana with the British detective Duggan.

Two art lovers are admiring the Police Box – how its line and colour counterpoint the redundant vestiges of its function – when the Doctor, Romana and Duggan barge through the gallery and into the TARDIS. The critics watch with delight as it fades away quite exquisitely.

- **NOTES** The TARDIS's return to the art gallery was shot using the roll-back-and-mix technique. Its subsequent departure was done with a split-screen effect, though, the Police Box on the right being obscured by fading in a view of the empty room as John Cleese and Eleanor Bron continue to act on the left. A soft join was aligned with the corner of the background wall.
- When the Doctor entered the gallery the previous night (a studio set) the windows either side of the door had their blinds down. When he exits the next morning (filmed on location), those windows are clear.
- The Doctor has met Shakespeare, probably prior to Landing 98. That Count Scarlioni owns the first draft of Hamlet, dating from somewhere between the 1580s and 1600s, suggests one of his splinters was around then, but which? It depends how long-lived the Jagaroth were and whether Scaroth's facets overlap. They're evidently not spread evenly across the 400 million years between his ship exploding and 1979 or the first eleven would exist before humans evolved. Even if the first was the one who showed Man "the true use of fire" (whatever that is) around 100,000BC, an even distribution of his other selves would place them at intervals above 9,000 years. For Tancredi and Scarlioni to be barely 500 years apart, there must be a decreasing differential, making an overlap, or another facet between those two, highly unlikely. We can also assume each splinter's consciousness progresses at the same rate – Scarlioni doesn't know what Tancredi has learned about the Doctor until they have one of their mental catch-ups – and that when the Count is killed Scaroth's other facets also die or evaporate at equivalent points in their existences. So if Tancredi expires in 1505, shortly after encountering the Doctor, Scarlioni can't have been around for more than 474 years, but at least 300 in order to have purloined the original Hamlet. It must be he who also acquired an original Gainsborough in the mid-to-late-1700s, while Tancredi – who would have popped into being between 1031 and 1205 – must have stashed some Gutenberg bibles in the 1450s.

LANDING 164

SPACE Earth
TIME 400,000,000BC
TRAVELLERS The Doctor, K9, Romana, Duggan
EPISODES City of Death 4

Following a faint trail left by Scaroth as he uses his time bubble to travel back to when his spaceship originally landed on Earth, the TARDIS arrives a short distance from the spherical Jagaroth vessel. Emerging into the desolate landscape, Duggan cannot comprehend where they are – "This will be the middle of the Atlantic Ocean," speculates the Doctor – and even less that the pools of black goo around them are the organic soup from which life will spring once it is energised with a suitable dose of radiation.

With the Jagaroth spaceship preparing to take off using its warp drive (its atmospheric thrust motors being disabled), the Doctor ushers Romana and Duggan back to the TARDIS before its inevitable – and life-bringing – explosion. The Ship dematerialises just as the craft begins to rise into the blood-red sky.

- **NOTES** Model shots of the TARDIS arriving and leaving were filmed (using the miniature built for *Pyramids of Mars*) but the director found them unconvincing. Instead the full-size prop was recorded in the studio using the roll-back-and-mix technique. Shot from a distance on the primeval Earth set, the boundaries of the set were masked by a foreground glass painting.
- The Doctor has presumably again overridden the randomiser in order to follow Scaroth's trail, yet there's still no sign of the Black Guardian.
- If the TARDIS is following Scaroth's trail, how come it appears to arrive before he does? Maybe once it approached the correct period it was able to home in on the warp drive of the Jagaroth ship. Then again, we don't see Scaroth's arrival from the future so perhaps he gets there before the TARDIS but has to walk a further distance. Indeed, given the extent of tectonic movement over the past 400 million years, he's lucky to be anywhere near his spaceship.
- In our history, life is estimated to have begun on Earth around four billion years ago, ten times earlier than in the *Doctor Who* universe. Presumably human civilisation occurs at a similar time owing to the additional push given it by Scaroth – along with Fendahl and the Dæmons. If we assume that conditions on Earth for life to form were the same, whenever that was, then there would indeed have been a solid crust and the planet was cool enough for liquid water to form oceans. But the atmosphere wouldn't have been breathable, certainly for Duggan if not the two Time Lords or Scaroth, as it lacked oxygen. Does the TARDIS provide a bubble of breathable air, extending out to the Jagaroth spaceship?

LANDING 165

SPACE Earth, France, Paris, [Denise René art gallery]
TIME As Landing 163
TRAVELLERS The Doctor, K9, Romana, Duggan
EPISODES City of Death 4

The TARDIS returns to Paris 1979 to drop off Duggan, who accompanies the Doctor and Romana on a final trip to the top of the Eiffel Tower. The two Time Lords soon decide to move on, even though the randomiser means they have no idea where they are going.

- **NOTES** It's likely, but not stated, that the TARDIS returns to the same spot in the art gallery. Sadly, the dialogue makes it improbable that there have been unseen landings with Duggan. It is possible that, after taking their leave of Duggan, the Doctor and Romana continue their holiday in Paris.

LANDING 166

SPACE Chloris
TIME Unknown
TRAVELLERS The Doctor, K9, Romana
EPISODES The Creature from the Pit 1,4

K9 has recovered his voice, although it sounds different, and the Doctor has him exercise it by reading from 'The Tale of Peter Rabbit'. Romana has been clearing out number four hold and hauls into the control room a crate of objects she considers junk. One is a mark three emergency transceiver, for sending and receiving distress calls. K9 disputes the Doctor's assertion that it is broken, so the latter admits he removed it because it was a nuisance.

To prove his point, he has Romana attach the transceiver to the console and it immediately picks up a signal. The control room tips as the TARDIS is automatically redirected, landing in a lush, steamy jungle on the planet Chloris. Next to it is the source of the distress call, a section of a giant egg-shaped object woven from an aluminium compound and emitting an inaudible low-frequency sound.

The Doctor and Romana go out to examine the egg shell, the former tapping it with a spoon, touching it with a horseshoe magnet, and listening to it with a stethoscope. As he does so he is attacked by a pack of wolfweeds, thorny spherical plants, that try to smother him. They are called off by a whip-wielding huntsman as soldiers capture Romana. Their commander, Karela, quizzes the Doctor about his business in this Place of Death and the nature of the large blue box nearby. He offers to show her how it travels but the old woman has him secured in a pillory and leads the pair away for questioning by Lady Adrasta.

Shortly after, K9 detects the sound of his mistress's dog whistle and leaves the TARDIS to find her.

Later that day, the three travellers return to the Ship, bringing with them the shield-like device through which Erato, an ambassador from Tythonus, communicates. Freed from the pit in which it was trapped for fifteen years by Lady Adrasta, it has re-woven its egg-shaped spaceship and takes off to rendezvous with a neutron star that its fellow Tythonians have directed at Chloris's sun in retribution. Watching on the scanner, Romana dematerialises the TARDIS.

- **CONTROLS** The Doctor idly adjusts unseen controls on panel C3 (including the right-hand rotary handle and one of the two large sliders), possibly some in the bottom-right corner of panel C4, and the centre dial on panel C2. Romana plugs the emergency transceiver into its new connector on the bottom-right plate of panel C1. The Doctor operates the scanner with, it seems, the right-hand dial on panel C2 and opens the main doors from the same panel.
- Romana detects the neutron star "on band six" from panel C3, seemingly the lower-right display, then dematerialises using one or both of the large sliders on the same panel.
- The randomiser has been removed from panel C1 but the small grille it covered is now missing and the red-knobbed lever added below has reverted to a black-handled slider (with an additional piece of red tape on it). Next to this is the new connection for the emergency transceiver, replacing the controls previously there. This consists of a clear plastic disc with four protruding rods around the circumference and one in the middle. The transceiver prop slots inside the outer rods. This is a silver hemisphere with an octagonal base, red markings and a domed light.
- **LORE** The TARDIS has at least four cargo holds.
- The console is usually fitted with a mark three emergency transceiver, although the Doctor has disconnected his because it was a nuisance. This may be because it can direct the TARDIS automatically on receiving a distress call.
- K9 implies TARDIS is an initialism for Time And Relative Dimensions In Space. This is the first time the expansion has been given on screen since *The War Games* (Landing 68).
- **NOTES** The miniature Police Box built for *Pyramids of Mars* was used for the first shot of the TARDIS in flight. The swirling yellow overlay is possibly intended to represent the Vortex. Then again, during the immediately following control room scene, the central column of the console is stationary. It moves briefly when the distress call is received then stops when the TARDIS materialises. It's possible, therefore, the Police Box has materialised in space and is drifting through some nebular matter causing it to spin. The same miniature is used in the model shot of the TARDIS in the jungle beside the egg shell. Note the Police Box is much less obscured by foliage than in the following studio shot of the full-size prop, where the roof lamp is hidden by a leafy branch (or possibly missing).
- This story was the first produced for Season 17, in April 1979, so the first time the control room set and console were required after almost five months in storage. The angles of the walls are more acute than usual, giving the control room a cramped feel. A new hatstand is seen, here holding the Doctor's grey and brown coats, waistcoat, cape and deerstalker from *The Talons of Weng-Chiang* and what looks like a spare pair of trousers.
- Oops! As Lalla Ward pulls the crate of junk through the interior doorway, a hand can be seen helping to push it into shot.
- Romana's junk collection also includes a large ball of string, used to help Theseus navigate the Minotaur's labyrinth; the jawbone of an ass, suggested as being that with which Samson slew a thousand Philistines; and the barrel of the hyperspace projector the Doctor built in *The Stones of Blood* (Landing 150).
- The emergency transceiver is said to be for sending and receiving distress calls, yet Romana supposes the Doctor "kept getting calls from Gallifrey all the time" with requests or instructions for missions, which is not the same thing. Were the Time Lords using the Doctor as a field agent to respond to calls for help they

had received, or is the transceiver intended for Time Lords taking investigative trips in a TARDIS to request assistance? The only time it seems likely the Doctor was contacted this way would be just after control of the TARDIS was returned to him and his exile lifted during his third incarnation, particularly after they'd helped him track down the Daleks on Spiridon. Did he find his freedom restored but his help constantly sought, until he got fed up, removed the transceiver and hid it deep in the Ship? Even without the emergency transceiver the console can detect distress calls, most recently in *The Armageddon Factor* (Landing 156).

- It's possible the emergency transceiver is intended to override the randomiser here (and perhaps in the next story – see Landing 169), but given the latter is no longer visible on the console and the numerous intentional landings in the previous story, it's feasible the Doctor has simply disconnected it already. Perhaps dealing with Scaroth reminded him he often needs to direct the TARDIS; perhaps he comes to realise that now the White Guardian has restored the cosmological balance it'll be some time before the Black Guardian has enough of an upper hand again to come after him. Neither he nor the randomiser are even mentioned again until the latter is explicitly disposed of in *The Leisure Hive* (Landing 183), even after which it's a long time before the Black Guardian seeks his revenge. If the Doctor has recently decided to dispense with the randomiser after all, it would explain his displeasure at the idea of being at the beck and call of the emergency transceiver so soon.
- The roundels either side of the main doors are painted a paler shade of grey than the rest of the wall. When the control room is next used, for *Destiny of the Daleks*, they have been repainted.
- When the Doctor and Romana exit the control room, you can see through the zigzag gaps of the main doors' hinged edge that they immediately turn right. When K9 later leaves, although it's just off camera, it sounds like and his shadow indicates he collides with the edge of the doorway and gets stuck on the angled frame.
- K9 operates the main doors by extending his probe towards the edge of the console and, presumably, emitting a signal that activates the required control.

LANDING 167

SPACE Space, Chloris's solar system
TIME As above
TRAVELLERS The Doctor, K9, Romana
EPISODES The Creature from the Pit 4

The TARDIS instantly rematerialises close to the path of the neutron star, which Erato's ship is also approaching. It projects a gravity tractor beam towards the star, slowing its progress for Erato to get near enough to weave an aluminium shell around it and reduce its gravitational pull. The TARDIS shudders under the enormous stress.

It takes just seconds for Erato to encase the star, but as Romana is about to switch off the gravity beam its control circuit explodes preventing it from being deactivated. A second explosion on the console throws her and the Doctor to the floor. With the neutron star now being pulled towards the TARDIS, the Doctor struggles to reach the dematerialisation control but manages to move the Ship just in time.

He and Romana watch on the scanner as the star moves away on a new trajectory that will miss Chloris's sun. Erato, speaking through K9, is impressed but the Doctor claims the odds against success of 74,384,338 to one were the same as his lucky number.

- **CONTROLS** Romana activates the gravity tractor beam with the left-hand large slider on panel C3, then the Doctor does the same with the large slider on panel C1. He uses this same slider to dematerialise.
- The first explosion comes from the keyboard in the middle of panel C5, which has been fitted upside down. The second is in the top-right corner of the same panel and leaves a scorch mark on the collar around the top of the console and on the central column.
- The socket for the Key to Time tracer is still visible at top-right of panel C5 before the explosion there, but during and after the dial previously on panel C1 covers it, perhaps added to hide the explosive charge.
- **LORE** The TARDIS can generate a gravity tractor beam powerful enough to retard the motion of a super-dense neutron star for a few seconds, although not without considerable strain.
- **NOTES** The shots of the Police Box model in space were filmed reflected in a sheet of flexible mirrored material which was distorted to represent the stress on the Ship. Although obscured by a video effect for the gravity beam, these used the miniature built for *Pyramids of Mars*. Oddly, however, the one shot of the TARDIS dematerialising to avoid the neutron star used the *Hand of Fear* model.
- As in episode one, the central column is stationary in the last TARDIS scene as we see the neutron star moving away on the scanner, so it's arguable the Ship has rematerialised again out of its path. But in this story the column only moves during the moment of landing or take-off, so it's possible in this instance the TARDIS is in flight.
- The odds of success is a combination of the phone number of Television Centre and script editor Douglas Adams' extension. This was as scripted (almost certainly added by Adams) rather than the actors substituting a figure they'd find easier to remember.

LANDING 168

SPACE Chloris, Adrasta's palace
TIME As above
TRAVELLERS The Doctor, K9, Romana
EPISODES The Creature from the Pit 4

The TARDIS returns briefly to Chloris, materialising in the late Adrasta's throne room, where her ex-astrologer Organon is consulting his crystal ball. The Doctor hands over to the huntsman, who is now in charge, a draft contract from Erato for a trade agreement between Chloris and Tythonus.

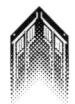

While Organon eavesdrops to convince the huntsman of his predictive abilities, securing his position under this new regime, the Doctor and Romana slip back into the TARDIS and take off.

NOTES The TARDIS's arrival is achieved using a split-screen effect, with Organon on the left and the Police Box on the right. A view of the empty room, masked off down the centre of the screen, initially obscures the latter and is then faded out as Organon looks up.

PREVIOUS LANDINGS

SPACE Unknown
TIME Late-21st/early-22nd century
TRAVELLERS The Doctor, [unknown companions]
EPISODES Recalled by the Doctor in Nightmare of Eden 1

The Doctor attended a seminar given by Professor Stein, who was working on developing a Continuous Event Transmuter machine.

NOTES This was before the TARDIS landed on the Empress, by which time Stein was deceased. The Doctor is interrupted before he can say what the seminar was about, but given he knows Stein had "toyed with an idea like this [the CET machine]" we can assume that was the subject of his talk.

LANDING 169

SPACE Earth space liner Empress, orbiting Azure
TIME [2116]
TRAVELLERS The Doctor, K9, Romana
EPISODES Nightmare of Eden 1-4

Responding to another distress call, the TARDIS lands aboard the Empress, a cruise liner travelling from Station Nine to the planet Azure. Part of the hull shimmers where a second ship, the Hecate, has cut across it when they collided while the Empress was emerging from warp. The travellers examine the matter interface which K9 warns is highly unstable. The Doctor elects to find the captain and offer their help.

Later, the Doctor collects a portable demat unit from the TARDIS, connected to it via a cable, which he sets up beside the Ship and aims at the nearby matter interface. Shortly after, Romana arrives to activate it, projecting energy into the interface to excite the molecules while the Hecate's pilot Dymond fires his engines in an attempt to pull free. His ship risks being damaged, however, and he shuts down before the two vessels can uncouple.

For a second attempt, K9 operates the demat unit, activating it on the sound of the Doctor's dog whistle. It fires an energy beam into the interface as both spaceships power their engines and successfully separate.

Marauding Mandrells have been herded back into their habitat on Eden, stored on a laser crystal in Tryst's Continuous Event Transmuter, and the Doctor has dismantled the dubious device. He and Romana collect all its crystals with the intention of returning the flora and fauna contained on them to their native planets, using machinery in the TARDIS that is rather more sophisticated than the unstable CET. They take their leave of Della and Stott, who promise to keep secret the knowledge that the Mandrells are a source of the drug Vraxoin.

LORE External monitors can be tuned to view the inside of the TARDIS [via the scanner].

NOTES The date Galactic Insurance went out of business is shown as 2096, which Captain Rigg says was 20 years ago, so depending how precise he's being it could now be a couple of years either side of 2116.

- The rotating blue light, last seen in *The Armageddon Factor* (Landing 155) has returned to the Police Box prop following the removal (and possible loss) of the original lensed lamp for *Destiny of the Daleks* (Landing 159). The front of the prop is marked with chalk dust following a photo shoot for a series of greetings cards, part of the centre post has split off at the bottom, and the base has been painted black. The left-hand 'Police box' sign box has slightly paler, smoother paintwork than the rest of the box so might have been refurbished, and a metal eyelet has been screwed into the left side next to the window, although there's no apparent need for it in this story (or the next and it had gone by the time *Shada* began recording).

- The TARDIS inconsiderately materialises in front of a doorway.

- Although we don't see inside the control room, might we assume the mark three emergency transceiver is still attached to the console and picked up the Empress's mayday? The last we saw of it in *The Creature from the Pit*, it was resting on the console but not in its connector. Perhaps the Doctor agreed to keep it activated for a while, although the console can pick up distress calls without it, as in *Planet of Evil* (Landing 110), *The Invisible Enemy* (Landing 133) and *The Armageddon Factor* (Landing 156).

- For the view on the Empress bridge monitor of Romana in the TARDIS, just one wall was erected for Lalla Ward to stand in front of (with staggered roundels). The Doctor presses a switch on the bridge control before speaking to Romana but we can assume she has previously tuned the Ship's scanner to the Empress's communications system rather than the other way round; the Doctor is perhaps accepting the connection or turning on the microphone at his end. The scanner has previously been used as a videophone in *The Three*

Doctors (by the same writer) but that was achieved via either Time Lord technology or mental projection (see Landing 91); this is the first time the TARDIS is seen to connect with a basic video system.
- The demat machine has a cable leading into the TARDIS but it's not certain if it's a component of the Ship or a separate device, although the fact it has a carry handle suggests the latter. It has an extendable barrel that projects an alternating pink/green ray.
- Given the Doctor plans to "project [the creatures on the crystals] back to their own planets" and Romana talks of "far more sophisticated stuff in the TARDIS" than the CET machine, we can assume they use the Ship or some equipment within it to return the samples rather than visiting each planet. If not, there may be further landings on Brus, Darp, Eden, Gidi, Lvan, Ranx, Vij and Zil (some of these names may be abbreviations).

LANDING 170

SPACE Space, sector L75, midway between Skonnos and Aneth
TIME Unknown
TRAVELLERS The Doctor, K9, Romana
EPISODES The Horns of Nimon 1-2

The Doctor completely immobilises the TARDIS, including dismantling half the control systems and the dematerialisation circuits, in order to modify the conceptual geometer. However, K9 reports and the console confirms that the Ship is still moving very fast, caught in a strong gravitational field (unknown to them, this is being generated by a focused gravity beam from nearby Skonnos). Romana urges the Doctor to put the console back together but before he can do so the defence shields burn out. The scanner shows a Skonnon battle cruiser in their path and the TARDIS collides with it, jamming up against the struts of the aged vessel.

In order to board the ship, the Doctor extrudes the main doors' defence shield into a corridor leading from the Police Box to an exterior hatch on the Skonnon craft, and the three travellers gingerly make their way along it. Moments later, K9 returns alone with instructions to assess the damage to the TARDIS.

When the Doctor joins him shortly after, the robot dog is buried under his own ticker-tape readouts. He reports that in addition to the inoperative dematerialisation circuits and defence shield, the dimensional stabiliser is fused but the gravitic anomaliser is functioning. The Doctor takes the last and some other items with which to upgrade the Skonnon spaceship's engines and enable it to escape the strengthening gravitational well. When he has delivered these to Romana, he returns to the TARDIS to move it into the ship's cargo hold.

Before he can, Romana completes her work and the Skonnon pilot sets his ship in motion, leaving the TARDIS at the centre of the gravitational well. This is pulling in other clumps of matter – including a 96.4-kilometer-wide, 220-million-tonne asteroid approaching at a speed of mach 9.3. Unable to dematerialise and with no defence shields, the Doctor sets the TARDIS spinning so that it deflects off the rotating asteroid like a bowled cricket ball, knocking it clear of the gravitational field.

To compensate for the missing gravitic anomaliser, the Doctor connects other components to the exposed mechanism of the central column and tries to take off. His first attempt fails – with a bang and a bizarre series of noises – but on the second go the TARDIS smoothly dematerialises.

- **CONTROLS** Romana indicates that the TARDIS is still moving by gesturing at panel C3 – possibly the left-hand quartered display – which the Doctor confirms by turning the bottom-right rotary handle on that panel and the left-hand dial on panel C2. The dematerialisation circuits are connected to panel C1, where there's also a motion indicator. The Doctor extends the doors' defence shield from panels C3 and C4 (including turning the silver dial on the right of the latter).
- The keyboard in the centre of panel C5 has lost all its buttons, leaving only the surrounding case (still upside down). Despite these being the centre of an explosion in *The Creature from the Pit*, they were still there in *Destiny of the Daleks* (recorded after) so their absence here can't be to do with damage caused in the former story. Panel C2 has lost its centre dial.
- Two explosions go off beneath panel C5, and when the TARDIS collides with the Skonnon ship something on fire falls off. Later when first trying to dematerialise, the explosion is from a visible piece of guncotton at top-right of panel C5. This again scorches the collar above it, as in *The Creature from the Pit* (Landing 167).
- Although the randomiser has disappeared since the last time the console was used in the studio for *Destiny of the Daleks*, the red-knobbed lever added to the slider control at the bottom centre of panel C1 is retained.
- The Doctor sets the TARDIS spinning from panel C2.
- **LORE** Modification of the conceptual geometer requires the Ship to be totally immobilised, with even the dematerialisation circuits deactivated.
- The defence shield on the main doors is on a different circuit to those protecting the Ship itself. This can be extruded to form a passageway.
- The gravitic anomaliser is a silver sphere with four protruding connectors. It can be removed and connected into alien drive systems to boost their power, or be used to enhance transmat equipment.
- The TARDIS exterior can be made to spin on a horizontal axis (rather than vertically as when in flight).
- **NOTES** The first shots of K9 with his probe extended to the underside of the console reveal the charge placed there for the first explosion later in the scene.
- The book used as the TARDIS manual — different from that previously seen in *The Pirate Planet* (Landing 146) – was actually a Bible. Here it's titled 'Tardis Handbook Type 40' so may be a alternative tome to the previously referenced "manual".

- Although the inner rim of the collar around the central column of the console is painted black, the absence of the usual glass drum reveals the rougher, unpainted wood below it.
- The model shots of the TARDIS were all videotaped during the studio recording. These feature a new Police Box miniature based closely on that from *Pyramids of Mars*, but with a deeper bottom rail on the side panelling and steps below the 'Police box' signs. These have white lettering on a black rather than blue background, and the windows have a frame as well as bars. The corner posts project higher above the sign boxes but the roof has only one, flat step.
- The spinning of the TARDIS's exterior causes the control room to rotate too, although not as violently. The hatstand stays upright, even after the Doctor has let go and fallen to the floor, and some of the detached components on the console remain in place (are the rest flung off to unseen corners of the room?).
- The sequence of sound effects – including car horns, springs and a twanged ruler – accompanying the failed take-off is *not* a reuse of the 'Major Bloodnok's stomach' effect created for 1950s BBC Radio comedy *The Goon Show*, although special sounds creator Dick Mills may have been inspired by his earlier effort.

LANDING 171

SPACE Skonnos, outside Power Complex; moved elsewhere
TIME As above
TRAVELLERS The Doctor, K9
EPISODES The Horns of Nimon 2-3

As the TARDIS approaches Skonnos, the scanner shows an aerial view of the Nimon's power complex and surrounding buildings, built in an arid region of the planet away from any other habitation. The largest of the octagonal pyramid structures is surmounted by two amber spires. It reminds the Doctor of a positronic circuit, so he plans to land there. K9 points out, however, that it is protected by a hemispherical defence shield of 7,300 megazones.

The Doctor therefore materialises the TARDIS at the entrance to the power complex – although not as discreetly as he hoped. On leaving the Ship he is immediately arrested by two armed guards who lead him away for questioning. Two Skonnon councillors examining the Police Box are startled when the Doctor runs past being chased by guards and technocrat Soldeed. The Time Lord is backed up against the hidden entrance to the Nimon's complex; Soldeed speaks the phrase to activate it and the Doctor falls through.

In the TARDIS, K9 observes on the scanner as Soldeed and guard captain Sorak speculate about the Ship and try, unsuccessfully, to break in. He exits when he hears his master's dog whistle but is immobilised by an energy blast from Soldeed's crystal-headed staff. K9 is taken to Soldeed's laboratory and the TARDIS placed under guard. Soldiers and councillors alike are distracted when the sky glows red as the horn-like spires on the Nimon's complex throb with power and emit an energy beam towards the gravitational well, opening a hyperspatial tunnel to another artificial black hole far across the universe. A jubilant Soldeed strides past and into the complex.

After the Nimon's complex has been destroyed by its exploding nuclear furnace, the Doctor persuades new leader Sorak to let the surviving Anethans return home in a Skonnon spaceship, painted white to show its peaceful intent. He, Romana and K9 then slip away in the TARDIS.

◉ CONTROLS On approach to Skonnos, the Doctor operates controls on panels C3 and C4, including the bottom-left rotary handle on the former and silver dial on the latter.

- **NOTES** Oops! When the Doctor emerges from the TARDIS, the curtain across the rear of the Police Box prop is not fully drawn and the set behind can be seen through the open door.
- Soldeed and Sorak look up towards the Police Box's roof lamp, then the scanner displays a high-angle view of them, the first indication the scanner camera is in the lamp since *The Daleks' Master Plan* (Landing 26).
- The control room is extended to the left of the main doors with a section of wall with aligned roundels.
- The TARDIS is no longer outside the entrance to the power complex when the Doctor and his friends emerge ahead of the explosion, so the Skonnons must have moved it, perhaps to somewhere more secure fearing there might be more K9s inside. How long the Doctor loitered to see the Anethans safely on their way home is uncertain, but likely just long enough to browbeat Sorak into letting them go.

LANDING 172

SPACE Space, near Skonnos
TIME As above
TRAVELLERS The Doctor, K9, Romana
EPISODES The Horns of Nimon 4

No sooner have they left Skonnos than the Doctor parks the TARDIS in space again to complete his modifications to the conceptual geometer. This time he completely removes the central column and connects K9 into the console. The Doctor and Romana watch on the scanner as Crinoth, at the other end of the hyperspatial tunnel, explodes and a Skonnon ship takes the Anethans back home.

- **NOTES** The TARDIS must be somewhere between Skonnos and Aneth as the scanner shows Seth's ship on its way – perhaps it's back where the Doctor originally parked in Landing 169 now the gravitational well is gone. It's not stated how far away Crinoth is – the Doctor says the hyperspatial tunnel allows the Nimons to "[leap] across the universe as far as they want instantaneously" but this doesn't mean Crinoth itself is that distant; it might make more sense for the Nimon to make relatively small jumps with each migration. Then again, the Skonnon empire is said to have covered a hundred star systems but Sezom on Crinoth hasn't heard of it, so the two must be many light years apart. Perhaps, then, the scanner is displaying information received via the hyperspatial tunnel before it collapses.

▤ The hatstand has been positively overloaded in this story, with four of the Doctor's previous coats hung on it. Here it's also draped with an illuminated cable.

LANDING 173

SPACE Earth, England, Cambridge, St Cedd's College, Professor Chronotis's rooms (P14)
TIME October, [early-1980s]
TRAVELLERS The Doctor, K9, Romana
EPISODES Shada 1-2

The Doctor receives a signal from his old friend Professor Chronotis, a Time Lord who has been living out his retirement secretly in Cambridge since the 17th century. The TARDIS materialises in the corner of the professor's book-lined study at St Cedd's College. The Doctor hopes they are in time for the festivities of May Week, but its being held in June has confused the Ship and they have arrived in October. The aged academic is out so the Doctor and Romana decide to explore the town, maybe take a punt on the river. Chronotis returns, unperturbed by the appearance of a Police Box in his rooms. Shortly after, he is visited by post-grad student Chris Parsons, taking up the professor's offer to borrow some books on carbon dating.

The Doctor and Romana call again and, over tea and crackers with Marmite, Chronotis recalls that he wanted the Doctor to take back to Gallifrey a book the professor took when he left. They search for it among the packed shelves but cannot find it – a problem because the book is *The Worshipful and Ancient Law of Gallifrey*, an artefact from the time of Rassilon of unknown power and potentially very dangerous in the wrong hands. After much memory searching, Chronotis recalls Parsons borrowed some books, so the Doctor leaves to try to find him.

While Romana is in the TARDIS fetching fresh milk for more tea, Skagra arrives at the professor's rooms and demands Chronotis give him the Gallifreyan book. When the professor dissembles, Skagra drains his mind of all its knowledge via a floating spherical device. Romana returns with the milk and K9 to find Chronotis in a coma. Parsons comes back to ask about the mysterious book he took and Romana sends him to retrieve a medical kit from the TARDIS. This contains a collar that takes over the unconscious professor's autonomic functions, freeing that part of his brain for cognition. Still unable to speak, he instead controls the rhythm of his heart to beat out a coded message. K9 amplifies the sound so Romana can translate but all she gets is a warning about Skagra and the sphere and to "beware Shada" before Chronotis dies.

K9 detects the babble of voices the sphere emits when it is active, and which the Doctor and Romana heard earlier, so Romana decides to take the TARDIS to its source.

▬ **LORE** Type 40 TARDISes have kitchens. They're inconveniently far from the control room.
▤ **NOTES** Chris Parsons graduated in 1978 and is now studying for a master's or a doctorate, so the story is probably contemporary with its intended broadcast.
▤ The Doctor's previous visits to Cambridge were prior to Landing 145 as Romana is only now introduced to Professor Chronotis.
▤ The centre post on the front of the Police Box prop has been repaired at the bottom where part had split off. The paintwork is slightly paler here so it's likely just a section was replaced rather than the whole thing. The pane in the right-hand window on the left side is still missing a piece, however. The paint has also been removed from the brass Yale lock on the door.
▤ The TARDIS medical kit is kept in a canvas bag on the top shelf of a white cupboard in a room three corridors from the control room.

LANDING 174

SPACE Earth, England, Cambridge, alley
TIME As above
TRAVELLERS K9, Romana
EPISODES Shada 3

The TARDIS materialises at the sphere's location, where the mind-draining device is closing in on the Doctor as he tries to escape under a locked wire gate. Fortunately the Ship's arrival disorients the sphere and it backs off.

Saved from the sphere, the Doctor dashes into the TARDIS and immediately takes off again. He admits to having found the book but then lost it while being chased by the sphere, and is shocked to learn that Professor Chronotis is dead.

▤ **NOTES** This and subsequent control room scenes were scheduled to be recorded at the end of a two-day studio session on Monday 19 and Tuesday 20 November 1979. The sets for both days were erected overnight in Studio 6 at BBC Television Centre and rehearsals were run during the Monday morning. At lunchtime, however, the studios were locked owing to a dispute between management and the technicians' union and none of the scenes were recorded.
▤ The scene of the TARDIS landing in the alley was later used in *The Five Doctors* to represent the freeing of the Doctor's fourth incarnation from the Vortex and return to his time-stream. We might suppose the time that passed between the Doctor's punting and his rescue here is the duration of events in *The Five Doctors* and that Rassilon returned this incarnation to the point his Cambridge adventure would have reached had he not been Time Scooped. Either his return reinstated those events he missed while trapped in the Vortex, as if he had never been snatched away, or the failure to Time Scoop him left him in a dual state of being both trapped and continuing his adventure in Cambridge.

- The Doctor's scarf getting caught in the doors was done deliberately by Tom Baker, in agreement with the director, to highlight his hurry to get away.
- Although in the unrecorded scene Romana explains that K9 traced the sphere, it's not clear why she follows it in the TARDIS. She knows the professor's mind has been drained, to "beware the sphere" and she has heard a faint babble of voices, but she has neither seen nor learned anything that connects these. She might presume Chronotis's warning about a sphere indicates some such object was involved in draining his mind, so perhaps when K9 detects the babble of voices he discerns the professor's among them (as he does later with the Doctor's, although he hasn't yet heard Chronotis speak unless he was eavesdropping via the scanner) and Romana simply hopes to recover his mind somehow if they find the source of the voices, not knowing they come from the sphere, which just happens to be menacing the Doctor at that very moment.
- According to the script, the TARDIS was supposed to materialise between the Doctor and the approaching sphere, which "both baffles and dismays it".

LANDING 175

SPACE Earth, England, Cambridge, St Cedd's College, Professor Chronotis's rooms
TIME As above
TRAVELLERS The Doctor, K9, Romana
EPISODES Shada 3

The TARDIS returns to Chronotis's rooms, where Parsons reports the professor's body has just that minute vanished. The Doctor supposes the old Time Lord was no longer able to regenerate. He decides to find Skagra and asks K9 to alert him when the trace of the sphere becomes strong enough to track. They all, including Parsons, wait inside the TARDIS.

They sit around the control room dozing, but soon enough the voices become detectable as the sphere absorbs another mind. The Doctor enters the distance and bearing given by K9 and the Police Box fades away from the professor's study.

- **NOTES** Photos of the studio in preparation reveal the control room set had a partial ceiling across the angle of the two roundels walls, presumably to allow for low-angle shooting using the camera crane also visible. As well as an aligned-roundels wall to the right of the interior door, as seen in *Destiny of the Daleks*, there was a second placed beyond the main doors, rather than the usual black curtain (we can't know if this would have been moved or covered before recording). The console has its panels out of order – arranged 1-4-5-6-2-3 clockwise – with panel 6 facing the doors. Although not seen in these photos, it's reported the Doctor and company would be sitting in deckchairs while waiting for K9 to track the sphere.

LANDING 176

SPACE Earth, England, Cambridge outskirts
TIME As above
TRAVELLERS The Doctor, K9, Romana, Chris Parsons
EPISODES Shada 3-4

The trace leads the TARDIS to a meadow just outside Cambridge where Skagra's concealed spaceship is parked. The Doctor emerges just in time to spot the sphere seemingly vanish as it enters the invisible ship. K9 can see the vessel but the others cannot and feel their way along it. They spot an incongruous strip of red carpet on the grass, and K9 informs them a door is opening in the ship. They climb an invisible ramp and disappear inside.

A short while later, Skagra emerges with Romana his captive and followed by the hovering sphere. He walks her over to the TARDIS, unconcerned when she refuses to open the door as he has the Doctor's key. Skagra pushes her inside and the sphere glides in after them. Romana insists only she and the Doctor can pilot the TARDIS, but the sphere settles on the console, Skagra puts a hand on it and with the other correctly operates the controls. She tries to pull him away from the console but he shoves her aside and takes off. The Police Box vanishes from the field.

Romana continues trying to bluff Skagra about the complexity of flying the TARDIS but with the contents of the Doctor's mind in the sphere (although Skagra does not realise he has only a partial copy) he can access all the knowledge he needs. The globe rises threateningly when Romana tries to approach the console, so instead she quizzes Skagra about his intentions. He mentions the name Salyavin, but then goes quiet as he concentrates on landing the Ship.

- **NOTES** Christopher Neame, playing Skagra, opens the Police Box door using the upper Yale lock but forgets to remove the key and it's still in the keyhole when the door closes behind him.

LANDING 177

SPACE Krarg spaceship
TIME As above
TRAVELLERS Romana, Skagra
EPISODES Shada 4-5

Skagra materialises the TARDIS on the flight deck of his command ship. Romana is escorted out and confronted by the tall, imposing, coal-black figure of a Krarg. She tries again to get Skagra to reveal his plans; he gestures to the wide forward window that dominates the flight deck, looking out into deep space, and hints at a desire to bring order to the chaos of universal entropy.

The sphere attaches to a control console and Skagra scans the Doctor's mind for the secret of how to read the coded text in *The Worshipful and Ancient Law of Gallifrey*. He soon accepts the Doctor did not know, but realises a

Time Lord artefact would be related to time. He scans the Doctor's memories and locates his discovery in Parson's lab that time is flowing backwards for the book. He takes it into the TARDIS and, to Romana's dismay, discovers that turning the pages causes the central column to respond; he reasons that turning the last page will transport them to Shada, the long-forgotten Time Lord prison, where Salyavin is confined. They return to the flight deck.

Some time later, many more Krargs have been generated, some of which have captured the Doctor, Parsons and K9, recently arrived in Skagra's ship. The Doctor tries to convince the villain the universe is not worth taking over but learns he does not plan to: Skagra intends to unite all life into a single mind – his. The Doctor makes a feint for the TARDIS and when the Krargs move to stop him he and the others escape through an exit.

Skagra takes Romana into the TARDIS along with three Krargs and takes off. Inside he turns the pages of the book one by one, directing the Ship towards Shada.

- **NOTES** There's no indication that the TARDIS travels in time to get to the Krarg command ship – presumably Skagra intended to go there in his own ship before the Doctor turned up – so this landing must be in the same time period as on Earth.
- Script directions indicate that under the influence of the book the TARDIS engines would have a smoother, more melodious sound than usual.

LANDING 178

SPACE Shada
TIME Unknown
TRAVELLERS Romana, Skagra, three Krargs
EPISODES Shada 5-6

They arrive in the gloomy central hall of the Time Lord's prison. Skagra activates a console and locates which cell Salyavin is in: chamber T, cabinet nine. Leaving two Krargs guarding the TARDIS, he takes the other and Romana to meet the greatest ever Time Lord criminal.

Later, Skagra returns with a gaggle of released prisoners, and Chris Parsons, all with spheres attached to their heads that unify their minds with his. They and the three Krargs enter the TARDIS and it dematerialises.

Heading back to the Krarg command ship, Skagra is puzzled when a control on the console explodes. He determines something in the Vortex is jamming the TARDIS and operates the scanner to reveal Professor Chronotis's college rooms travelling alongside. This other TARDIS is generating a forcefield that has enveloped the Police Box. Skagra is unconcerned, however, as the field is already weakening and will not last more than two minutes. Finally it collapses and the two time machines are flung away from each other. Skagra has Parsons and some of the prisoners help him at the console to bring the bucking TARDIS under control and, with one mind, they succeed.

Unknown to them, the Doctor has traversed the Vortex and finds himself aboard his TARDIS, in an equipment room. He gathers together various components which he uses to construct an eccentric helmet.

- **LORE** By manipulating the vortex shields it is possible to create a traversable tunnel between two TARDISes while they are in flight.
- **NOTES** As Skagra was planning to travel to Shada in the Krarg command ship before he fortuitously gained access to a TARDIS, it may be that the scenes on Shada are set in the same time as the rest of the story. However, given we only see people get there by TARDIS – the Doctor's under instructions from the book and Chronotis's following it – it's possible some time travel is involved.
- The camera script listed the prisoners who would be released as: Lucretia Borgia, Boadicea, Lady Macbeth, Salome, Rasputin, Emperor Nero, Genghis Khan, a [Roman] gladiator, an executioner and three "space monsters". Rumours at the time of production suggested these last may be a Dalek, a Cyberman and a Zygon, but this was just fans guessing and it's more likely they would have been random aliens cobbled together from existing costumes. Either way, it's a peculiar bunch for the Time Lords to consider worth locking up for all eternity (or are we to presume they were all renegades from Gallifrey?). Certainly it would have been a tight squeeze in the cramped control room set for all twelve plus Skagra, Chris and three Krargs.
- Model shots of the two TARDISes in the Vortex were completed in the first recording block using the Police Box miniature built for *Pyramids of Mars* and a model of the exterior of Chronotis's college rooms.
- The equipment room was composed of wall flats reused from the Think Tank set, plus metal shelving units and a workbench. In the studio this was set up next to the control room with a short corridor section of the same wall pieces leading directly to the interior door.

LANDING 179

SPACE Krarg spaceship
TIME Shortly after Landing 177
TRAVELLERS Skagra, Chris Parsons, three Krargs, prisoners
EPISODES Shada 6

The TARDIS materialises back on the Krarg command ship and the occupants file out, Skagra bringing up the rear. Ships like his own are prepared to take the prisoners to different population centres and from there begin the spread of Skagra's mind across the universe.

Inside the TARDIS, the Doctor has completed his helmet contraption and makes his way to the control room. He checks the scanner and sees Skagra and the prisoners gathered around the entrance to Chronotis's TARDIS: a wooden door within the flight deck wall. He goes outside to confront them, donning and activating the helmet. This gives him control over Parsons and the prisoners because their spheres contain a copy of his mind. Skagra fights back and regains dominance over some of them.

As the two mentally duel, Romana empties the heavy gas from the Krarg generation vats so that it pours across the floor of the flight deck. When she applies a current across it, all the Krargs begin to dissolve. This distracts Skagra and the Doctor gains the upper hand, turning all the prisoners on the villain. He runs from the flight deck and heads for his spaceship.

Released from the spheres, the prisoners are in shock but the Doctor is confident he can return their minds to them, then return them to their cells on Shada.

- **NOTES** In scripted dialogue the Doctor says that, unlike him, the TARDIS was "built" for travelling through the space-time Vortex. This could simply mean 'constructed' but equally can be taken to mean 'suited'.

LANDING 180

SPACE Shada
TIME As Landing 178
TRAVELLERS The Doctor, prisoners, [K9, Skagra]
EPISODES Shada 6

The Doctor takes the TARDIS back to Shada with the prisoners aboard and places them back in their cells before they wake up. He also recovers the body of Professor Chronotis.

- **NOTES** This journey is not shown (or wouldn't have been had the serial been completed) but the Doctor says he plans to take the prisoners back to Shada and leave them for the Time Lords to sort out. He and Romana wonder if Chronotis is still alive – last seen being attacked by a sphere on Shada – but as he appears in the following scene back at Cambridge, the Doctor must have found him and restored his mind (and stabilised whatever time-field tangling brought him back from the dead). But does he need to turn the pages of the book again to direct the TARDIS back to Shada or can he simply reverse the last journey?
- It's possible the Doctor also takes Skagra as it would be more secure to lock him up on Shada than leave him in his ship's brig – although how much of a threat he'd be were someone to find and release him is debatable. If so, it seems likely he'd want K9 with him to keep the villain in check. Meanwhile, presumably, Romana takes Chronotis's TARDIS back to Cambridge, with Chris Parsons and Clare Keightley.

LANDING 181

SPACE Earth, England, Cambridge, St Cedd's College, Professor Chronotis's rooms
TIME As Landing 173
TRAVELLERS The Doctor, Chronotis, [K9]
EPISODES Shada 6

With Professor Chronotis's rooms back in place in St Cedd's college, the TARDIS returns there from Shada, settling back in the corner of his study where it first arrived.

The Doctor is reading aloud from Charles Dickens' *The Old Curiosity Shop* when a policeman enters to investigate a report by the college's porter that the professor's room had been stolen. When he notices the Police Box, the Doctor and Romana say hurried goodbyes to Chronotis, Chris and Clare and take their leave in the TARDIS.

- **NOTES** Now we know the professor's rooms are also a TARDIS, that means when the Doctor first arrived he parked his TARDIS inside another (apparently unknowingly as he is later surprised to learn the truth). The last time we saw this happen, in *The Time Monster* (Landing 87), it was said to be "appallingly dangerous" and produced an infinite loop of each TARDIS being within the other. Chronotis's is said to be "very ancient" and "rescued…literally from the scrap heaps" so perhaps it's less dimensionally complex than later models, making it safer to materialise in. Given all we see of it is the study (which contains its controls) and the suggestion of a kitchen and one other room, we can't be sure it's dimensionally transcendental even and may have only as much space as the college rooms it appears to be. Nor is it clear what external form it takes: when it materialises elsewhere it appears as just a wooden door within a pre-existing wall (so what if it landed in a field?), yet for the shots in the Vortex of the Doctor crossing between TARDISes, a model was made showing a stone facade with windows and ivy, as if a section of the college building had been removed. There can't be a whacking great hole in St Cedd's, though, or Wilkin would be telling the police about more than just a stolen room. Perhaps it doesn't occupy any space within the college building, then, and the door is just a portal to the professor's rooms in another dimension. But someone over the past 300 years would surely have noticed if the door led to rooms where there physically couldn't be any – such as if it were in an external wall – so it must occupy some plausible amount of space (even if it has more rooms beyond those anyone but the professor ever sees). And where is the entrance when it's parked in Cambridge anyway? The black outer door Wilkin finds a shimmering blue haze behind is not the same as the plain wooden door that leads into Chronotis's study and which appears when his TARDIS materialises elsewhere. As seen when Clare first calls on him, between the two is a vestibule with a hat rack. This isn't there when the door appears on the Think Tank or Shada so it cannot be part of the TARDIS. Why, then, doesn't Wilkin just find himself in a vestibule leading nowhere?
- Components of Chronotis's TARDIS include an interfacial resonator, a conceptual geometer relay with an agronomic trigger and field separator, vortex shields, and sub-neutron circuits.

IT LOOKS JUST LIKE A POLICE BOX

THE YARDLEY-JONES BOX 1
1980-1982

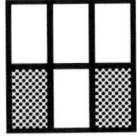

Along with numerous other revamps that new producer John Nathan-Turner implemented when he took over in 1980, he decided a new Police Box prop was required. This task fell to Tom Yardley-Jones as the assigned designer for the first story of Season 18 into production, *The Leisure Hive*.

Unlike previous boxes that had been constructed from wood, this was the first to be made from fibreglass, to minimise its weight. The design reintroduced features missing from the Newbery box, such as the steps below the sign boxes and a roof section with deeper levels and a steeper pitch, on top of which the lamp sat directly. This looked the same as that originally used on the Newbery box, with a lensed casing and a metal domed cap on three supports, although blue rather than white. The box's corner posts were narrower, giving a taller, slimmer silhouette than the previous prop, and for the first time the sign boxes had an even-width frame, rather than being wider at the ends (although that was how they were drawn on the design plans). The lettering was in white on blue translucent acrylic, fitted behind beading around the inner edge of the frames.

Like the Newbery box, the new prop was composed of several sections bolted together: a base on castors, two sides including corner posts and sign boxes (cast separately then bonded together), front and rear sign boxes including steps below and a ledge above, two pairs of doors, four acrylic signs with 'Police box' lettering, the roof and the lamp. It thus returned to having rear and front doors (all opening inwards despite being drawn hinging outwards on the plans), rather than an open back like the Newbery box. Each pair was the same: the right-hand doors fitted with the centre post onto which a handle was screwed, and the left-hand doors featuring a Yale lock. One also had the 'Police telephone' plaque, which had white seriffed lettering on a blue background and a second smaller handle on its frame.

OUTWARD BOUND

The new prop was seen in the very first scene of *The Leisure Hive*, filmed on Brighton Beach on Thursday 20 March 1980. By the time it was taken into the studio for recording on Thursday 3 April it had already undergone its first adjustment. The doors were too short and didn't tuck behind the stepped lintel (this may have been deliberate so that when closed the doors' centre post sat flush with the lowest step above it, as on the sides, or it could have been a consequence of the sides and doors being produced from the same mould then either cut or bonded as needed). With no stop, the doors would bow outwards and there was a slight gap above them. Before the studio recording, therefore, two extra strips were fixed to the bottom step of the front lintel, either side of the centre post, to overlap the tops of the doors.

Prior to filming for *Full Circle* in late July, the 'Police box' sign on the left side of the prop was replaced with a paler one with darker lettering – possibly cut out from opaque film stuck to clear acrylic – while the sign box on the rear was empty (the sign lost or just not fitted). The sign on the front and the new one on the left were now placed in front of the frame's beading and thus almost flush with the frame, whereas that on the right was still inset. The rear of the box is glimpsed during *The Keeper of Traken* and has its 'Police box' sign again, but this was possibly moved from the right-hand side, which isn't seen. In *Logopolis* the sign box on the back was again empty while one of the sign inserts had new lettering

Left The telephone plaque returned to its original wording
Right Yardley-Jones prop front elevation and section

IT LOOKS JUST LIKE A POLICE BOX

IT LOOKS JUST LIKE A POLICE BOX

in a bolder typeface (matching the revamped Newbery box's signs). For the day of filming at the lay-by, this was placed on the front above the doors (which were missing their handle), while in the later studio recordings it was on the right-hand side and flush rather than inset.

The prop's paintwork was also badly scuffed by the time of *Full Circle*'s studio recording in August 1980, as is very noticeable on screen, so this was touched up before it was needed for *Warriors' Gate* in early October. The strip added above the right-hand door had gone missing by the time *The Keeper of Traken* was recorded a month later. The main change for *Logopolis*, however, was the addition of a thick square block under the roof lamp, seemingly to make it more closely match the changes made to the Newbery prop for its appearance as a genuine Police Box (even though the point of the story is that the TARDIS doesn't look exactly like a Police Box). This block was retained throughout Season 19.

The first half of 1982's stories were recorded out of order owing to delays with the script for Peter Davison's debut. This meant changes made to the Police Box prop during production appeared and disappeared when the episodes were shown in their intended order.

First into the studio was *Four to Doomsday*, in which the box appeared as it had done in *Logopolis* three months earlier. The only change was to replace the additional fourth step below the front sign box with a single, full-width strip. Without a gap for the centre post, the doors didn't shut properly and pushed against the back of the steps. This is clearest in shots from the press photocall for the reveal of Davison's costume, held on Thursday 16 April 1981 after the first studio recording for *Four to Doomsday*. In these photos the whole front sign box is pushed up and away from the corner posts. At this time the bolder 'Police box' sign was fitted on the right.

The Visitation was produced next, with filming at Ealing involving the Police Box prop taking place just three days after its last use in studio for *Four to Doomsday*. Yet now the bolder sign was placed on the left side of the prop. Damage to the window bars on this side matches shots in the previous story, verifying the box had been erected the same way – that is, the sides weren't swapped over, only the sign graphics were switched. This confirms the signs were detachable and, given later adjustments, may have been prone to falling out. The prop then appeared the same when filmed on location the following week.

The Police Box was needed only for one day's studio recording for *Kinda*, on Wednesday 12 August 1981, for which at least two sides were given mottled paintwork to suggest sunlight filtering through the trees of Deva Loka. More notable is that the rear of the prop was used as the entrance on screen for the first time, evidenced by there being only three steps above the doors and the side with the damaged window bars usually seen on the left now appearing as the right-hand side of the box. Why the prop was deployed this way round is unknown but one consequence was that a new telephone plaque was needed to allow the rear door to appear as the front (indicating that the existing plaque was fixed to the front door and couldn't simply be moved). This had slight differences in its wording and layout (see page 260), most significantly changing 'Urgent calls' to 'All calls' – which would later be mimicked on the 21st century props. It also had no handle. Photos taken around this time by Richard Farley for the book *The Making of a Television Series* by Alan Road show the mottled paintwork and a plaque on the rear door but its lettering not yet painted.

GAINING STRENGTH

During the three weeks between recording *Kinda* and filming the Pharos Project scenes for *Castrovalva*, some alterations were made to the prop (which means they disappear for the following three stories as broadcast – if only they'd waited until after this brief outing). The main purpose of this appears to have been to add some internal bracing, as bolt heads become visible on the front and rear corner posts, suggesting crossbars were added to reinforce the sides. On the face seen in *Castrovalva* these bolts were level with the upper and lower edges of the windows, while on the opposite side they were further apart, level with the bottom lintel step and the top edge of the panel below the windows (visible in *Earthshock*). Repairs were made to broken window bars and the sign boxes had a wider retaining frame added that overlapped the edges of the lettered inserts. The signs themselves were newly made from clear (or pale translucent) acrylic with a blue film applied from which the lettering was cut out; as such they were less legible than the previous white-lettered signs.

By the time *Earthshock* was recorded in November, one face of the Police Box had acquired one of the deep, wide-ended sign boxes from the Newbery box, which had recently been used in *Black Orchid* (when it was missing its left-side sign). It's likely one of the regular sign boxes was damaged or lost so a replacement was taken from the spare prop. As these were slightly shorter, the steps below it had to be extended so there was no gap above the doors, and strips were again added either side of the centre post, as had been done during Season 18. This odd addition is more noticeable in *Time-Flight* but can be spotted in *Earthshock* when the Doctor first exits the TARDIS in the caves; shots in episode two show the opposite face with the usual sign and the wider-spaced bolts in the corner posts. The bottom lintel-step on this face had a notch cut for the centre post, while the telephone plaque had lost its handle and now also had the 'All cars' wording.

With the Police Box prop now effectively double-fronted, little attention was paid to its orientation. While scenes on the freighter in *Earthshock* made use of the face with the regular sign box, in *Time-Flight* the other was favoured, no one seeming to notice (or care) about the oddity of the Newbery sign box – even the publicity

IT LOOKS JUST LIKE A POLICE BOX

Above From *Logopolis* the prop gained a block under the roof lamp. Strengthening work during Season 19 saw bolt heads appear on the corner posts. Both faces now had telephone plaques and the sign boxes gained wider fascias to hold in the signs

photos taken at Heathrow Airport focused on this atypical side of the prop. In this story, the TARDIS again appeared on its back, in Concorde's hold, requiring the cast to clamber into it from above. Unlike in *Castrovalva*, the main Yardley-Jones box was used, evidently sufficiently sturdy. This can't be purely because of the internal bracing as this had been added before *Castrovalva* was recorded. Perhaps being in the studio and lying squarely on its back put less stress on the box than it would have been subject to for the woodland setup in the earlier story.

Despite or perhaps because of this strengthening required during Season 19, it was decided to retire the prop and build a new one for the following year (see page 306). Box 1's last known appearance was on Thursday 18 March 1982 (the same day its replacement was commissioned) in London's Trafalgar Square, where it was set up for filming a publicity item to promote *Doctor Who* in Australia – or so Peter Davison was led to believe. In fact, when he emerged from the box that evening, the cameras were from Thames Television and he was confronted by Eamonn Andrews and his big red *This Is Your Life* book. The story of Davison's life and career was then recorded at the nearby New London Theatre and broadcast the following week on 25 March.

It was long assumed this 1980 original had survived through to the end of the 20th-century series but this now appears not to be the case. As there's no evidence of two Yardley-Jones-style boxes co-existing until after a third was made in 1983, it's likely this one was junked in favour of its replacement.

IT LOOKS JUST LIKE A POLICE BOX

WORDS WHICH MIGHT BRING SALVATION TO EVERYONE

The initial 'Police telephone' plaque on the Yardley-Jones box was the most accurate in its wording and layout, compared to a genuine Metropolitan Police Box, since the original Brachacki box. The lettering was all in a serif typeface, although a plainer Times-based font without the idiosyncrasies of the original. 'Free' and 'Public' were on their own lines, the latter written larger as were 'Police telephone' and 'Pull to open'. There were no ampersands and 'Officers' responded to 'Urgent calls' (see page 256).

When a second plaque (below left) was added to the rear of the box between production of *The Visitation* and *Kinda*, its lettering was a strange mixture of the front plaque's and that on the Newbery box. The first half of the wording was still serifed but 'Police telephone' was smaller and 'Free' larger to match 'Public', these two words given extended-width letters. The second half was then in sans-serif lettering and used ampersands in 'Advice & assistance' and 'Officer [singular] & cars'. This last phrase was split across only two lines rather than three so, seemingly to make it fit, 'Urgent calls' was shortened to 'All calls' for the first time. 'Pull to open' was elongated making it the largest lettering on the plaque.

When the Yardley-Jones and Newbery boxes were remodelled prior to being used in *Castrovalva*, their plaques were standardised with this newer form of wording and layout. Both sides of the Yardley-Jones box display the new wording in *Earthshock*; the scenes are too dark to make out details but a close-up shot of the plaque in *Time-Flight* reveals subtle differences in the letter spacing between this and the refitted Newbery box plaque (as they were all hand-painted).

In 1982 ahead of production on Season 20 a new Yardley-Jones box was struck from the original moulds to replace the previous one. This would also see both its sets of doors used as the entrance so it too needed two telephone plaques (both can be glimpsed in *Resurrection of the Daleks*). The one with the extended 'Public' lettering was taken from the old box, but the other (below right) seems to be new, or at least repainted, as a close-up of the plaque's first appearance in *Snakedance* reveals differences from the one seen in *Time-Flight*. Neither had a handle on its frame. The face of the box with the former plaque was used as the entrance in *Arc of Infinity*, *Mawdryn Undead* and studio scenes for *The Five Doctors*, then *The Awakening* and *Resurrection of the Daleks* the next year; the other face was favoured in *Snakedance*, *Enlightenment*, *The King's Demons*, *The Five Doctors* (on location), *Warriors of the Deep* and *Frontios*.

When an additional Police Box prop was constructed in 1983 prior to *Planet of Fire*, it was given only one telephone plaque that could be fitted to either face (hooking onto four pin heads in the corners of the inset panel). At the end of *Attack of the Cybermen*, when the TARDIS lands in Cyber-control, both front and rear doors are seen and only the former carries a plaque. This new sign saw a return to the correct wording and layout, looking almost identical to the original from Season 18 (because the designer's plans for it were copied directly from Tom Yardley-Jones's 1980 blueprints).

Throughout Season 22 in 1985 both props were used, Box 2 with the 'All calls' plaques (extended 'Public' on one face, normal on the other), Box 3 with its new 'Urgent calls' plaque. This was the last time the extended-'Public' version was seen. The Box 3 plaque was used throughout Season 23 (bar one deleted scene) after which the other 'All calls' plaque from Box 2 became the standard. It was now detachable and switched between whichever of the two props was being used.

Above The second plaque added in *Kinda* (left) copied the Newbery box's wording but had widened letterforms for 'Free' and 'Public'. This was transferred to Box 2 from Season 20, joined on the opposite face by a new plaque (right) that was subtly different from previous ones seen during Season 19. This would become the main plaque on both Boxes 2 and 3

IT'S BIGGER ON THE INSIDE

THE RUSCOE EXPANSION
1980-1983

Barry Newbery's interpretation of the traditional white control room had been a compact set, as requested by producer Graham Williams, even though scenes in the TARDIS were becoming more common. By the time John Nathan-Turner took over, it was usual for the set to be seen not just at the start and end of an adventure but often returned to throughout as well. Perhaps with this is mind and anticipating even greater exploration of the TARDIS to come, the new producer had the set expanded for Season 18.

The first story into production that would feature the control room was *State of Decay*, for which the allocated designer was Christine Ruscoe – who had already tweaked the TARDIS set once before when working on *Pyramids of Mars*. To create more space she replaced Newbery's two staggered-roundels walls with three: two that had three columns of staggered circles and one with two columns of aligned circles. These were simple flats with circular holes, fitted with more of the same ridged fibreglass roundels Newbery had designed for the 1976 set,. They were connected by two new slimmer slatted columns. Initially the walls had a strip along the top to match the existing Newbery walls but by *Full Circle* only one of the three-column walls retained this, and by *The Keeper of Traken* all three had lost it. The extra sections expanded the space around the console by flattening the angles between them and moving the main doors and scanner (reused from the previous set) further apart.

The second change was to have the interior door (again reused) positioned in line with the scanner, rather than angling back in around the console, with a third wide slatted column between them. With an existing aligned-roundels wall placed to the right of the interior door, also at 180 degrees, this created more floor space on that side of the set for wider camera angles. Indeed, some of director Peter Moffat's shots for *State of Decay* required a second aligned-roundels wall to be placed to the left of the main doors too. (Although not on the original set plan, this wall was probably available because it had been intended to position it beyond the main doors – as studio photos suggest was done for *Shada*. There's only one instance on screen of this actually being done, though, so it's not certain if this was a permanent fixture.)

Ruscoe also formalised the area beyond the interior door slightly, with another wall of three columns of staggered circles leading to a second inner door. This had three translucent roundels set into it and a silver doorknob like the control room interior door (the latter also had two metal push plates added above and below the handle). Next to this was a new piece with a single column of roundels so that camera shots through the door from the control room didn't show the studio wall.

Although only the control room itself was needed for *Meglos*, one brief glimpse of the second inner door indicates the corridor sections were erected anyway. These were also needed for *Full Circle* as we were introduced to Romana's bedroom. For this designer Janet Budden had two further walls with four columns of staggered translucent roundels made. One of these became the corridor section between the two interior doors, which both gained new, square handles (the push plates were moved to the second door, on either side below its handle).

The single-column wall was placed to the right of the interior door in *Full Circle*; by *The Keeper of Traken* an aligned-roundels section was back in this position. But for *Logopolis* even more space was required for the scenes with a Police Box inside the control room, so both the single-column wall and an aligned-roundels section were used to extend the set to the right. In fact, with the corridor/bedroom set elsewhere in the studio incorporating two other aligned-roundels walls, this is the first evidence that at least three of these walls survived after 1977 (debunking the 'warped in storage' claim). Behind the interior door was one of Newbery's 3½-column walls from the previous control room set (half-roundels on the left) and the double-curved slats that formed part of Romana's room in *Full Circle*.

EXTENDING CORRIDORS

Logopolis and its follow-up story *Castrovalva* featured more action in TARDIS corridors than ever before, requiring most of the accumulated stock of walls to be used. The control room itself underwent one change after the former serial was made: the main doors wall was rebuilt as the horizontal join above the doors had become increasingly weak and visible over the previous year. The first serial of Season 19 into production was *Four to Doomsday* in April 1981 so this new wall was supervised by designer Tony Burrough. The double doors themselves were again retained (now eighteen years old) although the cam mechanism for opening them was able to be completely hidden. The new wall around them was built to the same dimensions as the previous one but the arrangement of roundels was different, now completely surrounding the doors.

The remaining walls were unchanged except for the three roundels walls regaining the strip across the top.

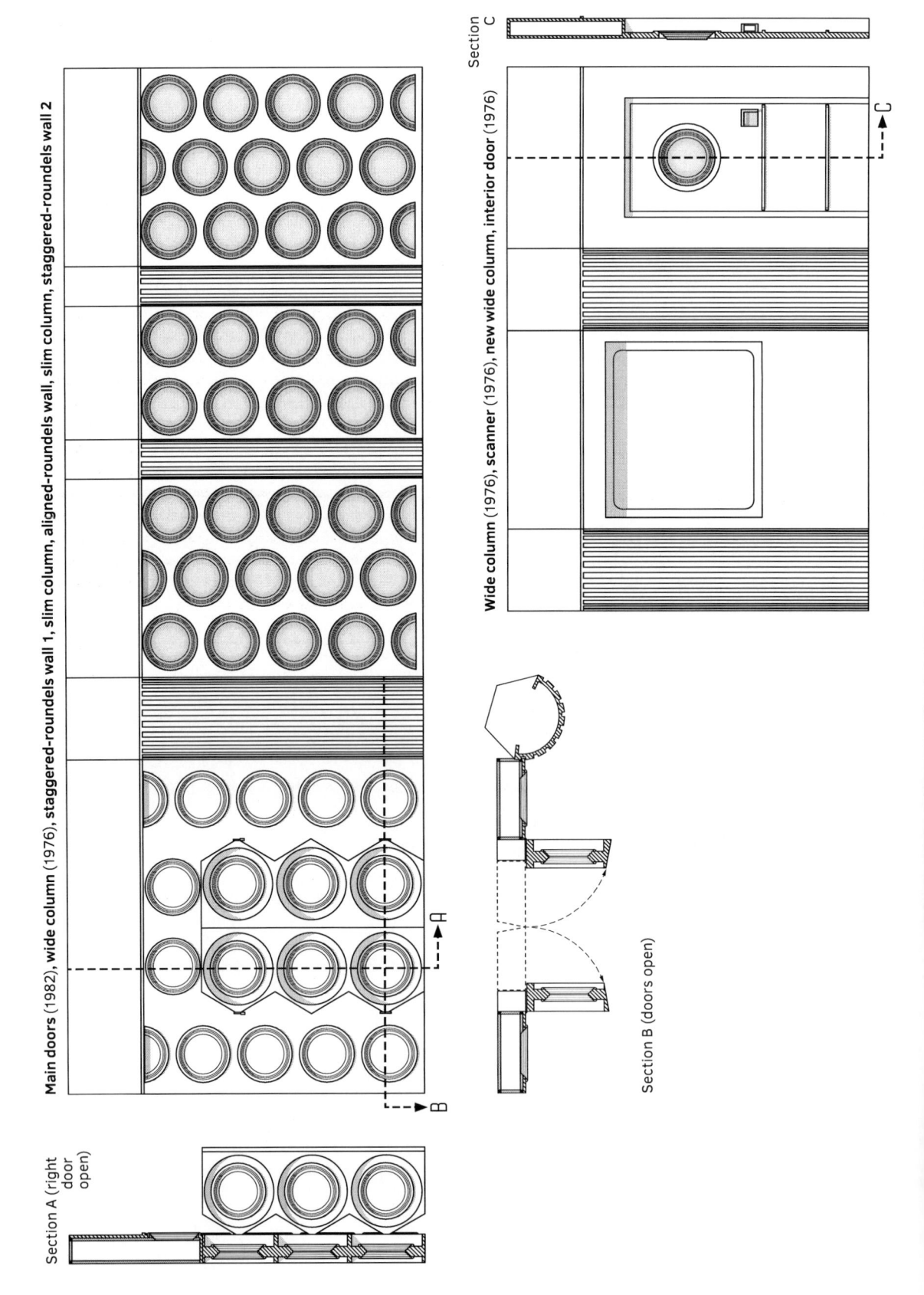

IT'S BIGGER ON THE INSIDE

Main doors (1982), wide column (1976), staggered-roundels wall 1, slim column, aligned-roundels wall, slim column, staggered-roundels wall 2

Section A (right door open)

Section B (doors open)

Wide column (1976), scanner (1976), new wide column, interior door (1976)

Section C

IT'S BIGGER ON THE INSIDE

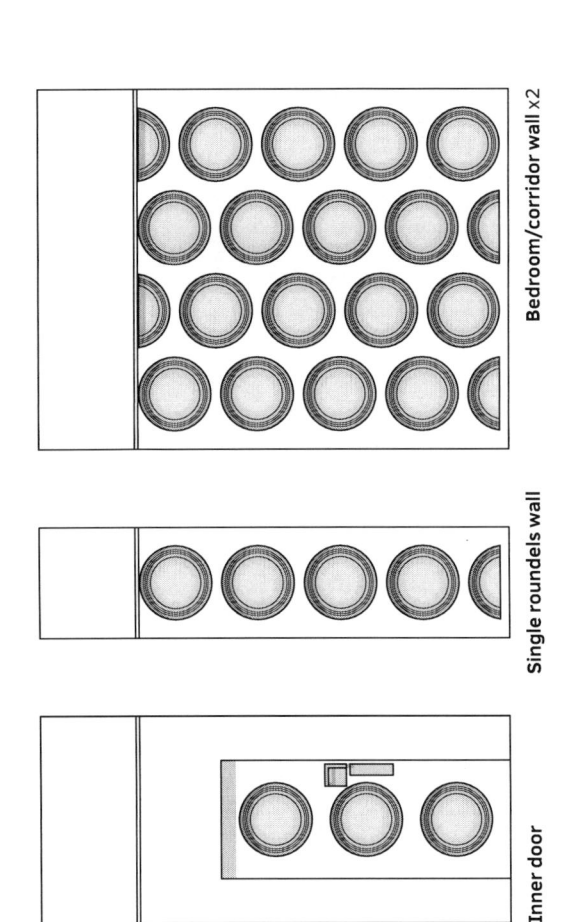

Bedroom/corridor wall ×2

Single roundels wall

Inner door

Aligned-roundels wall (1976) ×3

The layout of these and the scanner (which now had a single shutter) remained the same but the interior doorway was brought in at a less obtuse angle (and the door reversed and hinged on the right). To the right of this was another slim slatted column and a wall with translucent roundels (possibly the single-column section), except in *Castrovalva* where these were replaced by plain flats, probably because all other pieces were needed for the corridors set. From *The Visitation*, the interior door gained two horizontal battens below its roundel.

This is how the control room remained until its replacement in 1983 – except for in *Time-Flight*, when for unknown reasons the centre two-column roundels wall was omitted and one of the 1977 walls with 3½ columns of circles made an unexpected reappearance in the control room. This and other pre-existing walls continued to be used for corridor and bedroom scenes, notably in *The Visitation*, *Arc of Infinity* and *Terminus*. After the set was redesigned in 1983, scenes in other sections of the TARDIS became rarer and featured new walls, suggesting all earlier ones were scrapped.

This control room set was erected one last time at the Longleat 20th anniversary celebration weekend on the 3rd and 4th of April 1983, along with its outgoing console, on display for visiting fans to admire. This was just three days after recording on the new set for *The Five Doctors* had concluded.

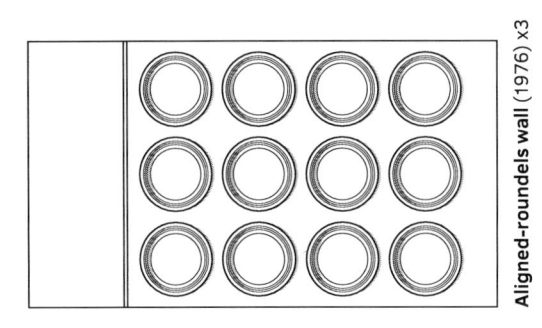

WHAT ARE ALL THESE KNOBS?

PANELS Cii
1980-1981

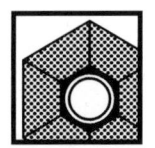

② **SCANNER** (195,196)
③ **CHAMELEON CIRCUIT PROGRAMMER** (196,207)

PANEL C1
① **IMAGE TRANSLATOR SLOT** (191)

PANEL C2

The console's appearance during Season 18 was much as it had been for the previous three years apart from a major change to one panel. For *State of Decay*, panel 5 was adapted to include a mechanism for printing out the Record of Rassilon. All components bar the light strip at the bottom were removed and a copper-coloured plate incorporating a teleprinter was added in the centre. This was a working unit with a moving print head and scrolling roll of paper, although the text on this was pre-printed. To the right of this was added a slot for the Doctor to feed in punchcards. This was also practical, with rollers beneath to smoothly pull the cards into the console. Some of the panel's previous controls were then refitted: the coloured buttons were placed below the printer plate; the red dome and silver dial (later replaced) swapped sides; and the red grille was placed vertically at top-left of the panel. The hole for the tracer was filled and painted over.

Logopolis required a further significant addition: the chameleon circuit programmer. The keyboard from a 1970s Honeywell data-conversion machine was fitted onto an extending rod. This was operated manually from below the console by one of the scenic crew pushing it up and then pulling on a straightening rod to pivot the keyboard down. The angle of this mechanism required one of the recesses of the console's pedestal to be given a new face flush with the corner fins, with the top third projecting even further forward. Panel 1 was chosen to accommodate this new feature in place of the upper metal plate. A slot was cut in the panel and covered with a board that had a metal flap (also operated from beneath) covering the hole for the programmer to rise through.

While the console was being modified, some cosmetic changes were also made. Panel 6 gained stripes below the screen and its tape border was changed from blue to yellow, while panel 2 received a similar border in white and panel 3 one in pale blue, with the existing tape strips in the bottom corners renewed in the same colour. This panel also had the buttons above the two sliders replaced and the two pushbuttons either side changed to flick switches, plus red and yellow circles stuck at the top of its metal plate. Another red circle was placed above the green plastic control on panel 5 (added in *Warriors' Gate*), and on panel 1 the six outer rings were replaced with blue circles. Finally the collar was given red lines along both top and bottom edges. From *Logopolis* the layout changed, with panels 3 & 4 and 5 & 6 switched, as they would be (bar a couple of exceptions) through to 1983.

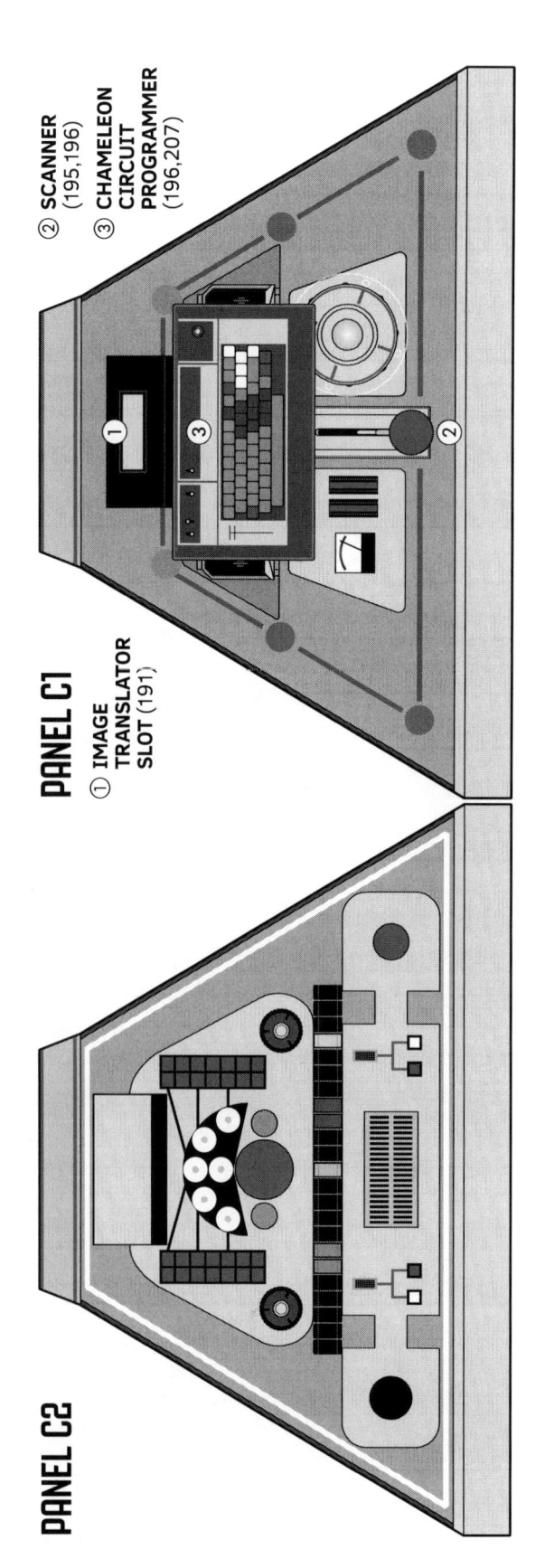

WHAT ARE ALL THESE KNOBS?

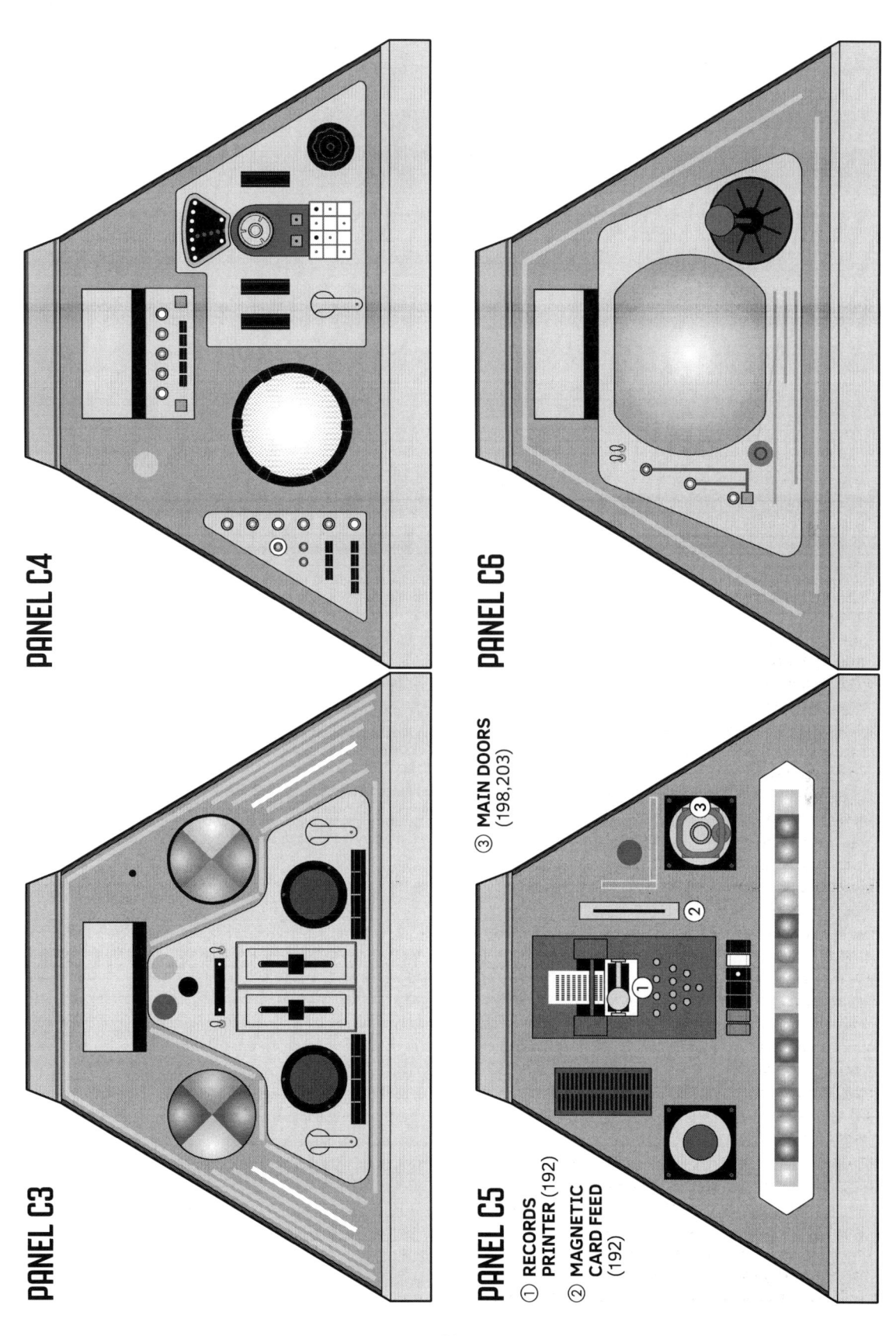

PANEL C4

PANEL C6

PANEL C3

PANEL C5

① **RECORDS PRINTER** (192)
② **MAGNETIC CARD FEED** (192)
③ **MAIN DOORS** (198, 203)

PREVIOUS LANDINGS

SPACE Logopolis
TIME Unknown
TRAVELLERS The Doctor, [unknown companions]
EPISODES Mentioned by the Doctor in Logopolis 1

The Doctor visited Logopolis and met the Monitor, learning about the ability to model space-time events through block transfer computation. At this time the Logopolitans had not created their copy of the Pharos Project radio-telescope dish and control room. They did, however, offer to rectify the TARDIS's chameleon circuit if the Doctor could provide precise measurements of a genuine Police Box.

- **NOTES** This was before the Doctor met Adric, and thus before the TARDIS fell into E-space. It was after the Doctor left Gallifrey as the Monitor says he "continue[s] to roam the universe".
- The claim that "time has changed little for either of us" could indicate the Doctor was in his fourth incarnation, although it's possible the Monitor can see past a Time Lord's outward appearance. If the Doctor visited Logopolis before his exile, when he couldn't control the TARDIS, it might explain why he didn't return with the required measurements sooner. If not, he was presumably just distracted by other adventures, until something inspired him (prior to Landing 196) to follow up on the offer.

SPACE Earth, [England]
TIME 19th century
TRAVELLERS The Doctor, [unknown companions]
EPISODES Mentioned by the Doctor in Logopolis 3

The Doctor met naturalist Thomas Huxley and considered him a friend.

- **NOTES** The Doctor misquotes Huxley's address 'A Liberal Education; and Where to Find It' given at the opening of the South London Working Men's College (of which he was principal) on 4 January 1868: "The chess board is the world, the pieces are the phenomena of the universe...The player on the other side...never overlooks a mistake, or makes the smallest allowance for ignorance." It's possible the Doctor attended the opening, or may simply know the quote and met Huxley at another time in his life.

SPACE Earth, England, London, Heathrow Airport
TIME [Late-20th century]
TRAVELLERS The Doctor, [unknown companions]
EPISODES Mentioned by the Doctor in Four to Doomsday 1

The Doctor visited Heathrow Airport at a time when "they were doing strange things to Terminal Three".

- **NOTES** Heathrow Terminal 3 was opened in November 1961 but called the Oceanic Terminal until 1968, so the Doctor's use of the later title may suggest he was there after that date – perhaps when it was expanded in 1970, or during refurbishment at the end of the 1980s.
- See Landing 212 for a theory about what the Doctor was dealing with on this visit.

SPACE Earth, England, Devon, Plymouth
TIME July 1588
TRAVELLERS The Doctor, [unknown companions]
EPISODES Claimed by the Doctor in Four to Doomsday 2

The Doctor was friends with Sir Francis Drake around the time he was preparing to combat the Spanish Armada, and recalls him saying "something like, there's time enough to get to Terminal Three and beat the Armada too".

- **NOTES** The Doctor's paraphrases Drake's reported (but almost certainly apocryphal) remark made while finishing a game of bowls on Plymouth Hoe as the Spanish fleet approached, suggesting he knew the man at this time.
- In the Big Finish audio play *The Marian Conspiracy*, the Doctor again name-drops Drake, claiming to have thrown a bowls match to allow the Vice Admiral to leave in time to meet the Armada.

SPACE Earth, Australia
TIME After 17th century
TRAVELLERS The Doctor, [unknown companions]
EPISODES Claimed by the Doctor in Four to Doomsday 4

The Doctor played for the New South Wales cricket team and took five wickets by bowling a left-arm unorthodox spin known as a chinaman.

- **NOTES** If true, this was probably during the Doctor's fourth incarnation, the only one so far to have shown an interest in cricket, so after Landing 119. As he makes the claim in Adric's presence, it probably predates their meeting.

LANDING 182

SPACE Earth, England, Brighton, beach
TIME [Late-20th century]
TRAVELLERS The Doctor, K9, Romana
EPISODES The Leisure Hive 1

The Doctor plans to visit the opening of the Brighton Pavilion, having once before missed the event, so bypasses the randomiser and programmes the controls himself. He manages to get the venue more or less correct, and the TARDIS materialises on the pebbles of Brighton beach amid a long row of striped beach tents. But his timing is way out: instead of 1850, the Ship arrives in the latter half of the 20th century. Worse, the seaside town is not even in season and a harsh wind blows in off the sea.

Disappointed, the Doctor bundles up in his coat, scarf and hat and settles into a deckchair to sulk and snooze. Romana takes a walk along the beach towards the West Pier, accompanied by K9 who recites a list of alternative recreation facilities in this galaxy.

The pair are on their way back to the TARDIS by the time K9 reaches the end of his catalogue, Romana now thoroughly fed up. She throws a beachball for K9 to fetch and he obediently follows even when it rolls into the sea and the water makes his control panel explode. Romana retrieves him and carries him back to the Doctor, dropping the disabled robot dog into the sleeping Time Lord's lap.

As an alternative to freezing on Brighton beach, Romana suggests visiting the Leisure Hive on Argolis. Once she has stopped the Doctor dozing off again, he agrees and they take K9 back to the TARDIS and take off.

- **NOTES** With only two Time Lords and a robot dog travelling in the TARDIS, innumerable landings could have occurred since they departed Cambridge as we wouldn't necessarily notice how much older they were. Certainly the Doctor seems more weary than when he visited Professor Chronotis and has adopted a more muted outfit.
- No date for this landing is given on screen but production documents indicate it was 1903. However, it must be after 1975 when the West Pier was closed and 'Danger' signs were erected, yet no later than 2002 as it's still standing. A date contemporary with the story's filming in March 1980 is therefore more likely.
- The Doctor hoped to see the "opening of the Brighton Pavilion", more properly the Royal Pavilion, by which he presumably means its opening to the public in either June 1850 when it was purchased from the Crown or January 1851 after some restoration work had been done. It's often assumed the Doctor's first attempt at visiting the Pavilion was in *Horror of Fang Rock*, but see Landing 132 for why that can't be the case.
- Romana notes how "dangerous it is bypassing the randomiser", yet the Doctor has been doing this perfectly well since Landing 162. Why should his navigation skills desert him now? Is this an early sign that his fourth body is beginning to wear a bit thin?
- The spacing of the beach tents suggests the TARDIS has materialised around one rather than in an otherwise atypically wide gap between them.

LANDING 183

SPACE Milky Way galaxy, Argolis, Leisure Hive, Generator hall
TIME Two days in [2290]
TRAVELLERS The Doctor, K9, Romana
EPISODES The Leisure Hive 1-4

As a dazzling radioactive dust storm howls outside the windows of the Leisure Hive, the TARDIS materialises in the hall where a group of human tourists are watching a demonstration by the youngest Argolin, Pangol, of the Recreation Generator. This uses tachyonics to manipulate solid projections, and the Doctor and Romana are quietly impressed – until one visitor takes his turn in the Generator and is torn apart just like his on-screen tachyon duplicate. Offering his help, the Doctor is mistaken for a human scientist called Hardin and, with Romana, is invited to an audience with the Argolin's leader (and Pangol's mother) Mena.

A short while later, the pair sneak back to the TARDIS but the Doctor is distracted by the Generator and goes inside. Romana watches horrified as his image, manipulated by an unseen Foamasi infiltrator, is also torn apart. The real Doctor is fine, however, having used his sonic screwdriver to escape through the back of the Generator cubicle. He and Romana are again taken away for questioning.

That evening, Hardin's assistant Stimson enters the darkened Generator hall and is killed by the Foamasi. His body is found with the Doctor's scarf around its neck, so the Time Lord is arrested on suspicion of murder. As a form of trial by combat, he is used as a test subject for Romana and Hardin's modifications to turn the Recreation Generator into an effective rejuvenator. However, a malfunction results in the Doctor aging 500 years. While he and Romana are confined, Pangol continues with his own adaptations to the Generator.

Hardin frees the Doctor and Romana, and they return to the hall. The men distract the Argolin working there – causing one to faint from the complexity of the warp mechanics equations the Doctor chalks on the side of the TARDIS – while Romana slips into the Generator cubicle to investigate Pangol's work. Another Foamasi helps her escape before Pangol, believing the Doctor is inside, can use it to age her by 2,000 years.

As dawn breaks, Pangol gathers the Argolin in the Generator hall to announce a new era for their race. The Doctor slips into the TARDIS to retrieve the randomiser and then sneaks into the Generator cubicle. Romana tries to stop Pangol activating the machine but he uses himself as the template for an army of tachyon duplicates. Romana is taken away as his clone army files out.

The duplicates are unstable, however, and soon disappear. Pangol plans a second attempt but Hardin is determined to try rejuvenating the near-dead Mena and places her in the Generator. Pangol pulls the scientist away but when he goes in to remove his mother's body the door closes behind him and the machine activates. The Doctor interrupts the sequence by destroying the viewscreen, and a younger Mena emerges from the cubicle with a crying baby Pangol.

The Doctor is left holding the baby as Mena leaves to restore relations with the legitimate Foamasi ambassador. He quickly passes it to Hardin and advises Romana they make a quick exit. She is worried about leaving without the randomiser but the Doctor is dismissive of the threat from the Black Guardian. They board the TARDIS and it dematerialises.

- **NOTES** The war against the Foamasi is stated as being in 2250, which Pangol says was "forty years ago". But the

Argolin are also said to have undertaken "forty years' work on tachyonics" in an attempt, it's suggested, to overcome their post-war sterility (although it's possible they were building on pre-war theoretical work). It's also implied they didn't construct the Hive until after the war, to protect them from the fallout. So this story may be set a year or two after 2290, with references to the war being rounded down from just over 40 years and to the development of tachyonics being rounded up.

- *The Leisure Hive* featured the first use in *Doctor Who* of digital image processing using the Quantel DPE 5000. One shot this device enabled was of the TARDIS materialising while the camera appeared to be moving. In fact this was initially shot as a static split-screen mix. With the camera in a fixed position, Pangol was recorded explaining anti-gravity squash. The Police Box prop was then moved into place and the shot resumed, initially with the TARDIS on the left of the picture masked off by the recording of Pangol – look closely and you can see where part of the 'Police box' sign has not been covered completely. This overlay was faded out to reveal the TARDIS just as the camera began to pan down to show the Doctor emerging. All this was stored in the Quantel 5000, allowing the shot to begin slightly zoomed into the top-left of the picture, then carefully timed to zoom out to full frame just as the downward pan began. This gives the impression of the camera pulling back from Pangol as the TARDIS materialises and then, in one smooth motion, moving down.
- The Doctor's warp mechanics equations consist of indecipherable symbols chalked on the right-hand door, window and corner post. He also writes 'Beware of the Dog' below the window on the left-hand door.
- Here the randomiser is a larger, more complex unit than was fitted to the console in *The Armageddon Factor* (Landing 158), although it does have a strip of flashing lights that could be interpreted as the previous unit attached to a larger component.
- When the Doctor enters the TARDIS to collect the randomiser, the chalk equations are still there, but when he and Romana go to leave Argolis they have gone. Who rubbed them off?
- So farewell to the randomiser. But really, what was the point of it? As we've seen, after installation it's mentioned twice and then is quietly ignored. The idea may have been to return some disorder to the TARDIS's landings, as in the series' early days, but the writers quickly realised that if the plot requires the Doctor to go somewhere then he needs to be able to pilot the Ship. Besides, most viewers probably didn't even remember the randomiser by the time Season 17 began, let alone Season 18. So why bring it back just to get rid of it? Because the people who *would* remember were the increasingly organised fans, and this is perhaps an early sign of the influence they would gain over the programme through its new producer John Nathan-Turner.

LANDING 184

SPACE Prion system, Tigella, jungle
TIME [Late-20th century]
TRAVELLERS The Doctor, K9, Romana
EPISODES Meglos 1-2,4

The Doctor is repairing the sea-damage that befell K9 and has Romana set the TARDIS to hover in space rather than land, to avoid jolts while he performs the delicate work. They are in the Prion star system, which has two habitable planets: Zolfa-Thura, now barren and lifeless, and Tigella, which the Doctor recalls he has visited before. He contacts his friend Zastor and learns the Tigellans' power source, the Dodecahedron, has become erratic. He agrees to visit and take a look once he has finished fixing K9.

But as Romana completes the repairs, the TARDIS is trapped in a chronic hysteresis, looping through the same moment over and over. The Doctor and Romana are aware of what is happening and can move freely when the loop resets, but are powerless as time repeatedly jumps back. With no known technological procedure for escaping the hysteresis, the Doctor hopes they can throw it out of phase by performing their actions ahead of the cycle.

The loop is successfully broken and the Doctor proceeds with their visit to Tigella while Romana changes out of her bathing costume. The TARDIS lands not in sector eight of the underground city, as the Doctor intended, but on the surface amid dense jungle, containing some carnivorous plants. A short distance away is a Gaztak spacecraft, the landing rockets of which have burnt parts of the foliage. The Doctor and Romana, along with the now operational K9, head for the city entrance 22 degrees north, 36.4 degrees west.

A few hours later they return, Romana carrying K9, whose batteries are depleted. With them are two Tigellan engineers, Deedrix and Caris, and they all enter the TARDIS to follow Meglos and his Gaztak mercenaries who have stolen the Dodecahedron.

- **CONTROLS** Romana adjusts controls on the triangular plate on the left of panel C4 and unseen others on the right when she puts the TARDIS into hover mode. She also turns the silver dial now on the right of panel C5.
- When trying to determine what's causing time to repeat, Romana adjusts the right-hand black dial on panel C2 while the Doctor turns the silver dials on panels C4 and C5.
- **LORE** The TARDIS can hover: remaining in flight but with the exterior appearing in four-dimensional space. We've seen it do this several times before, and it may account for the confusion of Landing 56, but this is the first time it's referred to as a specific mode.
- Stopping the time rotor is a "terrible idea" for escaping a chronic hysteresis. (There's no indication from the actors that they're referring to the central column.)
- **NOTES** The Doctor is repairing K9 after his dip in the sea at Brighton and Romana is still wearing the same outfit, so it's unlikely there have been further landings since leaving Argolis.

- As that planet is in the Milky Way and close enough to Earth for a regular shuttle service, and the Gaztaks transport a human "across the galaxy" to Zolfa-Thura, the Prion star system is probably also in our galaxy.
- A relative Earth date isn't given but the human the Gaztaks kidnap appears to be from a time contemporary with the serial's production, going by his suit and spectacles. There's no indication the Gaztaks' ship has time-travel capability so the events on Tigella and Zolfa-Thura are in the same time period.
- Although built for *State of Decay*, recorded prior to *Meglos*, this is the first time viewers saw the remodelled control room on screen. The two walls with 3½ columns of circles have been replaced by a pair of walls with just three columns of staggered translucent roundels, separated by a section with two columns of aligned roundels. These are joined by two slatted columns slimmer than those by the main doors and scanner walls. The hatstand is another new model with just four rather than the more usual six hooks, here holding the Doctor's current coat, scarf and hat while he works on K9, plus Romana's straw hat. The Doctor later hangs up his apron.
- The Doctor specifically tells Romana not to land during K9's repair but that "hovering will do" and the central column continues to oscillate. Later the TARDIS's hover function will be used more frequently, often with the Police Box shown floating in the sky (with or without its lamp flashing). As a new mode separate from being in flight (column moving and lit) or materialised (column still and unlit), a policy was adopted to indicate the Ship was hovering by having the central column stationary (usually in its lowest position) but still illuminated. We will tend to list these instances as separate landings.
- How does K9 have a manual? It's usually assumed that Professor Marius designed and built the original K9 from scratch, but all he says in *The Invisible Enemy* is, "I had K9 made up." This could mean from his own specifications or it could mean from a kit (even if subsequently adapted). At the very least it implies others were involved in the actual work of constructing K9. Either way, it's unlikely a specific manual for the finished unit existed, and there's no evidence Marius gave the Doctor a copy when K9 boarded the TARDIS. The second K9 is presumed to have been put together by the Doctor (who's hardly the type to bother with documentation), although he's contained in a cardboard box stencilled 'K9 MII' which could suggest he was acquired. And the third K9 given to Sarah Jane Smith is only said to be a gift from the Doctor, not specifically made by him. So could there actually be many K9s, sold in kit or complete form, with operating manuals?
- Not only does Meglos have the technology to put the TARDIS into a chronic hysteresis, he can also monitor inside the control room. The Doctor has previously described a time loop as passing "continually through the same points in time"; the difference with a chronic hysteresis might be the period of free movement as the loop resets. This can perhaps be taken as having the same duration as the repeated section, although the on-screen action doesn't quite fit this theory. Usually in science fiction a time loop is presented as a continual effect in which those affected have no awareness of their predicament (except perhaps for one sensitive character who comes to realise their déjà vu is something more); a chronic hysteresis is arguably worse if its victims know they're trapped and are briefly lucid but doomed to keep looping back. This might be a consequence of the Doctor and Romana being Time Lords, however, as with their awareness of the time slips in *City of Death* (Landing 161), allowing them to re-enact the repeated actions during the respite and thus throw the hysteresis out of phase. It's not really clear how this leads to "phase cancellation" – why should their actions while free to move affect those during the loop, even if they are (mostly) the same?
- The image duplication and shifting zoom representing the cancellation of the chronic hysteresis were accomplished using the Quantel DPE 5000.

LANDING 185

SPACE Prion system, Zolfa-Thura
TIME As above
TRAVELLERS The Doctor, K9, Romana, Caris, Deedrix
EPISODES Meglos 4

The TARDIS materialises at night on Zolfa-Thura, tucked discreetly in the shadows behind one of the five giant pentagonal screens that are arranged around a central tower. Atop this is the Dodecahedron, the energy from which is being absorbed by the screens and lighting up the sky. The Doctor insists on exploring alone as he can pretend to be Meglos, given the Zolfa-Thuran has already been impersonating him. After he has left them, however, Romana and Caris decide they want a closer look at the screens and approach along with Deedrix and a recharged K9.

They all return to the TARDIS shortly after as Brotadac counts down to activation of the Dodecahedron beams, unaware that the Doctor has inverted the target settings. The Doctor's hope for a swift getaway in unfulfilled, however, as the Ship struggles to dematerialise. But as the tower descends into the ground the TARDIS successfully takes off.

- **NOTES** The arrival of the TARDIS was a model shot recorded on video. The scene, set at night, is too dark to be sure but this seems to be a new Police Box miniature in scale with the screens. It has a flashing light and white 'Police telephone' plaque but darkened windows. The full-size Police Box prop was then shot against black drapes representing either the night sky or the back of the screen.
- Although the model setup shows the TARDIS landing right next to one of the screens, the subsequent studio scenes suggest it's a short walk away from the action.

Notably, Romana says she thinks they should take a closer look, as if she's not standing right under one of the panels. She's next seen creeping round behind the Gaztak spaceship, so did she look at the screens or not?

▌ Any amazement Caris and Deedrix had at the inside of the TARDIS must have been expressed during the brief journey as they show no astonishment once they arrive on Zolfa-Thura. Quite why they come along is unclear as the Doctor handles things perfectly well on his own. Did he just want some backup because K9 was rundown (even though he has recharged by the time they arrive)?

▌ Why is the TARDIS sluggish at taking off? It's implied this is just the Ship being unreliable – the Doctor says it needs "a thorough overhaul" – but this hasn't been the case since the 1960s episodes, and then it was never clear whether it was the TARDIS or the Doctor at fault. Another case of fans' memories (mis)guiding the production? Or perhaps the Ship is being affected by the energy from the Dodecahedron, given we know the Zolfa-Thurans' technology is advanced enough to affect it in other ways, such as the chronic hysteresis. The stuttering take-off sound effect is that first heard in *The War Games* (Landing 71) and later, with additions, in *Spearhead from Space* (Landing 73).

▌ Is Zolfa-Thura destroyed? It's implied the planet visible in the sky is Tigella, and the two must be in similar orbits if they're both capable of supporting humanoid life. So were one to explode the other would surely be catastrophically affected, which doesn't appear to be the case. There's a suggestion at the end of the countdown that Meglos is attempting to instigate a chronic hysteresis – part of Grugger and Brotadac's dialogue is repeated – to postpone the destruction, and note that the picture doesn't completely white-out. So is the planet left intact but trapped in a five-second loop of imminent destruction until Meglos can figure out how the Doctor broke a hysteresis? Good luck getting those Gaztaks to remember their lines.

LANDING 186

SPACE Prion system, Tigella, jungle
TIME Shortly after Landing 184
TRAVELLERS The Doctor, K9, Romana, Caris, Deedrix, unnamed human
EPISODES Meglos 4

The TARDIS returns safely to Tigella, where Zastor's people are now forced to reclaim the surface without the Dodecahedron to power their underground city. Romana alerts the Doctor that they have received a message from Gallifrey instructing them to return home but he offers to take the human back to Earth first.

▌ **NOTES** It's not said how the Time Lords deliver their message (mentally? Via the console?) but it does suggest they now know where the TARDIS is at any time.

LANDING 187

SPACE Earth, [England]
TIME As above (approximately)
TRAVELLERS The Doctor, K9, Romana, unnamed human
EPISODES Full Circle 1

The TARDIS lands on Earth to return the man who was kidnapped by the Gaztaks, at around the same time as he was originally snatched, give or take 20 minutes, so he can make it home to his wife as promised.

Romana has time during the journey to change her clothes but the Doctor does not hang about, accepting the order to return to Gallifrey. He has K9 set the coordinates to 10-0-11-0-0 by 02 from galactic zero centre and the robot dog himself dematerialises the TARDIS by initialising the spatial drive.

◉ **CONTROLS** The Doctor pushes the left-hand large slider on panel C3 downwards and presses the push-button just above it, while operating unseen controls on the left of panel C4.

▌ **NOTES** Presumably the unnamed man tells the Doctor when and where he was grabbed by the Gaztaks (he's English but could be living anywhere). Although the Doctor mused on getting him back before he left, it's likely he simply drops him off just after he was snatched, as if he'd never been away; or possibly 20 minutes later at his front door to save him a journey.

▌ The TARDIS is stationary in the opening scene of *Full Circle* episode one and the Doctor says, "Now we've dropped off our Earth friend we can be on our way," confirming they do indeed take the man home and he doesn't decide to stay on Tigella after all.

LANDING 188

SPACE E-space, Alzarius, forest; carried to cave
TIME Unknown
TRAVELLERS The Doctor, K9, Romana
EPISODES Full Circle 1-2

Romana does not want to go back to Gallifrey but the Doctor says they have no choice. However, as K9 pilots the TARDIS it passes through a charged vacuum emboitement and emerges in the smaller universe of Exo-space. K9 regains control and reports there has been no damage.

The TARDIS materialises, seemingly at the programmed coordinates, the scanner showing the outer wilderness of Gallifrey. But when the Doctor goes outside he finds they are in a lush forest. It is a clear, sunny day, although the air is cool. Not far away is a grounded spaceship and signs of habitation by a lake.

The Doctor returns to the control room, where the scanner still shows Gallifrey and K9 confirms they are at the correct coordinates. The Doctor ducks under the console to try to figure out what is wrong with the scanner but only causes a small explosion.

Within no time he has pulled out wiring and circuit boards from the console's pedestal and is hammering at something inside. Nevertheless, Romana thinks she hears a noise from outside and when she opens the doors a teenage boy stumbles in and faints. They take him to Romana's room and put a dressing on his wounded knee. He wakes and warns them of Mistfall. Intrigued, the Doctor plans to take a look outside until Romana reminds him about the console and scanner. He deduces the image translator is displaying the absolute coordinate values, suggesting wherever they have landed has negative coordinates. He and K9 head out, leaving Romana to tidy up the console.

Shortly after, the boy, Adric, decides he must warn his friends about the oncoming Mistfall, his knee having already healed. Romana gives him a homing device in case he needs to find his way back to the TARDIS.

She finishes work on the console and is pondering a universe of negative coordinates when Adric returns with his brother Varsh and two friends, Keara and Tylos, taking shelter from the mist that is beginning to envelop the planet and change its atmosphere. Romana is worried for the Doctor but before she can leave to find him the control room is rocked as the Police Box is carried off by creatures that have risen from the marshy lake. When it eventually comes to a rest, the scanner still shows a Gallifreyan landscape so Romana peers out through the door. The Ship is now in a cave overlooking the Starliner spaceship some five kilometres away. She ducks back inside as Marshmen approach and begin beating at the Police Box with clubs. They are distracted by the arrival of K9, who has tracked the TARDIS to its new location, but one of the creatures strikes at him and knocks his head off.

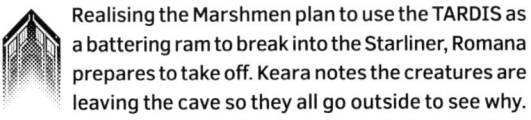

Realising the Marshmen plan to use the TARDIS as a battering ram to break into the Starliner, Romana prepares to take off. Keara notes the creatures are leaving the cave so they all go outside to see why. The Marshmen have been frightened away by large spiders that are bursting out of river fruit. These skitter across the cave floor and the teenagers take refuge in the TARDIS, closing the doors and leaving Romana stranded outside. When Adric tries to open the main doors he accidentally dematerialises the Ship.

- **CONTROLS** Romana adjusts controls on panels C1 and C2 after passing through the CVE. The Doctor operates the scanner with the rotary handle on panel C4.
- When the Doctor is working at the console innards, there are drop-down flaps beneath panels C2 and C3. The components on these are different from those seen on a similar flap beneath panel C5 in *The Invasion of Time* (Landing 144). There's no sign of these flaps in earlier shots of the console's underside so they were probably just hung in position to appear to have dropped down. The black inset of the pedestal below panel C2 has also been replaced with a gold panel (that looks rather like brickwork) which is presumably intended to be internal circuitry.
- Just before the TARDIS is carried off by Marshmen, Romana reaches across to the top-left of panel C1 (to open the main doors?) and twists her hand as if turning a dial, although there's no rotating control in that area.

She later flicks the switch that is there to open the doors. Tylos then uses the flick switch on the right of the same plate to close them, and when Adric flicks the left-hand one again the TARDIS dematerialises.
- When preparing to take off, Romana turns the bottom-right black dial and rotary handle on panel C4.
- **LORE** The image translator reads the absolute value of the Ship's landing coordinates and displays that location on the scanner. It has square ends joined at the corners by rods enclosing a crystal attached by coiled wires.
- The TARDIS is said to weigh 5,000,000 kilograms in Earth-equivalent gravity.
- **NOTES** This is the first time we've seen any of the TARDIS's domestic quarters since *The Chase* (Landing 17). Here, Romana's room is just beyond the control room's interior door, past one of the white-painted aligned-roundels walls. The set draws heavily on the look of the control room, with two new walls each with four columns of 4½ translucent roundels, another aligned opaque-roundels wall, a doorway with three roundels set into the door, and slatted columns (one wide, one narrow and one with a double curve). The room contains a bed, soft chairs, lots of cushions, a potted fern, a white hatstand with dresses hanging on it, a wooden screen carved in tree-like shapes, several paintings, a chess set with abstract chrome pieces, a chrome-and-glass shelving unit and hanging lamps.
- The hatstand in the control room is the same as in *Meglos*, now holding the oatmeal-coloured coat last worn by the Doctor in *The Horns of Nimon* and his cape from *The Talons of Weng-Chiang*.
- K9 says the Ship is 32 minutes from Gallifrey just before it encounters the CVE. It then materialises mere moments after emerging into E-space; there must have been some contraction of time while passing through.
- The model shots of the TARDIS in space use the new miniature built for *The Horns of Nimon*. We can now see it too has a white 'Police telephone' plaque, like previous models but not the full-size prop since 1969. Note it has holes in the front-left corner post, perhaps where it was supported for its debut shoot. The effect of passing through the CVE was again achieved using the Quantel DPE 5000.
- When the Doctor moves to work under the console, the flash charge goes off underneath panel C2. This produced light and smoke but not much heat, so as to cause little damage.
- It's indicated here that the image translator interprets coordinates and then displays on the scanner what's supposed to be at that space-time location. The implication is that Alzarius is at the same coordinates in E-space as Gallifrey is in N-space (even though E-space is much smaller and surely can't have the same 'galactic zero centre' reference point) but because the image translator can't read negative coordinates it just shows the positive equivalent. Although this might explain some of the scanner's previously seen capabilities – such as looking beyond the immediate area in *The Reign of Terror* (Landing 9) or showing far-away

planets in *The Horns of Nimon* (Landing 172) – it's contrary to the more common indication that the scanner essentially works like a camera showing what's directly outside the Ship (among other functions). The view of Gallifrey also changes when the Police Box is moved, so perhaps the scanner is receiving a view of what's outside as usual but this data is still processed through the image translator, which is misinterpreting it and outputting the wrong result.

▪ This is also the first use of a TARDIS homing device since Landing 17. Here it's a faceted green crystal with a circular base, not totally unlike what was glimpsed in *The Chase*. It just happens to be sitting on the console, which is handy. It's not clear why Romana gives it to Adric as he has already found the TARDIS once and why would she expect him to need to come back?

▪ Oops! When the camera image is tilted to represent the rocking control room, the top of the set can be glimpsed. Why is there an echoey grinding sound when the Marshmen move the TARDIS? It's not as if the Ship has taken off, they're just carrying the outer Police Box. And how/why are they rocking it around so much that the occupants are constantly thrown from one side of the room to the other?

▪ Romana tells Adric the TARDIS weighs "five times ten to the six kilos in your gravity". As Alzarius appears to have roughly the same gravity as Earth, that's 5,000 tonnes – as heavy as 400 double-decker buses. There's no evidence the Marshmen are so strong that half a dozen of them could lift that, and it has been man-handled by a similar number of mere humans before. It would be rather dim of Romana to be giving the total weight of the Ship's interior if that's irrelevant to the effort involved in moving the Police Box, which is what they're discussing, so maybe she's estimating in Gallifreyan kilos which are smaller than Earth kilos.

▪ The actors playing the Marshmen beat rather gently at the Police Box so as not to damage the prop with their clubs (or perhaps vice versa).

▪ In the shot of the TARDIS's roof lamp flashing as it begins to take off, the front and left-side 'Police box' signs are starting to pop out of their frames. The dematerialisation uses a split-screen effect, allowing Lalla Ward to continue acting on the right of the picture as an overlaid shot of the Police Box on the left is faded out.

LANDING 189

SPACE E-space, Alzarius, Starliner
TIME As above
TRAVELLERS Adric, Varsh, Keara, Tylos
EPISODES Full Circle 3

Following Romana's preset coordinates, the teenagers are helpless as the TARDIS takes them to the Starliner, materialising right next to the Doctor in the lobby by the main entrance. He is startled as one by one the four teenagers emerge, Adric admitting that Romana is not with them.

The Doctor bundles the lad back inside and prepares to take the TARDIS back to the cave, although he is uncertain such a short reverse trip will be possible. Showing Adric how to cross his fingers for luck, he dematerialises the Ship.

○ **CONTROLS** When setting the reverse trip, the Doctor turns the black dial on panel C4, the left-hand rotary handle on panel C3 then moves this panel's left-hand large slider upwards. He adjusts the silver dial on panel C4, the rotary handle below it and the black dial again.

▪ **NOTES** Adric says Romana programmed the flight, presumably when she was seen preparing to take off from the cave. Having learned of the Starliner, she no doubt thought that would be the most likely place to find the Doctor.

▪ The TARDIS's materialisation was again done using a split screen, with a shot of the empty lobby overlaid on the left of the picture to obscure the Police Box. This has a soft join aligned with the angle in the wall behind and is faded out while Tom Baker reacts as if the prop he's already standing next to has just appeared.

▪ Why should the Doctor be concerned by making a reverse journey when he has done so often before, most recently from Zolfa-Thura back to Tigella (Landing 186)? Perhaps he's less certain because of the restricted nature of E-space.

LANDING 190

SPACE E-space, Alzarius, cave
TIME Shortly after Landing 188
TRAVELLERS The Doctor, Adric
EPISODES Full Circle 3

The short journey is successful and the TARDIS reappears in the cave right on the spot it previously occupied. The Doctor and Adric find Romana sitting peacefully but strangely subdued and unaware of who they are. While Adric collects a dead spider along with K9's body – his head is missing – the Doctor helps Romana into the Ship and takes her to her room to lie down.

He returns to the control room and sets the TARDIS in flight, then checks on Romana only to find her in a deep sleep. He notices a bite on her cheek and theorises the spiders might inject a psycho-chemical.

LANDING 191

SPACE E-space, Alzarius, Starliner
TIME Shortly after Landing 189
TRAVELLERS The Doctor, K9 (body only), Romana, Adric
EPISODES Full Circle 3-4

The TARDIS returns to the lobby of the Starliner so the Doctor can use the ship's laboratory to examine the spider. Its arrival startles a maintenance team working on a nearby control panel. As they emerge, the Doctor assures Adric that Romana will be safe alone in the Ship.

However, she wakens when scientist Dexter begins to operate on a captured young Marshman. The veins in her face glow with the chemical that links her mentally to the creatures. As the Marshman attacks Dexeter and smashes his lab, so Romana overturns her room. She stumbles out of the TARDIS, leaving a trail of torn clothing and the broken image translator. Adric returns to check on her but finds her missing so he fetches the Doctor. They survey the damage, suspecting Marshmen have broken into the Ship, before leaving to search for Romana.

Varsh and his two friends have been placed on repair detail and, under supervision, work on a panel near the TARDIS. Marshmen have got into the Starliner and approach the teenagers from two directions. Varsh distracts the creatures by throwing his satchel of spare parts over the floor. He and Keara escape but Tylos is killed.

The Doctor finds Tylos's body and is approached by a Marshman carrying K9's head on the end of its club. The Doctor snatches it but is soon encircled by more of the creatures. They back off when Romana appears behind him. She tries to claw at his face but he calls on her recognition of K9 and the TARDIS to soothe her, and slips away as she strokes the familiar blue box.

She soon succumbs again and joins the Marshmen on their rampage. Adric, Varsh and a group of Alzarians find Tylos's body by the TARDIS as they fend off Marshmen by releasing pure oxygen from canisters to weaken them. The group escapes down a corridor but the bulkhead will not close so Varsh stays to hold off the creatures. His canister expires, however, and he is killed before Adric can return with fresh supplies. As Adric mourns his brother, the Doctor tells Decider Login to flood the Starliner with oxygen to drive out the Marshmen.

Adric is waiting by the TARDIS with a new image translator taken from the lab. When he hears the Doctor approaching he slips inside, leaves the component on the console and hides beyond the control room. After showing the Deciders how to fly the Starliner, the Doctor and a recovered Romana return to the Ship and take off.

Romana reattaches K9's head before noticing the image translator. The Doctor plugs it into the console and checks the scanner, which shows a green-tinged starscape proving they are in E-space. He retunes the view to Alzarius, where the Starliner is at last lifting off. The TARDIS, however, is trapped in this universe unless they can find another CVE, one of the rarest space-time events.

✪ **CONTROLS** After dematerialising, the Doctor presses a button below the silver dial on panel C4 and one of the pushbuttons on the left-hand triangular plate. He operates the scanner using a flick switch on panel C1 and refocuses it from the same panel.

✪ The image translator slots into the block at the top of panel C1 (here facing the scanner).

📄 **NOTES** When the Doctor leaves Romana's room he doesn't go straight to the control room, the door to which can be seen behind Adric and remains closed. So they must look for her inside the TARDIS first before returning to the Starliner.

📄 Romana repairs K9 awfully quickly. The Ship appears to have only just dematerialised as the Doctor hasn't yet removed his coat and the image translator on the console is still unnoticed. Yet she has reattached K9's head and got him fully working. Impressive work.

📄 As the scanner shutters begin to open, the blue CSO flat can be seen behind them, although it's unlit so appears dark enough to look like it could be the view of space that's subsequently shown. This might be why the screen images were overlaid during editing rather than keyed in while recording – note they have square rather than round corners and take up a larger area than the scanner window.

LANDING 192

SPACE E-space, unnamed planet, forest
TIME Two days in unknown [future]
TRAVELLERS The Doctor, K9, Romana, Adric
EPISODES State of Decay 1,3-4

Romana worries about being trapped in E-space but the Doctor is interested in exploring while they seek a way out. K9 detects a habitable planet with Earth-like gravity, rotation and orbital period so the Doctor directs the TARDIS there. As they approach, K9 registers one localised reading of metal that could indicate high technology, although low energy levels suggest primitive life.

The Doctor lands the TARDIS as close to this concentration of energy as he can, materialising one afternoon in a wood on a coastal headland. Beyond the tree line, beside a small lake, is a pointed metal tower – in fact an ancient spaceship – atop a rocky outcrop and at its base is a cluster of simple mud-walled dwellings. The Doctor leaves K9 on guard in the TARDIS while he and Romana make their way to this village.

Shortly after they have left, Adric comes out of hiding. His presence and intention to follow the Doctor are challenged by K9 but Adric argues that because he is a stowaway who should not be in the TARDIS it is better that he leave immediately.

At dusk the next day, the Doctor returns to the Ship to look up the Record of Rassilon. He attaches K9 to the console with cables to search the TARDIS's databanks but they contain no mention of the Record, nor of vampires. K9 reminds his master that the Ship has a magnetic card system so the Doctor retrieves this and feeds punchcards into the console, producing a text printout.

Having learned about his people's war against vampires, the disappearance of their king – now known to have escaped through the CVE – and the only way to destroy them, the Doctor realises he will need the help of the rebel villagers if he is to kill the Great Vampire. He decides to use the TARDIS to impress them and dematerialises.

✪ **CONTROLS** While in flight, the Doctor adjusts unseen controls on panel C3 and the two black dials on panel

C2. Romana operates the scanner with the right-hand rotary handle on panel C3.

- When the Doctor returns to the TARDIS he adjusts controls on panel C3, including the two pushbuttons and the right-hand rotary handle. After attaching K9 to the console, by clipping cables to the emergency transceiver socket on panel C1, he turns the rotary handle again and moves the two large sliders downwards. He makes further adjustments on this panel and turns dials on panels C2 and C4 as K9 searches the databanks.
- The punchcards are fed into the new slot on panel C5 and the information is output on a roll of paper by the adjacent printer (see page 264).
- When preparing the TARDIS for a short hop, the Doctor presses the two pushbuttons on panel C3 simultaneously, adjusts the right-hand rotary handle again, and the left-hand black dial on panel C2.

LORE Type 40 TARDISes carry a copy of the Record of Rassilon on magnetic cards. One contains details of the war the ancient Time Lords fought to eradicate a race of powerful vampires, and an emergency instruction that any Time Lord who encounters the sole survivor, the king vampire, must destroy it even at the cost of his own life. Another gives information on how to kill the vampires.

The TARDIS has a memory core with searchable databanks of information, including 18,348 emergency instructions but no information on vampires.

NOTES Romana is still fretting about being marooned in E-space and says, "Supposing there aren't any other planets here," so it sounds like there haven't been any further landings since leaving Alzarius – although she has changed her outfit. Adric hasn't revealed himself yet but could be lost while exploring the TARDIS.

The Hydrax must have left Earth in our future, and it's said the three officers/lords have ruled this planet for a thousand years, but it's not impossible that passage through the CVE and/or the Great Vampire's powers involved some time displacement, so this could be set in our past. The Hydrax's log has a page listing the ship's three officers which is labelled 'Data file: 12/12/1998' but this surely can't be an origin date.

This was the first serial to use Christine Ruscoe's expanded control room set, although it would be seen on screen in *Meglos* and *Full Circle* beforehand. Here the corridor wall beyond the interior door has three columns of staggered translucent circles and the adjacent door with three roundels has a different handle from that seen in *Full Circle*. The hatstand is the model first seen in *The Invisible Enemy* and holds the Doctor's brown and oatmeal coats.

The model shot of the TARDIS flying through E-space uses the miniature built for *Pyramids of Mars*. The stars are superimposed over the top of the model footage using the green-tinged space image representing E-space. (Indeed, the lighting and movement of the model Police Box are similar to the footage shot for *Pyramids of Mars* and may be old film rather than newly shot for *State of Decay*, given visual effects designer Tony Harding struggled to complete filming of the tower model in the time allocated.)

We can assume K9 closes the control room doors behind the Doctor as he is seen extending his antenna towards the console after his master has left. But who opens them when Adric leaves? Neither he nor K9 touches the console. K9's ears twitch when considering Adric's argument so he can perhaps now control the TARDIS remotely, as in Landing 151, and opens the doors on concluding the boy's logic is sound?

The databanks seem to be different from the memory bank mentioned in *The Edge of Destruction* (Landing 4), holding general information rather than specifically a log of journeys, although this might all be stored in the same memory core.

The wooden trolley the Doctor wheels out carries stacks of punchcards, books, sheaves of paper and packs of playing cards.

LANDING 193

SPACE E-space, unnamed planet, burrow
TIME As above
TRAVELLERS The Doctor, K9
EPISODES State of Decay 4

The TARDIS materialises in the rebels' underground headquarters, startling the assembled men. The Doctor explains their predicament and tries to rouse them into battle but their scientist, Kalmar, is hesitant. To convince him, the Doctor uses the scanning equipment they salvaged to display the Great Vampire awakening beneath the tower and pick up the sound of its heartbeat.

Kalmar contacts the head man of the village, Ivo, who joins them to plan an attack on the tower. The rebels will overcome the guards, with the aid of K9, while the Doctor hopes to use one of the tower's pointed scout ships as a bolt of steel to kill the vampire.

The next morning everyone returns to the rebels' headquarters. The Doctor gets the last of the equipment working so the villagers can regain lost knowledge and advance their society at last. He must leave to take Adric straight back to the Starliner and joins him, Romana and K9 in the TARDIS, which promptly dematerialises.

NOTES The shot of the TARDIS dematerialising is not a reverse of that of it materialising, but a separate roll-back-and-mix shot – note the equipment in the background is positioned differently in the frame.

For the first time K9 is shown exiting the Police Box. Previously his wheels had been unable to cope with the prop's step but prior to this story's production he had been refitted by the Visual Effects department with larger front wheels. A ramp was also used to reduce the drop K9 had to travel over (this was covered in dirt to match the floor and make it less noticeable, although you can see it buckle as K9's weight moves onto it).

LANDING 194

SPACE Charged vacuum emboitement
TIME None
TRAVELLERS The Doctor, K9, Romana, Adric
EPISODES Warriors' Gate 1-2,4

The TARDIS appears to be caught in a time rift from which neither Romana nor the Doctor can break it free. Adrift and unable to navigate, they consider if a random action would resolve their situation. Adric tosses a coin to choose a switch and presses it, which ends the Ship's shuddering. The main doors open, even though the TARDIS is still in flight, and the bright light of the Time Winds falls across the console, causing a small explosion. It also burns the Doctor's hand and strikes K9, who begins to smoke alarmingly. A time-sensitive Tharil, Biroc, enters the control room, although he is out of phase on a different timeline. He fumbles at the console and seems to stabilise, enough to warn the travellers not to trust those who are coming, before he runs back out and disappears into the white void surrounding the Ship.

Checking the console, the Doctor finds the coordinates are locked off at zero – they must be at or near the intersection of positive normal space and negative E-space. K9 is operating but damaged by the Time Winds, so the Doctor follows Biroc outside alone while Romana attempts to repair the robot dog. His memory wafers are aged to dust but otherwise he is functional, if a little erratic, and warns of three humans approaching the TARDIS.

The three men are from a spaceship also stranded in the void (a ship composed of dense dwarf-star alloy, the mass of which is contracting space-time around it) and have located the TARDIS using a mass detector. Romana decides to speak to them as they may have spare memory wafers for K9, and goes out as they are trying to kick in the door. She talks them into letting her assess the damage to their ship and they head off in the direction indicated by the mass detector. Watching on the scanner, Adric worries she is in danger so he and K9 follow.

Some indeterminate time later, the Doctor, Romana, Adric and a powerless K9 return to the TARDIS. Before they can decide how to help the enslaved Tharils aboard the humans' spaceship, the whole domain shudders as the now-much-closer freighter manoeuvres so that its warp motors are aimed at the Tharils' gateway. The Doctor and Romana head back to try to disable its power lines, leaving Adric with strict instructions to dematerialise if they fail to return within thirteen-and-a-half minutes.

When they do return Biroc is with them. Romana has decided to stay to help free his people. The Doctor gives her K9 as he will be restored beyond the gateway, then takes off before the back-blast from the spaceship destroys both itself and the gateway. As the TARDIS departs through the CVE, it appears briefly in the Tharils' domain. The Doctor and Adric are watching the scanner as this view fades, indicating that the image translator the Doctor acquired from the Starliner is no longer working because they are back in normal space.

- **CONTROLS** When trying to free the TARDIS from the time rift, Romana reaches for the right-hand black dial on panel C2 as the Doctor flicks one of the switches at top-left of panel C6. He then moves to panel C2 and turns the same dial. He later plays with the small lights on panel C6. When considering pressing a button at random, he reaches for the right-hand flick switch on the upper plate of panel C1 – which activates the reverse bias – before Romana stops him. Adric presses the lower-left of the three pushbuttons on the triangular plate on panel C4 as his random choice.
- Biroc touches various controls on the upper plate of panel C2. After he leaves, the red dome newly added to this panel goes missing. The TARDIS scenes were scheduled to be recorded at the end of the serial's first studio block, on Friday 26 September 1980, but not all were completed and those after Biroc's departure had to be resumed at the start of the next recording session on Thursday 2 October. The dome was presumably dislodged in the interim. In the first session, panel C2 is facing the doors; in the second, panel C3 is.
- The Doctor and Romana check the coordinates by turning the rotary handle on panel C4.
- In the episode one control room scenes recorded in the earlier studio block, the recessed face of the console's pedestal below panel C5 is missing, revealing the 'brickwork' inner workings glimpsed below panel C2 in *Full Circle* (Landing 188). That below panel C4 must also be loose or missing as the studio floor and Adric's shadow can be seen through the gap.
- The three red tubes in the central column each gain a silver dome at the top. The wires connecting the strip lights inside emerge from these and feed down through the triangular central core of the mechanism.

LORE Activating the reverse bias during flight would be catastrophic.

TARDIS navigation possibly works by digitally modelling time-cone isometry parallel-bussed into the image translator, with local motion mapped into each refresh cycle (if Romana isn't just spouting technobabble to confuse Rorvik and his men).

NOTES Despite the Doctor insisting he would take Adric back to the Starliner at the end of *State of Decay*, there's no mention of doing so here – indeed, Romana expresses concern about taking him out of E-space – so it seems they are resigned to his staying aboard. This might be because of further landings during which he proved useful to have around. They must also have shown him some basic TARDIS operations if they expect him to dematerialise without them (and in the next story he is said to be "getting the hang of this console").

It's not made explicit where the Tharils' gateway is. The Doctor calls it a micro-universe while Romana says, "We are in the theoretical medium between the striations of the continuum." So that's clear. Given the zeroed coordinates they are presumably within the CVE, and what we see fits with the Monitor's description of them in *Logopolis* as "voids into other universes".

- The shots of a wireframe Police Box on the spaceship's viewscreen and in Biroc's eye are not computer graphics as they might appear. The systems of the time weren't capable of producing the appearance of a rotating 3D object, so a model was built from balsa wood, recorded and then treated electronically.
- The video effect representing the light entering the control room as the doors open is poorly applied, the shape intended to cut around the console being badly aligned with the picture. The clear tube feeding smoke into K9 is also plainly visible, particularly when it turns white as the smoke is fed along it (they could have hidden it behind Tom Baker).
- One consequence of the control room scenes needing a second day to complete was that different hatstands were used in each session, changing mid-episode from the new model introduced to *Meglos* to the one first seen in *The Invisible Enemy*. In both instances they carry the Doctor's oatmeal coat and old multi-coloured scarf along with his current burgundy hat.
- When watching on the scanner as the spaceship turns to aim its engines at the gateway, one shot is actually taken through the scanner window, with the camera behind the set.
- The model Police Box used during filming of the gateway and spaceship appears to be the one built for *Pyramids of Mars* (with its windows now darkened) rather than the more recent *Horns of Nimon* miniature, although the latter is used for the shot of the TARDIS hovering in the Tharils' domain, which was recorded later in the studio.
- This brief appearance of the TARDIS can't be considered a landing, even in hover mode, as its roof lamp flashes and the engine sound is heard throughout (and is part of the take-off sound effect rather than the landing one – note the rising background whine).

LANDING 195

SPACE Metulla Orionsis system, Traken, grove
TIME Two days in unknown [before late-20th century]
TRAVELLERS The Doctor, Adric
EPISODES The Keeper of Traken 1-4

The TARDIS emerges from the CVE in the region of the star Metulla Orionsis and its system of planets. A number form the peaceful Traken Union, which the Doctor has heard of but never visited. He and Adric are surprised to discover the coordinates have been set for Traken itself, although not by either of them, and they are already heading there.

As the TARDIS orbits the planet, it is visited by the Keeper of Traken: a wizened old man in an ornate chair. The Doctor deduces he has commandeered the Ship, using the power he draws from the minds of everyone in the Union. The Keeper, nearing the end of his incumbency, seeks the Doctor's help with an impending threat and uses the scanner to show recent events: the arrival of a statuesque Melkur, immobilised by the beatific atmosphere, and its tending by a young girl called Kassia; and the now-adult Kassia's wedding to fellow consul Tremas, and their blessing by the Keeper, who assigns Tremas's daughter Nyssa to take over caring for Melkur. The Keeper tells the Doctor he senses some evil centred on these three and warns him he will face life-threatening power, then vanishes.

The Doctor retrieves some old journals to see if he has been to Traken before after all. He passes one volume to Adric but the boy struggles with both the temporal shifts in narrative and the handwriting.

The TARDIS materialises at twilight on Traken among the rich foliage of the grove, close to where Melkur stands. Adric is unnerved by the statue but the Doctor reckons it is safely calcified. They leave the grove and are immediately apprehended by armed fosters. Left alone, Melkur's eyes glow red and fire a volley of energy bolts at the TARDIS that shifts it in time slightly, rendering it intangible.

The next morning, the Doctor uses a TARDIS homing device to determine the Ship is still there but displaced by the current time cone. He builds a foldback flow inducer to create a standing wave for the TARDIS systems to home in on. He, Adric and Tremas enter the grove and, despite taunting from Melkur, the inducer works and the TARDIS reappears. But Kassia prevents them entering and they are caught in an electrified net then taken to the cells.

Kassia reports to Melkur, pleased her husband cannot now become the next Keeper but concerned when the statue suggests she could take his place. Kassia catches Nyssa eavesdropping and orders her home but the girl is more loyal to her father and determines to help him. Later, Melkur is displeased to learn the Doctor has escaped and punishes Kassia before ordering her to kill him.

The Doctor and his friends eventually make it back to the grove hoping to take refuge in the TARDIS but they are apprehended. Before the fosters can carry out their orders to kill the fugitives, a storm breaks and the ground shakes as the old Keeper perishes. The fosters flee while the Doctor's group struggle against the wind. The turmoil dies away as Kassia takes over the Keepership. Melkur tries unsuccessfully to intimidate the Doctor, who heads for the sanctum. Unseen, the Melkur statue dematerialises with the grinding sound of a TARDIS.

Adric and Nyssa are sent back to the Ship for safety but he finds the drives are being blocked so they cannot take off. Instead, they begin constructing a device to short-circuit the Source Manipulator, the bioelectronic system that supplies the Keeper's power. When they have completed this, they leave to connect it to the Source.

With Melkur destroyed and a new Keeper in place, the Doctor and Adric make a swift return to the TARDIS. The drives are now working and they leave Traken, although the Doctor admits the Ship needs an overhaul.

- **CONTROLS** For the first time since *Underworld* (not counting the unbroadcast *Shada*), the console's six panels have been positioned in a different order from usual, arranged 1-4-3-6-5-2 clockwise with panel C6 facing the main doors.
- Adric reads their destination from panel C1, seemingly

by looking at the slot in the top block that was added for the image translator. The Doctor turns the left-hand black dial on panel C2 which closes the scanner, but on landing he opens it again by pulling the red-knobbed lever on panel C1.
- The collar above panel C1 has lost its strip of red tape along the bottom edge.
- On returning to the TARDIS, Adric closes the main doors by moving the left-hand large slider on panel C3 downwards, then later opens them by sliding it back up. When testing the drives he flicks switches and wiggles the lever on panel C6.
- **LORE** The TARDIS can be penetrated and controlled by powerful entities such as the Keeper of Traken. (The Doctor says, "There can't be many people in the universe with the capacity of just dropping in like this," implying there are others.)
- From within his own TARDIS, the Master can block the engines of the Doctor's TARDIS and prevent it dematerialising.
- **NOTES** The story begins with what seems to be Adric's first view of N-space so there have been no additional landings since the TARDIS escaped E-space.
- While the Doctor and Adric view Metulla Orionsis on the scanner the stars are moving past them and the background hum of the control room is the 'in-flight' sound effect, even though the central column when briefly glimpsed on the left of screen is stationary. This may have not been visible on broadcast and so, given the other evidence, on balance it's likely the TARDIS has not materialised in space but is still in flight. After they notice the coordinates have been set for Traken, the Police Box is shown spinning through space and the column is seen oscillating.
- In *Logopolis*, Traken and Metulla Orionsis are extinguished by the entropy field unleashed by the Master. While the early Earth-bound scenes in that story are set in 1981, those on Logopolis, from where the Master initiates the unravelling, and back on Earth at the Pharos Project could be in a different time period (a decade or two either side). And although entropy is presented as spreading fast – Adric and Nyssa are outside space and time altogether when they view the effects so who knows what timescale they're seeing – it could take many years before reaching Traken. Although Nyssa's plea for help finding her missing father is received by the Doctor just after he leaves Earth in 1981, we've seen the TARDIS get signals from other time periods before. So the events on Traken could happen long before the planet's destruction.
- The model shot of the TARDIS spinning towards Traken uses the miniature built for *The Horns of Nimon*. The holes in the front-left corner post evident in *Full Circle* have been filled in but can still be made out. This was shot against a green background with the stars and planets added in via CSO.
- The original hatstand from *The Invisible Enemy* is again in use, holding the Doctor's cape from *The Talons of Weng-Chiang* for the last time, and with numerous books scattered around its base. Has Adric been boning up about N-space?
- The shot of the Keeper flitting around the control room used multiple split-screen effects. Denis Carey in his chair was first recorded on the left of the set. With the camera in a locked position, he was then moved to the right-hand side and joined by Tom Baker and Matthew Waterhouse. They were recorded initially with overlays of the earlier material placing Carey on the left and masking his new position on the right, then briefly removing him altogether before revealing his current position on the other side of the room. Dialogue was dubbed over to fit the timing of the movements. For his final vanishing, Baker and Waterhouse held their kneeling positions while Carey's chair was moved out of shot and then recording continued. The actors freeze well but, to soften a slight movement, in video editing parts of the second shot were mixed in over a couple of frames immediately before the cut.
- Oops! After the Keeper disappears and the camera moves up as Baker and Waterhouse stand, it reveals the top of the set and white cyclorama behind it, which are visible for the rest of the scene.
- Special sound designer Dick Mills introduces a soft chime as the central column comes to a rest on materialisation, perhaps to cover the change in background hum between in-flight and stationary modes.
- The Doctor carries the same homing device prop previously given to Adric in *Full Circle*.
- When Adric tests the TARDIS drives the stuttering grinding sound effect used for the failed take-off in *Spearhead from Space* (Landing 73) is faintly heard.
- Nyssa gets to ask the immortal question, "Why is it so much bigger inside than it is outside?" on seeing the TARDIS control room. Adric replies, "The Doctor told me that was because it was dimensionally transcendental," the first utterance of that precise phrase since *Colony in Space* (Landing 81).

PREVIOUS LANDINGS

SPACE Earth, England, London, Croydon
TIME 1978
TRAVELLERS The Doctor, [unknown companions]
EPISODES Mentioned by K9 III in K9 & Company
The Doctor produces a third K9 as a gift for Sarah Jane Smith. He instructs the robot dog to pass on the Doctor's his fondest love and tell her that he remembers her, then packs him in a crate and leaves it in the attic of Sarah's house in Croydon.
- **NOTES** K9 says the Doctor last spoke (to him) in 1978, suggesting this is when he was delivered to Croydon. If the crate had been left in view then surely Sarah or her aunt Lavinia would have opened it before the events of *K9 & Company*, so the Doctor must have deliberately put it in the attic.

Perhaps having landed in 1978, which could be before he first met Sarah or while she was travelling with him, he didn't want it found until after she had left the TARDIS.

▤ It's likely the Doctor was still in his fourth incarnation as later ones tend to overlook their previous companions. It may be after realising he has left K9s with both Leela and Romana that he thinks to gift one to Sarah too, in which case this is the last opportunity before his regeneration (and recalling his time with her in younger days may be why he's mooching in the cloisters). But perhaps a more likely point is shortly after *The Invasion of Time* (Landing 144), when he has just left the first K9 behind and got a replacement for himself. His memories of Sarah and how he never returned for her (and where she lived) would be fresher, plus the date tallies with that story's airing.

SPACE Jaconda
TIME Unknown [before 2300]
TRAVELLERS The Doctor, [unknown companions]
EPISODES Mentioned by the Doctor in
   The Twin Dilemma

While in his fourth incarnation, the Doctor visited his old teacher and mentor Azmael, a Time Lord who ruled the bird-people of Jaconda. Azmael showed him tunnels under the palace where ancient murals told the myth of the giant Gastropods. On the Doctor's last night there he pushed Azmael into a fountain to sober his friend up as he had drunk "like twenty giants".

▤ **NOTES** The Doctor in *The Twin Dilemma* says he has regenerated twice since he last met Azmael so must have been in his fourth incarnation (thus, after Landing 119). He recognises his friend's face so presumably Azmael has not regenerated since that meeting. Being a Time Lord too, he could have been in this (his last) incarnation for some time, so this visit could be several hundred years before the events of *The Twin Dilemma*.

LANDING 196

SPACE Earth, England, Hertfordshire, A1 Barnet bypass
TIME 28 February 1981
TRAVELLERS The Doctor, Adric
EPISODES Logopolis 1

The Doctor broods in the TARDIS's cloisters. He is reluctant now to return to Gallifrey and explain Romana's absence, so he decides to try fixing the chameleon circuit that controls the Ship's external appearance. This will require visiting Earth to measure a genuine Police Box, and then Logopolis where mathematicians use block transfer computations to remodel physical objects, as he tells Adric when the lad tracks him down.

While they make their way through the Ship's corridors to the control room, the cloister bell briefly tolls but the Doctor dismisses it and continues explaining to Adric the operation of the chameleon circuit. Back at the console, he activates the circuit's programmer and shows via the scanner how, whatever disguise he sets, such as a pyramid, the system reverts to a Police Box.

The TARDIS materialises on a grey, drizzly day in a lay-by off the Barnet bypass just north of London, 2.6 metres from a genuine Police Box that provides for roadside assistance. Indeed, not far away a red sports car has pulled up, but the two women occupants are too busy trying to change a tyre to notice there is now a pair of Police Boxes in the lay-by.

The Doctor is unsurprised but disappointed to have missed the target coordinates, expecting to have materialised around the Police Box rather than next to it. However, he is confident of being able to perform a short hop and swiftly dematerialises.

◉ **CONTROLS** The console's six panels are repositioned again, arranged 1-2-4-3-6-5 clockwise with panel C1 facing the main doors. This becomes the norm for the remainder of this console's use (with a couple of exceptions) so perhaps the panels were renumbered on the underside in this new order.

◉ The keyboard for programming the chameleon circuit rises from behind a new upper plate on panel C1. The Doctor uses the red-knobbed lever below to open the scanner. He later seems to operate the scanner from panel C2, possibly using the left-hand black dial, and checks and resets the landing coordinates from there. Adric reaches for the red-knobbed lever on panel C1 to open the main doors before the Doctor stops him.

▤ **LORE** The TARDIS has cloisters: an octagonal space with flagstones and grey walls, some of which have roundels (some illuminated). A number of archways provide multiple ways to access other areas of the Ship. In the centre is a square colonnade of eight stone arched pillars hung with ivy. There are also a couple of stone benches and potted plants.

▤ The cloister bell is an alarm system that chimes when the TARDIS is facing a "wild catastrophe". It can be rung manually.

▤ The chameleon circuit controls the outer plasmic shell of the TARDIS and should be able to mould it into any form. The exterior is the only part of the Ship that exists as a real space-time event [when it materialises], mapped onto one of the interior continua. The user interface for the chameleon circuit is a keyboard that emerges from inside the console and allows instructions to be entered in machine code. Results can be viewed on the scanner.

▤ The TARDIS needed repairing at the time the Doctor "borrowed" it and left Gallifrey for "pressing reasons".

▤ **NOTES** Although there is continuity from *The Keeper of Traken* with the returns of Nyssa and the Master, it's possible there have been further landings for the Doctor and Adric since leaving Traken.

- The date is stated in *Four to Doomsday* when the Doctor (mistakenly) believes he has finally got Tegan back to Heathrow Airport in time for her flight.
- When the Newbery Police Box prop was brought out of retirement for this story, it was modified to more closely match the Yardley-Jones prop and/or a genuine Police Box. But it also underwent some more subtle changes during production. In the opening scene, the right door with the Yale lock opens, as was usual for this box, and the centre post is attached to the left-hand side, which now has an opening telephone door with handle and a telephone (a black GPO No.332 model, the same as the Doctor had in his limbo-fridge in *The Pirate Planet* – see Landing 146) in a cubbyhole behind it. In subsequent scenes in the lay-by and on the control room set, however, the left side has become a practical door with a lock, while the centre post is fixed to the right-hand door. For shots of the left-hand door being used (such as when Tegan and Vanessa each enter), the telephone cubbyhole was removed. For the later studio scenes this needed to be reattached, so the right-hand door had to be used – note it's always slightly ajar as the centre post prevents it closing fully when the left-hand door is shut. Production documentation shows filming at the lay-by location was done over three days: the opening scene of the Master's arrival and shots of the TARDIS landing beside the Police Box (plus some of the Watcher in the field opposite) were filmed on Wednesday 17 December 1980; the crew returned on Friday the 19th but it seems this day may have been rained off; then the bulk of the scenes with the Doctor, Adric, Tegan and the police detective were filmed on Monday the 22nd. It's likely the left-hand door was made an actual door before filming started, but the swapping over of the lock and centre post was done during that first location day – they change between scenes shot in the morning (cycle policeman's murder) and afternoon (TARDIS arriving off target). Why this was felt necessary is unclear; presumably they wanted the two props to match even more closely for their side-by-side scene.
- The Doctor refers to "the time column…wheezing like a grampus" (a genus of dolphin). It's not explicit that he means the central column of the console, although that's no doubt the intention (an in-joke about the noisiness of the prop's drive mechanism).
- Why does the cloister bell toll in episode one? The TARDIS isn't in any immediate danger and although it's already heading for Earth, if it was detecting impending trouble surely it would have rung before countless prior landings. Could it be, if the Watcher is a pre-echo of the Doctor's regeneration caused by the Master's interference with the causal nexus, that this is when he is incarnated? The TARDIS senses this but when the Watcher manifests on Earth – as we see a few scenes later – it thinks the threat is gone and stops ringing the cloister bell. If, alternatively, the Ship has detected that the Master's TARDIS has already materialised around the Police Box the Doctor has programmed it to materialise around, then why would it stop chiming the bell? This could be why the TARDIS initially lands at slightly different coordinates, only for the Doctor to force it to relocate.
- Only one corridor set was built, then shot from a number of angles to suggest more. This had a continuous zigzagging wall on one side, consisting of a section with four columns of staggered translucent roundels, one with aligned opaque roundels, two plain flat sections, then another four-column translucent-roundels wall, with slim or wide slatted columns joining each section. Opposite these but not continuous were a plain flat with four vertical slats (similar sections were used in the cloister set), a plain section with a three-roundels doorway leading to Romana's room, and a plain flat with a wide slatted column at one end.
- Romana's room appears rather reduced from its previous appearance in *Full Circle*, although it contains the same shelving unit, sofa chairs, wooden screen and hatstand. The last holds Romana's costumes from *The Leisure Hive* and *Nightmare of Eden*. The painting on the wall (a single aligned opaque-roundels section) is different from those seen in *Full Circle*, however.
- The Doctor says the TARDIS was "in on Gallifrey for repair when I borrowed her" and that he "should have waited until they'd done the chameleon conversion", yet the chameleon circuit is stuck "in a totter's yard". We know the TARDIS could change its appearance for some time between leaving Gallifrey and landing on prehistoric Earth (Landing 2), so the chameleon circuit can't have been completely inoperable when the Doctor took the Ship. Perhaps the term 'conversion' suggests it was simply due an upgrade.
- The on-scanner animation of a pyramid and Police Box is the first use of computer graphics in *Doctor Who*. These were *not* produced on a BBC Micro, as is commonly claimed, a computer that wasn't developed until later in 1981. They may have been created on the DEC VAX 11/750 platform used by the BBC Computer Graphics Workshop (which later produced the opening titles for *The Tripods*) or on another microcomputer such as an Acorn Atom or Apple II.
- The Doctor talks of some Police Boxes "in the North [of Britain] that are still in use" despite their being "more or less obsolete by the time we'll be arriving there" (a reference to surviving boxes in Glasgow and Edinburgh, although of a different design from the Metropolitan box the TARDIS is based on). Yet when he says this he has already set the coordinates for the Barnet box just outside London (confirmed in *Mawdryn Undead* as being on the Barnet bypass). Even if he knows the Scottish boxes aren't a suitable match, why not land earlier in the 20th century when Police Boxes were more commonplace?
- When this story was being written and planned, it was hoped the last surviving Metropolitan Police Box in London – box S63 beside the Barnet bypass by Dyrham Park – might be used for filming the scenes set in the lay-by. Both writer Christopher H Bidmead and

director Peter Grimwade visited the site, and although the box was vandalised it was reckoned it could be cleaned up enough to be usable. But on 19 November 1980, just a month before filming was planned, the box was demolished. Some sources claim this was because of upcoming construction of the M25, which crosses the A1 Barnet bypass a mile north of the Police Box's site. However, this junction had already been expanded in the early-1970s when a section of the motorway to the east was built, connecting to the then-A6 to the west. (In fact, this work covered the site of another Police Box, S65, that had stood at Bignell's Corner where St Albans Road crosses the A1 and was removed in April 1970.) This idea may have arisen because photos of the Barnet Box believed to be have been taken shortly before its removal (although it appears in good condition) show it surrounded by piles of soil. If this dating is correct, it may be the box was removed owing to road-widening works and/or the building of the pedestrian bridge that now crosses the bypass at the box's former location. Whatever the reason, it's a mystery how this box survived ten years beyond when most London Police Boxes were demolished.

- Would the production team really have used the Barnet Box had it survived? There's only one brief shot where two boxes are seen together, and while the script argues they should be different, which is why the Doctor needs to measure a genuine Police Box, the production spent effort to make its two props appear the same. Both the Yardley-Jones box and the old Newbery box were altered to look more similar, presumably so the latter could be used to represent both a true Police Box and the TARDIS. Indeed, Police Boxes were significantly larger than the TARDIS prop, so how would the shot of the TARDIS materialising around the Barnet Box have been achieved? Also, how would the Barnet Box have been represented in the studio when it needed to appear in the control room? Would the Newbery box have been more extensively adapted to look closer to a real Police Box? While the survival of the Barnet Box may have inspired some aspects of the story, it's possible the production team would have chosen not to feature it even if it hadn't been inopportunely demolished.
- The lay-by scenes were ultimately filmed on the A413 Amersham Road just outside Gerrards Cross to the west of London (the Chalfont No.2 viaduct carrying the Chiltern Main Line railway can be seen in the shot of Tegan's car entering the lay-by). As a nod to the original planned location, producer John Nathan-Turner suggested placing a 'Barnet Borough Council' sign beside the Police Box prop (reading 'Please take your litter home' even though there's a rubbish bin right next to it). This location *was* affected by the building of the M25 – the section between junctions 16 and 17 constructed between 1983 and 1985 – the lay-by being where the motorway now crosses the Amersham Road.
- In the lay-by scenes only, the Yardley-Jones box is missing the handle on the front centre post and the front 'Police box' sign is a new replacement that otherwise featured on the right-hand side of the prop. The lettering on this is in the same typeface as the refurbished Newbery box but different from the Yardley-Jones prop's other signs. Possibly this was moved so the two boxes looked more alike in the shots of them together, where only the front of the newer prop is seen.
- One of the slats is missing from the large corner column next to the main doors wall.
- The view on the scanner of Tegan and Vanessa working on their car beyond the Police Box, doesn't quite match the position the TARDIS was shown landing in.

LANDING 197

SPACE Earth, England, Hertfordshire, A1 Barnet bypass (2.6m from previous location)
TIME As above
TRAVELLERS The Doctor, Adric
EPISODES Logopolis 1-2

The Doctor shifts the TARDIS slightly and rematerialises around the Police Box (causing the bicycle leaning against it to fall over), unaware the Master has earlier done the same. The box appears within the control room and Adric takes measurements while the Doctor explains about block transfer computation.

An instrumentation failure on the console and an alarm indicate they are being affected by a gravity bubble. The Doctor checks outside to confirm it is localised on the TARDIS, noting the two women by the sports car, then spotting a spectral white figure staring at him from the far side of the road. Disturbed by this, he returns inside where Adric is trying to pick the Police Box's door lock with the pin of his badge. It opens but when they go inside they find themselves in a darker version of the control room.

Outside, the younger woman, Tegan, has given up on the car and agrees to seek help from a garage. Intending to wheel the flat tyre along with her, she stops when she notices the Police Box and its plaque offering help. It reads 'Pull to open' but when she reaches out the door swings inwards. Noticing something peculiar, she ventures inside.

The Police Box inside the control room vanishes just before Tegan enters. The doors close behind her and, surveying the complex console, she tries a switch she hopes is an intercom but the only reply to her enquiry is the chiming of the cloister bell. She ventures further into the Ship in search of a crew but is soon lost in the maze of corridors.

The Doctor and Adric proceed through ever-darkening versions of the control room, hoping to reach the gravity bubble's nucleus but fearful that it could be an infinite regression, caused by another TARDIS materialising before them in the same location. They too hear the cloister bell, distorted, but must go on. Fortunately they emerge from the back of the TARDIS into the lay-by, where a police detective and two constables have found the abandoned sports car and two shrunken corpses.

The police try to take the Doctor away for questioning but Adric distracts them by pretending to have fallen off the abandoned bicycle. When the constables go to assist him, the Doctor slips back into the TARDIS, Adric dashes after him, and the doors slam in the policemen's faces.

Back in the primary control room, they notice the Police Box has gone and the cloister bell still ringing, but the Doctor decides to dematerialise before investigating. The engines are sluggish so he uses the architectural configuration system to jettison Romana's room, providing the power to take off. The Doctor sends Adric to answer the cloister bell – although it stops before he can reach the cloister – while he listens to a transmission the console has received.

- **CONTROLS** When the gravity bubble hits, the six lights on the new plate on panel C1 flash. The Doctor pushes the red-knobbed lever below this upwards and flicks switches on the plate to its left, then adjusts the right-hand dial on panel C2. He moves the lever back down and thumps the console to confirm the bubble. Touching the button at bottom-left of the plate on panel C6 appears to shut off the alarm that sounds, and the Doctor flicks one of the switches above. He knocks the lever at bottom-right to open the main doors.
- When trying to find an intercom, Tegan flicks the right-hand switch above the sliders on panel C3.
- When responding to the cloister bell, the Doctor flicks the two switches at top-left of panel C6 and seemingly closes the doors with the lower-left rotary handle on panel C3. He dematerialises (or tries to) by pushing one or both large sliders on this panel upwards. He adjusts controls on panels C1, C2 and C4 – including flick switches on the bottom-left plate of the first – when discussing the architectural configuration, then jettisons Romana's room with an unseen control on panel C4. When receiving the message, he moves the two large sliders on panel C3 downwards, flicks the two switches above and turns the left-hand rotary handle before putting his ear to the top block.
- **LORE** The architectural configuration system controls the interior allocation of space and allows specific rooms to be jettisoned [converted to energy].
- **NOTES** Briefly, the TARDIS appears to be in two places at once. The genuine Police Box's roof lamp flashes and its telephone door closes before the TARDIS to its right has completely vanished, suggesting the Ship is materialising around the Police Box *as* it's dematerialising from the lay-by.
- It also changes appearance as it rematerialises. Yes, this is because in real life different props were used to represent the TARDIS, but given the whole point is that the TARDIS doesn't precisely match the genuine Police Box, why didn't they swap the Newbery prop (playing the Police Box) for the Yardley-Jones prop (playing the TARDIS) when the Ship repositions, reinforcing the idea that the latter has enveloped the former?
- After the material filmed on Wednesday 17 December, the telephone plaque on the Newbery box became much dirtier, almost obscuring the lettering. Was this just a result of the prop repeatedly being transported to and from the location, or was it deliberate to hide the fact the two boxes had differently worded plaques?
- Note this manoeuvre is quite different from when the Master arrived. There's no distortion and the dangling telephone and open door fade as the TARDIS materialises around the Police Box. Previously the box shimmered but the small door remained open and the telephone inside was still accessible, although the connection was cut. Despite what Adric supposes, has the Master actually materialised his TARDIS *inside* the Police Box, in some dimensionally clever way such that their doors are linked so he can pull unsuspecting policemen inside? This might explain why there's no time-ram-like catastrophe when the Doctor's TARDIS materialises around the Police Box and why only the Doctor's control room is caught in a loop, rather than alternating with the Master's as happened in The Time Monster (Landing 87). And it seems clear the Doctor and Adric are measuring the genuine Police Box, not the Master's TARDIS. So by hiding inside the Police Box, the Master can successfully infiltrate the Doctor's TARDIS once it has materialised around them both.
- Nonetheless, there's some strange dimensional trickery going on. Even after the gravity bubble has been initiated (by the Master, not automatically, as the Doctor and Adric are measuring the Police Box for some time before it kicks in), the Doctor can go outside, so does that mean if he retraced his steps through brightening control rooms he would get back to the primary one? This must still 'be' somewhere as Tegan is wandering around it. Perhaps the vanishing of the Police Box from this primary interior locks them into the regression, but how does it dematerialise? The slightly modulated sound effect (first heard in The Keeper of Traken for Melkur's comings and goings) indicates we're seeing the Master's TARDIS taking off, but if that was around (or inside) the Police Box wouldn't it just leave the real box behind (and thus still inside the Doctor's TARDIS)? So where is the Police Box at this point? Not being a trans-dimensional object, presumably it can only exist in one control room at a time, so each time the Doctor and Adric go through into a further iteration of their control room the Police Box ceases to exist in the previous one. The first time they go through, the Box shifts into the next nested control room and disappears from the first, leaving the Master's TARDIS behind. This then dematerialises just before Tegan enters, and rematerialises in the lay-by around the outer plasmic shell of the Doctor's TARDIS (which may be why the cloister bell sounds). Vanessa ventures inside (to her misfortune), before the Master moves his TARDIS back into the Doctor's somewhere, later relocating to the cloister. As his plan is to hitch a lift to Logopolis, the gravity bubble must just be to distract the Doctor, not trap him forever, so the iterations are finite and eventually he and Adric emerge into the outside world (somehow from the back of the TARDIS). After re-entering through the front door to escape the police, they note the Police Box is missing from the primary control

room – still in the darkest iteration, now inaccessible. The dimensionally nested control rooms drag on the Ship, however, requiring the Doctor to convert part of the interior into energy. This enables it to dematerialise, collapsing the gravity bubble and leaving the Police Box back in the real world to confound the police.

- How does measuring a genuine Police Box help fix the chameleon circuit? Is the inaccuracy of the TARDIS's impression a symptom of the circuit's failure? If so, perhaps comparing (in all 37 dimensions) a real Police Box with what the chameleon circuit has produced would reveal what corrections need to be made. The Doctor says, "The Logopolitans convert [the measurements] into a precise mathematical model…to overlay it on the TARDIS," which could suggest they or the Ship itself then adjust the chameleon circuit so its output matches the accurate model, thereby resetting it. In his novelisation of the story, script writer Christopher Bidmead has the Doctor explain: "The dimensional interference patterns will shake the thing loose."
- The 'Police box' sign on the right-hand side of the Newbery prop is not an original as on the front and left, being shallower and lacking a raised frame.
- The Doctor uses a set of spiralling wooden library steps while measuring the Police Box, with four triangular steps around a spindle topped with a brass knob. Although these are present when the gravity bubble forms, they do not appear to be in the duplicate control rooms, unlike the hatstand.
- When reading the 'Police telephone' plaque, Tegan says, "Officers and cars respond to urgent calls," (as scripted) even though on the Newbery prop she's looking at it reads 'Officer and cars'.
- Beyond the control room's interior door is one of the walls from the previous set with 3½ columns of translucent roundels. To the right of this, seen in episode four, is the double-curved slatted section previously used in *Full Circle*.
- The "sluggish" take-off is indicated by the juddering sound effect recently reintroduced in *The Keeper of Traken* (Landing 195).
- For the shot of the inside of the genuine Police Box after the TARDIS has dematerialised, the Newbery prop was given a back for the first time. This was just a plain flat with no windows, painted black, and with a small ledge to hold a clipboard and two amber beacons.

LANDING 198

SPACE Earth, England, London, above river Thames
TIME [As above]
TRAVELLERS The Doctor, Adric, Tegan Jovanka, the Master
EPISODES Logopolis 2

Tegan finds herself in the cloister and takes a rest. But its peaceful atmosphere is disturbed by the appearance of the Master's TARDIS, still disguised as a Police Box. The door creaks open and an ominous chuckle unnerves Tegan so she resumes trying to find a way out. She ends up back in the cloister and, sobbing in desperation, does not notice the Police Box vanish. Steeling herself for another try, she leaves the cloister. Behind her, the Master's TARDIS reappears, now disguised as a tall potted bush.

The Doctor tells Adric he has received information from Traken that Nyssa's father has vanished, evidently taken by the dying Master to renew himself. Realising they cannot risk going to Logopolis while the Master's TARDIS is somewhere aboard, the Doctor decides to flush him out by materialising underwater and opening the doors.

The TARDIS materialises hovering above London while Adric helps the Doctor shut down all its systems so that it drops towards the Thames below. It lands with a thump but when the Doctor finds there is no water pressure on the doors, the pair go outside and discover they are on a floating pier. Watching from a bridge above is the spectral white figure the Doctor glimpsed at the roadside. It signals him to approach and Adric watches as they talk.

A sombre Doctor returns and programmes the TARDIS to take them to Logopolis after all, having learned a chain of events has already been set in motion. The Police Box fades from the river pier.

○ **CONTROLS** When preparing to shut down the TARDIS systems, the Doctor and Adric each twist the black dials on panel C2. While the Doctor adjusts further unseen control on panels C2 and C3, Adric folds back the omega configuration by pressing buttons on the left of panel C4 then disables the other systems from beneath the console. The Doctor flicks switches on the bottom-left plate of panel C1 to "partially materialise". Adric opens the doors by sticking his finger in the middle tube of the green plastic control on panel C5; he does the same to close them later.

○ Although Tom Baker's hands move over the console and sound effects are heard when setting the coordinates for Logopolis, it doesn't look like he actually adjusts any of the controls (except possibly the right-hand dial on panel C2).

▮ **LORE** The omega configuration can be folded back, the exponential cross-field halted, pathways seven to seventeen closed, and main and auxiliary drives ended. Even with all these systems deactivated, the TARDIS can still materialise.

▮ **NOTES** There's nothing to specify this is the same time period as the scenes in the lay-by – it's now sunnier for one thing – but equally no reason the Doctor would have moved in time. It must be between 1908 and 1985 as the White City Stadium is visible in the aerial view of London on the scanner (a photo from Aerofilms).

▮ The Doctor later says Nyssa "contacted me and begged me to help you find your father" but surely her society doesn't possess the technology to direct a transmission so specifically across untold space and time, and he didn't hang around on Traken long enough to leave behind something like a space-time telegraph, nor have any reason to do so. So her plea must have been conveyed via the Keeper, although his influence may

not extend much beyond the Traken Union, which would explain why the Doctor's reception is faint.
- 📘 Although the Doctor says his plan is to "materialise the TARDIS underwater" he then proceeds to hover above the Thames and seemingly intends to let the Ship drop. Surely the first method would be easier and safer? While the aerial view of the city needn't be live, the central column isn't moving (but is flashing) and Dick Mills introduces a new 'hovering' background hum, so it's safe to assume the Police Box has materialised in the sky (does anyone spot it?). Yet the Doctor then says, "We'll partially materialise so there'll be a slight jolt," which indeed there is. But as the TARDIS hasn't actually dropped into the water and sunk to the bottom, why is there a second jolt? If it did plummet from a height onto the pier, surely it would smash through the wooden decking, yet there's no hint of damage when the Doctor and Adric go outside. At the very least it would displace the floating pier, yet there's nary a ripple nor splash. So perhaps this is like Landing 58 in *Fury from the Deep*: the TARDIS materialises in the sky then performs a controlled descent – the partial materialisation (and in that earlier landing the engine groan was heard throughout) – to the water, or in this case the pier. The second jolt may be a drop from just a metre or two after the Ship is confused by not settling on the river surface after all.
- 📘 Why do the Doctor and Adric brace themselves against the main doors? Do they really plan to hold them, letting water wash in slowly, until the whole TARDIS is full? After all, they won't be able to swim out until the pressure has almost equalised – that could take some time. Might it not be better to stand to either side of the doors and let the incoming water rush past them until it has slowed enough for them to escape? Even if the interior of the Ship is finite and able to be flooded, how will that flush out the Master's TARDIS? It's not going to float out through the doors – it wouldn't fit through the interior doorways let alone the main doors (unless the Doctor's expecting it to go into siege mode – see Landing 644, vol.2). And even if it did, how will the Doctor and Adric recover the Ship once they've swum to the surface? Okay, materialising underwater is a silly plan. It seems clear the TARDIS reaches the same conclusion and deliberately lands on the pier instead.
- 📘 The doors strain to open with the Doctor and Adric leaning on them and it sounds like the mechanism cuts out after a few seconds. They remain closed when the force against them is released but then open normally of their own accord moments later. Presumably they have a safety cut-out that resets after a few seconds then resumes the initial operation.
- 📘 The shot of the Master's TARDIS dematerialising is a split-screen effect, with the Police Box on the right being faded out from a shot of Tegan sobbing on the otherwise empty cloister set.
- 📘 Why does the Master's TARDIS vanish before reappearing as a bush? Later we see it changing its disguise without dematerialising.

LANDING 199

SPACE Logopolis, above main city
TIME [Late-20th century]
TRAVELLERS The Doctor, Adric, Tegan, the Master
EPISODES Logopolis 2

The TARDIS materialises in the pink-hued sky above the main cluster of rough stone dwellings of Logopolis. Overlooking these is a large radio-telescope dish, which the Doctor notes is a new addition since he was last here. He prepares to relocate the Ship to the planet's surface, just as Tegan finally gets back to the control room – and she is not happy.

- ⚙ **CONTROLS** The Doctor possibly uses the left-hand black dial on panel C2 to close the scanner, then adjusts other unseen controls on that panel.
- 📘 **NOTES** The TARDIS is seen to appear in the sky above Logopolis (although silently) and the central column is stationary, so this must be a full materialisation. The model Police Box was inserted into the shot of the Logopolis model using the Quantel DPE 5000.
- 📘 There's nothing on screen to suggest the visit to Logopolis is in the same time period as recent landings on Earth. It's said the Logopolitans "can model any space-time event in the universe" so even their copy of the Pharos Project could be a logical prefiguration of the future. But as the Doctor stabilises the CVE from late-20th century Earth, it's probable the events on Logopolis are contemporary.
- 📘 Tom Baker and Matthew Waterhouse speak and act as if they're viewing Logopolis on the scanner, but a moment later the screen's shutters are seen to be closed. One could interpret Baker's movements at the console as closing it but no sound effect is heard.

LANDING 200

SPACE Logopolis, terrace; carried to Central Register
TIME As above
TRAVELLERS The Doctor, Adric, Tegan, the Master
EPISODES Logopolis 2

A group of Logopolitans and their spokesman the Monitor have gathered in an open area to view the arrival of the TARDIS, unaware that inside an impatient Tegan is loudly demanding explanations from a shocked Doctor and Adric. When the Doctor realises her aunt has been murdered by the Master, he accepts responsibility for her.

The Master moves his TARDIS from the Doctor's cloister and rematerialises outside, behind the cluster of Logopolitans who greet the Doctor and his friends as they emerge. The Monitor leads the new arrivals away towards the Central Register, and once the crowd has dispersed the Master's TARDIS changes its appearance into a fluted stone column before dematerialising once more.

A short time later the Doctor returns to the TARDIS with a print-out of the code needed to reset the chameleon circuit. He chooses to proceed alone, however, and leaves Adric and Tegan under the Monitor's protection while he enters the numbers into the console. Unaware the Master has corrupted the code, the Doctor's friends, now joined by Nyssa, watch helplessly as the TARDIS glows with a shimmering blue light and starts to shrink. The contraction stops when the Police Box is just a few feet tall and the Monitor has it carried to the Central Register.

While he and Adric search for the error in the code, a pair of sonic projectors is placed around the TARDIS to hold it in a zone of stasis. Inside, the dimensional instability is affecting both the Ship and the Doctor. He cannot dematerialise but fortunately the scanner is on and he can see but not hear his friends trying to reassure him. The projectors arrest the dimensional spiral, allowing the Doctor to focus. He too tries to identify the error in the dimension subroutine but requires help from outside. Fortunately, the Monitor has identified the incorrect numbers and Tegan holds them up for the scanner to see. The Doctor enters the corrections and the TARDIS is restored to full size. He emerges unscathed, only to learn that Adric and Nyssa have gone looking for the Master.

Tegan and the Monitor are alone in the Central Register when the Master appears. He positions one of the sonic projectors in front of the input console and emits a sound-cancelling wave that silences the whispered calculations of all Logopolitans. The Monitor warns him that without them the structure of the planet and thence the universe will collapse. The Master is dismissive, believing the effect of his device is only temporary, but when he switches it off the silence persists. They all head out into the already crumbling streets and so do not see the TARDIS dematerialise.

○ **CONTROLS** The Doctor seemingly enters the code to correct the chameleon circuit using the row of buttons across the middle of panel C2. He presses these again after adjusting the right-hand dial when entering the corrected numbers.

- **NOTES** The TARDIS's arrival is a split-screen effect, with the Logopolitans on the left moving on an empty set as a separate shot of the Police Box prop is faded in over the right-hand side of the picture. Owing to the close positioning of the elements, the line between the two parts of the image is sharp rather than softened, making it more visible than usual, and the rock behind the TARDIS shifts noticeably during the transition.
- The shot of the Doctor taking Adric aside to discuss Tegan is taken through the open control room doors.
- Why does the Master need to hitch a ride in the Doctor's TARDIS in order to reach Logopolis? Is its location a mystery known only to a few, or is it protected by some kind of barrier that he knows the Doctor will be allowed through? Is this why the TARDIS has to pause above the planet first, while it awaits clearance? (In his novelisation of the story, script writer Christopher Bidmead indicates the Doctor is politely announcing his presence and intention to land but this doesn't answer why the Master couldn't travel there alone.)
- In the shot of the Doctor asking the Monitor to look after Adric and Tegan, the rear doors of the Police Box prop in the background can be seen to be open, and the rear sign box is missing its lettered insert.
- The Doctor insists on being alone when he implements the chameleon circuit correction as if he's expecting something dangerous to happen. We might assume that the Watcher warned him of this when they conversed on Albert Bridge, but then the Doctor seems to be surprised by the TARDIS shrinking and can't resolve it without help from outside. Maybe the Watcher only revealed that he would shortly regenerate owing to the Master's scheming but not exactly when and how, so the Doctor is simply being cautious by leaving Adric and Tegan out of it.
- The Quantel DPE 5000 was used for the shots of the TARDIS shrinking and later growing, both to change the size of the image of the miniature Police Box and to overlay the shimmering blue glow – a defocused shot of some small lights. The miniature was recorded against a green background to be placed onto a view of the Logopolis set via CSO. As the shot of the Police Box is a static one manipulated electronically, rather than the camera tracking back to make it smaller (note the perspective doesn't change), using the full-size prop would have produced a more convincing effect; presumably it was quicker to move the model onto the green set than the main prop.
- The shrunken Police Box was a new model about a quarter the size of the main prop, so similar to the 3-foot miniature from the 1960s. It appears to be modelled on the Yardley-Jones box, with matching roof levels and a uniform-width frame around the 'Police box' signs. It even has front and back door handles, although not on the centre posts as they are on the main prop. There are fewer steps above the doors, and the 'Police telephone' wording is just painted on the indented panel, but with the same spelling and layout as the main prop. What mostly stands out, though, are the darker window frames and pale window panes, which contrast much more than on the full-size box. It also lacks the thick block under the roof lamp that was latterly added to the main prop. After this sole appearance in the series, the model was kept. It was taken on location to Lanzarote in 1983 while *Planet of Fire* was being filmed although it doesn't appear in the finished serial, just press photographs taken at the time (see Landing 255). In 1990 it was modified to have opening front doors for a brief appearance in BBC Schools programme *Search Out Science*, also gaining a telephone plaque with frame and handle.
- The actors look at the lamp on top of the miniature Police Box when trying to speak to the Doctor, and the view of them on the scanner also suggests this is where the image is captured.
- The script implies it's the sonic projectors that stop the TARDIS shrinking further – "They've arrested the dimensional spiral" – but in execution it stops after the cliffhanger effects shot.

The scenes inside the shrunken TARDIS used a fish-eye lens on the camera to distort the view – the resulting blackness in the corners would have been less noticeable on the curved CRT televisions of the time than they are on today's flat screens. Awkwardly, Tom Baker is shot lying right by the cable running across the set floor to power the console. Although this is covered with white tape, it's still obvious. The circuit boards the Doctor later tinkers with can also be seen propped against the console's pedestal. In some shots it's clear the scanner is closed, even though cutaways show it open.

PREVIOUS LANDINGS

SPACE Metulla Orionsis system, Traken
TIME Shortly after Landing 195
TRAVELLERS The Watcher
EPISODES During Logopolis 2-3

While the Ship is empty, the spectral white figure can respond to Nyssa's plea for help finding her missing father. With uncanny familiarity with the controls, he dematerialises the TARDIS and returns to Traken, some days after its previous visit, since when Consul Tremas has been missing. The white figure beckons to Nyssa who, feeling unafraid of him and familiar with the TARDIS, takes this as the Doctor's acceptance of her request for help and enters the Ship.

SPACE Logopolis, terrace
TIME As Landing 200
TRAVELLERS The Watcher, Nyssa
EPISODES During Logopolis 2-3

They return to Logopolis, landing the TARDIS in the instant after it left, as if it had never moved. The white figure leads Nyssa outside and indicates she should search the streets for the Doctor, while he watches events from a distance.

▤ **NOTES** It's not made explicit how Nyssa travels to Logopolis. She simply says, "A friend of the Doctor's brought me," and later identifies the Watcher as "the man who brought me from Traken". A respectable girl like she is would doubtless not be in the habit of wandering off with silent, ethereal figures, so his being with the TARDIS would convince her he was sent by the Doctor. In dialogue cut from episode four, Adric asked her, "What did he say when he fetched you from Traken?" to which Nyssa replied, "He didn't say anything, just beckoned. But I wasn't afraid of him." In episode three, when the TARDIS is moved by someone other than the Doctor, she deduces its pilot "must be the man who brought me to Logopolis", suggesting she has seen the Watcher operating the Ship before. This trip can only be while the Doctor is occupied in the Central Register, the Watcher having waited until the Master had vacated the Ship.

LANDING 201

SPACE Logopolis, terrace
TIME As above
TRAVELLERS The Watcher
EPISODES Logopolis 3-4

The spectral white figure pilots the TARDIS back to its original landing spot on the terrace overlooking the plains of Logopolis, where the Doctor ushers his three young friends inside for safety while he allies with the Master to find a way of stopping the spread of entropy the villain has unleashed.

After the two Time Lords have followed the Monitor back to the Central Register, Tegan exits the TARDIS despite Adric's objections, determined that sticking with the Doctor is her only sure way of getting back to Earth. She watches as Adric goes back inside and the Police Box fades away.

LANDING 202

SPACE Outside universe
TIME None
TRAVELLERS Adric, the Watcher, Nyssa
EPISODES Logopolis 4

Adric and Nyssa watch from outside the control room as the spectral white figure operates the console, unsetting the coordinates and disconnecting the entire subsystem to take the TARDIS out of space and time altogether. Seemingly safe, the two youngsters retreat to the cloister.

The white figure follows them there and beckons to Adric. He tells the boy something of what is to come and instructs him to take the TARDIS to the Pharos Project on Earth, in sector 80-23 of the third quadrant. As Adric sets the coordinates, Nyssa notices on the scanner a view of the entire universe – and the dark spread of entropy across a large portion, including her home solar system.

- **CONTROLS** The Watcher somehow disconnects the coordinate subsystem simply by touching the lights on the new upper plate of panel C1 and one of the switches (without flicking it) just below.
- When setting the coordinates for Earth, Adric works at panels C4, C2 and C1, although it's not clear if he actually adjusts any controls other than moving the red-knobbed lever on the last downwards and flicking a switch to its left, one of which seems to operate the scanner. Nyssa flicks the two blue buttons on the left of the group in the middle of panel C5.
- ▤ **LORE** The TARDIS can be taken outside of time and space by "unsetting" the coordinates.
- ▤ **NOTES** The effect of the shift out of space and time was achieved, you guessed it, with the Quantel DPE 5000. The initial flip of the image into negative, however, was done in camera by overexposing the picture.
- ▤ Again, the central column is stationary so we must assume the TARDIS materialises somewhere, outside the space-time continuum of our universe.

WHAT ARE ALL THESE KNOBS?

PANELS Cii
1982

Another year and another revamp for the now seven-year-old control panels. They were painted in a darker grey and each given a thick white border in place of the thinner multi-coloured stylings applied in *Logopolis*. Changes to the controls were minimal at first: three lights and a few rocker switches were added to panel 2 while the black semi-circle in the centre lost its radiating lines, and extra square buttons were stuck on panels 3, 5 and 6. The teleprinter on panel 5 lost its triangle of round buttons and was painted a light grey.

The script for *Castrovalva* – the opening serial of Season 19 but the fourth to be recorded – introduced the Index File, a database that required a screen from which the characters could read information. Panel 6 was chosen as the location for this, its screen replaced with a working television monitor. In fact, the whole metal plate on this panel was remade, matching the shape of the previous one and retaining the lever in the bottom-right corner but with a smaller cut-out in the centre, just large enough for the back of the monitor to fit through. This sat within an angled housing with a projecting keypad below. To the left was a digital numeric readout and the rest of the panel was supplemented with pushbuttons. All this, of course, disappeared for the next few stories as broadcast, which had been recorded earlier, but was also absent from those made after. The hole for the monitor was simply covered by a black-painted board with a cowl around it. The digital readout was also removed.

The latter stories of this season saw changes to panel 1. *Earthshock* required a gauge to detect an electromagnetic field so a large circular display with an illuminated green screen was fitted in place of the emergency transceiver socket on the bottom-right plate. On the other side of the red-knobbed lever – now consistently used as the main doors control – a silver block was added while the adjacent plate gained a new control beneath its three flick switches. This may have been to cover a hole that somehow appeared in the panel, which is visible in *Time-Flight* as the new control had gone missing. On panel 3, a rotating stalk was added above the left-hand quartered display, while the bottom-right rotary handle, having been loosened for the Doctor to accidentally pull off in *The Visitation*, disappeared thereafter.

In *Time-Flight*, characters had to remove components from the console's pedestal. Rather than cut or remove the recessed faces, a larger inset was added between the fins of the pedestal, making the recess shallower. Two sides of the pedestal were thus amended.

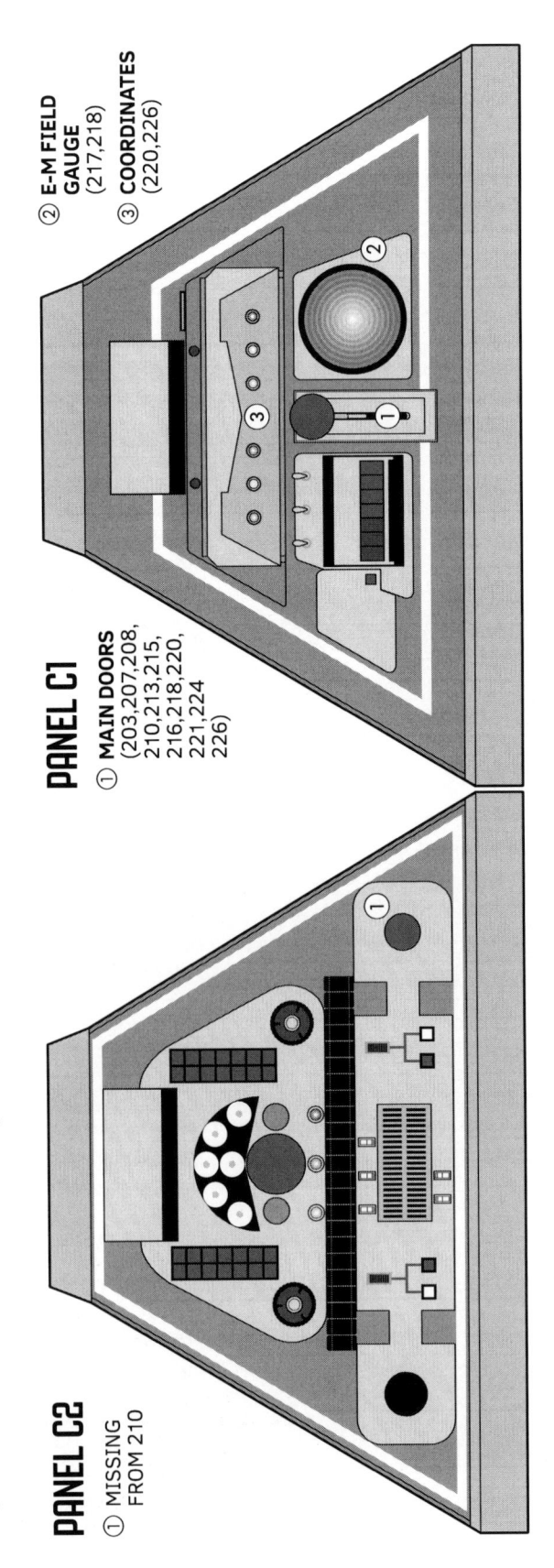

PANEL C1
② E-M FIELD GAUGE (217,218)
③ COORDINATES (220,226)
① MAIN DOORS (203,207,208, 210,213,215, 216,218,220, 221,224, 226)

PANEL C2
① MISSING FROM 210

WHAT ARE ALL THESE KNOBS?

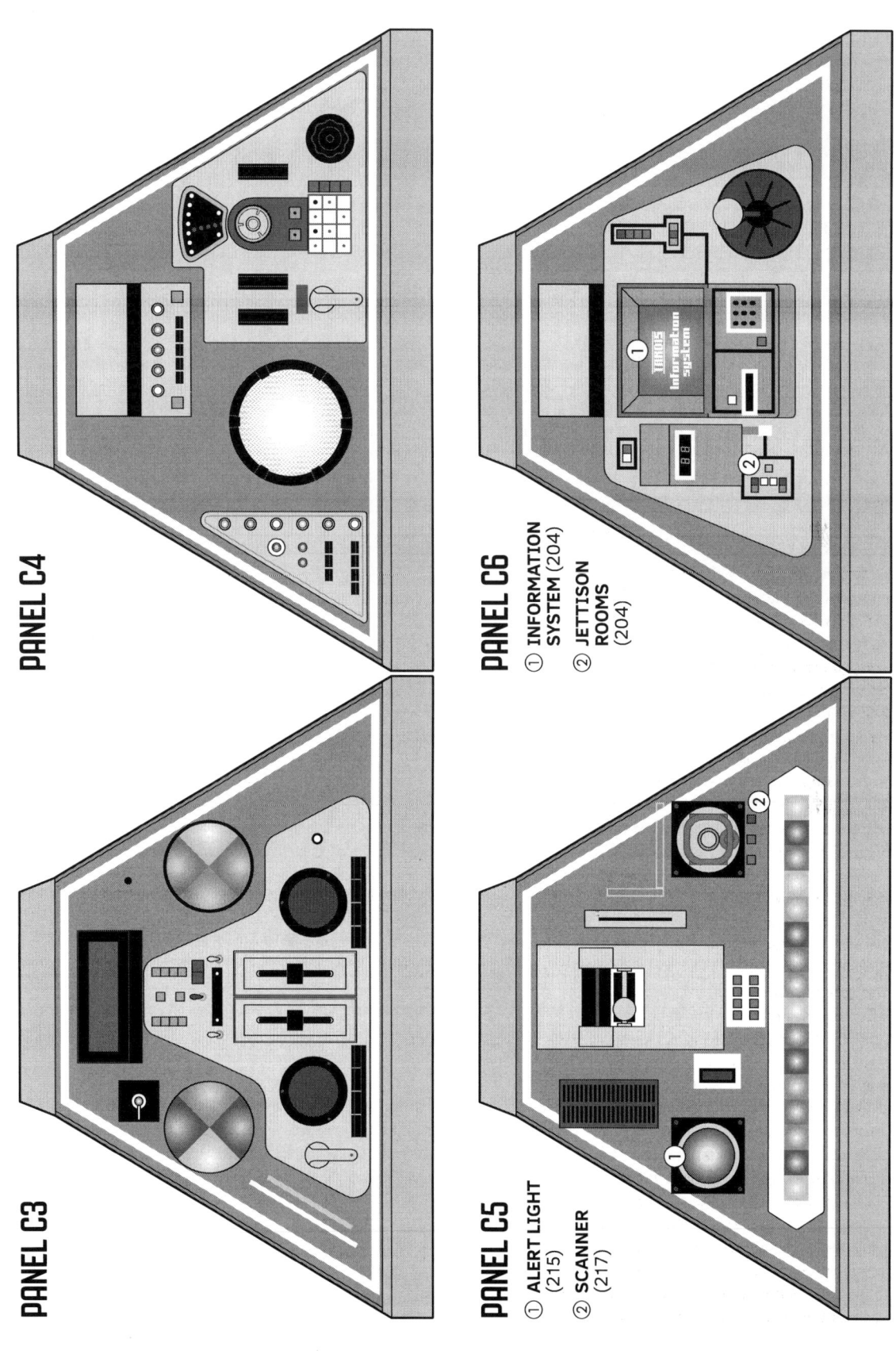

PANEL C4

PANEL C6
① **INFORMATION SYSTEM** (204)
② **JETTISON ROOMS** (204)

PANEL C3

PANEL C5
① **ALERT LIGHT** (215)
② **SCANNER** (217)

LANDING 203

SPACE Earth, England, East Sussex, Pharos Project
TIME [Late-20th century]
TRAVELLERS Adric, the Watcher, Nyssa
EPISODES Logopolis 4; Castrovalva 1

Adric completes the coordinate entry, moves the TARDIS back into space-time and materialises on Earth in the early morning. They are near the base of a radio-telescope dish exactly like the one on Logopolis. He explains to Nyssa the Pharos Project is seeking proof of extraterrestrial intelligences, so they expect to be welcomed, although on leaving the Ship they duck out of sight of two patrolling guards. As they move on in search of the Doctor, they are watched from the doorway by the spectral white figure – perhaps aware that the Doctor is at that moment looking from the window of the nearby control centre. Moments later, he, the Master and Tegan pass close by as they head for the radio dish.

Shortly after an ambulance pulls up sharply beside the TARDIS. Tegan and Nyssa assist a confused, freshly regenerated Doctor inside and close the doors as the chasing Pharos security guards and ambulance men reach them. Adric is apprehended and the women watch on the scanner as the Master's TARDIS appears and stuns the guards with a burst of energy. It dematerialises leaving Adric alone and the women bring him into the Ship – unaware the real Adric had been kidnapped by the Master and this is a block-transfer projection. He programs a course and sets the TARDIS in motion, followed by the Master's craft.

○ **CONTROLS** Adric touches controls on panel C2 then pushes the red-knobbed lever of panel C1 upwards – although it immediately drops back down – and flicks a switch to its left.

○ After landing on Earth, Adric presses the green plastic control on panel C5. This coincides with the sound effect of the scanner closing but it's possible Matthew Waterhouse was intending it to open the main doors – as in previous scenes – which they do moments later with no other control being pressed.

○ Nyssa closes the doors with the red-knobbed lever on panel C1 – as now becomes the norm – and activates the scanner with the rotary handle on panel C4. Adric programmes the Ship's course from panel C2 and seemingly uses the black dial at bottom-right of panel C4 to dematerialise.

▤ **NOTES** The Pharos Project's location isn't specified in *Logopolis*, but in the follow-on scenes in *Castrovalva* the ambulance that arrives for the injured Doctor is from the East Sussex Area Health Authority.

▤ The materialisation of the TARDIS on Earth is a model shot, recorded during *Logopolis*'s final studio session on Saturday 24 January 1981. This featured the 3-foot model of the radio dish in the background, in front of which was a diorama of trees and bushes in scale with the Police Box miniature built for *The Horns of Nimon*. Sadly this was a poor match for the location filming of the full-size prop, which was positioned in a more open shrubby area rather than among thick bushes.

▤ In the model shot, the TARDIS lands in front of the radio dish, but when Adric and Nyssa view it on the scanner it's shown from behind. This suggests the Pharos Project has more than one large dish, unlike Jodrell Bank on which it's based.

▤ Unusually for the Yardley-Jones box at this point, the right-hand door is used. Because this had the centre post attached so couldn't be closed while the left-hand door was shut, it's ajar before Waterhouse emerges and Sarah Sutton is unable to close it properly behind her.

▤ The shots of everyone running towards the dish, with the TARDIS in the background, show the prop from behind, revealing the rear 'Police box' sign is missing. Light shining through the front sign can be seen through the gap.

▤ From *Castrovalva*, the scanner has a single rising shutter, rather than two sections meeting in the centre. The close-up of the scanner activating, however, uses CSO to insert a flat grey colour that wipes vertically to reveal the outside view. This and later similar inserts were created in a studio gallery effects session after recording was completed.

▤ As well as changes to the console, the hatstand has disappeared between Adric and Nyssa leaving the control room and she and Tegan returning with the regenerated Doctor. Did the Watcher do a quick bit of spring cleaning?

▤ Nyssa mentions Adric taking off in the TARDIS "once before…but that was by mistake". This refers to his accidental operation of the Ship in *Full Circle* (Landing 188), something he presumably told Nyssa about when they were hanging around in the cloister.

LANDING 204

SPACE Space
TIME Unknown
TRAVELLERS The Doctor, Tegan, Nyssa, Adric projection
EPISODES Castrovalva 1-2

The Doctor wanders the TARDIS corridors in confusion, leaving a trail of his clothing – his coat, unravelled scarf, shoes and torn waistcoat – as he searches for the Zero Room in which to recuperate. The imitation Adric catches up to assist him but then abandons the Doctor and makes his own way through the maze-like corridors.

In the control room, Nyssa and Tegan are mystified by the TARDIS controls and fear the Ship will eventually crash into something. They discover the Information System, though, and after working out how to access it they learn the Ship is safely on a programmed flight so decide to track down the Doctor and Adric.

The women follow the trail of discarded clothing as far as it leads, after which Tegan marks their route with lipstick on the walls. Meanwhile the Doctor dons a new outfit he finds in a room made out as a cricket pavilion. As he assesses his look in a mirror, he hears the Zero Room door slam and, trying to trace it, bumps into Nyssa and Tegan. Together they find the room and the Doctor sleeps while levitating so his synapses can stabilise.

As he does so, a projection of the real Adric briefly appears to warn the women about a trap the Master has laid. Nyssa returns to the control room to investigate the coordinates, learning they are set for Event One: the creation of the universe. Because they are travelling backwards in time, this manifests as an enormous inrush of hydrogen. As the Ship's engineering tolerances are exceeded it begins to heat up. Even in the balanced environment of the Zero Room the Doctor wakes and senses something is wrong. The cloister bell starts chiming but the Doctor is still too weak to venture outside the room so Tegan offers to investigate.

She joins Nyssa in the steaming and stifling control room and learns of their predicament. They check the scanner but it shows only the laughing face of the Master, watching from his TARDIS, where he has Adric imprisoned in a web of hadron power lines. Determined to help, the Doctor leaves the Zero Room but collapses. However, he finds an electric wheelchair to transport him to the control room as the heat, smoke and adrenaline affect his brain chemistry, enabling him to concentrate.

He sends Nyssa to vent the thermo buffer to reduce the temperature inside the Ship and get the console working again, then shows Tegan how to programme the architectural configuration systems to delete rooms and provide the energy required to escape the inrush: he calculates they need to convert 25% of the Ship to generate 17,000 tons of thrust. Before he can explain how to avoid jettisoning the control room, however, he passes out again.

As the TARDIS flies into the centre of the inrush, Tegan activates the deletion programme and the Ship successfully escapes the maelstrom, control room intact. It enters into hover mode in deep space while its systems recover.

Tegan reads up on regeneration from the Information System and learns of Castrovalva, a place with similar properties to a Zero environment where the Doctor can convalesce – unaware this is a fabrication entered by the imitation Adric as part of the Master's trap. While Nyssa wheels the Doctor back to the Zero Room, Tegan also finds instructions for piloting the TARDIS and, with a lurch, sets the Ship in motion – or so she believes. These too were entered by the Adric projection and the destination is already set.

◉ **CONTROLS** The control panels are arranged in their usual order, but the console is oriented so panel C5 is facing the doors, rather than C1 as usual at this time.

◉ Nyssa identifies the switches on the triangular plate on panel C4 as comprising the mean-free path tracker, and seemingly the whole of panel C3 as a referential difference. Tegan operates the scanner with the rotary handle on panel C4 (singeing her finger in the process) and Nyssa uses the same to turn it off (seemingly unburnt. Given she keeps her fur-lined jacket on throughout this journey, Trakenites may not feel the heat as much as humans). As the console heats up, Nyssa flicks the left-most of the three rocker switches above the grille on the bottom plate of panel C2 and adjusts a control above the left-hand large lever on panel C3 while Tegan presses a button below the green plastic control on the right of panel C5. The Doctor uses his coat-tail to protect his fingers as he turns the silver dial on the right on panel C4 then presses buttons on the left. He also flicks one of the black switches on the upper plate. When Tegan thinks she is setting the TARDIS on course for Castrovalva she presses an unseen control on the right of panel C3.

◉ The Information Systems interface is a new screen on panel C6 with a nine-button keypad labelled A to I and a digital readout to its left. This disappears in subsequent stories – some were recorded before *Castrovalva*, and in those recorded after it was replaced by a simpler screen – so it's tempting to suppose the entire interface is a block transfer projection, except that it's there even before the Master captures Adric to appropriate his mathematical skills. Then again, so is Tegan's handbag, which was last seen in the cloister room in *Logopolis*. Did the Watcher adapt the console and move the handbag?

◉ The databank screen used a working monitor to display its Teletext-programmed wording. This whole panel was refitted for *Castrovalva* (including repainting the handle on the bottom-right lever silver), so reverts to its prior appearance in *Four to Doomsday* and *The Visitation* as they were recorded first but broadcast after.

◉ Although there's talk of using the architectural reconfiguration system to delete rooms, the pop-up console on panel C1 isn't used (although the operating rods are still in place and can be glimpsed later when the control room lurches). Tegan jettisons rooms by pressing the red button to the left of the screen on panel C6.

▌ **LORE** A databank labelled 'TARDIS Information System' can be accessed via a screen on the console, although it can be programmed with false records.

▌ The Zero Room is a neutral environment isolated from the rest of the universe. As its energy is perfectly balanced against the environment outside the room – even its gravity – it cannot be detected by the architectural configuration system, yet can still be jettisoned. It's an octagonal pyramid-shaped room with large circles in the walls that emit a pink light. It smells of roses.

▌ A roundel in the wall outside the Zero Room can be opened to access a medicine cabinet (marked with a red cross) containing labelled vials and cotton pads.

▌ In the event of the TARDIS overheating (due to outside influence) the thermo buffer can be vented manually by turning an arrow-shaped lever behind a roundel in a corridor. As the temperature drops a light behind the lever changes from red to yellow to green to blue.

▌ Many of the TARDIS's systems run automatically but can be overridden and controlled by the pilot.

▌ The TARDIS interior may be extensive but not infinite, as the Doctor can assign a quarter of it to be deleted.

▌ **NOTES** The imitation Adric spent less than ten seconds at the console when taking off, yet apparently programmed a course to Event One, entered false information into the databanks about how to fly the TARDIS and Castrovalva, and programmed the Ship to go there should it survive the hydrogen inrush. The latter course could be entered later, while the others are in the Zero Room, but must still be done before the Ship flies into the Big Bang as the control room is always occupied thereafter. Clearly the Master isn't very confident of his first plan working – he even talks of "a trap behind that trap that would have been a joy to spring" – yet seems surprised when indeed it doesn't.

- Although the Master has taken control of the Doctor's scanner before (see Landing 87) that was then their two TARDIS's were inside each other. Presumably here the scanner's showing the inside of the Master's TARDIS is achieved through Adric, as he is allowing the Master to see inside the Doctor's TARDIS also. It's not clear if the Master is also flying towards Event One to maintain his spying on the Doctor, or if Adric can achieve this from a safe distance.

- It's not explained what happens to the imitation Adric. We last see him wandering the corridors, viewed by the Master who thinks the projection is trying to escape his control, later admitting, "These simulated projections are real enough to have a will of their own. Almost." The Doctor hears running footsteps just before the sound of the Zero Room door slamming, suggesting faux-Adric has found his way there, perhaps hoping the isolated environment will free him from the Master's influence. Yet the room is empty when the others arrive, and the slamming door is heard a second time beforehand, so the imitation Adric must have left again. When the real Adric projects an image of himself into the Zero Room to warn Tegan and Nyssa, he believes the Master won't be able to detect it but is proven wrong. So it could be that the villain regains power over the imitation Adric even while he's in the Zero Room and directs him back to the control room to input the course to Castrovalva. Possibly the Master then deletes him once his usefulness is over, or if he's a continuous projection from the captured Adric's mind he perhaps fades out as the TARDIS is obscured by the high energies of Event One.

- The control room, corridor and Zero Room sets were erected in Studio 3 at BBC Television Centre for two days' recording on Tuesday 15 and Wednesday 16 September 1981. They were arranged almost as a single composite set, representing the largest TARDIS layout to date (excluding the locations used in *The Invasion of Time*). While this made full use of existing walls and several plain flats, it still required new walls to be constructed. The corridor set was erected immediately beyond the control room's interior door and incorporated: two of the aligned-roundels walls originally built for the 1976 control room; a wall from the 1977 control room with half-roundels on the left-hand edge (previously seen in *Logopolis*); the one-roundel-wide wall from *State of Decay*; and one of the four-roundels-wide walls that formed Romana's room in *Full Circle*.

As well as three plain sections, there were two new inner doorways (with no roundels inset so different from that for Romana's room) leading to a cricket pavilion and a store room. Two three-roundels-wide walls (in addition to the two that now form the control room) were used in the corridor set, one a free-standing section that was moved out of the way for some shots, as was an additional section with two columns of aligned translucent roundels.

- The area outside the Zero Room comprised a new section with four columns of four aligned translucent roundels, the centre two forming a pair of doors through to the Zero Room itself. Either side of this were two more three-roundels-wide walls (probably new constructions). Then to the left the 1977 wall was placed, now with one of its roundels fitted out as the medicine cabinet and another further down given a removable roundel (made of resin and thicker than usual so it could contain a green light) behind which was the thermo buffer control. A further wall to the left of this was probably the free-standing three-roundels-wide wall. All these wall sections were connected with numerous wide and narrow slatted columns, with more free-standing, notably outside the Zero Room. There was also a free-standing pillar with smooth curves in a four-leaf clover formation. Immediately in front of the Zero Room doors was another slatted column surrounded by a sloping hexagonal parapet. The room beyond had a short entrance tunnel leading to an octagonal space with tapering walls each with three circular cutouts.

- The hatstand in the corridor on which the Doctor finds his beige coat and Panama hat is not one seen before in the control room. It also holds a cricket bat and stands next to a pair of green rubber boots.

- The Zero Room set was later painted black and used as the interior of the Master's TARDIS.

- For the first time the control room is referred to as the 'console room', initially by the Doctor – "This should get you back to the console room when the time comes" – so perhaps it's just a preference of this incarnation. Tegan also adopts the term without having heard it from anyone else.

- As Nyssa and Tegan get the hang of using the Information System, a shot looking up at them suggests the arrangement of control room walls to the left of the main doors is the same as to their right. This shot was recorded separately from those of them standing at the console, using the regular walls as a background.

- While the scanner isn't in use it has its physical shutter covering the screen. But when it's shown opening at the end of episode one, the rising shutter is again overlaid using CSO.

- The model shots of the TARDIS use the miniature built for *The Horns of Nimon*.

- Although the Doctor relates 25% of the architecture to 17,000 tonnes of thrust, that doesn't mean the mass of the TARDIS is 68,000 tonnes (far more than suggested by Romana in *Full Circle* – see Landing 188) as the unit is not a measurement of force, lacking velocity and time components.

- It's suggested the TARDIS materialises after escaping Event One. The central column is stationary, although in its raised position with its lights flashing. Dick Mills also uses the 'hovering' background hum introduced in *Logopolis* rather than either the 'in-flight' or 'stationary' sound effects. The column then begins to oscillate and the hum changes when Tegan sets the Ship on course for Castrovalva. The Police Box is also briefly seen on the Master's scanner as being stationary in space.
- Nyssa reads off the databank screen about the Dwellings of Simplicity, then says, "Castrovalva. Where's that?" Well it says so right there on the display: 'The central habitation of the planet that forms the Andromedan Phylox Series.'

LANDING 205

SPACE Andromeda galaxy, Phylox series, orbit of unnamed planet
TIME Unknown
TRAVELLERS The Doctor, Tegan, Nyssa
EPISODES Castrovalva 2

Tegan learns about landing procedures from the invented instructions in the Information System as the TARDIS approaches the pink-hued planet where Castrovalva is located, materialising in high orbit.

Meanwhile, the Doctor and Nyssa discover the Zero Room was among the 25% of the TARDIS jettisoned to escape Event One. Only the entrance doors remain, which the Doctor has Nyssa unscrew using his sonic screwdriver so they can use them to construct a new Zero Room.

- **NOTES** Again the central column is lit but stationary and the 'hovering' sound effect is heard as the TARDIS overlooks the planet, indicating it materialises in orbit. Tegan doesn't give the impression she has done anything with the controls at this point, but given so far her only experience of the TARDIS landing has been on Logopolis, where it went into hover mode first, she might assume this is normal procedure. Then again, the flight has supposedly been pre-programmed by the projection of Adric. Would the Master really instruct him to have the Ship hover first before landing quite some distance from Castrovalva itself? Perhaps Tegan's tinkering, or the Ship itself, has adjusted the settings. Or did the false Adric have enough free will to alter the Master's instructions himself?
- Although Castrovalva is often taken to be the name of the planet, the information on the databank screen and dialogue in later episodes make clear it's just the cliff-top settlement. Although this is a block transfer projection created by Adric, and its people and history a fiction invented by the Master, the planet itself is real. It's not clear if the pig-like animals the Castrovalvans hunt are native or projections, and it's possible celery grows there naturally.

LANDING 206

SPACE Unnamed planet (as above)
TIME Two days in unknown (as above)
TRAVELLERS The Doctor, Tegan, Nyssa
EPISODES Castrovalva 2,4

Believing she has discovered how to land from the Information System, Tegan has a go at bringing the Ship down safely on the planet. It successfully materialises in an area of woodland but immediately topples over onto a thick bed of ferns. The interior of the Ship lists also, forcing Tegan to edge up the sloping floor to reach the main doors. She clambers out of the Police Box and climbs a nearby tree to survey the terrain, spying the walls of Castrovalva built atop a rocky outcrop several kilometres away.

Meanwhile, Nyssa uses the detached Zero Room doors to construct a cabinet that provides the same neutral environment as the deleted room. This the Doctor can seal himself in to recuperate while the two women carry him to Castrovalva; he promises to levitate so they will have only the weight of the cabinet to contend with.

Just getting the cabinet out of the leaning TARDIS is an effort, and while Tegan rests Nyssa changes out of her cumbersome Traken skirts into a sturdier pair of trousers from the wardrobe. She rejoins Tegan outside and they use the electric wheelchair to transport the cabinet in the direction of Castrovalva.

The next day, a refreshed Doctor leads Nyssa, Tegan and a rescued Adric in a jog back to the TARDIS. Seeing its inclination, he is dismissive of Tegan's claims to have landed it, saying there are no instructions for doing so in the databank. He deduces that Adric must have programmed its journey as part of the Master's trap. They all clamber aboard and the Police Box dematerialises.

- **NOTES** We've known the TARDIS interior is directly affected by the orientation of the exterior since as far back as *The Romans* (Landing 13) but this is the first time we've seen that it doesn't automatically right itself. See Landing 220 for a further example of this.
- The Newbery Police Box prop was taken on location for filming at Birchden Wood near Royal Tunbridge Wells. It's not clear why this was used rather than the newer Yardley-Jones Box, which had already featured in earlier filming for the Pharos Project scenes. It's possible this wooden prop was considered sturdier than the fibreglass one to allow for the cast to climb in and out while it rested at an angle, although the newer Box seems to have received some reinforcement prior to *Castrovalva* and is fine in a similar situation in *Time-Flight*. Whatever the reason (if it wasn't just chance), the prop wasn't easy to keep steady on its back and a stagehand had to crouch inside to counterbalance it as the cast squeezed inside.
- The closing scene as filmed was slightly longer, showing Nyssa, Tegan then the Doctor climbing inside (rather shakily) and the TARDIS dematerialising.

LANDING 207

SPACE Urbankan spaceship approaching Earth, laboratory
TIME 4.15pm 28 February 1981
TRAVELLERS The Doctor, Adric, Tegan, Nyssa
EPISODES Four to Doomsday 1,3

The Doctor has Adric set the coordinates – "Six three zero niner in the inner spiral arm of Galaxia Kyklos", also known as the Milky Way – to return Tegan to Heathrow Airport in time for the flight she was due to begin her stewarding career on before she was unexectedly carried away in the TARDIS. However, a strong magnetic field diverts the Ship and it materialises aboard a massive spaceship four days' flight from Earth. The atmosphere is thin, with reduced oxygen and nitrogen, traces of a mercury compound and high photon activity, so the Doctor decides to investigate alone. He dons a space-pack helmet to help him breathe as he explores the laboratory outside – observed by a floating spherical camera, a Monopticon.

As they wait, Tegan frets about losing her job while Adric taunts her and Nyssa reads. When the Doctor returns he invites the others to don space packs and examine the machinery outside, warning them they are being watched. He gives Tegan a key to the TARDIS so she can get back in should the party be separated. They are unaware the TARDIS is being scanned by the ship's computer.

The instrumentation in the lab is highly advanced, Nyssa identifying a resonant stroboscope, a matter densifier, an interferometer for measuring gravitation waves (incorporating a laser key and directional cobalt flux) and a graviton crystal detector, some made of non-corrosive alloys and saturated polymers. The Doctor's request via the Monopticon for an audience with the ship's occupants seems granted when a door on the upper level opens, so he and Tegan leave Nyssa and Adric working on the interferometer. It is too heavy for them to move into the TARDIS in order to use it on the time-curve circuits, so Adric goes inside to fetch them. He uses the console to locate them. Outside, Nyssa is approached by a man in Ancient Greek attire who leads her away. When Adric emerges from the TARDIS to ask for her help with the circuits, he demands of the Monopticon to know where his friend is and a different doorway opens. He passes through, after closing the TARDIS door to keep out the prying Monopticon.

A short time later, a breathable atmosphere is restored to the laboratory as Monarch, the Urbankan sovereign, arrives to examine the TARDIS. He tries using the laser key and directional cobalt flux to unlock the door but neither succeeds. Frustrated by the seeming ability of an Earth object to withstand his technology, he leaves.

Tegan returns alone to the Ship in a fluster and begins operating random controls, desperate to reach Earth and warn of Monarch's invasion plan. She become increasingly frustrated at the console's unresponsiveness until eventually the TARDIS dematerialises, still watched by the Monopticon.

● **CONTROLS** Adric is standing at panel C1 when the TARDIS materialises, although he seems surprised the Ship has stopped so he may not be piloting it. The Doctor touches controls on the triangular plate on panel C4 when checking the local time, seemingly reading the results from the circular display, then operates the scanner with the rotary handle to its right. When Adric confirms the coordinates he indicates the clear disc on panel C1 (originally the emergency transceiver socket) and the Doctor notes the magnetic field shift from the gauge on the opposite plate. He opens the doors by pulling the red-knobbed lever downwards. It remains in that position until he returns when the lever is suddenly up and Adric pulls it down again to close the doors. The Doctor closes the scanner with one of the flick switches to the left of this lever. When everyone goes out, the doors open on their own.

● When the Doctor mentions the Piccadilly Line, the red-knobbed lever on panel C1 is in its downward position. Yet after the shot of Tegan for her line of dialogue, it has been moved upwards. Perhaps Peter Davison noticed it was in the wrong position for his later opening of the doors so surreptitiously reset it while the camera was off him.

● Adric activates the circuit programmer by flicking the left-most switch on the bottom-left plate of panel C1; the keyboard rises with the same sound effect used in *Logopolis*. He uses one of its upper switches to turn on the scanner, although now the device operates as a general circuit tracer.

● When Tegan returns to the TARDIS, she closes the doors with the red-knobbed lever on panel C1, flicks switches on the plate to its left – deactivating the circuit programmer – and presses the newly added rocker switches and turns the left-hand black dial on panel C2

▮ **LORE** The TARDIS's course can be deflected by a sufficiently strong magnetic field.

▮ The molecular structure of the TARDIS exterior registers – at least to Urbankan scanners – as consistent with being of Earth origin.

▮ The time-curve circuits are affected by or perhaps cause gravitational waves. They must be part of the time-curve indicator (see Landing 31) as Adric later says Nyssa was intending to repair this.

▮ The TARDIS lock is resistant to a laser key ray and a directional cobalt flux beam.

▮ Adric understands the word TARDIS to be "short for Time And Relative Dimensions In Space". He tells Monarch the interior is "in a different dimension" and is "quite large", containing a power room (see Landing 61), bathroom (see Landing 144) and cloisters (see Landing 196).

▮ **NOTES** Although the Doctor is trying to get Tegan back to Earth to catch her flight (A778 due to leave Heathrow at 5.30pm), and her panic while he explores shows she's keen to do so, it's not impossible there has been a landing or two since defeating the Master.

▮ The Doctor suggests the Urbankan ship's "dense magnetic field" caused "a fluctuation of my artron energy".

This was established in *The Deadly Assassin* as a form of energy Time Lord brains possess, so it's not clear why a disturbance of this would affect the TARDIS's navigation. Only later does it become a catch-all term for the Ship's power as well as enabling bodily regeneration.

- Although the TARDIS is diverted from landing on Earth, there's no indication the reported time period is off so we can take the date and time the Doctor reads from the console as accurate.
- Nyssa is reading the third of three volumes of Alfred North Whitehead and Bertrand Russell's *Principia Mathematica*, a second edition published by Cambridge University Press in 1927 (reprints with the dust jacket seen here date from 1950 onwards, most recently at time of production in 1978). The other two volumes rest on the console, although they disappear while Adric and Nyssa talk alone, then are back when the Doctor returns. Has Tegan taken up Adric's suggestion to try reading "Bert" Russell's work after all?
- Another new hatstand appears in the control room, which remains for much of the next two series. It's generally bare, used only occasionally by the Doctor to hang his hat (when it's not rolled up in his pocket) or, later in this story, Tegan's space-pack helmet.
- At this point the TARDIS carries at least four space packs: helmets with two gas cylinders on the rear, connected by tubes to a mouthpiece that can be positioned in front of the face. They have visors but these can be detached if not needed.
- Oops! When the Doctor returns to the control room after collecting a space pack, the camera angle reveals the edge of the corridor set beyond the interior door and the white curtain backing it.
- The on-scanner images of circuitry were not computer generated but handmade graphics, with slots cut to allow sections to slide across.
- Most of Tegan's attempts to get the TARDIS moving involve pressing the same controls repeatedly, as she doesn't move from panel C2. Does the Ship give in and dematerialise itself just to get her to stop?

LANDING 208

SPACE Urbankan spaceship, recreation area
TIME As above
TRAVELLERS The Doctor, Tegan
EPISODES Four to Doomsday 4

The TARDIS does not get far, held close to the Urbankan craft by its magnetic field. Tegan finds the control for the scanner but is reluctant to risk attempting to return the TARDIS to the spaceship. She tries reading the Type 40's handbook but cannot understand it.

The Doctor attempts to reach the Ship by leaping from an exterior hatch wearing only a space pack to help with breathing, as his body can withstand the near-zero temperature for up to six minutes. Two bids fail as he loses momentum and must pull himself back to the Urbankan ship with a rope. On his third go, however, Monarch's minister of enlightenment unties the line and the Doctor is stranded between the two craft. Fortunately he carries a cricket ball, which he throws at the spaceship and catches on the rebound, its momentum propelling him towards the TARDIS. Clambering aboard and recovering from the vacuum of space, he sets the controls to return to the Urbankan vessel.

The TARDIS materialises amid the commotion of dancing androids in the recreation area. Carrying their space-pack helmets, the Doctor and Tegan emerge to find themselves face to face with an enraged Monarch. They run away as the Urbankan orders the spaceship's control system to shut down life support as he returns to his throne room to await his enemies' suffocation.

The Doctor and his friends have donned helmets, however, and they return to the TARDIS with a sample of Monarch's matter-shrinking poison for analysis on their journey to Earth. But Monarch restores life support and reaches the Ship ahead of them. The Doctor throws the flask of poison at the Urbankan who, not yet having converted himself to an android like the rest of his people, is reduced to just a few inches in height, and the Doctor traps him under his helmet.

Tegan is keen to depart and the Doctor accedes. He offers to take Bigon and the other cultural leaders with him to Earth but they elect to find another planet where they can establish a new society. They watch as the TARDIS fades away.

○ **CONTROLS** Tegan first activates the scanner with the top button on the triangular plate of panel C4, but later uses the rotary handle on the right, after pressing two of the left-hand buttons. She moves back to panel C2 to try moving the Ship again but thinks better of it before operating any controls. After the manual proves no help, she operates the scanner again with an unseen control on panel C2.

○ When the Doctor boards, he closes and subsequently opens the main doors with the red-knobbed lever and presses switches on panels C1 and C2 (so Tegan was in the right area).

- **NOTES** While the Police Box is stuck in space its roof lamp flashes and in the control room the central column oscillates and the background him is the 'in-flight' sound effect. The TARDIS has not 'landed', therefore, and is still trying to escape the Urbankan craft's magnetic field even though it's physically present and the Doctor can climb aboard. This is thus the first time we've seen someone gain access while the Ship is 'in motion', and note Tegan isn't sucked out when the main doors open like Salamander was in *The Enemy of the World* (Landing 55). Along with the recently introduced hover mode, the TARDIS is gaining more modes of operation beyond simply materialised or travelling. So when we've previously seen model shots of the Police Box spinning through space, this perhaps wasn't just a representation of its travelling through space-time but may be considered more literally.

- Unlike in episode one, the opening of the scanner wasn't a recorded action but done electronically. A still frame of the open scanner had a plain grey colour keyed into its CSO screen to appear as the shutter, which was then 'raised' via a vertical wipe to show a view of the Urbankan ship.
- The 'Tardis Handbook Type 40' that Tegan reads is the same as seen in *The Horns of Nimon* (Landing 170). Has the Doctor shown her where the real manual is kept after her being fooled by the false instructions in the Information System? She describes its contents as "Pommie mumbo jumbo".
- For the spacewalk sequence, the *Horns of Nimon* model Police Box was used, superimposed against stars using CSO, as was Peter Davison. For the final shot of him entering the TARDIS, however, the full-size prop had to be used – made to look like it's floating by rotating the image slightly using the Quantel DPE 5000.
- To avoid a complicated materialisation shot amid so many moving extras, the TARDIS is only heard landing as the camera follows Monarch walking across the set to arrive at the in-position Police Box. Similarly it's only heard, not seen, departing.
- The Doctor and Tegan leave the TARDIS door wide open yet Monarch, who earlier was keen to see inside, makes no attempt to enter. Later it has swung closed but is still ajar, so that's two missed chances.

LANDING 209

SPACE Deva Loka, forest
TIME Three days in unknown [future]
TRAVELLERS The Doctor, Adric, Tegan, Nyssa
EPISODES Four to Doomsday 4; Kinda 1,4

The TARDIS is barely on course for Heathrow when Nyssa faints from mental disorientation. The Doctor diverts the Ship to somewhere more tranquil where they can all take a rest, materialising in a sun-dappled forest on the undeveloped world Deva Loka. There are fruit-bearing trees, including apples, and singing birds.

Nyssa faints again so when she recovers the Doctor sends his friends outside for some fresh air. Tegan takes a walk while Adric and Nyssa sit playing draughts, although she cannot concentrate and he wins the game easily. Meanwhile the Doctor constructs a delta wave augmenter, incorporating his sonic screwdriver as a delta wave generator, to put Nyssa into a deep sleep and let her recover. While she slumbers, the others explore their surroundings.

They return to the TARDIS just as Nyssa wakes from her 48 hours of rest. The Doctor says farewell to the scientist Todd he has formed a bond with and joins his young friends as they enter the Ship and leave paradise behind.

○ CONTROLS After taking off from the Urbankan spaceship, the Doctor seems to turn the right-hand black dial on panel C2 and presses two of the lights on the cover of the circuit programmer on panel C1 as if they're buttons.

- **NOTES** Adric seems doubtful of reaching Heathrow Airport because "Nyssa never repaired the time-curve indicator". Is this why, at the start of *The Visitation*, the TARDIS lands in the wrong time period?
- It's not stated that the survey team on Deva Loka is from Earth but it's not an unreasonable assumption, which if correct places this story in the future.
- Although we only see scenes on Deva Loka set during daylight, the delta-wave augmenter is said to induce 48-hours' sleep for Nyssa. At the start of episode two, the caged Todd says she, the Doctor and Adric have been "locked up in here all night" so the rest of the story must be set during the second day. The Doctor and friends presumably then stay a second night after the Mara has been banished, perhaps helping Hindle and Sanders recover knowing they can't leave before Nyssa is awake anyway.

LANDING 210

SPACE Earth, England, Middlesex, Harmondsworth, woodland
TIME 1 September 1666
TRAVELLERS The Doctor, Adric, Tegan, Nyssa
EPISODES The Visitation 1,3-4

After her traumatic encounter with the Mara, Tegan is relieved to be going home at last. The Doctor has promised to get her to Heathrow Airport in time for her flight, just half an hour after she first entered the TARDIS. She is understandably upset, therefore, when an apparent fault in the lateral balance cones causes the Ship to land in the correct location but just over 300 years too early. It materialises in woodland on a balmy summer's day. Dismissing the Doctor's excuses, Tegan storms outside. Slightly reluctantly, the Doctor follows to apologise. They notice the smell of sulphur, and Adric points out smoke drifting among the trees. The four travellers head off to seek its source.

Some time later, Nyssa returns to the TARDIS alone to modify the sonic booster with a frequency accelerator as a defence against the Terileptian android the travellers have encountered at the manor house in a nearby village. She clears space to work in her bedroom and drags the heavy booster there from the control room, so she can test it without risking damage to the console.

As she works, Adric returns with news that Tegan has been captured by the android. He tries to help Nyssa by fetching tools and components, but is anxious to find the Doctor and insists on leaving to look for him. Nyssa objects, and sure enough no sooner has he set out than he is caught by hostile villagers.

Nyssa finishes work on the sonic booster and connects it to the console with a heavy-duty power cable. She briefly switches it on as a test and the whole bedroom shudders. She is tidying up her tools when she notices on the scanner Adric returning alone. She goes outside to greet him but the android has been tracking him and emerges from behind the Police Box. Nyssa manages to slip back inside ahead of it but Adric is knocked down when he tries to wrestle with the robot. It pushes its way into the TARDIS and follows Nyssa through to her room, firing its finger-mounted laser. She turns on the booster and the android staggers in the doorway as it is struck by sonic waves. It tries to shoot the booster with no effect, and as the vibrations increase its aim goes wild, striking the power cable. The android begins to smoke then explodes into pieces. Nyssa struggles to turn off the booster and has to rip out the cable connection.

Adric recovers and finds her mourning the destruction of such an impressive creation. He is still worried about the Doctor and Tegan but with villagers patrolling the darkening woods they cannot risk going outside. So Adric persuades a reluctant Nyssa they should pilot the TARDIS to the manor house where Tegan is being held.

- **CONTROLS** While the Doctor berates Adric, he flicks the three switches on the lower-left plate on panel C1 then turns the left-hand black dial on panel C2. When the alarm sounds to indicate a fault in the lateral balance cones, Adric points to the far-right light on the circuit programmer cover on panel C1 (although it's not visibly flashing) and the Doctor shuts off the sound by flicking rocker switches on panel C2. He then turns both black dials on that panel and an unseen control on panel C4.
- Adric is aware they have missed their destination before the Doctor, perhaps from the clear disc on Panel C1 as in *Four to Doomsday* (Landing 207). Neither noticeably operates a control to activate the scanner, and when they look up the shutter is fully open even though the sound effect can still be heard. The Doctor seems to close it with the right-hand black dial on panel C2.
- The control that comes off in the Doctor's hand when he admits the TARDIS "isn't always reliable" is the right-hand rotary handle on panel C3 (this happened by accident in rehearsals and was deliberately repeated during recording). Perhaps because of this, the handle goes missing from subsequently recorded stories (so including *Castrovalva*) and is replaced with a silver knob. The big red button at bottom-right of panel C2 also goes missing here.
- The red-knobbed lever on panel C1 is repeatedly used to open and close the main doors.
- The power cable for the sonic booster is attached to the console below panel C4.
- In later control room scenes in episode four, the strip at the bottom of panel C5 is covered with black tape.
- **LORE** A temperamental solenoid on the lateral balance cones might cause a slip in temporal coordinates.
- The TARDIS carries a sonic booster, a thick disc with a central core projecting above and below, protected by a square metal frame.
- **NOTES** If the TARDIS does land on the site of the future airport, then the locals are unlikely to be from Heath Row itself, which at the time was a hamlet of barely half a dozen houses. The village we see has a manor house and mill, and enough inhabitants to warrant appointing a headman; perhaps Longford, which as the name indicates was where the main road from London to Bath crossed the river Colne. However, contemporary maps indicate most of the surrounding area was cultivated or moorland, not woodland, so the TARDIS may have landed further east. Either way, Tegan is unlikely to be able to stake a claim on the land, which by 1666 had been in the possession of the Paget family for over 100 years.
- Nyssa is reading a copy of *Woman's Journal* magazine. She must have found this aboard the Ship as she has had no opportunity to visit a newsagent. Did Sarah Jane leave it behind? (The edition is unidentified but likely contemporary with this story's production in May 1981, which means Sarah could have bought it after the events of *The Seeds of Doom* perhaps.)
- Tegan might subconsciously want to stay aboard the TARDIS as she leaves her uniform hat behind on her dressing table.
- The interior configuration beyond the control room has changed again since *Castrovalva* (a reorganisation owing to losing a quarter of the architecture?). To the left of the interior door is one of the 1977 control room walls with half-roundels down the right-hand edge (not seen since *The Horns of Nimon*), a plain flat section, then the door to the bedroom. This has three translucent roundels inset into it, a square handle and a push plate, as seen in *Full Circle*. The bedroom is not the same as Romana's (which was jettisoned in *Logopolis*); it's comprised of plain flat walls with just one featuring translucent roundels (four columns wide), and wide slatted columns at each corner. In the room are a potted plant, a hatstand, metal-and-glass shelving units, two brass-framed beds, a side table, a dressing table with mirror, and two wicker chairs.
- Nyssa detaches the sonic booster from the console, so is it part of the control desk, perhaps normally housed within the pedestal (as scripted)? This attachment is a thin coiled cable, whereas she later powers the booster with a thicker heavy-duty cable plugged into the console, so perhaps she is initially just charging the control circuitry. She finds a metal toolkit from somewhere (she later stashes this behind the console so maybe it was there all along) and the library steps seen in *Logopolis* (Landing 197). Just outside her room is a handy case of fire extinguishers; they're there even before the TARDIS lands so someone's concerned about safety on board.
- When Nyssa goes out to greet Adric's return, the library steps are still in the control room. But moments later when the android enters they have gone.
- This is the first time we've seen an enemy penetrate the TARDIS since the Sontarans in *The Invasion of Time* (Landing 144), having missed out on Skagra's hijacking in the unfinished *Shada* (Landings 177-179). The android can also fire its weapon inside the Ship. It places its skull mask on the console but it's no longer there when Adric comes in moments later. He's later revealed to have kept it.

LANDING 211

SPACE Earth, England, Middlesex, Harmondsworth, manor house
TIME As above
TRAVELLERS Adric, Nyssa
EPISODES The Visitation 4

Adric dematerialises the TARDIS and gets it to home in on the Doctor, but the Ship has trouble rematerialising. It flickers in and out of view and the central column jams. Mimicking the Doctor's approach to piloting, Adric thumps the console and the TARDIS finally solidifies in the manor house's dining room.

The Doctor is uncharitable about being saved a long walk back to the woods, but appreciative of Nyssa's success with the sonic booster. With the travellers back together, along with itinerant actor Richard Mace, the Doctor takes off again – thumping the console himself to get the central column moving – to search for the Terileptils that built the android.

◯ CONTROLS When trying to land, Adric presses lights on the upper plate on panel C1 and is heard to flick switches, presumably those on the bottom-left plate. Preparing to take off, the Doctor flicks rocker switches on panel C2 and adjusts the right-hand black dial.

▤ NOTES We've seen Adric programme coordinates and land the TARDIS before, so what causes the problem this time? Although it's presented as just the Ship being unreliable, perhaps Nyssa was right and the sonic booster did cause some slight damage.

▤ The main doors close silently and without the red-knobbed lever being moved.

▤ Although Richard Mace thinks the TARDIS's interior "isn't possible" but "quite amazing", he has already seen a craft seemingly bigger inside than out when he earlier entered the Terileptil escape pod.

LANDING 212

SPACE Earth, England, London, Pudding Lane
TIME 2 September 1666
TRAVELLERS The Doctor, Adric, Tegan, Nyssa, Richard Mace
EPISODES The Visitation 4

Knowing the Terileptil leader has decamped to London, the Doctor scans the city for indications of anything anomalous to the 17th century. He detects an electrical emission from a piece of scientific equipment in a street on the north bank of the Thames just east of the bridge and sets the TARDIS down close by. It materialises opposite a bakery, outside which stands the horse and cart of the miller from the village. Deducing the Terileptils must be inside, the Doctor leads his friends into the bakery.

Shortly after, they emerge in a hurry as a fire breaks out. The Terileptils are still inside when their soliton gas machine explodes from the heat. As the fire takes hold, the travellers unload the boxes of plague virus from the cart and throw them into the flames.

Mace sends a nightwatchman to wake the street and fetch fire-fighters, so the Doctor decides the travellers should leave before their presence raises too many questions. He offers to take Mace somewhere safer but the actor believes helping to fight the blaze will be much less dangerous. The Doctor gives him a control circuit from the Terileptil equipment at the manor house as a keepsake, then joins his companions in the TARDIS and takes off.

◯ CONTROLS The Doctor flicks rocker switches on panel C2 when the scanner detects the Terileptil base, and seems to refine the scan with the left-hand black dial (although he also briefly touches the black dial at bottom-right of panel C4).

◯ After dematerialising, the Doctor flicks the switches on the lower-left plate of panel C1 and turns the right-hand black dial on panel C2.

▤ NOTES The scanner displays John Norden's 1593 map of London, so it's somewhat out of date, although the street layout had changed little by 1666. (A copy of Norden's map with additional streets indexed was produced in 1653 but minor differences show the scanner is displaying the original.) Why a map is shown rather than an aerial view, as in *Logopolis* (Landing 198), isn't clear (beyond real-world production choices). A whim of the Doctor's, or even the Ship's, perhaps? The scan lines slightly miss Pudding Lane, highlighting a spot just to the south-east, closer to Botolph Lane.

▤ Although Nyssa earlier noted, "It's beginning to get dark," it was still daylight when the TARDIS arrived at the manor house. In our history the fire at Thomas Farynor's bakery broke out between midnight and 2am, and the TARDIS materialises only minutes beforehand (a bell peals four times as the travellers emerge but it can't be 4am – the fire was spreading to other houses by then – so this may be the end of the midnight toll). Sunset on 1 September 1666 was around 6.20pm, so has the Doctor been scanning London for anomalies for six hours or so? If he'd detected technology earlier he could have arrived at Pudding Lane well ahead of the Terileptil leader, so perhaps there was nothing to detect. Is it only when the leader arrives and the three Terileptils turn on their machine for a puff of soliton that the Doctor is able to locate them?

▤ When does the Doctor twig that the fire will become the Great Fire of London? If the console tells him the date and time when the TARDIS lands, he goes into the bakery knowing there's a good chance he or his friends will start the fire. If not, he probably spots the street sign at some point. Is this why he doesn't try harder to save the Terileptils, because he can't risk derailing a crucial moment in history? (At the start of *Black Orchid* he says the fire would have started with or without them, so it's presumably one of those fixed points in time.) Of course, if his statement in *Pyramids of Mars* is to be believed, he has previously been blamed for starting the fire, possibly from having been present during its aftermath (see Previous to Landing 98).

- Nyssa points out that leaving Mace with a piece of sophisticated technology might confuse any archaeologists who find it, but as is often noted, as far as we know the Doctor has left a cellar full of equipment and a sizeable escape pod in situ back in the village. We can imagine the former went undiscovered, perhaps buried when the empty manor house falls to ruin, is levelled and built over. But the escape pod was out in the open and bound to cause a stir once all the villagers were released from mind control. It's unlikely they could dismantle it and would probably have considered it the devil's work, so maybe they dug down and buried it completely. When Heathrow Airport was expanded, was this the cause of the "strange things" happening around Terminal Three (see previous to Landing 182)?

LANDING 213

SPACE Earth, England, [Wiltshire], Cranleigh Halt station; moved to local police station
TIME 3pm 11 June 1925
TRAVELLERS The Doctor, Adric, Tegan, Nyssa
EPISODES Black Orchid 1-2

The TARDIS materialises on the northbound platform of Cranleigh Halt railway station just after the departure of a train from London. The Doctor is puzzled by the return to Earth, having stopped trying to reach Heathrow, but Tegan is keen to look around.

On leaving the station, the four travellers are met by a chauffeur sent by Lord Cranleigh. He mistakes the Doctor for a friend of his lordship owing to his cricketing garb and drives them to join in a local match.

It is not long before the station porter spots the Police Box that has appeared on his platform. He calls for a constable, who arranges for the box to be removed to the police station yard but no key can be found to unlock it.

Later that afternoon the Doctor, with his friends, is brought to the police station under suspicion of murder. Pleased to find the TARDIS there, he unlocks it and shows Chief Constable Sir Robert Muir and Sergeant Markham inside to prove his claim of owning a time machine. When news arrives that a second body has been discovered at Dalton Hall, the Doctor offers to get Sir Robert back there quicker than by car, and dematerialises the Ship.

- **CONTROLS** After the TARDIS lands, the Doctor adjusts controls on panel C2 including the left-hand black dial, while Adric flicks a switch on panel C1 and again appears to use the clear disc on the lower-right plate as a coordinates readout; the Doctor does the same to learn the date. He reaches across to panel C4 to open the scanner, probably using the usual rotary handle, and touches unseen controls on the left of panel C1 before going out, perhaps to check atmospheric conditions. The red-knobbed lever opens the main doors.

- This was the first story recorded after *Castrovalva* and the Information System screen and keypad on panel C6 have been removed. They're replaced with a plainer black cowl. The digital readout to its left is also gone.
- **NOTES** Nyssa mentions "what we've just done to London" which the Doctor says was "all part of Earth's history". This is obviously intended to refer to the Great Fire, implying this is their very next landing, but they could be taking about, say, an encounter with Boudicca that led to her sacking the city. Tegan has now decided she wants to stay, despite spending most of the past day as a mind-controlled prisoner. So it's possible there have been one or two landings since leaving the 17th century – probably on Earth given the two we see hardly count as a "compulsion" for the planet as the Doctor bemoans – which have led Tegan to believe she's not getting home soon so may as well make the most of travelling with the Doctor.
- Although there is a village called Cranleigh in Surrey, south-east of Guildford, this one must be further west as it's served by the Great Western Railway. The badge on Sergeant Markham's helmet is for the Wiltshire constabulary.
- The TARDIS lands at 3pm and sunset on 11 June 1925 was at 9.26pm, so the cricket match, party and fire all occur within six hours.
- The Police Box has its doors angled towards the platform edge but the view on the scanner is aimed at the station building. Does the scanner automatically select whichever viewing angle will give the most information about a landing site?
- Nobody locks the TARDIS when leaving, Tegan just pulls the door shut (by clinging to the telephone plaque's frame as there's no handle on the left-hand door). So it must lock automatically if the police can't get in and it requires the Doctor's key to open.
- The local police seem oddly familiar with Police Boxes given the idea of a kiosk with an emergency telephone for public use was limited to Glasgow and Sunderland at this time, and the Metropolitan Police Box wouldn't be designed for several years to come. It's possible Cummings is simply calling it by what's written above the doors, and perhaps thinks it's some new innovation brought up on the train from London.

LANDING 214

SPACE Earth, England, [Wiltshire], Dalton Hall, driveway
TIME A few days from 11 June 1925
TRAVELLERS The Doctor, Adric, Tegan, Nyssa, Sir Robert Muir, Sergeant Markham
EPISODES Black Orchid 2

The TARDIS achieves the short journey smoothly, materialising on the front driveway of Dalton Hall. As everyone emerges, Ann Talbot runs into Sir Robert's arm in tears, having just learned the truth about her first fiancé from his mother and brother. They all head into the house.

The Ship remains outside the hall for a few days while the travellers stay on to attend George Cranleigh's funeral. Afterwards they say goodbye to his family, taking with them gifts of their fancy dress costumes and a copy of George's book about his discovery of the black orchid.

NOTES Although not named in the final episode, a cut scene from episode one showed the travellers being driven towards the hall through a gateway bearing the name Dalton Hall. This was also used is press publicity for the serial.

LANDING 215

SPACE Earth, cave
TIME 2526
TRAVELLERS The Doctor, Adric, Tegan, Nyssa
EPISODES Earthshock 1-2

Adric tells the Doctor he wants to return to his people on Terradon, which would mean taking the TARDIS back into E-space. This the Doctor flatly refuses to do even though Adric is confident he can do the necessary calculations. They argue and the Doctor makes a seemingly random landing so he can go for a walk.

The TARDIS materialises in a small, chilly cave somewhere on Earth, around 26 metres below the surface. In some places fossilised dinosaur bones are exposed and a low level of light comes from a phosphorescent element in the rock. The Doctor emerges in a huff and Tegan and Nyssa follow to calm him down.

As Adric performs his calculations in the TARDIS he keeps an eye on the others via the scanner, noting when they wander away from the Ship into a larger cavern. He is distracted, however, when the console detects a signal being transmitted from the vicinity. Adric cannot trace its source so he heads out to find the Doctor.

The discovery of a powerful bomb brings everyone hurrying back to the Ship. The Doctor has Adric set the coordinates to zero so he can trace the remote signal that is controlling the bomb's arming procedure and jam it, giving him time to deactivate the device. While he works, the signal increases in power, pushing the jamming transmitter to maximum output. However, the Doctor succeeds in disabling the bomb and the arming signal ceases.

Having located the area of space from which the signal originated, the Doctor is keen to find out who was controlling the androids that were guarding the bomb. Palaeontology professor Kyle and military lieutenant Scott, who were investigating the caves, insist on helping fight whoever is threatening their planet. Reluctantly, the Doctor agrees they can come along and he dematerialises the Ship.

- **CONTROLS** When Adric asks to use the computer he moves to panel C5 and later looks down as if reading data from a display although there is none. The Doctor pushes the red-knobbed lever upwards to open the main doors rather than the more usual downwards, as Adric later does (so it didn't reset when the doors closed). When Adric tries to trace the transmission signal, he checks the black screen on panel C6 and flicks switches on panel C3. The red dome on the left of panel C5 flashes when the signal's power increases and Nyssa presses the buttons below the teleprinter.
- A new circular display has been added to the bottom-right plate on panel C1 in place of the clear disc (the sticky pads used to secure the latter can still be seen though). This has a deep black surround and a green illuminated screen which acts as the electromagnetic field gauge. A connection for the jamming cable is fixed to the top edge of the upper plate on this panel. The block at the top of panel C3 has an additional fascia with a thick frame and there is a new control to the left of it – a rotating stalk with an orange light on the end – but the right-hand quartered display has now lost its black cowl. The flick switch the Doctor uses is also new. A component board and attached ribbon cable are slung below this panel for the Doctor to use when jamming the bomb's activation signal. One of the buttons below the teleprinter on panel C5 is missing.
- The pedestal beneath panel C1 still has a flat flush face, cut off two-thirds of the way up (from the fitting of the circuit programmer mechanism for *Logopolis*), and in one shot the inner workings of the console prop are visible, as are the cables that power it.
- **LORE** The TARDIS has limitless power (or so Tegan believes) but certain components are restricted in how much they can channel.
- A transmitter can emit a signal to jam other transmissions in the Ship's vicinity.
- **NOTES** Although the Doctor is reading his copy of *Black Orchid* (by George Cranleigh, not Terence Dudley's Target book) at the start, he may be returning to it after intervening landings. As with Tegan's decision to stay, Adric's moroseness is rather out of the blue given he was last seen happily stuffing his face at a party, suggesting more time has passed in which he has been increasingly teased.
- Here we see Adric's bedroom for the first time. The door is solid but with a ring where a roundel would usually be, and the walls all have a raised triangular pattern. This is also a rare instance of seeing a ceiling in the TARDIS. In fact, the room is much pokier than Nyssa and Tegan's so it's no wonder he feels they get better treatment. There's a bed, a table on wheels, a desk and chair, shelf and drawer units, and storage crates. On the wall is a chart of the stars visible from Earth's northern and southern hemispheres (which the Doctor will later make use of – see Landing 273) and among Adric's belongings are a Kinda necklace, the Terileptian android's skull mask and his costume from the Cranleigh's fancy dress ball. The corridor outside the room is two of the solid aligned-roundels walls.
- The hatstand, this model only introduced in *Four to Doomsday*, has by now lost one of its hooks, leaving the broken stem sticking out.

- The Doctor has upgraded his toolkit since *The Visitation*. The new one has a smart black case containing a magnetic clamp, probe, laser cutter and magnetic drone.
- On venturing beyond the control room, Scott notes the TARDIS is "bigger than you think".

LANDING 216

SPACE Space sector 16, freighter, hold
TIME As above
TRAVELLERS The Doctor, Adric, Tegan, Nyssa, Professor Kyle, Lieutenant Scott, three troopers
EPISODES Earthshock 2-4

En route, the Doctor and Adric reconcile after their earlier argument, the lad admitting he does not really want to return home just yet but has at least proved it is possible.

The TARDIS materialises in the cargo hold of a freighter docked at a space station, surrounded by ranks of cylindrical containers. Uncertain if this is the origin of the arming signal or just a relay point, the Doctor elects to reconnoitre, joined by Adric.

Shortly after they have gone, the console alerts the others that the freighter has got underway using a warp drive. Scott is soon itching to follow the Doctor but Nyssa cautions him when an unusually large electromagnetic field is detected, coinciding with a drain on the freighter's power systems. Eventually this weakens and Nyssa lets Scott and his troopers go out. Tegan insists on joining them and borrows Kyle's overalls. Scott gives Nyssa a radio to contact him should the Doctor return first.

Nyssa and Kyle wait anxiously. Keeping an eye on the scanner, they spot two armed Cybermen patrolling nearby. Scott calls in to say his party is returning but they have lost Tegan. They are spotted approaching on the scanner and, with no sign of the Cybermen, Nyssa opens the doors. But as the troopers enter, one of the robotic creatures emerges from behind the Police Box and grabs and kills the rear solider. It then enters the TARDIS but is blasted down by Scott and the other two troopers. Nyssa pulls the door control as another Cyberman tries to force its way in. Caught in the closing doors, it fires and kills Professor Kyle before Scott manages to kill it. Now with two of the Cybermen's own weapons boosting their armaments, the troopers head out again.

Scott contacts Nyssa to say the Cybermen appear to have evacuated the freighter; she warns him the electromagnetic field is functioning again. Shortly after, the Doctor and Tegan return but without Adric, just two Cybermen, one their leader. Under duress, the Doctor dematerialises the TARDIS.

- **CONTROLS** The Doctor and later Nyssa use the red-knobbed lever on panel C1 to open and close the main doors. An unseen control on panel C5 gives an audio alert when the freighter enters warp drive. When the electromagnetic field is detected the new display on panel C1 glows green and Nyssa flicks a switch on the lower-left plate and another on panel C3.
- A charge at the top of panel C3 explodes when the Cyberman trapped in the doorway fires, even though this is on the far side of the central column.
- **LORE** The TARDIS can be detected and identified while in flight, at least by the Cybermen's deep space probes and possibly by standard radar.
- **NOTES** Initially only two troopers are seen on the control room set but just before they leave, and while exploring the freighter, there are three.
- A model shot of the Police Box travelling through space was planned but never filmed. This would presumably have been inserted before the scene where the Cyberman reports their deep space probes have identified the TARDIS.
- Oops! The sole female trooper is grabbed by a Cyberman outside the TARDIS, but then she is seen entering the control room (recorded two weeks earlier) and one of the other male troopers is missing. Subsequent scenes on the freighter feature the two male troopers.
- Scott leaves Nyssa with the bodies of Kyle and a Cyberman yet these are gone when the Doctor returns. Nyssa could, perhaps, have dragged the Cyberman outside but presumably moves Kyle to another room and lets Scott take her body when they return to his time. She's not having a good day even before Adric dies.

LANDING 217

SPACE Solar system, near Earth, freighter escape pod
TIME 65,000,000BC
TRAVELLERS The Doctor, Tegan, Nyssa, two dead Cybermen
EPISODES Earthshock 4; before Time-Flight 1

Under the Cyberleader's orders, the Doctor follows the freighter on its programmed course to crash into the Earth. In desperation, Tegan presses a random control causing the TARDIS to lurch; the Doctor brings it to rest and berates her rash action.

Watching the freighter on the scanner, they see it flicker and disappear as it begins to travel backwards through time. The Cyberleader orders the Doctor to follow and land back on the freighter but its temporal coordinates are constantly changing so he cannot get a fix. However, he reluctantly admits it is locked onto the same spatial coordinates and will still crash.

As the freighter approaches Earth it comes out of warp drive, ending its shift through time. The scanner shows an escape pod launching, and the Doctor notes they have travelled back some 65 million years to the time when history records the dinosaurs were wiped out by a collision from space: evidently the anti-matter-powered freighter. Scott contacts them from the escape pod to alert them that Adric is still aboard the freighter.

Seeing its plans have failed, the Cyberleader prepares to shoot the Doctor but Tegan distracts it long enough for the Doctor to crush Adric's gold-edged badge into its chest plate. As the Cyberleader is affected it fires its weapon randomly, striking the console, until the Doctor grabs the gun and shoots the creature at point-blank range. With the console damaged, the Doctor struggles to land the TARDIS aboard the freighter. The second Cyberman returns from searching the Ship and Nyssa shoots it with the leader's weapon as the Doctor works frantically at the controls. But they can only watch the scanner helplessly as the freighter plunges into Earth's atmosphere and explodes.

Once he has got the console operating, the Doctor materialises the TARDIS aboard the escape pod to collect Scott and the other survivors. They reveal that Adric chose to stay behind believing he could avert the collision.

○ **CONTROLS** Tegan presses one of the buttons below the teleprinter on panel C5, causing the TARDIS to lurch; the Doctor presses several of them to reset it. The Doctor directs Nyssa's gaze at panel C5 when noting the time shift. After the console is damaged, Nyssa flicks switches on panel C1 while the Doctor flicks a switch on panel C3 and buttons on C5; then buttons on C6, the left-hand rotary handle on C3 and twists his hand as if rotating the red dome on panel C5. He closes the scanner with the right-most button below the green plastic control on the right of that panel.

▤ **NOTES** The scanner can display the freighter's exterior while it's in warp drive (which is presumably distorting space-time but not pushing the craft into a different dimension such as hyperspace or the Vortex) and as it plunges back through time (on and off as it catches up then loses it again). But the TARDIS is constantly in flight throughout. Even when the freighter drops out of warp and approaches Earth, and the Cyberleader instructs, "Hold this position," there's no evidence the Police Box has materialised as the central column continues to oscillate and the control room's hum is the 'in-flight' sound effect.

▤ The hatstand topples over when Tegan attacks the controls and makes the room tilt. It's still lying on the floor when the freighter slips backwards in time and although everyone is focused on the scanner someone has evidently righted it before the next scene.

▤ Tegan's shriek when the Cyberleader shoots the console is reportedly genuine as she is struck by flying sparks.

▤ The size of the escape pod is uncertain but there must be more to it than the empty vestibule the evacuees initially enter. The detailing on the model as it ejects from the freighter makes it seem a sizeable vessel, big enough for the TARDIS to materialise aboard.

▤ There'd be no point taking the bodies of the two Cybermen back to the future so it's likely they were left behind in the escape pod.

LANDING 218

SPACE [Earth]
TIME As Landing 215
TRAVELLERS The Doctor, Tegan, Nyssa, Scott, trooper, Captain Briggs, Berger
EPISODES Time-Flight 1

The TARDIS returns to the 26th century with the troopers and freighter crew. They alert Earth's authorities to the approaching Cyber fleet, which is successfully dispersed.

The Doctor, Tegan and Nyssa return to the TARDIS, still fraught over the loss of Adric. Tegan argues for attempting a rescue by landing aboard the freighter before its destruction but the Doctor angrily insists there are rules even he cannot break.

In an attempt to cheer them up, the Doctor proposes a visit to the opening of the Great Exhibition at the Crystal Palace in London's Hyde Park in 1851, and programmes the coordinates. No sooner has he set the TARDIS in motion than it is buffeted by cross-tracing on the time-space axis caused by a Concorde aeroplane being hijacked along a time contour.

○ **CONTROLS** The console's panels are arranged in a different order to normal in this story, with panel C1 facing the doors as usual but then positioned 1-6-3-5-2-4 clockwise. This at least gives us a clearer view of panels C2 and C4, which so far this season have been hidden on the far side of the console. The pedestal is also oriented differently. The side with no recess usually below panel C1 (and now extended upward to fill the gap visible in *Earthshock* – see Landing 215) is now under panel C5 and thus facing away from the main doors. The two sides below panels C4 and C1 now have much shallower recesses, formed by placing larger black faces into them with fold-down flaps to reveal prop circuitry behind, for the scenes of the Doctor and Master retrieving components from beneath the console. There was perhaps a reason to choose these sides of the pedestal for modification, and thus for it to be rotated so they faced the camera. This would have placed the now-familiar red-knobbed main doors lever on the far side of the console, so panels C1, C3 and C5 were swapped around.

○ The Doctor closes the main doors with the usual red-knobbed lever of panel C1. He sets the coordinates from the same panel, seemingly by twisting the lights on the upper plate and the top two lights on the triangular plate of panel C4, plus an unseen control on panel C6. Nyssa reads the destination by looking over his shoulder somewhere towards the left of panel C1. The Doctor dematerialises by sliding an unseen control on panel C5. Nyssa flicks switches on panel C1 to confirm the Ship's systems are functioning, and the Doctor checks for feedback from the solar comparator by pressing the upper-right red buttons on panel C2.

▤ **LORE** Shaking of the Ship in flight might be caused by malfunctioning of the dimensional stabilisers, a problem with the relative drift compensator or feedback from the solar comparator.

▤ **NOTES** The Doctor only mentions the crew of the freighter being returned to their own time, but it's likely he took them to Earth as that's where they were originally heading, and the planet would need to be warned of the Cybermen's planned attack. The Doctor would be bound to stay and help repulse the

Cyber fleet, although the grieving women may have remained in the TARDIS; Tegan has changed out of Kyle's overalls and back into her airline uniform when we first see her in *Time-Flight*. We might also assume Professor Kyle's body was returned to her family and the travellers may even have attended her funeral to help with their own grief – if they had the decency to attend George Cranleigh's burial surely they would do the same for Kyle, someone they actually interacted with and whose death visibly upset Nyssa.

- To be honest, Tegan's plan for rescuing Adric sounds perfectly feasible. Materialise aboard the freighter moments before it crashes, grab the boy and leave (it should even be possible to materialise around him). Freighter smashes into Earth, major extinction event, history proceeds as recorded. There might be an issue with the TARDIS being present twice at the same point in time in close proximity, although Nyssa believes the Ship can do it, and this isn't a problem in *The Two Doctors* (see previous to Landing 73 and Landing 272). Yet the Doctor reacts angrily and claims, "There are some rules that cannot be broken even with the TARDIS." So it's more the case that he shouldn't rather than can't; might it be one of the Time Lords' only-ever-mentioned-when-they're-being-contravened Laws of Time? If so it's surprising the Doctor chooses to obey in this situation, almost as if he didn't want to save Adric.
- Throughout *Time-Flight* the control room set is slightly different from normal. The narrow section with two columns of aligned roundels is missing, so the two three-column walls are adjacent, and to their right before the scanner wall is one of the 1977 control room walls with half-circles down the right-hand edge. An hour's delay on the day of recording owing to an incorrect setting of the TARDIS set indicates the change was not deliberate and it may be that the difference in alignment was at odds with the usual lighting plan or area of painted studio floor for the set. The hatstand also reverted to that first seen in *The Invisible Enemy*, although this would be its final appearance.
- The TARDIS is destabilised the moment it departs the 26th century en route for the 19th, yet the Concorde is being transported from the late-20th century back 140 million years. The Ship's journey may not be a linear one, therefore, but a jump into the Vortex at a point that happens to intersect with the time contour.

LANDING 219

SPACE Earth, England, London, Heathrow Airport, above runway
TIME [January 1982]
TRAVELLERS The Doctor, Tegan, Nyssa
EPISODES Time-Flight 1

The proximity of another time-travelling craft threatens to draw the TARDIS into spatial convergence so the Doctor materialises to prevent being destroyed. Expecting to be hovering above Hyde Park in the 19th century, the scanner reveals the Ship has actually reached Heathrow Airport in the 1980s at last.

However, it is floating above the main runway right in the path of incoming aircraft. The Doctor ducks under the console to active the coordinate override and relocate the TARDIS to avoid a collision. The Police Box disappears from the sky above the airport, and from the air traffic controller's radar screen.

- **CONTROLS** No one appears to intentionally activate the scanner, unless it's Nyssa doing so discretely from panel C1, but the Doctor closes it by turning a control on panel C3, likely the bottom-left rotary handle.
- The coordinate override is said to be a device, as opposed to a procedure. It's located beneath panel C5, either under the panel itself of within the pedestal.
- **LORE** The coordinate override allows the TARDIS to ignore the programmed destination and materialise in the nearest safe location in the event of possible collision with another craft. Is this what the hostile action displacement system activates (see Landing 65)?
- **NOTES** Tegan confidently claims this to be the 1980s (changed from the scripted 1982), seemingly based solely on the appearance of Terminal One and the passengers therein. Or she might just be assuming the TARDIS has finally got her back in time for her flight as intended. Certainly it's winter as we later see there is snow on the ground (although not in the aerial view on the scanner), which could be February 1981 or a year or two later. The copy of *The Times* the Doctor reads is the Wednesday 6 January 1982 edition, the day on which those scenes were filmed.
- Visual effects designer Peter Logan recalls that for the shot of the TARDIS hovering above the runway he made a new Police Box miniature. This was 2½ inches tall with sides made from photographs of the full-size prop and a flashing roof light. However, a similar shot of the TARDIS hovering in episode four used the six-inch model built for *The Horns of Nimon* – seen in studio recording footage – and on screen the two appear the same, so Logan may have been thinking of another story or his new model wasn't featured after all.
- The scanner's shutter is again overlaid electronically.

LANDING 220

SPACE Earth, England, London, Heathrow Airport, Terminal One; loaded into Concorde GAC hold; taken to citadel, central chamber
TIME As above; transported back 140,000,000 years
TRAVELLERS The Doctor, Tegan, Nyssa
EPISODES Time-Flight 1-3

The TARDIS materialises in the same general time and place but a much safer location: in Terminal One on an upper level overlooking the passenger concourse. The Doctor prepares to move on momentarily, then notices a readout on the console and instead pops outside. Puzzled, Tegan and Nyssa follow.

The Doctor has found a newspaper and is catching up with the English cricket results when he is approached by airport security. To avoid explaining about the TARDIS, the Doctor cites his old UNIT credentials and, once these are verified, he is invited to assist with the mystery of the disappearance of Concorde Golf Victor Foxtrot.

Suspecting a connection with the time contour, the Doctor has the TARDIS loaded by forklift truck into the rear cargo bay of another Concorde, Golf Alpha Charlie, and all three travellers take seats aboard as it takes off. They find the TARDIS on its side in the cramped hold so the Doctor enters first to realign the interior. As the Concorde loops back towards London on the same course as the missing plane and begins its descent, it too is pulled along the time contour and the Doctor returns to the cockpit.

The plane emerges 140 million years in the past and lands on a dry, rocky plain with scrub vegetation and no sign of life. Nearby is the missing Concorde, and beyond it a stone-built citadel and the wreck of a Xeraphin spaceship. While the Doctor and the Alpha Charlie crew explore, a group of hypnotised passengers from Victor Foxtrot unload the TARDIS from the newly arrived Concorde and wheel it into the citadel, depositing it in a central chamber before Kalid, seemingly an ancient Arabian mystic.

The Doctor arrives and Kalid demands he hand over the TARDIS key. When the Doctor refuses the magician imperils the Concorde crew, but a disruption of the Xeraphin psychic powers Kalid is drawing on causes him to collapse. He quickly recovers and reveals himself to be the Master in disguise. He threatens to shoot the crew with his tissue compressor, forcing the Doctor to give him the key to the Ship. He enters and the TARDIS dematerialises.

○ **CONTROLS** In a shot cut from the final episode, the Doctor opened the scanner with the bottom-right rotary handle on panel C3. When preparing to leave, he presses the buttons below the teleprinter on panel C5 and looks at the printer head as if it's a display. He opens the main doors with (you guessed it) the red-knobbed lever on panel C1. To reorient the room, the Doctor flicks the left-most switch on the triangular plate of panel C4. Nyssa points at the teleprinter when noting they're travelling through time, and fiddles with the printer head which seems to fade the audio alert.
○ There's a sizeable hole in panel C1 to the left of the centre lever. New controls were added here prior to *Earthshock*. As the original plate appears to have been cut down in size, the panel may have been severely damaged and needed the new controls to cover the hole but which have now gone missing.

▮ **LORE** If the outer Police Box is not upright, the interior can be reoriented to the horizontal.
▮ An alarm sounds on the console if the Ship travels through time (other than the standard forward flow) owing to an outside force rather than its own engines.
▮ The Doctor admits that his TARDIS is "not exactly the first-class end of the market" but considers it "a serviceable vehicle".

▤ **NOTES** Having finally reached her own time, and Heathrow Airport to boot, Tegan is very keen to move on. She seems worried about the authorities finding the TARDIS but that's hardly a major problem, so perhaps she's just really eager to see the Great Exhibition.
▤ What does the Doctor see on the console that causes him to hurry out and find a newspaper? It can only be the date, which spurs him to catch up on the cricket results. (In the script, he spots a news-stand on the scanner with a notice of 'some amazing cricketing development'.) He is seen reading a report on the on-going fourth test of the 1981/82 series between India and England (headlined 'Perfect prelude to the final act') but it's not like this was a remarkable or historic match that he might have heard about. It ultimately ended in a draw, with India going on to win the series 1-0 – presumably what makes the Doctor bemoan "what English cricket is coming to".
▤ The Police Box seen on its side in the Concorde hold is the newer Yardley-Jones prop although at this point it has one of the old Newbery sign boxes above one set of doors, here facing upwards. In this position the doors wouldn't stay shut so two stagehands had to crouch inside and hold them up.
▤ It's all very well for the Doctor to lower himself along the upright control room floor to reach the console and realign the interior space but how much weirder must it be for Nyssa and Tegan? Bear in mind the Police Box is still on its side, so they have to climb onto it and lower themselves feet first through the doors as the Doctor did, yet they trot into the control room without any hint of the gravitational flip-flopping they must have gone through between the outer and inner doors. Similarly they walk out as normal but then must somehow climb upwards out of the Police Box doors.
▤ Also, what a mess the inside of the TARDIS must now be. The hatstand in the control room is seen to have toppled over (the direction makes a point of showing the Doctor setting it upright), and in *Castrovalva* we saw the loose Zero Room doors tip as the Ship landed askew. So all those ornaments in the companions' bedrooms must be scatted everywhere, the mirror seen in *Castrovalva* has probably shattered, and what about the water in the swimming pool? If the interior dimension can be rotated to compensate – or even if just its gravity is shifted – wouldn't it be better for this to be automatic rather than requiring a switch to be flicked? (Indeed, the script called it an 'automatic gravity control'.) Maybe this is just another malfunction of the Doctor's TARDIS.
▤ The Doctor estimates the time contour has taken them "some a hundred and forty million years ago", "definitely Jurassic" and not "far off the Pleistocene era". In our history the Jurassic ended 145 million years ago so they should be in the Cretaceous period, but there's a margin of error for such boundaries and the Doctor may know better. The Pleistocene epoch, however, began less than three million years ago so that "nip in the air" is a long way off. Brontosaurus is believed to

have gone extinct towards the end of the Jurassic, and besides lived in what would become North America.
- The Doctor tells Stapley they're "where you thought we were" and doesn't contradict the captain's, "Heathrow?" But what does this mean given 140 million years of continental drift and changing sea levels? If he's suggesting this is the bedrock that will later form southern England, then it may only recently (in geological terms) have emerged after sea levels fell at the end of the Jurassic, which could explain the absence of fauna (it would later be submerged again).
- How do the hypnotised passengers retrieve the TARDIS from Concorde's hold, which required a forklift to be loaded? They have only minutes while the flight crew are off hallucinating the M4 in which to climb five metres to the bay doors, unlock and open them, and unload the Police Box (which they could just push out and let fall to the ground). They then shift it onto a trolley that appears to be lashed together from logs, even though there are no trees anywhere in sight. Why couldn't Kalid simply send his protein cloud to carry it off as he does with Bilton and Scobie? The supporting artists playing the passengers were encouraged to make it seem the Police Box was incredibly heavy but make little effort to do so.
- The Master finds the Doctor's Police Box is locked but who locked it? The Doctor leaves Tegan and Nyssa in the control room, then we next seem them disembarking after the plane has landed. Tegan may still have the key given her in *Four to Doomsday* but she has no reason to lock the Ship behind her. The Doctor is clearly suspicious of their apparent return to Heathrow so presumably he popped down to the hold and locked the TARDIS to be on the safe side. He may have quickly checked the console to see what time period they're in, hence his certainty it's 140 million years ago.

LANDING 221

SPACE Earth, citadel, central chamber
TIME As above
TRAVELLERS The Master
EPISODES Time-Flight 3

The TARDIS swiftly returns to its precise departure point because the coordinate override is still operating. Unperturbed, the Master retrieves components from his own TARDIS that he had used to augment the Xeraphin control sphere, planning to install them in the Doctor's to bypass the limitation. While he works, Alpha Charlie's captain Stapley and first officer Bilton sneak out of hiding and into the TARDIS.

They hope to lock out the Master but cannot comprehend the vehicle's complex controls. They manage to turn on the scanner and see him returning, so hide behind the interior door. The Master enters with a handful of components that he inserts under the console. He tries to take off but the central column freezes and the TARDIS will not dematerialise.

When the Master steps outside, Stapley and Bilton hope to cause further problems for the villain by swapping around circuit boards within the console. But they are caught in the act and the Master simply removes the components he needs – including what he believes is the temporal limiter – presets the controls and leaves before the TARDIS dematerialises.

- **CONTROLS** The consistent use over this season of the red-knobbed lever on panel C1 to operate the main doors allows for a joke where Captain Stapley reaches for this lever to close the doors but Bilton discourages him, saying, "I wouldn't have thought it was that."
- Stapley subsequently flicks the upper-left switch on panel C3 to no effect, then operates the scanner with the bottom-left rotary handle. Even the Master knows the red-knobbed lever closes the doors. He presses buttons at the top of panel C3 and flicks the upper-right switch when trying to get the TARDIS working. Before leaving, he presses a button to the right of the screen on panel C6.
- The Master inserts his components into the pedestal beneath panel C1. A domed item slots onto a shelf immediately below the console. Stapley later pulls circuit boards out from behind a fold-down flap in the recess.
- **LORE** The Master's TARDIS has a dynomorphic generator that he has exhausted of power and plans to replace with the Xeraphin nucleus. That Nyssa understands this is feasible, and the Doctor talks of the Master's "own" generator, both suggesting the Doctor's TARDIS contains one too.
- **NOTES** The rematerialisation of the TARDIS is the same recording of its last dematerialisation played in reverse. This is used again for its failing to take off and finally dematerialising.
- A new sound effect is used for the stalled TARDIS, with some of the usual groans supplemented by a descending whine.
- The scanner shutter is again inserted electronically but note, instead of a simple vertical wipe as previously, it is here rotated slightly to match the changing perspective in the camera shot of the scanner wall.
- The corridor beyond the interior door is formed from two of the solid aligned-roundels walls.
- What exactly is the problem with the TARDIS? At first it takes off fine, just returning to where it left because of the coordinate override. Surely the Master could just turn this off so presumably he doesn't realise and jumps to the conclusion it's a fault of the Doctor's "third-rate" machine. He adds some components of his own and then the TARDIS won't take off at all, so he's just made the problem worse. Or are the Xeraphin using their power to keep him out of the sanctum? Is this why, even though extracting different circuits gets the Ship working again, at least within this time zone, the Master just sends it off with Stapley and Bilton aboard? It's not clear whether he needs these circuits to repair his own TARDIS or he's just sabotaging the

Doctor's; perhaps both as he needs the temporal limiter but later willingly returns the other parts. Was it his plan to leave the TARDIS hovering nearby, unable to help the Doctor but recoverable should the Master need it after all? Or did the Xeraphin use their mental powers to keep it close?

LANDING 222

SPACE Earth, above citadel
TIME As above
TRAVELLERS Captain Stapley, First Officer Andrew Bilton
EPISODES Time-Flight 3-4

The TARDIS rematerialises hovering above the citadel. Stapley tries to find the controls for landing but his attempts just cause the Ship to shudder. He suggests finding a radio to contact the Doctor when a psychic projection of Professor Hayter, a passenger aboard Victor Foxtrot, appears and takes control of the TARDIS.

⦿ **CONTROLS** Trying to land the TARDIS, Stapley pushes both large levers on panel C3 upwards (in fairness, they're not unlike a commercial jet's throttle controls) but this just causes the Ship to shudder and whine.

LANDING 223

SPACE Earth, citadel, inner sanctum
TIME As above
TRAVELLERS Stapley, Bilton, Professor Hayter
EPISODES Time-Flight 4

Hayter, now part of the Xeraphin amalgam, is able to operate the TARDIS and materialises it inside the sealed sanctum that until recently contained the physical nucleus of the Xeraphin, and where the Doctor, Nyssa and Tegan are now trapped. They greet the Concorde pilots and the Doctor is impressed by Stapley's ability to fly the Ship, until he explains it was not him but the professor, who has now disappeared.

▣ **NOTES** The Doctor describes the Xeraphin as being "highly developed" with "immense mental power" and that their amalgamated form has "immeasurable intelligence", so perhaps its ability to pilot the TARDIS isn't unreasonable. We know the Ship is partly telepathic.

LANDING 224

SPACE Earth, citadel, outer sanctum
TIME As above
TRAVELLERS The Doctor, Tegan, Nyssa, Stapley, Bilton
EPISODES Time-Flight 4

The Doctor resumes control of his Ship and relocates it by a few metres, materialising just outside the sanctum. He is disappointed to find the Master's TARDIS is no longer there, having co-opted the Xeraphin nucleus as a new power source, but is confident it cannot have gone far.

Learning from Alpha Charlie's flight engineer Roger Scobie that the Master took Victor Foxtrot's passengers with him in his TARDIS, the Doctor hurriedly returns to the control room and sets the coordinates to take the Ship back to the Concorde's hold. Entrusting Nyssa to implement the journey, he leaves with Tegan to look for the Master.

⦿ **CONTROLS** The Doctor sets the coordinates by twisting the lights on the upper plate of panel C1 and the top two on the triangular plate on panel C4, as he did at the start of episode one (Landing 218). Nyssa reaches for the red-knobbed door control as the Doctor leaves.

LANDING 225

SPACE Earth, Concorde GAC hold
TIME As above
TRAVELLERS Nyssa, Stapley, Bilton,
   Flight Engineer Roger Scobie
EPISODES Time-Flight 4

The TARDIS returns to Alpha Charlie's cargo hold, the Police Box materialising on its back owing to the restricted space. Nyssa and the flight crew emerge to prepare the plane for take-off.

Some time later, the Doctor returns with the components the Master took and refits them, although the latter has withheld the quantum accelerator. The Doctor also connects a 115-volt power cable from the Ship to the Concorde to start its engines. Nyssa informs him when the plane is ready, and Tegan warns that the Master is threatening to shoot passengers if the Doctor does not soon give him a working temporal limiter as promised. He leaves to make the exchange, having programmed an inhibition factor into the limiter to delay the Master's journey back along the time contour.

The Doctor refits the quantum accelerator then heads to the flight deck for take-off. Once the Concorde is airborne, he dematerialises the TARDIS, reversing the time contour and propelling the plane back to its own time and original flight path.

⦿ **CONTROLS** The Doctor replaces the circuit boards into the pedestal below panel C1. He slots the quantum accelerator into the shelf where the Master previously placed a domed unit. When returning to the Ship in the hold, he presses lights on the upper plate of panel C1 then adjusts unseen controls on panel C5.
⦿ The hole in panel C1 is particularly noticeable at the start of the shot of Nyssa rolling out the cable.
▣ **LORE** Removal of the temporal limiter restricts a TARDIS to its current time zone. This device is programmable and can be set with an inhibitor to extend flight time.
▣ The Ship can still function even without the time-lapse compressor or quantum accelerator installed.

▤ **NOTES** We can assume Nyssa activates the reorientation control when the TARDIS lands horizontally (if it's not now set to automatic), having seen the Doctor do so earlier, although she and the flight crew still have to lift themselves out of the upward-facing Police Box doors. In reality they're climbing up a metal stepladder, which can be heard creaking. The cargo hold was a raised set with a hole beneath the Police Box to allow the actors to climb up through it.

▤ The Doctor checks the control unit in the central chamber and notes the Master has "taken everything with him, including the bits of my TARDIS". But how does he know they're missing? Stapley hasn't had an opportunity to tell him and he only later learns of the captain's attempted sabotage. As the TARDIS can still relocate within this time zone, perhaps he knows the only way the Master could have bypassed the coordinate override was to remove certain components. And yet it transpires he took the time-lapse compressor instead of the temporal limiter, so what cancelled the override? And how stupid is it of the Master to mix them up? The time-lapse compressor, if one of the items he took, is a slim circuit board whereas the temporal limiter is a much bulkier unit.

▤ Equally, when did the Master pinch the Doctor's quantum accelerator? Like the temporal limiter, this is a larger multi-component unit quite unlike the three circuit boards we see him remove and later return.

LANDING 226

SPACE Earth, England, London, Heathrow Airport
TIME One day after Landing 219
TRAVELLERS The Doctor, Tegan, Nyssa
EPISODES Time-Flight 4

The TARDIS arrives back at Heathrow on the top level of a car park beside the departures building of Terminal Three. Alpha Charlie passes overhead as it comes in to land. The Master's TARDIS tries to materialise but cannot because the Doctor's is already at precisely the same coordinates. It is forced back into the Vortex, on a course that the Doctor has arranged will take it to the Xeraphin home world.

He goes outside to find where Tegan has wandered off to, only to be confronted by two policemen. The Alpha Charlie flight crew arrive with the airport controller, but the latter also demands explanations. The Doctor pops back into the TARDIS to "make a quick phone call" and clear up matters but promptly dematerialises – leaving behind a surprised Tegan.

○ **CONTROLS** The Doctor repels the Master's TARDIS by twisting the right-hand black dial on panel C2. Nyssa closes the scanner with the rotary handle on panel C3.

▤ **NOTES** The shot of the Police Box fading as it repels the Master's fluted column uses the same film footage as for its arrival moments earlier.

▤ Why does the TARDIS fade in and out when it's not moving anywhere – indeed, if it did surely that would allow the Master to land? Like the column appearing in the sky rather than where the Police Box is, let's put this down to visual distortion due to temporal dynamics.

▤ The Police Box's roof lamp doesn't flash when it dematerialises at the end of the story.

▤ So does the Doctor deliberately leave Tegan on Earth? After dealing with the Master he does wonder where she is, then seems simply to forget in the fluster of avoiding the authorities. But if Nyssa has told him about Tegan's earlier wistfulness, or if he assumes this was where she wanted to be all along, he may have chosen to save her the dilemma of choosing.

IT LOOKS JUST LIKE A POLICE BOX

THE YARDLEY-JONES BOX 2
1983-1989

By the end of Season 19 the Police Box prop was in a poor state after two years of rough handling during transport, assembly, dismantling and storage. It had undergone some internal strengthening towards the ends of August 1981, but in March 1982 it was decided the box should be replaced.

It has long been debated among TARDIS aficionados whether the prop seen from Season 20 onwards was new or merely a refurbishment of the 1980 box. Supporting the former argument were some curious differences that suggested if it wasn't entirely new then it must have had a significant rebuild, while for the latter was a lack of evidence that a new prop was commissioned and the knowledge that only two props survived the end of the series in 1989, one of which was the box made in 1984.

It's accepted that the Season 20 box had new doors, with the centre post now affixed to the left-hand one, so the right door opened first. This was the same on both front and rear, and they were taller so the stepped lintel above correctly acted as a doorstop at last. The right-hand doors featured a Yale lock and handle below, while each left-hand door had a telephone plaque with the 'All calls' wording that debuted in *Kinda* (see page 260).

More puzzling were the top ledges above the sign boxes, which gained a stub in the middle, in line with the centre posts between the windows as if these continued up to the top of the box. Why would a refurbishment add this detail unless these pieces were new mouldings? With the original 1980 box, the ledges were either cast in fibreglass as one with the sign boxes or made separately then bonded together. On the two faces with doors, the stepped lintel below was also part of this piece, while on the sides they were bonded with the walls and corner posts. If the additional centre-post stubs appeared only on the front and rear, it would be reasonable to assume that just these two sign boxes with ledge above and steps below were remade. But because they also feature on the sides, it raised the question whether the entire side walls including corner posts (which no longer exhibited the bolts added during Season 19) were recast, or were the top ledges cut from the existing sides and fresh fibreglass sections bonded in their place?

In fact, recently unearthed production documentation indicates that a new Police Box prop *was* commissioned. The first story of Season 20 to be made was *Snakedance*, the assigned designer for which was Jan Spoczynski. He was keen to have the serial's sets constructed by outside contractors, as he considered them more cost-effective, but his request was initially declined by the BBC design department. He persisted after being disappointed with the in-house sets for the filmed scenes in *Snakedance* and finally gained approval, although with little time left before recording was due to begin. The new TARDIS was therefore contracted out to George Block at Thorn-EMI Elstree Studios. He was proficient in working with fibreglass and had produced weapons and costume parts for *The Empire Strikes Back* when it filmed there in 1979. The commission was approved on 22 March 1982 with a due date barely two weeks later of the 8th of April, to be ready for recording on the 12th.

The order specified using the existing moulds from the 1980 prop, and they must have been given that Boxes 1 and 2 were so alike they've widely been assumed to be one and the same. Only the changes to the doors and those top-ledge stubs distinguish the new box – the latter still a puzzling addition as they didn't feature on the old moulds. Were they added for extra strength in the centre of the ledges to help with supporting the roof? One other change was to the sign box frames, which were made even wider than those added prior to *Castrovalva* to hold in the lettered inserts more securely; this created a narrower indent little taller than the signs' lettering. The acrylic inserts themselves were probably transferred from the previous box, along with the lamp (back to sitting directly on the pitched roof). Two new bases were also commissioned, no doubt because this was a damage-prone part of the prop, and like the remedial bracing added to Box 1, a steel subframe inside gave extra support to the tops of the wall and sign boxes.

The old box was to be delivered to the contractor so its texture and colouration could be reproduced, although in the event the new prop was painted in a darker, greyer shade of blue. If any parts were cannibalised, this would have led to the remainder being scrapped, explaining why there's no hint of two boxes existing at this time.

FORWARDS AND BACKWARDS

The TARDIS exterior makes only a brief appearance in *Snakedance*, and is mostly hidden by drapes. It does, however, afford a close-up of the newly painted telephone plaque with regular-width letters for 'Free' and 'Public'. With the box having usable doors on both faces, talk of a front and rear becomes redundant as it could be, and was, deployed in both orientations. The only way to

Right Recast Yardley-Jones prop front elevation and section

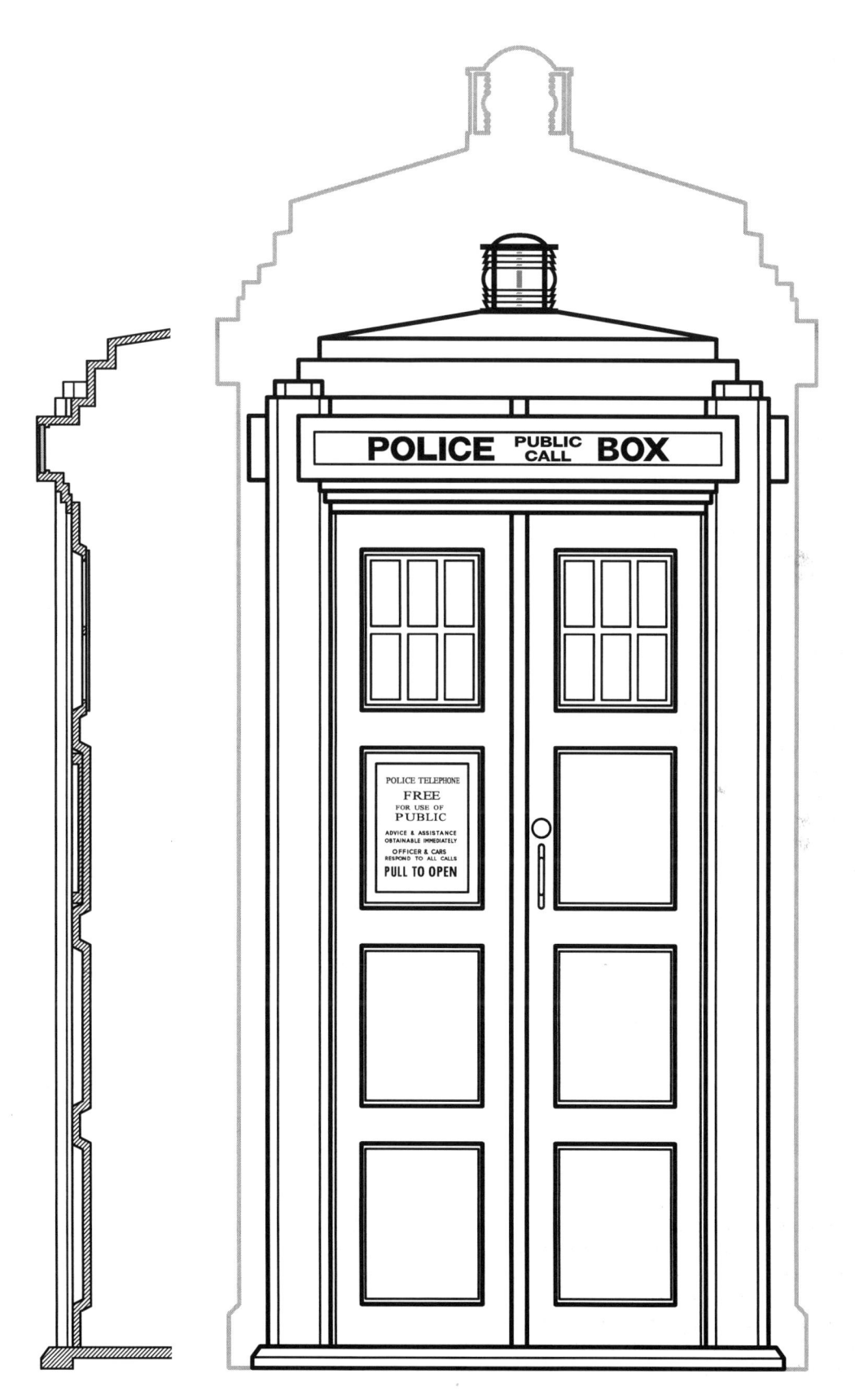

IT LOOKS JUST LIKE A POLICE BOX

POLICE PUBLIC CALL BOX

POLICE TELEPHONE
FREE
FOR USE OF
PUBLIC
ADVICE & ASSISTANCE
OBTAINABLE IMMEDIATELY
OFFICER & CARS
RESPOND TO ALL CALLS
PULL TO OPEN

differentiate the two is by which plaque is seen and spotting marks on the window panes – other signifiers like scuffs and flakes tend to disappear with repeated repaints. There's also the possibility that at times the doors were attached to opposite sides of the frame, although the sections were numbered on the reverse so there's a good chance the prop was assembled consistently. As this face was used first, let's call it the front.

For its next two appearances in *Arc of Infinity* and *Mawdryn Undead* the 'rear' of the box with the wider-'Public' plaque was used as the entrance. The prop doesn't appear in *Terminus* and in *Enlightenment* episode four the front is seen; in episode one it's too dark to be sure but careful examination suggests it's the same face. This is certainly the case in *The King's Demons* when the TARDIS arrives and departs at the end, although the scene in episode two where Tegan slips inside and takes off uses the rear. The new box was already showing signs of wear by then, with part of the right-side sign box frame missing – clearly visible in the location footage – and the bottom step above the front doors damaged in the middle where the centre post strikes it.

In *The Five Doctors* the front was used on location (at least for the Eye of Orion scenes – the box isn't seen close up in the Death Zone scenes) but in the studio, when it arrives in the Tomb of Rassilon, the rear was used. This shows the damage to the right-side sign box frame (now appearing on the left) had been repaired, but the first sign of a crack at the top of the rear-left corner post can be discerned – something that will become a useful identifier. The box continued to be rotated at random throughout the first half of Season 21, with the front used as the entrance in *Warriors of the Deep*, *Frontios* and on location for *Resurrection of the Daleks*, but the rear in *The Awakening* and the studio scenes of the Dalek story. At this point it also gained a new, thicker base – perhaps the additional one that had been commissioned in 1982.

A SIBLING TO SHARE WITH

A third fibreglass Police Box prop was constructed prior to *Planet of Fire* (see page 352) but this time supplementing rather than replacing the existing box. Even so, Box 2 didn't reappear in the rest of Season 21 but was set up in Hammersmith Park on Tuesday 10 January 1984 for a press photocall to reveal Colin Baker's costume. He posed in the rear doorway of the prop, with the crack in the left-hand corner post now very noticeable. This wasn't helped by the box being badly assembled, the sign boxes in particular being poorly attached.

Box 2 was back on screen in *The Two Doctors*, when it was shipped to Spain for location filming in August 1984, then returned to the studio at the end of the month for both Doctors' arrivals in Shockeye's kitchen. The younger favoured the rear of the prop but the front was used for the elder, even though another large crack was now evident in the stile next to the right-hand window.

By this time the box had also regained its thinner base. Having emerged from storage once, it was subsequently used in *Timelash* and *Revelation of the Daleks* (each time favouring the rear, perhaps because of the damage to the front-right door).

A scene of the TARDIS materialising on Ravolox was recorded for the opening segment of *The Trial of a Time Lord* and, although cut from the final episodes, this shows Box 2 was taken on location. The crack in the front right-hand door was gone but rather than a repair this might indicate the door was replaced with one of the old ones from Box 3, which was fitted with new doors at this time. This certainly seems to be the case on the rear, where markings on the left-hand door's window panes now match those previously seen on Box 3, visible when it arrives on Thoros Beta. Here it was missing its telephone plaque, perhaps forgotten in the hurry to erect the prop before the tide came in – although this was also missing when the box (in dire need of a repaint) was next used for the photocall introducing Sylvester McCoy to the press on Monday 2 March 1987 at the Langham Hotel garden on Cavendish Place.

Box 2 was used only in *Delta and the Bannermen* during McCoy's first season, when it appeared as both the TARDIS and a genuine Police Box. For this it needed a cubbyhole and telephone fitting behind the plaque for the first time – its frame consequently regaining a handle, missing since *The Visitation* – and the windows again indicate this was on the rear doors. It also had brackets added at the top and bottom of the sides to more securely attach them to the roof and base.

From here on Box 2 became the main prop again, used in all but one story each of Seasons 25 and 26. While only briefly seen in the first two serials produced, *Remembrance of the Daleks* and *The Greatest Show in the Galaxy*, it appears much more prominently in *Silver Nemesis*, for which it was repainted in a brighter shade of blue. The rear (still with the crack in the left corner post) was used as the entrance, and for shots of the arrow embedded in it a temporary right-hand door made of wood was fitted. This had a handle but no lock and the width of its panels was slightly narrower. By now some of the 'Police box' sign inserts were held in with four pins at the corners.

The box's appearance in *Battlefield* saw the front favoured once more (markings on the left-hand window panes match those seen as far back as Season 20), although the right-hand door was missing its handle. Next to be recorded was *Survival* when both front and rear faces are seen. Curiously, the back had no centre post; the lock and handle being on the right-hand door suggest the left one had been replaced. This is also evident in *Ghost Light*, the prop's final appearance on television.

After the series ended in 1989, Box 2 was eventually sold to fan Andrew Beech, a former DWAS coordinator and collector of screen-used props and costumes, who owns it to this day. 📞

WHAT ARE ALL THESE KNOBS?

CONSOLE Ciii
1983

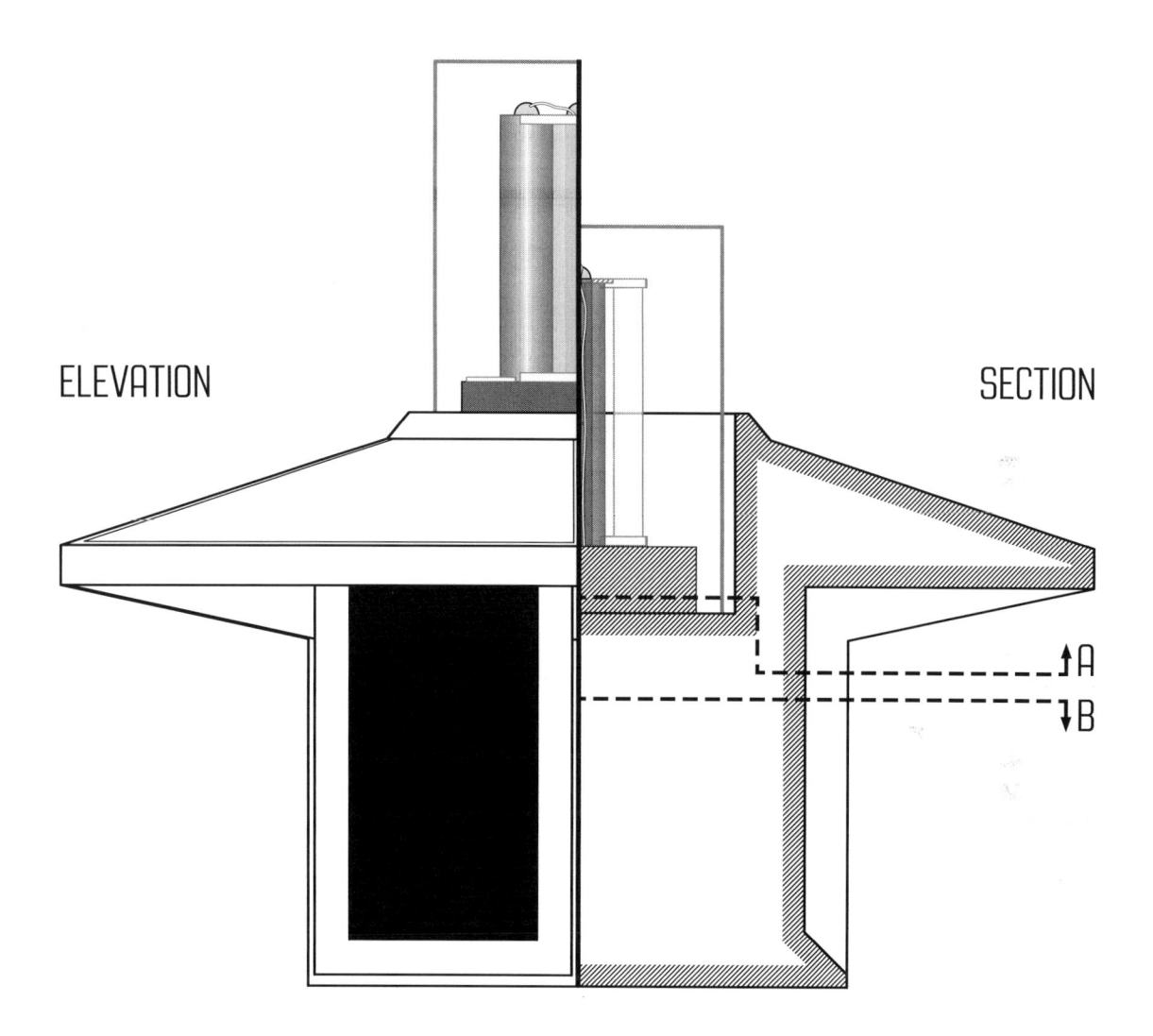

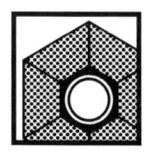

ELEVATION

SECTION

↑A
↓B

Doctor Who's twentieth season was to be the last regular appearance of Console C, although that wasn't known when preparations for recording began and the prop's control panels were given a more thorough overhaul than previous cosmetic changes. While the broad layout and appearance of the controls remained, the overall look was refreshed, almost giving the impression this was a whole new console.

The panels were returned to a lighter grey, with the collar and rim in a paler silvery shade. Those with damage to their bottom corners were covered by triangular pieces also in silver as if to make a feature of them. The most notable additions were the new units at the top of five of the six panels, in place of the silver blocks previously seen. These had a moulded angular shape with a wide opening inset with purple foil.

On panel 1 the flap for the circuit programmer was replaced with a fixed plate fitted with lights and a raised golden square with grooved sides (looking rather like an upside-down ashtray), several of which would be used on other panels. The hole to the left of the red-knobbed lever had a yellow illuminated display fitted into it and later, prior to *Terminus*, a flap for the safety cut-out was added on the right of the panel.

Panel 2 lost the two black dials from its upper plate,

WHAT ARE ALL THESE KNOBS?

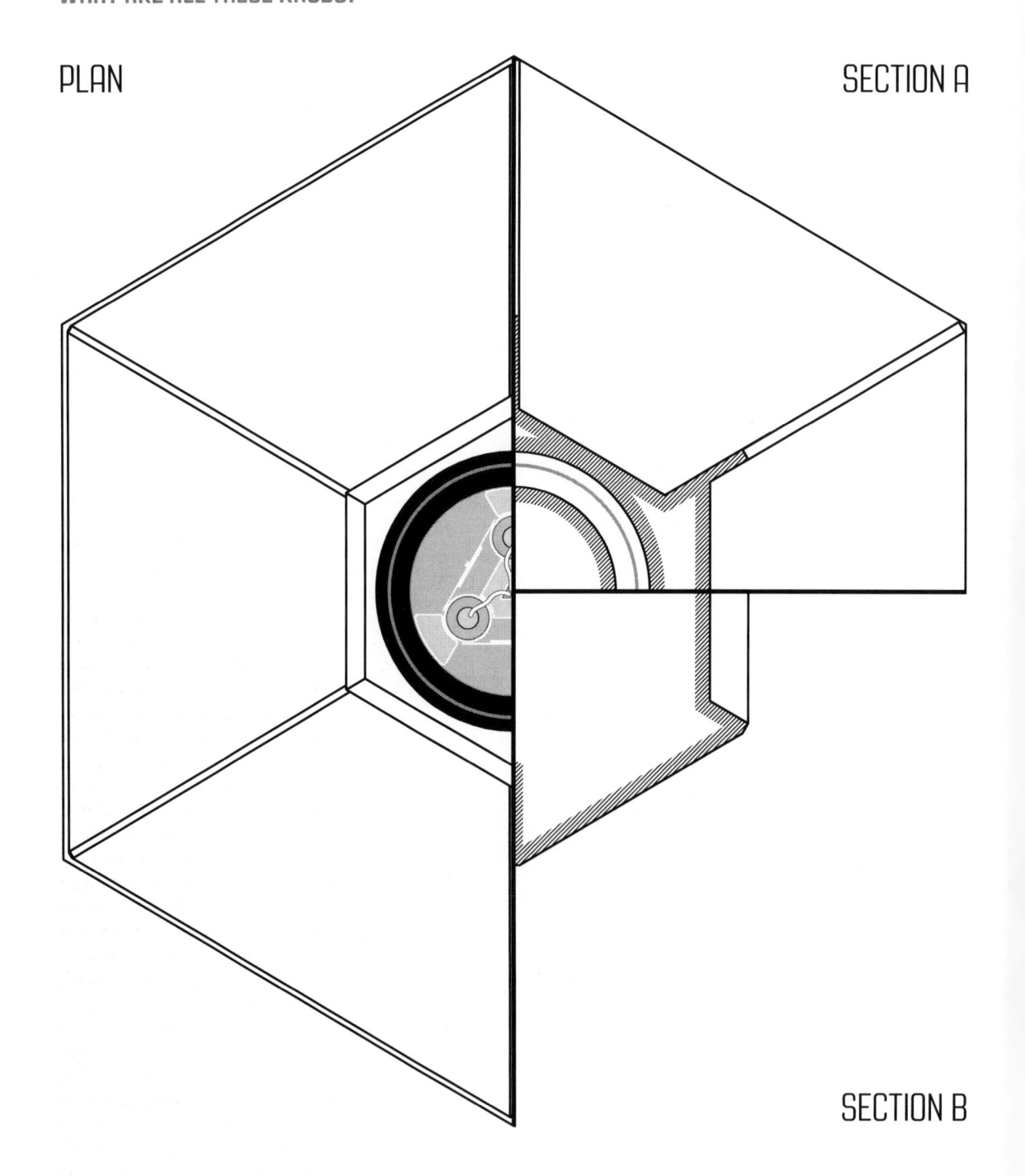

PLAN

SECTION A

SECTION B

WHAT ARE ALL THESE KNOBS?

although one was moved down to the bottom-right corner in place of the red button; the black dome on the opposite side was painted gold. The row of black buttons in the centre had silver foil added to brighten them, although the grille beneath was repainted from red to black. The right-hand quartered display on panel 3 finally lost its cowl (the left-hand one having been missing since 1978) and the buttons above the two large sliders (resprayed gold) were rearranged and another golden square added. Both rotary handles were now missing and the holes from their shaft pins were covered by square stick-on buttons. The two round displays either side of the sliders were enlivened with coloured backgrounds and decorative detailing.

Panel 4 had its main metal plate recreated in a gold-coloured material and while the shape was similar it wasn't exactly the same. The controls here also broadly matched those they replaced but were all new except for the black dial. The top plate was also replaced and the triangular plate on the left lost its buttons but gained new decorations, while the circular display gained a vertical red stripe. The main addition was a fluorescent orange plastic object under a clear dome in the top-left corner, which had a flashing light inside – used when magnetic radiation is detected in *Arc of Infinity*.

Panel 5 was chosen as the location for the illuminated pyramidal recall circuit, to the left of the teleprinter, which had two large black blocks added to its lower plate. Two more golden squares were placed between this and the two outer-edge controls, which had their surrounding black squares trimmed into octagons. The strip of coloured lights at the bottom was replaced with a different strip of unilluminated coloured squares.

Finally panel 6 was given a proper screen again after the one in *Castrovalva* had been replaced with a mock-up display. This was a working television monitor (used in *Arc of Infinity*) within a thick angled frame and a set of buttons on a ridge below. New buttons and blocks were added either side while the bottom-right lever gained a domed surround in gold with black decoration.

Although this was the most significant refit the console had received since it was reintroduced in 1977, the prop was on its last legs. During production of *Enlightenment*, visual effects designer Mike Kelt was exasperated with the state of the console (perhaps not helped by his needing to set off several explosive charges on it) and persuaded producer John Nathan-Turner to commission a new prop. Console C was subsequently put on display, along with the control room walls, at the Longleat celebration weekend in April 1983. Here the panels were finally back in numerical order although with panel 3 facing the main doors (so panels 4 and 5 were largely hidden from the viewing public).

After this the body of the console was scrapped but the control panels and central column were kept in storage – fortuitously as it allowed them to make one last appearance on television in 1985's *The Two Doctors*. For scenes of the Doctor's second incarnation in the TARDIS, these controls were considered a closer match to the 1960s console than the current prop was (even though the post-1983 control room set had to be used, including its anachronistic large wall-mounted scanner screen). With only the panels surviving, the pedestal had to be reconstructed and ended up wider than the original with shallower recesses (which were painted black even though this style wasn't introduced until 1977). This may be because the older-style panels were simply placed on the newer console's metal framework; while the footprint of its pedestal was no larger than the previous prop's, because its underside sloped down from the horizontal, oversized cladding might have been required to hide the frame. Or it's possible this new construction was just made bigger to comfortably cover the existing plinth.

The panels were fitted to the new console's frame in their post-*Logopolis* order: panel 1 facing the main doors then, clockwise, 2, 4, 3, 6 and 5. This meant the last two were mainly presented to the cameras and panel 5 was amended to meet the needs of the script. The remote control device was encased in a hinged clear dome on the right where the green plastic control introduced in *Logopolis* had been. To the left, in place of the punchcard slot added for *State of Decay*, the left-hand large slider from panel 3 was relocated for the Doctor to struggle with. The two golden squares were removed (or had since fallen off), the left one replaced by the fluorescent orange plastic object from panel 4 (without its dome).

The panels went back into storage and eventually were kept by BBC Enterprises, which ran the Longleat and Blackpool exhibitions for many years. They were subsequently salvaged by Mark Barton Hill, who refurbished and rebuilt the whole console using as many of the original parts as had survived. This was put on show at the Doctor Who Experience in Cardiff for several years, as well as appearing in the specially shot trailer for the 50th anniversary special *The Day of the Doctor* and in a new coda for the 2017 DVD/Blu-ray release of *Shada*.

WHAT ARE ALL THESE KNOBS?

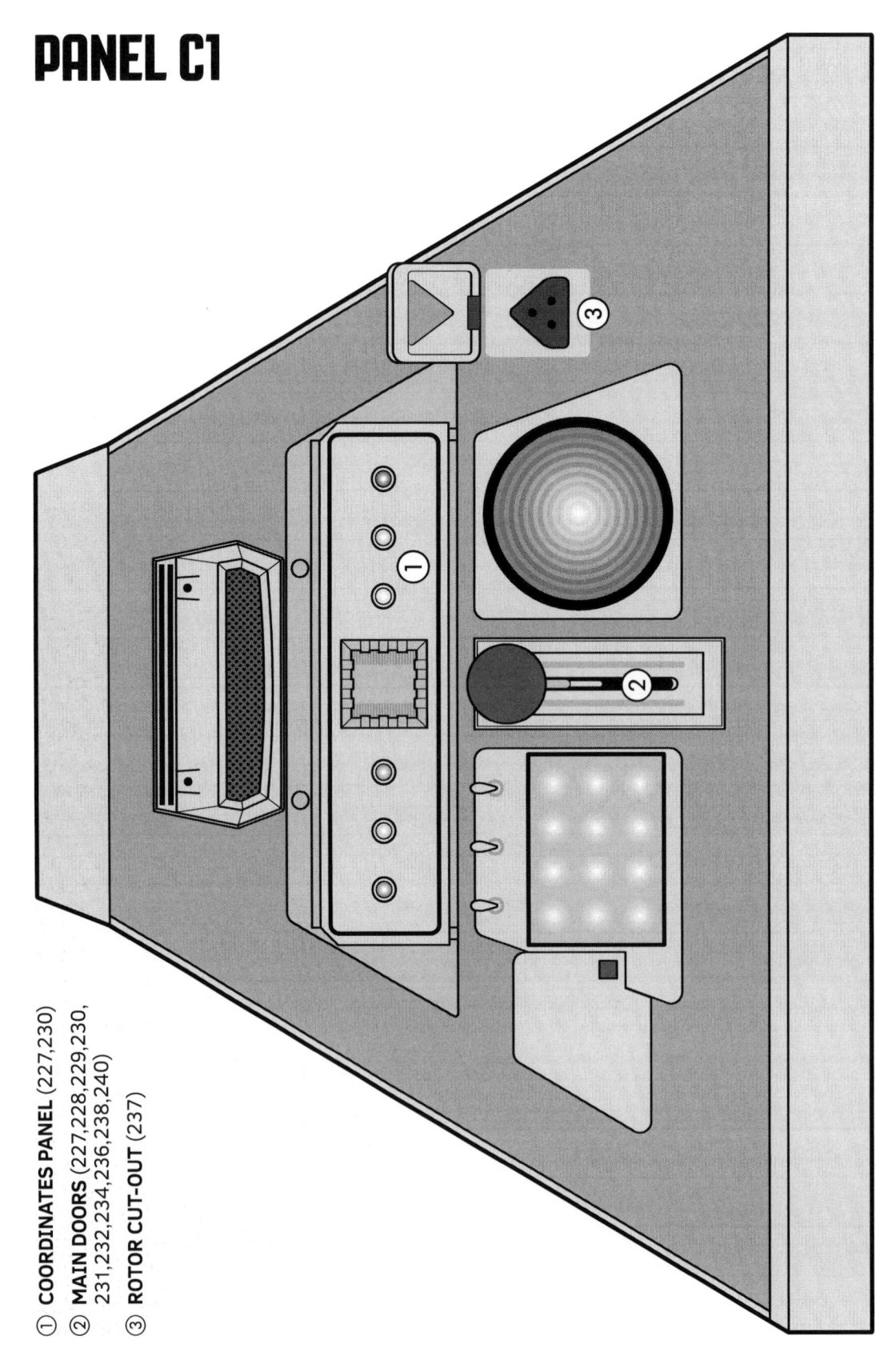

PANEL C1

① **COORDINATES PANEL** (227,230)
② **MAIN DOORS** (227,228,229,230, 231,232,234,236,238,240)
③ **ROTOR CUT-OUT** (237)

PANEL C2

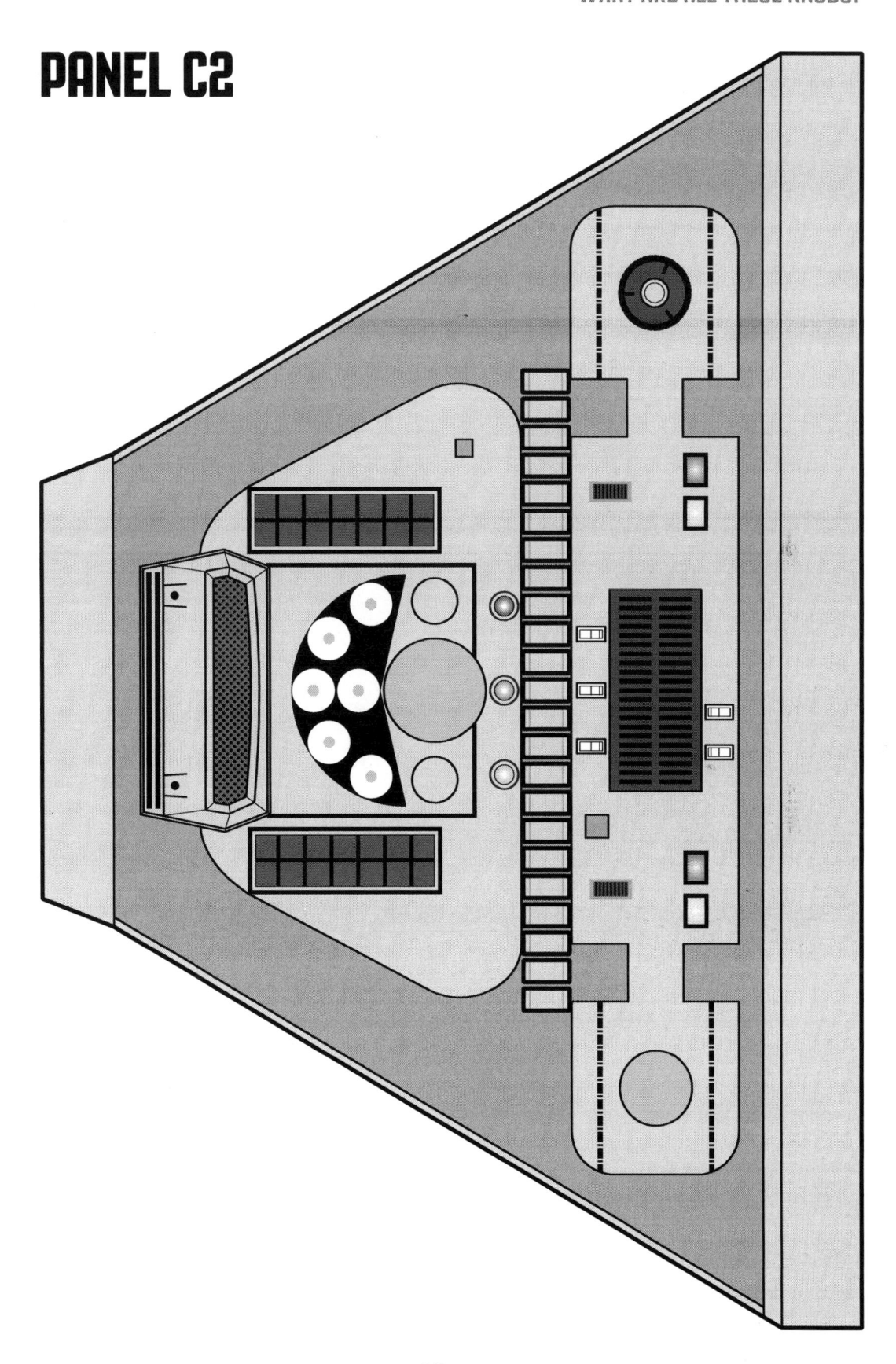

WHAT ARE ALL THESE KNOBS?

WHAT ARE ALL THESE KNOBS?

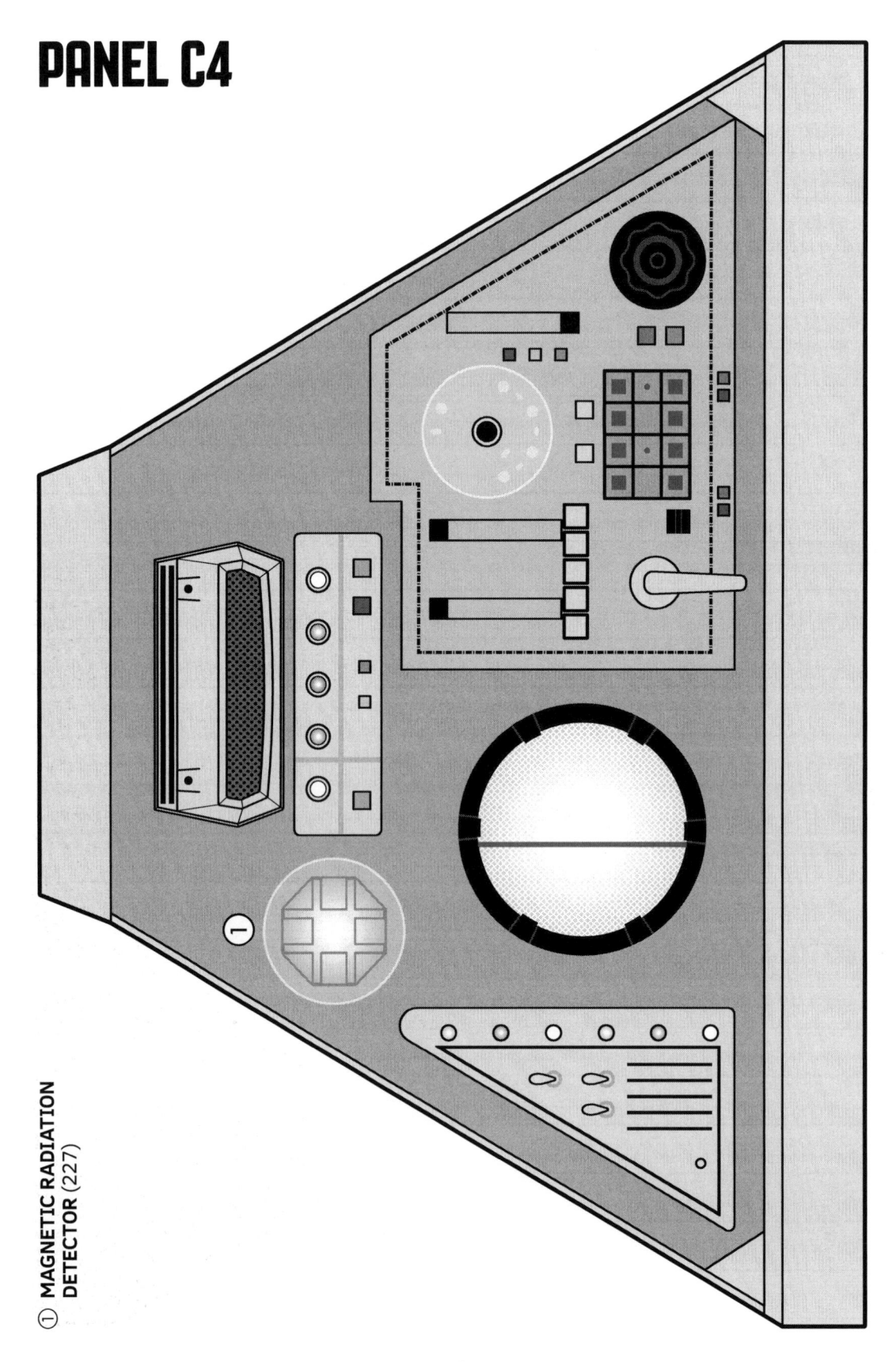

PANEL C4

① **MAGNETIC RADIATION DETECTOR** (227)

WHAT ARE ALL THESE KNOBS?

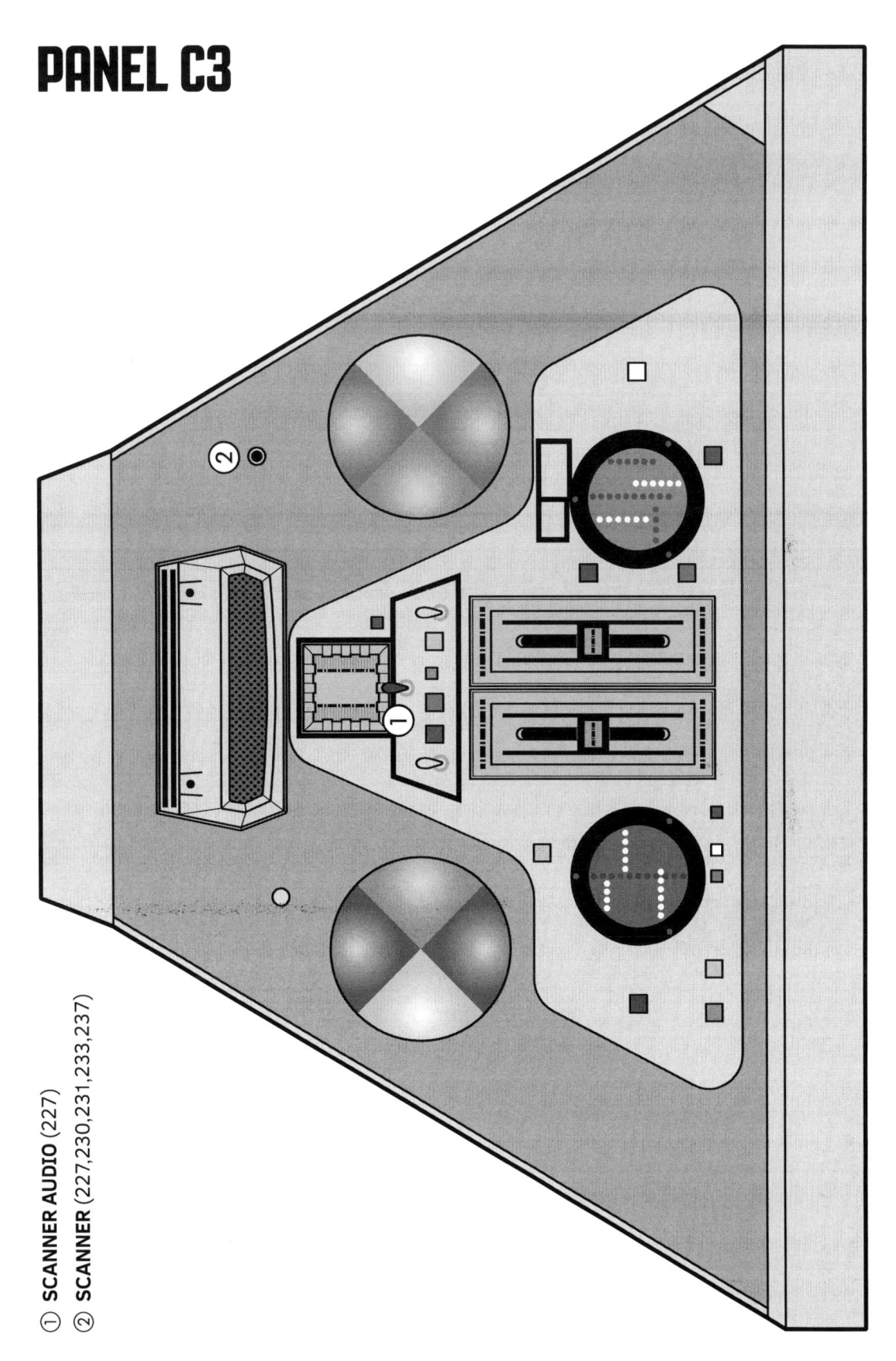

PANEL C3

① **SCANNER AUDIO** (227)
② **SCANNER** (227, 230, 231, 233, 237)

WHAT ARE ALL THESE KNOBS?

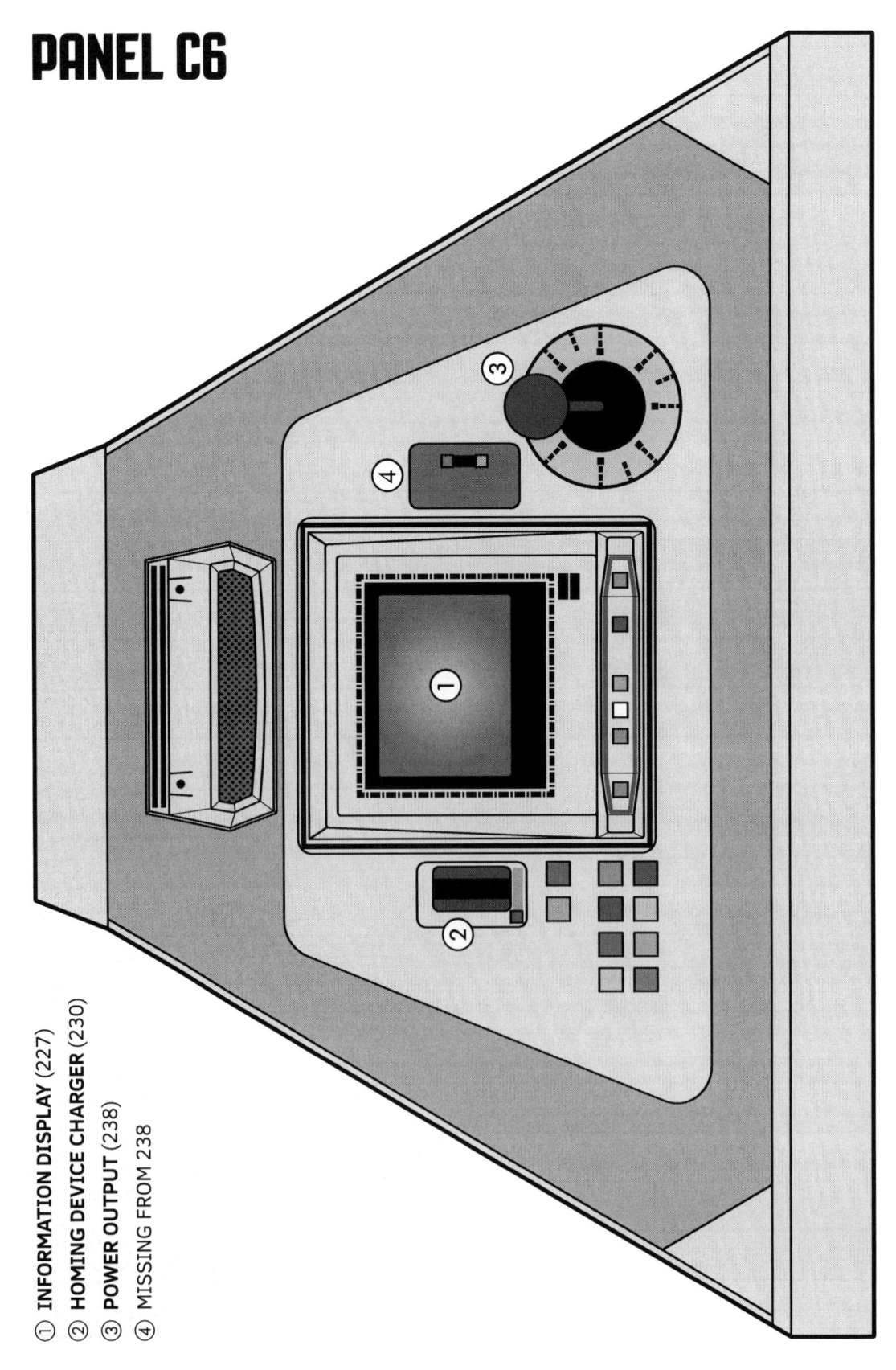

PANEL C6

① **INFORMATION DISPLAY** (227)
② **HOMING DEVICE CHARGER** (230)
③ **POWER OUTPUT** (238)
④ MISSING FROM 238

PANEL C5

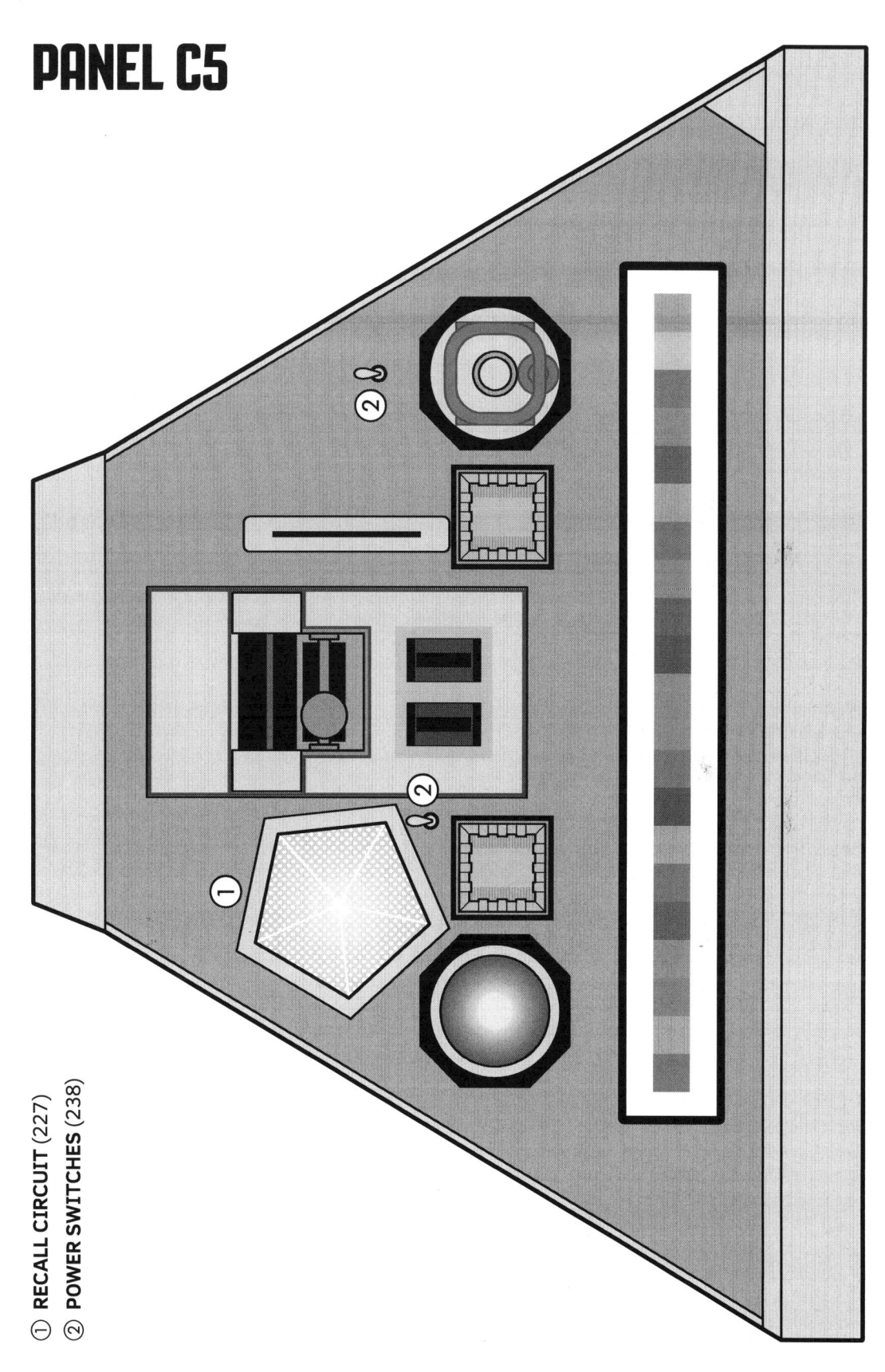

WHAT ARE ALL THESE KNOBS?

① **RECALL CIRCUIT** (227)
② **POWER SWITCHES** (238)

LANDING 227

SPACE Gallifrey, Citadel, security compound
TIME Unknown (after Landing 144)
TRAVELLERS The Doctor, Nyssa
EPISODES Arc of Infinity 1-4

The Doctor and Nyssa repair the audio connection for the scanner so they can hear and see what is outside, which for now is nothing but deep space. Passing through an empty region at star chart reference 92 63.72 C2, called Rondel but colloquially known as the Arc of Infinity, the console detects unusually high levels of quad magnetic radiation, the result of a collapsed Q star. The Doctor tries to direct the TARDIS elsewhere but it is drawn closer and he loses control of the Ship. It converges with the core of the magnetism which breaches the TARDIS, causing the interior dimensions to warp. A figure composed of anti-matter is using the magnetic forces to shield itself and tries to temporally bond with the Doctor – to align its molecules to his so it can exist in the normal universe – but the attempt fails and the creature retreats.

The transgression is detected by the Time Lords and they activate the TARDIS's recall circuit to bring the Ship back to Gallifrey. Under their control, it materialises in a security compound deep within the Citadel. The Doctor and Nyssa emerge to find themselves locked in, so he attempts to override the door control. The door opens but the Doctor doubts his tinkering would have succeeded so quickly and suspects outside help. Worried the Time Lords plan to kill him as the simplest way to prevent the anti-matter creature's bonding with him, he and Nyssa leave before guards can arrive.

The pair are soon caught, however, and returned to the TARDIS by Commander Maxil. The wounded Doctor is taken to Nyssa's bedroom to recover, while Maxil removes the main space-time element from the console to prevent escape. Shortly after, the commander returns to escort the Doctor and Nyssa to an audience with the High Council.

The Doctor is brought back under guard and under sentence of death. Nyssa and an old friend of the Doctor's, Damon, gain permission to visit him. Maxil plants a listening device under the console so the Castellan can eavesdrop, but the three friends trick the commander into letting them retire to Nyssa's room. Maxil does not give them much time to talk and has the Doctor's guests removed. Not long after, he returns to take the Doctor to the termination chamber.

With the Doctor believed dead, Damon is able to gain access to the TARDIS to fit a replacement space-time element. A grieving Nyssa joins him there but they are soon taken my Maxil to see the Castellan while his guards search the Ship for the Doctor.

Nyssa returns alone to wait for the Doctor, who eventually returns and sets the coordinates for Earth, having learned that Tegan is a prisoner of Omega. The Time Lords distract Omega, who is in control of the Matrix, so that the TARDIS can leave Gallifrey without being detected.

- **CONTROLS** The Doctor flicks a switch at the top of panel C3 to reactivate the scanner's audio link, and the button in the top-right corner to close the scanner. The pink dome at top-left of panel C4 flashes to indicate magnetic radiation nearby, although the Doctor takes readings from panel C3 (from the block at the top if what he points to later is any indication) and presses two buttons at the bottom. He sets course with the lights on the upper plate of panel C1 while Nyssa views the screen on panel C6 and presses buttons to its left.
- When the recall circuit it activated, the pentagonal pyramid on panel C5 flashes. The Doctor's statement that it's been used "only twice before in our history" could be a fannish reference to *The War Games* and *The Deadly Assassin* if by "our history" he means his past dealings with the Time Lords rather than his people's entire existence. Only in the former was the TARDIS forcibly returned to Gallifrey, though, and then only because the Doctor had already revealed his location to the Time Lords.
- The space-time element is fitted in the pedestal beneath panel C5, behind a panel within the shallow recess. It comprises two connected blocks filled with circuitry and bridged by a clear tube containing a red fluid.
- The flat face of the pedestal below panel C1 has again lost its top third revealing the mechanism for the circuit programmer (although it's doubtful the new upper plate still opens). This is noticeable when Maxil reaches under to remove the space-time element.
- Although the Doctor moves the left-hand large slider on panel C3 up then down just as the main doors are heard opening, this is him confirming the console isn't working, not opening the doors to let Maxil enter.
- On returning to the TARDIS, the Doctor closes the doors with the usual lever on panel C1, flicks switches to its left and sets coordinates on the plate above. He dematerialises by twisting the two outermost lights on this plate (plus giving the console a thump).

LORE The TARDIS is vulnerable to quad magnetism, which can distort its dimension but decays rapidly.

The Time Lords can remotely take control of a TARDIS and bring it back to Gallifrey by activating the recall circuit, although this has only been done twice before.

Removal of the space-time element stops the TARDIS from travelling (and dims the control room lights).

NOTES Nyssa says it'll be nice to have audio on the scanner "again" but we haven't seen it working since she joined the TARDIS crew. It was last seen playing sound in *The Keeper of Traken* (Landing 195) but was then being controlled by the Keeper; before that it hasn't relayed audio since *City of Death* (Landing 162).

This is the first time we see exposed wiring and circuitry behind a wall roundel, having previously only seen cupboards or controls (see Landing 204). It makes the TARDIS seem more of a mundane machine rather than a mysterious marvel.

When the Doctor switches off the scanner, its closing shutter is again overlaid via CSO. After a cutaway shot of Nyssa, the physical shutter is in place.

- When discussing further repairs, Nyssa says, "The TARDIS used to be in a state of temporal grace, you said. Guns couldn't be fired." The Doctor simply replies, "Nobody's perfect." Is he admitting he lied about it (although why lie if it's no longer working?) or does the 'nobody' refer to the Ship? We've seen that this state may have never existed – see Landings 125 and 144 – and later the Doctor openly confesses to lying in *Let's Kill Hitler* (Landing 519, vol.2).
- For the first time we see the corridor wall to the right of the interior door. It's formed from a section with aligned opaque roundels and the two walls from the 1977 control room with 3½ columns of staggered translucent roundels (in one shot damage to their skirting is clear). The sections are joined by slatted columns. To the left of the door is a plain flat wall, a slatted column (possibly the double-curved slats later used in the bedroom set) and the section with translucent roundels that the Doctor was working at.
- The hatstand in the control room has fallen over before the distortion from the Arc of Infinity strikes. This warping effect was achieved simply by recording the reflection of the action in a sheet of flexible mirrored material then flipping the image electronically. The stand was another new one (although possibly the same as seen in Romana's room in Season 18, repainted brown), first used in *Snakedance*, which was recorded before *Arc of Infinity*.
- A distorted version of the TARDIS's materialisation sound is used for Omega's TARDIS.
- Nyssa's room contains many of the elements last seen in *The Visitation* (Landing 210), including the brass bed, metal hatstand, shelf unit, dressing table with mirror, and wicker chairs. The configuration of walls is different, though, more akin to Romana's room in *Full Circle* (Landing 188): to the right of the plain door is a section with four columns of translucent roundels and one with aligned opaque roundels, while to the left are the double-curved slats then a plain flat wall.
- The Doctor asks for a replacement space-time element "preferably without a recall circuit", which, if achieved, could explain why the Time Lords have to use different measures to ensnare the TARDIS in *The Trial of a Time Lord* (Landing 283). Damon checks "the coding for a type forty time rotor" but there's no indication this refers to the central column.
- Omega's TARDIS interior is, of course, composed of existing wall sections, including the control room interior door, the two 1977 walls with 3½ columns of translucent roundels (abutting but with their half-circles on opposite sides) and the double-curved slats.

LANDING 228

SPACE Earth, Netherlands, Amsterdam
TIME [Early-1980s] (after Landing 226)
TRAVELLERS The Doctor, Nyssa
EPISODES Arc of Infinity 4

During the journey to Earth, the Doctor constructs a device to disrupt the fusion booster that Omega is using to store energy for his transfer from anti-matter to normal matter, while Nyssa calibrates a meter with which to detect the presence of anti-matter.

The TARDIS materialises on target – to the Doctor's surprise – on a bridge over one of Amsterdam's many canals. He and Nyssa head out to search for where Tegan is being held, their only clue: 'JHC'.

When they eventually return to the Ship, Tegan is only too happy to rejoin them in their travels, having lost her job. The Doctor soon comes round to the idea.

- **CONTROLS** Nyssa glances at panel C5 to determine the TARDIS is close to materialising. She operates the scanner with an unseen control at the top of either panel C3 or C4. The Doctor opens the main doors with the usual lever on panel C1.
- **NOTES** The view on the scanner is taken from Prinsengracht looking north along Reguliersgracht to the Kerkstraat bridge. This was filmed on the morning of Wednesday 5 May 1982.
- No date is given for the scenes on Earth but they are after Tegan was left behind in *Time-Flight*. She has lost her job as an air steward, presumably as a result of going AWOL for almost a year, and says she decided to "go and see my favourite cousin [to] cheer myself up", suggesting these events happened in short order. So it could be only a month after she returned to Earth or longer if she's been down in the dumps for a while.
- It's possible the TARDIS remains in Amsterdam for some time. Tegan says her cousin Colin will be out of hospital "in a couple of days" and she is likely to want to stick around to see him onto his plane home, having come all the way from Australia to spend time with him. And she's sure to make certain the Doctor doesn't leave without her this time.
- Indeed, this is what happens in Big Finish's 2016 audio play *The Waters of Amsterdam* by Jonathan Morris, in which the three travellers foil a plot by the water-based Teldak. This dates Tegan's return to 1983.

LANDING 229

SPACE Scrampus system, Manussa
TIME Two days in unknown [future]
TRAVELLERS The Doctor, Nyssa, Tegan
EPISODES Snakedance 1-2

The Doctor teaches Nyssa and Tegan how to read the star charts. He asks one of them to read out some coordinates so he can demonstrate how to set a course, and Tegan selects a destination.

Later, as Tegan sleeps, the TARDIS lands not on Earth as expected but on Manussa, listed in the manual as planet G139901KB in the Scrampus system. It has atmosphere and gravity close to that of Earth (98% and 96% respectively), making it a type 314S planet. The Police Box is hidden behind drapes and crates in a quiet corner near a market street. When Nyssa reads this was once the home world of the Sumaran empire, the Doctor suspects Tegan has been subconsciously manipulated to bring them here.

Tegan wakes from a nightmare, one she has had repeatedly. When she correctly guesses where they have landed, both she and the Doctor realise the Mara is still in her mind, hidden below the threshold of conscious thought. It is stronger when she is asleep but even when awake it can affect her actions. The Doctor uses a small device with an earpiece to put Tegan into a trance and return to the dream so she can describe it to him, but the Mara speaks through her to warn him off. The Doctor adjusts the device to inhibit the brainwaves associated with dreaming and keep the Mara in Tegan's mind dormant. The three travellers then venture out into the town to find the cave carved like a snake's mouth that appeared in her dream.

The Doctor and Nyssa return without Tegan, having lost her in the marketplace and hoping she might find her own way back. Soon impatient with waiting, and not knowing what the Mara wants on Manussa, the pair head out again to seek Tegan and answers.

They return as night falls. The Doctor has a small blue crystal that he believes can transform thought into energy. He and Nyssa try to focus their minds on the gem. There is no reaction so the Doctor readjusts the brainwave inhibitor device to block out external noise, allowing him to concentrate harder. He focuses his thoughts and this time the blue crystal glows with an inner light. Convinced the Mara is planning to use the much larger Great Crystal to bring about its reincarnation, the Doctor tells Nyssa to stay in the TARDIS while he warns the authorities.

The next morning, with no sign of the Doctor, Nyssa leaves the Ship and follows him to the Federator's palace.

The Mara is completely expunged from Tegan's mind and she is keen to leave Manussa after the harm she feels she has done. As the traditional celebrations of the Mara's destruction continue with a renewed purpose, the three travellers slip back to the TARDIS and depart.

- **CONTROLS** The red-knobbed lever on panel C1 is used to open and close the main doors.
- **NOTES** There's nothing explicit to relate events here to Earth's history. Manussa is now classified as a colony, suggesting the Federation that defeated the Mara and took control 500 years earlier was established elsewhere. It rules only three worlds, of which Manussa is its third, so these could all be in the Scrampus system. It's said that Lon's ancestor "defeated the Mara and founded the Federation", that the Mara was destroyed "by the Federation", or it was banished "by the founders of the Federation"; these aren't contradictory but suggest the Federation was founded less than a generation before the Sumaran Empire was vanquished. Perhaps the original Manussan Empire – "a highly civilised people" who "had mastered the techniques of molecular engineering in a zero-gravity environment" – founded a colony on one of the other planets in its system, which survived after the home world fell to the Mara. This group expanded to a second planet and later was able to reclaim its roots, uniting all three worlds as a federation. The Great Crystal is said to be 800 years old, and the reign of the Mara it brought into being ended 500 years previously, yet Ambril says "the Federation record begins some six hundred years" after the collapse of the Manussan civilisation; either the records don't begin until 300 years after the Federation's founding or, more likely, the age of the crystal has been underestimated.
- The bedroom seen here is the same as in *Arc of Infinity* (or rather, vice versa as this story was recorded first) except that the wall behind the bed has roundels rather than being flat. The furniture is generally consistent too, although the dressing table is absent.
- Nyssa finally changes out of the brown velvet Traken outfit that she has worn since joining the TARDIS crew. Presumably the Ship has laundry facilities, therefore, or her fellow travellers would surely have made her change sooner.
- The book Nyssa reads from is a large hardback with a light grey cover and silver foil markings. Nearly five months after recording *Snakedance*, this was used in a publicity photoshoot of Sarah Sutton and Mark Strickson by which time it had the title 'Tardis Manual' awkwardly stencilled on the cover. In this story it appears to be more of a gazetteer containing information about planets.

LANDING 230

SPACE Spaceship in Earth orbit
TIME [Spring] 1983
TRAVELLERS The Doctor, Nyssa, Tegan
EPISODES Mawdryn Undead 1-2

Tegan is fretful that the Mara may still be lurking inside her as she continues to have bad dreams, but the Doctor assures her its influence is gone and her mind is merely processing the trauma. Nevertheless, she asks to return to Earth for a rest in familiar surroundings.

The Doctor concurs but the TARDIS lurches as it nears a spaceship in a warp ellipse: a fixed orbit in time as well as space. With the TARDIS at risk of colliding with the vessel but caught in the warp ellipse too, the Doctor has no option but to land on board. The Police Box materialises at the foot of a staircase in ornate surroundings that Tegan likens to a luxury cruise liner. With no sign of occupants, they start to explore.

They return to the TARDIS and try to dematerialise but the spaceship's transmat capsule has just returned and its signal – which has not cut out owing to a faulty receptor on the planet below – jams the Ship's ability to take off. The Doctor checks circuity under the console and deduces the problem, heading back outside to rectify it, Tegan and Nyssa following. Once they have gone, a schoolboy who arrived in the transmat capsule, Turlough, emerges from behind the Police Box and steps inside.

He is examining the controls when the Doctor returns. Turlough claims to have innocently stumbled into the transmat capsule and the Doctor takes him at his word, for now. He programmes the TARDIS to follow the capsule to Earth once he has taken it there. Nyssa and Tegan are more suspicious of the boy but he leaves with the Doctor before they can quiz him further. After a short wait while the Doctor disconnects the transmat beam, the Ship dematerialises.

- **CONTROLS** When the TARDIS is caught in the warp ellipse, the Doctor presses unseen controls on panel C3 and buttons at bottom-left of panel C6. Nyssa operates the scanner with the button at top-right of panel C3. Trying to move out of the spaceship's way, the Doctor smacks a control on panel C4 and turns another. He pushes up the right-hand large slider on panel C3 and has Nyssa hold it there while he turns an unseen control on panel C2 (likely the bottom-right dial) to materialise.
- The homing device used later is already visible on the console, seemingly plugged into the box to the left of the screen on panel C6 (recharging it, perhaps?).
- When the Doctor hurries back to the control room, he presses two switches on panel C1, one on panel C3 then views the screen on panel C6. He twists the lights on the upper plate of panel C1 to finish setting the coordinates.
- **LORE** Transmat signals can interfere with the TARDIS's ability to dematerialise if both capsules are dimensionally similar. The console sounds an alarm when this happens.
- A TARDIS within a warp ellipse can't escape without programming a temporal deviation (that is, travelling through time).
- **NOTES** Dialogue about the Mara in the first TARDIS scene suggests events follow closely on from *Snakedance*, although Tegan does say she is "still having terrible dreams" so she has required at least one period of sleep since leaving Manussa. It could be that there has been a landing in the meantime, perhaps somewhere peaceful to help Tegan recover.
- The nature of the spaceship's flight path and the warp ellipse are not entirely clear. Are they the same thing or is the latter a phenomenon that has interrupted the former? Mawdryn says, "Every seventy years the beacon guides us to within transmit distance of a planet and…one of our company may leave the ship to seek help," which suggests they travel to different planets hoping to find a civilisation that can cure their mutation. Nyssa says the ship is in "perpetual orbit" and the Doctor learns from a flight indicator that it has "been in orbit three thousand years". The use of the word 'orbit' implies it's on a fixed path around a specific object. So does it pass the same planets repeatedly, calling in to see if one has advanced sufficiently to help its occupants? The Doctor does say, "A vehicle in a warp ellipse would be travelling for a very long time." Yet the warp ellipse is said to indicate "an object in a fixed orbit in time as well as space". That can't mean it's stuck at one point in time relative to the universe outside (like a time loop) as it clearly interacts with different time zones during its visit to Earth; nor can it be that one cycle of its orbit brings it back to its starting time, or the planets it passes would never progress. Time on the ship passes at the same rate as on Earth – the transmat is reported to have beamed down "almost six years" prior to the TARDIS's arrival (which is why the ship scenes must be set in 1983, before June) and the span between younger and older Brigadiers is repeatedly given as six years. Yet there's clearly some time factor involved as it affects the TARDIS and requires a "temporal deviation" to escape. One object trapped near Earth passing "continuously through the same points in time" possibly around 1977 is Axos. Is the warp ellipse a local effect caused by the accidental interaction of this time loop with Mawdryn's ship (or even the TARDIS)?

LANDING 231

SPACE Earth, England, hilltop near Brendon School
TIME 7 June 1977
TRAVELLERS Nyssa, Tegan
EPISODES Mawdryn Undead 2-3

The TARDIS follows the transmat capsule to Earth but even with a dead reckoning alignment in the coordinates the Ship is affected by the warp ellipse. It appears briefly in 1983 when the Doctor is but is then drawn backwards in time and fully materialises in the same location six years earlier.

The Police Box sits in the shadow of trees at the top of a hill on a breezy summer's day. Nearby stands a tall obelisk but there is no sign of the Doctor. Nyssa and Tegan go out to look for him and moments later the transmat capsule materialises. Inside they find a horribly burned man whom they mistake for the Doctor, injured by the transmat process. They drag him into the TARDIS and try to keep him warm. Tegan checks the capsule again for Turlough but he is not to be found and Nyssa fears he may have been atomised. With no Zero Room to help restore the man, Tegan decides to seek help from the building in the valley below, and takes a homing device.

While Nyssa waits, the man recovers, his body healing incredibly rapidly. She thinks the Doctor may be regenerating again, but when he demands to be taken back to the spaceship she begs him to wait for Tegan and goes outside to look for her. Fortunately she is just that minute returning up the hill with the Doctor's old friend Brigadier Lethbridge-Stewart. Tegan's suspicion that the man is not the Doctor after all is strengthened when they find him fully restored but not as human in appearance, with his skull split open and his brain exposed.

The man, Mawdryn, knows of the Time Lords and their regenerative powers so is able to play on the others' doubts about his identity enough to convince them to help him. He insists they take the

TARDIS back to the spaceship and Nyssa is about to operate the controls when the communications system detects a transmission from 1983. It soon cuts out, so despite Tegan's fears Nyssa dematerialises the Ship.

- **CONTROLS** Nyssa again uses the button at top-right of panel C3 to operate the scanner and the usual lever to open the main doors. She twists the right-most light on the upper plate of panel C1 either to "activate sequential regression" as Mawdryn instructs or to dematerialise.
- **NOTES** Turlough calls Brendon an "English public school" in *Planet of Fire*. The location for filming was at Trent Park in North London but fictionally the school might be somewhere more remote if the Brigadier wanted to keep a low profile (see below).
- Although the 25th anniversary of Queen Elizabeth's accession to the throne was on 6 February 1977, the main public celebrations for the Silver Jubilee were on a special bank holiday on Tuesday 7 June. It's the Doctor who comes up with the date but the Brigadier doesn't correct him. As he's trying to pinpoint exactly when the TARDIS landed and later gets a signal through to it, he must be right.
- Why does the TARDIS arrive in the wrong time? Turlough suggests a "tangential deviation coming out of the warp ellipse" but the Doctor disagrees. He later says he may have "miscalculated the offset" so it could be his fault. Or is it because the transmat beam receptor he tries to repair explodes so the TARDIS locks onto the original signal of the transmat capsule beaming down in 1977?
- Although the Police Box does achieve full solidity in 1983 for a split second, this can't be counted as a proper landing. Its materialisation sound doesn't finish before the take-off sound kicks in, and Nyssa and Tegan are unaware of any pause in their journey so we can assume the central column doesn't stop then start moving again.
- The scanner's physical shutter is recorded opening for once, rather than being superimposed. The angle of view doesn't match the Police Box's position relative to the obelisk, and the second time it's operated the view has changed to one looking down the hill.
- Why does Tegan take a homing device when the obelisk beside the TARDIS is plainly visible from a distance?
- As any fan knows, this story contradicts previous continuity (such as it was) by stating the Brigadier retired from UNIT in 1976. For this to be true, the Doctor's exile on Earth must have been contemporary with those stories' original broadcast, even though the intention was they were set slightly into the future; most notably, Sarah Jane Smith said she hailed from 1980 (see Landing 114). It's not as if there weren't already inconsistencies. There's a strong argument that *The Invasion* is set in 1979 (see Landing 63), which would mean the Doctor's entire exile was between then and 1980. So fudges already had to be made in dating the UNIT era but this is the story that really put the Tharil among the Chronovores. There's no way to satisfactorily produce a single timeline that fits all the on-screen 'facts'; something has to be ignored or explained away. Some fans happily take the UNIT stories as broadly contemporary with their transmission, disregarding the vague dating of a couple of 1960s stories and Sarah's claim in favour of the more specific dates in *Mawdryn Undead*. Others see this story as the outlier to be explained given the 1970s production teams' intention that the UNIT stories were set around five years ahead. My preferred theory is that the Doctor took a recently retired Brigadier from the early-1980s on a trip in the TARDIS but accidentally returned him to 1976. Realising he mustn't interfere with his past, the Brigadier hid himself away teaching maths at a minor public school. Shortly after, an encounter with his own future caused a mental breakdown and he came to believe his own cover story, until he reached that same future and regained his memories. He soon organised a reunion to catch up with friends he hadn't seen for several years (although for them it had been fewer), as seen in *The Five Doctors*. Note the 'incongruous' backstory is only given by the older, muddled Brigadier in *Mawdryn Undead*; his retirement and the whereabouts of Benton and Harry could be an attempt to make sense of his patchy recollection. His younger self may be keen to help Tegan because he's hoping her Doctor will be able to take him back to his proper time, but they never meet before he has his breakdown. There are, of course, (many) other theories.

LANDING 232

SPACE Spaceship in Earth orbit
TIME Shortly after Landing 230
TRAVELLERS Nyssa, Tegan, Mawdryn, Brigadier Lethbridge-Stewart
EPISODES Mawdryn Undead 3-4

The Police Box materialises back on the orbiting spaceship in the same location and time as its last visit. Mawdryn orders the others to stay while he goes outside but Tegan refuses to let him leave alone in case he reactivates the transmat beam and grounds the TARDIS again. He starts to weaken and begs for release; the Brigadier and Nyssa relent and open the doors. Shortly after, however, the Brigadier decides to follow and keep an eye on him.

Tegan tires of waiting and is about to go looking for the Doctor when he turns up by himself, having used the homing device that the Brigadier took from Tegan in 1977 to enable the transmat capsule to follow the TARDIS back to the spaceship. He brought Turlough and an older Brigadier from 1983 with him, although he has now lost them both. When he learns the Brigadier from 1977 is also aboard, he insists both iterations must be found and kept apart, so everyone leaves to look for them. Turlough therefore finds the TARDIS empty and attempts to operate the controls but his master the Black Guardian appears and orders the boy to find the younger Brigadier and keep him away from his older self.

⬛ The Doctor, Tegan, Nyssa and the older Brigadier return intending to leave Mawdryn and his associates to their self-inflicted fate. Hoping Turlough is somewhere aboard too, the Doctor prepares to take off when Nyssa spots the boy approaching on the scanner. The Doctor intercepts him outside and instructs him to find the younger Brigadier and use the transmat capsule, still attuned to the TARDIS, to travel to the centre of the Ship and stay there until the older version has been returned to 1983. The Doctor returns inside and takes off.

- ◉ **CONTROLS** Both Nyssa and the Doctor operate the main doors with the usual lever on panel C1. When trying to work the TARDIS, Turlough flicks a switch on the same panel and others on panels C2 and C3. Prior to dematerialising, the Doctor turns the dial at bottom-right of panel C2 and flicks switches on the left of panel C1.
- ▤ **NOTES** The console wobbles noticeably when Turlough thumps it while talking to the Black Guardian.
- ▤ When the Doctor first tries to leave he pulls the lever to close the main doors and we hear them whirr, but you can just see over the Brigadier's shoulder that they don't actually shut until moments later. To be fair, this wouldn't have been visible on televisions at the time.
- ▤ We know the TARDIS interior is finite as a quarter of it was jettisoned (see Landing 204), which means it's feasible it has a centre for the transmat capsule to beam to. In *Journey to the Centre of the TARDIS* this is implied to be the engine room, but here we might presume the Doctor simply means somewhere deep within the Ship away from the control room.

LANDING 233

SPACE Spaceship in Earth orbit
TIME As above
TRAVELLERS The Doctor, Nyssa, Tegan, Brigadier Lethbridge-Stewart
EPISODES Mawdryn Undead 4

The Doctor sets course for Brendon School but passing out of the warp ellipse involves the TARDIS moving through time. As it does do, Nyssa and Tegan begin to age fast.

⬛ The Doctor reverses course and the women return to their normal state as the TARDIS lands back aboard the spaceship, watched by Mawdryn and his gathered fellow scientists. The Doctor deduces that Nyssa and Tegan have been infected with a viral side-effect of Mawdryn's condition, which is inhibiting their ability to time travel.

▲ Seemingly unable to escape the warp ellipse without programming a temporal deviation and harming the women, the Doctor tries another tack involving reversing the polarity of a neutron flow. The younger Brigadier finds his way back to the Ship just in time to see it dematerialise without him.

- ◉ **CONTROLS** When first escaping the warp ellipse the Doctor flicks a switch at the top of panel C3; to reverse course he reaches across to unseen controls on panels C1 and C2. After landing he presses the button at top-right of panel C3 to operate the scanner – the sound effect of it opening is omitted but is played when he closes the scanner moments later.
- ▤ **NOTES** The Brigadier watching the TARDIS disappear is achieved by a split-screen effect, with the Police Box overlaid on the right of the picture while Nicholas Courtney runs onto the empty set, pauses while he probably waits for a signal that the TARDIS has been faded out, then proceeds forwards.

LANDING 234

SPACE Spaceship in Earth orbit
TIME As above
TRAVELLERS The Doctor, Nyssa, Tegan, Brigadier Lethbridge-Stewart
EPISODES Mawdryn Undead 4

⬛ Travelling out of the warp ellipse in the opposite direction simply produces an opposite effect, Nyssa and Tegan reverting to childhood. The Doctor is forced to return to Mawdryn's ship once more in order to restore them to their correct age.

As the TARDIS materialises, the console sounds an alert that the transmat capsule is trying to beam into the Ship but cannot do so while it is aboard the alien vessel, instead returning to its terminal on the bridge.

With no way to leave the spaceship without harming Nyssa and Tegan, the travellers all go outside to face Mawdryn. The only cure for the women is the same as that for the alien scientists: for the Doctor to pass on his regenerative ability at the cost of no longer being able to regenerate himself. For his friends, he submits and they depart for the laboratory.

The transmat having failed to return him to Earth, the younger Brigadier returns to the TARDIS but finding it empty he heads out again to search for the Doctor.

The time differential of the two iterations of the Brigadier is short-circuited when they touch, releasing a huge burst of energy (possibly from the TARDIS). Afterwards, Turlough slips aboard and hides, believing his bargain with the Black Guardian is over and that the Doctor is his best chance of getting away from Earth.

Nyssa brings a dazed older Brigadier to the Ship and takes him well away from the control room. The Doctor and Tegan then return with the unconscious younger Brigadier and take off as the spaceship begins to destabilise.

- ◉ **CONTROLS** Red-knobbed lever opens main doors.
- ▤ **NOTES** The console noticeably wobbles again when the Doctor discusses being stuck on the spaceship.
- ▤ Oops! During the journey when Nyssa and Tegan revert to children, the control room hum remains the soft tremolo of the 'stationary' sound effect, rather than the higher hum of the 'in-flight' noise.

- Again, when the Doctor tells Nyssa to take the Brigadier "right to the centre" of the TARDIS he must mean somewhere secure rather than the absolute centre point – assuming she knows where that is, it would surely take a long time to get there and back.
- The Doctor says the energy discharge came "from the TARDIS really", although "the two Brigadiers just shorted-out the time differential". This might suggest the Ship was maintaining or restraining a temporal potential energy within the Brigadiers, as a consequence of it transporting one from 1977 to 1983. Alternatively, because the other Brigadier arrived via transmat, was the potential actually within these two capsules? If the discharge was between them, it might explain why the spaceship proceeds to destabilise and explode, and why in other situations where two iterations of the same person touch – Rose in *Father's Day* or Amy in *The Big Bang* – there isn't a discharge, because they weren't brought into proximity by such mechanical means. (Note that in the latter story, two iterations of the same sonic screwdriver do spark when touched as they were present owing to the TARDIS and a vortex manipulator.)

LANDING 235

SPACE Earth, England, hilltop near Brendon School
TIME Shortly after Landing 231
TRAVELLERS The Doctor, Nyssa, Tegan, two Brigadiers Lethbridge-Stewart, Vizlor Turlough
EPISODES Mawdryn Undead 4

The TARDIS materialises at its previous location beside the obelisk on the hill. The Doctor and Tegan carry out the younger Brigadier originally transported from 1977 and lay him gently on the grass. Not far away, the school's medical doctor calls out as he looks for the retired solider.

The two travellers dash back into the Ship and it dematerialises just as the Brigadier comes round and sits up. He will recall it leaving even though his memory is addled by the temporal discharge.

LANDING 236

SPACE Earth, England, hilltop near Brendon School
TIME As Landing 230
TRAVELLERS The Doctor, Nyssa, Tegan, Brigadier Lethbridge-Stewart, Turlough
EPISODES Mawdryn Undead 4

The older Brigadier is allowed back to the control room after his short tour of the Ship with Nyssa. The same cause of his earlier memory loss has restored his faculties. The TARDIS lands on the hilltop again but now six years later.

The Brigadier's goodbyes are cut short when the others realise Turlough cannot have left the spaceship in the transmat capsule as planned and must still be aboard. The Doctor, Nyssa and Tegan hurry back into the TARDIS intending to rescue the boy, only to find him examining the console. The Doctor agrees to let him come with them.

- **CONTROLS** Tegan gets the chance to open the main doors for once, using the usual lever.
- **NOTES** So the Doctor is prepared to travel to a spaceship that's about to explode in order to rescue Turlough, a slippery character he's barely said hello to, but wasn't willing to do the same to save Adric? Is Peter Grimwade trolling Eric Saward?
- The TARDIS isn't seen departing at the end of the story, and with Turlough safe it's possible the travellers rejoin the Brigadier outside after their interrupted farewell. The Doctor perhaps spends some time with him to make sure he's fully recovered and to reminisce about old times (now the Brigadier can remember them).

LANDING 237

SPACE Space, docked to Lazar ship
TIME Unknown [future]
TRAVELLERS The Doctor, Nyssa, Tegan, Turlough
EPISODES Terminus 1,4

Turlough is still under the dominion of the Black Guardian, who directs the boy to a roundel deep in the TARDIS behind which are safety switches that he deactivates. Tegan comes looking for him so she can show him to his bedroom, Adric's old room. She has suspicions about her new travelling companion and the pair bicker, so she leaves to express her concerns to Nyssa. Turlough sneaks into the empty control room and, instructed by the Black Guardian, yanks the space-time element from its housing beneath the console.

The TARDIS begins to break up, areas of fizzing dimensional instability appearing in the vicinity of Nyssa's room. The Doctor arrives in the control room and notes the rotor is jamming so activates the safety cut-out. He uses the scanner to contact Nyssa and finds she is completely surrounded by the instability. However, the TARDIS locks on to a nearby spaceship and partially merges with it in order to stabilise. One wall of Nyssa's room transforms into that of the vessel and swings opens. The Doctor urges her to go through to escape the instability. The TARDIS quickly recovers and the opening begins to close but the Doctor arrives just in time to jam it with a chair. He enters the spaceship to retrieve Nyssa and, against orders, Tegan and Turlough follow him.

Some time later, after the spaceship has docked with the large Terminus complex at the centre of the known universe, Turlough rediscovers the section of wall that leads back to the TARDIS and returns to the control room hoping to escape alone. However, the Black Guardian is displeased with his failure to kill the Doctor and stuns the boy. He wakes just before the Doctor and Tegan return, having reluctantly yielded to Nyssa's desire to stay behind and help reform the running of Terminus.

- **CONTROLS** The space-time element is now behind a hatch in the pedestal below panel C6. This is a full-depth recess rather than one of the false-front shallow recesses used to hide circuitry in *Time-Flight* and *Arc of Infinity*, so the base of the console must have been modified. An alarm sounds as other components are removed to gain access to the space-time element. The prop matches that seen in *Arc of Infinity* (Landing 227). Once removed, the central column stops moving and its internal lights flash.
- The side of the pedestal with the flat face, usually beneath panel C1, is here below panel C3.
- The rotor cut-out is a removable three-pin plug beneath a (newly added) flap on the right of panel C1. This causes the lights to go out in the central column.
- Prior to operating the cut-out, the Doctor twists his hand on the left side of panel C2 as if turning a control, and Dick Mills adds in a sound effect. But there's no longer a rotary control in this area and it may just be Peter Davison placing his hand on the desk as he walks around it rather than deliberately operating a control.
- The Doctor operates the scanner with the button at top-right of panel C3 then refocuses it on the interior of the Ship using unseen controls on panel C2 and, seemingly, touching the top unit on panel C1 (are these telepathic inputs?). As the disintegration continues he presses buttons on panel C1 including that on the bottom-left block. Later, when Turlough tries to steal the Ship, he flicks a switch at the top of panel C3 and prepares to use the right-hand large slider.

- **LORE** Operating two blue switches behind a roundel in one of the corridors enables the removal of the space-time element during flight. Doing so causes the central column to jam and the TARDIS to begin breaking up. A fail-safe system enables the Ship to lock on to a nearby spaceship in order to stabilise itself.
- If the central column, or rotor, jams then a component can be removed from the console to cut off the power to it safely. (In *The Visitation* a thump on the console was enough to unstick the central column so it probably depends on the cause of the jam.)
- The scanner can be refocused to show areas inside the TARDIS, with audio communication also.

- **NOTES** Although Turlough hasn't spent time exploring the TARDIS before now, and presumably hasn't slept in it as he's yet to be allocated a room, there could have been a landing or two since leaving Earth. We've previously seen the Doctor and friends go through several consecutive adventures apparently without any rest, or they might have spent a night on a planet. Turlough and Tegan, who barely met during *Mawdryn Undead*, have had time to size each other up and decide they are "unreliable" and "rude" respectively.
- The corridors are again comprised of walls and columns from stock, although arranged at less regular angles than in previous stories. They include a section from the 1977 control room with half-circles down the right-hand edge, a section with four columns of staggered translucent roundels, a narrower one with three columns of roundels, and two with three columns of aligned opaque circles. One of these last has a roundel (centre column, second up) that folds down on a motorised hinge at the bottom to reveal circuitry and illuminated pushbuttons. These are not the same workings as last seen behind a roundel in *Arc of Infinity*.
- This is the first time the circles patterning the TARDIS walls are referred to in dialogue as "roundels", a descriptor coined by fans and now incorporated into the programme itself.
- Adric's old room is pleasingly faithful to its last appearance in *Earthshock* (Landing 215), although very slightly smaller and the wall bracings and trim have been painted brown instead of white. The star chart is still on the wall and the arrangement of furniture is largely the same (a black trolley has been added and some storage cases are gone), but most of the knick-knacks are different. The door has lost its ring and has a different handle but retains the ridged panels around the outside. The adjacent wall now has staggered translucent roundels rather than aligned opaque ones.
- The room Nyssa is practising her chemistry in is different from the previously seen bedrooms in *Arc of Infinity* (Landing 227) and *The Visitation* (Landing 210), yet some of the same furniture is present: the brass beds, dressing table, wicker chair and metal shelves.
- The space-time element was previously removed safely in *Arc of Infinity* when the TARDIS was stationary; removing it while in flight is understandably more dangerous. The break-up of the Ship's interior dimensions may be a direct result of this, or caused by the stresses of being shunted out of the Vortex improperly.
- The corridor in which Tegan finds the Doctor has the same arrangement of walls on one side as the control room, indicating this was recorded on that set with an extra wall section on the left to obscure the console.
- The Doctor says, "The rotor's jamming," while looking towards the central column, the first on-screen indication that they are one and the same (although still not 'time rotor').
- It's not entirely clear whether the safety cut-out just disables the central column and the fail-safe that allows the TARDIS to lock on to the nearest spaceship is an automatic response to break-up, or if activating the former leads to the latter. The Doctor is initially alarmed that "the outside universe is breaking through" but later knows about the fail-safe – was he worried it wouldn't kick in fast enough or just, as he says (somewhat flippantly), that "it never worked before"? We might assume the Ship itself chooses Nyssa's room as the location of the interface with the spaceship deliberately to save one of its occupants. The section of spaceship wall appears to gain some chameleon properties from the TARDIS, and there's no evidence it was built as a doorway (it doesn't look like the vessel's internal doors nor the exit hatch) so its opening may by the Ship performing some structural reconfiguration to enable Nyssa to escape. The dimensional instability vanishes as soon as the TARDIS merges with the spaceship so

- presumably it just needed some contact with a real-word object to restabilise itself.
- Turlough must replace the space-time element before the TARDIS can detach from the spaceship. The Doctor is sure to investigate what went wrong, so does Turlough leave the element slightly loose to imply it was accidentally dislodged not deliberately removed? Perhaps the Doctor concludes Damon didn't fit it correctly back on Gallifrey.

LANDING 238

SPACE Solar system, near Venus, The Shadow, hold; hidden in Doctor's mind; released to wheelhouse
TIME Unknown
TRAVELLERS The Doctor, Tegan, Turlough
EPISODES Enlightenment 1,4

The TARDIS begins losing power and the Doctor determines it is not leaking away but being tapped. He initially blocks the demand on energy but when the White Guardian tries to contact him the Doctor realises he must increase the power output so that the ethereal being can complete his message. The Guardian appears and warns of danger, giving the Doctor a set of coordinates. For a moment everything freezes as the Black Guardian manifests to mock the Doctor. Time flows again and Turlough, fearing the smoking console will explode, cuts the power.

The Doctor enters the coordinates – galactic north six degrees by nine zero seven seven – which include a time override that causes the TARDIS to lurch then materialise instantly. To all appearances it is in the dark wooden hold of an Edwardian sailing ship, the vessel even rolling as if at sea; in fact it is in space, travelling through Earth's solar system under the command of Eternals, beings from beyond time. The Doctor and Turlough take torches and explore, leaving Tegan to wait for further contact from the White Guardian.

He appears and Tegan boosts the power but he can only warn, "Winner takes all." As the console sparks, Tegan notices she is being watched from the scanner screen by a naval officer, who suddenly drops out of view. She ventures outside to make sure he is not hurt but is captured and taken away.

The captain of the ship, Striker, senses the Doctor's concern for keeping the TARDIS out of the Eternals' hands and amuses himself by hiding it within the Doctor's mind. Later, he releases it so the Doctor can prevent his rival, Captain Wrack, from winning their race. The Police Box reappears in the ship's wheelhouse and the Doctor enters alone and dematerialises.

- **CONTROLS** As in *Terminus*, the side of the pedestal with a flat face is under panel C3 and that below panel C6 has the hatch behind which was the space-time element (here hanging open). The Doctor works beneath panel C5.
- While gauging the power drain, the Doctor operates unseen controls on panel C4. When turning up the power, he throws the two flick switches on panel C5 repeatedly. The power lever he has Tegan operate is that at bottom-right of panel C6 and, as the central column smokes, Turlough presses two buttons below the screen. The Doctor isn't seen entering the coordinates but he's standing at panel C1 when sound effects are heard. Turlough is nowhere near the console when declaring the air to be breathable but looks towards panel C6, so its screen may be displaying atmospheric conditions. After landing, the Doctor flicks the right-hand switch at the top of the plate on panel C3 and opens the main doors with the usual lever.
- The metal surround for the punchcard slot on panel C5 has been broken by this point. On panel C6 the unit to the right of the screen is missing and the bar below the screen has gained two blue buttons.
- **NOTES** Although the Black Guardian ends the previous story telling Turlough he is on his last chance to kill the Doctor, the villain is prone to hyperbole so there could have been further landings during which Turlough has failed to do the deed. There is also mention of his running away on Terminus, so it's unlikely there have been many stop-offs since.
- As the Doctor works under the console, Tegan is shining a torch to help him. Yet when she moves it away and turns it off, the light on the pedestal takes several moments to fade out, betraying the fact a studio lamp was used to augment the weak torchlight.
- The chess board and pieces Turlough plays with are different from previous sets seen in *The Sun Makers* (Landing 140) and *The Androids of Tara* (Landing 151).
- The corridor beyond the interior door consists of the double-curved slats, a 1977 control room wall (half-roundels on the left), a slatted column and one of the four-circles-wide walls.
- It's suggested Marriner has climbed onto the Police Box roof and can see into the control room via the lamp, although his hand and body movements don't really match this and he could just be looking through one of the windows. The apparent fall could be a feint to lure Tegan outside.

LANDING 239

SPACE Solar system, The Buccaneer, below decks
TIME As above
TRAVELLERS The Doctor
EPISODES Enlightenment 4

The TARDIS makes the short trip to Wrack's galleon The Buccaneer, materialising outside the power room from where the captain summons the aid of her master, the Black Guardian.

Moments later, after a struggle with Wrack and her first mate Mansell in which the two Eternals are ejected into space, the Doctor and Turlough pass the Police Box on their way to the wheelhouse to bring the ship into harbour and win the race themselves.

After Tegan has crossed from The Shadow and Turlough has banished the Black Guardian, freeing him from their contract, the three travellers return to the TARDIS to fulfil the boy's wish to return to his home planet.

LANDING 240

SPACE Earth, England, by Fitzwilliam Castle; transported into castle bailey, then into main hall
TIME 4 March 1215
TRAVELLERS The Doctor, Tegan, Turlough
EPISODES The King's Demons 1-2

The TARDIS materialises in the meadow outside the walls of Fitzwilliam Castle, where a jousting tournament is in progress. The Police Box's noisy arrival startles the horses, as well as the assembled nobles and peasants, although not their king, John. Inside, the Doctor senses something is awry as he did not set the Ship to come here, and decides to take a quick look outside, followed by his two friends.

They are greeted as demons by the king and invited to join him in viewing the joust. The monarch's champion Sir Gilles charges Lord Ranulf's son Hugh and dislodges him from his horse. The Doctor persuades the king to spare the young noble's life, to the boy's dishonour. With the tournament over, they all repair to the castle.

Not long after, Sir Gilles supervises as the TARDIS is dragged onto a cart and transported into the confines of the castle walls.

Later, men-at-arms manhandle the Police Box into the main hall. When the Doctor and Tegan are brought in and questioned about the whereabouts of Ranulf's cousin Sir Geoffrey, Tegan offers to release him from the "blue engine" but once inside she dematerialises the Ship. The distraction allows the Doctor to escape his captors.

- **CONTROLS** The Doctor reads the date from panel C1, possibly the display to the left of the centre lever. He doesn't appear to operate the scanner when it's heard opening but Turlough has just moved around the console so he presumably does it out of shot. The Doctor uses the usual lever to open the main doors.
- When she returns to the TARDIS, Tegan closes the main doors with the usual lever and handles the flick switches to its left.
- **NOTES** Turlough seems to suspect the Doctor of deliberately landing on Earth rather than his home planet, suggesting the latter was his expectation, as requested at the end of *Enlightenment*. He later says, "We were on our way to my planet, actually," but is easily wooed by the prospect of visiting the Eye of Orion so seems to be in no hurry. (We later learn Turlough is a political exile, unaware that he has since been pardoned, so has he told the Doctor he's from a different planet? In *Planet of Fire*, Turlough admits Trion is his home planet, which the Doctor says he has never mentioned before.) Tegan is still wary of the Black Guardian but has changed her outfit (having not previously done so since she rejoined the TARDIS) and a thick woollen coat has appeared on the hatstand, so there could have been some brief intervening landings.
- The Doctor's adamance that he didn't set the coordinates for Earth and his feeling that "something certainly isn't right" might be taken to imply the Master has drawn the TARDIS off course. Yet later the villain says, "Your arrival here was most timely," so that can't be the case. The Ship ending up somewhere unplanned is nothing new, but what causes the Doctor's wariness? Perhaps he's sensing the perception filter the Master is using to appear as Sir Gilles.
- Fitzwilliam Castle is said to be four hours' ride from London, which at a gallop could be up to 200km (Sir Geoffrey is talking about warning the king so would be estimating a fast pace). That would place it either in the south-west — somewhere in western Dorset or central Somerset — or anywhere in an arc from Herefordshire across the Midlands to Lincolnshire.
- A thick coat for Tegan is handily hanging on the hatstand before the travellers have even discovered where they've landed. This is the last use of the stand first seen in *Four to Doomsday*.
- The travellers emerge from the left-hand door, unusual at this stage as this side had the centre post attached meaning the right door should open first. Thus, when the Doctor pulls the door to, it doesn't close fully.
- The movements of the TARDIS are a little confused. We see the Master (as Sir Gilles) have it brought into the castle courtyard, then later he has Ranulf's men bring it to the hall. Meanwhile, having discovered the Ship has been moved, Tegan says the castle doors aren't big enough for it to be brought inside and the Doctor points out the Master could pilot it to "the same place he keeps the king"; Ranulf seems to confirm this, saying it was "with the king". But if the Master wanted to stow it in the king's chamber, why not pilot it there from the field outside rather than bring it into the bailey first, where he's more likely to be seen entering it? And if it's too big to fit through the outer doors, as Tegan claims, how is it moved from the king's room — which only has a small door — to the hall? It's clearly set there by guards, not relocated by the Master, who's occupied having Sir Geoffrey killed. Besides, the king is resting: would Ranulf dare enter his chamber on the off-chance the "blue engine" is there, let alone risk disturbing his liege by having it moved? This does seem to have been the intention, supported by the novelisation, but if we accept the Master took the TARDIS into the king's room, he must also have piloted it out again to somewhere within easy reach of the hall, of which there's no evidence or seemingly opportunity. It's simpler all round if the Master left the Police Box in the courtyard, perhaps outside the king's chamber window, and from there it was taken into the hall through an entrance unknown to Tegan or the Doctor. Besides, despite the Doctor's musing,

there's no reason to believe the Master can get into the TARDIS, having specifically required the Doctor's own key the last time he entered it in *Time-Flight*.
- The Police Box's dematerialisation was achieved with a double split-screen effect, with a recording of the prop overlaid in the centre third of the picture and the actors keeping to either side. The image of the prop was faded out, allowing the soldiers to then move into the already empty space.
- Does Tegan intend to take off? The Doctor tells her to "get into the TARDIS" and although he mentions "the coordinates will be set" (which could mean for the king's room if he does believe the Master has previously taken the Ship there, but could equally mean back to the outer meadow where they first arrived) that doesn't mean he intends her to leave him behind; surely he would be hoping to follow her. She simply wants to "distract them somehow" and may set the TARDIS in motion by mistake.

LANDING 241

SPACE Earth, England, Fitzwilliam Castle, king's chamber
TIME As above
TRAVELLERS Tegan
EPISODES The King's Demons 2

An alarm sounds once Tegan has set the TARDIS in motion. Unable to figure out what is causing it, she thumps the console in frustration – and the Ship completes its journey, materialising in the king's chamber just as the Doctor and the Master are battling for control of the shape-changing robot Kamelion.

The distraction allows the Doctor to gain the upper hand and Kamelion takes on the form of Tegan. The Doctor ushers it into the TARDIS while Turlough holds off Ranulf and his men at sword point, then enters the Ship. The Master mutters oaths as the Police Box vanishes.

Tegan is uncertain about Kamelion staying on board but the robot is keen and the Doctor and Turlough both agree. The Doctor takes Tegan's complaints as a desire to go home and sets coordinates supposedly for Earth. When she insists she would rather go to the Eye of Orion as he wanted, the Doctor admits that is where they are really heading.

- **CONTROLS** As the alarm sounds, Tegan moves round to panel C3 and holds but not does move the two large sliders. She later presses two of the rocker switches on, then thumps, panel C2. After taking off, the Doctor turns the black dial in the bottom-right corner of the same panel and also presses a switch, while Turlough presses a button below the left-hand round display on panel C3. The Doctor flicks switches on that panel and possibly adjusts one or both of the large sliders. He sets the coordinates from panel C6.
- The control room scene in episode one was recorded on Monday 20 December 1982 but delays owing to problems with the Kamelion prop meant the scenes for episode two had to be postponed until Sunday 16 January 1983. In the former session, the console's panels were placed in their usual order – or at least with panel 5 to the right of panel 1, the only two visible on screen – but in the later studio they were rearranged clockwise 1-6-5-3-2-4.
- **NOTES** What is the cause of the alarm that sounds after Tegan takes off? She doesn't appear to mishandle the controls, and must have picked up some basic operational knowledge by now anyway. Even when she was frantically pressing buttons in *Four to Doomsday* (Landing 208) there was no alarm. So is there an outside cause? There's no reason the Master's TARDIS should produce interference, and if the psychokinetic energies around Kamelion are cause for concern they ultimately don't stop the TARDIS landing in proximity. Perhaps the coordinates are still set for the arrival site outside the castle but the Ship itself is trying to override them knowing the Doctor needs her. The intention of the script seems simply to delay the TARDIS's arrival in the king's chamber until the opportune moment, so perhaps it's the plot contrivance alert.

IT'S BIGGER ON THE INSIDE

THE THORNTON RECTIFICATION 1983-1988

Series producer John Nathan-Turner had consented to a new console being built for the series' 20th anniversary special *The Five Doctors* and it was decided the control room around it should also be freshened up. Although this was the first completely new set since 1976, it wasn't a radical rethink by the special's designer Malcolm Thornton and he retained the now-established pale-grey walls with illuminated circles set around the console with main doors on the left, scanner and interior door on the right. But there were some innovations too.

Although the main doors wall had been reconstructed less than two years earlier, this was replaced again, along with – for the first time after close on 20 years of use – the doors themselves. Both were made to match the previous set precisely, with the same arrangement of roundels around the doorway, and deep indents in the doors larger than the roundels placed into them, front and rear. The slight offset of the centre gap was rectified, however, and the points of the middle zigzags were flattened like those fitted with hinges. The rear side was also extended well beyond the hinges so when the doors were open the zigzag edge couldn't be seen. This helped directors with the producer's instruction to no longer allow cameras to see through the doorway to what was beyond.

The control room returned to two main walls with staggered circles but now four columns wide. These were seemingly based on the previous design so again the roundels were spaced further apart horizontally than they were vertically, unlike the interlocking arrangement of the original 1963 walls. Also, because the half-roundels were proper semicircles (rather than slightly less to account for the gap between roundels), their straight edge was level with the top or bottom of the full circle in the adjacent column, meaning alternate columns of roundels were fractionally misaligned.

The scanner wall was also new, wider than before with six decorative strips placed on each side of the screen bay. This deep recess had angled sides but the squarer window now filled it edge to edge, although there was a lip above and below. It still had a single shutter but more often than not shots of the scanner opening were achieved electronically rather than raising the physical shutter.

The new interior doorway had solid roundels around the door to mirror the main doors wall opposite, with half-circles down each side, a full circle above and a return of quarter-circles in the top corners. The door itself had three translucent roundels held in place by rings with their outer rim sitting slightly proud. This opened outwards from the control room, hinged on the right, and had a thin vertical handle (actually two square-ended handles abutting).

While the control room retained slatted columns in the corners between wall sections, these were square rather than round. Their footprint was actually a trapezium as the sides splayed slightly so they sat at right angles to the walls, which were angled at approximately 130 degrees to each other. The slats on the faces of the columns – seven on the front and three on each side – had chamfered ends and those at the sides shortened like the ones around the scanner. Six of these columns featured in the control room but several more were made for use in other areas of the TARDIS.

The other main change was the reintroduction of a projecting cornice across the top of the walls, an idea last seen in 1975. This had a sloping underside then a vertical face with a decorative strip, and featured on all walls including the main and interior doors.

CORRIDORS AND BEDROOMS

Beyond the interior door was a wall section, a square slatted column and an inner door: plain with a square handle and set within a plain flat doorway (possibly reused from the previous set but not hard to reproduce). In *The Five Doctors* this corridor wall section had indented roundels (possibly an older piece reused) but by *Warriors of the Deep* it was a plain flat wall, and in *Frontios* it had aligned opaque roundels.

Planet of Fire reintroduced a bedroom set for the first time since the control room redesign and for this and the corridor new wall sections were made. These had three columns of four staggered circles but more widely spaced horizontally than usual. While the roundels were translucent, their rims sat on the front of the wall, like the solid wall, rather than being indented. At least three are seen in *Planet of Fire*, and by *Attack of the Cybermen* there are four making up corridors and rooms. In this latter case, several had roundels removed as the Doctor worked on circuitry behind them.

The wall with aligned opaque roundels had three columns of four circles, mimicking those of the 1976 set. Indeed, although the circles are lower down the wall, this may be one of the old walls trimmed down to remove damage to its bottom edge. This also had one roundel with its centre disc removed to allow circuitry to be placed behind it for characters to access. This was first performed for *The Awakening* but the scene was later

IT'S BIGGER ON THE INSIDE

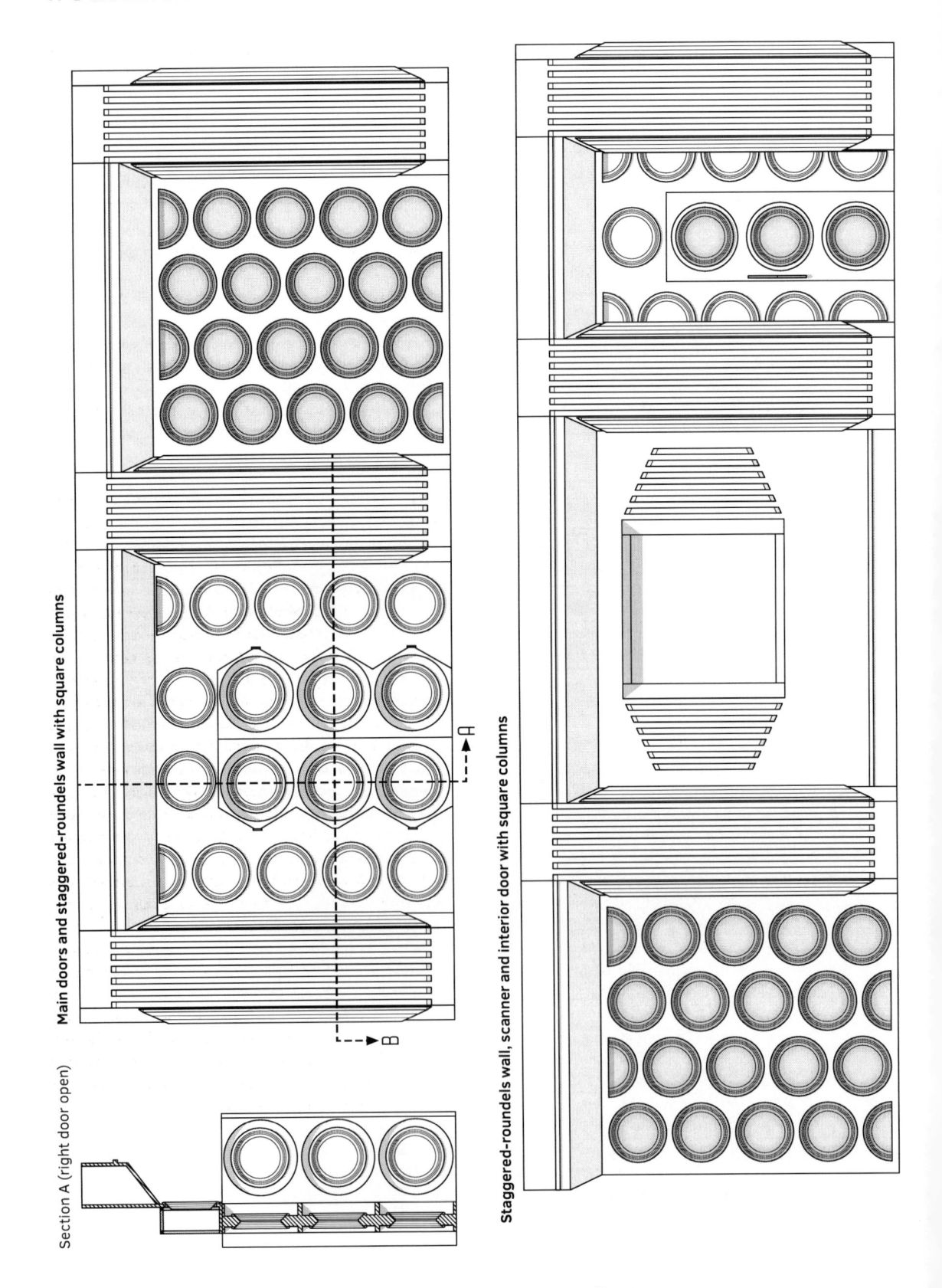

Main doors and staggered-roundels wall with square columns

Staggered-roundels wall, scanner and interior door with square columns

Section A (right door open)

IT'S BIGGER ON THE INSIDE

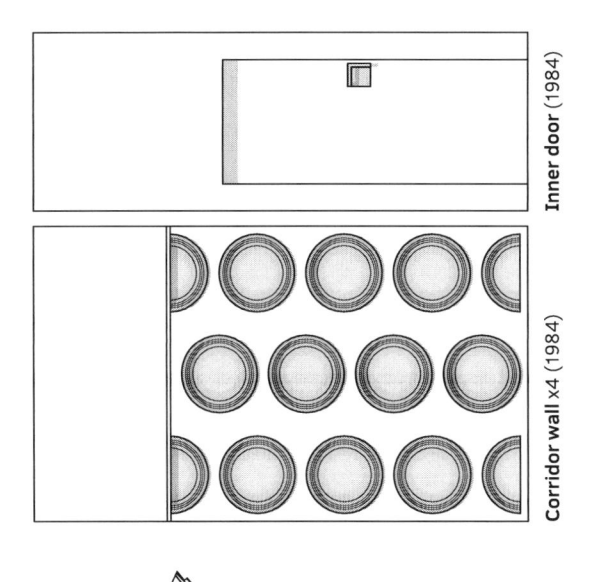

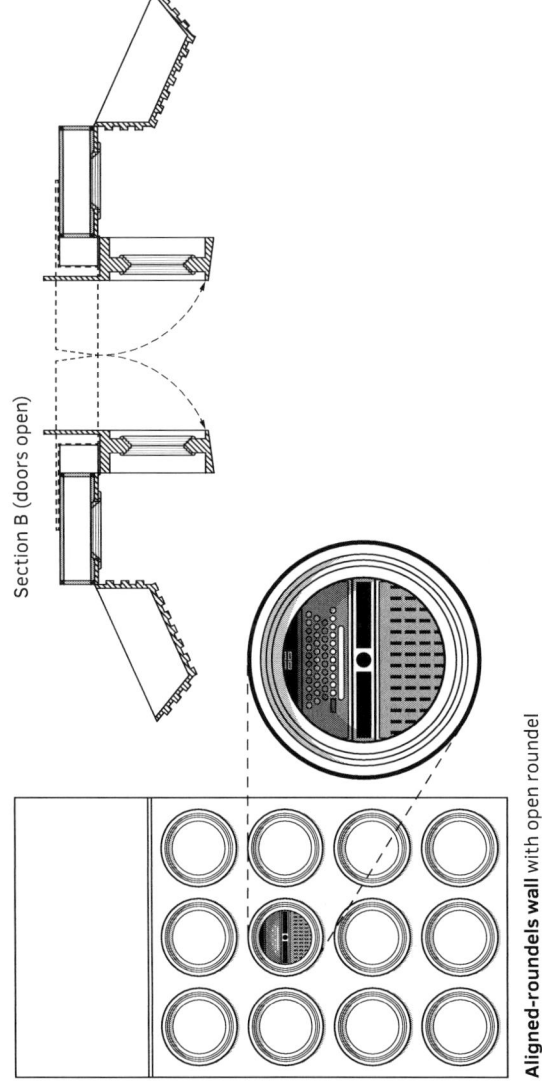

cut from the broadcast episode so it wasn't seen on screen until *Planet of Fire*. (There may have been two of these aligned-roundels walls as one does appear without an opening, but could simply be the same wall modified.)

The control room itself remained admirably consistent throughout its five years of use thanks to the new corner columns keeping the walls at fixed angles. The first modification was required for *Frontios* when the room was augmented with blocks of polystyrene rocks. In *Planet of Fire* the set was painted black to represent the Master's TARDIS (as it was again in *The Trial of a Time Lord*). One consequence of this appears to be that when it was cleaned up (the paint used was water based) the three translucent roundels in the interior door were painted over with grey (did the black paint not wash off these well enough?). This door was also rehung so it hinged on the left (still opening outwards), although this reverted from 1986 onwards.

DIMINISHING SIGHTS

For the last few years of the original series the control room was used less often. Its last appearance was in *The Greatest Show in the Galaxy*, erected in a tent in the car park at Elstree Studios owing to a temporary closure of BBC Television Centre's studios. The only control room scene in the 1989 season was in *Battlefield*, when it was discovered the set was unavailable – reports differ but it had either not been returned to the scenery store after recording at Elstree and likely scrapped, or was discovered to be damaged when required for *Battlefield*. Whichever the case, a substitute was hurriedly knocked up: simple flats with circular holes cut out and a back-lit backcloth placed behind (with wrinkles evident on screen). Some attempt was made to replicate the columns too although careful examination of the episode reveals these had no slats. To hide the fact this wasn't the proper set, the lighting was reduced to minimum and the script amended to explain why the TARDIS was dark – prophetic given the more moodily lit control rooms of future series.

While the main set walls may have gone, at least one of the supplementary sections survived in the BBC's scenery store. In 1990 the BBC Schools programme *Search Out Science* – which featured Sylvester McCoy as the Doctor, Sophie Aldred as Ace and John Leeson voicing K9 as they answered questions about astronomy – saw the wall with aligned opaque roundels make one last appearance on television.

WHAT ARE ALL THESE KNOBS?

CONSOLE E
1983-1989

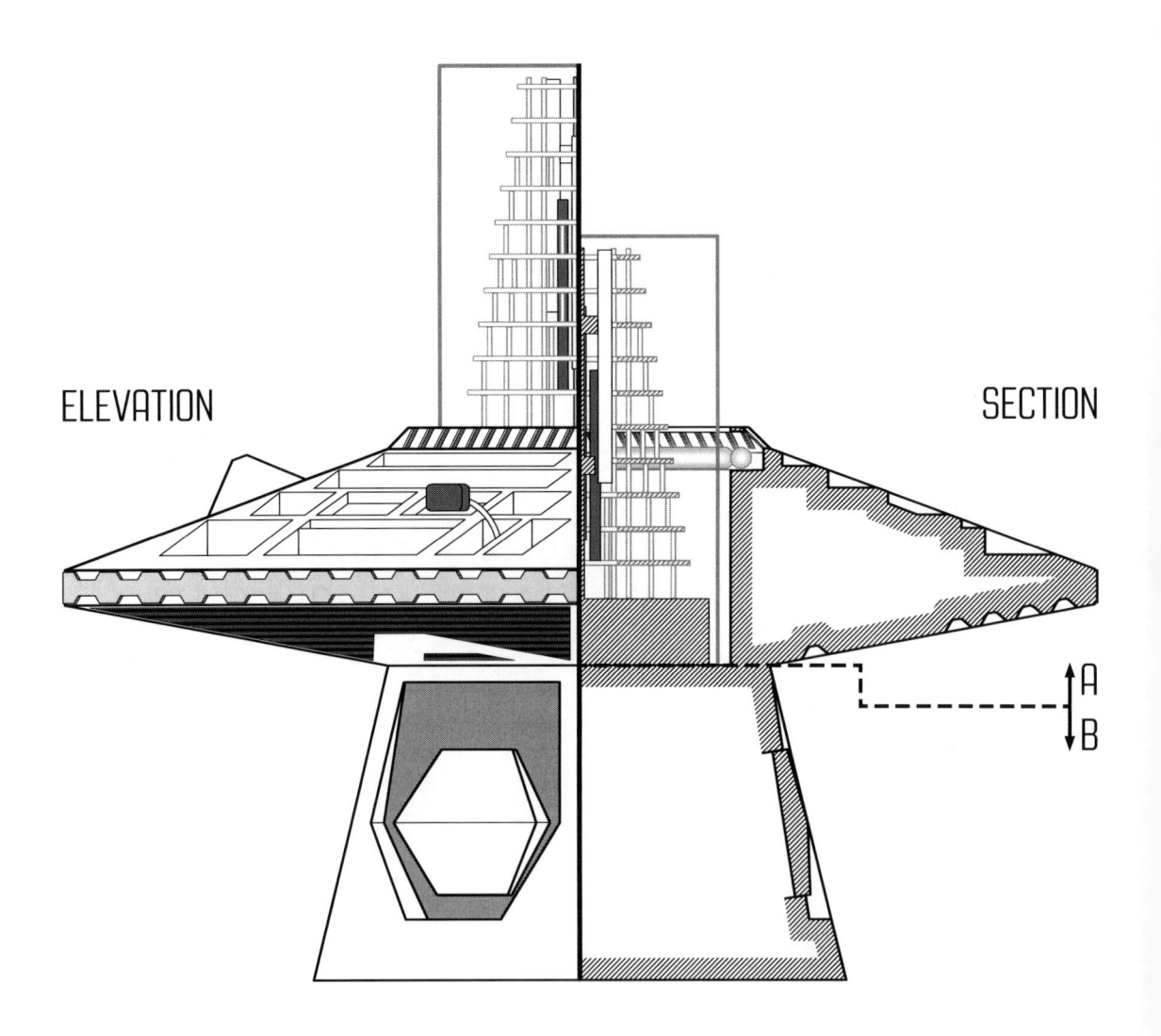

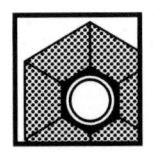

ELEVATION

SECTION

Visual effects designer Mike Kelt encountered the dilapidated state of the previous console and its mechanics while working on *Enlightenment* in January 1983. He convinced producer John Nathan-Turner that setting up the prop and keeping it functioning cost valuable studio time, and gained permission to design and build a new console to debut in the upcoming 20th anniversary special *The Five Doctors*. Kelt's brief was to preserve the size and general shape of the control desk, with six sloping panels, and to keep certain controls.

A chief concern was to make the new console more robust than the previous wooden one, so Kelt constructed an aluminium framework that supported the internal workings like the monitors and central column mechanism. This included the stepped band around the rim, behind which the lips of the upper and lower panels tucked. These panels were made from fibreglass and could be detached for storage, as could the pedestal.

The detailing of the pedestal, now with sloping sides, was inspired by the shape of the console itself, with embossed hexagons on each side and the recesses in which they sat shaped accordingly. At least some of these hexagonal pieces were removable to enable the cables powering the prop to be plugged in and, occasionally, characters to tinker inside the pedestal. This also supported the

WHAT ARE ALL THESE KNOBS?

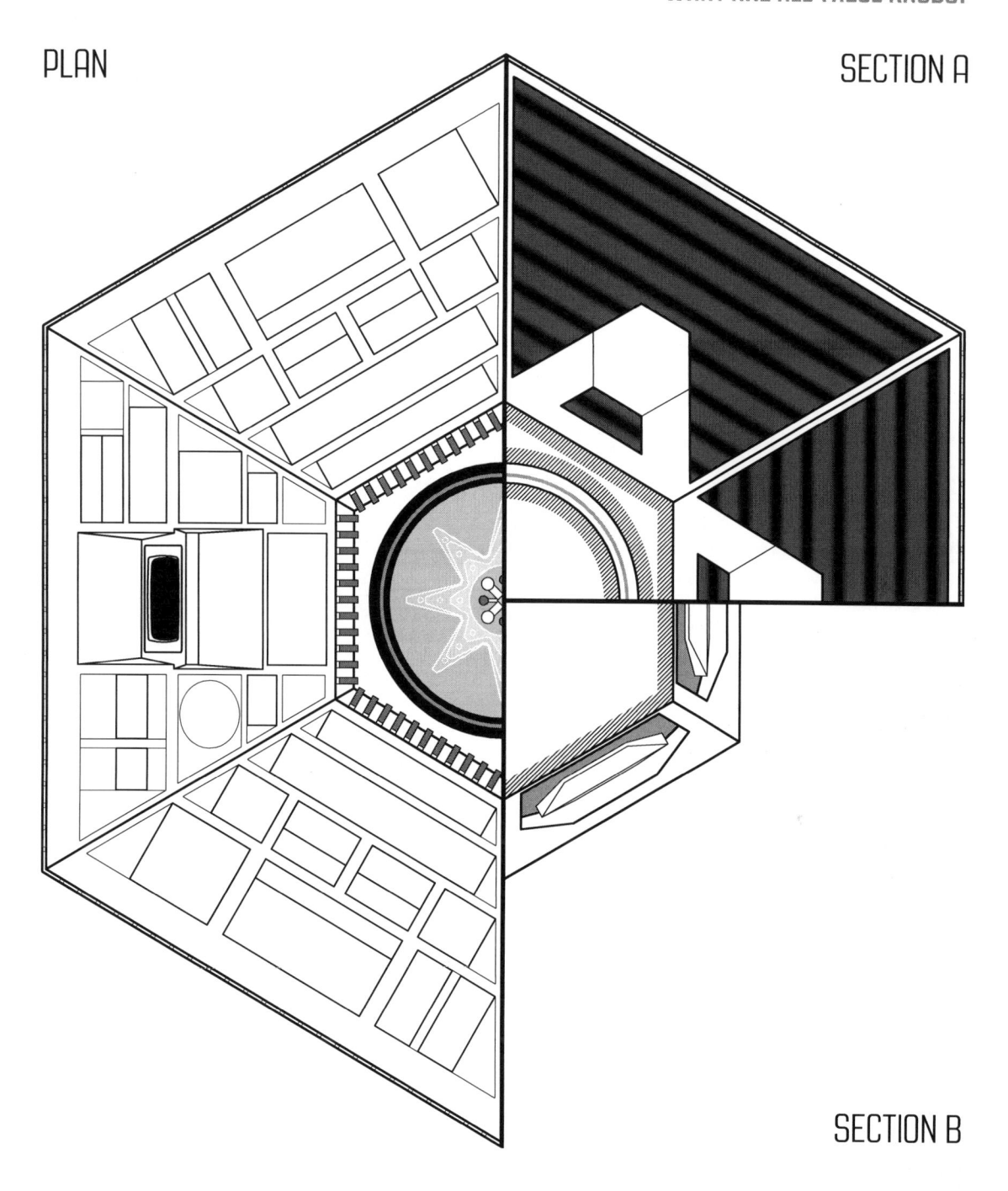

PLAN

SECTION A

SECTION B

mechanism for moving the central column up and down. The inner structure of the column was inspired by Kelt's construction of the glowing city in *Enlightenment*, with clear acrylic rods supporting ten tiers of eight-pointed-star-shaped pieces in decreasing size. In the centre were four fluorescent tubes and four red rods to add colour.

The underside of the console was also sloped, as Console D's had been, although not as steeply as the top, and had a pattern of ridges. At least one of these panels had a removable hexagonal section, as seen in *The Awakening*. The six upper control panels were each a single piece including the collar, which had eleven vertical slots cut out and backed by red film to be illuminated by six more fluorescent tubes fitted below the rim of the collar – although the bright overhead studio lighting usually hid this and it was only noticeable when the control room was darkened in *Battlefield*. The main face of the panels was moulded with a series of hollows

WHAT ARE ALL THESE KNOBS?

that provided a level base for controls. These were short and shallow near the top, getting taller and thus deeper towards the bottom. Two layouts were made: one had four rows of niches, the upper two almost full width, the lower two divided into four, with the deep bottom-centre cavity given an extra shelf; the second layout had a central housing for a television monitor with a deep recess in front, shallower ones either side and a circular depression on the right. Three of each style were cast and, in all but one instance (see Landing 249), were arranged alternately. In the following diagrams, panel 1 faced the main doors and the others are numbered clockwise around the console.

Only two of the panels with monitor housings had screens fitted into them as the third was generally on the side of the console facing the rear walls and therefore hidden from the cameras (except for a few times, most noticeably in *Attack of the Cybermen*). This retained its flat face whereas the other two had cutouts into which a television monitor was placed, both usually fed with the same graphics or text from a BBC Micro computer. In the adjacent circular depression, one panel had the five-sided illuminated pyramid from the previous console, another had an illuminated display (later replaced with a mesh to suggest a speaker) and the third, on the screen-less panel, was left empty.

The other style of panel was slightly more uniform. Two had pairs of illuminated displays in their centre niches, and the two deep, narrow hollows in the bottom-right corner were given sliding black discs – except one that had an oblong red handle that pulled outwards on a curved rod to mimic the red-knobbed lever that had become the standard control to operate the main doors on the previous console.

For the bulk of controls Kelt went for a contemporary technological feel with computer-like keypads. One style were flat square coloured buttons with a round dip in the middle; another were thick black keys with white tops on which some had letters, numbers or words like 'Clear', 'Enter' and 'Return'. None of these buttons was operational, though, being solid and glued to the console rather than sprung like a real keyboard. Other controls did have movement, notably the silver rocker switches and flip switches, and it's these the actors tended to favour. Finally there were a number of shiny black squares that had sequenced flashing lights beneath.

With the controls being smaller and often protected by their niches, this console was less prone to damage than previous ones and survived its six years of use largely unchanged. The most structural was that prior to *Planet of Fire* the blank screen housing gained a cavity moulded into its top, covered by two flaps (which disappeared from Season 24 onwards). Further component housings were added for this story but removed immediately after, as were the loops for the seatbelts in *Timelash*. A late addition was the connector for the advertising robot in *The Greatest Show in the Galaxy* to link itself to the console. The console survived the apparently accidental loss of its control room set after this story and last appeared in *Battlefield* episode one, backed by makeshift walls in low lighting. It was then kept in storage.

For 1993's Children In Need *Doctor Who*/*EastEnders* tie-up *Dimensions in Time*, parts of the prop were used to represent the Rani's TARDIS console. While the frame and pedestal were from storage, with areas covered in black adhesive vinyl, the control panels themselves were newly formed in black fibreglass using the original moulds. These had clusters of computer keyboard buttons sprayed red fitted in most niches, rather than the variety of controls on the regular console, and only two of the screen housings had working monitors fitted – in fact, the third panel with this arrangement didn't even have the raised housing for a screen. The walls were provided by organisers of the Doctor Who Appreciation Society, for which they had been constructed as stage dressing for its annual PanoptiCon convention.

The console parts were sold to fan Andrew Beech, a former DWAS coordinator and collector of screen-used props and costumes. He later became curator of the Doctor Who Experience, first in London Olympia then in Cardiff, and the console went on display there from 2011 until the exhibition closed in 2018.

PANEL E1

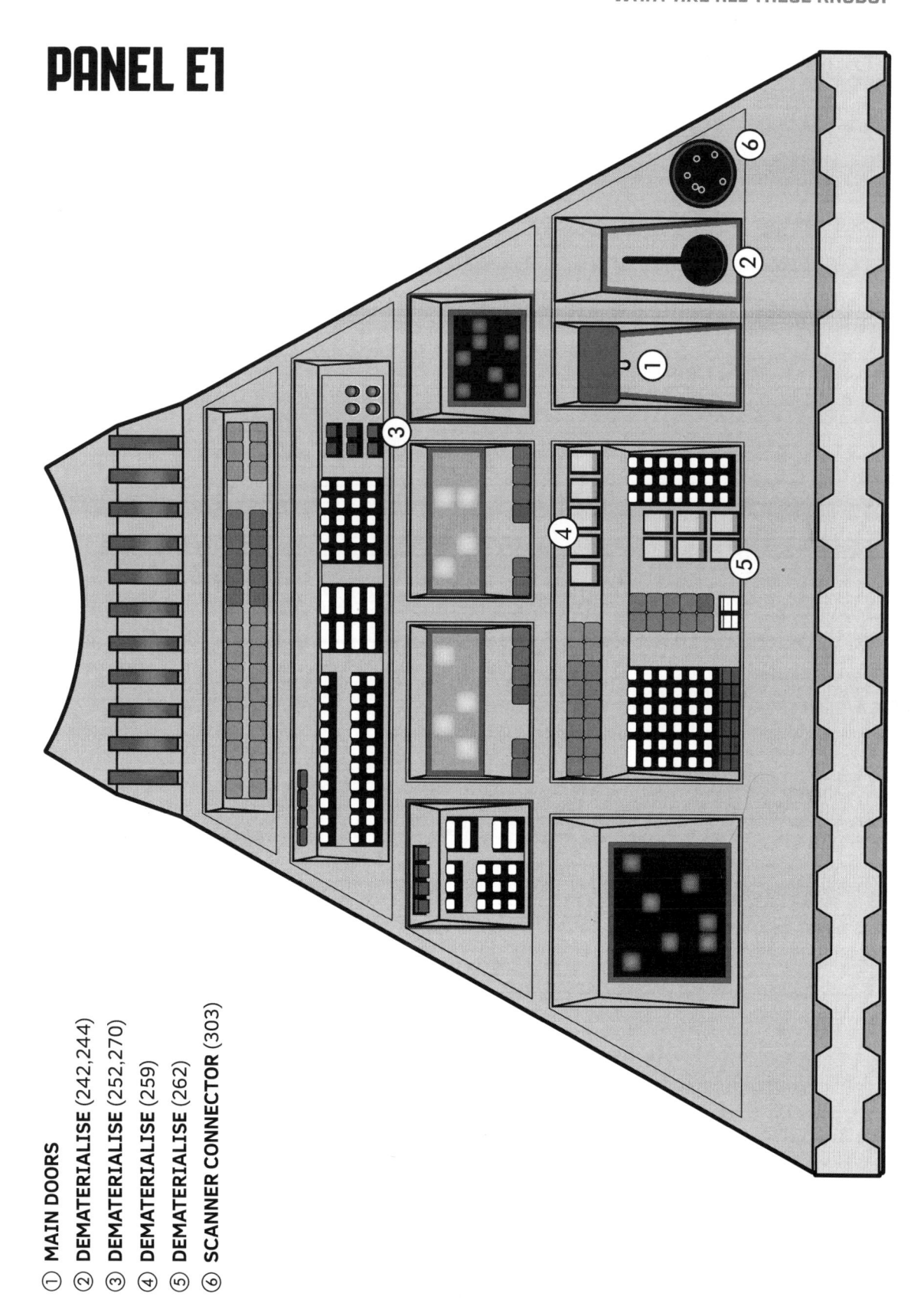

WHAT ARE ALL THESE KNOBS?

① **MAIN DOORS**
② **DEMATERIALISE** (242, 244)
③ **DEMATERIALISE** (252, 270)
④ **DEMATERIALISE** (259)
⑤ **DEMATERIALISE** (262)
⑥ **SCANNER CONNECTOR** (303)

WHAT ARE ALL THESE KNOBS?

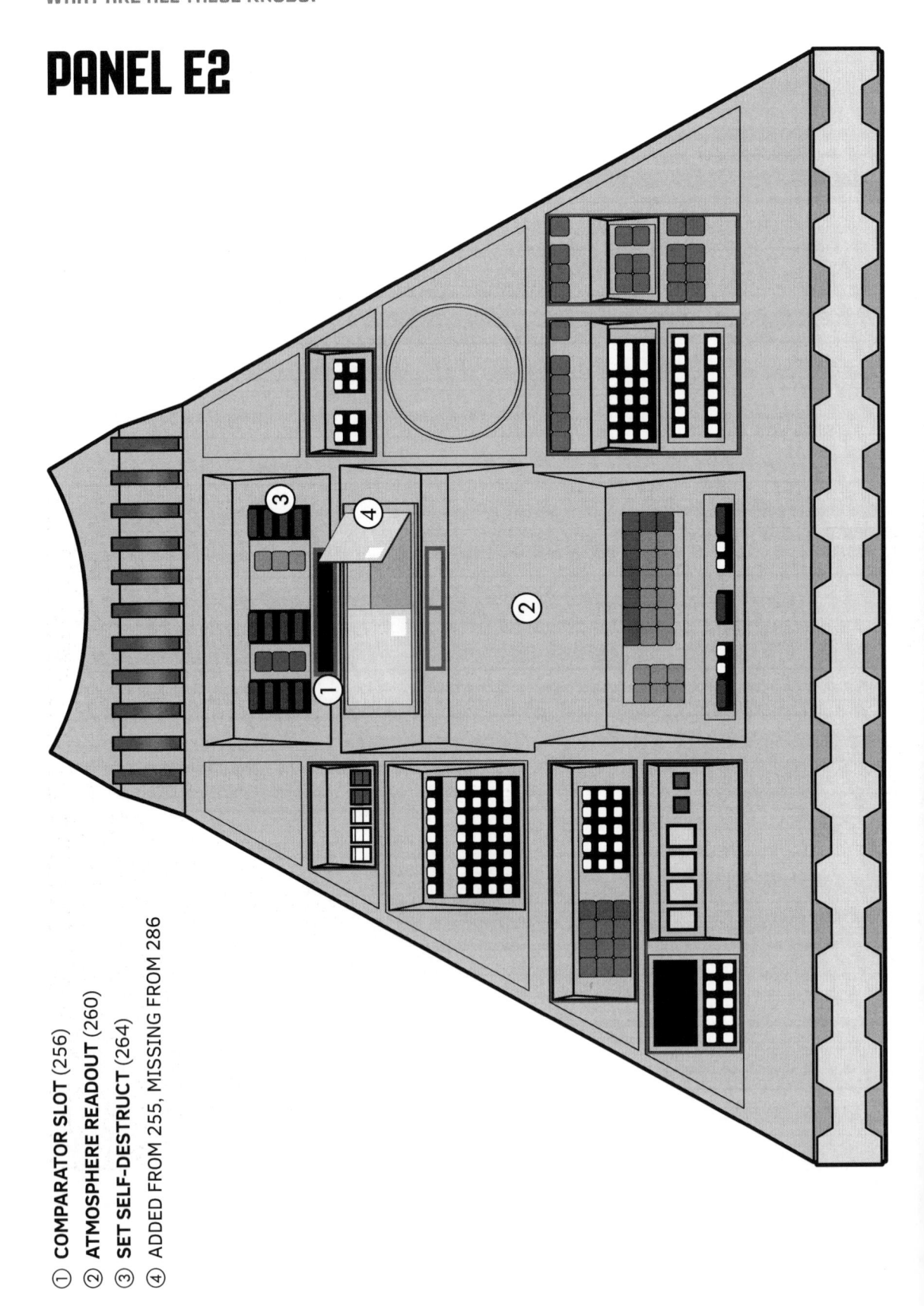

PANEL E2

① **COMPARATOR SLOT** (256)
② **ATMOSPHERE READOUT** (260)
③ **SET SELF-DESTRUCT** (264)
④ ADDED FROM 255, MISSING FROM 286

PANEL E3

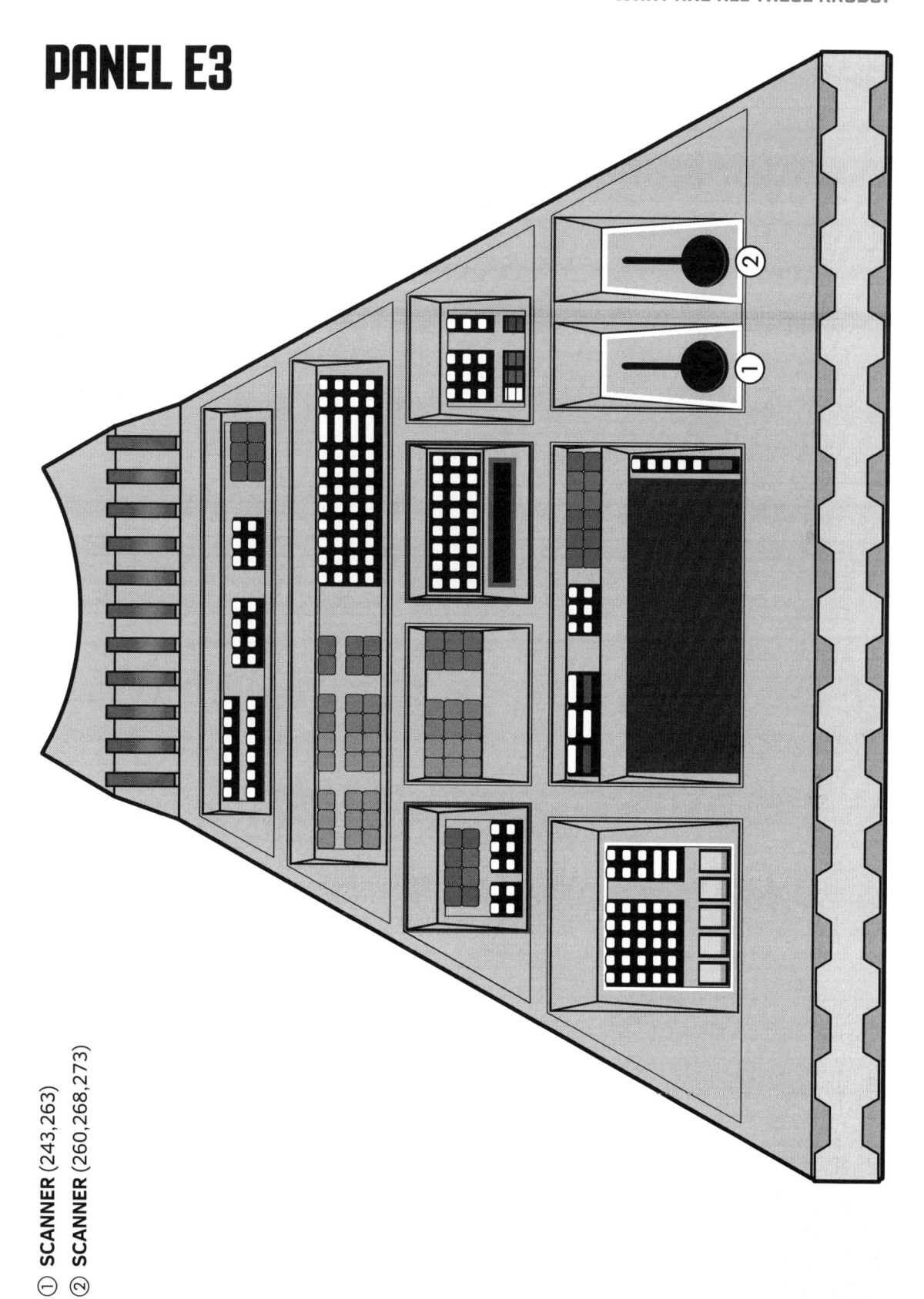

WHAT ARE ALL THESE KNOBS?

① **SCANNER** (243, 263)
② **SCANNER** (260, 268, 273)

WHAT ARE ALL THESE KNOBS?

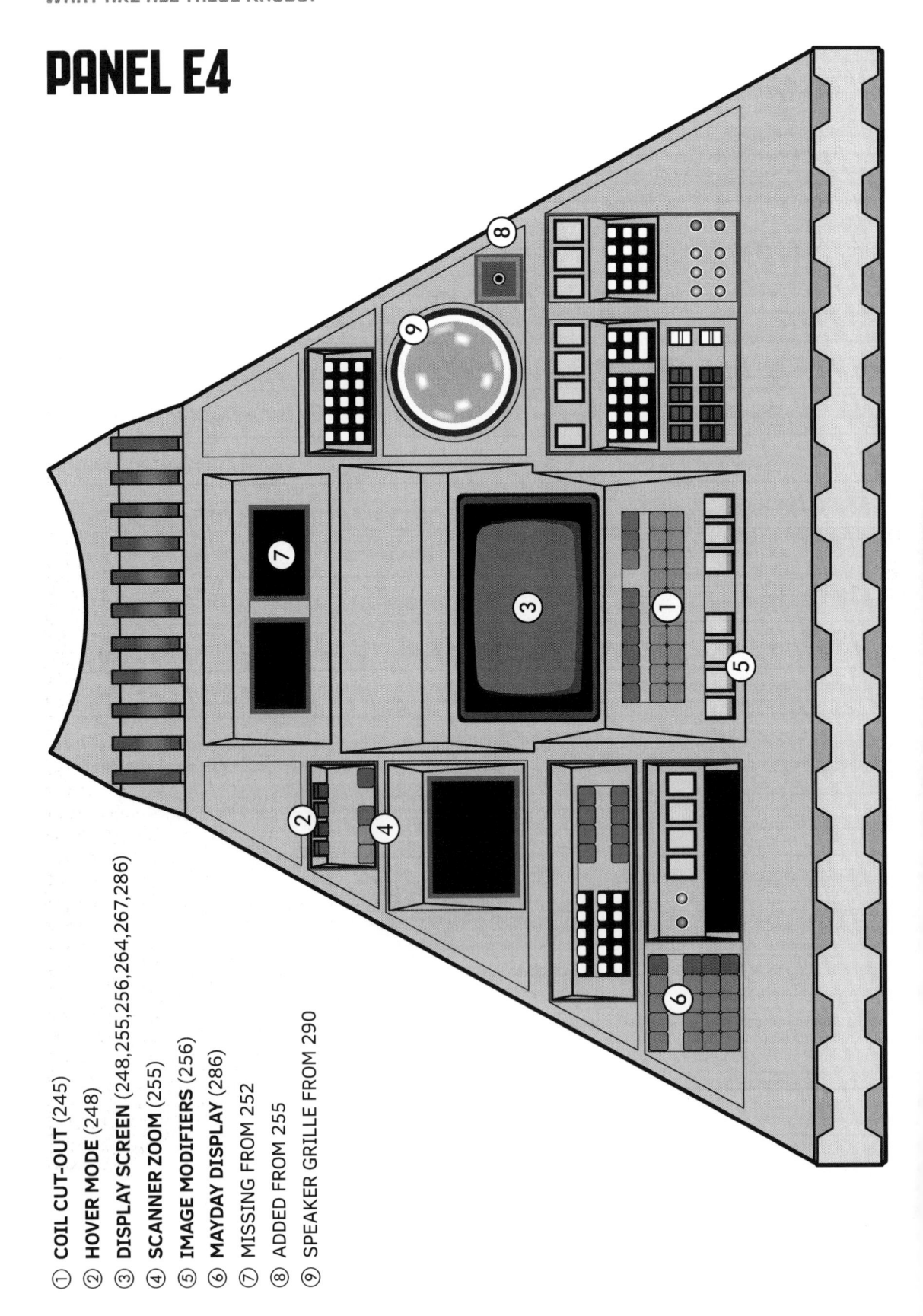

PANEL E4

① **COIL CUT-OUT** (245)
② **HOVER MODE** (248)
③ **DISPLAY SCREEN** (248, 255, 256, 264, 267, 286)
④ **SCANNER ZOOM** (255)
⑤ **IMAGE MODIFIERS** (256)
⑥ **MAYDAY DISPLAY** (286)
⑦ MISSING FROM 252
⑧ ADDED FROM 255
⑨ SPEAKER GRILLE FROM 290

WHAT ARE ALL THESE KNOBS?

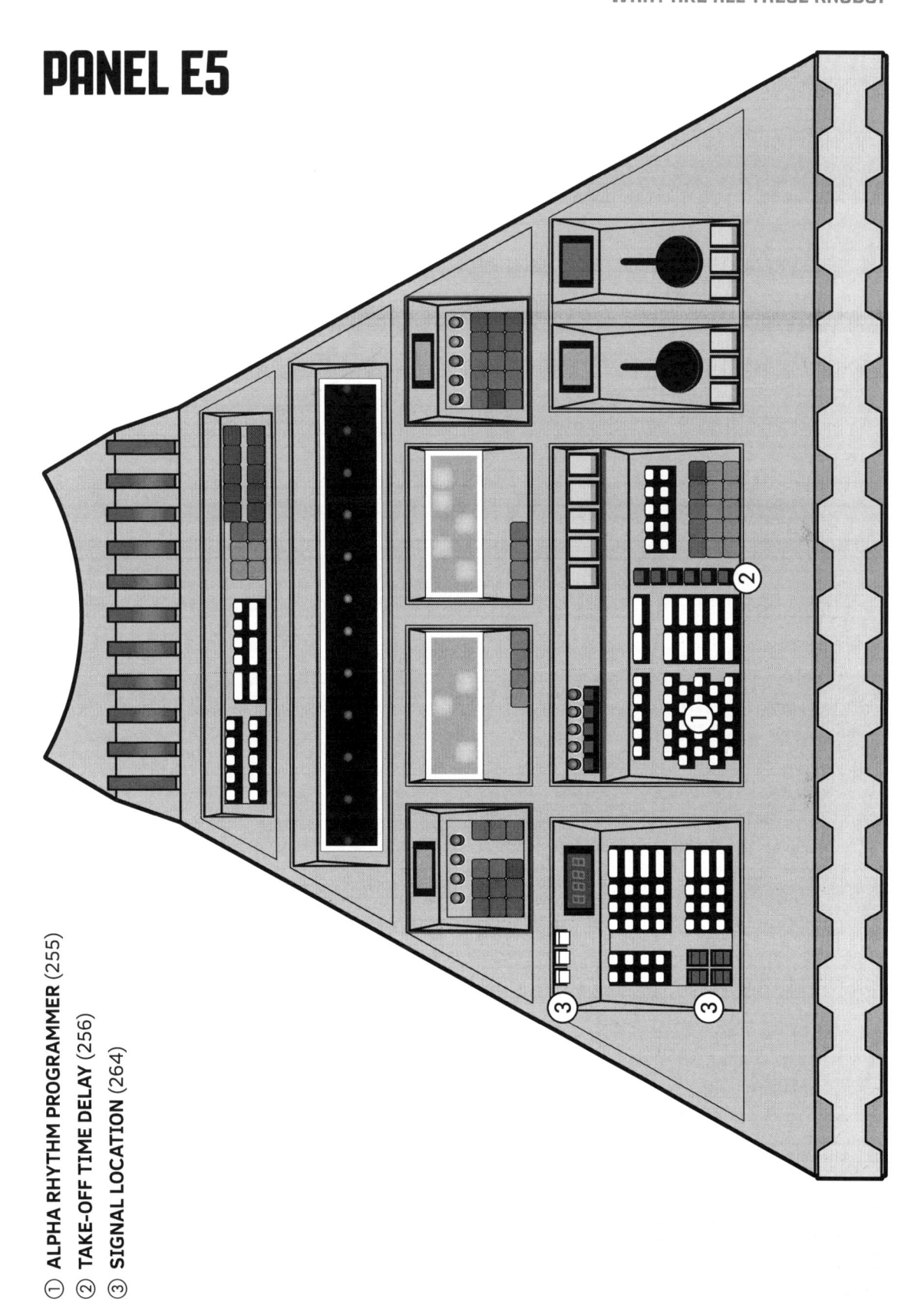

PANEL E5

① **ALPHA RHYTHM PROGRAMMER** (255)
② **TAKE-OFF TIME DELAY** (256)
③ **SIGNAL LOCATION** (264)

WHAT ARE ALL THESE KNOBS?

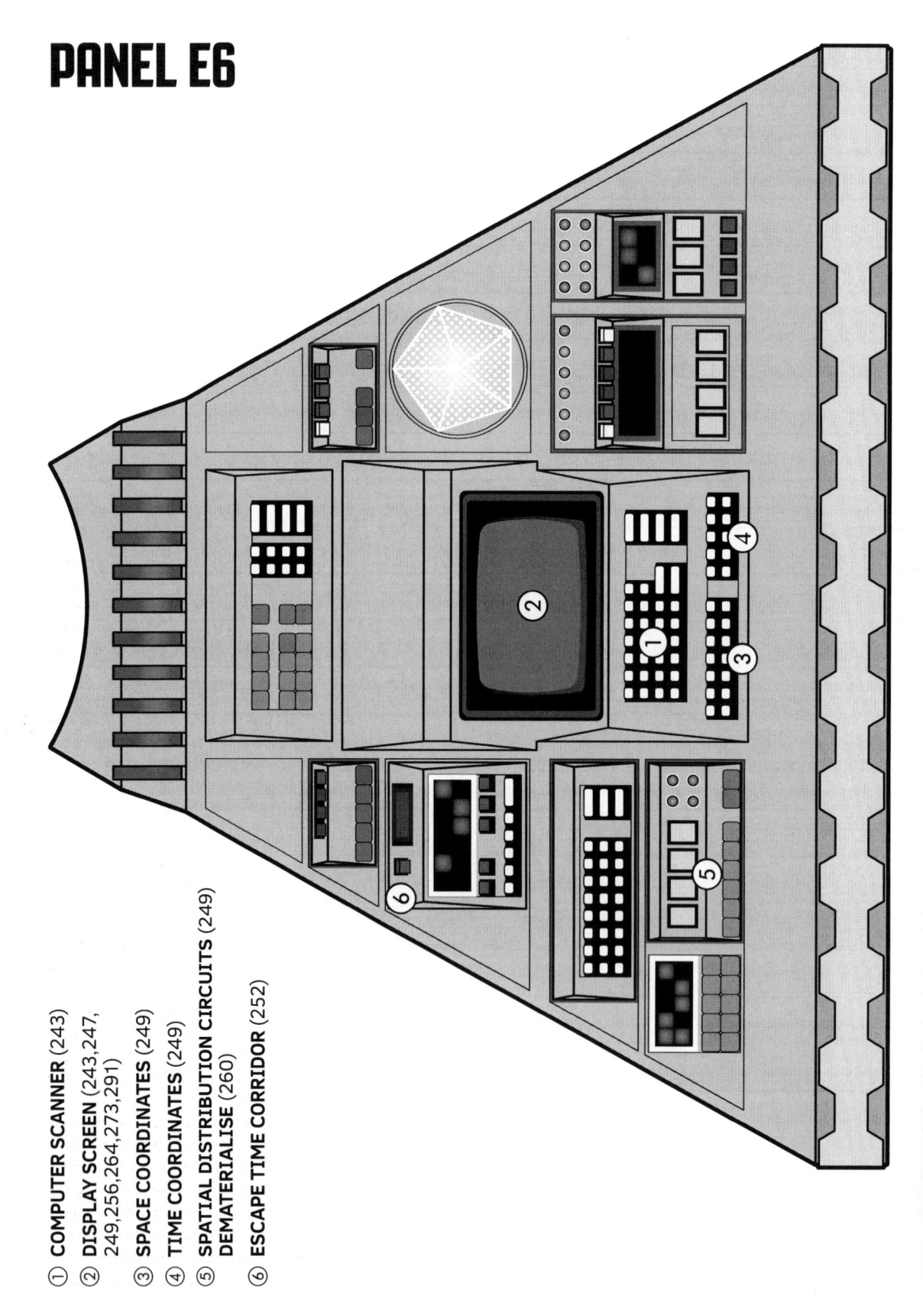

PANEL E6

① **COMPUTER SCANNER** (243)
② **DISPLAY SCREEN** (243, 247, 249, 256, 264, 273, 291)
③ **SPACE COORDINATES** (249)
④ **TIME COORDINATES** (249)
⑤ **SPATIAL DISTRIBUTION CIRCUITS** (249) **DEMATERIALISE** (260)
⑥ **ESCAPE TIME CORRIDOR** (252)

LANDING 242

SPACE Eye of Orion
TIME Unknown
TRAVELLERS The Doctor, Tegan, Turlough, (Kamelion)
EPISODES The Five Doctors

The TARDIS arrives on an Earth-like planet where a high bombardment of positive ions creates a relaxing atmosphere ("like Earth after a thunderstorm"). It settles among the ruins of a stone building on a hillside overlooking a wide valley with mountains beyond.

The Doctor refurbishes the control room, including remodelling the console with numerous keypads and screens. He is pleased with the results even before he has tested all the systems, but is compelled to admit to Tegan that the TARDIS may not be any more reliable – he has to thump the console to get the doors control to work.

They join Turlough outside, where he is sketching the view. The Doctor starts feeling sharp pangs as he senses his earlier incarnations being removed from his past one by one. Tegan and Turlough help the weakened Doctor back to the TARDIS and he takes off with only a vague sense of needing to find his other selves. Moments after, however, he faints.

- **CONTROLS** When showing off the console to Tegan, the Doctor flips up one of the switches in the top-left niche of panel E4. He opens the main doors with the red handle on panel E1 (after a coaxing thump), as will be the norm throughout this console's use. To dematerialise, he pushes forward the black slider in the bottom-right niche next to the door control while pressing buttons in the top niche, then reaches for the buttons below the middle-right display on panel E5 before collapsing.
- **LORE** The Doctor describes the TARDIS as "more than a machine" and "like a person, it needs coaxing, persuading, encouraging" in order to perform as desired.
- **NOTES** The TARDIS was on course for the Eye of Orion at the end of *The King's Demons* and is seen there at the start of *The Five Doctors* so it's unlikely there have been further landings in between. Tegan asks if they can stay awhile, which suggests they've only recently arrived. Later control room redecorations will be accomplished in less than a day so it may not take the Doctor long to perform this refit, although he could have been doing it en route.
- Beyond the interior door of this new-look control room is another wall with staggered translucent roundels and a square slatted column. Beyond this, glimpsed in the very last scene, is another grey wall with a white grating (like those used extensively in the prison sets for *Resurrection of the Daleks*).
- The control room seemingly gains a new hatstand, now painted white, but this is actually the one first used in *Meglos*, although extra hooks have been added. The Doctor has conveniently laid out a fur coat for Tegan to wear. Later Susan hangs up her mackintosh and places her grandfather's cane in the stand.
- Although Kamelion is presumably somewhere aboard the TARDIS, he is not seen or mentioned again until *Planet of Fire* (Landing 255, but see also Landing 247). Given this, it's not impossible the Doctor has deposited him somewhere or left him deactivated.

LANDING 243

SPACE Gallifrey, Death Zone
TIME After Landing 227
TRAVELLERS The Doctor, Tegan, Turlough, (Kamelion)
EPISODES The Five Doctors

Unconscious on the control room floor, the Doctor's body briefly fades away then returns just before the TARDIS lands in an open expanse of moorland ringed my mountains in the Death Zone on Gallifrey. Turlough checks the scanner, which shows a view of the monumental Tomb of Rassilon, yet his understanding of the console readout is that they are "nowhere and no time".

One of the Doctor's past incarnations is stuck in the Vortex, causing his current one to fade in and out of view. The Doctor stabilises long enough to wake and determine he must send a signal to bring his earlier selves to him, but collapses again before he can do so.

By chance, his first incarnation, with his granddaughter Susan, comes across the TARDIS in the wasteland. They enter and are surprised to find it occupied. The younger-looking elder Doctor recovers, strengthened by the presence of his older-looking younger self, although Tegan realises from recent events with two Brigadiers that this sort of duplication is dangerous.

While she and Turlough reluctantly fetch some refreshments for the new arrivals, the two Doctors discuss what to do next. The younger is happy with the original plan to send a signal to bring their intervening incarnations to the TARDIS, but the elder is still concerned about temporal instability and determines to investigate the Tomb. Together they set up a scan of the tower and surrounding area, which reveals three entrances and a forcefield holding the TARDIS, generated from within the Tomb. The elder Doctor leaves, with Tegan and Susan, intending to disable the forcefield so the younger Doctor can pilot the Ship to the tower. As he and Turlough wait, the scan picks up traces of two further incarnations.

Tegan and Susan return without the Doctor, who transmatted away to escape an ambush by Cybermen working with the Master. The youngest Doctor decides to go to the tower himself and reluctantly accedes to Tegan's company as Susan has injured her ankle.

She and Turlough follow the others' slow progress on the console screen. They hear a battering from outside and on the scanner see Cybermen. Unable to break in, the Cybermen position four large coffin-shaped bombs around the Police Box and wire them to a detonator. Fortunately, by the time they are ready, the Doctors in the tower have released the forcefield and the TARDIS dematerialises just as the bombs explode.

- **CONTROLS** Turlough reaches across to panel E3 to open the scanner. He later closes it from here too, seemingly with one of the black sliders in the bottom-right corner. When checking their location, he taps at the keypad in front of the screen on panel E6.
- The new central column retains the soft chime introduced in *The Keeper of Traken* when it comes to a stop and its lights go out as the TARDIS materialises.
- Susan automatically knows how to close the main doors even though the console is entirely different from how it looked when she travelled in the Ship. Presumably Time Lords can see past any cosmetic differences and divine a control's function.
- When setting up the computer scan, the younger Doctor works at controls in the bottom-left corner of panel E6 while the elder presses buttons above the bottom-right niches and those on the shelf of the bottom-centre niche of panel E5. He taps (although careful examination shows the keypads are fixed and don't depress) the third key down in the group of four on the right of the bottom-centre niche of panel E6 to bring up the results on the screen above. He then taps the lettered keys forming the top-left group in front of the screen, presses the seven silver rocker switches and four buttons at the very bottom-right of panel E6 and some of the red flip switches in the bottom-left niche of panel E5.

LORE The computer scanner can be programmed to display a crude representation of the surrounding area.

NOTES Does the TARDIS arrive in the Death Zone under its own steam or is it time-scooped? There's no visual evidence for the latter – we don't see the Police Box engulfed by the black trapezium – but Borusa knows when it has arrived and has statuettes of the three travellers ready for his game board. Otherwise, it's possible the Doctor telepathically directs the Ship to find his earlier incarnations when he takes off, or it's drawn to their location anyway.

- Surprisingly given the set is brand new and the scanner's shutter mechanism recently refitted, the cutaway shot of the scanner opening is achieved electronically, with a vertical wipe to represent the rising shutter (although cleverly twisted as it nears the top to match the angle of the top edge of the scanner window).
- Tegan and Turlough's idea of refreshments is ice cream, fruit (including pineapple, grapes and avocado) and drinks of blue and green liquids. Unless it has been majorly upgraded, this doesn't come out of the food machine so was probably prepared in the kitchen, as mentioned in *Shada* (Landing 173). The TARDIS also contains three bamboo chairs and a side table.
- The Doctor suggests setting up the computer scanner to see what dangers may be lurking outside but then all it does is register his others incarnations, being keyed to his brain patterns. Shouldn't it be warning of the Yeti, Raston Warrior Robot and numerous Cybermen roaming the Death Zone? The Doctor also says the scan has located the forcefield generator although this isn't displayed. Are the scanner's graphic representations of the environment automatically generated or programmed by the Doctor in a hurry? They're very basic: a rough outline of Rassilon's tower and simple triangles to indicate mountains. One might think a map showing the route would be more useful but then the tower seems to be visible from pretty much anywhere in the Zone anyway.
- Susan recognises the Cybermen, which could imply an unseen landing prior to Landing 11, possibly even before Landing 1. However, she may have encountered them on post-Dalek-invasion Earth, or simply know of them from Time Lord records given the Doctor also seems to be aware of their nature in *The Tenth Planet*. In a cut scene (included in the Special Edition released on VHS and DVD) Susan acknowledges that she can pilot the TARDIS.
- The scanner shows a view from above of the Cybermen outside, obviously intended to suggest the camera is in the Police Box's roof lamp, yet the angle of view is clearly greater than the height of the box.
- The TARDIS's dematerialisation is a cut as the bombs are exploded. One might expect that the Police Box prop would be removed before the explosions were set off, but stepping through each frame reveals it was still in place as a first set of pyrotechnics in front of it were detonated, then the picture cuts to a second set of explosions without the box.

LANDING 244

SPACE Gallifrey, Death Zone, Tomb of Rassilon
TIME As above
TRAVELLERS Turlough, Susan, (Kamelion)
EPISODES The Five Doctors

The TARDIS lands in the central chamber of Rassilon's mausoleum, where the legendary Time Lord's body is laid out on a stone altar carved with blank faces. Susan and Turlough join Tegan, Sarah and the Brigadier who have also been brought to the Death Zone, while the Doctor's first three incarnations try to contact their eldest iteration in the Capitol.

He arrives via transmat with Lord President Borusa, who is responsible for the gathering and has control over the eldest Doctor's mind through the Coronet of Rassilon he wears. The three younger incarnations concentrate their minds and in combination are able to free their future self. A vision of Rassilon himself appears and agrees to provide Borusa with the gift of immortality: preserved for eternity as one of the carvings on his altar. His trap sprung, Rassilon releases the Doctor's fourth incarnation from the Vortex and spirits away the Master.

The three youngest Doctors make their farewells and each steps into the TARDIS with their respective companion. The Police Box appears to split into four as Rassilon returns them to their proper times. The Doctor's fifth incarnation, Tegan and Turlough are joined by Chancellor Flavia and a squad of guards. Flavia informs the Doctor he has been appointed president in Borusa's stead. He therefore orders her to transmat back to the Capitol and assemble the High Council while he follows in his TARDIS.

The Doctor hurries his two friends into the Ship and proceeds to dematerialise. Turlough and Tegan expect to be sent home but the Doctor assures them he has no intention of returning to Gallifrey. He is once more on the run from his own people.

- **CONTROLS** The Doctor again dematerialises by pushing the black slider on panel E1 forwards while holding buttons in the top niche. (In the Special Edition he's seen closing the doors with the red handle.)
- **NOTES** The departure of the earlier Doctors is odd as it seems they're all returned home in the TARDIS despite not having arrived in the Death Zone that way. The grinding sound kicks in anew each time a Police Box image splits away. The impression is given that four instances of the TARDIS from different times in its life have been merged together. Did Rassilon reach back to the points each incarnation of the Doctor was snatched from and bring their iterations of the TARDIS to the Death Zone too (even though it was nowhere near in at least one case), just in order to send everyone home in them? Why do that when he sends the Master away with a simple fade from view? And surely the Doctors can't be expected to return their companions using the TARDIS: the first would be unable to navigate correctly (and there's no evidence Susan rejoins his travels for a time) and the third is already travelling with a younger Sarah Jane (he recognises her so must have been snatched after *The Time Warrior*). The splitting-TARDISes effect is not just for the audience, either, as the Doctor tells Tegan to watch, implying she sees the same. The Special Edition tries to remedy the issue by having the Timescoop emerge from the TARDIS as it whisks away the first three incarnations (but not their companions), but then reinstates a cut line from the Doctor about "clever" Rassilon using "temporal fission", a term that better fits with the original visual effect.
- Do the travellers resume their holiday at the Eye of Orion? Knowing the Doctor's short attention span, perhaps not, unless Tegan insists.

LANDING 245

SPACE Earth orbit
TIME [2084]
TRAVELLERS The Doctor, Tegan, Turlough, (Kamelion)
EPISODES Warriors of the Deep 1

Turlough has decided to stay aboard the TARDIS rather than go home, for the time being, so the Doctor promises to show Tegan what Earth is like a little into her future. They are on course but the Ship materialises sooner than the Doctor expected. He finds they are orbiting the planet just above the atmosphere, towards the end of the 21st century.

An automated weapons platform, Sentinel Six, detects and scans the TARDIS, demanding a security clearance code under threat of being shot down. It is unresponsive to the Doctor's requests for time to reset coordinates and, determining the Ship is a threat, fires a radiating energy pulse. The TARDIS lurches as it falls out of control towards the planet below.

The travellers cling onto the console and the Doctor attempts to perform a materialisation flip-flop to arrest their fall. The control room rights itself as he dematerialises the Ship before diving under the control desk to complete stage two.

- **CONTROLS** The Doctor operates each of the group of three rocker switches in the bottom-right corner of panel E6, two of the flip switches in the top-left niche of panel E4, one of the rocker switches at bottom-centre of this panel, and flip switches in the middle-far-left niche of panel E3. After the TARDIS materialises he flips these last again and some in the top-right niche of panel E2. He operates the scanner from the top-left of panel E1 and, when waiting for Sentinel Six's response, he presses a button at the top of panel E3.
- The display in the bottom-right niche of panel E5 shows digital numbers that can briefly be seen counting up from 4047.
- Turlough resets the coil cut-out using the blue buttons below the screen on panel E4. He taps here again when Sentinel Six gives its final warning.
- When trying to move the Ship on, the Doctor presses at least two of the rocker switches on the shelf of the bottom-centre nice on panel E1 and has Tegan hold a button on the left of the upper niche while he presses other controls on the same panel. After the Sentinel fires, the Doctor reaches over to controls on panel E2 and E5 (the buttons below the middle-right illuminated display) and then dematerialises using an unseen control on panel E2.
- The cables powering the console are connected to the pedestal beneath panel E3. The hexagonal cover on this side is detached and resting against the base but this may be deliberate for the shot of the Doctor checking under the console.
- **LORE** The TARDIS can be affected by certain external energy bursts. These can disable some controls and, if the Ship is materialised in orbit of a planet, cause gravity compensators to fail.
- There's a 'danger' lighting mode for the control room in which the illuminated wall roundels go dark and the room is bathed in red light.
- **NOTES** The Doctor later says the year is "about twenty eighty-four" but if he was generalising surely he'd pick a round number like 2080. So he may know precisely and is just being casual about it.
- Tegan wants to see "a little of her planet's future" but for some reason 100 years ahead is considered "too far advanced". What was the Doctor aiming for then: 50 years hence, 20 years? Would he really agree to show Tegan a period that, should he eventually return her

to her own time, she will be likely to live through? Isn't that inviting temptation to try to change things if she learns something unpleasant is going to occur? Maybe she hopes to pick up the next 30 years' worth of sporting results so that when she gets home she can clean up at the bookie's.
- ▤ The Doctor doesn't explain why the TARDIS has materialised later than intended other than it's his fault. His musing that he "should have changed it for a type fifty-seven while I had the chance" would seem to suggest he wishes he'd swapped TARDISes at some point and abandoned this old Type 40. That seems rather harsh after all they've been through together and given his usual fondness for the Ship, and what we later learn about its affection for him. And when was this chance? None was evident in either *Arc of Infinity* or *The Five Doctors*.
- ▤ Oops! When Turlough moves to the console after the Sentinel appears on the scanner, a camera cable can be seen snaking across the floor behind Tegan.
- ▤ While the Doctor addresses the scanner when talking to Sentinel Six his voice and its must be relayed via the console. The scanner has had audio since *Arc of Infinity* (Landing 227) but that can't be in use here as the Sentinel can't be broadcasting sound in space.
- ▤ Sentinel Six must have unusually powerful weaponry to affect the TARDIS. This is the first time the Ship has been shot down by an energy pulse (as opposed to a missile). The Doctor later mentions the need for repairs that "will take some time" so the burst must have done some considerable damage.

LANDING 246

SPACE Earth, SeaBase Four
TIME As above
TRAVELLERS The Doctor, Tegan, Turlough, (Kamelion)
EPISODES Warriors of the Deep 1-2

The Doctor successfully gets the TARDIS to materialise safely, within an underwater military base while a missile test run is underway. The travellers venture outside to establish whether they are on Earth. They deduce from the metallic structure and chilly air they are in a submersible of some kind and head up a spiral staircase to explore further, the Doctor wanting to get permission to stay while he repairs the Ship.

Their presence is soon detected and armed guards search the base. Two led by an officer called Preston discover the Police Box and, finding the door unlocked, check inside. Discovering the large control room within, Preston sends the guards to search beyond the interior door while she reports to Commander Vorshak that the craft is clearly not of Earth origin. She recalls the guards and leaves one on duty outside while she and the other return to the base's bridge.

As Sea Devil warriors break through the airlocks and storm the base, the guard is called away to help with the defence. Later, hexachromite gas spreads throughout the Seabase via the ventilation system, killing the Sea Devils and their Silurian generals. With the threat ended, but most of the base's crew dead, the Doctor completes repairs to the TARDIS and the travellers depart.

- ▤ **NOTES** Tegan is the last one to exit the TARDIS so she's to blame for leaving the door open, although it's unusual for the Doctor not to check. Preston and the guards are puzzled but not freaked out by the larger interior, and ready to accept it's alien technology, so humans by this period presumably have some awareness of extraterrestrials.
- ▤ The Doctor has met Ichtar previously, recognising him as "the surviving leader of the noble Silurian triad" from when he "tried to mediate between you and the people of Earth" during which Ichtar's "supreme wish was to live at peace with the other inhabitants of this planet", but the Doctor "thought he'd been killed". He also knows about the Myrka and can identify a Silurian battlecruiser. This doesn't really tally with either *The Silurians* or *The Sea Devils*. While there are three main (unnamed) Silurian characters in the former, there's no suggestion they form a ruling triumvirate – the 'old' Silurian (with whom the Doctor tries to negotiate a peace) is in charge until the 'young' Silurian kills him and takes over, liaising with the Silurian 'scientist' who is happy to arrange ways to wipe out the humans. When the scientist goes back into hibernation, the young Silurian tells him, "When our people revive, you will be the leader. See that the apes are destroyed." They're set to reawaken after 50 years, so perhaps – if they were just entombed rather than destroyed by UNIT – the Doctor encountered the scientist (who may be Ichtar or just joined with Ichtar and another to form the triad) and the Myrka in the mid-2020s. He later meets another group of Silurians from a shelter under Wales in 2020 (see Landing 455, vol.2).
- ▤ With most of the base personnel dead and the computer inoperative, it's possible the Doctor uses the TARDIS to take Bulic and any other survivors to their homeland as they seem to have no way to contact the surface to arrange their recovery. He may also take the opportunity to help resolve the differences between the two power blocs, perhaps using Bulic's testimony to convince their leaders to work together. Certainly representations of the 22nd century in the series show humans began to venture beyond the solar system in this period, which suggests resources are no longer being devoted to maintaining a power balance.

LANDING 247

SPACE Earth, England, Little Hodcombe, disused church, crypt
TIME Summer 1984
TRAVELLERS The Doctor, Tegan, Turlough, (Kamelion)
EPISODES The Awakening 1-2

Tegan asks to visit her grandfather, Andrew Verney, who lives in the English village of Little Hodcombe. As the TARDIS approaches, however, it detects time distortion and shudders as it passes through an energy field permeating the area. Unknown to the Doctor, the Ship lands near the focus of the energy in an abandoned church on the outskirts of the village, materialising in the crumbling crypt.

The scanner reveals falling masonry but, rather than relocate, the Doctor dashes outside when he spots someone amid the rubble. He searches the crypt with a small torch but the man slips past and hurries up some steps. Tegan notices the fugitive is wearing historical clothes but Turlough assures her they are in 1984. They follow the Doctor as he ventures upstairs to explore the church, unaware the man has reappeared back in the crypt.

When Tegan and Turlough return to the TARDIS they find a psychic projection is already forming inside the control room. They quickly leave again to tell the Doctor.

With the Malus in the church above gathering strength, by the time the Doctor returns to the TARDIS with Tegan, Turlough, villagers Jane Hampden and Ben Wolsey, and Will Chandler, a peasant boy transported from 1643, the projection is gaining substance: a smaller copy of the full Malus creature, clinging to the wall. The Doctor tries to lock the signal conversion unit onto the frequency of the psychic energy in order to redirect it. Tegan notices on the scanner that the sadistic Sergeant Willow and a trooper have followed them into the crypt so she closes the main doors. The two soldiers are puzzled to discover the Police Box but, finding it locked, try to break down the door with a chunk of masonry. Turlough and Verney arrive and knock them both out.

Inside, the Malus projection is solidifying and starting to move. The Doctor succeeds in blocking its ability to feed on the psychic energy being generated in the village and the creature begins to dissolve. Seeing the soldiers outside have been subdued, everyone heads up to the church to deal with the Malus itself. The trooper recovers and groggily follows them, as does Willow once he wakes.

The Doctor ushers everyone back down to the crypt and into the TARDIS as the Malus prepares to use its remaining energy reserves to obliterate as much as it can. With stonework beginning to fall all around it, the Police Box dematerialises. The Doctor confirms the Malus has destroyed itself and prepares to drop off the villagers then take Will back to the 17th century. Tegan reminds him she came to spend time with her grandfather and he reluctantly agrees to stay awhile.

- **CONTROLS** Turlough tinkers with the internal workings of the console beneath panel E6, wherein an orange light flashes (also illuminating gaps between the panel edges and console rim).
- The Doctor presses the four rocker switches at bottom-left of panel E6 to determine time distortion is still present, then the third-from-left of the group of four rockers on the right-hand side. He operates a control near the top of panel E2 – probably one of the switches in the top-left niche – while Turlough uses the keypad on the left of the bottom-centre niche of panel E1.
- When trying to block the Malus's psychic projection, the Doctor flips the red switches in the middle-far-left niche of panel E1, then presses pushbuttons on the right of the upper niche and the red button below the middle-left display. He operates further unseen controls on panels E2 and E1: judging from the sounds they make, these are the four rocker switches at bottom-left of the former panel, then three of the same on the shelf of the bottom-centre niche of the latter, one of the flip switches at the bottom of this niche, and the pushbuttons in the upper niche again. Tegan operates the scanner unseen from panel E3 while the Doctor presses further controls on panel E2 and uses the keypad below the screen on panel E6.
- Jane Hampden opens the main doors with the red lever, having seen Tegan use it to close them.
- When preparing to take off, the Doctor operates controls on panels E1, E2 and E3, then dematerialises by seeming to twist two controls on the last (even though none on this console rotate). While explaining about the Malus, he idly operates controls on panel E3.

- **LORE** The time monitor displays the current date for where the Ship has landed (another name for the yearometer, perhaps).
- The signal conversion unit can be tuned to specific energy frequencies.
- **NOTES** Sir George says a Civil War battle took place at Little Hodcombe on 13 July 1643, which he is now re-enacting. As he's at pains to recreate events precisely to revive the Malus, it may be the same date in 1984. Then again, Tegan is made to take the role of Queen of the May, suggesting it could be 1 May.
- A scene in the TARDIS featuring Kamelion was recorded but cut from the final episode (it can be viewed on the DVD release of the story). Tegan discovered the robot accessing controls behind a wall roundel in a corridor and expressed her distrust of him. This featured the wall with aligned opaque roundels, one of which had its central disc cut out and backed by two sideways-sliding shutters behind which was another sliding upwards. Inside was a screen with a keyboard beneath. The rest of the corridor comprised two translucent-roundels walls (the last appearance of any pre-1983 sections) and three of the new moulded square columns (additional to those in the control room as that set was erected elsewhere in the studio).
- The scenes in the control room had the console placed closer to the walls, making the room seem smaller than usual. The roundels weren't as brightly backlit as in other stories, revealing the mottled texture of the fibreglass. The hatstand is present but all but invisible, being painted the same grey as the walls. It's the model seen in *Arc of Infinity* and *Snakedance*.
- The Malus's psychic energy can manifest inside the TARDIS even though Turlough audibly shuts the Police Box door behind him when stepping out into the crypt (although in a cut scene, he and Tegan find

the doors open when they return). The initial sparkles were created using a BBC Micro, then the Malus itself was a puppet superimposed onto shots of the column to the right of the main doors (note, its shadow doesn't follow the contours of the slatted column). Although it spews copious amounts of green slime, presumably this vanishes along with the Malus projection once the psychic energy is blocked.
- The briefly glimpsed opening shutter of the scanner was achieved electronically rather than raising the physical shutter.
- The left-hand Police Box door is closed when everyone leaves the TARDIS after Willow has been clobbered (Will is last out and seems to leave the other door open). Yet when they all return to escape the church's destruction both doors are wide open.
- It's implied Turlough hasn't drunk tea since he was at Brendon School, so the TARDIS may not have tea-making facilities. It does by the time of the TV movie.

PREVIOUS LANDINGS

SPACE Earth, England, Little Hodcombe
TIME As Landing 247
TRAVELLERS The Doctor, Tegan, Turlough, Will Chandler, Sergeant Willow, Jane Hampden, Ben Wolsey, Andrew Verney, (Kamelion)
EPISODES Intended in The Awakening 2

After escaping the exploding church, the TARDIS rematerialises in Little Hodcombe to drop off the villagers who have helped defeat the Malus and allow Tegan to spend some time with her grandfather. Turlough is also looking forward to drinking tea again.
- **NOTES** Although the Doctor's intention is to drop everyone back at Little Hodcombe immediately, we don't see this in the serial, so for all we know something goes wrong with the TARDIS and the eight of them have a string of adventures together before eventually getting home.
- More likely is that the Ship makes the short trip to the village and everyone gets their lives back to normal after Sir George's war games. Tegan presumably spends at least a few days visiting her grandfather, and probably Turlough too given he "wouldn't mind staying for a while". How long the Doctor allows himself to relax is uncertain.

SPACE Earth, England, Little Hodcombe
TIME After 13 July 1643
TRAVELLERS The Doctor, Will Chandler, [Tegan, Turlough], (Kamelion)
EPISODES Intended in The Awakening 2

The Doctor takes Will back to his own time, dropping him off at Little Hodcombe after the battle between Cavaliers and Roundheads is well past.
- **NOTES** The Doctor states his intention to return Will to the 17th century but again we don't see it. Whether they leave Little Hodcombe with Tegan and Turlough, after all spending some time in 1984, or the Doctor alone returns himv to 1643 before returning for his friends, there's scope for further unseen adventures with Will.

SPACE Sirius system, Androzani Minor
TIME Unknown (before Landing 259)
TRAVELLERS The Doctor, [unknown companions]
EPISODES Mentioned by the Doctor in The Caves of Androzani 1

The Doctor visited Androzani Minor at a point after its seas had gone and the surface was "nothing but sand". He learned about its core of super-heated primeval mud and its tendency to erupt when passing close to its twin planet Androzani Major, but not about the fauna living in the caves. While Minor was uncolonised, Major was "becoming quite developed" so he may have encountered people from there (or visited it also).
- **NOTES** Androzani Major has a well-developed population by the time of the Doctor's return to the system so presumably this landing was earlier.
- This is before the Doctor meets Peri, and likely long before his fifth incarnation as his recollection seems like an old memory. He mentions having once tried to keep a diary of his travels, so this may have been while he was in his second incarnation.

SPACE Unnamed planet
TIME Unknown
TRAVELLERS The Doctor, [unknown companions]
EPISODES Mentioned by the Doctor in The Two Doctors 1

The Doctor fished on a stretch of river where gumblejack swam. He claims to have caught four magnificent examples in under ten minutes, which when cleaned, skinned and pan-fried were memorably delicious.
- **NOTES** This was before the Doctor met Peri. Even if the impressiveness of his haul is apocryphal there's no reason to disbelieve the fishing expedition occurred. He has shown most interest in fishing during his fourth incarnation so this may have been then, perhas shortly after his aborted fishing holiday on Tara (Landing 151).

SPACE Earth, Spain, Seville
TIME After 1588
TRAVELLERS The Doctor, [unknown companions]
EPISODES Mentioned by the Doctor in The Two Doctors 2

The Doctor spent some time in Seville during which he became familiar with the sound of the 25 bells of the Catedral de Santa Maria de la Sede, in particular the largest, Santa Maria La Mayor.

- **NOTES** This was before the Doctor met Peri, who hadn't visited Seville before she went with him. As he doesn't seem to remember his visit while in his second incarnation, when he was affected by Dastari's operation, this is presumably a different occasion.
- The Santa Maria is indeed the largest of the 24 bells in the belfry of the Giralda (the 25th is in the clock tower above), with a diameter of 2.1m and weighing approximately 5.4kg. It dates from 1588.

LANDING 248

SPACE Veruna system, near Frontios
TIME Far future
TRAVELLERS The Doctor, Tegan, Turlough, (Kamelion)
EPISODES Frontios 1

The Doctor is noisily clearing up somewhere in the TARDIS when he decides to remove the hatstand from the control room as it is rarely used. Just then the console warns of a time-parameter boundary error – the Ship has drifted too far into the future – so the Doctor materialises in hover mode in the Veruna system.

They are close to the planet Frontios, where one of the last groups of human refugees from the destruction of the Earth by its sun have settled. Tegan asks to visit but the Doctor is concerned any interference could destabilise the fledgling colony.

As the TARDIS drifts closer to the planet, gravitational fluctuations begin to pull on it. The stabilisers fail and the console jams, preventing the Doctor from switching off hover mode. Asteroids from nearby are also being pulled down to the planet, bombarding the surface at one location. The TARDIS is in danger of joining them until, with a thump, the Doctor frees the console and manages to dematerialise.

- **CONTROLS** The console's panels are fitted in a different order from usual; clockwise from the main doors they are arranged 1-3-2-6-5-4. This is the only time panels with the same layout are positioned adjacently.
- The message 'Boundary Error Time Parameters Exceeded' appears on the screen of panel E4. The Doctor puts the TARDIS into hover mode by flipping the switches in the top-left niche of this panel (and uses them again later to exit hover mode). Turlough presses some of the rocker switches and buttons below the screen, while Tegan reads their location from the screen on panel E6 (although it's only showing the 'Boundary error' message too). When trying to escape the gravitation pull, the Doctor presses controls near the top of panel E1.
- The structure inside the central column is missing most of its upper two tiers and these are not replaced until *Planet of Fire*.

- **NOTES** The TARDIS records state the humans in the Veruna system were "*fleeing* from the imminence of a *catastrophic* collision with the sun" and are "a group of refugees from the *doomed* planet Earth" (Turlough's italics). The Doctor also calls them "one of the last surviving groups of mankind", suggesting there were others. We perhaps saw another of these groups aboard the Ark, although they claimed to be carrying "the Earth's full population, human and animal" during what they called the 57th segment of time, which the Doctor estimated to be at least ten million years beyond even the fifth millennium (see Landing 35). We later learn (and see) in *The End of the World* (Landing 322, vol.2) that the Earth is ultimately consumed by the sun around the year five billion, by which time humans have spread across the universe, evolving and interbreeding with so many species that few pure-blood Earthlings are thought to exist. In *The Ark* we only see the planet's atmosphere boiling away so it's not impossible the Guardians were mistaken about the Earth being "swallowed in the pull of the sun"; perhaps it was the same anticipated collision as mentioned here (which arguably doesn't sound like the ultimate expansion of the sun itself) but which was actually averted. It's unlikely to be the shifting of the Earth by the Time Lords around the year two million (and back again shortly after, perhaps undone altogether) as they wouldn't have given anyone notice to prepare an escape (see Landing 281). Nor is it likely to be any of the solar flare events mentioned in *The Ark in Space* (Landing 107) or *The Beast Below* (Landing 444, vol.2).
- For the TARDIS to have boundaries on its travels and the Doctor to limit his knowledge "this far and no further" suggests, perhaps, that this occurs around the native time of his generation of Time Lords and that their laws forbid them from travelling into their future. The Doctor only ventures (or returns) to five billion and beyond when he believes Gallifrey destroyed and the Time Lords extinct. Even once he knows they're both back, they're hiding out near the end of the universe and he only travels even further forward out of desperation to deliberately escape them (and that's in a different TARDIS).
- Beyond the control room's interior door is a wall with aligned roundels. If this is the same as used in but cut from *The Awakening* (Landing 247) then its opening roundel has been replaced with a standard one.
- This story sees the (temporary) removal of a hatstand from the control room so it's perhaps odd that a never-before-seen model was used. Most notably the hooks' stems are almost horizontal and the upper hoop is below them rather than above as on previous stands. It also has no middle hoop for holding umbrellas. This was presumably chosen to look more convincing when Turlough later pretends it's a weapon. The Doctor does say he thinks he has another like it and it's possible this is glimpsed in the gloomy control room in *Battlefield*.
- This is the second time recently that the TARDIS has materialised above a planet and then plummeted out

of control towards it, forcing the Doctor to perform a quick landing on the surface in order to escape collision (see Landing 245). Does he again execute a materialisation flip-flop here?

LANDING 249

SPACE Frontios
TIME As above
TRAVELLERS The Doctor, Tegan, Turlough, (Kamelion)
EPISODES Frontios 1,4

The TARDIS lands at the impact site of the meteorites just as the bombardment is ending. A massive spaceship sits nearby, its bow crumpled and half buried in a hillside. Around a hatch in the hull are lean-to shelters amid salvaged wreckage and equipment, forming an arena with the surrounding rocks. The travellers emerge from the Ship as the darkened sky begins to clear and, noticing injured people on the ground, help carry them into the crashed colony ship.

Tegan and Turlough return to the TARDIS with instructions to collect a mu-field activator and five argon discharge globes, but they find the interior door jammed and cannot get beyond the control room.

Another bombardment of meteorites begins, slamming into the ground around the spaceship. The gravitational beams attracting them also pull on the Police Box and it is sucked through the soil. In fact, they are so strong they breach the Ship's outer plasmic shell and its interior is dispersed underground, merged into the surrounding earth and only exposed where tunnels bore through the slaty bedrock.

Fortunately the control room remains self-contained, although interwoven with outcrops of rock. Escaping the gravity-manipulating Tractators, the Doctor, Turlough and the colonists' leader Plantagenet discover the control room but find the console inoperable. Tegan joins them and warns the dominant Tractator, the Gravis, is just outside. The Doctor lures it into the control room and convinces it to use its gravitational powers to reassemble the TARDIS. As the sections are pulled together, the plasmic outer walls seal the interior into its own dimension once more, separating the Gravis from the other Tractators. The creature is exhausted by the effort and collapses.

With the Tractators in the tunnels now harmless, Plantagenet returns to the surface to quell the growing discord and the colonists' science officer Range examines the dormant Gravis. The Doctor and Tegan take a short trip to deposit the creature somewhere he cannot cause trouble.

◉ **CONTROLS** When the Doctor is working beneath the console, Turlough directs his hand to the buttons below the recall unit on panel E6.
◉ The Doctor tells the Gravis (so he may be lying) that all the main TARDIS functions are controlled from panel E6. He points to the two clusters of keys at the very bottom below the screen as the inputs for the time (on the right) and space (on the left) coordinates. The spatial distribution circuits are controlled by either the group of four rocker switches to the left or the row of blue buttons below them: the Doctor seems to indicate the former but when the Gravis reaches for them these don't move (because the costume's flippers aren't firm enough) so he may be pressing the latter. This activates the autoscan on the adjacent screen.

▌ **LORE** The Doctor reiterates the TARDIS is "an old type forty Time And Relative Dimension [singular] In Space machine".

▌ The spatial distributions circuits optimise the packing efficiency of the real-time envelope. An autoscan system can detect where TARDIS sections are located.

▌ **NOTES** The Tractators' ability to breach the TARDIS's dimensions with their gravity manipulation is unprecedented. The Ship is later seen to withstand close proximity to supernovae and black holes, yet a bunch of insects can concentrate gravity to such an extent that the TARDIS is pulled apart. We later see the Ship's interior intruded upon in a collision with the spaceship Titanic after the Doctor accidentally leaves the shields down (see Landing 392, vol.2) so are these deactivated here, either before arrival or as a consequence of the Tractators' pulling power?

▌ We only see the control room and a few walls among the tunnels, but presumably all the TARDIS rooms and their contents are scattered around underground, including Kamelion. That the Ship can locate and reassemble its own structure is conceivable, but how do its contents remain inside once the outer plasmic shell reseals (and what's so special about the hatstand that it's initially left behind and not pulled back into the TARDIS when it's recombined)? What happens to the Police Box exterior is not shown; perhaps it's simply somewhere in the tunnels, an empty shell as in *Father's Day* (see Landing 332, vol.2).

▌ When Tegan first finds parts of the TARDIS walls, one contains the main doors, and these are still visible behind the Gravis when he approaches her. Yet she backs away against the interior door and slips through into the control, where the main doors are. So are the first pair from an alternative control room? Or is there some spatial distortion going on such that the doors appear in two places at once?

▌ Although Turlough says, "None of the controls are functional," the screens are displaying text and all the lights are on. The autoscan is also working. (He simply means the flight controls?)

▌ Owing to the incorrect placement of panels, the view of the console through the interior door reveals the screen housing on panel E2 has no monitor fitted.

▌ Presumably once the TARDIS is reformed it's recombined with the Police Box exterior somewhere within the tunnels. It's possible the Doctor rematerialises it above ground before dropping off Turlough and Plantagenet, and allowing Range to examine the Gravis, but equally he may let them out underground. It's surprising Turlough stays behind while the Doctor and Tegan dispose of the Gravis as there must be a good chance they won't return. Maybe his ancestral fear of the Tractators makes him unwilling to travel with one, or perhaps he's happy to stay with Norna should the TARDIS not come back for him.

LANDING 250

SPACE Kolkokron
TIME Unknown
TRAVELLERS The Doctor, Tegan, Gravis, (Kamelion)
EPISODES Frontios 4

The Doctor selects the uninhabited planet Kolkokron, in an unoccupied system, on which to maroon the Gravis. He and Tegan leave the Tractator with nothing but rocks and boulders to play with.

- **NOTES** Although we don't directly see this landing, the Doctor explicitly takes the Gravis there and Tegan discusses the planet's appearance. There's no plausible scope for unseen landings after, either.
- While Tegan notes, "All the planets are deserted according to the TARDIS scanner," it's perhaps risky to leave the Gravis on a rocky world with plenty of boulders to manipulate with his gravitational powers. Should any spaceship happen to pass, the Tractator could fling rocks at it and potentially bring it down as with the human colony ship. And we know the creatures were able to survive almost 500 years on the similarly barren Frontios before the humans approached. So has the Doctor picked Kolkokron because he knows it's never visited by any intelligent lifeforms?

LANDING 251

SPACE Frontios
TIME Shortly after Landing 249
TRAVELLERS The Doctor, Tegan, (Kamelion)
EPISODES Frontios 4

The TARDIS returns to Frontios to collect Turlough, materialising once again in the arena outside the colony ship (although in a different spot from its earlier landing). The Doctor offers Plantagenet his hatstand as a farewell token.

The colonists entreat the travellers to stay awhile but the Doctor is wary of the Time Lords ever learning about his involvement, so he's keen to depart. Tegan and Turlough take their leave of Plantagenet, Range and his daughter Norna, who watch as the Police Box dematerialises.

- **NOTES** Damage to the corners of the 'Police box' sign on the right-hand side of the prop is very noticeable in the shot of the TARDIS materialising.
- The Doctor must have discussed with Turlough his plan to gift the colonists his unwanted hatstand before he left, as Turlough informs Plantagenet the Doctor has a present for him.

LANDING 252

SPACE Earth, England, London, wharf by Tower Bridge
TIME [Autumn] 1984
TRAVELLERS The Doctor, Tegan, Turlough, (Kamelion)
EPISODES Frontios 4; Resurrection of the Daleks 1-2

No sooner has the TARDIS departed Frontios than the engines begin making a harsh grating sound. The Doctor assures the others there is nothing wrong with them, even though Turlough notes the Ship is travelling "far too fast". The control room jolts as the TARDIS intersects with a time corridor and is dragged along it, heading towards "the middle of the universe".

The shaking gets worse, flinging the travellers around the control room. The movement eases slightly as the TARDIS weaves in time and the Doctor tries to find a way to materialise without risking the Ship breaking up. As the room lurches again, the cloister bell briefly tolls. The Doctor waits until the time stress on the TARDIS eases and makes his attempt to break free. The shuddering worsens and the room tilts as the travellers grip the console, but the TARDIS escapes the corridor and flies smoothly.

As the Doctor makes repairs beneath the console, Turlough notices they are travelling parallel to the time corridor, one end of which is on 20th century Earth. The TARDIS materialises close to its locus, on the south side of the River Thames, just downstream from Tower Bridge. The travellers head towards some disused and dilapidated warehouses to investigate who is operating the corridor.

The Doctor returns to the TARDIS with Stien, a soldier from the future who escaped to Earth via the time corridor. The Doctor uses the console to locate the Dalek battle cruiser at the other end of the time corridor, where Turlough has been transported, but the moment he sets the Ship in motion it lurches as it is ensnared in the corridor again.

- **CONTROLS** When first trying to pull against the time corridor, the Doctor flips switches in the top-left niche of panel E4 (previously used to go into hover mode so maybe he's trying to materialise) and presses rocker switches along the bottom. As the shuddering worsens, he thumps the top of the screen housing on panel E6 (now back adjacent to panel E1) and uses the keypad below it and unseen controls to the right. He presses buttons on the right of the upper niche of panel E1 before being flung away from the console.
- In *Resurrection of the Daleks* the console panels are back in their usual configuration, creating a continuity error with *Frontios*. The right-hand black square from the top of panel E4 has also gone missing.
- The Doctor presses rocker switches on panel E1 (probably those on the shelf of the bottom-centre niche), other buttons in that niche, his favoured buttons in the upper niche, some in the upper-left niche of panel E6, and keys below the screen again. To break free of the time corridor he flips the red switch on the side of the middle-left niche of this panel.

- After landing, the Doctor presses a button on the right of the upper niche of panel E1, the left-most red button in the middle-left niche of panel E6 and one of the blue buttons at bottom-far-left of this panel. Later when locating the Dalek ship, he presses the latter two again. To dematerialise, he presses the right red button on the right of the upper niche of panel E1.
- **NOTES** Putting aside the question of whether the universe even has a definable middle, the idea that the TARDIS is being dragged towards the centre of everything isn't explained or even supported by events in *Resurrection of the Daleks*, where the Doctor announces out of the blue that they're caught in a time corridor. So perhaps it's just that Earth is nearer this middle than Frontios, so the Ship is moving generally in that direction.
- Indeed, how is the TARDIS caught in the time corridor at all? No sooner has it left Frontios in the distant future, with all of time and space to explore, than it's ensnared in a single thread connecting two specific points less than three millennia apart. Then again, there was a similarly unlikely entanglement across disparate time periods in *Time-Flight* (Landing 218) It's later indicated the Daleks deliberately targeted the TARDIS but how did they track its location from so far in the past relative to it?
- Why does the cloister bell briefly chime? It hasn't sounded since *Castrovalva* (Landing 204) – not when the TARDIS was breaking up in *Terminus*, nor when the interior was being torn out of its dimension by Tractators. Even here it tolls once then is silent although the Ship is still stuck in the time corridor, and doesn't ring again during either of the further occasions the TARDIS is travelling along the corridor.
- Watch the traffic on Tower Bridge as the TARDIS materialises: the cars disappear.
- The Doctor says, "I think it's nineteen eighty-four," but notes, "The instruments are still affected by turbulence." However, as Tegan decides it's okay for her to stay behind in this time period we can assume the Doctor is correct. The weather is grey and wet so it's likely autumn (the location filming was in September); if it were spring Tegan would be returning to Earth before her earlier visit to Little Hodcombe, which could be awkward.
- As the Doctor and Stein walk back to the TARDIS, a telephone plaque can just be made out below the left-hand window on the side facing them, even though the opposite side of the Police Box was used as the entrance in the scene of it arriving. This proves the prop was fitted with plaques on both faces at this time..
- A cut scene featured the Doctor and Stien entering the control room, with the Doctor noting "it's bigger inside than out" before Stien can mention it. The experience makes the soldier wonder if he's going mad.
- When the Doctor presses the button to dematerialise, rather enthusiastically, the panel flexes noticeably.

LANDING 253

SPACE Dalek battle cruiser
TIME [4590] (at least 90 years after Landing 159)
TRAVELLERS The Doctor, Stien, (Kamelion)
EPISODES Resurrection of the Daleks 2-4

The TARDIS is pulled along the time corridor to the Dalek's spaceship in the future. It materialises in a reception area adjacent to the terminal for the corridor. There is no sign of Turlough, only troopers, and the Doctor successfully disarms one but is then held at gunpoint by Stien, who reveals that he is in fact a Dalek agent. Daleks arrive to exterminate the Doctor but are stopped by Lytton, a mercenary assisting them, who informs them that the Supreme Dalek has ordered the Doctor be duplicated, so he is led away to the duplication chamber.

Tegan is transported alone via the time corridor and arrives on the Dalek battle cruiser, emerging into the deserted reception area. She is discovered by Mercer, the security officer from the prison station with which the cruiser is docked. He is about to shoot her but is stopped from doing so by the arrival of Turlough, who is hoping to use the corridor to return to Earth. Tegan insists they find the Doctor first, pointing to the Police Box in the corner as proof he is somewhere on the ship. They move off, unaware they are being observed by Davros in the station's laboratory.

All three return to the TARDIS with the Doctor and Stien. The Doctor has programmed the Ship to return to Earth but decides he must first execute Davros himself. Stien and Mercer go with him.

Shortly after, however, the TARDIS dematerialises and proceeds on its programmed course, the Doctor having set a timer to keep Tegan and Turlough safe should he not return. The Ship lurches as it is again caught in the time corridor.

- **CONTROLS** On returning to the TARDIS, the Doctor flips switches on the side of the middle-left niche of panel E1 before even closing the main doors. As he doesn't appear to operate any other controls before leaving again, he presumably set the return course to Earth on arrival (to allow for a quick getaway, knowing he would be facing Daleks), so is this switch activating the take-off timer?
- **LORE** Dematerialisation of the TARDIS can be delayed on a timer and then a preset destination travelled to automatically.
- **NOTES** No date is given on screen for the time period in which the Daleks are recovering Davros, only that he has been in his frozen prison for 90 years. However, the script indicates the date is 4590.
- Although the TARDIS is said to be "caught in the time corridor", it materialises under its own power rather than appearing in the terminal as others using the corridor do. Either the Doctor breaks free or the Ship is again travelling parallel to the corridor but constrained to follow it.

- Further control room scenes were cut from the final episodes. One had the Doctor and Stien viewing the reception area on the scanner before going out to look for Turlough. After the Doctor leaves to kill Davros, Turlough was ready to abandon him but Tegan insisted on waiting. And before the TARDIS took off, Daleks fired at it; watching on the scanner, Tegan reassured Turlough they couldn't break in.
- Davros orders his Daleks to secure the TARDIS, seemingly recognising the Police Box on his security monitor. Yet he has no opportunity to see it in either *Genesis of the Daleks* (when the TARDIS is not present on Skaro) or *Destiny of the Daleks*. In the latter story, however, he does receive an update on the history of the Dalek-Movellan war, which might include details about the Doctor and his time machine if he has been involved in the conflict in an unseen adventure (he does briefly turn up during a battle in *The Pilot* – see Landing 695, vol.2). Davros also now knows the Doctor is a Time Lord. Alternatively, the Doctor may have been present while Davros was being tried on Earth, during which the villain learned these details. In either case, the Doctor must have been in his fourth incarnation as Davros seems unaware Time Lords can regenerate.

LANDING 254

SPACE Earth, England, London, warehouse
TIME Shortly after Landing 252
TRAVELLERS Tegan, Turlough, (Kamelion)
EPISODES Resurrection of the Daleks 4

The TARDIS arrives back on Earth, in the warehouse where the time corridor terminates although on the floor below. Tegan insists on going out to recover cylinders of the Movellan virus that the Daleks have secreted here, Turlough reluctantly assisting. They bring back one of the blue canisters but cannot open it. The Doctor returns, having travelled via the time corridor, and takes the cylinder outside where factions of Daleks and troopers are massacring each other. He releases the virus then slips back into the Ship, just evading a shot from Lytton's gun.

The travellers watch on the scanner as the infected Daleks die messily. The image is interrupted by the Supreme Dalek, who claims to have human duplicates in strategic positions around the world, but the Doctor is confident these are unstable and not a threat.

They venture out into the now-quiet warehouse to make sure no danger persists. Although Turlough suggests informing the authorities, the Doctor prepares to leave. But Tegan announces she wants to stay on Earth, sick of all the death she has witnessed, and runs off in tears. A chastened Doctor ushers Turlough into the TARDIS and it takes off.

NOTES One last cut control room scene showed the Ship coming to rest as it exited the time corridor. The scanner displayed a view of the warehouse and Tegan was keen to think of a way to help the Doctor.
- In views of the scanner, its shutter isn't fully raised so the CSO area is a different proportion to usual. While the view of the Supreme Dalek was superimposed during recording (against a white background because the battle cruiser bridge set wasn't ready, not otherwise being required until a later recording session), the preceding view of the dying Daleks hadn't yet been recorded. This was added later, overlaid on the picture and slightly larger than the CSO area.
- This is the first time the scanner has displayed an unsolicited videocall from a distant party. In *The Three Doctors* the Doctor contacted Omega in his castle, but that whole domain was conjured from the latter's mind so this may have been a telepathic link (see Landing 91). And in *Nightmare of Eden* the Doctor was able to talk to Romana in the TARDIS via a monitor on the Empress's bridge, she having likely connected to the liner's communications system (see Landing 169). But otherwise we've only seen the Doctor converse with others immediately outside the TARDIS via two-way audio, even though he might look at the scanner to see who he's talking to. Here, though, the screen is receiving a direct transmission from the Supreme Dalek located in a different space and time altogether and relaying back the Doctor's responses (can the Dalek see into the control room too?).
- How is the scanner showing a view of the exploding prison station and Dalek cruiser when the TARDIS is on Earth and thousands of years in the past? It last displayed a far distant event in *The Horns of Nimon* (Landing 172) so we know this is possible. Perhaps, knowing the coordinates of the Dalek ship, the Doctor set the scanner to display that point in space-time; or this final image was detectable through the time corridor as it (presumably) collapsed.

IT LOOKS JUST LIKE A POLICE BOX

THE YARDLEY-JONES BOX 3
1984-1989

During production of Season 21 in the latter half of 1983 it was decided another Police Box prop would be constructed, again from fibreglass to Tom Yardley-Jones' 1980 design. Unlike the last time a new box was produced, though, this was to supplement rather than replace the existing box.

Quite why is not clear: there was no narrative need for two TARDISes to appear together (as in *Logopolis*, for example) nor any obvious reason why having two props available would make scheduling recordings easier (there's no known situation where both boxes were in use at the same time). Even though the existing box was already beginning to look rundown after less than two years' use (see page 306), it continued to be repaired and employed until the end of the original series. Was Box 3 a replacement for the Newbery box, which had been brought out of retirement as a backup prop during Season 19 but unused since and last seen at the Longleat celebration in April 1983? Perhaps with a new control room having recently been introduced it was felt the outside of the TARDIS should be upgraded too.

Unlike the uncertainty whether Box 2 was new or a major refurbishment of Box 1 until the recent discovery of paperwork proving the former, we know Box 3 was a new construction as plans exist for a 'New demountable fibreglass Tardis', drawn by design assistant Gina Parr for Malcolm Thornton, the designer assigned to *Planet of Fire* (although misconceptions about its use in this story persist – see Landing 255 for the truth). This serial was chosen for the new Police Box's debut perhaps because the extensive location filming meant fewer studio sets were needed so the designer's budget would cover the cost of the new prop. The plans were drawn up on 20 September for completion by the 30th as it needed to be ready to ship to Lanzarote for filming two weeks later. These were a direct copy of the drawings by Tom Yardley-Jones from 1980, down to the wording of the annotations (the only difference is in the plan view the doors are correctly shown opening inwards). Similarly, when it came to forming the fibreglass sections, these were precise duplicates of the existing box, so it's likely the original moulds had been kept after their reuse in 1982. The sign boxes even had the wide retaining frame on the front to secure the lettered inserts. One influence the redrawn plans did have was that the wording of the 'Police telephone' plaque reverted to 'Officers and cars' responding to 'Urgent calls' – initially the only way to tell Boxes 2 and 3 apart at a glance.

Box 3 became the primary prop for the rest of Season 21 and into Season 22. When production travelled to Spain for *The Two Doctors*, however, Box 2 was used for the location filming and subsequent studio recording. While Box 3 was back for *The Mark of the Rani* it was mothballed for the remainder of the season (although the switch in transmission order of these two serials meant the Box 3 and Box 2 stories were grouped together).

ENTRANCES AND EXITS

Both boxes were stored away while *Doctor Who* was on hiatus but at some point prior to the series' return Box 3 was refurbished despite its relative lack of use. The biggest change was that the prop received new front and rear doors. Previously these had both opened the same way – that is, right-hand first as the left-hand door had the centre post attached, matching Box 2 – but now one set was switched to open left door first. Both had their locks positioned below the handle, these being on the door without the centre post, enabling Box 3 to be more clearly distinguished from its older sibling. The prop also inherited the thicker base that had been seen on Box 2 during Season 21, while the sign boxes' wide retaining frames were removed (as they were on Box 2 too).

These changes and the pristine look of the refurbished box have led some to presume this was another new prop but this time there are no design plans or (as yet) documents indicating a new build was commissioned, and no evidence there were ever three boxes in existence. Of course, similar arguments applied to Box 2's appearance in Season 20 and were later disproved but here we can be more certain. For one thing, there are on-screen indicators that Box 2 was used through to 1989, so why would the newer prop be the one to be replaced?

Despite this refit of Box 3 (or perhaps because it was in progress), Box 2 was used for location filming of the first segment of *The Trial of a Time Lord* (in a scene that was later cut). The arrival of the TARDIS aboard the court space station was remounted during production of the second segment, 'Mindwarp', using Box 3, so it's not known which prop was used for the first recording. This restaging was recorded the same day as the Doctor's snatching from Thoros Beta, on Friday 13 June 1986, so we know the prop's refit was completed by then. Both these scenes used the face with right-door

Right Front elevation and section of the prop Malcolm Thornton had built to match Yardley-Jones's original

IT LOOKS JUST LIKE A POLICE BOX

POLICE PUBLIC CALL BOX

POLICE TELEPHONE
FREE
FOR USE OF
PUBLIC
ADVICE AND ASSISTANCE
OBTAINABLE IMMEDIATELY
OFFICERS AND CARS
RESPOND TO
URGENT CALLS
PULL TO OPEN

IT LOOKS JUST LIKE A POLICE BOX

Above Prior to Season 23 in 1986, the prop was refurbished, including replacing both pairs of doors. These now had alternate opening priority – right door first on the 'front' (left) and left door first on the 'rear' (right). The box also gained a thicker base

priority as the entrance so let's call this the front and the left-door-priority face the rear. Although the location scenes for 'Mindwarp' were recorded just a few days later on Monday 16 June, Box 2 was used, perhaps so as not to risk water damage to the newer, smarter prop.

Next to be recorded were the scenes in the atrium outside the courtroom for the final two episodes of *The Trial of a Time Lord*, when the left-door-priority rear of the Police Box was favoured (making a continuity error with episode one when the front was seen, with the lock and handle on the right). Only here and in *The Happiness Patrol* (plus an appearance on *Blue Peter* on 2 March 1987 to introduce Sylvester McCoy) is this face used as the entrance; the right-hand front door was used in all Box 3's other appearances. These were fewer than might be expected. While Box 3 was used throughout Season 24 bar *Delta and the Bannermen* (and during a press photocall on Thursday 13 August 1987 to announce Sophie Aldred's casting as Ace), it appeared only once the following year (partially repainted pink) and one final brief time in 1989's *The Curse of Fenric*.

Why the older prop stayed in favour isn't known; perhaps it was just chance determining which happened to be pulled from storage. Both Yardley-Jones boxes were kept by the BBC after the series ended in 1989. Box 3 was used for promotional purposes – including an appearance in the 1999 Comic Relief spoof *The Curse of Fatal Death* (with new signage) and being positioned outside BBC Television Centre for some years, during which it became increasingly damaged. It was then meticulously restored by Mark Barton Hill (although made to match Box 1 during Season 18) for display at the Doctor Who Experience, first in London Olympia in 2011, then in Cardiff until the exhibition closed in 2018.

LANDING 255

SPACE Earth, Canary Islands, Lanzarote
TIME [May/June 1984/1985]
TRAVELLERS The Doctor, Turlough, Kamelion
EPISODES Planet of Fire 1

Kamelion has plugged himself into the TARDIS databank via a wall roundel not far from the control room. He is suddenly incapacitated by an unidentified signal and screams in pain, attracting the attention of the Doctor and Turlough. The disoriented robot senses someone trying to contact him. Turlough returns to the control room to programme an alpha rhythm that will calm Kamelion, just as a distress call is detected. He recognises it as coming from Trion, his home planet, and rips out components from under the console to make it stop. When the Doctor discovers this, Turlough claims there was a random emission he feared was affecting Kamelion. They notice the robot has reset the coordinates.

The TARDIS materialises close to the source of the distress call, on a sunny beach on the island of Lanzarote. The signal is coming from an alien object on a boat just off shore, having recently been recovered from a sunken vessel. The Doctor and Turlough change their clothes to suit the heat of the day – Turlough donning a loose shirt and shorts (over swimming trunks), the Doctor losing his coat and jumper in favour of an embroidered waistcoat – then head out to trace the source using a handheld receiver.

While they are gone, Kamelion uses the console to locate whoever is trying to contact him. But Turlough, returning to get a second reading on the distress call's bearing, angrily disables the robot and removes him from the control room. When he returns he notices on the scanner a girl struggling in the sea and, after a moment's hesitation, dashes outside and swims out to rescue her. He brings her back to the TARDIS and puts her to bed in Tegan's old room, noticing in her bag of belongings the object sending the distress call. This has the same triangular emblem as is branded on Turlough's arm. He takes the unit to the control room and removes its data core. The Doctor returns having detected the signal's change of location and finds Turlough with the dismantled unit, which he claims to have found on the shore. The Doctor connects the data core to the console so the computer can decode it but it burns out.

Meanwhile, the sleeping girl, Peri, dreams of her stepfather Howard, causing Kamelion to take on the man's appearance and reactivate. He reconnects himself to the TARDIS, closes the main doors and dematerialises. Only then does the Doctor discover he seemingly has two new passengers.

○ **CONTROLS** When programming the alpha rhythm, Turlough uses the left keypad in the bottom-centre niche of panel E5. The screen on panel E4 seems to display some information about the distress call and Turlough presses the keypad in the niche to the right of this to try to switch it off. He unclips a drop-down section under panel E6 that holds circuit boards and wiring, which he pulls out to kill the signal. When the Doctor returns, he presses one of the green buttons and two of the rocker switches on the shelf of the bottom-centre niche of panel E1 then flips one of the switches in the middle-left niche. It's when he presses buttons on the right of the upper niche of this panel that he discovers Turlough's sabotage.

○ Several modifications were made to the console to meet the requirements of the script. A drop-down panel was added for Turlough to access internal circuitry, with a similar trapezium shape to the underside sections but only about half the size. This was simply clipped on to avoid cutting into the console prop. A small drawer was slung under the left side of panel E1 to house the temporal stabiliser and a slot was cut into the top of panel E2 above the screen housing for the comparator to sit in. This raised housing also gained a pair of flaps to cover a new hollow in its top (intended for the comparator?). Finally, a red square control was added to panel E4 to the right of the circular display. Given the other changes were script led, was this intended as a connector for the distress beacon's data core?

○ Turlough punches at unseen controls (possibly the keypad below the screen on panel E6) to "finish" Kamelion, perhaps by cancelling the alpha rhythm given the robot screams again. When he returns to the control room, he presses the left-most of the group of four rocker switches to the right of the screen on panel E4, then buttons in the top-left niche to zoom the scanner image. When trying to decode the Trion data core, the Doctor flips an unseen switch on panel E3.

▤ **NOTES** The Doctor is brooding over the Daleks and admits he's missing Tegan, suggesting this story follows directly from the last, but it's possible there has been a landing or two since leaving Earth. Turlough seems finally to be relaxing now that Tegan isn't around: he's removed his tie for the first time.

▤ It's after October 1983 judging from Peri's passport stamps (although while this has her photo, the name is not hers, has a date of birth 15 November 1940, and expired in 1977). Peri reminds Howard her return to "college in the fall" is "in three months' time". Fall semesters in American colleges tend to start in late August or early September, placing this in early summer – in fact, possibly not long after she finished spring term, meaning she's bored pretty quickly. No year is given but it's typical for companions to come from the year of transmission. In *Timelash*, however, the Doctor suggests returning Peri to 1985 and in the following story *Revelation of the Daleks* she still anticipates going back to college, so even by then the plan is still to get her home before the next semester.

▤ Beyond the control room interior door is one of the wide-spaced translucent-roundels walls (see page 329), a square slatted column, then a plain door leading initially to the area where Kamelion is connected. This has a column behind the door, then the aligned opaque-roundels wall used for but cut from *The Awakening* (Landing 247) with its roundel open (although the circuitry behind it is different), another column and a second wide-spaced-roundels wall. After the scenes with Kamelion were recorded, the set was rearranged to form Tegan's old bedroom. This has the wide-spaced-roundels walls to the right of the door, while to the left is a unique piece with two faces at an obtuse angle, each with nine moulded slats (so wider than the columns which only have seven slats on their fronts), forming a corner with a third wide-spaced translucent-roundels section. (This plethora of new walls strongly suggests none of those from pre-1983 sets were kept.) The bedroom contains previously seen furniture including the brass-framed bed, wicker chairs and metal shelf unit with china ornaments. Because of this rearrangement of the set, on screen the two rooms appear to occupy the same space (or at least overlap) within the TARDIS.

- Publicity photos for this serial taken on location in Lanzarote feature a miniature Police Box (the quarter-size model from *Logopolis*) in several false-perspective shots of the main cast. It was therefore long assumed that the scenes of the TARDIS on the beach used this same prop – being easier to transport than the full-size box – and that this was why it was only seen close up, again creating a false perspective. However, production documentation indicates sections of the TARDIS prop *were* taken to the location and careful examination of the dimensions, paint textures and details of the Police Box on screen prove it's the newly built prop. In the episodes only the front doors and one side are seen (and never above the level of the windows), but attached to the base judging from the transport itinerary. This is presumably why the miniature was taken on location too, to allow for press photos with a complete Police Box.
- When in the guise of Howard, Kamelion says to the Doctor, "We meet again," but how does he know the Doctor has encountered the real professor? It can't be from Peri's mind as she wasn't present when the two met on the quayside. Howard-Kamelion also says he saw Turlough rescue Peri but the robot was inactive and out of sight of the scanner at that time (although that could have been from Peri's memories).

LANDING 256

SPACE Sarn, ruin
TIME [As above]
TRAVELLERS The Doctor, Turlough, Kamelion, Perpugilliam 'Peri' Brown
EPISODES Planet of Fire 1-4

Programmed by Kamelion, the TARDIS materialises on the volcanically active planet Sarn, among the ruins of a building with stone columns and alcoves. The Ship's computer indicates there is no imminent eruption nearby so the Doctor and Turlough go outside to determine where they are. When they discover a triangular mark matching that on the distress unit, Turlough realises this must be a colony planet of his own people and persuades the Doctor to seek out any inhabitants. They do not notice the Master's TARDIS materialising as a stone pillar.

Kamelion is now free to transmute into the Master and commandeer the TARDIS. When Peri tries to leave he grabs her, but her fear overwhelms the robot's personality circuits and he transforms back into his natural form. As the Master tries to regain control, Kamelion takes on Howard's appearance again, removes the comparator from the console and gives it to Peri. Before he can let her out, however, he succumbs to the Master and is ordered to go to his TARDIS, taking Peri with him. As they cross the ruin, an earth tremor causes the Master's TARDIS to topple over and a falling stone knocks out Kamelion, allowing Peri to run after the Doctor and Turlough.

Kamelion recovers but is unable to right the Master's TARDIS so is ordered to materialise the Doctor's inside it instead. He notices the comparator is missing, however, so heads off after Peri to retrieve it.

Some time later, Master-Kamelion returns with Peri and a group of Sarns including their chief elder Timanov. With the promise of gifts, he gets them to raise the fallen stone pillar then takes Peri inside, just as the Doctor and Turlough arrive. The Doctor plans to materialise his TARDIS around the Master's, and Turlough gives him the comparator he received from Peri. His plan is foiled, however, because Kamelion has removed the temporal stabiliser. The Doctor watches on the scanner as the stone pillar dematerialises, and discovers the two TARDISes' navigational systems have been remote-paralleled by Kamelion – this allowed the Master to follow him to Sarn but means he can also follow wherever the Master has gone now, if he had the temporal stabiliser.

The ruins are shaken by a localised earthquake and while most of the gathered Sarns scatter Turlough ushers Timanov and the elders into the TARDIS for safety. There, with rebel Amyand's help, the Doctor has produced an image of the Sarns' god, Logar – actually just a figure in a thermal suit – to win over the elders' trust. The console detects that the Master is in a control centre inside the volcano and when the seismic scanner alerts of activity there everyone goes outside to view the mountain, which is emitting a blue flame of numismaton gas from its crater. They all head back to the Sarns' settlement.

Later, Turlough replaces the temporal stabiliser with that from the Master's TARDIS then programmes a fifteen-second time-delayed take-off. The captain of a rescue ship from Trion confronts him but Turlough ushers him out before the main doors close and the Ship takes off.

○ CONTROLS After landing, the Doctor flips switches at the bottom-right of panel E4 and seemingly operates the scanner from panel E3. Howard-Kamelion operates four unseen controls (all sounding like rocker switches) on panels E4, E5 and E6 before closing the main doors. After transforming, Master-Kamelion uses

unseen controls on panel E6 and presses a button in the middle-left niche of panel E5.
- ● Howard-Kamelion takes the comparator from the hole above the screen on panel E2. This panel is rarely seen but can be glimpsed in *Frontios* where it appears to have no slot, so it was presumably added for this purpose.
- ● The Doctor tries to dematerialise from panel E1, seemingly by flipping the switches in the middle-far-left niche. After the Master's TARDIS vanishes, the Doctor presses rocker switches at bottom-left of panel E4 and below the left-hand slider at bottom-right of panel E5. He produces an image of Logar on the screen on panel E4 using the rocker switches below, pressing the same to display the image on panel E6's screen also. When the Master's TARDIS is located, the Doctor flips the rightmost switch in panel E4's top-left niche.
- ● After refitting the temporal stabiliser, Turlough presses a rocker switch on panel E1, unseen controls on panels E2 and E4, and two of the red buttons in the bottom-centre niche of panel E5 – after these last, the alert for the time-delayed take-off sounds.
- ▊ **LORE** The TARDIS is "useless" without the comparator.
- ▊ Removal of the temporal stabiliser prevents the Ship from dematerialising.
- ▊ The seismic scanner detects local geological vibrations.
- ▊ The main doors can be operated by short-circuiting wires in the console's pedestal.
- ▊ **NOTES** It's not explicit that events on Sarn are in the same time period as on Earth, but the Trion captain who arrives knows of Turlough and his exile. Malkon is said to have been an infant when his father's ship crashed on Sarn and is now in his mid-teens. But Turlough, who was exiled at the same time, can't have been attending Brendan School for that long prior to *Mawdryn Undead*, so either he was a little boy when sent to Earth and has been brought up in a number of institutions prior to boarding at Brendan or, given he never suggests this, he was already a young teenager during the Trion civil war. He must have been at Brendan for a while to develop so much hatred of it, perhaps from ages twelve to seventeen (arriving in 1978 after the Brigadier's breakdown). Events on Sarn may then be around the year 1994 and Malkon has almost caught up in age with a brother who should be around ten years his senior.
- ▊ The Master is shrunk when experimenting with his tissue compression eliminator and Kamelion senses his pain and screams. Moments later, the TARDIS detects a signal from a Trion distress beacon on Earth. Turlough recognises this as being from "a Trion ship" rather than his home world itself; is the beacon meant to be from his father's ship, fallen to Earth into the sea and settled amid an ancient wreck? The Master wants to get to Sarn to heal himself in the numismaton flame, so is it a coincidence that this is where the beacon directs the Doctor's TARDIS? Or, given the beacon explodes when plugged into the console and it's implied Kamelion takes control of the Ship, is the distress call irrelevant and the Master simply has his robot slave rendezvous with him on Sarn to assist with his restoration? In either case, why does the Master need to follow the Doctor's TARDIS in order to get there?
- ▊ We don't see Master-Kamelion remove the Doctor's temporal stabiliser but this was probably done after he discovered the comparator was missing. Nor do we see the Doctor replace the latter component but we can assume he has because when the TARDIS refuses to take off he immediately checks the stabiliser drawer.
- ▊ The Master's control room is simply the usual set painted black. The console is also modified with strips of black tape between the red insets around the collar and down the panel edges. The rim and the hexagonal reliefs on the pedestal are also coloured black. Note that the console retains the additional temporal stabiliser drawer and drop-down circuitry panel even though only the former is needed.
- ▊ The slot in the bevelled edge of the pedestal of the Master's console is actually just a strip of black tape, made to appear to be a gap through the CSO overlay of Anthony Ainley climbing over a short wall. The circuitry inside is a model onto which Ainley is superimposed, with further wiring overlaid in front of him. Note when he creates a puff of smoke it's only visible in front of his body, not the foreground or background.
- ▊ Oops! The low-angle shot of the Doctor and co looking down into the Master's control box accidentally shows the top of the control room set behind them.

LANDING 257

SPACE Sarn, volcano, control centre
TIME As above
TRAVELLERS None
EPISODES Planet of Fire 4

With the TARDIS's navigational system still remote-paralleled to the Master's, the Police Box rematerialises in the control centre within the volcano in the same spatial relation to the stone pillar as they were at the ruin. The Doctor and Peri are already there, having climbed the volcano, and he sends her inside the Ship for safety while he confronts the Master, now restored by the numismaton flame.

The gas flow is interrupted and the Master appears to burn away to nothing in the fire. The systems controlling the volcano begin to overload and the Doctor dashes into the TARDIS and takes off as the control centre is destroyed by the eruption.

- ● **CONTROLS** After dematerialising, the Doctor presses a button on the right of the upper niche of panel E1.
- ▊ **NOTES** This is the first time the TARDIS has travelled unoccupied since *The Android Invasion* (Landing 119) and only the fourth time seen in the series so far.
- ▊ To make it easier for Peri to enter the Police Box via the left-hand door, this is set with its centre post behind the right-hand door, meaning the TARDIS materialises with its door ajar.

LANDING 258

SPACE Sarn, ruin
TIME As above
TRAVELLERS The Doctor, Peri
EPISODES Planet of Fire 4

The TARDIS returns to its previous location in the ruin, where the last of the Sarns are boarding the nearby Trion ship. Turlough sends his brother, Malkon, to join them while he says goodbye to the Doctor. He is reluctant to end his travels aboard the TARDIS but must take this opportunity to return home now his exile has been rescinded.

The Doctor prepares to take Peri back to Earth but she asks if she can travel with him as she still has three months of vacation left. The Doctor agrees and dematerialises the Ship, none too smoothly.

○ **CONTROLS** The Doctor presses rocker switches on the shelf of the bottom-centre niche of panel E1 before closing the main doors. He moves to panel E4 and operates further unseen controls, including one to dematerialise the Ship.

LANDING 259

SPACE Sirius system, Androzani Minor
TIME Unknown future
TRAVELLERS The Doctor, Peri
EPISODES The Caves of Androzani 1,4

The TARDIS materialises on a sandy plain on the planet Androzani Minor. While this had seas billions of years earlier, now the surface is nothing but desert dunes and rocky hills, although its core is a mass of viscous super-heated mud. Periodically, when the planet's orbit brings it closer to its twin, the populated Androzani Major, the gravitational pull forces hot mud up along underground shafts to burst across the surface.

Peri finds clumps of glass nearby – or rather fused silica caused by the rockets of a landing spacecraft, the Doctor deduces. They also notice tracks where a laden monoskid left the ship then returned empty, which the Doctor decides to follow towards some cave openings.

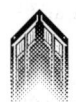

A mud burst begins, with sprays of boiling sludge erupting from below the surface. These get closer to the TARDIS as the Doctor struggles back carrying an unconscious Peri. Both have contracted toxemic poisoning from touching raw spectrox deposited by the bats that live in the caves, but the Doctor has a vial of curative milk extracted from a queen bat. Exhausted, he reaches the Police Box but as he takes the key from his pocket he drops the vial and spills some of the milk. He hurriedly saves what's left, heaves himself and Peri inside, and takes off just as columns of mud burst from the area where the TARDIS stood.

○ **CONTROLS** The Doctor presses the rocker switches on the shelf of the bottom-centre niche of panel E1 to dematerialise.

○ The drawer under panel E1 and hinged section under panel E6 added for *Planet of Fire* have been removed.

▮ **LORE** The TARDIS carries oxygenators.

▮ **NOTES** Peri is wearing the same outfit she had on in *Planet of Fire* and comments that super-heated mud "makes a change from lava", suggesting it's not long since they left Sarn. In *The Twin Dilemma* she knows how to activate the TARDIS scanner and where on the console to take atmospheric readings, so if there haven't been further landings the Doctor must show her how to do that here.

▮ Events on Androzani Major take place across two days – Morgus sends his agent to the Northcawl copper mining facility to complete his task "by the morning" before the president arrives "at five" [pm], then Timmin reports an explosion "early this morning". There's no indication of a night shift on Androzani Minor, however, so it's probably daytime throughout here. Given their names, it's likely Minor is smaller than Major but there's no way to tell by how much – although the Doctor calls them twin planets some definitions of this ignore the bodies' sizes, and we don't know if they're orbiting each other around a barycentre or are just similar distances from their star. It's said Major's pull bringing mud to the surface of Minor is why the latter is uninhabited, whereas Major is highly populated so the reverse attraction must be less catastrophic. They must also be close enough for consistent travel and communication between them, and for mud bursts to be regular enough to deter colonisation – there's some suggestion they occur at least monthly.

▮ An opening scene in the control room was to have had the Doctor explain he wanted some sand but that Androzani Minor's didn't look suitable for the glass-blowing technique he'd learned in a Thuringian monastery. Peri asked why he was in a monastery but he refused to tell her as he didn't yet know her well and she was too young; she commented he's a pain like her step-father. Director Graeme Harper ran out of studio time to record the scene so the script was rewritten with a new conversation to be heard over stock film of Monument Valley in Utah. Note this gives Peri a different excuse to call the Doctor a pain to tie in with the already filmed dialogue of him denying this.

LANDING 260

SPACE Titan Three
TIME Unknown future [August 2300]
TRAVELLERS The Doctor, Peri
EPISODES The Caves of Androzani 4;
The Twin Dilemma 1-3

The Doctor feeds Peri all the remaining bat's milk and she quickly recovers. His only chance, however, is to regenerate. He seems unsure this will happen but he hears his recent companions encouraging him to survive, and the

Master eager for him to die. With a final outburst of energy he regenerates and sits bolt upright.

The renewed Doctor is soon on his feet and admiring his new face. He heads to the wardrobe to replace his mud-splattered clothing but has a momentary breakdown. Recovering, he adopts a garish new outfit of clashing colours and fabrics at which Peri expresses her displeasure. He returns to the control room while she changes, childishly dismissing her own choice of dress.

The Doctor sets the coordinates for Vesta 95 where they can both rest, having for the moment forgotten the coordinates for the Eye of Orion. He has another psychotic episode, however, and attacks Peri. She fends him off and when he recovers he has no memory of his behaviour, but seeing how scared she is he turns manic again and redirects the TARDIS to Titan Three, a desolate asteroid where he can withdraw and repent – although Peri is not thrilled at the idea of being his disciple.

The Police Box comes to rest in a gully amid sandy dunes and rocky outcrops across which, though the atmosphere is thin, a harsh wind blows. As the Doctor declares he must find a less comfortable place than the TARDIS in which to perform his contemplation, a loud explosion is heard from outside and the two travellers venture out to discover a spaceship has crash-landed on their doorstep. They find the unconscious pilot thrown clear of the burning wreckage and carry him into the Ship.

Lieutenant Hugo Lang wakes and accuses the Doctor of shooting down his ship, but passes out again before he can fire his weapon. Peri takes the power-pack from the gun and hides it in the wardrobe then brings the medical kit so the Doctor can, reluctantly, tend to Lang's wounds.

The Doctor senses something amiss and deduces from Lang's mutterings that there are children in danger somewhere. He checks the scanner and notices a dome that is far too regular in shape to be natural. Despite the console indicating a worrying level of radiation, he determines to investigate, a hesitant Peri following. At the top of the gully they find an access point to some service ducts which they hope will let them enter the dome undetected.

Left alone in the TARDIS, Lang wakes and finds his gun disarmed so searches for the power-pack. He finds his way to the wardrobe and decides to change his scorched uniform, by happy chance choosing the very jacket in the pocket of which Peri hid the power-pack.

As Lang tries to find a way out of the Ship, Peri suddenly appears, transmatted from the dome by the Doctor. She fears his attempt to follow has failed as she watches the dome explode on the scanner. However, a simple mistiming has placed him ten seconds into the future, so he uses the console to resync himself with Peri and Lang. The Doctor convinces the lieutenant he can help recover the twin boys Lang was pursuing and sets the TARDIS on course for Jaconda.

- **CONTROLS** While setting course for Vesta 95, the Doctor presses the two left-most silver rocker switches on the shelf of the bottom-centre niche of panel E1 then flips switches in the middle-far-left niche of this panel, those in the top-left niche of panel E2 and in the bottom-right niche of panel E6, as well as pressing various buttons. When redirecting to Titan Three, he stabs at the controls in the bottom-centre niche of panel E1, causing the Ship to shake violently.
- After the TARDIS lands on Titan Three, one shot reveals the hexagon on the face of the pedestal beneath panel E3 has been removed to allow the console's power cable to be plugged in.
- Peri and the Doctor check the outside atmosphere, and later the radiation level, by looking at the (non-existent) screen on panel E2, the latter pressing unseen buttons on either side. She operates the scanner by twisting the right-hand black slider on panel E3.
- To resync his time with Peri's, the Doctor presses rocker switches on panel E1 and two of the red buttons on the left of the upper niche (before presumably moving back across the room to where he reappears).
- The Doctor dematerialises by pressing the rocker switches at bottom-left of panel E6, then flips switches in the middle-far-left niche of panel E1 and some in the top-right of E6.
- **LORE** The TARDIS can be detected while in flight by the scanners of a modified Spacehopper mark three freighter.
- **NOTES** This is only the second of the Doctor's regenerations to take place inside the TARDIS, although his third happened just outside. While there seems to be an outpouring of energy, this doesn't harm Peri or destroy the control room, as will later become common.
- The control room interior door has been rehung with the hinges now on the left, handle on the right (but still opening outwards), and its three roundels have been painted over to match the surrounding wall. This would seem to be a consequence of them having been painted black when the set was used as the Master's TARDIS in *Planet of Fire*.
- Although in the studio the wardrobe set was just along from the control room, on screen no one is shown directly walking from one to the other so it could be taken as being elsewhere in the TARDIS – although for Lang to find his way there so readily it must be close. Otherwise, the wardrobe is in the same location as the bedroom seen just two stories previously in *Planet of Fire*, which could suggest the Ship telepathically discerns what room an occupant wants and the architectural configuration system shifts the interior around so that room is easily accessible.
- The wardrobe is comprised of two of the wide-spaced-roundels walls, two square columns and the angled slats seen in *Planet of Fire*. It contains racks of clothing of different styles, a full-length mirror and a bamboo stool. When last seen in *The Androids of Tara* (Landing 151) the outfits were labelled with their planet of origin – does that mean there's a world out there where everyone is dressed in clashing colours like the outfit the Doctor selects? Let's hope Lang's choice of jacket is from the same society, otherwise there's more than one with horrendous fashion sense.

- No date is given on screen for the events of the story but the script set them in 2300. The computer record for Azmael's freighter reads 'Last contact: 12-99' which Elena says was "eight months ago" (that is, December 2299), suggesting it's now August.
- Oops! When the Doctor first moves to leave the control room and explore Titan Three, the sound of the main doors opening plays even though he hasn't operated their control and the doors themselves remain shut.
- Although the Doctor calls Titan Three an asteroid, it's large enough to hold a breathable atmosphere and is warm enough to support human life on its surface. As such, and despite the name, it must be in a different solar system from Earth. Azmael's freighter and the Interplanetary Pursuit squadron require warp drive to reach it, although the gap between the freighter first going to warp and Lang apparently getting shot down, by which time he's near Titan Three, is short so either their warp drives are very fast or Titan Three's system is relatively close to Earth's.
- In publicity photos of Colin Baker taken during the location filming at Springwell chalk quarry near Rickmansworth, Hertfordshire, the paintwork of the Police Box looks badly scuffed. In fact, this is just mud from when the sections of the prop were laid out on the ground prior to assembly. Once it was wiped down ready for filming it looked much better.
- The medical kit has the same case as the previously seen toolkit. The bamboo chair and table brought out when tending to Lang are different from those seen in *The Five Doctors*.
- When the Doctor and Peri leave the TARDIS a second time there's no sign of the wreckage of Lang's ship. They do head away from the Police Box in a different direction, so it's possible the debris is just out of shot.
- After the dome explodes, the scanner closes without sound or anyone operating a control.
- Irrespective of how the Doctor uses the revitalising modulator to get back to the TARDIS (it's not well explained; perhaps he tells Peri any old nonsense to get her to cooperate), 27 seconds pass between Peri's and his departures from the dome, and the same between her arrival in the control room and his first fleeting appearance. But the dome explodes only fourteen seconds after Peri returns to the Ship. So she must travel forward by at least thirteen seconds, not back by ten as the Doctor told her, or he'd be dead before he left. He then slips further into the future: he says ten seconds again but at least 20 pass for Peri before the Doctor properly rejoins her. Wouldn't it have been easier to de-randomise the proper transmat?

LANDING 261

SPACE Jaconda
TIME As above
TRAVELLERS The Doctor, Peri, Lieutenant Hugo Lang
EPISODES The Twin Dilemma 3

The TARDIS arrives on the surface of Jaconda. The Doctor expects them to be in a pleasant grove but, although the sun shines, what greets the travellers is acres of barren soil. All that remains of the trees are blackened trunks stripped of foliage and even their bark. The Doctor spots a slime trail across the arid ground and realises only the Gastropods – a species of sentient man-sized slug-like creatures believed to be mythological – could have caused such devastation.

They return to the TARDIS to consider their next move. The Doctor is still struggling to settle his mind and begins to feel sorry for himself. Peri implores him to take Lang to the palace where the twins are likely to be held but it takes the lieutenant's gun to his head to get the Doctor to comply.

○ CONTROLS The Doctor operates unseen controls on panels E1 and E6 as the TARDIS dematerialises.

LANDING 262

SPACE Jaconda, underground passage near palace
TIME As above
TRAVELLERS The Doctor, Peri, Lang
EPISODES The Twin Dilemma 3-4

The Ship relocates a short distance to a tunnel that leads to the Jacondan's palace – a more discrete landing site than the throne room, the Doctor points out. Lang is happy to search for the twins alone, distrusting his new acquaintances, but Peri and the Doctor persuade him he will need all the help he can get. They head off towards the palace, unaware of a Gastropod slithering along behind them.

The Jacondan chamberlain finds the Police Box and the dominating Gastropod Mestor projects his mental powers from his throne room and unlocks the door. The chamberlain and two guards enter and search the Ship.

Peri and Lang return with the rescued twins. While she goes back to find the Doctor, the lieutenant ushers the Jacondans – now meek following the death of their mind-controlling master – out of the TARDIS at gunpoint.

When Peri returns with the Doctor, Lang informs them he has decided to stay on the planet and help the Jacondans – who are already turning on the remaining Gastropods – rebuild their society. They must return the twins to Earth, though, and depart in the TARDIS. Peri is upset at the Doctor's rudeness to Lang but he assures her his personality has now stabilised and she will just have to live with it.

○ CONTROLS Peri closes the scanner with an unseen control on the left of panel E3. Preparing for departure, the Doctor presses buttons on the far right of the upper niche of panel E1, unseen controls to the left of the screen on panel E2, and dematerialises using the bottom-left rocker switch in the bottom-centre niche of panel E1.

▌ LORE The TARDIS door can be unlocked by someone with sufficient mental powers.

▌**NOTES** If strangling Peri wasn't bad enough, this new Doctor calling the TARDIS's Police Box disguise "utterly hideous" is almost as unforgivable.

▌The control room scenes for episodes three and four were recorded three weeks after those for the first two episodes. In this second studio session, the interior door wall was mistakenly erected back to front. Note there are no roundels around the doorway, those in the door are indented and the handle is back on the left, and the door itself is recessed into the wall.

PREVIOUS LANDING

SPACE Earth
TIME As Landing 260
TRAVELLERS The Doctor, Peri, Romulus and Remus Sylvest
EPISODES Intended in The Twin Dilemma 4

The TARDIS briefly returned to Earth to drop off the genius twins with their worried father and, possibly less concerned, mother.

▌**NOTES** The Doctor states his intention to get the twins back to Earth and they're gone by *Attack of the Cybermen*, although given his scatterbrained state at this point it's possible he simply forgets they're aboard and there could be a whole series of adventures involving Romulus and Remus before they are returned home.

LANDING 263

SPACE Earth, England, London, [Shoreditch,] 76 Totter's Lane
TIME 1985
TRAVELLERS The Doctor, Peri
EPISODES Attack of the Cybermen 1

Still invigorated by his recent regeneration, the Doctor decides to repair the chameleon circuit once and for all. He uses a sonic lance on circuitry behind several roundels in the corridor outside the control room and in an adjacent room where he has a jumble of components connected together. He takes one of these and (re)fits it into the console. But when he selects a destination where both he and Peri can have a rest, the TARDIS careers out of control.

The Doctor stabilises the Ship and confirms it is undamaged. Checking the scanner reveals they are passing close to Halley's comet as its orbit brings it in view of Earth in 1985. The Doctor finishes making further adjustments to the console, although a circuit in an open roundel on the wall blows out with a shower of sparks. Nervous about being so close to the comet, Peri tries to calm her fears by at least closing the scanner. Just then the console picks up an intergalactic distress signal that is evidently being transmitted from Earth.

Homing in on the signal, the TARDIS materialises between two disused vans in IM Foreman's junkyard at 76 Totter's Lane in London. The Doctor carries a handheld detector that is tracking the signal. As he and Peri head for the street, the Police Box makes a whirring sound as the chameleon circuit engages and transforms into a tall decorated-tile masonry heater.

Not long after, the Doctor and Peri return having deduced the local source of the signal is just a relay point and that its origin is elsewhere. For a moment they struggle to find a way into the heater until the Doctor discovers an entrance at the back. They are spied on by Lytton's two troopers disguised as policemen, who watch as the TARDIS dematerialises.

◉ **CONTROLS** The Doctor inserts a component into a space beneath the black square in the middle-left niche of panel E4, which has a small circuit fixed to its underside. He then presses the two red pushbuttons on the right of the upper niche of panel E1. After stabilising the TARDIS, he presses one of these again and buttons above them. He operates unseen controls at top-left of panel E3 and activates the scanner by twisting one of the black sliders at bottom-right; Peri later closes it with the left-hand of these. He appears to read the date from the black square on the right of panel E1, then presses the top-right buttons *again*.

◉ The shots of the scanner displaying Halley's comet are taken from further round the console than usual, providing us with a rare view of panel E2. This confirms the screen housing has no monitor inserted (as glimpsed in *Frontios*) and the circular depression to its right it blank. Although just out of shot, the Doctor clearly closes two flaps over the hollow in the top of this panel's screen housing.

◉ When the distress signal is heard, Peri flips the red switch in the bottom-centre niche of panel E1 – from which the sound seems to be emanating – and the Doctor then flips the two white switches to its right and those in the middle-far-left niche, followed by unseen controls on panel E5 before moving back to panel E1 and flicking more switches.

▌**NOTES** Peri says the Doctor has "only recently regenerated" and he suggests landing somewhere restful "after the bleakness of Jaconda" as they've "both spent too long in the TARDIS", indicating that if there have been any landings since leaving the twins on Earth (assuming they did) they have been brief and without much to see. Indeed, Peri says, "In the past couple of days you've called me Tegan, Zoe, Susan." The first of these we hear him do in *The Twin Dilemma*, so it may only be two days since they were on Titan Three.

▌The TARDIS corridor is formed of the three wide-spaced translucent-roundels walls first seen in *Planet of Fire*. Each has an open roundel with the ridged rim in place but the centre disc removed and circuitry behind. These walls are positioned in an L shape to the right of the control room interior door and joined by square slatted columns. Opposite these is the plain inner door leading to a new room. To its left is the angled slatted piece also from *Planet of Fire* and a new fourth wide-spaced translucent-roundels wall (also with one open); to the right of the door is another square column, a new narrow wall with slats mimicking the columns, and then the aligned opaque-roundels wall. On the corridor side of the inner door to its right is another square column (backed against the angled slats) and returning from this, glimpsed at the end of the episode, is a wall that has along one side three half-roundels and quarter-circles at the top and bottom. This doesn't appear to be the back of the wall forming the side room so must be a new section.

▪ The Doctor's repairs to the chameleon circuit appear only to involve tinkering with circuitry in the walls, there's no mention of block transfer computations. Perhaps he has already applied the corrections provided by the Logopolitans – having failed to do so throughout his previous incarnation – and is now just resetting some components. As the new console has no shortage of keyboards, presumably the previous pop-up circuit controller is redundant.

▪ The TARDIS has apples, unless Peri picked up one when they dropped off the Sylvest twins on Earth.

▪ There's no suggestion that the sudden turmoil in flight is a consequence of the Ship's proximity to Halley's comet so must be, as the Doctor guesses, because he "crossed a wire" during his repairs. The shimmering effect is achieved by the old method of recording the reflection in a sheet of mirrored material rather than the picture being rippled electronically.

▪ Why does the TARDIS materialise in the Totter's Lane junkyard? The Doctor's handheld detector leads him away from there to a different location, and although this turns out to be a relay point and not the true source, there's no indication the signal is also being relayed via the junkyard. Now the chameleon circuit is (kind of) working again, has the Ship deliberately returned to the last place it operated? Or given Lytton's signal is beaming from an entirely different scrap merchant's, is it just a mix-up?

▪ Of course, this junkyard looks nothing like that glimpsed in the dark in *An Unearthly Child* (Landing 1), that being a studio set and this being filmed on location. The street outside is also quite different, so is this another previously unseen entrance to the yard? Neither the Doctor nor the script makes any significance of the location (so one could ask why bother to use this setting?); a more notable return to Totter's Lane is seen in *Remembrance of the Daleks*, although not by the TARDIS.

▪ When the Master's TARDIS changed its appearance after landing in *Logopolis* it also made a sound, although different from that heard here. The delay between landing and changing is put down to the Ship "thinking about it"; for its next few landings its form will change automatically on materialisation.

▪ Despite Peri's laughter and the Doctor's claim the Ship is out of practice, is a European-style tiled room heater that incongruous in a junkyard? It doesn't look that out of place among the barrels, tires and pallets. In fact, why does the chameleon circuit switch in at all at this point? In 1985, over a decade since they went out of use, a Police Box would fit perfectly among a scrap merchant's detritus.

▪ The script suggested the TARDIS change into an Egyptian pillar but this may have been deliberately ignored owing to the Master's TARDIS often taking the form of a fluted pillar. In the event, designer Marjorie Pratt chose a suitably sized object from stock.

LANDING 264

SPACE Earth, England, London, garage
TIME As above
TRAVELLERS The Doctor, Peri
EPISODES Attack of the Cybermen 1-2

Although the signal is being bounced around London to give its sender a chance to assess anyone responding to it, the Doctor succeeds in tracing its true origin and the TARDIS materialises outside the garage of a scrap metal merchant. It adopts the appearance of a small pipe organ, to the Doctor's dismay, although he plays a quick tune.

Using his handheld detector, he locates the equipment sending the distress call. The travellers are held at gunpoint by the two fake policemen, whom they overcome, knocking one out and leaving the other handcuffed to a pipe. They find a maintenance pit has been knocked through to gain access to the sewer system, and venture down there in search of whoever sent the signal. Shortly after, the two policemen are retrieved by Cybermen and taken away for conversion.

Three Cybermen investigating the detection of time distortion trace it to the TARDIS at the garage and are able to gain access. One waits on guard in the control room while the other two search further inside the Ship. When the Doctor and Peri return with an undercover detective called Russell, they are attacked. Russell kills one Cyberman with his pistol, then another with the first's more advanced weapon, but the third Cyberman breaks his neck with one blow. Two more Cybermen and a Cyberleader push their way into the Ship, along with Lytton and his accomplice Griffiths.

The Cyberleader orders that Peri be killed so the Doctor quickly sets the TARDIS to self-destruct after a countdown of 20 seconds. The Cybermen are forced to relent. They command the Doctor to set coordinates for their base of operations on Telos, and the organ fades away from the scrap yard.

○ **CONTROLS** The Doctor now traces the distress signal from panel E5, flipping switches in the bottom-left niche while looking at the wide black display. He locks on to its coordinates from panel E1.

○ The Doctor sets the self-destruct – or at least displays a countdown – with controls at the top of panel E2 and right of the upper niche of panel E1 (although watch closely and you can see Colin Baker's finger misses any of the buttons and presses the panel itself). It takes rather more effort to stop the countdown, the Doctor pressing buttons below the screen on panel E2, one under the middle-left illuminated display on panel E1 and a key on the left of the bottom-centre niche of this panel. He then sets coordinates from the same panel, pressing a button below the middle-right illuminated display and rocker switches on the shelf of the bottom-centre niche.

- **LORE** The disguise a TARDIS adopts can operate as that object should.
- The TARDIS can be set to self-destruct, by some undisclosed means, after a short countdown (unless the Doctor is bluffing).
- **NOTES** It's not clear how the Doctor finds the garage. He says it could take days to trace back through all the relay points to the true source, but how does knowing someone is watching them help? Does the Doctor locate the two policemen, who we do see returning to the garage just before the TARDIS arrives?
- Oops! Just before the scanning grid comes up on the console screen (panel E6), a page of the BASIC code for the graphics can be glimpsed.
- This time the TARDIS was scripted as taking the form of a wardrobe. Although an organ is an odder choice of disguise, it is in the yard of a scrap metal dealer so not very likely to draw anyone's attention. It's notable that the organ can be played as we have yet to see the Police Box's telephone being used (or if it even has one), although it will be in the revived series.
- The TARDIS's defences must be in poor condition by now. Once even an innocuous Zarbi was automatically repelled but now dangerous Cybermen can pile inside unhindered. Does the entrance only lock when the Ship's in the form of an object with a lockable door?
- The charge ignited when Russell accidental discharges the Cyberman's gun leaves a scorch mark on the column, which can be seen in earlier scenes that were recorded after this one. The sparking around the main doors control as Peri reaches for it may be caused by a Cyberman outside firing to stop her closing the doors, although the usual sound effect and blue ring aren't applied. If it's just a coincidental fault it can't affect the doors as they're closed moments later.
- What happens to Russell's body? At the start of episode two it's no longer there (to save paying actor Terry Molloy extra money). The main doors close after the Cybermen enter and don't open again before take-off, so Russell and the dead Cyberman can't be left outside (and are not seen when the TARDIS dematerialises). While the Doctor and company are being locked up, the bodies must be moved to elsewhere in the TARDIS. Assuming the Doctor disposes of them later, one hopes Peri persuades him to treat the detective with dignity rather than just dumping him into space.
- Does the Doctor really set the Ship to "cease to exist"? When he tries a similar trick in *Journey to the Centre of the TARDIS* he admits he was faking it with a countdown and a stern expression, so it's possible he does the same here. If he's genuinely setting the Ship to be destroyed in some way (and with this incarnation's personality he might not be bluffing) then it takes a worrying few control operations to initiate. Even if he's just setting a fake countdown, it only requires a couple of button presses, unless some telepathic communication is taking place.
- Between the control room scenes for episodes one and two, the double-handle on the interior door changes, from the original square-ended one to two thicker handles with angled ends and baseplates (still placed one above the other). This is odd as all the TARDIS interior scenes were recorded on the same day, Thursday 21 June 1984.

LANDING 265

SPACE Telos, Cybermen tombs
TIME Unknown [future]
TRAVELLERS The Doctor, Peri, Griffiths, Lytton, Cyberleader, four Cybermen
EPISODES Attack of the Cybermen 2

During the journey, the Cybermen secure their four prisoners in the side room where the Doctor was working earlier. He accesses the circuitry behind a roundel and transmits a signal revealing their destination, then tries to adjust the coordinates marginally to avoid landing where the Cybermen expect. The signal is detected, however, and the Cyberleader has the Doctor brought to the control room to disable it.

Thanks to the Doctor's tinkering, the TARDIS materialises not in the Cybermen's control centre but some distance away, deep in the freezing hibernation complex. This time the chameleon circuit selects the disguise of a pair of ornate iron gates. The Cyberleader ushers his prisoners outside, seemingly disturbed to find they are in the 'tombs'. It leads them away to an audience with the Cybercontroller, leaving the other two Cybermen guarding the Ship.

Peri returns escorted by two Cryons, the natives of Telos, who are intent on preventing the Cybermen gaining control of the TARDIS. As they ponder how to deal with the guard barring the gates, the Doctor finds them and activates the distress signal in a dormant Cyberman to bring out the second guard inside the Ship so the Cryons can shoot them both. The plan succeeds but the Doctor learns that Lytton was actually working to help the Cryons so agrees to try to rescue him before leaving Telos. He and Peri depart in the TARDIS.

- **NOTES** Six Cybermen enter the TARDIS: the leader, a black 'stealth' Cybermen and four regular silver ones. Russell shoots two of the last but later three are seen intimidating the Doctor in the control room. Was a seventh on guard inside the Ship or was the one shot by a Cyber-weapon revived? Perhaps both as the one that escorts Peri while she changes is also silver. Two Cybermen and the leader exit the TARDIS when it arrives on Telos while two more stay on guard, so perhaps there were four silver troops (plus the one whose head explodes). The black Cyberman isn't seen again after the cliffhanger – does it change its colour during the journey?

- The Cyberman that reports the detection of a transmission stands at the console and appears to be pressing buttons, as if the message is being relayed there. But surely the TARDIS controls are beyond the Cybermen's understanding. Perhaps this one hears the message from Cyber-control via an internal receiver and is just pressing random controls to see what they do. Then again, later it can tell when the Ship is about to materialise and is heard operating controls.
- Does the Doctor send the signal? He doesn't mention it when tinkering in the roundel, just that he's adjusting the Ship's course. Yet neither does he seem surprised nor feign ignorance when the Cyberleader orders him to disconnect the transmission. So did he initiate it while setting the coordinates and dematerialising? If so, who is he transmitting to? The Cybermen on Telos guess he's trying to contact the Time Lords but later the Doctor is angered by the idea he's being used as an unwitting agent for them. Besides, how can they have manipulated him into doing their dirty work? He goes to Telos under duress from the Cybermen; before that it was his choice to visit Earth. And it's hardly unusual for him to stumble across villains' plans just in time to stop them. Or is the turbulence in episode one caused by the Time Lords retroactively taking control of the TARDIS and directing it to Earth at an opportune time? (If so, did they choose the Totter's Lane landing site?)
- Also, why does the Doctor need to fiddle behind a roundel to shift the Ship slightly off course? Why didn't he simply adjust the coordinates he was, presumably, given by the Cyberleader as he input them? (If the Cybermen can operate the console, they might have double-checked them.)
- The Cybermen call the TARDIS control centre the "console room". They haven't heard any of the crew use the term, though, so presumably choose it themselves. All the more reason to stick with the original 'control room' – you wouldn't want to side with Cybermen, would you?
- Again, the silver gates the chameleon circuit selects, while not matching the design of the Cyber-tombs, don't look especially out of place. All in all, the Ship hasn't done that badly given she's been stuck in the same form for so long.

LANDING 266

SPACE Telos, Cybermen control centre
TIME As above
TRAVELLERS The Doctor, Peri
EPISODES Attack of the Cybermen 2

The TARDIS materialises in the deserted control centre, reverting to its usual Police Box form. The Doctor finds Lytton in a conversion alcove, already halfway to becoming a Cyberman. As he tries to free the mercenary, the Cybercontroller returns. Lytton stops it killing the Doctor but is himself fatally struck down. The Doctor fends off more Cybermen with the Controller's weapon before turning it on the Controller itself.

Peri views the carnage on the scanner and dashes out to see if she can help Lytton but he is dead. The Doctor regrets misjudging the mercenary. He hurries Peri back into the Ship and dematerialises before the control centre is destroyed.

NOTES No explanation is given for why the TARDIS becomes stuck as a Police Box again (although see next landing). Did the coldness of the Cybermen's tombs affect the Ship or were the Doctor's repairs insufficient? He must decide he likes the blue box after all as he never attempts to fix the circuit again.

LANDING 267

SPACE Space, between Cetus and Sculptor
TIME Unknown
TRAVELLERS The Doctor, Peri
EPISODES Vengeance on Varos 1

The Doctor has been performing further repairs and adjustments to the TARDIS, although Peri is getting tired of some of the unintended consequences: "Three electrical fires, a total power failure and a near collision with a storm of asteroids." They are both disturbed when a fault in the power transmission system causes the Ship to stall, materialising in deep space. With no power getting through to the transitional elements, the TARDIS is immobilised.

The Doctor's initial response is to sulk so Peri unearths the TARDIS manual, propping open a vent in the workshop, in the hope it will inspire him to track down the problem. As he idly flicks through the book, the central column briefly moves with some vestigial power.

With Peri's help, the Doctor finds the power conversion factor is stable, with a correct orthogonal TR reading from the IV table in the hyper-time ratio section of ZS+101EQ, meaning the energy is being blocked somewhere. He succeeds in activating the emergency power booster and the TARDIS begins moving.

○ CONTROLS The Doctor operates the scanner from the bottom-right of panel E3 (probably the right-hand black control as in the next landing). He checks the power conversion factor on the screen on panel E4 while pressing unseen controls around it. He activates the emergency power booster with controls on either side of the screen on panel E2.

▌ LORE The emergency power booster provides a burst of energy for a limited flight.

- **NOTES** Peri lists the Doctor's activities "since we left Telos", suggesting no eventful landings have happened in the interim. However, in a cut continuation of the first TARDIS scene, Peri went on to note the Ship materialised "on the frozen plains of Ewan Nine". Having recently been in the frozen tombs of Telos, they presumably didn't stay long.
- On screen we don't find out what the Doctor was doing under the console but in further cut dialogue he said he'd "stabilised the chameleon circuit" so that the Ship would stay as a Police Box ("I think"). Peri thought this better than the pyramid it appeared as on Ewan Nine.
- Among the litany of the Doctor's errors, those involving specific TARDIS systems are wiping the flight computer memory and jettisoning three-quarters of the storage hold.
- When the TARDIS stalls, the central column stops moving but stays illuminated, suggesting the Ship has gone into hover mode.
- The wall beyond the interior door is back to being the aligned-roundels wall, as in *Frontios*.
- This incarnation has changed his taste in furniture and instead of wicker or bamboo there is now a pink metal-framed chair with blue padding in the control room. The Doctor boasts about how busy he's been, so has Peri just been sitting around doing nothing?
- Here we have yet another instruction book, a large black hardback with the title 'Tardis Type 40 Handbook' printed in white on the front. This is not the same as the book Nyssa read from in *Snakedance*, which may not have been a manual (see Landing 229), nor the smaller 'Tardis Handbook Type 40' referenced in *The Horns of Nimon* (Landing 170) and *Four to Doomsday* (Landing 208). It's more like the manual, title unseen, in *The Pirate Planet* (Landing 146), although less battered.
- The Doctor last used the emergency power booster to escape the void the TARDIS landed in after he'd activated the emergency unit (see Landing 61).

LANDING 268

SPACE Cetus constellation, Varos, punishment dome; moved to prison control centre, then elsewhere
TIME Late-23rd century
TRAVELLERS The Doctor, Peri
EPISODES Vengeance on Varos 1-2

The transitional elements have lost their capacity to generate orbital energy and the transpower system needs relining with zeiton-7. This element can only be found on the planet Varos, fortunately in a nearby constellation, but with limited power the Doctor has one chance of reaching the period when zeiton ore was being mined there.

The TARDIS successfully materialises in an underground level of one of the habitation domes of a human colony. The travellers watch on the scanner as a helmeted guard approaches, fires his gun at the Police Box then turns away when the energy bolts bounce off harmlessly.

The Doctor detects a nearby power source and when they go outside they find a prisoner is chained to the wall awaiting disintegration by a large, high-powered laser emitter. They help him knock out the guard and use the laser to break his chains. Four more guards arrive at the TARDIS, blocking their return, so the Doctor swings the laser in their direction then escapes another way. One of the guards is obliterated before the power is cut, and the others give chase.

Guards move the Police Box to the prison control centre but attempts to force it open with a laser rifle fail. A captured Peri is brought in as the bank of transmission screens show the Doctor apparently dying due to a hallucination of being lost in a desert. Peri is too distraught to answer the questions of the Varosian governor and his chief of staff, but denies the accusations of Sil, the representative of the Galatron Mining Corporation, that she is from a rival company. The governor escorts her to his office for further questioning.

The TARDIS is moved out of the control centre. Later, with the more bloodthirsty Varosian officers eradicated and the people's prospects improved by the promise of a fair price being paid for their zeiton, the Doctor and Peri return to the Ship with a generous supply of the ore, a gift from the governor. The Doctor soon gets the TARDIS operational again and they leave Varos.

- **CONTROLS** The Doctor closes the scanner with the right-hand black slider at bottom-right of panel E3. Peri reads external atmospheric details from the same panel, while the Doctor detects a nearby power source from panel E5, pressing one of the red buttons in the middle-far-left niche.
- **LORE** The transitional elements generate orbital energy. The transpower system is lined with the rare element zeiton-7 found only on Varos.
- **NOTES** Although no date is given on screen, in cut dialogue the Doctor told Peri they were in "the latter half of the twenty-third century". This makes sense of Peri's otherwise apparent guesswork that she's from a time "nearly three centuries" before the governor was born. He says there has been a stable society on Varos "for more than two hundred years" so if their ancestors are from Earth (they call themselves human) they must have been one of the earliest colonies in the late-21st century (and seemingly exploited by the Galatron Mining Corporation from the start). Although Sil mentions "every known solar system" crying out for zeiton-7 "to drive their space-time craft" this doesn't necessarily mean time-travelling vessels. The governor disbelieves Peri's claim to have come from another century so time travel can't be common. Sil's reference could just be to ships that distort space-time in order to travel interstellar distances quickly.
- The Doctor worries about missing Varos's mining era but even if they did would it really be beyond the travellers' ability to trace and dig up some zeiton themselves? Surely the TARDIS has facilities for any refining required. After all, it's said Galatron does the

refining of the zeiton-7 ore it buys from Varos, so what the governor gives the Doctor must be the raw ore. Perhaps he should worry more about where on Varos they land as there's no evidence of habitation beyond the small cluster of domes we see.
- The Varosians might have better luck breaking into the TARDIS if they fired their laser at the door rather than the edge of the corner post.
- A closing scene in the control room was cut, in which the Doctor confirmed "orthogonal readings haven't altered" thanks to "new elements on linings on the orbital transmission".

LANDING 269

SPACE Earth, England, Northumberland, Killingworth, slag heap; transported to and thrown down pit shaft; retrieved and moved to workshop
TIME Early-19th century
TRAVELLERS The Doctor, Peri
EPISODES The Mark of the Rani 1-2

En route to a royal open day at Kew Gardens, the TARDIS is drawn off course in space but not time, yet indications of time distortion suggest another time machine is nearby. The Police Box materialises in the north of England, on a slag heap just outside the colliery at Killingworth. Using a handheld detector, the Doctor and Peri head off to trace the cause of the time distortion.

Eight miners – whose brain chemistry has been altered so they can no longer sleep, leaving them with heightened aggression – load the Police Box onto a cart and wheel it through the countryside to the colliery. They push it to the head of a pit shaft and tip it down.

The colliery's engine-wright George Stephenson organises 40 men to recover the TARDIS from the bottom of the shaft and carry it back to his workshop. There he and the mine's owner Lord Ravensworth speculate about the box before the Doctor and Peri arrive to take their leave. The two men watch bemused as the TARDIS fades away.

○ CONTROLS The Doctor presses buttons on panel E3 when he notices the Ship is off course. He tries to override this from panel E6, pressing rocker switches at bottom-left and bottom-right, keys in the lower-left niche and flipping a switch in the top-right niche. He then moves back to panel E3 and presses unseen controls.

▮ LORE A TARDIS key may open more than one time capsule.

▤ NOTES No date is given on screen but the presence of George Stephenson at the Killingworth colliery puts it, most likely, in the 1810s when he was supervisor of all machinery and developing his ideas for steam locomotives. This decade was also the peak period of Luddite activity. In our history, Lord Ravensworth only became so titled from July 1821 (previously merely Sir Thomas Liddell). While Stephenson was increasingly involved with the Stockton and Darlington Railway from around the same time, he remained engine-wright at Killingworth until the following summer, so this story could be set as late as spring 1822.
- An opening scene in the control room was cut. This explained that Peri had found the dress she wears specifically for visiting the royal open day at Kew Gardens (a botanic garden from 1759) before the Ship shakes as it's drawn off course. Visible here but not in the televised scene is that the plain inner door was mistakenly erected in place of the usual interior door wall with roundels. The scene was cut for timing reasons, not because a microphone and its shadow were visible, as has been reported. A later shot of the TARDIS materialising and the Doctor stepping out was also cut.
- It's not specified how the Master "overrode the controls" to "force the TARDIS off course". Has he acquired a navigational guidance systems distorter like the Rani uses in *Time and the Rani* (Landing 286)? In fact, could she have got hers from him? Once the Rani gets her TARDIS under control, she presumably agrees to return the Master to Earth to collect his TARDIS, perhaps taking the distorter in exchange.
- Peri simply pulls the door shut behind her when leaving the TARDIS but at the end of the story the Doctor needs his key to let them back in.
- The Master draws a surprisingly precise picture of the Police Box when persuading the miners it's a dangerous machine, yet gets the window bars wrong (a common problem among artists over the years).
- The shot of the TARDIS being tipped down the mine was achieved with models of the Police Box and the shaft. The setup had an angled mirror beneath so the camera could shoot as if looking upwards.
- Does the Doctor's use of his key to get into the Rani's TARDIS mean hers is also a Type 40? If so, its interior decor may be available in the Doctor's TARDIS also.
- Both the Doctor and the Master credit the Rani with devising the means of operating her TARDIS remotely, even though the former identifies it as a Stattenheim remote control. He is also seemingly forgetting that his TARDIS was fitted with one of these for a time (see Previous to Landing 73) and that the Time Lords have frequently taken control of his Ship from afar, particularly during his exile to Earth. Even the Master overrode the controls of the Doctor's TARDIS and forced it to land here, a kind of remote control, so his praising the Rani is odd too.
- We've seen the Police Box moved by fewer than 40 people before – and those in *Time-Flight* were far from being stout colliery workers – so the extra work needed here may have been to manoeuvre the Ship along mine tunnels or winch it back up the pit shaft.
- The TARDIS dematerialising uses a split-screen effect, allowing Terence Alexander and Gawn Grainger to continue acting on the left of the picture as a shot of the empty set is overlaid on the right making the Police Box appear to fade out. Note the two men's shadows on the back wall disappear along with the TARDIS.

LANDING 270

SPACE Unnamed planet
TIME Unknown
TRAVELLERS The Doctor, Peri
EPISODES The Two Doctors 1

The TARDIS lands in a hot, sunny region where the Doctor spends a few hours fishing, although the river is unforthcoming of the abundant large tasty gumblejack he claims to have previously caught here. Instead all he hooks is a tiddler that would make barely a mouthful. He throws it back and a bored Peri convinces him to move on.

Returning to the TARDIS, the Doctor suggests they try instead to land one of the train-length congas in the great lakes of Pandatorea. But he is suddenly racked with pain as he senses himself being put to death in an earlier incarnation. He fears his past has been altered and that, if killed earlier in his life, he is now just a "temporal tautology", existing only until his timeline synchronises.

Peri suggests he consult a doctor and from a wallet of calling cards he selects Joinson Dastari, a geneticist on space station Camera in the Third Zone. The Ship dematerialises with a jolt.

- **CONTROLS** The Doctor sets course using buttons across panel E1 and dematerialises using one of the red pushbuttons on the right of the upper niche. Once underway he uses unseen controls on panels E2 and E3.
- The black display in the bottom-left corner of panel E1 has lost its cover, revealing the grid of lights beneath.
- **NOTES** The Doctor and Peri each suggest they're still getting used to the former's latest incarnation so there are unlikely to have been many landings in the gaps between stories.
- The pink-and-blue chair seen in *Vengeance on Varos* is still in the control room.
- Why is the Doctor affected by his earlier incarnation apparently being tortured when it's later revealed that was just an illusion?
- The Doctor's collection of accomplished names doesn't mean he has visited them all in the TARDIS, despite his flippant comments about Archimedes and Columbus. Certainly there's doubt over whether he has yet met Leonardo da Vinci (see Landing 162) and his first encounter with Dastari may have been before he absconded from Gallifrey (see Previous to Landing 73). Does that mean the entire wallet of cards is a holdover from his Gallifreyan days, perhaps a list of people he wanted to meet when he was dreaming of escaping his people's parochial practices?

LANDING 271

SPACE Third Zone, space station Camera, kitchen
TIME [1980s]
TRAVELLERS The Doctor, Peri
EPISODES The Two Doctors 1-2

The space station is dark and silent as the TARDIS approaches and the Doctor fears it has been struck by a comet or some such natural disaster. The Ship materialises in the exact same spot in the galley as it once did long ago, and yet only ten or so days earlier. Although there is still a breathable atmosphere, the air is ripe with the stench of decaying food and bodies – a dead Androgum cook lies nearby unnoticed in the gloom – turning Peri's stomach. The Doctor is keen to find out what happened so they make for director Dastari's office.

They come back to the kitchen a short time later, when the station's computer has restored the lights so it can track them and thus attempt to incapacitate them. The Doctor uncovers a chute leading into the infrastructure via which they can reach the computer's control centre undetected in order to deactivate it.

On returning to the TARDIS, the travellers are accompanied by the Doctor's past companion Jamie McCrimmon, who has been hiding in the station's infrastructure since the incarnation he arrived with was abducted by Sontarans. He takes a bath and changes into fresh Highland dress while the Doctor prepares to leave for Earth, having telepathically contacted his earlier self and, faintly hearing the Santa Maria bell of Seville Cathedral, deduced where he must be. The take-off is another bumpy one.

- **CONTROLS** When preparing to leave, the Doctor presses keys on panel E2, and dematerialises using controls on the same panel.
- **NOTES** See Previous to Landing 73 for dating notes.
- The materialisation sound effect fades out early, losing the final groan.
- A large crack is evident in the Police Box prop across the stile beside the right-hand door's window. This wasn't there when the box (the 1983 version) was taken to Spain for filming so may have happened during transit back to the studios.
- The Doctor mentions Time Lords have symbiotic nuclei and Peri immediately jumps to the conclusion that he controls the TARDIS through symbiosis. Earlier she didn't know what an attosecond was. At this point the Doctor neither confirms nor denies her spurious theory, but see next landing for further discussion.

LANDING 272

SPACE Earth, Spain, 4km outside Seville
TIME As above
TRAVELLERS The Doctor, Peri, Jamie
EPISODES The Two Doctors 2-3

The TARDIS materialises in the hot and sunny Andalusian countryside, where the Police Box is spied by English restaurant owner/failed actor Oscar Botcherby and his Spanish friend Anita, who have been out hunting moths. Mistaking the travellers for plain-clothes Interpol officers, Oscar reports seeing an aircraft crash nearby, which the Doctor realises was a

Sontaran battle sphere. He persuades the couple to show them the way to the hacienda towards which they saw survivors heading.

It is much later in the day when the Doctor and Peri get back to the Ship. The Doctor has now lost his appetite for fishing and decided that a healthy vegetarian diet is best for the both of them.

▤ **NOTES** How accurate is all the talk of symbiotic nuclei? The only thing we know for sure, which the Doctor volunteers without apparent reason to lie, is that "no one can travel through time without a molecular stabilisation system". The idea that Time Lords are provided with this via a symbiotic link with their TARDISes, which is embedded in their physiology and yet can be extended to anyone travelling with them, is purely Chessene's theorising, which the Doctor dismisses as "guesswork". The older Doctor explains to Jamie (and an eavesdropping Stike) that priming a time capsule's briode nebuliser with this "symbiotic print within the physiology of a Time Lord" will allow anyone to use it, but later admits "none of it was strictly true". Nonetheless, he does have to tinker with the briode nebuliser to allow one successful trip in the Kartz-Reimer module, so that at least is a necessary component – using the machine without it does nasty things to Stike and Chessene. We've seen plenty of people and creatures travel in the TARDIS without ill effect, and other races develop their own means of time travel, particular after the Time Lords vanish in the Last Great Time War. Do they all have symbiotic nuclei? It seems unlikely. Is it possible the Time Lords surreptitiously seeded the false idea that time travel is only possible with this genetic ability in order to deter professors Kartz and Reimer? When this failed they sent the Doctor, not expecting anyone to kidnap him and cut him up to extract it? The briode nebuliser could simply be part of the necessary molecular stabiliser, which TARDISes are also installed with (the Doctor's claim to have taken it "because it contains my symbiotic print" could be a lie to convince Chessene to use the module and get her "just desserts").

LANDING 273

SPACE Karfel, citadel, inner sanctum
TIME Unknown
TRAVELLERS The Doctor, Peri
EPISODES Timelash 1

The Doctor is planning a visit to Andromeda when the TARDIS is drawn towards a kontron tunnel, "a time corridor in space". He discerns that one end of the tunnel is located on Earth in 1179. Keen to avoid colliding with the phenomenon, he tinkers with circuitry behind a corridor wall roundel as Peri monitors the tunnel on the console.

Realising they cannot evade the kontron tunnel, the Doctor digs out a set of safety belts that he and Peri use to strap themselves to the console just as the Ship is pulled in and begins to shake violently. Eventually the TARDIS stabilises with the tunnel and settles down. A ghostly image of a woman, Vena, passes through the control room as she travels along the time corridor, although the Doctor notes the Ship's presence will have deflected her from reaching the 12th century.

The TARDIS proceeds in the opposite direction but as it nears the mouth of the tunnel the console sparks and the Ship begins shaking again. The terminus is a tall pyramidal cabinet – known to the Karfelons as the Timelash – in the inner sanctum of the citadel from where the ruling council presides over the planet. The TARDIS starts to materialise automatically, fading in and out of view as it emerges from the cabinet and moves across the room before solidifying.

The Doctor recognises their destination from a previous visit of his "a regeneration or three back", but is concerned the kontron tunnel should be centuries beyond the Karfelons' technological capability. He and Peri are greeted by newly promoted council leader Tekker, who takes them for refreshments.

The Doctor is escorted back to the TARDIS alone, under threat of harm to Peri if he does not retrieve Vena and the amulet she was carrying. Inside, he calculates that the Ship would have deflected her some 706 years after 1179 and sets course accordingly.

⚙ **CONTROLS** The Doctor enters data from the star chart (laid over panel E1) via panel E3, including flipping one of the switches in the middle-far-right niche. He reaches for controls on panel E4 when threatening to set course for Earth.

⚙ The right-hand flap on top of the screen housing on panel E2 is missing in some scenes, revealing the hollow beneath.

⚙ The Doctor turns off the scanner by twisting the right-hand black slider at the bottom-right of panel E3. He then operates controls on panel E2 and E3, learning the date of the tunnel's exit from the latter.

⚙ Peri monitors the kontron tunnel via the screen on panel E6 which displays a grid with a rotating white line across it.

⚙ The Doctor operates unseen controls on panels E1 and E3 as the console sparks: a flash charge ignited behind the right-hand display in the middle of panel E5, which has been refitted imprecisely. After landing, this is back in position properly but that niche is still scorched.

▤ **LORE** Collision with a kontron time corridor risks a realignment of the TARDIS's interior dimension, causing an implosion.

▤ Safety belts can be clipped to the underside of the console to offer some restraint when the Ship is being buffeted.

▤ **NOTES** Peri is hankering for somewhere she can "spend some time and relax" suggesting, perhaps, that there have been more adventures since defeating the Sontarans and that the break they took for the Doctor to indulge in some fishing is long past. The Doctor

- offers to take her to "Earth, 1985" which could either be the date they were last there (in *The Two Doctors*) or the date she met the Doctor on Lanzarote and he intends to fulfil their original deal of getting her back in time to resume her college course.
- There's no indication of when the events on Karfel are set so could be our future or past. Even though the kontron tunnel terminates in 12th-century Scotland, this could be projecting forwards in time, although as Vena is diverted to 1885 it's perhaps more likely that's between 1179 and the Karfel future (another 706 years, in 2591 maybe?).
- The star chart the Doctor uses is the same one that was pinned to Adric's bedroom wall, as seen in *Earthshock* (Landing 215) and *Terminus* (Landing 237). If the Doctor's aiming for Andromeda then he's looking in the wrong place on the chart, initially tapping near Altais in the Draco constellation, then pointing to somewhere in Ursa Major when he tells Peri where he's planning to take her.
- The second TARDIS scene had lines cut at the start – the Doctor pointing out to Peri the kontron tunnel on the scanner – and at the end, when his description of "the effect that time particles colliding within a multi-dimensional implosion field can have" was expanded from "pow!" to add: "The interior of the TARDIS will attempt to realign itself. As it does, there will be an external implosion."
- The corridor beyond the interior door is formed from one of the wide-spaced-roundels walls and a slatted column. Where the Doctor is working, the entire roundel is removed, not just its centre disc as in *Attack of the Cybermen* (Landing 263), and a tangle of multi-coloured cables hangs out. There is also a brass eagle lectern on which are pages of notes and various electrical components. It's possible this is the same one seen in *The Pirate Planet* (Landing 146).
- In a cut scene, the Doctor sent Peri to the magenta store room to get the trunk with the safety belts in. This also appears to contain the grey top hat the Doctor wore in his second incarnation when partly transformed into an Androgum in *The Two Doctors*.
- There are many previous times when safety harnesses would have been welcome as the TARDIS was being buffeted, notably the last time it was caught in a time corridor in *Resurrection of the Daleks* (Landing 252). On those occasions the disturbance was a surprise, whereas here the Doctor can anticipate and prepare for it.
- The distortions as the TARDIS is caught in the kontron tunnel were effected using Quantel's Mirage digital video manipulator (DVM 8000), which could distort the picture within a three-dimensional space. This was also used to place images on the Borad's angled monitor screen.
- A high-angle shot of the console as Vena passes through gives a rare view of the tube lights that illuminate the inside of the collar section.
- When the console sparks and the Doctor declares, "Velocity override," it's not clear whether he's naming the component that has just burned out, citing the cause of that, or explaining the course of action he needs to take to compensate for it.
- The Police Box shown emerging from the Timelash was recorded against black and superimposed over the shot of the inner sanctum (hence why its shadows are see-through). Contrary to reports, this is plainly not the main prop but a model. It's not one seen before, unless it's that used in *The Mark of the Rani* when the TARDIS is tipped down a coal shaft. The final materialisation is the full-size prop in a standard roll-back-and-mix shot.
- Why does the Doctor assume he has arrived at a time when "Karfel should be centuries from [time corridor] technology" and not simply that he's arrived a long time after his previous visit? Perhaps the architecture and style of clothing are close to those he remembers so he's guessing less than a century has passed.

LANDING 274

SPACE Earth, Scotland, near Inverness
TIME Summer 1885
TRAVELLERS The Doctor
EPISODES Timelash 1

Following the course of the kontron tunnel, the TARDIS lands beside a cottage in the Highlands close to Inverness. The Doctor finds Vena with a young would-be writer called Herbert – the Time Lord not yet aware his full name is Herbert George Wells – who is experimenting with spiritualism, although talk of a time machine attracts his greater interest.

While the Doctor persuades Vena to return the amulet she took, Herbert slips into the Police Box unseen. Vena insists on returning to Karfel to help stand against the despotic Borad so the Doctor allows her into the TARDIS and dematerialises.

- **NOTES** Although the script gives Herbert's age as "about 25 years old", he would have been only nineteen in the summer of 1885. At that time he had completed his first year studying biology and training to be a teacher at the Normal School of Science in South Kensington, London. Wells came from a modest family working in trade, service or on the land (although his father was also a cricketer) and living in the south of England, so none of his four paternal nor sole maternal uncles seems likely to have owned a cottage in the Highlands. A second-cousin of his mother's was known as Uncle Tom, a prosperous innkeeper in Windsor where Herbert and his two elder brothers spent teenage summer holidays, and his brother-in-law as Uncle (Arthur) Williams, who briefly took on a fourteen-year-old Wells as a pupil-teacher at his school in Wookey, Somerset. Might one of these have had a Scottish getaway?
- A scene was cut of Vena entering the control room and expressing her amazement at getting to travel in "the famous TARDIS".

LANDING 275

SPACE Karfel, citadel, corridor
TIME Shortly after Landing 273
TRAVELLERS The Doctor, Herbert George Wells, Vena
EPISODES Timelash 1-2

The TARDIS slips back into the time corridor on its return journey to Karfel. Only then does Herbert reveal himself, much to the Doctor's displeasure. They are already nearing their destination, however, and the Ship shakes again as it escapes the tunnel to materialise in a corridor near the inner sanctum.

Its arrival is heard by Tekker, who demands the amulet be returned to him; with Peri still captive, Vena accedes. Rebels including her fiancé Mykros are dragged past on their way to be disposed of in the Timelash, and the new arrivals follow.

The Doctor and a freed Peri return to the TARDIS as a Bandril missile with a bendalypse warhead approaches Karfel. He tries to convince her to leave so as not to distract him but she is reluctant to abandon him. As they argue, Herbert sneaks aboard and hides under the console. The Doctor resorts to physically ejecting Peri, promising he will be back shortly, and sets the Ship in motion.

- **CONTROLS** The Doctor operates unseen controls on panel E2 and at the top of panel E3, and others on the latter panel as the Ship nears Karfel.
- While arguing with Peri, he operates controls on the same two panels, then dematerialises from panel E3.
- **NOTES** The TARDIS presumably travels along the kontron tunnel, which is why the Doctor can't take Herbert straight home, although he expresses it as having "no time" to do so. The onset of distortion as the Ship "transcend[s] the time vortex" may be it breaking free before it reaches the Timelash cabinet to allow the Doctor to materialise outside the inner sanctum.
- Herbert marvels at the TARDIS being "bigger inside than it is outside". Others have boggled at the interior dimensions but none has used that wording since Nyssa in *The Keeper of Traken* (Landing 195).
- The debate with Peri, and its re-enactment with Herbert, were extended by script editor Eric Saward as episode two was under-running (can you tell?). They were recorded five weeks after the rest of the serial, during production of *Revelation of the Daleks*, by which time Colin Baker's hair had grown noticeably.

LANDING 276

SPACE Karfel, citadel, corridor
TIME As above
TRAVELLERS The Doctor, Herbert
EPISODES Timelash 2

As soon as the Ship has dematerialised Herbert shows himself. With no time to return him to safety on Karfel, the Doctor warns they may not make it back at all. His plan is to use the TARDIS to intercept the Bandril missile before it reaches the planet. He tries to ignore Herbert's wittering as he carefully pilots the Ship, then braces for impact. The missile explodes harmlessly in the planet's stratosphere.

The TARDIS is also unharmed and returns to Karfel. As Herbert leaves, the Doctor notices a calling card he has dropped bearing his full name. Although the young man is eager to stay, the Doctor insists on taking him back home, knowing the future that awaits the budding writer.

- **NOTES** The TARDIS doesn't appear to materialise in the path of the missile – the central column continues to oscillate – so this must be an instance of it in flight but within normal space.
- When Peri asks how the Doctor avoided being blown up, he simply says, "I'll explain one day. It's a neat trick." Yet we know the TARDIS has a forcefield and can withstand pretty much any impact, so why not simply cite the old 'indestructible ship' excuse?

PREVIOUS LANDING

SPACE Earth, Scotland, near Inverness
TIME As Landing 274
TRAVELLERS The Doctor, Peri, Herbert George Wells
EPISODES Intended in Timelash 2

The TARDIS returned to the Highlands safely once the kontron tunnel had been collapsed, and deposited Herbert back at his uncle's cottage to resume his life, although with a few new ideas perhaps.

- **NOTES** We know HG Wells must get home eventually but despite the Doctor clearly intending to take him straight there, who's to say he doesn't do a Harry, give the helmic regulator a twist and send the TARDIS halfway across the universe for a few adventures first?

LANDING 277

SPACE Necros
TIME Unknown future (after Landing 253)
TRAVELLERS The Doctor, Peri
EPISODES Revelation of the Daleks 1

The Doctor hears news that an old friend, agronomist Professor Arthur Stengos, is near to death and has had himself put into suspended animation at the funerary facility Tranquil Repose on Necros. Suspicious that the respected scientist would submit to such a process, the Doctor decides to investigate.

The TARDIS materialises on Necros some distance from Tranquil Repose, beyond its boundary wall and the reach of its security cameras, so the travellers can enter covertly. The ground is covered in snow and the air frosty. The Doctor has Peri dress in a blue overcoat and beret, this being the official colour of mourning on the planet, as their cover story will be they have come to pay their respects to Stengos.

While he finds a long blue cloak to cover his colourful coat, Peri steps outside into the cold and wanders down the bank of a nearby river. Disappointed with the nut roast roll the Doctor has prepared, she throws it into the frozen water, where some creature under the surface snatches it. The Doctor assures her the local voltrox and speelsnape won't harm them and leads the way to Tranquil Repose.

The pair return later that day, the Doctor promising to take Peri somewhere more fun, such as—

▤ **NOTES** When the Police Box prop was taken on location for filming, it was found the roof lamp had been forgotten so a makeshift replacement was put together. This was a tall, thin cylinder with a much wider circular cap and two thin struts. It was kept largely off-camera in the final episode but can be seen in location photos. Due to the unexpected snowfall the night before filming, the crew had to erect the prop with as little disturbance to the surrounding snow as possible.

▤ Although slightly obscured in the final edit by the fade from the establishing shot of Necros (actually a tinted photo of Earth), the materialisation of the TARDIS was achieved as a standard film mix.

LANDING 278

SPACE Zaurak Minor
TIME Unknown
TRAVELLERS The Doctor, Peri
EPISODES Slipback 1

The TARDIS lands on Zaurak so the Doctor can ask for directions. He and Peri visit a bar "full of very strange people" where they sample the local beverage voxnic. The Doctor ends up drinking three bottles of the liquor. Peri manages to get the drunken Time Lord back to the Ship and to take off before he collapses into bed.

LANDING 279

SPACE Space, alongside Vipod Mor
TIME Unknown
TRAVELLERS The Doctor, Peri
EPISODES Slipback 1

While the Doctor restlessly sleeps off his overindulgence, the TARDIS detects a time ripple and automatically materialises alongside the enormous census spaceship Vipod Mor from which it emanated. The ship's sentient computer probes the sleeping Doctor's mind to lure him aboard. The console starts to "wink, flash and grunt like some dirty old man in a park", according to Peri when she wakes the Doctor. An alarm indicates time spillage and the Doctor fears someone aboard the spaceship is experimenting dangerously with time.

▤ **LORE** There is a limit to how much the scanner can show of nearby objects. Peri says the freighter they are alongside is "so large I can't get the scanner screen to zoom out far enough to get it all in".

LANDING 280

SPACE Vipod Mor, service duct
TIME As above
TRAVELLERS The Doctor, Peri
EPISODES Slipback 1,6

The Doctor moves the TARDIS inside the spaceship, materialising in a service duct so he can investigate discreetly. As he and Peri explore, however, a large, hairy, slavering, carnivorous Maston gets between them and the Ship and gives chase as they run.

The Doctor, Peri and an art thief called Shellingborne Grant hurry back to the TARDIS – evading the still roaming Maston – both to escape an imminent outbreak of mors immedicabilis, a virus known as 'the incurable death', and to try to prevent the Vipod Mor's schizoid computer from taking the ship back in time to before life began in this galaxy in order to guide it along more peaceful lines.

The Doctor plans to materialise the TARDIS inside the computer's memory banks but an alarm indicates the Vipod Mor is already travelling through time. The voice of a Time Lord High Councillor warns him not to interfere or the universe will never exist. It explains a mistake in the computer's calculation will take the ship not to the birth of the galaxy but the heart of the super-condensed matter from which the cosmos was formed, where it will explode and initiate the Big Bang. The Doctor concedes his mistake and takes off, leaving the Vipod Mor to its destiny.

▤ **NOTES** *Slipback* was broadcast on BBC Radio 4 in the summer after the announcement that *Doctor Who* on television would be taking a longer break than usual. As an audio drama no TARDIS sets or console were used, but we do hear the usual control sound effects and a new stereo version of the materialisation sound.

PREVIOUS LANDING

SPACE Unknown
TIME As Landing 278
TRAVELLERS The Doctor, Peri, Shellingborne Grant
EPISODES Intended in Slipback 6

A contrite Doctor was determined to seek out "the largest library I can find" to refresh his knowledge of universal history, and to drop off Grant.

▤ **NOTES** We only hear the Doctor state his intent and can't be certain he follows through at once.
▤ The Doctor later knows of a planet-sized library (see Landing 405, vol.2), so this may be when he first visits.

LANDING 281

SPACE Stellian galaxy, Ravolox (Earth, England, London, near Marble Arch)
TIME After 2002000
TRAVELLERS The Doctor, Peri
EPISODES The Trial of a Time Lord 1

The Doctor is intrigued to learn of the planet Ravolox, which has the same mass, axial tilt and period of rotation as the Earth, an extremely rare occurrence. Gallifreyan records also indicate it was devastated by a solar fireball. Arriving around 500 years after this event, he and Peri find the world far from scorched, with surprisingly abundant overgrowth and copious precipitation.

Beneath the ground is a shelter where an Andromedan L3 robot, powered by a black light converter on the surface, governs a group of surviving humans. Strictly limited to 500 people, some have evaded being culled by escaping outside, where they have formed an Iron Age society.

In fact, Ravolox is Earth. The Time Lords used a magnotron to move the planet several light years across space when they discovered three Andromedans based there had been stealing secret knowledge from the Matrix. Anticipating this, the thieves put themselves into suspended animation in the shelter, built into the old tunnels of the London Underground, guarded over by the L3, Drathro.

Once the underground dwellers have been liberated and Drathro destroyed, the Doctor and Peri return to the TARDIS intent on discovering who moved the Earth and what the now-deceased Andromedans' secrets were.

▌ **LORE** The Matrix can record event data from within the collection range of a TARDIS, not just that directly experienced by Time Lords. This is said to be a "new surveillance system" possibly post-dating the origination of the Doctor's TARDIS ("an old model"), which he posits has "been bugged without my knowledge". We've seen he doesn't know everything about his Ship, but if this isn't a function that's always been in action when might the Time Lords have added it? There's no evidence of them doing so during *Arc of Infinity*, the last time they were seen to have access to the TARDIS, and why would they when they were intending to execute the Doctor thus ending his travels? More likely is in *The War Games*, where we see two technicians working on the console, so the Time Lords can keep a broader eye on events via the TARDIS while the Doctor is exiled.

▌ **NOTES** The Doctor postulates to Peri that "your planet and its entire constellation managed to shift itself a couple of light years across space". But this makes little sense as constellations, in our parlance at least, are groups of stars as visible from Earth. He can't mean the entire Milky Way (or Mutter's Spiral in the Time Lord lexicon) was moved as a shift of two light years would be all but imperceptible compared to the size of the galaxy (over 100,000 light years across). He might mean Earth's whole solar system was relocated. Even then, just two light years is less than half the distance to the nearest star so the Andromedans would need to be bad navigators not to find it. None of which explains why the Valeyard says 'Ravolox' is in the Stellian galaxy. He can't mean the Earth has really been moved to a different galaxy altogether, as that would be a lot more than two light years, so is this an alternative Time Lord name for the Milky Way?

▤ The Doctor estimates the date, from looking at his pocket watch, as "two million years or more" after Peri's native time. At that time scale the margin of error could be tens of thousand of years, but the "or more" suggests it's at least beyond the 2,002nd millennium.

▤ It's debatable whether the "solar fireball" happened or is just part of the fiction of 'Ravolox'. The Doctor cites Gallifreyan records, which understandably would have been falsified, and the human survivors only know what they've been told by Drathro to keep them underground, believing the surface is still ablaze. Glitz also says there was a "fireball five hundred years ago" but his sources may be suspect too (in dialogue cut from an early trial room scene, the Doctor notes, "The fireball that destroyed Ravolox is documented in *Extinct Civilisations* by Waris Bossard," but who's to say that author wasn't misled by the Time Lords' cover story?) or he's playing up to Katryca's beliefs to gain access to the black light converter. The only potentially reliable first-hand witness is Drathro, who says, "Only part of the planet was enveloped by fire." This is in response to learning there's abundant vegetation in the immediate area above the shelter, so is he saying the fire was elsewhere (how would he know?) or is he making a logical deduction to explain the presence of trees? As Peri notes, "Any soil left after the visitation of a fireball would be sterile," and even the Doctor admits re the fireball, "I think someone exaggerated." Yet come episode thirteen he's citing the shifting of Earth as "causing the fireball which nearly destroyed the planet"; when a magnotron is later used by the Daleks to drag the Earth across space there's no consequent combustion. So if there was no fire, why would the Time Lords feature a solar fireball in their fake history of Ravolox? It's just going to pique the curiosity of a certain wayward traveller.

▤ A scene showing the TARDIS materialising was shot on location but cut from the final episode. In it Peri emerged to find it raining but instead of going back inside she stood there getting wet until the Doctor brought out her jacket and a multi-coloured golfing umbrella. He proceeded to walk off with it until she called him back to share its cover.

LANDING 282

SPACE Thordon
TIME 2379
TRAVELLERS The Doctor, Peri
EPISODES Before The Trial of a Time Lord 5

The Doctor and Peri encounter a dying warlord who pleads for more "beams that kill" to be sent from Thoros Beta. Knowing that to be the home planet of the money-grubbing Mentors, and that the warlords' CD phaser weapons are beyond their technological capability, the Doctor decides to take a stand against such immoral interference.

- **NOTES** It's not explicitly stated where the TARDIS landed but the Doctor refers to meeting "a warlord of Thordon" and we later learn from Kiv that on "this Thordon world, the Krontep warriors have succeeded in subduing the massed hordes of the Tonkonp Empire". It might seem that Krontep and Tonkonp are two regions/countries at war on Thordon, but Yrcanos twice says, "On my planet of Krontep." So are the Krontep invading Thordon, or are they and the Tonkonp both trying to add the planet to their respective empires? Is the Doctor there to help the Thordon warlords resist being taken over? He may not be fully aware of the situation, however, as when ingratiating himself with Sil, he says of Yrcanos, "Why should I follow a mad warlord of Thordon?" suggesting he believes the king is from that planet.
- See next landing for dating discussion but these events are strongly suggested to happen directly before the Doctor and Peri visit Thoros Beta.

LANDING 283

SPACE Thoros Beta, beach; beamed to caves, then Time Lord court
TIME 3 July 2379
TRAVELLERS The Doctor, Peri
EPISODES The Trial of a Time Lord 5,8

The TARDIS materialises on a shoreline where the waters of a pink sea wash over lilac rocks beneath a green sky. Visible on the horizon is the twin-ringed planet Thoros Alpha. Although the tide is going out, the Doctor and Peri have to wade through the water to reach dry land.

As the scientist Crozier finally succeeds in transferring the contents of one mind into the brain of a different body, the Time Lord High Council decides to take matters into its own hands and remove the Doctor from the situation. They use an extraction beam first to move the TARDIS from the beach to the nearby caves, where the Doctor is drawn inside, then to take it out of time and bring it to a massive judiciary vessel in space.

- **NOTES** The Valeyard gives the time period as "twenty-fourth century, last quarter, fourth year, seventh month, third day". This gives the date above in Earth's calendar but arguably there's no reason a Time Lord court would use that so he might be referencing a Thorosian time scale.
- When Peri closes the left-hand Police Box door it's clear the telephone plaque is missing. As there's consequently no handle on this side, Nicola Bryant has to pull on the edge of the inset panel. Because the centre post is fixed to this door, she has to leave it slightly ajar. (It's a good job the Thorosian tide is going out rather than coming in or the Ship would be flooded.)
- In reality, when recording on the shore, the production crew discovered a mistake had been made in the tide timings and the sea *was* coming in rather than going out. The scene had to be filmed quickly in order to dismantle the Police Box prop before it was washed away.
- The appearance of the TARDIS to collect the Doctor was achieved using a split-screen effect. A shot of the empty tunnel was superimposed over the Police Box on the right of the picture, then faded out as Colin Baker ran past the prop, stopped and walked backwards into it. Stagehands inside the box opened and closed the doors. A bright light was shone onto the Police Box, enhanced with an overlaid white beam to match that in the following model shot. Note the prop is missing its roof lamp (or this has possibly been masked for some reason) and that just as the doors open there is a quick cross-fade, perhaps to speed up their opening or to cut a glimpse of someone inside.
- The impressive model shot of the TARDIS being pulled into the Time Lords' space court, reused from episode one, features a new miniature Police Box. This was constructed by Mike Tucker, at the time a student on secondment to the BBC Visual Effects department. This was a good match for the full-size prop except that it had an unusually deep gap between the 'Police box' signs and the tops of the windows. This was filmed separately from the space station model using the same computer-controlled camera movements then optically matted into the background footage.

LANDING 284

SPACE Time Lord court
TIME Unknown
TRAVELLERS The Doctor
EPISODES The Trial of a Time Lord 1,13-14

The TARDIS is brought into the judiciary vessel and remotely piloted to the atrium outside the court where a jury of high-ranking Time Lords is gathered to hear the case against the Doctor. Once released from the extraction beam, he stumbles from the Ship and has nowhere else to go but into the courtroom, where the prosecuting Valeyard awaits.

As the trial approaches sentencing, the extraction beam is used to bring two capsules containing Glitz and the Doctor's future companion Melanie Bush to the court as witnesses to support his defence, passing the TARDIS as they enter the courtroom.

Shortly after, as it is revealed that the Valeyard is a future aspect of the Doctor himself, the prosecutor runs into the atrium, summons the Seventh Door to the Matrix, opens it with a copy of the Keeper's key and enters. The Doctor and Glitz follow hot on his heels, leaving the Inquisitor to preside over an empty court.

After witnessing the Time Lords' unwillingness to involve themselves with events occurring inside the Matrix, Mel snatches the Keeper's key and hurries through the Seventh Door to save the Doctor from sacrificing himself. She returns to warn the jury they are the Valeyard's true target and should evacuate the courtroom. Eventually the Doctor too emerges from the Matrix and, having saved his peers, finds the charges against him have been dismissed. He returns to the TARDIS with Mel and they depart.

▤ **NOTES** Although the Doctor is said to have been "taken out of time" this need not imply the court itself is outside of time, merely that the extraction beam lifted him from the 24th century and deposited him whenever the trial is being held. Equally, however, shots of the space station in space don't automatically mean it's not in some form of extra-dimensional flight, as when we see the Police Box spinning past stars.

▤ The TARDIS materialises outside the courtroom with its usual grinding noise and no beam of light, unlike the witness capsules later, so presumably the extraction beam brings it to a reception area from where it's moved under its own power to the court atrium. The Doctor emerges fractionally before the Ship has completely solidified.

▤ When the TARDIS arrives its handle and lock are on the right-hand door, from which the Doctor emerges, and the centre post is attached to the left door. Yet when he and Mel leave, the handle and lock are now on the left and the post is attached to the right door (because the prop has been positioned back to front).

▤ The Master's TARDIS control room used the usual set painted black, including an aligned-roundels wall and the inner door beyond the control room's interior door. The console had the same application of black tape and paint as in *Planet of Fire* (Landing 256), with a box slung underneath panel E1 for the Master to slot the Matrix cassette into. The pyramidal recall unit is missing, with just a flat clear acrylic pentagon in its place. The Master activates the sensory bombardment with an unseen control on panel E1 and presses a button on the right of the upper niche to load the cassette.

▤ So where next for the Doctor and Mel? It's generally assumed he takes her home to Pease Pottage or wherever she was extracted from, which might have been during a future adventure with the Doctor. Yet he states no intention to do so when leaving the court and she seems eager to resume her life aboard the TARDIS ("We'll get you back on the exerciser"). We know from stories like *Day of the Daleks* that future timelines are not immutable, and given the Valeyard's ambitions this must apply to the Doctor's personal timeline too. We've now seen that the Doctor doesn't become the Valeyard during his first regeneration cycle (although "somewhere between your twelfth and final incarnation" has become a much bigger gap than was assumed at the time), so what if the Valeyard's presence during his past has already changed his future. Did the Doctor 'originally' save Peri from Crozier's mind-swap, later part with her amicably, meet Mel, encounter the Vervoids and eventually beget the Valeyard? In that guise he then travelled back and convinced the High Council to try his younger self, this very act altering the Doctor's future (the trial can't have happened in the Valeyard's past or he would know he loses). Peri is now left to her fate and the Doctor first meets Mel at the court, the Master having lifted her from the 'original' timeline (perhaps before it changed). As such she knows who the Doctor is and he knows about her from having selected his defence case (and if it's problematic that the Matrix has details of events yet to happen, maybe the answer lies in the fact that these are in the Valeyard's past so the Matrix might now have his knowledge – assuming he hasn't made the whole adventure up to frame the Doctor; note in episode fourteen it's only the Valeyard's Matrix facsimile of Mel who recalls events on the Hyperion III, not the real Mel). She resumes/begins her travels with the Doctor, with memories of adventures together that they may now never have, stays through his sixth regeneration and leaves to hang out with Glitz. (Given this outcome, it's tempting to suggest the Master snatches both of them from her post-TARDIS life, but while their initial lack of recognition could be amnesia from being taken out of time, neither questions why the Doctor is in his sixth incarnation.) The Doctor knows better than to quiz her about their now-erased time together and if he tries to explain what's happened to her she's likely to say, "Sure, whatever, let's have some carrot juice."

PREVIOUS LANDINGS

SPACE Spaceship
TIME Some years before 2986
TRAVELLERS The Doctor, [unknown companions]
EPISODES Discussed by the Doctor and Travers in The Trial of a Time Lord 9

The Doctor encountered Tonker Travers aboard the ship he was captaining and resolved a "web of mayhem and intrigue" (although he may have contributed to putting the ship in danger in the first place). Travers learned about the TARDIS.

▤ **NOTES** This was before Travers was promoted to commodore prior to his commanding the Hyperion III, and before the Doctor was travelling with Mel.

SPACE Milky Way (Perseus Arm), Mogar
TIME Unknown [before 2986]
TRAVELLERS The Doctor, [unknown companions]
EPISODES Mentioned by the Doctor in The Trial of a Time Lord 10

The Doctor visited the planet, despite it having no atmospheric oxygen, and learned of its abundant natural resources, including vionesium.

▣ **NOTES** Mel doesn't seem to know about Mogar so the Doctor's visit must have been before he travelled with her. At his trial he knows about the planet so it's likely he'd already been by then (although he did review events on the Hyperion III earlier). In the trial evidence, from 2986, the humans are said to be "stripping [the] planet bare" and the richness of natural resources the Doctor recalls "will soon be exhausted", so his previous visit must have been before then.

▣ Both these landings were before the events shown at the Doctor's trial, but as those are in his future so could these trips. If so, Mel's absence might indicte they are from an aborted timeline (see above).

LANDING 285

SPACE Hyperion III
TIME 2986
TRAVELLERS The Doctor, Melanie Bush
EPISODES The Trial of a Time Lord 9-12

The TARDIS is travelling in the vicinity of Mogar, in the Perseus Arm of the Milky Way, when it receives a mayday call from an intergalactic liner that has recently left the planet en route to Earth. The signal has been directed specifically at the Ship but is anonymous and incomplete, mentioning only the need to identify a traitor before the liner reaches its destination.

Encouraged by Mel, the Doctor responds immediately and materialises the TARDIS in the cargo hold of the liner, the Hyperion III. One end of the hold is cordoned off and limited to infra-spectrum light only. Before they can explore further they are captured by armed guards and escorted to the bridge. Once they have left, the sender of the mayday, an investigator called Hallet currently disguised as a helmeted Mogarian, breaks into the restricted area.

Doland, one of Professor Sarah Lasky's team of agronomists, discovers the break-in and returns shortly after with Lasky herself and their colleague Bruchner. When the other two have gone, Doland electrifies the entrance.

Mel hopes to explore the hydroponics centre in the hold but is found there by communications officer Edwardes. He agrees to let her look around but when he opens the entrance gate he is electrocuted. Mel is caught by two guards, one of whom takes her for questioning; the other is killed by a newly sprouted Vervoid.

Hallet, still posing as a Mogarian, searches the hydroponics centre again but finds all the large pods there are now empty. Bruchner and Doland arrive and are horrified to discover the same. Hallet tries to slip away but is glimpsed by Bruchner. He sneaks around the hold then makes a break for the door, the two scientists following.

The Doctor and Mel visit the cargo hold again having learned of the now-dead Hallet's presence and guessing it was he who sent them the mayday. The Doctor has a leaf he took from the investigator and compares it to the empty pods in the hydroponics centre but is unable to tell what came out of them. They return to the passenger area.

Bruchner comes to the hold to destroy the records of his team's work, fearing what they have unleashed. Doland finds him and locks him inside their lab cubicle before fetching Lasky. She berates Bruchner but he attacks her and runs off, passing the Doctor who has come looking for Lasky. She tells him Bruchner intends to destroy the ship and they hurry after him.

After Bruchner is prevented from pitching the Hyperion into a black hole, Doland brings the Doctor to the hold to look for an incriminating recording, only to pull a gun on him. But the Doctor has already deduced Doland is the one behind a string of murders and alerted Commodore Travers, who arrives to arrest the scientist.

With Vervoids roaming the ship and picking off more of the passengers and crew, the Doctor, Mel and Lasky check the lab for herbicidal chemicals but find none. A group of Vervoids corners them. Mel leads the Doctor into the ventilation ducts but Lasky insists on trying to reason with the plant creatures, only to be killed.

Once the Vervoids have been reduced to mulch, Travers and the stewardess Janet say goodbye to the Doctor and Mel by the TARDIS – the commodore hoping he will never need the Doctor's help again. As the Doctor performs a burst of Leoncavallo's aria 'Vesti la giubba', the Police Box fades away.

◉ **CONTROLS** To display the mayday message on the screen on panel E4 (although it also shows on panel E6's screen), the Doctor tells Mel to press a red button but then presses a different coloured one himself. The only red buttons are those at bottom-left, which means the Doctor must press one of the adjacent green ones.

◉ In cut shots, the Doctor traced the signal by pressing keys in the bottom-centre niche of panel E5 and buttons on the shelf of the same niche of panel E1.

◉ As when used for the Master's TARDIS in episode fourteen, recorded two weeks before the episode nine scenes, panel E6 is missing the five-sided pyramid. On panel E5 the two left-most flip switches in the bottom-left corner are missing, as are the flaps on top of the screen housing of panel E2, revealing the deep hollow in its top (also visible in episode fourteen).

▣ **LORE** The TARDIS carries an exercise bike and either cartons of carrot juice or fresh carrots and a squeezer.

▣ **NOTES** The Doctor gives the year when introducing his evidence in the court. The communications room aboard the Hyperion III has a display reading '164 2986'. As the last four digits match the year, the first three could indicate day and month – 16th of April – or number of days elapsed – making it the 13th of June.

▣ Mel's surname is never given on screen during her travels in the TARDIS but she was named Bush in the character outline the production team wrote.

▣ How does Hallet know the contact on the radar screen is the TARDIS when all it shows is a plain block and

specifically says 'Unidentified craft' and 'No ID possible'?
- Although the Doctor pulls the TARDIS door shut behind him on arrival, it's ajar when Lasky's trio arrive to investigate the break-in of the hydroponics centre. It's fully closed again by the end of the story.
- The TARDIS's departure was achieved using a split-screen effect. Bonnie Langford was recorded entering the Police Box. The prop was then removed from the set and actors Michael Craig and Yolande Palfrey took their positions on the right of the picture. The recording of the TARDIS was overlaid on the left (note the box's shadow is cut off just to the left of Craig's feet) and then faded out, allowing the two actors to cross the already empty floor in front of them.
- Does this adventure still happen? Regardless of theories about whether the Valeyard made the whole story up or the evidence is from a timeline that has been rewritten (see Landing 284), surely if or when the Doctor finds himself receiving a mayday from the Hyperion III he'll remember what's going on and immediately sort it out, saving the lives of all the murder victims. Or he may pre-empt matters and stop the initial development of the Vervoids. At the very least, wouldn't he find a way to avoid committing genocide? If these events occur at all, they must proceed very differently from what is presented during the trial.

LANDING 286

SPACE Lakertya
TIME Unknown
TRAVELLERS The Doctor, Mel
EPISODES Time and the Rani 1,4

The TARDIS is buffeted by energy bolts and forced into landing on the desolate planet Lakertya. The Doctor and Mel are knocked unconscious. The Rani enters with the navigational guidance systems distorter she used to bring down the TARDIS and orders her Tetrap servant Urak to take the Doctor's body to her laboratory. Injured or affected by the earlier bombardment, the prone figure regenerates. Urak hoists the now-shorter Doctor over his shoulder and carries him out.

One of the Lakertyans, Ikona, witnesses the arrival of the TARDIS and approaches after the Rani and Urak have departed. They have left the door open so he slips inside. Finding Mel still insensible, he assumes she is a colleague of the Rani's and takes her as a hostage to bargain for the release of his people's leader Beyus.

A revived Doctor – although affected by an amnestic drug injected by the Rani – returns accompanied by his fellow Time Lord, who is disguised as Mel to elicit his compliance. He tests her patience by trying on numerous outfits before making a final selection; she has to forcibly remind him they came to collect a radiation wave meter with which to diagnose why the equipment in 'his' laboratory is not working. While the Doctor retrieves the device from the tool room, the Rani receives word from Urak that he has found the real Mel. She tunes the scanner to his viewpoint and convinces the Doctor they are watching the Rani as she is caught in a spinning bubble trap and disappears over a crest. Believing her destroyed, they return to the laboratory.

Mel, Ikona and Beuys' wife Faroon shepherd the confused geniuses kidnapped by the Rani to the TARDIS for safety. Other Lakertyans gather round the Police Box as the Rani launches her rocket but the Doctor assures them the delay in its launch means it will miss its target: a strange matter asteroid passing near the planet. The gathered geniuses watch on the scanner as the rocket streaks harmlessly into space, before the Doctor ushers them further inside to await their return home. He goes back out to collect Mel and give the Lakertyans the antidote to the toxic sting of the insects the Rani used to ensure their subservience, although Ikona pours this away believing his people must overcome such challenges themselves. The Doctor and Mel say their goodbyes and depart.

○ CONTROLS The Rani operates the scanner with an unseen control on the left of panel E4; later the Doctor closes it from the middle-right of panel E3.
- The recall circuit pyramid is back in place on panel E6 while the red flip switch in the niche to the left of this panel's screen has been replaced with a white rocker switch. On panel E1, one of the red buttons in the upper niche has come off and a red rectangle has been added to the right of those remaining, extending to the width of keypad below.
- The pedestal is missing the hexagonal cover below panel E2, even though the console's power cable is attached beneath panel E3.

▮ LORE The scanner can be synched to an external [Gallifreyan] device to relay images from another source.

▤ NOTES It's not entirely clear whether the TARDIS is physically dragged down to Lakertya or materialises of its own accord – it appears to be a mixture of both. We see it being struck by energy bolts as it tumbles through space, emitting a high-pitched version of its usual grinding, so presumably at that point the Ship is in flight (sadly the shot inside doesn't show whether the central column is oscillating). The Doctor later says of the Rani's navigational guidance systems distorter, "This'd force any passing spaceship into landing here," but suggesting the TARDIS is as vulnerable as any old spacecraft feels rather mundane. We've seen it snared in mid-flight before, notably in *The Web Planet* (Landing 14) and *The Web of Fear* (Landing 56), but that was by mystical entities with strong mental powers, not a hi-tech rifle. Besides, surely the Rani wasn't standing outside aiming the distorter blindly into the sky. For one thing, the energy bolts fly at the TARDIS from all directions, sometimes two at a time, so is she pursuing in her own capsule, driving the Doctor's towards Lakertya? Next we see the Police Box sweep across the sky, held in a multi-coloured beam (is this being emitted by the distorter?). It could still be in flight as we've seen it moving through the air before, sort of (see Landing 58), and will do again (see Landing 361, vol.2). Certainly it's present in normal space as Ikona watches it pass. Yet when the beam touches the ground (not where the Rani's standing but she must be close by) the TARDIS doesn't travel along the beam but fades into view like a materialisation, and there's a burst of the usual sound effect's closing thump.

- Not counting the chameleon circuit demonstration in *Logopolis*, the opening shots of *Time and the Rani* offer the first ever computer-generated Police Box images used in the series – and the last until the 21st century revival. These, as with the new title sequence, were produced by Gareth Edwards at CAL Video.
- On waking, the Doctor muses, "There's a bicentennial refit of the TARDIS to book in." Previously he has said the Ship was overdue its 500 year service (see Landing 118), so he could mean that's now 200 years late or that the aging TARDIS needs more frequent maintenance.
- The wardrobe is simply a black void with hanging quilts. There are two triangular green metal frames with wide canvas panels forming a V-shape on which items of clothing are draped or hung, a large wooden trunk, a full-length mirror in a carved wooden frame, an easel, a carpet bag and other bits of paraphernalia.
- We only see the Rani press a control to open the scanner but can assume her wrist-worn control device is wirelessly connected to the console and relaying Urak's point of view. We don't learn enough about the Tetraps to know how the Rani can tap into their vision but some sort of implant wouldn't be beyond her skills.
- Only five geniuses are seen running from the Rani's lair yet later there are eleven inside the TARDIS.

PREVIOUS LANDINGS

SPACE Various planets including Earth
TIME Various including 4th/5th century, 19th century and 20th century
TRAVELLERS The Doctor, Mel, 11 geniuses
EPISODES Intended in Time and the Rani 4

The Doctor took all the geniuses who had been kidnapped by the Rani back to their proper times and places. He may or may not have explained some of how the TARDIS works to Einstein on the way.

- **NOTES** Only three of the geniuses are named, all from Earth: Hypatia, Pasteur and Einstein. The rest are humanoid bipeds, although one has vulpine features, another might be from Argolis, and the face of a third is hidden by a visor. That leaves five who could be from Earth of indeterminate periods, although one appears to be an Ancient Greek. In Pip and Jane Baker's novelisation of their story, Charles Darwin is also one of the kidnapped geniuses.
- Hypatia was an Egyptian philosopher and mathematician who lived in Alexandria from the mid-4th century until 415. As she would be violently murdered by an angry mob, she may have preferred to stay on Lakertya. She is presumably the lady in the multi-tiered headwear and long white robes.
- Louis Pasteur appears here grey-bearded and balding so was presumably snatched later in his life. Yet the Doctor says, "He will rid his world of a major scourge," implying Pasteur hasn't done so yet. If this is referring to his development of vaccines for the likes of cholera and anthrax, then he must have been taken before the late-1870s and be aged under 55. He is likely returned to Paris.
- Albert Einstein is also grey haired but doesn't look elderly, so is perhaps in his late-50s/early-60s (his moustache was darker before then). This would mean he was kidnapped after his emigration to America in the 1930s. While the Doctor may have met Einstein before (see Previous to Landing 145) the scientist wouldn't recognise this incarnation.

LANDING 287

SPACE Paradise Towers
TIME Unknown future (after 21st century)
TRAVELLERS The Doctor, Mel
EPISODES Paradise Towers 1-4

The Doctor has acquired a video prospectus of Paradise Towers, an enormous urban living complex with clean white walls and shining glass. While he is intrigued by its architectural reputation, Mel is keen to take a dip in the rooftop swimming pool being shown on the scanner.

When the TARDIS arrives, however, the travellers find themselves in dingy, dilapidated surroundings, with rubbish-strewn, rat-infested corridors, graffiti-sprayed walls and grimy windows. The Police Box stands in the corner of a square with dimly lit corridors leading off two sides and a staircase to a second-level walkway. The pair are accosted by a gang of young women with red hair and clothes calling themselves the Red Kangs and wielding crossbows. The Doctor convinces them he is friendly, although they are less sure of Mel as she is dressed in blue. When the travellers try to slip back to the TARDIS, though, the Kangs become suspicious, having heard them talk of "the great pool in the sky". They tie up the newcomers while checking the route back to their hideout is clear, but when they prepare to leave a group of middle-aged caretakers arrives and the girls scatter; Mel runs with them but the Doctor is caught and taken to see the chief caretaker.

Mel finds her way back to the square, accompanied by Pex who has promised to take her to the pool. He leads the way, unaware they are being tracked by Blue Kangs. Despite having now found a map of the building, Mel and Pex end up in the square again and discover the TARDIS doors have been graffitied with 'Red Kangs are best'. They continue their search for the pool.

With the brain of the Towers' psychotic architect Kroagnon transplanted into the chief caretaker's body, Pex is tasked with leading him into a trap. They pass through the square where the TARDIS stands, accompanied by two deadly cleaning robots.

Having overcome their differences and worked together to destroy Kroagnon, all the inhabitants of Paradise Towers gather in the square to mourn Pex, who sacrificed himself to save everyone. The Kangs have washed their graffiti from the TARDIS, and they make the Doctor an honorary Kang by giving him a blue-and-red scarf. He and Mel depart, the fading Police Box revealing 'Pex lives' scrawled on the wall behind.

● CONTROLS The Doctor closes the scanner from panel E1, possibly using the bottom-right black slider. When preparing to land, he presses keys in the bottom-centre and bottom-left niches of panel E5, buttons in the middle-right niche, and switches in the top-left and bottom-left niches of panel E4. He directs Mel to operate an unseen control on panel E6 and she flips a switch in its top-right niche also.
● Panel E1 flexes noticeably when Sylvester McCoy releases the main doors lever.
▌ LORE The Doctor jettisoned the TARDIS's swimming pool because it was leaking (at some point after he began travelling with Mel).
▉ NOTES We're not told where Paradise Towers are or when the Doctor arrives. He says this "remarkable architectural achievement…won all sorts of awards way back in the twenty-first century" so it's later than that. The inhabitants are said to have been moved into the Towers while most of the adult population went to fight a war "or something", which may have been shortly after the complex was completed; Tabby agrees she's been there "from the beginning… Ever since the Great Architect finished Paradise Towers and all the youngsters and all the oldsters were moved here." This could mean she lived there before the others arrived, though. If people thought they'd successfully disposed of Kroagnon and the Towers had won awards, it's likely they would be inhabited for at least some time before the war began; the adults wouldn't billet their children there if it was known to be dangerous. It's only since the elderly and young were left to fend for themselves, no more than 20 years, that the Towers have fallen into disrepair and Kroagnon's brain has gained control of the cleaning robots. If Tabby was one of the first to move in (as a child?) it's no more than 50 years since the Towers were completed.
▉ Where did the Doctor get the illustrated prospectus? Later in the story we see a copy on disc that was issued to residents; does the TARDIS have a DVD player (it does by *Blink* – see Landing 386, vol.2) or is it receiving a transmission from somewhere? It wouldn't be out of character for this incarnation of the Doctor to send himself the video at the end of his visit to Paradise Towers in order to lure himself there in the first place. Alternatively, the central column isn't moving in the first control room scene so the TARDIS may still be wherever the last of the Rani's kidnapped geniuses to be dropped off lives and the Doctor has picked up a copy of the prospectus there.
▉ The shots of the swimming pool that Mel views on the scanner were taken as part of the location recording at Elmswell House between Chalfont St Giles and Little Chalfont in Buckinghamshire. The artwork labelled 'Paradise Towers' is actually of Ville Radieuse (the Radiant City), an idealised plan for urban living in the modernist style published in 1933 by Swiss architect Charles-Édouard 'Le Corbusier' Jeanneret. This image was taken from a 1980 documentary series *The Shock of the New* by Robert Hughes; the fourth episode, 'Trouble in Utopia', broadcast on BBC2 on 12 October. (Further shots from this and episode eight, 'The Future That Was', were used for prospectus shots later in the story.) The final image of a cluster of tower blocks, which also appeared at the start of the following three episodes, was created by Oliver Elmes of the BBC Graphics Unit, who had designed the computer-animated title sequence for this season.
▉ The jettisoned swimming pool is usually taken to be that seen in *The Invasion of Time* (Landing 144) although then it's referred to only as the bathroom. The Ship will have regained a pool by the time of the Doctor's twelfth regeneration (see Landing 441, vol.2).
▉ Now the Doctor has taken to wearing a hat regularly again, there's a hatstand back in the control room. Rather than a traditional bentwood-style one, though, this is comprised of chrome tubes with open-hooped ends (see page 209). It's thankfully never seen again.
▉ What floor of the 304-storey Towers does the TARDIS arrive on? Tilda and Tabby's apartment is on floor 109, which is where Mel ends up after first running from the caretakers. Only then does she notice the Doctor isn't behind her so surely can't have gone far from the square? However, when Kroagnon sets the cleaning robots to fumigating the Towers from the basement upwards, we see him marking off floors 117 and 163 before Pex offers to show him where the Doctor is hiding. Their route takes them past the TARDIS, which must be above the level of decontamination as the Kangs are tracking them. That places the square on a floor in the high hundreds or two-hundreds. If Mel had gone down the best part of 100 flights of stairs during her earlier escape she'd have surely noticed the Doctor was missing sooner, so did she get bundled into a lift by the Red Kangs and assume the Doctor would be in the next one?

LANDING 288

SPACE Tollport G715
TIME Unknown future
TRAVELLERS The Doctor, Mel
EPISODES Delta and the Bannermen 1

The TARDIS arrives at a tollport for spacecraft, which appears to have been abandoned. The Doctor and Mel fear it has been attacked by space pirates but are relieved to learn they are, in fact, its one-billionth customers and have won a place on a Nostalgia Trips visit to Disneyland on Earth in 1959. A party of purple, tentacled Navarinos pass through a transformation arch to disguise themselves as humans and board a Hellstrom Two space cruiser converted to look like a beat-up 1950s charabanc.

The Doctor leaves Mel to travel with them while he follows in the TARDIS. He watches as the bus revs up its Hellstrom Fireball engine just as a Bannerman spacecraft arrives at the port, pursued by another that overshoots the landing pad. Delta, the last Chimeron queen, exits the first craft and boards the bus. The Doctor watches as it takes off, then tracks it in the Ship.

▪ **NOTES** Although on screen there's nothing to indicate how soon after the visit to *Paradise Towers* this is, in a cut line of dialogue Mel said their "last holiday wasn't exactly ice hot", a term used by the Kangs.

▪ The Navarinos are said to be travelling "back to 1959" so they must originate in the future. Nostalgia Trips is "the most notorious travel firm in the five galaxies", one of which might be our own. Intergalactic travel is evidently easy at this time so there's no way to tell how close the tollport is to the tri-polar moon Navarro, although Murray is a regular pilot for Nostalgia Trips and knows the tollmaster so perhaps this is the moon's local tollport. It's also only a short flight from Delta's planet Chumeria. It has been remarked that Nostalgia Trips' access to time travel is unusual as the Time Lords generally restrict such capabilities in other species, but this may not be technological time travel. The bus hardly seems powerful enough and Gavrok follows it to 1959 in his spaceship – if the Bannermen were time travellers the Time Lords surely would put a stop to them. So there may be a stable wormhole nearby leading to 20th century Earth, which would explain the Navarinos' fondness for its music and culture.

▪ A scene in the control room as the TARDIS approaches the tollport was cut from the final episode. The Doctor bemoaned how tollports were rare in some galaxies but common in others, blaming the lack of "a consistent three-dimensional planning policy". Mel worried the port appeared abandoned, the Doctor more about how to pay the toll as their kitty was empty. This was an old Cerebos Table Salt can, stored on a shelf under the console (below panel E6 – see Landing 290).

LANDING 289

SPACE Earth, Wales, South Glamorgan, Shangri-La holiday camp
TIME Two days (Wednesday to Thursday) in summer 1959
TRAVELLERS The Doctor
EPISODES Delta and the Bannermen 1-3

As the Nostalgia Trips bus approaches Earth it collides with a recently launched artificial satellite. The Doctor sees what has happened on the scanner so applies the TARDIS's vortex drive to generate an anti-gravity spiral around the bus and slow its descent, although it still comes down with a thump – not in Florida as planned but on the forecourt of the Shangri-La holiday camp in south Wales.

The TARDIS materialises more smoothly nearby as the tour party stagger from the bus. They are mistaken by the camp's director Burton for a genuine holiday group and shown the way to the chalets. After removing the battered satellite from the bus's front grille, the Doctor finds it has jammed the navigational pod and broken its quarb crystal. He fetches a replacement from the TARDIS but pilot Murray breaks the fragile item while trying to insert it. The Doctor returns to the Ship where he has a thermo-booster he can use to grow another crystal within 24 hours.

The next morning, having learned the Bannermen are on their way, the Doctor shows Burton inside the TARDIS to convince him his warning of attacking aliens is true and to evacuate the camp. The crystal is nearly ready and he leaves the thermo-booster with Murray while he goes in search of Delta. The camp staff get on a coach to take them to safety. Once the crystal is complete, Murray fits it in the navi-pod and the Navarinos board their bus. Before they can take off, however, the Bannermen arrive and destroy the vehicle. Mel and Burton are taken prisoner.

The Bannermen's leader, Gavrok, detects that the Police Box by the camp gates is something more than it appears so places a sonic cone on the roof, projecting a barrier around the Ship that atomises anything that touches it. After the Bannermen have left to search for Delta, the Doctor and his friends return to the camp. He spots the sonic cone and marks the reach of its beam on the ground, considering whether he can tunnel his way inside in order to deactivate it.

Before he can, the Bannermen return to storm the camp. But the Doctor has souped up a loudspeaker to amplify the newly hatched Chimeron princess's 'singing', which deafens the attackers. Gavrok staggers in pain near the TARDIS and stumbles into the beam of the sonic cone, atomising him and draining its power.

With Delta safely on her way back to her home to rebuild her race, the Doctor and Mel say their goodbyes outside the TARDIS. The arrival of the Skegness Glee Club provides a distraction, allowing them to slip inside and dematerialise.

● **CONTROLS** The Doctor uses the keypad below the screen on panel E6 when the bus is hit by the satellite; something in the niche above the screen explodes. He operates unseen controls on panel E1 (some with his foot) and uses his umbrella to press a key on the left of the top niche of panel E5 (which also explodes) to create an anti-gravity spiral to slow the bus's descent.

● A hole has appeared in one of the faces of the pyramid on panel E6 (did Sylvester McCoy accidentally put the tip of his umbrella through it during rehearsals?).

- **LORE** The vortex drive can be applied to generate an anti-gravity spiral in the vicinity of the Ship.
- The Doctor says TARDIS is "an acronym for Time And Relative Dimensions In Space".
- **NOTES** Gavrok's scanner shows the mercenary's signal came from South Glamorgan (a little west of Barry Island, where the holiday camp recording location was). Yet Burton plans to evacuate his staff to Llandrindod Wells, more than 50 miles to the north on the other side of the Brecon Beacons. Surely Cardiff would be a better destination.
- A poster for 'Dance nite' gives the day as Wednesday. The Doctor says the crystal will need "around twenty-four hours" to form and it's ready early the next morning, so it must be before midday when the bus and TARDIS arrive. The meal we see being served could be lunch at one or supper at six; the latter might be a bit late for Burton to be reminding everyone of the dance that evening so it's probably the former. (In a cut line, Burton says the dance is "eight till late" but the poster reads '7.30-10pm'.)
- The model shot of the TARDIS and bus falling towards Earth used the miniature Police Box built for *The Trial of a Time Lord*'s opening sequence.
- For its appearance as a genuine Police Box (strange for a London Metropolitan box to be situated in the Welsh countryside), the prop was fitted with a telephone in a cubbyhole behind the plaque on the left-hand door. Some sources claim this was a replacement wooden door to avoid cutting out the panel from one of the fibreglass doors, but this is unproven and markings on the window panes match those seen previously (although the panes could have been transferred to the temporary door).
- The shot of the TARDIS dematerialising at the end of the story is the same as that of its arrival only in reverse.

PREVIOUS LANDINGS

SPACE Earth, England, Birmingham
TIME 25th century
TRAVELLERS The Doctor, [unknown companions]
EPISODES Mentioned by the Doctor in
 The Happiness Patrol 3

The Doctor encountered a Stigorax, a rat-like creature the size of a small dog with long fur and spines along its back. Whether alien or a mutation, they were ruthless, intelligent predators.
- **NOTES** Ace doesn't seem familiar with Fifi the Stigorax so this must have been before she boarded the TARDIS.
- According to Captain Maitland in *The Sensorites*, London was subsumed into Central City, covering "the whole lower half of England" during the 24th century, so Birmingham is doing well to survive into the next.

SPACE Earth, England, Berkshire, Windsor
TIME Late-11th century
TRAVELLERS The Doctor, [unknown companions]
EPISODES Mentioned by the Doctor in
 Silver Nemesis 1

The Doctor was present during the construction of Windsor Castle.
- **NOTES** The original keep at Windsor was instigated by William the Conqueror in the decade after 1066 but the castle has been expanded and remodelled several times since so the Doctor could be referring to one of these phases.

SPACE Earth, England, Berkshire, Windsor
TIME November 1638
TRAVELLERS The Doctor, [Mel]
EPISODES Related by the Doctor in
 Silver Nemesis 1-3

An asteroid containing a quantity of the destructive living metal validium fell into the meadow behind Lady Peinforte's house in Windsor. She had the silvery substance fashioned into a statue of herself firing a bow and arrow; these were detachable and without them there was not the critical mass of validium needed for it to animate. It told Peinforte secrets of the Doctor's past.

While she fought off a force of Parliamentarians on the 23rd of the month, the Doctor placed the main body of the statue back in the asteroid and fitted rockets to launch it back into space and prevent the ruthless lady from wielding its power. His hurried calculations, however, meant the asteroid would go into an elliptical orbit, passing close to Earth every 25 years, but which would decay and after 350 years the statue would return to Earth in the same meadow. The Doctor set an alarm on his pocket watch to remind him to be around when this happened, knowing Peinforte had learned from the statue some rudimentary knowledge of how to time travel.
- **NOTES** The Doctor only says he launched the statue on 23 November 1638 so it's not clear if he arrived some time earlier and witnessed Peinforte's discovery of the validium or learned about that after the fact and was just present to dispose of it (although its revelations about him to Peinforte perhaps suggest for former).
- Lady Peinforte refers to the Doctor she encountered at this time as a "predictable little man" and recognises his seventh incarnation on sight (although Richard doesn't) so this is likely to be after Landing 286, in which case the Doctor must have been travelling with Mel (as it's before he travels with Ace). Then again, in the initial edit Peinforte didn't identify the Doctor at first but grew suspicious he and his "wench" had changed their faces, then was convinced only when she spotted the TARDIS. If, as implied, the Doctor

programmed his pocket-watch reminder immediately after the events, he can only have been in his first, sixth or seventh incarnation as the others didn't carry such a watch. The second of these could hardly be described as a little man, and the first is perhaps too long ago for him to recall the events so clearly (although the original script made mention of his granddaughter). Such forward planning is much more a characteristic of the Doctor's seventh incarnation anyway, and perhaps encountering the validium from Gallifrey is what reminds him the Hand of Omega still needs dealing with (see Landing 291).

SPACE Earth
TIME Around 501,800
TRAVELLERS The Doctor, [unknown companions]
EPISODES Mentioned by the Doctor in
The Curse of Fenric 3-4

The Doctor visited a time when humans had evolved into blood-drinking Haemovores. The world was dying, its "surface just a chemical slime". He may have encountered the Ancient One, who would eventually be the last living creature on Earth before being taken back to the 9th century in a time storm engineered by Fenric.

- **NOTES** The Doctor says this is after "half a million years of industrial progress". He perhaps means since the Industrial Revolution when chemical manufacturing on a large scale began. He also expresses this as "thousands of years in the future", which is understating it if the former is accurate.
- The Doctor has seen this future even though it is later, seemingly, erased when the Ancient One kills Fenric rather than initiating a chemical spill. He similarly visits alternative Earth timelines in *Day of the Daleks*, *Pyramids of Mars* (briefly) and *Orphan 55*, although only the second was in the TARDIS.
- Then again, although the Doctor tells the Ancient One that Fenric's order to "destroy the Earth's water with chemicals" is the "act [that] will be the beginning of your end" and "destroy your future", can averting this one action really prevent the half-million years of industrial pollution? Is the suggestion that once the seas are poisoned, Man gives up any attempt at environmental protection and progresses without regard for further contamination? Some might argue surviving another 500,000 years is a better prospect than we currently face in the real world. We were told in the *The Mutants* that Earth of just the 30th century is already "slag, ash and clinker"; how much worse can the timeline that leads to the Haemovores be if life persists until the 5,001st? Perhaps it's not the Earth's environmental destruction that's prevented by disobeying Fenric but simply Man's evolution into the Haemovores.

SPACE Earth, Asia
TIME 3rd century
TRAVELLERS The Doctor, [unknown companions]
EPISODES Related by the Doctor and Fenric in
The Curse of Fenric 4

The Doctor confronted Fenric (as the evil force from before the birth of the universe would later be called) and challenged him to a game of chess, using pieces he carved from bones pulled from the desert sands. The Doctor's tactics confused Fenric and it could not win. Rather than forcing its defeat and destruction, the Doctor banished Fenric to a shadow dimension held within a small flask.

- **NOTES** This was before the Doctor began travelling with Ace, a meeting engineered by Fenric so perhaps, for the Doctor, not that long after their initial encounter. Then again, when resetting the game in *The Curse of Fenric*, he struggles to recall where the pieces go as "it was so long ago".
- The flask in which Fenric is imprisoned is referred to as an "oriental treasure" from "the silk lands in the east", suggesting the Doctor's confrontation with Fenric was somewhere in modern-day China.
- Fenric says he's been trapped for seventeen centuries before finally being released in the 20th.

LANDING 290

SPACE Svartos, Iceworld, frozen-food section
TIME Unknown future [after Landing 281]
TRAVELLERS The Doctor, Mel
EPISODES Dragonfire 1,3

The Doctor detects a tracking signal somewhere in Iceworld, a trading outpost on the permanently dark side of Svartos. Intrigued, he and Mel view the planet on the scanner as they approach. The TARDIS materialises in a freezer centre where various species are shopping for frozen goods. Spotting a restaurant, the Doctor takes Mel for some refreshment.

All the shoppers are herded out of Iceworld by Kane's band of defrosted mercenaries so the freezer centre is deserted when the Doctor, Mel and a human girl called Ace return to the TARDIS. The Doctor searches a star chart on the scanner for the planet Proamon but it no longer exists, having been consumed when its red-giant star turned supernova 2,000 years earlier.

After they have left, Glitz looks for them in the freezer centre but encounters only a lucky survivor of the evacuation looking for her young daughter.

Iceworld lifts off from Svartos when its power source is restored, the outpost having been a spacecraft all along. With Kane evaporated, Glitz takes command of the vessel to replace his own destroyed ship. Mel decides to travel with him but persuades the Doctor to invite Ace aboard the TARDIS as she does not belong in this time period. The young woman is only too happy to join him as he proceeds to head for her home in 20th-century Perivale via "the scenic route".

- **CONTROLS** The Doctor looks at the screen on panel E6 when discussing the tracking signal (although we can't see what it's showing). He later opens the scanner from panel E2 but seems to close it from panel E4, where he operates unseen controls.
- When preparing to leave, the Doctor presses buttons below the screen on panel E4 and unseen controls at the top and bottom-left of panel E3.
- The middle niche to the left of the screen on panel E6 is missing the cover of the readout on its back face, and the hole behind appears to have been accidentally enlarged. The small black square in the bottom-left corner is missing, revealing the grid of lights beneath. The circular display to the right of the screen on panel E4 has been replaced with a speaker-like mesh. In the niche below this, the double-width key is missing.
- The shelf added under panel E6 to hold the kitty tin in *Delta and the Bannermen*, in a cut scene, is here visible as the control room scenes for both stories were recorded on the same day, Wednesday 12 August 1987. (Thus the above changes were also present but unseen in *Delta*.)
- **LORE** Mel explains how the TARDIS is "bigger on the inside than on the outside" by saying it's "transcendentally dimensional". As she has an "amazing ability for almost total recall", this must be how the Doctor has expressed it to her at some point (probably after his sixth regeneration as his subsequent persona was more prone to getting his words muddled).
- The TARDIS has access to or can generate star charts for any area of space in the time period it has landed.
- **NOTES** Glitz remembers Mel so for him this is after he met her at the Doctor's trial. After his acquittal, the Doctor asked the Time Lords to be lenient with the thief once they released him from the limbo atrophier, and it's reasonable to assume they would return him to his proper time period. The opening segment of *The Trial of a Time Lord* indicates this is over two million years in the future, although it's later revealed Glitz was working with the Master, who could have taken him forward in time in his TARDIS. The Doctor seems to think that Perivale at this time has "lush green fields and a village blacksmith", which may be a reference to the Iron Age-level society of the Tribe of the Free on Ravolox/Earth.
- The Doctor has ditched the gaudy chrome hatstand for a rather dull one comprised of bent white metal poles (see page 209). It also appears in the cut scene from *Delta and the Bannermen* episode one.
- The TARDIS's materialisation used a split-screen effect assembled in post-production. The scene of shoppers perusing the freezers was recorded without the Police Box on set. A separate shot of the TARDIS in position was then faded in over the right of the picture. Its departure was done in a similar way, with a shot of the girl looking at the Police Box having its right-hand side overlaid with a view of the empty set.
- Although the Doctor simply pulls the door closed when exiting the TARDIS, when he returns to check his star charts he has to unlock it with his key.
- We don't see it but presumably the Doctor lets Ace pick up some belongings from her room before the TARDIS leaves, as the rucksack she had earlier is seen again in later stories. (Although this raises the question of just how long Stellar's mother has been searching for her.) Perhaps she already owned the baseball bat and ghetto blaster featured in *Remembrance of the Daleks* then.

LANDING 291

SPACE Earth, England, London, Shoreditch, near Coal Hill School
TIME At least two days [between September and November] 1963
TRAVELLERS The Doctor, Ace
EPISODES Remembrance of the Daleks 1,3-4

The Doctor decides to finally deal with the Hand of Omega he left behind on Earth long ago when in his first incarnation. He returns to London in 1963, materialising the TARDIS in a pedestrian alleyway by an apartment block across the street from Coal Hill School. While the Doctor investigates a van with a curious aerial, Ace heads the opposite way to a café to get some breakfast.

She returns with Sergeant Mike Smith, who does not notice the for-once inconspicuous Police Box while he explains pre-decimal currency to her. They join the Doctor and Professor Rachel Jensen in the van when alerted to an incident at Totter's Lane.

The Doctor and Ace pass the TARDIS again when heading back to the school from Ratcliffe's builder's yard, closely pursued by three 'renegade' Daleks. These soon retreat along the alleyway when they detect an Imperial Dalek shuttle approaching the school.

After a recce to ascertain the Imperial Daleks have successfully regained the Hand of Omega, the Doctor pauses by the TARDIS as he watches their shuttle lift off for its return journey to their mothership.

He and Ace stay to mourn Mike's death and attend his funeral, although they slip away before the ceremony begins and head back to the TARDIS.

- **NOTES** The sign outside confirms Coal Hill (Road) secondary school is in Shoreditch. This tallies with the Daleks' maps, which show the area west of Great Eastern Street.
- Calendars in both Harry's café and Ratcliffe's office are turned to November. Yet, as noted under Landing 1, the bright weather and people's light clothing suggest a warmer month – in our universe November 1963 was wet and windy with temperatures no higher than sixteen degrees. Ratcliffe's calendar may not have been touched since the previous year, but Harry's reads 'November 1963' – is it set to remind him of some

upcoming event? The copy of the *Daily Mirror* that Mike reads in the café is from Saturday 7 September 1963 (headlined 'Give your passport to police' about Christine Keeler's arrest for perjury); as it's a school day it can't be earlier than Monday the 9th therefore (whereas the paper could be an old one that has been sitting around the café for a while). The vicar says the grave has "been ready for a month" but could have been dug before the Doctor "had to leave suddenly". Does that mean the undertaker has had the casket as long? Surely they would worry about decomposition (having not had a body to embalm) and would have notified the police once it hadn't been claimed and buried within a week? So perhaps the Doctor originally told Martin's governor and the vicar there was no corpse, he merely wanted to bury some scientific equipment for an experiment; this would also explain the occasional noise from the casket. In that case it could be longer than a month since he kidnapped the teachers and it's only recently the grave has finally been dug – we don't know who instigated this. If the Doctor originally left in March, as speculated under Landing 1, it could now be anytime between April (which would fit the weather as that's when the location recording was done) and, at a push, September (perhaps in the *Doctor Who* universe the events reported in the newspaper happened earlier in the year). Alternatively, it could only be a week or two since Barbara and Ian's discovery of the TARDIS forced the Doctor to leave, perhaps in October and it's now early November – no one mentions Kennedy's assassination and no days are crossed off Harry's calendar.

- Long shadows indicate it's early morning when the Doctor and Ace arrive and the children are being called in for assembly. After dealing with the Dalek at Totter's Lane, they return to the school where the headmaster is still about. We don't see any children but wouldn't if they were all in class; although no science lessons are currently timetabled judging from the empty lab the Doctor and Ace peruse. When Gilmore's troops arrive to clear away the dead Dalek from the cellar, they likely send everyone home. The next day, the Group Captain has arranged to have the area evacuated so the school's being empty doesn't mean it's now Saturday – despite what the television announcer says (he has to be ignored as he claims "the time is a quarter past five" when it's explicitly before lunch time; is this a test broadcast or part of the D-notice cover story?). The Doctor and Ace stay around for a day or two longer until Mike's funeral.
- The Doctor knows Harry's wife will give birth to twins but he has had many occasions while being on Earth in subsequent decades when he could have learned this, either from Harry, his wife or the children themselves. Given he directs Ace to the café, he must have visited it before and met Harry then, perhaps during his first incarnation while in London with Susan; he may even have had cause to assist with an early ultrasound scan of Harry's pregnant wife.

LANDING 292

SPACE Terra Alpha, Forum Square
TIME Unknown future
TRAVELLERS The Doctor, Ace
EPISODES The Happiness Patrol 1,3

The Doctor has heard rumours of disturbing happenings in the human colony on Terra Alpha and lands the TARDIS in the main township at nightfall in order to investigate. Ace immediately takes a dislike to the cheesy music that is playing from speakers all around the square and along the streets.

A Happiness Patrol squad led by Daisy K arrives in the square and proceeds to paint over the dreary dark blue of the Police Box with a much more uplifting bright pink. The Doctor and Ace deliberately get themselves arrested by the Patrol and are taken to a waiting zone on the other side of the square, guarded by Priscilla P. They escape in one of the Patrol's buggies.

Later that night, the Doctor has visiting student Earl bring a group of demonstrators to the square and pretend to party, their apparent jollity preventing the Happiness Patrol from killing them. Daisy K's disappointed squad is consequently arrested by Priscilla P.

The colony's tyrannical leader Helen A heads for the rocket port to escape the uprising. The Doctor tries to convince her happiness without sadness has no meaning but she remains pitiless – until she spots her fatally injured pet Fifi and breaks down in tears.

With the Happiness Patrol disbanded, its former members are charged with repainting the TARDIS. As dawn breaks, the Doctor and Ace say goodbye to their friends and prepare to leave, Ace quickly covering one final patch of pink on the Police Box's door with blue paint.

- **NOTES** The only indication of time period is that the Doctor tells Ace the colony settled on Terra Alpha "some centuries in your future" but we don't know how long it has been there at this point. He refers to encountering a Stigorax like Fifi in the 25th century, suggesting they're not in that time now. According to Trevor Sigma, Earth is now a "miserable sort of place".
- The Police Box prop is initially missing the telephone plaque from its left-hand door, presumably to avoid its lettering getting painted over. It's only affixed for the final scene as Ace paints the rail below it blue.
- When the (quite short) Happiness Patrol is first seen painting the TARDIS they've managed to reach up to the ledge above the 'Police box' signs (nice of them not to paint over the sign lettering) seemingly without a ladder. They ultimately paint at least the right-hand side too, right up to the roof.
- One might think it would have been easier to pre-paint two sides of the Police Box prop pink, then simply rotate it when it needs to switch colours. However, the scene of its arrival was recorded first, after which it was repainted while on the set. The water-based pink paint was then washed off prior to the final scene of the

story, bar one bit for Sophie Aldred to slap blue paint over. Because of the different arrangement of handles and locks on either side of the prop, we can see that the door the travellers emerge from is the same as is later painted by the Happiness Patrol.

- The TARDIS is actually on screen in episode two but you have to turn the brightness right up to see it. In the scene where the Doctor meets Trevor Sigma again, the Police Box is in the deep shadows at the back of the shot, all but invisible because it's still blue. At this point in the story it should be pink but this scene was one of the first recorded, before the prop was repainted.
- That the TARDIS needs a further coat of paint to return it to its usual blue hue suggests the pink paint would remain once the Ship dematerialised – not slough off or vaporise in the Vortex. If the chameleon circuit were working, surely this doesn't mean whatever form the TARDIS took on its next landing would also be coated in pink paint? So perhaps it only persists because the Ship can't change its appearance. The very next story confirms an object stuck to the Police Box exterior is transported with it but see also *Aliens of London* (Landing 327, vol.2), *Utopia* (Landing 388) and *Vincent and the Doctor* (Landing 459).

LANDING 293

SPACE Earth, England, Berkshire, Windsor, riverbank
TIME Wednesday 23 November 1988
TRAVELLERS The Doctor, Ace
EPISODES Silver Nemesis 1

The TARDIS lands on an uncommonly sunny and warm late-November day beside a small river near Windsor. By luck or judgement, just beyond the trees is a pub garden where live jazz is being played so the Doctor and Ace settle down for a relaxed afternoon of music.

The Doctor's pocket watch chimes to remind him of an impending danger but he has forgotten what it is so must return to the TARDIS to check. As the pair approach the Ship they are shot at and fall into the river. Unharmed, they scramble onto the bank to dry out. The Doctor retrieves from the TARDIS a tape deck he built for Ace, which is also a scanner; he enters the details from his pocket watch to discover the planet facing imminent destruction is Earth.

- **NOTES** Although the Doctor forgets what he set his alarm for, he's evidently in the right place and time. Coincidence or has he subconsciously landed where he needs to be? It's not stated where the pub garden is but it must be near Windsor given the Cyber-controlled gunmen are in the vicinity. The edition of the *Daily Mirror* that Ace reads is dated Tuesday 22 November 1988 but the Doctor's watch countdown indicates it's only 51 minutes until (presumably) the Nemesis comet makes landfall, so they must have arrived on Wednesday the 23rd and Ace has found a copy of yesterday's *Mirror*. (The newspaper cover is a mock-up but the back page is from the Monday 14 October 1985 edition, which does mention Charlton Athletic but only in regard to moving their home ground from the Valley to share Selhurst Park with Crystal Palace.)

LANDING 294

SPACE Earth, England, Berkshire, Windsor Castle, cellar
TIME As above
TRAVELLERS The Doctor, Ace
EPISODES Silver Nemesis 1

The Doctor moves the TARDIS a short distance in space but not time, materialising in a vaulted cellar beneath Windsor Castle, filled with statues, furniture and ornaments. This is where all the gifts the royals receive on foreign trips are stored but the Doctor is looking for one in particular: a silver bow.

While he and Ace search, the cellar is shaken as nearby the Nemesis comet slams into the ground. Its orbit has finally decayed after circling the Earth every 25 years since the Doctor launched it into space in 1638.

Ace finds an empty case for the bow beside a drawing of the statue it was part of. A notice explains that the bow disappeared in 1788 but unless a place is kept for it the silver statue will return to destroy the world. The lights flicker as something drains power across the area but the Doctor has somewhere else he wants to be.

- **NOTES** The stairs to the vault at Arundel Castle, where the Windsor castle scenes were recorded, were so narrow it was tricky to get the Police Box prop down them, even with it in sections. The ceiling was only just high enough for the prop to be erected.

LANDING 295

SPACE Earth, England, Berkshire, Windsor, Lady Peinforte's house
TIME December 1638
TRAVELLERS The Doctor, Ace
EPISODES Silver Nemesis 1

The TARDIS causes a draught as it materialises on the landing of Lady Peinforte's house near Windsor Castle. Downstairs in the study, the Doctor and Ace discover the body of a scholar who correctly calculated when the orbiting Nemesis would return to Earth. He was then killed by Peinforte and his blood added to the potion that, along with the silver arrow in her possession, has enabled her to travel in time to 1988.

The Doctor explains that the silver statue of Lady Peinforte firing a bow and arrow was formed from validium, a destructive living metal that fell into the meadow behind her house, and which he later sent into space. They head back to the 20th century.

- **LORE** The arrival of the TARDIS can sometimes disturb the air around it.

- **NOTES** The Doctor earlier indicated his original dealings with Lady Peinforte and the Nemesis were on 23 November 1638. This return visit is explicitly still in 1638 yet the Doctor says it's "a matter of months since I was last here". It may have taken time for Peinforte to secure the services of a mathematician and prepare to travel to the time of the statue's return, but the Doctor must be exaggerating that it's more than a month later.
- This time the ceiling of St Mary's in Bramber, West Sussex, where the scenes in Lady Peinforte's house were recorded, was too low for the Police Box prop and it had to be erected without its roof lamp. The flashing was added electronically in post-production.
- The candles blowing out as the TARDIS materialises, suggesting it displaces the air, is the first time the Ship is shown having such an impact on landing.

LANDING 296

SPACE Earth, England, Berkshire, Windsor Castle, outer wall
TIME As Landing 293
TRAVELLERS The Doctor, Ace
EPISODES Silver Nemesis 1

Returning to Windsor Castle, this time the TARDIS materialises at the base of a tower in the curtain wall, unnoticed by a group of visitors filing past a Coldstream Guard on sentry duty beside an entrance. Ace recognises the castle from an earlier school trip but cannot remember her way around so she and the Doctor attach themselves to the tourist party in order to get into the grounds.

Having failed to secure the Queen's help in getting the assistance of the armed forces, and pursued by two security guards, they return to the Ship.

- **NOTES** The TARDIS's arrival was achieved using a split-screen effect. The shot of the tourists was overlaid on the left with a separate shot of Sophie Aldred and Sylvester McCoy emerging from the Police Box. The tour party was comprised of friends and members of the *Doctor Who* production team, including actor Nicholas Courtney (in the flat cap). So did the Brigadier just miss another encounter with the Doctor?

LANDING 297

SPACE Earth, England, Berkshire, Windsor, waste ground
TIME As above
TRAVELLERS The Doctor, Ace
EPISODES Silver Nemesis 1-2

The TARDIS moves a few hundred yards to the patch of rough ground where the Nemesis comet has made landfall, materialising beside a large concrete barn. The comet itself has now cooled but the police sent to investigate it have been gassed by Cyberman technology. A group of paramilitaries lead by a surviving Nazi officer called De Flores now surround the comet. They have the silver bow, which makes the statue inside react, but without the arrow as well there is not the critical mass of validium needed to animate it. De Flores demands the Doctor tell him where the arrow is, threatening to shoot Ace, but is prevented by the arrival of the Cybermen in their spacecraft.

They and the paramilitaries get into a gun fight. Lady Peinforte watches from a distance, occasionally killing Cybermen with gold-tipped arrows. The Doctor and Ace hide behind the comet in its crater as the battle rages.

With gunfire getting dangerously close, they decide to leave. The Doctor grabs the silver bow and the pair dash back to the TARDIS. Peinforte spots them and tries to hit the Doctor with a poisoned arrow but it embeds in the door and fades away along with the Police Box.

- **LORE** Sharp items can stick into the TARDIS's outer shell [when disguised as something soft enough].
- Any such objects will be transported with it when the TARDIS dematerialises.
- **NOTES** It's said the meadow outside Lady Peinforte's house is "a few hundred yards" from Windsor Castle, although the establishing shots in 1638 show the castle a much greater distance away. The Nemesis was both launched from and returns to that meadow, and indeed Peinforte sees the police approach the newly arrived comet from the window of her house (although surely an impact anywhere in the vicinity of Windsor Castle, especially when the Queen was in residence, would see the whole area swamped with soldiers). At the start of the story, the Nazis' computer somewhere in South America locates the landing site to 'Grid ref: 74W 32N'. This can't be a latitude and longitude as 32 degrees north, 75 degrees west is in the Atlantic Ocean, some 400 miles off the coast of South Carolina. Equally, it can't be a direction from their current location, as 32 degrees south, 75 degrees east of Windsor would put them in east India, about 50 miles from Mumbai.
- The recording location was on the Greenwich peninsula in London, in the grounds of the decommissioned East Greenwich Gas Works – later the site of the Millennium Dome (although the specific location is now under car parks). The distinctive parabolic-roofed barn was part of the Phoenix Wharf chemical works and built in the 1956. Constructed from pre-cast, pre-stressed concrete, it could store up to 10,000 tons of ammonium sulphate, used to remove ammonia from the raw manufactured gas. When the site was being considered for the Dome, efforts were made to have this shed listed in order to preserve it as an example of concrete engineering, and making it a music venue was proposed owing to its excellent acoustics. Site owner British Gas had it pulled down before these could be actioned, claiming illegal raves were being held there.
- The shot of the arrow striking the TARDIS door was recorded with the arrow in position then tugged out on a length of wire; this was then played in reverse

during editing. Freeze-frame the picture and you can see the chink from the arrow tip before it hits. The door has no lock and seemingly joins between its rails and stiles, suggesting it's a wooden replacement for the usual fibreglass door. The struck panel may have been a foam insert, hence its slightly darker appearance.

LANDING 298

SPACE Earth, England, Berkshire, countryside near Windsor
TIME As above
TRAVELLERS The Doctor, Ace
EPISODES Silver Nemesis 2-3

The TARDIS – the arrow still stuck in its door – relocates to a nearby area of parkland to avoid any risk of the Cybermen commandeering it. The Doctor uses the pulsing glow of the silver bow to direct him towards the bulk of the validium. He and Ace, carrying her Nitro-9-filled rucksack and the tape-deck scanner, head towards a large castellated tower in the distance.

A pall of smoke rises above the treetops in that direction when the Cybermen's spacecraft is destroyed.

Having reanimated the Nemesis by bringing the statue, arrow and bow together, the Doctor and Ace hurry back to the TARDIS. They still have the bow, knowing the Nemesis will follow them in order to be complete.

NOTES The mix shot of the TARDIS arriving and departing is the same, one played in reverse.

The public footpath signpost is a genuine part of the location, not a prop, but the tower on the horizon was added in electronically during editing.

A scene prior to this landing was cut, in which the travellers returned to Lady Peinforte's house in 1638. They discovered the scholar's body had gone and the Doctor burned a note that, it's suggested, gave the mathematician a start for his calculations. The implication is it was the Doctor who helped him.

LANDING 299

SPACE Earth, England, Berkshire, Windsor, Lady Peinforte's house
TIME After Landing 295
TRAVELLERS The Doctor, Ace
EPISODES Silver Nemesis 3

The Doctor briefly revisits Lady Peinforte's house in the 17th century, the night after her departure, ostensibly to collect the scholar's calculations and prevent others from benefiting from them, although he spends most of the visit moving pieces around a chess board. When they leave, Ace takes a bag of gold coins with her.

NOTES We don't see the TARDIS in this scene but can presume it lands on the upstairs landing again.

LANDING 300

SPACE Earth, England, Berkshire, Windsor, barn on waste ground
TIME Shortly after Landing 298
TRAVELLERS The Doctor, Ace
EPISODES Silver Nemesis 3

Returning to 1988 moments after their previous departure, the TARDIS materialises inside the large barn where the Cybermen left the comet after cutting out the statue. The Nemesis arrives and settles back into the comet. The Doctor gives it the bow then reprogrammes the rockets to take it into the heart of the Cyber fleet orbiting the moon.

Meanwhile Ace holds off the Cybermen using the gold coins and a catapult. These soon run out, however, and she finds herself surrounded by three Cybermen on a walkway high above the floor of the barn. She disables the leader with her last coin and ducks as the other two shoot, hitting each other and tipping over the rail. They smash to pieces close by the TARDIS below.

The Doctor instructs the Nemesis to destroy the Cyber fleet before taking back the bow. Two last Cybermen are destroyed when the Doctor lures them into range of the rocket jets as they test-fire. De Flores arrives and takes the bow but is killed by the Cyberleader. Lady Peinforte also arrives with her servant Richard and threatens to reveal the Doctor's secrets if he does not give her the bow. He confounds her by giving it to the Cyberleader, who is not interested in her knowledge. As the comet readies for launch, Peinforte leaps into the cavity with the Nemesis and is absorbed. The rockets fire and the comet is shot back into space.

The others watch on the tape-deck scanner as the Nemesis flies into the Cyber fleet and destroys every ship. The Cyberleader is about to shoot the Doctor in retaliation but Richard snatches the gold-tipped arrow from the TARDIS door and plunges it into the creature's chest unit, killing it. In thanks, the Doctor promises to take Richard back to his proper time.

NOTES The TARDIS was originally intended to land outside the barn and the Doctor pulled the arrow from its door, but overruns during location recording meant this had to be reworked. The Police Box was now set up inside the barn but there wasn't time to record a mix shot of its arrival so this was indicated by playing the sound effect over an exterior view of the barn.

LANDING 301

SPACE Earth, England, Berkshire, Windsor, Lady Peinforte's house
TIME After Landing 299
TRAVELLERS The Doctor, Ace, Richard Maynarde
EPISODES Silver Nemesis 3

The TARDIS returns to the 17th century one last time to bring Richard home. The Doctor and Ace spend a little time there, playing chess and listening to contemporary music in lieu of modern jazz.

▨ **NOTES** The Doctor and Ace are seen in the garden of Peinforte's house, so the TARDIS perhaps landed on its landing again. Richard and his lady friend seem quite relaxed so is he planning to take over the household?

LANDING 302

SPACE Segonax
TIME Unknown [future]
TRAVELLERS The Doctor, Ace
EPISODES The Greatest Show in the Galaxy 1

The Doctor practises his juggling skills in the control room while Ace searches for her lost rucksack. They are disturbed by the appearance of an advertising robot that connects itself to the console and activates the scanner to display an invite to the Psychic Circus on Segonax and its talent contest. Ace is reluctant, finding clowns creepy, but the Doctor's wish to show off his spoon playing – and a little taunting from the robot – makes her acquiesce.

The TARDIS materialises on a narrow sandy ridge amid the dusty deserts of Segonax, several miles from the circus itself. Nearby, however, is a stall selling local produce so the Doctor and Ace approach the vendor to ask for directions.

Once the circus has been released from the dominance of the Gods of Ragnarok, the survivors prepare to set up a new act. The Doctor is not tempted by an offer to join them, however, having his own travels to resume.

◉ **CONTROLS** A circular socket was added in the bottom-right corner of panel E1 for the ad robot's connector. The scanner opens automatically when this is plugged in and closes when Ace removes it.

▨ **NOTES** No dating evidence is given in the story so its setting depends on whether the circus folk are as human as they appear; if so, and they've developed robot technology and interplanetary travel, it must be in the future. This also raises the question of whether the stall holder is a native of Segonax or descended from earlier human colonists.

▨ This serial was unable to be recorded in the studios at BBC Television Centre as usual because they were closed at short notice for the removal of asbestos. Producer John Nathan-Turner and the serial's designer David Laskey arranged instead to have a large metal-framed marquee erected in the car park at the BBC's Elstree Studios as a makeshift studio. The TARDIS control room was thus erected outside a genuine studio for the first time ever (although see Landing 143). The full set, including working console and CSO backdrop for the scanner, were set up as usual – their only appearance in this season of stories, and the last sighting of the wall sections. Beyond the interior doorway were plain flats and the door itself was omitted. Prop components for the Doctor to tinker with, plus a cord to hold the juggling instruction book, were hung from the lighting gantry above, as was just the top section of a hatstand.

▨ The Doctor is reading *Juggling for the Complete Klutz* by John Cassidy and BC Rimbeaux (illustrated by Diane Waller), the UK paperback edition published by Fontana in 1984. One of the scenery crew standing on the lighting gantry used a fishing net to catch the Doctor's 'disappearing' juggling ball, a suggestion made by Sylvester McCoy.

▨ *The Greatest Show in the Galaxy* was made before but broadcast after *Silver Nemesis*. Consequently, Ace seems to have forgotten her rucksack full of Nitro-9 hasn't vanished: she used it to blow up the Cybermen's ship.

▨ Unused model shots were filmed of the ad robot approaching the spinning TARDIS. These used the miniature Police Box built for *The Trial of a Time Lord*.

▨ In *Pyramids of Mars* the Doctor claimed "nothing can enter the TARDIS" unless of unimaginable mental force, so how does the ad robot materialise in the control room? Has the Doctor's tinkering diminished the Ship's protective forcefield? Or is the robot transported by the powers of the Gods of Ragnarok to draw victims to them? Alternatively, given Ace's suspicion by the end of events that this "was [the Doctor's] show all along", has he arranged for the robot to provide a pretext for them to visit Segonax so he can deal with the Gods? His confrontation with them arguably feels pre-planned. In cut dialogue Ace asked of the robot's appearance, "Is that unusual?" to which the Doctor replied, "Almost without precedent."

▨ The shot of the robot attaching itself to the console was recorded with the connector initially plugged in then yanked out on a wire. This was then played in reverse when the episode was edited.

▨ The Doctor would seem not to have visited Segonax before as he says on exiting the TARDIS, "Not quite the green and pleasant land we'd been led to expect," although it's not clear where he got that idea from as it looks the same on the circus advert. He goes on to say, "I've had good reports of the friendliness of the natives." When and from whom? The stall holder sells 'Plaup from Vulpana' so evidently there's trade with people from other planets; perhaps the Doctor heard about the Segonax natives from them.

LANDING 303

SPACE Earth, England, near Carbury
TIME At least two days in [1990s]
TRAVELLERS The Doctor, Ace
EPISODES Battlefield 1

The control room is in darkness as the console picks up an unknown signal: "A cry for help, perhaps a summoning." The Doctor traces its origin to Earth even though the transmission seems to be rippling across time and sideways to other universes. He deciphers one word: "Merlin."

The TARDIS materialises on the verge of a woodland lane, beside a signpost indicating it is four kilometres to Lake Vortigern, from the depths of which the signal is transmitting. The Doctor and Ace walk up to a busier road to thumb a lift.

Ancelyn, a knight from an alternative Earth who has crossed dimensions in search of Merlin, finds the TARDIS, which he recognises. He hides behind it as a UNIT Range Rover passes by, driven by Brigadier Winifred Bambera with the Doctor and Ace her passengers.

Bambera is passing back along the lane to rejoin her convoy when she receives notification over the radio to be on the lookout for a police telephone box. She pulls up by the TARDIS and is checking it when Ancelyn confronts her. Suddenly, three rival knights attack. Ancelyn fights off their leader, Mordred, with his sword while the Brigadier shoots at another. Ancelyn gains the upper hand and takes the opportunity to leave, the others following. Bambera is left stranded with one of her tyres shot out. She sets off on foot back the way she came.

After spending some time with his old friend Brigadier Alastair Lethbridge-Stewart, the Doctor returns with Ace to the TARDIS.

- **○ CONTROLS** The Doctor operates numerous buttons and switches on all panels bar E5. Although the actors behave as if the voice message is emanating from panel E1, the cutaway shot of the speaker grille is that recently added to panel E4.
- ○ This is the last appearance of Console E in the series.
- **▮ NOTES** The Doctor tells Ace the signal comes from "a few years in your future", at a time when the UK apparently has a king, £5 coins are acceptable currency and distances on road signs are given in kilometres. Despite these not coming to pass in our universe, the production team intended it to be the mid-to-late-1990s.
- ▮ Why is the control room dark, asks Ace? Because the regular set walls were found to be missing – likely lost or junked after being taken to Elstree to record *The Greatest Show in the Galaxy* – so simple replacements had to be hurriedly made. (Presumably the additional walls made for the likes of *Attack of the Cybermen* were also junked by then.) These were just plywood with circles cut out and backed with fabric, which was lit from behind. Effort was taken to mimic the proper set, however, with two walls of four columns of staggered roundels separated by square columns (although without vertical slats). There was also a hatstand, holding the Doctor's hat and coat and Ace's bomber jacket. It's hard to tell but some aspects indicate this was the same or very similar to the one used in *Frontios* – well, the Doctor did say that was one of a pair.
- ▮ The final scene of the story sees everyone hanging out at Lethbridge-Stewart's country home, but how did they get there? It would be an awful coincidence if he just happened to live close to where the action had been, and the helicopter flight to London then out to Carbury perhaps suggests otherwise. There's no indication the Doctor used the TARDIS, although it's possible – if not he and Ace will have to travel back to Carbury – so did they all squeeze into Bessie? And how long after the defeat of Morgaine is it? Given the events of that confrontation, the potential length of the journey and the fact it's still early enough for the girls to go for an afternoon drive, it must be at least the day after by now. Ancelyn talks of "the silence after battle" as if that was recent. Ace is wearing the same clothes, understandably, but so too is Shou Yuing. But if they all went straight there from Carbury, why is Bambera with them? Shouldn't she be heading the clearing-up operation? There's still a nuclear missile to dispose of and no doubt plenty of "inch-thick forms" to be filled out. Is she slacking off while on duty? All this suggests the Doctor has, for once, hung around for a few days – unusual for him but plausible for the chance to catch up with Lethbridge-Stewart (especially after fearing he'd been killed earlier). Could the young women really not find a change of clothes, though, and does Ancelyn have no duties to return to?

LANDING 304

SPACE Earth, England, Middlesex, Perivale, Gabriel Chase
TIME Two days in 1883
TRAVELLERS The Doctor, Ace
EPISODES Ghost Light 1-3

Ace has told the Doctor about a deserted house she broke into for a dare when she was thirteen but was frightened away by an aura of intense evil. He decides to go there, without telling her, to investigate the cause.

The TARDIS materialises in the observatory turret of Gabriel Chase, a mansion in the small village of Perivale, shortly before six o'clock in the evening and a hundred years before Ace lived in the area. The cramped space is packed with old children's toys and scientific equipment, including chemicals used in taxidermy. After a quick look round, they descend the circular staircase to explore the rest of the house.

A sedated Reverend Ernest Matthews is brought to the observatory. As dawn breaks, he is awoken by a gunshot as a decaying Josiah Samuel Smith takes pot shots at a photo of Queen Victoria. The reverend is beginning to de-evolve into a lower primate, and when Gwendoline joins them Josiah has her put Matthews to sleep for good. He is placed in a display cabinet and covered with a dust sheet. During the day, Josiah, Gwendoline and Mrs Pritchard sit like statues beneath sheets.

Towards sundown, Ace and Inspector Mackenzie find the three dormant figures, and the monkey-like Matthews. As the clock strikes six, the women awaken and grab Ace, while Mackenzie is held by the husk of Josiah's last form. A newly evolved, stronger version of him emerges, no longer sensitive to light. They all head downstairs.

The Doctor has released the being known as Light so Josiah and the two women retreat to the observatory, bringing Redvers Fenn-Cooper with them. Hoping Light and the Doctor will keep each other busy, Josiah sends the others to continue with his plans.

The house is empty when the Doctor and Ace return to the TARDIS, its surviving occupants departed in the spaceship buried under the house. Light has dispersed, its aura imbuing the building with the hateful feelings that led Ace to burn it down in 1983. Now she only wishes she had blown it up instead.

▤ **NOTES** The year is given on screen. Mrs Pritchard says it's "almost first light" at 4.35am and it must get dark shortly after 6pm given how keen Mrs Grose is to leave before then. This makes April or September the most likely times of year.

▤ The TARDIS lands with its doors facing the wall, forcing Ace and the Doctor to squeeze out. Usually it seems able to determine the best orientation relative to its landing site; has the Doctor been allowing Ace to pilot the Ship as part of her initiative test? The flashing of the (not visible) roof lamp was added electronically.

▤ Although it's hard to see on screen, the Doctor has a new TARDIS key. Created by the BBC Visual Effects department, this featured the Prydonian seal above a fan-shaped blade. The Doctor also uses it to lock the Police Box door in *Survival* (Landing 306).

LANDING 305

SPACE Earth, England, [North] Yorkshire, naval base
TIME Two days (Saturday to Sunday) in [May] 1943
TRAVELLERS The Doctor, Ace
EPISODES The Curse of Fenric 1

Ace wants to go rock climbing so the Doctor takes her to the north-east coast of England during World War Two, for which she dons suitable period clothing. The TARDIS materialises in a quiet corner of a naval camp, its arrival not going unnoticed by the troops. The Doctor clearly has a specific intention in mind for coming to this time and place, however.

With Fenric once more banished and Ace having overcome some of her emotional issues regarding her mother, the travellers return to the TARDIS.

▤ **NOTES** In the 9th century, when the Vikings with the flask are said to have "sought haven in Northumbria... at a place called Maiden's Bay", that kingdom covered all of northern Britain, including the east coast from the Forth to the Humber. Norse incursion and settlement was mostly south of the Tees, however, so the naval base is somewhere in the north or east riding of Yorkshire. (The script indicated local characters had North Riding accents, and Ian Briggs' novelisation of his story set it explicitly in North Yorkshire.)

▤ Ace mentions the year and the script suggested it was 'probably May'. The Doctor and Ace find a bunk for the night after their arrival, and a church service the next morning indicates this is a Sunday.

LANDING 306

SPACE Earth, England, London, Perivale
TIME Sunday, [summer 1989]
TRAVELLERS The Doctor, Ace
EPISODES Survival 1,3

Ace idly wonders how her old friends are doing so the Doctor takes her home to Perivale, landing the TARDIS in a quiet residential street one Sunday morning. She is none too thrilled about being back in the "boredom capital of the universe" but they head towards Horsenden Hill, where her gang used to hang out.

Bewitched by the planet of the Cheetahs, Ace gains the ability to teleport home and brings the Doctor, two of her friends and Sergeant Paterson back to Earth. They appear beside the TARDIS, which Ace now considers her only home. Believing herself free of the influence, she is all for moving on, but the Doctor reminds her the Master must also have been brought back to Perivale by Midge. They head towards the lad's home.

The Master tries to pick the lock of the TARDIS but the Doctor interrupts him. They struggle and the Master teleports them back to the Cheetah's planet. A briefly infected Doctor manages to return before that world destroys itself, appearing mid-sentence beside his beloved Ship. He goes to find Ace and bring her home to the TARDIS; they still have danger, injustice and cold tea to combat.

▤ **NOTES** A street sign for Bleasdale Avenue, the real-life location on which the Police Box prop was erected (on the corner with Colwyn Avenue), appears on camera in episode three but isn't quite legible. As the story is specifically set in Perivale, however, this can be taken as the in-fiction location of the TARDIS's arrival.

▤ No date is given on screen, the Doctor telling Ace she has "been away as long as you think you have". The newspaper Len is reading mentions American preacher Billy Graham, who visited London from Wednesday 14 June 1989, three days after the mini-market scenes were recorded. (Boxing event posters at the youth centre are clearly old and for inspiration more than information, but promote bouts as late as March 1989.)

▤ The TARDIS's arrival is a subtle split-screen shot so that the cat can still be seen running away on the right of the picture as the Police Box begins to appear in the centre. This also means the moving shadows on the wall to the right don't blur as they would in a simple mix.

▤ The Police Box prop's rear doors are very slightly ajar when it's shown materialising. They move fractionally as the Doctor pulls the front doors closed, and have been properly closed before the next shot of Ace walking away from the TARDIS.

IT LOOKS JUST LIKE A POLICE BOX

THE HUDOLIN BOX
1996

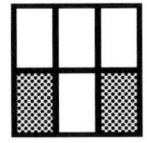

Throughout the long gestation of the BBC/Universal TV movie simply titled *Doctor Who*, there was no suggestion the TARDIS should appear as anything other than an old Metropolitan Police Box. This is perhaps surprising given the movie was primarily targeted at an American audience.

In the earliest script treatments by John Leekley, the time machine's shape was seemingly taken as read, even when it had belonged to the Doctor's late grandfather Barusa (sic) whose life essence now inhabited its power crystals (!). In Robert DeLaurentis's revised script it changed into a Police Box when it landed in London during the Blitz, after which it simply stayed that way. This idea was dropped once the movie's ultimate writer Matthew Jacobs was brought in, and the TARDIS just appeared in its familiar form without any introduction.

Once pre-production for the movie got underway at the end of November 1995, it fell to designer Richard Hudolin to arrange the construction of a new Police Box prop. In this he was assisted by schematics provided by the BBC. These were likely the design drawings for Tom Yardley-Jones's fibreglass box as its dimensions closely match those on the blueprints for the movie prop. There are some minor variations, though, in the height of the base and roof stacks and position of the lock. The plans also indicate only the front doors were made to open, with no access at the back.

Further alterations were made when the box was constructed, once more from wood rather than fibreglass. The base became even taller and the sign boxes were deeper than even the Newbery box's. These also reverted to having a narrower sign inset, with a the frame wider at the ends. The signs themselves had white lettering on a black background and were illuminated from behind. The steps below the sign box on the front no longer acted as a doorstop but formed a solid lintel. Similarly, the centre post attached to the left-hand door was flush with its edge, no longer overlapping the gap between the doors. This door also carried a 'Police telephone' plaque, which was hinged on the right and had a handle on its frame on the left – an arrangement last seen on the later-stage Brachacki box and reintroduced on the 2018 TV prop. The plaque's lettering was hand-painted and matched the original Yardley-Jones box in wording if not font choice (Souvenir with some adaptations). The right-hand door had a handle on its inner stile with the lock above. This was a vertical slot for the shield-shaped key, hidden behind a disc with a Yale keyhole.

The windows had two panes fitted with mottled glass, although which pair varied on each window – for example, the left-hand door had its lower left and right panes pebbled, but on the right-hand door it was the lower left and upper right panes. The inside of the box was painted black and the windows covered. The roof lamp was a modified handheld lantern with a blue flashing light. According to plans, this was initially freestanding but ultimately was given a square cap with corner struts, even though the lantern already had bars protecting its lens.

STUNT DOUBLE

A second Police Box was also built solely for the shot of the motorcycle cop driving into and out of the TARDIS. This was the same depth as the main prop but sixteen inches wider to provide clearance for the stunt rider. So there wasn't a step to mount, it also didn't have a full-width base. Indeed, the prop was basically an archway, with two sides matching the main prop (incorporating a narrow section of base) joined by an oblong roof. The sign box on the front was proportionately elongated, although the inset was the same width as the sides (presumably so all the 'Police box' graphics could be made the same size). A pair of front doors was fitted but fixed in an open position; these were the same width as the main prop's so as not to distort the panelling, thus they wouldn't have met in the middle had they been able to close. Filmed from the side as the rider passes through and back again, the extra width wasn't noticeable, and the space behind the box was overlaid in post-production with a view of the empty street to complete the illusion.

It's not known what happened to these Police Boxes after filming, particularly once the option to produce a series expired. The stunt prop was likely junked, but the main prop was rumoured to have been kept by producer Philip Segal, although he has since denied this.

Right Hudolin prop front elevation and section
Left The telephone plaque restored the genuine wording and adapted its typeface to mimic some of the original's letter forms

IT LOOKS JUST LIKE A POLICE BOX

POLICE PUBLIC CALL BOX

POLICE TELEPHONE
FREE
FOR USE OF
PUBLIC
ADVICE AND ASSISTANCE
OBTAINABLE IMMEDIATELY
OFFICERS AND CARS
RESPOND TO
URGENT CALLS
PULL TO OPEN

IT'S BIGGER ON THE INSIDE

THE HUDOLIN CATHEDRAL
1996

From the outset of his bid to revive *Doctor Who*, executive producer Philip Segal wanted the TARDIS interior to "mimic the feel of the Victorian era", inspired by the dark-wood appearance of Barry Newbery's 1976 control room set. Early concept artwork by Matthew Codd took a Gothic approach with high vaulting columns and lancet arches, ideas production designer Richard Hudolin retained only for the cloisters where the Eye of Harmony was housed. For the control room itself he followed Segal's instruction that "every aspect of the TARDIS was to feel dated and antique", with a number of architectural styles incorporated.

Some concepts from initial writer John Leekley's format document also survived. This had the central "five-sided console" surround by different chambers linked to each panel's function: the Doctor's quarters and library, from where he navigated using a "magic lantern" that gave "a 360 degree view of the galaxy"; an engineering and environmental control section; a science laboratory; cloisters, with "stained glass depicting the mythology of Gallifrey" (and where the hologramatic Barusa would appear – don't ask); and finally, 'cosmos', "a simple wooden railing which overlooks the galaxy through a vast and invisible lens". Fortunately Hudolin did better research and stuck with a traditional six-sided console, but the idea of different areas surrounding the central control section was adopted, in a scaled-down form.

The final set was a full 360-degree stage, broadly circular centred on the console, although only two solid wall sections were built. The rest was comprised of colonnades and open archways that gave the impression of the room extending into infinity. The main entrance was housed in a cracked and flaking marble wall. Between two Ionic columns were a pair of large double doors that featured rows of squares in relief with circular indentations, one of the few nods to the roundels of previous TARDIS designs. Beyond these was an anteroom with more ranks of circles but this went unseen in the finished programme as it proved difficult to light effectively. Above the doors was the knotted Time Lord emblem originally designed by Roger Murray-Leach for the Vogans in *Revenge of the Cybermen* (1975) but repurposed by him in his Panopticon sets for *The Deadly Assassin* (1976) and subsequently used as a general symbol for all things Time Lordy. Two statues of a figure holding up a lamp flanked the doors, before which was a platform with a rug and three steps leading down to the main floor of the control room.

Main doors (columns and architrave continue to left to form arcade)

To the right of the doors wall was the library. This was a long, straight section formed from five thick stepped buttresses supporting tall I-beam girders. Fitted between these were wooden bookcases. Above was a metal-railed walkway suspended from the girders, which rose past large windows before curving over as the top of the wall angled inwards at 45 degrees. The shelves were stacked with books while the ledges of the buttresses were dressed with candlesticks and ornaments. In front of this was placed the rococo fanback armchair in which the Doctor relaxes, plus various lamps and small tables.

At the right-hand end of the library was a panelled section below the walkway that abutted a large cabinet with 30 filing drawers, labelled alphabetically. The Master retrieves bags of gold dust from the 'G' drawer, while 'D' contained a detached Dalek sucker arm (intended to be seen in the movie but lack of time meant it went unfilmed). Continuing from this was a balustrade with an

IT'S BIGGER ON THE INSIDE

Library

Conservatory

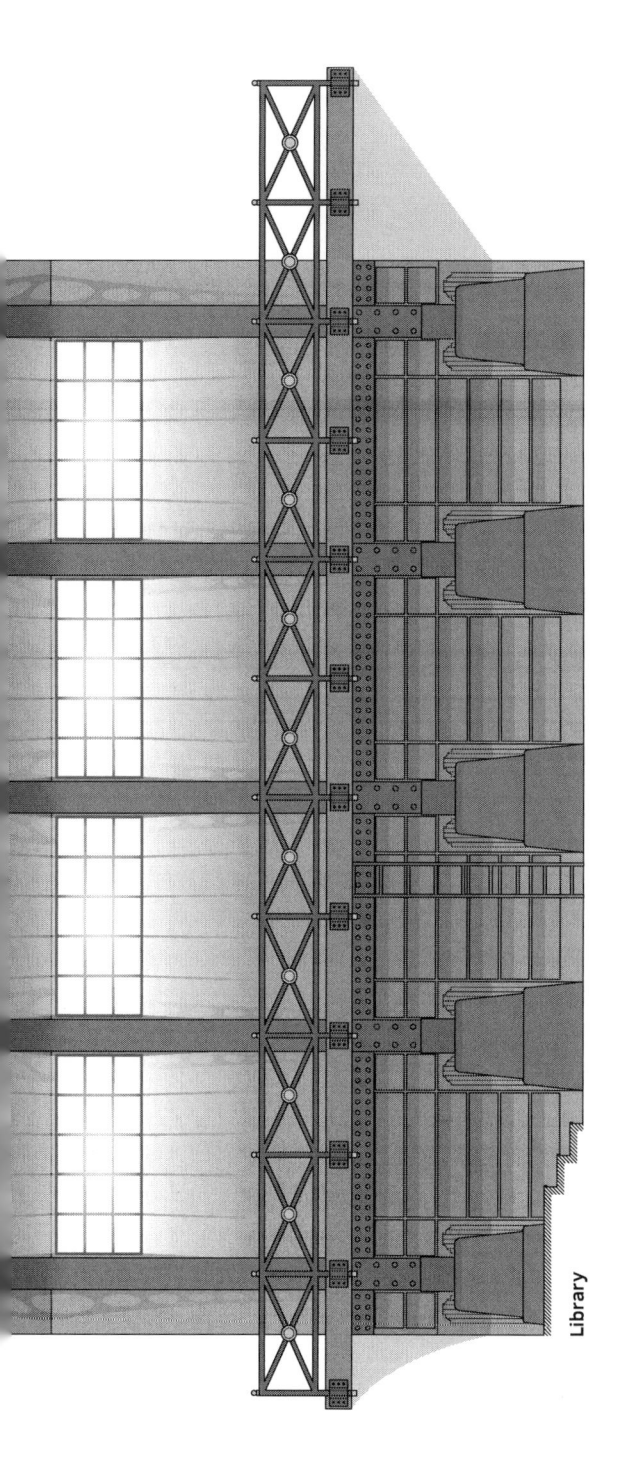

archway leading into a conservatory containing houseplants and a collection of clocks and musical instruments.

The rest of the room comprised three ranks of colonnades. The first, closest to the console area, was wooden with illuminated recesses in its columns and more instances of the circular Time Lord emblem along its entablature. Behind this were taller Ionic columns supporting an architrave that continued along the top of the main doors.

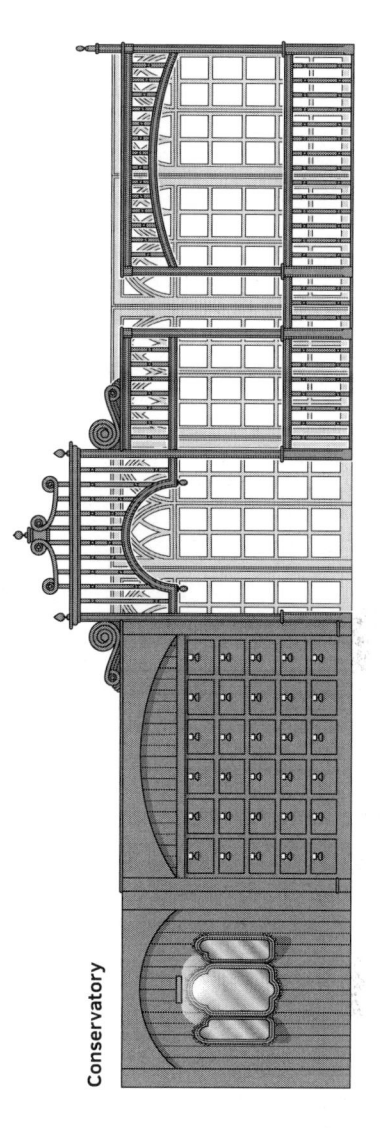

Lastly a series of high Doric pillars formed an arched arcade around the outside of the room. One of these arches housed another Time Lord emblem and acted as the entrance to the cloister room; through another was a second seating area, with an armchair and standard lamp. Circling almost the entire set, but most noticeable beyond the conservatory, was a tall dark-green curtain.

Overall the control room was a complete departure from those seen in the original series, even the 1976 set. With low lighting, the room's shape and layout were hard to discern on screen, giving it a more cavernous feel. Despite being countered by the home comforts strewn around the space, this arguably makes the extent of the TARDIS feel smaller as everything the Doctor needs is accessible in this one room. Nonetheless, this control room design had more influence on those that were to follow than any previous look.

WHAT ARE ALL THESE KNOBS?

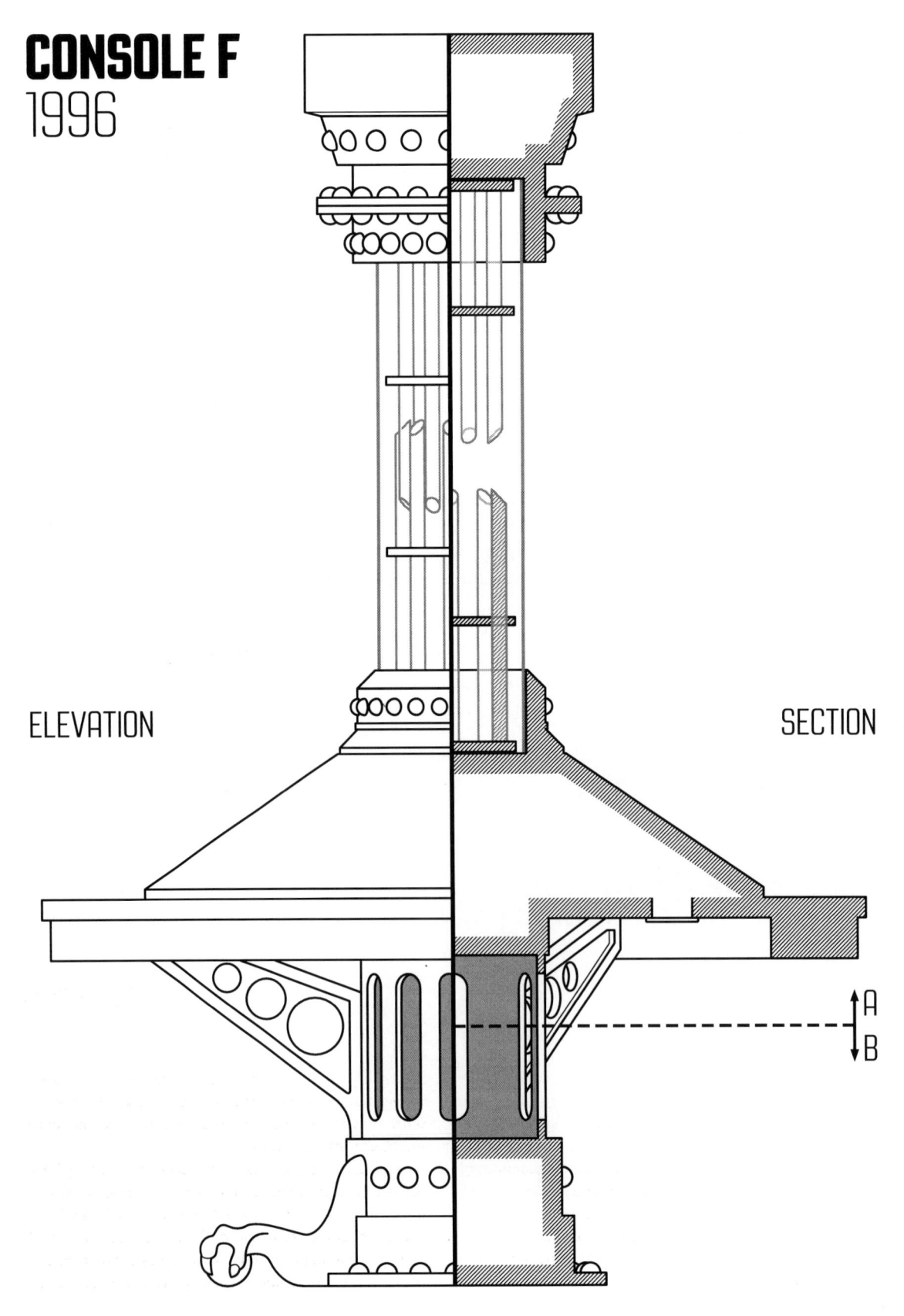

CONSOLE F
1996

ELEVATION

SECTION

A
B

WHAT ARE ALL THESE KNOBS?

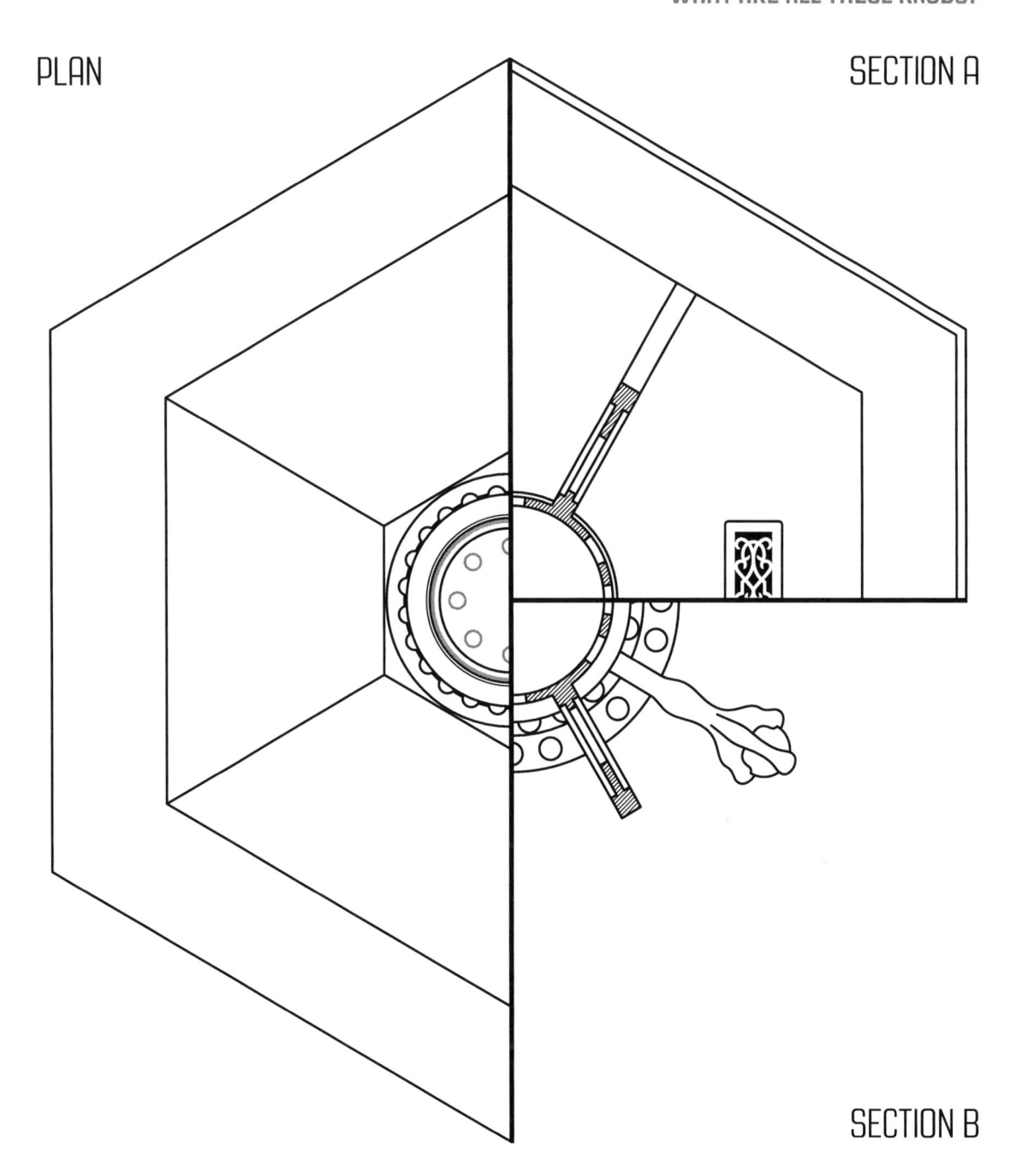

PLAN

SECTION A

SECTION B

In 1994 when John Leekley was writing his format document for the planned TV movie, he described a five-sided console with "the gigantic crystals that power all the generators" in the centre, extending "outward and upward, into deep space and beyond". This was visualised in accompanying artwork by Matthew Codd as a steep-sided pentagonal pyramid with a cluster of tall glass spires in the centre, the whole thing descending into the floor during flight. Once designer Richard Hudolin joined the production this was fortunately revised as a more familiar hexagonal console on a plinth with a central glass column. But that's not to say he didn't introduce his own innovations.

The brief from executive producer Philip Segal was for something timeless, avoiding any sort of futuristic look, with "old-fashioned knobs and switches". He wanted a "Jules Verne approach" like Barry Newbery's 1976 control room, although both were perhaps thinking more of the representation of Captain Nemo's Nautilus

WHAT ARE ALL THESE KNOBS?

Above For the first time the central column was connected above to the confluence of six pylons around the console's platform

submarine in the 1954 Disney film adaptation of *20,000 Leagues Under the Sea* rather than Verne's original novel, particularly with the riveted ironwork of Hudolin's final set. Concept sketches from December 1995 initially show a freestanding console with a traditionally short central column, although connected by a thinner tube (or possibly a beam of energy) to an overhead unit that may have been intended to move up and down. The console stood on a hexagonal platform with railings on three sides, akin to the 1976 set. This was soon reworked to include the six large arching pylons that connected to the upper unit and a full-height central column.

The console itself was made from oak, with the outer surfaces given a red-mahogany veneer. The panels were at a steeper angle than usual (like Console D) and the controls were largely taken from old radios and electrical testing equipment, such as galvanometers, potentiometers and capacitance bridges (some still bearing the name of their manufacturer, Leeds & Northrup Co of Philadelphia). One such was the large central dial on the panel facing the main doors (therefore designated here as panel 1), which also had a reading lamp on a flexible stalk, usually angled over panel 2. This was the panel for navigation, with six-sided drums displaying era, planet, date and time, rotated using adjacent thumbwheels. As well as the Rassilon and Humanian Eras seen on screen, the four others were Manussian, Sumaron, Kraaiian and Sensorian. In addition to Gallifrey and Earth, planet options were Argolis, Calufrax, Manussa and Sarn (all locations from previous stories). Months ranged from November to April and dates from 1 to 3 and 29 to 31; times were any combination of 12/22/23/24/00/01 : 47/58/59/00/01/02 : 37/58/59/00/01/02; and years ranged from 1998 to 2000 and 5725.1 to 5725.3. This panel also had a squeeze-grip brake handle and three clocks, one of which was seen winding backwards (operated manually). On panel 3, either side of a board of rheostats, were two lights fitted into badges from a 1920s Sonora radio phonograph. Panel 5 had a rotating crank handle, while panel 6 had three lights fitted into glass insulators from a telegraph pole, below which was the large horizontal lever that activated the overhead scanner. This had a carved wooden knob and operated the sequence of lights above and below its slot. In fact many of the lights were wired to controls, making this the most functional console to date.

Initial design drawings show just three projecting shelves on alternate sides but during construction these were expanded to a full shelf around the rim. Only panel 2 had any controls fitted in this extra space, however:

the keyboard from a mechanical adding machine and a small telephone plug board, which lifted out to allow the beryllium chip prop to be inserted. Beneath this shelf were screwed the three pieces that formed the underside of the console. These were removable to provide access to the console's electrics and each had a slot for ventilation (and for Grace to pull wires from when re-routing the power) covered by a filigreed brass grille. Between the three sections and aligned with alternate edges of the hexagonal desk were tapered struts with circular holes in them that joined to the pedestal.

The core of the pedestal was formed from plastic resin and had vertical slots to reveal lighting and wiring inside. Around the base were wooden rings with domed 'rivet heads' and three projecting feet sculpted from foam, each with a three-fingered claw clutching a globe. These were aligned with the console's corners but not symmetrically between the three struts. The whole pedestal was textured and painted to look like cast iron.

A similar 'riveted-iron' ring sat on top of the console around the base of the central column, which was now static and only the illuminated rods inside oscillated while the TARDIS was in flight. Eight rose from within the console, interlocking with eight descending from above. At the top of the glass column was another set of mock-iron cylinders joining with six large girders that arched over the console and down to the edges of the hexagonal platform on which it stood. These had circular holes in their sides (a nod to the traditional wall roundels) and crossed struts on their front and rear faces. At their bases were hinge-like half-cylinders that gave the impression the structure could move. A dodecagon around the dais was painted to look like parquet flooring.

While the console had a traditional feel harking back to the series' first, with its hands-on knobs, switches and levers, the ironwork structure around it was different from any previous design. This would be echoed, however, in the buttresses of the 2005 control room, which also retained the central column connecting to the ceiling.

Once it was decided an ongoing series wouldn't follow from the TV movie, the console went into storage at the Vancouver props company that had been contracted to build it. In 2007 the firm's owner was looking to dispose of the bulky prop and, through mutual friends, was put in touch with Californian film producer and *Doctor Who* fan Paul J Salamoff. Astonished the console had survived and in remarkably good condition after a decade, he was more than happy to take possession of it. The central column wasn't included, so Salamoff built a (static) reproduction, but the electrics for all the lights still worked and all but a handful of controls were in situ.

When it was announced the main cast and producer of the TV movie would be at the Gallifrey One convention in February 2012, Salamoff decided to properly restore the console so it could be displayed at the event. With help from friends Brian Uiga and Bob Mitsch, he gave the prop a thorough overhaul, repairing damage, replacing missing controls (notably the crank handle), swapping the hot halogen lights for safer LEDs, and inserting a speaker to play sound effects from the movie when certain controls are operated. They also fitted it onto a new wheeled platform so it could be moved without the risk of damaging the fragile feet. After three months of painstaking work, the console made its impressive return at Gallifrey One 23 to the admiration of all, and continues to go on display at conventions around the world.

WHAT ARE ALL THESE KNOBS?

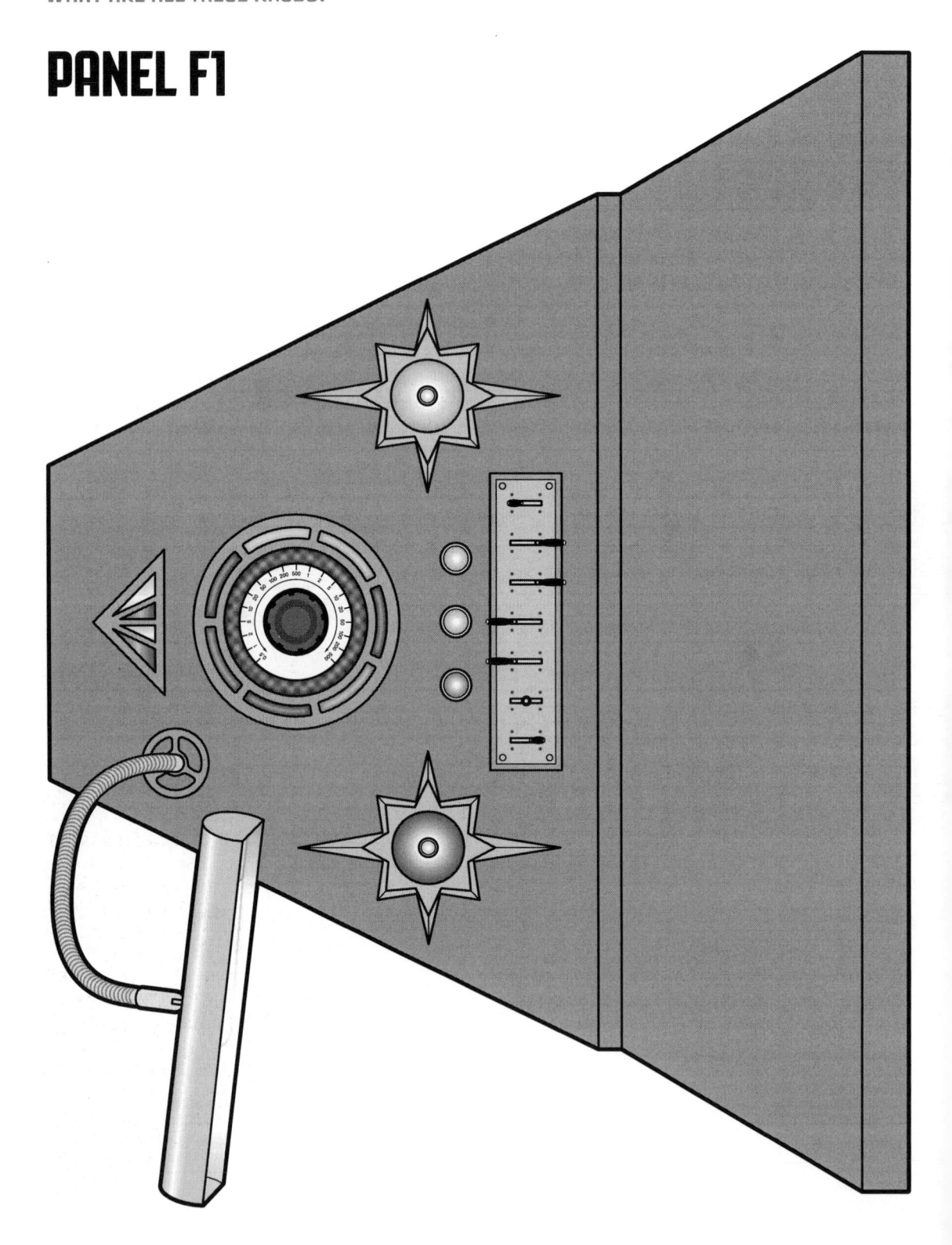

PANEL F1

WHAT ARE ALL THESE KNOBS?

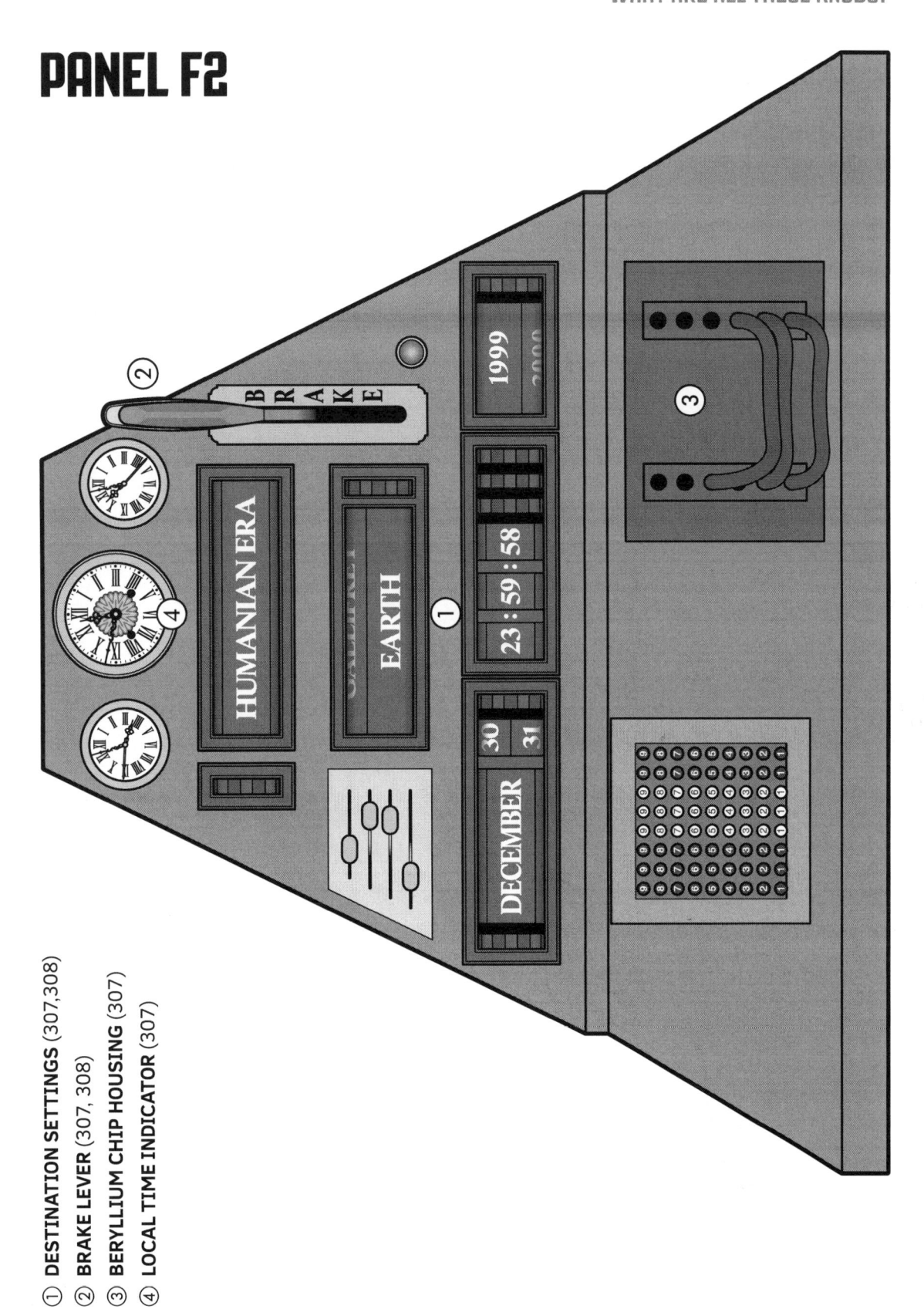

PANEL F2

① **DESTINATION SETTINGS** (307, 308)
② **BRAKE LEVER** (307, 308)
③ **BERYLLIUM CHIP HOUSING** (307)
④ **LOCAL TIME INDICATOR** (307)

WHAT ARE ALL THESE KNOBS?

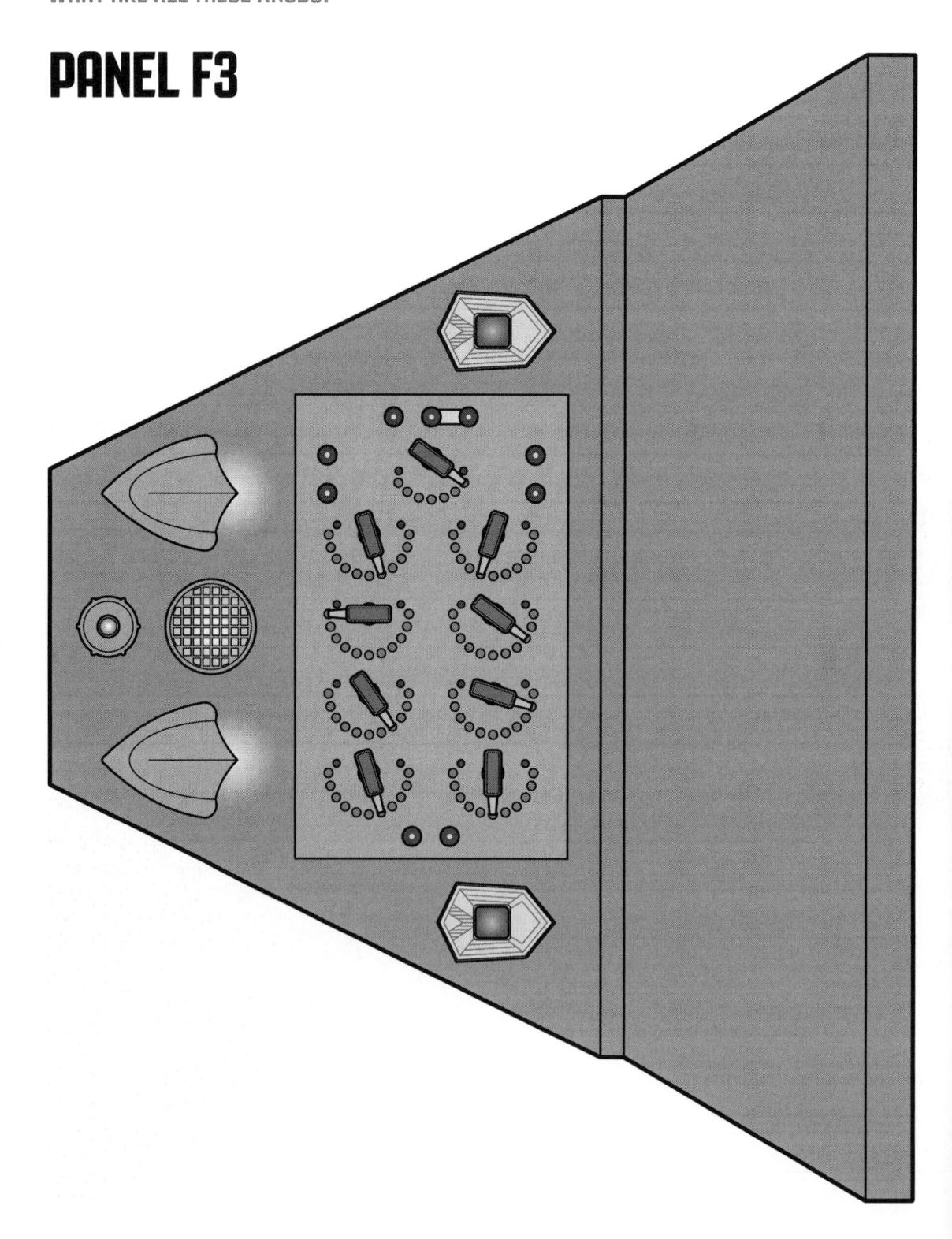

PANEL F3

PANEL F4

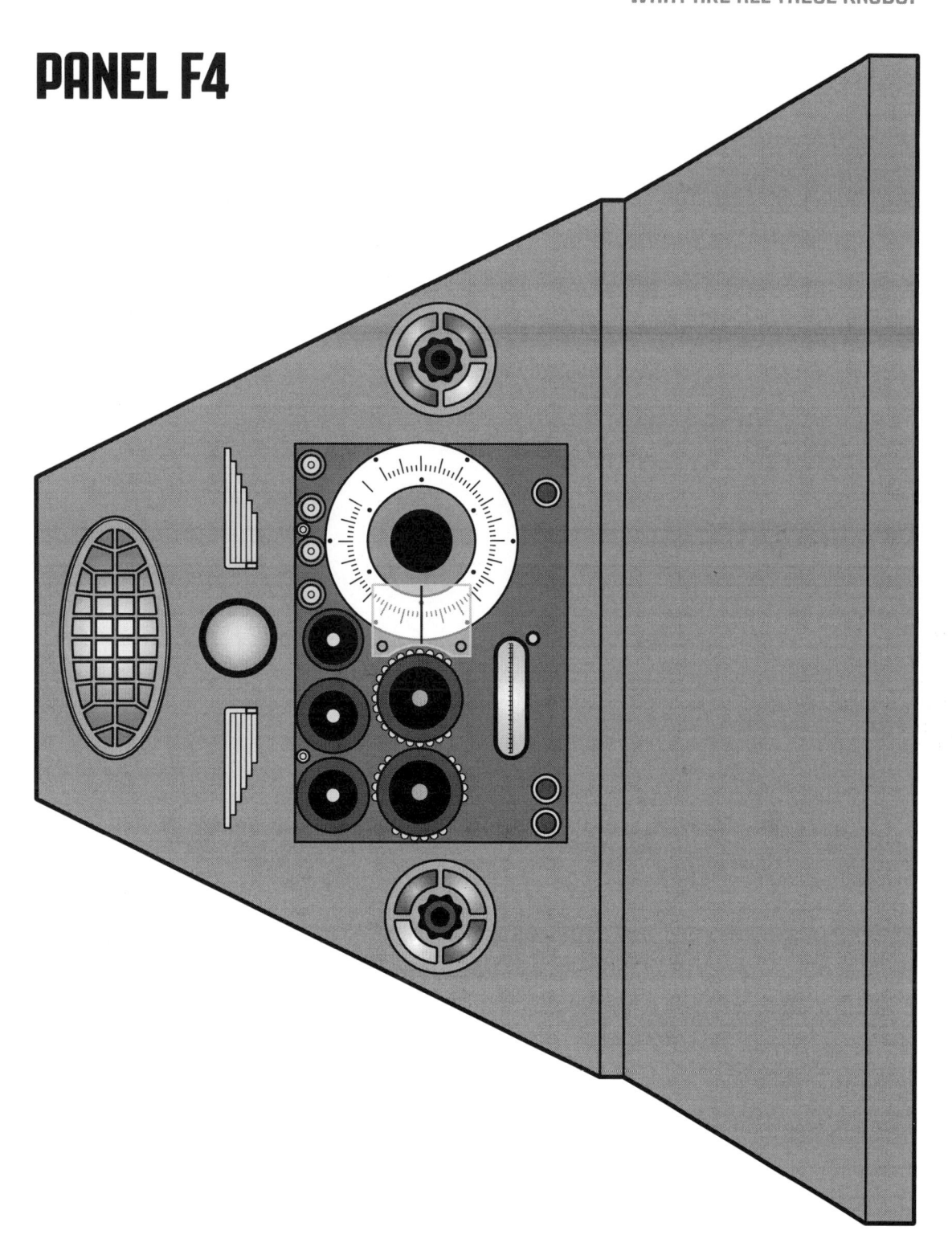

WHAT ARE ALL THESE KNOBS?

WHAT ARE ALL THESE KNOBS?

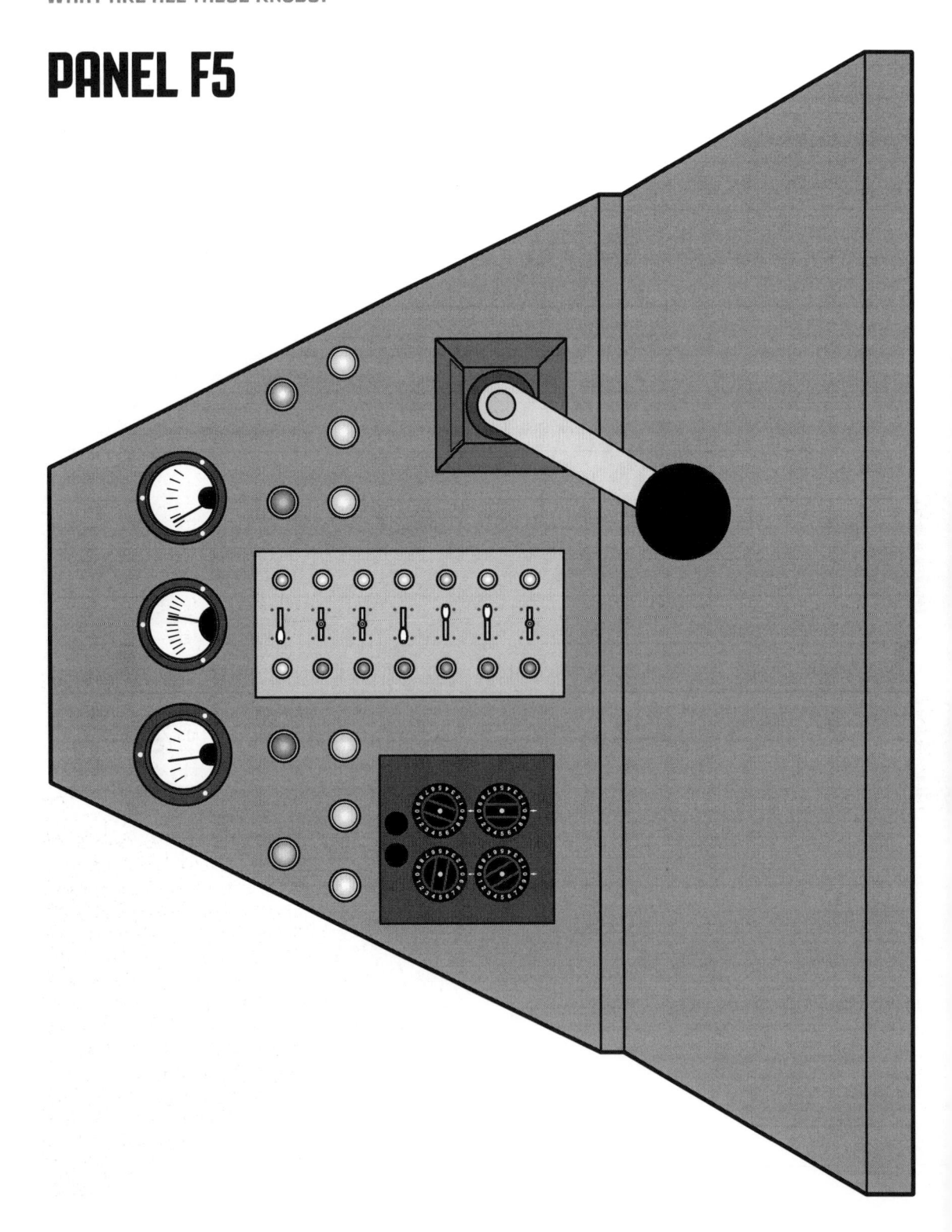

PANEL F5

PANEL F6

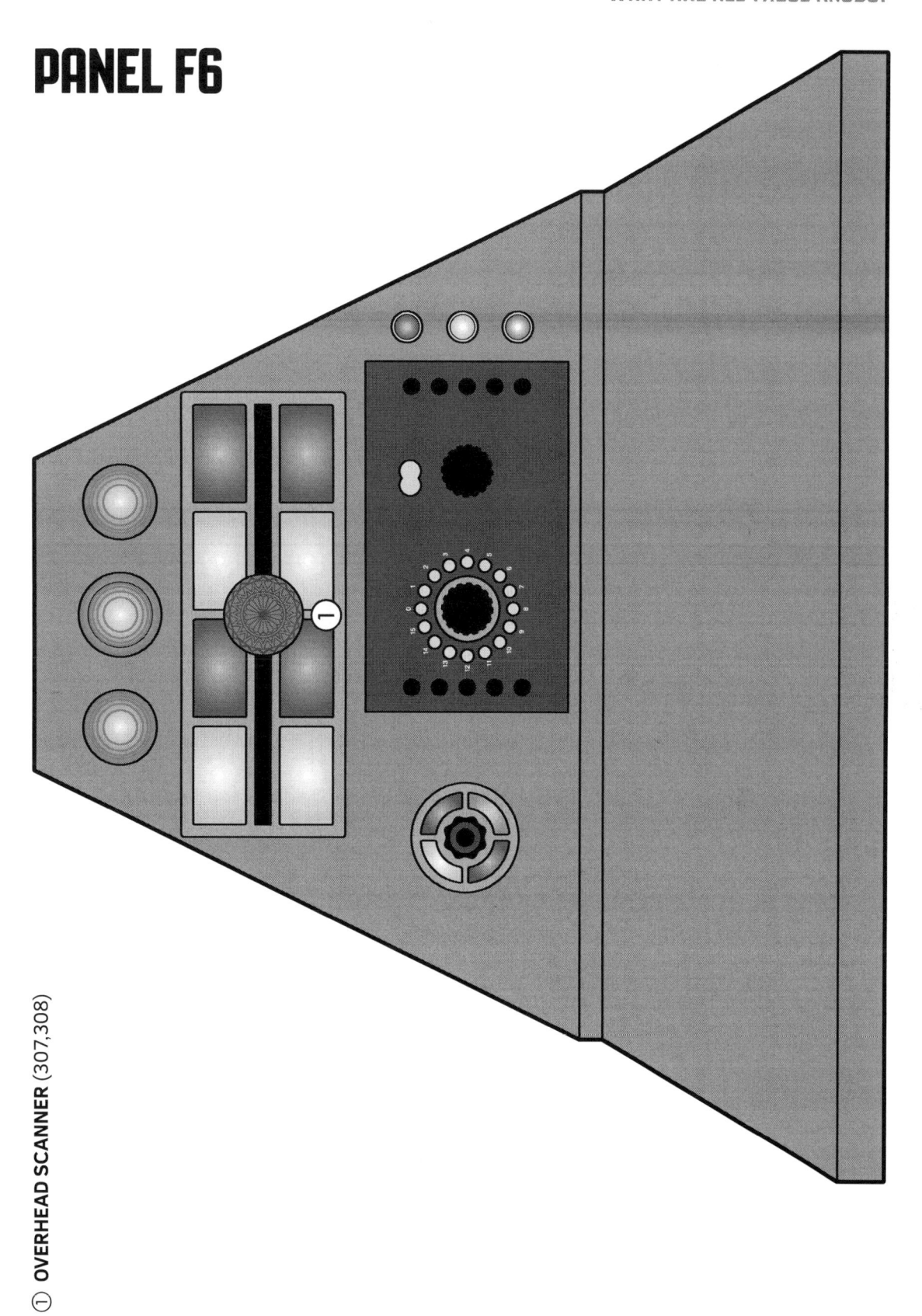

WHAT ARE ALL THESE KNOBS?

① **OVERHEAD SCANNER** (307, 308)

PREVIOUS LANDINGS

SPACE Earth, Italy
TIME Late-15th century
TRAVELLERS The Doctor, [unknown companions]
EPISODES Claimed by the Doctor in Doctor Who (Movie)

The Doctor met Leonardo da Vinci at a time when the artist had a cold while he was sketching the face of a young woman.

NOTES This was before the Doctor's seventh regeneration but after his third. For Leonardo it's likely to be before he was commissioned by Captain Tancredi in 1505 to reproduce six further copies of the Mona Lisa (see Landing 162).

SPACE Earth, Belgium, Brussels
TIME November 1924
TRAVELLERS The Doctor, [unknown companions]
EPISODES Mentioned by the Doctor in Doctor Who (Movie)

The Doctor was with the opera composer Giacomo Puccini shortly before he died, leaving his last work, Turandot, unfinished.

NOTES Puccini, a heavy smoker, was diagnosed with laryngeal cancer on 2 November 1924 and travelled from his home in Viareggio, Tuscany, to Brussels to begin radiation therapy, taking with him notes and musical sketches for the finale of Turandot. The treatment using radium was effective but, following surgery on the 24th, the composer died on the 29th after a heart attack the evening before. The Doctor only says he was with Puccini "before he died" but as he talks of it being "so sad" it's likely he was in Brussels that final week rather than Italy earlier. His talk of Franco Alfano completing Turandot based on Puccini's notes may just be from knowledge rather than implying he stayed on for the debates over who should be appointed to finish the work, which didn't premiere until April 1926.

SPACE Earth, Austria, Vienna
TIME Late-19th/early-20th century
TRAVELLERS The Doctor, [unknown companions]
EPISODES Claimed by the Doctor in Doctor Who (Movie) and The Curse of the Black Spot

The Doctor met and got on very well with Sigmund Freud. The psychoanalyst had a comfy sofa.

NOTES The Doctor could have met Freud at any point in his life but given he refers to psychoanalytical terms it may have been after the neurologist published those theories and began putting them into practice with his patients.

SPACE Earth, France, Paris
TIME Early-20th century
TRAVELLERS The Doctor, [unknown companions]
EPISODES Claimed by the Doctor in Doctor Who (Movie)

The Doctor knew Marie Curie "intimately".

NOTES Given Grace refers to "Madame Curie" and the Doctor doesn't correct her, we can assume he met Marie after her marriage to Pierre in July 1895. Depending how intimate he was, it may have been after Monsieur Curie's death in 1906.

SPACE Earth, America, California, Los Angeles
TIME 2009
TRAVELLERS The Doctor, [unknown companions]
EPISODES Related by the Doctor in Doctor Who (Movie)

The Doctor met Gareth Fitzpatrick, head of the seismology unit of the University of California, Los Angeles, when he devised a system to accurately predict earthquakes. He learned that as a student Gareth had answered the second question on a mid-term exam in 2000 even though the third looked easier. The Doctor may have been given reason to believe this choice was because of advice given to Gareth on New Year's Eve 1999 by a strange man he met at the Institute for Technological Advancement and Research in San Francisco.

NOTES Gareth is only credited by his first name at the end of the episode but his surname is given in the shooting script and Gary Russell's novelisation of the story.

SPACE Skaro
TIME Unknown
TRAVELLERS The Doctor
EPISODES Suggested in Doctor Who (Movie)

The Doctor learned the Master had been captured, tried and executed by the Daleks. His old enemy's last request was to have his remains returned to Gallifrey and the Doctor agreed to go to Skaro to collect them.

NOTES We can't be sure the TARDIS landed on Skaro – the Master's urn might have been transmatted to the Ship or collected from a Dalek saucer – but the opening narration of the episode says his request was one "they [the Daleks] should never have granted", which perhaps suggests they permitted the Doctor to come and go unmolested. Gary Russell's novelisation of the story has the Doctor intending to "get there unnoticed, sneak in unannounced, collect the Master's remains unobtrusively and leave again unnoticed".

LANDING 307

SPACE Earth, America, California, San Francisco, Chinatown
TIME 30 to 31 December 1999
TRAVELLERS The Doctor
EPISODES Doctor Who (Movie)

The Doctor has the Master's remains in a small urn, which he locks away in a metal casket, sealed using a new sonic screwdriver from the toolkit. He programmes the TARDIS for Gallifrey in the Rassilon era, local dateline 5725.2, then settles back in an armchair with a book, a cup of tea and music playing on a gramophone.

The gelatinous form the Master has become breaks out of its casket, slithers across the floor and penetrates the console, where it causes a critical timing malfunction. The Doctor works the controls but the central column jams and an emergency landing is automatically instigated.

The TARDIS materialises with a great gust of wind in a San Franciscan side street behind Kim Loo's Grocery late at night. A gang of youths, who had been about to shoot Chang Lee before the Police Box blocked their aim, fire instead at the new arrival. Their bullets bounce off harmlessly, but when the Doctor steps out he is shot three times in the chest and collapses.

The gang hurries away as sirens sound. Lee emerges from behind the TARDIS and tends to the Doctor, who spots goo emerging from the Police Box's keyhole then loses consciousness. Lee waves down an approaching ambulance and the paramedic, Bruce, gets the Doctor onto a stretcher to take him to hospital – unaware the amorphous Master has hitched a ride also. Police tape off the area around the TARDIS as a crime scene.

The next afternoon the Master, now possessing Bruce's body, returns just ahead of Lee, who has the Doctor's key. The Master claims the Ship is his, stolen from him by the Doctor along with his body, and offers Lee riches if he helps to get it back before Bruce's body decays. Together they open the Eye of Harmony in the cloister room which connects with the regenerated Doctor. They see his view of Grace, who Lee recognises as a surgeon from the hospital, and learn the Doctor plans to acquire an atomic clock to fix the Ship's timing mechanism. When Grace telephones the hospital for help, convinced the Doctor is an escaped psychiatric patient, the Master and Lee set out to find her in Bruce's ambulance, leaving the Eye open.

The Doctor returns with Grace as midnight approaches. As he uses a spare key to open the TARDIS doors, a motorcycle cop approaches along the alley. His brakes have failed and he drives straight into the Police Box, emerging moments later and speeding away.

Inside, the cloister bell is tolling and the Doctor hurries to fit into the console the beryllium chip he took from the atomic clock, to correct the timing malfunction. The bell stops and the Eye closes but it has been open too long and the consequent collapse of matter is inevitable. The Doctor sets coordinates for one minute after midnight to see what will happen and a view of space projected above the control room shows every star and planet exploding.

He proposes travelling back in time and preventing the Eye ever being opened but it has already drained the TARDIS of power. He devises a plan to pre-set the coordinates for 30 December then divert power from the Eye into the time rotor to jump-start the Ship. As he begins work, however, the Master and Lee appear and Grace is possessed by the former. She knocks out the Doctor.

They shackle him in the cloister room. The Doctor convinces Lee the Master has lied to him and the boy refuses to open the Eye again. The Master kills him, releases Grace from her possession and forces her to open it. He then stands opposite the Doctor as the Eye pins them in beams of light that enable the Master to begin absorbing his rival's life force.

Now the Master cannot move, however, Grace is free to return to the control room and complete the Doctor's plan. With the cloister bell chiming again, she tugs at wires below the console and, as midnight strikes, finds the correct connection to restart the central column. Crackling with energy, the TARDIS dematerialises.

- **CONTROLS** When the console malfunctions, the Doctor turns the centre dial on panel F1 and flicks switches below. He taps the keypad on the outer rim of panel F2 and pulls the brake lever.
- The Doctor connects the beryllium chip to wires under the plug board on the outer rim of panel F2, which can be flipped up. To activate the overhead scanner he twists the centre dial on panel F6 then moves the large wood-knobbed lever from left to right, which illuminates the adjacent lights. (Note that in the shots either side of this close-up of panel F6, the Doctor is standing at panel F2.)
- When preparing to jump-start the time rotor, the Doctor has Grace operate the top small lever on the left of panel F2.
- **LORE** Damage to the timing mechanism causes a critical timing malfunction and the need to instigate an emergency landing (this seems to happen automatically but may require some manual intervention). This can be repaired by replacing a beryllium microchip with one from a sufficiently advanced atomic clock.
- The cloisters have bats nesting in them.
- The portal to the Eye of Harmony in the Doctor's TARDIS can only be opened by scanning a human retina. Leaving the Eye open drains power from the Ship but this can be re-routed back to the time rotor to get it going again.
- The Doctor gives the expansion of the acronym TARDIS as "Time And Relative Dimension In Space". He also reiterates the Ship is a Type 40.
- At this point the Doctor keeps a spare door key in a cubbyhole in the top of the front sign box, above the P of 'Police box'.
- The overhead scanner can display a view of space and be set to show the [near] future. Its image occupies the entire ceiling of the control room from the top of the inner wooden colonnade upwards.

NOTES The TARDIS toolkit makes a reappearance, last seen in use in *Vengeance on Varos*, although it was in the control room in *Time and the Rani*. Here it's housed in a Gladstone bag but has the same utensils, plus several pocket watches and other bric-a-brac.

▪ Both the scanner and the console indicate the destination is Gallifrey in the Rassilon era, the latter also suggesting an arrival date of 30 December at 22:47.

▪ The Police Box seen in the opening titles of the TV movie was a detailed model that closely matched the full-size prop at a tenth its size (so approximately 27cm tall) with internal illumination. This was filmed on a motion-control rig so it could spin as it approached then retreated from the camera. The footage was then matted with the computer-generated vortex.

▪ As if the signage of nearby streets weren't enough, a television newsreader later confirms "last night's shooting" was in Chinatown. Later an effects shot shows a plume of dust rising into the sky from the Port of San Francisco Ferry Building but this can't be where the tardis is as Chinatown is further inland behind the Financial District.

▪ The TARDIS materialisation is augmented with a wisp of blue smoke at its centre as the Police Box is faded in. This landing also has added whooshing noises and disturbs the air even before the TARDIS appears. The next landing is more like normal (although still with the wisp) so this additional noise and wind is presumably a result of the timing malfunction and/or emergency landing.

▪ The Doctor's shield-shaped key is reintroduced, last seen in *The Robots of Death* (Landing 130). The slot for this is hidden behind the Yale keyhole.

▪ The main doors repeatedly close by themselves after people have entered the control room. This may be a function the Doctor initiated once the console was moved further from the entrance.

▪ How does the Master get inside the TARDIS when Lee has the key? In earlier versions of the script the Master followed Lee after he had unlocked the door, which is just about possible *if* there's a space between the Police Box and control room doors (the set was built with one but it wasn't shown on screen). The Master might slip in after Lee's first entrance and hide in the darkness outside the control room as the boy goggles at the huge space inside. When Lee steps out again to walk around the Police Box, the Master moves over to the far side of the console.

▪ The cloisters are a large, cathedral-like room strewn with dried leaves. There's an arched doorway at one end and a staircase at the other. This leads up between two balconies to a large lancet arch and window, with the Time Lord emblem at its apex, then branches left and right. In the centre is a diamond dais with steps at each corner and a shallow dome covering the Eye of Harmony in the middle, also carved with the emblem. Above this is a framework of stone arches – a model built to match the full-size set and matted in during post-production; the starry background beyond was computer-generated (as were the bats).

▪ The Eye of Harmony was said to be located on Gallifrey in *The Deadly Assassin*. In *Journey to the Centre of the TARDIS* it's again shown within the Ship. It seems the original was the one powering Gallifrey but that each TARDIS contains its own Eye of Harmony. The Master says, "Everything gets its power from here," so this may be the "heart of the machine" that the Doctor refers to in *The Edge of Destruction* (Landing 4).

▪ This Eye can be opened by a human looking into the beam of light from beneath the reflector staffs. This seems an unlikely restriction for the Time Lords to apply so the Doctor may have adapted his, knowing he generally has a reliable human travelling with him. He says it hasn't been opened "in seven hundred years" (since he stole the TARDIS?) and although he asks the Master how he did it, he may be fishing for how much his rival knows rather than expressing genuine ignorance. It's not clear if the Master already knew a human retinal structure was needed and that's why he got Lee on his side, or if he just began to suspect when he saw how much "the TARDIS really likes" the boy. He implies the Doctor's being only half human is insufficient to open the Eye but this is likely a guess. Is it merely one of the Doctor's retinas that has a human structure, part of his modifications to secure the Eye in his TARDIS from the Time Lords? This might be why some incarnations have used a monocle or worn glasses. (Although the Doctor himself admits half-human heritage – "On my mother's side" – he may be being flippant while he distracts Professor Wagg and steals his security pass.)

▪ How does the Doctor know where the TARDIS is parked? He barely had time to glimpse the alleyway before he was shot and bundled unconscious into an ambulance. It's just about feasible that when he was at Grace's house he heard the TV news report of a gang shooting in Chinatown (he was talking over it at the time) and concluded it related to his injury, so asked Grace to direct him to the district then drove around until they spotted the Police Box. Or perhaps he can sense when he's getting close to it, or the open Eye.

▪ The Doctor explains the TARDIS's Police Box appearance as a result of its "cloaking device" being stuck. This term is familiar from the various *Star Trek* series, although there it's usually deployed to make spaceships invisible rather than disguise them.

▪ Throughout the story, but most noticeable when the Doctor returns to the control room, is a corked blue bottle on the rim of the console. Did he like a bit of a tipple towards the end of his seventh incarnation?

▪ Although not named on screen, the cloister bell is the same as previously heard (taken from a commercial CD of *Doctor Who* sound effects) and the Doctor notes it's "a warning. The TARDIS is dying."

▪ Although the Doctor talks of diverting power "into the time rotor here" he simply nods towards the console and doesn't specifically indicate the central column.

▪ Oops! Shots of the console sparking as the Master

begins draining the Doctor's life force show the toolkit sitting on the rim, where the Doctor left it when he was knocked out. But in the immediately preceding overhead shot the toolkit bag isn't there.

- As the TARDIS takes off, the coordinates panel on the console reads 'December 31, 23:59:59, 1999'. Wasn't the Doctor supposed to reset them to before his arrival on the 30th?
- The central column makes an intermittent wheezing sound as it begins moving. There's an element of the traditional grinding effect but the Police Box vanishes in a flash rather than fading slowly.

LANDING 308

SPACE Earth, America, California, San Francisco, park
TIME 1 January 2000, just after midnight
TRAVELLERS The Doctor, Grace Holloway, Chang Lee
EPISODES Doctor Who (Movie)

The TARDIS immediately goes into a temporal orbit, which reverses the energy transfer and causes the Master to decay again. Grace releases the Doctor but the Master kills her. He and the Doctor struggle until the Master stumbles into the Eye of Harmony. The Doctor tries to save him but the Master refuses his help and is consumed by the Eye.

Before it closes, a golden energy emanates from the Eye and resurrects Grace and Lee. The Doctor takes them back to the control room and they check the overhead scanner to confirm the future of the universe is assured. He offers to drop them off on the 29th of December but neither wants to repeat the last two days.

The Doctor therefore shifts the coordinates ahead to where they took off from and the TARDIS rematerialises in a small park just after midnight in what people are calling a new millennium. There are fireworks in the sky and the sound of celebration all around as the Doctor takes his leave of Lee and Grace. He allows Lee to keep the bags of gold dust that the Master gave him, and is a little sad when Grace turns down his offer to travel with him.

The Doctor kisses Grace and returns to the Ship, taking one last look back as she waves him goodbye. He enters and the Police Box fades away. Inside, he plays music on the gramophone and finishes repairing the console with his sonic screwdriver, then settles down with a fresh cup of tea as he returns to reading his book – unaware of the chaotic war to come...

- **CONTROLS** After re-routing the power, Grace flicks switches at the bottom of panel F1 and turns the centre dial. It sounds like she pulls the brake lever on panel F2.
- The Doctor uses the lever on panel F6 to activate the overhead scanner again, operates an unseen control on panel F1 (probably the centre dial) and presses the keypad on the outer rim of panel F2 to "see where we are". He resets the destination date on this panel then operates unseen controls and the rotary lever on panel F5. He's then seen turning dials on panel F3.

- **NOTES** It's never explained what a 'temporal orbit' means. Is the TARDIS suspended outside of time or looping through a fixed period? A clock on the console begins winding backwards, suggesting the TARDIS is moving back in time even though we proceed to see Earth spaghettified as midnight strikes on the American west coast. We then see the coordinates rolling back to 'December 30' and by the time the Doctor returns to the control room they read 'December 29'. But if the Ship itself just travels back a couple of days, how is that preventing the events already seen? The implication seems to be that the whole planet/universe is reversed and the timeline from the moment the TARDIS lands is erased. This happens in *Father's Day* and *Journey to the Centre of the TARDIS* but in those instances the Doctor's timeline is reset also and he no longer remembers the erased events. That can't happen here else he would degenerate into his seventh incarnation. Perhaps that's ultimately why the Doctor doesn't land on the 29th but jumps ahead to the New Year, to protect his own timeline more than Grace's and Lee's. So for those in the TARDIS during the temporal orbit the last two days did happen as we've seen, but to the rest of the world/universe they didn't. This likely leaves some anomalies. It's probably wisest to assume there aren't duplicates of Grace and Lee who never met the Doctor living through the reset timeline; instead they just disappeared for the two days before New Year. People likely assume Lee was in hiding from rival gangs but Grace's situation is a bit more complicated. From the hospital's point of view she never quit, so at least she has a job to go back to, but without her running off in the middle of the opera did Brian still leave? That was probably just the last straw for him, so her going AWOL for two days could have had the same effect. The hospital will also have no records of the Doctor's operation and death, so that's fortunate, but what about his advice to Gareth, which he was now not there to give? Is that why we never did get a reliable way to predict earthquakes in 2009? And is there a beryllium chip still in Professor Wagg's atomic clock or not?
- For the shot of the clock on the console winding backwards, someone under the prop rotated the hands manually, hence their rather jerky motion (watch the hour hand in particular).
- It's not clear whether Grace and Lee are resurrected because time (outside) has rolled back to a point when they were alive or, more plausibly, because of the energy from the Eye. Note this is a twinkly amber light similar to what will later represent the Doctor's regenerations and comes to be labelled artron energy, so perhaps in hindsight this can be considered the same. The Doctor does imply it's deliberately released by the Ship, calling it "a sentimental old thing".
- The Doctor advises Lee not to be in San Francisco next Christmas, suggesting he has previously visited the city at that time and knows there will be danger. Grace is with them when he says this but he doesn't direct the same advice at her, so is he trusting she'll do the

same or does he know she needs to be there? Perhaps they met and that's how he knows about her reason for becoming a doctor and that she'll "do great things". If so it must have been before Landing 286 as Grace doesn't recognise the Doctor's seventh incarnation.
- According to the console, the lone Doctor is heading for 31 December on Earth in the Kraaiian Era – unfortunately the year setting is obscured.

THE TIME WAR BEGINS

As the Doctor continues his erratic travels, the long-lasting enmity between the Time Lords and the Daleks escalates into all-out war. The Doctor tries to keep his distance from both but the increasing efforts of each time-travelling species to eradicate the other begin to affect other planets and their peoples. He starts to sense this is interfering with even his own timeline, as sometimes he remembers travelling with Izzy, Fey and Destrii; or was it Sam, Fitz, Anji and Trix? Then his memory shifts again and he recalls being with Charley, C'rizz, Lucie, Molly, Tamsin, Liv and Helen. The war gets harder to avoid but the Doctor remains determined only to help where he can, not to fight.

LANDING 309

SPACE Spaceship plummeting towards Karn
TIME Unknown [future]
TRAVELLERS The Doctor
EPISODES The Night of the Doctor

The TARDIS picks up a distress call from a gunship that is heading out of control towards the planet Karn. It materialises in a compartment towards the rear of the ship – the safest place given the front will hit the ground first. The Doctor heads to the flight deck.

He is on his way back with the sole remaining crewmember, Cass – who has teleported the rest to safety – when an emergency hatch cuts them off from the TARDIS. The Doctor opens it with his sonic screwdriver but when he tells Cass the Police Box is bigger inside she realises it is a TARDIS and that he is a Time Lord. She closes the hatch again, deadlock-sealing her off from the Doctor and his Ship, believing his people to be as terrible as the Daleks they are warring against. The Doctor refuses to leave her to die but she will not be persuaded and the gunship smashes into the rocky surface of Karn. Members of the Sisterhood of Karn come to retrieve the Doctor's dead body from the wreckage.

When he returns for the TARDIS he has regenerated for an eighth time, with help from one of the Sisterhood's potions. He no longer considers himself to be 'the Doctor', however, just a nameless warrior as he prepares at last to take a stand in the Time War.

- **NOTES** There's no way to tell when this takes place – if, indeed, dates mean much during a Time War – given the Sisterhood appear as ageless as Time Lords. But if Cass is as human as she seems it's likely to be in the future for her to be crewing a spaceship.
- Recorded in 2013 as a prequel to the 50th anniversary special *The Day of the Doctor*, this mini-episode used one of the Police Box props designed and built for the revived series. This was Prop 1c, constructed in 2007 and most recently used in the special as the Warrior's battered TARDIS (see vol.2).
- As the TARDIS's Police Box appearance has been refreshed, might we assume that this incarnation of the Doctor has also changed the control room decor to the coral-with-roundels look by this point? It's unlikely the determined Warrior would be concerned with such aesthetics (although it could have been necessitated by some damage caused during the Time War). If so, then the Warrior joins only the Doctor's second, sixth and tenth incarnations not to redecorate the control room during their occupancy.
- The CGI shot of the Police Box flying after the gunship, however, used the post-2010 model with white window frames and a St John Ambulance emblem.

INDEX

NAMED CONTROLS AND COMPONENTS

NAME	LANDING
2LO	5
Architectural configuration	197,204
Astral map	14,23,43
Astro-sextant rectifier	123
Automatic drift control	22
Automatic oxygen supply	94
Autoscan	249
Auxiliary drives	198
Calibrators	120
Camouflage unit	22
—see also *Chameleon circuit*	
Chameleon circuit	196,197,202,263-266
—see also *Volume 2*	
Circuit programmer	196,207
Cloaking device	307
—see also *Chameleon circuit*	
Cloister bell	196,197,204,252,307
—see also *Volume 2*	
Coil cut-out	245
Communication circuit	91
Comparator	256
Computer scanner	243
Conceptual geometer	170,172
Coordinate override	219,221
Course circuit	78
Databanks	192,204,205,255
Defence shields	170
—see also *Forcefield*	
Dematerialisation circuit	77c,80,82,91,170
—see also *Landing circuit*	
Dematerialising control	22
Dimensional control	22
Dimensional stabiliser	156,170,218
—see also *Relative dimensional stabiliser*	
Directional unit	31
Double-curtain trimonic barrier	128
Drift compensators	108
—see also *Relative drift compensator*	
Dynomorphic generator	223
Electromagnetic field gauge	215,216
Emergency power booster	61,267
Emergency transceiver	166
Emergency unit	60,61
Exponential cross-field	198
Extreme Emergency	88,91

NAME	LANDING
Fail-safe switch	144
Fast return switch	4
Fault indicator	59
Fault locator	3,4,10
Flight computer	267
Fluid link	3,14,59,60
—see also *Volume 2*	
Food machine	3,4,16
Forcefield	14,23,91,148
—see also *Defence shields, Safety barrier*	
—see also *Volume 2*	
Forcefield generator	91
Gravitational bearing	37
Gravitic anomaliser	170
—see also *Volume 2*	
Gravity dilation meter	147
Gravity tractor beam	167
Helmic regulator	107
—see also *Volume 2*	
Hostile action displacement system (HADS)	65
—see also *Volume 2*	
Image translator	188,191,194
Interstitial beam synthesiser	83
Landing circuit	62,63
—see also *Dematerialisation circuit*	
Lateral balance cones	210
Linear calculator	118
Main switch	31
Main unit	4
Master switch	37
Mean-free path tracker	204
Memory bank	4
Memory core	192
Molecular stabiliser	150
Multi-loop stabiliser	146,147
Omega configuration	198
Pause control	118
Quantum accelerator	225
Radiation meter	3
Randomiser	158,159,161,182,183

INDEX

NAME	LANDING
Recall circuit	227
Referential difference	204
Refraction tube	144
Relative continuum stabiliser	113
Relative dimensional stabiliser	135,142,144
—see also *Dimensional stabiliser*	
Relative drift compensator	218
—see also *Drift compensators*	
Reverse bias	194
Rotor cut-out	237
Safety barrier	37
—see also *Forcefield*	
Safety circuits	144
Seismic scanner	256
Signal conversion unit	247
Solar comparator	218
Sonic booster	210
Space-time coordinate programmer	96,102
Space-time element	227,237
Spatial distribution circuits	249
Spatial drive	187
Stabiliser(s)	78,144,248
Storage unit	75
Synchronic feedback	146,147
Take-off delay timer	256
Telepathic circuits	87,88,93
—see also *Volume 2*	
Telepathic field	138
Temporal grace	125,227
—see also *Volume 2*	

NAME	LANDING
Temporal limiter	221,225
Temporal stabiliser	256
Thermo buffer	204
Thermo couplings	126
Time control unit	68,117
Time-curve circuits	207
Time-curve indicator	28,29,31,209
Time-lapse compressor	225
Time/timing mechanism	6,20,307
Time monitor	247
—see also *Yearometer*	
Time-path detector	17
Time ram control	89
Time rotor	18,184,227,307
Time scanner	49
Time setting	86
Time-vector generator	59,73
Tracers	129
Trachoid time crystal	126
Transitional elements	268
Transmitter	215
Transpower system	268
Tri-gamma circuits	75
Visual orientation circuits	132
Visual stabiliser circuit	63
Vortex drive	289
Warp oscilloscope	147
Yearometer	2
—see also *Time monitor*	

Printed in Great Britain
by Amazon